THE LAST TSAR'S WARRIORS
Volume II: P – Z

Andris J. Kursietis

THE LAST TSAR'S WARRIORS

A Biographical Dictionary of the Senior Officers
of the Imperial Russian Armed Forces under Tsar Nikolai II
1894 - 1917

Volume II: P - Z; Illustrations; Order of Battle

Aspekt Publishers

THE LAST TSAR'S WARRIORS - Volume II: P – Z

© Andris J. Kursietis
© 2017 Uitgeverij ASPEKT / Aspekt Publishers
Amersfoortsestraat 27, 3769 AD Soesterberg, The Netherlands
info@uitgeverijaspekt.nl – http://www.uitgeverijaspekt.nl

Cover: Maarten Bakker
Inside: Maarten Bakker

ISBN: 9789463382045
NUR: 680

All rights reserved. No reproduction copy or transmission of this publication may be made without written permission.

INDEX

Introduction ……………………………………………………………………..…… 599

Generals & Admirals of Imperial Russia, 1894 - 1917:
    Table of ranks …………………………………………………………………… 601
    Alphabetical listing of Generals and Admirals (P - Z) …………………………. 602

Illustrations ……………………………………………………………………….… 1005

Order of Battle of the Imperial Russian Armed Forces:
    Supreme Command …………………………………………………………....... 1025
    Section I: Army Administration
        Minister of War ………………………………………………………… 1025
        Chief of the General Directorate of the General Staff ………………….. 1025
        Chief of the Main General Staff of the Imperial Russian Army ……….... 1026
        Chief of the Main Artillery Directorate …………………………………. 1026
        Chief of the Main Military Technical Directorate ………………………. 1026
        Chief of the Main Intendant Directorate ………………………………… 1026
        Chief of the Main Directorate for Military Schools …………………….. 1026
        Chief of the Main Military Medical Directorate ………………………... 1026
        Chief of the Main Military Justice Directorate ………………………….. 1027
        Chief of the Main Directorate for Cossack Troops ……………………… 1027
        Chief of the Main Directorate for Troop Billeting ……………………..... 1027
        Chief of the Army Veterinary Directorate ………………………………. 1027
        Chief of the Directorate of the Orthodox Army and Naval Chaplaincy ….. 1027
        Commanding General, Corps of Gendarmerie …………………………....... 1027
    Section II: Field Army
        Fronts …………………………………………………………………… 1028
        Armies …………………………………………………………………… 1028
        Military Districts ………………………………………………………… 1031
        Corps:
            Guards, Grenadier, Army Corps ……………………………………. 1035
            Cavalry Corps ………………………………………………………. 1046
        Divisions and Brigades:
            Guards, Grenadier Divisions ……………………………………….. 1048
            Infantry Divisions …………………………………………………... 1056
            Rifle Divisions ……………………………………………………… 1128
            Guards Cavalry Divisions ………………………………………….. 1144
            Cavalry Divisions ………………………………………………….. 1147
            Cossack Divisions …………………………………………………... 1160
            Ussuri Mounted Division …………………………………………... 1167
        Independent Brigades:
            Infantry Brigades …………………………………………………… 1168
            Rifle Brigades ……………………………………………………….. 1168
            Cavalry Brigades …………………………………………………… 1173
            Cossack Brigades …………………………………………………… 1174

Section III: Naval Administration
    Minister of the Navy 1176
    Chief of the Main Naval Staff 1176
    Chief of the Naval General Staff 1176
    Chief of the Main Directorate of Shipbuilding & Logistics 1176
Section IV: Naval Units
    Baltic Fleet 1177
    Black Sea Fleet 1177
    Pacific Fleet/Squadron 1177

List of Primary Sources.. 1178

Introduction

In October 1894, Tsar Aleksandr III died at the early age of 49, and his son Nikolai ascended the throne of the Russian Empire as Nikolai II, Emperor and Autocrat of All the Russias. He inherited an empire that spanned three continents, almost 9 million square miles, extending from the Arctic Ocean in the north to the Black Sea in the south, from the Baltic Sea in the west to the Pacific Ocean in the east. As can be imagined, such a vast territory required a significantly-sized military to maintain order in the interior and to protect its borders from foreign aggressors. The size of the imperial armed forces can be judged by the fact that over 6,400 generals and admirals served the last Tsar of Russia during the 23-year period of his reign, 1894 – 1917. A study of the annual rank lists published by the Ministry of War shows that well over 1,000 generals were on active duty each year. This book attempts to provide an overview of the empire's military commanders, a task made all the more difficult by the lack of any detailed material in the English language, and the destruction of countless Russian-language records during the revolution in 1917 and the years that followed. Many senior officers were murdered by the revolutionaries, by unorganized mobs that did not keep records of whom they killed or when; others were lucky to flee the country and scatter to all corners of the planet, where they lived out their remaining years in obscurity and anonymity, wishing to avoid recognition and potential assassination by Communist agents. Accordingly, the dates when many of the generals and admirals listed in this book died have been lost to posterity, and the reader will frequently see a question mark in place of an officer's death date.

Structure of the armed forces

During peacetime, command of the army at the highest level was overseen by the Minister of War, with the Minister of the Navy holding an equivalent responsibility over the Navy. Their ministries were divided into several Main Directorates, all headed by senior officers. In addition, the army and navy both had general staffs that oversaw the day-to-day administration of the military.

The highest peacetime army unit was the Military District, of which there were twelve in number. These Military Districts remained active even during wartime, serving mainly as bases for conscription, especially during World War I. Upon mobilization in July 1914, troops from the Military Districts were used to create Armies which were then sent to the various theaters of operations. These armies were grouped under "Fronts" that were designated according to their respective theaters (for example, Northwestern Front).

Subordinated to the Military Districts in peacetime, and to the Armies during the war, were corps of various designations: Guards Corps, Grenadier Corps, Army (= infantry) Corps, and Cavalry Corps. These units comprised Divisions, which in turn were made up of Brigades. A typical Infantry Division comprised two Infantry Brigades and an Artillery Brigade, while Cavalry Divisons were composed of two Cavalry Brigades and a Horse Artillery Battalion.

The Russian Navy had three main spheres of activity: the Baltic Sea, Black Sea and the Pacific. After the Pacific Fleet was destroyed by the Japanese in 1905, naval operations in the Far East effectively ceased, and the focus of attention switched to the Baltic and Black

Sea. During World War I, naval activities in the Baltic were mainly defensive in nature, while the Black Sea Fleet became dominant in its area of operations throughout the war.

Conclusion

During Nikolai's reign, Russia was involved in two significant conflicts, the Russo-Japanese War in 1904-1905, and World War I. Despite the size of its armed forces, Russia was soundly beaten by the Japanese and forced to sue for peace. Unfortunately for the Russian Empire, any lessons learned from the poor showing of its army and navy in the fight against Japan were not put to constructive use. Although Russia possessed the largest army in the world, the initial battles of World War I on the Eastern Front resulted in yet another series of decisive defeats at the hands of the Germans, and matters did not improve as war dragged on. A combination of poor training, inadequate supplies, abysmal morale, and ineffective leadership, both at the front and in the high command, led to the Russian army suffering significant losses for no military tactical or strategic gain.

A total of 15 million men served in the Russian Army during World War I, of which an estimated 1.8 million were killed and a further 2.8 million wounded. These are only approximations, with different sources providing figures ranging from 1.5 million dead to 2.2 million. The lack of accurate statistics is regrettable but not surprising given the chaotic conditions in the front lines and the change in regime in 1917. By most accounts over 2 million Russian soldiers were captured and became prisoners of war.

Eventually, this sapping of manpower and the ever-decreasing morale of the soldiers in the trenches led to conditions that were ripe for revolution, and that is indeed what occurred in February 1917. Tired of the sacrifices of war, both at home and in the front lines, the Russians revolted in protest, and within a week the last Russian emperor's reign was over. Bowing to the inevitable, on March 2, 1917 (date based on the Julian calendar that was still in use in Russia at that time), Nikolai II abdicated and the four-hundred year old Russian Empire was no more. The fate of the last Tsar and his family, and indeed of Russia itself, is well known.

Generals & Admirals of Imperial Russia, 1894 - 1917

This list includes all officers who held the rank of General or Admiral during 20 October 1894 - 2 March 1917*, from the ascension of Tsar Nikolai II to the throne until the Russian Empire ceased to exist upon his abdication.

(* These dates correspond to the Julian calendar that was in effect during the period in question.)

Table of ranks

Генерал-фельдмаршал	General Field Marshal
Генерал-адмирал	General-Admiral
Генерал от артиллерии	General of Artillery
Генерал от кавалерии	General of Cavalry
Инженер-генерал	General of Engineers
Генерал от инфантерии	General of Infantry
Генерал по адмиралтейству	General of the Admiralty
Генерал флота	General of the Fleet
Генерал корпуса гидрографов	General of the Hydrographic Corps
Адмирал	Admiral
Действительный тайный советник	Actual Privy Councillor
Генерал-лейтенант	Lieutenant-General
Генерал-лейтенант по адмиралтейству	Lieutenant-General of the Admiralty
Генерал-лейтенант флота	Lieutenant-General of the Fleet
Генерал-лейтенант корпуса гидрографов	Lieutenant-General of the Hydrographic Corps
Вице-адмирал	Vice-Admiral
Тайный советник	Privy Councillor
Протопресвитер военного и морского духовенства	Protopresbyter, army and naval clergy
Генерал-майор	Major-General
Генерал-майор по адмиралтейству	Major-General of the Admiralty
Генерал-майор флота	Major-General of the Fleet
Генерал-майор корпуса гидрографов	Major-General of the Hydrographic Corps
Контр-адмирал	Rear-Admiral
Действительный статский советник	Actual State Councillor
Главные священники округов	Chief District Chaplain
Полковник	Colonel
Капитан 1-го ранга	Captain 1st Class (Navy)

Note: The rank of Генерал-адъютант *(General-Adjutant) was accorded to officers of General rank and was used as an honorable distinction for senior military officials, giving them the right to report directly to the Emperor.*

Major-General Vladimir Aleksandrovich **Pakhalen** (27 Mar 1847 - ?)
19 Aug 1896:	Promoted to *Major-General*
19 Aug 1896 - 13 Nov 1896:	Commander, 2nd Brigade, 4th Cavalry Division
13 Nov 1896 - 2 Aug 1903:	Commander, 1st Brigade, 11th Cavalry Division

Major-General Vladimir Karlovich **Palander** (15 Dec 1860 - 7 Jul 1933)
4 Dec 1908 - 11 Apr 1911:	Commander, 5th Infantry Regiment
11 Apr 1911:	Promoted to *Major-General*
11 Apr 1911:	Retired
1915 - 17 May 1915:	Recalled; Commander, State Militia Brigade
17 May 1915 - 10 Sep 1916:	Reserve officer, Minsk Military District
10 Sep 1916 - 19 Oct 1916:	Reserve officer, Caucasus Military District
19 Oct 1916 - 2 Jul 1917:	Special Assignments General, Logistics Department, Caucasus Army
2 Jul 1917:	Dismissed

Lieutenant-General Aleksandr Khristoforovich **Paleolog** (4 Jan 1853 - ?)
16 Aug 1900 - 4 May 1917:	Chief of Bureau, Imperial Stables
6 Dec 1902:	Promoted to *Major-General*
6 Dec 1915:	Promoted to *Lieutenant-General*
4 May 1917:	Dismissed

Major-General Pyotr Pavlovich **Palibin** (27 Jun 1862 - 9 Apr 1938)
12 May 1910:	Promoted to *Major-General*
12 May 1910 - 12 Feb 1913:	Commander, 1st Brigade, 25th Infantry Division
12 Feb 1913 - 8 Feb 1914:	Commander, 2nd Brigade, 27th Infantry Division
8 Feb 1914 - 13 May 1914:	Commander, 1st Brigade, 27th Infantry Division
13 May 1914 - 1 Nov 1914:	Commander, 3rd Rifle Brigade
1 Nov 1914 - 1917:	Special Assignments General, 8th Army
1917:	Chief of Staff, Military Governor of Occupied Austro-Hungarian Areas

Major-General Vladimir Petrovich **Palibin** (9 Oct 1851 - ?)
29 Jan 1897 - 1907:	Chief of Police, St. Petersburg
1906:	Promoted to *Major-General*

Major-General Yalmar Karlovich **Palin** (12 Jul 1848 - 9 Nov 1907)
1880 - 25 Nov 1888:	Chief of Staff, Military Section, Office of the Governor-General of Finland
30 Aug 1888:	Promoted to *Major-General*
25 Nov 1888 - 31 Dec 1896:	Governor of Uusimaa Province
31 Dec 1896 - 1899:	Senator, Imperial Finnish Senate
1899:	Resigned

Lieutenant-General Aleksandr Stepanovich **Palitsyn** (21 May 1842 - 1913)
13 Feb 1896 - 23 Aug 1896:	Transferred to the reserve
7 Aug 1896:	Promoted to *Major-General*
23 Aug 1896 - 18 Feb 1902:	Commander of Gendarmerie, Volyn Province

18 Feb 1902:   Promoted to *Lieutenant-General*
18 Feb 1902:   Retired

Major-General Dmitry Pavlovich **Palitsyn** (21 May 1830 - ?)
26 Jul 1887:   Promoted to *Major-General*
26 Jul 1887 - 9 Nov 1889:   At the disposal of the Main Engineering Directorate
9 Nov 1889 - 1894:   At the disposal of the Commanding General, Warsaw Military District

General of Infantry Fyodor Fyodorovich **Palitsyn** (28 Oct 1851 - 20 Feb 1923)
19 Nov 1891 - 19 Apr 1895:   Deputy Chief of Staff, St. Petersburg Military District
30 Aug 1894:   Promoted to *Major-General*
19 Apr 1895 - 31 May 1895:   Chief of Staff, Guards Corps
31 May 1895 - 28 Jun 1905:   Chief of Staff, Inspector-General of Cavalry
6 Dec 1900:   Promoted to *Lieutenant-General*
28 Jun 1905 - 2 Dec 1908:   Chief of the General Directorate of the General Staff
6 May 1907:   Promoted to *General of Infantry*
13 Dec 1908 - Oct 1917:   Member of the State Council
10 Nov 1917:   Retired

Major-General Nikolai Fyodorovich **Palitsyn** (13 Dec 1843 - ?)
9 Dec 1900 - 5 Jan 1904:   Commander, 18th Artillery Brigade
6 Dec 1901:   Promoted to *Major-General*

Lieutenant-General Vladimir Aleksandrovich **Palitsyn** (29 May 1845 - 13 Feb 1906)
2 Aug 1891:   Promoted to *Major-General*
2 Aug 1891 - 6 Sep 1891:   Commander, 1st Brigade, 12th Cavalry Division
6 Sep 1891 - 15 Apr 1893:   Commander, 2nd Brigade, 2nd Cavalry Division
15 Apr 1893 - 13 Feb 1906:   At the disposal of the Inspector of Remounts
6 Dec 1900:   Promoted to *Lieutenant-General*

Major-General Andrey Fedorovich **Palkin** (29 Nov 1858 - ?)
22 Oct 1914 - 3 Nov 1916:   Deputy Chief, Kazan Gunpowder Factory
6 Dec 1914:   Promoted to *Major-General*
3 Nov 1916 - 1917:   Reserve officer, Petrograd Military District

General of the Fleet Sergey Ilich **Paltov** (5 Nov 1843 - ?)
2 Apr 1895:   Promoted to *Rear-Admiral*
12 Jun 1896 - 19 Feb 1901:   Junior Flagman, Black Sea Fleet
19 Feb 1901 - 22 Jul 1903:   Junior Flagman, 2nd Naval Division
22 Jul 1903:   Promoted to *Lieutenant-General of the Admiralty*
22 Jul 1903 - 1916:   Honorary Trustee, Board of Trustees, Empress Maria Institutions
28 Dec 1909:   Promoted to *General of the Admiralty*
8 Apr 1913:   Redesignated *General of the Fleet*

Major-General Andrey Ivanovich **Panafutin** (12 Sep 1859 - ?)
4 Jul 1910 - 19 Dec 1912:   Commander, 189th Infantry Regiment

19 Dec 1912:	Promoted to *Major-General*
19 Dec 1912:	Retired
1915 - 1916:	Recalled; Commander, 19th State Militia Brigade
1916 - 5 Aug 1916:	Commander, 6th State Militia Brigade
5 Aug 1916 - 1917:	Commander, Brigade, 7th Siberian Rifle Division
1917 - 8 Jul 1917:	Reserve officer, Minsk Military District
8 Jul 1917:	Dismissed

Lieutenant-General Yevgeny Alekseyevich **Panchulidzev** (17 Sep 1853 - 10 Feb 1917)
24 Oct 1900 - 26 Nov 1903:	Commander, 52nd Dragoon Regiment
26 Nov 1903:	Promoted to *Major-General*
26 Nov 1903 - 28 May 1905:	Attached to the Chief of the General Staff
28 May 1905 - 18 Oct 1905:	Attached to the C-in-C, 2nd Manchurian Army
18 Oct 1905 - 17 Apr 1906:	Attached to the Chief of the General Staff
17 Apr 1906 - 12 May 1910:	Commander, 2nd Brigade, 6th Cavalry Division
12 May 1910 - 17 Sep 1912:	Commander, 1st Brigade, 13th Cavalry Division
17 Sep 1912:	Promoted to *Lieutenant-General*
17 Sep 1912:	Retired
7 Oct 1914 - 29 Jan 1916:	Recalled; Chief of the Sanatory Section, 8th Army
29 Jan 1916 - 1916:	Reserve officer, Kiev Military District
1916 - 10 Feb 1917:	Attached to the Commander-in-Chief of the Army

Major-General of the Fleet Konstantin Aleksandrovich **Panferov** (25 Oct 1860 - 1919)
1 Nov 1911 - 1917:	Commandant, Kronstadt Naval Sub-Depot
6 Feb 1913:	Promoted to *Major-General of the Fleet*

Major-General Nikolai Dmitriyevich **Panfilov** (26 Oct 1861 - Dec 1920)
29 Jun 1907 - 1917:	Chairman of the Remount Commission, Voronezh Region
6 Dec 1913:	Promoted to *Major-General*

Major-General Pyotr Petrovich **Panfilov** (20 Dec 1865 - ?)
5 May 1912 - 16 Jan 1916:	Commander, 34th Siberian Rifle Regiment
6 Dec 1915:	Promoted to *Major-General*
16 Jan 1916 - 1917:	Commander, Brigade, 27th Infantry Division
1917 - 12 May 1917:	Commander, Brigade, 1st Siberian Rifle Division
12 May 1917 - 20 Sep 1917:	Commander, 5th Grenadier Division
20 Sep 1917 - 1918:	Reserve officer, Minsk Military District

Lieutenant-General Sergey Nikolayevich **Panin** (14 Feb 1834 - ?)
12 Nov 1884 - 31 May 1888:	Ataman, 2nd Military Division, Terek Cossack Army
30 Aug 1886:	Promoted to *Major-General*
31 May 1888 - 14 Jan 1893:	Ataman, Sunzha Division, Terek Region
14 Jan 1893 - 21 Jul 1895:	Commander, Terek Cossack Brigade
21 Jul 1895 - 16 Nov 1895:	Deputy Military Commander, Terek Region, Ataman, Terek Cossack Army
16 Nov 1895 - 15 Jan 1899:	Commander, 2nd Caucasus Cossack Division
14 May 1896:	Promoted to *Lieutenant-General*

Major-General Vladimir Semyonovich **Pankov** (19 Jun 1856 - ?)
31 Dec 1913 - 15 Jun 1917:   Commander of Artillery, St. Petersburg Garrison,
                              Commandant, St. Petersburg Artillery Depot
6 Apr 1914:   Promoted to *Major-General*
15 Jun 1917:   Retired
7 Aug 1917 - ?:   Recalled; Commander of Artillery, Fortress Petrograd,
                              Commandant, Petrograd Artillery Depot

Major-General Filipp Petrovich **Panov** (11 Oct 1870 - 2 Aug 1960)
11 Sep 1913 - 22 Jan 1916:   Commander, 9th Turkestan Rifle Regiment
5 Oct 1915:   Promoted to *Major-General*
22 Jan 1916 - 29 Feb 1916:   Chief of Staff, 3rd Infantry Division
29 Feb 1916 - 12 Apr 1917:   Chief of Staff, VI. Army Corps
12 Apr 1917 - 15 Oct 1917:   Commander, 2nd Turkestan Rifle Division
15 Oct 1917 - Nov 1917:   Reserve officer, Moscow Military District
Nov 1917:   Dismissed

Major-General Ivan Ardalionovich **Panov** (29 Nov 1866 - ?)
26 May 1914 - 1917:   Military Judge, Caucasus Military District Court
6 Dec 1914:   Promoted to *Major-General*

Major-General Vladimir Vasilyevich **Panpushko** (18 May 1866 - ?)
31 Oct 1915 - 1918:   Commander, 2nd Amur Artillery Brigade
26 Aug 1916:   Promoted to *Major-General*

General of Infantry Aleksandr Ilich **Panteleyev** (26 Jun 1838 - 17 Jan 1919)
17 Feb 1882 - 8 Dec 1890:   Commander, Life Guards Semyonov Regiment
30 Aug 1882:   Promoted to *Major-General*
8 Dec 1890 - 4 Feb 1897:   Director of the Imperial School of Jurisprudence,
                              Member, Supreme Military Tribunal
30 Aug 1893:   Promoted to *Lieutenant-General*
4 Feb 1897 - 20 Apr 1900:   Deputy Commanding General, Corps of Gendarmerie,
                              Deputy Minister of Internal Affairs
31 Jan 1898 - 20 Apr 1900:   Commanding General, Corps of Gendarmerie
20 Apr 1900 - 13 May 1903:   Governor-General of Irkutsk
6 May 1903 - 1 May 1917:   Member of the State Council
28 Mar 1904:   Promoted to *General of Infantry*
21 Nov 1905:   Promoted to *General-Adjutant*
1 May 1917:   Dismissed

Lieutenant-General Mitrofan Alekseyevich **Panteleyev** (22 Oct 1853 - 23 Sep 1906)
29 Dec 1898 - 22 Apr 1904:   Ataman, 2nd Don District, Don Cossack Army
6 May 1900:   Promoted to *Major-General*
22 Apr 1904 - 1906:   Ataman, Rostov District, Don Cossack Army
1906:   Promoted to *Lieutenant-General*

Lieutenant-General Vsevolod Fyodorovich **Panyutin** (20 Jan 1833 - 12 Jan 1895)
18 Feb 1878 - 4 Aug 1883: Commander, Kexholm Grenadier Regiment
17 Apr 1879: Promoted to *Major-General*
4 Aug 1883 - 25 Nov 1884: Commander, 1st Brigade, 3rd Guards Infantry Division
25 Nov 1884 - 17 Jan 1890: At the disposal of the Commanding General, Warsaw Military District
17 Jan 1890 - 6 Jun 1890: Commander, 6th Infantry Division
6 Jun 1890 - 12 Jan 1895: Commander, 11th Infantry Division
30 Aug 1890: Promoted to *Lieutenant-General*

Lieutenant-General Nikolai Georgiyevich **Papa-Afanasopulo** (14 Oct 1848 - ?)
16 Dec 1899: Promoted to *Major-General*
16 Dec 1899 - 8 Mar 1907: Commander, 1st Brigade, 2nd Cavalry Division
8 Mar 1907 - 1 May 1910: Commander, 15th Cavalry Division
22 Apr 1907: Promoted to *Lieutenant-General*

Major-General of the Fleet Georgy Nikolayevich **Papa-Fedorov** (26 Jul 1865 - 8 Oct 1926)
1914 - 1915: Commandant, Port of Nikolayev
1915 - 1917: Commandant, Port of Odessa
6 Dec 1915: Promoted to *Major-General of the Fleet*

Major-General Mikhail Nikolayevich **Papa-Fedorov** (16 May 1868 - 1960)
27 Jun 1915: Promoted to *Major-General*
27 Jun 1915 - 12 May 1916: Commander, Caucasus Grenadier Artillery Brigade
12 May 1916 - 29 Apr 1917: Commander, Life Guards 3rd Artillery Brigade
29 Apr 1917 - 1917: Inspector of Artillery, XXXII. Army Corps

Major-General of the Admiralty Vasily Dmitryevich **Papayegorov** (22 Sep 1854 - ?)
1 Oct 1908 - ?: Attached to Black Sea Naval Depot
?: Promoted to *Major-General of the Admiralty*

Lieutenant-General Pavel Oskarovich **Papengut** (10 Feb 1854 - 17 Oct 1935)
20 Sep 1901: Promoted to *Major-General*
20 Sep 1901 - 23 Dec 1902: Chief of Staff, Trans-Baikal Region
23 Dec 1902 - 16 Jul 1905: Chief of Staff, II. Siberian Army Corps
16 Jul 1905 - 25 Nov 1906: Commander, 3rd Siberian Infantry Division
25 Nov 1906 - 15 Jun 1910: Commander, 28th Infantry Division
31 May 1907: Promoted to *Lieutenant-General*
15 Jun 1910: Retired
Aug 1914 - 16 Sep 1914: Recalled; Commander, 41st State Militia Brigade
16 Sep 1914 - 18 Apr 1917: Commander, 18th Infantry Division
18 Apr 1917 - Oct 1917: Reserve officer, Dvinsk Military District

Lieutenant-General Aleksandr Aleksandrovich **Parchevsky** (13 Jan 1838 - 1895)
13 May 1864 - 6 Nov 1877: Commander, 4th Battalion, 19th Artillery Brigade
15 Sep 1877: Promoted to *Major-General*
6 Nov 1877 - 28 May 1883: Commander, 19th Artillery Brigade
28 May 1883 - 3 Apr 1886: Deputy Commander of Artillery, Caucasus Military

	District
3 Apr 1886 - 1895:	Commander of Artillery, Caucasus Military District
30 Aug 1886:	Promoted to *Lieutenant-General*

Lieutenant-General Pavel Antonovich **Parchevsky** (8 Jan 1854 - ?)

3 Feb 1903:	Promoted to *Major-General*
3 Feb 1903 - 17 Apr 1905:	Chief of Staff, Trans-Baikal Region
7 Dec 1904 - 17 Apr 1905:	Acting Intendant-General, Manchurian Army
17 Apr 1905 - 16 May 1906:	Intendant-General, Rear Areas, Manchurian Army
16 May 1906 - 11 Jul 1906:	Intendant-General, Rear Areas, Far East
11 Jul 1906 - 18 Apr 1907:	Intendant-General, Irkutsk Military District
18 Apr 1907 - 17 Oct 1910:	Commander, 48th Replacement Infantry Brigade
17 Oct 1910 - 31 Dec 1913:	Commander, 2nd Brigade, 6th Infantry Division
31 Dec 1913:	Promoted to *Lieutenant-General*
31 Dec 1913 - 15 May 1916:	Commander, 5th Infantry Division
15 May 1916 - 18 Apr 1917:	Commanding General, XXXV. Army Corps
18 Apr 1917 - Oct 1917:	Reserve officer, Minsk Military District

Vice-Admiral Aleksandr Nikolayevich **Parenago** (18 Jan 1847 - 22 Jul 1908)

1899:	Promoted to *Rear-Admiral*
1904 - ?:	Supervisor of Ship Construction, Port of St. Petersburg
1907:	Promoted to *Vice-Admiral*
1907:	Retired

General of Infantry Pyotr Dmitriyevich **Parensov** (5 Jul 1843 - 25 Aug 1914)

16 Apr 1878 - 4 Jul 1879:	At the disposal of the High Command
23 Dec 1878:	Promoted to *Major-General*
4 Jul 1879:	Retired
29 Mar 1880 - 11 Sep 1880:	Recalled; Attached to the Commanding General, St. Petersburg Military District
11 Sep 1880 - 6 Sep 1881:	Unassigned
6 Sep 1881 - 7 Oct 1884:	Chief of Staff, II. Army Corps
7 Oct 1884 - 14 Mar 1886:	Reserve officer, General Staff
14 Mar 1886 - 19 Apr 1887:	At the disposal of the Chief of the General Staff
19 Apr 1887 - 26 Jul 1887:	Commandant of Warsaw
26 Jul 1887 - 19 Feb 1890:	Deputy Chief of Staff, Warsaw Military District
19 Feb 1890 - 7 Dec 1898:	Commander, 6th Cavalry Division
30 Aug 1890:	Promoted to *Lieutenant-General*
7 Dec 1898 - 5 Jun 1902:	Commandant of Fortress Warsaw
1 Apr 1901:	Promoted to *General of Infantry*
5 Jun 1902 - 5 Jan 1906:	At the disposal of the Minister of War
5 Jan 1906 - 31 Dec 1913 :	Commandant of Peterhof
31 Dec 1913:	Retired

General of Artillery Pyotr Fridrikhovich von **Parkau** (7 Oct 1851 - ?)

29 Nov 1895 - 4 Jul 1905:	Ministry of War Representative, Caucasus Military District Council
6 Dec 1900:	Promoted to *Major-General*

4 Jul 1905 - 1 Jan 1908:	Military Governor, Batum Region
1 Jan 1908 - 24 Jun 1912:	Military Governor, Kars Region
6 Dec 1906:	Promoted to *Lieutenant-General*
24 Jun 1912:	Promoted to *General of Artillery*
24 Jun 1912:	Retired
19 Nov 1914 - 1917:	Recalled; Reserve officer, Kiev Military District

Lieutenant-General Dmitry Nikolayevich **Parkhomov** (5 Sep 1871 - 16 Mar 1925)

4 Dec 1914 - 3 Aug 1915:	Commander, 47th Infantry Regiment
16 May 1915:	Promoted to *Major-General*
3 Aug 1915 - 22 Mar 1916:	Commander, 1st Brigade, 12th Infantry Division
22 Mar 1915 - 7 Jun 1916:	Chief of Staff, 100th Infantry Division
7 Jun 1916 - 15 Jun 1917:	Chief of Staff, XI. Army Corps
15 Jun 1917 - 7 Oct 1917:	Commander of Land Forces attached to the C-in-C, Baltic Fleet
1 Jul 1917:	Promoted to *Lieutenant-General*
7 Oct 1917 - 1918:	Chief of Staff, Northern Front

Lieutenant-General of the Admiralty Aleksandr Ivanovich **Paromensky** (15 Aug 1850 - 10 Aug 1922)

1900:	Promoted to *Major-General of the Admiralty*
1900 - 1908:	Commandant, Naval Engineering College
1907:	Promoted to *Lieutenant-General of the Admiralty*
1908:	Dismissed

Major-General of Naval Artillery Nikolai Dorimedontovich **Parshintsov** (12 Oct 1867 - ?)

13 Nov 1909 - ?:	Commander of Naval Artillery, Port of Sevastopol
6 Dec 1914:	Promoted to *Major-General of Naval Artillery*

Lieutenant-General Dmitry Pavlovich **Parsky** (17 Oct 1866 - 20 Dec 1921)

17 Jun 1910:	Promoted to *Major-General*
17 Jun 1910 - 31 Jan 1915:	Commander, 2nd Brigade, 46th Infantry Division
31 Jan 1915 - 9 Aug 1915:	Commander, 80th Infantry Division
16 May 1915:	Promoted to *Lieutenant-General*
9 Aug 1915 - 17 Oct 1915:	Unassigned
17 Oct 1915 - 20 Feb 1916:	Commander, 55th Infantry Division
20 Feb 1916 - 20 Jul 1917:	Commanding General, Grenadier Corps
20 Jul 1917 - 9 Sep 1917:	C-in-C, 12th Army
9 Sep 1917 - Nov 1917:	C-in-C, 3rd Army

Lieutenant-General Vasily Ignatyevich **Parutsky** (28 Feb 1847 - ?)

5 Aug 1899:	Promoted to *Major-General*
5 Aug 1899 - 21 Apr 1903:	Commander, 2nd Brigade, 22nd Infantry Division
21 Apr 1903 - 1 Jun 1904:	Unassigned
1 Jun 1904 - 1906:	Commander, 1st Brigade, 78th Infantry Division
1906 - 8 Nov 1907:	At the disposal of the Commanding General, Kazan Military District
8 Nov 1907:	Promoted to *Lieutenant-General*

8 Nov 1907: Retired

Major-General Aleksey Grigoryevich **Pashchenko** (30 Oct 1869 - 27 Oct 1909)
24 Jan 1909: Promoted to *Major-General*
24 Jan 1909 - 27 Oct 1909: Commander, 3rd Artillery Brigade

Major-General Ivan Grigoryevich **Pashchenko** (1 Jul 1872 - ?)
3 Jun 1916 - 1917: Commander, 10th Artillery Brigade
25 Aug 1916: Promoted to *Major-General*
1917 - 30 Sep 1917: Reserve officer, Kiev Military District
30 Sep 1917 - 1918: Inspector of Artillery, 9th Army

Lieutenant-General Vasily Grigoryevich **Pashchenko** (9 Mar 1868 - 20 Apr 1932)
27 Jul 1907 - 18 Mar 1909: Commander of Artillery, Fortress Libau
13 Apr 1908: Promoted to *Major-General*
18 Mar 1909 - 23 Mar 1914: Special Purposes General, Inspectorate-General of Artillery
1913: Promoted to *Lieutenant-General*
23 Mar 1914 - 15 Jan 1915: Commander of Artillery, Fortress Kronstadt
15 Jan 1915 - 7 Aug 1917: Commandant of Fortress Sveaborg
7 Aug 1917 - Dec 1917: Inspector of Artillery, IV. Caucasus Army Corps

Lieutenant-General Count Vladimir Lvovich **Pashchenko-Razvadovsky** (29 Sep 1834 - 1894)
17 Sep 1877 - 14 Jul 1883: Commander, 24th Dragoon Regiment
14 Jul 1883: Promoted to *Major-General*
14 Jul 1883 - 29 Oct 1890: Commander, 1st Brigade, 6th Cavalry Division
29 Oct 1890 - 1894: Special Assignments General, Moscow Military District
30 Aug 1893: Promoted to *Lieutenant-General*

Lieutenant-General Mikhail Alekseyevich **Pashkov** (17 Dec 1853 - Jan 1908)
18 Mar 1892 - 7 Nov 1894: Commander, 13th Dragoon Regiment
7 Nov 1894: Promoted to *Major-General*
7 Nov 1894 - 20 Mar 1899: General for Special Assignments, Warsaw Military District
20 Mar 1899 - 27 Jan 1901: Commander, Life Guards Lithuanian Regiment
3 Aug 1900 - 27 Jan 1901: Commander, 1st Brigade, 3rd Guards Infantry Division
27 Jan 1901 - 22 Jun 1905: Governor of Livonia
1 Jan 1903: Promoted to *Lieutenant-General*
22 Jun 1905 - Jan 1908: Honorary Trustee, Tsarina Maria Board of Trustees

Major-General Gilyary-Ivan-Sigizmund Stanislavovich **Pashkovsky** (11 Jan 1853 - ?)
24 Feb 1900 - 19 Jun 1905: Commander, 12th Rifle Regiment
19 Jun 1905: Promoted to *Major-General*
19 Jun 1905 - 1906: Commander, 2nd Brigade, 3rd Rifle Division

Major-General Yevgeny Aleksandrovich **Pashkovsky** (9 Jan 1866 - ?)
? - 10 Jul 1916: Commander, 279th Infantry Regiment

10 Apr 1916: Promoted to *Major-General*
10 Jul 1916 - 22 Apr 1917: Commander, Brigade, 36th Infantry Division
22 Apr 1917 - 1917: Commander, 36th Infantry Division

Major-General Mikhail Semyonovich **Paskevich** (23 Mar 1851 - ?)
7 Jun 1906 - 21 Nov 1907: Commander, 39th Artillery Brigade
6 Dec 1906: Promoted to *Major-General*
21 Nov 1907 - 25 Jul 1910: Commander of Artillery, Omsk Military District
25 Jul 1910 - 10 Mar 1912: Inspector of Artillery, XXIV. Army Corps

Major-General Anatoly Petrovich **Paskin** (27 Nov 1842 - 14 May 1899)
24 Nov 1882 - 1899: Chief of the Fire Service, St. Petersburg
30 Aug 1893: Promoted to *Major-General*

Major-General Vladimir Petrovich **Paskin** (18 May 1849 - ?)
17 Jan 1903: Promoted to *Major-General*
17 Jan 1903 - 1905: Commander, Tambov Regional Brigade

Major-General Anton Petrovich **Passover** (13 Jun 1851 - ?)
23 May 1908 - 1910: Commander, 25th Infantry Regiment
1910: Promoted to *Major-General*
1910: Retired
1914 - 1915: Recalled; Commander, State Militia Brigade
1915 - 1916: Commander, 498th Infantry Regiment
1916: Dismissed

Major-General Aleksandr Nikolayevich **Pastukhov** (24 Aug 1840 - ?)
2 May 1882 - Jan 1901: Company Commander, Palace Grenadiers
2 Apr 1895: Promoted to *Major-General*

Major-General of the Fleet Yevgeny Alekseyevich **Pastukhov** (14 Aug 1863 - ?)
1911 - 13 Jun 1917: Deputy Chief of Mine Division, Main Directorate of Shipbuilding
6 Apr 1914: Promoted to *Major-General of the Fleet*
13 Jun 1917 - 1917: Chief of Mine Division, Main Directorate of Shipbuilding

Major-General Aleksandr Mikhailovich **Pasypkin** (18 Aug 1839 - 1903)
17 Sep 1896 - 1903: Deputy Commander of Engineers, Vilnius Military District
6 Feb 1897: Promoted to *Major-General*

Major-General Nikolai Aleksandrovich **Pataraki** (4 Aug 1863 - 13 Aug 1933)
2 Mar 1908 - 17 Jun 1910: Chief of Staff, III. Siberian Army Corps
13 Apr 1908: Promoted to *Major-General*
17 Jun 1910: Retired
1915 - 1916: Recalled; Commander, State Militia Brigade
1916 - 18 Sep 1916: Commander, 21st State Militia Brigade

18 Sep 1916 - 1917: Commander, 114th State Militia Brigade

Major-General Mikhail Grigoryevich **Patsevich** (28 Sep 1865 - 13 Feb 1916)
8 Sep 1913 - 13 Feb 1916: Commander, 39th Infantry Regiment
1916: Posthumously promoted to *Major-General*

Major-General Nikolai Petrovich **Patsevich** (5 Apr 1849 - ?)
3 Nov 1903 - 1907: Chief of Gendarmerie, Grodno
28 Mar 1904: Promoted to *Major-General*

Rear-Admiral Pyotr Ivanovich **Patton-Fanton de Verrayon** (24 Apr 1866 - 7 Sep 1941)
13 Jan 1914 - ?: Deputy Commander, Training Detachment, Black Sea Fleet
6 Dec 1915: Promoted to *Rear-Admiral*
? - 13 Apr 1917: Chief of Navigation, Defense Vessels, Northwestern Black Sea
13 Apr 1917 - Oct 1917: Reserve officer, Black Sea Fleet

Lieutenant-General of the Admiralty Yakov Ivanovich **Pavlinov** (2 Oct 1849 - ?)
9 Apr 1900: Promoted to *Major-General of the Admiralty*
10 Jul 1906 - 29 Oct 1909: Member, Volunteer Fleet Committee
22 Apr 1907: Promoted to *Lieutenant-General of the Admiralty*
29 Oct 1909 - Mar 1913: Member, Supreme Naval Tribunal

Major-General Pavel Nikolayevich **Pavlishchev** (11 Jul 1870 - ?)
25 Mar 1916 - 1917: Commander, 1st Brigade, 2nd Cavalry Division
21 Dec 1916: Promoted to *Major-General*

Lieutenant-General Aleksandr Aleksandrovich **Pavlov** (7 Oct 1856 - ?)
14 Feb 1904 - 6 Aug 1908: Commandant, Military Electrotechnical School
6 Dec 1904: Promoted to *Major-General*
6 Aug 1908 - 15 Oct 1912: Chief of Electrotechnical Section, Chief Engineer's Office
6 Dec 1910: Promoted to *Lieutenant-General*
15 Oct 1912: Retired

Lieutenant-General Aleksandr Aleksandrovich **Pavlov** (11 Jul 1867 - 7 Dec 1935)
4 Sep 1907: Promoted to *Major-General*
4 Sep 1907 - 10 Mar 1910: Commander, Life Guards Uhlan Regiment
10 Mar 1910 - 24 Sep 1914: General à la suite
24 Sep 1914: Promoted to *Lieutenant-General*
24 Sep 1914 - 10 Sep 1915: Commander, 2nd Consolidated Cossack Division
10 Sep 1915 - 17 Nov 1915: At the disposal of the C-in-C, Northern Front
17 Nov 1915 - 25 Apr 1917: Commanding General, VI. Cavalry Corps
25 Apr 1917 - 7 Jun 1917: Commanding General, 1st Caucasus Cavalry Corps
7 Jun 1917 - 20 Sep 1917: At the disposal of the Supreme Commander-in-Chief
20 Sep 1917 - Oct 1917: Reserve officer, Kiev Military District

Lieutenant-General Aleksandr Fyodorovich **Pavlov** (21 Aug 1851 - ?)
12 Feb 1909 - 22 Oct 1912:	Engineer Inspector, Omsk Military District
29 Mar 1909:	Promoted to *Major-General*
22 Oct 1913 - 31 Dec 1913:	Chief of Troop Billeting, Omsk Military District
31 Dec 1913:	Promoted to *Lieutenant-General*
31 Dec 1913:	Retired

Major-General Aleksandr Nikolayevich **Pavlov** (14 Jan 1856 - ?)
1 Jan 1893 - 5 Jul 1905:	Section Chief, Main Artillery Directorate
5 Oct 1904:	Promoted to *Major-General*
5 Jul 1905 - Jul 1907:	Deputy Commander of Artillery, St. Petersburg Military District
Jul 1907:	Retired

Major-General Aleksandr Prokofyevich **Pavlov** (21 Jul 1862 - ?)
5 Jan 1908 - 1914:	Attached to the Ministry of Internal Affairs
6 Dec 1910:	Promoted to *Major-General*
1914 - 19 May 1915:	Reserve officer, Dvinsk Military District
19 May 1915 - 1917:	Chairman of the Evacuation Commission, Southwestern Front

Major-General Aleksey Fyodorovich **Pavlov** (26 Oct 1852 - ?)
16 Sep 1897 - 27 Feb 1906:	Military Judge, Warsaw Military District Court
1 Jan 1901:	Promoted to *Major-General*
27 Feb 1906 - 1906:	Military Judge, Moscow Military District Court

Lieutenant-General Andrey Pavlovich **Pavlov** (22 Jul 1855 - ?)
8 May 1906 - 5 Jun 1914:	General for Special Assignments, Caucasus Military District
30 Jun 1906:	Promoted to *Major-General*
5 Jun 1914:	Promoted to *Lieutenant-General*
5 Jun 1914:	Retired

Lieutenant-General Dmitry Petrovich **Pavlov** (20 Sep 1861 - ?)
22 Nov 1911:	Promoted to *Major-General*
22 Nov 1911 - 5 Jul 1915:	Commander, 2nd Brigade, 12th Infantry Division
5 Jul 1915 - 1917:	Commander, 49th Infantry Division
10 Apr 1916:	Promoted to *Lieutenant-General*

Major-General Georgy Aleksandrovich **Pavlov** (7 Apr 1850 - 22 Mar 1929)
5 Nov 1904:	Promoted to *Major-General*
5 Nov 1904 - 8 Aug 1906:	Commander, Ussuri Mounted Brigade
8 Aug 1906 - 1906:	Commander, Urals-Trans-Baikal Division
1906:	Retired
28 Mar 1915 - 28 Dec 1915:	Recalled; Chief of Staff, Don Cossack Foot Brigade
28 Dec 1915:	Retired

Major-General Iosif Vladimirovich **Pavlov** (9 Sep 1866 - ?)
14 May 1913: Promoted to *Major-General*
14 May 1913 - 12 Oct 1915: Commandant of Krasnoselsky
12 Oct 1915 - 1917: Chief of Evacuation Section, Military Medical Department, Petrograd Military District

Major-General of Naval Engineers Ivan Pavlovich **Pavlov** (8 Oct 1852 - ?)
1893 - 8 Sep 1908: Deputy Chief, Baltic Factory
6 Dec 1907: Promoted to *Major-General of Naval Engineers*
8 Sep 1908 - Mar 1913: Member of the Board, Baltic Factory

General of Infantry Ivan Petrovich **Pavlov** (18 Dec 1830 - 24 Sep 1909)
6 Feb 1868 - 25 Oct 1870: Intendant, Riga Military District
17 Apr 1870: Promoted to *Major-General*
25 Oct 1870 - 23 Jun 1873: Unassigned
23 Jun 1873 - 30 Aug 1875: Intendant, Kharkov Military District
30 Aug 1875 - 18 Mar 1885: Intendant, Warsaw Military District
1 Jan 1880: Promoted to *Lieutenant-General*
18 Mar 1885 - 15 Feb 1888: Transferred to the reserve
15 Feb 1888 - 14 May 1896: Deputy Intendant-General of the Army
14 May 1896: Promoted to *General of Infantry*
14 May 1896 - 24 Sep 1909: At the disposal of the Minister of War

Major-General Mikhail Andreyevich **Pavlov** (6 Sep 1852 - 2 Oct 1915)
30 Dec 1900 - 2 Oct 1915: Deputy Chief of Staff of Horse Breeding Establishments, Don Army
31 May 1907: Promoted to *Major-General*

Lieutenant-General Mikhail Ivanovich **Pavlov** (17 Sep 1848 - ?)
7 Feb 1900 - 9 Nov 1913: Commandant, Technical Artillery School
1 Apr 1901: Promoted to *Major-General*
9 Nov 1913 - 31 May 1917: Chief of the Artillery Department, Military Technical College
6 Dec 1913: Promoted to *Lieutenant-General*
31 May 1917: Dismissed

Major-General Nikifor Damianovich **Pavlov** (4 Feb 1867 - 19 Jun 1929)
18 Dec 1908 - 1918: Chief of Topographical Section, Omsk Military District
14 Apr 1913: Promoted to *Major-General*

General of Infantry Platon Petrovich **Pavlov** (26 Aug 1834 - 22 Nov 1904)
14 Apr 1868 - 11 Nov 1870: Deputy Chief of Staff, Caucasus Military District
11 Nov 1870: Promoted to *Major-General*
11 Nov 1870 - 28 Oct 1872: Chief of Caucasus Mountains Administration
28 Oct 1872 - 17 Apr 1875: Deputy Commander, Terek Region
17 Apr 1875 - 15 Nov 1882: Chief of Staff, Caucasus Military District
8 Nov 1878: Promoted to *Lieutenant-General*
15 Nov 1882 - 4 Nov 1883: Reserve officer, General Staff

4 Nov 1883 - 9 Apr 1889:	Commanding General, VI. Army Corps
9 Apr 1891 - 17 Jun 1891:	Commanding General, VII. Army Corps
17 Jun 1891 - 19 Oct 1894:	Deputy Commanding General, Warsaw Military District
30 Aug 1891:	Promoted to *General of Infantry*
19 Oct 1894 - 22 Nov 1904:	Member of the Military Council

Lieutenant-General Vladimir Petrovich **Pavlov** (31 Aug 1851 - 27 Dec 1906)

10 Dec 1888 - 9 Sep 1894:	MilitaryJudge, St. Petersburg Military District Court
30 Aug 1893:	Promoted to *Major-General*
9 Sep 1894 - 14 Aug 1905:	Military Prosecutor, St. Petersburg Military District
6 Apr 1903:	Promoted to *Lieutenant-General*
14 Aug 1905 - 27 Dec 1906:	Chief Military Prosecutor, Chief of the Main Military Justice Directorate

Major-General Gerasim Semonovich **Pavlovsky** (1 Mar 1850 - ?)

20 Feb 1904 - 1910:	Intendant, Fortress Kaunas
6 Dec 1909:	Promoted to *Major-General*
1910:	Retired

Major-General of the Fleet Iosif Dmitriyevich **Pavlovsky** (1 Apr 1858 - 1920)

16 Oct 1906 - 1917:	Senior Deputy Captain, Port of Sevastopol
14 Apr 1913:	Promoted to *Major-General of the Fleet*

Lieutenant-General Mikhail Yemelyanovich **Pavlovsky** (8 Nov 1856 - 4 Apr 1916)

16 May 1895 - 4 Apr 1916:	Chief of the St. Petersburg Gun Factory
6 Dec 1906:	Promoted to *Major-General*
14 Apr 1913:	Promoted to *Lieutenant-General*

General of Infantry Nikolai Akimovich **Pavlovsky** (15 Feb 1845 - 17 Dec 1927)

24 Nov 1894 - 21 May 1898:	Commander, Life Guards 4th Rifle Battalion
6 Dec 1895:	Promoted to *Major-General*
21 May 1898 - 27 Aug 1900:	Commander, Life Guards Izmailovo Regiment
27 Aug 1900 - 26 Mar 1903:	Commander, 2nd Brigade, 1st Guards Infantry Division
26 Mar 1903 - 19 May 1906:	Commander, 1st Grenadier Division
6 Apr 1903:	Promoted to *Lieutenant-General*
19 May 1906:	Promoted to *General of Infantry*
19 May 1906:	Retired

Major-General Nikolai Grigoryevich **Pavlovsky** (9 Nov 1865 - ?)

6 Dec 1914:	Promoted to *Major-General*
6 Dec 1914 - 1917:	Official, Inspectorate of Gunpowder & Ammunition Depots

Lieutenant-General Ivan Vladimirovich **Pavsky** (31 Aug 1870 - 4 Dec 1948)

6 Dec 1905 - 25 Sep 1912:	Chief of Military Communications Section, General Staff Directorate
6 Dec 1911:	Promoted to *Major-General*
25 Sep 1912 - 30 Nov 1912:	Chief of Communications, Amur Military District

30 Nov 1912 - 14 Jun 1914:	Chief of Communications, Odessa Military District
14 Jun 1914 - 19 Jul 1914:	Deputy Chief of Communications Section, General Staff
19 Jul 1914 - 8 Oct 1916:	Chief of Communications, Southwestern Front
8 Oct 1916 - 28 Sep 1917:	Deputy Chief of Supplies, Southwestern Front
2 Apr 1917:	Promoted to *Lieutenant-General*
28 Sep 1917 - Nov 1917:	Reserve officer, Odessa Military District

Major-General of the Fleet Yevgeny Andreyevich **Pchelnikov** (? - ?)

?:	Promoted to *Major-General of the Fleet*

Major-General Vasily Mikhailovich **Pechenkin** (22 Mar 1863 - 5 Jun 1920)

4 Dec 1914 - 5 Jun 1916:	Commander, 1st Orenburg Cossack Regiment
2 Apr 1916 - 15 May 1916:	Acting Commander, 2nd Brigade, 10th Cavalry Division
5 Jun 1916 - 12 Oct 1916:	Medical leave
12 Oct 1916 - 21 Mar 1917:	Reserve officer, Kiev Military District
23 Jan 1917:	Promoted to *Major-General*
21 Mar 1917 - 23 Apr 1917:	Commander, 1st Brigade, 2nd Orenburg Cossack Division
23 Apr 1917 - 17 May 1917:	Commander, 2nd Orenburg Cossack Division

Major-General Mikhail Antonovich **Pechkovsky** (23 Feb 1865 - 7 Apr 1918)

15 Jul 1910 - 14 Mar 1916:	Commander, 1st Siberian Railway Battalion
6 Dec 1915:	Promoted to *Major-General*
14 Mar 1916 - 1917:	Commander, 2nd Railway Brigade

Lieutenant-General Anton Filippovich **Pedin** (12 Feb 1836 - ?)

3 Aug 1891:	Promoted to *Major-General*
3 Aug 1891 - Dec 1899:	Commander, 2nd Brigade, 1st Caucasus Cossack Division
Dec 1899:	Promoted to *Lieutenant-General*
Dec 1899:	Retired

Lieutenant-General Ivan Karlovich **Peltser** (19 Apr 1850 - ?)

7 Feb 1901:	Promoted to *Major-General*
7 Feb 1901 - 6 Nov 1902:	Commander, 1st Brigade, 17th Infantry Division
6 Nov 1902 - 2 Sep 1904:	Commander, 2nd Brigade, 18th Infantry Division
16 Aug 1906 - 7 Nov 1907:	Commander, 25th Infantry Division
22 Apr 1907:	Promoted to *Lieutenant-General*

Lieutenant-General Lev Konstantinovich **Pengo** (18 Feb 1844 - ?)

2 Sep 1905 - 4 Jun 1910:	Deputy Commander of Engineers, Vilnius Military District
6 Dec 1905:	Promoted to *Major-General*
4 Jun 1910:	Promoted to *Lieutenant-General*
4 Jun 1910:	Retired

Lieutenant-General Vasily Konstantinovich **Penkin** (17 Dec 1858 - ?)

28 Jan 1906 - 13 Sep 1906:	Military Judge, Warsaw Military District Court

2 Apr 1906:	Promoted to *Major-General*
13 Sep 1906 - 9 Mar 1912:	Military Judge, Caucasus Military District Court
9 Mar 1912 - 22 Apr 1917:	Military Judge, Kiev Military District Court
22 Apr 1917:	Promoted to *Lieutenant-General*
22 Apr 1917:	Retired

Lieutenant-General Vladimir Vasilyevich **Pensky** (6 Jan 1844 - ?)
9 Dec 1890:	Promoted to *Major-General*
9 Dec 1890 - 2 Sep 1899:	Commander, Life Guards Semyonov Regiment
2 Sep 1899 - 17 Feb 1900:	Commander, 1st Brigade, 1st Guards Infantry Division
17 Feb 1900:	Promoted to *Lieutenant-General*
17 Feb 1900 - 12 Sep 1904:	Commander, 1st Infantry Division
12 Sep 1904 - Sep 1905:	At the disposal of the Commanding General, Moscow Military District

Major-General Aleksey Gavrilovich **Pentyukhov** (17 Mar 1836 - ?)
23 Mar 1889:	Promoted to *Major-General*
23 Mar 1889 - 23 Mar 1894:	Commander, 2nd Brigade, 2nd Consolidated Cossack Division
23 Mar 1894 - 1901:	Attached to the Kuban Cossack Army

Major-General Ali-Bek **Penzulayev** (20 Feb 1823 - ?)
15 Sep 1859 - 1910:	Attached to the Caucasus Military District
15 May 1883:	Promoted to *Major-General*

Lieutenant-General Nikolai Mikhailovich **Pepelyayev** (6 May 1858 - 21 Nov 1916)
18 Oct 1911:	Promoted to *Major-General*
18 Oct 1911 - 11 May 1915:	Commander, 2nd Brigade, 8th Siberian Rifle Division
11 May 1915 - 25 Aug 1916:	Reserve officer, Dvinsk Military District
25 Aug 1916:	Promoted to *Lieutenant-General*
25 Aug 1916:	Retired

Major-General Konstantin Ivanovich **Perdzinsky** (12 May 1862 - ?)
19 Nov 1914 - 1917:	Commander, 11th Sapper Battalion
30 Jul 1916:	Promoted to *Major-General*

Major-General Viktor Aleksandrovich **Perebaskin** (19 Jan 1847 - ?)
24 Oct 1899:	Promoted to *Major-General*
24 Oct 1899 - Jul 1906:	Commander, 2nd Brigade, 12th Infantry Division

General of Infantry Andrey Aleksandrovich **Perekrestov** (30 Nov 1851 - ?)
20 Sep 1901:	Promoted to *Major-General*
20 Sep 1901 - 10 Jun 1908:	Chief of Staff, IX. Army Corps
10 Jun 1908:	Promoted to *Lieutenant-General*
10 Jun 1908 - 31 Dec 1913:	Commander, 5th Infantry Division
31 Dec 1913:	Promoted to *General of Infantry*
31 Dec 1913:	Retired
3 Feb 1915 - Oct 1917:	Recalled; Reserve officer, Kiev Military District

Lieutenant-General Sergey Vasilyevich **Perekrestov** (12 May 1863 - ?)
5 May 1905 - 31 Dec 1913:	Section Chief, Main Artillery Directorate
6 Dec 1908:	Promoted to *Major-General*
31 Dec 1913 - 28 Mar 1915:	Deputy Commander of Artillery, Warsaw Military District
28 Mar 1915 - 27 Nov 1916:	Chief of the Artillery Directorate, Minsk Military District
27 Nov 1916 - 1917:	Deputy Chief of Artillery Logistics, Western Front
6 Dec 1916:	Promoted to *Lieutenant-General*

Admiral Pavel Aleksandrovich **Pereleshin** (27 Jun 1821 - 28 Feb 1901)
May 1861 - 1864:	Captain, Port of Baku
Aug 1863:	Promoted to *Rear-Admiral*
1864 - 11 Apr 1866:	Mayor of Taganrog
11 Apr 1866 - 8 Apr 1873:	Chief of Navigation, Azov Sea
1 Jan 1872:	Promoted to *General-Adjutant*
8 Apr 1873:	Promoted to *Vice-Admiral*
13 Aug 1873 - 1881:	Governor of Sevastopol
1881 - 1883:	Director of the Inspection Department, Ministry of the Navy
1883 - 28 Feb 1901:	Member of the Admiralty Board
21 Apr 1891:	Promoted to *Admiral*

Lieutenant-General of the Fleet Vladimir Platonovich **Pereleshin** (? - 27 May 1908)
?:	Promoted to *Major-General of the Fleet*
?:	Promoted to *Lieutenant-General of the Fleet*
1904:	Head of Odessa Commercial Port

Major-General Kirill Ivanovich **Perepechin** (29 Mar 1852 - 20 Sep 1918)
25 Aug 1905:	Promoted to *Major-General*
25 Aug 1905 - 1 Nov 1907:	Commander, 1st Brigade, 8th East Siberian Rifle Division
1 Nov 1907 - Aug 1908:	Commander, 1st Brigade, 2nd East Siberian Rifle Division
Aug 1908:	Retired

Major-General of the Admiralty Yakov Nikolayevich **Perepelkin** (25 Feb 1874 - 16 Jun 1935)
31 Dec 1907 - 5 Apr 1910:	Deputy Chief of Obukhov Steelworks
5 Apr 1910:	Retired
1916:	Promoted to *Major-General of the Admiralty (Retired)*

Lieutenant-General Vasily Grigoriyevich **Perepelovsky** (18 Feb 1818 - 1908)
10 Dec 1870 - 28 Nov 1881:	Ataman, Ekaterinodar Section, Kuban Cossack Army
1871:	Promoted to *Major-General*
28 Nov 1881 - 1908:	Attached to the Kuban Cossack Army
6 Oct 1888:	Promoted to *Lieutenant-General*

Major-General Nikolai Mikhailovich **Pereverzev** (2 May 1866 - ?)
31 Jul 1909 - 26 Apr 1915:	Commander, 1st Detachment, Amur District Borderguard Corps
6 Dec 1910:	Promoted to *Major-General*
26 Apr 1915 - 1917:	Commander, 2nd Detachment, Amur District Borderguard Corps

Major-General Mikhail Pavlovich **Perevoshchikov** (26 Jul 1866 - 9 Mar 1929)
12 Jan 1914 - 26 Jul 1915:	Commander, 2nd Hussar Regiment
26 Jul 1915:	Promoted to *Major-General*
26 Jul 1915 - 14 Apr 1917:	Commander, 1st Brigade, 14th Cavalry Division
14 Apr 1917 - 18 May 1917:	Reserve officer, Dvinsk Military District
18 May 1917:	Dismissed

Major-General Pyotr Andreyevich **Pereyaslavtsev** (26 Jul 1855 - 18 Feb 1915)
19 Jun 1897 - 6 Dec 1914:	Chief of Police, Imperial Moscow Theaters
6 Dec 1914:	Promoted to *Major-General*
6 Dec 1914 - 18 Feb 1915:	Attached to the Ministry of the Imperial Court

Major-General Mikhail Apollonovich **Perfilyev** (23 Oct 1866 - ?)
28 Oct 1907 - 16 Mar 1914:	Commander, 1st Regiment, Trans-Baikal Cossack Army
16 Mar 1914:	Promoted to *Major-General*
16 Mar 1914 - 2 Aug 1914:	Commander, 2nd Brigade, 1st Turkestan Cossack Division
2 Aug 1914 - 14 Nov 1915:	Commander, 1st Brigade, Orenburg Cossack Division
14 Nov 1915 - 16 Apr 1916:	Reserve officer, Kiev Military District
16 Apr 1916 - 28 May 1917:	Special Purposes General, Irkutsk Military District
28 May 1917:	Dismissed

Lieutenant-General Sergey Apollonovich **Perfilyev** (27 Jul 1853 - 19 Oct 1918)
16 Jan 1909:	Promoted to *Major-General*
16 Jan 1909 - 25 Jul 1910:	Commander, 34th Artillery Brigade
25 Jul 1910 - 23 Sep 1912:	Commander, 15th Artillery Brigade
23 Sep 1912 - 27 Jul 1913:	Commander, 6th Artillery Brigade
27 Jul 1913:	Promoted to *Lieutenant-General*
27 Jul 1913:	Retired
12 Jan 1916:	Recalled to duty with the rank of *Major-General*
12 Jan 1916 - 18 Apr 1917:	Inspector of Artillery, XLIII. Army Corps
4 Apr 1917:	Promoted to *Lieutenant-General*
18 Apr 1917 - 28 May 1917:	Reserve officer, Dvinsk Military District
28 May 1917:	Dismissed

Lieutenant-General Dmitry Ivanovich **Perlik** (8 Feb 1853 - ?)
25 Apr 1901:	Promoted to *Major-General*
25 Apr 1901 - 19 Mar 1903:	Chief of Staff, XI. Army Corps
19 Mar 1903 - 20 Aug 1905:	Commander, 1st Brigade, 40th Infantry Division
20 Aug 1905 - 26 Jun 1906:	Commander, East Siberian Reserve Brigade
26 Jun 1906 - 1911:	Commander, 57th Replacement Infantry Brigade

3 Oct 1909: Promoted to *Lieutenant-General*

General of Infantry Pyotr Timofeyevich **Perlik** (22 Feb 1836 - 12 Sep 1914)
12 Dec 1874 - 12 May 1878: Commander, 82nd Infantry Regiment
2 Nov 1877: Promoted to *Major-General*
12 May 1878 - 20 Apr 1881: Commander, 2nd Brigade, 40th Infantry Division
20 Apr 1881 - 13 Apr 1883: Commander, 2nd Brigade, 21st Infantry Division
13 Apr 1883 - 3 May 1887: Chief of Staff, II. Caucasus Army Corps
2 May 1887 - 6 Oct 1889: Chief of Staff, Kazan Military District
30 Aug 1887: Promoted to *Lieutenant-General*
6 Oct 1889 - 29 Apr 1896: Chief of Staff, Caucasus Military District
29 Apr 1896 - 16 Mar 1898: Commanding General, IV. Army Corps
16 Mar 1898 - 6 Dec 1901: Deputy Commanding General, Vilnius Military District
6 Dec 1899: Promoted to *General of Infantry*
6 Dec 1901 - Sep 1905: Member, Committee for Wounded Veterans

Major-General Aleksandr Aleksandrovich **Perren** (9 Dec 1844 - ?)
23 Dec 1889 - 11 Sep 1899: Commander of Gendarmerie, Ryazan Province
13 Apr 1897: Promoted to *Major-General*
11 Sep 1899 - 1901: Staff officer, Corps of Gendarmerie

Major-General Yevgeny Vasilyevich **Perret** (17 Jul 1876 - 19 Jul 1940)
25 Mar 1916 - 8 Oct 1916: Commander, 2nd Battalion, Life Guards Rifle Artillery Brigade
1916: Promoted to *Major-General*
8 Oct 1916 - 1917: Commander, 4th Finnish Rifle Artillery Brigade
1917: Inspector of Artillery, I. Guards Corps

Major-General Ivan Ivanovich **Pertsev** (15 Sep 1856 - ?)
16 Feb 1916 - 1917: Commander, 167th Infantry Regiment
27 Dec 1916: Promoted to *Major-General*

Major-General Sergey Nikolayevich **Pertsov** (4 Mar 1867 - ?)
3 Nov 1914 - 1917: Special Assignments General, Petrograd Military District
6 Dec 1915: Promoted to *Major-General*

Major-General Mikhail Grigoryevich **Pervushin** (22 May 1860 - ?)
8 Jul 1911 - 17 Aug 1914: Commander, 1st Infantry Regiment
17 Aug 1914 - 1916: POW
6 Apr 1916 - 22 Mar 1917: Reserve officer, Petrograd Military District
6 May 1916: Promoted to *Major-General*
22 Mar 1917: Dismissed

Major-General Fridrikh Adolfovich **Perzeke** (14 May 1863 - ?)
28 Feb 1908 - 28 Mar 1913: Military Judge, Amur Military District Court
6 Dec 1908: Promoted to *Major-General*
28 Mar 1913 - Jul 1914: Military Judge, Vilnius Military District Court

Jul 1914 - 1917:	Military Judge, Dvinsk Military District Court

Lieutenant-General Avgustin Ottonovich **Perzhkhaylo** (28 Aug 1864 - ?)
1914 - 26 Feb 1915:	Deputy Commander, 2nd Finnish Rifle Regiment
6 Dec 1914:	Promoted to *Major-General*
26 Feb 1915- 3 Apr 1916:	Commander, 10th Finnish Rifle Regiment
3 Apr 1916 - 15 Aug 1916:	Reserve officer, Kiev Military District
15 Aug 1916 - 1917:	Commander, Brigade, 41st Infantry Division
1917 - 15 Apr 1917:	Commander, 35th Replacement Infantry Brigade
15 Apr 1917 - 25 Aug 1917:	Commander, 2nd Amur Borderguard Infantry Division
25 Aug 1917:	Promoted to *Lieutenant-General*
25 Aug 1917 - ?:	Commanding General, VII. Army Corps

Lieutenant-General Georgy Ivanovich **Peshchansky** (4 Jun 1851 - Mar 1913)
31 May 1898:	Promoted to *Major-General*
31 May 1898 - 2 Apr 1899:	Deputy Chief of Staff, Caucasus Military District
6 Mar 1899 - 14 May 1899:	Acting Chief of Staff, Caucasus Military District
2 Apr 1899 - 6 Mar 1900:	General Staff officer, Caucasus Military District
6 Mar 1900 - 2 Sep 1904:	Commander, 62nd Replacement Infantry Brigade
2 Sep 1904 - 6 Feb 1907:	Commander, 2nd Infantry Division
6 Dec 1904:	Promoted to *Lieutenant-General*
6 Feb 1907:	Retired

Major-General of the Hydrographic Corps Eduard Osipovich **Peshkansky** (1 Mar 1862 - 12 Dec 1916)
28 Feb 1911 - 12 Dec 1912:	Chief of Hydrographic Survey, Murmansk Coast
30 Jul 1916:	Promoted to *Major-General of the Hydrographic Corps*

Major-General Fyodor Nikolayevich **Peshkov** (14 Nov 1859 - 1910)
3 Jun 1906 - 1910:	Head of the Tsarskoye Selo Palace Administration
6 Dec 1906:	Promoted to *Major-General*

Lieutenant-General Nikolai Nikolayevich **Peshkov** (4 Apr 1857 - ?)
17 Jun 1899 - 19 Oct 1902:	Attached to the Chief of the General Staff
9 Apr 1900:	Promoted to *Major-General*
19 Oct 1902 - 5 Apr 1904:	Chief of Staff, VII. Army Corps
5 Apr 1904 - 3 Jan 1906:	Chief of Staff, II. Cavalry Corps
3 Jan 1906 - 6 Oct 1908:	Governor of Kharkov
6 Dec 1906:	Promoted to *Lieutenant-General*
6 Oct 1908:	Retired
20 Mar 1916 - 20 Aug 1916:	Recalled; Reserve officer, Caucasus Military District
20 Aug 1916 - 8 Feb 1917:	Military Governor of Occupied Territories, Turkey
8 Feb 1917 - 31 May 1917:	Reserve Officer, Petrograd Military District
31 May 1917:	Retired

Lieutenant-General Sergey Vasilyevich **Peskov** (19 Mar 1838 - 1909)
9 Oct 1889 - 1900:	Chief of Odessa Military Hospital
25 May 1892:	Promoted to *Major-General*

1900: Promoted to *Lieutenant-General*
1900: Retired

Major-General Yevgeny Filimonovich **Pestich** (13 Feb 1866 - 5 Sep 1919)
11 Jul 1910: Promoted to *Major-General*
11 Jul 1910 - 17 Aug 1914: Chief of Staff, XIII. Army Corps
17 Aug 1914 - 1918: POW, Germany

Major-General Nikolai Sergeyevich **Pestrikov** (11 May 1867 - 6 Jan 1934)
14 Aug 1910 - 1917: Inspector of Classes, Vladimir Military School
6 Dec 1913: Promoted to *Major-General*

Major-General Mikhail Ilariyevich **Pestrzhetsky** (10 May 1869 - 20 Dec 1941)
17 May 1911 - 10 Nov 1914: Commander, 12th Grenadier Regiment
1914: Acting Commander, 2nd Brigade, 3rd Grenadier Division
10 Nov 1914 - 6 Sep 1915: Commander, Brigade, 37th Infantry Division
3 Mar 1915: Promoted to *Major-General*
6 Sep 1915 - 20 Mar 1917: Duty General, 11th Army
20 Mar 1917 - 28 Apr 1917: Chief of Staff, XVII. Army Corps
28 Apr 1917 - 2 Jun 1917: Commander, 157th Infantry Division

Major-General Yuly Gustavovich **Petander** (9 Jan 1835 - ?)
16 Dec 1878 - 1899: Deputy Military Governor of Kars Province
30 Aug 1885: Promoted to *Major-General*

General of Infantry Ernest-Yakov Kasparovich **Peterov** (19 Nov 1851 - ?)
2 Sep 1899 - 26 May 1904: Commander, 15th Grenadier Regiment
1 Jun 1904: Promoted to *Major-General*
1 Jun 1904 - 28 Jul 1906: Commander, 1st Brigade, 54th Infantry Division
28 Jul 1906 - 7 Mar 1908: Commander, 2nd Brigade, 39th Infantry Division
7 Mar 1908 - 15 Jul 1910: Commander, 64th Reserve Infantry Brigade
15 Jul 1910 - 16 Nov 1911: Commander, 2nd Turkestan Rifle Brigade
16 Nov 1911: Promoted to *Lieutenant-General*
16 Nov 1911 - 31 Dec 1913: Commander, 52nd Infantry Division
31 Dec 1913: Promoted to *General of Infantry*
31 Dec 1913: Retired

Major-General Konstantin-Gugo Kasparovich **Peterov** (7 Jan 1854 - ?)
25 Mar 1905: Promoted to *Major-General*
25 Mar 1905 - 28 Feb 1907: Commander, Brigade, 69th Infantry Division
28 Feb 1907 - 12 Nov 1907: Commander, 2nd Brigade, 32nd Infantry Division

Lieutenant-General Aleksandr Fyodorovich von **Peters** (23 Feb 1836 - 7 Jun 1895)
13 Oct 1877: Promoted to *Major-General*
13 Oct 1877 - 8 Nov 1881: Member of the Tsar's retinue
8 Nov 1881 - 13 Aug 1883: Trustee to Grand Duke Mikhail Mikhailovich
13 Aug 1883 - 8 Dec 1885: Member of the Tsar's retinue
8 Dec 1885 - 9 Oct 1890: Conference Member, Mikhailovsky Artillery Academy

30 Aug 1890: Promoted to *Lieutenant-General*
9 Oct 1890 - 7 Jun 1895: Senator

Major-General Garri Karlovich **Peters** (31 Oct 1859 - 28 Apr 1915)
19 Oct 1910 - 28 Apr 1915: Commander, 1st Infantry Regiment, Amur Borderguard District
12 Jun 1916: Posthumously promoted to *Major-General*

Major-General Vladimir Nikolayevich **Peters** (11 Aug 1864 - 8 Jan 1938)
14 Aug 1910 - 29 Jul 1914: Commander, Yelizavetgrad Cavalry School
1 Sep 1910: Promoted to *Major-General*
29 Jul 1914 - 13 May 1915: Commander, 1st Brigade, 5th Cavalry Division
13 May 1915 - 4 Feb 1916: Commander, 14th Cavalry Division
4 Feb 1916 - 9 Jul 1916: Reserve officer, Minsk Military District
9 Jul 1916 - 20 Jul 1916: Reserve officer, Petrograd Military District
20 Jul 1916 - 7 Aug 1917: Commandant of the Imperial Military Academy
7 Aug 1917 - 1918: Reserve officer, Petrograd Military District

Major-General Yevgeny Konstantinovich **Petersen** (17 Nov 1860 - ?)
14 Sep 1910 - 11 Apr 1916: Chief of Subsection 3, Duty Section, General Staff
10 Apr 1911: Promoted to *Major-General*
11 Apr 1916 - Oct 1917: Deputy Duty General, General Staff

Major-General Stepan Ivanovich **Petin** (5 Oct 1861 - ?)
11 Mar 1912 - 22 Jun 1917: Attached to the Kuban Cossack Army
2 Sep 1915: Promoted to *Major-General*
22 Jun 1917: Retired

General of Artillery Aleksandr Nikolayevich **Petrakov** (23 Aug 1844 - ?)
23 Dec 1898: Promoted to *Major-General*
23 Dec 1898 - 22 Jun 1902: Commander, 28th Artillery Brigade
22 Jun 1902 - 1910: Commander of Artillery, Turkestan Military District
17 Apr 1905: Promoted to *Lieutenant-General*
1910: Promoted to *General of Artillery*
1910: Retired

Lieutenant-General Nikolai Georgiyevich **Petrakov** (19 Dec 1833 - 9 Jun 1903)
15 Jul 1891: Promoted to *Major-General*
15 Jul 1891 - Dec 1899: Commander, 36th Artillery Brigade
Dec 1899: Promoted to *Lieutenant-General*
Dec 1899: Retired

Major-General Mikhail Ivanovich **Petrandi** (2 Sep 1864 - ?)
7 Sep 1913 - 30 Jun 1916: Deputy Chief of Lugansk Cartridge Factory
6 Dec 1913: Promoted to *Major-General*
30 Jun 1916 - 1917: Chief of Lugansk Cartridge Factory

Major-General Aleksandr Konstantinovich **Petrashkevich** (6 Oct 1851 - ?)
5 Jan 1890 - 4 Jul 1902: Military Judge, Caucasus Military District Court
6 Dec 1898: Promoted to *Major-General*
4 Jul 1902 - 1905: Military Judge, Amur Military District Court

Major-General Aleksandr Yevstafyevich **Petrenko** (13 Aug 1870 - ?)
7 May 1913 - 10 Oct 1916: Commander, 1st Caucasus Mortar Artillery Battalion
16 Jul 1916: Promoted to *Major-General*
10 Oct 1916 - 1917: Commander, 2nd Caucasus Rifle Artillery Brigade

Major-General Ivan Vladimirovich **Petrichenko** (28 Mar 1854 - 25 Jun 1916)
28 Aug 1905 - 19 May 1906: Commander, 10th East Siberian Rifle Artillery Brigade
19 May 1906 - 14 Mar 1907: Unassigned
14 Mar 1907 - 1 Aug 1909: Commander, 1st Reserve Artillery Brigade
31 May 1907: Promoted to *Major-General*
1 Aug 1909 - 7 Oct 1911: Commander, 14th Artillery Brigade
7 Oct 1911: Retired

Major-General Nikolai Ivanovich **Petropavlovsky** (31 Mar 1853 - ?)
27 May 1897 - 1913: Staff Officer, Weapons Inspectorate, Caucasus Military District
1913: Retired
29 Aug 1915 - 1917: Recalled; Commander, 66th Park Artillery Brigade
1915: Promoted to *Major-General*

General of Infantry Aleksandr Karpovich **Petrov** (30 Aug 1856 - ?)
25 Nov 1899 - 29 Jan 1905: Commander, 107th Infantry Regiment
6 Dec 1904: Promoted to *Major-General*
29 Jan 1905 - 20 Aug 1909: Commandant of Fortress Zegrze
20 Aug 1909 - 9 Mar 1917: Commandant of Fortress Vyborg
30 Jun 1910: Promoted to *Lieutenant-General*
6 Dec 1916: Promoted to *General of Infantry*
2 Apr 1917 - 17 Dec 1917: Reserve officer, Petrograd Military District
17 Dec 1917: Retired

Lieutenant-General Aleksandr Konstantinovich **Petrov** (1 Sep 1854 - ?)
2 Nov 1899: Promoted to *Major-General*
2 Nov 1899 - 17 Feb 1904: Chief of Staff, III. Army Corps
17 Feb 1904 - 17 Sep 1905: Commander, 2nd Rifle Brigade
17 Sep 1905 - 10 Mar 1906: Attached to the Chief of the General Staff
10 Mar 1906 - 11 Jun 1910: Commander, 2nd Rifle Brigade
3 May 1910: Promoted to *Lieutenant-General*

Major-General of the Fleet Aleksandr Vasilyevich **Petrov** (10 Dec 1860 - 1918)
5 Sep 1911 - 8 May 1917: Commander, Rifle Training Units, Oranienbaum
14 Apr 1913: Promoted to *Major-General of the Fleet*
8 May 1917 - 22 Jul 1917: Reserve officer, Ministry of the Navy
22 Jul 1917: Dismissed

Major-General of Naval Engineers Aleksandr Viktorovich **Petrov** (7 Jun 1867 - ?)
19 Oct 1911 - 1917: Deputy Chief of Mechanical Department, Main Shipbuilding Directorate
6 Dec 1912: Promoted to *Major-General of Naval Engineers*

Lieutenant-General Andrey Nikolayevich **Petrov** (1837 - 9 Sep 1900)
30 Aug 1885: Promoted to *Major-General*
30 Aug 1885 - 9 Sep 1900: Member of the Military Education Committee, General Staff
6 Dec 1898: Promoted to *Lieutenant-General*

Major-General of Naval Engineers Andrey Pavlovich **Petrov** (16 Oct 1859 - ?)
5 Oct 1909: Promoted to *Major-General of Naval Engineers*
25 Apr 1911 - Mar 1913: Member of the Board, Obukhov Steelworks & Izhora Factory
Sep 1915 - 1917: Attached to 2nd Baltic Naval Depot

Vice-Admiral Dmitry Dmitriyevich **Petrov** (17 Sep 1857 - ?)
6 Dec 1909: Promoted to *Rear-Admiral*
1909 - 22 Aug 1911: Captain, Port of Sevastopol
22 Aug 1911 - Jul 1913: Commander of Training Units, Black Sea Fleet
23 Sep 1913: Promoted to *Vice-Admiral*

Major-General Dmitry Nikolayevich **Petrov** (11 Dec 1862 - 1941)
11 Feb 1909 - 1918: Chief of Warsaw Railway Gendarmerie
6 Dec 1915: Promoted to *Major-General*

Major-General Dormidont Fyodorovich **Petrov** (6 Sep 1842 - ?)
24 Oct 1894 - 1897: Duty General, Warsaw Military District
14 May 1896: Promoted to *Major-General*

Major-General Fyodor Vasilyevich **Petrov** (12 Feb 1866 - 15 Oct 1920)
17 Mar 1913 - Jul 1914: Military Judge, Vilnius Military District Court
14 Apr 1913: Promoted to *Major-General*
Jul 1914 - 1917: Military Judge, Dvinsk Military District Court

Major-General of Naval Engineers Ivan Martinianovich **Petrov** (7 Jan 1867 - ?)
1912 - 1917: Member, Baltic Sea Shipbuilding Commission
1915: Promoted to *Major-General of Naval Engineers*

Major-General Ivan Nikolayevich **Petrov** (1 Jan 1856 - 1 Dec 1916)
3 Aug 1909 - 12 Mar 1913: Chief of Vilnius Railway Gendarmerie
6 Dec 1912: Promoted to *Major-General*
12 Mar 1913 - 1 Dec 1916: Chief of Perm Railway Gendarmerie

Major-General Mikhail Ivanovich **Petrov** (25 Jun 1846 - ?)
30 Jan 1899 - 4 Jun 1901: Commander of Gendarmerie, St-Petersburg-Warsaw

	Railway
9 Apr 1900:	Promoted to *Major-General*
4 Jun 1901 - 1907:	Commander of Gendarmerie, Moscow-Kiev Railway

Major-General Mitrofan Petrovich **Petrov** (2 Jun 1847 - ?)
17 Feb 1900 - 5 Apr 1904:	Commander, 11th Artillery Brigade
1 Jan 1901:	Promoted to *Major-General*

General of Infantry Nikolai Ivanovich **Petrov** (20 Oct 1841 - 24 Dec 1905)
1 Jan 1880 - 1 Aug 1882:	Chief of Staff, Eastern Siberian Military District
1 Apr 1880:	Promoted to *Major-General*
1 Aug 1882 - 7 Sep 1883:	Attached to the General Staff
7 Sep 1883 - 4 Jan 1884:	Ataman, Astrakhan Cossack Army, Governor of Astrakhan
4 Jan 1884 - 10 Feb 1893:	Chief of Staff, Corps of Gendarmes
30 Aug 1891:	Promoted to *Lieutenant-General*
10 Feb 1893 - 22 Jul 1895:	Director of the Police Department
22 Jul 1895 - 1 Jan 1903:	Chief of Posts & Telegraphs Main Directorate
21 Sep 1901:	Promoted to *General of Infantry*
1 Jan 1903 - 24 Dec 1905:	Member of the State Council

General of Engineers Nikolai Pavlovich **Petrov** (1 May 1836 - 15 Jan 1920)
1867 - 15 Dec 1888:	Professor, Nikolaev Engineering Academy
30 Aug 1878:	Promoted to *Major-General*
30 Aug 1888:	Promoted to *Lieutenant-General*
15 Dec 1888 - 7 May 1892:	Chairman, Engineering Council of the Ministry of Railways
7 May 1892 - 9 Apr 1900:	Deputy Minister of Communications
9 Apr 1900:	Promoted to *General of Engineers*
9 Apr 1900 - 1917:	Member of the State Council

Major-General of the Fleet Nikolai Pavlovich **Petrov** (19 Oct 1865 - ?)
1912 - 1917:	Senior Deputy Captain, Port of Sevastopol
6 Dec 1915:	Promoted to *Major-General of the Fleet*

Major-General Platon Andreyevich **Petrov** (17 Jul 1846 - ?)
30 Nov 1899:	Promoted to *Major-General*
30 Nov 1899 - 12 Dec 1901:	Commander, Irkutsk Regional Brigade
12 Dec 1901 - 1907:	Commander, Saratov Regional Brigade

Lieutenant-General Viktor Aleksandrovich **Petrov** (12 Dec 1858 - 1944)
21 Feb 1900 - 29 Dec 1901:	Inspector of Classes, Aleksandrov Military School
6 Dec 1901:	Promoted to *Major-General*
29 Dec 1901 - 1907:	Director, 2nd Moscow Cadet Corps
30 Jul 1916:	Promoted to *Lieutenant-General*

Major-General of Naval Artillery Vladimir Ivanovich **Petrov** (8 Jul 1864 - ?)
26 Nov 1912 - 1916:	Deputy Chief, Obukhov Steel Factory

6 Dec 1912:   Promoted to *Major-General of Naval Artillery*
1916 - 1917:   Attached to 2nd Baltic Naval Depot

Vice-Admiral Nikolai Arkadyevich **Petrov-Chernyshin** (13 Mar 1860 - 1 Dec 1944)
1911 - 1916:   Chief of Staff, Port of Sevastopol
6 Dec 1911:   Promoted to *Rear-Admiral*
1916 - 1917:   Deputy Chief of the Naval General Staff
1917:   Promoted to *Vice-Admiral*
1917:   Retired

Major-General Danilo Aleksandar **Petrović-Njegoš**, Crown Prince of Montenegro (29 Jun 1871 - 24 Sep 1939)
15 Aug 1910:   Promoted to *Major-General*
15 Aug 1910 - 1917:   General à la suite

General-Field Marshal Nikola I Mirkov **Petrović-Njegoš**, King of Montenegro (7 Oct 1841 - 1 Mar 1921)
15 Aug 1910:   Promoted to *General-Field Marshal*
28 Aug 1910 - 26 Nov 1918:   King of Montenegro

Major-General Nikolai Grigoryevich **Petrovich** (6 Dec 1846 - ?)
28 Feb 1901:   Promoted to *Major-General*
28 Feb 1901 - 1 Mar 1906:   Commander of Artillery, Fortress Libau
1 Jan 1903 - 21 Apr 1903:   Acting Commandant, Fortress Libau

Lieutenant-General Sergey Georgiyevich **Petrovich** (5 Jul 1869 - Jan 1926)
24 Sep 1910 - 24 Oct 1916:   Head of Teaching, Artillery Training Schools
6 Dec 1910:   Promoted to *Major-General*
24 Oct 1916 - Apr 1917:   Professor, Artillery Academy
Apr 1917 - Mar 1919:   Commandant of the Artillery Academy
1917:   Promoted to *Lieutenant-General*

Major-General Boris Mikhailovich **Petrovo-Sololovo** (3 Sep 1861 - 1925)
24 Sep 1905 - 11 Aug 1907:   Commander, Life Guards Hussar Regiment
6 Dec 1905:   Promoted to *Major-General*
11 Aug 1907 - 30 Nov 1907:   Unassigned
30 Nov 1907 - 24 Jan 1914:   Commander, 1st Brigade, 1st Guards Cavalry Division
8 Feb 1914 - 25 Jul 1914:   Marshal of the Nobility, Ryazan Province
25 Jul 1914 - 22 Jul 1917:   Special Assignments General, Supreme Commander-in-Chief
22 Jul 1917:   Retired

General of Cavalry Aleksandr Fyodorovich **Petrovsky** (26 Feb 1832 - 19 Dec 1908)
27 Jul 1875:   Promoted to *Major-General*
27 Jul 1875 - 6 Oct 1875:   Commander, 1st Brigade, 12th Cavalry Division
6 Oct 1875 - 20 Apr 1880:   Commander, 2nd Brigade, 11th Cavalry Division
20 Apr 1880 - 2 Jul 1890:   Commander, 2nd Reserve Cavalry Brigade
6 May 1884:   Promoted to *Lieutenant-General*

2 Jul 1890 - 28 Mar 1896:	Commander, 7th Reserve Cavalry Brigade
28 Mar 1896 - 1906:	At the disposal of the Minister of War
6 Dec 1897:	Promoted to *General of Cavalry*
1906:	Retired

Major-General Kozma Timofeyevich **Petrovsky** (23 Dec 1861 - ?)
4 Jun 1910 - 23 Apr 1915:	Commander, 192nd Infantry Regiment
23 Apr 1915 - Jul 1918:	POW
24 May 1915:	Promoted to *Major-General*

Lieutenant-General Nikolai Ivanovich **Petrovsky** (22 Feb 1865 - ?)
11 Aug 1905 - 8 Oct 1914:	Section Chief, Main Artillery Directorate
6 Dec 1908:	Promoted to *Major-General*
8 Oct 1914 - 17 Sep 1915:	Deputy Chief of Economic Section, Main Artillery Directorate
17 Sep 1915 - 27 Apr 1917:	Chief of 1st Economic Section, Main Artillery Directorate
6 Dec 1916:	Promoted to *Lieutenant-General*
27 Apr 1917 - Oct 1917:	Reserve officer, Petrograd Military District

Major-General Vasily Ivanovich **Petrovsky** (9 Apr 1858 - ?)
20 Dec 1913 - 31 Jul 1915:	Commander, 180th Infantry Regiment
31 Jul 1915 - 5 Aug 1916:	Reserve officer, Minsk Military District
5 Aug 1916:	Promoted to *Major-General*
5 Aug 1916:	Retired

Major-General Nikolai Andreyevich **Petrusha** (8 May 1857 - Dec 1920)
20 May 1904 - 1906:	Commander, 27th East Siberian Rifle Regiment
1906:	Retired
11 Jun 1916 - 1917:	Recalled; Commander, 3rd State Militia Brigade
8 Sep 1916:	Promoted to *Major-General*

Lieutenant-General of the Fleet Aleksandr Germanovich von **Petts** (29 Jan 1861 - ?)
6 Dec 1912:	Promoted to *Major-General of the Admiralty*
6 Dec 1912 - 2 May 1916:	Commandant, Kronstadt Naval Cadet School
8 Apr 1913:	Redesignated *Major-General of the Fleet*
2 May 1916:	Promoted to *Lieutenant-General of the Fleet*
2 May 1916:	Retired

Lieutenant-General Aleksandr Yakovlevich **Petunin** (1 Aug 1851 - ?)
21 Feb 1907 - 17 Dec 1908:	Commander, 40th Artillery Brigade
31 May 1907:	Promoted to *Major-General*
17 Dec 1908 - 25 Jul 1910:	Commander, 2nd Grenadier Artillery Brigade
25 Jul 1910 - 1912:	Inspector of Artillery, V. Army Corps
1912:	Promoted to *Lieutenant-General*
1912:	Retired

Major-General Vasily Dmitriyevich **Petunin** (12 Mar 1858 - ?)
19 May 1912:	Promoted to *Major-General*
19 May 1912 - 3 Aug 1915:	Commander, 11th Artillery Brigade
3 Aug 1915 - 8 Sep 1916:	Inspector of Artillery, XLI. Army Corps
8 Sep 1916:	Dismissed

Major-General Aleksandr Leontyevich **Pevnev** (23 Nov 1875 - 14 May 1936)
9 Jan 1914 - 20 Jan 1916:	Commander, 1st Brigade, 2nd Caucasus Cossack Division
6 Apr 1914:	Promoted to *Major-General*
Nov 1914:	Acting Commander, 2nd Caucasus Cossack Division
20 Jan 1916 - 8 May 1916:	Chief of Staff, 5th Caucasus Cossack Division
8 May 1916 - 4 Jul 1916:	Chief of Staff, Caucasus Cavalry Corps
4 Jul 1916 - 22 Jun 1917:	Second Deputy Quartermaster-General, General Staff
22 Jun 1917 - Jul 1918:	At the disposal of the Chief of the General Staff

Lieutenant-General Aleksandr Aleksandrovich **Pevtsov** (3 Jun 1861 - ?)
29 Dec 1906 - 4 Apr 1911:	Deputy Chief of Lugansk Cartridge Factory
29 Mar 1909:	Promoted to *Major-General*
4 Apr 1911 - 5 Apr 1916:	Chief of Izhevsk Army Factory
5 Apr 1916 - 26 Nov 1916:	Reserve officer, Odessa Military District
26 Nov 1916:	Promoted to *Lieutenant-General*
26 Nov 1916:	Dismissed

Major-General Mikhail Vasilyevich **Pevtsov** (21 May 1843 - 25 Feb 1902)
16 Dec 1888 - 15 Nov 1896:	At the disposal of the Chief of the General Staff
30 Aug 1891:	Promoted to *Major-General*
15 Nov 1896 - 1901:	Attached to the General Staff

Major-General Nikolai Nikolayevich **Peyker** (14 Jan 1844 - 16 May 1902)
13 May 1887 - 30 Aug 1887:	Attached to the Ministry of Internal Affairs
30 Aug 1887:	Promoted to *Major-General*
30 Aug 1887 - 15 May 1897:	Transferred to the reserve
15 May 1897 - 16 May 1902:	Special Assignments General, Ministry of Internal Affairs

Major-General Dmitry Nikolayevich **Pfeyfer** (28 Mar 1870 - 26 Aug 1914)
19 Jan 1913:	Promoted to *Major-General*
19 Jan 1913 - 26 Aug 1914:	Commander, Life Guards 2nd Rifle Regiment

Major-General Robert Emilyevich von **Pfeylitser-Frank** (31 Jan 1864 - 25 May 1915)
16 Mar 1913 - 25 May 1915:	Intendant, Amur Military District
14 Apr 1913:	Promoted to *Major-General*

Major-General Nikolai Aristarkhovich **Pichugin** (11 Apr 1843 - ?)
9 Apr 1900:	Promoted to *Major-General*
9 Apr 1900 - 22 Apr 1903:	Commander, 19th Artillery Brigade
22 Apr 1903:	Retired

Major-General Mikhail Favstovich **Pigulevsky** (15 Aug 1855 - ?)
30 Nov 1908 - 3 Feb 1913:	Commander, 5th Finnish Rifle Regiment
1 Jan 1913:	Promoted to *Major-General*
3 Feb 1913 - 1915:	Commander, 2nd Brigade, 50th Infantry Division
1915 - 6 Jul 1916:	General for Assignments, Moscow Military District
6 Jul 1916 - 25 Apr 1917:	Commander, 42nd Replacement Infantry Brigade
25 Apr 1917 - Oct 1917:	Reserve officer, Moscow Military District

Major-General Vsevolod Stepanovich **Pigulovich** (23 Jan 1836 - 16 Sep 1898)
2 Dec 1889 - 23 Jun 1896:	Intendant, Odessa Military District
30 Aug 1890:	Promoted to *Major-General*
23 Jun 1896 - 1898:	Deputy Intendant-General, Ministry of War

Major-General of the Fleet Aleksandr Karlovich **Pik** (28 Apr 1873 - ?)
3 Feb 1910 - ?:	Judge, Port of Kronstadt Naval Court
6 Dec 1915:	Promoted to *Major-General of the Fleet*

Major-General Konstantin Konstantinovich **Pilkin** (27 May 1870 - 30 Nov 1948)
23 Jan 1914:	Promoted to *Major-General*
23 Jan 1914 - 12 May 1916:	Commander, 13th Artillery Brigade
12 May 1916 - 18 Feb 1917:	Commander of Artillery, III. Army Corps
18 Feb 1917 - 1918:	Commander, 167th Infantry Division

Admiral Konstantin Pavlovich **Pilkin** (26 Dec 1824 - 12 Jan 1913)
1 Jan 1872:	Promoted to *Rear-Admiral*
1 Jan 1872 - 18 Feb 1874:	Captain, Port of Kronstadt
18 Feb 184 - 1874:	At the disposal of the Minister of the Navy
1874 - 26 Dec 1877:	Commander, Mine Training Detachment
26 Dec 1877 - 1883:	Commander of Fleet Mines
15 May 1883:	Promoted to *Vice-Admiral*
1883 - 1885:	Senior Flagman, Training Squadron
1885 - 1887:	Commander, Baltic Training Squadron
1886:	Chief Inspector of Mines
1886:	Senior Flagman, Baltic Fleet
1 Jan 1888 - 1896:	Chairman of the Naval Technical Committee
30 Aug 1889 - 10 Aug 1909:	Member of the Admiralty Board
14 May 1896:	Promoted to *Admiral*
10 Aug 1909 - 12 Jan 1913:	Attached to retinue of the Tsar

Admiral Pyotr Pavlovich **Pilkin** (29 Jun 1829 - 15 Oct 1911)
22 Feb 1882 - 1 Jan 1886:	Commander, 6th Naval Depot
30 Aug 1882:	Promoted to *Rear-Admiral*
1 Jan 1886 - 4 Mar 1891:	Junior Flagman, Baltic Fleet, Commander, Artillery Training Detachment
30 Aug 1889:	Promoted to *Vice-Admiral*
4 Mar 1891 - 1904:	Member, Supreme Naval Tribunal
1902:	Promoted to *Admiral*
1904 - 1905:	Chairman, Supreme Naval Tribunal

Rear-Admiral Vladimir Konstantinovich **Pilkin** (11 Jul 1869 - 6 Jan 1950)
1911 - 1916:   Commander, Battleship "Pyotropavlovsk"
1916 - 1917:   Commander, 1st Cruiser Brigade, Baltic Fleet
6 Dec 1916:   Promoted to *Rear-Admiral*

Major-General Aleksandr Mechislavovich **Pilsudsky** (31 Aug 1841 - 2 May 1895)
3 Jun 1880 - 17 Feb 1891:   Commander, 8th Dragoon Regiment
17 Feb 1891:   Promoted to *Major-General*
17 Feb 1891 - 2 May 1895:   Commander, 1st Brigade, 4th Cavalry Division

Major-General of the Fleet Vladimir Gordeyevich **Pimenov** (30 Jun 1859 - 30 May 1918)
6 Dec 1913:   Promoted to *Major-General of the Fleet*
1913 - 1916:   Commander, Sevastopol Naval Sub-Depot
1916 - 1917:   Commandant, Port of Mariupol

Lieutenant-General of Naval Engineers Georgy Nikolayevich **Pio-Ulsky** (24 Jan 1864 - 12 Aug 1938)
1906 - 1914:   Professor of Shipbuilding, Polytechnic Institute
10 Apr 1911:   Promoted to *Major-General of Naval Engineers*
1914 - Oct 1917:   Chief of Mechanical Section, Central Technical Laboratory, Ministry of War
?:   Promoted to *Lieutenant-General of Naval Engineers*

General of Infantry Bronislav-Adolf Ignatyevich **Piotrovsky** (7 Jul 1849 - ?)
24 Sep 1904:   Promoted to *Major-General*
24 Sep 1904 - 20 Mar 1906:   At the disposal of the C-in-C, 1st Manchurian Army
20 Mar 1906 - 4 Apr 1912:   Commander, Irkutsk Regional Brigade
6 Dec 1908:   Promoted to *Lieutenant-General*
4 Apr 1912 - 31 Dec 1913:   Commander, Orenburg Regional Brigade
31 Dec 1913:   Promoted to *General of Infantry*
31 Dec 1913:   Retired

Lieutenant-General Konstantin Andreyevich **Piradov** (29 Nov 1855 - 18 Oct 1918)
13 May 1911:   Promoted to *Major-General*
13 May 1911 - 1 Nov 1913:   Commander, 44th Artillery Brigade
1 Nov 1913:   Promoted to *Lieutenant-General*
1 Nov 1913:   Retired

Lieutenant-General Aleksandr Semyonovich **Pisarenko** (11 Dec 1842 - ?)
17 Sep 1894 - 31 Mar 1899:   Deputy Chief of Staff, Turkestan Military District
14 Nov 1894:   Promoted to *Major-General*
31 Mar 1899 - 25 Sep 1899:   Chief of Staff, II. Caucasus Army Corps
25 Sep 1899 - 22 Jul 1902:   Commander, 56th Reserve Infantry Brigade
22 Jul 1902 - 28 Dec 1905:   Commander, 32nd Infantry Division
6 Dec 1902:   Promoted to *Lieutenant-General*

Major-General Sergey Nikolayevich **Pisarev** (17 Apr 1866 - ?)
28 Jul 1910 - 17 Jun 1914:   Military Commander, Samara District

17 Jun 1914:	Promoted to *Major-General*
17 Jun 1914 - 2 Nov 1914:	Commander, Perm Local Brigade
2 Nov 1914 - 21 Feb 1916:	Commander, 17th Replacement Infantry Brigade
21 Feb 1916 - 1917:	Commander, Vologda Local Brigade

Major-General Stepan Ivanovich **Pisarev** (5 Jul 1846 - ?)
1 Jul 1888 - 1904:	Senior Deputy Commander, Terek Region
6 May 1897:	Promoted to *Major-General*

Major-General Mikhail Petrovich **Pisarevsky** (5 Sep 1859 - ?)
22 Aug 1913 - 1914:	Military Commander, Cherkassy District
1914 - 28 Nov 1915:	Ministry of War Representative, Dvinsk Military District Council
6 Dec 1914:	Promoted to *Major-General*
28 Nov 1915 - 10 Sep 1916:	Reserve officer, Kiev Military District
10 Sep 1916:	Dismissed

Lieutenant-General Nikolai Petrovich **Pisarevsky** (14 Aug 1841 - 5 Apr 1907)
30 Aug 1890:	Promoted to *Major-General*
30 Aug 1890 - 30 Sep 1899:	At the disposal of the Chief Engineer's Office
30 Sep 1899 - 5 Apr 1907:	Inspector for the Construction of Military Schools
28 Mar 1904:	Promoted to *Lieutenant-General*

Rear-Admiral Ivan Nikolayevich **Pistol** (7 May 1862 - ?)
?:	Promoted to *Rear-Admiral*

Major-General Erik-Gergardt Avgustovich von **Pistolkors** (13 Nov 1853 - 8 Nov 1935)
3 Feb 1906 - 10 Jun 1906:	Special Assignments General, Ministry of Internal Affairs
1906:	Promoted to *Major-General*
10 Jun 1906 - 30 Apr 1907:	Transferred to the reserve
30 Apr 1907 - 19 Mar 1912:	General for Special Assignments, Main Directorate of Horse Breeding
19 Mar 1912 - 1917:	Attached to the Main Directorate of Horse Breeding

General of Artillery Mikhail Ivanovich **Pivovarov** (28 Jul 1834 - 14 Jan 1906)
7 Aug 1889:	Promoted to *Major-General*
7 Aug 1889 - 14 Jan 1891:	Commander, 3rd Artillery Brigade
14 Jan 1891 - 1902:	Commandant of Fortress Sevastopol
6 Dec 1898:	Promoted to *Lieutenant-General*
1902:	Promoted to *General of Artillery*
1902:	Retired

General of Infantry Vadim Vasilyevich **Plaksin** (21 Oct 1832 - 29 Sep 1908)
4 May 1872 - 26 Apr 1878:	Commander, 127th Infantry Regiment
21 Jun 1877:	Promoted to *Major-General*
26 Apr 1878 - 26 Mar 1882:	Commander, 1st Brigade, 2nd Grenadier Division
26 Mar 1882 - 14 Jan 1887:	Commander, 1st Brigade, 14th Infantry Division

14 Jan 1887 - 6 Jun 1890:	Commander, 11th Infantry Division
30 Aug 1887:	Promoted to *Lieutenant-General*
6 Jun 1890 - 2 Sep 1895:	Commander, 32nd Infantry Division
2 Sep 1895 - 7 Aug 1901:	At the disposal of the Commanding General, Kiev Military District
6 Dec 1901:	Promoted to *General of Infantry*
7 Aug 1901 - Sep 1905:	Member, Committee for Wounded Veterans
Sep 1905:	Retired

Vice-Admiral Konstantin Antonovich **Planson** (30 Nov 1861 - 1921)
1912 - 28 Jan 1913:	Commander, Mine Division, Black Sea Fleet
6 Dec 1912:	Promoted to *Rear-Admiral*
28 Jan 1913 - 1916:	Chief of Staff, Black Sea Fleet
30 Jul 1915:	Promoted to *Vice-Admiral*
1916 - 1917:	Member, Board of Admiralty

Major-General Lev Antonovich **Planson-Rostkov** (11 Apr 1858 - ?)
31 Jan 1907 - Jul 1914:	Military Judge, Warsaw Military District Court
22 Apr 1907:	Promoted to *Major-General*
Jul 1914 - 1917:	Military Judge, Minsk Military District Court

General of Artillery Florenty Nikolayevich **Platonov** (19 Jan 1839 - 15 Nov 1914)
15 Jun 1884 - 30 May 1888:	Military Prosecutor, Moscow Military District
30 Aug 1887:	Promoted to *Major-General*
30 May 1888 - 26 Jan 1897:	Chairman of the Moscow Military Court
26 Jan 1897 - 30 Jul 1905:	Commandant, Aleksandr Military Law Academy
6 Dec 1897:	Promoted to *Lieutenant-General*
30 Jul 1905 - 15 Nov 1914:	Senator
6 Jun 1907:	Promoted to *General of Artillery*

Major-General Leonid Nikolayevich **Platonov** (30 Sep 1834 - ?)
7 Jul 1890:	Promoted to *Major-General*
7 Jul 1890 - 19 Oct 1892:	Commander, 8th Artillery Brigade
19 Oct 1892 - Dec 1899:	Commander, 2nd Grenadier Artillery Brigade

Major-General Nikolai Florentyevich **Platonov** (16 Jun 1870 - Jul 1916)
27 Aug 1915 - Feb 1916:	Commander, 88th Artillery Brigade
Feb 1916 - Jul 1916:	Reserve officer, Kiev Military District
2 Mar 1916:	Promoted to *Major-General*

Major-General Sergey Aleksandrovich **Platov** (20 Nov 1865 - 1920)
6 Jan 1913:	Promoted to *Major-General*
6 Jan 1913 - 27 Aug 1913:	Commander, 1st Brigade, 2nd Consolidated Cossack Division
27 Aug 1913:	Retired
29 Nov 1915 - 12 Feb 1917:	Recalled; Reserve officer, Minsk Military District
12 Feb 1917 - 25 Aug 1917:	Inspector of Cavalry, 10th Army
25 Aug 1917 - Oct 1917:	General for Assignments, 10th Army

Major-General Nikolai Sergeyevich **Plautin** (21 Jan 1868 - 13 Nov 1918)
8 Apr 1910 - 14 Nov 1914:	At the disposal of the Commanding General, St. Petersburg Military District
6 Apr 1914:	Promoted to *Major-General*
14 Nov 1914 - 29 Apr 1917:	Commander, 2nd Brigade, 2nd Consolidated Cossack Division
29 Apr 1917:	Retired

Major-General Agaton Vikentyevich **Plavsky** (23 Dec 1854 - 1916)
31 Dec 1904 - 1907:	Commander, 140th Infantry Regiment
1907:	Promoted to *Major-General*
1907:	Retired
1914 - 1916:	Recalled; Special Assignments General, Omsk Military District

Major-General Aleksandr Eduardovich **Plavsky** (18 Sep 1856 - 1921)
2 Apr 1910 - 6 Dec 1911:	Commander, 3rd Border Infantry Regiment, Amur Military District
6 Dec 1911:	Promoted to *Major-General*
6 Dec 1911:	Retired
25 Aug 1915 - 1917:	Recalled; Commander, 98th Temporary Supply Train Battalion

Lieutenant-General Anton Nikolayevich **Plazovsky** (21 Dec 1831 - ?)
17 Nov 1884:	Promoted to *Major-General*
17 Nov 1884 - 7 Oct 1893:	Commander, 38th Artillery Brigade
7 Oct 1893 - 27 Oct 1899:	Commander of Artillery, XVI. Army Corps
14 Nov 1894:	Promoted to *Lieutenant-General*

Lieutenant-General Dmitry Stepanovich **Pleshko** (29 Dec 1844 - 24 Sep 1912)
8 Aug 1891 - 1907:	Chief of Peterhof Palace Administration
14 May 1896:	Promoted to *Major-General*
11 Aug 1904:	Promoted to *Lieutenant-General*
1907:	Retired

Major-General Aleksandr Georgiyevich **Pleshkov** (30 Aug 1866 - ?)
2 Sep 1912 - 13 Apr 1916:	Commander, 3rd Turkestan Rifle Regiment
1916:	Promoted to *Major-General*
13 Apr 1916 - 6 Mar 1917:	Commander, Brigade, 7th Turkestan Rifle Division
6 Mar 1917 - 20 May 1917:	Commander, 8th Rifle Division

Lieutenant-General Fyodor Yemelyanovich **Pleshkov** (15 Jun 1855 - ?)
25 Mar 1904:	Promoted to *Major-General*
25 Mar 1904 - 2 Dec 1904:	Commander, 1st Brigade, 2nd Siberian Infantry Division
2 Dec 1904 - 5 May 1906:	Commander, 2nd Brigade, 13th Infantry Division
5 May 1906 - 27 Oct 1908:	Commander, 1st Brigade, 19th Infantry Division
27 Oct 1908 - 23 Jul 1911:	Commander, 2nd Brigade, 18th Infantry Division
23 Jul 1911:	Promoted to *Lieutenant-General*

23 Jul 1911: Retired

General of Cavalry Mikhail Mikhailovich **Pleshkov** (1 Nov 1856 - 21 May 1927)
25 Jan 1902: Promoted to *Major-General*
25 Jan 1902 - 15 Jun 1907: Commander, 2nd Brigade, 2nd Cavalry Division
15 Jun 1907: Promoted to *Lieutenant-General*
15 Jun 1907 - 11 May 1912: Commander, 7th Cavalry Division
11 May 1912 - 3 Jul 1917: Commanding General, I. Siberian Army Corps
14 Mar 1913: Promoted to *General of Cavalry*
3 Jul 1917 - Oct 1917: Reserve officer, Minsk Military District

General of Cavalry Pavel Adamovich **Pleve** (30 May 1850 - 28 Mar 1916)
27 Jan 1893: Promoted to *Major-General*
27 Jan 1893 - 23 Jun 1895: Quartermaster-General, Vilnius Military District
23 Jun 1895 - 30 Jun 1899: Commandant, Cavalry School
30 Jun 1899 - 20 Nov 1901: Commander, 2nd Cavalry Division
6 Dec 1900: Promoted to *Lieutenant-General*
20 Nov 1901 - 7 Mar 1905: Chief of Staff, Don Army
7 Mar 1905 - 4 Jul 1905: Commandant, Fortress Warsaw
4 Jul 1905 - 18 Mar 1906: Commanding General, XIII. Army Corps
18 Mar 1906 - 17 Mar 1909: Deputy Commanding General, Vilnius Military District
6 Dec 1907: Promoted to *General of Cavalry*
17 Mar 1909 - 19 Jul 1914: Commanding General, Moscow Military District
19 Jul 1914 - 14 Jan 1915: C-in-C, 5th Army
14 Jan 1915 - 8 Jun 1915: C-in-C, 12th Army
8 Jun 1915 - 6 Dec 1915: C-in-C, 5th Army
6 Dec 1915 - 6 Feb 1916: C-in-C, Northern Front
6 Feb 1916 - 28 Mar 1916: Member of the State Council

Major-General Dmitry Viktorovich **Plotnikov** (21 Oct 1852 - 14 Mar 1910)
20 May 1903 - 14 Mar 1910: Member of the Economic Board, Orenburg Cossack Army
2 Apr 1906: Promoted to *Major-General*

Lieutenant-General Vladimir Ivanovich **Plotnikov** (1 Aug 1847 - ?)
5 Jun 1903: Promoted to *Major-General*
5 Jun 1903 - 4 Jun 1904: Commander, 6th Reserve Artillery Brigade
4 Jun 1904 - 11 Mar 1906: Commander, 61st Artillery Brigade
11 Mar 1906 - 5 Apr 1907: Commander, 6th Reserve Artillery Brigade
5 Apr 1907 - 10 Oct 1908: Commander of Artillery, II. Siberian Army Corps
31 May 1907: Promoted to *Lieutenant-General*

Major-General Yakov Petrovich **Plume** (22 Feb 1855 - 3 Jul 1931)
? - 1910: Commander, 116th Infantry Regiment
1910: Promoted to *Major-General*
1910: Retired

Lieutenant-General Aleksandr Fyodorovich **Plyutsinsky** (6 Mar 1844 - 17 Feb 1900)
18 Jun 1885 - 28 Feb 1898:	Professor, Nikolaev Engineering Academy
30 Aug 1890:	Promoted to *Major-General*
28 Feb 1898 - 4 Aug 1899:	Commandant of Fortress Osovets
4 Aug 1899 - 17 Feb 1900:	Commander, 34th Infantry Division
6 Dec 1899:	Promoted to *Lieutenant-General*

Lieutenant-General Vladimir Fyodorovich **Plyutsinsky** (10 Feb 1842 - ?)
29 Sep 1900 - 1906:	Commander, Fortress Dvinsk Artillery Depot
6 Dec 1901:	Promoted to *Major-General*
1905:	Promoted to *Lieutenant-General*

Major-General Nikolai Vyacheslavovich **Pnevsky** (14 Aug 1874 - 1928)
20 Aug 1915 - 6 May 1916:	Quartermaster-General, 11th Army
Mar 1916:	Promoted to *Major-General*
6 May 1916 - 7 Jan 1917:	C-in-C of the Air Force
7 Jan 1917 - 22 Apr 1917:	Chief of Staff, 3rd Turkestan Rifle Division
22 Apr 1917 - 17 Aug 1917:	Commander, 48th Infantry Division
17 Aug 1917 - 15 Dec 1917:	Chief of Staff, 1st Army
15 Dec 1917 - 27 Dec 1917:	Acting C-in-C, 1st Army

General of Infantry Vyacheslav Ivanovich **Pnevsky** (8 Dec 1848 - ?)
10 Mar 1895:	Promoted to *Major-General*
10 Mar 1895 - 18 Sep 1899:	Chief of Staff, Deputy Commanding General, Warsaw Military District
18 Sep 1899 - 13 Oct 1901:	Chief of Staff, Don Cossack Army
6 May 1901:	Promoted to *Lieutenant-General*
13 Oct 1901 - 2 Aug 1906:	Commander, 25th Infantry Division
2 Aug 1906:	Promoted to *General of Infantry*
2 Aug 1906:	Retired

Major-General Nikolai Markovich **Pobilevsky** (8 May 1858 - ?)
4 Mar 1916 - 1917:	Commander, 253rd Infantry Regiment
26 Feb 1917:	Promoted to *Major-General*

Major-General Vyacheslav Frantsevich **Poboyevsky** (25 Oct 1862 - 11 Jul 1927)
23 Feb 1915 - 29 Jun 1915:	Commander, 190th Infantry Regiment
27 May 1915:	Promoted to *Major-General*
29 Jun 1915 - 14 Jul 1915:	Commander, 2nd Brigade, 107th Infantry Division
14 Jul 1915 - 20 Mar 1916:	Chief of Land Defenses, Fortress Sveaborg
20 Mar 1916 - 5 Apr 1917:	Commander, 116th Infantry Division
5 Apr 1917 - 7 Sep 1917:	Reserve officer, Dvinsk Military District
7 Sep 1917 - 17 Dec 1917:	Reserve officer, Petrograd Military District
17 Dec 1917:	Retired

Major-General Aleksandr Alekseyevich **Podcherkov** (5 Jun 1856 - 1911)
16 Oct 1906 - 1911:	Attached to Main Engineering Directorate
1911:	Promoted to *Major-General*

Major-General Leonid Gavrilovich **Podgoretsky** (11 Feb 1864 - 1919)
22 Nov 1911 - 12 May 1916: Commander, 1st Battalion, 41st Artillery Brigade
20 Jan 1915: Promoted to *Major-General*
12 May 1916 - 1917: Commander, 41st Artillery Brigade

Major-General Aleksey Dmitriyevich **Podgursky** (17 Mar 1862 - ?)
13 Jul 1912 - 30 Mar 1916: Military Governor of Kars
6 Dec 1915: Promoted to *Major-General*
30 Mar 1916 - 1917: Commander, 1st Caucasus Supply Train Brigade

Lieutenant-General Fyodor Aleksandrovich **Podgursky** (2 Dec 1860 - 1929)
6 Oct 1901 - 20 Mar 1905: Section Chief, General Staff
1904: Promoted to *Major-General*
20 Mar 1905 - 25 Apr 1906: Chief of Section 2, General Staff
25 Apr 1906 - 16 Jul 1910: Duty General, Amur Military District
16 Jul 1910 - 5 Sep 1915: Commander, 2nd Brigade, 10th Siberian Rifle Division, Commandant of Nikolayevsk
19 Jul 1914: Promoted to *Lieutenant-General*
5 Sep 1915 - Nov 1917: Commander, 1st Siberian Rifle Division
Nov 1917 - Jun 1918: Reserve officer, Minsk Military District

Rear-Admiral Nikolai Lyutsianovich **Podgursky** (13 Aug 1877 - 1 Nov 1918)
4 Nov 1916 - Apr 1918: Commander of Protection Detachment, Gulf of Bothnia
6 Dec 1916: Promoted to *Rear-Admiral*

Lieutenant-General Pavel Yakovlevich **Podtyagin** (10 Jan 1836 - 28 Dec 1913)
16 Sep 1887 - 18 Feb 1893: Commander of Artillery, Fortress Mikhailov
30 Aug 1890: Promoted to *Major-General*
18 Feb 1893 - 6 Nov 1897: Commandant of Fortress Mikhailovsk
6 Nov 1897: Promoted to *Lieutenant-General*
6 Nov 1897: Retired

Major-General of the Fleet German Semyonovich **Podushkin** (24 Dec 1857 - 28 Oct 1924)
?: Promoted to *Major-General of the Fleet*

General of Infantry Nikolai Ivanovich **Podvalnyuk** (23 Jul 1848 - ?)
15 Feb 1900: Promoted to *Major-General*
15 Feb 1900 - 6 Oct 1903: Commander, 2nd Brigade, 44th Infantry Division
6 Oct 1903 - 1 Jun 1904: Commander, 61st Replacement Infantry Brigade
1 Jun 1904 - 3 Mar 1906: Commander, 61st Infantry Division
3 Mar 1906 - 19 Jun 1910: Commander, 41st Infantry Division
12 Jun 1906: Promoted to *Lieutenant-General*
19 Jun 1910 - 7 Aug 1911: Commanding General, V. Siberian Army Corps
7 Aug 1911 - 13 Dec 1912: Commanding General, XI. Army Corps
6 Dec 1912: Promoted to *General of Infantry*
13 Dec 1912 - 1917: Member, Committee for Wounded Veterans

Major-General Vitaly Ivanovich **Podyapolsky** (25 Apr 1864 - ?)
21 Sep 1913 - 1917: Chief Map Editor, Topographical Section, General Staff
22 Mar 1915: Promoted to *Major-General*

Major-General Aleksandr Aleksandrovich **Podymov** (8 Dec 1869 - 11 May 1915)
16 Oct 1913 - 11 May 1915: Commander, 173rd Infantry Regiment
23 Apr 1915: Promoted to *Major-General*

General of Engineers Aleksandr Dormidontovich **Podymov** (17 Nov 1824 - 8 Nov 1909)
12 Apr 1874 - 17 Jul 1882: Deputy Commander of Engineers, Kiev Military District
30 Aug 1875: Promoted to *Major-General*
17 Jul 1882 - 28 Nov 1895: Commander of Engineers, Caucasus Military District
15 May 1883: Promoted to *Lieutenant-General*
28 Nov 1895 - 31 Dec 1895: Member of the Engineer Committee, Main Engineering Directorate
31 Dec 1895 - 3 Jan 1906: Member of the Military Council
14 May 1896: Promoted to *General of Engineers*
3 Jan 1906: Retired

Major-General Boris Aleksandrovich **Podymov** (23 Aug 1866 - 9 Feb 1931)
24 Mar 1911 - 20 Feb 1916: Commander, Life Guards Sapper Battalion
6 Dec 1912: Promoted to *Major-General*
2 Feb 1916 - 11 Sep 1916: Commander, Life Guards Sapper Regiment
11 Sep 1916 - 11 Apr 1917: General à la suite
11 Apr 1917 - 9 Jun 1917: Reserve officer, Kiev Military District
9 Jun 1917: Dismissed

Major-General Koloman Ferdinandovich **Poganko** (5 Sep 1852 - ?)
5 Feb 1910: Promoted to *Major-General*
5 Feb 1910 - 5 Sep 1912: Commander, 6th Artillery Brigade
5 Sep 1912: Retired

Lieutenant-General of Naval Engineers Aleksey Ivanovich **Pogodin** (17 Mar 1857 - ?)
29 May 1900 - 1917: Inspector of Classes, Naval Engineering School
29 Mar 1909: Promoted to *Major-General of Naval Engineers*
22 Mar 1915: Promoted to *Lieutenant-General of Naval Engineers*

Major-General Vasily Lvovich **Pogodin** (20 Nov 1870 - ?)
8 Jul 1914 - 1917: Military Judge, Irkutsk Military District Court
6 Dec 1915: Promoted to *Major-General*

Major-General Pyotr Ivanovich **Pogorelov** (19 Dec 1855 - ?)
15 Mar 1904 - 18 May 1907: Commander, 4th Grenadier Regiment
6 Dec 1906: Promoted to *Major-General*

Lieutenant-General Sergey Timofeyevich **Pogoretsky** (10 Oct 1856 - ?)
1 Jun 1904: Promoted to *Major-General*

1 Jun 1904 - 29 Mar 1906:	Commander, 1st Brigade, 71st Infantry Division
29 Mar 1906 - 10 Dec 1908:	Commander, 2nd Brigade, 44th Infantry Division, Governor-General of Cherkassy
10 Dec 1908 - 5 Jul 1910:	Commander, 54th Reserve Infantry Brigade
5 Jul 1910 - 24 Aug 1914:	Commander, 48th Infantry Division
17 Oct 1910:	Promoted to *Lieutenant-General*
?:	Acting Commanding General, XXIV. Army Corps
24 Aug 1914 - 19 Dec 1914:	Transferred to the reserve
19 Dec 1914 - 21 Feb 1915:	Commander, 13th Infantry Division
21 Feb 1915 - 1 May 1915:	Reserve officer, Kiev Military District
1 May 1915 - Nov 1916:	Commander, 18th Replacement Infantry Brigade
Nov 1916 - Mar 1917:	Commandant of Orenburg Garrison

Lieutenant-General Vladimir Gustavovich **Pogoretsky** (18 Nov 1852 - ?)
6 Sep 1908:	Promoted to *Major-General*
6 Sep 1908 - Dec 1912:	Commander, 1st Brigade, 9th East Siberian Rifle Division
Dec 1912:	Promoted to *Lieutenant-General*
Dec 1912:	Retired

Lieutenant-General Leonard-Karl Alekseyevich **Pogossky** (16 Nov 1860 - 3 Aug 1917)
25 Mar 1916 - 8 Jun 1917:	Commander, Brigade, 48th Infantry Division
18 Jan 1916:	Promoted to *Major-General*
8 Jun 1917 - 2 Aug 1917:	Commander, 103rd Infantry Division
14 Aug 1917:	Posthumously promoted to *Lieutenant-General*

Major-General Viktor Vikentyevich **Pogossky** (23 Feb 1858 - 30 Jan 1930)
1915 - 1916:	Commander, 53rd State Militia Brigade
1916:	Promoted to *Major-General*
1916 - 28 Aug 1916:	Commander, 54th State Militia Brigade

Major-General Vladislav Vikentyevich **Pogossky** (5 Jun 1859 - 1920)
15 Feb 1907 - 1915:	Military Judge, Kazan Military District Court
22 Apr 1907:	Promoted to *Major-General*
1915:	Chairman of the Military Court, XXVII. Army Corps
1915 - 1916:	Chairman of the Military Court, 1st Army
1916 - 27 Apr 1917:	Military Judge, Kazan Military District Court
27 Apr 1917 - 1918:	Chairman of the Military Court, Kazan Military District

Major-General Pyotr Nestorovich **Pogrebnoy** (1872 - Aug 1916)
24 May 1916 - Aug 1916:	Commander, 4th Siberian Mortar Artillery Battalion
23 Jan 1917:	Posthumously promoted to *Major-General*

Major-General Nikolai Antonovich **Pogrebnyakov** (19 Jun 1871 - 1920)
21 Feb 1916 - 1917:	Commander, 26th Artillery Brigade
25 Aug 1916:	Promoted to *Major-General*

Major-General Sergey Antonovich **Pogrebnyakov** (6 Jul 1870 - ?)
14 Nov 1901 - 26 Feb 1916: Staff Officer for Testing, Main Artillery Polygon
6 Dec 1915: Promoted to *Major-General*
26 Feb 1916 - 1917: Deputy Commander, Main Artillery Polygon

Rear-Admiral Sergey Sergeyevich **Pogulyayev** (1 Mar 1873 - 13 Mar 1941)
29 Feb 1916: Promoted to *Rear-Admiral*
29 Feb 1916 - Oct 1916: Commander, 1st Battleship Brigade
Oct 1916 - Apr 1917: Chief of Staff, Black Sea Fleet

Major-General Dmitry Viktorovich **Pokatilov** (9 Aug 1842 - 1899)
1 Jan 1882 - 1899: Inspector of Construction, Main Directorate for Military Schools
30 Aug 1887: Promoted to *Major-General*

Major-General Pyotr Danilovich **Pokhitonov** (6 May 1859 - ?)
5 Dec 1910 - 26 May 1915: Commander, 2nd Vladivostok Fortress Artillery Brigade
6 Dec 1911: Promoted to *Major-General*
26 May 1915 - 1917: Commander of Artillery, Fortress Kronstadt

Lieutenant-General Emmanuil Borisovich **Pokhvisnyev** (27 Jun 1860 - ?)
30 Nov 1904 - 10 Apr 1907: Commander, 15th Artillery Brigade
6 Dec 1906: Promoted to *Major-General*
10 Apr 1907 - 1 Jul 1914: Commandant, Konstantinov Artillery School
6 Dec 1910: Promoted to *Lieutenant-General*
1 Jul 1914 - 29 Jul 1914: Commander of Artillery, Warsaw Military District
29 Jul 1914 - 10 Jul 1916: Chief of Artillery Logistics, Northwestern Front
10 Jul 1916 - Oct 1917: Chief of Artillery Logistics, Western Front

General of Cavalry Vasily Ivanovich **Pokotilo** (8 Aug 1856 - ?)
12 Feb 1900 - 11 Dec 1904: Director, 1st Cadet Corps
6 Dec 1901: Promoted to *Major-General*
11 Dec 1904 - 28 Jul 1907: Military Governor of Ferghana
28 Jul 1907 - 7 Oct 1908: Military Governor of Semirechensk, Ataman, Semirechensk Cossack Army
1908: Promoted to *Lieutenant-General*
7 Oct 1908 - 1 Jan 1910: Military Governor of Ural Region, Ataman, Ural Cossack Army
1 Jan 1910 - 22 Oct 1912: Deputy Governor-General of Turkestan, Deputy Commanding General, Turkestan Military District
22 Oct 1912 - 4 May 1916: C-in-C, Don Cossack Army
14 Apr 1913: Promoted to *General of Cavalry*
4 May 1916 - 20 Oct 1916: Chief of Logistics, Northern Front
20 Oct 1916 - 4 Apr 1917: Member of the Military Council
4 Apr 1917: Retired

Major-General Aleksey Matveyevich **Pokrovsky** (13 Mar 1847 - ?)
6 Sep 1899: Promoted to *Major-General*
6 Sep 1899 - 30 Apr 1905: Commander, 2nd Brigade, 39th Infantry Division

Vice-Admiral Andrey Georgiyevich **Pokrovsky** (14 Aug 1862 - 1944)
7 Dec 1911 - 28 Jan 1913: Chief of Staff, Black Sea Fleet
25 Mar 1912: Promoted to *Rear-Admiral*
28 Jan 1913 - 1916: Commander, Mine Division, Black Sea Fleet
1916 - 28 Jun 1916: Chief of Staff, Black Sea Fleet
10 Apr 1916: Promoted to *Vice-Admiral*
28 Jun 1916 - 1917: Commander, 2nd Battleship Brigade, Black Sea Fleet
1917 - Oct 1917: Commandant, Port of Nikolayev

Major-General Grigory Vasilyevich **Pokrovsky** (9 Oct 1871 - 16 Jan 1968)
20 Oct 1913 - 9 Aug 1915: Commander, 129th Infantry Regiment
9 Aug 1915: Promoted to *Major-General*
9 Aug 1915 - 25 Sep 1916: Chief of Staff, I. Turkestan Army Corps
25 Sep 1916 - 1917: Quartermaster-General, 8th Army
1917 - 25 Aug 1917: Chief of Staff, 8th Army
25 Aug 1917 - 1918: Reserve officer, Kiev Military District

Lieutenant-General Aleksandr Karlovich **Pol** (28 Aug 1843 - ?)
26 Feb 1894: Promoted to *Major-General*
26 Feb 1894 - 12 Aug 1902: Commander, 2nd Brigade, 1st Infantry Division
12 Aug 1902: Promoted to *Lieutenant-General*
12 Aug 1902 - 2 Nov 1904: Commander, 7th Infantry Division

Major-General Aleksey Andreyevich **Polenov** (18 Jun 1833 - ?)
8 Mar 1879 - 1894: Deputy Chief of Police, Warsaw Region
15 May 1883: Promoted to *Major-General*

Major-General Konstantin Fyodorovich **Poletika** (21 May 1858 - ?)
1915 - 1916: Commander, Artillery Brigade
16 Jul 1916: Promoted to *Major-General*

Major-General of the Fleet Sergey Apollonovich **Polikarpov** (25 Sep 1866 - ?)
Oct 1911 - 1917: Deputy Chief, Main Naval Economic Directorate
6 Apr 1914: Promoted to *Major-General of the Fleet*

Major-General Anastasy Yegorovich **Polityev** (1 Sep 1856 - ?)
31 Mar 1912 - 1913: Commander, 125th Infantry Regiment
1913: Promoted to *Major-General*
1913: Retired
19 Jun 1916 - Jul 1916: Recalled; Commander, 228th Reserve Infantry Regiment
Jul 1916 - 1917: Deputy Commander, 5th Replacement Infantry Brigade

General of Infantry Aleksey Andreyevich **Polivanov** (4 Mar 1855 - 25 Sep 1920)
30 Aug 1899 - 16 Nov 1904:	Chief Editor, "Military Digest" Journal and "Russian Invalid" Gazette
6 Dec 1899:	Promoted to *Major-General*
16 Nov 1904 - 18 Jan 1905:	Director-General, Main Committee on Fortresses
18 Jan 1905 - 28 Jun 1905:	Deputy Quartmaster-General, General Staff
28 Jun 1905 - 14 Apr 1906:	Chief of the General Staff
2 Apr 1906:	Promoted to *Lieutenant-General*
14 Apr 1906 - 24 Apr 1912:	Deputy Minister of War
10 Apr 1911:	Promoted to *General of Infantry*
1 Jan 1912 - 1917:	Member of the State Council
13 Jun 1915 - 15 Mar 1916:	Minister of War

Major-General Apollon Nikolayevich **Polivanov** (20 Nov 1839 - ?)
3 Nov 1896 - 1906:	Inspector of Classes, 2nd Moscow Cadet Corps
6 Dec 1903:	Promoted to *Major-General*

Major-General Matvey Mikhailovich **Polivanov** (10 Aug 1837 - 23 Aug 1897)
25 Oct 1889:	Promoted to *Major-General*
25 Oct 1889 - 4 Jun 1892:	Commander, 1st Brigade, 40th Infantry Division
4 Jun 1892 - 26 May 1893:	Commander, 2nd Brigade, 22nd Infantry Division
26 May 1893 - 23 Aug 1897:	Commander, 2nd Brigade, 37th Infantry Division

Major-General Pyotr Vasilyevich **Polkovnikov** (19 Nov 1850 - 4 Nov 1906)
7 Aug 1900:	Promoted to *Major-General*
7 Aug 1900 - 28 Feb 1901:	Commander, 3rd Siberian Infantry Brigade
28 Feb 1901 - 9 Mar 1905:	Commander, 4th Rifle Brigade
9 Mar 1905 - 16 Jul 1905:	Commander, 3rd Siberian Infantry Division
16 Jul 1905 - 27 Feb 1906:	Commander, 5th East Siberian Rifle Division
27 Feb 1906 - 4 Nov 1906:	Commander, 9th Infantry Division

Major-General Yakov Ivanovich **Polman** (9 Jun 1836 - 2 Nov 1906)
6 Dec 1904:	Promoted to *Major-General*
6 Dec 1904 - 1906:	At the disposal of the Commanding General, St. Petersburg Military District

Major-General Nikolai Aleksandrovich **Polochaninov** (14 Nov 1856 - 1912)
23 Aug 1909 - 1912:	District Commander, Bugulminsk
1912:	Promoted to *Major-General*

Major-General Erast Andreyevich **Polonsky** (4 Jan 1856 - ?)
14 Nov 1908 - 28 Jan 1913:	Chief of St. Petersburg Weapons Depot
6 Dec 1908:	Promoted to *Major-General*
28 Jan 1913 - 31 Dec 1913:	Commander of Artillery, Fortress St. Petersburg, Commandant, St. Petersburg Artillery Depot
31 Dec 1913 - 11 Dec 1915:	Deputy Commander of Artillery, Kiev Military District
11 Dec 1915 - 1917:	Commander of Artillery, Kiev Military District

Major-General Andrey Petrovich **Polovtsov** (12 Aug 1868 - ?)
18 Sep 1909 - 6 Oct 1914:	Deputy Chief of Cabinet to the Tsar
6 Dec 1912:	Promoted to *Major-General*
6 Oct 1914 - 1 Feb 1916:	Deputy Military Governor of Galicia
1914:	Acting Military Governor of Galicia
1 Feb 1916 - 10 May 1917:	Deputy Chief of Cabinet to the Tsar
10 May 1917:	Discharged

Major-General Nikolai Petrovich **Polovtsov** (23 May 1873 - 27 Sep 1941)
28 Jun 1914 - 12 Sep 1915:	Commander, 13th Hussar Regiment
12 Sep 1915:	Promoted to *Major-General*
12 Sep 1915 - 18 Apr 1916:	Chief of Staff, V. Caucasus Army Corps
18 Apr 1916 - 10 Aug 1916:	Chief of Staff, XLVI. Army Corps
10 Aug 1916 - 25 Sep 1916:	Chief of Staff, XLVII. Army Corps
25 Sep 1916 - 10 Jul 1917:	Chief of Staff, VIII. Army Corps
10 Jul 1917 - 1918:	Commander, Amur Cavalry Division

Major-General Aleksandr Aleksandrovich **Polozov** (19 Mar 1864 - 1908)
23 Jan 1905 - 26 Jan 1907:	Commander, 82nd Infantry Regiment
26 Jan 1907 - 1908:	Unassigned
1908:	Promoted to *Major-General*
1908:	Retired

Lieutenant-General Vasily Nikolayevich **Polozov** (24 Dec 1851 - ?)
11 Nov 1907 - 21 Oct 1910:	Ataman, 1st Military Division, Orenburg Cossack Army
29 Mar 1909:	Promoted to *Major-General*
21 Oct 1910 - 17 Jul 1917:	Senior Member of the Military Board, Orenburg Cossack Army
17 Jul 1917:	Promoted to *Lieutenant-General*
17 Jul 1917:	Retired

Major-General Aleksey Vladimirovich **Poltoratsky** (30 Dec 1860 - ?)
4 Mar 1910 - 13 Mar 1917:	Chief of Bureau, Inspectorate-General of Military Schools
6 Dec 1912:	Promoted to *Major-General*
13 Mar 1917:	Retired

Major-General Iosif Suleymanovich **Poltorzhitsky** (6 Dec 1846 - ?)
31 Oct 1899:	Promoted to *Major-General*
31 Oct 1899 - 29 May 1903:	Commander, 1st Brigade, 27th Infantry Division
29 May 1903 - 5 Mar 1905:	Commander, 53rd Reserve Infantry Brigade
5 Mar 1905 - 1906:	Commander, 53rd Infantry Division

Major-General Konstantin Semyonovich **Polyakov** (15 May 1859 - ?)
26 Jun 1910 - 18 Dec 1913:	Commander, 13th Don Cossack Regiment
18 Dec 1913:	Promoted to *Major-General*
18 Dec 1913 - 6 Oct 1914:	Commander, 2nd Brigade, 1st Don Cossack Division
6 Oct 1914 - 4 May 1917:	Commander, 1st Brigade, 5th Don Cossack Division

4 May 1917 - 1917:   Attached to the High Command

Lieutenant-General Nikolai Maksimovich **Polyakov** (8 May 1846 - 19 Jul 1918)
3 May 1900 - 1908:   Commander of Gendarmerie, Mogilev Province
6 Dec 1907:   Promoted to *Major-General*
1908:   Retired
2 Apr 1915 - 1917:   Recalled; Reserve officer, Dvinsk Military District
1917:   Promoted to *Lieutenant-General*
1917:   Retired

Lieutenant-General Platon Alekseyevich **Polyakov** (9 Apr 1832 - 1903)
19 Apr 1886:   Promoted to *Major-General*
19 Apr 1886 - 22 Jun 1888:   Cherkassy District Ataman, Don Cossack Army
22 Jun 1888 - 1896:   Rostov District Ataman, Don Cossack Army
1896:   Promoted to *Lieutenant-General*
1896:   Retired

Major-General Pyotr Vasilyevich **Polyakov** (19 Jan 1856 - ?)
14 Jul 1910 - 19 Jan 1914:   Commander, 2nd Battalion, 13th Artillery Brigade
19 Jan 1914:   Promoted to *Major-General*
19 Jan 1914:   Retired
1915 - 29 Feb 1916:   Recalled; Commander, Artillery Battalion
29 Feb 1916 - 1917:   Commander, 50th Artillery Brigade

General of Infantry Vladimir Alekseyevich **Polyakov** (9 Jul 1852 - ?)
23 Jun 1896 - 16 Aug 1899:   Deputy Intendant, Moscow Military District
6 May 1897:   Promoted to *Major-General*
16 Aug 1899 - 13 Apr 1902:   Intendant, Warsaw Military District
13 Apr 1902 - 18 Apr 1903:   Intendant, Moscow Military District
18 Apr 1903 - 6 Jun 1908:   Deputy Intendant-General, Ministry of War
28 Mar 1904:   Promoted to *Lieutenant-General*
6 Jun 1908 - 7 Aug 1909:   Intendant-General, Ministry of War,
                                 Chief of the Main Intendant Directorate
7 Aug 1909 - 13 Oct 1909:   At the disposal of the Minister of War
13 Oct 1909 - 25 Jan 1911:   Member of the Military Council
25 Jan 1911:   Promoted to *General of Infantry*
25 Jan 1911:   Retired

Major-General Mikhail Pavlovich **Polyanovsky** (24 Jun 1842 - ?)
11 Mar 1900 - 1904:   Chief of the Military Topographical Section, Amur
                                 Military District
1 Apr 1901:   Promoted to *Major-General*
1904:   Retired

Lieutenant-General Aleksey Sergeyevich **Polyansky** (5 Feb 1858 - ?)
15 Jul 1910:   Promoted to *Major-General*
15 Jul 1910 - 23 Jul 1914:   Commander, 2nd Brigade, 11th Siberian Rifle Division
23 Jul 1914 - 22 Apr 1915:   Commander, 1st Caucasus Rifle Brigade

22 Apr 1915 - 10 Jan 1917: Commander, 24th Infantry Division
13 Jun 1915: Promoted to *Lieutenant-General*
10 Jan 1917 - 1917: Reserve officer, Petrograd Military District

Major-General Vasily Amfianovich **Polyansky** (15 Nov 1834 - ?)
6 Sep 1891: Promoted to *Major-General*
6 Sep 1891 - 5 Feb 1897: Commander, 1st Brigade, 17th Infantry Division

Lieutenant-General Pyotr Aleksandrovich **Polzikov** (28 Jul 1855 - ?)
19 May 1912: Promoted to *Major-General*
19 May 1912 - Aug 1914: Commander, 1st Artillery Brigade
Aug 1914 - 14 Mar 1916: Inspector of Artillery, XIII. Army Corps
14 Mar 1916 - 1917: Commander, 1st Artillery Brigade
1917 - 31 May 1917: Reserve officer, Dvinsk Military District
31 May 1917: Promoted to *Lieutenant-General*
31 May 1917: Retired

General of Infantry Pyotr Vladimirovich **Polzikov** (23 Feb 1854 - 11 Jun 1938)
15 May 1904: Promoted to *Major-General*
15 May 1904 - 30 Jan 1907: Commander, 2nd Brigade, 37th Infantry Division
30 Jan 1907 - 22 Sep 1910: Commander, 1st Finnish Rifle Brigade
22 Sep 1910: Promoted to *Lieutenant-General*
22 Sep 1910 - 13 Nov 1914: Commander, 3rd Infantry Division
13 Nov 1914 - 1915: Reserve officer, Minsk Military District
1915: Promoted to *General of Infantry*
1915: Retired

Major-General Dmitry Nikanorovich **Pomerantsev** (20 Feb 1863 - ?)
16 Mar 1912 - 29 Nov 1915: Commander, 19th Turkestan Rifle Regiment
15 Jun 1915: Promoted to *Major-General*
29 Nov 1915 - 1917: Commander, Brigade, 5th Turkestan Rifle Division

Major-General Dmitry Semyonovich **Pomerantsev** (3 Feb 1853 - ?)
18 May 1902 - ?: Commander of Gendarmerie, Saratov Province
6 Dec 1909: Promoted to *Major-General*
? - 10 Apr 1916: Commander of Gendarmerie, Moscow
10 Apr 1916: Dismissed

General of Infantry Iliodor Ivanovich **Pomerantsev** (29 Aug 1847 - 1 May 1921)
2 May 1894 - 20 Mar 1903: Chief of Geodesic Section, Military Topographical Department, General Staff
14 May 1896: Promoted to *Major-General*
20 Mar 1903 - 8 Apr 1911: Commandant of the Military Topography School
6 Dec 1904: Promoted to *Lieutenant-General*
8 Apr 1911 - 19 Apr 1917: Chief of Military Topographical Department, General Staff
6 Dec 1914: Promoted to *General of Infantry*
19 Apr 1917: Retired

Lieutenant-General Pyotr Petrovich **Pomorsky** (17 Aug 1854 - ?)
7 Dec 1907 - 12 Jun 1909:	Commander of Engineers, Fortress Mikhailovsky
13 Apr 1908:	Promoted to *Major-General*
12 Jun 1909 - 2 Aug 1911:	Deputy Commander of Engineers, Amur Military District
2 Aug 1911 - 22 Oct 1912:	Commander of Engineers, Amur Military District
22 Oct 1912 - 1 Sep 1913:	Chief of Troop Billeting, Amur Military District
1 Sep 1913:	Promoted to *Lieutenant-General*
1 Sep 1913:	Retired
21 Jan 1914 - 20 Mar 1914:	Recalled; Attached to the Ministry of War
20 Mar 1914 - 1917:	Member, Barracks Committee, Main Directorate of Troop Billeting

Major-General Mikhail Mikhailovich **Pomortsev** (12 Jul 1851 - 19 Jun 1916)
9 Dec 1898 - Feb 1907:	Professor of Topography, Mikhailovsky Artillery School
2 Apr 1906:	Promoted to *Major-General*
Feb 1907:	Retired

Major-General Ivan Loginovich **Ponkratov** (5 Jan 1842 - ?)
26 May 1895 - 1905:	Military Judge, Kazan Military District Court
6 Dec 1900:	Promoted to *Major-General*

Lieutenant-General Georgy Logginovich **Ponomarev** (23 Apr 1857 - 10 Nov 1932)
16 Feb 1907 - 31 Dec 1913:	Commander, Life Guards Cossack Regiment
22 Apr 1907:	Promoted to *Major-General*
31 Dec 1913 - 14 Jan 1915:	Commander, 3rd Brigade, 1st Guards Cavalry Division
14 Jan 1915 - 12 May 1915:	District Ataman, 1st Don Cossack District
12 May 1915 - 18 Apr 1916:	Commander, 2nd Separate Don Cossack Brigade
19 Feb 1916:	Promoted to *Lieutenant-General*
18 Apr 1916 - Nov 1917:	Commander, 6th Don Cossack Division

Major-General Khrisanf Vasilyevich **Ponomarev** (17 Mar 1839 - ?)
1 Jul 1887:	Promoted to *Major-General*
1 Jul 1887 - 1898:	Ataman, Ust-Medveditsk District, Don Cossack Army

Lieutenant-General of the Fleet Vladimir Fyodorovich **Ponomarev** (8 Jul 1860 - Oct 1927)
5 Oct 1909 - 4 Apr 1917:	Commander, 1st Baltic Naval Depot
7 May 1911 - 4 Apr 1917:	Commandant, Peterhof Naval Base
6 Dec 1911:	Promoted to *Rear-Admiral*
6 Dec 1915:	Promoted to *Lieutenant-General of the Fleet*
4 Apr 1917 - 25 Apr 1917:	Reserve officer, Ministry of the Navy
25 Apr 1917:	Dismissed

Major-General Yevgeny Vladimirovich **Ponomarevsky-Svidersky** (17 Mar 1867 - 1920)
22 Nov 1914 - 27 Feb 1917:	Commander, Life Guards 1st Artillery Brigade
23 Apr 1915:	Promoted to *Major-General*

27 Feb 1917 - 1917: Inspector of Artillery, VII. Army Corps

Major-General Apollon Iosifovich **Poplavsky** (26 Jul 1875 - 1916)
1913 - 1916: Attached to 48th Infantry Regiment
26 Feb 1917: Posthumously promoted to *Major-General*

Lieutenant-General Aleksandr Andreyevich **Popov** (19 Jul 1834 - 1 Aug 1900)
3 Feb 1895 - 29 Apr 1900: Commander of Gendarmerie, Mogilev Province
2 Apr 1895: Promoted to *Major-General*
29 Apr 1900: Promoted to *Lieutenant-General*
29 Apr 1900: Retired

General of Cavalry Aleksandr Fyodorovich **Popov** (17 Nov 1852 - ?)
2 Jun 1906 - 16 Sep 1910: General for Special Assignments, Don Cossack Army
31 May 1907: Promoted to *Major-General*
16 Sep 1910 - 25 May 1914: Deputy Military Ataman, Siberian Cossack Army
1912: Promoted to *Lieutenant-General*
25 May 1914: Promoted to *General of Cavalry*
25 May 1914: Retired

Major-General Aleksandr Konstantinovich **Popov** (16 Aug 1851 - ?)
4 Jul 1907 - 28 Jun 1910: Commander, 27th Infantry Regiment
28 Jun 1910: Retired
1 Jun 1916 - 1917: Recalled; Reserve officer, Minsk Military District
6 Dec 1916: Promoted to *Major-General*

General of Infantry Aleksandr Nikolayevich **Popov** (23 Nov 1839 - 4 May 1910)
1 Jul 1888: Promoted to *Major-General*
1 Jul 1888 - 11 Apr 1890: Chief of Staff, South Ussuria Sector
11 Apr 1890 - 15 Jun 1892: Commander, 5th East Siberian Rifle Brigade
1 Jun 1892 - 15 Sep 1892: At the disposal of the Chief of the General Staff
15 Sep 1892 - 10 Jan 1898: Commander, Finnish Rifle Brigade
14 May 1896: Promoted to *Lieutenant-General*
10 Jan 1898 - 7 Jun 1898: Commander, 1st Grenadier Division
7 Jun 1898 - 14 Jun 1902: Deputy Commanding General, Amur Military District
14 Jun 1902 - 4 Oct 1905: At the disposal of the Minister of War
4 Oct 1905: Promoted to *General of Infantry*
4 Oct 1905: Retired

Lieutenant-General Aleksandr Nikolayevich **Popov** (1 Aug 1852 - ?)
2 Oct 1903: Promoted to *Major-General*
2 Oct 1903 - 28 May 1907: Commander, 36th Artillery Brigade
28 May 1907 - 29 May 1908: Commander of Artillery, I. Siberian Army Corps
2 Oct 1907: Promoted to *Lieutenant-General*

Major-General Dmitry Dmitriyevich **Popov** (21 Jan 1860 - 1 Apr 1915)
23 Jan 1914: Promoted to *Major-General*
23 Jan 1914 - 1 Apr 1915: Commander, 44th Artillery Brigade

Major-General Dmitry Petrovich **Popov** (22 Oct 1847 - ?)
27 Mar 1901 - 1912: Attached to the Don Cossack Army
1912: Promoted to *Major-General*
1912: Retired

Major-General Ippolit Ivanovich **Popov** (11 Aug 1857 - ?)
8 Jun 1907: Promoted to *Major-General*
8 Jun 1907 - 1907: Chief of Staff, Fortress Novogeorgiyevsk

Major-General Ivan Danilovich **Popov** (24 Feb 1864 - Feb 1920)
11 Sep 1914 - 23 Apr 1916: Commander, 9th Don Cossack Regiment
27 Nov 1915: Promoted to *Major-General*
23 Apr 1916 - 8 Jun 1917: Commander, 1st Brigade, 6th Don Cossack Division
8 Jun 1917 - Dec 1917: Commander, 8th Don Cossack Division

Major-General Ivan Dmitriyevich **Popov** (7 Oct 1853 - 13 May 1928)
12 Jun 1907 - 1917: Ataman, Pyatigorsk Division, Terek Region
6 Dec 1912: Promoted to *Major-General*

Lieutenant-General Ivan Ivanovich **Popov** (28 Aug 1866 - Jul 1918)
24 Sep 1908 - 17 Nov 1912: Commander, 56th Infantry Regiment
3 May 1912: Promoted to *Major-General*
17 Nov 1912 - 1 Nov 1913: Commander, 1st Brigade, 41st Infantry Division
1 Nov 1913 - 18 Jul 1914: Quartermaster-General, Kazan Military District
18 Jul 1914 - 4 Mar 1915: Quartermaster-General, 4th Army
4 Mar 1915 - 14 Oct 1916: Chief of Staff, 10th Army
30 Jul 1916: Promoted to *Lieutenant-General*
14 Oct 1916 - 18 Apr 1917: Commander, 32nd Infantry Division
18 Apr 1917 - Nov 1917: Reserve officer, Kazan Military District

Major-General Ivan Vasilyevich **Popov** (5 Jan 1851 - 17 Apr 1906)
15 Nov 1897: Promoted to *Major-General*
15 Nov 1897 - 17 Apr 1906: Commander, Kuban Light Infantry Brigade

Major-General of Naval Engineers Konstantin Nikolayevich **Popov** (6 Mar 1867 - 24 Feb 1918)
5 Nov 1911 - 1917: Chief Engineer, Battleship "Panteleimon"
1917: Promoted to *Major-General of Naval Engineers*

Major-General Mikhail Ivanovich **Popov** (11 Jan 1843 - 11 Mar 1916)
? - 1900: Attached to the Ministry of War
1900: Promoted to *Major-General*
1900: Retired

Major-General Mikhail Vasilyevich **Popov** (24 Dec 1856 - ?)
21 Sep 1913 - 1917: Senior Engineer Inspector, Main Military-Technical Directorate
6 Dec 1916: Promoted to *Major-General*

Major-General Nikolai Konstantinovich **Popov** (14 Nov 1854 - ?)
29 Jan 1911 - 1912: Commander, 16th Siberian Rifle Regiment
1912: Retired
9 Feb 1915 - 1917: Recalled; Reserve officer, Caucasus Military District
10 Jul 1916: Promoted to *Major-General*

Major-General Nikolai Petrovich **Popov** (13 Apr 1858 - 3 Jun 1926)
1 Aug 1905 - 6 Sep 1911: Director, Petrovsky Poltava Cadet Corps
13 Apr 1908: Promoted to *Major-General*
6 Sep 1911: Dismissed
1916 - 1917: Recalled; Reserve officer, Caucasus Military District

Major-General Pyotr Kharitonovich **Popov** (10 Jan 1867 - 7 Oct 1960)
10 Jun 1910 - Jan 1918: Commandant, Novocherkassk Cossack School
14 Mar 1913: Promoted to *Major-General*

Major-General Pyotr Ksenofontovich **Popov** (20 Dec 1868 - ?)
11 Feb 1915 - 1917: Staff Officer for Special Assignments, Minister of Internal Affairs
6 Dec 1915: Promoted to *Major-General*

Major-General Vasily Fyodorovich **Popov** (20 Dec 1871 - ?)
7 Sep 1915 - 17 Oct 1916: Commander, 8th Finnish Rifle Regiment
17 Oct 1916 - 1918: Chief of Stff, 59th Infantry Division
6 Dec 1916: Promoted to *Major-General*

Major-General Viktor Lukich **Popov** (4 Nov 1864 - ?)
17 Dec 1915 - 6 Nov 1916: Chief of Staff, 14th Siberian Rifle Division
27 Apr 1916: Promoted to *Major-General*
6 Nov 1916 - 29 Jan 1917: Chief of Staff, XIII. Army Corps
29 Jan 1917 - 20 Sep 1917: Commander, 182nd Infantry Division
20 Sep 1917 - 14 Dec 1917: Reserve officer, Dvinsk Military District

Major-General Viktor Vasilyevich **Popov** (28 Oct 1844 - ?)
18 Sep 1898: Promoted to *Major-General*
18 Sep 1898 - 16 Sep 1902: Commander, 1st Brigade, 21st Infantry Division

Major-General of the Fleet Vladimir Aleksandrovich **Popov** (8 Apr 1857 - ?)
29 Sep 1909 - 1917: Commander of Pilots, Port of Kronstadt, Commander, London Lightship
6 Dec 1909: Promoted to *Major-General of the Admiralty*
4 Feb 1913: Redesignated *Major-General of the Hydrographic Corps*

Major-General Vladimir Mikhailovich **Popov** (26 Nov 1863 - 20 Apr 1926)
1915 - 29 Mar 1916: Commander, 78th Infantry Regiment
1916: Promoted to *Major-General*
29 Mar 1916 - 1917: Reserve officer, Dvinsk Military District

Lieutenant-General of Naval Engineers Vladimir Nikolayevich **Popov** (15 Feb 1865 - 18 Aug 1947)
18 Jul 1910 - 11 Apr 1919:	Chief Mechanical Engineer, Port of Sevastopol
22 Aug 1911:	Promoted to *Major-General of Naval Engineers*
1916:	Promoted to *Lieutenant-General of Naval Engineers*

Major-General Vladimir Nikolayevich **Popov** (22 Sep 1874 - ?)
13 Nov 1915 - 1917:	Commander, 2nd Brigade, 5th Cavalry Division
14 Nov 1915:	Promoted to *Major-General*
1917:	Chief of Staff, Inspector of Cavalry
1917 - 30 Nov 1917:	Special Assignments General, 5th Army
30 Nov 1917 - 1918:	Reserve officer, Odessa Military District

Major-General Vladimir Petrovich **Popov** (25 Jan 1877 - 17 Oct 1935)
5 Mar 1916 - 1917:	Chief of Staff, 1st Don Cossack Division
1917:	Promoted to *Major-General*
1917 - Jun 1917:	Chief of Staff, III. Cavalry Corps
Jun 1917 - 1918:	Commander, 1stv Don Cossack Division

Major-General Vladimir Platonovich **Popov** (9 Feb 1863 - ?)
28 Apr 1914 - 27 Jul 1914:	Deputy Chief of Troop Billeting, Vilnius Military District
27 Jul 1914 - 1917:	Reserve officer, Dvinsk Militatary District
6 May 1915:	Promoted to *Major-General*

Major-General Vladimir Vasilyevich **Popov** (21 Apr 1841 - 31 Oct 1896)
22 Aug 1881 - 1894:	Deputy Commander of Engineers, St. Petersburg Military District
7 May 1887:	Promoted to *Major-General*

Lieutenant-General Yakov Kozmich **Popov** (9 Oct 1844 - 1918)
21 Nov 1894:	Promoted to *Major-General*
21 Nov 1894 - 12 Jul 1896:	Head of the Izhevsk Machine-Building Plant
12 Jul 1896 - 18 Apr 1900:	Transferred to the reserve
18 Apr 1900 - 23 Sep 1905:	At the disposal of the Minister of War
17 Apr 1905:	Promoted to *Lieutenant-General*
23 Sep 1905:	Retired

Major-General Yevgeny Iosifovich **Popov** (17 Jan 1865 - ?)
30 Aug 1910 - 30 Apr 1914:	Clerk, Engineering Committee, Main Engineering Directorate
6 Dec 1911:	Promoted to *Major-General*
30 Apr 1914 - 1917:	Commander of Engineers, Fortress Ivangorod

Lieutenant-General Ivan Yuryevich **Popovich-Lipovats** (14 Jun 1856 - 17 Aug 1919)
24 Dec 1904 - 18 Oct 1905:	At the disposal of the C-in-C, 1st Manchurian Army
4 Sep 1905:	Promoted to *Major-General*
18 Oct 1905 - 20 Apr 1908:	At the disposal of the Chief of the General Staff

20 Apr 1908:	Retired
29 Aug 1914 - 17 Oct 1914:	Recalled; Commander, 2nd Brigade, 9th Infantry Division
17 Oct 1914 - 19 Dec 1914:	Commander, Brigade, 60th Infantry Division
19 Dec 1914 - 10 Apr 1915:	Commander, 1st Brigade, 9th Infantry Division
10 Apr 1915 - Jun 1915:	Commander, 2nd Brigade, 48th Infantry Division
8 Jul 1915 - 17 Apr 1917:	Reserve officer, Minsk Military District
24 Jan 1916:	Promoted to *Lieutenant-General*
17 Apr 1917 - 1917:	At the disposal of the Minister of War

Lieutenant-General Georgy-Karl-Vilgelm-Yakov Vasilyevich von **Poppen** (16 Feb 1851 - 16 Mar 1924)

1 Nov 1897:	Promoted to *Major-General*
1 Nov 1897 - 30 Apr 1900:	Chief of Staff, XVIII. Army Corps
30 Apr 1900 - 12 Jan 1904:	Chief of Staff, I. Army Corps
12 Jan 1904 - 2 May 1904:	Commander, 9th Infantry Division
28 Mar 1904:	Promoted to *Lieutenant-General*
2 May 1904 - 17 Jan 1906:	Commander, 45th Infantry Division

General of Artillery Mikhail Grigoryevich **Popruzhenko** (3 Aug 1854 - 13 Feb 1917)

18 May 1898 - 8 Jan 1905:	Director, Vladimir-Kiev Cadet Corps
1 Jan 1901:	Promoted to *Major-General*
8 Jan 1905 - 13 Feb 1917:	General for Special Assignments, Main Directorate for Military Schools
22 Apr 1907:	Promoted to *Lieutenant-General*
14 Feb 1917:	Posthumously promoted to *General of Artillery*

Major-General Yevgeny Aleksandrovich **Poray-Koshits** (6 Sep 1851 - ?)

18 Dec 1904 - 13 Jun 1905:	Attached to the C-in-C, Manchurian Army
25 Mar 1905:	Promoted to *Major-General*
13 Jun 1905 - 25 Aug 1905:	At the disposal of the General Staff
25 Aug 1905 - 25 Sep 1907:	Commander, 1st Brigade, 39th Infantry Division
25 Sep 1907:	Retired
10 Nov 1915 - 1917:	Recalled; Reserve officer, Dvinsk Military District

Lieutenant-General of Naval Engineers Fyodor Yakovlevich **Porechkin** (19 Sep 1849 - Nov 1928)

1904 - 18 Apr 1910:	Inspector of Naval Mechanical Engineers
1 Jan 1905:	Promoted to *Major-General of Naval Engineers*
18 Apr 1910:	Promoted to *Lieutenant-General of Naval Engineers*
18 Apr 1910 - Jul 1911:	Chief Inspector of Naval Mechanical Engineers
Jul 1911:	Retired
1914 - 1917:	Recalled; Attached to the 2nd Baltic Naval Depot
1916 - 1917:	Ministry of the Navy Representative, England

Rear-Admiral Kazimir Adolfovich **Porembsky** (5 Nov 1872 - 20 Jan 1933)

10 Apr 1916 - 10 Nov 1916:	Commander, Cruiser Brigade, Black Sea Fleet
19 Apr 1916:	Promoted to *Rear-Admiral*

10 Nov 1916: Transferred to the reserve

General of Infantry Aleksandr Nikolayevich **Poretsky** (13 Apr 1855 - 25 Mar 1915)
10 Jul 1904: Promoted to *Major-General*
16 Jul 1904 - 11 Feb 1908: Commander, Life Guards Izmailovo Regiment
11 Feb 1908 - 24 Sep 1913: Commander, 1st Brigade, 2nd Guards Infantry Division
24 Sep 1913: Promoted to *Lieutenant-General*
24 Sep 1913 - 18 Sep 1914: Commander, 26th Infantry Division
18 Sep 1914 - 25 Mar 1916: Sick leave
23 Mar 1915: Promoted to *General of Infantry*

Major-General Nikolai Nikolayevich **Porokhov** (1855 - 1909)
1908: Attached to 1st Reserve Artillery Brigade
1908: Promoted to *Major-General*
1908: Retired

Major-General Aleksandr Sergeyevich **Porokhovshchikov** (10 Feb 1865 - ?)
Dec 1914 - Jun 1915: Commander, 335th Infantry Regiment
5 Jun 1915: Promoted to *Major-General*
Jun 1915 - 5 Jan 1916: Commander, Brigade, 64th Infantry Division
5 Jan 1916 - 24 May 1916: Chief of Staff, 18th Infantry Division
24 May 1916 - 1917: At the disposal of the Chief of the General Staff
1917: Attached to the C-in-C, Southwestern Front

Major-General Nikolai Vyacheslavovich **Poroshin** (28 Jan 1854 - 19 May 1910)
? - 1910: Chief of Gendarmerie, Baku
1910: Promoted to *Major-General*

Lieutenant-General Yakov Afinogenovich **Poroshin** (23 Oct 1855 - Sep 1916)
23 May 1904 - 5 Mar 1907: Commander of Engineers, Fortress Libau
6 Dec 1904: Promoted to *Major-General*
5 Mar 1907 - 29 Nov 1912: Commander of Engineers, Caucasus Military District
6 Dec 1910: Promoted to *Lieutenant-General*
29 Nov 1912 - 10 Jul 1915: Inspector of Engineers, Caucasus Military District
10 Jul 1915 - Sep 1916: Head of Caucasus District Railways

Lieutenant-General Ilya Titovich **Poslavsky** (2 Aug 1853 - 13 Nov 1914)
Jan 1900 - 8 Mar 1901: Inspector of Engineering Projects, Turkestan Military District
6 Dec 1900: Promoted to *Major-General*
8 Mar 1901 - 27 Mar 1903: Deputy Commander of Engineers, Turkestan Military District
27 Mar 1903 - 22 Oct 1912: Commander of Engineers, Turkestan Military District
22 Apr 1907: Promoted to *Lieutenant-General*
22 Oct 1912 - 13 Nov 1914: Chief of Troop Billeting, Turkestan Military District

Major-General Stepan Semyonovich **Poslavsky** (17 May 1861 - 22 Aug 1914)
24 Jan 1909 - 9 Dec 1910: Class V Member, Technical Committee, Main Artillery

	Directorate
29 Mar 1909:	Promoted to *Major-General*
9 Dec 1910 - 22 Aug 1914:	Head of the Technical Committee, Main Artillery Directorate

Lieutenant-General Pavel Ippolitovich **Posnikov** (19 Feb 1837 - ?)
13 Nov 1894:	Promoted to *Major-General*
13 Nov 1894 - 30 Jan 1900:	Commander, 11th Artillery Brigade
30 Jan 1900:	Promoted to *Lieutenant-General*
30 Jan 1900:	Retired

Major-General Sergey Dmitriyevich **Posnikov** (4 Jul 1858 - ?)
6 Dec 1911:	Promoted to *Major-General*
6 Dec 1911 - 4 Jul 1915:	Special Assignments General, Ministry of War
4 Jul 1915 - Oct 1917:	Reserve officer, 6th Army

Major-General Andrey Andreyevich **Posokhov** (5 Oct 1872 - 19 Apr 1931)
Nov 1914 - 24 Oct 1915:	Quartermaster-General, 2nd Army
14 Jan 1915:	Promoted to *Major-General*
24 Oct 1915 - 9 Apr 1917 :	Quartermaster-General, 3rd Army
9 Apr 1917 - Oct 1917:	Chief of Staff, 12th Army

Rear-Admiral Sergey Andreyevich **Posokhov** (15 Oct 1866 - 2 Feb 1935)
27 Feb 1915 - 31 Oct 1916:	Commander, Mine Training Detachment, Baltic Fleet
30 Sep 1916:	Promoted to *Rear-Admiral*
31 Oct 1916 - Apr 1917:	Chief of Staff, Arctic Ocean Flotilla
Apr 1917 - 6 Oct 1917:	Reserve officer, Ministry of the Navy
6 Oct 1917:	Dismissed

Lieutenant-General Sergey Matveyevich **Pospelov** (30 Nov 1854 - ?)
9 Mar 1904 - 18 Jul 1905:	Commander, 13th East Siberian Rifle Regiment
1905:	Promoted to *Major-General*
18 Jul 1905 - 8 Oct 1907:	Commander, 2nd Brigade, 3rd East Siberian Rifle Division
8 Oct 1907 - 4 Jul 1910:	Commander, 8th Turkestan Rifle Brigade
4 Jul 1910 - 23 Dec 1911:	Commander, 6th Turkestan Rifle Brigade
23 Dec 1911:	Promoted to *Lieutenant-General*
23 Dec 1911 - 16 Apr 1917:	Commander, 2nd Siberian Rifle Division
16 Apr 1917 - 29 May 1917:	Commanding General, XXXI. Army Corps
29 May 1917 - 8 Aug 1917:	Unassigned
8 Aug 1917:	Dismissed

Lieutenant-General Aleksandr Ivanovich **Postovsky** (7 Jan 1861 - 23 Mar 1941)
24 Jun 1904 - 28 Feb 1907:	Chief of Staff, VI. Siberian Army Corps
27 Sep 1904:	Promoted to *Major-General*
28 Feb 1907 - 19 Oct 1907:	Chief of Staff, XVI. Army Corps
19 Oct 1907 - 17 Nov 1912:	Chief of Communications, Moscow Military District
17 Nov 1912:	Promoted to *Lieutenant-General*

17 Nov 1912 - 29 Jul 1915:	Commander, 1st Grenadier Division
29 Jul 1915 - 2 Dec 1915:	Reserve officer, Dvinsk Military District
2 Dec 1915 - 22 Dec 1916:	Reserve officer, Petrograd Military District
22 Dec 1916 - 8 Oct 1917:	At the disposal of the Minister of War
8 Oct 1917:	Retired

General of Artillery Ivan Konstantinovich **Postovsky** (27 Jul 1828 - 1906)
4 Nov 1872 - 30 Aug 1888:	Commander, 7th Artillery Brigade
1 Jan 1878:	Promoted to *Major-General*
30 Aug 1888:	Promoted to *Lieutenant-General*
30 Aug 1888 - 8 Jul 1900:	Commander of Artillery, XV. Army Corps
8 Jul 1900:	Promoted to *General of Artillery*
8 Jul 1900:	Retired

Lieutenant-General Pyotr Ivanovich **Postovsky** (22 Sep 1857 - ?)
6 Aug 1906:	Promoted to *Major-General*
6 Aug 1906 - 3 Dec 1908:	General for Special Assignments, Warsaw Military District
3 Dec 1908 - 9 Apr 1913:	Quartermaster-General, Warsaw Military District
9 Apr 1913 - 19 Jul 1914:	Commander, 1st Caucasus Rifle Brigade
19 Jul 1914 - 7 Oct 1914:	Chief of Staff, 2nd Army
8 Oct 1914 - 11 Nov 1914:	Commander, 76th Infantry Division
11 Nov 1914 - 5 Jul 1915:	Commander, 65th Infantry Division
23 Mar 1915:	Promoted to *Lieutenant-General*
5 Jul 1915 - 22 Dec 1915:	Reserve officer, Kiev Military District
22 Dec 1915 - 11 Nov 1916:	At the disposal of the Chief of the General Staff
11 Nov 1916 - Oct 1917:	Head of Main Committee for Conscription, General Staff

Major-General Dmitry Vladimirovich **Potapchin** (30 Jan 1839 - ?)
29 Jan 1901:	Promoted to *Major-General*
29 Jan 1901 - 1906:	Commander, Poltava Regional Brigade

Major-General Aleksey Stepanovich **Potapov** (17 Mar 1872 - ?)
8 Feb 1911 - 16 Aug 1912:	Chief of Staff, 47th Infantry Division
16 Aug 1912:	Promoted to *Major-General*
16 Aug 1912:	Retired
8 Dec 1914 - 1915:	Recalled; Reserve officer, Dvinsk Military District
1915 - 18 Jan 1916:	Commander, Cavalry Detachment
18 Jan 1916 - 14 Jan 1917:	Commander, Brigade, 64th Infantry Division
14 Jan 1917 - 1 Mar 1917:	Reserve officer, Kiev Military District
1 Mar 1917 - 4 Mar 1917:	Member of the Military Commission, Provisional Committee of the State Duma
4 Mar 1917 - Apr 1917:	Chairman of the Military Commission, Provisional Committee of the State Duma
Apr 1917 - 20 Jun 1917:	Special Assignments General, Ministry of War
20 Jun 1917 - 1918:	Reserve officer, Petrograd Military District

Major-General Nikolai Aleksandrovich **Potapov** (23 Sep 1862 - ?)
20 May 1910 - 1917: Military Judge, Caucasus Military District Court
6 Dec 1910: Promoted to *Major-General*

Lieutenant-General Nikolai Mihailovich **Potapov** (2 Mar 1871 - 1946)
10 Jun 1903 - Aug 1916: Military Attaché, Montenegro
2 Feb 1912: Promoted to *Major-General*
10 Aug 1916 - 13 Apr 197: Chief of Evacuation Section, General Staff
13 Apr 1917 - 23 Nov 1917: Quartermaster-General, General Staff
1917: Promoted to *Lieutenant-General*
23 Nov 1917 - May 1918: Chief of the General Directorate of the General Staff, Deputy Minister of War

Major-General Stepan Zakharovich **Potapov** (30 Jul 1860 - ?)
19 Dec 1912 - 29 May 1916: Commander, 189th Infantry Regiment
26 Mar 1916: Promoted to *Major-General*
29 May 1916 - 22 Jan 1917: Commander, 1st Brigade, 10th Infantry Division
22 Jan 1917 - 7 Sep 1917: Commander, 56th Infantry Division
7 Sep 1917 - 1918: Commander, 62nd Infantry Division

Lieutenant-General Aleksandr Platonovich **Pototsky** (26 Feb 1846 - 1918)
12 Apr 1892 - 1 Aug 1905: Director of the Poltava Cadet Corps
30 Aug 1893: Promoted to *Major-General*
6 Dec 1904: Promoted to *Lieutenant-General*
1 Aug 1905: Retired

General of Infantry Ivan Platonovich **Pototsky** (1 Feb 1848 - 19 Sep 1912)
5 Apr 1893 - 2 Mar 1895: Chief of Staff, Trans-Baikal Region
2 Jun 1893: Promoted to *Major-General*
2 Mar 1895 - 18 Oct 1896: Deputy Chief of Staff, Irkutsk Military Region
18 Oct 1896 - 24 Oct 1899: Chief of Staff, Fortress Brest-Litovsk
24 Oct 1899 - 10 Aug 1900: Commander, 47th Replacement Infantry Brigade
10 Aug 1900 - 22 Jul 1902: Commander, 7th Infantry Division
6 Dec 1900: Promoted to *Lieutenant-General*
22 Jul 1902 - 17 Sep 1903: Commander, 26th Infantry Division
17 Sep 1903 - 7 Feb 1906: At the disposal of the Chief of the General Staff
7 Feb 1906: Promoted to *General of Infantry*
7 Feb 1906: Retired

General of Artillery Nikolai Platonovich **Pototsky** (1 Mar 1844 - 10 Feb 1911)
26 Feb 1891 - 27 Feb 1901: Professor, Mikhailovsk Artillery Academy
30 Aug 1891: Promoted to *Major-General*
27 Feb 1901 - 1906: Member of the Artillery Committee, Main Artillery Directorate
14 Apr 1902: Promoted to *Lieutenant-General*
1906: Promoted to *General of Artillery*
1906: Retired

General of Artillery Pavel Platonovich **Pototsky** (12 Dec 1857 - 26 Aug 1938)
3 Mar 1904 - 17 Nov 1904:	Commander, 22nd Artillery Brigade
17 Nov 1904 - 21 Nov 1907:	Commander, 25th Artillery Brigade
17 Apr 1905:	Promoted to *Major-General*
21 Nov 1907 - 3 Jul 1908:	Commander of Artillery, XIII. Army Corps
3 Jul 1908 - 24 Jul 1910:	Commander of Artillery, Guards Corps
29 Mar 1909:	Promoted to *Lieutenant-General*
24 Jul 1910 - 27 Dec 1914:	Inspector of Artillery, Guards Corps
27 Dec 1914 - 21 Aug 1916:	Commander, 2nd Guards Infantry Division
21 Aug 1916 - 13 Sep 1916:	Commanding General, XXV. Army Corps
13 Sep 1916 - 2 Apr 1917:	Commanding General, I. Guards Corps
6 Dec 1916:	Promoted to *General of Artillery*
2 Apr 1917 - 22 Apr 1917:	Reserve officer, Kiev Military District
22 Apr 1917 - Oct 1917:	Reserve officer, Petrograd Military District

General of Infantry Pyotr Platonovich **Pototsky** (8 Jun 1855 - ?)
17 May 1903:	Promoted to *Major-General*
17 May 1903 - 14 Mar 1904:	Chief of Staff, XI. Army Corps
14 Mar 1904 - 24 Sep 1905:	Chief of Staff, XXI. Army Corps
24 Sep 1905 - 11 May 1907:	Chief of Staff, Fortress Warsaw
11 May 1907 - 2 Jul 1910:	Commander of Artillery, Fortress Warsaw
2 Jul 1910:	Promoted to *Lieutenant-General*
2 Jul 1910 - 23 Apr 1913:	Commander, 28th Infantry Division
23 Apr 1913 - 22 Oct 1914:	Commander, 35th Infantry Division
Aug 1914:	Acting Commanding General, XVII. Army Corps
22 Oct 1914 - 2 May 1915:	Reserve officer, Kiev Military District
2 May 1915:	Promoted to *General of Infantry*
2 May 1915:	Retired

Major-General Yevgeny Pavlovich **Pototsky** (2 May 1844 - ?)
23 Jun 1909:	Promoted to *Major-General*
23 Jun 1909 - 1911:	Attached to the Independent Corps of Gendarmes

Major-General Aleksandr Vasilyevich **Potto** (28 Feb 1866 - 21 Jan 1917)
4 Jun 1915 - 21 Jan 1917:	Commander, 2nd Brigade, 2nd Caucasus Cossack Division
6 Dec 1915:	Promoted to *Major-General*

Lieutenant-General Vasily Aleksandrovich **Potto** (1 Jan 1836 - 29 Nov 1911)
18 Feb 1896 - 29 Nov 1911:	Chief of Military History Department, Caucasus Military District
14 May 1896:	Promoted to *Major-General*
22 Apr 1907:	Promoted to *Lieutenant-General*

Major-General Pyotr Petrovich **Potulov** (10 Apr 1855 - ?)
22 Jun 1902 - 30 Mar 1904:	Commander, 3rd Grenadier Artillery Brigade
3 Oct 1902:	Promoted to *Major-General*

Lieutenant-General Aleksandr Nikolayevich **Povalo-Shveykovsky** (6 Apr 1834 - 28 Jan 1903)
28 Feb 1886:   Promoted to *Major-General*
28 Feb 1886 - 20 Mar 1887:   Commander, 1st Brigade, 13th Infantry Division
20 Mar 1887 - 25 Nov 1891:   Commander, 2nd Brigade, 28th Infantry Division
25 Nov 1891 - 31 Dec 1892:   Chief of Staff, Grenadier Corps
31 Dec 1892 - 30 Jun 1893:   Chief of Staff, Turkestan Military District
30 Jun 1893 - 1898:   Military Governor of Fergana Province,
                                Military Commander, Fergana Province
14 May 1896:   Promoted to *Lieutenant-General*
1898:   Retired

Major-General Nikolai Alekseyevich **Povalo-Shvyykovsky** (26 Dec 1860 - ?)
14 Aug 1906 - 11 Oct 1911:   Military Prosecutor, Irkutsk Military District
6 Dec 1906:   Promoted to *Major-General*
11 Oct 1911 - Jul 1914:   Military Judge, Vilnius Military District Court
Jul 1914 - 1918:   Military Judge, Dvinsk Military District Court

General of Infantry Ivan Maksimovich **Povolotsky** (20 Jul 1842 - 15 Oct 1914)
5 Nov 1890:   Promoted to *Major-General*
5 Nov 1890 - 17 Mar 1895:   Chief of Staff, X. Army Corps
17 Mar 1895 - 17 Feb 1902:   Chief of Staff, Vilnius Military District
6 Dec 1897:   Promoted to *Lieutenant-General*
17 Feb 1902 - 12 Mar 1903:   At the disposal of the Minister of War
12 Mar 1903 - 30 Dec 1906:   Commanding General, II. Army Corps
6 Dec 1906:   Promoted to *General of Infantry*
30 Dec 1906 - 15 Oct 1914:   Member of the Military Council

General of Cavalry Ippolit Apollonovich **Pozdeyev** (12 Mar 1845 - ?)
17 Dec 1893:   Promoted to *Major-General*
17 Dec 1893 - 17 Feb 1896:   Commander, Life Guards Ataman Regiment
17 Feb 1896 - 28 Mar 1897:   Attached to the Don Cossack Army
28 Mar 1897 - 18 Sep 1900:   Commander, 2nd Brigade, 15th Cavalry Division
18 Sep 1900 - Apr 1907:   Commander, 1st Don Cossack Division
6 May 1901:   Promoted to *Lieutenant-General*
Apr 1907:   Retired
3 Mar 1917:   Promoted to *General of Cavalry*

Major-General Iosif Fomich **Pozharsky** (2 Jul 1866 - ?)
24 Apr 1916 - 1917:   Commander, Guard Battalion, Supreme High Command
11 Oct 1916:   Promoted to *Major-General*
1917:   Commander, Marine Division, Black Sea Fleet
1917 - 9 Jan 1918:   Commander, 30th Infantry Division

Lieutenant-General Nikolai Prokofyevich **Pozhidayev** (28 Oct 1844 - ?)
24 Oct 1899:   Promoted to *Major-General*
24 Oct 1899 - 12 Jul 1902:   Commander, 1st Brigade, 30th Infantry Division
12 Jul 1902 - 6 Sep 1906:   Commandant of Fortress Mikhailov

6 Sep 1906:	Promoted to *Lieutenant-General*
6 Sep 1906:	Retired
19 Dec 1915 - 18 May 1917:	Recalled; Chief of Kazan District Evacuation Points

Lieutenant-General Ignaty Nikolayevich **Poznansky** (28 Mar 1835 - 1897)

6 Apr 1882 - 10 Apr 1895:	Commander of Gendarmerie, Nizhny Novgorod Province
8 Apr 1884:	Promoted to *Major-General*
10 Apr 1895 - 1897:	Commander, Siberian Gendarmerie District
14 May 1896:	Promoted to *Lieutenant-General*

Major-General Georgy Avetikovich **Pozoyev** (20 Oct 1858 - ?)

1 Aug 1910 - 11 Jan 1916:	Commander, 2nd Battalion, 3rd Grenadier Artillery Brigade
22 Oct 1915:	Promoted to *Major-General*
11 Jan 1916 - 23 Jun 1917:	Commander, 46th Artillery Brigade
23 Jun 1917 - 1918:	Inspector of Artillery, XXXIII. Army Corps

Lieutenant-General Leon Avetikovich **Pozoyev** (6 Jan 1855 - ?)

15 May 1907 - 26 Jul 1910:	Commander, 1st Turkestan Artillery Brigade
31 May 1907:	Promoted to *Major-General*
26 Jul 1910 - 17 Aug 1914:	Inspector of Artillery, I. Turkestan Army Corps
14 Apr 1913:	Promoted to *Lieutenant-General*
17 Aug 1914 - 1917:	Commander of Artillery, Turkestan Military District

Major-General Ruben Avetikovich **Pozoyev** (16 Nov 1856 - ?)

1 Jun 1910 - 12 May 1916:	Commander, 1st Battalion, 20th Artillery Brigade
11 Aug 1915:	Promoted to *Major-General*
12 May 1916 - Nov 1917:	Commander, 6th Artillery Brigade

Lieutenant-General Vladimir Porfiryevich **Prasalov** (6 Oct 1856 - 1 Aug 1917)

11 Apr 1902:	Promoted to *Major-General*
11 Apr 1902 - 29 Aug 1907:	Commandant of Fortress Kushka
30 Jul 1907:	Promoted to *Lieutenant-General*
29 Aug 1907 - 18 Nov 1910:	Commandant of Fortress Kerch
18 Nov 1910 - 11 Mar 1912:	Attached to the General Staff
11 Mar 1912 - 13 May 1915:	Commander, 38th Infantry Division
22 Jul 1915 - 20 Aug 1915:	Commander, 119th Infantry Division
20 Aug 1915 - 1917:	POW, Germany

General of Cavalry Nikolai Alekseyevich **Pratasov-Bakhmetev** (28 Mar 1834 - 25 Oct 1907)

16 Jan 1871 - 17 May 1875:	Commander, Life Guards Horse Regiment
28 May 1871:	Promoted to *Major-General*
18 Dec 1873 - 31 Jan 1876:	Commander, 1st Brigade, 1st Guards Cavalry Division
31 Jan 1876 - 1877:	General à la suite
1877 - 1878:	Commander, Consolidated Cossack Division
1878 - 25 May 1880:	General à la suite

25 May 1880 - 18 Jul 1882:	Governor of Astrakhan, Ataman, Astrakhan Cossack Army
30 Aug 1881:	Promoted to *Lieutenant-General*
18 Jul 1882 - 29 Jul 1889:	Attached to the Minister of Internal Affairs
29 Jul 1889 - 2 Apr 1906:	Chief Superintendent, Chancellery of the Board of Trustees, Empress Maria Institutions
21 May 1890 - 2 Apr 1906:	Member of the State Council
6 Dec 1895:	Promoted to *General of Infantry*
1 Jan 1896:	Redesignated *General of Cavalry*

Major-General Dmitry Aleksandrovich **Pravikov** (16 Oct 1863 - 1 Feb 1941)
26 Sep 1913 - 22 Apr 1917:	Deputy Chief of Staff, Corps of Gendarmerie
22 Mar 1915:	Promoted to *Major-General*
22 Apr 1917 - 2 Jun 1917:	Reserve officer, Moscow Military District
2 Jun 1917:	Retired

Major-General Nikolai Viktorovich **Pravotorov** (18 Apr 1864 - ?)
1 May 1914 - 24 Mar 1915:	Commander, 10th Grenadier Regiment
16 Feb 1915:	Promoted to *Major-General*
24 Mar 1915 - 1917:	Commander, Brigade, 3rd Grenadier Division

General of Infantry Aleksandr Eduardovich **Preskott** (23 Mar 1846 - 16 Dec 1904)
15 Mar 1889:	Promoted to *Major-General*
15 Mar 1889 - 23 Jun 1897:	Commander, 3rd Sapper Brigade
23 Jun 1897 - 1 Jan 1898:	Commander, 42nd Reserve Infantry Brigade
1 Jan 1898 - 22 Jun 1904:	Commander, 42nd Infantry Division
6 Dec 1898:	Promoted to *Lieutenant-General*
22 Jun 1904 - 16 Dec 1904:	Commanding General, III. Army Corps
11 Jan 1905:	Posthumously promoted to *General of Infantry*

General of Engineers Nikolai Edgarovich **Preskott** (2 Feb 1851 - ?)
26 Aug 1897 - 4 Dec 1901:	Commander, Life Guards Sapper Battalion
6 Dec 1898:	Promoted to *Major-General*
4 Dec 1901 - 19 May 1907:	Commander, 1st Sapper Brigade
6 Dec 1904:	Promoted to *Lieutenant-General*
1906:	Promoted to *General-Adjutant*
19 May 1907 - Oct 1917:	Reserve officer, Engineer Corps
6 Dec 1914:	Promoted to *General of Engineers*

Major-General of the Hydrographic Corps Konstantin Ivanovich **Prestin** (24 Jul 1864 - ?)
1911 - 1917:	Director of Lighthouses & Navigation, White Sea
1915:	Promoted to *Major-General of the Hydrographic Corps*

Major-General Aleksandr-Erast Ioganovich **Preys** (7 Nov 1844 - ?)
20 Feb 1902 - 1 Dec 1904:	Commander of Artillery, Fortress Kerch
6 Dec 1902:	Promoted to *Major-General*

General of Artillery Konstantin Pavlovich **Prezhbyano** (14 Sep 1840 - 24 Jul 1905)
24 May 1893:	Promoted to *Major-General*
24 May 1893 - 5 Dec 1899:	Commander, 24th Artillery Brigade
5 Dec 1899 - 14 Sep 1903:	Commander of Artillery, XI. Army Corps
1 Apr 1901:	Promoted to *Lieutenant-General*
14 Sep 1903:	Promoted to *General of Artillery*
14 Sep 1903:	Retired

Lieutenant-General Aleksandr Bogdanovich **Prezhentsov** (25 Jan 1859 - 11 Nov 1915)
2 Mar 1904 - 2 Jul 1905:	At the disposal of the Commanding General, Finland Military District
28 Mar 1904:	Promoted to *Major-General*
2 Jul 1905 - 16 Oct 1906:	Chief of Staff, XXII. Army Corps
16 Oct 1906 - 15 Apr 1907:	Attached to the General Staff
15 Apr 1907 - 24 Feb 1909:	Quartermaster-General, Vilnius Military District
24 Feb 1909:	Promoted to *Lieutenant-General*
24 Feb 1909 - 29 Apr 1913:	Chief of Staff, Vilnius Military District
29 Apr 1913 - 17 Aug 1914:	Commander, 36th Infantry Division
17 Aug 1914 - 11 Nov 1915:	POW, Germany

General of Cavalry Yakov Bogdanovich **Prezhentsov** (24 Aug 1854 - 10 Jun 1911)
7 Feb 1898 - 25 May 1903:	Commander, Life Guards Cuirassier Regiment
6 Dec 1898:	Promoted to *Major-General*
25 May 1903 - 12 Oct 1904:	Commander, 2nd Brigade, 2nd Guards Cavalry Division
12 Oct 1904 - 20 Jul 1905:	General for Special Assignments, St. Petersburg Military District
20 Jul 1905 - 21 May 1908:	Chief of Staff, Inspectorate-General of Cavalry
6 Dec 1906:	Promoted to *Lieutenant-General*
21 May 1908 - 30 Dec 1908:	Commander, 9th Cavalry Division
30 Dec 1908:	Promoted to *General of Cavalry*
30 Dec 1908:	Retired

Lieutenant-General Aleksey Alekseyevich **Prigorovsky** (12 Feb 1853 - ?)
22 May 1910:	Promoted to *Major-General*
22 May 1910 - 10 Aug 1910:	Commander, 2nd Brigade, 28th Infantry Division
10 Aug 1910 - Feb 1913:	Commander, 2nd Brigade, 27th Infantry Division
Feb 1913:	Retired
12 Nov 1914 - 25 Aug 1915:	Recalled; Commander, 2nd Brigade, 8th Infantry Division
25 Aug 1915 - 18 Apr 1917:	Commander, 8th Infantry Division
18 Apr 1917 - 9 Sep 1917:	Reserve officer, Dvinsk Military District
19 Jun 1917:	Promoted to *Lieutenant-General*
9 Sep 1917:	Retired

Major-General Dmitry Dmitriyevich **Prikhodkin** (30 Oct 1870 - 1944)
3 Jun 1915 - 11 Jun 1916:	Commander, 10th Hussar Regiment
11 Jun 1916 - 24 Feb 1917:	Chief of Staff, Consolidated Cavalry Divsiion
6 Dec 1916:	Promoted to *Major-General*

24 Feb 1917 - 4 Mar 1917:   Chief of Staff, VI. Cavalry Corps

Major-General Pyotr Ivanovich **Prilukov** (3 Apr 1847 - 19 Sep 1902)
21 Jul 1901:   Promoted to *Major-General*
21 Jul 1901 - 19 Sep 1902:   Commander, 1st Brigade, 9th Infantry Division

Lieutenant-General Dmitry Vasilyevich **Primo** (24 Jul 1832 - ?)
11 Jan 1878 - 11 Oct 1885:   Commander, 31st Infantry Regiment
15 May 1883:   Promoted to *Major-General*
11 Oct 1885 - 13 May 1886:   Commander, 2nd Brigade, 14th Infantry Division
13 May 1886 - 31 Aug 1894:   Commander, 1st Brigade, 7th Infantry Division
31 Aug 1894 - 1896:   Commander, 48th Reserve Infantry Brigade
14 May 1896:   Promoted to *Lieutenant-General*

Major-General Pyotr Petrovich **Printz** (28 Dec 1838 - ?)
10 Mar 1884 - 10 Feb 1891:   Commander, 155th Infantry Regiment
7 Jun 1890:   Promoted to *Major-General*
10 Feb 1891 - 4 Nov 1896:   Commander, 2nd Brigade, 8th Infantry Division
4 Nov 1896 - 1901:   Commander, 48th Reserve Infantry Brigade

Major-General Baron Aleksandr-Konstantin-Oskar Filippovich von **Pritvits** (30 Aug 1838 - 1915)
23 Aug 1896 - 1902:   Commander, St. Petersburg Railway Gendarmerie
1 Jan 1901:   Promoted to *Major-General*
1902:   Retired

Lieutenant-General Baron Nikolai Karlovich **Pritvits** (11 Mar 1835 - 27 Nov 1896)
27 Jul 1875 - 1 Jul 1883:   Commander, Life Guards Uhlan Regiment
1 Jan 1878:   Promoted to *Major-General*
1 Jul 1883 - 27 Nov 1896:   Commander, 1st Replacement Cavalry Brigade
30 Aug 1886:   Promoted to *Lieutenant-General*

Major-General Porfiry Gerasimovich **Probenko** (26 Feb 1854 - ?)
9 Apr 1900:   Promoted to *Major-General*
9 Apr 1900 - 16 Aug 1900:   Chief of Staff, Fortress Novogeorgiyevsk
16 Aug 1900 - 11 Mar 1904:   Chief of Staff, Deputy Commanding General, Warsaw Military District
11 Mar 1904 - 1905:   Commander, 60th Replacement Infantry Brigade

Major-General Karl Karlovich **Proffen** (7 Sep 1847 - ?)
16 May 1902 - 12 Sep 1905:   Deputy Intendant, Caucasus Military District
6 Dec 1904:   Promoted to *Major-General*
12 Sep 1905 - 1907:   Intendant, Amur Military District

Major-General Viktor Alekseyevich **Prokhorov** (8 Jan 1843 - ?)
26 Apr 1884 - 8 Dec 1895:   Commander of Engineers, Fortress Kiev
30 Aug 1891:   Promoted to *Major-General*
8 Dec 1895 - 1896:   Engineer Inspector, Transcaspian Region

Major-General Vladimir Afanasyevich **Prokhorovich** (25 Jun 1850 - ?)
4 Jun 1904 - 18 Mar 1906: Commander, 71st Artillery Brigade
17 Apr 1905: Promoted to *Major-General*
18 Mar 1906 - 14 Nov 1906: Commander, 2nd Artillery Brigade

Major-General of Naval Engineers Iosif Petrovich **Prokofyev** (26 Jan 1849 - 1912)
13 Oct 1896 - 1909: Attached to the 2nd Baltic Naval Depot
6 Dec 1907: Promoted to *Major-General of Naval Engineers*

Major-General Mikhail Savvich **Prokofyev** (1 Oct 1857 - ?)
25 Aug 1912 - 1918: Military Commander, Kiev District
6 Dec 1916: Promoted to *Major-General*

Lieutenant-General Fyodor Fyodorovich **Prokope** (27 Oct 1840 - 9 Aug 1916)
23 Nov 1894: Promoted to *Major-General*
23 Nov 1894 - 27 Mar 1903: Deputy C-in-C of the Finnish Army, Special Purposes General to the Governor-General of Finland
27 Mar 1903 - 1905: Commander, Vladikavkaz Regional Brigade
1905: Promoted to *Lieutenant-General*
1905: Retired

General of Infantry German Berntovich **Prokope** (6 Feb 1841 - 22 Sep 1905)
19 Feb 1890: Promoted to *Major-General*
19 Feb 1890 - 7 Feb 1894: Commander, 2nd Brigade, 12th Infantry Division
7 Feb 1894 - 20 Mar 1900: Commander, 50th Reserve Infantry Brigade
20 Mar 1900: Promoted to *Lieutenant-General*
20 Mar 1900 - 9 Feb 1904: Commander, 8th Infantry Division
9 Feb 1904: Promoted to *General of Infantry*
9 Feb 1904: Retired

General of Infantry Viktor Berntovich **Prokope** (25 Jul 1839 - 10 Sep 1906)
27 Oct 1877 - 11 Nov 1884: Commander, Life Guards 3rd Finnish Rifle Battalion
12 Dec 1878: Promoted to *Major-General*
11 Nov 1884 - 16 Aug 1888: Military Commander of Vaasa
16 Aug 1888 - 1 Dec 1888: Military Commander of Uusimaa
1 Dec 1888 - 22 Jul 1891: Commanding General, Finnish Militia
11 Sep 1889: Promoted to *Lieutenant-General*
22 Jul 1891 - 11 Mar 1900: Deputy Minister of State for the Grand Duchy of Finland
13 Jun 1898 - 29 Aug 1899: Acting Minister of State for the Grand Duchy of Finland
11 Mar 1900: Promoted to *General of Infantry*
11 Mar 1900: Retired

Major-General Yulian Vasilyevich **Prokopenko** (20 Jun 1857 - ?)
3 May 1910 - 2 Nov 1914: Commander, 15th Grenadier Regiment
2 Nov 1914 - 14 Nov 1915: Reserve officer, Minsk Military District
3 Apr 1915: Promoted to *Major-General*

14 Nov 1915 - 18 Feb 1917:	Commander, 2nd Brigade, 105th Infantry Division
18 Feb 1917 - 25 Apr 1917:	Commander, 155th Infantry Division
25 Apr 1917 - 1917:	Reserve officer, Kiev Military District

Major-General Iosif Vikentyevich **Prokopovich** (11 Nov 1855 - 29 Nov 1931)
15 May 1908 - 11 Nov 1911:	Commander, 16th Hussar Regiment
11 Nov 1911:	Promoted to *Major-General*
11 Nov 1911:	Retired
1 Sep 1914 - Dec 1914:	Recalled; Commander, 59th State Militia Cavalry Brigade
Dec 1914 - 1915:	Commandant, Tsarskoye Selo Garrison
1915 - 29 Nov 1915:	Commander, Independent Cavalry Brigade
29 Nov 1915 - 1917:	Commander, 2nd Independent Baltic Cavalry Brigade

Major-General Dmitry Nikolayevich **Promtov** (13 Aug 1864 - 1 Sep 1935)
27 Mar 1913 - 1914:	Battalion Commander, Sergievsky Artillery School
14 Apr 1913:	Promoted to *Major-General*
1914 - 30 May 1915:	Chairman, Commission for the Construction of 4th Artillery School, Kiev
30 May 1915 - 1918:	Commandant, Nikolayev Artillery School

Lieutenant-General Mikhail Nikolayevich **Promtov** (12 Jul 1857 - 4 Jul 1950)
16 Jul 1910 - 16 Feb 1911:	Deputy Commander, 30th Artillery Brigade
16 Feb 1911:	Promoted to *Major-General*
16 Feb 1911 - 2 Nov 1914:	Commander, 32nd Artillery Brigade
2 Nov 1914 - 7 Apr 1917:	Commander, 82nd Infantry Division
19 Feb 1915:	Promoted to *Lieutenant-General*
Jun 1916 - 7 Apr 1917:	Commanding General, Combined Army Corps
7 Apr 1917 - 9 Sep 1917:	Commanding General, XXIII. Army Corps
9 Sep 1917 - 1 Dec 1917:	C-in-C, 11th Army

Major-General Vatslav-Martsely Lavrentyevich **Prosinsky** (5 Oct 1849 - ?)
8 Oct 1901 - 19 Jun 1905:	Commander, 161st Infantry Regiment
2 Apr 1905:	Promoted to *Major-General*
19 Jun 1905 - 2 Dec 1906:	Commander, 1st Brigade, 3rd Rifle Division
2 Dec 1906 - 19 Mar 1908:	Commander, 2nd Brigade, 21st Infantry Division

General of Infantry Aleksandr Pavlovich **Protopopov** (3 Jul 1849 - 13 Oct 1909)
18 Jan 1893 - 4 Feb 1898:	Deputy Chief of Staff, Odessa Military District
30 Aug 1894:	Promoted to *Major-General*
4 Feb 1898 - 29 Jan 1904:	Chief of Staff, Odessa Military District
6 Dec 1900:	Promoted to *Lieutenant-General*
29 Jan 1904 - 22 Dec 1905:	Deputy Commanding General, Odessa Military District
22 Dec 1905 - 10 Jan 1907:	Attached to the Ministry of War
31 Dec 1906 - 13 Oct 1909:	Member, Council of State for Defense
10 Jan 1907 - 13 Oct 1909:	Chairman, Main Fortress Committee
6 Dec 1907:	Promoted to *General of Infantry*

General of Infantry Nikolai Ivanovich **Protopopov** (17 Nov 1853 - ?)
20 Apr 1902 - 19 Dec 1904:	Military Attaché, Bulgaria
6 Apr 1903:	Promoted to *Major-General*
19 Dec 1904 - 2 Mar 1907:	Quartermaster-General, Vilnius Military District
2 Mar 1907 - 23 Dec 1909:	Deputy Commanding General of Cossack Troops
23 Dec 1909:	Promoted to *Lieutenant-General*
23 Dec 1909 - 23 Sep 1912:	Chief of Staff, Moscow Military District
23 Sep 1912 - 6 Oct 1914:	Commander, 31st Infantry Division
6 Oct 1914 - 28 May 1916:	Commanding General, X. Army Corps
10 Apr 1916:	Promoted to *General of Infantry*
28 May 1916 - 12 Aug 1917:	Deputy Commanding General, Moscow Military District
Apr 1917 - 31 May 1917:	Acting Commanding General, Moscow Military District
12 Aug 1917:	Retired

Lieutenant-General of the Fleet Veniamin Nikolayevich **Protopopov** (5 Feb 1864 - 5 Mar 1917)
14 Oct 1909 - 10 Apr 1914:	Deputy Commandant, Port of Sveaborg
6 Apr 1914:	Promoted to *Major-General of the Fleet*
10 Apr 1914 - 5 Mar 1917:	Commandant, Port of Sveaborg
1 Jan 1917:	Promoted to *Lieutenant-General of the Fleet*

Lieutenant-General Aleksandr Petrovich **Protsenko** (23 Nov 1836 - ?)
1 Jan 1878 - 24 May 1878:	Attached to the General Staff
1878:	Promoted to *Major-General*
24 May 1878 - 23 Nov 1883:	Military Governor, Semipalatinsk Region
23 Nov 1883 - 22 Dec 1887:	Military Governor, Turgay Region
22 Dec 1887 - 21 Oct 1891:	Transferred to the reserve
21 Oct 1891 - 5 Jan 1898:	Chief of Asian Section, General Staff
28 May 1892 - 1 May 1903:	Member of the Military-Scientific Committee, General Staff
30 Aug 1892:	Promoted to *Lieutenant-General*
1 May 1903 - 1906:	Committee Member, General Staff

Major-General Aleksandr Ivanovich **Protsykov** (17 Aug 1849 - ?)
17 Sep 1910 - 20 Jan 1914:	Inspector of Works, Troop Billeting Department, Caucasus Military District
14 Apr 1913:	Promoted to *Major-General*
29 Jan 1914:	Retired
29 Apr 1915 - 1917:	Recalled; Reserve officer, Caucasus Military District

General of Cavalry Stepan Mironovich **Prozorkevich** (28 Mar 1835 - ?)
18 Feb 1885:	Promoted to *Major-General*
18 Feb 1885 - 31 Jul 1893:	Commander, 1st Brigade, 1st Caucasus Cossack Division
31 Jul 1893 - 20 Apr 1898:	Commander, 1st Caucasus Cossack Division
14 Nov 1894:	Promoted to *Lieutenant-General*
20 Apr 1898 - 12 May 1900:	At the disposal of the Commanding General, Caucasus Military District

12 May 1900: Promoted to *General of Cavalry*
12 May 1900: Retired

Major-General Aleksey Ivanovich **Prozorov** (28 Feb 1860 - 1920)
30 May 1912 - Oct 1917: Intendant-General, Omsk Military District
1913: Promoted to *Major-General*

Major-General Mikhail Dmitriyevich **Prozorovsky** (6 Nov 1847 - ?)
14 Jul 1903 - 1906: Commander of Gendarmerie, Penzensk Province
28 Mar 1904: Promoted to *Major-General*

Major-General Nikolai Konstantinovich **Prussak** (8 Aug 1867 - ?)
28 Oct 1910 - 13 Jun 1913: Section Chief, Main Engineering Directorate
6 Dec 1910: Promoted to *Major-General*
13 Jun 1913 - 30 Apr 1914: Commander of Engineers, Fortress Mikhailov
30 Apr 1914 - 31 Oct 1915: Commander of Engineers, Fortress Sveaborg
31 Oct 1915 - 1917: Reserve officer, St. Petersburg Military District

Lieutenant-General Vladimir Konstantinovich **Prussak** (8 Sep 1868 - 1913)
1 May 1903 - 1913: Deputy Chief Editor, "Military Digest" & "Russian Invalid"
6 Dec 1910: Promoted to *Major-General*
1913: Promoted to *Lieutenant-General*

General of Cavalry (Prussian *Generalfeldmarschall*) Prince Friedrich Wilhelm Nikolaus Albrecht of **Prussia**(8 May 1837 - 13 Sep 1906)
10 Mar 1875: Promoted to *General of Cavalry*

Lieutenant-General Mikhail Andreyevich **Pryaslov** (23 Feb 1856 - ?)
25 May 1904 - 14 Mar 1906: Commander, 1st Brigade, 61st Infantry Division
1 Jun 1904: Promoted to *Major-General*
14 Mar 1906 - 17 Dec 1908: Commander, 1st Brigade, 40th Infantry Division
17 Dec 1908 - 6 Jul 1910: Commander, 58th Replacement Infantry Brigade
6 Jul 1910 - 5 Jul 1915: Commander, 49th Infantry Division
1910 - 1914: Commandant of Perm Garrison
17 Oct 1910: Promoted to *Lieutenant-General*
5 Jul 1915 - 4 Nov 1915: Commander, 109th Infantry Division
4 Nov 1915 - 2 Apr 1917: Reserve officer, Petrograd Military District
2 Apr 1917: Retired

Major-General Vladimir Andreyevich **Pryaslov** (6 Jul 1859 - 1 Nov 1919)
29 Jan 1914: Promoted to *Major-General*
29 Jan 1914 - 12 May 1916: Commander, 21st Artillery Brigade
12 May 1916 - 1917: Inspector of Artillery, XXXVII. Army Corps

Major-General Mitrofan Yemelyanovich **Przhelutsky** (23 Oct 1863 - 30 Dec 1940)
2 Dec 1911 - 1 May 1915: Commander, 28th Infantry Regiment
14 Nov 1914: Promoted to *Major-General*

1 May 1915 - 22 Apr 1917:	Commander, 17th Replacement Infantry Brigade
22 Apr 1917 - 1918:	Reserve officer, Kazan Military District

Major-General Aleksandr Nikolayevich **Przhetslavsky** (24 Aug 1848 - ?)
20 Sep 1901:	Promoted to *Major-General*
20 Sep 1901 - 23 Sep 1904:	Commander, 2nd Brigade, 27th Infantry Division

Major-General Aleksandr Severinovich **Przhetslavsky** (1 Nov 1846 - ?)
30 Jun 1903:	Promoted to *Major-General*
30 Jun 1903 - 5 Mar 1905:	Commander, 2nd Brigade, 19th Infantry Division
5 Mar 1905 - 18 May 1906:	Commander, 1st Brigade, 53rd Infantry Division
18 May 1906 - 16 Dec 1906:	Commander, 1st Brigade, 38th Infantry Division
16 Dec 1906:	Retired
28 May 1915 - 1917:	Recalled; Reserve officer, Dvinsk Military District

Major-General Nikolai Nikolayevich **Przhetslavsky** (17 Jan 1854 - 1913)
8 Jan 1909:	Promoted to *Major-General*
8 Jan 1909 - 9 Nov 1913:	Commander, 2nd Brigade, 26th Infantry Division

General of Infantry Mikhail Alekseyevich **Przhevalsky** (5 Nov 1859 - 13 Dec 1934)
2 Jun 1905 - 5 May 1906:	Chief of Staff, Kuban Cossack Army
2 Apr 1906:	Promoted to *Major-General*
5 May 1906 - 13 Dec 1908:	Chief of Staff, Terek Cossack Army
13 Dec 1908 - 3 Feb 1915:	Commander, Kuban Cossack Infantry Brigade
19 Jul 1914:	Promoted to *Lieutenant-General*
3 Feb 1915 - 3 Apr 1917:	Commanding General, II. Turkestan Army Corps
19 Nov 1916:	Promoted to *General of Infantry*
3 May 1917 - 11 Sep 1917:	C-in-C, Caucasus Army
31 May 1917 - 28 Dec 1917:	C-in-C, Caucasus Front

Lieutenant-General Vladimir Alekseyevich **Przhevalsky** (10 Oct 1847 - 11 Nov 1918)
29 Sep 1902 - 1909:	Commander, Kuban Cossack Horse Artillery Brigade
28 Mar 1904:	Promoted to *Major-General*
1909:	Promoted to *Lieutenant-General*
1909:	Retired

Lieutenant-General Yevgeny Mikhailovich **Przhevalsky** (15 Jan 1844 - 10 Sep 1925)
7 Jun 1866 - 1908:	Mathematics Teacher, 3rd Aleksandr Military School
17 Apr 1905:	Promoted to *Major-General*
1908:	Promoted to *Lieutenant-General*
1908:	Retired
13 Aug 1914 - 1917:	Recalled; Honorary Trustee, Empress Maria Institutions

Lieutenant-General Konstantin Yefimovich **Przhevlotsky** (13 Nov 1847 - ?)
14 Mar 1895:	Promoted to *Major-General*
14 Mar 1895 - 25 Jan 1900:	Commander, 2nd Brigade, 7th Cavalry Division
25 Jan 1900 - 10 Jun 1903:	Commander, 1st Brigade, 7th Cavalry Division
10 Jun 1903 - 23 May 1907:	Commander, 6th Cavalry Division

6 Dec 1903: Promoted to *Lieutenant-General*

Major-General Vladislav Antonovich **Przhibylsky** (26 Jun 1854 - ?)
12 Sep 1910 - 1912: Commander, 59th Infantry Regiment
1912: Promoted to *Major-General*
1912: Retired
2 Feb 1915 - 8 Apr 1917: Recalled; Reserve officer, Kiev Military District
8 Apr 1917: Dismissed

Major-General Mitrofan Yemelyanovich **Przhilutsky** (23 Oct 1863 - 30 Dec 1940)
2 Dec 1912 - 1 May 1915: Commander, 28th Infantry Regiment
14 Nov 1914: Promoted to *Major-General*
1 May 1915 - 1917: Commander, 17th Replacement Infantry Brigade

Lieutenant-General Vladimir Yemelyanovich **Przhilutsky** (21 Feb 1860 - ?)
15 Jan 1909: Promoted to *Major-General*
15 Jan 1909 - 14 Oct 1912: Commander, 2nd Brigade, 44th Infantry Division
14 Oct 1912 - 15 Nov 1913: Commander, 5th Rifle Brigade
15 Nov 1913: Promoted to *Lieutenant-General*
15 Nov 1913: Retired
14 Nov 1914: Recalled with the rank of *Major-General*
14 Nov 1914 - 26 Aug 1916: Commander, 67th Infantry Division
15 Jun 1915: Promoted to *Lieutenant-General*

Major-General Nikolai Sokratovich **Pugovichnikov** (17 May 1856 - ?)
21 Sep 1907 - 29 Jun 1912: Commander, 12th Dragoon Regiment
29 Jun 1912: Promoted to *Major-General*
29 Jun 1912: Retired
22 May 1916 - 1917: Recalled; Reserve officer, Kiev Military District

Major-General Manuil Platonovich **Pukalov** (22 Jan 1843 - ?)
1 Jan 1887 - 26 Nov 1895: Deputy Governor of Samarkand
30 Aug 1890: Promoted to *Major-General*

Major-General Vasily Ivanovich **Pupyrev** (27 Jan 1862 - ?)
16 Aug 1914 - 6 Oct 1916: Commander, 305th Infantry Regiment
6 Dec 1915: Promoted to *Major-General*
6 Oct 1916 - 1917: Reserve officer, Minsk Military District

Major-General Georgy Mikhailovich **Purtseladze** (29 Oct 1867 - 1922)
17 Mar 1915 - 1917: Commander, 84th Infantry Regiment
12 Dec 1916: Promoted to *Major-General*

Lieutenant-General of Naval Engineers Nikolai Nikolayevich **Pushchin** (9 May 1861 - ?)
6 May 1909: Promoted to *Major-General of Naval Engineers*
10 May 1910 - 11 Oct 1911: Chief Inspector of Shipbuilding
11 Oct 1911 - 1914: Chief of Shipbuilding Section, Main Shipbuilding Directorate

14 Apr 1913: Promoted to *Lieutenant-General of Naval Engineers*
1914 - 1917: Attached to Petrograd Port Office

Major-General Vladimir Vasilyevich **Pushechnikov** (25 Oct 1859 - 20 Dec 1941)
29 Sep 1906 - 1917: Commander, 14th Sapper Battalion
12 Jul 1915: Promoted to *Major-General*
1917 - 4 Apr 1917: Commander, 14th Sapper Regiment

General of Cavalry Aleksandr Aleksandrovich **Pushkin** (6 Jul 1833 - 19 Jul 1914)
1 Jul 1880: Promoted to *Major-General*
1 Jul 1880 - 31 Oct 1881: Commander, 1st Brigade, 13th Cavalry Division
31 Oct 1981 - 28 Feb 1891: General à la suite
30 Aug 1890: Promoted to *Lieutenant-General*
28 Feb 1891: Retired
27 May 1895 - 19 Jul 1914: Recalled as Privy Councillor; Honorary Trustee, Moscow Board of Empress Maria Institutions
16 Sep 1898 - 1913: Member of the Board, Catherine & Alexander Women's Institute
22 Apr 1908: Promoted to *General of Cavalry*

Lieutenant-General Mikhail Savvich **Pustovoytenko** (3 Nov 1865 - ?)
6 Dec 1913: Promoted to *Major-General*
6 Dec 1913 - 19 Jun 1914: Chief of Staff, I. Siberian Army Corps
19 Jun 1914 - Jul 1914: First Deputy Quartermaster-General, General Staff
Jul 1914 - 19 Jul 1914: Quartermaster-General, General Staff
19 Jul 1914 - 1 Apr 1915: Quartermaster-General, Southwestern Front
1 Apr 1915 - 30 Aug 1915: Quartermaster-General, Northwestern Front
30 Aug 1915 - 6 Dec 1916: Quartermaster-General to the Supreme Commander-in-Chief
8 Nov 1916: Promoted to *Lieutenant-General*
6 Dec 1916 - 21 Oct 1917: Commander, 12th Infantry Division
21 Oct 1917 - 1918: Commanding General, XLVI. Army Corps

Lieutenant-General Pavel Ivanovich **Pustynsky** (14 Jan 1852 - ?)
9 Aug 1902 - 24 Apr 1904: Commander, Verzhbolov Borderguard Brigade
24 Apr 1904 - 1 Jan 1911: Commander, Sandomirsk Borderguard Brigade
6 Dec 1908: Promoted to *Major-General*
2 May 1913: Promoted to *Lieutenant-General*
2 May 1913: Retired

Lieutenant-General Nil Nilovich **Putilov** (14 Jun 1853 - Dec 1915)
7 Jan 1905: Promoted to *Major-General*
7 Jan 1905 - 2 Jul 1913: Commander, 1st Brigade, 11th Infantry Division
2 Jul 1913: Promoted to *Lieutenant-General*
2 Jul 1913: Retired
11 Sep 1914 - 31 Dec 1914: Recalled; Commander, 3rd Replacement Infantry Brigade
31 Dec 1914 - 15 Feb 1915: Reserve officer, Kiev Military District

15 Feb 1915 - 20 Sep 1915:   Commander, 73rd State Militia Brigade
20 Sep 1915 - Dec 1917:   Reserve officer, Kiev Military District

Lieutenant-General Pavel Nikolayevich **Putilov** (16 Apr 1854 - 12 Dec 1919)
22 Feb 1904:   Promoted to *Major-General*
22 Feb 1904 - 9 Mar 1905:   Commander, 2nd Brigade, 5th East Siberian Rifle Division
9 Mar 1905 - 6 Jul 1905:   Commander, 4th Rifle Brigade
6 Jul 1905 - 29 May 1906:   Commander, 1st Brigade, 10th East Siberian Rifle Division
29 May 1906 - 28 Oct 1906:   Commander, 1st Brigade, 6th East Siberian Rifle Division
28 Oct 1906 - 15 Aug 1911:   Commander, 2nd Brigade, 6th Siberian Rifle Division
15 Aug 1911:   Promoted to *Lieutenant-General*
15 Aug 1911:   Retired

Lieutenant-General Yevfim Semonovich **Putilov** (28 Mar 1853 - ?)
22 Jun 1900 - 8 Jul 1913:   Ataman, 3rd Division, Trans-Baikal Cossack Army
6 Apr 1903:   Promoted to *Major-General*
8 Jul 1913:   Promoted to *Lieutenant-General*
8 Jul 1913:   Retired

General of Artillery Pyotr Flegontovich **Putintsev** (5 Aug 1850 - ?)
28 Mar 1903 - 27 Sep 1906:   Commander, 28th Artillery Brigade
6 Dec 1903:   Promoted to *Major-General*
27 Sep 1906 - 5 Feb 1908:   Commander of Artillery, VI. Army Corps
6 Dec 1907:   Promoted to *Lieutenant-General*
5 Feb 1908 - 5 Aug 1913:   Commander of Artillery, Kiev Military District
5 Aug 1913:   Promoted to *General of Artillery*
5 Aug 1913:   Retired
29 Mar 1915 - Oct 1917:   Recalled; Reserve officer, Kiev Military District

Major-General Viktor Dmitriyevich **Putintsev** (9 Oct 1866 - 7 Aug 1939)
12 Jul 1910 - 12 Oct 1915:   Chief of Staff, 5th Turkestan Rifle Brigade
12 Oct 1915 - 20 Jun 1916:   Commander, Brigade, 4th Caucasus Rifle Division
31 Oct 1915:   Promoted to *Major-General*
20 Jun 1916 - 31 Jul 1916:   Chief of Staff, 5th Turkestan Rifle Division
31 Jul 1916 - 9 Jun 1917:   Chief of Staff, II. Turkestan Army Corps
9 Jun 1917 - Oct 1917:   Commander, 7th Caucasus Rifle Division

Major-General Platon Iosifovich **Putsyato** (23 May 1853 - ?)
24 Jul 1905 - 1906:   Military Judge, Amur Military District Court
6 Dec 1905:   Promoted to *Major-General*

Lieutenant-General Dmitry Vasilyevich **Putyata** (24 Feb 1855 - 3 Feb 1915)
6 Dec 1897:   Promoted to *Major-General*
6 Dec 1897 - 14 Jan 1898:   At the disposal of the Chief of the General Staff
14 Jan 1898 - 30 Mar 1902:   Chief of Asia Section, General Staff

8 Oct 1898 - Nov 1898:	Acting Deputy Chief of the General Staff
30 Mar 1902 - 15 Aug 1906:	Military Governor, Amur Region
17 Apr 1905:	Promoted to *Lieutenant-General*
15 Aug 1906 - 27 Dec 1906:	Unassigned
27 Dec 1906 - 9 Mar 1907:	Attached to the Chief of the General Staff
9 Mar 1907 - 3 Feb 1915:	Commander, Odessa Regional Brigade

Major-General Grigory Vasilyevich **Putyata** (30 Jan 1854 - 1925)
19 Sep 1901 - 15 Jan 1918:	Inspector of Classes, Odessa Military School
25 Mar 1912:	Promoted to *Major-General*

Lieutenant-General Prince Aleksey Petrovich **Putyatin** (2 Sep 1844 - 24 Dec 1912)
8 Jan 1900:	Promoted to *Major-General*
8 Jan 1900 - 18 Jan 1901:	Commander, 1st Brigade, 42nd Infantry Division
18 Jan 1901 - Sep 1903:	General for Special Assignments, Kiev Military District
Sep 1903:	Promoted to *Lieutenant-General*
Sep 1903:	Retired

Lieutenant-General Prince Mikhail Sergeyevich **Putyatin** (2 Jan 1861 - 24 May 1938)
1 Jan 1911 - 5 Jun 1917:	Head of the Tsarskoye Selo Palace Administration
10 Apr 1911:	Promoted to *Major-General*
5 Jun 1917:	Promoted to *Lieutenant-General*
5 Jun 1917:	Retired

Rear-Admiral Prince Nikolai Sergeyevich **Putyatin** (22 Aug 1862 - 24 Jul 1927)
6 Dec 1913:	Promoted to *Rear-Admiral*
6 Dec 1913 - 1917:	Commander, Training Detachment, Black Sea Fleet
1917:	Retired

Major-General Mikhail Vladimirovich **Puzanov** (26 Feb 1847 - ?)
30 Jan 1899 - 4 Jun 1901:	Commander of Moscow-Kiev Railway Gendarmerie
18 Apr 1899:	Promoted to *Major-General*
4 Jun 1901 - 1905:	Commander of St. Petersburg-Warsaw Railway Gendarmerie

Major-General Nikolai Aleksandrovich **Puzanov** (13 Dec 1853 - ?)
6 Dec 1901 - 8 Aug 1908:	Inspector of Classes, Tiflis Cadet Corps
13 Apr 1908:	Promoted to *Major-General*
8 Aug 1908 - Oct 1917:	Director, Orenburg Neplyuev Cadet Corps

General of Infantry Aleksandr Kazimirovich **Puzyrevsky** (3 Feb 1845 - 10 May 1904)
1 Oct 1879 - 14 Oct 1889:	Professor, Nikolai General Staff Academy
20 Apr 1882 - 4 Jan 1884:	Chief of Staff, 2nd Guards Cavalry Division
24 Apr 1887:	Promoted to *Major-General*
14 Oct 1889 - 19 Jan 1890:	Deputy Chief of Staff, Ministry of War
19 Jan 1890 - 24 Mar 1901:	Chief of Staff, Warsaw Military District
30 Aug 1893:	Promoted to *Lieutenant-General*
24 Mar 1901 - 28 Mar 1904:	Deputy Commanding General, Warsaw Military District

24 Mar 1901: Promoted to *General of Infantry*
28 Mar 1904 - 10 May 1904: Member of the State Council

Major-General of Naval Engineers Nil Alekseyevich **Puzyrevsky** (22 Oct 1861 - ?)
18 Aug 1905 - 1917: Commander, 1st Reserve Detachment & Training Detachment, Black Sea Fleet
6 Dec 1911: Promoted to *Major-General of Naval Engineers*

Major-General Pyotr Ivanovich **Puzyrov** (1 Oct 1855 - ?)
5 Jun 1903 - 24 Oct 1904: Commander, 25th Artillery Brigade
6 Dec 1903: Promoted to *Major-General*
24 Oct 1904 - 24 Feb 1905: Commander, 27th Artillery Brigade

General of Infantry Nikolai Appolonovich **Pykhachev** (13 Oct 1851 - Oct 1932)
24 Nov 1899 - 2 Jun 1904: Commander, Life Guards Moscow Regiment
9 Apr 1900: Promoted to *Major-General*
2 Jun 1904 - 23 Jan 1905: Commander, 1st Brigade, 2nd Guards Infantry Division
23 Jan 1905 - 9 Oct 1906: At the disposal of the Commanding General, St. Petersburg Military District
9 Oct 1906 - 16 Apr 1908: Commander, 23rd Infantry Division
22 Apr 1907: Promoted to *Lieutenant-General*
16 Apr 1908 - Feb 1917: Commanding General, Borderguard Corps
21 Nov 1911: Promoted to *General of Infantry*
Feb 1917: Retired

Lieutenant-General Viktor Apollonovich **Pykhachev** (7 Apr 1855 - ?)
27 Oct 1904 - 22 Dec 1908: Commander of Engineers, Fortress Kerch
17 Apr 1905: Promoted to *Major-General*
22 Dec 1908 - 23 Aug 1909: At the disposal of the Main Engineering Directorate
23 Aug 1909 - 31 Dec 1910: Commander of Engineers, Fortress Modlin
31 Dec 1910 - 22 Dec 1912: Commander of Engineers, Warsaw Military District
10 Apr 1911: Promoted to *Lieutenant-General*
22 Dec 1912 - Jul 1914: Chief of Troop Billeting, Warsaw Military District
Jul 1914 - 1917: Chief of Troop Billeting, Minsk Military District

Major-General Isaak Pavlovich **Pylkov** (14 Feb 1846 - ?)
15 May 1885 - 1903: Chief of Mikhailovsky Shostensky Gunpowder Factory
1894: Promoted to *Major-General*

Rear-Admiral Aleksandr Mikhailovich **Pyshnov** (27 Aug 1873 - 1929)
1917: Promoted to *Rear-Admiral*
1917 - 19 May 1917: Commander, 2nd Cruiser Brigade, Baltic Fleet
19 May 1917 - Oct 1917: Reserve officer, Ministry of the Navy

Rear-Admiral Mikhail Yakovlevich **Pyshnov** (1841 - 1912)
?: Promoted to *Rear-Admiral*

Major-General Mikhail Ivanovich **Pyzhevsky** (18 Nov 1869 - ?)
25 Jun 1914 - 28 Apr 1917: Commander, 80th Artillery Brigade
27 Jun 1915: Promoted to *Major-General*
28 Apr 1917 - 12 Aug 1917: Inspector of Artillery, XXX. Army Corps

General of Infantry Rudolf Samoylovich von **Raaben** (10 Apr 1843 - ?)
19 Jan 1883 - 6 Oct 1894: General for Special Assignments, Don Cossack Army
30 Aug 1886: Promoted to *Major-General*
6 Oct 1894 - 3 Jan 1895: Deputy Chief of Staff, Moscow Military District
3 Jan 1895 - 17 Dec 1898: Chief of Staff, Don Army
14 May 1896: Promoted to *Lieutenant-General*
17 Dec 1898 - 10 Jul 1899: Commander, 26th Infantry Division
10 Jul 1899 - 4 May 1903: Governor of Bessarabia
4 May 1903 - 24 Feb 1904: Attached to the Ministry of Internal Affairs
24 Feb 1904 - 5 Mar 1905: Attached to the Ministry of War
5 Mar 1905 - Oct 1917: Member, Committee for Wounded Veterans
6 Dec 1906: Promoted to *General of Infantry*

Major-General of Naval Artillery Vasily Georgiyevich **Rachinsky** (1 Jun 1867 - 1942)
?: Commandant, Nikolayev Naval Arsenal
13 Oct 1914: Promoted to *Major-General of Naval Artillery*
13 Oct 1914 - 1 May 1916: Commander, Peter the Great Naval Fortress Artillery Brigade
1 May 1916 - 1917: Deputy Chief, Petrograd Ammunition Factory

Major-General Vladimir Vladimirovich **Rachinsky** (30 Jan 1866 - ?)
12 Jul 1915 - 22 Apr 1917: Deputy Chief of Petrograd Cartridge Factory
6 Dec 1916: Promoted to *Major-General*
22 Apr 1917 - Jan 1918: Reserve officer, Petrograd Military District
Jan 1918: Dismissed

Lieutenant-General Ernest-Avgust Ferdinandovich **Raddats** (18 Jun 1868 - 6 Mar 1918)
4 Feb 1915 - 25 May 1916: Commander, Siberian Cossack Brigade
28 May 1915: Promoted to *Major-General*
25 May 1916 - 1918: Commander, 1st Caucasus Cossack Division
1917: Promoted to *Lieutenant-General*

Major-General of the Admiralty Konstantin Ivanovich **Radetsky** (5 Jun 1859 - ?)
7 Jan 1908 - 27 Sep 1912: Commandant, Nikolayev Port Repair School
27 Sep 1912: Promoted to *Major-General of the Admiralty*
27 Sep 1912: Retired

Major-General Pavel Ottokarovich **Radetsky** (22 Dec 1856 - ?)
2 Sep 1910 - 1 Jun 1912: Commander, 8th Uhlan Regiment
1 Jun 1912: Promoted to *Major-General*
1 Jun 1912: Retired

Rear-Admiral Viktor Ivanovich **Radetsky** (29 Jan 1855 - Dec 1920)
?:   Commander, 28th Naval Depot
?:   Promoted to *Rear-Admiral*

Major-General Mikhail Mikhailovich **Radkevich** (5 Nov 1868 - ?)
11 Nov 1915 - 1917:   Commander, 5th Siberian Rifle Artillery Brigade
4 Nov 1916:   Promoted to *Major-General*
1917 - 19 Apr 1917:   Commander, 203rd Artillery Brigade
19 Apr 1917 - 1918:   Inspector of Artillery, 12th Army

Lieutenant-General Nikolai Aleksandrovich **Radkevich** (28 Jul 1857 - ?)
30 Jul 1906 - 14 Nov 1914:   Director, Odessa Cadet Corps
6 Dec 1906:   Promoted to *Major-General*
6 Dec 1913:   Promoted to *Lieutenant-General*
14 Nov 1914 - 17 Jun 1915:   Commander, 2nd Brigade, 8th Cavalry Division
17 Jun 1915 - 1918:   Reserve officer, Dvinsk Military District

General of Infantry Yevgeny Aleksandrovich **Radkevich** (16 Sep 1851 - 1930)
3 Oct 1902:   Promoted to *Major-General*
3 Oct 1902 - 27 May 1905:   Commander, 10th Artillery Brigade
27 May 1905 - 3 Feb 1906:   Commander, 72nd Infantry Division
3 Feb 1906 - 14 Jun 1908:   Commander, 10th Infantry Division
31 May 1907:   Promoted to *Lieutenant-General*
14 Jun 1908 - 1 Sep 1912:   Commanding General, III. Siberian Army Corps
1 Sep 1912:   Promoted to *General of Infantry*
1 Sep 1912:   Retired
7 Aug 1914 - 25 Apr 1915:   Recalled; Commanding General, III. Siberian Army Corps
25 Apr 1915 - 12 Oct 1916:   C-in-C, 10th Army
12 Dec 1916 - 25 Apr 1917:   Member of the Military Council
25 Apr 1917 - 29 Apr 1917:   Deputy Commanding General, Petrograd Military District
29 Apr 1917 - 6 May 1917:   Acting Commanding General, Petrograd Military District
6 May 1917 - Oct 1917:   Member of the Military Council

General of Infantry Radko Dmitrievich **Radko-Dmitriev** (24 Sep 1859 - 18 Oct 1918)
26 Jul 1914:   Transferred from the Bulgarian Army
26 Jul 1914:   Promoted to *Lieutenant-General*
26 Jul 1914 - 3 Sep 1914:   Commanding General, VIII. Army Corps
3 Sep 1914:   Promoted to *General of Infantry*
3 Sep 1914 - 20 May 1915:   C-in-C, 3rd Army
3 Jun 1915 - 11 Oct 1915:   Commanding General, II. Siberian Army Corps
11 Oct 1915 - 20 Mar 1916:   Commanding General, VII. Siberian Army Corps
20 Mar 1916 - 20 Jul 1917:   C-in-C, 12th Army
20 Jul 1917:   Transferred to the reserve

General of the Fleet Otto Leopoldovich **Radlov** (27 Nov 1849 - 1916)
2 Apr 1906:	Promoted to *Major-General of the Admiralty*
2 Apr 1906 - 10 Nov 1908:	Chief of Facilities Section, Main Directorate of Shipbuilding & Equipment
10 Nov 1908 - 17 Sep 1913:	Chairman, Volunteer Fleet Committee
6 Dec 1909:	Promoted to *Lieutenant-General of the Admiralty*
8 Apr 1913:	Redesignated *Lieutenant-General of the Fleet*
17 Sep 1913:	Promoted to *General of the Fleet*
17 Sep 1913:	Retired

Major-General Aleksandr Stanislavovich **Radovsky** (31 Mar 1859 - ?)
6 Mar 1913 - 22 Jan 1916:	Commander, 9th Rifle Regiment
21 May 1915:	Promoted to *Major-General*
22 Jan 1916 - 1917:	Commander, 38th Replacement Infantry Brigade

Major-General Lev Apollonovich **Radus-Zenkovich** (21 Feb 1874 - 12 Apr 1946)
16 Feb 1916 - 6 Jan 1917:	Chief of Staff, 10th Siberian Rifle Division
10 Apr 1916:	Promoted to *Major-General*
6 Jan 1917 - 9 May 1917:	Quartermaster-General, 6th Army
9 May 1917 - 10 Sep 1917:	Chief of Staff, 6th Army
10 Sep 1917 - 23 Oct 1917:	Commander, 22nd Infantry Division
23 Oct 1917 - 1918:	Chief of Staff, 6th Army

Lieutenant-General Olgerd-Antony Viktorovich **Radvan-Rypinsky** (13 Dec 1853 - 20 Jul 1925)
19 Jun 1905:	Promoted to *Major-General*
19 Jun 1905 - 9 Jan 1906:	Commander, 1st Brigade, 4th Rifle Divisoin
9 Jan 1906 - 25 Feb 1909:	Commander, 2nd Brigade, 7th East Siberian Rifle Division
25 Feb 1909 - 23 Jul 1910:	Commander, 4th Turkestan Rifle Brigade
23 Jul 1910 - 13 Dec 1913:	Commander, 3rd Turkestan Rifle Brigade
13 Dec 1913:	Promoted to *Lieutenant-General*
13 Dec 1913:	Retired

Lieutenant-General Ivan Ivanovich **Radzishevsky** (15 Jul 1837 - ?)
26 Nov 1891:	Promoted to *Major-General*
26 Nov 1891 - 11 Jan 1900:	Commander, 2nd Brigade, 28th Infantry Division
11 Jan 1900:	Promoted to *Lieutenant-General*

Lieutenant-General Konstantin Ivanovich **Radzishevsky** (15 May 1843 - ?)
30 Dec 1897:	Promoted to *Major-General*
30 Dec 1897 - 17 May 1903:	Commander, 1st Brigade, 31st Infantry Division
17 May 1903:	Promoted to *Lieutenant-General*
17 May 1903:	Retired

Major-General Pyotr Stanislavovich **Radzishevsky** (23 Aug 1862 - ?)
24 Oct 1914 - 16 Apr 1917:	Military Judge, Minsk Military District Court
6 Dec 1914:	Promoted to *Major-General*

16 Apr 1917: Dismissed

Major-General Pyotr Alekseyevich **Rafailov** (10 Jun 1848 - ?)
13 Oct 1905 - 27 Feb 1916: Chief of Cartographic Institutions, Topographical Section, General Staff
29 Mar 1909: Promoted to *Major-General*
27 Feb 1916 - Oct 1917: Chief of Military Surveying, Petrograd & Finland

Major-General Aleksandr Ferdinandovich **Rafalovich** (15 Aug 1861 - 26 Apr 1932)
May 1915 - 1 Jul 1916: Commander, 2nd Brigade, 1st Caucasus Cossack Division
15 Jun 1915: Promoted to *Major-General*
1 Jul 1916 - 21 Oct 1916: Commander, Siberian Cossack Brigade
21 Oct 1916 - 23 Dec 1916: Commander, Kuban Consolidated Cossack Division
23 Dec 1916 - 5 Sep 1917: Commander, 3rd Kuban Cossack Division
5 Sep 1917 - 1918: Reserve officer, Caucasus Military District

Major-General Nikolai Ferdinandovich **Rafalovich** (11 Mar 1866 - 14 Apr 1930)
14 Apr 1907 - 21 Oct 1911: Inspector of Classes, 2nd Moscow Cadet Corps
1 Jun 1907 - 1 Aug 1907: Acting Director, 2nd Moscow Cadet Corps
28 Dec 1908 - 8 Jan 1909: Acting Director, 2nd Moscow Cadet Corps
6 Dec 1910: Promoted to *Major-General*
23 Dec 1910 - 7 Jan 1911: Acting Director, 2nd Moscow Cadet Corps
9 Jun 1911 - 7 Aug 1911: Acting Director, 2nd Moscow Cadet Corps
3 Oct 1911 - 21 Oct 1911: Acting Director, 2nd Moscow Cadet Corps
21 Oct 1911 - 1917: Director, Yaroslavl Cadet Corps

Major-General Grigory Mikhailovich **Rafalsky** (10 Jan 1860 - ?)
3 Nov 1915 - 15 Aug 1916: Commander, 126th Infantry Regiment
5 Aug 1916: Promoted to *Major-General*
15 Aug 1916 - 22 Apr 1917: Commander, Brigade, 32nd Infantry Division
22 Apr 1917 - 1918: Commander, 32nd Infantry Division

General of Infantry Aleksandr Frantsevich **Ragoza** (8 Jun 1858 - 29 Jun 1919)
2 Mar 1904: Promoted to *Major-General*
2 Mar 1904 - 22 Oct 1904: Commander, 1st Brigade, 27th Infantry Division
22 Oct 1904 - 16 Jun 1906: Chief of Staff, III. Army Corps
16 Jun 1906 - 17 Mar 1909: Commandant of Fortress Ust-Dvina
13 Apr 1908: Promoted to *Lieutenant-General*
17 Mar 1909 - 27 Sep 1914: Commander, 19th Infantry Division
27 Sep 1914 - 30 Aug 1915: Commanding General, XXV. Army Corps
6 Dec 1914: Promoted to *General of Infantry*
30 Aug 1915 - 21 Nov 1917: C-in-C, 4th Army

Lieutenant-General Aleksandr Nikolayevich **Ragozin** (14 Aug 1856 - ?)
16 Mar 1900 - 20 Jun 1901: Commander, Life Guards 2nd Rifle Battalion
1 Apr 1901: Promoted to *Major-General*
20 Jun 1901 - 28 Nov 1904: Commander, Life Guards Grenadier Regiment

28 Nov 1904 - 10 Sep 1907:	Commandant, Officers Rifle School
10 Sep 1907:	Promoted to *Lieutenant-General*
10 Sep 1907 - 11 Nov 1908:	Commander, 8th East Siberian Rifle Division
11 Nov 1908:	Retired
11 Oct 1914 - Oct 1917:	Recalled; Commanding General, VII. Militia Corps

Lieutenant-General Sergey Platonovich **Rakeyev** (26 Apr 1859 - 14 Mar 1938)
14 Mar 1909:	Promoted to *Major-General*
14 Mar 1909 - 9 Apr 1914:	Commander of Engineers, Fortress Sveaborg
9 Apr 1914 - 1918:	Chief of Troop Billeting Department, Irkutsk Military District
22 Mar 1915:	Promoted to *Lieutenant-General*

Lieutenant-General Konstantin Konstantinovich **Rakhmanin** (5 Feb 1839 - ?)
21 Aug 1877 - 8 Jul 1900:	Commandant of Tiflis Artillery Depot
30 Aug 1889:	Promoted to *Major-General*
8 Jul 1900:	Promoted to *Lieutenant-General*
8 Jul 1900:	Retired

Lieutenant-General Mitrofan Ivanovich **Rakhubovsky** (7 Jun 1841 - 1911)
22 Jul 1892 - 27 Jan 1906:	Military Judge, Warsaw Military District
6 Dec 1899:	Promoted to *Major-General*
27 Jan 1906:	Promoted to *Lieutenant-General*
27 Jan 1906:	Retired

Major-General Aleksandr Aleksandrovich **Rakilevich** (10 Sep 1858 - ?)
17 Aug 1914 - 1917:	Commander, 1st Siberian Heavy Artillery Brigade
24 May 1915:	Promoted to *Major-General*

Major-General Vladimir Aleksandrovich **Rakint** (15 Jan 1855 - ?)
24 Jul 1908:	Promoted to *Major-General*
24 Jul 1908 - 19 Oct 1910:	Commander, Omsk Sapper Brigade
19 Oct 1910 - 29 Nov 1912:	Inspector of Field Engineers, Kazan Military District
29 Nov 1912 - 17 Aug 1915:	Inspector of Engineers, Kazan Military District
17 Aug 1915 - 15 Nov 1916:	Commander, 8th Siberian Sapper Battalion
15 Nov 1916 - 1917:	Chief of Works Section, Engineer Department, 6th Army

Lieutenant-General Vladislav Iosifovich **Rakint** (1 Jun 1853 - ?)
6 Jan 1902 - 1910:	Commander of Engineers, Fortress Kronstadt
6 Dec 1902:	Promoted to *Major-General*
11 Nov 1910:	Promoted to *Lieutenant-General*

Major-General Nikolai Vasilyevich **Rakovich** (27 Oct 1858 - ?)
1 Aug 1915 - 8 May 1916:	Commander, 19th Artillery Brigade
23 Nov 1915:	Promoted to *Major-General*
1916:	Dismissed

Major-General Nikolai Pavlovich **Ralgin** (13 May 1848 - ?)
30 Jun 1899: Promoted to *Major-General*
30 Jun 1899 - 10 Feb 1903: Commander, 1st Brigade, 40th Infantry Division
10 Feb 1903 - 15 Sep 1904: Commander, 63rd Reserve Infantry Brigade

Major-General Valery Eduardovich **Rambakh** (15 Feb 1843 - 24 Sep 1907)
1 Apr 1902 - 1907: Chairman of the Remount Commission, Tambov Region
6 Dec 1904: Promoted to *Major-General*

Lieutenant-General Vladimir Dmitriyevich **Rambakh** (8 Jan 1837 - ?)
29 Dec 1890 - 19 Feb 1900: Commander of Engineers, Fortress Kerch
30 Aug 1891: Promoted to *Major-General*
19 Feb 1900: Promoted to *Lieutenant-General*
19 Feb 1900: Retired

Major-General Allan Gustavovich **Ramzay** (19 Dec 1839 - ?)
21 Jun 1894: Promoted to *Major-General*
10 Sep 1894 - 16 Jan 1901: Commander, 1st Brigade, 7th Infantry Division

General of Infantry Baron Georgy Eduardovich **Ramzay** (7 Sep 1834 - 5 Jul 1918)
17 Apr 1874 - 24 Oct 1877: Commander, Life Guards 3rd Finnish Rifle Battalion
12 Oct 1877: Promoted to *Major-General*
24 Oct 1877 - 7 Apr 1879: Commander, Life Guards Semenov Regiment
7 Apr 1879 - 12 Aug 1880: At the disposal of the Governor-General of Finland
12 Aug 1880 - 1 Feb 1902: Commander-in-Chief of the Finnish Army
30 Aug 1886: Promoted to *Lieutenant-General*
1 Feb 1902: Promoted to *General of Infantry*
1 Feb 1902: Retired

Major-General Vasily Vladimirovich **Rantsev** (28 May 1865 - ?)
25 Nov 1908 - 3 May 1914: Commander, 14th Grenadier Regiment
3 May 1914: Promoted to *Major-General*
3 May 1914: Retired
21 Oct 1915 - 20 Apr 1917: Recalled; Commander, 424th Infantry Regiment
20 Apr 1917 - Oct 1917: Commander, Brigade, 7th Infantry Division

Major-General Nikolai Nikiforovich **Raspopov** (9 May 1862 - 4 Apr 1917)
31 Mar 1912: Promoted to *Major-General*
31 Mar 1912 - 19 Apr 1915: Commander, 1st Brigade, 11th Siberian Rifle Division
19 Apr 1915 - 10 Nov 1915: Chief of Staff, XXXIV. Army Corps
10 Nov 1915 - 4 Apr 1917: At the disposal of the Chief of the General Staff

Major-General Georgy Nikolayevich **Rastorguyev** (5 Feb 1860 - 17 Apr 1943)
3 May 1916 - 21 Aug 1916: Commander, 18th Turkestan Rifle Regiment
2 Jun 1916: Promoted to *Major-General*
21 Aug 1916 - 1917: Commander, Brigade, 6th Caucasus Rifle Division

Major-General Mark Iasonovich **Ratinsky** (1 Jan 1848 - ?)
12 Mar 1902 - 1908: Military Judge, Caucasus Military District Court
14 Apr 1902: Promoted to *Major-General*

Major-General Vasily Aleksandrovich **Ratko** (10 May 1861 - 25 Nov 1931)
12 Jun 1912 - 6 Sep 1914: Commander, 32nd Infantry Regiment
6 Sep 1914: Promoted to *Major-General*
6 Sep 1914: Retired
13 May 1916 - 15 Apr 1917: Recalled; Reserve officer, Petrograd Military District
15 Apr 1917: Dismissed

Major-General of the Fleet Konstantin Mikhailovich **Ratkov** (15 Dec 1861 - 1919)
23 Nov 1915 - 16 Mar 1917: Commander, Archangelsk Naval Sub-Depot
10 Apr 1916: Promoted to *Major-General of the Fleet*

Lieutenant-General of the Admiralty Savery Ksaveryevich **Ratnik** (28 Nov 1852 - 1924)
1893 - 1905: Director, Baltic Shipbuilding Works
9 Apr 1900: Promoted to *Major-General of the Admiralty*
1905 - 14 Mar 1907: Chief Inspector of Shipbuilding
14 Mar 1907: Promoted to *Lieutenant-General of the Admiralty*
14 Mar 1907: Retired
10 Nov 1908 - 1911: Recalled; Chairman of the Board, Baltic Shipbuilding Works

Major-General Sergey Mikhailovich **Ratsul** (12 May 1861 - 1910)
22 Jan 1909 - 1910: Commander, 33rd East Siberian Rifle Regiment
1910: Promoted to *Major-General*

Major-General Nikolai Iosifovich **Rattel** (3 Dec 1875 - 3 Mar 1939)
1 May 1915 - 5 Jun 1916: Commander, 12th Infantry Regiment
21 Jan 1916: Promoted to *Major-General*
5 Jun 1916 - 2 Jun 1917: Deputy Quartermaster-General, Southwestern Front
2 Jun 1917 - 7 Aug 1917: Quartermaster-General, Southwestern Front
7 Aug 1917 - 10 Sep 1917: Quartermaster-General, Western Front
10 Sep 1917 - Jul 1918: Chief of Military Communications, Theater of Operations

General of Cavalry Georgy Ottonovich von **Raukh** (19 Aug 1860 - 30 Nov 1936)
26 Oct 1905 - 22 Dec 1906: Quartermaster-General, St. Petersburg Military District
2 Apr 1906: Promoted to *Major-General*
22 Dec 1906 - 9 Sep 1908: Chief of Staff, St. Petersburg Military District
9 Sep 1908: Promoted to *Lieutenant-General*
9 Sep 1908 - 29 Jan 1912: Commander, 10th Cavalry Division
29 Jan 1912 - 11 Oct 1914: Commander, 2nd Guards Cavalry Division
11 Oct 1914 - 23 Dec 1914: At the disposal of the C-in-C, Northwestern Front
23 Dec 1914 - 14 Nov 1915: Chief of Staff, 6th Army
14 Nov 1915 - 8 Dec 1915: Commanding General, II. Cavalry Corps
8 Dec 1915 - 27 May 1916: Commanding General, I. Guards Corps

27 May 1916 - 22 Apr 1917:	Reserve officer, Kiev Military District
22 Apr 1917 - Nov 1917:	Reserve officer, Petrograd Military District
10 Jun 1917:	Promoted to *General of Cavalry*
Nov 1917:	Retired

General of Cavalry Baron Yevgeny Aleksandrovich **Raush von Traubenberg** (11 Jun 1855 - 14 Mar 1923)

7 Apr 1899:	Promoted to *Major-General*
7 Apr 1899 - 18 Dec 1900:	Commander, Life Guards Cuirassier Regiment
18 Dec 1900 - 16 Jun 1904:	Chief of Staff, Guards Corps
16 Jun 1904 - 12 Sep 1907:	Chief of Staff, Moscow Military District
17 Apr 1905:	Promoted to *Lieutenant-General*
12 Sep 1907 - 29 May 1910:	Commander, 5th Cavalry Division
29 May 1910 - 15 Aug 1913:	Commanding General, XXIII. Army Corps
10 Apr 1911:	Promoted to *General of Cavalry*
15 Aug 1913 - 19 Jul 1914:	Deputy Commanding General, Warsaw Military District
19 Jul 1914 - 3 Mar 1917:	Commanding General, Minsk Military District
3 Mar 1917 - 31 Mar 1917:	Unassigned
31 Mar 1917 - 9 Nov 1917:	Reserve officer, Kiev Military District
9 Nov 1917:	Retired

Lieutenant-General Genrikh Ivanovich **Rautsman** (1 Jul 1852 - 14 Mar 1924)

16 Jun 1906 - 20 Nov 1909:	Special Assignments General, Inspectorate of Remounts & Cavalry Replacement
13 Apr 1908:	Promoted to *Major-General*
20 Nov 1909 - 1917:	Special Assignments General, Chief of the Army Remount Directorate
1913:	Promoted to *Lieutenant-General*

Major-General Arkady Vladimirovich **Rayevsky** (22 Dec 1861 - ?)

22 Mar 1913 - 1917:	Chairman of the Remount Commission, Kharkov Region
6 Dec 1916:	Promoted to *Major-General*

Major-General Vladimir Aleksandrovich **Rayevsky** (24 Aug 1851 - Dec 1910)

4 Dec 1907:	Promoted to *Major-General*
4 Dec 1907 - Dec 1910:	Commander, 1st Brigade, 22nd Infantry Division

Major-General Vikenty Logginovich **Raykovsky** (5 Apr 1856 - Oct 1912)

25 Feb 1912:	Promoted to *Major-General*
25 Apr 1912 - Oct 1912:	Commander, 1st Brigade, 46th Infantry Division

General of Infantry Pyotr Animpodistovich **Razgildeyev** (25 Nov 1833 - 26 Dec 1900)

3 Aug 1877:	Promoted to *Major-General*
3 Aug 1877 - 10 Sep 1877:	Commander, 1st Brigade, 2nd Infantry Division
10 Sep 1877 - 5 Jan 1878:	Sick leave
5 Jan 1878 - 2 Mar 1878:	Attached to the High Command
2 Mar 1878 - 1 Dec 1879:	Commander, 1st Brigade, 32nd Infantry Division

1 Dec 1879 - 8 Mar 1880:	Military Commander, Kamenetz-Podolsky
8 Mar 1880 - 24 Sep 1881:	Military Commander, Kiev
24 Sep 1881 - 8 May 1887:	Commander, 14th Local Brigade
30 Aug 1886:	Promoted to *Lieutenant-General*
8 May 1887 - 18 Sep 1890:	Commander, 8th Infantry Division
18 Sep 1890 - 9 Aug 1894:	Commander, 3rd Guards Infantry Division
9 Aug 1894 - 20 Mar 1897:	Commanding General, XIII. Army Corps
20 Mar 1897 - 26 Dec 1900:	Deputy Commanding General, Warsaw Military District
6 Dec 1898:	Promoted to *General of Infantry*

Major-General Vadim Petrovich **Razgildeyev** (20 Jan 1871 - 1929)
27 Jan 1916 - 31 Oct 1916:	Commander, 98th Infantry Regiment
18 Jul 1916:	Promoted to *Major-General*
31 Oct 1916 - 1917:	Commander, Life Guards Lithuanian Regiment
1917 - 7 Sep 1917:	Commander, Brigade, Guards Rifle Division
7 Sep 1917 - 1918:	Commander, 3rd Guards Infantry Division

General of Infantry Konstantin Iosifovich **Razgonov** (7 Mar 1843 - 18 Apr 1911)
1 Apr 1887 - 2 May 1896:	Commander, Amu Darya Detachment
9 Dec 1888:	Promoted to *Major-General*
2 May 1896 - 20 Jun 1898:	Chief of Staff, XVI. Army Corps
20 Jun 1898 - 26 Sep 1898:	Commander, 26th Infantry Division
26 Sep 1898 - 16 Apr 1903:	Commander, 41st Infantry Division
6 Dec 1898:	Promoted to *Lieutenant-General*
16 Apr 1903 - 22 Jul 1904:	Commanding General, III. Army Corps
22 Jul 1904 - 28 Sep 1904:	Commanding General, XVI. Army Corps
28 Sep 1904 - Sep 1906:	Member, Committee for Wounded Veterans
Sep 1906:	Promoted to *General of Infantry*
Sep 1906:	Retired

Major-General Nikanor Vasilyevich **Raznatovsky** (1 Feb 1861 - ?)
15 Jul 1906 - 1909:	Commander, 8th Rifle Regiment
1908:	Promoted to *Major-General*

General of Infantry Nikolai Iosifovich **Razgonov** (6 Dec 1831 - Apr 1902)
5 May 1878 - 6 Apr 1884:	Deputy Chief of Staff, Turkestan Military District
30 Aug 1878:	Promoted to *Major-General*
6 Apr 1884 - 28 Nov 1892:	Chief of Staff, Turkestan Military District
30 Aug 1888:	Promoted to *Lieutenant-General*
28 Nov 1892 - 1896:	Commandant of Fortress Kerch
1896:	Promoted to *General of Infantry*
1896:	Retired

Major-General Viktor Vasilyevich **Raznatovsky** (6 Aug 1857 - 2 Aug 1904)
27 Apr 1900 - 3 Feb 1904:	Commander, 9th East Siberian Rifle Regiment
25 Oct 1903:	Promoted to *Major-General*
3 Feb 1904 - 2 Aug 1904:	Chief of Staff, III. Siberian Army Corps
14 Mar 1904 - 15 May 1904:	Acting Chief of Staff, Kwantung Fortified Area

Lieutenant-General Aleksandr Pavlovich **Razumikhin** (12 Feb 1861 - ?)
24 Jan 1906 - 15 Feb 1907:   Military Judge, Kazan Military District Court
2 Apr 1906:   Promoted to *Major-General*
15 Feb 1907 - 27 Jul 1914:   Military Prosecutor, Omsk Military District
14 Apr 1913:   Promoted to *Lieutenant-General*
27 Jul 1914 - 9 Oct 1917:   Military Prosecutor, Kazan Military District
9 Oct 1917 - 31 Aug 1918:   Reserve officer, Kazan Military District

Major-General Leonid Pavlovich **Razumikhin** (20 Jun 1868 - ?)
19 Jun 1910 - 5 Jan 1916:   Intendant, XXIV. Army Corps
5 Jan 1916:   Promoted to *Major-General*
5 Jan 1916:   Retired

Lieutenant-General Sergey Ivanovich **Razumov** (14 Jul 1854 - ?)
26 Jul 1910:   Promoted to *Major-General*
26 Jul 1910 - 22 Oct 1913:   Commander, 7th Siberian Rifle Artillery Brigade
22 Oct 1913:   Promoted to *Lieutenant-General*
22 Oct 1913:   Retired

Lieutenant-General Nikolai Stepanovich **Razumovsky** (7 May 1850 - ?)
21 Apr 1906 - 31 Dec 1913:   Commandant, Tiflis Artillery Depot
6 Dec 1906:   Promoted to *Major-General*
31 Dec 1913:   Promoted to *Lieutenant-General*
31 Dec 1913:   Retired

Lieutenant-General Dmitry Aleksandrovich **Razvadovsky** (26 Oct 1854 - 28 Dec 1920)
21 Nov 1907:   Promoted to *Major-General*
21 Nov 1907 - 30 Apr 1910:   Commander, 1st Artillery Brigade
30 Apr 1910 - 24 Apr 1913:   Commander, 5th Artillery Brigade
24 Apr 1913 - 19 Oct 1916:   Inspector of Artillery, XVII. Army Corps
6 Dec 1913:   Promoted to *Lieutenant-General*
19 Oct 1916 - 1917:   Reserve officer, Odessa Military District
1917 - Oct 1917:   Commandant of Bender Garrison

Major-General Aleksandr Aleksandrovich **Razvozov** (22 Mar 1844 - ?)
2 Apr 1899 - 1906:   Commander, Nerchinsk Penal Colony
6 Dec 1905:   Promoted to *Major-General*

General of Infantry Aleksandr Alekseyevich **Rebinder** (27 Jan 1826 - 31 Aug 1913)
17 Apr 1863:   Promoted to *Major-General*
17 Apr 1863 - 23 Mar 1869:   Attached to the Inspector of Rifle Battalions
23 Mar 1869 - 30 Aug 1873:   General à la suite
30 Aug 1873:   Promoted to *Lieutenant-General*
30 Aug 1873 - 1880:   At the disposal of the Commanding General, St. Petersburg Military District
1881 - 14 Oct 1888:   Special Assignments General, St. Petersburg Military District

14 Oct 1888 - 26 Oct 1905:	Deputy Commanding General, St. Petersburg Military District
30 Aug 1889:	Promoted to *General of Infantry*
26 Oct 1905 - 1907:	At the disposal of the Commanding General, St. Petersburg Military District
1907:	Retired

General of Cavalry Aleksandr Maksimovich **Rebinder** (7 Jul 1838 - 4 Mar 1909)

30 Aug 1874 - 29 May 1880:	Commander, 4th Dragoon Regiment
19 Dec 1877:	Promoted to *Major-General*
29 May 1880 - 14 Jul 1883:	Commander, 2nd Brigade, 4th Cavalry Division
14 Jul 1883 - 10 Aug 1886:	Commander, Life Guards Cuirassier Regiment
10 Aug 1886 - 23 Nov 1887:	Commander, 2nd Brigade, 1st Guards Cavalry Division
23 Nov 1887 - 27 Mar 1897:	Commander, 10th Cavalry Division
30 Aug 1888:	Promoted to *Lieutenant-General*
27 Mar 1897 - 21 Jun 1905:	Commanding General, XIII. Army Corps
6 Dec 1899:	Promoted to *General of Cavalry*
21 Jun 1905 - 3 Jan 1906:	Member, Committee for Wounded Veterans
3 Jan 1906:	Retired

Lieutenant-General Aleksey Maksimovich **Rebinder** (14 Jan 1853 - 1923)

7 Dec 1904 - 15 Jan 1909:	Commander, 12th Grenadier Regiment
15 Jan 1909:	Promoted to *Major-General*
15 Jan 1909 - 14 Jan 1913:	Commander, 1st Brigade, 1st Grenadier Division
14 Jan 1913:	Promoted to *Lieutenant-General*
14 Jan 1913:	Retired

Major-General Baron Nikolai Ottonovich **Rebinder** (20 Apr 1851 - ?)

25 Mar 1904:	Promoted to *Major-General*
25 Mar 1904 - 9 Mar 1905:	Commander, 2nd Brigade, 3rd Siberian Infantry Division
9 Mar 1905 - 28 May 1905:	Attached to the General Staff
28 May 1905 - 4 Nov 1906:	Commander, 1st Brigade, 3rd Grenadier Division

General of Infantry Aleksandr Fyodorovich **Rediger** (31 Dec 1853 - 26 Jan 1920)

20 Mar 1884 - 21 Jan 1897:	Clerk, Chancellery of the Ministry of War
24 Oct 1884 - 11 May 1898:	Professor, Nikolai General Staff Academy
30 Aug 1893:	Promoted to *Major-General*
21 Jan 1897 - 30 Jun 1898:	Assistant Chief of Chancellery, Ministry of War
30 Jun 1898 - 20 Jun 1905:	Chief of Chancellery, Ministry of War
6 Dec 1900:	Promoted to *Lieutenant-General*
21 Jun 1905 - 15 Jul 1905:	Deputy Minister of War
21 Jun 1905 - 1 May 1917:	Member of the Military Council
15 Jul 1905 - 11 Mar 1909:	Minister of War
4 Nov 1905 - 1 May 1917:	Member of the State Council
6 May 1907:	Promoted to *General of Infantry*
1 May 1917 - 25 Oct 1917:	Unassigned
25 Oct 1917:	Retired

Lieutenant-General Nikolai Fyodorovich **Rediger** (29 Jun 1848 - ?)
4 Apr 1900:	Promoted to *Major-General*
4 Apr 1900 - 23 Jul 1902:	Commander, 2nd Brigade, 3rd Infantry Division
23 Jul 1902 - 1908:	Member, Main Military Sanitation Committee
6 Dec 1906:	Promoted to *Lieutenant-General*

General of Infantry Pyotr Timofeyevich **Redkin** (1 May 1841 - 9 Sep 1916)
14 Aug 1896:	Promoted to *Major-General*
14 Aug 1896 - 28 Apr 1899:	Commander, 2nd Brigade, 39th Infantry Division
28 Apr 1899 - 22 May 1901:	Commander, 2nd Brigade, 3rd Grenadier Division
22 May 1901 - 1904:	Commandant of Fortress Ust-Dvinsk
6 Dec 1901:	Promoted to *Lieutenant-General*
1904:	Promoted to *General of Infantry*
1904:	Retired

Lieutenant-General Aleksey Yefimovich **Redko** (12 Mar 1862 - ?)
7 Sep 1905:	Promoted to *Major-General*
7 Sep 1905 - 23 Aug 1906:	Commander, 2nd Brigade, 2nd Siberian Rifle Division
23 Aug 1906 - 27 Nov 1906:	Commander, 2nd Brigade, 4th East Siberian Rifle Division
27 Nov 1906 - 23 Jul 1910:	Commander, 2nd Siberian Reserve Infantry Brigade
23 Jul 1910 - 19 Jul 1914:	Commander, 4th Turkestan Rifle Brigade
19 Jul 1914 - 7 Aug 1914:	Commander, 14th Siberian Rifle Division
7 Aug 1914 - 6 Apr 1917:	Commander, 8th Siberian Rifle Division
22 Jan 1915:	Promoted to *Lieutenant-General*
6 Apr 1917 - Jul 1917:	Commanding General, III. Siberian Army Corps

Lieutenant-General Iosif Ilich **Regulsky** (15 Mar 1854 - ?)
11 Dec 1903:	Promoted to *Major-General*
11 Dec 1903 - 15 Mar 1914:	Commander, 2nd Brigade, 2nd Infantry Division
15 Mar 1914:	Promoted to *Lieutenant-General*
15 Mar 1914:	Retired
3 Aug 1914 - 7 Mar 1915:	Recalled; Commander, 1st Brigade, 2nd Infantry Division
7 Mar 1915 - 13 Apr 1917:	Commander, 9th Siberian Rifle Division
13 Apr 1917 - 1918:	Reserve officer, Odessa Military District

Lieutenant-General Nikolai Aleksandrovich **Rekhenberg** (23 Oct 1846 - 1908)
14 Jan 1898:	Promoted to *Major-General*
14 Jan 1898 - 31 Dec 1899:	Commander, 1st Brigade, 42nd Infantry Division
31 Dec 1899 - 14 Aug 1902:	Governor of Vyborg
14 Aug 1902:	Promoted to *Lieutenant-General*
14 Aug 1902:	Retired
20 Feb 1906 - 12 Mar 1907:	Recalled; Governor of Vyborg
12 Mar 1907:	Retired

Major-General Aleksandr Vilgelmovich **Remer** (11 Oct 1868 - 28 Jun 1926)
13 Oct 1913 - 9 Nov 1915:	Military Judge, Kiev Military District Court
6 Dec 1913:	Promoted to *Major-General*

9 Nov 1915 - 1917: Chief of Legal Section, Logistics Department, Southwestern Front
1917: Attached to the Legal Service, Caucasus Front

Lieutenant-General of Naval Artillery Fyodor Demyanovich **Remesnikov** (9 Aug 1866 - ?)
19 Nov 1907 - ?: Chairman of the Naval Artillery Committee
6 Dec 1910: Promoted to *Major-General of Naval Artillery*
6 Dec 1916: Promoted to *Lieutenant-General of Naval Artillery*

Major-General Aleksandr Kondratyevich **Remezov** (10 Dec 1869 - ?)
25 Dec 1914 - 5 Jul 1915: Commander, 194th Infantry Regiment
1 May 1915: Promoted to *Major-General*
5 Jul 1915 - 5 May 1916: Commander, Brigade, 81st Infantry Division
5 May 1916 - 5 Jun 1916: Chief of Staff, 75th Infantry Division
5 Jun 1916 - 18 Apr 1917: Chief of Staff, XXXI. Army Corps
18 Apr 1917 - 19 Nov 1917: Commander, 16th Siberian Rifle Division
19 Nov 1917 - 1918: Commander, 2nd Siberian Rifle Division

Major-General Nikolai Mitrofanovich **Remezov** (8 Dec 1864 - 30 Oct 1916)
14 Jan 1914: Promoted to *Major-General*
14 Jan 1914 - 29 Jul 1914: Commander, 2nd Brigade, 10th Infantry Division
29 Jul 1914 - 1915: Commander, 1st Brigade, 35th Infantry Division
Oct 1914: Acting Commander, 35th Infantry Division
1915 - 20 Jan 1916: Reserve officer, Kiev Military District
20 Jan 1916 - 30 Oct 1916: Commander, 1st Brigade, 35th Infantry Division

Lieutenant-General Aleksandr Aleksandrovich **Remi** (25 Feb 1858 - ?)
12 Jul 1903: Promoted to *Major-General*
12 Jul 1903 - 15 Sep 1904: Commander, 2nd Brigade, 20th Infantry Division
15 Sep 1904 - 8 Oct 1908: Commander, 2nd Brigade, 18th Infantry Division
8 Oct 1908 - 1909: Commander, 51st Reserve Infantry Brigade
1909: Promoted to *Lieutenant-General*
1909: Retired

Major-General Arnold Aleksandrovich von **Remlingen** (13 Dec 1841 - 29 Sep 1900)
23 Dec 1896 - 29 Jul 1899: Deputy Chief of Staff, Turkestan Military District
6 Dec 1897: Promoted to *Major-General*
29 Jul 1899 - 29 Sep 1900: Commander, 2nd Brigade, 36th Infantry Division

Actual Privy Councillor Adolf Aleksandrovich **Remmert** (14 Jul 1835 - 26 Jul 1902)
1878: Promoted to *Actual State Councillor*
1878 - ?: Chief of Medical Units, Tiflis-Alexandrov-Kars-Erzerum
? - Sep 1887: Chief Military Medical Inspector, Caucasus Military District
Sep 1887 - 26 Jul 1902: Chief, Main Military Medical Directorate
1888: Promoted to *Privy Councillor*
1898: Promoted to *Actual Privy Councillor*

Lieutenant-General of the Fleet Aleksandr Adolfovich **Remmert** (28 Jun 1861 - 1931)
24 Nov 1911 - 10 Apr 1916:	Chief of Mine Division, Main Shipbuilding Directorate
1 Jan 1913:	Promoted to *Major-General of the Admiralty*
8 Apr 1913:	Redesignated *Major-General of the Fleet*
10 Apr 1916:	Promoted to *Lieutenant-General of the Fleet*
10 Apr 1916 - Oct 1917:	Reserve officer, Ministry of the Navy

Major-General Boris Aleksandrovich **Rengarten** (14 Aug 1853 - ?)
25 Nov 1894 - 22 Sep 1910:	Military Judge, Amur Military District
6 Dec 1901:	Promoted to *Major-General*
22 Sep 1910 - 1917:	Military Judge, Kiev Military District

Major-General Ivan Aleksandrovich **Rengarten** (5 Oct 1846 - ?)
4 Jan 1893 - 21 Dec 1896:	Commander, 122nd Infantry Regiment
14 May 1896:	Promoted to *Major-General*
21 Dec 1896 - 23 Oct 1897:	Commander, 2nd Brigade, 9th Infantry Division
23 Oct 1897 - 25 Jan 1900:	Commander, 2nd Brigade, 24th Infantry Division
25 Jan 1900 - 24 Nov 1901:	Commander, 54th Reserve Infantry Brigade
24 Nov 1901 - Jul 1906:	At the disposal of the Commanding General, Kazan Military District

General of Cavalry Pavel Georg Karlovich Edler von **Rennenkampf** (17 Apr 1854 - 1 Apr 1918)
25 Nov 1899 - 24 Jul 1901:	Chief of Staff, Transbaikal Region
9 Apr 1900:	Promoted to *Major-General*
24 Jul 1901 - 1 Feb 1904:	Commander, 1st Independent Cavalry Brigade
1 Feb 1904 - 31 Aug 1905:	Commander, Transbaikal Cossack Division
30 Jun 1904:	Promoted to *Lieutenant-General*
31 Aug 1905 - 9 Nov 1905:	Attached to the C-in-C, Far East
9 Nov 1905 - 9 Jun 1906:	Commanding General, VII. Siberian Army Corps
9 Jun 1906 - 27 Dec 1906:	Commanding General, III. Siberian Army Corps
27 Dec 1906 - 20 Jan 1913:	Commanding General, III. Army Corps
6 Oct 1910:	Promoted to *General of Cavalry*
5 Oct 1912:	Promoted to *General-Adjutant*
20 Jan 1913 - 19 Jul 1914:	Commanding General, Vilnius Military District
19 Jul 1914 - 18 Nov 1914:	C-in-C, 1st Army
18 Nov 1914 - 6 Oct 1915:	At the disposal of the Minister of War
6 Oct 1915:	Retired

Lieutenant-General Konstantin Ivanovich **Renvald** (13 Aug 1831 - 12 Sep 1909)
22 Sep 1871 - 4 Jul 1878:	Commander, 94th Infantry Regiment
1878:	Promoted to *Major-General*
4 Jul 1878 - 23 Sep 1878:	Unassigned
23 Sep 1878 - 10 Oct 1889:	Commander, 1st Brigade, 23rd Infantry Division
10 Oct 1889 - 1894:	Deputy C-in-C of the Finnish Army
30 Aug 1891:	Promoted to *Lieutenant-General*
1894:	Retired

Lieutenant-General Nikolai Afanasyevich **Repin** (22 Oct 1837 - 28 Apr 1905)
27 Apr 1885 - 30 Oct 1901:	Director, Voronezh Cadet Corps
30 Aug 1887:	Promoted to *Major-General*
30 Oct 1901 - 28 Apr 1905:	Board Member, Ministry of National Education
29 Feb 1902:	Promoted to *Lieutenant-General*

Major-General Dmitry Ivanovich **Repyev** (18 Dec 1866 - ?)
12 Feb 1910 - 1917:	Chief of Military Topographical Department, Turkestan Military District
25 Mar 1912:	Promoted to *Major-General*

Major-General Mikhail Ivanovich **Repyev** (14 Sep 1865 - 29 Apr 1937)
1914 - 3 Jul 1915:	Commander, 1st Battalion, 37th Artillery Brigade
19 Jun 1915:	Promoted to *Major-General*
3 Jul 1915 - 18 Feb 1917:	Commander, 37th Artillery Brigade
18 Feb 1917 - 1917:	Commander, 166th Infantry Division
1917 - 1918:	Commanding General, XVIII. Army Corps

Major-General Fyodor Petrovich **Rerberg** (9 Oct 1868 - 14 Sep 1928)
21 Oct 1909 - 10 Jul 1912:	Commander, 3rd Grenadier Regiment
10 Jul 1912:	Promoted to *Major-General*
10 Jul 1912 - 30 Jun 1915:	Chief of Staff, X. Army Corps
30 Jun 1915 - 12 Jul 1915:	Reserve officer, Kiev Military District
12 Jul 1915 - 5 Oct 1917:	Chief of Staff, Fortress Sevastopol
5 Oct 1917 - 1918:	Reserve officer, Odessa Military District

Lieutenant-General Fyodor Sergeyevich **Rerberg** (17 Feb 1860 - ?)
24 Feb 1909:	Promoted to *Major-General*
24 Feb 1909 - 3 Jul 1911:	Chief of Communications, Vilnius Military District
3 Jul 1911 - 19 Jul 1914:	Chief of Communications, Kiev Military District
19 Jul 1914 - 6 Nov 1914:	Chief of Economics Staff, 3rd Army
6 Nov 1914 - 23 Nov 1914:	Deputy Commander, Kuban Cossack Division
23 Nov 1914 - 6 Apr 1917:	Commander, 7th Cavalry Division
22 Mar 1915:	Promoted to *Lieutenant-General*
6 Apr 1917 - 20 Nov 1917:	Commanding General, VII. Cavalry Corps
19 Jul 1917 - 29 Aug 1917:	Acting C-in-C, 11th Army
20 Nov 1917 - 13 Dec 1917:	C-in-C, Special Army

General of Engineers Pyotr Fyodorovich **Rerberg** (6 Oct 1835 - 22 May 1912)
19 Jan 1867 - 20 Jun 1879:	Commander of Engineers, Caucasus Military District
29 Jan 1867:	Promoted to *Major-General*
8 Nov 1877:	Promoted to *Lieutenant-General*
20 Jun 1879 - 12 Mar 1881:	Commander, Caucasus Infantry Division
12 Mar 1881 - 22 Mar 1883:	Commander, Trans-Caspian Region
22 Mar 1883 - 6 Jul 1885:	Commander, 25th Infantry Division
6 Jul 1885 - 29 May 1893:	Commanding General, VIII. Army Corps
26 Feb 1886 - 14 Mar 1886:	Acting Commanding General, Odessa Military District
29 Jun 1886 - 14 Aug 1886:	Acting Commanding General, Odessa Military District

7 Oct 1886 - 31 Oct 1886:	Acting Commanding General, Odessa Military District
18 Feb 1887 - 19 Mar 1887:	Acting Commanding General, Odessa Military District
17 May 1887 - 26 Jun 1887:	Acting Commanding General, Odessa Military District
11 Jan 1888 - 1 Mar 1888:	Acting Commanding General, Odessa Military District
8 Jul 1888 - 10 Aug 1888:	Acting Commanding General, Odessa Military District
26 Jun 1889 - 10 Aug 1889:	Acting Commanding General, Odessa Military District
29 Aug 1889 - 28 Sep 1889:	Acting Commanding General, Odessa Military District
16 May 1890 - 18 Jun 1890:	Acting Commanding General, Odessa Military District
26 Oct 1890 - 4 Dec 1890:	Acting Commanding General, Odessa Military District
15 Feb 1891 - 19 Mar 1891:	Acting Commanding General, Odessa Military District
15 Jun 1891 - 1 Aug 1891:	Acting Commanding General, Odessa Military District
30 Aug 1891:	Promoted to *General of Engineers*
2 Jan 1892 - 9 Feb 1892:	Acting Commanding General, Odessa Military District
11 Jul 1892 - 1 Aug 1892:	Acting Commanding General, Odessa Military District
2 Jan 1893 - 26 Feb 1893:	Acting Commanding General, Odessa Military District
29 May 1893 - 22 May 1912:	Member of the Military Council
3 Jul 1893 - 8 Aug 1893:	Acting Commanding General, Odessa Military District

Lieutenant-General Nikolai Petrovich **Reshchikov** (17 Nov 1853 - ?)
10 May 1904:	Promoted to *Major-General*
10 May 1904 - 7 Jul 1908:	General for Special Assignments, Kiev Military District
7 Jul 1908 - 12 Jul 1910:	Chief of Staff, IX. Army Corps
12 Jul 1910:	Promoted to *Lieutenant-General*
12 Jul 1910 - 19 Apr 1915:	Commander, 24th Infantry Division
19 Apr 1915 - 15 May 1916:	Commanding General, XXXV. Army Corps
15 May 1916 - 30 Jul 1917:	Reserve officer, Petrograd Military District
30 Jul 1917:	Retired

Lieutenant-General Nikolai Lavrentyevich **Reshetin** (21 Nov 1842 - 7 Apr 1914)
1 Oct 1897:	Promoted to *Major-General*
1 Oct 1897 - 20 Oct 1898:	Deputy Commander of Artillery, Amur Military District
20 Oct 1898 - 11 Jan 1900:	At the disposal of the Commanding General, Amur Military District
11 Jan 1900 - 4 Mar 1903:	Commander of Artillery, Amur Military District
4 Mar 1903 - Oct 1905:	Commander of Artillery, Caucasus Military District
28 Mar 1904:	Promoted to *Lieutenant-General*
Oct 1905 - Dec 1905:	Attached to the Governor of the Caucasus
Dec 1905:	Retired

Lieutenant-General Aleksandr Alekseyevich **Resin** (21 Apr 1857 - 24 Jun 1933)
6 Jul 1904:	Promoted to *Major-General*
6 Jul 1904 - 24 Feb 1905:	Commander, 1st Brigade, 16th Infantry Division
24 Feb 1905 - 4 Mar 1909:	Commander, Life Guards Kexholmsky Regiment
4 Mar 1909 - 3 May 1910:	Commander, 2nd Brigade, 3rd Guards Infantry Division
3 May 1910 - 19 Jan 1913:	Commander, Guards Rifle Brigade
17 Oct 1910:	Promoted to *Lieutenant-General*
19 Jan 1913 - 4 Nov 1914:	Commander, 2nd Guards Infantry Division
4 Nov 1914 - 12 Feb 1915:	Reserve officer, Kiev Military District

12 Feb 1915 - 6 Jun 1915:	Commanding General, X. Militia Corps
6 Jun 1915 - 23 Dec 1915:	Commanding Geneal, XLII. Army Corps
23 Dec 1915 - 25 Jan 1916:	Reserve officer, Dvinsk Military District
25 Jan 1916 - 14 Feb 1917:	Reserve officer, Petrograd Military District
14 Feb 1917 - 1 Aug 1917:	Reserve officer, Dvinsk Military District
1 Aug 1917:	Retired

Major-General Aleksey Alekseyevich **Resin** (31 Jan 1866 - ?)
14 Aug 1914 - 28 May 1917:	Commander, His Majesty's Own Consolidated Infantry Regiment
6 Dec 1914:	Promoted to *Major-General*
28 May 1917:	Dismissed

Lieutenant-General Pyotr Fodorovich **Retivov** (5 Oct 1853 - ?)
10 Feb 1907 - 22 Jun 1908:	Attached to Main Intendant Directorate
31 May 1907:	Promoted to *Major-General*
22 Jun 1908 - 14 Oct 1912:	Deputy Intendant, Vilnius Military District
14 Oct 1912:	Promoted to *Lieutenant-General*
14 Oct 1912:	Retired

Vice-Admiral Mikhail Alekseyevich **Reunov** (8 Nov 1841 - 11 Feb 1904)
1894:	Promoted to *Rear-Admiral*
12 Oct 1896 - 1898:	Junior Flagman, Pacific Squadron
1898 - 6 Dec 1901:	Deputy Chief of the Main Naval Staff
6 Dec 1901:	Promoted to *Vice-Admiral*
6 Dec 1901:	Retired

Major-General of the Fleet Vladimir Ksenofontovich **Revelioti** (28 Sep 1859 - 7 Apr 1929)
3 Jan 1911 - ?:	Deputy Commander, Sevastopol Naval Depot
?:	Promoted to *Major-General of the Fleet*

Major-General Ivan Ivanovich **Reyman** (30 Aug 1850 - ?)
2 Sep 1899:	Promoted to *Major-General*
2 Sep 1899 - 6 Mar 1900:	Commander, 2nd Brigade, 30th Infantry Division
6 Mar 1900 - 5 Jul 1903:	Commander, 64th Reserve Infantry Brigade

Rear-Admiral Nikolay Gotlibovich **Reyn** (2 Sep 1870 - 1 Mar 1917)
29 Jun 1915 - 31 Oct 1916:	Commander, Minelayer Detachment, Baltic Fleet
30 Jul 1916:	Promoted to *Rear-Admiral*
31 Oct 1916 - 1 Mar 1917:	Commander, Training-Mine Detachment, Baltic Fleet

Major-General Anatoly Anatolyevich **Reynbot** (1914: **Rezvoy**) (4 Feb 1868 - ?)
6 Nov 1905 - 7 Jan 1906:	Acting Governor of Kazan
7 Jan 1906:	Promoted to *Major-General*
7 Jan 1906 - 11 Dec 1907:	Mayor of Moscow
11 Dec 1907 - 12 Nov 1908:	Member of the Tsar's retinue
12 Nov 1908:	Dismissed
4 Apr 1914 - 2 Dec 1914:	Recalled; At the disposal of the Minister of War

2 Dec 1914 - 1915:	Chief of Sanatory Department, Northwestern Front
1915 - 6 Jul 1916:	Special Assignments General, Logistics Department, Northwestern Front
6 Jul 1916 - 30 Apr 1917:	Commander, 40th Infantry Division
30 Apr 1917 - 1918:	Reserve officer, Odessa Military District

Lieutenant-General Aleksandr Georgiyevich **Reyneke** (4 Jun 1833 - 26 Jan 1911)

22 Oct 1885 - 19 Aug 1888:	Director, 3rd Moscow Cadet Corps
30 Aug 1886:	Promoted to *Major-General*
19 Aug 1888 - 22 Oct 1892:	Director, Siberian Cadet Corps
22 Oct 1892 - 19 Jun 1900:	Director, Nizhny Novgorod Count Arakcheyev Cadet Corps
19 Jun 1900:	Promoted to *Lieutenant-General*
19 Jun 1900:	Retired

Lieutenant-General Ivan Aleksandrovich **Reyngard** (11 Aug 1864 - ?)

20 Aug 1905 - 1914:	Deputy Governor of Radom
6 Dec 1908:	Promoted to *Major-General*
21 Jun 1914:	Promoted to *Lieutenant-General*

General of Artillery Vladimir Yakovlevich **Reyntal** (5 Oct 1838 - 15 Jan 1913)

12 Jul 1886 - 25 Jan 1893:	Commander of Artillery, Fortress Dunaburg
30 Aug 1888:	Promoted to *Major-General*
25 Jan 1893 - 16 Nov 1904:	Inspector of Fortress & Siege Artillery
6 Dec 1898:	Promoted to *Lieutenant-General*
16 Nov 1904 - 12 Jun 1909:	Member, Main Fortress Committee, Member of the Artillery Committee, Main Artillery Directorate
12 Jun 1909 - 13 Oct 1909:	At the disposal of the Main Artillery Directorate
13 Oct 1909 - 15 Jan 1913:	Member of the Military Council
6 Dec 1909:	Promoted to *General of Artillery*

Lieutenant-General Viktor Aleksandrovich **Reys** (22 Feb 1864 - ?)

30 Oct 1903 - 15 Dec 1904:	Commander, 27th East Siberian Rifle Regiment
22 Oct 1904:	Promoted to *Major-General*
15 Dec 1904 - 30 Jun 1906:	Chief of Staff, Kwantung Fortified Area
30 Jun 1906 - 2 Apr 1908:	Attached to the General Staff
2 Apr 1908:	Dismissed
10 Apr 1916:	Promoted to *Lieutenant-General*

Lieutenant-General Ivan Nikolayevich **Reyter** (2 Sep 1837 - 1911)

8 Mar 1894:	Promoted to *Major-General*
8 Mar 1894 - Sep 1904:	Commandant of Tiflis
14 Apr 1902:	Promoted to *Lieutenant-General*
Sep 1904:	Retired

Admiral Nikolai Karlovich **Reytsenstein** (7 Aug 1854 - 27 Nov 1916)
16 Jan 1904 - Feb 1904:	Commander, Vladivostok Cruiser Detachment, Pacific Fleet
9 Mar 1904 - 9 Oct 1906:	Commander, Cruiser Group, Pacific Squadron
12 Jul 1904:	Promoted to *Rear-Admiral*
9 Oct 1906 - 26 Mar 1907:	Junior Flagman, 2nd Division, Baltic Fleet
26 Mar 1907 - 28 Aug 1909:	Commander of Training & Naval Artillery, Baltic Fleet
28 Aug 1909:	Promoted to *Vice-Admiral*
28 Aug 1909 - 21 Jun 1916:	Member of the Admiralty Board
14 Apr 1913:	Promoted to *Admiral*
21 Jun 1916:	Retired

Major-General Konstantin Mikhailovich **Rezanov** (1820 - 1898)
22 Sep 1866 - 1897:	Chief of Tambov Factory Horse Depot
30 Aug 1879:	Promoted to *Major-General*
1897:	Retired

Major-General Vasily Savvich **Reznikov** (17 Jul 1859 - 19 Apr 1927)
23 Jan 1913 - 15 Jan 1916:	Commander, 11th Uhlan Regiment
15 Jan 1916 - 10 Jul 1916:	Reserve officer, Kiev Military District
3 Feb 1916:	Promoted to *Major-General*
10 Jul 1916:	Retired

General of Artillery Orest Pavlovich **Rezvoy** (21 Feb 1811 - 29 Jan 1904)
25 Aug 1847 - 15 Apr 1853:	Member, Artillery Section, Military-Scientific Committee
6 Dec 1851:	Promoted to *Major-General*
15 Apr 1853 - 13 Jul 1859:	Member, Training Committee, Main Directorate for Military Schools
19 Apr 1853 - 23 Jan 1857:	Commandant, Mikhailovsky Artillery School
18 Jul 1859 - 10 Mar 1863:	Member, Artillery Committee
30 Aug 1860:	Promoted to *Lieutenant-General*
10 Mar 1863 - 8 May 1867:	Member, Main Military-Scientific Committee
8 May 1867 - 25 Nov 1870:	Member, Technical Committee, Main Artillery Directorate
25 Nov 1870 - 29 Jan 1904:	Honorary Member, Mikhailovsky Artillery Academy
20 Aug 1871:	Promoted to *General of Artillery*
20 Aug 1871 - 29 Jan 1904.	Member of the Military Council

General of Infantry Dmitry Modestovich **Rezvy** (1 Feb 1843 - 29 Nov 1912)
4 Feb 1891 - 5 Apr 1895:	Commander, Life Guards Kexholmsky Regiment
30 Aug 1891:	Promoted to *Major-General*
5 Apr 1895 - 28 Oct 1899:	Commander, 1st Brigade, 3rd Guards Infantry Division
28 Oct 1899 - 9 Oct 1904:	Commander, 21st Infantry Division
6 Dec 1899:	Promoted to *Lieutenant-General*
9 Oct 1904 - 23 May 1905:	Commanding General, XIX. Army Corps
23 May 1905 - 29 Nov 1912:	Member, Committee for Wounded Veterans
6 Dec 1907:	Promoted to *General of Infantry*

Major-General Pyotr Petrovich **Ribas** (5 May 1842 - ?)
10 Jul 1889 - 1904:	General for Special Assignments, Main Directorate of Horsebreeding
2 Apr 1895:	Promoted to *Major-General*

General of Infantry Aleksandr Nikolayevich **Ridiger** (23 Jul 1838 - Jun 1910)
25 Aug 1883:	Promoted to *Major-General*
25 Aug 1883 - 26 Apr 1884:	Commander, 2nd Brigade, 21st Infantry Division
26 Apr 1884 - 12 Nov 1886:	Commander, 2nd Brigade, 35th Infantry Division
12 Nov 1886 - 20 Nov 1889:	Commander, 2nd Rifle Brigade
20 Nov 1889 - 28 Jan 1895:	Commandant, Infantry Officers School
30 Aug 1894:	Promoted to *Lieutenant-General*
28 Jan 1895 - 4 Feb 1906:	Inspector of Riflemen
28 Jan 1895 - Jun 1910:	Member of the Artillery Committee, Main Artillery Directorate
6 Dec 1904:	Promoted to *General of Infantry*
21 Jun 1905 - Jun 1910:	Member of the Military Council

Major-General Count Aleksandr Alekseyevich **Ridiger-Belyaev** (8 Feb 1867 - 1939)
6 Dec 1915:	Promoted to *Major-General*
6 Dec 1915 - 1917:	Attached to Grand Duke Andrey Vladimirovich

Lieutenant-General Vladimir Karlovich **Rike** (25 May 1848 - 29 May 1907)
13 Apr 1885 - 4 May 1897:	Military Judge, St. Petersburg Military District Court
30 Aug 1892:	Promoted to *Major-General*
4 May 1897 - 15 Feb 1898:	Military Prosecutor, Kazan Military District Court
15 Feb 1898 - 4 Jun 1898:	Military Judge, Moscow Military District Court
4 Jun 1898 - 14 Feb 1900:	Military Judge, St. Petersburg Military District Court
14 Feb 1900:	Promoted to *Lieutenant-General*
14 Feb 1900:	Retired

General of Infantry Aleksandr Karlovich **Rikhter** (26 Apr 1834 - 31 Dec 1896)
23 Aug 1872:	Promoted to *Major-General*
23 Aug 1872 - 4 Feb 1879:	Commander, 3rd Sapper Brigade
4 Feb 1879 - 25 Jul 1885:	Commander, 16th Infantry Division
30 Aug 1881:	Promoted to *Lieutenant-General*
25 Jul 1885 - 17 Feb 1891:	Commander, 2nd Guards Infantry Division
17 Feb 1891 - 31 Dec 1896:	Commanding General, XVI. Army Corps
6 Dec 1895:	Promoted to *General of Infantry*

General of Infantry Gvido Kazimirovich **Rikhter** (25 Jun 1855 - 17 Mar 1919)
18 Nov 1899 - 11 Feb 1903:	Chief of Staff, Orenburg Cossack Army
1 Apr 1901:	Promoted to *Major-General*
11 Feb 1903 - 17 Oct 1904:	Chief of Staff, Fortress Kovno
17 Oct 1904 - 18 Aug 1905:	At the disposal of the C-in-C, 2nd Manchurian Army
18 Aug 1905 - 17 Jul 1906:	Chief of Staff, Consolidated Rifle Corps
17 Jul 1906 - 1 May 1910:	Chief of Staff, Turkestan Military District
22 Apr 1907:	Promoted to *Lieutenant-General*

1 May 1910 - 13 Aug 1914:	Commander, 16th Infantry Division
13 Aug 1914 - 27 Aug 1914:	Unassigned
27 Aug 1914 - 30 Aug 1914:	Acting Commanding General, VI. Army Corps
30 Aug 1914 - 1915:	Unassigned
1915:	Promoted to *General of Infantry*
1915:	Retired

General of Infantry Otton Borisovich **Rikhter** (1 Aug 1830 - 2 Mar 1908)

30 Aug 1858 - 12 Apr 1865:	Attached to the Tsarevich, Grand Duke Nikolai Aleksandrovich
19 Apr 1864:	Promoted to *Major-General*
12 Apr 1865 - 19 May 1866:	General à la suite
19 May 1866 - 9 Oct 1866:	Chancellor of the Imperial Headquarters
9 Oct 1866 - 9 Sep 1867:	Chief of Staff, St. Petersburg Military District
9 Sep 1867 - 4 Apr 1871:	Member, Main Committee on Troop Training
4 Apr 1871 - 1 May 1879:	Commander, 13th Infantry Division
5 Oct 1871:	Promoted to *General-Adjutant*
10 Sep 1872:	Promoted to *Lieutenant-General*
1 May 1879 - 2 Sep 1881:	Commanding General, VII. Army Corps
2 Sep 1881 - 13 Jun 1898:	Commanding General of the Imperial Headquarters
30 Aug 1886:	Promoted to *General of Infantry*
13 Jun 1898 - 2 Mar 1908:	Member of the State Council

Rear-Admiral Baron Otton Ottonovich **Rikhter** (26 Jun 1871 - 1920)

23 Jun 1915 - 12 Dec 1916:	Commander, Abo-Åland Islands Detachment, Peter the Great Naval Fortress
12 Nov 1915:	Promoted to *Rear-Admiral*
12 Dec 1916 - 10 Aug 1917:	Reserve officer, Ministry of the Navy
10 Aug 1917:	Dismissed

Rear-Admiral Fyodor Voinovich **Rimsky-Korsakov** (13 May 1863 - 28 Sep 1923)

18 Dec 1909 - 26 Aug 1913:	Deputy Commander, 2nd Baltic Naval Depot
26 Aug 1913:	Promoted to *Rear-Admiral*
26 Aug 1913:	Retired

Major-General Mikhail Nikolayevich **Rimsky-Korsakov** (7 Nov 1864 - ?)

1915 - 27 Jul 1915:	Deputy Commander of Artillery, Fortress Novogeorgiyevsk
27 Jul 1915:	Promoted to *Major-General*
27 Jul 1915 - 7 Aug 1915:	Commander of Artillery, Fortress Novogeorgiyevsk
7 Aug 1915 - Aug 1918:	POW

Vice-Admiral Nikolai Alexandrovich **Rimsky-Korsakov** (23 Apr 1852 - 12 Jan 1907)

1900:	Promoted to *Rear-Admiral*
17 Dec 1901 - 26 Apr 1904:	Governor of Archangelsk
26 Apr 1904 - 7 Aug 1906:	Commandant of the Imperial Naval Academy, Director of the Marine Corps
7 Aug 1906 - 12 Jan 1907:	Deputy Minister of the Navy

14 Nov 1906: Promoted to *Vice-Admiral*

Rear-Admiral Pyotr Voinovich **Rimsky-Korsakov** (30 Jan 1861 - 1927)
4 Feb 1913: Promoted to *Rear-Admiral*
4 Feb 1913 - 1917: Commandant, Port of Vladivostok

Major-General Sergey Nikolayevich **Rimsky-Korsakov** (6 Apr 1852 - ?)
1 Dec 1904: Promoted to *Major-General*
1 Dec 1904 - 5 Sep 1907: Commander of Artillery, Fortress Kerch

Lieutenant-General Vladimir Valerianovich **Rimsky-Korsakov** (14 Jul 1859 - 8 Nov 1933)
11 Aug 1903 - 6 Dec 1903: Military Judge, Vilnius Military District Court
6 Dec 1903: Promoted to *Major-General*
6 Dec 1903 - 18 Apr 1904: Inspector of Classes, 1st Moscow Cadet Corps
18 Apr 1904 - 28 Aug 1917: Director, 1st Moscow Cadet Corps
6 Dec 1909: Promoted to *Lieutenant-General*
28 Aug 1917: Dismissed

Major-General Ivan Mikhailovich **Rinkevich** (29 Aug 1854 - 18 Sep 1906)
12 May 1905 - 6 Mar 1906: Military Judge, Turkestan Military District Court
6 Dec 1905: Promoted to *Major-General*
6 Mar 1906 - 18 Sep 1906: Military Prosecutor, Turkestan Military District Court

Major-General Fyodor Aleksandrovich **Rittikh** (20 Mar 1871 - 27 Nov 1923)
17 Jun 1906 - 14 May 1917: Inspector of Classes, Corps of Pages
6 Dec 1911: Promoted to *Major-General*
9 Nov 1916 - 14 May 1917: Acting Director, Corps of Pages
14 May 1917: Dismissed

Lieutenant-General Anton Yegorovich **Rizenkampf** (25 Apr 1849 - 13 Sep 1919)
16 Mar 1893: Promoted to *Major-General*
16 Mar 1893 - 22 Apr 1897: Commander, Life Guards Dragoon Regiment
22 Apr 1897 - 1907: At the disposal of the Commanding General, St. Petersburg Military District
1907: Promoted to *Lieutenant-General*
1907: Retired

Major-General Fridrikh-Magnus Yegorovich **Rizenkampf** (13 Mar 1839 - ?)
25 Sep 1892 - 1902: Military Commander, Barnaulsk County
1902: Promoted to *Major-General*
1902: Retired

Major-General Ivan Vasilyevich **Rklitsky** (3 Jan 1835 - ?)
30 Jan 1893: Promoted to *Major-General*
30 Jan 1893 - 9 Apr 1897: Commander, 6th Artillery Brigade
9 Apr 1897 - 29 Oct 1899: Commander, 7th Artillery Brigade
29 Oct 1899: Retired

General of Infantry Gotlib-Vilgelm Pavlovich **Rode** (3 Nov 1858 - 5 Mar 1935)
5 Nov 1904:	Promoted to *Major-General*
5 Nov 1904 - 29 Jan 1913:	Chief of Staff, I. Caucasus Army Corps
29 Jan 1913:	Promoted to *Lieutenant-General*
29 Jan 1913 - 23 Apr 1915:	Commander, 42nd Infantry Division
23 Apr 1915 - 5 Jun 1915:	Special Assignments General, ? Army
5 Jun 1915 - 12 Jul 1915:	Commander, 42nd Infantry Division
12 Jul 1915 - 11 Oct 1915:	Commanding General, VII. Siberian Army Corps
11 Oct 1915 - 9 Sep 1917:	Reserve officer, Petrograd Military District
9 Sep 1917:	Promoted to *General of Infantry*
9 Sep 1917:	Retired

Vice-Admiral Aleksandr Rostislavovich **Rodionov** (1849 - 1910)
1902:	Promoted to *Rear-Admiral*
1902 - 1906:	Chief of Structures Section, Main Shipbuilding Directorate
1906 - 26 Feb 1907:	Acting Chief of the Main Directorate of Shipbuilding & Supply
26 Feb 1907:	Promoted to *Vice-Admiral*
26 Feb 1907:	Retired

General of Cavalry Aleksey Viktorovich **Rodionov** (14 Jul 1853 - 4 Sep 1919)
11 Dec 1902:	Promoted to *Major-General*
11 Dec 1902 - 30 Jun 1904:	Special Assignments General, Ataman of the Don Cossacks
30 Jun 1904 - 10 Feb 1907:	Commander, Life Guards Cossack Regiment
10 Feb 1907 - 14 Sep 1911:	Commander, 3rd Brigade, 1st Guards Cavalry Division
14 Sep 1911:	Promoted to *Lieutenant-General*
14 Sep 1911 - 31 Dec 1913:	Commander, 2nd Consolidated Cossack Division
13 Dec 1913:	Promoted to *General of Cavalry*
13 Dec 1913:	Retired
6 Mar 1914:	Recalled with the rank of *Lieutenant-General*
6 Mar 1914 - 3 Oct 1917:	Honorary Trustee, St. Petersburg Board of Trustees, Empresss Maria Institutions
3 Oct 1917:	Promoted to *General of Cavalry*
3 Oct 1917:	Retired

Major General Nikolai Petrovich **Rodionov** (? Apr 1861 - ?)
1916 - 5 Jun 1917:	Commander, Brigade, 1st Rifle Division
30 Jul 1916:	Promoted to *Major-General*
5 Jun 1917 - 1918:	Commander, 1st Rifle Division

Major-General of the Fleet Sergey Viktorovich **Rodionov** (23 Sep 1859 - ?)
3 Jun 1913:	Promoted to *Major-General of the Fleet*
3 Jun 1913 - 1917:	Senior Deputy Commander, Port of Vladivostok

Major-General Vasily Matveyevich **Rodionov** (31 Dec 1859 - 7 Jun 1934)
14 Nov 1914:	Promoted to *Major-General*

14 Nov 1914 - 31 Jan 1915:	Commander, 5th Don Cossack Regiment
31 Jan 1915 - 13 Nov 1915:	Commander, 2nd Brigade, 5th Cavalry Division
13 Nov 1915 - 28 Aug 1917:	Commander, 1st Brigade, 4th Don Cossack Division
28 Aug 1917 - 1918:	Commander, 4th Don Cossack Division

Lieutenant-General Viktor Alekseyevich **Rodionov** (29 Oct 1821 - 24 Oct 1906)
1 Jan 1866 - 15 Jan 1869:	Commander, Life Guards Ataman Regiment
30 Aug 1868:	Promoted to *Major-General*
30 Aug 1868 - 31 Aug 1875:	General à la suite
31 Aug 1875 - 7 May 1877:	Commander, 2nd Brigade, Independent Don Cossack Division
7 May 1877 - 21 Oct 1878:	Commander, 2nd Don Cossack Division
21 Oct 1878 - 24 Oct 1906:	General à la suite
30 Aug 1881:	Promoted to *Lieutenant-General*

Major-General Vladimir Pavlovich **Rodionov** (9 Sep 1861 - 16 Dec 1912)
20 Oct 1906 - 16 Dec 1912:	Director of the Pskov Cadet Corps
31 May 1907:	Promoted to *Major-General*

Major-General Vladimir Ivanovich **Rodzevich** (17 Apr 1836 - ?)
31 May 1888 - 1897:	Ataman, Temryuk Division, Kuban Cossack Army
6 May 1894:	Promoted to *Major-General*

Major-General Vyacheslav Mikhailovich **Rodzevich** (10 Apr 1866 - 2 Jun 1938)
10 Jul 1914 - 1917:	Commandant, Tiflis Arsenal
6 Dec 1914:	Promoted to *Major-General*

Lieutenant-General Nikolai Vladimirovich **Rodzyanko** (21 Sep 1852 - 1918)
12 Sep 1893 - 1 Feb 1898:	Chief of Mobilization, Main Cossack Directorate
6 Dec 1895:	Promoted to *Major-General*
1 Feb 1898 - 15 Feb 1898:	Section Chief, Main Cossack Directorate
15 Feb 1898 - 18 Jul 1901:	Deputy Chief, Main Cosack Directorate
25 Sep 1900 - 16 Oct 1900:	Acting Chief, Main Cosack Directorate
18 Jul 1901 - 11 Jul 1902:	Chief of Staff, Finland Military District
11 Jul 1902 - 16 May 1905:	At the disposal of the Minister of War
28 Mar 1904:	Promoted to *Lieutenant-General*
16 May 1905 - 1908:	Ataman, Ural Cossack Army

Major-General Pavel Vladimirovich **Rodzyanko** (27 May 1856 - 8 Aug 1930)
1904 - 1917:	Master of the Horse of the Imperial Court
1917:	Promoted to *Major-General*

General of Infantry Aleksandr Ivanovich **Rogovskoy** (2 Jul 1848 - 19 Apr 1917)
24 Apr 1885 - 19 Jul 1896:	Adjutant to Prince of Oldenburg
30 Aug 1893:	Promoted to *Major-General*
19 Jul 1896 - 15 Mar 1897:	Governor of Lomzhinsky
15 Mar 1897 - 9 Apr 1902:	Director, Imperial School of Law
6 Dec 1900:	Promoted to *Lieutenant-General*

9 Apr 1902 - 19 Apr 1905:	At the disposal of the Minister of War
19 Apr 1905:	Promoted to *General of Infantry*
19 Apr 1905:	Retired
14 Jan 1911 - 19 Apr 1917:	Recalled; Honorary Trustee, Board of Trustees, Empress Maria Institutions

Lieutenant-General Nikolai Mikhailovich **Rogovsky** (29 Jul 1840 - 12 Mar 1903)

20 Oct 1884 - 16 Sep 1894:	Commander, 1st Brigade, 5th Cavalry Division
30 Aug 1886:	Promoted to *Major-General*
16 Sep 1894 - 4 Jul 1902:	Commander, 7th Cavalry Division
14 May 1896:	Promoted to *Lieutenant-General*
4 Jul 1902 - 12 Mar 1903:	Commanding General, II. Army Corps

Major-General Nikolai Osipovich **Rogovsky** (9 May 1852 - ?)

26 Dec 1903 - 14 Feb 1909:	Commander, Izmail Borderguard Brigade
14 Feb 1909:	Promoted to *Major-General*
14 Feb 1909:	Retired

General of Artillery Nikolai Fedotovich **Rogovtsev** (26 Dec 1844 - ?)

9 Dec 1891 - 4 May 1912:	Member of the Artillery Committee, Main Artillery Directorate
30 Aug 1892:	Promoted to *Major-General*
1 Apr 1901:	Promoted to *Lieutenant-General*
4 May 1912:	Promoted to *General of Artillery*
4 May 1912:	Retired

Rear-Admiral Yevgeny Petrovich **Rogulya** (1854 - ?)

7 Nov 1905 - 25 Apr 1906:	Mayor of Sevastopol
?:	Promoted to *Rear-Admiral*

General of Infantry Ivan Andreyevich **Romanenko** (20 Sep 1854 - 20 Mar 1922)

13 Oct 1893 - 21 Feb 1898:	General for Special Assignments (4th Class), Ministry of War
14 May 1896:	Promoted to *Major-General*
21 Feb 1898 - 2 May 1902:	Section Chief, Main Department of Cossack Troops
2 May 1902 - 28 Apr 1903:	Attached to the St. Petersburg Military District
28 Apr 1903 - 19 Apr 1904:	Commander, 2nd Brigade, 22nd Infantry Division
19 Apr 1904.	Promoted to *Lieutenant-General*
19 Apr 1904 - 21 Jun 1906:	Commander, 24th Infantry Division
21 Jun 1906 - 9 Jan 1907:	Commander, 2nd Guards Infantry Division
9 Jan 1907 - 26 Jul 1914:	Commanding General, VIII. Army Corps
18 Apr 1910:	Promoted to *General of Infantry*
26 Jul 1914 - 1 Jan 1915:	At the disposal of the Commanding General, Odessa Military District
1 Jan 1915 - 12 Oct 1917:	Member of the Mililtary Council
12 Oct 1917:	Retired

Admiral Grand Duke Aleksandr Mikhailovich **Romanov** (1 Apr 1866 - 26 Feb 1933)
1 Jan 1903:	Promoted to *Rear-Admiral*
1 Jan 1903 - Oct 1905:	Junior Flagman, Black Sea Fleet
Nov 1902 - Oct 1905:	Director-General, General Directorate of Merchant Shipping and Ports
Oct 1905 - 1909:	Junior Flagman, Baltic Fleet
Oct 1905 - 1910:	Commander, Destroyer Detachment, Baltic Fleet
22 Jul 1909:	Promoted to *Vice-Admiral*
22 Jul 1909:	Promoted to *General-Adjutant*
1910 - Dec 1916:	C-in-C, Imperial Air Force
1915:	Promoted to *Admiral*
Dec 1916 - 22 Mar 1917:	Inspector-General of the Field Air Force
22 Mar 1917:	Retired

General-Admiral Grand Duke Aleksei Aleksandrovich **Romanov** (2 Jan 1850 - 1 Nov 1908)
9 Jun 1877:	Promoted to *Rear-Admiral*
1877 - 1878:	Commander, Danube Naval Command
19 Feb 1880:	Promoted to *General-Adjutant*
1 Jan 1881 - 1 Nov 1908:	Member of the State Council
13 Jul 1881 - 2 Jun 1905:	Commander-in-Chief of the Navy, Chairman of the Admiralty Board
26 Feb 1882:	Promoted to *Vice-Admiral*
15 May 1883:	Promoted to *General-Admiral*
1 Jan 1888:	Redesignated *Admiral*
2 Jun 1905:	Resigned

Major-General Grand Duke Andrei Vladimirovich **Romanov** (2 May 1879 - 30 Oct 1956)
5 Jul 1915 - 4 Mar 1917:	Commander, Life Guards Horse Artillery
15 Aug 1915:	Promoted to *Major-General*

Major-General Grand Duke Boris Vladimirovich **Romanov** (12 Nov 1877 - 8 Nov 1943)
20 Mar 1914 - 17 Sep 1915:	Commander, Ataman Tsarevich Life Guards Regiment
23 Nov 1914:	Promoted to *Major-General*
17 Sep 1915 - 7 Aug 1917:	Ataman of Cossack Troops attached to the Supreme Commander-in-Chief
7 Aug 1917:	Dismissed

General of Cavalry Grand Duke Dmitry Konstantinovich **Romanov** (1 Jun 1860 - 29 Jan 1919)
14 May 1896:	Promoted to *Major-General*
14 May 1896 - 28 Dec 1903:	Commander, Life Guards Horse-Grenadier Regiment
16 Aug 1896 - 30 Aug 1896:	Acting Commander, 2nd Guards Cavalry Division
28 Dec 1903 - 23 Mar 1905:	Commander, 1st Brigade, 2nd Guards Cavalry Division
6 Dec 1904:	Promoted to *Lieutenant-General*
6 Dec 1904:	Promoted to *General-Adjutant*
23 Mar 1905 - 25 Apr 1917:	Member of the Tsar's retinue
6 Dec 1914:	Promoted to *General of Cavalry*
25 Apr 1917:	Retired

Lieutenant-General Grand Duke Georgy Mikhailovich **Romanov** (11 Aug 1863 - 29 Jan 1919)

13 Apr 1895 - 6 Sep 1915:	Director of the Russian Museum
6 May 1903:	Promoted to *Major-General*
22 Jul 1909:	Promoted to *Lieutenant-General*
22 Jul 1909:	Promoted to *General-Adjutant*
6 Sep 1915 - Mar 1917:	Attached to the Supreme Commander-in-Chief

Rear-Admiral Grand Duke Kirill Vladimirovich **Romanov** (30 Sep 1876 - 12 Oct 1938)

23 Feb 1915:	Promoted to *Rear-Admiral*
16 Mar 1915 - Feb 1917:	Commander, Guards Naval Depot

General of Infantry Grand Duke Konstantin Konstantinovich **Romanov** (10 Aug 1858 - 2 Jun 1915)

6 Dec 1894:	Promoted to *Major-General*
6 Dec 1894 - 4 Mar 1900:	Commander, Life Guards Preobrazhensky Regiment
4 Mar 1900 - 13 Feb 1910:	Chief of Military Schools, Chief of the Main Directorate for Military Schools
6 Dec 1900:	Promoted to *Lieutenant-General*
1 Jan 1901:	Promoted to *General-Adjutant*
6 Dec 1907:	Promoted to *General of Infantry*
13 Feb 1910 - 2 Jun 1915:	Inspector-General of Military Schools

Lieutenant-General Grand Duke Mikhail Alexandrovich **Romanov** (22 Nov 1878 - 13 Jun 1918)

23 Aug 1914:	Promoted to *Major-General*
23 Aug 1914 - 4 Feb 1916:	Commander, Caucasus Native Cavalry Division
4 Feb 1916 - 19 Jan 1917:	Commanding General, II. Cavalry Corps
2 Jul 1916:	Promoted to *Lieutenant-General*
1 Sep 1916:	Promoted to *General-Adjutant*
19 Jan 1917 - 31 Mar 1917:	Inspector-General of Cavalry
31 Mar 1917:	Dismissed

General-Field Marshal Grand Duke Mikhail Nikolayevich **Romanov** (13 Oct 1832 - 18 Dec 1909)

26 Nov 1852:	Promoted to *Major-General*
26 Nov 1852 - 26 Aug 1856:	Commander, Guards Horse Artillery
20 Apr 1853 - 27 Aug 1856:	Commander of Artillery, Guards Infantry Corps, Commander of Artillery, Guards Reserve Cavalry Corps
25 Jan 1856:	Promoted to *General-Adjutant*
25 Jan 1856 - 1 Jan 1863:	Master-General of Ordnance
27 Aug 1856:	Promoted to *Lieutenant-General*
27 Aug 1856 - 16 Aug 1857:	Commander, 2nd Guards Light Cavalry Division
16 Aug 1857 - 9 Feb 1860:	Commander of Artillery, Separate Guards Corps
9 Feb 1860 - 1 Jan 1863:	Chief of Military Schools
30 Aug 1860:	Promoted to *General of Artillery*
6 Dec 1862 - 27 Jul 1881:	Viceroy of the Caucasus, C-in-C, Caucasus Army

1865 - 14 Jul 1881:	Commanding General, Caucasus Military District
16 Apr 1878:	Promoted to *General-Field Marshal*
11 Jun 1881 - 18 Dec 1909:	Master-General of Ordnance
14 Jul 1881 - 24 Aug 1905:	Chairman of the State Council
12 Feb 1892 - 18 Dec 1909:	Chairman, Committee of Wounded Veterans
26 Apr 1894 - ?:	Chairman, Commission for Coastal Defense
24 Aug 1905 - 5 Dec 1909:	Honorary Chairman of the State Council

General of Infantry Mikhail Yakovlevich **Romanov** (15 Oct 1848 - 15 Sep 1915)

14 Aug 1898:	Promoted to *Major-General*
14 Aug 1898 - 7 May 1901:	Deputy Chief of Staff, Amur Military District
7 May 1901 - 17 Feb 1902:	Commander, 3rd Siberian Infantry Brigade
17 Feb 1902 - 1 Jan 1903:	Chief of Staff, Siberian Military District
1 Jan 1903 - 3 Aug 1906:	Military Governor of Akmola Region
6 Dec 1905:	Promoted to *Lieutenant-General*
3 Aug 1906 - 20 Jan 1911:	Governor of Syr Darya Region
20 Jan 1911:	Promoted to *General of Infantry*
20 Jan 1911:	Retired

Colonel/Captain 1st Class (British *Admiral of the Fleet*, *Field Marshal*) Nikolai II (Nikolai Alexandrovich **Romanov)**, Emperor and Autocrat of All the Russias (18 May 1868 - 17 Jul 1918)

6 Aug 1892:	Promoted to *Colonel*
2 Jan 1893 - 20 Oct 1894:	Commander, 1st Battalion, Life Guards Preobrazhensky Regiment
20 Oct 1894 - 15 Mar 1917:	Emperor of Russia
28 May 1908:	Promoted to *Honorary Admiral of the Fleet* (British Royal Navy)
23 Aug 1915 - 2 Mar 1917:	Supreme Commander-in-Chief
18 Dec 1915:	Promoted to *Honorary Field Marshal* (British Army)

General of Infantry Grand Duke Nikolai Mikhailovich **Romanov** (14 Apr 1859 - 29 Jan 1919)

5 Feb 1894 - 15 Sep 1897:	Commander, 16th Grenadier Regiment
14 May 1896:	Promoted to *Major-General*
15 Sep 1897 - 30 Dec 1903:	Commander, Caucasus Grenadier Division
6 Aug 1901:	Promoted to *Lieutenant-General*
6 May 1903:	Promoted to *General-Adjutant*
30 Dec 1903 - 28 Jul 1914:	Unassigned
14 Apr 1913:	Promoted to *General of Infantry*
28 Jul 1914 - 16 Mar 1917:	At the disposal of the C-in-C, Southwestern Front
16 Mar 1917:	Retired

General of Cavalry Grand Duke Nikolai Nikolayevich **Romanov** (6 Nov 1856 - 5 Jan 1929)

30 Aug 1885:	Promoted to *Major-General*
10 Nov 1890 - 11 Dec 1890:	Commander, 2nd Brigade, 2nd Guards Cavalry Division
11 Dec 1890 - 6 May 1895:	Commander, 2nd Guards Cavalry Division
26 Feb 1893:	Promoted to *Lieutenant-General*

1894:	Promoted to *General-Adjutant*
6 May 1895 - 8 Jun 1905:	Inspector-General of Cavalry
6 Dec 1900:	Promoted to *General of Cavalry*
8 Jun 1905 - 26 Jul 1908:	Chairman, Council of National Defense
26 Oct 1905 - 20 Jul 1914:	Commanding General, St. Petersburg Military District
20 Jul 1914 - 23 Aug 1915:	Supreme Commander-in-Chief
23 Aug 1914 - 2 Mar 1917:	C-in-C, Caucasus Front
2 Mar 1917 - 11 Mar 1917:	Supreme Commander-in-Chief

General of Cavalry Grand Duke Pavel Aleksandrovich **Romanov** (21 Sep 1860 - 29 Jan 1919)

20 Nov 1890 - 11 Aug 1896:	Commander, Life Guards Cavalry Regiment
30 Aug 1893:	Promoted to *Major-General*
11 Aug 1896 - 25 Dec 1898:	Commander, 1st Guards Cavalry Division
6 May 1897:	Promoted to *General-Adjutant*
25 Dec 1898:	Promoted to *Lieutenant-General*
25 Dec 1898 - 14 Oct 1902:	Commanding General, Guards Corps
14 Oct 1902:	Dismissed from service, stripped of rank
4 Feb 1905:	Recalled; Promoted to *General-Adjutant*
4 Feb 1905 - 27 May 1916:	Unassigned
14 Apr 1913:	Promoted to *General of Cavalry*
27 May 1916 - 13 Sep 1916:	Commanding General, I. Guards Corps
13 Sep 1916 - 31 Mar 1917:	Inspector-General of Guards
31 Mar 1917:	Retired

Lieutenant-General Grand Duke Pyotr Nikolayevich **Romanov** (10 Jan 1864 - 17 Jun 1931)

23 Jun 1897 - 11 Sep 1904:	Member of the Board, Main Department of State Breeding
6 May 1903:	Promoted to *Major-General*
11 Sep 1904 - 6 Feb 1909:	Inspector-General of Engineers
13 Apr 1908:	Promoted to *Lieutenant-General*
13 Apr 1908:	Promoted to *General-Adjutant*
6 Feb 1909 - 16 Mar 1917:	Reserve officer, Guards Cavalry

Lieutenant-General Grand Duke Sergey Aleksandrovich **Romanov** (29 Apr 1857 - 4 Feb 1905)

26 Feb 1887:	Promoted to *Major-General*
26 Feb 1887 - 26 Feb 1891:	Commander, Life Guards Preobrazhensky Regiment
26 Feb 1891:	Promoted to *General-Adjutant*
26 Feb 1891 - 1 Jan 1905:	Governor-General of Moscow
12 Jun 1894 - 4 Feb 1905:	Member of the State Council
14 May 1896:	Promoted to *Lieutenant-General*
26 May 1896 - 4 Feb 1905:	Commanding General, Moscow Military District

General of Artillery Grand Duke Sergey Mikhailovich **Romanov** (25 Sep 1869 - 18 Jul 1918)

10 Mar 1904:	Promoted to *Major-General*
10 Mar 1904 - 16 Jun 1904:	At the disposal of the Master-General of Ordnance

16 Jun 1904 - 7 Sep 1904:	Commander, Guards Horse-Artillery Brigade
7 Sep 1904 - 2 Jul 1905:	Inspector of Artillery
2 Jul 1905 - 5 Jan 1916:	Inspector-General of Artillery
13 Apr 1908:	Promoted to *General-Adjutant*
13 Apr 1908:	Promoted to *Lieutenant-General*
6 Apr 1914:	Promoted to *General of Artillery*
5 Jan 1916 - 22 Mar 1917:	Field Inspector-General of Artillery, Supreme High Command
22 Mar 1917:	Retired

General of Infantry Grand Duke Vladimir Aleksandrovich **Romanov** (10 Apr 1847 - 4 Feb 1909)

30 Aug 1868:	Promoted to *Major-General*
1 Jun 1869 - 13 Jul 1869:	Commander, Life Guards Regiment
10 Apr 1872:	Promoted to *General-Adjutant*
16 Apr 1872 - 26 Apr 1906:	Member of the State Council
17 Apr 1872 - 30 Aug 1874:	Commander, Guards Rifle Brigade
16 Aug 1874:	Promoted to *Lieutenant-General*
30 Aug 1874 - 25 Jun 1877:	Commander, 1st Guards Infantry Division
25 Jun 1877 - 30 Jan 1878:	Commanding General, XII. Army Corps
30 Jan 1878 - 17 Aug 1880:	Commander, 1st Guards Infantry Division
17 Aug 1880 - 2 Mar 1881:	Commanding General, Guards Corps
30 Nov 1880:	Promoted to *General of Infantry*
2 Mar 1881 - 26 Oct 1905:	Commanding General, St. Petersburg Military District
27 Oct 1905:	Retired

Lieutenant-General Vladimir Aleksandrovich **Romanov** (27 Dec 1856 - 19 Nov 1919)

26 Jul 1894 - 10 Jul 1904:	Commandant of the Electro-Technical School
26 Nov 1899:	Promoted to *Major-General*
16 Apr 1904 - 21 Sep 1904:	Commander, 6th East Siberian Rifle Division
22 Jul 1906 - 2 May 1907:	Commander, 11th Infantry Division
2 May 1907:	Promoted to *Lieutenant-General*
2 May 1907:	Retired

Major-General Vladimir Romanovich **Romanov** (2 Jul 1868 - ?)

24 Nov 1908 - 1915:	Commander, 172nd Infantry Regiment
24 May 1915:	Promoted to *Major-General*
1915 - 7 Dec 1915:	Commander, Brigade, 8th Siberian Rifle Division
7 Dec 1915 - 17 Jan 1917:	Chief of Staff, XLIV. Army Corps
17 Jan 1917 - 5 May 1917:	Chief of Staff, V. Army Corps
5 May 1917 - 4 Sep 1917:	Commander, 7th Infantry Division

Major-General Boris Stepanovich **Romanovsky** (15 Jun 1870 - 30 Oct 1941)

23 Mar 1909 - Oct 1917:	Military Governor of Batum Region
1 Jul 1913:	Promoted to *Major-General*

Lieutenant-General Georgy Dmitriyevich **Romanovsky** (13 Nov 1877 - 1939)

3 Sep 1914 - 24 Oct 1915:	Commander, 20th Infantry Regiment

3 Apr 1915:	Promoted to *Major-General*
24 Oct 1915 - 12 Jul 1916:	Quartermaster-General, 7th Army
12 Jul 1916 - 23 Oct 1916:	Chief of Staff, XIII. Army Corps
23 Oct 1916 - 9 May 1917:	Chief of Staff, 11th Army
9 May 1917 - 22 Sep 1917:	Acting Chief of the General Staff
24 Aug 1917:	Promoted to *Lieutenant-General*
22 Sep 1917 - 29 Nov 1917:	Reserve officer, Petrograd Military District
29 Nov 1917 - 17 Aug 1918:	At the disposal of the Chief of the General Staff
17 Aug 1918:	Retired

Lieutenant-General Prince Georgy Maksimilianovich **Romanovsky**, Duke of Leuchtenberg (17 Feb 1852 - 20 Apr 1912)

17 Feb 1872 - 1904:	Attached to the Guards Corps
9 Apr 1900:	Promoted to *Major-General*
1904 - 20 Apr 1912:	General à la suite
18 Apr 1910:	Promoted to *Lieutenant-General*
1910:	Promoted to *General-Adjutant*

Major-General Ivan Pavlovich **Romanovsky** (16 Apr 1877 - 5 Apr 1920)

6 Aug 1915 - 14 Oct 1916:	Commander, 206th Infantry Regiment
14 Oct 1916 - 9 Apr 1917:	Quartermaster-General, 10th Army
5 Nov 1916:	Promoted to *Major-General*
9 Apr 1917 - 10 Jun 1917:	Chief of Staff, 8th Army
10 Jun 1917 - 10 Sep 1917:	First Quartermaster-General to the Supreme Commander-in-Chief
18 Jul 1917 - 26 Sep 1917:	Chief of the General Directorate of the General Staff
26 Sep 1917:	Dismissed

Lieutenant-General Nikolai Aleksandrovich **Romanovsky** (1 Sep 1860 - 3 Jun 1928)

3 Jun 1911:	Promoted to *Major-General*
3 Jun 1911 - 7 May 1915:	Commander, 40th Artillery Brigade
7 May 1915 - 12 May 1916:	Inspector of Artillery, XXXVI. Army Corps
15 Aug 1915:	Promoted to *Lieutenant-General*
12 May 1916 - 1918:	Inspector of Artillery, IX. Army Corps

General of Infantry Prince Yevgeny Maksimilianovich **Romanovsky**, Duke of Leuchtenberg (27 Jan 1847 - 18 Aug 1901)

3 Jul 1877:	Promoted to *Major-General*
3 Jul 1877 - 15 Dec 1877:	At the disposal of the C-in-C, Danube Army
15 Dec 1877 - 18 Apr 1880:	Commander, 2nd Brigade, 2nd Guards Cavalry Division
18 Apr 1880 - 14 Jun 1883:	Commander, 1st Brigade, Guards Cavalry Division
14 Jun 1883 - 1884:	At the disposal of the Inspector-General of Cavalry
1884 - 20 Jan 1888:	Attached to 37th Infantry Division
30 Aug 1886:	Promoted to *Lieutenant-General*
20 Jan 1888 - 21 Dec 1893:	Commander, 37th Infantry Division
21 Dec 1893 - 18 Aug 1901:	At the disposal of the Commanding General, St. Petersburg Military District
8 Jun 1897:	Promoted to *General-Adjutant*

29 May 1898: Promoted to *General of Infantry*

Lieutenant-General Andrey Vasilyevich **Romashev** (6 Oct 1854 - ?)
12 Nov 1907: Promoted to *Major-General*
12 Nov 1907 - 23 Jun 1914: Commander, 1st Brigade, 18th Infantry Division
23 Jun 1914: Promoted to *Lieutenant-General*
23 Jun 1914: Retired
27 Jul 1914 - 25 Jan 1915: Recalled; Commander, Brigade, 75th Infantry Division
25 Jan 1915 - 18 Apr 1915: Reserve officer, Kiev Military District
18 Apr 1915 - 1917: Commander, 3rd Siberian Replacement Rifle Brigade

Major-General Dmitry Iosifovich **Romeyko-Gurko** (23 Sep 1872 - 19 Aug 1945)
30 Aug 1914 - 28 May 1915: Commander, 18th Hussar Regiment
25 May 1915: Promoted to *Major-General*
28 May 1915 - 6 Aug 1915: Unassigned
6 Aug 1915 - 7 Apr 1917: Chief of Staff, XIV. Army Corps
7 Apr 1917 - 27 Aug 1917: Commander, 16th Cavalry Division
27 Aug 1917 - 1918: Reserve officer, Moscow Military District

General-Field Marshal Count Iosif Vladimirovich **Romeyko-Gurko** (28 Jul 1828 - 28 Jan 1901)
23 Apr 1866 - 16 Apr 1869: Commander, 4th Hussar Regiment
30 Aug 1867: Promoted to *Major-General*
16 Apr 1869 - 27 Jul 1875: Commander, Life Guards Horse-Grenadier Regiment
8 Jan 1874 - 27 Jul 1875: Commander, 1st Brigade, 2nd Guards Cavalry Division
27 Jul 1875 - 24 Jun 1877: Commander, 2nd Guards Cavalry Division
30 Aug 1876: Promoted to *Lieutenant-General*
24 Jun 1877 - 1878: Commanding General, Advance Detachment, Army of the Danube
3 Jul 1877: Promoted to *General-Adjutant*
19 Dec 1877: Promoted to *General of Cavalry*
1878 - 7 Apr 1879: Unassigned
7 Apr 1879 - 14 Feb 1880: Acting Governor-General of St. Petersburg, Deputy Commanding General, St. Petersburg Military District
9 Jan 1882 - 7 Jun 1883: Acting Governor-General of Odessa, Commanding General, Odessa Military District
7 Jun 1883 - 6 Dec 1894: Governor-General of Warsaw, Commanding General, Warsaw Military District
1886 - 28 Jan 1901: Member of the State Council
6 Dec 1894: Promoted to *General-Field Marshal*

General of Cavalry Vasily Iosifovich **Romeyko-Gurko** (8 May 1864 - 11 Feb 1937)
12 Feb 1904 - 25 Mar 1905: Staff Officer, Manchurian Army
26 Mar 1904 - 25 Mar 1905: Chief of Staff, I. Siberian Army Corps
30 Sep 1904: Promoted to *Major-General*
25 Mar 1905 - 20 Apr 1906: Commander, 2nd Brigade, Ural-Transbaikal Cossack Division

20 Apr 1906 - 30 Oct 1906:	Commander, 2nd Brigade, 4th Cavalry Division
10 May 1906 - 12 Mar 1911:	Chairman, Military Commission on the History of the Russo-Japanese War
6 Dec 1910:	Promoted to *Lieutenant-General*
12 Mar 1911 - 9 Nov 1914:	Commander, 1st Cavalry Division
9 Nov 1914 - 6 Feb 1916:	Commanding General, VI. Army Corps
6 Feb 1916 - 14 Aug 1916:	C-in-C, 5th Army
10 Apr 1916:	Promoted to *General of Cavalry*
14 Aug 1916 - 31 Mar 1917:	C-in-C, Special Army, Western Front
10 Nov 1916 - 17 Feb 1917:	Acting Chief of Staff to the Supreme Commander-in-Chief
31 Mar 1917 - 22 May 1917:	C-in-C, Western Front
22 May 1917 - 14 Oct 1917:	Unassigned
14 Oct 1917:	Dismissed

Lieutenant-General Modest Vladislavovich **Romishevsky** (17 Jul 1861 - 7 Oct 1930)

22 Apr 1907 - 25 Jul 1910:	Commander, 26th Artillery Brigade
31 May 1907:	Promoted to *Major-General*
25 Jul 1910 - 26 Oct 1910:	Inspector of Artillery, III. Caucasus Army Corps
26 Oct 1910 - 23 Sep 1915:	Inspector of Artillery, VII. Army Corps
31 May 1913:	Promoted to *Lieutenant-General*
23 Sep 1915 - 15 Sep 1916:	Inspector of Artillery, XXI. Army Corps
15 Sep 1916 - 1917:	Inspector of Artillery, IV. Army Corps

General of Infantry Vladislav Feliksovich **Romishevsky** (27 Jun 1818 - Sep 1905)

16 Oct 1863:	Promoted to *Major-General*
16 Oct 1863 - 12 Sep 1870:	Deputy Chief of Staff, 6th Infantry Division
12 Sep 1870 - 14 Jul 1872:	Commander, 2nd Rifle Brigade
28 Mar 1871:	Promoted to *Lieutenant-General*
14 Jul 1872 - 4 Nov 1883:	Commander, 4th Infantry Division
4 Nov 1883 - Sep 1905:	Member, Committee for Wounded Veterans
30 Aug 1886:	Promoted to *General of Infantry*

Lieutenant-General of the Naval Legal Corps Ivan Aleksandrovich **Ronzhin** (26 Nov 1867 - 28 Aug 1927)

28 Aug 1906 - 28 Nov 1911:	Procurator, Sevastopol Naval Court
13 Apr 1908:	Promoted to *Major-General of the Naval Legal Corps*
28 Nov 1911 - 24 Dec 1914:	Chairman of Sevastopol Naval Court
6 Dec 1912:	Promoted to *Lieutenant-General of the Naval Legal Corps*
24 Dec 1914 - 17 May 1917:	Member, Supreme Naval Tribunal
17 May 1917:	Dismissed

Lieutenant-General Sergey Aleksandrovich **Ronzhin** (14 Aug 1869 - 1929)

23 Apr 1911 - 9 Oct 1913:	Section Chief, General Staff
6 Dec 1912:	Promoted to *Major-General*
9 Oct 1913 - 22 May 1914:	Deputy Chief of Military Communications, General Staff

22 May 1914 - 19 Jul 1914:	Chief of Military Communications, General Staff
19 Jul 1914 - 16 Jan 1917:	Chief of Military Communications, Supreme Commander-in-Chief
6 Dec 1916:	Promoted to *Lieutenant-General*
16 Jan 1917 - 20 May 1917:	At the disposal of the Minister of War
20 May 1917 - Oct 1917:	Reserve officer, Odessa Military District

General of Infantry Khristofor Khristoforovich **Roop** (1 May 1831 - 1917)

30 Jun 1862 - 10 Aug 1864:	Quartermaster-General, Separate Guards Corps
17 Apr 1863:	Promoted to *Major-General*
10 Aug 1864 - 12 May 1865:	Chief of Staff, Kharkov Military District
12 May 1865 - 19 Mar 1866:	General for Special Assignments, Moscow Military District
19 Mar 1866 - 20 Aug 1875:	Chief of Staff, Moscow Military District
28 Mar 1871:	Promoted to *Lieutenant-General*
20 Aug 1875 - 16 Apr 1878:	Commander, 1st Grenadier Division
16 Apr 1878 - 21 Oct 1883:	Commanding General, VI. Army Corps
21 Oct 1883 - 8 Aug 1889:	Governor-General of Odessa
21 Oct 1883 - 12 Oct 1890:	Commanding General, Odessa Military District
30 Aug 1885:	Promoted to *General of Infantry*
12 Oct 1890 - 25 Oct 1917:	Member of the State Council
25 Oct 1917:	Retired

Lieutenant-General Vladimir Khristoforovich **Roop** (4 Jul 1865 - 30 Dec 1929)

13 Mat 1905 - 24 Feb 1907:	Commander, 26th Dragoon Regiment
24 Feb 1907 - 3 Mar 1912:	Commander, Life Guards Horse-Grenadier Regiment
31 May 1907:	Promoted to *Major-General*
3 Mar 1912 - 15 Nov 1913:	Commander, Independent Guards Cavalry Brigade
15 Nov 1913:	Promoted to *Lieutenant-General*
15 Nov 1913 - 8 Feb 1917:	Commander, 6th Cavalry Division
8 Feb 1917 - 2 Apr 1917:	Commanding General, II. Cavalry Corps
2 Apr 1917 - Apr 1917:	Reserve officer, Kiev Military District
Apr 1917 - Oct 1917:	Head of special mission to the USA

General of Cavalry Baron Nikolai Vasilyevich von der **Ropp** (12 Mar 1848 - 11 Sep 1916)

31 May 1899:	Promoted to *Major-General*
31 May 1899 - 26 Mar 1901:	Commander, 1st Brigade, 6th Cavalry Division
26 Mar 1901 - 8 Feb 1903:	Commander, 2nd Brigade, 13th Cavalry Division
8 Feb 1903 - 23 May 1907:	Commander, Separate Guard Cavalry Brigade
23 May 1907:	Promoted to *Lieutenant-General*
23 May 1907 - 1 May 1910:	Commander, 13th Cavalry Division
1 May 1910:	Promoted to *General of Cavalry*
1 May 1910:	Retired

Major-General Baron Rafail-Gavriil-Vilgelm Vilgelmovich von der **Ropp** (2 Jul 1849 - 20 Jan 1904)

11 Jun 1901:	Promoted to *Major-General*
11 Jun 1901 - 23 Mar 1902:	Special Assignments General, Turkestan Military

	District
23 Mar 1902 - 20 Jan 1904:	Commander, Amu-Darya District

Lieutenant-General Baron Yevgeny-Yuly-Nikolay Eduardovich von der **Ropp** (4 Aug 1867 - 3 Jan 1917)

24 Jan 1907 - 22 Nov 1911:	Commander, Amur Railway Brigade
6 Dec 1907:	Promoted to *Major-General*
22 Nov 1911 - 1 Dec 1913:	Chief of Trans-Caucasus Railway
1 Dec 1913 - 29 Sep 1915:	Chief of Main Military-Technical Directorate
21 Dec 1913:	Promoted to *Lieutenant-General*
29 Sep 1915 - 3 Jan 1917:	At the disposal of the C-in-C, Northern Front

Major-General of the Fleet Ilya Yakovlevich **Rorog** (17 Jul 1863 - ?)

25 Mar 1907 - ?:	Chief Engineer, Cruiser "Pamyat Merkuriya"
?:	Promoted to *Major-General of the Fleet*

Major-General Feliks Vikentyevich **Roshkovsky** (11 Nov 1834 - ?)

7 May 1893:	Promoted to *Major-General*
7 May 1893 - 31 Oct 1899:	Commander, 14th Artillery Brigade
31 Oct 1899:	Retired

Major-General Ivan Karlovich **Roshkovsky** (25 Nov 1855 - ?)

27 Jul 1902 - 1904:	Military Judge, Turkestan Military District Court
6 Dec 1902:	Promoted to *Major-General*

Major-General Mechislav-Konstantin Erazmovich **Roshkovsky** (11 Feb 1854 - ?)

2 Aug 1905 - 7 Dec 1908:	Commander, 13th Infantry Regiment
7 Dec 1908:	Promoted to *Major-General*
7 Dec 1908:	Retired

Major-General Mikhail Sergeyevich **Roslyakov** (14 Feb 1871 - 28 Oct 1929)

22 Nov 1911 - 12 May 1916:	Commander, 9th Mortar Artillery Battalion
22 Nov 1915:	Promoted to *Major-General*
12 May 1916 - 1918:	Commander, 5th Artillery Brigade

Major-General Yuly Nikolayevich **Rossevich** (23 Sep 1859 - ?)

6 Dec 1914:	Promoted to *Major-General*
6 Dec 1914 - 1916:	Deputy Chief of Okhtenskaya Explosives Factory
1916 - 1917:	Deputy Chief of Section 2, Technical Artillery Establishments, Main Artillery Directorate

Lieutenant-General Vladimir Andreyevich **Rossovsky** (29 Jun 1854 - 2 Apr 1907)

15 Oct 1891 - 1905:	Military Judge, Warsaw Military District Court
1 Jan 1901:	Promoted to *Major-General*
1905:	Promoted to *Lieutenant-General*
1905:	Retired

Major-General Aleksandr Alekseyevich **Rossysky** (6 Apr 1834 - Dec 1897)
19 Oct 1892:   Promoted to *Major-General*
19 Oct 1892 - Dec 1897:   Commander, 2nd Brigade, 6th Infantry Division

Major-General Aleksey Aleksandrovich **Rossysky** (9 Nov 1866 - 6 Oct 1914)
30 Jan 1913 - 6 Oct 1914:   Director, Vladikavkaz Cadet Corps
14 Apr 1913:   Promoted to *Major-General*

Major-General Mikhail Aleksandrovich **Rossysky** (7 Nov 1862 - 2 Mar 1910)
10 Dec 1904 - 1910:   Commander, 118th Infantry Regiment
1910:   Promoted to *Major-General*
1910 - 2 Mar 1910:   Chief of Staff, XIV. Army Corps

Major-General Yevgeny Aleksandrovich **Rossysky** (24 Jan 1865 - 11 Apr 1933)
18 Mar 1913:   Promoted to *Major-General*
18 Mar 1913 - 26 Apr 1916:   Commander, 2nd Brigade, 28th Infantry Division
26 Apr 1916 - 22 Jan 1917:   Commander, 56th Infantry Division
22 Jan 1917 - 31 Jul 1917:   Reserve officer, Kiev Military District
31 Jul 1917 - 28 Aug 1917:   Commander, 194th Infantry Division
28 Aug 1917 - 21 Sep 1917:   Reserve officer, Kiev Military District
21 Sep 1917 - 1918:   Commander, Brigade, 3rd Grenadier Division

General of Infantry Feliks Yakovlevich **Rostkovsky** (19 May 1841 - 1920)
9 Oct 1883 - 11 Jan 1890:   Ministry of War Representative, Odessa Military
                                      District Council
30 Aug 1886:   Promoted to *Major-General*
11 Jan 1890 - 11 Apr 1902:   Intendant-General, Moscow Military District
14 May 1896:   Promoted to *Lieutenant-General*
11 Apr 1902 - 20 Mar 1903:   Deputy Intendant-General, Ministry of War
20 Mar 1903 - 6 Jun 1908:   Intendant-General, Ministry of War,
                                      Chief of the Main Intendant Directorate
6 Dec 1906:   Promoted to *General of Infantry*
6 Jun 1908 - 1 Jan 1915:   Member of the Military Council
1 Jan 1915:   Retired

Major-General Aleksandr Vladimirovich **Rostovshchikov** (24 Aug 1863 - ?)
31 Dec 1913 - 12 Jul 1915:   Deputy Chief, St. Petersburg Ammunition Factory
6 Apr 1914:   Promoted to *Major-General*
12 Jul 1915 - 29 Apr 1917:   Chief, Petrograd Ammunition Factory
29 Apr 1917 - 1918:   Reserve officer, Petrograd Military District

Major-General Aleksandr Aleksandrovich **Rostovtsev** (11 Oct 1861 - Nov 1916)
11 May 1907 - Nov 1916:   Chief of the Court, Grand Duke Nikolai Nikolayevich
6 Dec 1910:   Promoted to *Major-General*

Major-General Dmitry Ivanovich **Rostovtsev** (31 Aug 1867 - 1937)
1915 - 17 Dec 1916:   Chief of Bureau, Palace Commandant
6 Dec 1916:   Promoted to *Major-General*

17 Dec 1916 - 1917: Special Assignments General, Palace Commandant

Major-General Konstantin Nikolayevich **Rostovtsov** (16 May 1854 - ?)
23 Oct 1904 - 17 May 1905: Commander, 67th Artillery Brigade
17 May 1905 - 2 Sep 1907: Commander, 8th Artillery Brigade
26 Nov 1906: Promoted to *Major-General*

Lieutenant-General Count Nikolai Yakovlevich **Rostovtsov** (28 Jan 1831 - 23 Jul 1897)
11 Jan 1881 - 4 Jan 1883: Unassigned
30 Aug 1882: Promoted to *Major-General*
4 Jan 1883 - 19 Mar 1890: Chief of Staff, VIII. Army Corps
19 Mar 1890 - 29 Jan 1891: Commander, 4th Rifle Brigade
29 Jan 1891 - 23 Jul 1897: Military Governor of Samarkand, Military Commander, Samarkand Province
30 Aug 1892: Promoted to *Lieutenant-General*

Major-General Karl-Fridrikh-Vilgelm-Iogann Velyaminovich **Rostsius** (18 Feb 1833 - ?)
18 Feb 1893: Promoted to *Major-General*
18 Feb 1893 - 9 Oct 1899: Commander, 1st Brigade, 20th Infantry Division

Lieutenant-General Georgy Petrovich **Rozalion-Soshalsky** (21 Apr 1861 - 29 Jul 1945)
2 Apr 1910 - 10 Jan 1913: Commander, 11th Uhlan Regiment
22 Jul 1912: Promoted to *Major-General*
10 Jan 1913 - 3 Nov 1915: Commander, 2nd Brigade, 11th Cavalry Division
3 Nov 1915 - 29 Apr 1917: Commander, Amur Cavalry Division
28 Aug 1916: Promoted to *Lieutenant-General*
29 Apr 1917 - 1918: Reserve officer, Kiev Military District

Lieutenant-General Sergey Nikolayevich **Rozanov** (24 Sep 1869 - 28 Aug 1937)
30 Sep 1914 - 19 Jan 1915: Commander, 2nd Brigade, 45th Infantry Division
23 Dec 1914: Promoted to *Major-General*
19 Jan 1915 - 18 Feb 1917: Chief of Staff, III. Caucasus Army Corps
18 Feb 1917 - 25 Aug 1917: Commander, 162nd Infantry Division
25 Aug 1917: Promoted to *Lieutenant-General*
25 Aug 1917 - 2 Sep 1917: Commanding General, XLI. Army Corps

Major-General Aleksandr Nikolayevich **Rozemond** (18 Aug 1856 - ?)
6 Oct 1910 - 22 Apr 1917: Deputy Chief of St. Petersburg Weapons Factory
6 Dec 1916: Promoted to *Major-General*
22 Apr 1917 - 1917: Reserve officer, PetrogradMilitary District

General of Infantry Baron Aleksandr-Stepan Fridrikhovich **Rozen** (11 Nov 1835 - 1921)
18 Feb 1889: Promoted to *Major-General*
18 Feb 1889 - 25 Feb 1891: Commander, 1st Brigade, 27th Infantry Division
25 Feb 1891 - 18 Jan 1893: Deputy Chief of Staff, Odessa Military District
18 Jan 1893 - 25 Sep 1899: Chief of Staff, Grenadier Corps
25 Sep 1899: Promoted to *Lieutenant-General*
25 Sep 1899 - 1906: Special Assignments General, Moscow Military District

1906:   Promoted to *General of Infantry*
1906:   Retired

Lieutenant-General Baron Grigory Aleksandrovich **Rozen** (5 Mar 1848 - 1920)
1 Apr 1892 - 23 Mar 1907:   Military Attaché, Switzerland
19 May 1896:   Promoted to *Major-General*
23 Mar 1907:   Promoted to *Lieutenant-General*
23 Mar 1907:   Retired

Major-General Baron Konstantin Oskarovich **Rozen** (5 Feb 1851 - ?)
11 Jul 1900:   Promoted to *Major-General*
11 Jul 1900 - 3 Jun 1903:   Commander, Life Guards Jaeger Regiment

Major-General Baron Nikolai Andreyevich **Rozen** (21 Jun 1856 - 1912)
17 Apr 1905:   Promoted to *Major-General*
17 Apr 1905 - 10 Oct 1907:   Special Assignments General to the Governor-General of St. Petersburg
10 Oct 1907 - 1912:   Attached to the Ministry of Internal Affairs

Lieutenant-General Baron Stepan Fyodorovich von **Rozen** (27 Feb 1838 - 1918)
15 Aug 1888 - 21 Jun 1894:   Commander, 5th Grenadier Regiment
21 Jun 1894:   Promoted to *Major-General*
21 Jun 1894 - 14 Oct 1894:   Commander, 1st Brigade, 4th Infantry Division
14 Oct 1894 - 25 Apr 1901:   Commander, 2nd Brigade, 1st Grenadier Division
25 Apr 1901:   Promoted to *Lieutenant-General*
25 Apr 1901:   Retired

General of Infantry Nikolai Ottonovich von **Rozenbakh** (12 Jun 1836 - 5 May 1901)
17 Sep 1870 - 19 Mar 1877:   Commander, Life Guards Pavlovsky Regiment
30 Aug 1872:   Promoted to *Major-General*
19 Mar 1877 - 7 Aug 1878:   Commander, 2nd Brigade, 2nd Guards Infantry Division
7 Aug 1878 - 11 Jan 1881:   Chief of Staff, Guards Corps
19 Feb 1880:   Promoted to *General-Adjutant*
11 Jan 1881:   Promoted to *Lieutenant-General*
11 Jan 1881 - 21 Feb 1884:   Chief of Staff, St. Petersburg Military District
21 Feb 1884 - 28 Oct 1889:   Governor-General of Turkestan, Commanding General, Turkestan Military District
28 Oct 1889 - 5 May 1901:   Member of the Military Council
21 Nov 1891 - 5 May 1901:   Member of the State Council
6 Dec 1895:   Promoted to *General of Infantry*

Major-General Baron Mikhail Fyodorovich von **Rozenberg** (27 Oct 1861 - Apr 1928)
18 Feb 1909 - 7 May 1909:   Senior Clerk, Artillery Committee, Main Artillery Directorate
29 Mar 1909:   Promoted to *Major-General*
7 May 1909 - Oct 1917:   Member of the Artillery Committee, Main Artillery Directorate
8 Oct 1914 - Oct 1917:   Chief of Section 1, Artillery Committee, Main Artillery

Directorate

Lieutenant-General Anatoly Nikolayevich **Rozenschild von Paulin** (11 Dec 1860 - 22 Nov 1929)
15 Jul 1905:	Promoted to *Major-General*
15 Jul 1905 - 19 Nov 1905:	Commander, 2nd Brigade, 10th East Siberian Rifle Division
19 Nov 1905 - 4 Dec 1907:	Commander, Life Guards 1st Rifel Battalion
4 Dec 1907 - 14 Feb 1909:	Commandant of the Infantry Officers School
14 Feb 1909 - 12 Oct 1911:	Commander, 2nd Brigade, 12th Infantry Division
12 Oct 1911 - 9 May 1914:	Commander, 1st Brigade, 42nd Infantry Division
9 May 1914:	Promoted to *Lieutenant-General*
9 May 1914 - 3 Apr 1915:	Commander, 29th Infantry Division
3 Apr 1915 - 1918:	POW, Germany

Vice-Admiral Zinovy Petrovich **Rozhestvensky** (11 Nov 1848 - 14 Jan 1909)
1898:	Promoted to *Rear-Admiral*
1898 - 4 Mar 1903:	Commander of Training & Naval Artillery, Baltic Fleet
4 Mar 1903 - Apr 1904:	Chief of the Main Naval Staff
Apr 1904 - 15 May 1905:	Commander, 2nd Pacific Squadron
Sep 1904:	Promoted to *Vice-Admiral*
15 May 1905 - Nov 1905:	POW, Japan
Nov 1905 - Feb 1906:	Chief of the Main Naval Staff
Feb 1906:	Dismissed

Major-General Leopold Ivanovich **Rozhnov** (11 Jun 1836 - ?)
3 Mar 1891:	Promoted to *Major-General*
3 Mar 1891 - 7 Oct 1899:	Commander, 1st Brigade, 27th Infantry Division

Major-General Nikolai Mikhailovich **Rozov** (4 Mar 1849 - ?)
14 Jun 1899 - 27 Feb 1904:	Commander, 38th Artillery Brigade
6 Dec 1899:	Promoted to *Major-General*

Major-General Nikolai Ivanovich von **Rubenau** (31 Dec 1863 - 20 Jun 1925)
22 Jul 1915 - 18 Apr 1917:	Chief of Staff, Caucasus Military District
6 Dec 1915:	Promoted to *Major-General*
18 Apr 1917 - 1918:	Reserve officer, Caucasus Military District

Major-General Andrei Mikhailovich **Rubert** (17 Jul 1863 - ?)
23 Jan 1916 - 1917:	Deputy Intendant, Western Front
6 Dec 1916:	Promoted to *Major-General*

General of Artillery Ivan Pavlovich **Rubets** (24 Jun 1834 - ?)
19 Oct 1886:	Promoted to *Major-General*
19 Oct 1886 - 29 Jul 1891:	Commander, 30th Artillery Brigade
29 Jul 1891 - 9 Jan 1900:	Commandant of Fortress Vyborg
14 May 1896:	Promoted to *Lieutenant-General*
9 Jan 1900:	Promoted to *General of Artillery*

9 Jan 1900:   Retired

Lieutenant-General Fyodor Vasilyevich **Rubets-Masalsky** (16 Sep 1865 - ?)
22 Jan 1911 - 16 Aug 1914:   Commander, 7th Dragoon Regiment
14 Apr 1913:   Promoted to *Major-General*
16 Aug 1914 - 7 Sep 1914:   Commander, 1st Brigade, 14th Cavalry Division
7 Sep 1914 - 8 Oct 1915:   Commander, 2nd Brigade, 7th Cavalry Division
8 Oct 1915 - 1917:   Reserve officer, Kiev Military District
1917 - 21 Apr 1917:   Chief of Staff, Petrograd Military District
2 Apr 1917:   Promoted to *Lieutenant-General*
21 Apr 1917 - 29 Jan 1918:   At the disposal of the Chief of the General Staff

Major-General Boris Aleksandrovich **Rudakov** (15 May 1857 - 21 Aug 1920)
7 Jun 1910:   Promoted to *Major-General*
7 Jun 1910 - 29 Jul 1914:   Commander, 1st Brigade, 48th Infantry Division
29 Jul 1914 - 18 Nov 1914:   Commander, Brigade, 83rd Infantry Division
18 Nov 1914 - 22 Nov 1914:   Commander, 1st Brigade, 48th Infantry Division
22 Nov 1914 - 20 Aug 1916:   Reserve officer, Kiev Military District
20 Aug 1916 - 16 Nov 1916:   Commander, 12th Labor Brigade, Southwestern Front
16 Nov 1916 - 13 Dec 1916:   Unassigned
13 Dec 1916:   Retired

Major-General Fyodor Nikolayevich **Rudakov** (3 Aug 1867 - ?)
21 Jan 1912 - 13 Jun 1915:   Deputy Chief of Mikhailovsk-Shostka Gunpowder Factory
25 Mar 1912:   Promoted to *Major-General*
13 Jun 1915 - 1917:   Deputy Chief of Sergievsk-Samara Explosives Factory

Major-General Vasily Andreyevich **Rudakov** (27 Jan 1865 - ?)
16 Apr 1912 - 24 Jun 1913:   Military Judge, Irkutsk Military District Court
14 Apr 1913:   Promoted to *Major-General*
24 Jun 1913 - 17 Apr 1917:   Military Judge, Caucasus Military District Court
17 Apr 1917:   Dismissed

Lieutenant-General Konstantin Adrianovich **Rudanovsky** (17 Jun 1849 - ?)
6 Sep 1899 - 23 Jan 1904:   Commander, Finland Life Guards Regiment
9 Apr 1900:   Promoted to *Major-General*
23 Jan 1904 - Apr 1907:   Commander, 2nd Brigade, 1st Guards Infantry Division
Apr 1907:   Promoted to *Lieutenant-General*
Apr 1907:   Retired

Lieutenant-General Konstantin Vasilyevich **Rudanovsky** (4 May 1834 - ?)
15 Feb 1878 - 15 Jan 1900:   Director of the Aleksandr Cadet Corps
30 Aug 1879:   Promoted to *Major-General*
11 Sep 1898:   Promoted to *Lieutenant-General*
15 Jan 1900 - 29 Jul 1900:   Deputy Chief of the Main Directorate for Military Schools
15 Jan 1900 - 4 Mar 1900:   Acting Chief of the Main Directorate for Military

	Schools
29 Jul 1900 - Sep 1905:	At the disposal of the Minister of War

Lieutenant-General Andrey Matveyevich **Rudenko** (2 Jul 1853 - ?)
1896 - 1 Sep 1910:	Chief of Veterinary Section, Main Military Medical Directorate
?:	Promoted to *Actual State Councillor*
?:	Promoted to *Privy Councillor*
1 Sep 1910 - Jul 1917:	Chief of the Army Veterinary Directorate
?:	Redesignated *Lieutenant-General*

Lieutenant-General Georgy Ivanovich **Rudenko** (25 Nov 1853 - ?)
4 Jul 1902 - 13 Feb 1906:	Military Judge, Siberian Military District Court
6 Dec 1902:	Promoted to *Major-General*
13 Feb 1906 - Jul 1914:	Military Judge, Warsaw Military District Court
Jul 1914 - 11 May 1917:	Military Judge, Minsk Military District Court
11 May 1917:	Promoted to *Lieutenant-General*
11 May 1917:	Retired

Lieutenant-General Vasily Ivanovich **Rudenkov** (5 May 1858 - 20 Feb 1917)
16 May 1901 - 31 Dec 1913:	Chief of Bureau, Main Artillery Directorate
6 Dec 1908:	Promoted to *Major-General*
31 Dec 1913 - 18 Dec 1915:	Deputy Commander of Artillery, St. Petersburg Military District
18 Dec 1915 - 20 Feb 1917:	Commander of Artillery, Petrograd Military District
6 Dec 1916:	Promoted to *Lieutenant-General*

Lieutenant-General Vladimir Ivanovich **Rudenkov** (19 Jun 1851 - ?)
16 Apr 1899 - 16 Feb 1902:	Military Judge, Moscow Military District Court
1 Jan 1901:	Promoted to *Major-General*
16 Feb 1902 - 25 Feb 1906:	Military Prosecutor, Kazan Military District
25 Feb 1906 - 1908:	Chairman of the Military Court, Kiev Military District
22 Apr 1907:	Promoted to *Lieutenant-General*

Major-General Sergey Afinogenovich **Rudkovsky** (7 Nov 1866 - ?)
8 Jul 1914 - 1917:	Military Judge, Irkutsk Military District Court
22 Mar 1915:	Promoted to *Major-General*

Major-General Ivan Nikolayevich **Rudnev** (16 Apr 1851 - ?)
27 Aug 1893 - 1 Jan 1905:	Deputy Chief of Police, Moscow
6 Dec 1903:	Promoted to *Major-General*
1 Jan 1905 - 1905:	Deputy Mayor of Moscow
1 Jan 1905 - 16 Jan 1905:	Acting Mayor of Moscow

Major-General Sergey Ivanovich **Rudnev** (24 Sep 1873 - 1920)
3 May 1916 - 1918:	Commander, 83rd Infantry Regiment
9 Feb 1917:	Promoted to *Major-General*

Major-General Sergey Vasilyevich **Rudnev** (17 Sep 1866 - ?)
24 Jun 1915 - 8 Jun 1917:   Commander, 3rd Grenadier Artillery Brigade
1 Sep 1915:   Promoted to *Major-General*
8 Jun 1917 - 1918:   Commander of Artillery, II. Caucasus Army Corps

Rear-Admiral Vsevolod Fyodorovich **Rudnev** (19 Aug 1855 - 7 Jul 1913)
10 Jun 1904 - Nov 1905:   Commander, 14th Naval Depot
Nov 1905:   Promoted to *Rear-Admiral*
Nov 1905:   Resigned

Major-General Edmund-Boleslav Ivanovich **Rudnitsky** (16 Mar 1849 - ?)
7 Apr 1902 - 24 Mar 1909:   Commander, 136th Infantry Regiment
6 Dec 1907:   Promoted to *Major-General*
24 Mar 1909 - 22 May 1910:   Commander, 2nd Brigade, 28th Infantry Division

Major-General Nikolai Kvintilyanovich **Rudnitsky** (3 Nov 1868 - ?)
19 Dec 1915 - 18 Feb 1917:   Chief of Staff, 13th Siberian Rifle Division
1916:   Promoted to *Major-General*
18 Feb 1917 - 17 May 1917:   Chief of Staff, XXXIV. Army Corps
17 May 1917 - 25 Mar 1918:   Unassigned
25 Mar 1918:   Dismissed

Major-General Platon Gavrilovich **Rudnitsky-Sipaylo** (18 Nov 1867 - 1918)
? - 1913:   Attached to Life Guards Volyn Regiment
2 Oct 1913:   Promoted to *Major-General*

Major-General Nikolai Petrovich **Rudov** (12 Oct 1845 - 1912)
4 Feb 1897 - 1906:   Commander of Gendarmerie, Chernigov Governorate
6 Dec 1905:   Promoted to *Major-General*

Major-General Aleksandr Konstantinovich von **Rukteshel** (26 Sep 1862 - ?)
20 Dec 1908 - 11 Jan 1916:   Commander of Artillery, Fortress Brest-Litovsk
6 Dec 1909:   Promoted to *Major-General*
11 Jan 1916 - 14 May 1917:   Commander, 7th Field Artillery Brigade
14 May 1917 - 1918:   Inspector of Artillery, XV. Army Corps

Major-General Nikolai Alekseyevich **Rulitsky** (12 Nov 1857 - 1911)
22 Jun 1898 - 4 Jul 1902:   Military Judge, Amur Military District Court
14 Apr 1902:   Promoted to *Major-General*
4 Jul 1902 - 1911:   Military Judge, Caucasus Military District Court

Major-General Iosif Frantsevich **Rumshevich** (4 Jul 1852 - ?)
31 Jan 1904 - 1905:   Commander, 2nd Siberian Infantry Regiment
1905:   Promoted to *Major-General*
1905:   Retired

Major-General Mikhail Alekseyevich **Rumyantsev** (12 Jan 1864 - 1920)
27 Feb 1909 - Oct 1917:   Military Judge, Omsk Military District Court

18 Apr 1910: Promoted to *Major-General*

Lieutenant-General Mikhail Alekseyevich **Runov** (3 Sep 1836 - 23 Feb 1899)
24 Jan 1879 - 19 May 1887: Deputy Intendant, St. Petersburg Military District
30 Aug 1882: Promoted to *Major-General*
19 May 1887 - 17 Jan 1894: Intendant, Warsaw Military District
30 Aug 1893: Promoted to *Lieutenant-General*
17 Jan 1894 - 1895: At the disposal of the Intendant-General of the Army
1895: Retired

General of Infantry Sergey Ivanovich **Rusanov** (7 Sep 1847 - 10 Oct 1910)
23 Jul 1898: Promoted to *Major-General*
23 Jul 1898 - 23 Jul 1900: Commander, 2nd Transcaspian Rifle Brigade
23 Jul 1900 - 12 Jan 1904: Commander, 7th Turkestan Rifle Brigade
12 Jan 1904 - 12 Aug 1904: Commander, 1st Rifle Brigade
12 Aug 1904 - 8 Sep 1904: Unassigned
8 Sep 1904 - 29 May 1906: Commander, 14th Infantry Division
6 Dec 1904: Promoted to *Lieutenant-General*
29 May 1906 - 22 Sep 1910: Commander, 12th Infantry Division
22 Aug 1910: Promoted to *General of Infantry*

Admiral Aleksandr Ivanovich **Rusin** (8 Aug 1861 - 17 Nov 1956)
29 Mar 1909: Promoted to *Rear-Admiral*
29 Mar 1909 - 17 Sep 1913: Commandant of the Imperial Naval Academy, Director of the Marine Corps
25 Mar 1912: Promoted to *Vice-Admiral*
17 Sep 1913 - Apr 1917: Chief of the Main Naval Staff
23 Feb 1914 - Apr 1917: Chief of the Naval General Staff
1 Jun 1915 - Mar 1917: Deputy Minister of the Navy
10 Apr 1916: Promoted to *Admiral*
1 Jul 1917: Discharged

Major-General Apollon Ivanovich **Rusinov** (30 Jul 1835 - ?)
20 Sep 1879 - 1894: Ataman, 2nd Military Division, Siberian Cossack Army
6 May 1886: Promoted to *Major-General*

Lieutenant-General Kesar Vikentyevich **Russiyan** (12 Feb 1854 - ?)
14 Nov 1909 - 12 Feb 1914: Commander, 2nd Brigade, 14th Infantry Division
22 May 1910: Promoted to *Major-General*
12 Feb 1914: Promoted to *Lieutenant-General*
12 Feb 1914: Retired

Major-General Vasily Arsenyevich **Rustanovich** (21 Sep 1871 - 27 Jun 1941)
13 Nov 1914 - 6 Oct 1915: Commander, 8th Rifle Regiment
6 Oct 1915 - 16 Apr 1916: Commander, Brigade, 71st Infantry Division
31 Oct 1915: Promoted to *Major-General*
16 Apr 1916 - 12 Jul 1916: Chief of Staff, 80th Infantry Division
12 Jul 1916 - 13 Apr 1917: Chief of Staff, VII. Army Corps

13 Apr 1917 - Oct 1917:   Commander, 9th Siberian Rifle Division

Lieutenant-General Aleksandr Konstantinovich **Rutkovsky** (18 Aug 1854 - ?)
29 Oct 1899 - 1 Mar 1903:   Commander, 30th Dragoon Regiment
1 Mar 1903:   Promoted to *Major-General*
1 Mar 1903 - 11 Oct 1903:   Special Assignments General, Kiev Military District
11 Oct 1903 - 14 Aug 1908:   Duty General, Kiev Military District
14 Aug 1908 - 1 May 1910:   Commander, 1st Brigade, 10th Cavalry Division
1 May 1910:   Promoted to *Lieutenant-General*
1 May 1910 - 6 Dec 1912:   Commander, 12th Cavalry Division

Major-General Ivan-Ignaty Stanislavovich **Rutkovsky** (19 Apr 1856 - 15 Aug 1904)
26 Jun 1896 - 22 Feb 1904:   Commander, 4th East Siberian Rifle Regiment
11 Nov 1903:   Promoted to *Major-General*
22 Feb 1904 - 15 Aug 1904:   Commander, 1st Brigade, 1st East Siberian Rifle Division

Major-General Mechislav Avgustovich **Rutkovsky** (1843 - ?)
8 Mar 1890 - 1901:   Attached to the Caucasus Military District
6 Dec 1899:   Promoted to *Major-General*

General of Cavalry Pyotr Konstantinovich **Rutkovsky** (28 Dec 1852 - ?)
14 Dec 1899 - 27 Nov 1902:   Chief of Staff, II. Caucasus Army Corps
9 Apr 1900:   Promoted to *Major-General*
27 Nov 1902 - 12 Jul 1904:   Chief of Staff, XII. Army Corps
12 Jul 1904 - 17 Oct 1906:   Chief of Staff, Amur Military District
2 Apr 1906:   Promoted to *Lieutenant-General*
17 Oct 1906 - 3 May 1910:   Commander, 11th Cavalry Division
3 May 1910:   Promoted to *General of Cavalry*

Major-General Vladimir Ignatyevich **Rutkovsky** (7 Feb 1857 - 3 Sep 1918)
4 Feb 1907 - 1917:   Chairman of the Remount Commission, Kiev Region
6 Dec 1912:   Promoted to *Major-General*
1917 - 16 Jul 1917:   Reserve officer, Moscow Military District
16 Jul 1917:   Dismissed

General of Engineers Yakov Konstantinovich **Rutkovsky** (2 Oct 1843 - 24 Dec 1904)
29 Dec 1890 - 8 Dec 1895:   Chief of Engineers, Transcaspian Region
30 Aug 1892:   Promoted to *Major-General*
8 Dec 1895 - 24 Dec 1904:   Commander of Engineers, Caucasus Military District
6 Dec 1899:   Promoted to *Lieutenant-General*
30 Dec 1904:   Posthumously promoted to *General of Engineers*

General of Infantry Nikolai Vladimirovich **Ruzsky** (6 Mar 1854 - 18 Oct 1918)
13 Dec 1896:   Promoted to *Major-General*
13 Dec 1896 - 10 Apr 1902:   Quartermaster-General, Kiev Military District
10 Apr 1902 - 28 Sep 1904:   Chief of Staff, Vilnius Military District
6 Apr 1903:   Promoted to *Lieutenant-General*

28 Sep 1904 - 6 Oct 1906:	Chief of Staff, 2nd Manchurian Army
6 Oct 1906 - 31 Jan 1909:	Commanding General, XXI. Army Corps
31 Jan 1909 - 19 Jul 1914:	Member of the Military Council
29 Mar 1909:	Promoted to *General of Infantry*
7 Feb 1912 - 19 Jul 1914:	Deputy Commanding General, Kiev Military District
19 Jul 1914 - 3 Sep 1914:	C-in-C, 3rd Army
3 Sep 1914 - 17 Mar 1915:	C-in-C, Northwestern Front
22 Sep 1914:	Promoted to *General-Adjutant*
17 Mar 1915 - 1917:	Member of the State Council
20 May 1915 - 1917:	Member of the Military Council
30 Jun 1915 - 18 Aug 1915:	C-in-C, 6th Army
18 Aug 1915 - 6 Dec 1915:	C-in-C, Northern Front
1 Aug 1916 - 25 Apr 1917:	C-in-C, Northern Front
25 Apr 1917:	Dismissed

Major-General Mikhail Nikolayevich **Ryabinin** (21 May 1857 - 1916)

7 Jan 1914 - 1916:	Military Commander, Kishinev District
3 May 1916:	Posthumously promoted to *Major-General*

Lieutenant-General Fyodor Trofimovich **Ryabinkin** (12 Aug 1859 - ?)

19 Jun 1905:	Promoted to *Major-General*
19 Jun 1905 - 30 Dec 1906:	Commander, 1st Brigade, 5th Rifle Division
30 Dec 1906 - 15 Apr 1915:	Special Purposes General, Caucasus Military District
15 Apr 1915 - 18 Jul 1915:	Chief of Staff, IV. Caucasus Army Corps
18 Jul 1915 - 2 Jan 1916:	Special Purposes General, Caucasus Army
2 Jan 1916 - 22 May 1916:	Commander, 39th Infantry Division
20 Mar 1916:	Promoted to *Lieutenant-General*
22 May 1916 - 1917:	Reserve officer, Caucasus Military District

Major-General Konstantin Trofimovich **Ryabinkin** (28 May 1849 - 1 Oct 1904)

2 Nov 1902:	Promoted to *Major-General*
2 Nov 1902 - 1 Oct 1904:	Commander, 1st Brigade, 9th Infantry Division

Major-General Pavel Petrovich **Ryabkov** (29 Jun 1855 - 1921)

25 Jun 1910:	Promoted to *Major-General*
25 Jun 1910 - 1915:	Commander, 2nd Brigade, 47th Infantry Division
1915:	Commander, 1st Brigade, ? Infantry Division
1915 - 7 Apr 1916.	Reserve officer, Kiev Military District
7 Apr 1916 - 1917:	Commander, 55th State Militia Brigade

Major-General Vladimir Pimenovich **Ryabov** (21 Oct 1847 - ?)

15 Jun 1891 - 19??:	Deputy Chief of Administration, St. Petersburg Court
26 Nov 1901:	Promoted to *Major-General*

Major-General of Naval Artillery Gavriil Fyodorovich **Ryazanin** (25 Mar 1857 - ?)

11 Oct 1902 - ?:	Deputy Chief Inspector of Naval Artillery
6 Dec 1908:	Promoted to *Major-General of Naval Artillery*

Major-General Aleksey Nikiforovich **Rybakov** (2 Mar 1861 - ?)
25 Aug 1915 - 10 Jan 1918: Special Assignments General, Omsk Military District
6 Dec 1916: Promoted to *Major-General*
10 Jan 1918: Dismissed

Major-General Aleksandr Grigoryevich **Rybalchenko** (11 Oct 1859 - ?)
4 Jun 1915 - 24 Jan 1917: Commander, 1st Brigade, 4th Caucasus Cossack Division
21 Jan 1916: Promoted to *Major-General*
24 Jan 1917 - ?: Commander, 4th Kuban Cossack Division

Major-General Yevgraf Grigoryevich **Rybalchenko** (14 Sep 1857 - ?)
Apr 1915 - 1917: Commander, 12th Artillery Brigade
16 May 1915: Promoted to *Major-General*

Major-General of the Fleet Anatoly Aleksandrovich **Rybaltovsky** (24 Apr 1868 - 1921)
29 Jan 1915 - 28 Apr 1917: Attached to the 1st Baltic Naval Crew
30 Jul 1916: Promoted to *Major-General of the Fleet*

Major-General Ippolit Aleksandrovich **Rybaltovsky** (17 Oct 1850 - ?)
5 Aug 1894 - 25 Apr 1905: Section Chief, Main Artillery Directorate
6 Dec 1901: Promoted to *Major-General*
25 Apr 1905 - 22 Aug 1908: Deputy Commander of Artillery, Caucasus Military District
22 Aug 1908: Retired

Lieutenant-General Veniamin Veniaminovich **Rychkov** (12 Dec 1867 - 22 Aug 1935)
19 Oct 1914 - 13 Apr 1915: Commander, 202nd Infantry Regiment
18 Mar 1915: Promoted to *Major-General*
13 Apr 1915 - 13 Dec 1916: Quartermaster-General, 1st Army
13 Dec 1916 - 20 May 1917: Commander, 45th Infantry Division
20 May 1917: Promoted to *Lieutenant-General*
20 May 1917 - Nov 1917: Commanding General, XXVII. Army Corps

General of Cavalry Konstantin Nikolayevich **Rydzevsky** (17 Mar 1852 - 11 Nov 1929)
6 May 1898: Promoted to *Major-General*
6 May 1898 - 28 Sep 1904: Chief of the Tsar's Cabinet
28 Sep 1904 - 24 May 1905: Deputy Minister of Internal Affairs, Commanding General, Corps of Gendarmerie, Chief of National Police
24 May 1905 - 1917: Senator
6 Dec 1906: Promoted to *Lieutenant-General*
6 Dec 1916: Promoted to *General of Cavalry*

Major-General Nikolai Nikolayevich **Rydzevsky** (26 Oct 1840 - 1918)
29 Jan 1878 - 1895: Commandant, Kiev Regional Arsenal
6 May 1884: Promoted to *Major-General*
1895: Retired

General of the Fleet Mikhail Aleksandrovich **Rykachev** (24 Dec 1840 - 14 Apr 1919)
6 Dec 1895:	Promoted to *Major-General of the Admiralty*
17 Apr 1896 - 1913:	Director, Main Physical Observatory
6 Dec 1903:	Promoted to *Lieutenant-General of the Admiralty*
8 Sep 1909:	Promoted to *General of the Admiralty*
8 Apr 1913:	Redesignated *General of the Fleet*

Lieutenant-General Stepan Vasilyevich **Rykachev** (18 Jun 1829 - 2 Nov 1899)
26 Jul 1877 - 19 Feb 1881:	Commander, 18th Infantry Regiment
20 Dec 1877:	Promoted to *Major-General*
1877 - 1878:	Acting Commander, 1st Brigade, 5th Infantry Division
19 Feb 1881 - 22 Sep 1886:	Commander, Life Guards Volyn Regiment
22 Sep 1886 - 4 Mar 1890:	Commandant, Pavlovsk Military School
30 Aug 1887:	Promoted to *Lieutenant-General*
4 Mar 1890 - 7 Mar 1891:	Commander, 27th Infantry Division
7 Mar 1891 - 21 Feb 1895:	Commander, 2nd Guards Infantry Division
21 Feb 1895 - 2 Nov 1899:	Member, Committee for Wounded Veterans

Major-General of the Fleet Aleksandr Nikolayevich **Rykov** (14 Aug 1874 - 7 Dec 1918)
6 Dec 1914:	Promoted to *Major-General of the Fleet*
? - Dec 1917:	Head of Emperor Pavel I Military Invalid Home

Major-General of the Admiralty Sergey Ivanovich **Rykov** (11 Sep 1841 - 24 May 1911)
1900:	Commander, Caspian Sea Port
1900:	Promoted to *Major-General of the Admiralty*
1900:	Retired

Major-General Aleksandr Nikodimovich **Rykovsky** (23 Oct 1856 - May 1916)
16 Feb 1904 - May 1916:	Commander of Gendarmerie, Kharkov
6 Dec 1911:	Promoted to *Major-General*

General of Infantry Aleksandr Mikhailovich **Ryleyev** (1830 - 3 Apr 1907)
1 Jan 1864 - 27 Mar 1881:	Commandant, Imperial Headquarters
30 Aug 1867:	Promoted to *Major-General*
30 Aug 1873:	Promoted to *General-Adjutant*
30 Aug 1876:	Promoted to *Lieutenant-General*
27 Mar 1881 - 3 Apr 1907:	General à la suite
30 Aug 1890:	Promoted to *General of Infantry*

General of Infantry Genrikh Danilovich **Rylke** (16 Nov 1845 - 1917)
22 Feb 1885 - 3 Oct 1905:	Military Prosecutor, Odessa Military District
30 Aug 1894:	Promoted to *Major-General*
6 Apr 1903:	Promoted to *Lieutenant-General*
3 Oct 1905 - 13 Sep 1906:	Chairman of the Military Tribunal, Odessa Military District
13 Sep 1906 - 15 Jan 1907:	Chairman of the Military Tribunal, St. Petersburg Military District
15 Jan 1907 - 8 Apr 1908:	Chief of the Main Military Justice Directorate

8 Apr 1908 - 1 Jan 1915:	Member of the Military Council, Chief of Codification Department, Military Council
29 Mar 1909:	Promoted to *General of Infantry*
1 Jan 1915:	Retired
2 Jan 1915 - 15 Nov 1915:	Recalled; Attached to the Ministry of War
15 Nov 1915 - 22 Mar 1918:	Chairman of the Preparatory Commission for Liquidation
22 Mar 1918:	Retired

Major-General Stanislav Danilovich **Rylke** (8 May 1843 - 4 Apr 1899)
31 Dec 1892 - 4 Apr 1899:	Chief of Topographical Survey, Southwest Frontier Region
14 May 1896:	Promoted to *Major-General*

Major-General Konstantin Iosifovich **Rylsky** (12 May 1871 - 1921)
20 Dec 1914 - 21 Dec 1915:	Commander, Life Guards Grenadier Regiment
22 Apr 1915:	Promoted to *Major-General*
21 Dec 1915 - 6 Apr 1917:	Chief of Staff, I. Guards Corps
6 Apr 1917 - 25 Apr 1917:	Commander, 154th Infantry Division
25 Apr 1917 - 8 Jul 1917:	Commander, 2nd Guards Infantry Division
8 Jul 1917 - 26 Aug 1917:	Commander, 122nd Infantry Division
26 Aug 1917 - 1918:	Chief of Staff, 12th Army

Lieutenant-General Vasily Osipovich **Rylsky** (27 Dec 1844 - 1913)
2 Aug 1898:	Promoted to *Major-General*
2 Aug 1898 - 24 Nov 1899:	Commandant of Abas-Tuman
24 Nov 1899 - 4 Dec 1901:	Commander, 1st Brigade, Caucasus Grenadier Division
4 Dec 1901 - 23 Sep 1904:	Commander, 2nd Caucasus Rifle Brigade
23 Sep 1904 - 7 Dec 1904:	Acting Commandant of Tiflis
7 Dec 1904 - 15 Mar 1906:	Commander, Caucasus Grenadier Division
15 Mar 1906 - 5 Sep 1906:	Commander, 34th Infantry Division
2 Apr 1906:	Promoted to *Lieutenant-General*
5 Sep 1906:	Retired

Major-General Yevgeny Grigoryevich **Rylsky** (8 Dec 1841 - ?)
6 Dec 1897:	Promoted to *Major-General*
6 Dec 1897 - 20 Feb 1902:	Commander of Artillery, Fortress Kerch

Lieutenant-General Fabian Osipovich **Rymashevsky** (9 Jan 1832 - ?)
23 Sep 1870 - 8 Jul 1889:	Commander, 4th Battery, 11th Artillery Brigade
8 Jun 1889:	Promoted to *Major-General*
8 Jul 1889 - 14 Nov 1899:	Commander, 20th Artillery Brigade
14 Nov 1899:	Promoted to *Lieutenant-General*
14 Nov 1899:	Retired

Lieutenant-General Aleksey Kondratyevich **Ryndin**: see **Zeland**

Lieutenant-General Mikhail Mikhailovich **Ryndin** (31 Mar 1859 - ?)
23 Feb 1901 - 30 Jul 1907: Senior Adjutant, Inspector-General of Cavalry
31 May 1907: Promoted to *Major-General*
30 Jul 1907 - 31 Dec 1913: Commander, Guards Replacement Cavalry Regiment
31 Dec 1913: Promoted to *Lieutenant-General*
31 Dec 1913 - 1917: Commander, 2nd Replacement Cavalry Brigade

Lieutenant-General Mikhail Nikolayevich **Ryndin** (25 Feb 1839 - 16 Dec 1912)
30 Sep 1877 - 1905: Chief of Section 1, Main Engineering Directorate
30 Aug 1889: Promoted to *Major-General*
1905: Promoted to *Lieutenant-General*
1905: Retired

Major-General Yefim Yefimovich **Rynkevich** (24 Feb 1846 - ?)
10 May 1888 - 14 May 1889: At the disposal of the Chief of the General Staff
14 May 1889 - 5 Jul 1889: Unassigned
27 May 1889: Promoted to *Major-General*
5 Jul 1889 - 22 May 1890: Commander, Life Guards Uhlan Regiment
22 May 1890 - 10 May 1895: Commander, Nikolayev Cavalry School
10 May 1895 - Dec 1896: Commander, Caucasus Cavalry Division

Major-General Vasily Kuzmich **Rytikov** (22 Mar 1839 - 14 Jul 1901)
12 Jan 1889 - 1901: Provincial Commander, Don Cossack Army
12 Feb 1895: Promoted to *Major-General*
1901: Promoted to *Lieutenant-General*
1901 - 14 Jul 1901: Commandant of Novocherkassk

Lieutenant-General Mikhail Nikolayevich **Ryumin** (23 Apr 1836 - 22 Jul 1916)
4 Feb 1883 - 23 Oct 1893: Commander of Artillery, Fortress Novogeorgiyevsk
30 Aug 1888: Promoted to *Major-General*
23 Oct 1893 - 1899: Deputy Commander of Artillery, Warsaw Military District
1899: Promoted to *Lieutenant-General*
1899: Retired

Major-General Anton Yakovlevich **Ryzhkov** (10 Feb 1859 - 1910)
2 Mar 1906 - 1909: Attached to 64th Infantry Regiment
1909: Promoted to *Major-General*
1909: Retired

Lieutenant-General Pyotr Nikolayevich **Ryzhov** (7 Jun 1864 - 1936)
9 Jul 1908: Promoted to *Major-General*
9 Jul 1908 - 29 Jan 1913: Chief of Staff, XV. Army Corps
29 Jan 1913 - 30 Mar 1915: Commander, 1st Brigade, 15th Cavalry Division
1915: Promoted to *Lieutenant-General*
1915: Retired

General of Cavalry Lyudomir Aleksandrovich **Rzhevusky** (15 Oct 1848 - 27 Oct 1932)
2 May 1899 - 20 May 1904:	Ataman, Pyatigorsk Division, Terek Cossack Army
6 May 1901:	Promoted to *Major-General*
20 May 1904 - 3 Aug 1907:	Deputy Commander, Terek Region, Ataman, Terek Cossack Army
3 Aug 1907:	Promoted to *Lieutenant-General*
3 Aug 1907 - 1 May 1910:	Commander, 2nd Caucasus Cossack Division
1 May 1910:	Retired
1914:	Promoted to *General of Cavalry*
3 May 1915 - 21 May 1916:	Recalled; Reserve officer, Dvinsk Military District
21 May 1916 - 9 May 1917:	Attached to the Terek Cossack Army
9 May 1917:	Dismissed

Major-General Gavriil Vikentyevich **Rzhesniovetsky** (19 Mar 1848 - ?)
16 Jan 1902 - 4 Jan 1905:	Commander, 124th Infantry Regiment
4 Jan 1905:	Promoted to *Major-General*
4 Jan 1905 - 9 Mar 1905:	Unassigned
9 Mar 1905 - 17 Aug 1906:	Commander, 1st Brigade, 31st Infantry Division

Major-General Vasily Petrovich **Sabaneyev** (3 Aug 1820 - ?)
14 May 1896:	Promoted to *Major-General*
14 May 1896 - 1903:	Staff Officer, Fortress St. Petersburg

Lieutenant-General Aleksandr Fyodorovich **Sablin** (8 Mar 1843 - ?)
5 Aug 1900 - 21 Jun 1906:	Commandant, Tbilisi Artillery Depot
14 Apr 1902:	Promoted to *Major-General*
21 Jun 1906 - 1909:	Commandant, Warsaw Artillery Depot
1909:	Promoted to *Lieutenant-General*
1909:	Retired

Major-General Ivan Alekseyevich **Sablin** (8 Aug 1846 - 18 Dec 1900)
21 Nov 1897:	Promoted to *Major-General*
21 Nov 1897 - 18 Dec 1900:	General for Special Assignments, Odessa Military District

Rear-Admiral Mikhail Pavlovich **Sablin** (17 Jul 1869 - 17 Oct 1920)
1914 - 21 Jul 1916:	Attached to the Black Sea Naval Depot
18 Apr 1915:	Promoted to *Rear-Admiral*
21 Jul 1916 - 31 Oct 1916:	Commander, 2nd Cruiser Brigade, Black Sea Fleet Acting Commander, Battleship Division, Black Sea Fleet
31 Oct 1916 - 21 Jul 1917:	At the disposal of the Minister of the Navy
21 Jul 1917 - Oct 1917:	Chief of Staff, Black Sea Fleet

Vice-Admiral Pavel Fyodorovich **Sablin** (26 Jul 1839 - 13 Aug 1914)
1 Jan 1894:	Promoted to *Rear-Admiral*
1 Jan 1894 - 17 Nov 1897:	Director of Lighthouses & Navigation, Caspian Sea, Commander, Baku Naval Port

Jan 1898 - 28 Jun 1899:   Junior Flagman, Baltic Fleet
28 Jun 1899:   Promoted to *Vice-Admiral*
28 Jun 1899:   Retired

General-Field Marshal Friedrich August Albert Anton Ferdinand Joseph Karl Maria Baptist Nepomuk Wilhelm Xaver Georg Fidelis von **Sachsen** (23 Apr 1828 - 19 Jun 1902)
1872:   Promoted to *General-Field Marshal*
29 Oct 1873 - 19 Jun 1902: King of Saxony

General of Cavalry Karl Alexander August Johann, Großherzog von **Sachsen-Weimar-Eisenach** (24 Jun 1818 - 5 Jan 1901)
?:   Honorary Colonel-in-Chief, 30th Dragoon Regiment
16 May 1884:   Promoted to *Major-General*
23 Oct 1888:   Promoted to *Lieutenant-General*
?:   Promoted to *General of Cavalry*

Major-General Aleksandr Petrovich **Safonov** (26 Aug 1852 - 1913)
13 Apr 1910 - 1913:   Staff Officer, Main Intendant Directorate
1913:   Promoted to *Major-General*
1913:   Retired

Lieutenant-General Ilya Ivanovich **Safonov** (20 Jul 1825 - 22 Aug 1896)
23 Nov 1879:   Promoted to *Major-General*
4 May 1884 - 16 Feb 1885:   Member, Committee for Cossack Forces
16 Feb 1885 - 14 Jan 1893: Commander, Terek Cossack Brigade
30 Aug 1893:   Promoted to *Lieutenant-General*
14 Jan 1893 - 16 Nov 1895: Commander, 2nd Caucasus Cossack Division
16 Nov 1895 - 22 Aug 1896: Attached to Caucasus Military District

Major-General Vladimir Petrovich **Sagatovsky** (26 Feb 1857 - ?)
23 Jul 1911:   Promoted to *Major-General*
23 Jul 1911 - 18 Aug 1912: Commander of Artillery, Fortress Modlin
18 Aug 1912 - 25 Jul 1914: Commander, 3rd Siberian Rifle Artillery Brigade
25 Jul 1914 - 1918:   Commander of Artillery, Fortress Vladivostok

Major-General Sergey Petrovich **Sakhansky** (2 Oct 1866 - ?)
3 Nov 1905 - 24 Jul 1914:   Commander, Guards Field Gendarmerie Squadron
6 Aug 1913:   Promoted to *Major-General*
24 Jul 1914 - 1917:   Commandant, Supreme Command Headquarters

Major-General Vasily Mikhailovich **Sakharov** (31 Dec 1845 - ?)
2 Dec 1901:   Promoted to *Major-General*
2 Dec 1901 - 13 Dec 1902:   Commander, 1st Brigade, 9th Cavalry Division

Lieutenant-General Viktor Viktorovich **Sakharov** (20 Jul 1848 - 22 Nov 1905)
27 Feb 1890 - 25 Sep 1892: Deputy Chief of Staff, Warsaw Military District
30 Aug 1890:   Promoted to *Major-General*
25 Sep 1892 - 22 Sep 1894: Quartermaster-General, Warsaw Military District

22 Sep 1894 - 20 Jan 1898:	Chief of Staff, Odessa Military District
6 Dec 1897:	Promoted to *Lieutenant-General*
20 Jan 1898 - 11 Mar 1904:	Chief of the General Staff
1903:	Promoted to *General-Adjutant*
7 Feb 1904 - 21 Jun 1905:	Minister of War

General of Cavalry Vladimir Viktorovich **Sakharov** (20 May 1853 - Aug 1920)

12 Nov 1897:	Promoted to *Major-General*
12 Nov 1897 - 30 Jun 1899:	Chief of Staff, V. Army Corps
30 Jun 1899 - 30 Jul 1900:	Chief of Staff, Independent Borderguards Corps
30 Jul 1900 - 16 Feb 1901:	Commander, Northern Manchuria
13 Jan 1901:	Promoted to *Lieutenant-General*
16 Feb 1901 - 7 May 1901:	Commander, Amur District Borderguards
7 May 1901 - 29 Nov 1903:	Commander, 4th Cavalry Division
29 Nov 1903 - 5 Apr 1904:	Commanding General, I. Siberian Army Corps
5 Apr 1904 - 18 Oct 1904:	Chief of Staff, Manchurian Army
18 Oct 1904 - 17 Mar 1905:	Chief of Staff, Land & Naval Forces operating against Japan
17 Mar 1905 - 3 Jan 1906:	Member, Committee for Wounded Veterans
3 Jan 1906 - 21 Apr 1906:	Attached to C-in-C of Land & Naval Forces operating against Japan
21 Apr 1906 - 10 Nov 1906:	Attached to the General Staff
10 Nov 1906 - 4 Nov 1911:	Commanding General, VII. Army Corps
13 Apr 1908:	Promoted to *General of Cavalry*
4 Nov 1911 - 13 Dec 1912:	Unassigned
13 Dec 1912 - 22 Aug 1915:	Commanding General, XI. Army Corps
22 Aug 1915 - 4 Sep 1915:	Governor of Orenburg, C-in-C, Orenburg Cossack Army
4 Sep 1915 - 25 Oct 1915:	Unassigned
25 Oct 1915 - 19 Oct 1916:	C-in-C, 11th Army
19 Oct 1916 - 12 Dec 1916:	C-in-C, Danube Army
12 Dec 1916 - 2 Apr 1917:	Deputy C-in-C, Romanian Front
2 Apr 1917 - Oct 1917:	Unassigned

General of Infantry Vsevolod Viktorovich **Sakharov** (18 Feb 1851 - 2 Mar 1935)

10 Jun 1896:	Promoted to *Major-General*
10 Jun 1896 - 27 Feb 1899:	Chief of Staff, Trans-Caspian Region
27 Feb 1899 - 14 Nov 1904:	Chief of Staff, Turkestan Military District
11 Jun 1901:	Promoted to *Lieutenant-General*
14 Nov 1904 - 1 Jan 1906:	Deputy Commanding General, Turkestan Military District, Deputy Governor-General of Turkestan
1 Jan 1906:	Promoted to *General of Infantry*
1 Jan 1906:	Retired

Major-General Vyacheslav Petrovich **Sakharov** (25 Jul 1853 - Dec 1915)

11 Aug 1910 - 22 Oct 1912:	Engineering Insepctor, Kazan Military District
6 Dec 1910:	Promoted to *Major-General*

22 Oct 1912 - Dec 1915: Chief of Troop Billeting, Kazan Military District

Major-General Aleksey Antonovich **Sakhatsky** (6 Dec 1839 - 5 Oct 1900)
8 Apr 1896: Promoted to *Major-General*
8 Apr 1896 - 5 Oct 1900: Commander, 5th Sapper Brigade

Major-General Akim Ivanovich **Sakhnovsky** (28 Jan 1831 - 11 Apr 1895)
20 Dec 1889 - 11 Apr 1895: Commander, Odessa Military District Artillery Depot
30 Aug 1890: Promoted to *Major-General*

Major-General Aleksandr Akimovich **Sakhnovsky** (11 Mar 1846 - ?)
17 Dec 1900: Promoted to *Major-General*
17 Dec 1900 - 11 Mar 1906: Commander, 2nd Brigade, Caucasus Grenadier Division

Lieutenant-General Pavel Grigoryevich **Sakhnovsky** (7 Feb 1853 - 14 Feb 1908)
14 Apr 1901: Promoted to *Major-General*
14 Apr 1901 - 4 Sep 1904: General for Special Assignments, Finland Military District
4 Sep 1904 - Jun 1906: Commander, 1st Finnish Rifle Brigade
Jun 1906: Promoted to *Lieutenant-General*
Jun 1906: Retired

Major-General Pyotr Petrovich **Sakovich** (10 Sep 1866 - ?)
24 Oct 1910 - 1913: Intendant, Amur Military District
1913: Promoted to *Major-General*
1913: Retired
2 Jan 1915 - 24 Jul 1917: Recalled; Chief of Intendant Service, Dvinsk Military District
24 Jul 1917: Retired

Major-General of the Admiralty Nikolai Aleksandrovich **Saks** (1 Feb 1860 - 23 Feb 1918)
1 Aug 1908 - 1910: Deputy Commander, Black Sea Naval Depot
1910: Promoted to *Major-General of the Admiralty*
1910: Retired

Major-General Mikhail Lyudvigovich **Salatko-Petrishche** (14 Sep 1869 - 19 May 1935)
31 Jan 1912 - 29 Aug 1916: Inspector of Classes, Yaroslavl Cadet Corps
6 Dec 1913: Promoted to *Major-General*
29 Aug 1916 - 1918: Inspector of Classes, Suvorov Cadet Corps

Major-General Serene Highness Prince Ivan Nikolayevich **Saltykov** (15 May 1870 - 1941)
1909 - 15 Apr 1914: Marshal of Nobility, St. Petersburg
23 Feb 1913: Promoted to *Major-General*
23 Feb 1913 - Mar 1917: General à la suite
1915 - 1916: Chief of the 13th Forward Detachment, Red Cross

Major-General Vladimir Vladimirovich **Saltykov** (18 Apr 1863 - 18 Dec 1917)
21 Nov 1907: Promoted to *Major-General*

21 Nov 1907 - 18 Jun 1908:	Commander, 39th Artillery Brigade
18 Jun 1908:	Retired
Aug 1914 - 29 Jun 1915:	Recalled; Commander, 9th State Militia Brigade
29 Jun 1915 - 6 Aug 1915:	At the disposal of the Commander, 114th Infantry Division
6 Aug 1915 - 18 Dec 1917:	POW

Major-General Vladimir Ivanovich **Samaryanov** (2 Jul 1856 - ?)
4 Jan 1908 - 1910:	Commander, Battalion, 138th Infantry Regiment
1910:	Promoted to *Major-General*
1910:	Retired
1915 - 13 Jun 1916:	Recalled; Commander, 166th Replacement Infantry Battalion
13 Jun 1916 - 1918:	Commander, 166th Replacement Infantry Regiment

Lieutenant-General Pavel Mitrofanovich **Samgin** (27 Aug 1854 - ?)
23 Jan 1904:	Promoted to *Major-General*
23 Jan 1904 - Jun 1907:	Commander, Life Guards Finland Regiment
Jun 1907:	Promoted to *Lieutenant-General*
Jun 1907:	Retired
6 Jun 1915 - 15 Apr 1917:	Recalled; Commander, 107th Infantry Division
15 Apr 1917 - Oct 1917:	Reserve officer, Petrograd Military District

Lieutenant-General Mikhail Petrovich **Samokhvalov** (21 Oct 1833 - ?)
27 Apr 1874 - 5 Nov 1886:	Commandant, 3rd Aleksandrov Military School
30 Aug 1878:	Promoted to *Major-General*
5 Nov 1886 - 22 Jun 1891:	Commander, 3rd Rifle Brigade
30 Aug 1888:	Promoted to *Lieutenant-General*
22 Jun 1891 - 11 Aug 1891:	Commander, 9th Regional Brigade
11 Aug 1891 - 16 Feb 1896:	Commander, 4th Infantry Division

Lieutenant-General Feofil Matveyevich **Samotsvet** (30 May 1834 - 27 Nov 1905)
21 Mar 1876 - 27 Nov 1905:	Director, Orenburg Neplyuevsky Cadet Corps
30 Aug 1880:	Promoted to *Major-General*
30 Jun 1900:	Promoted to *Lieutenant-General*

Lieutenant-General of the Admiralty Ivan Valerianovich **Samovich** (21 Aug 1854 - 1914)
1 Jan 1892 - Mar 1913:	Chief of Lighthouse Construction, Black & Azov Seas
29 Mar 1909:	Promoted to *Major-General of the Admiralty*
1913:	Promoted to *Lieutenant-General of the Admiralty*
1913:	Retired

Major-General Aleksandr Aleksandrovich **Samoylo** (23 Oct 1869 - 8 Nov 1963)
10 Sep 1915 - 1917:	Deputy Quartermaster-General, Western Front
6 Dec 1916:	Promoted to *Major-General*
1917 - 30 Sep 1917:	Quartermaster-General, 10th Army
30 Sep 1917 - 1917:	Chief of Staff, 10th Army
1917 - 4 Dec 1917:	Quartermaster-General, Western Front

Lieutenant-General Sergey Ivanovich **Samoylo** (4 Sep 1852 - 25 Jan 1913)
2 Apr 1902 - 21 Sep 1904:	Chief of Staff, I. Caucasus Army Corps
6 Dec 1902:	Promoted to *Major-General*
21 Sep 1904 - 8 Feb 1905:	Commander, 2nd Brigade, 20th Infantry Division
8 Feb 1905 - 10 Feb 1909:	Commander, 4th Turkestan Rifle Brigade
10 Feb 1909:	Promoted to *Lieutenant-General*
10 Feb 1909 - 1909:	Commandant of Fortress Viborg
1909:	Retired

Lieutenant-General Aleksandr Aleksandrovich **Samoylov** (19 Apr 1838 - ?)
10 Jan 1891 - 1905:	Special Assignments General, Ministry of Internal Affairs
21 Apr 1891:	Promoted to *Major-General*
14 Apr 1902:	Promoted to *Lieutenant-General*

Lieutenant-General Aleksey Aleksandrovich **Samoylov** (1 Jul 1841 - ?)
10 May 1896 - 26 Jan 1900:	Deputy Military Governor of Kutaisi
6 Dec 1897:	Promoted to *Major-General*
26 Jan 1900 - 1906:	Military Governor of Kars Region
17 Apr 1905:	Promoted to *Lieutenant-General*

Lieutenant-General Mikhail Konstantinovich **Samoylov** (19 Oct 1868 - 13 Jan 1940)
16 Jan 1913:	Promoted to *Major-General*
16 Jan 1913 - 4 Jul 1913:	Commander, 1st Brigade, 9th Siberian Rifle Division
4 Jul 1913 - 13 Apr 1915:	Commander, 2nd Detachment, Amur Military District Borderguard Corps
13 Apr 1915 - 11 Mar 1917:	Commander, 1st Amur Borderguard Infantry Division
1916:	Promoted to *Lieutenant-General*
11 Mar 1917 - 19 Jun 1917:	Commander, 194th Infantry Division
19 Jun 1917 - 7 Oct 1917:	Commander, XXXIII. Army Corps

Major-General Vladimir Konstantinovich **Samoylov** (7 Sep 1866 - 1 Feb 1916)
10 Jan 1906 - 1 Feb 1916:	Military Attaché, Japan
6 Dec 1909:	Promoted to *Major-General*

General of Cavalry Aleksandr Vasilievich **Samsonov** (2 Feb 1859 - 17 Aug 1914)
25 Jul 1896 - 15 Mar 1904:	Commandant, Elisavetgrad Cavalry School
14 Apr 1902:	Promoted to *Major-General*
15 Mar 1904 - 2 Sep 1904:	Commander, Ussuri Mounted Brigade
2 Sep 1904 - 24 Sep 1905:	Commander, Siberian Cossack Division
17 May 1905:	Promoted to *Lieutenant-General*
24 Sep 1905 - 3 Apr 1907:	Chief of Staff, Warsaw Military District
3 Apr 1907 - 17 Mar 1909:	C-in-C, Don Cossack Army
17 Mar 1909 - 19 Jul 1914:	Commanding General, Turkestan Military District, C-in-C, Semirechensk Cossack Army, Governor-General of Turkestan
6 Dec 1910:	Promoted to *General of Cavalry*
19 Jul 1914 - 17 Aug 1914:	C-in-C, 2nd Army

General of Infantry Gavriil Petrovich **Samsonov** (18 Apr 1814 - 1896)
2 May 1855 - 26 Oct 1857:	Commander, Life Guards Reserve Regiment
26 Aug 1856:	Promoted to *Major-General*
26 Oct 1857 - 2 Apr 1862:	Attached to the Guards Corps
2 Apr 1862 - 4 Aug 1864:	Deputy Commander, 22nd Infantry Division
4 Aug 1864 - 24 May 1865:	Deputy Commander, 23rd Infantry Division
24 May 1865 - 19 Feb 1877:	Commander, 25th Infantry Division
30 Aug 1865:	Promoted to *Lieutenant-General*
19 Feb 1877 - 7 Jan 1878:	Commanding General, II. Army Corps
7 Jan 1878 - 1 Jan 1881:	Transferred to the reserve
1 Jan 1881 - 1 Mar 1882:	Commandant of St. Petersburg
1 Mar 1882 - 1896:	Member, Committee for Wounded Veterans
15 May 1883:	Promoted to *General of Infantry*
12 Nov 1892 - 1896:	Director of Izmailovo Military Almshouses

Major-General Ivan Yakovlevich **Samsonov** (16 Aug 1831 - ?)
6 Dec 1904:	Promoted to *Major-General*
6 Dec 1904 - 1905:	At the disposal of the Chief of Main Cossack Directorate

Lieutenant-General of the Hydrographic Corps Konstantin Vasilyevich **Samsonov** (9 Sep 1860 - 1919)
29 Apr 1910 - 1917:	Director of Lighthouses & Navigation, Finland
10 Apr 1911:	Promoted to *Major-General of the Admiralty*
4 Feb 1913:	Redesignated *Major-General of the Hydrographic Corps*
6 Dec 1914:	Promoted to *Lieutenant-General of the Hydrographic Corps*
1917:	Chief of Main Pilotage Directorate

General of Infantry Aleksandr Genrikhovich **Sandetsky** (17 Aug 1851 - Dec 1918)
12 Apr 1895 - 12 Jul 1899:	Chief of Staff, Trans-Baikal Region
14 May 1896:	Promoted to *Major-General*
12 Jul 1899 - 25 Jan 1904:	Commander, 1st Brigade, 15th Infantry Division
25 Jan 1904 - 15 Mar 1906:	Commander, 34th Infantry Division
28 Mar 1904:	Promoted to *Lieutenant-General*
15 Mar 1906 - 24 Sep 1907:	Commanding General, Grenadier Corps
24 Sep 1907 - 7 Feb 1912:	Commanding General, Kazan Military District
18 Apr 1910:	Promoted to *General of Infantry*
7 Feb 1912 - 19 Jul 1914:	Member of the Military Council
19 Jul 1914 - 5 May 1915:	Acting Commanding General, Moscow Military District
5 May 1915 - 8 Aug 1915:	At the disposal of the Supreme Commander-in-Chief
8 Aug 1915 - 5 Mar 1917:	Commanding General, Kazan Military District
7 Mar 1917 - 27 Mar 1917:	Member of the Military Council
27 Mar 1917:	Retired

Lieutenant-General Izrayel Agaporunovich **Sandzhanov** (4 Jul 1835 - 1920)
24 Aug 1888:	Promoted to *Major-General*

24 Aug 1888 - 18 Aug 1899: Commander, 21st Artillery Brigade
18 Aug 1899: Promoted to *Lieutenant-General*
18 Aug 1899: Retired

Major-General of the Fleet Aleksandr Feliksovich **Sangovich** (30 Nov 1860 - 1923)
1908 - 1916: Commander, Imperial Yacht "Aleksandria"
6 Dec 1915: Promoted to *Major-General of the Fleet*

Lieutenant-General Aleksandr Sergeyevich **Sannikov** (18 Apr 1866 - 16 Feb 1931)
2 Apr 1910: Promoted to *Major-General*
2 Apr 1910 - 28 Feb 1913: Quartermaster-General, Amur Military District
28 Feb 1913 - 19 Aug 1913: Quartermaster-General, Odessa Military District
19 Aug 1913 - 28 Dec 1914: Chief of Staff, Amur Military District
6 Dec 1914: Promoted to *Lieutenant-General*
28 Dec 1914 - 2 Feb 1915: Chief of Staff, 2nd Army
2 Feb 1915 - 13 Apr 1917: Chief of Staff, 9th Army
13 Apr 1917 - 4 Jan 1918: Chief of Logistics, Romanian Front

General of Infantry Nikolai Ivanovich **Sannikov** (9 Nov 1837 - ?)
3 Aug 1877 - 15 Nov 1884: Commander, 48th Infantry Regiment
15 Nov 1884: Promoted to *Major-General*
15 Nov 1884 - 3 Nov 1890: General for Special Assignments, Kiev Military District
3 Nov 1890 - 30 Oct 1893: Governor of Akmola
30 Oct 1893 - 29 Dec 1902: Military Governor, Akmola Region
14 May 1896: Promoted to *Lieutenant-General*
29 Dec 1902: Promoted to *General of Infantry*
29 Dec 1902: Retired

Major-General Nikolai Sergeyevich **Sannikov** (4 Mar 1870 - Mar 1942)
28 Mar 1916 - 1 Apr 1917: Head of Administrative Department, Main Military-Technical Directorate
10 Apr 1916: Promoted to *Major-General*
1 Apr 1917 - Oct 1917: Deputy Chief of Main Military-Technical Directorate

General of Cavalry Sergey Ivanovich **Sannikov** (11 Apr 1838 - May 1920)
27 Jan 1883: Promoted to *Major-General*
27 Jan 1883 - 14 Nov 1888: Commander, 1st Brigade, 7th Cavalry Division
14 Nov 1888 - 17 Feb 1895: Commander, 2nd Brigade, 10th Cavalry Division
17 Feb 1895 - 25 Oct 1901: Commander, 11th Cavalry Division
6 Dec 1895: Promoted to *Lieutenant-General*
25 Oct 1901: Promoted to *General of Cavalry*
25 Oct 1901: Retired

Lieutenant-General Aleksey Vasilyevich **Sapozhnikov** (15 Mar 1868 - 23 Jul 1935)
15 May 1905 - 3 Aug 1914: Professor, Artillery Academy
6 Dec 1910: Promoted to *Major-General*
3 Aug 1914 - 1917: Section Chief, Central Scientific-Technical Laboratory, Ministry of War

6 Dec 1916: Promoted to *Lieutenant-General*
1917 - 1918: Professor, Artillery Academy

General of Infantry Ivan Dmitriyevich **Sapozhnikov** (11 Sep 1831 - 18 Mar 1909)
8 Oct 1879 - 3 Nov 1896: Section Chief, General Staff
30 Aug 1887: Promoted to *Major-General*
3 Nov 1896 - 21 Jun 1907: Chief Inspector of Prisoner Escort & Transport, General Staff
6 Dec 1897: Promoted to *Lieutenant-General*
21 Jun 1907: Promoted to *General of Infantry*
21 Jun 1907: Retired

Major-General Nikolai Pavlovich **Sapozhnikov** (13 Jan 1874 - 1938)
13 Jan 1916 - 7 Jun 1917: Chief of Staff, 33rd Infantry Division
6 Dec 1916: Promoted to *Major-General*
7 Jun 1917 - 25 Nov 1917: Chief of Staff, XXI. Army Corps

Vice-Admiral Aleksandr Dmitriyevich **Sapsay** (8 Mar 1860 - 1922)
18 Apr 1910: Promoted to *Rear-Admiral*
1910 - 24 Jan 1911: Chief of Staff, Black Sea Fleet
24 Jan 1911 - 11 Mar 1911: At the disposal of the Chief of the Naval General Staff
11 Mar 1911 - 15 Nov 1911: Deputy Chief of the Naval General Staff
15 Nov 1911 - 1915: Commander, Mine Training Detachment, Baltic Fleet
6 Dec 1914: Promoted to *Vice-Admiral*
1915 - 12 Apr 1917: Chief of Training Detachment, Baltic Fleet
12 Apr 1917 - 12 Dec 1917: Reserve officer, Ministry of the Navy

Lieutenant-General of the Fleet Isaak Abramovich **Sapsay** (30 May 1858 - 1920)
28 Dec 1909 - Sep 1912: Commandant, Port of Kerch
6 Dec 1910: Promoted to *Major-General of the Admiralty*
8 Apr 1913: Redesignated *Major-General of the Fleet*
1913: Promoted to *Lieutenant-General of the Fleet*
1913: Retired

Lieutenant-General Ivan Konstantinovich **Sarafov** (23 Mar 1856 - 25 Nov 1935)
1903 - 1908: Commander, 8th Bulgarian Infantry Division
1905: Promoted to *General-mayor* (Bulgarian Army)
1909 - 1913: Commander, 3rd Bulgarian Infantry Division
1913: Retired
3 Jul 1915: Transferred to the Imperial Russian Army
3 Jul 1915 - 26 Apr 1917: Commander, 103rd Infantry Division
5 Aug 1916: Promoted to *Lieutenant-General*
26 Apr 1917 - 23 Jun 1917: Commander, 101st Infantry Division
23 Jun 1917 - 1918: Commanding General, XXXII. Army Corps

Lieutenant-General Andrey Mikhailovich **Saranchev** (17 Jun 1862 - 5 Dec 1935)
11 Feb 1905: Promoted to *Major-General*
11 Feb 1905 - 1917: Director, Sumsk Cadet Corps

10 Apr 1911:   Promoted to *Lieutenant-General*
1917:   At the disposal of the Chief of Military Schools

General of Engineers Yevgraf Semyonovich **Saranchev** (10 Dec 1850 - ?)
22 Nov 1893 - 4 Aug 1899:   Commander, 1st Sapper Brigade
14 Nov 1894:   Promoted to *Major-General*
4 Aug 1899 - 24 Dec 1905:   Commandant, Nikolayev Engineering Academy
6 Dec 1902:   Promoted to *Lieutenant-General*
24 Dec 1905 - 6 Oct 1906:   Commander, 23rd Infantry Division
6 Oct 1906 - 9 May 1914:   Commanding General, XIX. Army Corps
6 Dec 1908:   Promoted to *General of Engineers*
9 May 1914:   Retired
11 Oct 1914 - 5 Dec 1917:   Recalled; Commanding General, III. Militia Corps
5 Dec 1917:   Retired

Lieutenant-General Ivan Semyonovich **Saranchov** (13 Nov 1830 - ?)
13 Jan 1885:   Promoted to *Major-General*
13 Jan 1885 - 11 Apr 1893:   Commander, 3rd Turkestan Line Brigade
11 Apr 1893 - 18 Apr 1895:   Commander, 30th Infantry Division
14 Nov 1894:   Promoted to *Lieutenant-General*

Lieutenant-General Ivan Vasilyevich **Sarandinaki** (5 Sep 1840 - 21 Oct 1915)
15 Mar 1881 - 26 Jul 1893:   Commandant of the Technical Artillery School
30 Aug 1889:   Promoted to *Major-General*
26 Jul 1893 - 1906:   Commandant, Bryansk Regional Arsenal
1906:   Promoted to *Lieutenant-General*
1906:   Retired

Admiral Vladimir Simonovich **Sarnavsky** (22 Dec 1855 - 8 Jan 1916)
1906:   Promoted to *Rear-Admiral*
10 Apr 1906 - 16 Aug 1906:   Commander, Mine Training Detachment, Baltic Sea
16 Aug 1906 - 4 Jun 1908:   Chief of Staff, Black Sea Fleet
4 Jun 1908 - 9 Oct 1909:   Commander, Black Sea Squadron
9 Oct 1909 - 7 Jun 1911:   C-in-C, Black Sea Fleet
27 Nov 1909:   Promoted to *Vice-Admiral*
30 May 1911 - 25 Apr 1913:   Commandant, Port of Sevastopol
7 Jun 1911 - 25 Apr 1913:   Governor-General of Sevastopol
11 Mar 1913 - 1917:   Member, Board of Admiralty
22 Mar 1915:   Promoted to *Admiral*

Lieutenant-General of the Fleet Vladimir Fyodorovich **Sarychev** (15 Oct 1859 - 14 Feb 1924)
1 Aug 1908 - 1914:   Commander, Libau Naval Sub-Depot
14 Apr 1913:   Promoted to *Major-General of the Fleet*
13 Jun 1917:   Promoted to *Lieutenant-General of the Fleet*
13 Jun 1917:   Retired

Major-General Eduard Iosifovich **Sassky** (16 Oct 1839 -?)
1 Aug 1888 - 23 Dec 1896: Commander, 41st Infantry Regiment
14 May 1896: Promoted to *Major-General*
23 Dec 1896 - Dec 1900: Commander, 2nd Brigade, 29th Infantry Division

Major-General Aleksandr Aleksandrovich **Satkevich** (22 Aug 1869 - 8 Jul 1938)
10 Jan 1903 - 4 Aug 1914: Professor, Nikolayev Engineering Academy
14 Apr 1913: Promoted to *Major-General*
4 Aug 1914 - Nov 1917: Commandant of Nikolayev Engineering Academy

Major-General Nikolai Porfiryevich **Savchenko** (9 May 1853 - ?)
30 May 1913 - 21 Sep 1916: Deputy Chief of Moscow Provincial Gendarmerie Administration
21 Sep 1916: Promoted to *Major-General*
21 Sep 1916: Retired

Major-General Sergey Nikolayevich **Savchenko** (18 Oct 1871 - 1963)
31 Jul 1916 - 21 May 1917: Chief of Staff, 3rd Grenadier Division
6 Dec 1916: Promoted to *Major-General*
21 May 1917 - 2 Jun 1917: Chief of Staff, XXV. Army Corps
2 Jun 1917 - 23 Oct 1917: Commander, 3rd Grenadier Division

Major-General Sevastyan Matveyevich **Savchenko** (18 Dec 1839 - ?)
5 Mar 1892 - 7 Apr 1894: Military Chief of Staff, Terek Cossack Army
30 Aug 1892: Promoted to *Major-General*
7 Apr 1894 - 1897: Commander, Light Infantry Brigade, Kuban Cossack Army

Lieutenant-General Nikolai Antonovich **Savelyev** (1 Nov 1866 - 24 May 1934)
16 Jan 1914 - 24 Jan 1916: Commander, 18th Siberian Rifle Regiment
11 Oct 1914: Promoted to *Major-General*
24 Jan 1916 - 22 Apr 1917: Commander, Brigade, 13th Siberian Rifle Division
22 Apr 1917 - 9 Sep 1917: Commander, 13th Siberian Rifle Division
9 Sep 1917 - 1918: Commanding General, XLIX. Army Corps
12 Oct 1917: Promoted to *Lieutenant-General*

Major-General Viktor Zakharovich **Savelyev** (2 Jan 1875 - 1943)
17 Oct 1915 - 12 Nov 1916: Commander, 9th Uhlan Regiment
20 Jan 1916: Promoted to *Major-General*
12 Nov 1916 - Feb 1918: Commandant, Elisavetgrad Cavalry School

Major-General Fyodor Andreyevich **Savenkov** (20 Apr 1852 - ?)
20 Jul 1895 - 26 Mar 1901: Commander, 17th Dragoon Regiment
26 Mar 1901: Promoted to *Major-General*
26 Mar 1901 - 9 Dec 1904: Commander, 1st Brigade, 10th Cavalry Division
9 Dec 1904 - Dec 1907: Commander, 1st Brigade, 4th Cavalry Division

Major-General Aleksandr Nikolayevich **Savich** (28 May 1859 - 19 Feb 1916)
5 Apr 1914: Promoted to *Major-General*
5 Apr 1914 - 18 May 1915: Commander, 29th Artillery Brigade
18 May 1915 - 19 Feb 1916: General for Assignments, Dvinsk Military District

Major-General Iosif Andrianovich **Savich** (26 Sep 1858 - ?)
27 Nov 1914 - 16 Sep 1916: Chief of Evacuation Section, Sanatory Department, Southwestern Front
16 Sep 1916: Retired
8 Oct 1916: Promoted to *Major-General*

Major-General Genrikh Aleksandrovich **Savich-Zablotsky** (13 Feb 1859 - 1920)
19 Sep 1912: Promoted to *Major-General*
19 Sep 1912 - 29 Jul 1914: Commander, 1st Brigade, 4th Infantry Division
29 Jul 1914 - 20 Jan 1915: Commander, Brigade, 42nd Infantry Division
20 Jan 1915 - 14 Sep 1915: Reserve officer, Kiev Military District
14 Sep 1915 - Oct 1917: Commander, 31st Replacement Infantry Brigade

Major-General Vasily Nikolayevich **Savinov** (7 Mar 1859 - ?)
16 Aug 1914 - 26 Apr 1916: Commander, 238th Infantry Regiment
26 Aug 1915: Promoted to *Major-General*
26 Apr 1916 - Jan 1917: Commander, Brigade, 44th Infantry Division
Jan 1917 - Oct 1917: Commander, 48th Reserve Brigade

Major-General Nikolai Kondratyevich **Savisko** (6 Dec 1852 - 7 Jan 1915)
18 Mar 1909 - 7 Jan 1915: Commandant, Lugansk Cartridge Factory
29 Mar 1909: Promoted to *Major-General*

Major-General Aleksandr Georgiyevich **Savitsky** (21 Mar 1864 - ?)
13 Nov 1913 - 18 Apr 1916: Commander, 1st Amur Cossack Regiment
6 Dec 1915: Promoted to *Major-General*
18 Apr 1916 - 23 Jun 1916: Commander, Brigade, Ussuri Cavalry Division
23 Jun 1916 - 1917: Reserve officer, Petrograd Military District
1917 - 20 Jan 1918: Inspector of Cavalry 11th Army

Lieutenant-General Ippolit Viktorovich **Savitsky** (31 Jan 1863 - 9 Oct 1941)
13 Jul 1910: Promoted to *Major-General*
13 Jul 1910 - 26 Oct 1915: Chief of Staff, II. Turkestan Army Corps
26 Oct 1915 - 12 Oct 1917: Commander, 66th Infantry Division
Apr 1917: Promoted to *Lieutenant-General*
12 Oct 1917 - Nov 1917: Commanding General, II. Turkestan Army Corps

Lieutenant-General Lyudvig Fyodorovich **Savitsky** (7 Oct 1837 - Aug 1905)
12 Mar 1887: Promoted to *Major-General*
12 Mar 1887 - 8 Jan 1897: Commander, 2nd Brigade, 38th Infantry Division
8 Jan 1897 - 1 Jan 1898: Commander, 45th Reserve Infantry Brigade
6 Dec 1897: Promoted to *Lieutenant-General*
1 Jan 1898 - 8 Apr 1904: Commander, 45th Infantry Division

8 Apr 1904 - Aug 1905: Member, Committee for Wounded Veterans

Major-General Marian Sobeslavovich **Savitsky** (2 Aug 1871 - ?)
26 Sep 1916 - 1 Oct 1917: Commander, Separate Caucasus Railway Brigade
6 Dec 1916: Promoted to *Major-General*
1 Oct 1917 - 1918: Reserve officer, Caucasus Military District

General of Infantry Mikhail Aleksandrovich **Savitsky** (8 Nov 1838 - 7 Dec 1908)
3 Apr 1885 - 7 Dec 1908: Chief of Military Topography, Grodno Province
6 Dec 1894: Promoted to *Major-General*
6 Dec 1902: Promoted to *Lieutenant-General*
1908: Promoted to *General of Infantry*

Major-General Sergey Viktorovich **Savitsky** (7 Oct 1866 - ?)
1 Mar 1915 - 1916: Chief of Legal Department, Corps of Gendarmerie
1916 - 14 Apr 1917: Chief of Gendarmerie, Moscow
10 Apr 1916: Promoted to *Major-General*
14 Apr 1917 - 1917: Reserve officer, Moscow Military District

Lieutenant-General Vasily Platonovich **Savitsky** (2 Apr 1846 - 17 Sep 1919)
6 May 1899 - 27 Apr 1910: Ataman, Yekaterinodarsk Division, Kuban Cossack Army
6 May 1901: Promoted to *Major-General*
27 Apr 1910: Promoted to *Lieutenant-General*
27 Apr 1910: Retired

Major-General Vit Stepanovich **Savitsky** (17 May 1847 - ?)
22 Sep 1895 - 16 Jan 1905: Secretary of the District Council, St. Petersburg Military District
6 Dec 1904: Promoted to *Major-General*
16 Jan 1905 - Jul 1906: At the disposal of the Commanding General, St. Petersburg Military District

Major-General Vladimir Mikhailovich **Savitsky** (26 Oct 1850 - 17 Apr 1907)
23 Dec 1902 - 28 Jun 1905: Commander, 14th East Siberian Rifle Regiment
22 Oct 1904: Promoted to *Major-General*
28 Jun 1905 - 15 Oct 1905: Commander, 1st Brigade, 47th Infantry Division
15 Oct 1905 - 17 Apr 1907: Commander, 1st Brigade, 4th East Siberian Rifle Division

Major-General Pavel Matveyevich **Savostyanov** (31 Aug 1859 - 4 Apr 1911)
16 Mar 1902 - 4 Apr 1911: Head of Izhevsk Arms Factory
13 Apr 1908: Promoted to *Major-General*

Lieutenant-General Nikolai Vasilyevich **Savoysky** (1 Dec 1854 - 1930)
31 Jul 1909 - 17 Nov 1910: Commander, 3rd Uhlan Regiment
17 Nov 1910: Promoted to *Major-General*
17 Nov 1910 - 1 Dec 1913: Commander, 2nd Brigade, 7th Cavalry Division

1 Dec 1913: Promoted to *Lieutenant-General*
1 Dec 1913: Retired

General of Artillery Anton Osipovich **Savrimovich** (9 May 1834 - ?)
5 Oct 1883 - 28 Jun 1889: Commander, West Siberian Artillery Brigade
6 May 1884: Promoted to *Major-General*
28 Jun 1889 - 15 Feb 1893: Commander, 5th Reserve Artillery Brigade
15 Feb 1893 - 29 Nov 1893: Commander of Artillery, Grenadier Corps
29 Nov 1893 - 1 Jan 1898: Commander of Artillery, Turkestan Military District
30 Aug 1894: Promoted to *Lieutenant-General*
1 Jan 1898 - 19 Jan 1898: Commander of Artillery, XX. Army Corps
19 Jan 1898 - 30 Jan 1900: Commander of Artillery, II. Army Corps
30 Jan 1900: Promoted to *General of Artillery*
30 Jan 1900: Retired

Major-General Iosif Aleksandrovich **Savrimovich** (8 Jun 1866 - 1954)
2 Mar 1912 - 13 Feb 1914: General for Assignments, Main Engineering Directorate
1913: Promoted to *Major-General*
13 Feb 1914 - Oct 1917: Chief of Fortress Section, Main Engineering Directorate
13 Mar 1914 - 1917: Member of the Fortress Commission, General Staff

General of Engineers Aleksandr Aleksandrovich **Savursky** (10 Jul 1827 - 31 Dec 1911)
17 Oct 1866 - 22 Jun 1886: Inspector of Classes, Nikolayev Academy of Engineering
30 Aug 1873: Promoted to *Major-General*
22 Jun 1886 - 31 Dec 1911: Member of the Conference, Nikolayev Academy of Engineering
30 Aug 1886: Promoted to *Lieutenant-General*
6 Dec 1904: Promoted to *General of Engineers*

Lieutenant-General Aleksandr Sergeyevich **Savvich** (29 Jan 1865 - 10 Jan 1951)
6 Sep 1914 - 4 Nov 1914: Commander, 1st Brigade, 31st Infantry Division
31 Oct 1914: Promoted to *Major-General*
4 Nov 1914 - 27 Aug 1915: Commander, 2nd Brigade, 31st Infantry Division
27 Aug 1915 - 1917: Commander, 81st Infantry Division
1917: Promoted to *Lieutenant-General*

General of Infantry Pavel Sergeyevich **Savvich** (15 Feb 1857 - ?)
12 Dec 1900: Promoted to *Major-General*
12 Dec 1900 - 10 Apr 1902: General for Special Assignments, Kiev Military District
10 Apr 1902 - 7 Sep 1903: Duty General, Kiev Military District
7 Sep 1903 - 18 Oct 1905: Governor of Kiev
18 Oct 1905 - 2 Nov 1905: Governor of Kostroma
2 Nov 1905 - 1 Jul 1906: Governor of Kiev
1 Jul 1906 - 11 Nov 1908: Chief of Staff, Irkutsk Military District
22 Apr 1907: Promoted to *Lieutenant-General*
11 Nov 1908 - 2 May 1910: Commander, 45th Infantry Division
2 May 1910 - 22 Sep 1911: Commander, 25th Infantry Division

22 Sep 1911 - 28 Dec 1913:	Commanding General, V. Siberian Army Corps
14 Apr 1913:	Promoted to *General of Infantry*
28 Dec 1913 - Oct 1917:	Member of the Military Council
Oct 1917:	Retired

General of Infantry Sergey Sergeyevich **Savvich** (1 Apr 1863 - Aug 1939)
25 Jan 1905 - 14 Oct 1907:	Chief of Staff, Special Corps of Gendarmes
6 Dec 1906:	Promoted to *Major-General*
14 Oct 1907 - 19 Dec 1908:	Commander, 1st Brigade, 42nd Infantry Division
19 Dec 1908 - 29 Dec 1909:	Chief of Staff, XXI. Army Corps
29 Dec 1909:	Promoted to *Lieutenant-General*
29 Dec 1909 - 7 Aug 1913:	Chief of Staff, Amur Military District
7 Aug 1913 - 10 Nov 1914:	Commandant of Fortress Vladivostok
7 Aug 1913 - 8 May 1915:	Commanding General, IV. Siberian Army Corps
4 Sep 1914 - 10 Nov 1914:	Acting Commanding General, Amur Military District, Acting Commander, Amur & Ussuri Cossack Army
8 May 1915 - 13 Dec 1915:	Chief of Staff, Southwestern Front
6 Dec 1915:	Promoted to *General of Infantry*
13 Dec 1915 - 8 Oct 1916:	Commanding General, XVI. Army Corps
8 Oct 1916 - 22 Oct 1916:	Commanding General, XVIII. Army Corps
22 Oct 1916 - 9 May 1917:	Chief of Logistics, Northern Front
9 May 1917:	Retired

Major-General Afanasy Semyonovich **Saychuk** (30 Jun 1858 - 15 Sep 1914)
24 Jan 1911 - 8 Jun 1914:	Commander, 203rd Infantry Regiment
16 Apr 1914:	Promoted to *Major-General*
8 Jun 1914 - 29 Jul 1914:	Unassigned
29 Jul 1914 - 18 Aug 1914:	Commander, 2nd Brigade, 1st Infantry Division
18 Aug 1914 - 15 Sep 1914:	POW, Germany

Major-General Aleksandr Aleksandrovich **Sazonov** (29 Jul 1833 - ?)
5 Oct 1882 - 1894:	Commandant, Pyrotechnical Artillery School, Member of the Artillery Committee, Main Artillery Directorate
15 May 1883:	Promoted to *Major-General*

Major-General Dmitry Petrovich **Sazonov** (28 Oct 1868 - 25 Apr 1933)
23 Sep 1915:	Promoted to *Major-General*
23 Sep 1915 - 23 Nov 1915:	Commander, Life Guards Ataman Regiment
28 Nov 1915 - Aug 1917:	General for Assignments, Don Cossack Army
Aug 1917 - Oct 1917:	Deputy Ataman, Don Cossack Army

Major-General Yakov Dmitriyevich **Sazonov** (23 Oct 1855 - 21 Apr 1913)
18 Mar 1909 - 21 Apr 1913:	Chief of Troop Billeting, Kuban
6 Jun 1913:	Posthumously promoted to *Major-General*

Major-General Mikhail Mikhailovich **Sedelnikov** (13 Nov 1859 - ?)
22 Mar 1911 - 6 Nov 1914:	Commander, 1st Battalion, 17th Artillery Brigade

2 Nov 1914: Promoted to *Major-General*
6 Nov 1914 - 18 Feb 1917: Commander, 4th Artillery Brigade
18 Feb 1917 - 1918: Inspector of Artillery, VI. Army Corps

Major-General Dmitry Karlovich **Sedergolm** (20 Feb 1869 - 1920)
21 May 1915 - 24 Apr 1917: Commander, 36th Infantry Regiment
24 Nov 1916: Promoted to *Major-General*
24 Apr 1917 - 13 Oct 1917: Reserve officer, Minsk Military District
13 Oct 1917 - 1918: Commander, Brigade, 28th Infantry Division

Lieutenant-General Karl Erikovich **Sedergolm** (25 May 1818 - 23 Mar 1903)
17 Nov 1865 - 3 Feb 1877: Chief of Fortifications Construction, Kerch
30 Aug 1869: Promoted to *Major-General*
3 Feb 1877 - 10 Dec 1882: Commandant of Fortress Kerch
30 Aug 1881: Promoted to *Lieutenant-General*
10 Dec 1882 - 26 Jul 1894: Commander of Engineers, Finland Military District
26 Jul 1894 - 23 Mar 1903: Member of the Engineering Committee, Main Engineering Directorate

Major-General Pavel Arkadyevich **Sedletsky** (25 Jun 1833 - ?)
19 Oct 1893: Promoted to *Major-General*
19 Oct 1893 - 29 Oct 1899: Commander, 8th Artillery Brigade

Major-General Boleslav Ippolitovich **Segen** (19 Oct 1861 - 1909)
6 Dec 1904 - 1909: Attached to Main Engineering Directorate
1909: Promoted to *Major-General*

Lieutenant-General Pyotr Vasilyevich **Sekerinsky** (17 Jul 1837 - 8 Apr 1907)
31 Jan 1897 - 1904 Commander of Gendarmerie, St. Petersburg Province
6 Dec 1898: Promoted to *Major-General*
1904: Promoted to *Lieutenant-General*
1904: Retired

Major-General Pyotr Ivanovich **Sekretev** (25 Feb 1877 - 28 Oct 1935)
15 Jan 1915 - Feb 1917: Commandant, Military Automotive School
22 Mar 1915: Promoted to *Major-General*

Lieutenant-General Aleksandr Fedorovich **Seletsky** (5 Jun 1856 - 24 Aug 1931)
23 Nov 1905 - Jul 1914: Military Judge, Warsaw Military District Court
6 Dec 1905: Promoted to *Major-General*
Jul 1914 - 9 Sep 1917: Military Judge, Minsk Military District Court
1917: Promoted to *Lieutenant-General*
9 Sep 1917: Dismissed

Major-General Vladimir Nilovich **Seleznev** (15 Jun 1857 - 1 Oct 1914)
2 Apr 1910 - 30 May 1912: Intendant, Omsk Military District
10 Apr 1911: Promoted to *Major-General*
30 May 1912 - 1 Oct 1914: Intendant, Caucasus Military District

Lieutenant-General Vladimir Ivanovich **Selivachev** (14 Jun 1868 - 17 Sep 1919)
2 Nov 1911 - 2 Apr 1914: Commander, 4th Finnish Rifle Regiment
22 Mar 1914: Promoted to *Major-General*
2 Apr 1914 - 12 May 1915: Commander, 4th Finnish Rifle Brigade
12 May 1915 - 6 Apr 1917: Commander, 4th Finnish Rifle Division
6 Apr 1917 - 26 Jun 1917: Commanding General, XLIX. Army Corps
22 Sep 1916: Promoted to *Lieutenant-General*
26 Jun 1917 - 9 Sep 1917: C-in-C, 7th Army
9 Sep 1917: Dismissed

General of Infantry Andrei Nikolayevich **Selivanov** (5 Aug 1847 - 15 Jul 1917)
30 Jun 1895: Promoted to *Major-General*
30 Jun 1895 - 10 Mar 1899: Quartermaster-General, Vilnius Military District
10 Mar 1899 - 4 Jul 1901: Chief of Staff, Amur Military District
31 Jan 1901: Promoted to *Lieutenant-General*
4 Jul 1901 - 24 Dec 1903: Commander, 16th Infantry Division
24 Dec 1903 - 23 Oct 1904: Commander, 13th Infantry Division
23 Oct 1904 - 18 Aug 1905: Commander, 37th Infantry Division
18 Aug 1905 - 25 Apr 1906: Commanding General, II. Combined Rifle Corps
25 Apr 1906 - 21 Jul 1910: Commanding General, Irkutsk Military District,
 Governor-General of Irkutsk,
 Military Ataman, Trans-Baikal Cossacks
6 Dec 1907: Promoted to *General of Infantry*
21 Jul 1910 - 15 Jul 1917: Member of the State Council
21 Oct 1914 - 5 Apr 1915: C-in-C, 11th Army

Major-General Vasily Ivanovich **Selivanov** (9 Jan 1852 - ?)
30 Nov 1899 - 1906: Military Commander, Bakhmut District
1906: Promoted to *Major-General*
1906: Retired

Major-General Ivan Ivanovich **Seliverstov** (3 Apr 1868 - Aug 1937)
21 Sep 1913 - 1918: Chief of Triangulation, Western Border Regions
6 Dec 1916: Promoted to *Major-General*

Major-General Vasily Petrovich **Seliverstov** (24 Feb 1867 - 1919)
21 Aug 1912 - 6 Apr 1916: Commander, Life Guards Rifle Artillery Battalion
23 Apr 1915: Promoted to *Major-General*
6 Apr 1916 - 17 Mar 1917: Commander, Life Guards Rifle Artillery Brigade
17 Mar 1917 - 1918: Inspector of Artillery, XVII. Army Corps

Major-General Aleksandr Karlovich **Sellinen** (23 Feb 1848 - Mar 1911)
11 Feb 1909: Promoted to *Major-General*
11 Feb 1910 - Mar 1911: Commander, 1st Brigade, 30th Infantry Division

Major-General Afanasy Andreyevich **Selyadtsev** (2 May 1849 - 21 Jan 1915)
11 Nov 1911 - 21 Jan 1915: Commander, 21st Infantry Regiment
13 May 1915: Posthumously promoted to *Major-General*

Lieutenant-General Yevgeny Yevstafyevich **Semashkevich** (12 Mar 1857 - ?)
6 Dec 1903:	Promoted to *Major-General*
6 Dec 1903 - 24 Jan 1907 :	Director, Simbirsk Cadet Corps
24 Jan 1907 - 1918:	Director, Vladimir-Kiev Cadet Corps
6 Dec 1909:	Promoted to *Lieutenant-General*

Major-General Andrey Ivanovich **Semashko** (18 Nov 1853 - ?)
11 Mar 1906 - 9 Mar 1912:	Military Judge, Caucasus Military District Court
2 Apr 1906:	Promoted to *Major-General*
9 Mar 1912 - 1918:	Military Judge, Odessa Military District Court

Major-General Aleksandr Konstantinovich **Semchevsky** (18 Nov 1834 - ?)
18 May 1887 - 1905:	Chief of Drawing, Main Engineering Directorate
30 Aug 1887:	Promoted to *Major-General*

Lieutenant-General Vasily Konstantinovich **Semchevsky** (1 Jan 1828 - ?)
22 Jun 1869 - 5 Sep 1878:	Commander of the Artillery Park, Caucasus Military District
1875:	Promoted to *Major-General*
5 Sep 1878 - 20 Oct 1878:	Unassigned
20 Oct 1878 - 16 Apr 1883:	Deputy Commander of Artillery, Caucasus Military District
16 Apr 1883 - 3 Apr 1886:	Commander of Artillery, I. Caucasus Army Corps
3 Apr 1886 - 4 Dec 1895:	Commander of Artillery, Caucasus Military District
30 Aug 1886:	Promoted to *Lieutenant-General*
4 Dec 1895 - 1897:	Attached to the Caucasus Military District

Major-General Filaret Lavrentyevich **Semenchuk** (17 Apr 1859 - ?)
7 Jul 1910 - 30 Aug 1913:	Deputy Commander, 36th Artillery Brigade
30 Aug 1913:	Promoted to *Major-General*
30 Aug 1913 - 6 Nov 1914:	Commander, 6th Artillery Brigade
6 Nov 1914 - 1918:	POW

General of Infantry Vladimir Savvich **Semeka** (14 Nov 1816 - 10 Apr 1897)
7 May 1856 - 11 Jan 1859:	Chief of Staff, III. Army Corps
26 Aug 1856:	Promoted to *Major-General*
11 Jan 1859 - 30 Sep 1861:	Quartermaster-General, 1st Army
30 Sep 1861:	Promoted to *Lieutenant-General*
30 Sep 1861 - 16 Apr 1872:	Commander, 6th Infantry Division
16 Apr 1872 - 11 Jan 1874:	Deputy Commanding General, Odessa Military District
5 Oct 1873:	Promoted to *General-Adjutant*
11 Jan 1874 - 1 Sep 1879:	Commanding General, Odessa Military District
1 Jan 1878:	Promoted to *General of Infantry*
1 Sep 1879 - 10 Apr 1897:	Member of the Military Council

Major-General Aleksandr Ivanovich **Semenov** (14 Aug 1853 - ?)
23 Apr 1910:	Promoted to *Major-General*
23 Apr 1910 - 25 Jul 1910:	Commander, Finland Artillery Brigade

25 Jul 1910 - 31 May 1912: Commander, 2nd Grenadier Artillery Brigade

Major-General Aleksandr Nikolayevich **Semenov** (27 Nov 1857 - 1910)
11 Jun 1901 - 1910: Intendant, Fortress Novogeorgiyevsk
6 Dec 1906: Promoted to *Major-General*

Major-General Ivan Stepanovich **Semenov** (5 Jan 1855 - ?)
26 Aug 1908 - 1913: Commander of Gendarmerie, Kurland
10 Apr 1911: Promoted to *Major-General*

Major-General Nikolai Ivanovich **Semenov** (12 Jan 1861 - ?)
25 Jun 1910: Promoted to *Major-General*
25 Jun 1910 - 18 Aug 1912: Commander, 2nd Brigade, 49th Infantry Division

Major-General Orest Lvovich **Semenov** (18 Dec 1841 - ?)
28 Oct 1895 - 1 Sep 1905: Director, Gatchina Orphan Institute
22 Jul 1899: Promoted to *Major-General*

Major-General Pavel Timofeyevich **Semenov** (12 Mar 1860 - 4 Aug 1932)
13 Apr 1912 - 1915: Chief of Bureau, Ataman of the Don Cossack Army
1915: Promoted to *Major-General*
1915: Retired

General of Artillery Sergey Semyonovich **Semenov** (23 Sep 1831 - 28 Jan 1906)
4 May 1868 - 1903: Member of the Artillery Committee, Main Artillery Directorate
1 Jan 1878: Promoted to *Major-General*
30 Aug 1888: Promoted to *Lieutenant-General*
1903: Promoted to *General of Artillery*
1903: Retired

Major-General Viktor Aleksandrovich **Semenov** (8 Oct 1856 - ?)
18 Jan 1901 - 1905: Commander, 231st Reserve Battalion
1905: Retired
1 Apr 1915 - 28 Nov 1916: Recalled; Commander, 84th State Militia Brigade
17 Jul 1916: Promoted to *Major-General*
28 Nov 1916 - 9 Feb 1917: Unassigned
9 Feb 1917: Dismissed

Major-General Vladimir Grigoryevich **Semenov** (1 Jul 1857 - Sep 1908)
30 Oct 1903 - 15 Oct 1905: Commander, 26th East Siberian Rifle Regiment
27 Jan 1905: Promoted to *Major-General*
15 Oct 1905 - 6 Jul 1906: Commander, 1st Brigade, 7th East Siberian Rifle Division
6 Jul 1906 - 14 Dec 1907: General à la suite
14 Dec 1907 - Sep 1908: Commander, 6th Turkestan Rifle Brigade

Major-General Iosif Vladimirovich **Semenov-Merlin** (22 Jul 1870 - 19 Jan 1942)
1915 - 3 Feb 1916:	Commander, 134th Infantry Regiment
27 Jan 1916:	Promoted to *Major-General*
3 Feb 1916 - 20 Aug 1916:	Commander, Brigade, 126th Infantry Division
20 Aug 1916 - 10 Jun 1917:	Commander, Life Guards 3rd Rifle Regiment
25 Apr 1917 - 10 Oct 1917:	Commander, 154th Infantry Division
10 Oct 1917 - 1918:	Commander, 125th Infantry Division

Major-General Ivan Aleksandrovich **Semensky** (18 Jul 1856 - ?)
27 Jul 1907 - 1917:	Military Commander, Eletsky District
1 Jul 1915:	Promoted to *Major-General*

Lieutenant-General Aleksandr Timofeyevich **Semplikevich** (5 Oct 1841 - ?)
1 Jan 1889 - 9 Jun 1892:	Military Judge, Kiev Military District Court
30 Aug 1891:	Promoted to *Major-General*
9 Jun 1892 - 24 Mar 1897:	Military Prosecutor, Warsaw Military District
24 Mar 1897 - 22 Feb 1898:	Military Prosecutor, Vilnius Military District
22 Feb 1898 - 1901:	Chairman of the Military Tribunal, Vilnius Military District
6 Dec 1900:	Promoted to *Lieutenant-General*

Major-General Ivan Timofeyevich **Semplikevich** (15 Sep 1842 - ?)
29 Dec 1899 - 15 Sep 1902:	Commander, 4th Artillery Brigade
9 Apr 1900:	Promoted to *Major-General*

Major-General Mikhail Konstantinovich **Semyakin** (20 Jan 1847 - 17 May 1902)
9 Apr 1896 - 9 Feb 1901:	Governor of Podolsk
10 Apr 1896:	Promoted to *Major-General*
9 Feb 1901 - 17 May 1902:	Governor of Mogilev

Major-General Viktor Vladimirovich **Senatorsky** (4 Nov 1857 - ?)
27 Jul 1916 - 1917:	Commander, 106th Artillery Brigade
26 Aug 1916:	Promoted to *Major-General*

Major-General Vladimir Ivanovich **Sencha** (9 Jul 1868 - 1 Dec 1954)
9 Jul 1912 - 5 Mar 1915:	Commander, 14th Dragoon Regiment
11 Feb 1915:	Promoted to *Major-General*
5 Mar 1915 - 25 Apr 1915:	Unassigned
25 Apr 1915 - 1 Apr 1916:	Chief of Staff, III. Cavalry Corps
1 Apr 1916 - Dec 1917:	Chief of Staff, VII. Cavalry Corps

Lieutenant-General Vasily Ivanovich **Sendetsky** (1 Jan 1838 - 17 Feb 1907)
26 Feb 1894:	Promoted to *Major-General*
26 Feb 1894 - 29 Apr 1898:	Commander, 2nd Brigade, 33rd Infantry Division
29 Apr 1898 - 28 Dec 1898:	Commander, 3rd Turkestan Brigade
28 Dec 1898 - 2 Jul 1899:	Commander, 2nd Turkestan Brigade
2 Jul 1899 - 23 Jun 1900:	Commander, Turkestan Regional Brigade
23 Jun 1900 - 9 Jun 1901:	Commander, 1st Turkestan Reserve Brigade

9 Jun 1901 - 15 Jan 1902: Transferred to the reserve
15 Jan 1902: Promoted to *Lieutenant-General*
15 Jan 1902 - 6 Sep 1904: Commander, 14th Infantry Division
6 Sep 1904 - 17 Feb 1907: Member, Committee for Wounded Veterans

Major-General Nikolai Mikhailovich **Senitsky** (4 Apr 1866 - ?)
2 Dec 1908 - 16 Nov 1913: Military Judge, Amur Military District Court
14 Apr 1913: Promoted to *Major-General*
16 Nov 1913 - 1917: Military Judge, Omsk Military District Court

General of Infantry Vikenty Vikentyevich **Sennitsky** (6 Apr 1847 - 1944)
13 May 1898: Promoted to *Major-General*
13 May 1898 - 1 Jun 1904: Commander, 2nd Brigade, 15th Infantry Division
1 Jun 1904 - 16 Jan 1906: Commander, 68th Infantry Division
6 Dec 1904: Promoted to *Lieutenant-General*
16 Jan 1906 - 15 May 1908: Commander, 32nd Infantry Division
15 May 1908 - 28 Nov 1908: Commander, 30th Infantry Division
28 Nov 1908: Promoted to *General of Infantry*
28 Nov 1908: Retired

Lieutenant-General Aleksey Ivanovich **Sensov** (2 Mar 1861 - 3 Feb 1917)
14 Apr 1913: Promoted to *Major-General*
14 Apr 1913 - 8 Jan 1914: At the disposal of the Chief of the General Staff
8 Jan 1914 - 3 Feb 1917: General for Assignments, General Staff
15 Feb 1917: Posthumously promoted to *Lieutenant-General*

Lieutenant-General Lev Sergeyevich **Senyavin** (4 May 1852 - 1913)
20 Jan 1901 - 3 Mar 1911: President of the Remount Commission, Western Steppes
1903: Promoted to *Major-General*
3 Mar 1911 - 1913: Special Assignments General to Chief of the Army Remount Administration
10 Apr 1911: Promoted to *Lieutenant-General*

Major-General Konstantin Ivanovich **Serbinovich** (21 May 1868 - 30 Jun 1932)
14 Jun 1916 - 16 Jan 1917: Chief of Staff, 104th Infantry Division
6 Dec 1916: Promoted to *Major-General*
16 Jan 1917 - 12 Jul 1917: At the disposal of the Chief of the General Staff
12 Jul 1917 - 1918: Reserve officer, Petrograd Military District

Major-General Mikhail Vladimirovich **Serdyukov** (2 Nov 1835 - ?)
16 Oct 1884 - 20 Jul 1893: Commander of Gendarmerie, Samara Province
28 Mar 1893: Promoted to *Major-General*
20 Jul 1893 - 1 Dec 1893: Commander of Gendarmerie, Olonets Province
1 Dec 1893 - 1894: Attached to Gendarmerie Command, Kiev Province

Major-General Adrian Georgiyevich **Serebrennikov** (26 Aug 1863 - ?)
28 Sep 1913 - Jul 1917: Chief of Troop Billeting, Amur Military District
6 Dec 1913: Promoted to *Major-General*

Jul 1917 - 1918: Chief of Troop Billeting, Turkestan Military District

Major-General Ivan Konstantinovich **Serebrennikov** (12 Oct 1865 - ?)
14 Sep 1912: Promoted to *Major-General*
14 Sep 1912 - 19 Jul 1914: Quartermaster-General, Moscow Military District
19 Jul 1914 - 6 Sep 1914: Quartermaster-General, 5th Army
6 Sep 1914 - 4 May 1915: General Staff officer, 5th Army
4 May 1915 - 17 Mar 1917: Chief of Staff, XXXVI. Army Corps
17 Mar 1917 - 21 Apr 1917: Commander, 191st Infantry Division
21 Apr 1917 - 29 Jan 1918: Chief of Staff, Petrograd Military District

General of Engineers Apollon Alekseyevich **Serebryakov** (23 Oct 1811 - 25 Mar 1895)
1831 - 20 Jan 1883: Attached to the Ministry of Railways
30 Aug 1858: Promoted to *Major-General*
20 May 1868: Promoted to *Lieutenant-General*
20 Jan 1883 - 25 Mar 1895: Council Member, Ministry of Railways
30 Aug 1888: Promoted to *General of Engineers*

Major-General Nikolai Akimovich **Sereda** (3 Feb 1838 - 1897)
14 Sep 1882 - 29 Jul 1891: Commander of Gendarmerie, Moscow Province
15 May 1883: Promoted to *Major-General*
29 Jul 1891 - 1897: Commander of Gendarmerie, Livonia Province

General of Artillery Aleksandr Vasilyevich **Sergeyev** (9 Mar 1853 - ?)
5 Aug 1903: Promoted to *Major-General*
5 Aug 1903 - 31 Jan 1906: Commander, 3rd Replacement Artillery Brigade
31 Jan 1906 - 27 Sep 1906: Attached to the Main Artillery Directorate
27 Sep 1906 - 3 Oct 1908: Commander, 28th Artillery Brigade
3 Oct 1908: Promoted to *Lieutenant-General*
3 Oct 1908 - 13 Jun 1914: Commander of Artillery, II. Army Corps
13 Jun 1914: Promoted to *General of Artillery*
13 Jun 1914: Retired

Major-General Georgy Fyodorovich **Sergeyev** (21 Feb 1848 - ?)
25 Mar 1905 - 24 Aug 1907: Commander, 6th Artillery Brigade
5 Jan 1906: Promoted to *Major-General*

Lieutenant-General of the Hydrographic Corps Ivan Semyonovich **Sergeyev** (14 Jun 1863 - 1919)
2 Nov 1910 - 20 Oct 1914: Chief of Arctic Ocean Hydrographic Survey
25 Mar 1912: Promoted to *Major-General of the Admiralty*
4 Feb 1913: Redesignated *Major-General of the Hydrographic Corps*
20 Oct 1914: Promoted to *Lieutenant-General of the Hydrographic Corps*
20 Oct 1914: Dismissed

Lieutenant-General of the Fleet Nikolai Mikhailovich **Sergeyev** (23 Nov 1861 - ?)
1908 - 11 Oct 1911:	Section Chief, Main Directorate of Shipbuilding
10 Apr 1911:	Promoted to *Major-General of the Admiralty*
11 Oct 1911 - 1915:	Chief of General Affairs, Main Directorate of Shipbuilding
8 Apr 1913:	Redesignated *Major-General of the Fleet*
22 Mar 1915:	Promoted to *Lieutenant-General of the Fleet*
1915 - 1917:	Inspector of Factories, Ministry of the Navy
1917:	Retired

Major-General of the Fleet Nikolai Nikolayevich **Sergeyev** (3 Aug 1871 - 6 Dec 1956)
1914 - 1917:	Vice-Chairman, Commission on Shipbuilding, Baltic Sea
6 Dec 1915:	Promoted to *Major-General of the Fleet*
1917:	Retired

Major-General Pavel Aleksandrovich **Sergeyev** (15 Feb 1870 - ?)
31 Jul 1912 - 1917:	Deputy Intendant, St. Petersburg Military District
10 Apr 1916:	Promoted to *Major-General*

Major-General of the Fleet Vladimir Nikolayevich **Sergeyev** (18 Mar 1864 - Sep 1918)
19 Jun 1912 - 1917:	Senior Deputy Commandant, Port of Kronstadt
22 Mar 1915:	Promoted to *Major-General of the Fleet*
1917:	Retired

Major-General Vladimir Petrovich **Sergeyev** (13 Jan 1861 - ?)
18 Aug 1915 - 1 Aug 1916:	Reserve officer, Kiev Military District
23 Nov 1915:	Promoted to *Major-General*
1 Aug 1916 - Oct 1917:	Commander, 1st Rifle Artillery Brigade

Lieutenant-General Vladimir Vladimirovich **Sergeyevsky** (9 Feb 1838 - ?)
26 Feb 1894:	Promoted to *Major-General*
26 Feb 1894 - 30 Jan 1897:	Commander, 1st Brigade, 38th Infantry Division
30 Jan 1897 - 9 Feb 1900:	Commander, 2nd Brigade, 38th Infantry Division
9 Feb 1900:	Promoted to *Lieutenant-General*
9 Feb 1900:	Retired

Major-General Nikolai Ivanovich **Sergiyevich** (27 Oct 1845 - ?)
3 Sep 1900 - 1905:	Director, Volsk Military School
1 Jan 1901:	Promoted to *Major-General*

Major-General Dmitry Dmitriyevich **Sergiyevsky** (10 Mar 1867 - 4 Jun 1920)
14 Jan 1911 - 4 Nov 1914:	Professor, Nikolayev Military Academy
14 Apr 1913:	Promoted to *Major-General*
4 Nov 1914 - 19 Feb 1915:	Special Assignments General, Logistics Department, Southwestern Front
19 Feb 1915 - 22 Sep 1917:	Chief of Bureau to Head of Logistics Department, Southwestern Front

22 Sep 1917 - 1919: Professor of Geodesy, General Staff Academy

Lieutenant-General Sigizmund Faddeyevich **Serzhpinsky** (4 Jun 1838 - ?)
16 Apr 1889: Promoted to *Major-General*
16 Apr 1889 - 20 Feb 1890: Commander, 1st Brigade, 3rd Infantry Division
20 Feb 1890 - 6 Sep 1899: Commander, 1st Brigade, 37th Infantry Division
6 Sep 1899 - 1905: Commander, Kharkov Regional Brigade
1 Apr 1901: Promoted to *Lieutenant-General*

Lieutenant-General Vasily Nikolayevich **Sevastyanov** (29 May 1852 - ?)
17 Feb 1900 - 12 Feb 1904: Commander, 2nd East Siberian Artillery Brigade
31 Jan 1901: Promoted to *Major-General*
12 Feb 1904 - 4 Oct 1906: Chief of Artillery, Kwantung Region
4 Oct 1906 - 28 Jan 1910: Commander of Artillery, Amur Military District
22 Apr 1907: Promoted to *Lieutenant-General*
28 Jan 1910: Retired

Major-General Konstantin Georgiyevich **Sezenevsky** (20 May 1853 - 15 Nov 1913)
? - 1908: Commander, 219th Reserve Infantry Regiment
1908: Promoted to *Major-General*
1908: Retired

Major-General Vasily Nikitich **Shabanov** (6 Mar 1857 - 23 Jun 1913)
24 Mar 1913 - 23 Jun 1913: Deputy Chief of Topographical Section, Amur Military District
22 Aug 1913: Posthumously promoted to *Major-General*

Lieutenant-General Pavel Nikolayevich **Shabelsky** (11 Oct 1860 - 1935)
17 Jul 1905 - 25 Mar 1906: Staff Officer for Special Assignments to the Governor-General of Finland
1905: Promoted to *Major-General*
25 Mar 1906 - 6 Jun 1907: Special Assignments General to the Minister of Internal Affairs
6 Jun 1907 - 27 May 1917: At the disposal of the Minister of Internal Affairs
6 Dec 1913: Promoted to *Lieutenant-General*
27 May 1917: Dismissed

Major-General Leonid Viktorovich **Shadursky** (29 Dec 1846 - ?)
1 Jul 1886 - 1894: Military Judge, Turkestan Military District Court
30 Aug 1892: Promoted to *Major-General*

Lieutenant-General Adolf Vilgelmovich von **Shak** (27 Nov 1828 - 22 Aug 1897)
28 Jul 1877: Promoted to *Major-General*
28 Jul 1877 - 2 Sep 1882: Commander, 2nd Brigade, Caucasus Grenadier Division
2 Sep 1882 - 20 Dec 1884: Commander, 2nd Brigade, 19th Infantry Division
20 Dec 1884 - 17 Jul 1893: Commander, 39th Infantry Division
30 Aug 1886: Promoted to *Lieutenant-General*
17 Jul 1893 - 22 Aug 1897: Commanding General, VIII. Army Corps

Major-General Nikita Grigoryevich **Shakhnazarov** (1 Oct 1837 - ?)
31 May 1893: Promoted to *Major-General*
31 May 1893 - 19 Sep 1898: Commander, 1st Brigade, 25th Infantry Division

Major-General Prince Nikolai Dmitriyevich **Shakhovskoy** (1844 - ?)
30 Aug 1894: Promoted to *Major-General*
30 Aug 1894 - 1895: Section Chief, Main Directorate for Cossack Forces

Rear-Admiral Prince Yakov Ivanovich **Shakhovskoy** (1846 - 1899)
1897: Promoted to *Rear-Admiral*
1897 - 1899: Commander, Guards Naval Depot

Major-General Vladislav Adolfovich **Shalevich** (10 Jun 1872 - 26 Aug 1914)
? - 26 Aug 1914: Commander, Battalion, Life Guards Moscow Regiment
26 Jun 1916: Posthumously promoted to *Major-General*

General of Infantry Mikhail Yakovlevich **Shalikov** (12 Nov 1831 - 21 Oct 1909)
20 Apr 1877 - 17 May 1878: Chief of Staff, Caucasus Military District
15 Jun 1877: Promoted to *Major-General*
17 May 1878 - 7 Sep 1878: Commander, Consolidated Kutaisi & Gori Infantry Brigade
7 Sep 1878 - 22 Mar 1880: At the disposal of the C-in-C, Caucasus Army
22 Mar 1880 - 22 Dec 1890: Governor of Erivan
30 Aug 1886: Promoted to *Lieutenant-General*
22 Dec 1890 - 30 May 1898: Military Governor of Kutaisi
30 May 1898 - 24 Nov 1898: At the disposal of the Commanding General, Caucasus Military District
24 Nov 1898 - 1905: At the disposal of the Commanding General, Vilnius Military District
1905: Promoted to *General of Infantry*
1905: Retired

Major-General Iosif Lyudvigovich **Shamota** (18 Sep 1857 - 1942)
16 Jul 1910 - 28 Jul 1913: Commander, 2nd Siberian Rifle Regiment
28 Jul 1913: Promoted to *Major-General*
28 Jul 1913 - 11 Sep 1917: Commander, 1st Brigade, 2nd Siberian Rifle Division
11 Sep 1917 - May 1918: Commander, Polish Rifle Division

General of the Admiralty Fridrikh Sevastyanovich von **Shants** (17 Dec 1836 - 1907)
1889: Promoted to *Rear-Admiral*
1890 - 1893: Captain, Port of Kronstadt
1893 - 1898: Junior Flagman, Baltic Sea Training Squadron
1896: Promoted to *Vice-Admiral*
1898 - 1905: Chairman of the Board, Obukhov Steelworks
1905: Promoted to *General of the Admiralty*
1905: Retired

Lieutenant-General Valerian Vasilyevich **Shapko** (1 Dec 1844 - 22 Mar 1915)
15 May 1900 - 1909:	Military Judge, Warsaw Military District Court
6 Dec 1901:	Promoted to *Major-General*
1905:	Military Judge, 3rd Manchurian Army Court
1909:	Promoted to *Lieutenant-General*
1909:	Retired

Lieutenant-General Konstantin Vasilyevich **Sharngorst** (27 Feb 1846 - 4 May 1908)
11 Jun 1881 - 3 May 1897:	Deputy Chief of Cartography Subsection, Military Topographical Section, General Staff
19 Mar 1882 - 4 May 1908:	Professor, Nikolayev General Staff Academy
30 Aug 1885:	Promoted to *Major-General*
14 May 1896:	Promoted to *Lieutenant-General*
3 May 1897 - 4 May 1908:	Map Editor, Military Topographical Section, General Staff

Lieutenant-General of the Fleet Spiridon Andreyevich **Sharygin** (12 Dec 1856 - ?)
1 Aug 1908 - 1914:	Commander, Black Sea Naval Depot
18 Apr 1910:	Promoted to *Major-General of the Admiralty*
8 Apr 1913:	Redesignated *Major-General of the Fleet*
1914:	Promoted to *Lieutenant-General of the Fleet*
1914:	Retired

Major-General Aleksandr Vladimirovich **Shashurin** (26 Jan 1852 - 8 Jul 1907)
4 Jan 1901:	Promoted to *Major-General*
4 Jan 1901 - 28 Apr 1903:	Commander, 3rd Artillery Brigade

General of Infantry Nikolai Pavlovich **Shatilov** (31 Jan 1849 - 1919)
23 Nov 1889 - 9 Dec 1896:	Commandant, Moscow Infantry Cadet School
30 Aug 1894:	Promoted to *Major-General*
9 Dec 1896 - 28 Aug 1899:	Director, 3rd Moscow Cadet Corps
28 Aug 1899 - 24 Nov 1901:	Commandant, Pavlovsk Military School
24 Nov 1901 - 10 Dec 1902:	Commander, 4th Infantry Division
6 Dec 1901:	Promoted to *Lieutenant-General*
10 Dec 1902 - 29 Jan 1906:	Commander, 10th Infantry Division
29 Jan 1906 - 15 Jan 1907:	Chief of Staff, Caucasus Military District
15 Jan 1907 - 24 Dec 1913:	Deputy Military Governor of the Caucasus
13 Apr 1908:	Promoted to *General of Infantry*
24 Dec 1913 - 1 May 1917:	Member of the State Council
1 May 1917 - Dec 1917:	Unassigned
Dec 1917:	Retired

Major-General Nikolai Petrovich **Shatilov** (19 Feb 1850 - ?)
27 Feb 1908:	Promoted to *Major-General*
27 Feb 1908 - 21 Dec 1908:	Commander, 4th Artillery Brigade

General of Infantry Vladimir Pavlovich **Shatilov** (15 May 1855 - 28 Nov 1928)
1 Oct 1899 - 25 Mar 1904:	Commander, 31st Infantry Regiment

25 Mar 1904:	Promoted to *Major-General*
25 Mar 1904 - 22 Sep 1904:	Commander, 2nd Brigade, 1st Siberian Infantry Division
22 Sep 1904 - 13 Dec 1906:	Commander, 2nd Brigade, 9th Infantry Division
13 Dec 1906 - 3 Dec 1908:	Commander, 7th Turkestan Rifle Brigade
3 Dec 1908:	Promoted to *Lieutenant-General*
3 Dec 1908 - 13 Dec 1911:	Commander, 2nd East Siberian Rifle Division
13 Dec 1911 - 1 May 1913:	Commander, 20th Infantry Division
1 May 1913 - 8 Jun 1915:	Commander, Caucasus Grenadier Division
8 Jun 1915 - 3 Sep 1915:	Reserve officer, Kiev Military District
3 Sep 1915 - 23 Feb 1916:	Reserve officer, Petrograd Military District
23 Feb 1916 - 22 Jan 1917:	Commanding General, XXXIV. Army Corps
10 Apr 1916:	Promoted to *General of Infantry*
22 Jan 1917 - 8 Feb 1917:	Reserve officer, Kiev Military District
8 Feb 1917 - 15 Apr 1917:	Reserve officer, Petrograd Military District
15 Apr 1917:	Retired

Major-General Nikolai Vladislavovich **Shatkovsky** (9 May 1872 - 14 Feb 1944)
1915 - 10 Jul 1916:	Commander, 52nd Infantry Regiment
15 Aug 1915:	Promoted to *Major-General*
10 Jul 1916 - Oct 1917:	Commander, 1st Brigade, 9th Infantry Division
Oct 1917 - 1918:	Commander, 19th Infantry Division

Lieutenant-General Mikhail Konstantinovich **Shatlev** (6 Nov 1838 - 27 Mar 1899)
10 May 1893:	Promoted to *Major-General*
10 May 1893 - 1898:	Commander of Dvinsk Artillery Depot, Vilnius Military District
1898:	Promoted to *Lieutenant-General*
1898:	Retired

Lieutenant-General Pavel Vasilyevich **Shatov** (6 Jan 1852 - ?)
26 Aug 1898 - 14 May 1910:	Commander of Gendarmerie, Ufa Province
6 Apr 1903:	Promoted to *Major-General*
14 May 1910:	Promoted to *Lieutenant-General*
14 May 1910:	Retired

Lieutenant-General Nikolai Konstantinovich **Shaufus** (**Schaffhausen-Schönberg-Eck-Schaufuss**) (7 Dec 1846 - 29 Nov 1911)
1 Nov 1899 - 1905:	Chief of the Nikolayev Railway
1 Feb 1900 - 1905:	Member of the Engineering Committee, Main Engineering Directorate
1 Apr 1901:	Promoted to *Major-General*
1905 - 25 Apr 1906:	Chief of Railway Department, Ministry of Communications
25 Apr 1906:	Promoted to *Lieutenant-General*
25 Apr 1906 - 11 Feb 1909:	Minister of Railways

Lieutenant-General Fyodor Oskarovich **Shauman** (29 Jul 1844 - 16 Sep 1911)
7 Nov 1885 - 4 Dec 1888:	Attached to the Minister of War

30 Aug 1886:	Promoted to *Major-General*
4 Dec 1888 - 3 Nov 1894:	Chief of Staff to the Governor-General of Finland
3 Nov 1894 - Dec 1898:	Commander, Vaasa Province
14 May 1896:	Promoted to *Lieutenant-General*
Dec 1898 - 1900:	Member of the Economic Department, Imperial Finnish Senate
24 Feb 1899:	Renamed *Privy Councillor*
1900:	Retired

Protopresbyter Georgy Ivanovich **Shavelsky** (6 Jan 1871 - 2 Oct 1951)
22 Apr 1911:	Promoted to *Protopresbyter*
22 Apr 1911 - 1917:	Chief, Directorate of the Orthodox Army and Naval Chaplaincy

Major-General Boris Vladimirovich **Shavrov** (4 Mar 1870 - ?)
4 Jun 1912 - Jul 1914:	Military Prosecutor, Vilnius Military District
6 Dec 1912:	Promoted to *Major-General*
Jul 1914 - 19 Sep 1915:	Military Prosecutor, Dvinsk Military District
19 Sep 1915 - 28 Apr 1917:	Chief of Military Legal Section, Northern Front
28 Apr 1917 - 1918:	Chairman of the Military Tribunal, Dvinsk Military District

Major-General Nikolai Rafailovich **Shavrov** (4 Jul 1857 - ?)
20 Aug 1905 - 1917:	Military Commander, Baku District
14 Apr 1913:	Promoted to *Major-General*

Major-General Yevgeny Dmitriyevich **Shaytanov** (5 Mar 1847 - ?)
20 Nov 1903:	Promoted to *Major-General*
20 Nov 1903 - 4 Feb 1904:	Unassigned
4 Feb 1904 - 1905:	Ataman, 2nd Military Division, Siberian Cossack Army

Lieutenant-General Vasily Vasilyevich **Shchagin** (23 Jan 1848 - ?)
16 Mar 1900:	Promoted to *Major-General*
16 Mar 1900 - 15 Nov 1903:	Commander, 2nd Brigade, 30th Infantry Division
15 Nov 1903 - 17 Feb 1907:	Commander, 59th Replacement Infantry Brigade
17 Feb 1907 - 11 Sep 1907:	Commander, 26th Infantry Division
22 Apr 1907:	Promoted to *Lieutenant-General*

Lieutenant-General Mikhail Mikhailovich **Shchastny** (23 Jul 1846 - 5 May 1918)
15 Oct 1902 - 9 Jul 1906:	Commandant, Kiev Artillery Depot
6 Dec 1902:	Promoted to *Major-General*
9 Jul 1906 - Jul 1908:	Deputy Commander of Artillery, Kiev Military District
Jul 1908:	Promoted to *Lieutenant-General*
Jul 1908:	Retired

Major-General Konstantin Fodorovich **Shchedrin** (21 Feb 1867 - 1941)
3 Mar 1911 - 15 Apr 1915:	Commander, 33rd Infantry Regiment
12 Dec 1914:	Promoted to *Major-General*

15 Apr 1915 - 26 Jun 1915:   Chief of Staff, XVIII. Army Corps
26 Jun 1915 - 21 Feb 1917:   Chief of Staff, XII. Army Corps
21 Feb 1917 - Oct 1917:   Commander, 164th Infantry Division

Major-General Vladimir Ivanovich **Shcheglov** (15 Feb 1864 - ?)
3 Apr 1912:   Promoted to *Major-General*
3 Apr 1912 - 22 Jul 1913:   Commander of Engineers, Fortress Ivangorod
22 Jul 1913 - Oct 1917:   Commander of Engineers, Tsar Peter the Great Naval Fortress

Vice-Admiral Eduard Nikolayevich **Shchensnovich** (25 Dec 1852 - 20 Dec 1910)
1905:   Promoted to *Rear-Admiral*
1905 - 19 Mar 1906:   Junior Flagman, Baltic Fleet
19 Mar 1906 - 1908:   Commander, Submarine Training Detachment, Baltic Fleet
1908 - 1909:   Commander, Mine Training Detachment
1908:   Promoted to *Vice-Admiral*
1908 - 20 Dec 1910:   Member of the Admiralty Board

Major-General Arkady Vladimirovich **Shcherbachev** (22 Nov 1873 - 23 Apr 1916)
25 Aug 1915 - 23 Apr 1916:   Commander, 40th Infantry Regiment
12 Jun 1916:   Posthumously promoted to *Major-General*

General of Infantry Dmitry Grigoryevich **Shcherbachev** (6 Feb 1857 - 18 Jan 1932)
10 May 1903:   Promoted to *Major-General*
10 May 1903 - 23 Jun 1906:   Commander, Pavlovsky Life Guards Regiment
23 Jun 1906 - 24 Jan 1907:   Commander, 1st Finnish Rifle Brigade
24 Jan 1907 - 14 Dec 1912:   Commandant, Imperial Military Academy
29 Nov 1908:   Promoted to *Lieutenant-General*
14 Dec 1912 - 5 Apr 1915:   Commanding General, IX. Army Corps
6 Dec 1914:   Promoted to *General of Infantry*
5 Apr 1915 - 19 Oct 1915 :   C-in-C, 11th Army
19 Oct 1915 - 11 Apr 1917:   C-in-C, 7th Army
7 Nov 1915:   Promoted to *General-Adjutant*
11 Apr 1917 - 25 Mar 1918:   Deputy C-in-C, Romanian Front

Lieutenant-General Nikolai Vladimirovich **Shcherbakov** (11 Jul 1842 - ?)
3 Apr 1881 - 29 Oct 1893:   Attached to the Customs Department, Ministry of Finance
22 Jan 1893:   Promoted to *Major-General*
29 Oct 1893 - 19 May 1895:   General for Assignments, Separate Borderguard Corps
19 May 1895 - 2 Jan 1898:   General for Assignments, Military-Judicial Department
2 Jan 1898 - 1911:   Chief of Military-Judicial Department, Borderguard Corps
1 Apr 1901:   Promoted to *Lieutenant-General*

Major-General Pyotr Sergeyevich **Shcherbakov** (10 Jan 1849 - ?)
14 Sep 1900:   Promoted to *Major-General*

14 Sep 1900 - 30 Apr 1905: Commander, 2nd Brigade, 1st Turkestan Cossack Division

General of Infantry Prince Aleksandr Petrovich **Shcherbatov** (1836 - ?)
Jan 1867 - 4 Aug 1977: Governor of Kalisz
21 Sep 1868: Promoted to *Major-General*
4 Aug 1877 - 2 Sep 1877: Commander, 2nd Brigade, 1st Grenadier Division
2 Sep 1877 - 3 Jun 1878: Attached to the C-in-C, Caucasus Army
8 Feb 1879 - 3 Jul 1884: Attached to St. Petersburg Military District
11 Jun 1886 - 20 Jan 1888: At the disposal of the Chief of the General Staff
20 Jan 1888 - 1 Jan 1898: Commander, 26th Infantry Division
30 Aug 1888: Promoted to *Lieutenant-General*
1 Jan 1898 - 4 Jul 1902: Commanding General, II. Army Corps
6 Dec 1899: Promoted to *General of Infantry*
4 Jul 1902 - 1904: Attached to the General Staff

Major-General Ivan Nikolayevich **Shcherbina** (7 Jan 1856 - ?)
17 Oct 1911 - 24 Aug 1912: Commandant, Irkutsk Artillery Depot
6 Dec 1911: Promoted to *Major-General*
24 Aug 1912 - 27 Oct 1912: Commandant, Tomylovsk Artillery Depot
27 Oct 1912 - 31 Dec 1913: Commandant, Kremenchug Artillery Depot
31 Dec 1913 - 1917: Deputy Commander of Artillery, Amur Military District
1917: Commander of Artillery, Amur Military District

General of Infantry Pavel Osipovich **Shcherbov-Nefedovich** (15 Feb 1847 - 9 Jan 1918)
23 May 1882 - 21 Sep 1894: Professor, General Staff Academy
30 Aug 1889: Promoted to *Major-General*
22 Jan 1890 - 5 May 1892: Deputy Chief of Bureau, Ministry of War
5 May 1892 - 8 Sep 1892: Commander, Brigade, 15th Infantry Division
8 Sep 1892 - 21 Jan 1897: Deputy Chief of Bureau, Ministry of War
21 Jan 1897 - 30 Jan 1907: Chief of Main Cossack Directorate
6 Dec 1897: Promoted to *Lieutenant-General*
6 Dec 1906: Promoted to *General of Infantry*
30 Jan 1907 - 9 Jan 1918: Member of the Military Council

Lieutenant-General Olgerd Karlovich **Shcherbovich-Vechor** (18 Feb 1843 - 13 Apr 1908)
12 Aug 1888 - 3 Sep 1901: Military Prosecutor, Caucasus Military District
30 Aug 1892: Promoted to *Major-General*
3 Sep 1901 - 3 Oct 1905: Chairman of the Military Tribunal, Siberian Military District
6 Dec 1901: Promoted to *Lieutenant-General*
3 Oct 1905 - 13 Jan 1907: Chairman of the Military Tribunal, Caucasus Military District
13 Jan 1907 - 13 Apr 1908: Member, Supreme Military Tribunal

Lieutenant-General Aleksandr Nikolayevich **Shchetinin** (20 Aug 1832 - 1913)
17 Apr 1890 - 4 Sep 1893: Commander of Gendarmerie, Tomsk Province
30 Aug 1890: Promoted to *Major-General*

4 Sep 1893 - 1896:	Commander of Gendarmerie, Vologodsk Province
1896:	Promoted to *Lieutenant-General*
1896:	Retired

Lieutenant-General Orest Vasilyevich **Shchetinin** (12 Dec 1836 - 11 Mar 1898)
14 Jan 1884:	Promoted to *Major-General*
14 Jan 1884 - 28 Apr 1887:	Deputy Chief of Staff, Omsk Military District
28 Apr 1887 - 23 Jan 1891:	Military Governor of Semipalatinsk
23 Jan 1891 - 13 Sep 1894:	Commandant of Fortress Bender
30 Aug 1894:	Promoted to *Lieutenant-General*
13 Sep 1894 - 11 Mar 1898:	Commandant of Fortress Ochakov

Lieutenant-General Nikolai Iosifovich **Shchetkin** (8 Apr 1860 - 2 Jan 1927)
25 Jun 1905 - 9 Mar 1909:	Chief of Geodesical Section, Military Topographical Directorate, General Staff
13 Apr 1908:	Promoted to *Major-General*
9 Mar 1909 - 1918:	Chief of Military Topographical Section, Caucasus Military District
14 Sep 1917:	Promoted to *Lieutenant-General*

Major-General of the Fleet Mikhail Borisovich **Shchigolev** (1 Dec 1863 - 18 Sep 1935)
1904 - 1917:	Commander of Mines, Port of Sevastopol
6 Apr 1914:	Promoted to *Major-General of the Fleet*

Major-General Vladimir Ivanovich **Shchigrovsky** (31 Dec 1859 - Mar 1917)
16 Jan 1913 - 5 Jun 1914:	Special Assignments General, Viceroy of the Caucasus
14 Apr 1913:	Promoted to *Major-General*
5 Jun 1914 - 6 Nov 1914:	Special Assignments General, Caucasus Military District
6 Nov 1914 - Mar 1917:	Reserve officer, Caucasus Military District

Major-General Boris Iosifovich **Shchutskoy** (11 Apr 1870 - 9 Apr 1964)
23 Feb 1913 - 5 Feb 1915:	Commander, 42nd Siberian Rifle Regiment
5 Feb 1915 - 21 Nov 1916:	Chief of Lines of Communication Section, 1st Army
23 Mar 1915:	Promoted to *Major-General*
21 Nov 1916 - 25 Mar 1917:	Commander, 3rd Caucasus Rifle Division
25 Mar 1917 - 1918:	Reserve officer, Odessa Military District

Lieutenant-General Mikhail Maksimovich **Shchutsky** (3 Sep 1844 - 17 Apr 1916)
9 Aug 1878 - 1899:	Military Judge, Moscow Military District Court
30 Aug 1888:	Promoted to *Major-General*
1899:	Promoted to *Lieutenant-General*
1899:	Retired

Major-General of Naval Engineers Mikhail Vasilyevich **Shebalin** (20 Sep 1866 - ?)
1914:	Promoted to *Major-General of Naval Engineers*
1914 - Sep 1915:	Chief Naval Engineer, Baltic Fleet

Lieutenant-General Apollon Grigoryevich **Shebanov** (1840 - ?)
13 Dec 1886:	Promoted to *Major-General*
13 Dec 1886 - 7 May 1892:	Attached to the Ministry of War
7 May 1892 - 23 Feb 1893:	At the disposal of the Chief of the General Staff
23 Feb 1893 - 22 Nov 1893:	Deputy Chief of Staff, Irkutsk Military District
22 Nov 1893 - 1896:	Chief of Staff, Irkutsk Military District
14 May 1896:	Promoted to *Lieutenant-General*

Lieutenant-General Lev Ivanovich **Shebeko** (18 Feb 1860 - ?)
28 Feb 1908 - 4 Jun 1912:	Military Judge, St. Petersburg Military District Court
13 Apr 1908:	Promoted to *Major-General*
4 Jun 1912 - 16 Nov 1913:	Military Prosecutor, St. Petersburg Military District Court
16 Nov 1913 - 22 Apr 1917:	Chief of Military Prison Section, Main Directorate of Military Justice
6 Dec 1914:	Promoted to *Lieutenant-General*
22 Apr 1917:	Dismissed

General of Cavalry Nikolai Ignatyevich **Shebeko** (15 Dec 1834 - 24 Dec 1904)
3 Jun 1871 - 27 Feb 1879:	Governor of Bessarabia
1 Jan 1878:	Promoted to *Major-General*
27 Feb 1879 - 11 Feb 1887:	Attached to the Ministry of Internal Affairs
11 Feb 1887 - 6 Apr 1887:	Attached to the Ministry of War
6 Apr 1887:	Promoted to *Lieutenant-General*
6 Apr 1887 - 22 Jul 1895:	Deputy Minister of Internal Affairs, Chief of Police, Commanding General, Corps of Gendarmerie
22 Jul 1895 - Sep 1904:	Member of the State Council, Senator
18 Apr 1899:	Promoted to *General of Cavalry*

Major-General Vadim Nikolayevich **Shebeko** (11 Jul 1864 - 12 Nov 1943)
25 Feb 1913 - 18 Oct 1913:	Deputy Governor of Saratov
14 Apr 1913:	Promoted to *Major-General*
18 Oct 1913 - 17 Feb 1916:	Governor of Grodno
17 Feb 1916 - 29 Apr 1917:	Mayor of Moscow
29 Apr 1917:	Retired

Major-General Ali Davletovich **Sheikhaliev** (Sheikh-Ali) (8 Oct 1845 - ?)
10 Jan 1900:	Promoted to *Major-General*
10 Jan 1900 - 31 Oct 1900:	Commander, 2nd Brigade, 1st Caucasus Cossack Division
31 Oct 1900:	Retired

Lieutenant-General Pyotr Konstantinovich **Shein** (23 Mar 1848 - ?)
29 Mar 1896 - 22 May 1898:	Commander, Gordzhinskoy Borderguard Brigade
22 May 1898 - 28 Jul 1906:	Commander, Aleksandrov Borderguard Brigade
14 Apr 1902:	Promoted to *Major-General*

28 Jul 1906 - 1909: Commanding General, 6th Borderguard District
13 Apr 1908: Promoted to *Lieutenant-General*

Major-General Fyodor Petrovich **Shelekhov** (11 Dec 1862 - 1937)
23 Feb 1913 - 8 Jun 1915: Special Assignments General, Main Intendant Directorate
8 Jun 1915 - 1917: Intendant, Amur Military District
6 Dec 1915: Promoted to *Major-General*

General of Infantry Ivan Yakovlevich **Shelkovnikov** (1 Apr 1836 - 2 Oct 1901)
27 Jan 1876 - 20 Apr 1885: Commander, 70th Infantry Regiment
15 May 1883: Promoted to *Major-General*
20 Apr 1885 - 30 Aug 1891: Commander, 1st Brigade, 17th Infantry Division
30 Aug 1891 - 28 Apr 1894: Commander, 9th Regional Brigade
28 Apr 1894 - 7 Aug 1900: Commander, 7th Infantry Division
30 Aug 1894: Promoted to *Lieutenant-General*
7 Aug 1900: Promoted to *General of Infantry*
7 Aug 1900: Retired

General of Engineers Nil Nikolayevich **Shelkovnikov** (14 Aug 1851 - ?)
11 Jan 1900 - 24 Jun 1910: Commander of Engineers, Fortress Kaunas
6 Dec 1901: Promoted to *Major-General*
24 Jun 1910 - 22 Oct 1912: Commander of Engineers, Moscow Military District
6 Dec 1910: Promoted to *Lieutenant-General*
22 Oct 1912 - 31 Dec 1913: Chief of Troop Billeting, Moscow Military District
31 Dec 1913: Promoted to *General of Engineers*

Major-General Vladimir Yakovlevich **Shelkovnikov** (21 Apr 1835 - ?)
13 May 1886: Promoted to *Major-General*
13 May 1886 - 14 Feb 1894: Commander, 2nd Brigade, 1st Infantry Division
14 Feb 1894 - 1899: Commander, 54th Reserve Infantry Brigade

Lieutenant-General of the Admiralty Nikolai Nikolayevich **Sheman** (31 May 1847 - ?)
12 Nov 1894 - 1909: Director of Navigation & Lighthouses, Finland
6 Dec 1899: Promoted to *Major-General of the Admiralty*
6 Dec 1906: Promoted to *Lieutenant-General of the Admiralty*

Major-General Viktor Yakovlevich **Shemanin** (6 Oct 1845 - ?)
23 Dec 1898 - 1903: Commander of Gendarmerie, Nizhegorod Province
6 Dec 1899: Promoted to *Major-General*

Lieutenant-General of Naval Artillery Mikhail Zakharovich **Shemanov** (8 Oct 1862 - ?)
1 Jan 1908 - 1917: Member of the Board, Obukhov and Izhora Steelworks
6 Dec1910: Promoted to *Major-General of Naval Artillery*
6 Dec 1915: Promoted to *Lieutenant-General of Naval Artillery*

Major-General Anatoly Dmitriyevich **Shemansky** (18 Nov 1868 - 1942)
4 Jul 1913 - 1915: Deputy Chief Editor of "Military Collection" and

	"Russian Invalid"
22 Mar 1915:	Promoted to *Major-General*
1915 - Jul 1915:	Acting Chief Editor of "Military Collection" and "Russian Invalid"
Jul 1915 - 12 Jul 1916:	Deputy Chief Editor of "Military Collection" and "Russian Invalid"
12 Jul 1916 - 8 Feb 1917:	Chief of Staff, 11th Infantry Division
8 Feb 1917 - 19 Jun 1917:	Chief of Staff, XLVI. Army Corps
19 Jun 1917 - 1918:	Chief of Staff, XI. Army Corps

Major-General Konstantin Yakovlevich **Shemyakin** (6 May 1864 - 1927)
13 Jul 1910:	Promoted to *Major-General*
13 Jul 1910 - 30 Aug 1914:	Chief of Staff, XX. Army Corps
30 Aug 1914 - 28 Mar 1915:	Chief of Staff, XXIX. Army Corps
28 Mar 1915 - 1918:	POW, Germany

Major-General Vladimir Petrovich **Shendyuk** (24 Sep 1852 - ?)
20 Feb 1902:	Promoted to *Major-General*
20 Feb 1902 - 1 Jun 1904:	Commander of Artillery, Fortress Sevastopol
1 Jun 1904 - 1906:	Commander of Artillery, Fortress Mikhailov

Lieutenant-General Iosif Aleksandrovich **Shendzikovsky** (2 Sep 1849 - ?)
11 Aug 1895 - 11 Aug 1902:	Professor, Aleksandr Military Law Academy
6 Dec 1898:	Promoted to *Major-General*
7 Nov 1901 - 28 Nov 1905:	Military Judge, St. Petersburg Military District Court
28 Nov 1905:	Retired
1909:	Promoted to *Lieutenant-General (Retired)*

Major-General Dmitry Platonovich **Shepatovsky** (2 Oct 1864 - Mar 1915)
27 Sep 1913 - Mar 1915:	Commander, 2nd Battalion, Caucasus Grenadier Artillery Brigade
18 Apr 1915:	Posthumously promoted to *Major-General*

General of Artillery Aleksandr Dmitriyevich **Shepelev** (14 Nov 1829 - ?)
5 Nov 1876 - 2 Jan 1877:	Commander, 5th Artillery Brigade
2 Jan 1877 - 8 Oct 1878:	Commander, 24th Artillery Brigade
30 Oct 1877:	Promoted to *Major-General*
8 Oct 1878 - 8 Oct 1886:	Commander, Guards Horse Artillery Brigade
30 Aug 1886:	Promoted to *Lieutenant-General*
8 Oct 1886 - 11 May 1889:	Commander of Artillery, XIII. Army Corps
11 May 1889 - 12 Aug 1892:	Commander of Artillery, Moscow Military District
12 Aug 1892 - 29 Mar 1903:	At the disposal of the Master-General of Ordnance
29 Mar 1903 - 1905:	Member, Committee for Wounded Veterans
6 Apr 1903:	Promoted to *General of Artillery*

Major-General Andrey Petrovich **Shepelev** (30 Nov 1863 - 17 Sep 1915)
1915 - 17 Sep 1915:	Deputy Commander, 61st Artillery Brigade
8 Nov 1915:	Posthumously promoted to *Major-General*

Lieutenant-General Nikolai Aleksandrovich **Shepelev** (8 Feb 1842 - ?)
27 Jan 1888: Promoted to *Major-General*
27 Jan 1888 - 2 May 1895: Senior Deputy Commander, Terek Region, Ataman, Terek Cossack Army
2 May 1895 - 19 Dec 1897: Chief of Staff, Omsk Military District
14 May 1896: Promoted to *Lieutenant-General*
19 Dec 1897 - 27 Jun 1902: Commander, 32nd Infantry Division
27 Jun 1902 - 3 Sep 1904: Commanding General, VI. Army Corps
2 Sep 1904 - Sep 1905: Member, Committee for Wounded Veterans

Major-General Pavel Vasilyevich **Shepelev** (2 May 1869 - ?)
19 Jul 1914 - 10 Jul 1916: Commander, 62nd Artillery Brigade
10 Jul 1916 - 12 Aug 1917: Commander, 13th Artillery Brigade
18 Oct 1916: Promoted to *Major-General*
12 Aug 1917 - Dec 1917: Inspector of Artillery, XXX. Army Corps

General of Artillery Vladimir Petrovich **Shepelev** (10 Nov 1845 - 24 Dec 1916)
6 Feb 1893 - 12 Jul 1915: Member of the Artillery Committee, Main Artillery Directorate,
 Chief of St. Petersburg Cartridge Factory
30 Aug 1893: Promoted to *Major-General*
29 Mar 1909: Promoted to *Lieutenant-General*
12 Jul 1915: Promoted to *General of Artillery*
12 Jul 1915: Retired
31 Jul 1915 - 24 Dec 1916: Recalled; Attached to the Ministry of War

Major-General Aleksandr Mikhailovich **Shepelev-Voronovich** (24 Aug 1854 - ?)
22 Jan 1902: Promoted to *Major-General*
22 Jan 1902 - 2 Oct 1903: Commander, 36th Artillery Brigade

Lieutenant-General Aleksandr Aleksandrovich **Shepetkovsky** (29 Aug 1848 - ?)
10 May 1895 - 4 May 1904: General for Special Assignments, Minister of War
6 Dec 1899: Promoted to *Major-General*
4 May 1904: Promoted to *Lieutenant-General*
4 May 1904: Retired

Lieutenant-General Aleksey Stepanovich **Shepilov** (14 Oct 1843 - ?)
19 May 1893 - 25 Apr 1896: Commander, 2nd Mortar Artillery Regiment
25 Apr 1896: Promoted to *Major-General*
25 Apr 1896 - 30 May 1901: Commander, 30th Artillery Brigade
30 May 1901 - 9 Jul 1906: Commander of Artillery, III. Army Corps
6 Dec 1903: Promoted to *Lieutenant-General*

Major-General Count Aleksandr Dmitriyevich **Sheremetev** (27 Feb 1859 - 18 May 1931)
6 May 1901 - 8 Sep 1914: General à la suite
27 Jun 1909: Promoted to *Major-General*
27 Jun 1909 - 8 Sep 1914: Chief of the Court Choir
8 Sep 1914 - 14 Apr 1917: Commander, Aviation-Automobile Group, 6th Army

14 Apr 1917: Retired

General of Cavalry Sergey Alekseyevich **Sheremetev** (24 Mar 1836 - 13 Dec 1896)
16 Apr 1872: Promoted to *Major-General*
16 Apr 1872 - 12 Aug 1876: Member of the Tsar's retinue
12 Aug 1876 - 21 Jan 1879: Commander, Consolidated Caucasus Cossack Division
27 Jun 1878: Promoted to *Lieutenant-General*
21 Jan 1879 - 27 Jun 1881: Commander, Caucasus Cossack Division
19 Feb 1879: Promoted to *General-Adjutant*
27 Jun 1881 - 23 Jan 1882: Unassigned
23 Jan 1882 - 8 Feb 1884: Commander, Kuban Region,
Ataman, Kuban Cossack Army
8 Feb 1884 - 3 Jun 1890: Deputy C-in-C of the Caucasus,
Commanding General, Caucasus Military District
3 Jun 1890 - 12 Dec 1896: C-in-C of the Caucasus,
Commanding General, Caucasus Military District
30 Aug 1891: Promoted to *General of Cavalry*
12 Dec 1896 - 13 Dec 1896: Member of the State Council

Major-General Mikhail Petrovich **Sheremetevsky** (14 Oct 1856 - May 1917)
28 May 1909 - Jul 1914: Military Judge, Vilnius Military District Court
6 Dec 1909: Promoted to *Major-General*
Jul 1914 - May 1917: Military Judge, Dvinsk Military District Court

Major-General Fyodor Ignatyevich **Sheremetko** (15 Jun 1830 - ?)
17 Apr 1871 - 6 Oct 1888: Staff Officer, Caucasus Military District
30 Aug 1888: Promoted to *Major-General*
6 Oct 1888 - 1897: Attached to the Caucasus Military District

Lieutenant-General Aleksandr Vasilyevich **Sheremetov** (23 Feb 1857 - ?)
10 Oct 1908 - 31 Dec 1913: Commander, Life Guards Lithuanian Regiment
29 Mar 1909: Promoted to *Major-General*
31 Dec 1913 - 30 Aug 1914: Commander, 2nd Rifle Brigade
30 Aug 1914: Promoted to *Lieutenant-General*
30 Aug 1914: Retired

Major-General Nikolai Nikolayevich **Sherfer** (27 Sep 1843 - ?)
16 Mar 1900: Promoted to *Major-General*
16 Mar 1900 - 29 Sep 1903: Commander, 1st Brigade, 38th Infantry Division

Major-General Ilya Ivanovich **Shestakov** (26 Apr 1854 - Jan 1916)
4 Jul 1906 - 19 Jul 1907: Chief of St. Petersburg Firearms Depot
6 Dec 1906: Promoted to *Major-General*
19 Jul 1907 - 11 Dec 1912: Commander of Artillery, Fortress St. Petersburg,
Chief of St. Petersburg Artillery Depot
11 Dec 1912 - Jul 1914: Deputy Commander of Artillery, Vilnius Military District
Jul 1914 - 17 Feb 1915: Deputy Commander of Artillery, Dvinsk Military

	District
17 Feb 1915 - Jan 1916:	Reserve officer, Dvinsk Military District

Major-General Vladimir Aleksandrovich **Shestakov** (24 Mar 1843 - ?)
27 Aug 1890:	Promoted to *Major-General*
27 Aug 1890 - 28 Jan 1891:	Commander, 1st Brigade, 8th Infantry Division
28 Jan 1891 - 23 Oct 1897:	Chief of Staff, V. Army Corps
23 Oct 1897 - 1898:	Chief of Staff, Kazan Military District

Lieutenant-General Ivan Ivanovich **Shevalye de la Serr** (3 Nov 1854 - 20 May 1912)
6 Nov 1901 - 31 Mar 1904:	Commander of Engineers, Fortress Libau
6 Apr 1903:	Promoted to *Major-General*
31 Mar 1904 - 16 Aug 1906:	Chief of Roads Administration, 1st Manchurian Army
16 Aug 1906 - 10 Jul 1910:	Deputy Commander of Engineers, Odessa Military District
10 Jul 1910 - 20 May 1912:	Commander of Engineers, Odessa Military District
6 Dec 1910:	Promoted to *Lieutenant-General*

Major-General Dmitry Ivanovich **Shevandin** (22 Oct 1856 - ?)
3 May 1910 - 5 Nov 1913:	Commander, 131st Infantry Regiment
5 Nov 1913:	Promoted to *Major-General*
5 Nov 1913 - 31 Dec 1913:	Commander, 2nd Brigade, 10th Infantry Division
31 Dec 1913 - 29 Jul 1914:	Commander, 1st Brigade, 5th Infantry Division
29 Jul 1914 - 1915:	Commander, Brigade, 58th Infantry Division
1915 - 25 Feb 1916:	Commander, State Militia Brigade
25 Feb 1916 - 2 Aug 1916:	Reserve officer, Kiev Military District
2 Aug 1916:	Retired

Lieutenant-General Ivan Antonovich **Shevelev** (20 Feb 1838 - 1908)
30 Feb 1896 - 22 Aug 1901:	Deputy Intendant, Warsaw Military District
30 Aug 1900:	Promoted to *Major-General*
22 Aug 1901 - 15 Jan 1905:	Intendant, Finland Military District
15 Jan 1905 - 1908:	Intendant, Odessa Military District
6 Dec 1906:	Promoted to *Lieutenant-General*

Lieutenant-General Ivan Timofeyevich **Shevelev** (22 Oct 1849 - ?)
7 Apr 1908:	Promoted to *Major-General*
7 Apr 1908 - 31 Dec 1913:	Commander, Saratov Regional Brigade
31 Dec 1913:	Promoted to *Lieutenant-General*
31 Dec 1913:	Retired

Lieutenant-General Pavel Arkadyevich **Shevelev** (6 Nov 1846 - ?)
3 Mar 1893 - 1917:	Chief of State Council Archives, Section Chief, State Chancellery
6 Dec 1902:	Promoted to *Major-General*
14 Apr 1913:	Promoted to *Lieutenant-General*

Major-General Pyotr Andreyevich **Shevelev** (1 Oct 1861 - ?)
25 Aug 1909 - 1917:   Chief of State Printing Works
14 Apr 1913:   Promoted to *Major-General*

Major-General Vladimir Georgiyevich **Shevelev** (14 Mar 1857 - ?)
25 Jun 1910 - 5 Aug 1915:   Commander, 14th Infantry Regiment
11 Nov 1914:   Promoted to *Major-General*
5 Aug 1915 - 25 Aug 1915:   Commander, 1st Brigade, 1st Finnish Rifle Division
25 Aug 1915 - 1917:   Commander, Brigade, 4th Infantry Division

Major-General Dmitry Dmitriyevich **Shevich** (14 May 1868 - 26 Mar 1932)
1915 - 21 May 1916:   Commander, 65th Infantry Regiment
21 May 1916 - 28 Apr 1917:   Commander, Life Guards Pavlovsky Regiment
6 Dec 1916:   Promoted to *Major-General*
28 Apr 1917 - Dec 1917:   Reserve officer, Kiev Military District
Dec 1917:   Dismissed

Major-General Georgy Ivanovich **Shevich** (23 Nov 1871 - 8 Oct 1966)
20 Apr 1911 - 24 Dec 1913:   Commander, 20th Finnish Dragoon Regiment
24 Dec 1913:   Promoted to *Major-General*
24 Dec 1913 - 11 Jul 1915:   Commander, Life Guards Hussar Regiment
11 Jul 1915 - 21 Nov 1915:   Commander, 1st Brigade, 2nd Guards Cavalry Division
21 Nov 1915 - 8 Feb 1916:   General à la suite
8 Feb 1916 - 14 Apr 1917:   At the disposal of the Governor-General of the Caucasus
14 Apr 1917 - Oct 1917:   Reserve officer, Caucasus Military District

General of Infantry Aleksandr Prokhorovich **Shevtsov** (9 Aug 1853 - 18 Oct 1918)
20 Jul 1898:   Promoted to *Major-General*
20 Jul 1898 - 24 Mar 1899:   Special Assignments General, Vilnius Military District
24 Mar 1899 - 12 Aug 1904:   Quartermaster-General, Vilnius Military District
12 Aug 1904 - 8 Sep 1904:   Commander, 1st Rifle Brigade
8 Sep 1904 - 24 Apr 1908:   Commander, 30th Infantry Division
6 Dec 1904:   Promoted to *Lieutenant-General*
8 Dec 1908:   Promoted to *General of Infantry*
8 Dec 1908:   Retired

Major-General Ivan Nikolayevich **Shevtsov** (4 Jul 1875 - 31 Aug 1915)
1915 - 31 Aug 1915:   Chief of Staff, 1st Siberian Rifle Division
12 Feb 1916:   Posthumously promoted to *Major-General*

Lieutenant-General Georgy Mikhailovich **Sheydeman** (1 Feb 1867 - 22 Jun 1940)
27 Oct 1912 - 19 Mar 1915:   Commander, 21st Mortar Artillery Battalion
19 Mar 1915 - 31 May 1916:   Commander, 33rd Artillery Brigade
16 May 1915:   Promoted to *Major-General*
31 May 1916 - 12 Sep 1916:   Inspector of Artillery, IV. Army Corps
12 Sep 1916 - 17 Jan 1917:   Inspector of Artillery, 5th Army
17 Jan 1917:   Promoted to *Lieutenant-General*

17 Jan 1917 - 5 Jun 1917:   Commanding General, XLVIII. Army Corps

General of Cavalry Sergey Mikhailovich **Sheydeman** (18 Aug 1857 - 1922)
21 Mar 1901 - 20 May 1902:   Deputy Chief of Staff, Moscow Military District
14 Apr 1902:   Promoted to *Major-General*
20 May 1902 - 27 Nov 1906:   Quartermaster-General, Moscow Military District
27 Nov 1906 - 31 Aug 1908:   Chief of Staff, Amur Military District
6 Dec 1907:   Promoted to *Lieutenant-General*
31 Aug 1908 - 15 May 1912:   Commander, 3rd Cavalry Division
15 May 1912 - 23 Aug 1914:   Commanding General, II. Army Corps
14 Apr 1913:   Promoted to *General of Cavalry*
21 Aug 1914 - 5 Dec 1914:   Acting C-in-C, 2nd Army
5 Dec 1914 - 4 Jun 1917:   Commanding General, I. Turkestan Army Corps
4 Jun 1917 - Nov 1917:   Unassigned
Nov 1917:   C-in-C, 10th Army

Major-General Mikhail Vladimirovich **Shidlovsky** (20 Jul 1856 - Aug 1918)
Dec 1914:   Promoted to *Major-General*
Dec 1914 - Apr 1917:   Commander, "Ilya Muromets" Air Combat Squadron
Apr 1917 - 20 Jun 1917:   Reserve officer, Petrograd Military District
20 Jun 1917:   Dismissed

Major-General Pyotr Yulianovich **Shidlovsky** (14 Jan 1846 - ?)
28 Dec 1893 - 1905:   Chief of Ammunition Depot, St. Petersburg Military
                                   District
6 Dec 1895:   Promoted to *Major-General*

Major-General Pavel Aleksandrovich **Shiff** (4 Oct 1846 - ?)
10 Mar 1902:   Promoted to *Major-General*
10 Mar 1902 - Jan 1906:   Commander, 1st Brigade, 24th Infantry Division

Lieutenant-General Pyotr Aleksandrovich **Shiff** (2 Nov 1848 - 1909)
1 Aug 1894 - 2 Sep 1901:   Inspector of Classes, Konstantinov Artillery School
1 Apr 1901:   Promoted to *Major-General*
2 Sep 1901 - 1906:   Professor, Mikhailovsky Artillery Academy
1906:   Promoted to *Lieutenant-General*

Lieutenant-General Meyngard Antonovich **Shifner** (1 Mar 1856 - 1918)
11 Apr 1907 - 25 Jul 1910:   Commander, Caucasus Reserve Artillery Brigade
31 May 1907:   Promoted to *Major-General*
25 Jul 1910 - 26 Oct 1910:   Commander, 51st Artillery Brigade
26 Oct 1910 - 15 Feb 1917:   Inspector of Artillery, III. Caucasus Army Corps
1912:   Promoted to *Lieutenant-General*
15 Feb 1917 - Oct 1917:   Reserve officer, Petrograd Military District

Lieutenant-General Ali Agha Ismail Agha Oglu **Shikhlinski** (23 Apr 1865 - 18 Aug 1943)
2 Jan 1913:   Promoted to *Major-General*
2 Jan 1913 - Jan 1915:   Deputy Commandant, Artillery School

Jan 1915 - 23 May 1915:	Chief of Heavy Artillery Combat Training, Northwestern Front
23 May 1915 - Aug 1915:	Attached to the C-in-C, Northwestern Front
Aug 1915 - 31 Oct 1915:	Attached to the C-in-C, Western Front
31 Oct 1915 - 16 Apr 1916:	Attached to the Supreme Commander-in-Chief
16 Apr 1916 - 9 Sep 1917:	Inspector of Artillery, Western Front
9 Sep 1917 - 15 Nov 1917:	C-in-C, 10th Army
2 Apr 1917:	Promoted to *Lieutenant-General*
15 Nov 1917:	Resigned

Lieutenant-General Konstantin Konstantinovich **Shildbakh** (**Litovtsev**) (24 Jan 1872 - 20 Feb 1939)

31 Dec 1913:	Promoted to *Major-General*
31 Dec 1913 - 24 Jun 1915:	Commander, Life Guards Lithuanian Regiment
24 Jun 1915 - 24 Jan 1916:	Commander, 1st Brigade, 3rd Guards Infantry Division
Sep 1915:	Acting Chief of Staff, Army Group Flug
24 Jan 1916 - 14 Oct 1916:	Chief of Staff, XXXIX. Army Corps
14 Oct 1916 - 10 Apr 1917:	Commander, 102nd Infantry Division
10 Apr 1917 - 7 May 1917:	Reserve officer, Kiev Military District
7 May 1917 - 1918:	Commander, 79th Infantry Division
1917:	Promoted to *Lieutenant-General*

Lieutenant-General Nikolai Karlovich **Shilder** (21 May 1842 - 6 Apr 1902)

5 Jun 1878 - 21 Jun 1879:	Special Assignments General, Field Army
15 Sep 1878:	Promoted to *Major-General*
21 Jun 1879 - 28 Jul 1879:	Attached to the Main Engineering Directorate
28 Jul 1879 - 14 Aug 1879:	Deputy Editor of the Engineering Journal
14 Aug 1879 - 26 Apr 1886:	Director, Gatchina Orphan Institute
26 Apr 1886 - 12 Jul 1899:	Commandant, Nikolayev Engineering Academy
30 Aug 1893:	Promoted to *Lieutenant-General*
12 Jul 1899 - 6 Apr 1902:	Director of the Imperial Public Library

General of Infantry Vladimir Aleksandrovich **Shilder** (24 May 1855 - Jul 1925)

25 Apr 1902 - 22 Aug 1906:	Director, Pskov Cadet Corps
1903:	Promoted to *Major-General*
22 Aug 1906 - 13 Jul 1907:	Commander, Life Guards Semyonovsky Regiment
13 Jul 1907 - 14 Sep 1910:	Director of the Corps of Pages
14 Sep 1910 - 21 Sep 1917:	Director, Imperial Aleksandr College
6 Dec 1910:	Promoted to *Lieutenant-General*
21 Sep 1917:	Promoted to *General of Infantry*
21 Sep 1917:	Retired

Major-General Adolf Donatovich **Shileyko** (19 Feb 1851 - ?)

25 Mar 1904:	Promoted to *Major-General*
25 Mar 1904 - 14 Nov 1906:	Commander, 1st Brigade, 3rd Siberian Infantry Division
14 Nov 1906 - 10 Dec 1908:	Commander, 54th Reserve Infantry Brigade

Admiral Nikolai Gustavovich **Shilling** (1 Oct 1828 - Dec 1910)
1859 - 1907:	Attached to Grand Duke Alexei Alexandrovich
1877:	Promoted to *Rear-Admiral*
1877 - 1910:	Admiral à la suite
1887:	Promoted to *Vice-Admiral*
1898:	Promoted to *Admiral*

Lieutenant-General Nikolai Nikolayevich **Shilling** (16 Dec 1870 - 1946)
16 Mar 1916 - 14 Jul 1916:	Commander, Brigade, 2nd Finnish Rifle Division
13 Jul 1916:	Promoted to *Major-General*
14 Jul 1916 - 26 Apr 1917:	Commander, Life Guards Izmailovo Regiment
26 Apr 1917 - 20 May 1917:	Commander, Brigade, 1st Guards Infantry Division
20 May 1917 - Jul 1917:	Commander, 4th Finnish Rifle Division
Jul 1917 - Feb 1918:	Commanding General, XVII. Army Corps
23 Aug 1917:	Promoted to *Lieutenant-General*

Major-General of Naval Engineers Vasily Nikolayevich **Shilov** (4 Apr 1864 - ?)
11 Apr 1905 - 1915:	Chief of Mechanical Engineers, Port of Emperor Aleksandr III (Libau)
6 Dec 1910:	Promoted to *Major-General of Naval Engineers*
1915 - 1917:	Inspector of Factories, Ministry of the Navy

Major-General of the Hydrographic Corps Ivan Dmitriyevich **Shilyayev** (30 Mar 1861 - ?)
23 Feb 1904 - 1917:	Chief of Navigators, Port of St. Petersburg
6 Dec 1912:	Promoted to *Major-General of the Admiralty*
4 Feb 1913:	Redesignated *Major-General of the Hydrographic Corps*

Lieutenant-General Yevgeny Stanislavovich **Shimanovsky** (8 Jan 1848 - 2 Jul 1899)
25 Sep 1892 - 6 Nov 1896:	Quartermaster-General, Kiev Military District
28 Mar 1893:	Promoted to *Major-General*
6 Nov 1896 - 13 May 1899:	Chief of Staff, Kiev Military District
21 Feb 1899:	Promoted to *Lieutenant-General*
13 May 1899 - 2 Jul 1899:	Commander, 33rd Infantry Division

Major-General Stefan Fyodorovich **Shimchenko** (14 Oct 1868 - 3 Jul 1915)
7 May 1915 - 3 Jul 1915:	Commander, 206th Infantry Regiment
30 Jun 1916:	Posthumously promoted to *Major-General*

Lieutenant-General Vsevolod Ivanovich **Shinkarenko** (30 Jan 1861 - 1918)
2 Mar 1906 - 24 Oct 1908:	Military Judge, Amur Military District Court
1906:	Promoted to *Major-General*
24 Oct 1908 - Jan 1917:	Military Prosecutor, Amur Military District
6 Dec 1914:	Promoted to *Lieutenant-General*
Jan 1917 - 17 Mar 1917:	Chairman of the Military Tribunal, Irkutsk Military District
17 Mar 1917:	Retired

General of Cavalry Nikolai Nikolayevich **Shipov** (17 Mar 1846 - 15 Mar 1911)
14 Jun 1884 - 16 Feb 1885:	At the disposal of the Commanding General, St. Petersburg Military District
30 Aug 1884:	Promoted to *Major-General*
16 Feb 1885 - 24 Feb 1893:	Military Governor of the Urals, Ataman, Urals Cossack Army
24 Feb 1893 - 11 Aug 1896:	Commander, 1st Guards Cavalry Division
30 Aug 1894:	Promoted to *Lieutenant-General*
11 Aug 1896 - 4 Mar 1899:	At the disposal of the Commanding General, St. Petersburg Military District
4 Mar 1899 - 8 Apr 1902:	Deputy Governor-General of Finland, Deputy Commanding General, Finland Military District
8 Apr 1902 - 15 Mar 1911:	Member of the Military Council
6 Dec 1904:	Promoted to *General of Cavalry*
1906:	Promoted to *General-Adjutant*

Major-General Nikolai Nikolayevich **Shipov** (6 Feb 1876 - 29 Mar 1958)
17 May 1916 - 28 May 1917:	Commander, Her Majesty's Guards Cavalry Regiment
6 Dec 1916:	Promoted to *Major-General*

Lieutenant-General Pavel Dmitriyevich **Shipov** (9 Oct 1860 - 23 Jul 1919)
6 May 1913:	Promoted to *Major-General*
6 May 1913 - 17 Oct 1914:	General à la suite
17 Oct 1914 - 19 Dec 1914:	Commander, 1st Brigade, 9th Infantry Division
19 Dec 1914 - 29 May 1917:	Commander, 74th Infantry Division
10 Oct 1915:	Promoted to *Lieutenant-General*
29 May 1917 - Oct 1917:	Reserve officer, Kiev Military District

Lieutenant-General Yevgeny Nikiforovich **Shirinkin** (16 Sep 1843 - 1914)
1884 - 25 Jun 1905:	Chief of the Palace Police
2 Apr 1895:	Promoted to *Major-General*
25 Jun 1905 - 1906:	Police Inspector, Kuban Cossack Army
6 Dec 1905:	Promoted to *Lieutenant-General*

Rear-Admiral Prince Sergey Aleksandrovich **Shirinsky-Shikhmatov** (5 Jul 1866 - 13 Aug 1916)
1910 - 12 Aug 1916:	Staff Officer for Assignments, Commander of Army Naval Battalions & River Flotillas
12 Aug 1916:	Promoted to *Rear-Admiral*
12 Aug 1916:	Retired

General of Cavalry Konstantin Antonovich **Shirma** (3 Nov 1851 - ?)
21 Feb 1896 - 11 Apr 1902:	Commander, Life Guards Ataman Regiment
6 Dec 1897:	Promoted to *Major-General*
11 Apr 1902 - 28 Dec 1903:	Commander, 1st Brigade, 2nd Guards Cavalry Division
28 Dec 1903 - 18 Feb 1904:	Commander, 1st Brigade, 1st Guards Cavalry Division
18 Feb 1904 - 24 May 1905:	Commander, 3rd Brigade, 1st Guards Cavalry Division
24 May 1905 - 19 Apr 1906:	Commander, 2nd Guards Cavalry Division

2 Apr 1906:	Promoted to *Lieutenant-General*
19 Apr 1906 - 20 Oct 1912:	At the disposal of the Inspector-General of Cavalry
20 Oct 1912:	Promoted to *General of Cavalry*
20 Oct 1912:	Retired

Lieutenant-General Ivan Zakharovich **Shirokov** (26 Sep 1847 - 1928)

18 Sep 1902 - 16 Aug 1906:	Ataman, Khopersk Division, Don Cossack Army
6 Dec 1904:	Promoted to *Major-General*
16 Aug 1906 - 5 Nov 1908:	Ataman, Ust-Medveditsk Division, Don Cossack Army
5 Nov 1908 - 17 Nov 1910:	Commander, 2nd Brigade, 7th Cavalry Division
17 Nov 1910:	Promoted to *Lieutenant-General*
17 Nov 1910:	Retired

Major-General Konstantin Ilich **Shirokov** (24 Nov 1842 - ?)

7 Jan 1891 - 1904:	Commander of Gendarmerie, Perm Province
1 Jan 1901:	Promoted to *Major-General*

Lieutenant-General Vasily Pavlovich **Shirokov** (23 Jan 1844 - ?)

6 Apr 1888 - 21 Dec 1894:	Commander of Engineers, Fortress Dvinsk
1894:	Promoted to *Major-General*
21 Dec 1894 - 4 Jun 1910:	Engineer Inspector, Kazan Military District
4 Jun 1910:	Promoted to *Lieutenant-General*
4 Jun 1910:	Retired

Lieutenant-General Viktor Pavlovich **Shirokov** (5 Nov 1860 - 1919)

6 Dec 1907:	Promoted to *Major-General*
6 Dec 1907 - 22 Oct 1914:	Chief of Staff, XVI. Army Corps
22 Oct 1914 - 24 Oct 1915:	Commander, 41st Infantry Division
28 May 1915:	Promoted to *Lieutenant-General*
24 Oct 1915 - 2 Apr 1917:	Commanding General, XXI. Army Corps
2 Apr 1917 - 11 Oct 1917:	Reserve officer, Petrograd Military District
11 Oct 1917 - 14 Nov 1917:	Reserve officer, Kazan Military District
14 Nov 1917 - 1918:	Commanding General, XXXIII. Army Corps

Lieutenant-General Mikhail Ivanovich **Shishkevich** (4 Feb 1862 - ?)

16 Jul 1910:	Promoted to *Major-General*
16 Jul 1910 - 8 Aug 1912:	Quartermaster-General, Moscow Military District
8 Aug 1912 - 24 Dec 1913:	Chief of Aeronautics Section, General Staff
24 Dec 1913 - 19 Jul 1914:	Quartermaster-General, Odessa Military District
19 Jul 1914 - 4 Nov 1914:	Quartermaster-General, 7th Army
4 Nov 1914 - 19 Apr 1915:	Chief of Staff, 7th Army
31 Jan 1915:	Promoted to *Lieutenant-General*
19 Apr 1915 - 19 Oct 1916:	Chief of Staff, 11th Army
19 Oct 1916 - 12 Dec 1916:	Chief of Staff, Danube Army
12 Dec 1916 - 8 Apr 1917:	Chief of Staff, Romanian Front
8 Apr 1917 - 28 Apr 1917:	Commanding General, VII. Army Corps
28 Apr 1917 - 22 Aug 1917:	Reserve officer, Odessa Military District
22 Aug 1917 - Oct 1917:	Reserve officer, Moscow Military District

Major-General Aleksey Matveyevich **Shishkin** (13 Mar 1845 - ?)
5 Dec 1890 - 19??: Ataman, 3rd Military Division, Siberian Cossack Army
6 May 1900: Promoted to *Major-General*

Lieutenant-General Apollon Alekseyevich **Shishkin** (30 Aug 1862 - ?)
9 Dec 1910: Promoted to *Major-General*
9 Dec 1910 - 27 Jan 1917: Commander of Engineers, Fortress Kronstadt
27 Jan 1917 - 1918: Inspector of Engineers, Petrograd Military District
2 Apr 1917: Promoted to *Lieutenant-General*

Lieutenant-General Mikhail Ivanovich **Shishkin** (27 Sep 1863 - ?)
24 Jul 1906 - 6 Oct 1910: Commander, 17th Rifle Regiment
6 Oct 1910: Promoted to *Major-General*
6 Oct 1910 - 9 Nov 1914: Commander, 2nd Brigade, 24th Infantry Division
9 Nov 1914 - 11 Dec 1914: Acting Commander, 24th Infantry Division
11 Dec 1914 - 29 Oct 1916: Commander, 22nd Infantry Division
12 Feb 1915: Promoted to *Lieutenant-General*
29 Oct 1916 - 22 Nov 1916: Reserve officer, Kiev Military District
22 Nov 1916 - 22 Jan 1917: Reserve officer, Petrograd Military District
22 Jan 1917 - 10 Sep 1917: Commander, 14th Siberian Rifle Division
10 Sep 1917 - 24 Oct 1917: Unassigned
24 Oct 1917: Dismissed

Major-General Vladimir Nikolayevich **Shishkin** (11 Jul 1862 - 1920)
20 Jan 1909 - 13 Mar 1915: Commander, 5th Orenburg Cossack Regiment
13 Mar 1915 - 24 Jan 1916: Reserve officer, Dvinsk Military District
24 May 1915: Promoted to *Major-General*
24 Jan 1916 - 5 May 1916: Commander, Independent Consolidated Cossack Brigade
5 May 1916 - 31 Dec 1916: Commander, 2nd Brigade, 6th Don Cossack Division
31 Dec 1916 - 1917: Commander, Orenburg Cossack Division
1917 - 1918: Commander, 1st Orenburg Cossack Division

Lieutenant-General Sergey Emmanuilovich **Shishko** (18 Sep 1853 - 18 Nov 1940)
13 Feb 1907 - 31 Jan 1912: Chairman of the Remount Commission, Penza Region
10 Apr 1911: Promoted to *Major-General*
31 Jan 1912 - 1917: Chairman of the Remount Commission, Astrakhan Region
1917: Promoted to *Lieutenant-General*

Major-General Konrad Karlovich **Shishkovsky** (26 Nov 1842 - ?)
14 Jun 1899: Promoted to *Major-General*
14 Jun 1899 - 5 Oct 1902: Commander, 3rd Reserve Artillery Brigade
5 Oct 1902 - 11 Feb 1905: Commander of Artillery, I. Siberian Army Corps
11 Feb 1905 - 1906: At the disposal of the Main Artillery Directorate

Lieutenant-General Nikolai Feofilovich **Shishkovsky** (25 Oct 1851 - ?)
30 Mar 1898: Promoted to *Major-General*

30 Mar 1898 - 3 Jun 1899:	Deputy Chief of Staff, Omsk Military District
3 Jun 1899 - 2 Nov 1902:	Chief of Staff, XXI. Army Corps
2 Nov 1902 - 24 Aug 1904:	Commander, 49th Reserve Infantry Brigade
24 Aug 1904 - 15 Mar 1906:	Commander, 20th Infantry Division
6 Dec 1904:	Promoted to *Lieutenant-General*
15 Mar 1906 - 1906:	Attached to the General Staff

General of Infantry Yakov Fyodorovich **Shkinsky** (4 Jun 1858 - 22 Apr 1938)

8 Mar 1899 - 18 Jun 1901:	Chief of Communications, Caucasus Military District
1 Jan 1901:	Promoted to *Major-General*
18 Jun 1901 - 2 Jul 1905:	Quartermaster-General, Caucasus Military District
2 Jul 1905 - 2 Apr 1906:	Chief of Military Transport, C-in-C, Far East
2 Apr 1906 - 14 May 1907:	Quartermaster-General, General Staff
6 Dec 1906:	Promoted to *Lieutenant-General*
14 May 1907 - 21 Feb 1908:	Commander, 18th Infantry Division
21 Feb 1908 - 7 Jun 1910:	Commander, 3rd Guards Infantry Division
7 Jun 1910 - 11 Apr 1911:	Commanding General, I. Siberian Army Corps
11 Apr 1911 - 22 Apr 1914:	Deputy Commanding General, Vilnius Military District
6 Dec 1912:	Promoted to *General of Infantry*
22 Apr 1914 - 7 Oct 1915:	Commanding General, XXI. Army Corps
7 Oct 1915 - 31 Mar 1917:	Commanding General, Irkutsk Military District, C-in-C, Trans-Baikal Cossack Army
31 Mar 1917:	Retired

General of Artillery Vladimir Nikolayevich **Shklarevich** (23 Jun 1835 - 1915)

21 Apr 1869 - 5 Sep 1885:	Advisory Member, Artillery Committee, Main Artillery Directorate
3 Feb 1882:	Promoted to *Major-General*
5 Sep 1885 - 9 Jan 1911:	Permanent Member, Artillery Committee, Main Artillery Directorate
25 Nov 1895 - 31 Dec 1913:	Honorary Member, Mikhailovsky Artillery Academy
30 Aug 1892:	Promoted to *Lieutenant-General*
9 Jan 1911:	Promoted to *General of Artillery*
9 Jan 1911 - 31 Dec 1913:	Honorary Member, Artillery Committee, Main Artillery Directorate
31 Dec 1913:	Retired

Lieutenant-General Semyon Afanasyevich **Shkurinsky** (28 Apr 1832 - ?)

22 Nov 1879 - 10 Apr 1889:	Chief of Staff, I. Army Corps
1880:	Promoted to *Major-General*
10 Apr 1889 - 22 Nov 1893:	Chief of Staff, Irkutsk Military District
30 Aug 1889:	Promoted to *Lieutenant-General*
22 Nov 1893 - 3 Oct 1899:	Commander, 18th Infantry Division

Major-General Vladimir Lyudvigovich **Shlegel** (20 Sep 1857 - ?)

1915 - 3 Jun 1916:	Commander, 1st Mountain Artillery Battalion
23 Nov 1915:	Promoted to *Major-General*
3 Jun 1916 - 1918:	Commander, 47th Artillery Brigade

Major-General Aleksandr Lyudvigovich **Shletynsky** (6 Apr 1845 - ?)
2 Jun 1892 - 4 Jun 1898:	Military Judge, Kazan Military District Court
30 Aug 1893:	Promoted to *Major-General*
4 Jun 1898 - 1905:	Military Judge, Moscow Military District Court

Major-General Adolf Aleksandrovich von **Shleyer** (21 Oct 1847 - ?)
20 Aug 1903:	Promoted to *Major-General*
20 Aug 1903 - 2 May 1904:	Commander, 9th Artillery Brigade
2 May 1904 - 30 Nov 1904:	Commander, 19th Artillery Brigade

Major-General of Naval Engineers Gustav Fyodorovich **Shlezinger** (9 Mar 1860 - 1939)
24 Dec 1902 - 1909:	Deputy Chief Inspector of Shipbuilding
6 Dec 1908:	Promoted to *Major-General of Naval Engineers*
1909:	Retired

Lieutenant-General Vasily Antonovich **Shlikhting** (1 Jan 1846 - ?)
15 Apr 1906 - 17 Apr 1913:	Commander of Gendarmerie, Tversk Province
6 Dec 1907:	Promoted to *Major-General*
17 Apr 1913:	Promoted to *Lieutenant-General*
17 Apr 1913:	Retired

Major-General Erast Alekseyevich **Shlyakhtin** (10 Nov 1855 - ?)
1 Jan 1911:	Promoted to *Major-General*
1 Jan 1911 - 10 Feb 1913:	Commander, 2nd Brigade, 6th Cavalry Division

Major-General Aleksandr Mikhailovich **Shmakov** (22 Jul 1842 - ?)
5 Mar 1901 - 5 Jul 1901:	Commander of Gendarmerie, Lomzhinsk Province
1 Apr 1901:	Promoted to *Major-General*
5 Jul 1901 - 1906:	Attached to the Staff, Corps of Gendarmerie

Major-General Aleksandr Adamovich **Shmerling** (5 Jan 1843 - ?)
8 Dec 1892 - 1910:	Military Judge, Caucasus Military District Court
6 Dec 1898:	Promoted to *Major-General*

Major-General Pyotr Petrovich **Shmidt** (6 Oct 1859 - ?)
5 Dec 1909 - 11 Mar 1911:	Chairman of the Remount Commission, Orenburg Region
6 Dec 1910.	Promoted to *Major-General*
11 Mar 1911 - 1917:	Chairman of the Remount Commission, Western Trans-Don Steppes

Major-General Vladimir-Albert Avgustovich **Shmidt** (21 Jan 1852 - ?)
30 Mar 1904 - 5 Apr 1907:	Commander, 2nd Replacement Artillery Brigade
2 Apr 1906:	Promoted to *Major-General*
5 Apr 1907 - 18 May 1908:	Deputy Commander of Artillery, Amur Military District

Admiral Vladimir Petrovich **Shmidt** (27 Feb 1827 - 25 Feb 1909)
17 Jul 1877:	Promoted to *Rear-Admiral*

17 Jul 1877 - 1878:	Attached to the retinue of the Tsar
1878 - 1 Jan 1879:	Deputy Chief of Naval Defenses, Finland
1 Jan 1879 - 1880:	Junior Flagman, Baltic Fleet
1880 - 1882:	Commander, 2nd Torpedo Boat Detachment, Gulf of Finland
1882 - 1883:	Commander, Skerry Detachment, Baltic Fleet
1883 - 8 Apr 1884:	Commander, Training Squadron, Baltic Fleet
8 Apr 1884 - 31 Oct 1887:	Senior Flagman, Baltic Fleet
1 Jan 1886:	Promoted to *Vice-Admiral*
31 Oct 1887 - 14 Dec 1889:	Commander, Pacific Squadron
1890 - 1 Jan 1892:	Senior Flagman, Baltic Fleet
1 Jan 1892 - 25 Feb 1909:	Member, Board of Admiralty
1898:	Promoted to *Admiral*

Lieutenant-General Yuly Aleksandrovich **Shmidt** (16 Jan 1844 - 14 Jul 1910)

8 Jun 1899 - 16 May 1905:	Chief of the Topographical Section, Siberian Military District
9 Apr 1900:	Promoted to *Major-General*
16 May 1905 - 1 Dec 1906:	Chief of the Topographical Section, 2nd Manchurian Army
1 Dec 1906 - 3 Dec 1908:	Chief of the Topographical Section, Omsk Military District
6 Dec 1906:	Promoted to *Lieutenant-General*
3 Dec 1908 - 14 Jul 1910:	Chief of the Military Topographic Survey, Kiev

Lieutenant-General Ivan Aleksandrovich **Shmidt von der Launits** (7 Jan 1861 - ?)

18 Feb 1909 - 28 May 1910:	Senior Clerk, Artillery Committee, Main Artillery Directorate
29 Mar 1909:	Promoted to *Major-General*
28 May 1910 - Oct 1917:	Member of the Artillery Committee, Main Artillery Directorate
8 Oct 1914 - Oct 1917:	Chief of Section 3, Artillery Committee, Main Artillery Directorate
10 Apr 1916:	Promoted to *Lieutenant-General*

General of Infantry Aleksandr Ottovich **Shmit** (19 Mar 1833 - 21 Apr 1916)

14 Mar 1873 - 10 Oct 1875:	Deputy Chief of Staff, Kiev Military District
30 Aug 1873:	Promoted to *Major-General*
10 Oct 1875 - 22 Apr 1878:	Commander, 2nd Brigade, 32nd Infantry Division
22 Apr 1878 - 4 Aug 1885:	Commander, 29th Infantry Division
4 Aug 1885 - 3 Nov 1893:	Commander, 16th Infantry Division
30 Aug 1885:	Promoted to *Lieutenant-General*
3 Nov 1893 - 1905:	At the disposal of the Minister of War
6 Dec 1904:	Promoted to *General of Infantry*
1905:	Retired

General of Cavalry Yevgeny Ottovich **Shmit** (31 Dec 1844 - 11 Oct 1915)

21 May 1892:	Promoted to *Major-General*

21 May 1892 - 7 Feb 1898:	Commander, Life Guards Cuirassier Regiment
7 Feb 1898 - 26 Apr 1900:	Commander, 1st Brigade, 2nd Guards Cavalry Division
26 Apr 1900 - 12 Jan 1905:	Commander, 12th Cavalry Division
22 May 1900:	Promoted to *Lieutenant-General*
12 Jan 1905 - 18 Mar 1906:	Commanding General, XII. Army Corps
18 Mar 1906 - 8 Jun 1908:	Deputy Commanding General, Kiev Military District
6 Dec 1907:	Promoted to *General of Cavalry*
8 Jun 1908 - 24 May 1915:	Commanding General, Omsk Military District, Governor-General of the Steppes, Ataman, Siberian Cossack Army
24 May 1915 - 11 Oct 1915:	Member of the State Council

Lieutenant-General of the Admiralty Yuly Mikhailovich **Shokalsky** (5 Oct 1856 - 26 Mar 1940)

4 Mar 1907 - 1912:	Chief of Hydrometeorological Section, Main Hydrographic Directorate
6 Dec 1907:	Promoted to *Major-General of the Admiralty*
21 Aug 1910 - 1917:	Professor, Nikolayev Naval Academy
25 Mar 1912:	Promoted to *Lieutenant-General of the Admiralty*

Major-General Vladimir Nikolayevich **Shokorov** (15 Jul 1868 - 11 Jul 1940)

13 Nov 1914 - 2 Jan 1915:	Commander, 55th Infantry Regiment
2 Jan 1915 - 14 Oct 1916:	Quartermaster-General, 10th Army
27 Jul 1915:	Promoted to *Major-General*
14 Oct 1916 - 10 Jul 1917:	Chief of Staff, XXXIX. Army Corps
10 Jul 1917 - 15 Oct 1917:	Commander, 46th Infantry Division

Major-General Aleksandr Gustavovich **Sholp** (11 May 1857 - 8 Jun 1938)

5 Nov 1913:	Promoted to *Major-General*
5 Nov 1913 - 13 Jul 1916:	Commander, 1st Brigade, 41st Infantry Division
13 Jul 1916 - 18 Apr 1917:	Commander, 3rd Infantry Division
18 Apr 1907 - 1918:	Reserve officer, Kiev Military District

Lieutenant-General Pyotr Mikhailovich **Shorokhov** (5 Oct 1840 - 1914)

17 Dec 1898:	Promoted to *Major-General*
17 Dec 1898 - 28 Dec 1898:	Commander, 2nd Turkestan Line Brigade
28 Dec 1898 - 23 Jul 1900:	Commander, 3rd Independent Turkestan Line Brigade
23 Jul 1900 - 18 Jun 1906:	Commander, 3rd Turkestan Rifle Brigade
18 Jun 1906:	Promoted to *Lieutenant-General*
18 Jun 1906:	Retired

Major-General Aleksey Petrovich **Shoshin** (31 Aug 1861 - 1924)

22 Nov 1911:	Promoted to *Major-General*
22 Nov 1911 - 28 Apr 1917:	Commander of Engineers & Construction, Fortress Vladivostok
28 Apr 1917 - 1918:	Commander of Engineers, Northern Front

Lieutenant-General Fyodor Aleksandrovich **Shostak** (17 Apr 1853 - 1 Nov 1912)
23 Nov 1899:	Promoted to *Major-General*
23 Nov 1899 - 8 Jan 1900:	At the disposal of the Chief of the General Staff
8 Jan 1900 - 11 Jan 1904:	Chief of Staff, VIII. Army Corps
11 Jan 1904 - 14 Oct 1908:	At the disposal of the Chief of the General Staff
22 Apr 1907:	Promoted to *Lieutenant-General*
14 Oct 1908 - 21 Dec 1908:	Commander, 24th Infantry Division
21 Dec 1908 - 1 Jan 1911:	Commander, 35th Infantry Division
1 Jan 1911 - 1 Nov 1912:	Military Governor, Transcaspian Region, Commanding General, II. Turkestan Army Corps

Major-General of Naval Engineers Alexander Ernestovich **Shott** (29 Oct 1854 - ?)
1902 - 1906:	Shipbuilding Engineer, Port of Nikolayev
1906:	Promoted to *Major-General of Naval Engineers*
1906:	Retired

Lieutenant-General Mikhail Nikolayevich **Shotten** (9 Apr 1836 - 4 Apr 1905)
5 Nov 1895 - 1 May 1903:	Special Assignments General (5th Class) to the Chief of the General Staff
14 May 1896:	Promoted to *Major-General*
1 May 1903 - Jan 1905:	Member, General Staff Committee
Jan 1905:	Promoted to *Lieutenant-General*
Jan 1905:	Retired

Lieutenant-General Karl Vilyamovich **Shpigel** (26 Nov 1853 - ?)
24 Jan 1907:	Promoted to *Major-General*
24 Jan 1907 - 17 Aug 1913:	Director, Simbirsk Cadet Corps
17 Aug 1913:	Promoted to *Lieutenant-General*
17 Aug 1913:	Retired

Major-General Anton Anastasyevich **Shpilevsky** (30 Jul 1855 - ?)
19 Aug 1910 - 1913:	Attached to 4th Artillery Brigade
1913:	Promoted to *Major-General*
1913:	Retired

Major-General Aleksey Logginovich **Shpiller** (8 Jan 1836 - ?)
10 Mar 1893:	Promoted to *Major-General*
10 Mar 1893 - 1899:	Commander of Artillery, Fortress Ivangorod
1899:	Retired

General of Artillery Rostislav Vladimirovich **Shpitsberg** (14 Feb 1841 - 11 Feb 1909)
4 May 1880 - 9 Apr 1908:	Permanent Member, Artillery Committee, Main Artillery Directorate
6 May 1884:	Promoted to *Major-General*
30 Aug 1894:	Promoted to *Lieutenant-General*
9 Apr 1908:	Promoted to *General of Artillery*
9 Apr 1908:	Retired

General of Cavalry Yevgraf Vladimirovich **Shpitsberg** (9 Dec 1843 - ?)
20 Sep 1879 - 23 Oct 1896: Commander, 1st Orenburg Cossack Regiment
14 Nov 1894: Promoted to *Major-General*
23 Oct 1896 - 14 Sep 1900: Commander, 1st Turkestan Cossack Brigade
14 Sep 1900 - 5 Jul 1906: Commander, 1st Turkestan Cossack Division
6 Dec 1900: Promoted to *Lieutenant-General*
5 Jul 1906 - 10 Nov 1906: Commanding General, VII. Army Corps
10 Nov 1906: Promoted to *General of Cavalry*
10 Nov 1906: Retired

Major-General of Naval Artillery Aleksandr Yermolayevich **Shpynev** (22 Mar 1856 - ?)
26 Nov 1902 - 1912: Commander of Naval Artillery, Port of Kronstadt
6 Dec 1909: Promoted to *Major-General of Naval Artillery*

General of Infantry Konstantin Fyodorovich **Shramm** (11 Mar 1835 - ?)
17 Mar 1887 - 29 Jul 1891: Chief of Gendarmerie, Livonia
5 Apr 1887: Promoted to *Major-General*
29 Jul 1891 - 2 Sep 1905: Chief of Gendarmerie, Moscow Province
14 May 1896: Promoted to *Lieutenant-General*
2 Sep 1905: Promoted to *General of Infantry*
2 Sep 1905: Retired

Major-General Aleksandr Fyodorovich **Shredel** (7 Apr 1862 - ?)
? - 25 Sep 1917: Chief of Gendarmerie, Kiev Province
6 Dec 1916: Promoted to *Major-General*
25 Sep 1917: Dismissed

Major-General Adolf Ottovich **Shreder** (8 Oct 1849 - ?)
25 Jan 1904: Promoted to *Major-General*
25 Jan 1904 - 20 Feb 1906: Commander, 2nd Brigade, 44th Infantry Division
20 Feb 1906 - 1907: Commandant of Fortress Kerch

Lieutenant-General Mikhail Dmitriyevich **Shreyder** (12 Dec 1858 - 10 May 1916)
20 Jun 1904 - 10 Aug 1907: Commander, 1st Battalion, Life Guards 3rd Artillery Brigade
31 May 1907: Promoted to *Major-General*
10 Aug 1907 - 13 Oct 1907: Commander, 2nd Replacement Artillery Brigade
13 Oct 1907 - 12 Nov 1910: Commander, Life Guards 3rd Artillery Brigade
12 Nov 1910 - 7 Apr 1915: Inspector of Artillery, XX. Army Corps
14 Apr 1913: Promoted to *Lieutenant-General*
7 Apr 1915 - 10 May 1916: POW, Germany

Lieutenant-General Pyotr Dmitriyevich **Shreyder** (1917: **Telezhnikov**) (31 Mar 1863 - ?)
1 Jun 1904 - 26 Jan 1909: Commander, 99th Infantry Regiment
26 Jan 1909 - 8 Mar 1909: Chief of Staff, Orenburg Cossack Army
29 Jan 1909: Promoted to *Major-General*
8 Mar 1909 - 15 Nov 1913: Commandant, Infantry Officers School
15 Nov 1913 - 21 Mar 1915: Commander, 5th Rifle Brigade

21 Mar 1915 - 19 Apr 1917:	Commander, 17th Infantry Division
2 Apr 1915:	Promoted to *Lieutenant-General*
19 Apr 1917 - 14 May 1917:	Reserve officer, Dvinsk Military District
14 May 1917 - 9 Sep 1917:	Commanding General, IX. Army Corps
9 Sep 1917 - 7 Oct 1917:	Reserve officer, Minsk Military District
7 Oct 1917 - 1918:	Reserve officer, Petrograd Military District

Major-General Konstantin Nikolayevich **Shreyterfeld** (23 Jan 1869 - ?)
18 Nov 1916 - 1917:	Military Judge, Odessa Military District Court
6 Dec 1916:	Promoted to *Major-General*

Lieutenant-General Yevstafy Aleksandrovich **Shtaden** (11 Dec 1848 - ?)
12 May 1898 - 31 May 1906:	Military Commander, Moscow District
2 Apr 1906:	Promoted to *Major-General*
31 May 1906 - 31 Dec 1913:	Commander, Tambov Regional Brigade
6 Dec 1912:	Promoted to *Lieutenant-General*

Vice-Admiral Baron Evald-Otto-Aleksandr Antonovich von **Shtakelberg** (9 Feb 1847 - 29 Aug 1909)
1896 - 1901:	Commander, Imperial Yacht "North Star"
1901:	Promoted to *Rear-Admiral*
Sep 1902 - 20 Jun 1903:	Junior Flagman, Pacific Squadron
20 Jun 1903 - 29 Jan 1904:	Commander, Cruiser Detachment, Pacific Squadron
Feb 1904 - 1907:	Junior Flagman, Baltic Fleet
1908:	Promoted to *Vice-Admiral*
1908:	Retired

General of Cavalry Baron Georgy Karlovich von **Shtakelberg** (30 Jul 1851 - 25 Jul 1913)
18 Aug 1886 - 5 Dec 1890:	Commander, 25th Dragoon Regiment
5 Dec 1890:	Promoted to *Major-General*
5 Dec 1890 - 1894:	Commander, Trans-Caspian Cossack Cavalry Brigade
1894 - 3 Dec 1897:	Commander, Trans-Caspian Cossack Brigade
3 Dec 1897 - 31 May 1899:	Commander, 15th Cavalry Division
31 May 1899 - 25 Apr 1901:	Commander, 10th Cavalry Division
6 Dec 1899:	Promoted to *Lieutenant-General*
25 Apr 1901 - 2 Nov 1902:	Commanding General, II. Siberian Army Corps
2 Nov 1902 - 2 Mar 1904 :	Commanding General, I. Cavalry Corps
2 Mar 1904 - 5 Apr 1904:	At the disposal of the C-in-C, Manchurian Army
5 Apr 1904 - 17 Mar 1905:	Commanding General, I. Siberian Army Corps
17 Mar 1905 - 25 Jul 1913:	Member, Committee for Wounded Veterans
6 Dec 1907:	Promoted to *General of Cavalry*

General of Cavalry Baron Konstantin Karlovich von **Shtakelberg** (15 Jun 1848 - 30 Mar 1925)
24 Aug 1882 - 7 Sep 1897:	Director of the Court Choir
28 Mar 1893:	Promoted to *Major-General*
7 Sep 1897 - 24 May 1917:	Director of the Court Orchestra
22 Apr 1907:	Promoted to *Lieutenant-General*

24 May 1917: Promoted to *General of Cavalry*
24 May 1917: Retired

Major-General Baron Nikolai Ivanovich von **Shtakelberg** (3 Oct 1870 - 20 Mar 1956)
17 May 1916 - 7 Sep 1917: Commander, Life Guards Kexholm Regiment
6 Dec 1916: Promoted to *Major-General*
7 Sep 1917 - 1917: Commander, Brigade, 3rd Guards Infantry Division
1917 - 1918: Commander, Guards Rifle Division

Major-General of the Fleet Aleksandr Viktorovich **Shtal** (17 Apr 1865 - 13 Aug 1950)
Oct 1910 - 1921: Deputy Commandant of the Naval Academy
6 Dec 1913: Promoted to *Major-General of the Fleet*

Lieutenant-General Nikolai Kornilovich **Shtalman** (31 Oct 1835 - 28 Jul 1905)
16 Jan 1888: Promoted to *Major-General*
16 Jan 1888 - 6 Dec 1901: At the disposal of the Main Engineering Directorate
6 Dec 1901: Promoted to *Lieutenant-General*
6 Dec 1901 - 28 Jul 1905: At the disposal of the Minister of War

Lieutenant-General Mikhail Ivanovich **Shtegelman** (3 Sep 1860 - 22 Sep 1929)
3 Jul 1905 - 30 Sep 1905: Commander, 1st Brigade, 22nd Infantry Division
30 Sep 1905 - 2 Nov 1906: Deputy Inspector of Engineers, 1st Manchurian Army
28 Feb 1906: Promoted to *Major-General*
2 Nov 1906 - 20 Feb 1912: Commander, 2nd Brigade, 45th Infantry Division
20 Feb 1912 - 19 Jul 1914: Commander, 2nd Brigade, 38th Infantry Division
19 Jul 1914 - 28 Apr 1917: Commander, 75th Infantry Division
2 Oct 1914: Promoted to *Lieutenant-General*
28 Apr 1917 - 1918: Reserve officer, Minsk Military District

Lieutenant-General Baron Nikolai Arkadyevich von **Shtempel** (22 Jun 1861 - 1944)
16 Feb 1907 - 23 Feb 1910: Commander, 9th Hussar Regiment
23 Feb 1910: Promoted to *Major-General*
23 Feb 1910 - 17 Oct 1910: Commander, 1st Brigade, 5th Cavalry Division
17 Oct 1910 - 23 Dec 1911: Commander, 1st Brigade, 1st Cavalry Division
23 Dec 1911: Retired
10 Feb 1913 - 1917: Recalled; Commander, 2nd Brigade, 6th Cavalry Division
1917 - 1918: Commander, 9th Cavalry Division
22 Oct 1917: Promoted to *Lieutenant-General*

General of Cavalry Baron Reyngold-Frants-Oskar Aleksandrovich von **Shtempel** (4 Nov 1839 - 24 Apr 1913)
13 Mar 1885 - 20 Sep 1894: Commander, 39th Dragoon Regiment
20 Sep 1894: Promoted to *Major-General*
20 Sep 1894 - 12 Dec 1900: Commander, 1st Brigade, 5th Cavalry Division
12 Dec 1900 - 31 May 1901: Attached to the Commanding General, Warsaw Military District
31 May 1901: Promoted to *Lieutenant-General*
31 May 1901 - 26 Jan 1907: Special Assignments General, Inspectorate-General of

	Cavalry
26 Jan 1907 - 29 Jun 1909:	Inspector of Remounts & Cavalry Replacement
29 Mar 1909:	Promoted to *General of Cavalry*
29 Jun 1909 - 21 Apr 1910:	Chief of the Army Remount Directorate
21 Apr 1910 - 24 Apr 1913:	Commandant of Krasnoye Selo

General of the Fleet Vasily Aleksandrovich **Shtenger** (31 Jul 1861 - 28 Mar 1933)
1906 - 10 Apr 1911:	Chief of Staff, Minister of the Navy
10 Apr 1911:	Promoted to *Major-General of the Admiralty*
10 Apr 1911 - 6 Oct 1917:	General for Special Assignments, Ministry of the Navy
8 Apr 1913:	Redesignated *Major-General of the Fleet*
?:	Chief of Logistics, Naval General Staff
6 Dec 1915:	Promoted to *Lieutenant-General of the Fleet*
6 Oct 1917:	Promoted to *General of the Fleet*
6 Oct 1917:	Retired

Major-General Aleksey Platonovich **Shterich** (4 Sep 1852 - ?)
10 Feb 1904 - 1908:	Commander, Kremenchug Artillery Depot
6 Dec 1904:	Promoted to *Major-General*

Lieutenant-General Emil Karlovich **Shternberg** (6 Apr 1860 - ?)
10 Feb 1907 - 29 Jan 1910:	Intendant, I. Caucasus Army Corps
13 Apr 1908:	Promoted to *Major-General*
29 Jan 1910 - 1 Sep 1913:	Intendant, II. Army Corps
1 Sep 1913 - ?:	Intendant, XV. Army Corps
9 May 1914:	Promoted to *Lieutenant-General*

Major-General Nikolai Kapitonovich **Shteynfeld** (6 Dec 1832 - ?)
7 Oct 1893:	Promoted to *Major-General*
7 Oct 1893 - 24 Oct 1896:	Commander, 4th Reserve Artillery Brigade
24 Oct 1896 - 31 Oct 1899:	Commander, 16th Artillery Brigade

General of Infantry Baron Vyacheslav Vladimirovich **Shteyngeyl** (12 May 1823 - 8 Sep 1897)
13 Feb 1858 - 1 Jun 1868:	Editor, Russian Military Chronicle
23 Apr 1861:	Promoted to *Major-General*
1 Jun 1868 - 13 Dec 1881:	Museum Director, Main Intendant Directorate
30 Aug 1869:	Promoted to *Lieutenant-General*
13 Dec 1881 - 8 Sep 1897:	Member, Military Research Committee, General Staff
30 Apr 1891:	Promoted to *General of Infantry*

Vice-Admiral Ivan Aleksandrovich **Shtorre** (27 May 1862 - ?)
1911 - 2 Dec 1915:	Commander, 1st Mine Division, Baltic Fleet
6 Dec 1912:	Promoted to *Rear-Admiral*
2 Dec 1915:	Promoted to *Vice-Admiral*
2 Dec 1915:	Retired

Lieutenant-General Konstantin Karlovich von **Shtrandman** (26 Oct 1829 - ?)
1847 - 15 May 1897:	Attached to Life Guards Cuirassier Regiment
30 Aug 1874:	Promoted to *Major-General*
15 May 1897 - 1 Aug 1905:	General for Special Assignments, Minister of Internal Affairs
6 Dec 1898:	Promoted to *Lieutenant-General*
1 Aug 1905 - Jul 1907:	Member of the Board, Ministry of Internal Affairs
Jul 1907:	Retired

Major-General Aleksandr Nikolayevich **Shtrik** (4 Dec 1840 - ?)
25 Mar 1890:	Promoted to *Major-General*
25 Mar 1890 - 16 Apr 1892:	Chief of Staff, IV. Army Corps
16 Apr 1892 - 28 Sep 1892:	At the disposal of the Minister of War
28 Sep 1892 - 1 Nov 1897:	Chief of Staff, XVIII. Army Corps

General of Infantry Otto Eduardovich von **Shtubendorf** (25 Jan 1837 - 23 Jul 1918)
2 May 1867 - 14 Jan 1897:	Chief of Cartography, Military Topographical Section, General Staff
17 Apr 1877:	Promoted to *Major-General*
30 Aug 1888:	Promoted to *Lieutenant-General*
14 Jan 1897 - 1 Jan 1903:	Chief of Military Topographical Section, General Staff
1 Jan 1903 - 1906:	Member of the Military Council
6 Apr 1903:	Promoted to *General of Infantry*
1906:	Retired

Major-General Lyudvig-Severin Ivanovich **Shukevich** (15 Jan 1840 - ?)
1 Oct 1897:	Promoted to *Major-General*
1 Oct 1897 - 20 Nov 1897:	Commander, 42nd Artillery Brigade
20 Nov 1897 - 19 Jan 1901:	Commander, 1st Artillery Brigade

Major-General Karl Konradovich **Shuld** (28 Dec 1829 - ?)
11 Dec 1892:	Promoted to *Major-General*
11 Dec 1892 - 2 Sep 1899:	Commander, 2nd Brigade, 30th Infantry Division

Major-General Nikolai Vasilyevich **Shulga** (24 Nov 1863 - 21 Oct 1929)
14 Apr 1909 - 13 Jan 1914:	Staff Officer for Special Assignments, Inspectorate-General of Artillery
14 Apr 1913:	Promoted to *Major-General*
13 Jan 1914 - 1918:	Special Assignments General, Inspectorate-General of Artillery

General of Infantry Aleksandr Nikolayevich **Shulgin** (17 Aug 1836 - 1911)
23 Apr 1876 - 25 Oct 1884:	Commander, 69th Infantry Regiment
25 Oct 1884:	Promoted to *Major-General*
25 Oct 1884 - 27 Nov 1884:	Unassigned
27 Nov 1884 - 13 Jul 1885:	Commander, Kexholm Grenadier Regiment
13 Jul 1885 - 26 Jul 1887:	Deputy Chief of Staff, Warsaw Military District
26 Jul 1887 - 11 Oct 1892:	Chief of Staff, Fortress Warsaw

11 Oct 1892 - 16 Aug 1894:	Commander, 48th Reserve Infantry Brigade
16 Aug 1894 - 16 Jan 1901:	Commander, 36th Infantry Division
14 Nov 1894:	Promoted to *Lieutenant-General*
16 Jan 1901:	Promoted to *General of Infantry*
16 Jan 1901:	Retired

General of the Fleet Grigory Ivanovich **Shulgin** (5 Mar 1855 - 1923)

22 Apr 1907:	Promoted to *Major-General of the Admiralty*
1907 - 19 Aug 1910:	Deputy Commandant, Nikolayev Naval Academy
19 Aug 1910 - 1917:	Commandant, Nikolayev Naval Academy
6 Dec 1911:	Promoted to *Lieutenant-General of the Admiralty*
8 Apr 1913:	Redesignated *Lieutenant-General of the Fleet*
1917:	Promoted to *General of the Fleet*
1917:	Retired

Lieutenant-General Mikhail Mikhailovich **Shulgin** (11 Apr 1834 - 22 Jul 1904)

22 Jan 1872 - 22 Feb 1879:	Commander, 103rd Infantry Regiment
1 Jan 1879:	Promoted to *Major-General*
22 Feb 1879 - 19 May 1881:	At the disposal of the Commanding General, Vilnius Military District
19 May 1881 - 24 Aug 1892:	Commander, 1st Brigade, 1st Infantry Division
24 Aug 1892 - 9 Jan 1900:	Commander, 1st Infantry Division
30 Aug 1892:	Promoted to *Lieutenant-General*
9 Jan 1900:	Retired

Lieutenant-General Vladimir Mikhailovich **Shulgin** (8 Jun 1838 - 3 Aug 1911)

2 Jan 1881 - 24 Jan 1885:	Chief, Military Topographical Branch, East Siberian Military District
15 May 1883:	Promoted to *Major-General*
24 Jan 1885 - 16 Apr 1887:	Chief, Military Topographical Branch, Amur Military District
16 Apr 1887 - 3 Aug 1911:	Chief of Topographical Survey, Northwest Border Area
6 Dec 1895:	Promoted to *Lieutenant-General*

Major-General Vasily Lvovich **Shulkevich** (27 Feb 1860 - ?)

1914 - 1916:	Attached to 11th Finnish Rifle Regiment
1916:	Promoted to *Major-General*
1916:	Retired
25 Feb 1917 - 5 Apr 1917:	Recalled; Commander, 33rd Replacement Infantry Brigade
5 Apr 1917 - 1918:	Special Assignments General, Kazan Military District

Major-General Arnold Khristoforovich **Shulman** (2 Sep 1855 - 9 Aug 1917)

2 Apr 1913:	Promoted to *Major-General*
2 Apr 1913 - 23 Apr 1915:	Commander, 48th Artillery Brigade
23 Apr 1915 - 1917:	POW

Major-General Karl Aleksandrovich **Shulman** (23 Aug 1852 - ?)
27 May 1901 - 16 May 1902: Deputy Intendant, Odessa Military District
6 Dec 1901: Promoted to *Major-General*
16 May 1902 - 1903: Intendant, Caucasus Military District

General of Infantry Karl-Avgust Aleksandrovich **Shulman** (16 Aug 1861 - 1918)
20 May 1903 - 22 Apr 1906: Commander, 50th Infantry Regiment
2 Apr 1906: Promoted to *Major-General*
22 Apr 1906 - 6 Mar 1909: Chief of Staff, Fortress Kronstadt
6 Mar 1909 - 14 Sep 1915: Commandant of Fortress Osovets
30 Jul 1911: Promoted to *Lieutenant-General*
14 Sep 1915 - Jan 1916: Commander, 30th Replacement Infantry Brigade
Jan 1916 - 17 Jun 1916: Commander, 36th Replacement Infantry Brigade
17 Jun 1916 - 10 Oct 1916: Commander, 102nd Infantry Division
10 Oct 1916 - 4 Mar 1917: Reserve officer, Kiev Military District
4 Mar 1917 - Oct 1917: Reserve officer, Petrograd Military District
1917: Promoted to *General of Infantry*

General of Infantry Nikolai Gustavovich **Shulman** (12 Sep 1828 - 26 Jul 1900)
6 Aug 1865 - 20 May 1871: Intendant, Eastern Siberian Military District
30 Aug 1866: Promoted to *Major-General*
20 May 1871 - 19 May 1878: Intendant, Caucasus Military District
18 Dec 1877: Promoted to *Lieutenant-General*
19 May 1878 - 12 Jul 1879: Unassigned
12 Jul 1879 - 11 Dec 1895: Deputy Intendant-General, Ministry of War
11 Dec 1895 - 26 Jul 1900: Member, Committee for Wounded Veterans
14 May 1896: Promoted to *General of Infantry*

Major-General Sergey Nikolayevich von **Shulman** (23 Oct 1869 - 6 Jul 1927)
17 Dec 1905 - 22 Apr 1917: Chief of Bureau, Main Military Legal Service Directorate
6 Dec 1911: Promoted to *Major-General*
22 Apr 1917 - 1918: Chief of Military Prisons Section, Main Military Legal Service Directorate

Lieutenant-General Anatoly Lvovich **Shults** (3 Aug 1860 - ?)
3 Jun 1903 - 4 Sep 1909: Ministry of War Representative, Omsk Military District
6 Dec 1908: Promoted to *Major-General*
4 Sep 1909 - 1918: Ministry of War Representative, Kazan Military District
6 Dec 1914: Promoted to *Lieutenant-General*

Major-General Dmitry Lvovich **Shults** (23 Oct 1853 - ?)
4 Jun 1903: Promoted to *Major-General*
4 Jun 1903 - 2 Mar 1904: Commander, 1st Brigade, 27th Infantry Division

Major-General Eduard Eduardovich von **Shults** (15 Jul 1841 - 1912)
8 Nov 1884 - 13 Sep 1895: Commander, 82nd Infantry Regiment
14 Nov 1894: Promoted to *Major-General*

13 Sep 1895 - 16 Jul 1901: Commander, 1st Brigade, 12th Infantry Division
16 Jul 1901: Retired

Major-General Ivan Aleksandrovich von **Shults** (26 Mar 1856 - Mar 1912)
8 Sep 1910: Promoted to *Major-General*
8 Sep 1910 - Mar 1912: Commander, 37th Artillery Brigade

Major-General Karl Eduardovich von **Shults** (29 Aug 1836 - 5 Jun 1896)
4 Dec 1888 - 5 Jun 1896: Attached to the Ministry of War
18 Feb 1889: Promoted to *Major-General*

Vice-Admiral Maksimilian Mikhail Fyodorovich von **Shults** (6 Jan 1862 - 1919)
5 Apr 1910 - 18 Mar 1913: Commander of Mine-Layer Detachment, Baltic Fleet
6 Dec 1911: Promoted to *Rear-Admiral*
18 Mar 1913 - 4 Nov 1913: Commander, Cruiser Brigade, Baltic Fleet
18 Nov 1913 - 4 Apr 1917: Commander, Siberian Flotilla
30 Jul 1915: Promoted to *Vice-Admiral*
4 Apr 1917 - 23 Jun 1917: Reserve officer, Ministry of the Navy
23 Jun 1917: Dismissed

Lieutenant-General Karl-Teofil-Mikhail-Nikolai Karlovich **Shultse** (15 Apr 1854 - 14 Jul 1935)
20 Apr 1904: Promoted to *Major-General*
20 Apr 1904 - 1913: Duty General, Odessa Military District
15 Apr 1913: Promoted to *Lieutenant-General*
1913: Retired

Major-General Aleksey Romanovich **Shulyachenko** (17 Mar 1841 - 29 May 1903)
23 Mar 1887 - 29 May 1903: Professor, Nikolayev Engineering Academy
30 Aug 1889: Promoted to *Major-General*
26 Sep 1890 - 20 Dec 1899: Inspector of Classes, Nikolayev Engineering Academy
21 May 1892 - 29 May 1903: Member of the Engineering Council, Ministry of Communications

Major-General Fyodor Danilovich **Shulyakovsky** (2 Sep 1851 - 1910)
17 Dec 1905 - 14 Aug 1906: Military Judge, Siberian Military District Court
2 Apr 1906: Promoted to *Major-General*
14 Aug 1906 - 1910: Military Judge, Omsk Military District Court

Major-General of the Admiralty Georgy Petrovich **Shumov** (7 Mar 1859 - 1 Jun 1929)
9 Nov 1908 - 1912: Attached to Sevastopol Naval Depot
1912: Promoted to *Major-General of the Admiralty*
1912: Retired

Major-General Pavel Andreyevich **Shupinsky** (6 Apr 1855 - ?)
22 Feb 1904: Promoted to *Major-General*
22 Feb 1904 - Sep 1905: Commander, 2nd Brigade, 2nd East Siberian Rifle Division

Major-General Ferdinand Matveyevich **Shushkevich** (24 Jul 1842 - ?)
17 Apr 1905:	Promoted to *Major-General*
17 Apr 1905 - 1909:	Member of the Engineering Committee, Main Engineering Directorate

General of Cavalry Nikolai Vasilyevich **Shutlevort** (20 Aug 1845 - ?)
24 Jul 1891:	Promoted to *Major-General*
24 Jul 1891 - 5 Jun 1896:	Chief of Staff, XIV. Army Corps
5 Jun 1896 - 13 Jan 1899:	Chief of Staff, Caucasus Military District
13 Jan 1899 - 9 Jun 1903:	Commander, 6th Cavalry Division
6 Dec 1899:	Promoted to *Lieutenant-General*
9 Jun 1903 - 11 Mar 1904:	Commander, 13th Cavalry Division
11 Mar 1904 - 2 Nov 1906:	Commanding General, I. Cavalry Corps
2 Nov 1906 - 30 Apr 1910:	Commanding General, V. Army Corps
6 Dec 1907:	Promoted to *General of Cavalry*
30 Apr 1910:	Retired

Major-General Count Andrey Petrovich **Shuvalov** (11 Nov 1865 - 1 Dec 1928)
25 Mar 1912:	Promoted to *Major-General*
25 Mar 1912 - Aug 1914:	General à la suite
Aug 1914 - 10 Dec 1915:	Attached to the C-in-C, 1st Army
10 Dec 1915 - Oct 1917:	Inspector of Medical Institutions, Petrograd

General of Infantry Count Pavel Andreyevich **Shuvalov** (13 Nov 1830 - 7 Apr 1908)
25 May 1863 - 24 Nov 1864:	Commander, Life Guards Rifle Battalion
30 Aug 1864:	Promoted to *Major-General*
24 Nov 1864 - 9 Sep 1867:	Commander, Life Guards Semyonov Regiment
9 Sep 1867 - 9 Aug 1877:	Chief of Staff, St. Petersburg Military District
17 May 1871:	Promoted to *General-Adjutant*
13 May 1873:	Promoted to *Lieutenant-General*
9 Aug 1877 - 17 Apr 1879:	Commander, 2nd Guards Infantry Division
1 Feb 1878 - 10 Aug 1878:	Acting Commanding General, Guards Corps
17 Apr 1879 - 14 Mar 1881:	Commanding General, Grenadier Corps
14 Mar 1881 - 1 Apr 1885:	Commanding General, Guards Corps
1 Apr 1885 - 13 Dec 1894:	Ambassador Extraordinary & Plenipotentiary Envoy in Germany
30 Aug 1887:	Promoted to *General of Infantry*
13 Dec 1894 - 12 Dec 1896:	Governor-General of Warsaw, Commanding General, Warsaw Military District
14 May 1896 - 7 Apr 1908:	Member of the State Council

Major-General Count Pavel Pavlovich **Shuvalov** (19 May 1859 - 28 Jun 1905)
20 Feb 1898 - 6 Mar 1903:	Mayor of Odessa
14 Apr 1902:	Promoted to *Major-General*
6 Mar 1903 - 18 Apr 1905:	General for Special Assignments, Ministry of Internal Affairs
18 Apr 1905 - 28 Jun 1905:	Mayor of Moscow

Major-General Count Pavel Petrovich **Shuvalov** (14 Feb 1847 - 12 Oct 1902)
10 Feb 1893:	Promoted to *Major-General*
10 Feb 1893 - 24 Nov 1894:	Commander, Life Guards 4th Rifle Battalion
24 Nov 1894 - 20 Nov 1895:	Commander, Life Guards Chasseur Regiment
20 Nov 1895 - 1898:	At the disposal of the Minister of War
1898:	Retired

General of Infantry Dmitry Savelyevich **Shuvayev** (12 Oct 1854 - 19 Dec 1937)
23 May 1899:	Promoted to *Major-General*
23 May 1899 - 10 Jan 1905:	Commandant, Kiev Military School
10 Jan 1905 - 21 May 1908:	Commander, 5th Infantry Division
6 Dec 1906:	Promoted to *Lieutenant-General*
21 May 1908 - 8 Aug 1909:	Commanding General, II. Caucasus Army Corps
8 Aug 1909 - 15 Mar 1916:	Intendant-General of the Army, Chief of the Main Intendant Directorate
27 Jul 1911:	Promoted to *General of Infantry*
15 Mar 1916 - 3 Jan 1917:	Minister of War
3 Jan 1917 - Oct 1917:	Member of the State Council
3 Oct 1917 - 1918:	Member of the Military Council

General of Engineers Boris Antonovich **Shvanebakh** (29 May 1823 - 8 Feb 1905)
19 Jul 1863 - 27 Apr 1874:	Director of the Alexander Cadet Corps
19 Apr 1864:	Promoted to *Major-General*
9 Oct 1863 - 27 Apr 1874:	Commandant, 3rd Aleksandr Military School
27 Apr 1874 - 8 Feb 1905:	Conference Member, Nikolai Engineering Academy
30 Aug 1874:	Promoted to *Lieutenant-General*
30 Aug 1892:	Promoted to *General of Engineers*

General of Infantry Leopold-Eduard Aleksandrovich **Shvank** (29 Oct 1849 - ?)
20 Nov 1899:	Promoted to *Major-General*
20 Nov 1899 - 28 Sep 1904:	Chief of Staff, VI. Army Corps
28 Sep 1904 - 14 Jan 1905:	Quartermaster-General, 2nd Manchurian Army
14 Jan 1905 - 25 Mar 1905:	At the disposal of the C-in-C of Imperial Forces against Japan
25 Mar 1905 - 6 Dec 1906:	At the disposal of the Chief of the General Staff
6 Dec 1906:	Promoted to *Lieutenant-General*
6 Dec 1906 - 16 Jan 1909:	Commander, 27th Infantry Division
16 Jan 1909 - 3 Jun 1910:	Commander, 24th Infantry Division
3 Jun 1910 - 1 Sep 1912:	Commanding General, VI. Army Corps
1 Sep 1912:	Promoted to *General of Infantry*
1 Sep 1912:	Retired

Major-General of the Fleet Maksimilian Fyodorovich **Shvank** (7 Apr 1867 - ?)
1911 - 1916:	Senior Clerk, Naval General Staff
30 Jul 1915:	Promoted to *Major-General of the Fleet*

Lieutenant-General Aleksey Vladimirovich von **Shvarts** (15 Mar 1874 - 27 Sep 1953)
13 Aug 1914 - 13 Nov 1915:	Commandant of Fortress Ivangorod

7 Nov 1914:	Promoted to *Major-General*
13 Nov 1915 - 23 Jul 1916:	Commandant of Fortress Kars
23 Jul 1916 - 22 Mar 1917:	Commander, Trebizond Fortified Area
22 Mar 1917 - Oct 1917:	Chief of Main Military Technical Directorate
24 Aug 1917:	Promoted to *Lieutenant-General*

Admiral Sergey Pavlovich **Shvarts** (18 Feb 1829 - 29 Mar 1905)
1 Jan 1868:	Promoted to *Rear-Admiral*
1 Jan 1868 - 26 Nov 1883:	Chairman, Artillery Branch, Naval Technical Committee
1880:	Promoted to *Vice-Admiral*
26 Nov 1883 - 30 Aug 1893:	Commander, Port of Kronstadt, Military Governor of Kronstadt
30 Aug 1893:	Promoted to *Admiral*
30 Aug 1893 - 29 Mar 1905:	Chairman, Supreme Naval Tribunal

Major-General of Naval Engineers Ivan Semyonovich **Shvedov** (1 Apr 1861 - ?)
6 Dec 1913:	Promoted to *Major-General of Naval Engineers*
1913 - 1917:	Attached the Guards Naval Depot
1917:	Retired

Major-General Konstantin Maksimovich **Shvedov** (13 May 1848 - ?)
27 Oct 1899:	Promoted to *Major-General*
27 Oct 1899 - 2 Sep 1905:	Commander, 1st Brigade, 2nd Caucasus Cossack Division
2 Sep 1905 - Nov 1906:	Commander, 2nd Caucasus Cossack Division

General of Artillery Nikolai Konstantinovich **Shvedov** (26 Feb 1849 - 18 Jun 1920)
39 Jun 1886 - 15 Oct 1893:	Deputy Inspector of Borderguards
1893:	Promoted to *Major-General*
15 Oct 1893 - 8 Apr 1894:	Unassigned
8 Apr 1894 - 4 Jul 1897:	Transferred to the reserve
4 Jul 1897 - 1 Jan 1917:	Attached to the Imperial Main Quarters
6 Apr 1903:	Promoted to *Lieutenant-General*
22 Dec 1915:	Promoted to *General of Artillery*
1 Jan1917 - Dec 1917:	Member of the State Council
Dec 1917:	Dismissed

Major-General Iosif Fyodorovich **Shvemberger** (24 Jul 1844 - 25 Jun 1899)
3 Jan 1895:	Promoted to *Major-General*
3 Jan 1895 - 24 Apr 1899:	Special Assignments General to the Ataman, Don Cossack Army
24 Apr 1899 - 25 Jun 1899:	Chief of Staff, Don Cossack Army

Major-General Konstantin Konstantinovich **Shverin** (24 Jul 1849 - 28 Apr 1906)
18 Feb 1904 - 16 Apr 1904:	Commander, 3rd East Siberian Rifle Artillery Brigade
16 Apr 1904 - 28 Apr 1906:	Commander of Artillery, III. East Siberian Army Corps

4 Jul 1904: Promoted to *Major-General*

Major-General Aleksandr Aleksandrovich **Shvetsov** (15 Jul 1865 - 22 Oct 1927)
4 Dec 1912 - 1915: Commander, 52nd Infantry Regiment
16 May 1915: Promoted to *Major-General*
1915 - 12 Apr 1917: Commander, Brigade, 23rd Infantry Division
12 Apr 1917 - 20 May 1917: Commander, 19th Siberian Rifle Division
20 May 1917 - 8 Jun 1917: Commander, 2nd Infantry Division
8 Jun 1917 - 1918: Commander, 19th Siberian Rifle Division

Major-General Andrey Aleksandrovich **Shvetsov** (27 Dec 1868 - 9 Oct 1934)
21 Nov 1914 - 1915: Commander, 177th Infantry Regiment
1915 - 7 Jul 1916: Reserve officer, Minsk Military District
7 Jul 1916 - 26 Jun 1917: Commander, Life Guards Grenadier Regiment
16 Jul 1916: Promoted to *Major-General*
26 Jun 1917 - 1918: Commander, Brigade, 2nd Guards Infantry Division

Lieutenant-General Pyotr Aleksandrovich **Shveykovsky** (17 Jun 1857 - ?)
15 Apr 1905 - 19 Sep 1906: Military Judge, Warsaw Military District Court
17 Apr 1905: Promoted to *Major-General*
19 Sep 1906 - 13 Feb 1907: Military Prosecutor, Omsk Military District
13 Feb 1907 - 24 Oct 1908: Military Prosecutor, Turkestan Military District
24 Oct 1908 - 1914: Chairman of the Military Tribunal, Irkutsk Military District
14 Apr 1913: Promoted to *Lieutenant-General*

Major-General Vladimir Gavrilovich **Sidelnikov** (11 Jun 1847 - ?)
10 Jun 1904: Promoted to *Major-General*
10 Jun 1904 - 1909: Commander, 1st Brigade, 13th Infantry Division

Admiral Aleksandr Karlovich **Sidensner** (25 Aug 1842 - ?)
6 Dec 1894: Promoted to *Rear-Admiral*
13 Jan 1897 - 9 Apr 1901: Junior Flagman, Black Sea Training Squadron
9 Apr 1901 - 6 Dec 1901: Junior Flagman, 1st Naval Division
6 Dec 1901: Promoted to *Vice-Admiral*
6 Dec 1901 - 9 Feb 1904: Senior Flagman, 2nd Naval Division
9 Feb 1904 - 19 Nov 1907: Senior Flagman, Baltic Fleet
19 Nov 1907: Promoted to *Admiral*
19 Nov 1907: Retired

Major-General Nikolai Maksimovich **Sidorenko** (1 Feb 1835 - ?)
16 Apr 1889: Promoted to *Major-General*
16 Apr 1889 - 18 Aug 1895: Commander, 1st Brigade, 33rd Infantry Division
18 Aug 1895 - 1897: Commander, 2nd Caucasus Reserve Infantry Brigade

General of Infantry Leonty Leontyevich **Sidorin** (12 Jun 1852 - 15 Feb 1918)
26 Nov 1902: Promoted to *Major-General*
26 Nov 1902 - 17 Jan 1904: At the disposal of the Chief of the General Staff

17 Jan 1904 - 16 Feb 1905:	Chief of Staff, VIII. Army Corps
16 Feb 1905 - 17 Jun 1905:	At the disposal of the C-in-C, 2nd Manchurian Army
17 Jun 1905 - 8 Feb 1914:	Commander, 1st Siberian Rifle Division
30 Jul 1907:	Promoted to *Lieutenant-General*
8 Feb 1914 - 22 Dec 1914:	Commanding General, V. Siberian Army Corps
6 Apr 1914:	Promoted to *General of Infantry*
22 Dec 1914 - 21 Mar 1915:	Reserve officer, Dvinsk Military District
21 Mar 1915 - Oct 1917:	Member, Committee for Wounded Veterans

General of Artillery Nikolai Petrovich **Sidorov** (10 Dec 1828 - 1902)
10 Jan 1867 - 7 Dec 1879:	Commander, Artillery Brigade
22 Jun 1875:	Promoted to *Major-General*
7 Dec 1879 - Sep 1899:	Commander of Artillery, V. Army Corps
6 May 1884:	Promoted to *Lieutenant-General*
Sep 1899:	Promoted to *General of Artillery*
Sep 1899:	Retired

Major-General Aleksandr Nikolayevich **Sigunov** (23 Nov 1838 - 1905)
31 May 1886 - 1905:	Deputy Editor of the Artillery Journal
30 Aug 1888:	Promoted to *Major-General*

Lieutenant-General Konstantin Vasilyevich **Sikstel** (22 Mar 1826 - 27 Jan 1899)
23 Mar 1880 - 8 Mar 1893:	Artillery Inspector, Omsk Military District
13 Feb 1883:	Promoted to *Major-General*
8 Mar 1893 - 27 Jan 1899:	Commander of Artillery, Moscow Military District
30 Aug 1893:	Promoted to *Lieutenant-General*

Major-General Emmanuil Viktorovich **Sila-Novitsky** (25 Mar 1852 - 26 Apr 1917)
29 Apr 1906 - 28 Dec 1908:	Commander, 221st Reserve Infantry Regiment
28 Dec 1908:	Promoted to *Major-General*
28 Dec 1908:	Retired
11 Sep 1914 - 26 Apr 1917:	Recalled; Commander, 11th Replacement Infantry Brigade

Vice-Admiral Fyodor Fyodorovich **Silman** (17 Jan 1854 - 12 Mar 1926)
11 Sep 1906 - 20 Sep 1911:	Director, Emperor Paul Invalid Home
26 Feb 1907:	Promoted to *Rear-Admiral*
13 Oct 1909 - 14 Feb 1910.	Member of the Finance Department, Finnish Senate
20 Sep 1911:	Promoted to *Vice-Admiral*
20 Sep 1911:	Retired

Lieutenant-General of the Fleet Nikolai Fyodorovich **Silman** (9 May 1858 - 6 Jan 1929)
26 Jan 1909 - 20 Nov 1913:	Commander, Sevastopol Naval Crew
6 Dec 1911:	Promoted to *Major-General of the Admiralty*
8 Apr 1913:	Redesignated *Major-General of the Fleet*
20 Nov 1913 - 5 Aug 1916:	Governor of Vaasa
22 Mar 1915:	Promoted to *Lieutenant-General of the Fleet*
5 Aug 1916 - 1917:	Governor of Fortress St. Michael

Major-General Pavel Petrovich **Silnitsky** (7 Apr 1845 - ?)
9 Feb 1899 - 1904:					Commander of Gendarmerie, Orlovsk Province
1 Jan 1901:						Promoted to *Major-General*

Major-General Konstantin Onufriyevich **Silvestrovich** (8 Jul 1836 - 2 Jun 1902)
4 May 1891:						Promoted to *Major-General*
4 May 1891 - Jul 1896:				Commander, 2nd Brigade, 20th Infantry Division
2 Oct 1891 - Jul 1896:				Chief of Grozny Military Hospital

Major-General Vladimir Yakovlevich **Simanov** (1 Jul 1856 - ?)
1916 - 1917:						Commander of Engineers, 7th Army
30 Jul 1916:						Promoted to *Major-General*

Major-General Ivan Dmitriyevich **Simanovsky** (4 Nov 1850 - ?)
18 Feb 1899 - 20 Sep 1915:			Attached to Technical Artillery Institutions
29 Mar 1909:						Promoted to *Major-General*
20 Sep 1915 - Oct 1917:				Inspector, Technical Artillery Institutions

Lieutenant-General Panteleymon Nikolayevich **Simansky** (30 Sep 1866 - 22 Apr 1938)
14 Feb 1907 - 16 Mar 1910:			Member, Military Commission on the history of the Russian-Japanese War
22 Jan 1909:						Promoted to *Major-General*
16 Mar 1910 - 24 Mar 1910:			At the disposal of the Minister of War
24 Mar 1910 - 19 Jul 1914:			Commander, 2nd Brigade, 35th Infantry Division
19 Jul 1914 - 7 Jul 1917:			Commander, 61st Infantry Division
7 Jul 1917 - 1917:					Reserve officer, Moscow Military District
1917:							Promoted to *Lieutenant-General*
1917:							Commanding General, XLVII. Army Corps

Major-General Aleksandr Vasilyevich **Simbirsky** (24 Dec 1851 - ?)
18 Jan 1902 - 28 May 1903:			Chief of Okhtenskaya Explosives Factory
14 Apr 1902:						Promoted to *Major-General*
28 May 1903 - 1908:				Chief of Mikhailovsky Shostensky Gunpowder Factory

General of Infantry Aleksandr Ivanovich **Simonov** (27 Jun 1829 - 1903)
21 Oct 1870 - 24 Sep 1881:			Military Commander, Livonia Province
21 Nov 1875:						Promoted to *Major-General*
24 Sep 1881 - 7 Oct 1892:			Commander, 4th Regional Brigade
30 Aug 1888:						Promoted to *Lieutenant-General*
7 Oct 1892 - 1899:					Commander, 5th (Vilnius) Regional Brigade
1899:							Promoted to *General of Infantry*
1899:							Retired

Major-General Leonid Yakovlevich **Simonov** (6 Apr 1862 - ?)
? - 24 Jun 1915:					Commander, 1st Battalion, 7th Siberian Rifle Artillery Brigade
19 Jun 1915:						Promoted to *Major-General*
24 Jun 1915 - 17 Mar 1917:			Commander, 68th Artillery Brigade

17 Mar 1917 - 1918: Inspector of Artillery, II. Army Corps

Major-General Mikhail Agafangelovich **Simonov** (29 Mar 1871 - ?)
8 Jul 1915 - 19 Oct 1917: Chief of Staff, XLIII. Army Corps
6 Dec 1915: Promoted to *Major-General*
19 Oct 1917 - 1918: Chief of Lines of Communication, 5th Army

Lieutenant-General Nikolai Alekseyevich **Simonov** (4 May 1851 - 1917)
31 Dec 1888 - 14 Jul 1900: Ataman, 1st Military Division, Siberian Cossack Army
14 May 1896: Promoted to *Major-General*
14 Jul 1900 - 18 Feb 1901: Commander, Siberian Cossack Division
18 Feb 1901 - 4 Feb 1904: Ataman, 1st Military Division, Siberian Cossack Army
4 Feb 1904 - 26 Jul 1904: Commander, Siberian Cossack Division
28 Mar 1904: Promoted to *Lieutenant-General*
26 Jul 1904 - 1907: At the disposal of the Ataman, Siberian Cossack Army
1907: Retired

Major-General David Petrovich **Simonson** (23 Mar 1859 - 13 Jan 1933)
31 Mar 1912 - 22 Nov 1915: Commander, 66th Infantry Regiment
22 Oct 1915: Promoted to *Major-General*
22 Nov 1915 - 19 Oct 1916: Commander, Brigade, 17th Infantry Division
19 Oct 1916 - 21 Jan 1917: Commander, Kaluga Infantry Brigade
21 Jan 1917 - 1917: Commander, 135th Infantry Division
1917 - 15 Oct 1917: Commander, 4th Special Infantry Division
15 Oct 1917 - 31 Oct 1917: Reserve officer, Dvinsk Military District
31 Oct 1917: Dismissed

Lieutenant-General Aleksandr Petrovich **Sinelnikov** (21 Oct 1851 - ?)
3 May 1903 - 1911: Chief of Moscow Military Hospital
1903: Promoted to *Major-General*
1911: Promoted to *Lieutenant-General*
1911: Retired

Major-General Nikolai Grigoryevich **Sineokov** (14 Nov 1873 - 1934)
10 Jun 1915 - 23 Jul 1916: Commander, 48th Artillery Brigade
25 Jul 1915: Promoted to *Major-General*
23 Jul 1916 - 31 Mar 1917: General for Assignments, Inspector-General of Artillery
31 Mar 1917 - 29 May 1917: Inspector of Artillery, II. Caucasus Army Corps
29 May 1917 - Oct 1917: Inspector of Artillery, 4th Army

General of Artillery Aleksandr Nikolayevich **Sinitsyn** (31 May 1849 - 9 Feb 1924)
9 Sep 1899 - 31 Dec 1913: Commandant of the Officers Artillery School
9 Apr 1900: Promoted to *Major-General*
30 Jul 1906: Promoted to *Lieutenant-General*
31 Dec 1913: Promoted to *General of Artillery*
31 Dec 1913: Retired
18 Jun 1915 - 30 Apr 1917: Recalled; Inspector of Artillery, XL. Army Corps
30 Apr 1917 - Oct 1917: Reserve officer, Petrograd Military District

Major-General Afanasy Kuzmich **Sinkevich** (18 Jan 1866 - ?)
25 Apr 1915 - 1917: Commander, 16th Infantry Regiment
12 Dec 1916: Promoted to *Major-General*

Lieutenant-General Mikhail Nikolayevich **Sipyagin** (12 Nov 1856 - ?)
29 Oct 1903 - 14 Apr 1904: Attached to the General Staff
6 Dec 1903: Promoted to *Major-General*
14 Apr 1904 - 1909: Chief of the Feldjaeger Corps
1909: Promoted to *Lieutenant-General*
1909: Retired

General of Infantry Leonid-Otto Ottovich **Sirelius** (14 May 1859 - 1920)
11 Jan 1897 - 3 Jun 1903: Military Attaché, Denmark & Sweden
14 Apr 1902: Promoted to *Major-General*
3 Jun 1903 - 18 Feb 1906: Commander, Life Guards Chasseur Regiment
18 Feb 1906 - 10 Jul 1908: Commander, 1st Brigade, 1st Guards Infantry Division
10 Jul 1908: Promoted to *Lieutenant-General*
10 Jul 1908 - 11 Jun 1910: Commander, 23rd Infantry Division
11 Jun 1910 - 18 Aug 1914: Commander, 3rd Guards Infantry Division
18 Aug 1914 - 30 Aug 1914: Commanding General, I. Army Corps
30 Aug 1914 - 5 Nov 1914: Reserve officer, Minsk Military District
5 Nov 1914 - 28 Dec 1914: Commanding General, XXIII. Army Corps
6 Dec 1914: Promoted to *General of Infantry*
28 Dec 1914 - 29 Apr 1915: At the disposal of the C-in-C, Northwestern Front
29 Apr 1915 - 3 Jun 1915: Commanding General, XXXVII. Army Corps
3 Jun 1915 - 2 Oct 1915: At the disposal of the C-in-C, Northwestern Front
2 Oct 1915 - 10 Apr 1917: Commanding General, IV. Siberian Army Corps
10 Apr 1917 - 28 Sep 1917: Reserve officer, Petrograd Military District
28 Sep 1917: Retired

Major-General Vladimir Mironovich **Sirotsynsky** (12 Jun 1832 - ?)
30 Aug 1882: Promoted to *Major-General*
30 Aug 1882 - 20 Jul 1884: Unassigned
20 Jul 1884 - 24 Apr 1889: Commander, 2nd Brigade, 26th Infantry Division
24 Apr 1889 - 18 Nov 1894: Commander, 2nd Brigade, 16th Infantry Division

Major-General Nikanor Fyodorovich **Sitnyakovsky** (1845 - 1 May 1910)
? - 1910: Chief of Military Topography Department, Turkestan Military District
1910: Promoted to *Major-General*

Major-General Aleksandr Aleksandrovich **Siverbrik** (11 Aug 1860 - 1911)
20 Aug 1908 - 1911: Commander, 2nd Battalion, 41st Artillery Brigade, Deputy Commander, 41st Artillery Brigade
1911: Promoted to *Major-General*

Lieutenant-General Aleksandr Mikhailovich **Sivers** (8 Dec 1868 - ?)
7 Oct 1911: Promoted to *Major-General*

7 Oct 1911 - 21 Mar 1913:	Commander, 14th Artillery Brigade
21 Mar 1913 - 7 Apr 1915:	Commander, Life Guards 2nd Artillery Brigade
7 Apr 1915 - 16 Apr 1916:	Inspector of Artillery, XX. Army Corps
23 Dec 1915:	Promoted to *Lieutenant-General*
16 Apr 1916 - 1918:	Inspector of Artillery, 10th Army

General of Infantry Faddei Vasilievich **Sivers** (18 Oct 1853 - ?)

31 Jul 1900:	Promoted to *Major-General*
31 Jul 1900 - 14 Dec 1900:	Chief of Staff, III. Siberian Army Corps
14 Dec 1900 - 7 Aug 1901:	Attached to the General Staff
7 Aug 1901 - 11 Aug 1902:	Chief of Staff, VII. Army Corps
11 Aug 1902 - 19 Nov 1904:	Chief of Staff, XVIII. Army Corps
19 Nov 1904 - 3 Dec 1906:	Commander, 27th Infantry Division
3 Dec 1906 - 21 Dec 1908:	Chief of Staff, Vilnius Military District
6 Dec 1906:	Promoted to *Lieutenant-General*
21 Dec 1908 - 3 Mar 1911:	Commanding General, XVI. Army Corps
3 Mar 1911 - 23 Sep 1914:	Commanding General, X. Army Corps
6 Dec 1912:	Promoted to *General of Infantry*
23 Sep 1914 - 25 Apr 1915:	C-in-C, 10th Army
25 Apr 1915:	Dismissed

Major-General Konstantin Lvovich **Sivers** (15 Sep 1856 - ?)

17 Jul 1900 - 25 Mar 1905:	Commander, 9th Grenadier Regiment
25 Mar 1905:	Promoted to *Major-General*
25 Mar 1905 - Jun 1907:	Commander, 1st Brigade, 16th Infantry Division

General of Artillery Count Mikhail Aleksandrovich **Sivers** (25 Oct 1834 - 1912)

8 Nov 1876 - 7 Aug 1888:	Commander, Life Guards 2nd Artillery Brigade
1 Jan 1878:	Promoted to *Major-General*
8 Nov 1879:	Promoted to *Major-General à la suite*
7 Aug 1888 - 28 Sep 1892:	Commander of Artillery, XIII. Army Corps
30 Aug 1888:	Promoted to *Lieutenant-General*
28 Sep 1892 - 4 Nov 1896:	Commander of Artillery, XVIII. Army Corps
4 Nov 1896 - 12 Feb 1897:	Commander, 24th Infantry Division
12 Feb 1897 - 2 Feb 1900:	Commander, 23rd Infantry Division
2 Feb 1900 - 1905:	Member, Committee for Wounded Veterans
9 Apr 1900:	Promoted to *General of Artillery*
1905:	Retired

Lieutenant-General Nikolai Nikolayevich **Sivers** (29 Sep 1869 - 1919)

14 May 1913:	Promoted to *Major-General*
14 May 1913 - 19 Jul 1914:	Duty General, Moscow Military District
19 Jul 1914 - 30 Jul 1914:	Duty General, 5th Army
30 Jul 1914 - Dec 1914:	Acting Quartermaster-General, 5th Army
Dec 1914 - 25 Jan 1915:	Chief of Staff, 5th Army
25 Jan 1915 - 19 Jun 1915:	Chief of Staff, 12th Army
19 Jun 1915 - 22 Nov 1915:	Unassigned
22 Nov 1915 - 25 Feb 1916:	Chief of Staff, 6th Army

25 Feb 1916 - 11 Aug 1916:	Chief of Staff, Northern Front
11 Aug 1916 - 22 Apr 1917:	Chief of Staff, Turkestan Military District
2 Apr 1917:	Promoted to *Lieutenant-General*
22 Apr 1917 - 31 Aug 1917:	Reserve officer, Pyotrogard Military District
31 Aug 1917 - 1918:	Deputy Chief of the General Staff

Major-General Andrey Andreyevich **Siversky** (24 Nov 1849 - ?)
23 Apr 1901:	Promoted to *Major-General*
23 Apr 1901 - 28 Jun 1901:	Commander, 2nd Brigade, 7th Infantry Division
28 Jun 1901 - 12 Nov 1907:	Commander, 1st Brigade, 5th Infantry Division

Lieutenant-General Mechislav Iosif Lyutsianovich **Sivitsky** (15 Sep 1849 - ?)
18 Dec 1904 - 18 Oct 1905:	At the disposal of the Land & Naval C-in-C, Forces operating against Japan
11 Apr 1905:	Promoted to *Major-General*
18 Oct 1905 - 27 Feb 1906:	At the disposal of the Chief of the General Staff
27 Feb 1906 - 6 May 1910:	Commander, 1st Brigade, 7th Infantry Division
6 May 1910 - 1917:	Deputy Commander, Special Amur Border District
6 May 1912:	Promoted to *Lieutenant-General*
1913:	Acting Commander, Special Amur Border District

Lieutenant-General Pyotr Nikolayevich **Sivitsky** (24 Jul 1855 - ?)
7 Mar 1908 - 10 Mar 1913:	Commander, 9th Infantry Regiment
30 Aug 1912:	Promoted to *Major-General*
10 Mar 1913 - 26 May 1915:	Commander, 1st Brigade, 22nd Infantry Division
26 May 1915 - 1917:	Commander, 23rd Replacement Infantry Brigade
1917 - 8 Oct 1917:	Reserve officer, Minsk Military District
8 Oct 1917:	Promoted to *Lieutenant-General*
8 Oct 1917:	Retired

General of Cavalry Dmitry Antonovich **Skalon** (27 Oct 1840 - 1919)
18 May 1878 - 22 Jul 1891:	Chief of Office, Inspector-General of Cavalry
30 Aug 1886:	Promoted to *Major-General*
22 Jul 1891 - 12 May 1895:	Chief of Cavalry Section, General Staff
12 May 1895:	Promoted to *Lieutenant-General*
12 May 1895 - 11 Apr 1916:	At the disposal of the Minister of War
6 Dec 1907:	Promoted to *General of Cavalry*
24 Feb 1914:	Promoted to *General-Adjutant*
11 Apr 1916 - 31 Mar 1917:	General à la suite
31 Mar 1917:	Retired

General of Cavalry Georgy Antonovich **Skalon** (24 Oct 1847 - Apr 1914)
7 Jan 1893 - 19 Aug 1894:	General for Special Assignments, Warsaw Military District
30 Aug 1893:	Promoted to *Major-General*
19 Aug 1894 - 2 Aug 1897:	Commander, Life Guards Uhlan Regiment
2 Aug 1897 - 2 Apr 1899:	Commander, 1st Brigade, 1st Guards Cavalry Division
2 Apr 1899 - 4 Apr 1901:	Commander, 4th Cavalry Division

6 Dec 1900:	Promoted to *Lieutenant-General*
4 Apr 1901 - 15 May 1905:	Commander, 2nd Guards Cavalry Division
15 May 1905 - 15 Aug 1905:	Deputy Commanding General, Warsaw Military District
15 Aug 1905 - 4 Mar 1914:	Governor-General of Warsaw, Commanding General, Warsaw Military District
17 Jan 1906:	Promoted to *General of Cavalry*

Major-General Mikhail Nikolayevich **Skalon** (19 Jan 1874 - 28 Feb 1940)
22 Apr 1915 - 5 Apr 1917:	Commander, Life Guards 4th Rifle Regiment
21 May 1915:	Promoted to *Major-General*
5 Apr 1917 - Jan 1918:	Commander, 33rd Infantry Division

General of Cavalry Nikolai Antonovich **Skalon** (1 Dec 1832 - 6 Sep 1903)
28 Oct 1866 - 8 Feb 1876:	Member of the Imperial Court
27 Jul 1870:	Promoted to *Major-General*
8 Feb 1876 - 1 Feb 1881:	General à la suite
30 Aug 1880:	Promoted to *Lieutenant-General*
1 Feb 1881 - 30 Aug 1894:	Equerry, Imperial Court
30 Aug 1894:	Promoted to *General of Cavalry*
30 Aug 1894 - 6 Sep 1903:	Chief Marshal of the Imperial Court

Major-General Pavel Nikolayevich **Skalon** (15 Jun 1868 - 14 Dec 1937)
1 Aug 1908 - 26 Jun 1917:	Inspector of Classes, Mikhailov Cadet Corps, Voronezh
6 Dec 1916:	Promoted to *Major-General*
26 Jun 1917 - Jan 1918:	Director, Irkutsk Cadet Corps

General of Infantry Vasily Danilovich **Skalon** (28 May 1835 - Jul 1907)
6 Oct 1873 - 19 Jun 1883:	Commander, Life Guards Sapper Battalion
18 Dec 1877:	Promoted to *Major-General*
19 Jun 1883 - 31 Jul 1889:	Commander, 5th Sapper Brigade
31 Jul 1889 - 30 Dec 1895:	Commander, 15th Infantry Division
30 Aug 1886:	Promoted to *Lieutenant-General*
30 Dec 1895 - 30 Mar 1896:	Commanding General, IV. Army Corps
30 Mar 1896 - 27 Sep 1897:	Commandant of Brest-Litovsk
27 Sep 1897 - 23 Jan 1901:	Commanding General, VIII. Army Corps
6 Dec 1898:	Promoted to *General of Infantry*
23 Jan 1901 - Jul 1907:	Member, Committee for Wounded Veterans

Major-General Vladimir Yevstafyevich **Skalon** (28 Nov 1872 - 29 Nov 1917)
25 Jul 1914 - 8 Nov 1917:	General for Administrative Matters attached to the Quartermaster-General, High Command
6 Dec 1916:	Promoted to *Major-General*
8 Nov 1917 - 29 Nov 1917:	Quartermaster-General, High Command

Vice-Admiral Aleksandr Nikolayevich **Skalovsky** (28 Aug 1852 - 1938)
6 Jan 1906 - 14 Jul 1908:	Director of Lighthouses & Navigation, Caspian Sea
6 Dec 1906:	Promoted to *Major-General of the Admiralty*
1907:	Redesignated *Rear-Admiral*

14 Jul 1908 - 20 Oct 1908:   Reserve officer, Ministry of the Navy
20 Oct 1908:   Promoted to *Vice-Admiral*
20 Oct 1908:   Retired

Major-General of the Fleet Mitrofan Mitrofanovich **Skalovsky** (13 Aug 1866 - 27 Mar 1928)
13 Aug 1914 - 17 Jun 1918:   Commander, Tugboat Detachment, Baltic Fleet
30 Jul 1916:   Promoted to *Major-General of the Fleet*
17 Jun 1918:   Dismissed

Major-General Aleksandr Aleksandrovich **Skalsky** (30 Aug 1843 - ?)
10 Nov 1899 - 8 Mar 1901:   Deputy Commander of Engineers, Warsaw Military District
9 Apr 1900:   Promoted to *Major-General*

Lieutenant-General Nikolai Dmitriyevich **Skaryatin** (26 Nov 1846 - ?)
18 May 1884 - 9 Mar 1891:   Commander, Life Guards 2nd Rifle Battalion
30 Aug 1889:   Promoted to *Major-General*
9 Mar 1891 - 5 Jan 1900:   Special Assignments General, Inspectorate of Riflemen
5 Jan 1900:   Promoted to *Lieutenant-General*
5 Jan 1900 - 15 Nov 1901:   Commander, 37th Infantry Division
15 Nov 1901 - 8 Nov 1903:   Commander, Guards Rifle Brigade

Lieutenant-General Vladimir Vladimirovich **Skaryatin** (2 Dec 1847 - 1919)
15 Jul 1892 - 1917:   Master of the Hunt, Imperial Court
6 Oct 1892:   Promoted to *Major-General*
6 Dec 1901:   Promoted to *Lieutenant-General*

Major-General Nikolai Georgiyevich **Skarzhinsky** (14 Jul 1849 - 1910)
5 Aug 1900 - 1910:   Chairman of Poltava Region Remount Commission
6 Dec 1901:   Promoted to *Major-General*

Major-General Ivan Borisovich **Skasyrsky** (11 Jan 1864 - ?)
25 Dec 1915 - 1917:   Chief of Tambov Powder Factory
6 Dec 1916:   Promoted to *Major-General*

Lieutenant-General Nikolai Pavlovich **Skerletov** (9 Mar 1827 - ?)
29 Jul 1879 - 25 Jun 1884:   Commander, 12th Artillery Brigade
30 Aug 1880:   Promoted to *Major-General*
25 Jun 1884 - 2 May 1890:   Commander, 15th Artillery Brigade
2 May 1890 - 17 May 1895:   Commander of Artillery, XII. Army Corps
30 Aug 1890:   Promoted to *Lieutenant-General*

Lieutenant-General Aleksandr Genrikhovich **Skersky** (18 Jun 1861 - ?)
2 Jan 1908 - 12 Jun 1910:   Quartermaster-General, General Staff
13 Apr 1908:   Promoted to *Major-General*
12 Jun 1910 - 30 Dec 1914:   Chief of Staff, XXI. Army Corps
30 Dec 1914:   Promoted to *Lieutenant-General*

30 Dec 1914:	Retired
30 Oct 1915 - 18 Apr 1917:	Recalled; Commander, 34th Replacement Infantry Brigade
18 Apr 1917 - 20 May 1917:	Commander, 31st Infantry Division
20 May 1917 - 1918:	Reserve officer, Kiev Military District

Major-General Leonard-Vilgelm Genrikhovich **Skersky** (26 Apr 1866 - Apr 1940)
10 Mar 1912 - 10 Mar 1915:	Commander, 2nd Battalion, Life Guards 3rd Artillery Brigade
11 Feb 1915:	Promoted to *Major-General*
10 Mar 1915 - 29 Apr 1917:	Commander, 7th Artillery Brigade
29 Apr 1917 - 1918:	Inspector of Artillery, V. Army Corps

Major-General Vasily Feodosiyevich **Sklifasovsky** (21 Jan 1873 - Jun 1915)
4 Oct 1913 - Jun 1915:	Commander, 1st Battalion, 51st Artillery Brigade
12 Jan 1916:	Posthumously promoted to *Major-General*

Major-General Dmitry Yepifanovich **Sklyarevsky** (10 Feb 1853 - 1913)
4 Nov 1910:	Promoted to *Major-General*
4 Nov 1910 - 1913:	Special Assignments General, Irkutsk Military District

Major-General Nikolai Vasilyevich **Sklyarov** (19 Dec 1875 - 4 Apr 1920)
30 Jul 1914 - 12 Dec 1916:	Commander, 2nd Regiment, Terek Cossack Army
12 Dec 1916 - 1918:	Commander, 2nd Brigade, 1st Terek Cossack Division
21 Dec 1916:	Promoted to *Major-General*

General of Infantry Vasily Yepifanovich **Sklyarevsky** (1 Jan 1855 - ?)
21 Dec 1906 - 11 Sep 1912:	Commander, 130th Infantry Regiment
3 May 1912:	Promoted to *Major-General*
11 Sep 1912 - 31 Dec 1913:	Commander, 2nd Brigade, 39th Infantry Division
31 Dec 1913 - 21 Oct 1914:	Commander, 1st Brigade, 52nd Infantry Division
21 Oct 1914:	Promoted to *Lieutenant-General*
21 Oct 1914:	Retired
18 Dec 1914:	Recalled with the rank of *Major-General*
18 Dec 1914 - 9 Dec 1915:	Commander, 1st Brigade, 52nd Infantry Division
9 Dec 1915 - 23 Jun 1917:	Commander, 2nd Grenadier Division
5 May 1916:	Promoted to *Lieutenant-General*
23 Jun 1917 - 14 Jul 1917:	Unassigned
14 Jul 1917:	Promoted to *General of Infantry*
14 Jul 1917:	Retired

Major-General Vladimir Stepanovich **Skobeltsyn** (12 Mar 1872 - 4 Jan 1944)
1913 - 4 Dec 1915:	Commander, 2nd Finnish Rifle Regiment
19 Oct 1914:	Promoted to *Major-General*
4 Dec 1915 - 6 Mar 1917:	Chief of Staff, XVII. Army Corps
6 Mar 1917 - 12 Apr 1917:	Commander, 2nd Turkestan Rifle Division
12 Apr 1917 - 18 Jul 1917:	Commander, 1st Finnish Rifle Division
18 Jul 1917 - Oct 1917:	Reserve officer, Kiev Military District

Major-General Aleksandr Aleksandrovich **Skopinsky-Shtrik** (6 Aug 1859 - ?)
28 May 1909: Promoted to *Major-General*
28 May 1909 - 7 Nov 1909: Commander, 2nd Brigade, 14th Infantry Division
7 Nov 1909 - 4 Nov 1910: Commander, Life Guards Moscow Regiment
4 Nov 1910 - 8 Jul 1913: Commander, 2nd Brigade, 30th Infantry Division
8 Jul 1913: Retired

Major-General Ignaty Iosifovich **Skorino** (2 Apr 1859 - ?)
1 Dec 1908 - 1915: Commander, 9th Borderguard Brigade
6 Dec 1912: Promoted to *Major-General*
1915 - 17 Dec 1915: Chief of Warsaw Evacuation Points
17 Dec 1915 - 1917: Chief of 27th Evacuation Points

Lieutenant-General Aleksandr Nikolayevich **Skornyakov** (11 Dec 1854 - ?)
15 Jun 1910: Promoted to *Major-General*
15 Jun 1910 - 29 Jul 1914: Commander, 2nd Brigade, 51st Infantry Division
29 Jul 1914 - 15 Jul 1915: Commander, Brigade, 62nd Infantry Division
15 Jul 1915 - 22 Apr 1917: Commander, 105th Infantry Division
22 Sep 1916: Promoted to *Lieutenant-General*
22 Apr 1917 - Oct 1917: Reserve officer, Kiev Military District

Lieutenant-General Viktor Ivanovich **Skorobogatov** (4 Nov 1856 - ?)
22 Jun 1904 - 1 Mar 1906: Commander of Artillery, Fortress Libau
17 Apr 1905: Promoted to *Major-General*
1 Mar 1906 - 18 May 1910: Commandant, Main Artillery Polygon
18 May 1910: Promoted to *Lieutenant-General*
18 May 1910 - 28 Sep 1912: Commander of Artillery, Turkestan Military District

Major-General Aleksandr Petrovich **Skorodinsky** (10 Aug 1870 - ?)
2 Jun 1906 - 12 Nov 1916: Senior Artillery Inspector, Main Artillery Directorate
12 Nov 1916 - 1918: Supervisor of Gunpowder and Ammunition Depots, Main Artillery Directorate
6 Dec 1916: Promoted to *Major-General*

Lieutenant-General Pavel Petrovich **Skoropadsky** (3 May 1873 - 24 Jun 1945)
4 Sep 1910 - 15 Apr 1911: Commander, 20th Dragoon Regiment
15 Apr 1911 - 3 Oct 1914: Commander, Life Guards Cavalry Regiment
6 Dec 1912: Promoted to *Major-General*
3 Oct 1914 - 29 Jul 1915: Commander, 1st Brigade, 1st Guards Cavalry Division
29 Jul 1915 - 2 Apr 1916: Commander, 5th Cavalry Division
1 Jan 1916: Promoted to *Lieutenant-General*
2 Apr 1916 - 22 Jan 1917: Commander, 1st Guards Cavalry Division
22 Jan 1917 - 2 Jul 1917: Commanding General, XXXIV. Army Corps
2 Jul 1917 - 6 Oct 1917: Commanding General, I. Ukrainian Army Corps

Major-General Pyotr Vasilyevich **Skosyrev** (2 Nov 1866 - 18 Mar 1936)
22 Jul 1913 - 1918: Military Judge, Irkutsk Military District Court
22 Mar 1915: Promoted to *Major-General*

Major-General Mikhail Ivanovich **Skrebkov** (24 Jan 1866 - 3 Feb 1910)
28 May 1908 - 3 Feb 1910: Military Judge, Odessa Military District
9 Dec 1909: Promoted to *Major-General*

Major-General Aleksey Aleksandrovich **Skryabin** (3 Mar 1858 - 1914)
10 Apr 1912: Promoted to *Major-General*
10 Apr 1912 - 1914: Commander, Irkutsk Regional Brigade

Major-General Dmitry Aleksandrovich **Skryabin** (16 Sep 1865 - ?)
10 Oct 1914 - 1917: Clerk of Technical Bureau, Main Artillery Directorate
6 Dec 1914: Promoted to *Major-General*

Admiral Nikolai Illarionovich **Skrydlov** (1 Apr 1844 - 4 Oct 1918)
30 Aug 1893: Promoted to *Rear-Admiral*
1894 - 21 Feb 1898: Director of the Torpedo Section, Naval Technical Department
21 Feb 1898 - 1899: Commander, Mediterranean Squadron
3 Jul 1900: Promoted to *Vice-Admiral*
1900 - 7 Feb 1902: Commander, Pacific Squadron
4 Mar 1903 - 1 Apr 1904: C-in-C, Black Sea Fleet
4 Apr 1904 - 7 Jan 1905: C-in-C, Pacific Fleet
7 Jan 1905 - 28 Jun 1906: Member of the Admiralty Board
28 Jun 1906 - 26 Mar 1907: C-in-C, Black Sea Fleet
26 Mar 1907 - Aug 1909: Member of the Admiralty Board
Aug 1909: Promoted to *Admiral*
Aug 1909: Retired

Major-General Nikolai Vladimirovich **Skrydlov** (14 Dec 1867 - Oct 1919)
1 Aug 1912 - 13 Mar 1915: Commander, 1st Battalion, 10th Artillery Brigade
3 Jan 1915: Promoted to *Major-General*
13 Mar 1915 - 16 May 1916: Commander, 10th Artillery Brigade
16 May 1916 - 13 Oct 1916: Reserve officer, Minsk Military District
13 Oct 1916 - 24 Jun 1917: Inspector of Artillery, Moscow Military District
24 Jun 1917 - 12 Apr 1918: Reserve officer, Moscow Military District
12 Apr 1918: Retired

General of Infantry Arkady Platonovich **Skugarevsky** (15 Jan 1847 - ?)
23 Oct 1889: Promoted to *Major-General*
23 Oct 1889 - 20 Mar 1895: Chief of Staff, Guards Corps
20 Mar 1895 - 28 Apr 1896: Commander, 4th Rifle Brigade
28 Apr 1896 - 19 Jun 1896: Unassigned
19 Jun 1896 - 26 Oct 1898: Commander, 58th Replacement Infantry Brigade
26 Oct 1898 - 3 Sep 1904: Commander, 27th Infantry Division
6 Dec 1898: Promoted to *Lieutenant-General*
3 Sep 1904 - 25 Apr 1905: Commanding General, VI. Army Corps
25 Apr 1905 - 7 May 1905: At the disposal of the C-in-C, Far East
7 May 1905 - 30 Dec 1906: Commanding General, VIII. Army Corps
6 Dec 1906: Promoted to *General of Infantry*

30 Dec 1906 - 24 Aug 1909: Chairman of the Army Education Committee
24 Aug 1909 - 27 Apr 1912: Member of the Military Council
27 Apr 1912: Retired

Lieutenant-General Yevstafy Aleksandrovich **Skupio** (11 Mar 1847 - 31 Jul 1910)
14 Jan 1898: Promoted to *Major-General*
14 Jan 1898 - 15 Feb 1907: Commander, 2nd Brigade, 43rd Infantry Division
15 Feb 1907: Promoted to *Lieutenant-General*
15 Feb 1907: Retired

General of Artillery Aleksandr Nikolayevich **Skvortsov** (10 Jul 1835 - 28 Jan 1905)
14 Apr 1878 - 27 Feb 1879: Commander, 13th Reserve Artillery Brigade
27 Feb 1879 - 29 Jul 1879: Unassigned
29 Jul 1879 - 27 May 1882: Commander, 41st Artillery Brigade
30 Aug 1882: Promoted to *Major-General*
27 May 1882 - 18 Apr 1883: Commander, 24th Artillery Brigade
18 Apr 1883 - 8 Nov 1885: Commander, 23rd Artillery Brigade
8 Nov 1885 - 17 Dec 1890: Commander, Life Guards 1st Artillery Brigade
17 Dec 1890 - 4 Feb 1893: Commander of Artillery, IV. Army Corps
30 Aug 1892: Promoted to *Lieutenant-General*
4 Feb 1893 - 19 Jan 1898: Commander of Artillery, III. Army Corps
19 Jan 1898 - 24 Jul 1900: Commander of Artillery, XX. Army Corps
24 Jul 1900: Promoted to *General of Artillery*
24 Jul 1900: Retired

Major-General Aleksandr Vasilyevich **Skvortsov** (2 Aug 1827 - ?)
7 Nov 1871 - 1905: Member of the Military Council, Astrakhan Cossack Army
14 Apr 1895: Promoted to *Major-General*

Major-General of the Fleet Dmitry Ivanovich **Skvortsov** (12 Oct 1862 - 1919)
10 Apr 1916: Promoted to *Major-General of the Fleet*
8 Aug 1916 - 1917: Deputy Commandant, Port of Sveaborg

Major-General of Naval Engineers Dmitry Vasilyevich **Skvortsov** (23 Oct 1859 - 20 Jul 1910)
1900 - 3 Sep 1908: Chief Naval Engineer, Port of St. Petersburg
19 Mar 1907: Promoted to *Major-General of Naval Engineers*
3 Sep 1908 - 20 Jul 1910: Senior Deputy Chief Inspector of Shipbuilding, Naval Technical Committee

Major-General Ivan Nikolayevich **Skvortsov** (5 Apr 1864 - 1910)
25 Jun 1902 - 1910: Attached to the Main Directorate of Engineering
1910: Promoted to *Major-General*

General of Infantry Nikolai Nikolayevich **Skvortsov** (7 Aug 1827 - 25 Jun 1895)
8 Sep 1864 - 21 Jul 1866: Deputy Chief of Staff, St. Petersburg Military District
27 Mar 1866: Promoted to *Major-General*

21 Jul 1866 - 21 Jun 1879:	Intendant, St. Petersburg Military District
1 Jan 1878:	Promoted to *Lieutenant-General*
21 Jun 1879 - 25 Jun 1895:	Chief of the Main Intendant Directorate, Chief Intendant, Ministry of War
30 Aug 1892:	Promoted to *General of Infantry*

Major-General Vladimir Ivanovich **Slabolitsky** (22 Mar 1866 - ?)

16 Aug 1914 - 7 Nov 1916:	Commander, 204th Infantry Regiment
9 Jan 1915:	Promoted to *Major-General*
7 Nov 1916 - 14 Apr 1917:	Commander, Brigade, 3rd Amur Border Infantry Division
14 Apr 1917 - 1918:	Commander, 113th Infantry Division

Major-General Vasily Ivanovich **Slansky** (4 Apr 1861 - 18 Oct 1914)

16 Aug 1914 - 18 Oct 1914:	Commander, 215th Infantry Regiment
3 Feb 1915:	Posthumously promoted to *Major-General*

Lieutenant-General Adam Ivanovich **Slavochinsky** (18 Aug 1855 - 18 Oct 1925)

25 Apr 1905 - 17 Apr 1906:	Commander, 85th Infantry Regiment
1906:	Promoted to *Major-General*
17 Apr 1906 - 28 Nov 1907:	Commander, 1st Brigade, 22nd Infantry Division
28 Nov 1907 - 16 Apr 1914:	Governor of Kutaisi
10 Apr 1911:	Promoted to *Lieutenant-General*
16 Apr 1914:	Retired
3 Sep 1914 - 27 Nov 1914:	Recalled; Reserve officer, Kiev Military District
27 Nov 1914 - 7 Apr 1916:	Commander, 1st Brigade, 45th Infantry Division
7 Apr 1916 - 2 Sep 1916:	Commander, Polish Rifle Brigade
2 Sep 1916 - 15 Oct 1917:	Commander, 5th Infantry Division
15 Oct 1917 - 1918:	Reserve officer, Petrograd Military District

Major-General Vladimir Tarasovich **Slepushkin** (10 Apr 1844 - ?)

11 Aug 1900 - May 1903:	Commander, 25th Artillery Brigade
1 Apr 1901:	Promoted to *Major-General*

Major-General Konstantin Maksimovich **Slesarev** (2 Sep 1870 - Mar 1921)

13 Jan 1908 - Oct 1917:	Commandant, Orenburg Cossack School
14 Mar 1913:	Promoted to *Major-General*

Lieutenant-General Aleksey Mikhailovich **Slezkin** (28 Dec 1852 - 1919)

6 Dec 1900 - 15 Feb 1905:	Commander, 40th Artillery Brigade
1 Jan 1901:	Promoted to *Major-General*
15 Feb 1905 - 3 May 1910:	Commander of Artillery, X. Army Corps
22 Apr 1907:	Promoted to *Lieutenant-General*
3 May 1910 - 26 Feb 1915:	Commander, 9th Siberian Rifle Division
1915:	Retired

Lieutenant-General Lev Mikhailovich **Slezkin** (10 May 1855 - ?)

9 Dec 1906 - 1917:	At the disposal of the Commanding General, Corps of

	Gendarmerie
22 Apr 1907:	Promoted to *Major-General*
6 Dec 1915:	Promoted to *Lieutenant-General*

Major-General Mitrofan Konstantinovich **Slonchevsky** (28 Sep 1842 - ?)
18 Sep 1898:	Promoted to *Major-General*
18 Sep 1898 - 17 Oct 1902:	Commander, 2nd Brigade, 21st Infantry Division

General of Engineers Kapiton Konstantinovich **Sluchevsky** (19 Jan 1843 - 14 Mar 1906)
19 Jun 1883 - 17 Sep 1889:	Commander, Life Guards Sapper Battalion
6 May 1887:	Promoted to *Major-General*
17 Sep 1889 - 15 Sep 1901:	Commander, 1st Sapper Brigade
14 May 1896:	Promoted to *Lieutenant-General*
15 Sep 1901 - 30 Oct 1904:	Commanding General, X. Army Corps
30 Oct 1904 - 22 Mar 1905:	At the disposal of the C-in-C, Forces operating against Japan
22 Mar 1905 - 3 Jan 1906:	Member of the Military Council
18 Jun 1905 - 3 Jan 1906:	Member, Council of National Defense
3 Jan 1906:	Promoted to *General of Engineers*
3 Jan 1906:	Retired

Major-General Viktor Alekseyevich **Slyusarenko** (26 Dec 1854 - ?)
5 May 1910:	Promoted to *Major-General*
5 May 1910 - 5 Jun 1914:	Commander, 8th Siberian Rifle Artillery Brigade
5 Jun 1914 - 21 Feb 1915:	Inspector of Artillery, II. Turkestan Army Corps
21 Feb 1915 - 17 Nov 1915:	Reserve officer, Kiev Military District
17 Nov 1915 - Oct 1917:	Commander, Mikhailov Fortress State Militia Brigade

General of Infantry Vladimir Alekseyevich **Slyusarenko** (2 May 1857 - 22 May 1933)
23 Aug 1905 - 20 May 1906:	Commander, 45th Artillery Brigade
20 May 1906 - 12 Sep 1907:	Commander, 2nd Grenadier Artillery Brigade
29 Jun 1906:	Promoted to *Major-General*
12 Sep 1907 - 21 Mar 1908:	Commander of Artillery, XIX. Army Corps
21 Mar 1908 - 15 May 1910:	Commander of Artillery, II. Caucasus Army Corps
29 Mar 1909:	Promoted to *Lieutenant-General*
15 May 1910 - 24 Oct 1915:	Commander, 43rd Infantry Division
24 Oct 1915 - Aug 1917:	Commanding General, XXVIII. Army Corps
6 Dec 1915:	Promoted to *General of Infantry*
Aug 1917:	Resigned

General of Cavalry Aleksey Alekseyevich **Smagin** (4 Jul 1857 - 20 Nov 1928)
20 Oct 1901 - 25 Jun 1903:	Military Governor of Kutaisi
6 Dec 1901:	Promoted to *Major-General*
25 Jun 1903 - 27 May 1905:	Governor of Kutaisi
27 May 1905 - 31 Jan 1906:	At the disposal of the Minister of War
31 Jan 1906 - 10 Jun 1906:	Chief of Staff, II. Turkestan Army Corps
10 Jun 1906 - 22 Mar 1915:	Chief of Staff, Don Cossack Army
6 Dec 1907:	Promoted to *Lieutenant-General*

22 Mar 1915: Promoted to *General of Cavalry*
22 Mar 1915 - 5 Sep 1916: Ataman, Don Cossack Army
5 Sep 1916 - 7 Dec 1917: Reserve officer, Minsk Military District

General of Artillery Aleksey Andreyevich **Smagin** (8 Feb 1829 - 10 Jun 1901)
3 Jun 1870 - 21 Apr 1875: Commander, Artillery Training Polygon, St. Petersburg Military District
30 Aug 1870: Promoted to *Major-General*
21 Apr 1875 - 11 Jan 1884: Commander of Artillery, Fortress Kronstadt
19 May 1875 - 11 Jan 1884: Member of the Artillery Committee, Main Artillery Directorate
30 Aug 1882: Promoted to *Lieutenant-General*
11 Jan 1884 - 5 Apr 1899: Commander of Artillery, Finland Military District
5 Apr 1899 - 1899: Attached to the Main Artillery Directorate
1899: Promoted to *General of Artillery*
1899: Retired

Major-General of Naval Engineers Sergey Semyonovich **Smaznukhin** (5 Jul 1865 - 25 Oct 1937)
1905 - 1917: Inspector of Mines
10 Apr 1916: Promoted to *Major-General of Naval Engineers*

Lieutenant-General Vsevolod Nikanorovich **Smelsky** (11 Feb 1831 - 1913)
30 Dec 1896 - 1905: Chief of Nikolayev Military Hospital, St. Petersburg
6 Dec 1897: Promoted to *Major-General*
1905: Promoted to *Lieutenant-General*
1905: Retired

Major-General Vladimir Andreyevich **Smirnitsky** (3 Mar 1862 - 13 Dec 1917)
9 Sep 1910 - 13 Dec 1917: Intendant, Turkestan Military District
6 Dec 1912: Promoted to *Major-General*

Lieutenant-General of the Admiralty Aleksandr Ivanovich **Smirnov** (30 May 1851 - 22 Nov 1910)
19 Jan 1887 - 1909: Chief of Electrical Engineers, Ministry of the Imperial Court
6 Apr 1903: Promoted to *Major-General of the Admiralty*
18 Apr 1910: Promoted to *Lieutenant-General of the Admiralty*

Major-General Ioasan Dmitriyevich **Smirnov** (23 Apr 1842 - ?)
19 Jan 1896: Promoted to *Major-General*
19 Jan 1896 - 16 Sep 1899: Director, Tiflis Cadet Corps
16 Sep 1899 - 22 Aug 1903: Director, 3rd Moscow Cadet Corps

Lieutenant-General Konstantin Nikolayevich **Smirnov** (19 May 1854 - 9 Nov 1930)
28 Jun 1899: Promoted to *Major-General*
28 Jun 1899 - 13 Jul 1900: Chief of Staff, Fortress Warsaw
13 Jul 1900 - 2 Feb 1904: Commander, 2nd Rifle Brigade

2 Feb 1904: Promoted to *Lieutenant-General*
2 Feb 1904 - 3 Feb 1906: Commandant, Fortress Port Arthur
3 Feb 1906 - 1908: At the disposal of the Chief of the General Staff
1908: Retired

Major-General Mikhail Nikolayevich **Smirnov** (5 Aug 1861 - 18 Apr 1933)
19 Jun 1900 - 28 Mar 1912: Chief of Pensions Department, Don Cossack Army
6 Dec 1911: Promoted to *Major-General*
28 Mar 1912 - 17 May 1913: Deputy Ataman for Civilian Affairs, Don Cossack Army
17 May 1913 - 2 Jun 1917: Ataman, Cherkassy District
2 Jun 1917: Dismissed

Major-General Nikolai Mikhailovich **Smirnov** (9 May 1836 - 11 Jul 1899)
4 Mar 1893 - 1896: Commander, 9th Don Cossack Regiment
14 May 1896: Promoted to *Major-General*
1896: Retired

Major-General Nikolai Pavlovich **Smirnov** (31 Oct 1840 - 16 Jan 1903)
16 May 1891 - 16 Jan 1903: Map Editor, Military Topographical Section, General Staff
6 Dec 1900: Promoted to *Major-General*

Major-General Sergey Vladimirovich **Smirnov** (3 Apr 1873 - 18 Jun 1915)
? - 18 Jun 1915: Commander, 122nd Infantry Regiment
17 Nov 1915: Posthumously promoted to *Major-General*

Major-General Vasily Stepanovich **Smirnov** (3 May 1861 - ?)
1915: Commander, 280th Infantry Regiment
3 Apr 1915: Promoted to *Major-General*
1915 - 7 Feb 1917: Commander, Brigade, 70th Infantry Division
7 Feb 1917 - 1917: Commander, 175th Infantry Division

General of Infantry Vladimir Vasilievich **Smirnov** (4 Jul 1849 - 18 Oct 1918)
26 Feb 1894: Promoted to *Major-General*
26 Feb 1894 - 4 Jul 1901: Chief of Staff, IX. Army Corps
4 Jul 1901 - 9 Jun 1906: Commander, 18th Infantry Division
6 Dec 1901: Promoted to *Lieutenant-General*
9 Jun 1906 - 28 Jul 1908: Commanding General, II. Siberian Army Corps
13 Apr 1908: Promoted to *General of Infantry*
28 Jul 1908 - 5 Dec 1914: Commanding General, XX. Army Corps
5 Dec 1914 - 8 Apr 1917: C-in-C, 2nd Army
8 Apr 1917 - 31 Mar 1917: C-in-C, Western Front
31 Mar 1917 - 22 Apr 1917: Unassigned
22 Apr 1917 - Oct 1917: Member of the Military Council

Major-General Yakov Semyonovich **Smirnov** (15 Nov 1853 - ?)
23 Dec 1907 - 1911: Commander, 68th Infantry Regiment
1911: Promoted to *Major-General*

1911:	Retired
1914 - 19 Apr 1915:	Recalled; Reserve officer, Kiev Military District
19 Apr 1915 - 1916:	Commander, Brigade, 21st Infantry Division
1916 - 1917:	Commander, 21st Replacement Infantry Brigade

Lieutenant-General Konstantin Ivanovich **Smirnsky** (12 May 1842 - 5 Feb 1913)
18 Jan 1893:	Promoted to *Major-General*
18 Jan 1893 - 14 Apr 1902:	Commander, 2nd Brigade, 2nd Grenadier Division
14 Apr 1902:	Promoted to *Lieutenant-General*
14 Apr 1902 - 12 Apr 1904:	Commander, 35th Infantry Division
12 Apr 1904 - 1 Jun 1904:	At the disposal of the Commanding General, Mosow Military District
1 Jun 1904 - 1906:	Commander, 73rd Infantry Division

General of Infantry Pavel Andreyevich **Smorodsky** (2 Sep 1856 - ?)
9 Apr 1899 - 17 Jan 1901:	Section Chief, General Staff
6 Dec 1899:	Promoted to *Major-General*
17 Jan 1901 - 27 May 1904:	Chief of Communications Section, General Staff
27 May 1904 - 3 Oct 1910:	General for Assignments, General Staff
2 Sep 1904 - 23 May 1905:	Acting Commander, 2nd Brigade, 2nd Guards Infantry Division
8 Jun 1905 - 1 Oct 1905:	Acting Commander, 2nd Brigade, 2nd Guards Infantry Division
6 Dec 1906:	Promoted to *Lieutenant-General*
3 Oct 1910 - 7 Jan 1914:	Chief of Pension Service, General Staff
7 Jan 1914 - 1917:	Managing Director, Committee for Wounded Veterans
22 Mar 1915:	Promoted to *General of Infantry*
1917 - 10 Sep 1917:	Reserve officer, Petrograd Military District
10 Sep 1917:	Retired

Lieutenant-General of Naval Engineers Aleksandr Adamovich **Smulsky** (21 Feb 1858 - ?)
29 May 1909:	Promoted to *Major-General of Naval Engineers*
21 Mar 1911 - 1917:	Deputy Chief Inspector of Naval Construction
14 Oct 1913:	Promoted to *Lieutenant-General of Naval Engineers*

Lieutenant-General Yevgeny Konstantinovich **Smyslovsky** (23 Nov 1868 - 4 Nov 1933)
4 Jun 1910:	Promoted to *Major-General*
4 Jun 1910 - 11 Jul 1912:	Commander, 3rd Grenadier Artillery Brigade
11 Jul 1912 - 17 Jun 1915:	Chief of Economic Department, Main Artillery Directorate
6 Dec 1914:	Promoted to *Lieutenant-General*
17 Jun 1915 - 29 Dec 1915:	Inspector of Artillery, VII. Siberian Army Corps
29 Dec 1915 - 18 Sep 1916:	Inspector of Artillery, I. Guards Army Corps
18 Sep 1916 - 29 Apr 1917:	Inspector of Artillery, Special Army
29 Apr 1917 - Oct 1917:	Reserve officer, Moscow Military District

Lieutenant-General Ivan Aleksandrovich **Snarsky** (8 May 1852 - 18 Oct 1911)
22 Nov 1904:	Promoted to *Major-General*

22 Nov 1904 - 19 Feb 1908:	Commander, 1st Brigade, Caucasus Grenadier Division
19 Feb 1908 - 12 Mar 1908:	Unassigned
12 Mar 1908 - 4 Nov 1910:	Commander, 1st Caucasus Rifle Brigade
4 Nov 1910 - 18 Oct 1911:	Commander, 52nd Infantry Division
1911:	Promoted to *Lieutenant-General*

Lieutenant-General Andrey Yevgenyevich **Snesarev** (1 Dec 1865 - 4 Dec 1937)
30 Dec 1914 - 28 Jan 1916:	Commander, 133rd Infantry Regiment
23 Dec 1915:	Promoted to *Major-General*
? - 18 Feb 1916:	Actng Commander, Brigade, 34th Infantry Division
28 Jan 1916 - 1 Mar 1917:	Chief of Staff, 12th Infantry Division
Sep 1916 - 23 Nov 1916:	Acting Commander, 64th Infantry Division
1 Mar 1917 - 12 Apr 1917:	Chief of Staff, XII. Army Corps
12 Apr 1917 - 9 Sep 1917:	Commander, 159th Infantry Division
9 Sep 1917 - Nov 1917:	Commanding General, IX. Army Corps
12 Oct 1917:	Promoted to *Lieutenant-General*

Major-General Fyodor Alekseyevich **Snessorev** (8 Feb 1860 - 9 Dec 1942)
27 Jul 1914 - 23 Jan 1917:	Commander, 1st Battalion, 65th Artillery Brigade
12 Dec 1916:	Promoted to *Major-General*
23 Jan 1917 - 1918:	Commander, 75th Artillery Brigade

Major-General Vladimir Nikolayevich **Snezhkov** (29 Aug 1848 - 14 Mar 1915)
28 Jun 1905:	Promoted to *Major-General*
28 Jun 1905 - 12 Mar 1907:	Commander, Brigade, 46th Infantry Division
12 Mar 1907 - 24 Apr 1909:	Commander, 1st Brigade, 3rd Infantry Division

Major-General Vladimir Aleksandrovich **Sobakinsky** (5 Oct 1857 - Dec 1918)
27 Oct 1911 - 1916:	Reserve officer, St. Petersburg Gendamerie Administration
1916 - 1917:	Chief of Gendarmerie, Radom Province
6 Dec 1916:	Promoted to *Major-General*

General of Infantry Leonid Nikolayevich **Sobolev** (28 May 1844 - 13 Oct 1913)
16 Jul 1878 - 11 Jul 1881:	Attached to the General Staff
30 Aug 1880:	Promoted to *Major-General*
11 Jul 1881 - 27 Oct 1883:	General Staff Officer, General Staff
27 Oct 1883 - 17 Feb 1891:	Commander, 1st Brigade, 37th Infantry Division
17 Feb 1891 - 14 Mar 1895:	Chief of Staff, Vilnius Military District
1 Jan 1894:	Promoted to *Lieutenant-General*
14 Mar 1895 - 1 Jun 1904:	Chief of Staff, Moscow Military District
6 Dec 1903:	Promoted to *General of Infantry*
1 Jun 1904 - 5 May 1906:	Commanding General, VI. Siberian Army Corps
Mar 1905 -1905:	Acting C-in-C, 2nd Manchurian Army
5 May 1906 - Jul 1906:	At the disposal of the Minister of War
Jul 1906:	Retired

Major-General Pyotr Petrovich **Sobolevsky** (23 Dec 1850 - ?)
1 Jun 1916 - 1917: Commander, 253rd Replacement Infantry Regiment
14 Jan 1917: Promoted to *Major-General*

Lieutenant-General Stepan Ivanovich **Sobolevsky** (14 Jan 1849 - ?)
12 Nov 1900 - 30 May 1901: Commander of Artillery, I. Siberian Army Corps
26 Feb 1901: Promoted to *Major-General*
30 May 1901 - 24 Oct 1904: Commander, 30th Artillery Brigade
24 Oct 1904 - 24 Dec 1905: Commander, 55th Artillery Brigade
24 Dec 1905 - 12 Apr 1907: Commander of Artillery, II. Army Corps
6 Dec 1906: Promoted to *Lieutenant-General*
12 Apr 1907: Retired

Lieutenant-General Aleksey Semyonovich **Sofiano** (4 Jan 1854 - 1929)
24 Jan 1909: Promoted to *Major-General*
24 Jan 1909 - 19 May 1912: Commander, 11th Artillery Brigade
19 May 1912 - 4 Jan 1914: Commander, 31st Artillery Brigade
4 Jan 1914: Promoted to *Lieutenant-General*
4 Jan 1914: Retired
18 Jul 1915 - 3 Feb 1916: Recalled; Commander, 90th Artillery Brigade
3 Feb 1916 - Dec 1916: Commander, 125th Artillery Brigade
Dec 1916 - 14 Nov 1917: Chairman, Commission for Verification of Military Service
14 Nov 1917: Retired

General of Artillery Leonid Petrovich **Sofiano** (12 Oct 1820 - 29 Jun 1898)
21 May 1865: Promoted to *Major-General*
21 May 1865 - 11 Feb 1873: Commander of Artillery, Eastern Siberia
11 Feb 1873 - 16 Jun 1881: Commander of Artillery, Caucasus Military District
30 Aug 1873: Promoted to *Lieutenant-General*
16 Apr 1878: Promoted to *General-Adjutant*
16 Jun 1881 - 6 Dec 1896: Deputy Master-General of Ordnance. Chief of the Main Artillery Directorate
30 Aug 1887: Promoted to *General of Artillery*
6 Dec 1896 - 29 Jun 1898: Member of the State Council

Major-General Nikolai Semyonovich **Sofiano** (5 Apr 1844 - 20 Jun 1902)
1901: Promoted to *Major-General*
1901: Retired

Major-General Georgy Ivanovich **Sokerin** (1 Apr 1843 - ?)
29 Feb 1888 - 20 Jul 1896: Member of the Artillery Committee, Main Artillery Directorate
5 Jul 1895: Promoted to *Major-General*
20 Jul 1896 - 1898: Chief of Izhevsk Arms Factory

Major-General Nikolai Ivanovich **Sokhansky** (15 Mar 1844 - 29 Dec 1900)
29 Dec 1899 - 29 Dec 1900: Commander, 3rd Artillery Brigade

9 Apr 1900:   Promoted to *Major-General*

Major-General Viktor Nikolayevich **Sokira-Yakhontov** (28 Aug 1874 - 1938)
5 Jun 1915 - 1917:   Commander, 25th Infantry Regiment
5 Mar 1917:   Promoted to *Major-General*
1917 - 1918:   Commander, 7th Infantry Division

Major-General Aleksandr Aleksandrovich **Sokolov** (17 Aug 1851 - ?)
11 May 1899 - 1909:   Chief of Artillery Section, Moscow Military District
1909:   Promoted to *Major-General*
1909:   Retired

Major-General Aleksandr Alekseyevich **Sokolov** (10 Aug 1869 - ?)
22 Mar 1915 - 1 Apr 1916:   Senior Engineer for Technical Artillery Research & Development, Artillery Committee, Main Artillery Directorate
6 Dec 1915:   Promoted to *Major-General*
1 Apr 1916 - 1917:   Member of the Artillery Committee, Main Artillery Directorate

Major-General Aleksandr Ivanovich **Sokolov** (1 Apr 1848 - 30 May 1909)
7 Feb 1900 - 1905:   Inspector of Classes, Technical Artillery School
1905:   Promoted to *Major-General*
1905:   Retired

Major-General Klavdy Petrovich **Sokolov** (10 Oct 1852 - ?)
29 Apr 1907 - 1917:   Ataman, Sunzha Department, Terek Region
6 Dec 1909:   Promoted to *Major-General*

General of Artillery Leonid Aleksandrovich **Sokolov** (22 Feb 1842 - 9 Oct 1916)
31 May 1879 - 27 Feb 1891:   Section Chief, Main Artillery Directorate
1889:   Promoted to *Major-General*
27 Feb 1891 - 19 Oct 1892:   Commander, 2nd Grenadier Artillery Brigade
19 Oct 1892 - 7 Oct 1893:   Commander, 4th Reserve Artillery Brigade
7 Oct 1893 - 1 Jan 1898:   Deputy Commander of Artillery, Vilnius Military District
1 Jan 1898 - 2 Mar 1901:   Commander of Artillery, Turkestan Military District
6 Dec 1899:   Promoted to *Lieutenant-General*
2 Mar 1901 - 1905:   Commander of Artillery, Moscow Military District
1905:   Promoted to *General of Artillery*
1905:   Retired

Major-General Olimp Petrovich **Sokolov** (6 Nov 1850 - ?)
24 Jul 1905 - 1909:   Military Judge, Turkestan Military District Court
6 Dec 1905:   Promoted to *Major-General*

Major-General Sergey Petrovich **Sokolov** (20 Oct 1858 - 24 Jan 1934)
28 Apr 1908 - 8 Jul 1913:   Commander, 146th Infantry Regiment

14 Apr 1913:	Promoted to *Major-General*
8 Jul 1913 - 29 Aug 1914:	Commander, 2nd Brigade, 30th Infantry Division
29 Aug 1914 - 1918:	POW

Lieutenant-General Vladimir Ivanovich **Sokolov** (2 Nov 1862 - 1919)
9 Mar 1909:	Promoted to *Major-General*
9 Mar 1909 - 3 May 1913:	Chief of Staff, Ural Cossack Army
3 May 1913 - 19 Nov 1914:	Chief of Staff, Grenadier Corps
19 Nov 1914 - 27 Mar 1915:	Chief of Staff, XVII. Army Corps
27 Mar 1915 - 30 Jul 1917:	Commander, 14th Infantry Division
27 Jan 1916:	Promoted to *Lieutenant-General*
30 Jul 1917 - Oct 1917:	Commanding General, IV. Siberian Army Corps

Major-General Yelisey Nikolayevich **Sokolov** (4 Jan 1861 - ?)
14 Jan 1913 - 13 Nov 1914:	Commander, 76th Infantry Regiment
28 Oct 1914:	Promoted to *Major-General*
13 Nov 1914 - 1917:	Reserve officer, Kiev Military District

Major-General Andrey Frantsevich **Sokolovsky** (12 Jan 1863 - 24 Dec 1943)
8 Oct 1913 - 31 Dec 1913:	Commander, 24th Infantry Regiment
31 Dec 1913:	Promoted to *Major-General*
31 Dec 1913:	Retired
1915 - 16 Nov 1915:	Recalled; Commander, State Militia Brigade
16 Nov 1915 - 11 Aug 1917:	Reserve officer, Kiev Military District
11 Aug 1917:	Dismissed

General of Cavalry Ivan Nikolayevich **Sokolovsky** (27 Jan 1858 - ?)
9 Dec 1901 - 28 May 1903:	Military Governor of Semipalatinsk Region
1 Jan 1903:	Promoted to *Major-General*
28 May 1903 - 20 Jun 1905:	Governor of Ufa
20 Jun 1905 - 8 Aug 1906:	At the disposal of the Minister of War
8 Aug 1906 - 21 Jul 1914:	Governor of Astrakhan, Ataman, Astrakhan Cossack Army
6 Dec 1907:	Promoted to *Lieutenant-General*
21 Jul 1914 - 8 Mar 1915:	POW, Germany
8 Mar 1915 - 3 Mar 1917:	Governor of Astrakhan, Ataman, Astrakhan Cossack Army
3 Mar 1917 - 6 Jun 1917:	Unassigned
6 Jun 1917:	Promoted to *General of Cavalry*
6 Jun 1917:	Retired

Major-General Nikolai Aleksandrovich **Sokolovsky** (8 Mar 1843 - ?)
3 Sep 1898 - 1904:	Chief of Emperor Aleksandr II School
6 Dec 1898:	Promoted to *Major-General*

Major-General Stanislav Vladislavovich **Sokolovsky** (8 Dec 1860 - ?)
22 Oct 1914 - 30 Jun 1916:	Commander, 266th Infantry Regiment
5 Jun 1915:	Promoted to *Major-General*

30 Jun 1916 - 1917: Reserve officer, Minsk Military District
1917: Special Assignments General, 3rd Army

Major-General Valerian Iosifovich **Sokolovsky** (8 Jun 1824 - ?)
30 Jul 1878 - 1894: Chancellery Clerk, Ministry of War
30 Aug 1882: Promoted to *Major-General*

Lieutenant-General Viktor Adamovich **Sokolovsky** (8 Mar 1844 - ?)
31 Mar 1893 - 10 Apr 1896: Chief of Staff, South Ussuri District
30 Aug 1893: Promoted to *Major-General*
10 Apr 1896 - 7 Nov 1897: Chief of Staff, VII. Army Corps
7 Nov 1897 - 13 Jun 1902: Commandant of Mikhailov
6 Dec 1901: Promoted to *Lieutenant-General*
13 Jun 1902 - 7 Oct 1906: Commander, 40th Infantry Division

Major-General Pavel Aleksandrovich **Sokolsky** (19 Jun 1852 - ?)
16 Aug 1908: Promoted to *Major-General*
16 Aug 1908 - 8 May 1910: Commander, 10th Artillery Brigade

Major-General Viktor Aleksandrovich **Sokolsky** (19 Apr 1869 - 16 May 1913)
4 Mar 1911 - 16 May 1913: Extraordinary Professor, Nikolai Engineering Academy
1913: Promoted to *Major-General*

Lieutenant-General Mikhail Alekseyevich **Sokovnin** (18 Oct 1863 - 1943)
23 Feb 1907 - 6 Oct 1910: Consul in Jilin
13 Apr 1910: Promoted to *Major-General*
6 Oct 1910 - 17 Oct 1910: Attached to the General Staff
17 Oct 1910 - 2 May 1913: Commander, 1st Brigade, 3rd Siberian Rifle Division
2 May 1913 - 8 Feb 1914: Commander, 1st Brigade, 27th Infantry Division
8 Feb 1914 - Jul 1914: Special Assignments General, Vilnius Military District
Jul 1914 - 6 Sep 1914: Special Assignments General, Dvinsk Military District
6 Sep 1914 - 8 Jan 1915: Chief of Staff, XXVI. Army Corps
8 Jan 1915 - 23 Sep 1915: Commander, 25th Infantry Division
23 Sep 1915 - 31 Oct 1916: Chief of Staff, 2nd Army
30 Sep 1915: Promoted to *Lieutenant-General*
31 Oct 1916 - 22 Apr 1917: Commanding General, XXXVIII. Army Corps
22 Apr 1917 - 30 Jul 1917: C-in-C, 1st Army
30 Jul 1917 - 17 Oct 1917: C-in-C, 8th Army
17 Oct 1917: Transferred to the reserve

Major-General Vsevolod Alekseyevich **Sokovnin** (22 Apr 1870 - 1922)
22 Apr 1914: Promoted to *Major-General*
22 Apr 1914 - 4 Nov 1914: General Staff officer, Odessa Military District
4 Nov 1914 - 22 Nov 1915: Quartermaster-General, 7th Army
22 Nov 1915 - Oct 1917: Quartermaster-General, 12th Army

Major-General of the Fleet Yakov Savvich **Soldatov** (2 Oct 1877 - 1935)
1917: Promoted to *Major-General of the Fleet*

1917: Senior Acceptance Inspector for Submarines

Major-General Dmitry Ivanovich **Solers** (13 Oct 1867 - ?)
4 Dec 1910 - 22 May 1915:	Commander, 87th Infantry Regiment
22 May 1915:	Promoted to *Major-General*
22 May 1915 - 5 Jun 1915:	Commander, Brigade, Infantry Division
5 Jun 1915 - 1917:	Commander, 1st Brigade, 22nd Infantry Division

Major-General Kazimir Ivanovich **Solini** (3 Mar 1853 - ?)
18 Feb 1904 - 4 Aug 1913:	Deputy Chief of Warsaw Palace Administration
6 Dec 1910:	Promoted to *Major-General*
4 Aug 1913 - 26 Sep 1914:	Chief of Warsaw Palace Administration
26 Sep 1914:	Retired

Lieutenant-General Edmund-Matsey-Marian Stanislavovich **Sollogub** (19 Aug 1857 - ?)
4 Aug 1909:	Promoted to *Major-General*
4 Aug 1909 - 17 Oct 1910:	Commander, Caucasus Sapper Brigade
17 Oct 1910 - 29 Nov 1912:	Inspector of Field Engineers, Caucasus Military District
29 Nov 1912 - 19 Jul 1915:	Deputy Inspector of Engineers, Caucasus Military District
19 Jul 1915 - 1917:	Inspector of Engineers, Caucasus Military District
10 Apr 1916:	Promoted to *Lieutenant-General*

General of Infantry Vasily Ustinovich **Sollogub** (23 Aug 1848 - 1 Feb 1917)
14 Apr 1890 - 5 Nov 1896:	Attached to the General Staff
30 Aug 1890:	Promoted to *Major-General*
3 Dec 1894 - 24 Nov 1900:	Professor, General Staff Academy
5 Nov 1896 - 25 Nov 1900:	Head of Military Research Committee, General Staff
6 Dec 1897:	Promoted to *Lieutenant-General*
25 Nov 1900 - 23 Mar 1905:	At the disposal of the Minister of War
23 Mar 1905 - 25 Oct 1905:	At the disposal of the C-in-C, Land and Naval Forces operating against Japan
25 Oct 1905 - 4 Dec 1905:	At the disposal of the Minister of War
4 Dec 1905 - 17 Oct 1906:	Acting Governor-General of the Baltic States
17 Oct 1906 - 16 May 1909:	At the disposal of the Minister of War
16 May 1909:	Promoted to *General of Infantry*
16 May 1909:	Retired

Major-General Vladimir Ustinovich **Sollogub** (20 Dec 1853 - 1907)
10 Aug 1900:	Promoted to *Major-General*
10 Aug 1900 - 7 Feb 1901:	Commander, 2nd Brigade, 7th Infantry Division
7 Feb 1901 - 29 Apr 1904:	Commander, 1st Brigade, 13th Infantry Division
29 Apr 1904 - 18 Jul 1905:	Commander, 3rd Rifle Brigade
18 Jul 1905 - 1907:	Unassigned

Major-General Konstantin Stepanovich **Solonenko** (6 Nov 1852 - ?)
19 Jul 1908:	Promoted to *Major-General*
19 Jul 1908 - 11 Sep 1912:	Commander, 2nd Brigade, 39th Infantry Division

11 Sep 1912:   Retired

Lieutenant-General Vladimir Konstantinovich **Solonina** (23 Jul 1851 - ?)
15 Oct 1902 - 19 Feb 1907:   Commander, 15th Infantry Regiment
12 Sep 1906:   Promoted to *Major-General*
19 Feb 1907 - 12 Nov 1907:   Commander, 1st Brigade, 45th Infantry Division
12 Nov 1907 - 23 Jul 1911:   Commander, 2nd Brigade, 4th Infantry Division
23 Jul 1911:   Promoted to *Lieutenant-General*
23 Jul 1911:   Retired

Major-General of the Fleet Aleksey Petrovich **Solovyev** (? - ?)
?:   Promoted to *Major-General of the Fleet*

Lieutenant-General Ivan Vasilyevich **Solovyev** (26 Sep 1848 - Jan 1914)
1 Feb 1898 - 6 Jul 1906:   Section Chief, Main Cossack Directorate
6 Dec 1904:   Promoted to *Major-General*
6 Jul 1906 - 1909:   Deputy Ataman, Terek Cossack Army
1909:   Promoted to *Lieutenant-General*
1909:   Retired

Major-General Konstantin Sergeyevich **Solovyev** (12 Apr 1853 - ?)
23 Feb 1898 - 1908:   Deputy Military Governor of Dagestan
6 Dec 1901:   Promoted to *Major-General*

General of Infantry Nikolai Ivanovich **Solovyev** (6 Sep 1850 - 19 May 1907)
17 Apr 1896 - 10 Nov 1901:   Chief of Mobilization, Main Intendant Directorate
14 May 1896:   Promoted to *Major-General*
12 May 1900 - 19 May 1907:   Chief of Intendant Training Courses
6 Dec 1902:   Promoted to *Lieutenant-General*
22 May 1907:   Posthumously promoted to *General of Infantry*

Major-General of the Fleet Pavel Pavlovich **Solovyev** (17 Sep 1856 - ?)
6 Dec 1913:   Promoted to *Major-General of the Fleet*
Sep 1915:   Attached to 2nd Baltic Naval Depot

Major-General Pyotr Nikolayevich **Solovyev** (4 Jan 1858 - ?)
14 Dec 1905 - 1912:   Commander of Northwest Railway Gendarmerie
29 Mar 1909:   Promoted to *Major-General*
1912 - 15 Apr 1917:   Chief of Moscow-Archangelsk Railroad Gendarmerie
15 Apr 1917 - 7 Jun 1917:   Reserve officer, Moscow Military District

Major-General Pyotr Petrovich **Solovyev** (25 Jul 1859 - ?)
16 Oct 1915 - 1917:   Chief of Petrograd Evacuation Points
10 Apr 1916:   Promoted to *Major-General*

General of Artillery Pavel Alekseyevich **Soltanov** (14 May 1839 - 7 Dec 1915)
15 Apr 1868 - 1 Mar 1880:   Chief of Bureau, Ministry of War
1878:   Promoted to *Major-General*

1 Mar 1880 - 4 Jan 1899:	Chief of Retirement Office, Ministry of War
30 Aug 1891:	Promoted to *Lieutenant-General*
4 Jan 1899 - 11 Sep 1904:	Chief Cashier, Retirement Department, Military Council
11 Sep 1904 - 7 Dec 1915:	Member of the Military Council
6 Dec 1904:	Promoted to *General of Artillery*

Major-General Stepan Mikhailovich **Solunskov** (1 Jan 1868 - 1941)
16 Jan 1914 - 25 Aug 1915:	Commander, 3rd Rifle Regiment
1 May 1915:	Promoted to *Major-General*
25 Aug 1915 - Sep 1915:	Commander, Brigade, 46th Infantry Division
Sep 1915 - 27 Oct 1915:	Commander, Brigade, 17th Infantry Division
27 Oct 1915 - 15 May 1916:	Chief of Staff, XXXIII. Army Corps
15 May 1916 - 13 Apr 1917:	Chief of Staff, XLV. Army Corps
13 Apr 1917 - 1918:	Commander, 124th Infantry Division

Lieutenant-General Nikolai Pavlovich **Somov** (12 May 1852 - ?)
17 Aug 1907:	Promoted to *Major-General*
17 Aug 1907 - 16 Aug 1914:	Chief of Okhtenskaya Explosives Factory
16 Aug 1914:	Promoted to *Lieutenant-General*
16 Aug 1914:	Retired
1915 - 1916:	Recalled; Attached to the State Militia
1916 - 1917:	Attached to the Main Artillery Directorate

Major-General Nikolai Sergeyevich **Somov** (14 Nov 1849 - ?)
16 Jan 1909:	Promoted to *Major-General*
16 Jan 1909 - 16 Jan 1911:	Commander, 45th Artillery Brigade
16 Jan 1911:	Retired
31 Oct 1914 - 1917:	Recalled; Reserve officer, Kiev Military District

Lieutenant-General Anton Grigoryevich **Sornetsky** (15 Jan 1850 - 27 Jan 1914)
30 Jul 1910 - 1 Jan 1914:	Deputy Commander of Engineers, Odessa Military District
6 Dec 1910:	Promoted to *Major-General*
1 Jan 1914:	Promoted to *Lieutenant-General*
1 Jan 1914:	Retired

Major General Vasily Alekseyevich **Sornev** (11 Apr 1843 - ?)
29 Dec 1899 - 5 Jun 1903:	Commander, 44th Artillery Brigade
1 Jan 1901:	Promoted to *Major-General*
5 Jun 1903:	Retired

Major-General Sergey Ivanovich **Sovazh** (18 Feb 1875 - 8 May 1916)
22 Aug 1915 - 8 May 1916:	Commander, Life Guards Semenov Regiment
18 Feb 1916:	Promoted to *Major-General*

Major-General Aleksandr Danilovich **Soymonov** (22 Jul 1849 - 1900)
8 Sep 1893 - 1900:	Ataman, 3rd Military Division, Trans-Baikal Cossack Army

6 May 1898: Promoted to *Major-General*

General of Infantry Ivan Gavrilovich **Soymonov** (10 Feb 1859 - 3 Feb 1919)
6 Nov 1902 - 19 Feb 1905: Director, Tiflis Cadet Corps
6 Apr 1903: Promoted to *Major-General*
19 Feb 1905 - 13 Aug 1906: Director, Voronezh Cadet Corps
13 Aug 1906 - 23 Jan 1913: Director, Vladikavkaz Cadet Corps
29 Mar 1909: Promoted to *Lieutenant-General*
23 Jan 1913: Promoted to *General of Infantry*
23 Jan 1913: Retired

Major-General Vladimir Fyodorovich **Sozanovich** (5 Aug 1865 - 18 Nov 1943)
Aug 1914 - 12 Nov 1914: Commander, 54th Artillery Brigade
12 Nov 1914 - 15 Jan 1915: Acting Commander, 3rd Artillery Brigade
15 Jan 1915 - 18 May 1917: Commander, 2nd Grenadier Artillery Brigade
30 Sep 1915: Promoted to *Major-General*
18 May 1917 - 1918: Inspector of Artillery, L. Army Corps

Major-General Andrey Klavdiyevich **Speransky** (10 Oct 1866 - Dec 1916)
18 Jan 1914 - 1915: Duty General, Amur Military District
6 Apr 1914: Promoted to *Major-General*
1915 - 1916: Acting Chief of Staff, Amur Military District
1916 - Dec 1916: Duty General, Amur Military District

Actual Privy Councillor Nikolai Vasilyevich **Speransky** (22 Oct 1840 - 1924)
1889: Promoted to *Active State Councillor*
1889 - 1893: Deputy Chief Military Medical Inspector, Vilnius Military District
1893 - 1896: Chief Military Medical Inspector, Don Cossack Army
1896 - 1899: Chief Military Medical Inspector, Kiev Military District
1898: Promoted to *Privy Councillor*
1899 - 11 Aug 1902: Deputy Chief, Main Military Medical Directorate
11 Aug 1902 - 23 May 1906: Chief, Main Military Medical Directorate
23 May 1906: Promoted to *Actual Privy Councillor*
23 May 1906: Retired

Lieutenant-General Sergey Ivanovich **Speransky** (2 Sep 1845 - 29 Jul 1914)
18 Aug 1891 - 29 Jul 1914: Chief of St. Petersburg Palace Administration
30 Aug 1894: Promoted to *Major-General*
17 Apr 1905: Promoted to *Lieutenant-General*

Major-General Aleksandr Yakovlevich **Speshnev** (23 Oct 1865 - 28 Nov 1933)
24 May 1906 - 1918: Military Commander, Skvirsky District
12 May 1915: Promoted to *Major-General*

Major-General Anatoly Yakovlevich **Speshnev** (29 Dec 1863 - ?)
28 Feb 1908 - 1917: Military Judge, St. Petersburg Military District Court
13 Apr 1908: Promoted to *Major-General*

Major-General Ivan Timofeyevich **Spevak** (27 Sep 1868 - 25 Aug 1916)
Aug 1916 - 25 Aug 1916: Commander, 3rd Amur Border Infantry Regiment
21 Jan 1917: Posthumously promoted to *Major-General*

Major-General Aleksandr Ivanovich **Spiridovich** (5 Aug 1873 - 30 Jun 1952)
1 Jan 1906 - 15 Aug 1916: Chief of Security, Tsarskoye Selo
6 May 1915: Promoted to *Major-General*
15 Aug 1916 - 1917: Mayor of Yalta

Lieutenant-General Yevgeny Stepanovich **Spokoysky-Frantsevich** (15 Mar 1835 - ?)
31 Dec 1892: Promoted to *Major-General*
31 Dec 1892 - 16 Mar 1897: Commander, 28th (Trancaspian) Regional Brigade
16 Mar 1897 - 23 Oct 1897: Commander, 2nd Transcaspian Rifle Brigade
23 Oct 1897 - 11 Oct 1899: Commander, 2nd Brigade, 9th Infantry Division
11 Oct 1899: Promoted to *Lieutenant-General*
11 Oct 1899: Retired

Major-General Artur-Robert-Gustav Valfridovich **Spore** (8 May 1862 - 12 Oct 1937)
13 May 1913 - 18 Sep 1917: Governor of Kuopio
6 Dec 1913: Promoted to *Major-General*
18 Sep 1917: Retired

Major-General Rafail Valfridovich **Spore** (11 Jan 1864 - 12 Jan 1943)
30 Oct 1911 - 18 May 1917: Governor of Tavasthus
6 Dec 1913: Promoted to *Major-General*
18 May 1917: Dismissed

Major-General German Ferdinandovich von **Staal** (4 Oct 1870 - ?)
19 Feb 1915 - 18 Apr 1916: Commander, 60th Infantry Regiment
18 Apr 1916 - 23 Apr 1917: Commander, Brigade, 12th Infantry Division
2 Jun 1916: Promoted to *Major-General*
23 Apr 1917 - 1918: Reserve officer, Kiev Military District

Lieutenant-General Count Gustav Ernestovich von **Stakelberg** (26 Aug 1853 - 15 Mar 1917)
10 Apr 1899: Promoted to *Major-General*
10 Apr 1899 - 1909: At the disposal of Grand Duke Vladimir Aleksandrovich
1909: Promoted to *Lieutenant-General*
1909: Retired

Major-General Nikolai Aleksandrovich **Stakhiyev** (11 Sep 1844 - 3 Dec 1902)
4 Apr 1900: Promoted to *Major-General*
4 Apr 1900 - 3 Dec 1902: Commander, 1st Brigade, 26th Infantry Division

Major-General Pyotr Aleksandrovich **Stakhiyev** (24 Jun 1843 - 14 Jun 1905)
1 Oct 1899: Promoted to *Major-General*
1 Oct 1899 - 15 Feb 1900: Commander, 1st Brigade, 41st Infantry Division

15 Feb 1900 - 16 Apr 1903:	Commander, 2nd Brigade, 24th Infantry Division
16 Apr 1903 - 27 Jun 1904:	At the disposal of the Commanding General, St. Petersburg Military District
27 Jun 1904 - 14 Jun 1905:	Commander, Arkhangelsk Regional Brigade

Major-General Aleksey Aleksandrovich **Stakhovich** (21 Jan 1856 - ?)
10 Apr 1905 - 1907:	At the disposal of the Governor of the Caucasus
17 Apr 1905:	Promoted to *Major-General*

Major-General Mikhail Parmenovich **Stakhovich** (18 Oct 1844 - 19 Aug 1895)
26 Jul 1893 - 19 Aug 1895:	Chief of Railway Gendarmerie, Finland
30 Aug 1893:	Promoted to *Major-General*

Lieutenant-General Pavel Aleksandrovich **Stakhovich** (14 Jan 1865 - ?)
16 Feb 1906 - 22 Dec 1906:	Commander, Life Guards Uhlan Regiment
6 Dec 1906:	Promoted to *Major-General*
22 Dec 1906 - 4 Oct 1908:	Quartermaster-General of Guards Troops, St. Petersburg Military District
4 Oct 1908 - 27 Nov 1912:	Commander, 2nd Independent Cavalry Brigade
27 Nov 1912 - 19 Jul 1914:	Special Assignments General, Inspectorate-General of Cavalry
14 Apr 1913:	Promoted to *Lieutenant-General*
19 Jul 1914 - 28 Jul 1915:	Commander, 1st Kuban Cossack Division
28 Jul 1915 - Jan 1917:	Head of State Horse Breeding
Jan 1917 - Oct 1917:	Chief Superintendent of State Horse Breeding

Lieutenant-General Baron Aleksey Ivanovich **Stal von Golshteyn** (24 Mar 1858 - 5 Dec 1941)
1 May 1891 - 6 Dec 1905:	Adjutant to Grand Duke Pyotr Nikolayevich
1905:	Promoted to *Major-General*
6 Dec 1905 - 19 Jun 1917:	Head of the Court of Grand Duke Pyotr Nikolayevich
31 May 1913:	Promoted to *Lieutenant-General*
19 Jun 1917:	Retired

Lieutenant-General Baron Vladimir Ivanovich **Stal von Golshteyn** (29 Jun 1853 - ?)
6 Dec 1904:	Promoted to *Major-General*
6 Dec 1904 - 9 Mar 1906:	At the disposal of the Commanding General, St. Petersburg Military District
9 Mar 1906 - 10 Nov 1906:	Special Assignments General to the Commanding General, St. Petersburg Military District
10 Nov 1906 - 5 Jul 1908:	At the disposal of the Commanding General, St. Petersburg Military District
5 Jul 1908 - 29 Jul 1914:	Deputy Commandant of Fortress St. Petersburg
31 Dec 1910:	Promoted to *Lieutenant-General*
29 Jul 1914 - 16 Sep 1914:	Commander, 1st Replacement Infantry Brigade
16 Sep 1914 - 15 Apr 1917:	Deputy Commandant of Fortress St. Petersburg
15 Apr 1917:	Dismissed

Lieutenant-General Aleksey Vasilyevich **Stanislavsky** (30 Nov 1853 - 12 Feb 1913)
20 Sep 1895 - 1908: Military Judge, Odessa Military District Court
1 Jan 1901: Promoted to *Major-General*
1908: Promoted to *Lieutenant-General*
1908: Retired

Lieutenant-General Adam Yuryevich **Stankevich** (17 Feb 1855 - 1918)
24 Nov 1908: Promoted to *Major-General*
24 Nov 1908 - 19 Jul 1914: Commander, 2nd Brigade, 22nd Infantry Division
19 Jul 1914 - 14 Nov 1914: Commander, 67th Infantry Division
14 Nov 1914: Promoted to *Lieutenant-General*
14 Nov 1914: Retired
19 Jun 1915 - 1917: Recalled; Commander, 106th Infantry Division

Lieutenant-General Silvestr Lvovich **Stankevich** (31 Dec 1866 - 11 Mar 1919)
9 Jun 1913 - 7 Aug 1915: Commander, 14th Rifle Regiment
16 Feb 1915: Promoted to *Major-General*
7 Aug 1915 - 9 Sep 1916: Commander, 1st Brigade, 4th Rifle Division
9 Sep 1916 - 25 Aug 1917: Commander, 4th Rifle Division
25 Aug 1917: Promoted to *Lieutenant-General*
25 Aug 1917 - 10 Jan 1918: Commanding General, II. Army Corps

Major-General Stepan Karlovich **Stankovsky** (22 Dec 1855 - 27 Feb 1920)
25 Sep 1904 - 1 Sep 1910: Commandant, Irkutsk Infantry Cadet School
1 Sep 1910: Promoted to *Major-General*
1 Sep 1910 - 8 Jun 1916: Commandant, Irkutsk Military School
8 Jun 1916 - Jan 1917: Commander, Brigade, 28th Infantry Division
Jan 1917 - 17 May 1917: Chief of Staff, XX. Army Corps
17 May 1917 - 4 Jul 1917: Reserve officer, Minsk Military District
4 Jul 1917 - Oct 1917: General for Assignments, Irkutsk Military District

Major-General Vladimir Andreyevich **Starchevsky** (14 May 1853 - 1916)
26 May 1910 - 1916: Military Commander, Kharkov District
4 Jul 1916: Posthumously promoted to *Major-General*

Major-General Fyodor Mitrofanovich **Starikov** (1 Jun 1842 - 5 Jan 1911)
7 Jul 1900 - 1907: Ataman, 2nd Verkhneuralsk Military Division, Orenburg Cossack Army
6 Apr 1903: Promoted to *Major-General*
1907: Retired

Major-General Konstantin Fyodorovich **Starikov** (1 Oct 1831 - ?)
21 Jul 1893: Promoted to *Major-General*
21 Jul 1893 - 16 Feb 1894: Commander, 1st Brigade, Caucasus Grenadier Division
16 Feb 1894 - 24 Nov 1899: Commander, 2nd Brigade, Caucasus Grenadier Division

Major-General of the Admiralty Nikolai Nikolayevich **Stark** (14 Dec 1863 - 1932)
30 Aug 1904 - 1912: Military Judge, Kronstadt Naval Court

10 Apr 1911:   Promoted to *Major-General of the Admiralty*
Mar 1912:   Attached to the 1st Baltic Naval Crew

Admiral Oskar Viktorovich **Stark** (16 Aug 1846 - 13 Nov 1928)
1896:   Promoted to *Rear-Admiral*
1 May 1898 - 7 Oct 1902:   Commandant of Port Arthur
7 Feb 1902 - 24 Feb 1904:   C-in-C, Pacific Fleet
6 Dec 1902:   Promoted to *Vice-Admiral*
24 Feb 1904 - 17 Apr 1905:   Unassigned
17 Apr 1905 - 14 Jan 1908:   Senior Flagman, Baltic Fleet
14 Jan 1908 - 1910:   Chairman of the Board, Obukhov & Izhorsk Plants
20 Oct 1908:   Promoted to *Admiral*
20 Oct 1908:   Retired
1914 - 1917:   Recalled; Commander, Siberian Squadron

Major-General Pavel Fedorovich **Stark** (9 May 1856 - 26 Jan 1926)
25 Oct 1907 - 1917:   Inspector of Classes, Kiev Military School
13 Apr 1908:   Promoted to *Major-General*

Major-General Viktor Fedorovich **Stark** (23 Nov 1859 - 1920)
9 Mar 1900 - 2 Feb 1914:   Deputy Chief of St. Petersburg Gun Factory
29 Mar 1909:   Promoted to *Major-General*
2 Feb 1914 - 29 Apr 1915:   Advisory Member of the Artillery Committee, Main
                                Artillery Directorate
29 Apr 1915 - 1917:   Advisory Member, Land Artillery Department,
                                Obukhov Steel Factory
1917 - 1918:   Chief of Technical Service, Petrograd Gun Factory

Major-General Iosif Mikhailovich **Starkovsky** (29 Feb 1860 - ?)
8 Feb 1906 - 31 Dec 1913:   Military Commander, Vinnitsa District
25 Mar 1912:   Promoted to *Major-General*
31 Dec 1913 - 1917:   Commander, Poltava Regional Brigade

Major-General Ivan Mikhailovich **Starkovsky** (15 Mar 1866 - 26 Aug 1938)
17 Jul 1908 - 3 Jul 1914:   Military Judge, Irkutsk Military District
6 Dec 1909:   Promoted to *Major-General*
3 Jul 1914 - Jul 1916:   Military Judge, Amur Military District
Jul 1916 - Oct 1917:   Military Judge, Turkestan Military District

Major-General Vladimir Pavlovich **Starov** (12 Jun 1871 - 17 Dec 1919)
1914 - 12 May 1916:   Commander, 84th Artillery Brigade
12 May 1916 - 1917:   Commander, 77th Artillery Brigade
8 Oct 1916:   Promoted to *Major-General*

Major-General Konstantin Sokratovich **Starynkevich** (17 Sep 1858 - 23 Sep 1906)
23 Jul 1903 - 6 Nov 1904:   Governor of Tomsk
6 Dec 1903:   Promoted to *Major-General*
6 Nov 1904 - 3 Jan 1906:   Governor of Kharkov

3 Jan 1906 - 25 Jul 1906:	Attached to the Ministry of Internal Affairs
25 Jul 1906 - 23 Sep 1906:	Governor of Simbirsk

General of Engineers Olimpiy Ivanovich **Starynkevich** (29 Oct 1837 - 1909)
18 Mar 1884 - 24 Dec 1890:	Commander of Engineers, Fortress Warsaw
9 Apr 1889:	Promoted to *Major-General*
24 Dec 1890 - 1909:	Member of the Engineering Committee, Main Engineering Directorate
6 Dec 1900:	Promoted to *Lieutenant-General*
1909:	Promoted to *General of Engineers*

Lieutenant-General Aleksey Dmitriyevich **Stashevsky** (25 Feb 1852 - ?)
20 Jan 1906 - 22 Oct 1908:	Commander, Moscow Artillery Depot
2 Apr 1906:	Promoted to *Major-General*
22 Oct 1908 - 31 Dec 1913:	Deputy Commander of Artillery, Kiev Military District
31 Dec 1913:	Promoted to *Lieutenant-General*
31 Dec 1913:	Retired

Lieutenant-General Arseny Dmitriyevich **Stashevsky** (30 Jan 1851 - Sep 1916)
4 Dec 1902 - 11 Mar 1906:	Commander, Orenburg Cossack Horse Artillery Brigade
11 Mar 1906:	Promoted to *Major-General*
11 Mar 1906 - 6 Feb 1910:	Commander, 3rd Replacement Artillery Brigade
6 Feb 1910 - 28 Jul 1910:	Commander of Artillery, XI. Army Corps
18 Apr 1910:	Promoted to *Lieutenant-General*
28 Jul 1910 - 7 Jan 1913:	Inspector of Artillery, XI. Army Corps
7 Jan 1913 - 21 Jan 1914:	Inspector of Artillery, IX. Army Corps
21 Jan 1914 - 13 Jan 1916:	Military Governor of Primorye Region, Ataman, Ussuri Cossack Army
13 Jan 1916 - 21 Jan 1916:	Reserve officer, Kiev Military District
21 Jan 1916 - 16 Apr 1916:	Inspector of Artillery, XXX. Army Corps
16 Apr 1916 - Sep 1916:	Inspector of Artillery, 11th Army

Major-General Nikolai Stepanovich **Stasyuk** (14 Nov 1859 - ?)
11 Sep 1913 - 3 Apr 1915:	Commander, 118th Infantry Regiment
11 Feb 1915:	Promoted to *Major-General*
3 Apr 1915 - 9 Sep 1916:	Commander, Brigade, 55th Infantry Division
9 Sep 1916 - 14 Aug 1917:	Reserve officer, Minsk Military District
14 Aug 1917 - 1918:	Commander, 7th Siberian Rifle Division

Lieutenant-General Vadim Platonovich **Statsenko** (29 Sep 1860 - 1918)
3 Dec 1902 - Oct 1917:	Professor, Nikolayev Engineering Academy
1906:	Promoted to *Major-General*
6 Dec 1914:	Promoted to *Lieutenant-General*

Lieutenant-General Pyotr Karpovich **Stavitsky** (28 Jun 1852 - 1911)
7 May 1899 - 7 Jan 1909:	Inspector of Construction, Port of Vladivostok
6 Dec 1904:	Promoted to *Major-General*
7 Jan 1909 - 1911:	Member of the Engineering Committee, Main

	Engineering Directorate
6 Dec 1910:	Promoted to *Lieutenant-General*

Lieutenant-General Mikhail Mitrofanovich **Stavrov** (29 Oct 1868 - 1922)
29 Dec 1914 - 7 Jul 1915:	Chief of Staff, V. Siberian Army Corps
11 Mar 1915:	Promoted to *Major-General*
7 Jul 1915 - 7 Feb 1917:	Quartermaster-General, 2nd Army
7 Feb 1917 - 12 May 1917:	Commander, 5th Grenadier Division
12 May 1917 - 29 Jul 1917:	Chief of Staff, 1st Army
29 Jul 1917 - 1918:	Commanding General, XXXV. Army Corps
23 Aug 1917:	Promoted to *Lieutenant-General*

Lieutenant-General Nikolai Grigoryevich **Stavrovich** (14 May 1857 - 25 Dec 1933)
1 Jun 1904:	Promoted to *Major-General*
1 Jun 1904 - 3 Dec 1904:	Commander, 2nd Brigade, 61st Infantry Division
3 Dec 1904 - 17 Oct 1906:	Chief of Staff, V. Siberian Army Corps
17 Oct 1906 - 1 May 1911:	Chief of Staff, XXII. Army Corps
15 Feb 1911:	Promoted to *Lieutenant-General*
1 May 1911 - 9 Dec 1915:	Commander, 2nd Grenadier Division
9 Dec 1915 - 10 Mar 1916:	Reserve officer, Minsk Military District
10 Mar 1916 - 18 Apr 1917:	Commander, 27th Infantry Division
18 Apr 1917 - 1918:	Reserve officer, Moscow Military District

General of Cavalry Konstantin Nikolayevich **Stavrovsky** (3 May 1846 - ?)
27 May 1891:	Promoted to *Major-General*
27 May 1891 - 10 Jul 1891:	Chief of Staff, Fortress Kaunas
10 Jul 1891 - 8 Jun 1892:	Chief of Staff, VII. Army Corps
8 Jun 1892 - 20 Nov 1893:	Chief of Staff, IV. Army Corps
20 Nov 1893 - 10 May 1899:	Deputy Chief of Staff, Borderguard Corps
10 May 1899 - 4 May 1905:	Military Governor of the Ural Region, Ataman, Ural Cossack Army
6 Dec 1899:	Promoted to *Lieutenant-General*
4 May 1905 - 21 Mar 1918:	Member of the Military Council
6 Dec 1907:	Promoted to *General of Cavalry*
21 Mar 1918:	Retired

Lieutenant-General Mikhail Ivanovich **Stavsky** (12 Jul 1853 - ?)
21 Aug 1908:	Promoted to *Major-General*
21 Aug 1908 - 28 Jul 1913:	Commander, 1st Brigade, 2nd East Siberian Rifle Division
28 Jul 1913:	Promoted to *Lieutenant-General*
28 Jul 1913:	Retired

Major-General Pavel Stepanovich **Stayev** (13 Mar 1870 - 1951)
2 Nov 1911 - 4 Mar 1915:	Commander, 1st Grenadier Regiment
20 Feb 1915:	Promoted to *Major-General*
4 Mar 1915 - 18 Sep 1916:	Quartermaster-General, 4th Army
18 Sep 1916 - 1 Oct 1917:	Commander, 1st Grenadier Division

1 Oct 1917 - 1918: Reserve officer, Moscow Military District

General of Infantry Iyeronim Ivanovich **Stebnitsky** (30 Sep 1832 - 29 Jan 1897)
1 Jun 1867 - 28 Nov 1885: Chief of Military Topographical Section, Caucasus Military District
1875: Promoted to *Major-General*
28 Nov 1885 - 6 Dec 1896: Chief of Military Topographical Section, General Staff
30 Aug 1886: Promoted to *Lieutenant-General*
6 Dec 1896: Promoted to *General of Infantry*
6 Dec 1896: Retired

Major-General Kazimir Albinovich **Stefanovich** (8 Apr 1868 - 24 Aug 1917)
29 Feb 1912 - 9 Jul 1915: Commander, 83rd Infantry Regiment
22 Jan 1915: Promoted to *Major-General*
9 Jul 1915 - 30 Apr 1917: Commander, Brigade, 21st Infantry Division
30 Apr 1917 - 24 Aug 1917: Commander, 108th Infantry Division

Major-General Pavel Spiridonovich **Stefanovich-Stasenko** (13 May 1869 - ?)
17 Jan 1915 - 20 Mar 1916: Commander, 15th Turkestan Rifle Regiment
20 Mar 1916 - 11 Mar 1917: Chief of Staff, 2nd Caucasus Rifle Division
10 Apr 1916: Promoted to *Major-General*
11 Mar 1917 - 1918: Chief of Staff, XL. Army Corps

Major-General Semyon Vasilyevich **Steletsky** (28 Aug 1844 - 1903)
1 Apr 1895 - 1903: Commander of Engineers, Fortress Warsaw
9 Apr 1900: Promoted to *Major-General*

General of Infantry Stanislav Feliksovich **Stelnitsky** (1 Dec 1854 - ?)
7 Sep 1905: Promoted to *Major-General*
7 Sep 1905 - 8 Mar 1907: Commander, 2nd Brigade, 3rd Siberian Infantry Division
8 Mar 1907 - 2 Jul 1907: Commander, 1st Brigade, 32nd Infantry Division
2 Jul 1907 - 8 Jun 1910: Commander, 49th Replacement Infantry Brigade
8 Jun 1910 - 24 Sep 1914: Commander, 3rd Finnish Rifle Brigade
24 Sep 1914: Promoted to *Lieutenant-General*
24 Sep 1914 - 18 Jun 1915: Commander, 58th Infantry Division
18 Jun 1915 - 14 Sep 1917: Commanding General, XXXIX. Army Corps
13 Jan 1916: Promoted to *General of Infantry*
14 Sep 1917 - 20 Nov 1917: C-in-C, Special Army

Major-General Count Pyotr Mikhailovich **Stenbok** (11 Apr 1869 - 31 Jul 1931)
3 May 1908 - 1911: Commander, 2nd Hussary Regiment
1911: Promoted to *Major-General*
1911: Retired
30 Jul 1914 - 1 Oct 1916: Recalled; Commander, Brigade, Ural Cossack Division
1 Oct 1916 - 1917: Commander, 1st Brigade, 16th Cavalry Division

Lieutenant-General Count Aleksey Aleksandrovich **Stenbok-Fermor** (3 Sep 1835 - 4 Oct 1916)
30 Aug 1875:	Promoted to *Major-General*
30 Aug 1875 - 30 Aug 1885:	General à la suite
30 Aug 1885:	Promoted to *Lieutenant-General*
30 Aug 1885 - 13 May 1895:	Transferred to the reserve
5 Apr 1887 - 4 Oct 1916:	Master of the Horse, Tsar's Court

Lieutenant-General Count German Germanovich **Stenbok-Fermor** (6 Dec 1847 - 8 May 1904)
29 Apr 1892:	Promoted to *Major-General*
29 Apr 1892 - 13 Oct 1900:	Attached to Grand Duke Sergey Aleksandrovich
30 Jul 1892 - 29 Dec 1894:	Head of the Palace of Grand Duke Sergey Aleksandrovich
29 Dec 1894 - 13 Oct 1900:	Attached to Grand Duke Sergey Aleksandrovich
13 Oct 1900 - 1 Feb 1903:	Commander, 3rd Grenadier Division
6 Dec 1900:	Promoted to *Lieutenant-General*
1 Feb 1903 - 14 Apr 1904:	Commander, 1st Guards Infantry Division

Major-General of the Admiralty Aleksandr Ivanovich **Stepanov** (21 Jan 1863 - ?)
1902 - 1917:	Senior Clerk, Naval General Staff
25 Mar 1912:	Promoted to *Major-General of the Admiralty*

Major-General Fyodor Vasilyevich **Stepanov** (13 May 1871 - 29 Aug 1917)
1914 - 15 Oct 1915:	Commander, 150th Infantry Regiment
13 Jun 1915:	Promoted to *Major-General*
15 Oct 1915 - 29 May 1916:	Special Assignments General, 12th Army
29 May 1916 - 12 Apr 1917:	Chief of Staff, VII. Siberian Army Corps
12 Apr 1917 - 1917:	Commandant of Fortress Ust-Dvinsk
1917 - 29 Aug 1917:	Commandant of Fortress Vyborg

Major-General Konstantin Savelyevich **Stepanov** (4 Jan 1834 - ?)
24 Apr 1889:	Promoted to *Major-General*
24 Apr 1889 - 28 Nov 1890:	Commander, 2nd Brigade, 26th Infantry Division
28 Nov 1890 - 23 Jan 1891:	Commandant of Fortress Bender
23 Jan 1891 - 3 Nov 1893:	At the disposal of the Commanding General, Vilnius Military District
3 Nov 1893 - 1898:	Commandant of Fortress Osovets

General of Cavalry Mikhail Petrovich **Stepanov** (10 Feb 1853 - 12 Dec 1917)
29 Apr 1891:	Promoted to *Major-General*
29 Apr 1891 - 7 Mar 1905:	Aide to Grand Duke Sergey Aleksandrovich
29 Apr 1900:	Promoted to *Lieutenant-General*
7 Mar 1905 - 2 Apr 1917:	Aide to Grand Duchess Elizaveta Feodorovna
6 Dec 1910:	Promoted to *General of Cavalry*
2 Apr 1917:	Retired

Major-General Nikolai Aleksandrovich **Stepanov** (2 May 1869 - 19 Jan 1949)
17 Oct 1915 - 27 Dec 1916:	General for Assignments, Supreme Commander-in-Chief
6 Dec 1915:	Promoted to *Major-General*
27 Dec 1916 - 30 Sep 1917:	Chief of Staff for Land Forces, C-in-C Baltic Fleet
30 Sep 1917 - 1918:	Chief of Staff, IV. Cavalry Corps

Major-General Nikolai Ivanovich **Stepanov** (19 Feb 1850 - ?)
6 Apr 1903 - 21 Jun 1910:	Section Chief, Main Cossack Forces Directorate
1906:	Promoted to *Major-General*
21 Jun 1910 - 6 Sep 1910:	Ataman, Kizlyar Department, Terek Region
6 Sep 1910 - 15 Oct 1917:	Senior Deputy Commander, Terek Region, Ataman, Terek Cossack Army
15 Oct 1917:	Dismissed

Major-General Nikolai Pavlovich **Stepanov** (3 May 1859 - ?)
29 Mar 1916 - 1917:	Chairman of the Remount Commission, Caucasus Region
6 Dec 1916:	Promoted to *Major-General*

Major-General Nikolai Petrovich **Stepanov** (23 Nov 1851 - ?)
9 Oct 1894 - 1 Mar 1899:	Commander, 19th Dragoon Regiment
1 Mar 1899:	Promoted to *Major-General*
1 Mar 1899 - 16 Jan 1901:	Commander, 1st Brigade, 9th Cavalry Division
16 Jan 1901 - 13 Jun 1905:	Commander, 2nd Independent Cavalry Brigade
13 Jun 1905 - 1905:	Attached to the General Staff

Lieutenant-General Pavel Feofilaktovich **Stepanov** (1 Nov 1839 - ?)
27 Feb 1895 - 12 Mar 1910:	Inspector of Surveying, Office of the C-in-C, Caucasus
6 Apr 1903:	Promoted to *Major-General*
12 Mar 1910:	Promoted to *Lieutenant-General*
12 Mar 1910:	Retired

Major-General Sergey Ivanovich **Stepanov** (26 Feb 1856 - ?)
26 Jan 1908 - 1913:	Commander, 13th Sapper Battalion
14 Apr 1913:	Promoted to *Major-General*

Major-General of the Fleet Veniamin Vasilyevich **Stepanov** (19 Jul 1860 - 23 Feb 1931)
5 Feb 1912 - 31 Oct 1916:	Intendant-General, Black Sea Fleet
1 Jan 1916:	Promoted to *Major-General of the Fleet*
31 Oct 1916 - Oct 1917:	Commandant of Machinist School, Black Sea Fleet

Major-General Yuri Nikolayevich **Stepanov** (25 Feb 1862 - 1913)
18 Nov 1908 - 1913:	Commander, 1st Finnish Rifle Regiment
1913:	Promoted to *Major-General*

Major-General Yevgeny Semyonovich **Stepantsov** (11 Aug 1867 - ?)
13 May 1916 - 1917:	Commander, 7th Siberian Rifle Artillery Brigade

26 Feb 1917: Promoted to *Major-General*

Major-General Adrian Danilovich **Stepura-Serdyukov** (12 Aug 1865 - 8 Jul 1915)
? - 8 Jul 1915: Attached to 277th Infantry Regiment
19 Nov 1915: Posthumously promoted to *Major-General*

Major-General Andrey Vasilyevich **Sterligov** (8 Nov 1842 - ?)
10 Nov 1891 - 28 Dec 1893: Commandant of Firearms Depot, St. Petersburg Miltary District
19 Nov 1891: Promoted to *Major-General*
28 Dec 1893 - 1905: Commandant of Artillery Depot, Moscow Military District

Major-General Boris Andreyevich **Sterligov** (12 Mar 1874 - 7 Jun 1915)
1914 - 7 Jun 1915: Attached to 284th Infantry Regiment
5 Oct 1915: Posthumously promoted to *Major-General*

Major-General Nikolai Fyodorovich **Sterligov** (28 Apr 1861 - ?)
18 May 1916 - 1 Dec 1916: Military Commander of Tambov District
1 Dec 1916: Promoted to *Major-General*
1 Dec 1916: Retired

Lieutenant-General Anatoly Mikhailovich **Stessel** (28 Jun 1848 - 18 Jan 1915)
26 Jan 1899 - 4 May 1903: Commander, 3rd East Siberian Rifle Brigade
22 May 1899: Promoted to *Major-General*
24 Apr 1901: Promoted to *Lieutenant-General*
4 May 1903 - 12 Aug 1903: Commander, 2nd Infantry Division
12 Aug 1903 - 30 Jan 1904: Commandant of Fortress Port Arthur
30 Jan 1904 - 16 Jul 1905: Commanding General, III. Siberian Army Corps
14 Feb 1904 - 16 Jul 1905: Commander, Kwantung Fortified Area
16 Jul 1905 - Sep 1906: Adjutant-General
Sep 1906: Dismissed

Admiral Konstantin Vasilyevich **Stetsenko** (21 May 1862 - 1920)
1909 - 11 Oct 1911: Chief of Staff, Baltic Fleet
18 Apr 1910: Promoted to *Rear-Admiral*
11 Oct 1911 - 14 Apr 1913: Commander, Siberian Flotilla
14 Apr 1913: Promoted to *Vice-Admiral*
14 Apr 1913 - 17 Apr 1914: At the disposal of the Minister of the Navy
17 Apr 1914 - 15 Jun 1917: Chief of the Naval General Staff
6 Dec 1916: Promoted to *Admiral*
7 Mar 1917 - 15 Jun 1917: Member of the Admiralty Board
15 Jun 1917: Dismissed

Admiral Vasily Alexandrovich **Stetsenko** (7 Dec 1822 - 1901)
28 Oct 1866: Promoted to *Rear-Admiral*
28 Oct 1866 - 1868: Member of the Tsar's retinue
1868 - 1874: Detachment Commander, Armored Squadron

7 Jan 1874:	Promoted to *Vice-Admiral*
1874 - 1877:	Member of the Tsar's retinue
1877 - 1883:	Commander of Defenses, Finnish Archipelago
1883 - 1901:	Member of the Admiralty Board
1 Jan 1893:	Promoted to *Admiral*

Lieutenant-General Nikolai Nikolayevich **Stogov** (10 Sep 1872 - 7 Dec 1959)
6 Nov 1914 - 15 Apr 1915:	Commander, 3rd Finnish Rifle Regiment
7 Feb 1915:	Promoted to *Major-General*
15 Apr 1915 - 25 Sep 1916:	Quartermaster-General, 8th Army
25 Sep 1916 - 2 Apr 1917:	Chief of Staff, 8th Army
2 Apr 1917 - 10 Sep 1917:	Commanding General, XVI. Army Corps
29 Apr 1917:	Promoted to *Lieutenant-General*
10 Sep 1917 - Oct 1917:	Chief of Staff, Southwestern Front

Lieutenant-General Yevgraf Yevgrafovich **Stogov** (17 Jul 1842 - ?)
30 Nov 1892:	Promoted to *Major-General*
30 Nov 1892 - 15 Oct 1895:	Commander, 40th Artillery Brigade
15 Oct 1895 - 5 Dec 1899:	Commander, 3rd Artillery Brigade
5 Dec 1899 - 1905:	Commander of Artillery, V. Army Corps
6 Dec 1900:	Promoted to *Lieutenant-General*

Major-General Prince Nikolai Pavlovich **Stokasimov** (10 May 1869 - ?)
6 Nov 1912 - 17 Nov 1914:	Commander, 177th Infantry Regiment
28 Oct 1914:	Promoted to *Major-General*
17 Nov 1914 - 15 Mar 1915:	Commander, 1st Brigade, 70th Infantry Division
15 Mar 1915 - Jan 1917:	Chief of Staff, 1st Turkestan Rifle Division
Jan 1917 - 23 Jul 1917:	Chief of Staff, 19th Siberian Rifle Division
23 Jul 1917 - 1918:	Commander, 3rd Amur Border Infantry Division

Major-General Boris Ivanovich **Stolbin** (23 Dec 1872 - 11 Dec 1937)
23 Apr 1915 - 5 Apr 1917:	Commander, 10th Siberian Rifle Artillery Brigade
3 Mar 1916:	Promoted to *Major-General*
5 Apr 1917 - 7 May 1917:	Attached to 201st Artillery Brigade
7 May 1917 - 14 Dec 1917:	Inspector of Artillery, IV. Siberian Army Corps
14 Dec 1917 - 8 Feb 1918:	Acting Commanding General, IV. Siberian Army Corps

Major-General Dmitry Grigoryevich **Stoletov** (22 Feb 1845 - 18 Aug 1899)
1 Apr 1891 - 27 Feb 1898:	Commander, Artillery Training Polygon, Kiev Military District
1894:	Promoted to *Major-General*
27 Feb 1898 - 13 May 1899:	Commander, 5th Artillery Brigade

General of Infantry Nikolai Grigoryevich **Stoletov** (1 Nov 1834 - 27 Jun 1912)
8 Sep 1875 - 1 Nov 1876:	Commander, 1st Brigade, 17th Infantry Division
12 Apr 1877 - 1 Jan 1878:	Commander, Bulgarian Militia
15 Jun 1877:	Promoted to *Major-General*
1 Jan 1878 - 5 Apr 1878:	Commander, 1st Brigade, 3rd Infantry Division

5 Apr 1878 - 26 May 1878:	At the disposal of the Commanding General, Turkestan Military District
26 May 1878 - 11 Apr 1881:	Chief of Mission to the Emir of Afghanistan
11 Apr 1881 - 27 Oct 1886:	Commander, 1st Rifle Brigade
30 Aug 1886:	Promoted to *Lieutenant-General*
27 Oct 1886 - 3 Nov 1893:	Commander, 18th Infantry Division
3 Nov 1893 - 14 Nov 1894:	Commanding General, XV. Army Corps
14 Nov 1894 - 29 May 1899:	Commanding General, XIV. Army Corps
6 Dec 1898:	Promoted to *General of Infantry*
29 May 1899 - 1 Jan 1911:	Member of the Military Council
1 Jan 1911 - 27 Jun 1912:	Member, Committee for Wounded Veterans

Lieutenant-General Georgy Petrovich **Stolitsa** (1 Apr 1856 - 23 Dec 1916)
18 Apr 1910:	Promoted to *Major-General*
18 Apr 1910 - 23 Dec 1916:	Special Assignments General, Main Directorate of the Gendarmerie Corps
1916:	Posthumously promoted to *Lieutenant-General*

Lieutenant-General Konstantin Akimovich **Stolitsa** (15 May 1839 - 16 Mar 1910)
10 May 1892:	Promoted to *Major-General*
10 May 1892 - 26 Jul 1899:	Commander, 1st Brigade, 26th Infantry Division
26 Jul 1899 - 14 Jul 1902:	Commander, 26th Infantry Division
6 Dec 1899:	Promoted to *Lieutenant-General*

Major-General Mikhail Stepanovich **Stolitsa** (27 Oct 1856 - 5 Apr 1907)
22 Feb 1904:	Promoted to *Major-General*
22 Feb 1904 - 7 Jan 1905:	Commander, 2nd Brigade, 3rd East Siberian Rifle Division
7 Jan 1905 - 24 Aug 1905:	Chief of Staff, I. Army Corps
24 Aug 1905 - 30 Apr 1907:	Commander, 37th Infantry Division

Major-General Yevgeny Mikhailovich **Stolitsa** (18 Dec 1845 - ?)
31 Oct 1899:	Promoted to *Major-General*
31 Oct 1899 - 28 Dec 1904:	Commander, 1st Brigade, 2nd Grenadier Division
28 Dec 1904 - 19 Jan 1906:	Commander, 1st Infantry Division

Major-General Leonid Nikolayevich **Stolyarevsky** (29 Mar 1859 - ?)
14 Feb 1906 - 1909:	Military Judge, Caucasus Military District Court
2 Apr 1906:	Promoted to *Major-General*

General of Artillery Arkady Dmitriyevich **Stolypin** (26 Dec 1822 - 17 Nov 1899)
17 Sep 1857 - 8 Apr 1862:	Ataman, Ural Cossack Army
1 Jan 1859:	Promoted to *Major-General*
8 Apr 1862 - 10 Jun 1869:	Transferred to the reserve
20 May 1868:	Promoted to *Lieutenant-General*
10 Jun 1869 - 23 Mar 1877:	Equerry, Imperial Court
2 Apr 1877 - 15 Aug 1878:	At the disposal of the C-in-C, Field Army
15 Aug 1878 - 13 Apr 1886:	Commanding General, IX. Army Corps

8 Aug 1879:	Promoted to *General-Adjutant*
15 May 1883:	Promoted to *General of Artillery*
13 Apr 1886 - 9 Apr 1889:	Commanding General, Grenadier Corps
9 Apr 1889 - 17 Nov 1899:	Member, Committee for Wounded Veterans
31 Mar 1892 - 17 Nov 1899:	Commandant of the Kremlin

Major-General Vitold-Mechislav Ignatyevich **Stomma** (13 Mar 1868 - ?)
22 Feb 1912 - 1917:	Deputy Chief of St. Petersburg Cartridge Factory
6 Dec 1915:	Promoted to *Major-General*

Major-General Andrey Mikhailovich **Stopchansky** (6 Jan 1839 - 6 Jan 1904)
18 Mar 1897 - 6 Jan 1904:	Commander of Gendarmerie, Kutaisi Province
14 Apr 1902:	Promoted to *Major-General*

Lieutenant-General Aleksandr Nikolayevich **Storozhenko** (23 Oct 1850 - 11 Mar 1913)
31 Jul 1903 - 9 May 1906:	Inspector of Artillery Remounts
1904:	Promoted to *Major-General*
9 May 1906 - 11 Apr 1907:	Commander, Caucasus Reserve Artillery Brigade
11 Apr 1907 - 1 Jul 1910:	Commander, 15th Artillery Brigade
1 Jul 1910:	Promoted to *Lieutenant-General*
1 Jul 1910 - 11 Mar 1913:	Inspector of Artillery, VIII. Army Corps

Lieutenant-General Mikhail Pavlovich **Stoyanov** (24 Oct 1845 - ?)
29 Mar 1901:	Promoted to *Major-General*
29 Mar 1901 - 20 Jul 1904:	Commander, 1st Brigade, 2nd Consolidated Cossack Division
20 Jul 1904 - 2 Sep 1905:	Commander, 1st Brigade, 4th Don Cossack Division
2 Sep 1905 - 18 May 1906:	Commander, 4th Don Cossack Division
18 May 1906 - 14 Oct 1906:	Attached to Kiev Military District
14 Oct 1906 - Nov 1907:	Commander, 2nd Consolidated Cossack Division
22 Apr 1907:	Promoted to *Lieutenant-General*

General of Artillery Nikolai Vladimirovich **Stoyanov** (16 Apr 1850 - ?)
29 Dec 1899 - 4 Jun 1904:	Commander, 33rd Artillery Brigade
1 Jan 1900:	Promoted to *Major-General*
4 Jun 1905 - 1 Mar 1906:	Commander of Artillery, V. Siberian Army Corps
8 Oct 1905:	Promoted to *Lieutenant-General*
1 Mar 1906 - 15 Apr 1914:	Commander of Artillery, Moscow Military District
15 Apr 1914:	Promoted to *General of Artillery*
15 Apr 1914:	Retired

Major-General Vladimir Ivanovich **Stoyanov** (26 May 1859 - ?)
4 Feb 1912 - ?:	Commander, 2nd Vladivostok Fortress Artillery Regiment
1916:	Promoted to *Major-General*
? - 1917:	Commander, 51st Militia Brigade

Lieutenant-General Konstantin Nikitich **Stoyanovsky** (21 May 1855 - ?)
2 Nov 1908 - 23 Jul 1910:	Commander, 1st Uman Regiment, Kuban Cossack Army
23 Jul 1910:	Promoted to *Major-General*
23 Jul 1910 - 31 Dec 1913:	Commander, 1st Brigade, 2nd Caucasus Cossack Division
31 Dec 1913:	Promoted to *Lieutenant-General*
31 Dec 1913:	Retired
22 Oct 1914:	Recalled with the rank of *Major-General*
22 Oct 1914 - 30 Dec 1915:	Commander, 3rd Trans-Baikal Cossack Brigade
30 Dec 1915 - 1917:	Reserve officer, Caucasus Military District

Major-General Alexey Ivanovich **Stradetsky** (5 Mar 1844 - ?)
15 Dec 1898 - 1904:	Commander of Artillery, Fortress Mikhailov
6 Dec 1899:	Promoted to *Major-General*

Major-General Aleksandr Khristianovich **Stradovsky** (24 Jun 1848 - May 1906)
4 Apr 1904:	Promoted to *Major-General*
4 Apr 1904 - 13 May 1906:	Commander, 2nd Brigade, 6th Infantry Division

Major-General Valerian Petrovich **Strakhov** (25 Aug 1846 - 14 Oct 1899)
13 Oct 1898:	Promoted to *Major-General*
13 Oct 1898 - 14 Oct 1899:	Commander, 5th Reserve Artillery Brigade

Lieutenant-General Vladimir Ivanovich **Strazhevsky** (22 Sep 1843 - ?)
9 Apr 1890 - 14 May 1893:	Commandant, Georgievsk Artillery Depot
14 May 1893:	Promoted to *Major-General*
14 May 1893 - 1903:	Commander of Artillery, Fortress Terek-Dagestan
1903:	Promoted to *Lieutenant-General*
1903:	Retired

General of Infantry Ivan Afanasyevich **Strelbitsky** (18 Jun 1828 - 15 Jul 1900)
15 Dec 1864 - 1899:	Attached to the Military Topographical Section, General Staff
19 Feb 1880:	Promoted to *Major-General*
30 Aug 1890:	Promoted to *Lieutenant-General*
1899:	Promoted to *General of Infantry*

Major-General Stanislav Antonovich **Streletsky** (1 Nov 1844 - ?)
6 Dec 1901:	Promoted to *Major-General*
1902 - 1904:	Deputy Commander of Engineers, Amur Military District

Lieutenant-General Fyodor Efimovch **Strelnikov** (2 Mar 1839 - 2 Dec 1906)
26 Oct 1872 - 30 May 1888:	Military Judge, Warsaw Military District Court
30 Aug 1886:	Promoted to *Major-General*
30 May 1888 - 23 Nov 1889:	Military Prosecutor, Warsaw Military District Court
23 Nov 1889 - 10 Dec 1905:	Chairman of the Military Court, Warsaw Military District

14 May 1896: Promoted to *Lieutenant-General*
10 Dec 1905 - 2 Dec 1906: Member, Supreme Military Tribunal

Lieutenant-General Nikolai Petrovich **Stremoukhov** (29 Aug 1861 - 8 Dec 1938)
30 Sep 1906: Promoted to *Major-General*
30 Sep 1906 - 21 Jun 1909: General for Special Assignments, Irkutsk Military District
21 Jun 1909 - 31 Oct 1914: Chief of Staff, XVII. Army Corps
31 Oct 1914 - 21 Mar 1915: Commander, 17th Infantry Division
22 Jan 1915: Promoted to *Lieutenant-General*
21 Mar 1915 - 19 May 1915: Reserve officer, Dvinsk Military District
19 May 1915 - 19 Oct 1915: Chief of Staff, 7th Army
19 Oct 1915 - 10 Mar 1916: At the disposal of the C-in-C, Southwestern Front
10 Mar 1916 - 4 Sep 1917: Commander, 34th Infantry Division
4 Sep 1917 - Oct 1917: Reserve officer, Odessa Military District

Major-General Aleksey Grigoryevich **Strizhev** (17 Mar 1846 - ?)
6 Feb 1886 - 1913: Artillery Inspector, Main Artillery Directorate
6 Dec 1904: Promoted to *Major-General*

General of Artillery Maksim Ivanovich **Strizhev** (8 Mar 1843 - ?)
9 Sep 1891: Promoted to *Major-General*
9 Sep 1891 - 25 Feb 1902: Commandant of Fortress Vladivostok
6 Dec 1899: Promoted to *Lieutenant-General*
25 Feb 1902 - 1 Aug 1905: Commandant of Fortress Sevastopol
1 Aug 1905 - 31 Dec 1913: Commandant of Fortress Warsaw
6 Dec 1907: Promoted to *General of Artillery*
31 Dec 1913: Retired

Major-General of the Fleet Nikolai Vasilyevich **Stronsky** (28 Apr 1863 - 2 Mar 1917)
29 Oct 1913 - 2 Mar 1917: Commander, 1st Baltic Naval Depot
3 Mar 1914: Promoted to *Major-General of the Fleet*

General of Cavalry Aleksandr Petrovich **Strukov** (18 Jul 1840 - 14 Oct 1911)
1 Feb 1873 - 2 Mar 1878: Adjutant to the Commanding General, St. Petersburg Military District
10 Jul 1877: Promoted to *Major-General*
2 Mar 1878 - 30 Aug 1881: Commander, Life Guards Uhlan Regiment
30 Aug 1881 - 26 Jun 1883: Commander, 3rd Brigade, 2nd Guards Cavalry Division
26 Jun 1883 - 7 Jan 1892: Commander, 4th Cavalry Division
30 Aug 1886: Promoted to *Lieutenant-General*
7 Jan 1892 - 24 Feb 1893: Commander, 1st Guards Cavalry Division
24 Feb 1893 - 18 Jan 1907: Inspector of Remounts & Reserve Cavalry Brigades
6 Dec 1898: Promoted to *General of Cavalry*
1903: Promoted to *General-Adjutant*
18 Jan 1907 - 14 Oct 1911: Reserve officer, Guards Cavalry

Major-General Dmitry Petrovich **Strukov** (4 Apr 1864 - 1920)
1912: Promoted to *Major-General*
16 Jul 1912 - 1919: Head of Artillery History Museum

Major-General Mikhail Ivanovich **Strukov** (22 Nov 1853 - 4 Jun 1915)
14 Feb 1907: Promoted to *Major-General*
14 Feb 1907 - 1907: Commander, Omsk Sapper Brigade

Major-General Aleksandr Petrovich **Strusevich** (30 Sep 1855 - ?)
3 Apr 1897 - 1906: Inspector of Classes, Simbirsk Cadet Corps
6 Dec 1903: Promoted to *Major-General*

Major-General Osip Osipovich **Strusevich** (9 Dec 1861 - 8 Sep 1914)
13 May 1913 - 8 Sep 1914: Commander, 108th Infantry Regiment
3 Feb 1915: Posthumously promoted to *Major-General*

Lieutenant-General of the Hydrographic Corps Ippolit Vladimirovich **Studnitsky** (13 Aug 1857 - 22 Feb 1929)
29 Sep 1909 - 1916: Chairman, Finnish Archipelago Review Committee, Main Hydrographic Directorate
6 Dec 1911: Promoted to *Major-General of the Admiralty*
4 Feb 1913: Redesignated *Major-General of the Hydrographic Corps*
6 Dec 1914: Promoted to *Lieutenant-General of the Hydrographic Corps*
6 Feb 1917 - 4 Apr 1917: Chief of Finnish Archipelago Hydrographic Survey
4 Apr 1917 - 5 Jul 1917: Reserve officer, Ministry of the Navy
5 Jul 1917: Dismissed

General of Artillery Aleksandr Ivanovich **Studzinsky** (11 Aug 1843 - 8 May 1907)
22 Aug 1882 - 2 Apr 1899: Chief of Okhtenskaya Explosives Factory
30 Aug 1888: Promoted to *Major-General*
10 Aug 1891 - 8 May 1907: Member of the Artillery Committee, Main Artillery Directorate
6 Dec 1898: Promoted to *Lieutenant-General*
2 Apr 1899 - 8 May 1907: Inspector of Powder Factories
8 May 1907: Promoted to *General of Artillery*

Major-General Nikolai Aleksandrovich **Studzitsky** (10 Jun 1842 - ?)
14 Jun 1899 - 15 Jun 1902: Commander, 5th Artillery Brigade
1 Jan 1900: Promoted to *Major-General*

Lieutenant-General Aleksandr Nikolayevich **Stupin** (28 Aug 1852 - ?)
6 Sep 1904: Promoted to *Major-General*
6 Sep 1904 - 12 Jan 1905: Commander, 1st Brigade, 69th Infantry Division
12 Jan 1905 - 11 Aug 1906: Commander, 1st Brigade, 52nd Infantry Division
11 Aug 1906 - 29 Jan 1907: Commander, 2nd Brigade, 15th Infantry Division
29 Jan 1907 - 30 Mar 1909: Commander, 52nd Reserve Infantry Brigade

30 Mar 1909 - 1 Sep 1910:	Commander, 56th Reserve Infantry Brigade
1 Sep 1910:	Promoted to *Lieutenant-General*
1 Sep 1910:	Retired

Lieutenant-General Georgy Vladimirovich **Stupin** (22 Jun 1860 - ?)

1 May 1910 - 20 Apr 1915:	Commander, 18th Infantry Regiment
17 Aug 1914:	Promoted to *Major-General*
20 Apr 1915 - 1915:	Commander, Consolidated Border Infantry Division
1915 - ?:	Commander, 2nd Amur Border Infantry Division
? - 25 Oct 1916:	Commander, Infantry Division
20 Oct 1916:	Promoted to *Lieutenant-General*
25 Oct 1916 - 18 Apr 1917:	Commanding General, VII. Siberian Army Corps
18 Apr 1917 - 11 Aug 1917:	C-in-C, 9th Army
11 Aug 1917 - 5 Oct 1917:	Reserve officer, Odessa Military District
5 Oct 1917 - 27 Oct 1917:	Reserve officer, Kiev Military District
27 Oct 1917:	Dismissed

General of Cavalry Aleksandr Nikolayevich **Styurler** (8 Sep 1825 - 21 May 1901)

17 Apr 1860:	Promoted to *Major-General*
17 Apr 1860 - 8 Jul 1872:	Member of the Tsar's retinue
20 May 1868:	Promoted to *Lieutenant-General*
8 Jul 1872 - 14 Dec 1875:	Master of the Horse, Court of the Tsarevich
14 Dec 1875:	Promoted to *General-Adjutant*
14 Dec 1875 - 14 May 1896:	Adjutant-General to the Tsar
15 May 1883:	Promoted to *General of Cavalry*
14 May 1896 - 21 May 1901:	Member of the State Council

Lieutenant-General Dean Ivanovich **Subbotich** (7 May 1851 - ?)

24 Mar 1894:	Promoted to *Major-General*
24 Mar 1894 - 11 Jun 1897:	Deputy Chief of Staff, Amur Military District
11 Jun 1897 - 29 Aug 1898:	Military Governor & Commander of the Maritime Region, Ataman, Ussuri Cossack Army
29 Aug 1898 - 3 Sep 1899:	Commander, Kwantung Peninsula
3 Sep 1899 - 7 Feb 1901:	Deputy Commander, Kwantung Region
12 Aug 1900:	Promoted to *Lieutenant-General*
7 Feb 1901 - 10 Apr 1901:	At the disposal of the Minister of War
10 Apr 1901 - 2 Nov 1902:	Commanding General, II. Turkestan Army Corps, Commander, Trans-Caspian Region
2 Nov 1902 - 7 Sep 1903:	Commanding General, Amur Military District, Governor-General of Amur, Ataman, Amur Cossack Army
7 Sep 1903 - 24 Nov 1905:	Member of the Military Council
24 Nov 1905 - 15 Aug 1906:	Governor-General of Turkestan, Commanding General, Turkestan Military District, Ataman, Semirechensk Cossack Army
15 Aug 1906:	Retired

Major-General of Naval Engineers Nikolai Aleksandrovich **Subbotin** (6 Oct 1838 - 3 May 1901)
1891 - 3 May 1901: Chief of Engineers, Port of St. Petersburg
1900: Promoted to *Major-General of Naval Engineers*

Major-General Vladimir Fyodorovich **Subbotin** (10 Mar 1874 - 4 Sep 1937)
5 Jan 1915 - 5 May 1916: Commander, 298th Infantry Regiment
5 Oct 1915: Promoted to *Major-General*
5 May 1916 - 11 Nov 1916: Commander of Engineers, 11th Army
11 Nov 1916 - 6 Jan 1917: Commander of Engineers, Danube Army
6 Jan 1917 - 20 Sep 1917: Commander of Engineers, Romanian Front
20 Sep 1917 - Oct 1917: Reserve officer, Petrograd Military District

Major-General Boris Ksaveryevich **Sudravsky** (24 Oct 1875 - 10 Jul 1915)
? - 10 Jul 1915: Battalion Commander, Life Guards Grenadier Regiment
26 Jun 1916: Posthumously promoted to *Major-General*

Major-General Vladimir Ksaveryevich **Sudravsky** (16 Dec 1872 - 6 Oct 1914)
1913 - 6 Oct 1914: Commander, 2nd Battalion, Life Guards Grenadier Regiment
26 Jun 1916: Posthumously promoted to *Major-General*

Major-General Dmitry Fedorovich **Sukachev** (29 Sep 1872 - 13 Aug 1914)
1909 - 13 Aug 1914: Attached to 122nd Infantry Regiment
24 May 1915: Posthumously promoted to *Major-General*

Major-General of the Fleet Nikolai Savelyevich **Sukhanov** (22 Apr 1863 - ?)
?: Promoted to *Major-General of the Fleet*
?: Professor, Black Sea Master Machinist School

Lieutenant-General Panteleymon Grigoryevich **Sukhanov** (29 Apr 1874 - ?)
19 Apr 1916 - 9 Jan 1917: Chief of Staff, 3rd Infantry Division
18 Jul 1916: Promoted to *Major-General*
9 Jan 1917 - 5 May 1917: Chief of Staff, XXXII. Army Corps
5 May 1917 - 12 Aug 1917: Commander, 105th Infantry Division
12 Aug 1917 - Nov 1917: Commanding General, XLV. Army Corps
23 Aug 1917: Promoted to *Lieutenant-General*

Major-General Vladimir Ivanovich **Sukhikh** (20 Feb 1864 - 24 Oct 1920)
17 Jun 1912 - 6 Oct 1915: Commander, 15th Rifle Regiment
6 Oct 1915 - Oct 1917: Commander, Brigade, 82nd Infantry Division
6 Dec 1915: Promoted to *Major-General*

Major-General Konstantin Ivanovich **Sukhin** (7 Aug 1860 - 1913)
24 Dec 1908 - 24 Dec 1911: Deputy Chief of Mikhailovsky-Shostensky Gunpowder Factory
18 Apr 1910: Promoted to *Major-General*
24 Dec 1911 - 1913: Deputy Chief of Okhtenskaya Explosives Factory

General of Artillery Aleksandr Vasilyevich **Sukhinsky** (16 Oct 1848 - ?)
17 Oct 1883 - 4 Jun 1899:	Deputy Chief of Okhtenskaya Explosives Factory
10 Aug 1891 - 1913:	Member of the Artillery Committee, Main Artillery Directorate
14 May 1896:	Promoted to *Major-General*
4 Jun 1899 - 1913:	Chief of Okhtenskaya Explosives Factory
29 Mar 1906:	Promoted to *Lieutenant-General*
1913:	Promoted to *General of Artillery*
1913:	Retired

General of Artillery Nikolai Vasilyevich **Sukhinsky** (1 Nov 1850 - ?)
4 Nov 1883 - 16 Jun 1905:	Section Chief, Main Directorate for Military Schools
6 Dec 1899:	Promoted to *Major-General*
16 Jun 1905 - 3 May 1910:	Special Assignments General, Main Directorate for Military Schools
22 Jun 1906:	Promoted to *Lieutenant-General*
3 May 1910:	Promoted to *General of Artillery*
3 May 1910 - 1 Sep 1911:	Transferred to the reserve
1 Sep 1911:	Retired
3 Sep 1911 - 1917:	Attached to the Ministry of War

Lieutenant-General Pyotr Vasilyevich **Sukhinsky** (9 Jan 1854 - 8 Mar 1916)
30 Mar 1904 - 2 May 1904:	Commander, 3rd Grenadier Artillery Brigade
2 May 1904 - 1 Jul 1908:	Commander, 9th Artillery Brigade
1 Apr 1905:	Promoted to *Major-General*
1 Jul 1908 - 28 Jul 1910:	Commander of Artillery, XII. Army Corps
3 Jul 1908:	Promoted to *Lieutenant-General*
28 Jul 1910 - 16 Jul 1915:	Inspector of Artillery, XII. Army Corps
16 Jul 1915 - 8 Mar 1916:	Reserve officer, Kiev Military District

Major-General Avenir Yeliseyevich **Sukhodolsky** (30 Oct 1845 - 20 Aug 1903)
24 Jul 1899 - 20 Aug 1903:	Member of the Artillery Committee, Main Artillery Direcorate
6 Dec 1899:	Promoted to *Major-General*

Major-General Lev Vladimirovich **Sukhodolsky** (3 Aug 1855 - 9 Oct 1914)
15 Oct 1904 - 4 May 1908:	Commander, 2nd Fortress Infantry Regiment
4 May 1908:	Promoted to *Major-General*
4 May 1908 - 22 Jul 1910:	Commander, Ussuri Railway Brigade
22 Jul 1910 - 9 Oct 1914:	Commander, 2nd Railway Brigade

Major-General of the Admiralty Vatslav Modestovich **Sukhomel** (9 Feb 1864 - Jan 1942)
30 Sep 1896 - 1918:	Professor, Naval Cadet Corps
14 Apr 1913:	Promoted to *Major-General of the Admiralty*

Lieutenant-General Semyon Andreyevich **Sukhomlin** (3 Feb 1867 - 1928)
21 Sep 1907 - 12 Jul 1912:	Commander, 72nd Infantry Regiment

12 Jul 1912:	Promoted to *Major-General*
12 Jul 1912 - 19 Jul 1914:	Quartermaster-General, Irkutsk Military District
19 Jul 1914 - 19 Apr 1915:	Chief of Staff, Kazan Military District
19 Apr 1915 - 18 Jul 1915:	Deputy Military Governor of Galicia
18 Jul 1915 - 6 Sep 1916:	Chief of Staff, 8th Army
6 Sep 1916 - 4 Oct 1916:	Reserve officer, Kiev Military District
1 Oct 1916:	Promoted to *Lieutenant-General*
4 Oct 1916 - 23 Oct 1916:	Deputy Military Governor of Occupied Austro-Hungarian Regions
23 Oct 1916 - 29 May 1917:	Chief of Staff, Southwestern Front
29 May 1917 - 6 Feb 1918:	Reserve officer, Petrograd Military District
6 Feb 1918:	Dismissed

General of Cavalry Nikolai Aleksandrovich **Sukhomlinov** (27 Jul 1850 - 1918)

3 Feb 1903:	Promoted to *Major-General*
3 Feb 1903 - 7 Jan 1909:	Commander, 1st Brigade, 9th Cavalry Division
7 Jan 1909 - 4 Sep 1911:	Commander, 9th Cavalry Division
6 Dec 1909:	Promoted to *Lieutenant-General*
4 Sep 1911 - 24 May 1915:	C-in-C, Orenburg Cossack Army, Governor of Orenburg
24 May 1915 - Mar 1917:	Commanding General, Omsk Military District, C-in-C, Siberian Cossack Army
10 Apr 1916:	Promoted to *General of Cavalry*
Mar 1917:	Retired

General of Infantry Vladimir Aleksandrovich **Sukhomlinov** (4 Aug 1848 - 2 Feb 1926)

10 Jan 1886 - 16 Apr 1897:	Commandant, Cavalry School
30 Aug 1890:	Promoted to *Major-General*
16 Apr 1897 - 25 May 1899:	Commander, 10th Cavalry Division
13 Jan 1898:	Promoted to *Lieutenant-General*
25 May 1899 - 12 Oct 1902:	Chief of Staff, Kiev Military District
12 Oct 1902 - 23 Oct 1904:	Deputy Commanding General, Kiev Military District
23 Oct 1904 - 2 Dec 1908:	Governor-General of Kiev, Podolska and Volyn
19 Oct 1905 - 2 Dec 1908:	Commanding General, Kiev Military District
6 Dec 1906:	Promoted to *General of Infantry*
2 Dec 1908 - 11 Mar 1909:	Chief of the General Directorate of the General Staff
11 Mar 1909 - 13 Jun 1915:	Minister of War
6 Dec 1911 - 8 Mar 1916:	Member of the State Council
1912:	Promoted to *General-Adjutant*
8 Mar 1916:	Retired

General of Cavalry Nikolai Nikolayevich **Sukhotin** (28 Jan 1847 - Jul 1918)

28 May 1881 - 24 Nov 1894:	Professor, Nikolayev General Staff Academy
30 Aug 1887:	Promoted to *Major-General*
30 Aug 1887 - 21 Jul 1891:	Member, Military Scientific Committee, General Staff
21 Jul 1891 - 24 Nov 1894:	Attached to the Minister of War
24 Nov 1894 - 17 Aug 1898:	Commander, 3rd Cavalry Division
14 May 1896:	Promoted to *Lieutenant-General*

17 Aug 1898 - 14 Apr 1901:	Commandant, General Staff Academy
14 Apr 1901 - 24 Apr 1906:	Governor-General of the Steppes, Commanding General, Siberian Military District, Ataman, Siberian Cossack Army
24 Apr 1906 - 25 Oct 1917:	Member of the State Council
6 May 1906:	Promoted to *General of Cavalry*

Major-General Nikolai Petrovich **Sukhotin** (8 Feb 1842 - 22 May 1924)
23 Dec 1904 - 30 Sep 1917:	Chancellor of Finland
18 Jan 1905:	Promoted to *Major-General*
30 Sep 1917:	Dismissed

Lieutenant-General Fridrikh Fridrikhovich **Sukin** (12 Sep 1823 - ?)
14 Feb 1879 - 31 Oct 1881:	Commander, 11th Uhlan Regiment
31 Oct 1881:	Promoted to *Major-General*
31 Oct 1881 - 22 Jun 1886:	Commander, 1st Brigade, 3rd Cavalry Division
22 Jun 1886 - 1898:	Commander, 5th Replacement Cavalry Brigade
30 Aug 1894:	Promoted to *Lieutenant-General*

General of Engineers Ivan Mikhailovich **Sukin** (12 Nov 1842 - ?)
2 Jun 1892 - 17 Sep 1896:	Commander of Engineers, Fortress Brest-Litovsk
30 Aug 1892:	Promoted to *Major-General*
17 Sep 1896 - 7 Jan 1897:	Commander of Engineers, Turkestan Military District
7 Jan 1897 - 31 Dec 1904:	Commander of Engineers, Finland Military District
6 Dec 1903:	Promoted to *Lieutenant-General*
31 Dec 1904 - 29 May 1905:	Commander of Engineers, Odessa Military District
29 May 1905 - 29 Jul 1910:	Deputy Chief of Main Engineering Directorate
29 Jul 1910:	Promoted to *General of Engineers*
29 Jul 1910:	Retired

Major-General Pyotr Iosafovich **Sukovkin** (29 Sep 1864 - 19 Nov 1939)
12 Oct 1911 - 4 Mar 1915:	Commander, 7th Hussar Regiment
22 Jan 1915:	Promoted to *Major-General*
4 Mar 1915 - 17 Oct 1915:	Commander, 1st Brigade, 16th Cavalry Division
17 Oct 1915 - 21 Oct 1917:	Reserve officer, Minsk Military District
21 Oct 1917:	Retired

Lieutenant-General Aleksandr Semyonovich **Sulevich** (29 Mar 1856 - ?)
15 Aug 1911 - 18 Feb 1917:	Commander, 2nd Brigade, 6th Siberian Rifle Division
18 Oct 1911:	Promoted to *Major-General*
18 Feb 1917 - 12 Oct 1917:	Commander, 22nd Siberian Rifle Division
27 Aug 1917:	Promoted to *Lieutenant-General*
12 Oct 1917 - 2 Aug 1918:	Reserve officer, Kiev Military District

Lieutenant-General Sigizmund-Mikhail Feliksovich **Sulikovsky** (6 Sep 1855 - ?)
31 Oct 1899 - 26 Nov 1901:	Commander, 14th Grenadier Regiment
26 Nov 1901:	Promoted to *Major-General*
26 Nov 1901 - 8 Oct 1902:	At the disposal of the Chief of the General Staff

8 Oct 1902 - 2 Jan 1908:	Chief of Staff, XIX. Army Corps
2 Jan 1908:	Promoted to *Lieutenant-General*
2 Jan 1908 - Dec 1908:	Commander, 4th East Siberian Rifle Division

Major-General Leonid Yulianovich **Sulima-Samuylo** (23 Apr 1862 - 4 Aug 1905)

28 Sep 1904:	Promoted to *Major-General*
28 Sep 1904 - 4 Aug 1905:	Duty General, 2nd Manchurian Army

Lieutenant-General Nikolai Ilich **Sulimov** (4 Dec 1855 - ?)

6 Jul 1904:	Promoted to *Major-General*
6 Jul 1904 - 15 Dec 1908:	Commander, 1st Brigade, 20th Infantry Division
15 Dec 1908 - 13 Feb 1909:	Commander, 65th Replacement Infantry Brigade
13 Feb 1909 - 13 Aug 1912:	Commander, 5th Rifle Brigade
30 May 1912:	Promoted to *Lieutenant-General*
13 Aug 1912 - 8 Aug 1914:	Commander, 7th Siberian Rifle Division
8 Aug 1914 - 12 Jul 1915:	Commander, 12th Siberian Rifle Division
12 Jul 1915 - 10 Nov 1915:	Reserve officer, Dvinsk Military District
10 Nov 1915 - 18 Apr 1917:	Commander, 109th Infantry Division
18 Apr 1917 - 4 May 1917:	Reserve officer, Dvinsk Military District
4 May 1917:	Dismissed

Major-General Leonid Ivanovich **Sulimovsky** (1 May 1854 - ?)

27 Mar 1904 - 1910:	Military Commander, Minsk District
1910:	Promoted to *Major-General*
1910:	Retired
10 Nov 1915 - 20 Nov 1916:	Recalled; Reserve officer, Kiev Military District
20 Nov 1916:	Dismissed

Major-General Mikhail Ippolitovich **Sulin** (8 Nov 1849 - ?)

27 Sep 1906 - 16 Jan 1909:	Commander, 45th Artillery Brigade
31 May 1907:	Promoted to *Major-General*

Lieutenant-General Matvey Aleksandrovich **Sulkevich** (20 Jul 1865 - 15 Jul 1920)

17 Oct 1910:	Promoted to *Major-General*
17 Oct 1910 - 14 Jun 1912:	Quartermaster-General, Irkutsk Military District
14 Jun 1912 - 23 May 1914:	Chief of Staff, VII. Army Corps
23 May 1914 - 26 Feb 1915:	Chief of Staff, 11th Army
26 Feb 1915 - 27 Feb 1917:	Commander, 33rd Infantry Division
8 Jan 1916:	Promoted to *Lieutenant-General*
27 Feb 1917 - 20 Sep 1917:	Commanding General, XXXVII. Army Corps
20 Sep 1917 - Oct 1917:	Reserve officer, Dvinsk Military District
Oct 1917:	Commanding General, I. Muslim Corps

Major-General Roman Petrovich **Sulmenev** (29 Jul 1864 - ?)

8 Aug 1909 - 1917:	Chief of Emperor Aleksandr II School
16 Oct 1912:	Promoted to *Major-General*

Major-General Nikolai Izmaylovich **Sumarokov** (19 Oct 1844 - ?)
29 Dec 1899 - 24 Feb 1905:   Commander, 14th Artillery Brigade
9 Apr 1900:   Promoted to *Major-General*

Major-General Nikolai Sergeyevich **Sumarokov** (14 Aug 1854 - 2 May 1906)
1900 - 2 May 1906:   Director, 2nd Cadet Corps
6 Dec 1901:   Promoted to *Major-General*

Lieutenant-General Aleksey Pavlovich **Surazhevsky** (17 Mar 1826 - 1900)
7 Aug 1888:   Promoted to *Major-General*
7 Aug 1888 - 10 Mar 1895:   Commander, 3rd Grenadier Artillery Brigade
10 Mar 1895 - 31 Jan 1900:   Commander, 1st Grenadier Artillery Brigade
31 Jan 1900 - 1900:   Honorary Trustee, Empress Maria Institutions
24 Sep 1900:   Promoted to *Lieutenant-General*

Major-General Stanislav-Silvestr Onufriyevich **Surin** (31 Dec 1858 - 11 Feb 1928)
25 Feb 1912 - 27 Aug 1915:   Commander, 6th Grenadier Regiment
27 Aug 1915:   Promoted to *Major-General*
27 Aug 1915 - 6 Dec 1917:   Commander, 1st Brigade, 8th Infantry Division

Major-General Vladimir Iosifovich **Surin** (23 Dec 1850 - ?)
2 Mar 1905 - 31 Jul 1907:   Commander, 21st Artillery Brigade
6 Dec 1906:   Promoted to *Major-General*

Major-General Pyotr Fyodorovich **Surkov** (11 Jun 1835 - ?)
22 Nov 1887 - 30 Jun 1889:   Commander of Artillery, Fortress Bobruysk
30 Jun 1889:   Promoted to *Major-General*
30 Jun 1889 - 1902:   Commandant of Artillery Depot, Kiev Military District

Major-General Aleksandr Andreyevich **Surov** (22 Nov 1860 - 28 Feb 1932)
2 Aug 1911 - 1916:   Deputy Chief of Cossack Section, General Staff
6 Dec 1911:   Promoted to *Major-General*
1916:   Retired

Major-General Nikolai Stepanovich **Surovetsky** (28 Apr 1851 - 17 Jul 1914)
12 Jun 1902 - 1906:   Ataman, Sunzha Division, Terek Cossack Army
6 Dec 1902:   Promoted to *Major-General*

Major-General Vladimir Dmitriyevich **Surovtsev** (23 Jan 1856 - 27 Sep 1900)
30 Sep 1894 - 23 Feb 1896:   Special Assignments Officer, Caucasus Military District
30 Aug 1895:   Promoted to *Major-General*
23 Feb 1896 - 27 Sep 1900:   Governor of Livonia

Major-General Vladimir Nikolayevich **Susanin** (1 Jun 1855 - Jun 1917)
23 Sep 1907 - 6 Feb 1911:   Military Governor of Ferghana Region
13 Apr 1908:   Promoted to *Major-General*
6 Feb 1911:   Retired
25 Apr 1914 - 15 Apr 1915:   Recalled; Special Assignments General, Main

	Directorate of Horse Breeding
15 Apr 1915 - Jun 1917:	Member of Council, Main Directorate of Horse Breeding

Major-General Aleksandr Ilyich **Sushchinsky** (31 Jul 1855 - 1 Jul 1933)
12 May 1908 - 28 Apr 1916:	Commander of Zagatala District
6 Dec 1914:	Promoted to *Major-General*
28 Apr 1916 - 1917:	Military Governor of Kars Region

Major-General Ivan Stepanovich **Sushchinsky** (7 May 1850 - ?)
17 Feb 1904:	Promoted to *Major-General*
17 Feb 1904 - 1905:	Commander, Caucasus Sapper Brigade

Major-General Vladimir Nikolayevich **Sushkov** (9 Apr 1866 - 1927)
24 Dec 1908 - 8 Mar 1915:	Commander, 162nd Infantry Regiment
7 Dec 1914:	Promoted to *Major-General*
8 Mar 1915 - 7 Jun 1916:	Chief of Staff, XI. Army Corps
7 Jun 1916 - 17 May 1917:	Chief of Staff, XXX. Army Corps
17 May 1917 - 1918:	Reserve officer, Odessa Military District

Major-General Andrey Nikolayevich **Suvorov** (30 Sep 1873 - 11 Feb 1938)
27 Aug 1915 - 20 Sep 1916:	Commander, 6th Grenadier Regiment
20 Sep 1916 - 12 Aug 1917:	Chief of Staff, 81st Infantry Division
22 Sep 1916:	Promoted to *Major-General*
12 Aug 1917 - 1918:	Chief of Staff, III. Army Corps

Major-General Mikhail Nikolayevich **Suvorov** (15 Aug 1877 - 1 Feb 1948)
16 Jan 1916 - 7 Sep 1916:	Chief of Staff, Guards Rifle Division
7 Sep 1916 - 22 Jun 1917:	Commander, 121st Infantry Regiment
1916:	Promoted to *Major-General*
22 Jun 1917 - 30 Jul 1917:	Chief of Staff, L. Army Corps
30 Jul 1917 - 1917:	Chief of Staff, 2nd Army
1917 - Dec 1917:	Attached to Petrograd Military District

Major-General Nikolai Andreyevich **Suvorov** (8 Apr 1846 - ?)
30 Jan 1891 - 7 Jul 1897:	Commander, 10th Grenadier Regiment
14 May 1896:	Promoted to *Major-General*
7 Jul 1897 - 11 Mar 1898:	Commander, 2nd Brigade, 34th Infantry Division

Major-General Pyotr Ivanovich **Suvorov** (1 Jan 1855 - ?)
12 Apr 1907 - 16 Jul 1912:	Commander, 41st Infantry Regiment
16 Jul 1912:	Promoted to *Major-General*
16 Jul 1912 - 20 Aug 1913:	Commander, 1st Brigade, 5th Siberian Rifle Division
20 Aug 1913:	Retired
11 Sep 1914 - 16 Jan 1917:	Recalled; Commander, 16th Replacement Infantry Brigade
16 Jan 1917 - 21 Oct 1917:	Reserve officer, Minsk Military District
21 Oct 1917:	Dismissed

Major-General Sergey Alekseyevich **Suyetin** (20 Mar 1860 - ?)
9 Jun 1913 - 1914:	Commander, 2nd Battalion, 19th Artillery Brigade
26 Feb 1915:	Promoted to *Major-General*
1914 - 13 May 1915:	Reserve officer, Kiev Military District
13 May 1915 - 1917:	Commander, 6th Replacement Artillery Battalion

General of Infantry Aleksandr Alekseyevich **Svechin** (17 Dec 1826 - 8 Mar 1896)
5 May 1861 - 10 Dec 1865:	Commander, 14th Grenadier Regiment
20 Jun 1864:	Promoted to *Major-General*
10 Dec 1865 - 6 Mar 1868:	Deputy Commander, Caucasus Grenadier Division
6 Mar 1868 - 25 Mar 1869:	Commander, 38th Infantry Division
25 Mar 1869 - 16 Apr 1878:	Commander, 29th Infantry Division
6 Dec 1872:	Promoted to *Lieutenant-General*
16 Apr 1878 - 17 Apr 1879:	Commander, 1st Grenadier Division
17 Apr 1879 - 9 Apr 1889:	Commanding General, X. Army Corps
20 Aug 1880:	Promoted to *General-Adjutant*
30 Aug 1886:	Promoted to *General of Infantry*
9 Apr 1889 - 8 Mar 1896:	Member, Committee for Wounded Veterans

Lieutenant-General Aleksandr Andreyevich **Svechin** (17 Aug 1878 - 29 Jul 1938)
23 Jul 1915 - 15 Jan 1917:	Commander, 6th Finnish Rifle Regiment
22 Sep 1916:	Promoted to *Major-General*
15 Jan 1917 - 26 Jan 1917:	Chief of Staff, 7th Infantry Division
26 Jan 1917 - 24 May 1917:	Section Chief, Black Sea Airborne Division
24 May 1917 - 22 Sep 1917:	Chief of Staff, 5th Army
22 Sep 1917 - Mar 1918:	Chief of Staff, Northern Front
Oct 1917:	Promoted to *Lieutenant-General*

Lieutenant-General Andrey Mikhailovich **Svechin** (21 Nov 1838 - 6 Mar 1903)
3 Apr 1886 - 27 Jan 1892:	Deputy Chief of Staff, Amur Military District
6 May 1887:	Promoted to *Major-General*
27 Jan 1892 - 8 Jun 1893:	Chief of Staff, XIII. Army Corps
8 Jun 1893 - 11 Mar 1897:	Commander, 1st Transcaspian Rifle Brigade
11 Mar 1897 - 11 Mar 1900:	Commander, 2nd Brigade, 18th Infantry Division
11 Mar 1900:	Promoted to *Lieutenant-General*
11 Mar 1900:	Retired

Lieutenant-General Ivan Nikolayevich **Svechin** (12 Feb 1863 - 17 Mar 1930)
23 Mar 1899 - 1 Aug 1905:	Governor of Tiflis
1904:	Promoted to *Major-General*
1 Aug 1905 - 13 Oct 1905:	Special Assignments General to the Minister of Internal Affairs
13 Oct 1905 - 31 Jan 1906:	Governor of Stavropol
31 Jan 1906 - 23 Jan 1910:	Attached to the Ministry of Internal Affairs
23 Jan 1910 - 28 Feb 1911:	Military Governor of Primorye Region, Ataman, Ussuri Cossack Army
28 Feb 1911 - 4 May 1917:	Attached to the Minister of Internal Affairs
14 Apr 1913:	Promoted to *Lieutenant-General*

Feb 1915 - 4 May 1917: Chief Inspector of Medical Institutions, Petrograd
4 May 1917: Dismissed

Lieutenant-General Mikhail Andreyevich **Svechin** (16 May 1876 - 15 Apr 1969)
19 Dec 1915 - 29 Mar 1917: Commander, Life Guards Cuirassier Regiment
1916: Promoted to *Major-General*
29 Mar 1917 - 12 May 1917: Chief of Staff, Guards Cavalry Corps
12 May 1917 - 9 Sep 1917: Commander, Consolidated Cavalry Division
9 Sep 1917 - 30 Dec 1917: Commanding General, I. Cavalry Corps
12 Oct 1917: Promoted to *Lieutenant-General*

Major-General Sergey Alekseyevich **Svechin** (16 Jun 1857 - ?)
12 Jun 1910 - 25 Mar 1911: Commander, 1st Infantry Regiment
25 Mar 1911: Promoted to *Major-General*
25 Mar 1911: Retired
13 Jun 1915 - 14 Apr 1917: Recalled; Commander, Brigade, 106th Infantry Division
14 Apr 1917 - 1917: Reserve officer, Dvinsk Military District

Lieutenant-General Lyudomir-Mikhail-Oktavian Vatslavovich **Sventorzhetsky** (22 Mar 1865 - ?)
10 Jan 1905 - 24 Aug 1916: Professor, Nikolayev Engineering Academy
18 Apr 1910: Promoted to *Major-General*
4 Mar 1911 - 24 Aug 1916: Member, Technical Committee, Main Technical Directorate
20 Feb 1915: Promoted to *Lieutenant-General*
24 Aug 1916 - 16 Oct 1917: Member of the Board, Ministry of Trade & Industry
16 Oct 1917: Retired

Major-General Vladimir Iosifovich **Sventsitsky** (24 Mar 1859 - ?)
4 Oct 1911 - 8 Sep 1913: Inspector of Classes, 2nd Moscow Cadet Corps
14 Apr 1913: Promoted to *Major-General*
8 Sep 1913 - 12 Oct 1917: Inspector of Classes, Alekseyev Military School
12 Oct 1917 - 1918: Director, 2nd Moscow Cadet Corps

General of Infantry Isidor Dmitriyevich **Sverchkov** (14 May 1837 - 17 Mar 1907)
20 Oct 1892 - 1 Mar 1898: Commandant, Vilnius Military Hospital
6 Mar 1894: Promoted to *Major-General*
1 Mar 1898 - 16 Mar 1901: Commander of Fortress Ust-Dvina
6 Dec 1900: Promoted to *Lieutenant-General*
16 Mar 1901 - 27 Jan 1904: Governor of Tavastgus
27 Jan 1904: Promoted to *General of Infantry*
27 Jan 1904: Retired

Major-General Arkady Aleksandrovich **Sveshnikov** (15 Aug 1837 - ?)
14 Mar 1895 - 1898: Commander of Artillery, Fortress Osovets
14 May 1896: Promoted to *Major-General*

Rear-Admiral Dmitry Aleksandrovich **Sveshnikov** (18 Nov 1864 - 23 Dec 1936)
25 Oct 1916 - 1917:	Commandant of Moonsund Fortified Position
10 Nov 1916:	Promoted to *Rear-Admiral*
7 Dec 1917:	Retired

Lieutenant-General Nikolai Lvovich **Sveshnikov** (19 Jul 1864 - 23 Nov 1934)
14 Jun 1908 - 14 Dec 1913:	Commander, 6th Hussar Regiment
14 Dec 1913:	Promoted to *Major-General*
14 Dec 1913 - 2 Aug 1914:	Commander, 2nd Brigade, 7th Cavalry Division
2 Aug 1914 - 18 Mar 1915:	Commander, Brigade, 4th Don Cossack Division
Oct 1914:	Acting Commander, 4th Don Cossack Division
18 Mar 1915 - 1915:	Reserve officer, Kiev Military District
1915 - 20 Sep 1915:	Commander, 4th Separate Cavalry Brigade
20 Sep 1915 - ?:	Reserve officer, Petrograd Military District
? - 19 Apr 1917:	Inspector of Remounts, 5th Army
19 Apr 1917 - 21 Aug 1917:	Commander, 4th Cavalry Division
21 Aug 1917 - 30 Sep 1917:	Unassigned
30 Sep 1917:	Promoted to *Lieutenant-General*
30 Sep 1917:	Retired

Lieutenant-General Konstantin Nikolayevich **Svetlitsky** (1842 - ?)
3 Feb 1881 - 12 May 1889:	Special Assignments General to the Commanding General, East Siberian Military District
30 Aug 1887:	Promoted to *Major-General*
12 May 1889 - 24 Jan 1897:	Governor of Irkutsk Province
24 Jan 1897 - 1897:	Governor of Yenisei Province
1897:	Promoted to *Lieutenant-General*
1897:	Retired

Major-General Nikolai Nikolayevich **Svetlitsky** (11 Jan 1836 - ?)
1 Feb 1875 - 22 Aug 1884:	Inspector of Classes, 3rd Aleksandr Military School
6 May 1884:	Promoted to *Major-General*
22 Aug 1884 - Dec 1902:	Director, Orlovsky-Bakhtina Cadet Corps

General of Infantry Nikolai Yegorovich **Svetlov** (1 Dec 1852 - ?)
24 Mar 1885 - 10 Feb 1902:	Section Chief, General Staff
10 Apr 1899:	Promoted to *Major-General*
10 Feb 1902 - 23 Nov 1904:	Commander, 1st Caucasus Rifle Brigade
23 Nov 1904 - 29 Apr 1906:	Commander, 21st Infantry Division
17 Apr 1905:	Promoted to *Lieutenant-General*
29 Apr 1906 - 1 Dec 1912:	Chief of Staff, Kazan Military District
1 Dec 1912:	Promoted to *General of Infantry*
1 Dec 1912:	Retired

Major-General Nikolai Ivanovich **Svetozarov** (15 Sep 1853 - ?)
28 Nov 1899 - 6 Jun 1902:	Chief of Staff, Grenadier Corps
6 Dec 1899:	Promoted to *Major-General*
6 Jun 1902 - 1906:	At the disposal of the Commanding General, Moscow

Military District

Major-General Grigory Aleksandrovich **Svidersky** (1 Sep 1870 - ?)
31 Dec 1913 - 17 Nov 1915:	Chief of Sub-Section, Main Artillery Directorate
22 Mar 1915:	Promoted to *Major-General*
17 Nov 1915 - 1918:	Deputy Chief of Section 1, Main Artillery Directorate

Lieutenant-General Bronislav Matveyevich **Svidzinsky** (5 Mar 1867 - 13 Dec 1916)
6 Dec 1909:	Promoted to *Major-General*
9 Dec 1909 - 13 Aug 1911:	Secretary of the Engineering Committee, Main Engineering Directorate
13 Aug 1911 - 17 Feb 1912:	Member, Engineering Committee, Main Engineering Directorate
17 Feb 1912 - 9 Feb 1914:	Member, Main Committee on Troop Billeting
9 Feb 1914 - 6 Apr 1916:	Head of the Engineering Committee, Chief Engineer's Office
6 Apr 1916 - 13 Dec 1916:	Commander of Engineers, Northern Front
6 Dec 1916:	Promoted to *Lieutenant-General*

General of Infantry Edmund-Leopold Ferdinandovich **Svidzinsky** (15 Nov 1848 - 1919)
19 May 1900:	Promoted to *Major-General*
19 May 1900 - 16 Aug 1901:	Commander, 1st Brigade, 19th Infantry Division
16 Aug 1901 - 21 Nov 1908:	Commander, 2nd Brigade, 42nd Infantry Division
21 Nov 1908:	Promoted to *Lieutenant-General*
21 Nov 1908 - 19 Jun 1910:	Commander, 11th Infantry Division
19 Jun 1910 - 16 Nov 1911:	Commander, 41st Infantry Division
16 Nov 1911:	Promoted to *General of Infantry*
16 Nov 1911:	Retired

General of Artillery Aleksandr Dmitriyevich **Svinin** (16 May 1831 - 23 Jul 1913)
1 Mar 1877 - 2 Sep 1878:	Commander, 1st Battery, 30th Artillery Brigade
28 Nov 1877:	Promoted to *Major-General*
2 Sep 1878 - 25 Aug 1879:	Deputy Commander of Artillery, Principality of Bulgaria
11 Sep 1879 - 24 Aug 1886:	Commander, 30th Artillery Brigade
24 Aug 1886 - 14 May 1889:	Commander of Artillery, VII. Army Corps
30 Aug 1886:	Promoted to *Lieutenant-General*
14 May 1889 - 14 Feb 1893:	Commander of Artillery, Guards Corps
14 Feb 1893 - 15 Oct 1893:	Inspector of Borderguards
15 Oct 1893 - 13 Apr 1908:	Commanding General, Borderguard Corps
6 Dec 1898:	Promoted to *General of Artillery*
13 Apr 1908 - 23 Jul 1913:	Member of the State Council

General of Engineers Dmitry Timofeyevich **Svishchevsky** (11 Feb 1840 - 1922)
17 Aug 1888:	Promoted to *Major-General*
17 Aug 1888 - 23 Feb 1898:	Commander, 2nd Sapper Brigade
14 May 1896:	Promoted to *Lieutenant-General*
23 Feb 1898 - 7 Aug 1909:	Member of the Engineering Committee, Chief

	Engineer's Office
23 Nov 1898 - 7 Aug 1909:	Inspector of Engineers
7 Aug 1909 - 13 Oct 1909:	At the disposal of the Minister of War
13 Oct 1909 - 1 Jan 1916:	Member of the Military Council
6 Dec 1909:	Promoted to *General of Engineers*
1 Jan 1916:	Retired

Major-General Vasily Alekseyevich **Svitushkov** (22 Mar 1857 - ?)
3 Jun 1907 - 31 Dec 1913:	Military Commander, Vyatka District
14 Apr 1913:	Promoted to *Major-General*
31 Dec 1913 - 29 Jul 1914:	Commander, Saratov Regional Brigade
29 Jul 1914 - 13 Apr 1915:	Commander, 14th Replacement Infantry Brigade
13 Apr 1915 - 30 Jul 1917:	Commander, Saratov Regional Brigade
30 Jul 1917:	Dismissed

Major-General Aleksandr Ivanovich **Svyatitsky** (1 Sep 1856 - 1910)
19 May 1908 - 1909:	Commander, 42nd Infantry Regiment
1909:	Promoted to *Major-General*
1909:	Retired

Lieutenant-General Anatoly Vladimirovich **Svyatlovsky** (3 May 1854 - ?)
23 Jun 1905 - 12 Jun 1906:	Deputy Commander of Reserve Artillery, Manchurian Army
6 Dec 1906:	Promoted to *Major-General*
12 Jun 1906 - 19 Jul 1907:	Commander of Artillery, Fortress St. Petersburg, Commandant, St. Petersburg Artillery Depot
19 Jul 1907 - 3 Jul 1908:	Deputy Commander of Artillery, St. Petersburg Military District
3 Jul 1908 - 26 Jul 1910:	Commander of Artillery, IV. Army Corps
1 Oct 1909:	Promoted to *Lieutenant-General*
26 Jul 1910 - 10 May 1916:	Inspector of Artillery, IV. Army Corps
14 Jun 1915 - ?:	Acting Commanding General, IV. Army Corps
10 May 1916 - 1918:	Inspector of Artillery, 6th Army

General of Infantry Prince Dmitry Ivanovich **Svyatopolk-Mirsky** (25 Oct 1826 - 18 Jan 1899)
12 Apr 1859:	Promoted to *Major-General*
12 Apr 1859 - 17 Oct 1860:	Chief of Staff, Caspian Territory Forces
17 Oct 1860 - 28 Apr 1861:	Deputy Commander of Forces, Kuban Region
28 Apr 1861 - 21 Sep 1861:	Deputy Commander of Forces, Terek Region
21 Sep 1861:	Promoted to *Lieutenant-General*
21 Sep 1861 - 17 Apr 1863:	Commanding General, Terek Region
17 Apr 1863 - 19 Apr 1867:	Governor-General of Kutaisi
15 Jun 1864:	Promoted to *General-Adjutant*
19 Apr 1867 - 14 Apr 1868:	Attached to the C-in-C, Caucasus Army
14 Apr 1868 - 25 Dec 1875:	Deputy C-in-C, Caucasus Army
30 Aug 1873:	Promoted to *General of Infantry*
25 Dec 1875 - 6 Jan 1880:	Deputy Viceroy of the Caucasus

6 Jan 1880 - 18 Jan 1899: Member of the State Council
13 Jan 1881 - 10 May 1882: Commanding General, Kharkov Military District, Acting Governor-General of Kharkov

General of Cavalry Prince Nikolai Ivanovich **Svyatopolk-Mirsky** (5 Jul 1833 - 27 Oct 1898)
21 Sep 1861 - 16 May 1865: Commander, 77th Infantry Regiment
1862: Promoted to *Major-General*
16 May 1865 - 9 Sep 1867: Unassigned
9 Sep 1867 - 2 Oct 1873: Commander, Life Guards Semenov Regiment
2 Oct 1873 - 1 Nov 1876: Commander, 1st Brigade, 1st Guards Infantry Division
16 Aug 1874: Promoted to *General-Adjutant*
30 Aug 1876: Promoted to *Lieutenant-General*
1 Nov 1876 - 28 Apr 1881: Commander, 9th Infantry Division
28 Apr 1891 - 15 Jul 1898: Ataman, Don Cossack Army
30 Aug 1890: Promoted to *General of Cavalry*
15 Jul 1898 - 27 Oct 1898: Member of the State Council

General of Cavalry Prince Pyotr Dmitriyevich **Svyatopolk-Mirsky** (18 Aug 1857 - 16 May 1914)
11 Jun 1895: Promoted to *Major-General*
11 Jun 1895 - 30 Dec 1897: Governor of Penza
30 Dec 1897 - 20 Apr 1900: Governor of Ekaterynoslav
20 Apr 1900 - 15 Sep 1902: Commanding General, Corps of Gendarmerie
8 May 1900 - 15 Sep 1902: Deputy Minister of Internal Affairs
11 Jun 1901: Promoted to *Lieutenant-General*
15 Sep 1902 - 26 Aug 1904: Governor-General of Vilnius, Grodno & Kiev
26 Aug 1904: Promoted to *General-Adjutant*
26 Aug 1904 - 18 Jan 1905: Minister of Internal Affairs
18 Jan 1905 - 16 May 1914: General à la suite
14 Apr 1913: Promoted to *General of Cavalry*

Lieutenant-General Vladimir Nikolayevich **Svyatsky** (4 Nov 1865 - ?)
26 Oct 1912: Promoted to *Major-General*
26 Oct 1912 - 27 Nov 1915: Commander, 2nd Brigade, 44th Infantry Division
27 Nov 1915 - 1918: Reserve officer, Petrograd Military District
22 Aug 1917: Promoted to *Lieutenant-General*

General of Infantry Arkady Valerianovich **Sychevsky** (21 Jan 1860 - 22 Nov 1927)
18 Dec 1904 - 9 Mar 1905: Commander, 19th Eastern Siberian Rifle Regiment
4 Jan 1905: Promoted to *Major-General*
9 Mar 1905 - 1 Mar 1906: Commander, 2nd Brigade, 9th Eastern Siberian Rifle Division
1 Mar 1906 - 22 Aug 1906: Military Governor of the Trans-Baikal Region
22 Aug 1906 - 23 Jul 1910: Military Governor of the Amur Region, Ataman, Amur Cossack Army
23 Jul 1910: Promoted to *Lieutenant-General*
23 Jul 1910 - 15 Feb 1911: Commander, 10th Siberian Rifle Division

15 Feb 1911 - 19 Feb 1913:	Commander, 35th Infantry Division
19 Feb 1913 - 28 Dec 1913:	Commander, Amur Military District Borderguard Corps
28 Dec 1913 - 8 Feb 1914:	Commanding General, V. Siberian Army Corps
8 Feb 1914 - 8 May 1915:	Commanding General, II. Siberian Army Corps
6 Dec 1914:	Promoted to *General of Infantry*
8 May 1915 - 1 Oct 1915:	Commanding General, IV. Siberian Army Corps
1 Oct 1915 - 19 Oct 1916:	Commanding General, XXIII. Army Corps
19 Oct 1916 - 5 Apr 1917:	Commanding General, VII. Army Corps
5 Apr 1917 - 4 May 1917:	Reserve officer, Odessa Military District
4 May 1917:	Retired

Lieutenant-General Yevgeny Aleksandrovich **Sykalov** (20 Jan 1845 - ?)

12 Mar 1892 - 19 Aug 1896:	Commander, 30th Dragoon Regiment
19 Aug 1896:	Promoted to *Major-General*
19 Aug 1896 - 22 May 1904:	Commander, 1st Brigade, 15th Cavalry Division
22 May 1904 - 23 May 1907:	Commander, 13th Cavalry Division
6 Dec 1904:	Promoted to *Lieutenant-General*
23 May 1907:	Retired

Lieutenant-General Anton Petrovich **Symon** (7 Apr 1862 - 18 Nov 1927)

30 Apr 1908 - 8 Jun 1913:	Commander, 19th Infantry Regiment
14 Apr 1913:	Promoted to *Major-General*
8 Jun 1913 - 29 Jul 1914:	Commander, 1st Brigade, 47th Infantry Division
29 Jul 1914 - 1915:	Commander, Brigade, 82nd Infantry Division
1915 - 26 Apr 1916:	Commander, 1st Brigade, 47th Infantry Division
26 Apr 1916 - 4 May 1917:	Commander, 117th Infantry Division
4 May 1917 - 25 Aug 1917:	Unassigned
25 Aug 1917 - 20 Sep 1917:	Commander, 47th Infantry Division
20 Sep 1917 - 7 Oct 1917:	Commanding General, XXXVII. Army Corps
7 Oct 1917 - 1918:	Commanding General, XIII. Army Corps
12 Oct 1917:	Promoted to *Lieutenant-General*

Lieutenant-General Nikolai Nikiforovich **Syngayevsky** (5 Oct 1836 - 1911)

12 Mar 1895 - 30 Dec 1896:	Commander, 2nd Battalion, 26th Artillery Brigade
14 May 1896:	Promoted to *Major-General*
30 Dec 1896 - 30 Jan 1900:	Commander, 13th Artillery Brigade
30 Jan 1900:	Promoted to *Lieutenant-General*
30 Jan 1900:	Retired

Major-General Aleksandr Petrovich **Syropyatov** (25 May 1855 - Jun 1915)

10 Jan 1903 - 14 Jul 1914:	Chief of St. Petersburg-Vindau Railway Gendarmerie
1906:	Promoted to *Major-General*
14 Jul 1914:	Transferred to the reserve
Aug 1914 - Jun 1915:	Recalled; Duty General, Kazan Military District

Major-General Ravil Shakh-Aydarovich **Syrtlanov** (29 Oct 1877 - 20 Jun 1916)

20 Jan 1916 - 20 Jun 1916:	Commander, 166th Infantry Regiment
29 Jul 1916:	Posthumously promoted to *Major-General*

Major-General Ivan Nikolayevich **Sysoyev** (27 Jan 1859 - ?)
9 Oct 1902 - 4 Jun 1907:   Military Attaché, Montenegro
2 Apr 1906:   Promoted to *Major-General*
4 Jun 1907 - 1907:   Commander 1st Brigade, 43rd Infantry Division

Lieutenant-General Mikhail Abramovich **Sytenko** (6 Jun 1835 - 30 Apr 1925)
17 Sep 1889 - 7 Apr 1899:   Commander, Railway Brigade
30 Aug 1890:   Promoted to *Major-General*
7 Apr 1899 - 1901:   At the disposal of the Main Engineering Directorate
1901:   Promoted to *Lieutenant-General*
1901:   Retired

Lieutenant-General Iulian Fyodorovich **Sytin** (15 Jul 1845 - ?)
12 Jul 1896 - 28 Apr 1910:   Commander of Gendarmerie, Kielce Province
6 Dec 1907:   Promoted to *Major-General*
28 Apr 1910:   Promoted to *Lieutenant-General*
28 Apr 1910:   Retired

Major-General Ivan Pavlovich **Sytin** (31 Oct 1873 - 23 Sep 1927)
28 Sep 1913 - 15 Apr 1915:   Chief of Staff, 18th Infantry Division
15 Apr 1915 - 11 May 1916:   Commander, 50th Infantry Regiment
13 Jul 1915:   Promoted to *Major-General*
11 May 1916 - 4 Nov 1916:   Chief of Staff, 35th Infantry Division
4 Nov 1916 - 25 Dec 1916:   Chief of Staff, XXXII. Army Corps
25 Dec 1916 - 1918:   Duty General, Romanian Front

Major-General Pavel Pavlovich **Sytin** (18 Jul 1870 - 22 Aug 1938)
8 Jul 1916 - 17 Oct 1917:   Commander, 79th Artillery Brigade
23 Jan 1917:   Promoted to *Major-General*
17 Oct 1917 - Dec 1917:   Commander, 37th Infantry Division

Major-General Georgy Fyodorovich **Syunnerberg** (28 Oct 1844 - 1901)
30 Nov 1888 - 7 Jan 1895:   Commander, Life Guards 3rd Finnish Rifle Brigade
30 Aug 1889:   Promoted to *Major-General*
7 Jan 1895 - 1901:   Commander, Nerchinsk Mountain Region

Major-General of the Admiralty Vladimir Vikentyevich **Tabulevich** (1845 - 1914)
? - 1 Aug 1905:   Attached to Main Shipbuilding Directorate
1 Aug 1905:   Promoted to *Major-General of the Admiralty*
1 Aug 1905:   Retired

Major-General Varlaam Stepanovich **Takayshvili** (11 Feb 1857 - ?)
17 Apr 1905:   Promoted to *Major-General*
17 Apr 1905 - 1905:   Chief of Military Communications, Caucasus Military District

Lieutenant-General Isaak Artemyevich **Takhatelov** (8 Feb 1853 - 21 Oct 1918)
31 Oct 1906 - 2 Oct 1910:   Commander, 2nd Vladivostok Fortress Artillery Brigade

26 Nov 1906: Promoted to *Major-General*
2 Oct 1910: Promoted to *Lieutenant-General*
2 Oct 1910: Retired

General of Artillery Mikhail Konstantinovich **Takhtarev** (7 Jan 1839 - ?)
15 Jan 1879 - 3 Sep 1913: Professor, Mikhailovsky Artillery Academy, Member of the Artillery Committee, Main Artillery Directorate
15 May 1883: Promoted to *Major-General*
30 Aug 1893: Promoted to *Lieutenant-General*
3 Sep 1913: Promoted to *General of Artillery*
3 Sep 1913: Retired

General of Cavalry Aleksandr Yakovlevich von **Tal** (18 Jul 1840 - 16 Oct 1911)
9 Dec 1887 - 21 May 1892: Commander, Life Guards Cuirassier Regiment
30 Aug 1888: Promoted to *Major-General*
21 May 1892 - 15 Dec 1894: Commander, 2nd Brigade, 1st Guards Cavalry Division
15 Dec 1894 - 4 May 1897: Commander, 3rd Brigade, 2nd Guards Cavalry Division
4 May 1897 - 22 May 1903: Commander, 13th Cavalry Division
6 Dec 1897: Promoted to *Lieutenant-General*
22 May 1903 - 1 Jun 1905: Commanding General, XI. Army Corps
1 Jun 1905 - 16 Oct 1911: Member, Committee for Wounded Veterans
6 Dec 1906: Promoted to *General of Cavalry*

Lieutenant-General Otto Germanovich von **Talberg** (5 Nov 1826 - ?)
14 Sep 1877: Promoted to *Major-General*
14 Sep 1877 - 1 Oct 1877: Commander, 1st Brigade, 14th Infantry Division
1 Oct 1877 - 12 Nov 1877: Unassigned
12 Nov 1877 - 28 Nov 1877: Commander, 2nd Brigade, 11th Infantry Division
28 Nov 1877 - 7 Apr 1878: Commander, 2nd Brigade, 35th Infantry Division
7 Apr 1878 - 9 Jan 1888: Commander, 2nd Brigade, 6th Infantry Division
9 Jan 1888 - 1895: Commander, 13th Regional Brigade
30 Aug 1888: Promoted to *Lieutenant-General*

Major-General Vladimir Pavlovich **Talgren** (14 Sep 1870 - Nov 1920)
7 Jan 1914: Promoted to *Major-General*
7 Jan 1914 - 19 Jul 1914: Special Assignments General, Odessa Military District
19 Jul 1914 - 4 Oct 1915: Chief of Economic Section, 8th Army
4 Oct 1915 - 29 Sep 1916: Commander, 35th Infantry Division
29 Sep 1916 - 31 Oct 1916: Chief of Logistics, XLVII. Army Corps
31 Oct 1916 - 14 Dec 1916: Chief of Logistics, Danube Army
14 Dec 1916 - Oct 1917: Deputy Chief of Logistics, Romanian Front

Major-General Aleksandr Osmanovich **Talkovsky** (14 May 1858 - 1921)
2 Jun 1906 - 31 May 1912: Commander, 25th Borderguard Brigade
6 Dec 1910: Promoted to *Major-General*
31 May 1912 - Jan 1915: Commander, 4th Borderguard Brigade
Jan 1915 - 18 Feb 1916: Commandant of Vindava Garrison

18 Feb 1916 - Jun 1918:Reserve officer, Petrograd Military District

Major-General of the Fleet Kesary Moiseyevich **Talyat-Kelpsh** (14 Aug 1857 - ?)
1909 - 1917:Professor, Naval Engineering School
1915:Promoted to *Major-General of the Fleet*

Major-General Asad-Bek **Talyshkhanov** (16 Nov 1857 - 1919)
25 Jul 1915 - 1917:Commander, 52nd Artillery Brigade
23 Nov 1915:Promoted to *Major-General*

Major-General Vasily Mikhailovich **Tamamshev** (26 Jul 1859 - 1 Mar 1932)
23 Feb 1913 - 6 Nov 1914:General for Assignments, Viceroy of the Caucasus
6 Dec 1913:Promoted to *Major-General*
6 Nov 1914 - Oct 1917:General for Assignments, Caucasus Army

Major-General Sergey Vasilyevich **Taneyev** (13 Jun 1841 - 15 Nov 1910)
20 Sep 1896 - 1906:Special Assignments Staff Officer, Main Intendant Directorate
1906:Promoted to *Major-General*
1906:Retired

Lieutenant-General Pyotr Grigoriyevich **Taranovsky** (16 Dec 1831 - ?)
24 Mar 1885 - 19 Oct 1895:Ministry of War Representative, Caucasus Military District Council
30 Aug 1887:Promoted to *Major-General*
19 Oct 1895 - 1902:Intendant, Caucasus Military District
14 May 1896:Promoted to *Lieutenant-General*

Major-General Viktor Petrovich **Taranovsky** (12 Oct 1864 - 7 Jan 1937)
11 Apr 1911 - 11 May 1915:Commander, 20th Rifle Regiment
3 Apr 1915:Promoted to *Major-General*
11 May 1915 - 26 Apr 1916:Commander, Brigade, 57th Infantry Division
26 Apr 1916 - 27 Jan 1917:Commander, 5th Rifle Division
27 Jan 1917 - Oct 1917:Commander, 2nd Special Infantry Division

Major-General Nikolai Fyodorovich **Tarasenkov** (5 Oct 1865 - ?)
2 Jul 1908 - 25 Jun 1909:Military Judge, Caucasus Military District Court
29 Mar 1909:Promoted to *Major-General*
25 Jun 1909 - Jul 1914:Military Judge, Warsaw Military District Court
Jul 1914 - 30 May 1915:Military Judge, Minsk Military District Court
30 May 1915 - 1917:Military Judge, Moscow Military District Court

Lieutenant-General Nikolai Vasilyevich **Tarasenkov** (21 Sep 1839 - ?)
28 Nov 1887 - 26 Oct 1892:Commander of Engineers, Fortress Ivangorod
22 Mar 1889:Promoted to *Major-General*
26 Oct 1892 - 23 Jan 1907:Deputy Commander of Engineers, Caucasus Military District
23 Jan 1907 - 1908:Commander of Engineers, Kiev Military District

22 Apr 1907: Promoted to *Lieutenant-General*

Major-General Aleksey Iosifovich **Tarasevich** (12 Jul 1848 - 1909)
27 Oct 1908: Promoted to *Major-General*
27 Oct 1908 - 1909: Commander, 1st Brigade, 30th Infantry Division

Lieutenant-General Gennady Nikolayevich **Tarkhanov** (8 Sep 1854 - ?)
24 Jun 1910 - 22 Oct 1912: Deputy Commander of Engineers, Caucasus Military District
6 Dec 1910: Promoted to *Major-General*
22 Oct 1912 - 1918: Chief of Troop Billeting, Caucasus Military District
6 Dec 1916: Promoted to *Lieutenant-General*

Major-General Aleksey Nikolayevich **Tarkhov** (17 May 1852 - ?)
12 Sep 1907: Promoted to *Major-General*
12 Sep 1907 - 17 Dec 1908: Commander, 2nd Grenadier Artillery Brigade

Major-General Nikolai Aleksandrovich **Tarkhov** (17 Apr 1852 - ?)
3 Jun 1894 - 1905: Commander, 72nd Park Artillery Brigade
1905: Promoted to *Major-General*
1905: Retired

Major-General Viktor Zakharovich **Tarkhov** (11 Apr 1854 - ?)
19 Feb 1904 - 1917: Chief of Gendarmerie, Kaluga Province
6 Dec 1912: Promoted to *Major-General*

Lieutenant-General Pavel Vladimirovich **Tarnagursky** (6 Jan 1854 - ?)
15 May 1906: Promoted to *Major-General*
15 May 1906 - 17 Oct 1910: Commander, 2nd Brigade, 6th Infantry Division
17 Oct 1910: Promoted to *Lieutenant-General*
17 Oct 1910: Retired

Lieutenant-General Zakhar Tselestinovich **Tarnovsky** (2 Sep 1845 - ?)
1 May 1891 - 12 Mar 1897: Commander, 27th Infantry Regiment
14 May 1896: Promoted to *Major-General*
12 Mar 1897 - 2 Feb 1900: Commander, 2nd Brigade, 8th Infantry Division
2 Feb 1900 - 11 Jan 1903: Commander, 63rd Reserve Infantry Brigade
11 Jan 1903 - 19 Mar 1906: Commander, 39th Infantry Division
28 Mar 1904: Promoted to *Lieutenant-General*

Major-General Petr Yakovlevich **Tatarov** (27 May 1858 - 24 Jun 1916)
1915 - 24 Jun 1916: Commander, 404th Infantry Regiment
11 Nov 1916: Posthumously promoted to *Major-General*

Lieutenant-General Count Dmitry Nikolayevich **Tatishchev** (1867 - 17 Aug 1919)
7 Jun 1909 - 25 Oct 1915: Governor of Yaroslavl
1910: Promoted to *State Councillor*
20 Oct 1915: Redesignated *Major-General*

20 Oct 1915 - 10 Jun 1917:	Commanding General, Corps of Gendarmerie
6 Dec 1916:	Promoted to *Lieutenant-General*
10 Jun 1917:	Dismissed

Lieutenant-General Ilya Leonidovich **Tatishchev** (11 Dec 1859 - 30 Jun 1918)
6 Dec 1905:	Promoted to *Major-General*
6 Dec 1905 - 18 Jul 1914:	Attached to Kaiser Wilhelm II of Germany
18 Jul 1914 - 2 Sep 1916:	Attached to Prince Aleksandr Petrovich Oldenburg
2 Sep 1916:	Promoted to *Lieutenant-General*
2 Sep 1916 - 18 Apr 1917:	Adjutant-General to the Tsar
18 Apr 1917:	Dismissed

General of Infantry Count Ivan Dmitriyevich **Tatishchev** (23 May 1830 - 24 Sep 1913)
30 May 1867 - 4 Jun 1878:	Military Commander, Moscow Province
30 Aug 1869:	Promoted to *Major-General*
22 Sep 1878 - 10 Apr 1879:	At the disposal of the Commanding General, Moscow Military District
10 Apr 1879 - 9 Apr 1889:	Commander, 40th Infantry Division
30 Aug 1879:	Promoted to *Lieutenant-General*
9 Apr 1889 - 9 Oct 1890:	Commanding General, XIII. Army Corps
9 Oct 1890 - 21 Jan 1897:	Deputy Commanding General, Caucasus Military District, Deputy Military Commander of the Caucasus
30 Aug 1893:	Promoted to *General of Infantry*
21 Jan 1897 - 24 Sep 1913:	Member of the Military Council
11 Aug 1904 - 24 Sep 1913:	Member of the State Council
19 Aug 1907:	Promoted to *General-Adjutant*

General of Infantry Count Nikolai Dmitriyevich **Tatishchev** (15 Feb 1829 - 16 Sep 1907)
1 Jan 1878:	Promoted to *Major-General*
1 Jan 1878 - 30 Apr 1878:	At the disposal of the C-in-C of the Field Army
Jan 1878 - Feb 1878:	Acting Commander, 1st Brigade, 3rd Infantry Division
30 Apr 1878 - 30 Jul 1879:	Commander, 2nd Brigade, 32nd Infantry Division
30 Jul 1879 - 28 Apr 1881:	Unassigned
28 Apr 1881 - 30 Aug 1890:	Commander, 2nd Brigade, 1st Grenadier Division
30 Aug 1890:	Promoted to *Lieutenant-General*
30 Aug 1890 - 17 Jan 1896:	Commander, 29th Infantry Division
17 Jan 1896:	Promoted to *General of Infantry*
17 Jan 1896:	Retired

Lieutenant-General Baron Aleksandr Aleksandrovich von **Taube** (9 Aug 1864 - Jan 1919)
7 Oct 1907 - 15 Sep 1914:	Chief of Communications, Irkutsk Military District
6 Dec 1907:	Promoted to *Major-General*
15 Sep 1914 - 19 Oct 1914:	Chief of Lines of Communication, 10th Army
19 Oct 1914 - 31 Jan 1915:	Chief of Lines of Communication, 1st Army
31 Jan 1915 - 26 Jul 1915:	Commander, 5th Siberian Rifle Division
28 May 1915:	Promoted to *Lieutenant-General*
26 Jul 1915 - 1 Jan 1916:	Reserve officer, Dvinsk Military District

1 Jan 1916 - 25 Mar 1916:	Commander, 121st Infantry Division
25 Mar 1916 - 31 May 1916:	Reserve officer, Petrograd Military District
31 May 1916 - 1917:	Chief of Staff, Omsk Military District

Lieutenant-General Baron Ferdinand Ferdinandovich von **Taube** (1 Mar 1838 - ?)
11 May 1887:	Promoted to *Major-General*
11 May 1887 - 8 Jul 1891:	Deputy Chief of Staff, Omsk Military District
8 Jul 1891 - 1 Mar 1897:	Commander, 2nd Rifle Brigade
1 Mar 1897 - 8 May 1898:	Commander, 2nd Infantry Division
6 May 1897:	Promoted to *Lieutenant-General*
8 May 1898 - 8 Jan 1902:	Commander, 17th Infantry Division
8 Jan 1902:	Retired

Lieutenant-General Baron Fyodor Fyodorovich von **Taube** (12 Jun 1857 - 23 Feb 1911)
10 Jun 1903:	Promoted to *Major-General*
10 Jun 1903 - 9 Apr 1906:	Chief of Staff, Orenburg Cossack Army
9 Apr 1906 - 17 Nov 1906:	Governor of Orenburg, Ataman, Orenburg Cossack Army
17 Nov 1906 - 17 Mar 1909:	Commanding General, Corps of Gendarmerie
6 Dec 1907:	Promoted to *Lieutenant-General*
17 Mar 1909 - 23 Feb 1911:	Ataman, Don Cossack Army

General of Artillery Baron Maksim Antonovich von **Taube** (25 Dec 1826 - 12 Jun 1910)
27 Mar 1866:	Promoted to *Major-General*
27 Mar 1866 - 16 Dec 1873:	Commandant of the Cavalry School
16 Dec 1873 - 27 Jul 1875:	Commander, 3rd Cavalry Division
27 Jul 1875 - 27 May 1881:	Commander, 5th Cavalry Division
30 Aug 1876:	Promoted to *Lieutenant-General*
22 Jul 1880 - 12 Aug 1880:	Acting Commanding General, V. Army Corps
27 May 1881 - 9 Apr 1889:	Commanding General, XII. Army Corps
6 Jan 1886 - 28 Feb 1886:	Acting Commanding General, Kiev Military District
10 Jun 1886 - 12 Aug 1886:	Acting Commanding General, Kiev Military District, Acting Governor-General of Kiev, Podolia & Volyn
18 Jul 1888 - 23 Oct 1888:	Acting Commanding General, Kiev Military District
9 Apr 1889 - 24 Oct 1889:	Deputy Commanding General, Kiev Military District
24 Oct 1889 - 26 Dec 1897:	Commanding General, Omsk Military District, Governor-General of the Steppes
30 Aug 1890:	Promoted to *General of Cavalry*
26 Dec 1897 - 11 Jul 1900:	Commanding General, Siberian Military District, Ataman, Siberian Cossack Army
11 Jul 1900 - 12 Jun 1910:	Member of the State Council
20 Sep 1900:	Redesignated *General of Artillery*

Major-General Aleksandr Vilgelmovich **Tavastsherna** (13 Jul 1863 - 30 Sep 1930)
31 Oct 1912 - 13 Oct 1913:	Military Judge, Kiev Military District Court
6 Dec 1912:	Promoted to *Major-General*
13 Oct 1913 - 1917:	Military Judge, St. Petersburg Military District Court

Lieutenant-General Iodor Vilgelmovich **Tavastsherna** (7 Nov 1855 - 22 Jul 1917)
16 Dec 1908: Promoted to *Major-General*
16 Dec 1908 - 31 Dec 1910: Commander of Engineers, Fortress Ivangorod
31 Dec 1910 - 2 Jan 1913: Commander of Engineers, Fortress Modlin
2 Jan 1913 - 28 Sep 1914: Inspector of Engineers, Turkestan Military District
28 Sep 1914: Promoted to *Lieutenant-General*
28 Sep 1914: Retired

Major-General Vladimir Vilgelmovich **Tavastsherna** (5 Nov 1861 - 20 Sep 1915)
31 Dec 1913 - 20 Sep 1915: Deputy Chief of Okhtenskaya Explosives Factory
22 Jan 1916: Posthumously promoted to *Major-General*

Major-General Igor Konstantinovich **Teleshev** (8 Sep 1862 - 13 Aug 1930)
27 Apr 1911 - 23 Jan 1914: Section Chief, Main Artillery Directorate
14 Apr 1913: Promoted to *Major-General*
23 Jan 1914 - 29 Feb 1916: Commander, 31st Artillery Brigade
29 Feb 1916 - 6 Nov 1916: Inspector of Artillery, III. Siberian Army Corps
6 Nov 1916 - Oct 1917: Inspector of Artillery, X. Army Corps

Major-General Mikhail Nikolayevich **Teleshev** (5 Nov 1854 - ?)
1 Nov 1900: Promoted to *Major-General*
1 Nov 1900 - 20 Jul 1904: Commander, 2nd Brigade, 15th Cavalry Division
20 Jul 1904 - 11 Aug 1905: Commander, 4th Don Cossack Division
11 Aug 1905 - 8 Mar 1911: Attached to the Don Cossack Army
8 Mar 1911: Dismissed

Lieutenant-General Leonid Arkadyevich **Telyakovsky** (9 Oct 1850 - 12 Dec 1912)
25 Mar 1894 - 2 Jul 1899: Commander, Lomzhinsk Borderguard Brigade
2 Jul 1899 - 8 Mar 1902: Commander, St. Petersburg Borderguard Brigade
9 Apr 1900: Promoted to *Major-General*
8 Mar 1902 - 28 Jul 1906: Commander, 6th Borderguard District
2 Apr 1906: Promoted to *Lieutenant-General*
28 Jul 1906 - 12 Dec 1912: Commander, 3rd Borderguard District

Lieutenant-General Temir Bulat **Temir-Bulat-Dudarov** (23 Sep 1844 - ?)
17 Feb 1900 - 1 Jul 1903: Commander, 2nd Turkestan Artillery Brigade
1 Jan 1901: Promoted to *Major-General*
1 Jul 1903 - 1904: Inspector of Artillery, II. Turkestan Army Corps
1904: Promoted to *Lieutenant-General*

Lieutenant-General Viktor Lvovich **Temnikov** (10 Feb 1856 - 1944)
15 Feb 1911 - 15 Jun 1912: Chief of Moscow General Military Hospital
6 Dec 1911: Promoted to *Major-General*
15 Jun 1912 - 18 Nov 1914: Military Commander, Belgorod District
18 Nov 1914 - 8 Mar 1915: Commander, 1st Moscow Evacuation Points
8 Mar 1915 - 7 Apr 1917: Commander, Kharkov Regional Brigade
7 Apr 1917 - 1918: Reserve officer, Kiev Military District
1917: Promoted to *Lieutenant-General*

Major-General Flegont Ivanovich **Temperov** (23 Feb 1853 - Mar 1916)
29 May 1913 - Mar 1916: Military Commander, Voronezh District
16 Mar 1916: Posthumously promoted to *Major-General*

Major-General Dmitry Eduardovich **Tenner** (5 Jul 1869 - 20 Dec 1921)
22 Jul 1906 - 30 Apr 1916: Deputy Director, Pedagogical Museum of Military Educational Institutions
6 Dec 1912: Promoted to *Major-General*
30 Apr 1916 - 1917: Commander, 26th Rear Area Evacuation Points

Major-General Eduard Karlovich **Tenner** (13 Mar 1842 - ?)
14 Jul 1891 - 1898: Member of the Artillery Committee, Main Artillery Directorate
30 Aug 1891: Promoted to *Major-General*

Lieutenant-General Yeremy Karlovich **Tenner** (8 Apr 1836 - 28 Sep 1903)
18 Jul 1878 - 7 May 1891: Commander, Finland Life Guards Regiment
30 Aug 1881: Promoted to *Major-General*
29 Sep 1888 - 8 Mar 1893: Temporary Member, Supreme Military Tribunal
4 Oct 1888 - 8 Mar 1893: Commander, 2nd Brigade, 2nd Guards Infantry Division
8 Mar 1893 - 27 Feb 1898: Attached to the Ministry of War
30 Aug 1893: Promoted to *Lieutenant-General*
27 Feb 1898 - 28 Sep 1903: Honorary Trustee, St. Petersburg Board of Trustees, Empress Maria Institutions

General of Artillery Aleksandr Ivanovich **Teodorovich** (22 Jan 1852 - ?)
15 Feb 1905 - 10 Oct 1908: Commander, 7th Artillery Brigade
17 May 1906: Promoted to *Major-General*
10 Oct 1908 - 31 Jul 1910: Commander of Artillery, II. Siberian Army Corps
17 May 1910: Promoted to *Lieutenant-General*
31 Jul 1910 - 24 Oct 1911: Inspector of Artillery, II. Siberian Army Corps
24 Oct 1911 - 22 Jan 1914: Commander of Artillery, Irkutsk Military District
22 Jan 1914: Promoted to *General of Artillery*
22 Jan 1914: Retired

Lieutenant-General Nikolai Nikolayevich **Teplov** (16 Feb 1828 - ?)
16 Oct 1873 - 20 Jan 1884: Commander of Artillery, Fortress Warsaw
17 Apr 1876: Promoted to *Major-General*
20 Jan 1884 - 16 Dec 1886: Deputy Commander of Artillery, Warsaw Military District
16 Dec 1886 - 6 Dec 1895: Commander of Artillery, Odessa Military District
30 Aug 1887: Promoted to *Lieutenant-General*

Lieutenant-General Vladimir Vladimirovich **Teplov** (9 Feb 1861 - 28 Sep 1924)
13 Apr 1913: Promoted to *Major-General*
13 Apr 1913 - 15 Mar 1915: Commander, Life Guards Finland Regiment
15 Mar 1915 - 8 Jun 1917: Commander, Brigade, 2nd Guards Infantry Division
8 Jun 1917 - 20 Jun 1917: Commander, 1st Turkestan Rifle Division

20 Jun 1917 - 1 Sep 1917:	At the disposal of the Minister of War
10 Jul 1917:	Promoted to *Lieutenant-General*
1 Sep 1917 - 4 Sep 1917:	Commanding General, Petrograd Military District
4 Sep 1917 - Oct 1917:	At the disposal of the Minister of War

Major-General Vagarmak Oganesovich **Ter-Akopov-Ter-Markosyants** (14 Oct 1865 - ?)
15 Feb 1912 - 1917:	Commander, 2nd Turkestan Sapper Battalion
30 Jul 1916:	Promoted to *Major-General*

Lieutenant-General Dmitry Bogdanovich **Ter-Asaturov** (20 Mar 1836 - 7 Jul 1897)
29 May 1877:	Promoted to *Major-General*
29 May 1877 - 10 Mar 1883:	Attached to the C-in-C, Caucasus Army
10 Mar 1883 - 10 Oct 1884:	Commander, 2nd Brigade, 2nd Caucasus Cavalry Division
10 Oct 1884 - 8 Feb 1895:	Commander, 11th Cavalry Division
30 Aug 1886:	Promoted to *Lieutenant-General*
8 Feb 1895 - 7 Jul 1897:	At the disposal of the Commanding General, Caucasus Military District

Lieutenant-General Mikhail Afrikanovich **Terentyev** (8 Jan 1837 - 19 Mar 1909)
10 Apr 1888 - 16 May 1895:	Military Judge, Warsaw Military District Court
30 Aug 1894:	Promoted to *Major-General*
16 May 1895 - 24 Oct 1900:	Military Judge, Turkestan Military District Court
24 Oct 1900 - 1902:	Military Judge, Vilnius Military District Court
1902:	Promoted to *Lieutenant-General*
1902:	Retired

Major-General Ivan Filippovich **Tereshchenko** (28 Mar 1837 - 20 Feb 1907)
11 Jun 1905:	Promoted to *Major-General*
11 Jun 1905 - 14 Jul 1905:	At the disposal of the Intendant-General, Ministry of War
14 Jul 1905 - 20 Feb 1907:	Chief of Moscow Specialized Workshops

Major-General Aleksandr Dmitriyevich **Terletsky** (28 Aug 1864 - ?)
20 Apr 1915 - 29 Nov 1916:	Commander, 18th Infantry Regiment
21 Oct 1915:	Promoted to *Major-General*
29 Nov 1916 - 1917:	Commander, Brigade, 129th Infantry Division
1917 - 1918:	Commander, 129th Infantry Division

Major-General Konstantin Semonovich **Terletsky** (10 Nov 1851 - 28 May 1907)
28 Feb 1904 - 6 Feb 1906:	Deputy Intendant, Siberian Military District
6 Dec 1904:	Promoted to *Major-General*
6 Feb 1906 - 17 Oct 1906:	Deputy Intendant, Odessa Military District
17 Oct 1906 - 28 May 1907:	Intendant, Turkestan Military District

Major-General Richard Iosipovich **Termen** (4 Feb 1870 - 5 Aug 1938)
20 Jan 1915 - 29 Nov 1915:	Commander, 80th Infantry Regiment
12 Aug 1915:	Promoted to *Major-General*

29 Nov 1915 - Jan 1916:	Reserve officer, Caucasus Military District
Jan 1916 - 20 Jun 1916:	Chief of Staff, 5th Turkestan Rifle Division
20 Jun 1916 - 26 Jul 1916:	Chief of Staff, Azerbaijani-Vansk Detachment
26 Jul 1916 - 1917:	Chief of Staff, Governor-General of Occupied Territories, Turkey

Major-General Leonid Prokofyevich **Ternavsky** (5 Aug 1857 - ?)
17 Nov 1912:	Promoted to *Major-General*
17 Nov 1912 - 19 Apr 1917:	Commander, 2nd Brigade, 43rd Infantry Division
Nov 1914:	Acting Commander, 43rd Infantry Division
19 Apr 1917 - 1917:	Reserve officer, Kiev Military District

Major-General Pavel Mikhailovich **Terpigorev** (1 Feb 1863 - ?)
1913 - 13 Oct 1916:	Commander, 4th Amur Border Infantry Regiment
2 Jun 1916:	Promoted to *Major-General*
13 Oct 1916 - 26 Apr 1917:	Commander, Brigade, 122nd Infantry Division
26 Apr 1917 - 1917:	Commander, 191st Infantry Division

Major-General Feliks Feliksovich **Terpilovsky** (22 Feb 1846 - 5 Jan 1907)
22 Jan 1902:	Promoted to *Major-General*
22 Jan 1902 - 23 Aug 1905:	Commander, 35th Artillery Brigade
23 Aug 1905 - 5 Jan 1907:	Commander of Artillery, XVII. Army Corps

Major-General Nikolai Gavrilovich **Tetruyev** (18 Aug 1864 - 1920)
31 Aug 1916 - 19 Jun 1917:	Chief of Staff, 67th Infantry Division
6 Dec 1916:	Promoted to *Major-General*
19 Jun 1917 - 1918:	Commander, 55th Infantry Division

Major-General Vasily Gavrilovich **Tetruyev** (8 Apr 1872 - 7 May 1915)
21 Mar 1915 - 7 May 1915:	Commander, 208th Infantry Regiment
27 May 1915:	Posthumously promoted to *Major-General*

General of Cavalry Nikolai Nikolayevich **Tevyashev** (31 Jun 1842 - 24 Nov 1905)
7 Jun 1881 - 28 Nov 1884:	Aide-de-Camp to the Tsar
30 Aug 1882:	Promoted to *Major-General*
28 Nov 1884 - 9 Mar 1889:	Commander, 1st Brigade, 2nd Cavalry Division
9 Mar 1889 - 1 May 1890:	Secretary of Special Commissions, Ministry of War
1 May 1890 - 17 Oct 1895:	Governor of Astrakhan, Ataman, Astrakhan Cossack Army
30 Aug 1892:	Promoted to *Lieutenant-General*
17 Oct 1895 - 14 Mar 1903:	Chief of the Main Intendant Directorate, Intendant-General of the Army
14 Apr 1902:	Promoted to *General of Cavalry*
14 Mar 1903 - 22 Jun 1904:	Member of the Military Council
22 Jun 1904 - 24 Nov 1905:	Governor-General of Turkestan, Commanding General, Turkestan Military District, Ataman, Semirechensk Cossack Army

Major-General of the Fleet Esper Konstantinovich **Teyle** (17 Apr 1869 - ?)
1909 - 1917:	Chief of the Naval Section, Independent Corps of Borderguards
14 Apr 1913:	Promoted to *Major-General of the Fleet*

Major-General Leonid Faddeyevich **Tigranov** (23 Nov 1871 - ?)
24 Jan 1916 - 11 Jan 1917:	Chief of Staff, 106th Infantry Division
6 Dec 1916:	Promoted to *Major-General*
11 Jan 1917 - 16 Apr 1917:	Chief of Lines of Communication, XLII. Army Corps
16 Apr 1917 - 15 Sep 1917:	Duty General, Petrograd Military District
15 Sep 1917 - Mar 1918:	Deputy Chief of Staff, Petrograd Military District

General of Cavalry Yevgraf Filippovich **Tikhanov** (10 Dec 1837 - 1908)
24 Jul 1884 - 19 Oct 1896:	Deputy Military Governor of Dagestan
30 Aug 1888:	Promoted to *Major-General*
19 Oct 1896 - 17 Nov 1901:	Governor, Black Sea Province
22 May 1900:	Promoted to *Lieutenant-General*
17 Nov 1901 - 15 Jun 1907:	Military Governor of Dagestan
15 Jun 1907:	Promoted to *General of Cavalry*
15 Jun 1907:	Retired

Lieutenant-General Sergey Vasilyevich **Tikhanovich** (25 Sep 1849 - 14 Oct 1910)
7 May 1895 - 21 Dec 1906:	Commander of Gendarmerie, Don Region
6 Dec 1904:	Promoted to *Major-General*
21 Dec 1906:	Promoted to *Lieutenant-General*
21 Dec 1906:	Retired

Major-General Georgy Mikhailovich **Tikhmenev** (30 Sep 1873 - 1943)
20 Dec 1914 - 25 Feb 1916:	Commander, 157th Infantry Regiment
27 Jan 1916:	Promoted to *Major-General*
25 Feb 1916 - 22 Aug 1916:	Special Assignments General, 1st Army
22 Aug 1916 - 1 Feb 1917:	Chief of Staff, 45th Infantry Division
1 Feb 1917 - 19 Apr 1917:	Chief of Staff, XIII. Army Corps
19 Apr 1917 - 1917:	Commander, 17th Infantry Division
1917 - 4 Mar 1918:	Attached to the Northern Front

Lieutenant-General Nikolai Mikhailovich **Tikhmenev** (27 Mar 1872 - 12 Jun 1954)
27 Sep 1913 - 12 Feb 1915:	Commander, 60th Infantry Regiment
28 Oct 1914:	Promoted to *Major-General*
12 Feb 1915 - 4 May 1915:	Commander, Brigade, 58th Infantry Division
4 May 1915 - 5 Oct 1915:	Deputy Chief of Transport, Southwestern Front
5 Oct 1915 - 8 Feb 1917:	Deputy Chief of Military Communications
8 Feb 1917 - 10 Sep 1917:	Chief of Military Communications
1917:	Promoted to *Lieutenant-General*
10 Sep 1917 - 1918:	Reserve officer, Odessa Military District

General of Infantry Valerian Pavlovich **Tikhmenev** (30 May 1851 - ?)
26 Jul 1899:	Promoted to *Major-General*

26 Jul 1899 - 21 Jan 1905:	Chief of Staff, I. Turkestan Army Corps
21 Jan 1905 - 19 Mar 1906:	Commander, 62nd Infantry Division
19 Mar 1906 - 2 Jan 1907:	Commander, 39th Infantry Division
6 Dec 1906:	Promoted to *Lieutenant-General*
2 Jan 1907 - 1 Jun 1911:	Chief of Staff, Omsk Military District
1 Jun 1911:	Promoted to *General of Infantry*
1 Jun 1911:	Retired

Major-General Leonid Abramovich **Tikhobrazov** (12 Apr 1862 - ?)
23 Nov 1904 - 1917:	Inspector of Classes, Pavlovsk Military School
6 Dec 1906:	Promoted to *Major-General*

Lieutenant-General Nikolai Dmitriyevich **Tikhobrazov** (3 Mar 1845 - ?)
1 Aug 1890 - 17 May 1895:	Chief of Artillery Training Polygon, Moscow Military District
30 Aug 1890:	Promoted to *Major-General*
17 May 1895 - 5 Dec 1899:	Commander, 33rd Artillery Brigade
5 Dec 1899 - 18 Jan 1902:	Commander of Artillery, IX. Army Corps
1 Jan 1900:	Promoted to *Lieutenant-General*
18 Jan 1902 - 6 Jan 1903:	Commander of Artillery, XIV. Army Corps
6 Jan 1903 - 10 Dec 1904:	Commander of Artillery, XVIII. Army Corps
10 Dec 1904 - 1906:	Inspector of Artillery, 3rd Manchurian Army

Major-General Nikolai Ivanovich **Tikhomirov** (1 May 1855 - ?)
14 Jul 1910:	Promoted to *Major-General*
14 Jul 1910 - 13 Feb 1913:	Commander, 2nd Brigade, 50th Infantry Division

Major-General Vadim Mikhailovich **Tikhomirov** (17 Jan 1872 - ?)
14 May 1909 - 11 May 1916:	Commander of Artillery, Fortress Ust-Dvinsk
10 Apr 1916:	Promoted to *Major-General*
11 May 1916 - 1917:	Commander, 15th Heavy Field Artillery Brigade
1917:	Inspector of Artillery, XIV. Army Corps

Major-General Pyotr Andreyevich **Tikhonovich** (15 Jan 1858 - 9 Jun 1917)
12 May 1910:	Promoted to *Major-General*
12 May 1910 - 16 Jan 1915:	Commander, 1st Brigade, 7th Infantry Division
16 Jan 1915 - 25 Aug 1915:	Commander, 26th Infantry Division
25 Aug 1915 - 9 Nov 1916:	Reserve officer, Dvinsk Military District
9 Nov 1916 - 9 Jun 1917:	Commander, 128th Infantry Division

Lieutenant-General Konstantin Ivanovich **Tikhonravov** (10 Aug 1857 - ?)
24 Jan 1909:	Promoted to *Major-General*
24 Jan 1909 - 13 Jun 1914:	Commander, 36th Artillery Brigade
13 Jun 1914 - 11 Mar 1917:	Inspector of Artillery, II. Army Corps
28 Feb 1915:	Promoted to *Lieutenant-General*
11 Mar 1917 - 24 Jun 1917:	Commander, 193rd Infantry Division
24 Jun 1917 - 14 Aug 1917:	Commanding General, II. Army Corps

Vice-Admiral Karl Mikhailovich **Tikotsky** (18 Oct 1845 - ?)
9 Aug 1899:	Promoted to *Rear-Admiral*
9 Aug 1899 - 5 Jun 1900:	Captain, Port of Nikolayev
5 Jun 1900 - 1 Jul 1900:	Military Governor of Nikolayev
1 Jul 1900 - 11 Oct 1902:	Mayor of Nikolayev
11 Oct 1902 - 1904:	Chief of Mine Detachment, Baltic Fleet
1904:	Promoted to *Vice-Admiral*
1904:	Retired

Lieutenant-General Aleksey Andreyevich **Tillo** (13 Nov 1839 - 30 Dec 1899)
24 Jul 1879 - 19 May 1883:	Unassigned
30 Aug 1882:	Promoted to *Major-General*
19 May 1883 - 10 Jan 1894:	Chief of Staff, I. Army Corps
10 Jan 1894 - 30 Dec 1899:	Commander, 37th Infantry Division
30 Aug 1894:	Promoted to *Lieutenant-General*

Major-General Pavel Eduardovich **Tillo** (12 Aug 1872 - 19 Jul 1931)
17 May 1916 - 16 Apr 1917:	Commander, Life Guards Semenov Regiment
6 Dec 1916:	Promoted to *Major-General*
16 Apr 1917 - 1917:	Commander, 1st Brigade, 1st Guards Infantry Division

Major-General Leonid Petrovich **Timashev** (10 May 1864 - 1932)
29 Jul 1912 - 25 Jul 1915:	Commander, 1st Orenburg Cossack Regiment
2 Jan 1915:	Promoted to *Major-General*
25 Jul 1915 - 24 Mar 1917:	Commander, 2nd Brigade, 10th Cavalry Division
24 Mar 1917 - Oct 1917:	Commander, 2nd Orenburg Cossack Division

Lieutenant-General Aleksandr Lvovich **Timchenko** (26 Jul 1863 - Jun 1917)
28 Jan 1909:	Promoted to *Major-General*
28 Jan 1909 - 6 Mar 1913:	Deputy Chief of Staff, Omsk Military District
6 Mar 1913 - 16 Mar 1916:	Commander, 1st Brigade, 19th Infantry Division
16 Mar 1916 - 17 Mar 1917:	Commander, 113th Infantry Division
10 Apr 1916:	Promoted to *Lieutenant-General*
17 Mar 1917 - Jun 1917:	Reserve officer, Kiev Military District

Major-General Aleksandr Lukich **Timchenko-Ostroverkhov** (11 Apr 1835 - ?)
19 Oct 1899:	Promoted to *Major-General*
19 Oct 1899 - 5 Aug 1900:	Special Assignments General to the Inspector-General of Cavalry
5 Aug 1900 - 1906:	Chairman of the Cavalry Remount Commission, Kiev Region

Lieutenant-General Nikolai Lukich **Timchenko-Ostroverkhov** (16 Feb 1829 - 21 Jan 1903)
9 Oct 1889 - 1896:	Commander, Kiev Military Hospital
30 Aug 1890:	Promoted to *Major-General*
1896:	Promoted to *Lieutenant-General*
1896:	Retired

Lieutenant-General Georgy Ivanovich **Timchenko-Ruban** (23 Apr 1861 - 14 Feb 1917)
4 Aug 1909 - 21 Sep 1913:	Chief of Bureau, Inspectorate-General of Engineers
6 Dec 1909:	Promoted to *Major-General*
21 Sep 1913 - 14 Feb 1917:	Chief of Engineering Acceptance, Main Military Technical Directorate
6 Dec 1916:	Promoted to *Lieutenant-General*

General of Infantry Nikolai Ivanovich **Timchenko-Ruban** (13 Nov 1849 - ?)
1 Jun 1904:	Promoted to *Major-General*
1 Jun 1904 - 4 Jul 1906:	Commander, 1st Brigade, 73rd Infantry Division
4 Jul 1906 - 8 Oct 1908:	Commander, 1st Brigade, 30th Infantry Division
8 Oct 1908 - 15 Jul 1910:	Commander, 1st Turkestan Reserve Brigade
15 Jul 1910 - 2 Oct 1911:	Transferred to the reserve
2 Oct 1911:	Promoted to *Lieutenant-General*
2 Oct 1911:	Retired
20 Jan 1912 - 20 Jan 1914:	Recalled; Commander, Turkestan Regional Brigade
20 Jan 1914:	Retired
17 Aug 1914 - 1916:	Recalled; Commander, 3rd West Siberian Replacement Brigade
1916:	Promoted to *General of Infantry*
1916:	Retired
7 Nov 1916 - 9 Sep 1917:	Recalled; Commander, 40th State Militia Brigade
9 Sep 1917 - 1918:	Commanding General, VI. State Militia Corps

General of Cavalry Nikolai Arkadyevich **Timiryazev** (3 Aug 1835 - 19 Jan 1906)
14 Jun 1884 - Oct 1891:	Commander, Guards Cavalry Regiment
30 Aug 1884:	Promoted to *Major-General*
14 Oct 1891 - 22 Jan 1892:	Commander, 1st Brigade, 1st Guards Cavalry Division
22 Jan 1892 - 3 Aug 1897:	Commander, 4th Cavalry Division
30 Aug 1894:	Promoted to *Lieutenant-General*
3 Aug 1897 - 19 Jan 1906:	Honorary Trustee, Board of Trustees, Empress Maria Institutions
4 May 1898 - 19 Jan 1906:	Chief, Nikolayev Orphan Institute
6 Dec 1904:	Promoted to *General of Cavalry*

Lieutenant-General Ivan Platonovich **Timkovsky** (1 Aug 1849 - ?)
10 Sep 1903 - 11 Sep 1910:	Member of the Artillery Committee, Main Artillery Directorate
6 Dec 1903:	Promoted to *Major-General*
11 Sep 1910:	Promoted to *Lieutenant-General*
11 Sep 1910:	Retired

Lieutenant-General Kornely Danilovich **Timkovsky** (19 May 1855 - ?)
22 Apr 1910:	Promoted to *Major-General*
22 Apr 1910 - 23 Jul 1911:	Duty General, Irkutsk Military District
23 Jul 1911 - 29 Oct 1913:	Commander, 2nd Brigade, 10th Infantry Division
29 Oct 1913:	Promoted to *Lieutenant-General*
29 Oct 1913:	Retired

29 Jul 1914: Recalled with the rank of *Major-General*
29 Jul 1914 - 1917: Commander, 8th Replacement Infantry Brigade
1917: Promoted to *Lieutenant-General*

Lieutenant-General Aleksandr Karlovich **Timler** (22 Aug 1837 - 8 Dec 1896)
1 Jan 1881 - 25 Jan 1887: Member, General Staff Committee
30 Aug 1886: Promoted to *Major-General*
25 Jan 1887 - 15 Mar 1890: Chief of Staff, IV. Army Corps
15 Mar 1890 - 10 Jan 1896: Commander, 1st Brigade, 15th Infantry Division
10 Jan 1896 - 8 Dec 1896: Commander, 15th Infantry Division
14 May 1896: Promoted to *Lieutenant-General*

Lieutenant-General Nikolai Petrovich **Timofeyev** (25 Jan 1841 - 5 Jun 1910)
16 Sep 1896 - 16 Dec 1901: Commander, 12th Grenadier Regiment
16 Dec 1901: Promoted to *Major-General*
16 Dec 1901 - 31 May 1906: Chief of Tiflis Military Hospital
31 May 1906: Promoted to *Lieutenant-General*
31 May 1906 - 19 Oct 1907: Commandant of Tiflis
19 Oct 1907: Retired

Lieutenant-General Nikolai Vasilyevich **Timofeyev** (8 Nov 1837 - 23 Mar 1905)
16 Aug 1889 - 1896: Commander of Gendarmerie, St. Petersburg
21 Apr 1891: Promoted to *Major-General*
1896: Promoted to *Lieutenant-General*
1896: Retired

Major-General Sergey Yakolevich **Timofeyev** (14 Oct 1853 - ?)
28 Jun 1905: Promoted to *Major-General*
28 Jun 1905 - 1906: Commander, 1st Brigade, 49th Infantry Division

Major-General Yegor Ivanovich **Timofeyev** (17 Feb 1838 - ?)
3 Jun 1882 - 1901: Advisory member of the Artillery Committee, Main Artillery Directorate
30 Aug 1889: Promoted to *Major-General*

Major-General of the Admiralty Ivan Ignatyevich **Timoshchuk** (27 Aug 1857 - ?)
18 Apr 1910: Promoted to *Major-General of the Admiralty*
19 Oct 1911 - ?: Senior Deputy Inspector of Naval Construction

Major-General Gotgard Gotgardovich von **Timrot** (8 Feb 1868 - 2 Nov 1942)
25 Aug 1915 - 12 Apr 1917: Commander, Brigade, 34th Infantry Division
11 Oct 1915: Promoted to *Major-General*
12 Apr 1917 - 1918: Commander, 15th Infantry Division

Lieutenant-General Karl Aleksandrovich **Timrot** (22 Dec 1833 - 6 Apr 1895)
25 May 1875 - 8 Jul 1883: Deputy Chief of Staff, Finland Military District
17 Apr 1876: Promoted to *Major-General*
8 Jul 1883 - 11 Feb 1887: Commander, 3rd Regional Brigade

30 Aug 1886:	Promoted to *Lieutenant-General*
11 Feb 1887 - 13 Mar 1891:	Chief of Staff, Finland Military District
13 Mar 1891 - 7 Dec 1892:	Commander, 27th Infantry Division
7 Dec 1892 - 6 Apr 1895:	Commanding General, V. Army Corps

Major-General of the Fleet Baron Nikolai Apollonovich **Tipolt** (1 Aug 1864 - 5 Jul 1948)
1 Oct 1916 - 31 Mar 1917:	Senior Deputy Commander, Port of St. Petersburg
6 Dec 1916:	Promoted to *Major-General of the Fleet*
31 Mar 1917 - 1917:	Reserve officer, Ministry of the Navy
1917:	Dismissed

Major-General of Naval Engineers Robert Yulevich **Tirnshteyn** (14 Oct 1841 - 28 Mar 1896)
1890 - 1895:	Senior Shipbuilder, Port of Nikolayev
1895:	Promoted to *Major-General of Naval Engineers*
1895:	Retired

Lieutenant-General Vladimir Konstantinovich **Tisheninov** (20 Jul 1853 - ?)
5 Jan 1899 - 20 Jul 1913:	Intendant, Grenadier Corps
1909:	Promoted to *Major-General*
20 Jul 1913:	Promoted to *Lieutenant-General*

Lieutenant-General Pavel Nikolayevich **Tishevsky** (8 May 1843 - ?)
24 Oct 1899:	Promoted to *Major-General*
24 Oct 1899 - 23 Jul 1900:	Commander, 1st Turkestan Line Brigade
23 Jul 1900 - May 1903:	Commander, 5th Turkestan Rifle Brigade
May 1903:	Promoted to *Lieutenant-General*
May 1903:	Retired

Major-General Sergey Sergeyevich **Tishin** (16 Jun 1867 - 6 Nov 1912)
14 Jul 1910:	Promoted to *Major-General*
14 Jul 1910 - 23 Jul 1912:	Commander, 2nd Brigade, 9th Infantry Division
23 Jul 1912 - 6 Nov 1912:	Commander, 2nd Brigade, 13th Infantry Division

Major-General of Naval Engineers Aleksandr Petrovich **Titov** (11 Apr 1870 - ?)
1912 - 1917:	Chief Naval Engineer, Port of Sevastopol
14 Apr 1913:	Promoted to *Major-General of Naval Engineers*

Lieutenant-General Roman Alekseyevich **Tizdel** (10 Dec 1852 - 1924)
6 Apr 1903:	Promoted to *Major-General*
6 Apr 1903 - 2 Oct 1905:	Attached to Prince Aleksandr Petrovich Oldenburg
2 Oct 1905 - 4 Aug 1913:	Chief of Warsaw Palace Administration
18 Apr 1910:	Promoted to *Lieutenant-General*
4 Aug 1913:	Retired
10 Jun 1914 - 9 Apr 1917:	Recalled; Attached to the Ministry of the Imperial Court
9 Apr 1917:	Retired

Major-General Baron Aleksandr Yevgenyevich **Tizengauzen** (9 Aug 1858 - ?)
20 Sep 1901:   Promoted to *Major-General*
20 Sep 1901 - Jul 1908:   Chief of Staff, XVII. Army Corps

Major-General Fyodor Gustavovich **Tizengauzen** (1 May 1857 - ?)
29 Nov 1904 - 1908:   Bureau Clerk, Main Fortress Committee
6 Dec 1906:   Promoted to *Major-General*

Major-General Ivan Mikhailovich **Tkhorzhevsky** (18 Nov 1842 - ?)
11 Jan 1900 - 1902:   Deputy Commander of Artillery, Amur Military District
1 Apr 1901:   Promoted to *Major-General*
1902:   Retired

Major-General Nikolai Nikolayevich **Tokarev** (31 Jan 1863 - ?)
25 Jan 1915 - 17 Oct 1915:   Commander, 2nd Life Guards Uhlan Regiment
17 Oct 1915 - 29 Jul 1916:   Reserve officer, Dvinsk Military District
29 Jul 1916:   Promoted to *Major-General*
29 Jul 1916:   Retired

Major-General Vladimir Nikolayevich **Tokarev** (23 Jun 1867 - 14 Jun 1915)
24 May 1913 - 5 Jun 1915:   Commander, 9th Grenadier Regiment
5 Jun 1915:   Promoted to *Major-General*
5 Jun 1915 - 14 Jun 1915:   Chief of Staff, VII. Siberian Army Corps

Major-General Vladimir Ivanovich **Tokmachev** (27 May 1857 - ?)
12 Mar 1904 - 31 Dec 1913:   Military Commander, Kostroma District
14 Apr 1913:   Promoted to *Major-General*
31 Dec 1913 - 29 Jul 1914:   Commander, Smolensk Local Brigade
29 Jul 1914 - 19 Sep 1914:   Commander, 9th Replacement Infantry Brigade
19 Sep 1914 - 1917:   Commander, Smolensk Local Brigade

Lieutenant-General Pyotr Ivanovich **Tolkushkin** (19 Feb 1859 - ?)
1 Jan 1898 - 1912:   Intendant, VIII. Army Corps
6 Dec 1904:   Promoted to *Major-General*
1912:   Promoted to *Lieutenant-General*
1912:   Retired

Major-General Aleksandr Alekseyevich **Tolmachev** (9 Apr 1860 - 17 Jan 1932)
1916 - 1918:   Chief of 42nd Line of Communications Area, Caucasus Army
6 Dec 1916:   Promoted to *Major-General*

Lieutenant-General Ivan Nikolayevich **Tolmachev** (5 Jan 1861 - 28 Jun 1932)
7 Feb 1904 - 30 Jun 1907:   Commander, 132nd Infantry Regiment
9 May 1907:   Promoted to *Major-General*
30 Jun 1907 - 26 Oct 1907:   General Staff officer, Kiev Military District
26 Oct 1907 - 2 Dec 1907:   Chief of Staff, XVI. Army Corps
2 Dec 1907 - 4 Nov 1911:   Mayor of Odessa

4 Nov 1911:	Promoted to *Lieutenant-General*
4 Nov 1911:	Retired
11 Sep 1914 - 17 Nov 1914:	Recalled; Commander, 1st Brigade, 70th Infantry Division
17 Nov 1914 - 6 Mar 1915:	Reserve officer, Minsk Military District
6 Mar 1915 - 18 Nov 1917:	General for Assignments to Chief of Logistics, Southwestern Front
18 Nov 1917:	Retired

Major-General of the Fleet Mikhail Dmitrievich **Tolmachev** (28 Oct 1859 - ?)

6 Dec 1908 - 1912:	Deputy Commander, Black Sea Naval Depot
?:	Promoted to *Major-General of the Fleet*
?:	Member of the Supervisory Commission, Economic Committee, Black Sea Fleet

Lieutenant-General Vladimir Aleksandrovich **Tolmachev** (4 Nov 1853 - 1932)

9 Mar 1900 - 16 Apr 1904:	Commander, 2nd Orenburg Cossack Regiment
4 Apr 1904:	Promoted to *Major-General*
16 Apr 1904 - 9 Jun 1906:	Commander, 2nd Brigade, Orenburg Cossack Division
9 Jun 1906 - 20 Jul 1906:	Attached to Warsaw Military District
20 Jul 1906 - 10 Jul 1907:	Commander, Trans-Baikal Cossack Brigade
10 Jul 1907 - 26 Jan 1912:	Commander, Ussuri Mounted Brigade
29 Mar 1909:	Promoted to *Lieutenant-General*
26 Jan 1912 - 25 Jan 1913:	Commanding General, Corps of Gendarmerie
25 Jan 1913 - 20 Aug 1913:	Attached to the Ministry of Internal Affairs
20 Aug 1913 - 20 Jan 1916:	Military Governor of Amur Region, Ataman, Amur Cossack Army
20 Jan 1916 - 11 Mar 1917:	Military Governor of the Maritime Region, Ataman, Ussuri Cossack Army
11 Mar 1917 - 14 Jun 1917:	Unassigned
14 Jun 1917:	Retired

Major-General Pavel Ustinovich **Tolochko** (26 Oct 1853 - ?)

28 Feb 1911:	Promoted to *Major-General*
28 Feb 1911 - 27 Sep 1913:	Commander, 1st Brigade, 10th Siberian Rifle Division

Lieutenant-General Anton Aleksandrovich **Tolpygo** (5 Jan 1858 - ?)

24 Mar 1903 - 6 Dec 1907:	Commander, 20th Dragoon Regiment
6 Dec 1907:	Promoted to *Major-General*
6 Dec 1907 - 29 May 1910:	Commander, 2nd Brigade, 4th Cavalry Division
29 May 1910 - 22 Jun 1912:	Commander, 3rd Independent Cavalry Brigade
22 Jun 1912 - 15 Oct 1914:	Commander, 4th Cavalry Division
6 Dec 1913:	Promoted to *Lieutenant-General*
15 Oct 1914 - 4 Feb 1916:	Reserve officer, Dvinsk Military District
4 Feb 1916 - 5 Apr 1917:	Commander, 14th Cavalry Division
5 Apr 1917 - 28 Apr 1917:	Reserve officer, Dvinsk Military District
28 Apr 1917:	Retired

Major-General Ivan Nikolayevich **Tolstikhin** (10 Dec 1867 - 1921)
24 Jul 1913 - 1917:   Ataman, 1st Military Division, Trans-Baikal Cossack
                                   Army
10 Apr 1916:   Promoted to *Major-General*

Lieutenant-General Aleksey Vladimirovich **Tolstoy** (13 Jul 1840 - 1907)
9 Jan 1889:   Promoted to *Major-General*
9 Jan 1889 - 1907:   At the disposal of Grand Duke Mikhail Nikolayevich
6 Dec 1899:   Promoted to *Lieutenant-General*

Rear-Admiral Count Nikolai Mikhailovich **Tolstoy** (17 Jul 1857 - 8 Mar 1915)
1901 - 21 Apr 1908:   Captain, *"Polar Star"*
6 Dec 1907:   Promoted to *Rear-Admiral*
21 Apr 1908 - 8 Mar 1915:   Commander, Guards Naval Depot

Major-General Pavel Ivanovich **Tolstoy** (2 Feb 1862 - Aug 1915)
29 Jul 1912 - Aug 1915:   Chief of Office, Commission for the Resolution of
                                   Accounts for the Russo-Japanese War, Military Council
6 Dec 1913:   Promoted to *Major-General*

Lieutenant-General Sergey Ivanovich **Tolstoy** (12 Mar 1838 - 23 Dec 1897)
29 Oct 1872 - 1 Jan 1878:   Chief of Section VI, General Staff
1877 - 1878:   Acting Deputy Chief of the General Staff
1 Jan 1878 - 23 Feb 1879:   Attached to the Ministry of Internal Affairs
30 Aug 1878:   Promoted to *Major-General*
23 Feb 1879 - 29 Apr 1884:   Governor of Plotsk
29 Apr 1884 - 13 Feb 1888:   Chief of Police, Warsaw
13 Feb 1888 - 2 Apr 1892:   Attached to the Ministry of Internal Affairs
1889:   Acting Mayor of Odessa
2 Apr 1892 - 23 Dec 1897:   Council Member, Ministry of Internal Affairs
30 Aug 1892:   Promoted to *Lieutenant-General*
1893:   Acting Deputy Minister of Internal Affairs

General of Cavalry Sergey Yevlampievich **Tolstoy** (14 Oct 1849 - Mar 1921)
4 Feb 1888 - 7 Jun 1895:   Ataman, 3rd Military Division, Ural Cossack Army
6 May 1893:   Promoted to *Major-General*
7 Jun 1895 - 23 Jul 1899:   Commander, Western Siberian Cossack Brigade
23 Jul 1899 - 1905:   Commander, Terek Province,
                                   Ataman, Terek Cossack Army
6 Dec 1900:   Promoted to *Lieutenant-General*
1905:   Promoted to *General of Cavalry*
1905:   Retired

Lieutenant-General Flavian Illarionovich **Tolstukhin** (15 Feb 1845 - ?)
8 Jan 1896 - 1906:   Ataman, 2nd Military Division, Ural Cossack Army
6 May 1901:   Promoted to *Major-General*
1906:   Promoted to *Lieutenant-General*

Lieutenant-General Mikhail Ilich **Tolubayev** (16 Aug 1854 - 18 May 1920)
4 Jun 1898 - 3 May 1909:	Military Judge, Kazan Military District Court
6 Dec 1901:	Promoted to *Major-General*
Oct 1904 - Oct 1905:	Military Prosecutor, 2nd Manchurian Army
3 May 1909 - 4 Jun 1912:	Military Prosecutor, Vilnius Military District Court
6 Dec 1909:	Promoted to *Lieutenant-General*
4 Jun 1912 - Jul 1914:	Chairman of the Military Tribunal, Vilnius Military District
Jul 1914 - 31 Mar 1917:	Chairman of the Military Tribunal, Dvinsk Military District
31 Mar 1917 - 1918:	Member, Supreme Military Tribunal

Lieutenant-General Vladislav Andreyevich **Tomashevich** (10 Jun 1857 - ?)
23 Jun 1897 - 26 Oct 1907:	Military Judge, St. Petersburg Military District Court
6 Dec 1900:	Promoted to *Major-General*
26 Oct 1907:	Promoted to *Lieutenant-General*
26 Oct 1907:	Retired

Major-General Makary-Tselestin Petrovich **Tomashevsky** (3 Jan 1848 - ?)
9 Dec 1904:	Promoted to *Major-General*
9 Dec 1904 - 6 Jul 1906:	Commander, Primorsk Regional Brigade
6 Jul 1906 - Sep 1908:	Commander, 2nd Brigade, 1st East Siberian Rifle Division

General of Artillery Nikolai Konstantinovich **Tomashevsky** (8 May 1854 - Dec 1916)
23 Oct 1904 - 13 Dec 1905:	Commander, 73rd Artillery Brigade
13 Dec 1905 - 29 May 1908:	Commander, 3rd East Siberian Rifle Artillery Brigade
6 Dec 1906:	Promoted to *Major-General*
29 May 1908 - 31 Jul 1910:	Commander of Artillery, I. Siberian Army Corps
31 Jul 1910 - 5 Jan 1914:	Inspector of Artillery, I. Siberian Army Corps
6 Dec 1910:	Promoted to *Lieutenant-General*
5 Jan 1914 - Dec 1916:	Inspector of Artillery, I. Caucasus Army Corps
20 Feb 1917:	Posthumously promoted to *General of Artillery*

Lieutenant-General Sergey Vladimirovich **Tomashevsky** (14 Sep 1857 - ?)
11 Dec 1907 - 23 Dec 1911:	Commander, 7th Uhlan Regiment
23 Dec 1911:	Promoted to *Major-General*
23 Dec 1911 - 21 Oct 1915:	Commander, Trans-Baikal Cossack Brigade
10 Oct 1915:	Promoted to *Lieutenant-General*
21 Oct 1915 - 15 Nov 1916:	Commander, 2nd Kuban Cossack Division
15 Nov 1916 - 2 Sep 1917:	Commander, 5th Caucasus Cossack Division
2 Sep 1917 - 1918:	At the disposal of the Kuban Cossack Army

Lieutenant-General Pyotr Ivanovich **Tomich** (11 Dec 1838 - 1 Jun 1911)
5 Oct 1883:	Promoted to *Major-General*
5 Oct 1883 - 22 Apr 1898:	Military Governor of Kars Region
30 Aug 1893:	Promoted to *Lieutenant-General*
22 Apr 1898 - 1 Jun 1911:	Member of the Board, Ministry of Internal Affairs

Major-General Pyotr Andreyevich **Tomilov** (20 Oct 1870 - 23 Jul 1948)
14 Dec 1914 - 31 Jan 1915: Acting Chief of Staff, IV. Caucasus Army Corps
31 Jan 1915 - 11 May 1917: Quartermaster-General, Caucasus Army
14 Apr 1915: Promoted to *Major-General*
11 May 1917 - 5 Oct 1917: Chief of Staff, Caucasus Front
5 Oct 1917 - 1918: At the disposal of the Chief of Staff, Caucasus Front

Major-General Pavel Petrovich **Tomilovsky** (14 Jan 1857 - ?)
3 Feb 1916 - 1917: Commander, 103rd Artillery Brigade
10 Oct 1916: Promoted to *Major-General*

Major-General Yevgeny Petrovich **Tomilovsky** (30 Jul 1860 - 1919)
5 Jul 1910 - 20 Aug 1916: Commander, Grenadier Sapper Battalion
6 Dec 1915: Promoted to *Major-General*
20 Aug 1916 - 1918: Commander, Replacement Engineer & Technical Brigade, Moscow Military District

Lieutenant-General Ivan Petrovich **Tomkeyev** (2 Feb 1859 - 6 Mar 1916)
1 Mar 1905 - 6 Mar 1916: Director, Tiflis Cadet Corps
2 Apr 1906: Promoted to *Major-General*
14 Apr 1913: Promoted to *Lieutenant-General*

Lieutenant-General Mikhail Ilich **Tomkeyev** (6 Nov 1858 - ?)
17 Apr 1905: Promoted to *Major-General*
17 Apr 1905 - 18 May 1908: Senior Clerk, Office of the Artillery Committee, Main Artillery Directorate
18 May 1908 - 19 Oct 1912: Deputy Commander of Artillery, Vilnius Military District
19 Oct 1912 - Oct 1917: Commander of Artillery, Kazan Military District
14 Apr 1913: Promoted to *Lieutenant-General*

Major-General Vasily Fyodorovich **Tompofolsky** (23 Dec 1832 - 28 Jun 1906)
16 Sep 1881 - 1900: Commander of Gendarmerie, Kherson Province
14 May 1896: Promoted to *Major-General*
1900: Retired

General of Cavalry Vladislav Ksaveryevich **Topchevsky** (7 Aug 1850 - 1910)
16 Sep 1896 - 16 Aug 1899: Commander, 52nd Dragoon Regiment
16 Aug 1899: Promoted to *Major-General*
16 Aug 1899 - 18 Jan 1907: Commander, 1st Brigade, 8th Cavalry Division
12 Jan 1907 - 1 May 1910: Commander, 12th Cavalry Division
22 Apr 1907: Promoted to *Lieutenant-General*
1 May 1910: Promoted to *General of Cavalry*
1 May 1910: Retired

Major-General Vikenty Nikolayevich **Topor-Rabchinsky** (4 Oct 1849 - ?)
13 Apr 1908: Promoted to *Major-General*
13 Apr 1908 - 24 Jul 1910: Intendant, Kiev Military District

24 Jul 1910 - 1912: Unassigned

General of Artillery Dmitry Andreyevich **Topornin** (19 May 1846 - 6 Jul 1914)
17 Nov 1879 - 25 May 1890: Commander, Orenburg Horse Artillery Brigade
6 May 1889: Promoted to *Major-General*
25 May 1890 - 11 Oct 1893: Commander, East Siberian Artillery Brigade
11 Oct 1893 - 9 Aug 1896: Commander of Artillery, Amur Military District
9 Aug 1896 - 19 Jan 1898: Commander of Artillery, II. Army Corps
19 Jan 1898 - 10 Apr 1901: Commander of Artillery, III. Army Corps
5 Apr 1898: Promoted to *Lieutenant-General*
10 Apr 1901 - 11 Dec 1903: Commanding General, I. Turkestan Army Corps
11 Dec 1903 - 28 Sep 1904: Commanding General, XIX. Army Corps
28 Sep 1904 - 23 Dec 1906: Commanding General, XVI. Army Corps
6 Dec 1906: Promoted to *General of Artillery*
23 Dec 1906: Retired

Major-General Dmitry Solomonovich **Topuriya** (11 Feb 1861 - ?)
16 Aug 1914 - 1917: Commander, 308th Infantry Regiment
1916: Promoted to *Major-General*

Major-General Nikolai Gavrilovich **Torchalovsky** (4 Dec 1852 - Aug 1915)
8 Jan 1899 - 1910: Commander, Battalion, 85th Infantry Regiment
20 Jul 1901 - 7 Sep 1901: Acting Commander, 87th Infantry Regiment
1910: Promoted to *Major-General*
1910: Retired
29 Dec 1914 - Aug 1915: Recalled; Commander, 1st Replacement Infantry Battalion

General of Infantry Fyodor-Emily-Karl Ivanovich von **Torklus** (19 Mar 1858 - ?)
11 Oct 1904: Promoted to *Major-General*
11 Oct 1904 - 1 Aug 1906: Commander, 1st Brigade, 62nd Infantry Division
1 Aug 1906 - 6 Oct 1906: Commander, 1st Brigade, 45th Infantry Division
6 Oct 1906 - 17 Oct 1910: Commander, 1st Brigade, 27th Infantry Division
17 Oct 1910: Promoted to *Lieutenant-General*
17 Oct 1910 - 31 Oct 1914: Commander, 6th Infantry Division
31 Oct 1914 - 16 Jan 1917: Commanding General, XV. Army Corps
6 Dec 1916: Promoted to *General of Infantry*
16 Jan 1917 - 21 May 1918: Member of the Military Council

Major-General Baron Aleksandr Georgiyevich **Tornau** (9 Aug 1857 - 17 Jan 1927)
30 Apr 1904 - 3 May 1908: Commander, 6th Dragoon Regiment
3 May 1908: Promoted to *Major-General*
3 May 1908 - 25 Jun 1915: Commander, 1st Brigade, 3rd Cavalry Division
25 Jun 1915: Retired

Major-General Sergey Pavlovich **Tovarishchev** (6 Oct 1870 - 8 May 1917)
26 Jan 1913 - 25 Jun 1915: Commander, 13th Lancer Regiment
16 May 1915: Promoted to *Major-General*

25 Jun 1915 - 2 Jul 1915:	Commander, 2nd Brigade, 13th Cavalry Division
2 Jul 1915 - 15 Oct 1916:	Chief of Staff, I. Cavalry Corps
15 Oct 1916 - 26 Nov 1916:	At the disposal of the Chief of the General Staff
26 Nov 1916 - 8 May 1917:	Chief of Staff, Orenburg Cossack Army

Major-General Vasily Grigoryevich **Tovstoles** (1 Aug 1857 - ?)
9 Nov 1915 - 1917:	Commander, 60th Artillery Brigade
23 Nov 1915:	Promoted to *Major-General*

Major-General Anton Iosifovich **Tovyansky** (4 Feb 1857 - 12 Mar 1924)
12 Aug 1909 - 21 Aug 1915:	Commander, 128th Infantry Regiment
14 Nov 1914:	Promoted to *Major-General*
21 Aug 1915 - 18 Sep 1916:	Reserve officer, Minsk Military District
18 Sep 1916 - 1918:	Commander, 80th State Militia Brigade

Lieutenant-General Yevgeny Georgiyevich **Trambitsky** (10 Feb 1859 - 6 Apr 1931)
26 Jan 1904 - 31 Dec 1906:	Commander, 17th Dragoon Regiment
31 Dec 1906:	Promoted to *Major-General*
31 Dec 1906 - Apr 1912:	Commander, 1st Independent Cavalry Brigade
Apr 1912:	Promoted to *Lieutenant-General*
Apr 1912:	Retired

Major-General Fyodor Nikolayevich **Trankovsky** (15 Aug 1862 - ?)
18 Aug 1912:	Promoted to *Major-General*
18 Aug 1912 - 29 Jul 1914:	Commander, 2nd Brigade, 3rd Siberian Rifle Division
29 Jul 1914 - 31 Jul 1915:	Commander, Brigade, 13th Siberian Rifle Division
31 Jul 1915 - 11 Aug 1917:	Commander, Consolidated Border Infantry Division
11 Aug 1917 - 1919:	Reserve officer, Amur Military District

Major-General Mikhail Petrovich **Trankvilevsky** (19 Nov 1861 - ?)
16 Apr 1904 - 1916:	Chairman of the Remount Commission, Warsaw Region
6 Dec 1910:	Promoted to *Major-General*
1916 - 1917:	Council Member, Main Directorate for State Horse Breeding

Lieutenant-General Otto Yegorovich von **Tranzege** (Georgy Georgiyevich von **Tranze**) (23 Apr 1845 - 1908)
13 Dec 1893 - 7 Apr 1899:	Commander, Life Guards Cuirassier Regiment
6 Dec 1895:	Promoted to *Major-General*
7 Apr 1899 - 17 Feb 1902:	Commander, 1st Brigade, 1st Guards Cavalry Division
17 Feb 1902 - 1908:	Commandant of Gatchina
6 Dec 1902:	Promoted to *Lieutenant-General*

Major-General of the Fleet Platon Platonovich **Travlinsky** (6 Nov 1864 - 1926)
24 Dec 1912 - ?:	Commander, Black Sea Naval Depot
30 Jul 1916:	Promoted to *Major-General of the Fleet*

Major-General Aleksandr Aleksandrovich **Tregubov** (18 Jan 1848 - ?)
24 Aug 1892 - 20 Nov 1895:   Commander, 36th Dragoon Regiment
25 Sep 1895:   Promoted to *Major-General*
20 Nov 1895 - 14 Apr 1901:   Commander, 2nd Brigade, 3rd Cavalry Division

Major-General of the Fleet Apollon Viktorovich **Tregubov** (4 Jan 1863 - 1925)
9 Jun 1913 - 1917:   Commandant, Port of Kerch
8 Sep 1914:   Promoted to *Major-General of the Fleet*

General of Artillery Nikolai Nikolayevich **Tregubov** (8 Jul 1835 - ?)
21 May 1887 - 16 Jan 1897:   Deputy Intendant-General, St. Petersburg Military District
30 Aug 1888:   Promoted to *Major-General*
14 May 1896:   Promoted to *Lieutenant-General*
16 Jan 1897 - 6 Sep 1904:   Intendant-General, St. Petersburg Military District
6 Sep 1904 - 3 Jan 1906:   Member, Committee for Wounded Veterans
3 Jan 1906:   Promoted to *General of Artillery*
3 Jan 1906:   Retired
2 Dec 1909 - 1917:   Recalled; Honorary Trustee, St. Petersburg Board of Trustees, Empress Maria Institutions

Lieutenant-General Yevgeny Emmanuilovich **Tregubov** (29 Oct 1862 - 1919)
14 Jul 1910:   Promoted to *Major-General*
14 Jul 1910 - 30 Sep 1914:   Chief of Staff, XXIV. Army Corps
30 Sep 1914 - 31 Jan 1915:   Chief of Staff, VI. Siberian Army Corps
31 Jan 1915 - 16 Apr 1917:   Commander, 16th Infantry Division
6 Dec 1915:   Promoted to *Lieutenant-General*
16 Apr 1917 - 1918:   Reserve officer, Kiev Military District

Major-General Nikolai Eduardovich **Trembinsky** (16 Jul 1861 - 1927)
1915 - 31 Jul 1915:   Commander, 47th Siberian Rifle Regiment
7 Mar 1915:   Promoted to *Major-General*
31 Jul 1915 - 1915:   Commander, 117th Infantry Regiment
1915 - 30 Mar 1916:   Reserve officer, Dvinsk Military District
30 Mar 1916 - 7 Nov 1916:   Reserve officer, Petrograd Military District
7 Nov 1916 - Mar 1917:   Commander, Special Replacement Brigade
Mar 1917:   Commandant of Novgorod Garrison

Major-General Dmitry Fyodorovich **Trepov** (2 Dec 1855 - 2 Sep 1906)
12 Sep 1896 - 1 Jan 1905:   Chief of Police, Moscow
9 Apr 1900:   Promoted to *Major-General*
1 Jan 1905 - 9 Jan 1905:   At the disposal of the C-in-C of forces operating against Japan
9 Jan 1905 - 24 May 1905:   Governor-General of St. Petersburg
24 May 1905 - 26 Oct 1905:   Deputy Minister of Internal Affairs, Commanding General, Corps of Gendarmerie
26 Oct 1905 - 2 Sep 1906:   Commandant of the Imperial Palace

General of Cavalry Fyodor Fyodorovich **Trepov** (13 May 1854 - 27 Mar 1938)
13 Feb 1892 - 11 Aug 1894:	Deputy Governor of the Ural Region
11 Aug 1894:	Promoted to *Major-General*
11 Aug 1894 - 9 Jul 1896:	Governor of Vyatsk
9 Jul 1896 - 17 Apr 1898:	Governor of Volyn
17 Apr 1898 - 5 Apr 1903:	Governor of Kiev
6 Dec 1901:	Promoted to *Lieutenant-General*
5 Apr 1903 - 31 Mar 1917:	Senator
17 Apr 1904 - 31 May 1905:	Chief of Sanitation Service, 1st Manchurian Army
15 Nov 1905 - 31 Mar 1917:	Member of the State Council
18 Dec 1908 - 15 Oct 1914:	Governor-General of Kiev, Podolia & Volyn
1 Jan 1909:	Promoted to *General of Cavalry*
28 Jun 1909:	Promoted to *General-Adjutant*
4 Oct 1916 - 31 Mar 1917:	Governor-General of Occupied Austro-Hungarian Territories
31 Mar 1917:	Retired

Major-General Aleksandr Yevgenyevich **Treshchenkov** (12 Jun 1873 - ?)
27 Apr 1916 - 30 Apr 1917:	Chief of Staff, 4th Infantry Division
6 Dec 1916:	Promoted to *Major-General*
30 Apr 1917 - 1 Aug 1917:	Chief of Staff, VI. Army Corps
1 Aug 1917 - Oct 1917:	Commander, 4th Finnish Rifle Division

Major-General Aleksandr Kapitonovich **Treskin** (30 Dec 1865 - Feb 1916)
12 Oct 1915 - Feb 1916:	Commander, 23rd Turkestan Rifle Regiment
3 Jul 1916:	Posthumously promoted to *Major-General*

Major-General Aleksandr Nikolayevich **Tretilov** (30 Oct 1861 - Jun 1917)
4 Jun 1912 - 9 Mar 1917:	Commander, 9th Hussar Regiment
10 Apr 1916:	Promoted to *Major-General*
9 Mar 1917 - Jun 1917:	General for Horse Inspection, 7th Army

Lieutenant-General Aleksandr Aleksandrovich **Tretyakov** (20 Oct 1847 - ?)
8 Mar 1901 - 27 Nov 1908:	Commander of Engineers, Fortress Ivangorod
6 Dec 1901:	Promoted to *Major-General*
27 Nov 1908 - ?:	Deputy Commander of Engineers, Warsaw Military District
27 Nov 1910:	Promoted to *Lieutenant-General*

Major-General Ivan Vasilyevich **Tretyakov** (27 Jan 1866 - 1 Jul 1919)
Jan 1916 - 1916:	Commander, 8th Kuban Light Infantry Battalion
1916 - 21 Sep 1916:	Reserve officer, Caucasus Military District
21 Sep 1916:	Promoted to *Major-General*
21 Sep 1916:	Dismissed

General of Engineers Nikolai Aleksandrovich **Tretyakov** (2 Oct 1854 - 5 Feb 1917)
27 Feb 1901 - 29 Jul 1905:	Commander, 5th Eastern Siberian Rifle Regiment
22 Oct 1904:	Promoted to *Major-General*

29 Jul 1905 - 17 Oct 1910:	Commander, 3rd Engineer Brigade
17 Oct 1910 - 28 Feb 1911:	Inspector of Field Engineers, Kiev Military District
6 Dec 1910:	Promoted to *Lieutenant-General*
28 Feb 1911 - 12 Oct 1911:	Commander, 10th Siberian Rifle Division
12 Oct 1911 - 12 Aug 1914:	Commander, 3rd Siberian Rifle Division
12 Aug 1914 - 5 Sep 1915:	Commander, 1st Siberian Rifle Division
5 Sep 1915 - 12 Sep 1915:	Commanding General, XXIII. Army Corps
12 Sep 1915 - Dec 1915:	Reserve officer, Dvinsk Military District
Dec 1915 - 20 Mar 1916:	Commanding General, XLII. Army Corps
20 Mar 1916 - 5 Feb 1917:	Commanding General, XXXVII. Army Corps
6 Dec 1916:	Promoted to *General of Engineers*

Major-General Pavel Petrovich **Tretyakov** (12 Jun 1864 - 16 Apr 1937)
31 Dec 1913 - 28 Jan 1916:	Deputy Chief, Tula Armaments Factory
6 Apr 1914:	Promoted to *Major-General*
28 Jan 1916 - Oct 1917:	Chief, Tula Armaments Factory

Lieutenant-General Mikhail Aleksandrovich **Treydler** (28 Oct 1849 - 1913)
7 Aug 1903 - 1907:	Commander, Odessa Fortress Artillery Depot
6 Dec 1904:	Promoted to *Major-General*
1907:	Promoted to *Lieutenant-General*
1907:	Retired

General of Infantry Vasily Vasilyevich **Treyter** (22 Mar 1830 - 10 Jun 1912)
6 May 1878:	Promoted to *Major-General*
6 May 1878 - 22 May 1878:	Commander, 2nd Brigade, 40th Infantry Division
22 May 1878 - 12 Dec 1880:	Commander, 1st Brigade, 38th Infantry Division
12 Dec 1880 - 16 Sep 1885:	Commander, 2nd Brigade, 20th Infantry Division
16 Sep 1885 - 19 Feb 1886:	Commander, 1st Brigade, 20th Infantry Division
19 Feb 1886 - 12 Oct 1895:	Commander, Caucasus Rifle Brigade
30 Aug 1888:	Promoted to *Lieutenant-General*
12 Oct 1895 - 5 Oct 1899:	Commander, 21st Infantry Division
5 Oct 1899:	Promoted to *General of Infantry*
5 Oct 1899:	Retired

Lieutenant-General Vladimir Vasilyevich **Treyter** (12 Jul 1840 - 10 May 1907)
5 Oct 1892 - 3 Jan 1899:	Intendant, IV. Army Corps
6 Dec 1897:	Promoted to *Major-General*
3 Jan 1899 - 6 May 1901:	Deputy Intendant, Caucasus Military District
6 May 1901 - 23 Nov 1906:	Deputy Intendant, St. Petersburg Military District
23 Nov 1906:	Promoted to *Lieutenant-General*
23 Nov 1906:	Retired

Major-General Avtonom Onufriyevich **Tridensky** (21 Sep 1857 - Feb 1916)
15 Jul 1910 - 29 Nov 1915:	Commander, 6th Caucasus Rifle Regiment
29 Nov 1915 - Feb 1916:	Commander, Brigade, 2nd Caucasus Rifle Division
8 Jan 1916:	Promoted to *Major-General*

Major-General Nikolai Vasilyevich **Tringam** (21 Oct 1860 - 29 Aug 1914)
20 Dec 1911 - 29 Aug 1914: Commander, 12th Hussar Regiment
17 Sep 1915: Posthumously promoted to *Major-General*

Major-General Aleksey Ivanovich **Tripolsky** (23 Feb 1849 - ?)
? - 1913: Intendant, Omsk Military District
1913: Promoted to *Major-General*
1913: Retired
14 Nov 1914 - 1917: Recalled; Reserve officer, Kiev Military District

Major-General Konstantin Iosifovich **Trishatnyy** (8 Jul 1869 - 19 Oct 1918)
27 Mar 1915 - 9 Jan 1916: Commander, 54th Infantry Regiment
9 Jan 1916 - 28 Apr 1917: Commander, Brigade, 37th Infantry Division
14 Nov 1916: Promoted to *Major-General*
28 Apr 1917 - ?: Commander, Brigade, 82nd Infantry Division
? - 10 Oct 1917: Commander, Brigade, 79th Infantry Division
10 Oct 1917 - 1918: Commander, 41st Infantry Division

General of Engineers Dmitry Stepanovich **Trizna** (15 Oct 1846 - ?)
10 Mar 1891 - 26 Aug 1905: Ministry of War Representative, Kiev Military District Council
14 May 1896: Promoted to *Major-General*
26 Aug 1905 - 16 Jun 1907: Intendant, Kiev Military District
6 Dec 1905: Promoted to *Lieutenant-General*
16 Jun 1907 - 15 Apr 1910: Special Assignments General (4th Class), Main Intendant Directorate
15 Apr 1910: Promoted to *General of Engineers*
15 Apr 1910: Retired

Major-General Vasily Mikhailovich **Trofimov** (24 Jul 1865 - 20 Feb 1926)
27 May 1910 - 1917: Commander, Main Artillery Polygon
6 Dec 1910: Promoted to *Major-General*
1917 - 1918: Member of the Artillery Committee, Main Artillery Directorate

Major-General Vladimir Andreyevich **Trofimov** (29 Apr 1862 - ?)
17 Mar 1910 - 1917: Intendant, Irkutsk Military District
6 Dec 1911: Promoted to *Major-General*

Lieutenant-General Vladimir Onufriyevich **Trofimov** (5 Aug 1860 - 20 Dec 1924)
5 May 1902 - 10 May 1905: Head of Chancellery, Viceroy of the Caucasus
6 Apr 1903: Promoted to *Major-General*
10 May 1905 - 2 Oct 1906: Governor of the Black Sea
2 Oct 1906 - 14 Jan 1914: Commander, 1st Brigade, 7th Siberian Rifle Division
14 Jan 1914 - 19 Jul 1914: Commander, 2nd Brigade, 7th Siberian Rifle Division
19 Jul 1914 - 8 Aug 1914: Commander, 12th Siberian Rifle Division
8 Aug 1914 - 25 Apr 1915: Commander, 7th Siberian Rifle Division
30 Sep 1914: Promoted to *Lieutenant-General*

25 Apr 1915 - 6 Apr 1917:	Commanding General, III. Siberian Army Corps
6 Apr 1917 - 1 Aug 1917:	Reserve officer, Minsk Military District
1 Aug 1917:	Retired

Major-General Mikhail Ivanovich **Troitsky** (1 Oct 1856 - ?)
11 Jun 1914:	Promoted to *Major-General*
11 Jun 1914 - 3 Aug 1915:	Commander, 1st Brigade, 12th Infantry Division

Major-General Nikolai Nikolayevich **Troitsky** (11 Jun 1847 - ?)
7 Feb 1901:	Promoted to *Major-General*
7 Feb 1901 - 11 May 1907:	Commander, 1st Brigade, 44th Infantry Division
11 May 1907 - Dec 1907:	Commander, 4th East Siberian Rifle Division
Dec 1907:	Retired

Major-General Pyotr Arkhipovich **Troitsky** (20 May 1834 - Jul 1895)
19 Aug 1885:	Promoted to *Major-General*
19 Aug 1885 - 19 Jul 1889:	Deputy Chief of Staff, Vilnius Military District
19 Jul 1889 - 14 Feb 1894:	Commander, 1st Turkestan Line Brigade
14 Feb 1894 - 20 Jan 1895:	Commander, 56th Reserve Infantry Brigade
20 Jan 1895 - Jul 1895:	Commander, 12th Infantry Division

Major-General Karl-Khristian Lvovich von **Trompeter** (6 Mar 1841 - ?)
8 Oct 1889 - 1898:	Commander, Warsaw Uyazdovsky Military Hospital
30 Aug 1890:	Promoted to *Major-General*

Lieutenant-General Dmitry Pavlovich **Trotsky** (28 Aug 1861 - ?)
16 Jan 1913:	Promoted to *Major-General*
16 Jan 1913 - 29 Jul 1914:	Commander, 1st Brigade, 44th Infantry Division
29 Jul 1914 - 11 Aug 1915:	Commander, Brigade, 79th Infantry Division
11 Aug 1915 - 25 Aug 1915:	Commander, 53rd Infantry Division
25 Aug 1915 - Oct 1917:	Commander, 65th Infantry Division
14 Jul 1917:	Promoted to *Lieutenant-General*

General of Infantry Vitaly Nikolayevich **Trotsky** (19 Dec 1835 - 9 May 1901)
1 Nov 1869 - 10 Jan 1873:	Deputy Commander, Syr-Darya Region
14 Aug 1870:	Promoted to *Major-General*
10 Jan 1873 - 5 May 1878:	Chief of Staff, Turkestan Military District
5 May 1878 - 18 Feb 1883:	Military Governor of Syr-Darya Region
30 Aug 1880:	Promoted to *Lieutenant-General*
18 Feb 1883 - 16 Mar 1883:	Commander, 23rd Infantry Division
16 Mar 1883 - 13 Aug 1889:	Chief of Staff, Caucasus Military District
13 Aug 1889 - 22 Jan 1890:	Commanding General, XVI. Army Corps
22 Jan 1890 - 25 Feb 1895:	Deputy Commanding General, Kiev Military District
30 Aug 1894:	Promoted to *General of Infantry*
25 Feb 1895 - 9 May 1901:	Commanding General, Vilnius Military District
1897 - 9 May 1901:	Governor-General of Vilnius, Kaunas & Grodno
6 Dec 1897:	Promoted to *General-Adjutant*

General of Infantry Vladimir Ioannikiyevich **Trotsky** (14 Jul 1847 - ?)
16 Feb 1900:	Promoted to *Major-General*
16 Feb 1900 - 10 May 1903:	Commander, Life Guards Pavlovsky Regiment
10 May 1903 - 21 Jun 1904:	Commander, 2nd Brigade, 2nd Guards Infantry Division
21 Jun 1904 - 25 Nov 1905:	Commander, 2nd Guards Infantry Division
25 Nov 1905 - 23 Mar 1914:	Commandant of St. Petersburg
6 Dec 1906:	Promoted to *Lieutenant-General*
1910:	Promoted to *General-Adjutant*
6 Dec 1912:	Promoted to *General of Infantry*
23 Mar 1914 - 10 Nov 1914:	Unassigned
10 Nov 1914 - 8 Apr 1916:	Commanding General, Kiev Military District
8 Apr 1916 - 21 Mar 1918:	Member of the Military Council
21 Mar 1918:	Retired

Major-General Viktor Viktorovich **Trotsky-Senyutovich** (12 Jul 1868 - ?)
15 Mar 1915 - 1917:	Director, Vladikavkaz Cadet Corps
6 Dec 1915:	Promoted to *Major-General*

Lieutenant-General Prince Georgy Ivanovich **Trubetskoy** (5 Nov 1866 - 27 Dec 1926)
10 Apr 1906 - 1 Jan 1914:	Chief of the Tsar's Escort
31 May 1907:	Promoted to *Major-General*
1 Jan 1914 - 18 Oct 1914:	Deputy Commander of the Imperial Home Apartments
18 Oct 1914:	Promoted to *Lieutenant-General*
18 Oct 1914 - 18 Apr 1917:	Commander, 2nd Cavalry Division
18 Apr 1917 - 1917:	Reserve officer, Minsk Military District
1917 - 16 Oct 1917:	Reserve officer, Kiev Military District

Major-General Prince Nikolai Andreyevich **Trubetskoy** (24 Jul 1857 - 1931)
6 Oct 1901 - 1905:	Commander, Life Guards 1st Rifle Battalion
1903:	Promoted to *Major-General*
1905:	Retired

Lieutenant-General Prince Nikolai Nikolayevich **Trubetskoy** (27 Aug 1837 - 20 Jul 1902)
11 Oct 1878 - 11 Feb 1886:	Special Assignments Officer, Class VI, Ministry of War
30 Aug 1879:	Promoted to *Major-General*
11 Feb 1886 - 20 Jul 1902:	Governor of Minsk
30 Aug 1891:	Promoted to *Lieutenant-General*

Rear-Admiral Prince Vladimir Vladimirovich **Trubetskoy** (18 Nov 1868 - 30 Jun 1931)
Aug 1916 - 1917:	Commander, Mine Brigade, Black Sea Fleet
6 Dec 1916:	Promoted to *Rear-Admiral*

Major-General Nikolai Aleksandrovich **Trubnikov** (4 Sep 1866 - 23 Jun 1916)
? - 23 Jun 1916:	Attached to 136th Infantry Regiment
12 Oct 1916:	Posthumously promoted to *Major-General*

Major-General Semyon Vasilyevich **Trubnikov** (26 Mar 1839 - 26 Jun 1906)
21 Apr 1895 - 1904:	Commander of Gendarmerie, Tavrichesky District

18 Apr 1899: Promoted to *Major-General*
1904: Retired

Vice-Admiral Pyotr Lvovich **Trukhachev** (10 Nov 1867 - Nov 1916)
1915 - 19 Dec 1915: Commander, Mine Division, Baltic Fleet
6 Aug 1915: Promoted to *Rear-Admiral*
19 Dec 1915 - Nov 1916: Commander, 1st Cruiser Brigade, Baltic Fleet
31 Oct 1916: Promoted to *Vice-Admiral*

Lieutenant-General Ivan Yevdokimovich **Trukhin** (17 Apr 1852 - 4 Dec 1922)
30 Jul 1904 - 24 Jul 1913: Ataman, 1st Military Division, Trans-Baikal Cossack Army
6 Dec 1909: Promoted to *Major-General*
24 Jul 1913: Promoted to *Lieutenant-General*
24 Jul 1913: Retired
3 Sep 1914 - 1915: Recalled; Commander, 2nd Separate Trans-Baikal Cossack Brigade
1915: Retired

Major-General Aleksey Aleksandrovich **Trusov** (17 Jan 1853 - ?)
2 Sep 1900 - 6 Jun 1902: Special Assignments General, Amur Military District
31 Jan 1901: Promoted to *Major-General*
6 Jun 1902 - 22 Feb 1904: Commander, 6th East Siberian Rifle Brigade
22 Feb 1904 - 16 Jul 1904: Commander, 6th East Siberian Rifle Division
16 Jul 1904 - 1904: Attached to the General Staff

Major-General Vladimir Aleksandrovich **Trusov** (2 Sep 1839 - ?)
28 Feb 1878 - 1896: Commander of Artillery, Fortress Tashkent
22 Aug 1890: Promoted to *Major-General*
22 Aug 1890 - 1896: Commander, Artillery Depot, Turkestan Military District

Lieutenant-General Pyotr Petrovich **Trut** (10 Aug 1847 - ?)
28 Jul 1899 - 26 Apr 1902: Deputy Intendant, Kazan Military District
6 Dec 1899: Promoted to *Major-General*
26 Apr 1902 - 1 Jun 1905: Intendant, Siberian Military District
1 Jun 1905 - 11 Jan 1906: At the disposal of the Intendant-General of the Army
11 Jan 1906: Promoted to *Lieutenant-General*
11 Jan 1906: Retired

Major-General Sergey Aleksandrovich **Tsabel** (29 Jul 1871 - ?)
26 Jan 1914 - 1918: Commander, 1st Railway Regiment
6 Dec 1914: Promoted to *Major-General*

Major-General Baron Iosif-Ernest Yakovlevich **Tsege von Manteyfel** (17 Feb 1834 - 1920)
12 Nov 1886 - 1899: Chief of Staff, Caucasus Cavalry Reserve
14 May 1896: Promoted to *Major-General*
1899: Retired

Major-General Vitaly Nikolayevich **Tsege von Manteyfel** (10 Jul 1868 - ?)
4 Aug 1911 - 16 Nov 1913:	Military Judge, Moscow Military District Court
6 Dec 1911:	Promoted to *Major-General*
16 Nov 1913 - 1915:	Military Prosecutor, St. Petersburg Military District
1915 - 1916:	Chief of Military Legal Section, ? Front
1916 - 24 Sep 1916:	Military Prosecutor, Petrograd Military District
24 Sep 1916 - 1917:	Chief of Military Legal Section, High Command Representation to the C-in-C of the French Army

Major-General Vitaly Platonovich **Tselebrovsky** (1 Apr 1854 - 1908)
9 Dec 1896 - 30 Nov 1901:	Senior Clerk, Military Research Committee, General Staff
6 Dec 1900:	Promoted to *Major-General*
30 Nov 1901 - 1 May 1903:	Head of Military Research Committee, General Staff
1 May 1903 - 9 Feb 1905:	Head of Department on Military Statistics of Foreign Countries, Military Statistics Office, General Staff, Chief of Military Intelligence
9 Feb 1905 - 1908:	Head of Main Fortress Committee, General Staff

General of Infantry Vladimir Mikhailovich **Tsemirov** (6 May 1834 - 13 May 1917)
1878 - 1 Jun 1884:	Military Judge, St. Petersburg Military District Court
30 Aug 1879:	Promoted to *Major-General*
1 Jun 1884 - 14 Aug 1894:	Chairman of the Military Tribunal, St. Petersburg Military District
30 Aug 1892:	Promoted to *Lieutenant-General*
14 Aug 1894 - 1905:	Member of the Supreme Military Tribunal
6 Dec 1903:	Promoted to *General of Infantry*
1905:	Retired

Lieutenant-General Konstantin Vikentyevich **Tserpitsky** (11 Dec 1849 - 14 Nov 1905)
26 Jul 1895 - 16 Mar 1897:	Commander, 2nd Transcaucausus Rifle Brigade
6 Dec 1895:	Promoted to *Major-General*
16 Mar 1897 - 11 Feb 1898:	Commander, 1st Transcaucausus Rifle Brigade
11 Feb 1898 - 23 Jun 1899:	Commander, 5th Rifle Brigade
23 Jun 1899 - 5 Jan 1900:	At the disposal of the Commanding General, Vilnius Military District
5 Jan 1900 - 23 Jun 1900:	Commander, 60th Replacement Infantry Brigade
23 Jun 1900 - 17 Jul 1900:	Commander, 1st Eastern Siberian Rifle Brigade
17 Jul 1900 - 20 Feb 1902:	Commander, 2nd Eastern Siberian Rifle Brigade
31 Oct 1900:	Promoted to *Lieutenant-General*
20 Feb 1902 - 11 Dec 1903:	Commander, 13th Infantry Division
11 Dec 1903 - 14 Nov 1904:	Commanding General, I. Turkestan Army Corps
14 Nov 1904 - 14 Nov 1905:	Commanding General, X. Army Corps

Major-General Valerian Kazimirovich **Tserpitsky** (27 Nov 1850 - 14 Nov 1906)
22 Feb 1904:	Promoted to *Major-General*
22 Feb 1904 - Dec 1905:	Commander, 2nd Brigade, 7th East Siberian Rifle Division

Dec 1905: Retired

Major-General Otton Lorentsovich **Tsetterman** (30 Aug 1842 - ?)
1 Feb 1888 - 8 Dec 1894: Commander, 119th Infantry Regiment
14 Nov 1894: Promoted to *Major-General*
8 Dec 1894 - 30 Aug 1902: Commander, 2nd Brigade, 16th Infantry Division

Major-General Nikolai Fyodorovich **Tseykhanovich** (22 Jul 1868 - ?)
23 Aug 1912 - 23 Jun 1916: Commander, 156th Infantry Regiment
23 Jun 1916 - 14 Aug 1917: Commander, Brigade, 4th Caucasus Rifle Division
5 Aug 1916: Promoted to *Major-General*
14 Aug 1917 - 1918: Commander, 4th Caucasus Rifle Division

Lieutenant-General Sergey Vladimirovich **Tseyl** *(19 Nov 1915:* **Pokatov***)* (4 Sep 1868 - 27 Sep 1934)
14 Feb 1907 - 26 Nov 1913: Chief of Asia Section, General Staff
30 Jun 1910: Promoted to *Major-General*
26 Nov 1913 - 3 Oct 1914: Attached to the Ministry of War
3 Oct 1914 - 26 Feb 1916: Chief of Staff, IX. Army Corps
26 Feb 1916 - 4 May 1917: Commander, 55th Infantry Division
4 Nov 1916: Promoted to *Lieutenant-General*
13 Dec 1916 - 8 Jan 1917: Acting Commanding General, XXXV. Army Corps
6 Mar 1917 - 7 Mar 1917: Acting Commanding General, XXXV. Army Corps
4 May 1917 - 25 Jun 1917: At the disposal of the Minister of War
25 Jun 1917 - 7 Dec 1917: Reserve officer, Petrograd Military District
7 Dec 1917: Retired

General of Infantry Nikolai Maksimovich von **Tseymern** (24 Apr 1839 - 11 Apr 1915)
3 May 1879 - 16 Oct 1883: Governor of Grodno
30 Aug 1879: Promoted to *Major-General*
1 Feb 1884 - 17 May 1888: Governor of Astrakhan,
 Ataman, Astrakhan Cossack Army
17 May 1888 - 3 Jun 1898: Member of the Board, Ministry of Internal Affairs
30 Aug 1889: Promoted to *Lieutenant-General*
3 Jun 1898 - 16 Oct 1901: Governor of Vladimir
16 Oct 1901 - 11 Apr 1915: Honorary Trustee, Board of Trustees, Empress Maria Institutions
14 Apr 1902: Promoted to *General of Infantry*

Lieutenant-General Avksenty Dmitriyevich **Tsibulsky** (13 Feb 1857 - ?)
22 Oct 1908: Promoted to *Major-General*
22 Oct 1908 - 18 Jan 1914: Commander, 16th Artillery Brigade
18 Jan 1914 - 5 Oct 1914: Inspector of Artillery, Grenadier Corps
5 Oct 1914 - 13 Mar 1917: Reserve officer, Minsk Military District
13 Mar 1917: Promoted to *Lieutenant-General*
13 Mar 1917: Retired

Major-General Aleksandr Nikolayevich **Tsigler** (11 Jan 1870 - 1927)
16 Jun 1912 - 1915:	Chief of Workshop, Izhevsk Arms Factory
1915 - 20 Apr 1915:	Deputy Chief of Izhevsk Arms Factory
22 Mar 1915:	Promoted to *Major-General*
20 Apr 1915 - 1917:	Inspector, Technical Artillery Institution

Major-General Mikhail Aleksandrovich von **Tsigler** (7 Sep 1867 - 22 May 1916)
3 Apr 1916 - 22 May 1916:	Commander, 9th Amur Border Infantry Regiment
5 Sep 1916:	Posthumously promoted to *Major-General*

Lieutenant-General Dmitry Andreyevich **Tsikeln** (23 Sep 1833 - May 1902)
31 May 1880 - 1 Jan 1889:	Section Chief, General Staff
30 Aug 1885:	Promoted to *Major-General*
1 Jan 1889 - May 1902:	Director, Main Military Sanitation Committee, General Staff
6 Dec 1895:	Promoted to *Lieutenant-General*

Lieutenant-General Yanuary Kazimirovich **Tsikhovich** (7 Sep 1871 - ?)
7 Dec 1910 - 8 Jul 1915:	Commander, 26th Siberian Rifle Regiment
15 Feb 1915:	Promoted to *Major-General*
8 Jul 1915 - 21 Oct 1915:	Commander, 1st Independent Infantry Brigade
21 Oct 1915 - 17 Dec 1915:	Reserve officer, Minsk Military District
6 Dec 1915:	Promoted to *Lieutenant-General*
17 Dec 1915 - 12 Jul 1917:	Commander, 44th Infantry Division
12 Jul 1917 - 11 Aug 1917:	Commanding General, X. Army Corps
11 Aug 1917 - 9 Sep 1917:	C-in-C, 3rd Army
9 Sep 1917 - 3 Dec 1917:	C-in-C, 7th Army

Major-General Valerian Mikhailovich **Tsiklaurov** (27 May 1854 - ?)
1 Jun 1916 - 1917:	Commander, 207th Replacement Infantry Regiment
29 Jul 1916:	Promoted to *Major-General*

Major-General Vasily Petrovich **Tsiklinsky** (28 Mar 1847 - ?)
1 Apr 1897 - 10 Mar 1899:	Commander of Fortress Artillery Depot, Odessa
6 Dec 1897:	Promoted to *Major-General*
10 Mar 1899 - 1903:	Commander, Main Artillery Polygon

Lieutenant-General Vasily Vladimirovich **Tsilliakus** (21 Sep 1840 - ?)
7 Sep 1889:	Promoted to *Major-General*
7 Sep 1889 - 16 Mar 1892:	Commander, 26th Artillery Brigade
16 Mar 1892 - 14 Feb 1899:	Commander, 29th Artillery Brigade
14 Feb 1899 - 1903:	Commander of Artillery, VI. Army Corps
6 Dec 1899:	Promoted to *Lieutenant-General*

Major-General Teofil Florianovich **Tsimkovich** (3 Nov 1849 - ?)
18 Mar 1916 - 1917:	Map Editor, Military Topographical Section, General Staff
6 Dec 1916:	Promoted to *Major-General*

Lieutenant-General Nikolai Yakovlevich **Tsinger** (19 Apr 1842 - 16 Oct 1918)
11 Dec 1874 - 1905:	Professor of Geodesy, Nikolayev General Staff Academy
30 Aug 1885:	Promoted to *Major-General*
14 May 1896:	Promoted to *Lieutenant-General*
1905:	Retired

Major-General Aleksey Pavlovich **Tsirg** (23 Dec 1836 - 7 Jan 1896)
15 Feb 1878 - 7 Jan 1896:	Inspector of Classes, Nikolayev Cavalry School
30 Aug 1885:	Promoted to *Major-General*

Lieutenant-General Aleksandr Andreyevich **Tsitsovich** (7 Oct 1853 - ?)
15 Jan 1909:	Promoted to *Major-General*
15 Jan 1909 - 8 Oct 1913:	Commander, 1st Brigade, 5th Infantry Division
8 Oct 1913:	Promoted to *Lieutenant-General*
8 Oct 1913:	Retired
30 Aug 1914 - 10 Nov 1914:	Recalled; Commander, Brigade, 31st Infantry Division
10 Nov 1914 - 16 Jan 1915:	Commander, 2nd Brigade, 32nd Infantry Division
16 Jan 1915 - 13 May 1915:	Commander, 1st Brigade, 11th Infantry Division
13 May 1915 - 20 Jul 1915:	Commander, 3rd State Militia Division
20 Jul 1915 - 23 Jul 1916:	Commander, 104th Infantry Division
23 Jul 1916 - 23 Sep 1917:	Reserve officer, Kiev Military District
23 Sep 1917 - Oct 1917:	Commandant of Kiev

Major-General Count Nikolai Mikhailovich **Tsukatto** (14 Nov 1845 - ?)
9 Feb 1901 - 1906:	Commander, Częstochowa Borderguard Brigade
14 Apr 1902:	Promoted to *Major-General*

Major-General Prince Georgy Davidovich **Tsulukidze** (23 Apr 1860 - 20 May 1923)
15 Feb 1916 - 7 Feb 1917:	Commander, Brigade, 5th Rifle Division
18 Feb 1916:	Promoted to *Major-General*
7 Feb 1917 - 22 Aug 1917:	Commander, 174th Infantry Division
22 Aug 1917 - 1918:	Commander, 67th Infantry Division

Major-General Prince Nestor Grigoryevich **Tsulukidze** (16 Sep 1855 - 2 Sep 1922)
? - 1910:	Attached to 8th Hussar Regiment
1910:	Promoted to *Major-General*
1910:	Retired

Major-General Prince Varden Grigoryevich **Tsulukidze** (8 Nov 1865 - 20 May 1923)
16 Nov 1914 - 8 Dec 1915:	Commander, 205th Infantry Regiment
8 Dec 1915 - 1918:	Reserve officer, Caucasus Military District
10 Apr 1916:	Promoted to *Major-General*

Major-General Konstantin-Karl Yulyevich **Tsumpfort** (27 Aug 1852 - ?)
31 Jul 1907:	Promoted to *Major-General*
31 Jul 1907 - Dec 1908:	Commander, 21st Artillery Brigade

Major-General Sergey Avgustovich von **Tsur-Milen** (1 Dec 1857 - ?)
30 Jan 1911 - 20 Jan 1914:   Military Commander, Vologda District
14 Apr 1913:   Promoted to *Major-General*
20 Jan 1914 - 1917:   Commander, Turkestan Local Brigade

General of Cavalry Afanasy Andreyevich **Tsurikov** (1 Jul 1858 - 23 May 1922)
16 Sep 1896 - 26 Mar 1901:   Commander, 51st Dragoon Regiment
26 Mar 1901:   Promoted to *Major-General*
26 Mar 1901 - 1 Nov 1902:   Commander, 2nd Brigade, 11th Cavalry Division
1 Nov 1902 - 14 Jun 1905:   Chief of Staff, X. Army Corps
14 Jun 1905 - 20 Feb 1906:   Attached to the General Staff
20 Feb 1906 - 18 Jan 1907:   Special Assignments General to the Inspector-General of Cavalry
18 Jan 1907 - 8 Mar 1907:   Commander, 15th Cavalry Division
8 Mar 1907 - 2 Jan 1914:   Commander, 2nd Cavalry Division
22 Apr 1907:   Promoted to *Lieutenant-General*
2 Jan 1914 - 12 Oct 1916:   Commanding General, XXIV. Army Corps
6 Apr 1914:   Promoted to *General of Cavalry*
12 Oct 1916 - 12 Dec 1916:   C-in-C, 10th Army
12 Dec 1916 - Dec 1917:   C-in-C, 6th Army
Dec 1917:   Retired

Lieutenant-General Vladimir Andreyevich **Tsurikov** (1 Feb 1851 - 25 Sep 1910)
7 May 1897 - 19 Dec 1902:   Commander, 6th Life-Dragoon Regiment
19 Dec 1902:   Promoted to *Major-General*
19 Dec 1902 - 3 Apr 1907:   Commander, 2nd Brigade, 11th Cavalry Division
3 Apr 1907 - 25 Sep 1910:   Commander, 3rd Replacement Cavalry Brigade
31 May 1907:   Promoted to *Lieutenant-General*

Major-General Aleksandr Andreyevich von **Tsurmilen** (12 Jun 1836 - ?)
27 Feb 1883 - 30 May 1888:   Transferred to the reserve
17 Aug 1886:   Promoted to *Major-General*
30 May 1888 - 24 Oct 1899:   Commander, 2nd Brigade, 41st Infantry Division

Major-General Konstantin Maksimovich **Tsurukanov** (14 Sep 1854 - ?)
1 Jun 1906 - 4 Nov 1911:   Commander, 8th Grenadier Regiment
4 Nov 1911:   Promoted to *Major-General*
4 Nov 1911:   Retired
? - 10 Jan 1917:   Recalled; Commander, 111th State Militia Brigade
10 Jan 1917 - ?:   Commander, 112th State Militia Brigade

Lieutenant-General Nikolai Viktorovich **Tsvetkov** (26 Aug 1841 - ?)
15 Oct 1895:   Promoted to *Major-General*
15 Oct 1895 - 14 Feb 1899:   Commander, 40th Artillery Brigade
14 Feb 1899 - 11 Aug 1900:   Commander, 29th Artillery Brigade
11 Aug 1900 - Aug 1904:   Commander of Artillery, XX. Army Corps
6 Dec 1903:   Promoted to *Lieutenant-General*

Lieutenant-General Konstantin Yegorovich **Tsvetkovsky** (18 May 1844 - ?)
17 Nov 1898: Promoted to *Major-General*
17 Nov 1898 - 18 Jan 1902: Commander, 35th Artillery Brigade
18 Jan 1902 - 1908: Commander of Artillery, IX. Army Corps
6 Dec 1904: Promoted to *Lieutenant-General*

Major-General Mikhail Viktorovich **Tsygalsky** (11 Aug 1874 - 1928)
14 Jan 1915 - 30 Sep 1916: Commander, 160th Infantry Regiment
24 Jul 1916: Promoted to *Major-General*
30 Sep 1916 - 12 May 1917: Chief of Staff, 83rd Infantry Division
12 May 1917 - 2 Jun 1917: Chief of Staff, XXXI. Army Corps
2 Jun 1917 - 1918: Commander, 130th Infantry Division

Major-General Viktor Mikhailovich **Tsygalsky** (11 Feb 1845 - ?)
25 Oct 1900 - 1904: Inspector of Classes, Kiev Military School
1 Apr 1901: Promoted to *Major-General*

General of Infantry Erast Stepanovich **Tsytovich** (28 Feb 1830 - 27 Jan 1898)
11 Nov 1870 - 28 Sep 1874: Chief of Staff, Kuban Cossack Army
30 Aug 1873: Promoted to *Major-General*
28 Sep 1874 - 7 Apr 1877: Commander, 1st Brigade, 41st Infantry Division
7 Apr 1877 - 7 Apr 1878: Commander, 1st Brigade, 39th Infantry Division
7 Apr 1878 - 12 Dec 1884: Commander, 39th Infantry Division
20 May 1881: Promoted to *Lieutenant-General*
12 Dec 1884 - 20 Mar 1896: Commandant of Fortress Brest-Litovsk
6 Dec 1895: Promoted to *General of Infantry*
20 Mar 1896 - 27 Jan 1898: Member of the Military Council

Major-General Nikolai Platonovich **Tsytovich** (6 Dec 1865 - ?)
4 Nov 1907 - 1918: Professor, Mikhailovsky Artillery Academy
18 Apr 1910: Promoted to *Major-General*

Major-General Vladimir Nikolayevich **Tsytovich** (9 Apr 1858 - 1941)
11 Sep 1900 - 1905: Attached to the Main Engineering Directorate
1905: Promoted to *Major-General*
1905: Retired
4 Sep 1915 - 1918: Recalled; Reserve officer, Petrograd Military District

Vice-Admiral Genrikh Faddeyevich **Tsyvinsky** (31 Jan 1855 - 6 Dec 1938)
1906: Promoted to *Rear-Admiral*
1906 - 1908: Commander, Training Squadron, Black Sea Fleet
1908 - 9 Aug 1910: Commander, Black Sea Naval Detachment
9 Aug 1910 - Nov 1911: Inpsector-General of Mines
6 Dec 1910: Promoted to *Vice-Admiral*
Nov 1911: Dismissed

Major-General Yulian Venediktovich **Tubilevich** (14 Apr 1838 - 1914)
10 Jun 1898: Promoted to *Major-General*

10 Jun 1898 - 1901:	Deputy Commander of Engineers, Amur Military District
1901:	Retired

Major-General Aleksandr Gavrilovich **Tuchapsky** (19 Nov 1869 - ?)
4 Sep 1911 - 1915:	Commander, 7th Siberian Rifle Regiment
11 Jun 1915:	Promoted to *Major-General*
1915 - 19 May 1916:	Commander, Brigade, 24th Infantry Division
19 May 1916 - 27 Aug 1917:	Commander, 21st Infantry Division

Lieutenant-General Aleksandr Davidovich **Tugan-Mirza-Baranovsky** (8 Jan 1847 - ?)
27 Mar 1897 - 4 Jun 1899:	Chief of Staff, Fortress Warsaw
6 May 1897:	Promoted to *Major-General*
4 Jun 1899 - 16 Aug 1900:	Commander, 2nd Brigade, 27th Infantry Division
16 Aug 1900 - 30 Jul 1903:	Commander, 4th Turkestan Rifle Brigade
30 Jul 1903 - 1 Jun 1904:	Commander, 2nd Turkestan Rifle Brigade
1 Jun 1904 - 27 May 1905:	Commander, 72nd Infantry Division
6 Dec 1904:	Promoted to *Lieutenant-General*
27 May 1905 - 18 Jun 1905:	Attached to the General Staff
18 Jun 1905 - 23 May 1906:	Commander, 12th Infantry Division

Lieutenant-General Ivan Davidovich **Tugan-Mirza-Baranovsky** (28 Mar 1853 - ?)
5 Oct 1908:	Promoted to *Major-General*
5 Oct 1908 - 30 Dec 1913:	Special Assignments General, Kiev Military District
30 Dec 1913:	Promoted to *Lieutenant-General*
30 Dec 1913:	Retired

General of Cavalry Prince Georgy Aleksandrovich **Tumanov** (24 Nov 1856 - 18 Oct 1918)
29 Dec 1901 - 20 Aug 1904:	General for Special Assignments, Warsaw Military District
6 Dec 1902:	Promoted to *Major-General*
20 Aug 1904 - 31 Dec 1905:	Commander, 2nd Brigade, Siberian Cossack Division
31 Dec 1905 - 4 Feb 1906:	Chief of Staff, X. Army Corps
4 Feb 1906 - 12 Jan 1907:	Chief of Staff, II. Cavalry Corps
12 Jan 1907 - 2 Feb 1907:	Chief of Staff, XVI. Army Corps
2 Feb 1907 - 1 May 1910:	General Staff officer, Warsaw Military District
1 May 1910:	Promoted to *Lieutenant-General*
1 May 1910 - 8 Mar 1916:	Commander, 13th Cavalry Division
8 Mar 1916 - 2 Apr 1917:	Commanding General, VII. Cavalry Corps
6 Dec 1916:	Promoted to *General of Cavalry*
2 Apr 1917 - Oct 1917:	Reserve officer, Kiev Military District

General of Infantry Prince Georgy Yevseyevich **Tumanov** (16 Mar 1839 - 30 May 1901)
2 Oct 1877 - 15 Jan 1887:	Commander, 1st Caucasus Sapper Battalion
1886:	Promoted to *Major-General*
15 Jan 1887 - 17 Sep 1889:	Commander, Railway Brigade
17 Sep 1889 - 21 Feb 1896:	Commander, 5th Sapper Brigade
21 Feb 1896 - 19 Dec 1897:	Commander, 32nd Infantry Division

14 May 1896:	Promoted to *Lieutenant-General*
19 Dec 1897 - 30 May 1901:	Commander, 5th Infantry Division
2 Jun 1901:	Posthumously promoted to *General of Infantry*

Lieutenant-General Prince Konstantin Aleksandrovich **Tumanov** (19 May 1862 - 4 Feb 1933)

16 Sep 1908 - 5 Dec 1912:	Commander, 5th Uhlan Regiment
5 Dec 1912:	Promoted to *Major-General*
5 Dec 1912 - 28 Feb 1916:	Commander, 1st Brigade, 9th Cavalry Division
28 Feb 1916 - 26 Mar 1917:	Commander, 1st Amur Cavalry Brigade
30 Jan 1917:	Promoted to *Lieutenant-General*
26 Mar 1917 - 6 Apr 1917:	Attached to the C-in-C, Southwestern Front
6 Apr 1917 - 30 Apr 1917:	Commander, 9th Cavalry Division
30 Apr 1917 - Oct 1917:	Commanding General, II. Cavalry Corps

Major-General Prince Mikhail Georgiyevich **Tumanov** (22 Jul 1848 - 30 Mar 1905)

27 Mar 1902 - 30 Mar 1905:	Commander of Gendarmerie, St. Petersburg-Vindau Railway
6 Dec 1902:	Promoted to *Major-General*

Lieutenant-General Prince Nikolai Georgiyevich **Tumanov** (22 Jul 1848 - ?)

3 Apr 1896 - 15 Nov 1905:	At the disposal of the Commandant of the Imperial Palace
6 Dec 1903:	Promoted to *Major-General*
15 Nov 1905 - 1917:	General for Special Assignments, Minister of Imperial Estates
6 Dec 1911:	Promoted to *Lieutenant-General*

Major-General Prince Nikolai Ivanovich **Tumanov** (13 Feb 1868 - ?)

21 Sep 1913 - 18 Apr 1915:	Senior Engineering Inspector, Main Military-Technical Directorate
6 Dec 1914:	Promoted to *Major-General*
18 Apr 1915 - 1917:	Deputy Inspector of Engineers, Moscow Military District

General of Engineers Prince Nikolai Yevseyevich **Tumanov** (24 Oct 1844 - 1917)

29 Jun 1882 - 7 Jan 1897:	Chief of Engineers, Fortress Kars
30 Aug 1892:	Promoted to *Major-General*
7 Jan 1897 - 20 Aug 1899:	Commander of Engineers, Trans-Caspian Region
20 Aug 1899 - 4 Dec 1904:	Commander of Engineers, Warsaw Military District
6 Dec 1899:	Promoted to *Lieutenant-General*
24 Jun 1903 - 4 Sep 1903:	Acting Commander, 38th Infantry Division
4 Dec 1904 - 26 Nov 1905:	Inspector of Engineers, 1st Manchurian Army
26 Nov 1905 - 7 Jul 1906:	Commander of Engineers, Warsaw Military District
7 Jul 1906 - 24 Jun 1910:	Commandant of Fortress Brest-Litovsk
6 Dec 1907:	Promoted to *General of Engineers*
24 Jun 1910 - Oct 1917:	Member of the Military Council
30 Aug 1914 - 14 Sep 1915:	Commanding General, Dvinsk Military District

14 Sep 1915 - 13 Jun 1916:	Commanding General, Petrograd Military District
13 Jun 1916 - 22 Mar 1917:	Chief of Logistics, Western Front

Major-General Fyodor Nikolayevich **Tumansky** (20 Apr 1833 - ?)
14 Mar 1887 - 23 Jan 1891:	Commander of Artillery, Fortress Bender
23 Jan 1891:	Promoted to *Major-General*
23 Jan 1891 - 19 Sep 1891:	Commander of Artillery, Fortress Sveaborg
19 Sep 1891 - 1899:	Commander of Artillery, Fortress Kiev

Major-General Anton Vasilyevich **Tumilo-Denisovich** (10 Jul 1850 - 22 Mar 1915)
15 Feb 1915 - 22 Mar 1915:	Attached to 281st Infantry Regiment
16 May 1915:	Posthumously promoted to *Major-General*

Lieutenant-General Adrian Ivanovich **Tumsky** (25 Jan 1860 - ?)
12 Nov 1911 - 29 Mar 1915:	Commander, 68th Infantry Regiment
2 Nov 1914:	Promoted to *Major-General*
29 Mar 1915 - 11 Mar 1916:	Commander, 3rd Turkestan Rifle Brigade
11 Mar 1916 - 15 Apr 1917:	Commander, 3rd Turkestan Rifle Division
16 Jan 1917:	Promoted to *Lieutenant-General*
15 Apr 1917 - 7 Dec 1917:	Reserve officer, Odessa Military District
7 Dec 1917:	Retired

Lieutenant-General Vladimir Dmitriyevich **Tunoshensky** (6 Jul 1838 - 30 Sep 1898)
14 Mar 1887 - 25 Jan 1893:	Commander of Artillery, Fortress Ivangorod
30 Aug 1887:	Promoted to *Major-General*
5 Jul 1891 - 25 Jan 1893:	Chief of Ivangorod Military Hospital
25 Jan 1893 - 30 Sep 1898:	Commander of Artillery, Fortress Dvinsk
Sep 1898:	Promoted to *Lieutenant-General*

Lieutenant-General Frants-Eduard Yegorovich **Tunzelman von Adlerflug** (19 Aug 1822 - 8 Nov 1899)
18 Apr 1885 - 16 May 1894:	Commander of Gendarmerie, Finland
24 Apr 1888:	Promoted to *Major-General*
16 May 1894 - 1894:	Attached to the Staff, Independent Corps of Gendarmerie
1894:	Promoted to *Lieutenant-General*
1894:	Retired

Lieutenant-General Nikolai Antonovich **Tunzelman von Adlerflug** (4 Mar 1828 - 21 Nov 1905)
17 Nov 1875 - 16 Sep 1885:	Commander, 111th Infantry Regiment
15 May 1883:	Promoted to *Major-General*
16 Sep 1885 - 7 Oct 1899:	Commander, 1st Brigade, 29th Infantry Division
7 Oct 1899:	Promoted to *Lieutenant-General*
7 Oct 1899:	Retired

Lieutenant-General Aleksandr Fedorovich **Turbin** (12 Jan 1858 - 9 Sep 1922)
13 Feb 1909:	Promoted to *Major-General*

13 Feb 1909 - 4 Feb 1914:	Commander, Life Guards Volyn Regiment
4 Feb 1914:	Promoted to *Lieutenant-General*
4 Feb 1914 - 21 Jul 1914:	Commandant of Warsaw
21 Jul 1914 - 26 Jul 1915:	Military Governor of Warsaw
29 Nov 1914 - 26 Jul 1915:	Commandant of Warsaw Citadel
26 Jul 1915 - 26 Aug 1915:	Commander of Vitebsk Garrison
26 Aug 1915 - 30 Oct 1915:	Commander of Bobruisk Garrison
30 Oct 1915 - 12 Apr 1917:	Commander, 6th Siberian Rifle Division
12 Apr 1917 - 26 Nov 1917:	Commanding General, V. Siberian Army Corps

General of Infantry Nikolai Matveyevich **Turbin** (4 Jun 1832 - ?)

14 Jan 1877 - 13 Mar 1889:	Deputy Chief of Staff, Moscow Military District
1 Jan 1878:	Promoted to *Major-General*
29 Apr 1887 - 13 Mar 1889:	Chief of Moscow Military Hospital
13 Mar 1889 - 17 Jun 1891:	Commandant of Fortress Vyborg
30 Aug 1889:	Promoted to *Lieutenant-General*
17 Jun 1891 - 31 Mar 1896:	Commander, 25th Infantry Division
31 Mar 1896 - 7 Jun 1898:	Deputy Commanding General, Amur Military District
7 Jun 1898 - 12 May 1902:	At the disposal of the Minister of War
12 May 1902:	Promoted to *General of Infantry*
12 May 1902 - 4 Jul 1905:	Deputy Commanding General, Finland Military District
4 Jul 1905 - 3 Jan 1906:	Governor-General of Finland, Member of the Military Council
3 Jan 1906:	Retired

Major-General Nikolai Vasilyevich **Turbin** (2 Sep 1844 - ?)

7 May 1900 - 1904:	Commander of Engineers, Fortress Kerch
1 Jan 1901:	Promoted to *Major-General*
1904:	Retired

Major-General Vasily Nikolayevich **Turchaninov** (18 Jul 1845 - ?)

2 Apr 1890:	Promoted to *Major-General*
2 Apr 1890 - 22 Jan 1894:	Commander, 1st Brigade, 1st Don Cossack Division
22 Jan 1894 - 20 Feb 1899:	Commander, 3rd Brigade, 1st Guards Cavalry Division
20 Feb 1899 - 15 Apr 1904:	Attached to the Commanding General, St. Petersburg Military District
15 Apr 1904 - 1906:	Attached to the Don Army

Lieutenant-General Zaurbek Dzhambulatovich **Turgiyev** (24 Jul 1859 - Jun 1915)

13 May 1911 - Jun 1915:	Commander, 1st Brigade, 1st Caucasus Cossack Division
25 Mar 1912:	Promoted to *Major-General*
Jul 1915:	Posthumously promoted to *Lieutenant-General*

Major-General Aleksandr Konstantinovich **Turkov** (8 Oct 1850 - ?)

6 Jul 1907:	Promoted to *Major-General*
6 Jul 1907 - 21 Oct 1908:	Commander, 2nd Brigade, 9th East Siberian Rifle Division
21 Oct 1908 - Oct 1910:	Commander, 1st Brigade, 3rd East Siberian Rifle

	Division
Oct 1910:	Retired

Lieutenant-General Mikhail Konstantinovich **Turkov** (8 Nov 1843 - ?)
23 Mar 1899 - 11 May 1910:	Chief of Warsaw-Uyazdov Military Hospital
14 Apr 1902:	Promoted to *Major-General*
11 May 1910:	Promoted to *Lieutenant-General*
11 May 1910:	Retired

Lieutenant-General Mikhail Andreyevich **Turkul** (28 Aug 1852 - 9 May 1917)
3 Jun 1898 - 15 Dec 1904:	Chief of Sub-Section, General Staff
6 Apr 1903:	Promoted to *Major-General*
15 Dec 1904 - 24 Nov 1907:	Duty General, Turkestan Military District
24 Nov 1907 - 2 Aug 1914:	Commander, Kiev Regional Brigade
6 Dec 1908:	Promoted to *Lieutenant-General*
2 Aug 1914 - 11 Sep 1914:	Commander, 3rd Replacement Infantry Brigade
11 Sep 1914 - 9 May 1917:	Commander, Kiev Regional Brigade

Major-General Eduard-Kipriyan Iosifovich **Turoboysky** (13 Oct 1855 - Dec 1915)
1 Oct 1910 - 1911:	Reserve officer, St. Petersburg District
1911:	Promoted to *Major-General*
1911:	Retired
20 Jan 1915 - 1915:	Recalled; Member of the Medical Commission, 2nd Warsaw Rear Evacuation Point
1915 - Dec 1915:	Staff officer, Medical Commission, 27th Rear Evacuation Points

Lieutenant-General Pyotr Nikolayevich **Turov** (20 Dec 1865 - ?)
12 Feb 1907 - 7 Jul 1914:	Commander, 161st Infantry Regiment
26 Jan 1914:	Promoted to *Major-General*
7 Jul 1914 - 29 Jul 1914:	Commander, 1st Brigade, 28th Infantry Division
29 Jul 1914 - 27 Aug 1914:	Commander, Brigade, 72nd Infantry Division
27 Aug 1914 - 13 May 1915:	Commander, 1st Brigade, 26th Infantry Division
18 Sep 1914 - 16 Jan 1915:	Acting Commander, 26th Infantry Division
13 May 1915 - 10 Oct 1915:	Commander, 38th Infantry Division
10 Oct 1915 - 12 Jan 1916:	Reserve officer, Dvinsk Military District
12 Jan 1916 - 26 Jun 1917:	Reserve officer, Petrograd Military District
26 Jun 1917:	Promoted to *Lieutenant-General*
26 Jun 1917:	Retired

Lieutenant-General Vladimir Dmitriyevich **Turov** (31 Jan 1858 - ?)
25 Aug 1905 - 20 Jul 1907:	Commander, 6th Mortar Artillery Battalion
10 Jul 1907:	Promoted to *Major-General*
20 Jul 1907 - 26 Jul 1910:	Commander, 31st Artillery Brigade
26 Jul 1910 - 11 Dec 1913:	Inspector of Artillery, V. Siberian Army Corps
6 Dec 1912:	Promoted to *Lieutenant-General*
11 Dec 1913:	Dismissed
8 Sep 1916 - 1917:	Recalled; Inspector of Artillery, V. Siberian Army Corps

Lieutenant-General Mikhail Aleksandrovich **Turoverov** (10 Nov 1863 - Mar 1918)
3 May 1901 - 28 Mar 1912: Chief of Bureau to the Ataman, Don Cossack Army
6 Dec 1910: Promoted to *Major-General*
28 Mar 1912 - Mar 1918: Deputy Ataman, Don Cossack Army
6 Dec 1916: Promoted to *Lieutenant-General*

Major-General Aristarkh Nikolayevich **Tushin** (15 Apr 1864 - ?)
3 Aug 1915 - 28 Apr 1917: Commander, 47th Infantry Regiment
21 Oct 1916: Promoted to *Major-General*
28 Apr 1917 - 1918: Reserve officer, Kiev Military District

General of Cavalry Ivan Fyodorovich **Tutolmin** (25 Oct 1837 - 7 Aug 1908)
10 Apr 1877 - 10 Oct 1878: Commander, 1st Brigade, Caucasus Cossack Division
2 Oct 1877: Promoted to *Major-General*
10 Oct 1878 - 22 Oct 1882: General for Special Assignments, Inspector-General of Cavalry
22 Oct 1882 - 29 Dec 1885: Commandant, Officers Cavalry School
29 Dec 1885 - 16 Jan 1893: Commander, 1st Caucasus Cossack Division
30 Aug 1886: Promoted to *Lieutenant-General*
16 Jan 1893 - 18 Apr 1895: Commander, Caucasus Cavalry Division
18 Apr 1895 - 1 Feb 1896: Commanding General, V. Army Corps
1 Feb 1896 - 19 Jul 1896: At the disposal of the Inspector-General of Cavalry
19 Jul 1896 - 7 Mar 1901: Deputy Inspector-General of Cavalry
6 Dec 1898: Promoted to *General of Cavalry*
7 Mar 1901 - 7 Aug 1908: Member of the Military Council

Major-General Vladimir Kazimirovich **Tutsevich** (15 Nov 1848 - ?)
23 Aug 1905 - 12 May 1907: Commander, 41st Artillery Brigade
6 Dec 1906: Promoted to *Major-General*

Major-General of the Fleet Leonid Dormidontovich **Tverdyy** (14 Dec 1872 - 21 Apr 1968)
1914 - 1918: Prosecutor, Sevastopol Naval Court
1915: Promoted to *Major-General of the Fleet*

Major-General Mikhail Ivanovich **Tyazhelnikov** (25 Sep 1866 - Dec 1933)
28 Jun 1910 - 23 Jun 1914: Commander, 11th Infantry Regiment
23 Jun 1914: Promoted to *Major-General*
23 Jun 1914: Retired
15 Aug 1914: Recalled with the rank of *Colonel*
15 Aug 1914 - 6 Aug 1915: Commander, 4th Grenadier Regiment
6 Aug 1915 - Mar 1917: Acting Chief of Staff, Petrograd Military District
6 Sep 1915: Promoted to *Major-General*
Mar 1917 - 26 Apr 1917: Reserve officer, Petrograd Military District
26 Apr 1917 - 1917: Reserve officer, Kiev Military District
1917 - 10 Jun 1917: Reserve officer, Caucasus Military District
10 Jun 1917: Retired

Lieutenant-General Vladimir Vasilyevich **Tyazhelov** (13 Jul 1831 - ?)
4 Mar 1877 - 27 Jan 1884:	Commander of Artillery, Fortress Ivangorod
15 May 1883:	Promoted to *Major-General*
27 Jan 1884 - 30 Jun 1884:	Commander of Artillery, Fortress Warsaw
30 Jun 1884 - 12 Jul 1886:	Commander of Artillery, Fortress Dinaburg
12 Jul 1886 - 26 Jan 1887:	Deputy Commander of Artillery, Odessa Military District
26 Jan 1887 - 27 Jul 1890:	Deputy Commander of Artillery, Warsaw Military District
27 Jul 1890 - 1898:	Commander of Artillery, Kiev Military District
26 Jan 1893:	Promoted to *Lieutenant-General*

Rear-Admiral Vladimir Dmitriyevich **Tyrkov** (22 Dec 1868 - 29 Mar 1915)
19 Dec 1911 - 1914:	Commander, Battleship "Emperor Paul I"
29 Mar 1915:	Posthumously promoted to *Rear-Admiral*

Lieutenant-General of the Admiralty Fyodor Fyodorovich **Tyrtov** (12 Apr 1854 - Jan 1911)
7 Jun 1899 - Jan 1911:	Chief of St. Petersburg River Police
17 Apr 1905:	Promoted to *Major-General of the Admiralty*
6 Dec 1910:	Promoted to *Lieutenant-General of the Admiralty*

Lieutenant-General Konstantin Petrovich **Tyrtov** (17 Jun 1845 - 3 Apr 1906)
21 May 1898:	Promoted to *Major-General*
21 May 1898 - 14 May 1901:	Commander, Life Guards 4th Rifle Battalion
14 May 1901 - 1 Jun 1904:	Commander, 1st Brigade, 2nd Guards Infantry Division
1 Jun 1904 - 3 Apr 1906:	Commander, 56th Infantry Division
6 Dec 1904:	Promoted to *Lieutenant-General*

Lieutenant-General Mikhail Alekseyevich **Tyrtov** (1 Dec 1864 - ?)
17 Jul 1908 - 27 Jul 1914:	Military Judge, Amur Military District Court
29 Mar 1909:	Promoted to *Major-General*
27 Jul 1914 - 27 Apr 1917:	Military Prosecutor, Irkutsk Military District Court
2 Apr 1917:	Promoted to *Lieutenant-General*
27 Apr 1917 - 1918:	Chairman of the Military Court, Irkutsk Military District

Admiral Pavel Petrovich **Tyrtov** (13 Jul 1836 - 4 Mar 1903)
1 Jan 1886 - 1887:	Deputy Chief of the Naval General Staff
13 Apr 1886:	Promoted to *Rear-Admiral*
1887 - 1890:	Commander, Training Squadron, Baltic Sea
1891 - 1892:	Commander, Pacific Squadron
30 Aug 1892:	Promoted to *Vice-Admiral*
1893 - 13 Jul 1896:	Chief of the Main Directorate of Shipbuilding and Logistics
1896:	Chairman, Naval Technical Committee
13 Jul 1896 - 4 Mar 1903:	Minister of the Navy
6 Dec 1896:	Promoted to *Admiral*
14 Apr 1902:	Promoted to *General-Adjutant*

Lieutenant-General of the Admiralty Pyotr Ivanovich **Tyrtov** (21 Nov 1856 - 30 Dec 1927)
17 Nov 1908 - Mar 1917:	Commandant, Naval Engineering School
29 Mar 1909:	Promoted to *Major-General of the Admiralty*
14 Apr 1913:	Promoted to *Lieutenant-General of the Admiralty*
Mar 1917:	Retired

Vice-Admiral Sergey Petrovich **Tyrtov** (19 Oct 1839 - 10 Jan 1903)
1 Jan 1888:	Promoted to *Rear-Admiral*
1 Jan 1888 - 16 May 1892:	Chief of Staff, Black Sea Fleet
16 May 1892 - 30 Nov 1892:	Junior Flagman, Black Sea Naval Division
30 Nov 1892 - 13 Mar 1895:	Commander, Pacific Squadron
1 Jan 1894:	Promoted to *Vice-Admiral*
13 Mar 1895 - 1 Jan 1896:	Commander, Joint Mediterranean & Pacific Squadrons
1 Jan 1896 - 6 May 1898:	Senior Flagman, 2nd Division, Baltic Fleet
1897:	Commander, Baltic Training Squadron
6 May 1898 - 4 Mar 1903:	C-in-C, Black Sea Fleet, Military Governor of Nikolayev

Lieutenant-General Vladimir Alekseyevich **Tyrtov** (3 Sep 1863 - ?)
7 May 1906 - 8 May 1907:	Military Judge, Irkutsk Military District Court
1906:	Promoted to *Major-General*
8 May 1907 - 17 Jul 1908:	Military Judge, Amur Military District Court
17 Jul 1908 - 19 Mar 1913:	Military Judge, Kazan Military District Court
19 Mar 1913:	Promoted to *Lieutenant-General*
19 Mar 1913:	Retired

Major-General Prokofy Semyonovich **Tyshkevich** (27 Feb 1852 - Apr 1904)
7 Aug 1900:	Promoted to *Major-General*
7 Aug 1900 - 20 Jan 1903:	Chief of Staff, Fortress Kaunas
20 Jan 1903 - Apr 1904:	Commander, 2nd Brigade, 4th Infantry Division

General of Cavalry Mikhail Stepanovich **Tyulin** (1 Sep 1862 - 1935)
9 Dec 1904 - 18 Aug 1908:	Duty General, Moscow Military District
17 Apr 1905:	Promoted to *Major-General*
18 Aug 1908 - 21 May 1912:	Commander, 2nd Brigade, 1st Cavalry Division
21 May 1912:	Promoted to *Lieutenant-General*
21 May 1912 - 23 Nov 1914:	Commander, 7th Cavalry Division
23 Nov 1914 - 17 Sep 1915:	Commander, 2nd Kuban Cossack Division
17 Sep 1915 - 17 Mar 1917:	Governor of Orenburg, Ataman, Orenburg Cossack Army
17 Mar 1917 - 26 Apr 1917:	Reserve officer, Caucasus Military District
26 Apr 1917 - 2 Oct 1917:	Reserve officer, Moscow Military District
2 Oct 1917:	Promoted to *General of Cavalry*
2 Oct 1917:	Retired

Major-General Mikhail Alekseyevich **Tyumenkov** (8 Sep 1850 - 31 May 1910)
1 Jun 1904:	Promoted to *Major-General*
1 Jun 1904 - 12 Nov 1907:	Commander, 2nd Brigade, 4th Infantry Division

12 Nov 1907:   Retired

Major-General Aleksey Aleksandrovich **Tyunegov** (19 Feb 1853 - ?)
23 Apr 1901:   Promoted to *Major-General*
23 Apr 1901 - 6 Apr 1907:   Commander, 1st Brigade, 2nd Infantry Division

Lieutenant-General Vasily Gavrilovich **Tyurin** (16 May 1861 - 31 Oct 1915)
2 Mar 1902 - 31 Oct 1915:   Professor, Nikolayev Engineering Academy
17 Apr 1905:   Promoted to *Major-General*
1913 - 31 Oct 1915:   Member, Technical Committee, Main Military-Technical Directorate
6 Dec 1914:   Promoted to *Lieutenant-General*

Major-General Yemelyan Filippovich **Tyurmorezov** (8 Aug 1826 - ?)
16 Aug 1889 - 1897:   Vice-Chairman, Don Region Military Charitable Societies
6 May 1891:   Promoted to *Major-General*

Lieutenant-General Ivan Ivanovich **Tyvalovich** (13 Sep 1836 - ?)
31 Jan 1876 - 5 Feb 1885:   Commander, 104th Infantry Regiment
15 May 1883:   Promoted to *Major-General*
5 Feb 1885 - 15 May 1885:   Commander, 2nd Brigade, 29th Infantry Division
15 May 1885 - 9 Dec 1892:   Chief of Staff, III. Army Corps
9 Dec 1892 - 18 Jan 1896:   Commander, 27th Infantry Division
30 Aug 1893:   Promoted to *Lieutenant-General*
18 Jan 1896 - 13 Apr 1896:   Commander, 29th Infantry Division

Major-General Ippolit Ivanovich **Uglichinin** (23 Jan 1859 - ?)
3 May 1909 - 1913:   Ataman, 3rd Military Division, Orenburg Cossack Army
10 Apr 1911:   Promoted to *Major-General*

Vice-Admiral Aleksey Petrovich **Ugryumov** (6 Jan 1859 - 14 Dec 1937)
1911 - 1913:   Deputy Chief of the Naval General Staff
6 Dec 1913:   Promoted to *Rear-Admiral*
1913 - 1 Jun 1915:   Vice-Chairman of the Naval Fortress Board, Emperor Peter the Great Naval Fortress
1 Jun 1915:   Promoted to *Vice-Admiral*
1 Jun 1915 - 27 Jun 1916:   Chief of Main Directorate of Shipbuilding
27 Jun 1916 - 10 Nov 1916:   C-in-C, Archangelsk & White Sea Naval Region
10 Nov 1916 - Oct 1917:   Chairman, Conference on Maritime Transport

Major-General Anatoly Aleksandrovich **Ugryumov** (5 Apr 1872 - 25 Sep 1929)
Jul 1914 - 1917:   Deputy Intendant, Dvinsk Military District
6 Dec 1916:   Promoted to *Major-General*

Lieutenant-General Andrey Aleksandrovich **Ugryumov** (1 Dec 1852 - ?)
16 Jun 1903:   Promoted to *Major-General*
16 Jun 1903 - 2 Jul 1910:   Chief of Staff, XIII. Army Corps

2 Jul 1910: Promoted to *Lieutenant-General*
2 Jul 1910 - 17 Aug 1914: Commander, 1st Infantry Division
17 Aug 1914 - 1918: POW, Germany

Major-General Nikolai Antonovich **Ukhach-Ogorovich** (7 May 1860 - ?)
16 Apr 1904 - 1907: Chief of Transport, 1st Manchurian Army
6 Dec 1904: Promoted to *Major-General*

Major-General Prince Aleksandr Vladimirovich **Ukhtomsky** (5 Dec 1857 - 13 Apr 1916)
25 Jul 1914 - 13 Apr 1916: Commander, 77th Artillery Brigade
1 Sep 1915: Promoted to *Major-General*

Vice-Admiral Prince Pavel Petrovich **Ukhtomsky** (10 Jun 1848 - 10 Sep 1910)
1901: Promoted to *Rear-Admiral*
1901 - Feb 1903: Chief of Staff, Port of Kronstadt
Feb 1903 - 31 Mar 1904: Junior Flagman, Pacific Squadron
31 Mar 1904 - 3 Apr 1904: Acting C-in-C, Pacific Fleet
3 Apr 1904 - 28 Jul 1904: Junior Flagman, Pacific Squadron
28 Jul 1904 - 24 Aug 1904: Acting Commander, Pacific Squadron
24 Aug 1904 - Sep 1904: At the disposal of the Viceroy, Far East
Sep 1904 - 1906: Commander, 12th Naval Depot
1906: Promoted to *Vice-Admiral*
1906: Retired

Major-General Sergey Gerasimovich **Ukke** (15 Dec 1858 - Mar 1917)
18 Mar 1909 - 24 Jul 1912: Deputy Chief of Sestroretsk Armory
18 Apr 1910: Promoted to *Major-General*
24 Jul 1912 - Jul 1916: Deputy Commandant, Kiev Arsenal
Jul 1916 - Mar 1917: Reserve officer, Kiev Military District

Major-General of the Fleet Semyon Semyonovich **Uklonsky** (28 May 1858 - ?)
1 Jul 1900 - Sep 1912: Senior Deputy Astronomer, Nikolayev Naval Observatory
6 Dec 1909: Promoted to *Major-General of the Fleet*

Major-General Tont Nauruzovich **Ukurov** (17 May 1865 - 1934)
1914 - 14 Aug 1915: Attached to 44th Infantry Regiment
14 Aug 1915: Promoted to *Major-General*
14 Aug 1915: Retired

Major-General Nikolai Alekseyevich **Ulyanin** (13 Aug 1850 - 29 May 1907)
26 Oct 1896 - 13 Jul 1902: Chief of Construction, Central Asian Railway
2 Nov 1900: Promoted to *Major-General*
13 Jul 1902 - 29 May 1907: Chief of the Central Asian Railway, Commander, Turkestan Railway Brigade

Lieutenant-General Afanasy Ivanovich **Ulyanov** (5 Jul 1846 - ?)
4 Sep 1905 - 19 Jul 1912: Chief of Tiflis Military Hospital

6 Dec 1906:	Promoted to *Major-General*
19 Jul 1912:	Promoted to *Lieutenant-General*
19 Jul 1912:	Retired
1915 - 28 May 1916:	Recalled; Commandant of Aleksandropol
28 May 1916 - 13 Apr 1917:	At the disposal of the C-in-C, Caucasus Army
13 Apr 1917 - 23 Jun 1917:	Chief of Sanitation, Caucasus Front
23 Jun 1917:	Dismissed

Major-General of the Fleet Zakhary Yakovlevich **Ulyanov** (5 Sep 1859 - ?)

29 Aug 1905 - 1917:	Senior Deputy Commander, Port of Nikolayev
6 Dec 1912:	Promoted to *Major-General of the Admiralty*
8 Apr 1913:	Redesignated *Major-General of the Fleet*

Major-General Yanuary Semyonovich **Ulyanovsky** (19 Sep 1868 - 13 Aug 1960)

1915 - 6 Dec 1915:	At the disposal of the Chief of the General Staff
6 Dec 1915:	Promoted to *Major-General*
6 Dec 1915 - 1917:	Inspector of Classes, Nikolayev Cavalry School
1917 - 8 Oct 1917:	Commandant of Nikolayev Cavalry School
8 Oct 1917:	Retired

Lieutenant-General Aleksandr Nikolayevich **Umanov** (23 Jul 1850 - ?)

4 May 1897 - 13 Apr 1909:	Military Commander, Brest-Litovsk District
13 Apr 1909:	Promoted to *Major-General*
13 Apr 1909 - 1917:	Commander, Warsaw Regional Brigade
6 Dec 1915:	Promoted to *Lieutenant-General*

General of Artillery Sergey Semyonovich **Unkovsky** (20 Sep 1829 - 1904)

2 Dec 1863 - 20 Feb 1875:	Commander, 36th Artillery Brigade
28 Mar 1871:	Promoted to *Major-General*
20 Feb 1875 - 15 May 1883:	Deputy Commandant of Moscow, Chief of Moscow Military Hospital
15 May 1883:	Promoted to *Lieutenant-General*
15 May 1883 - 17 Jul 1883:	Unassigned
17 Jul 1883 - 16 Jun 1886:	Commandant of Warsaw Citadel
16 Jun 1883 - 1904:	Commandant of Moscow
14 May 1896:	Promoted to *General of Artillery*

General of Engineers Pavel-Simon Fyodorovich **Unterberger** (9 Aug 1842 - 13 Feb 1921)

22 Sep 1884 - 1 Oct 1888:	Chief of Engineers, Amur Military District
30 Aug 1887:	Promoted to *Major-General*
1Oct 1888 - 7 May 1897:	Military Governor of the Maritime Region, Ataman, Ussuri Cossack Army
14 May 1896:	Promoted to *Lieutenant-General*
7 May 1897 - 8 Nov 1905:	Governor of Nizhny Novgorod
8 Nov 1905 - 6 Dec 1910:	Commanding General, Amur Military District, Governor-General of Amur
6 Dec 1906:	Promoted to *General of Engineers*
6 Dec 1910 - 1917:	Member of the State Council

Lieutenant-General of the Fleet Semyon Semyonovich **Uplonsky** (? - ?)
?:   Promoted to *Major-General of the Admiralty*
?:   Promoted to *Lieutenant-General of the Admiralty*

Major-General Pavel Nikolayevich **Urazov** (12 Jan 1853 - ?)
7 Sep 1904 - 31 Oct 1907:   Commander, 2nd Kuban Light Infantry Battalion
31 Oct 1907:   Promoted to *Major-General*
31 Oct 1907:   Retired
30 Mar 1915 - 13 Oct 1916: Recalled; Commander, 117th Replacement Infantry Battalion
13 Oct 1916 - 15 Oct 1917: Commander, 117th Replacement Infantry Regiment
15 Oct 1917:   Retired

Major-General Sergey Nikolayevich **Urnizhevsky** (19 May 1845 - ?)
26 Apr 1900:   Promoted to *Major-General*
26 Apr 1900 - 20 Jun 1906: Commander, 2nd Brigade, 5th Infantry Division
20 Jun 1906:   Retired

Major-General Prince Nikolai Valeryevich **Urusov** (27 Oct 1860 - 25 Dec 1912)
13 May 1910:   Promoted to *Major-General*
13 May 1910 - 24 Nov 1910: Commander, 2nd Brigade, 6th Cavalry Division
24 Nov 1910 - 27 Nov 1912: Commander, 2nd Brigade, 9th Cavalry Division

Lieutenant-General Prince Sergey Nikolayevich **Urusov** (12 May 1839 - 9 Feb 1906)
26 Feb 1894:   Promoted to *Major-General*
26 Feb 1894 - 22 Jan 1896: Commander, 1st Brigade, 13th Infantry Division
22 Jan 1896 - 23 Jun 1899: Commander, 1st Brigade, 15th Infantry Division
23 Jun 1899 - 17 Nov 1899: Commander, 2nd Brigade, 17th Infantry Division
17 Nov 1899:   Promoted to *Lieutenant-General*
17 Nov 1899:   Retired

Major-General Innokenty Vasilyevich **Uryadov** (1 Dec 1848 - ?)
28 Feb 1884 - 1908:   Commander, Khabarovsk Artillery Depot
6 Dec 1904:   Promoted to *Major-General*
1908:   Retired

Major-General Aleksandr Yakovlevich **Usachev** (17 Oct 1860 - 1 Apr 1943)
16 Jan 1911 - 1 Aug 1914:   Ataman, 2nd Military Division, Siberian Cossack Army
25 Mar 1912:   Promoted to *Major-General*
1 Aug 1914 - Feb 1915:   Commander, Brigade, Siberian Cossack Division
Feb 1915 - 1918:   POW, Germany

Major-General Kiprian Yakovlevich **Usachev** (2 Sep 1857 - 17 Feb 1918)
1915 - 23 Dec 1915:   Commander, 29th Don Cossack Regiment
27 Aug 1915:   Promoted to *Major-General*
23 Dec 1915 - 7 May 1917:   Commander, 2nd Brigade, 5th Don Cossack Division
7 May 1917 - Dec 1917:   Commander, 5th Don Cossack Division

Major-General Apollon Alekseyevich **Useltsev** (7 Dec 1851 - 20 Aug 1915)
8 Mar 1915 - 20 Aug 1915: Commander, 57th Kursk State Militia Squad
24 Mar 1916: Posthumously promoted to *Major-General*

Major-General Aleksandr Georgiyevich **Ushakov** (29 Sep 1868 - ?)
1914 - 19 Nov 1915: Commander, 290th Infantry Regiment
20 Jul 1915: Promoted to *Major-General*
19 Nov 1915 - Jul 1917: Commander, Brigade, 3rd Rifle Division
Jul 1917 - 4 Sep 1917: Commander, 10th Siberian Rifle Division
4 Sep 1917 - 1918: Commander, 103rd Infantry Division

Major-General Fyodor Alekseyevich **Ushakov** (19 Dec 1850 - 22 Oct 1914)
1 Jan 1887 - 1902: Company Commander, Pskov Cadet Corps
1902: Promoted to *Major-General*
1902: Retired

Major-General Ivan Yakovlevich **Ushakov** (16 Nov 1838 - ?)
20 Apr 1893 - 1 Nov 1895: Commander, 82nd Infantry Regiment
14 Nov 1894: Promoted to *Major-General*
22 Nov 1894 - 1 Nov 1895: Chief of Grodno Military Hospital
1 Nov 1895 - 4 Dec 1901: Commander, 2nd Caucasus Rifle Brigade
4 Dec 1901: Retired

General of Infantry Kirill Andreyevich **Ushakov** (20 Feb 1832 - 2 Dec 1907)
1 May 1874 - 13 Oct 1884: Military Judge, Kazan Military District Court
30 Aug 1881: Promoted to *Major-General*
13 Oct 1884 - 15 Jul 1890: Chairman of the Military Court, Odessa Military District
15 Jul 1890 - 1905: Member, Supreme Military Tribunal
30 Aug 1891: Promoted to *Lieutenant-General*
6 Dec 1902: Promoted to *General of Infantry*
1905: Retired

Major-General Konstantin Mikhailovich **Ushakov** (18 Jul 1871 - 1943)
17 Oct 1915 - 14 Oct 1916: Chief of Lines of Communication, 8th Army
6 Dec 1915: Promoted to *Major-General*
14 Oct 1916 - 23 Nov 1917: Chief of Military Communications, Northern Front

Lieutenant-General Mikhail Ivanovich **Ushakov** (29 Nov 1857 - ?)
11 Jul 1904: Promoted to *Major-General*
11 Jul 1904 - 29 May 1910: Attached to Grand Duke Mikhail Nikolayevich
24 Apr 1910: Promoted to *Lieutenant-General*
29 May 1910: Retired
5 Jun 1910 - 1917: Recalled; Honorary Trustee, St. Petersburg Board of Trustees, Empress Maria Institutions

Lieutenant-General Sergey Leonidovich **Ushakov** (23 Oct 1859 - 21 Oct 1918)
1 Dec 1908 - 19 Nov 1910: Commander, St. Petersburg Borderguard Brigade

19 Nov 1910:	Promoted to *Major-General*
19 Nov 1910 - 30 Mar 1911:	Special Assignments General of the Commanding General, Borderguard Corps
30 Mar 1911 - 1916:	Commander, 3rd Borderguard District
6 Dec 1915:	Promoted to *Lieutenant-General*
1916:	Dismissed

Major-General Adrian Vladimirovich **Usov** (27 May 1868 - ?)

24 Sep 1913:	Promoted to *Major-General*
24 Sep 1913 - 17 Dec 1915:	Commander, Life Guards 3rd Rifle Regiment
17 Dec 1915 - 29 Oct 1916:	Commander, 1st Brigade, Guards Rifle Division
29 Oct 1916 - 22 Aug 1917:	Commander, 22nd Infantry Division
22 Aug 1917 - Oct 1917:	Reserve officer, Dvinsk Military District

Lieutenant-General Nikolai Antonovich **Usov** (9 Sep 1833 - ?)

4 Mar 1883 - 27 Mar 1887:	Chief of Bessarabia Customs District
24 Mar 1885:	Promoted to *Major-General*
27 Mar 1887 - 1 Jul 1899:	Commander, Kalish Customs District,
2 Jan 1895 - 1 Jul 1899:	Special Purposes General, Ministry of Finance
14 May 1896:	Promoted to *Lieutenant-General*
1 Jul 1899 - Jul 1906:	Commander, 3rd Borderguard District

Lieutenant-General Nikolai Nikolayevich **Usov** (26 Jun 1866 - ?)

24 Feb 1907 - 14 Sep 1910:	Commander, Tver Cavalry School
1 Sep 1910:	Promoted to *Major-General*
14 Sep 1910 - 9 Nov 1916:	Director, Corps of Pages
9 Nov 1916 - 30 May 1917:	Deputy Military Governor-General of Occupied Austro-Hungarian Territories
6 Dec 1916:	Promoted to *Lieutenant-General*
30 May 1917 - 1918:	Director, Petrograd Cadet Corps

Major-General of Naval Engineers Viktor Alexeyevich **Usov** (28 Mar 1857 - ?)

18 Sep 1905 - 15 Mar 1910:	Chief of Shipbuilding Engineers, Port of Kronstadt
6 Dec 1908:	Promoted to *Major-General of Naval Engineers*
15 Mar 1910 - Jul 1913:	Attached to Port of St. Petersburg

General of Artillery Vladimir Stepanovich **Usov** (12 Jun 1841 - 9 Sep 1913)

4 Jul 1890:	Promoted to *Major-General*
4 Jul 1890 - 1 Feb 1895:	Commander, Horse Artillery Brigade, Orenburg Cossack Army
1 Feb 1895 - 29 Aug 1895:	Commander, 37th Artillery Brigade
29 Aug 1895 - 30 Dec 1896:	Commander, 23rd Artillery Brigade
30 Dec 1896 - 5 Dec 1899:	Commander, Life Guards 3rd Artillery Brigade
5 Dec 1899 - 8 Apr 1904:	Commander of Artillery, Don Cossack Army
1 Jan 1900:	Promoted to *Lieutenant-General*
8 Apr 1904 - 9 Sep 1913:	Member, Committee for Wounded Veterans
1906:	Promoted to *General of Artillery*
1906:	Retired

Vice-Admiral Ivan Petrovich **Uspensky** (1 Feb 1857 - ?)
27 Feb 1906 - 26 Feb 1907: Chief of Stores Section, Main Shipbuilding Directorate
2 Nov 1906: Promoted to *Rear-Admiral*
26 Feb 1907 - 9 Mar 1909: Chief of Main Directorate of Shipbuilding & Supply
9 Mar 1909 - 30 May 1911: C-in-C of Naval Forces, Pacific
18 Apr 1910: Promoted to *Vice-Admiral*
30 May 1911 - 27 Sep 1911: Attached to the Minister of the Navy
27 Sep 1911: Retired

Lieutenant-General Vladimir Vasilyevich **Uspensky** (4 Jun 1843 - ?)
31 May 1882 - 9 Jul 1897: Military Judge, Moscow Military District Court
30 Aug 1889: Promoted to *Major-General*
9 Jul 1897: Promoted to *Lieutenant-General*
9 Jul 1897: Retired

Major-General Vatslav Yevgenyevich **Ussakovsky** (5 Oct 1847 - ?)
27 Nov 1898 - 1914: Military Judge, Turkestan Military District Court
1 Jan 1901: Promoted to *Major-General*

General of Infantry Yevgeny Yevgenyevich **Ussakovsky** (15 May 1851 - 1935)
5 Apr 1892 - 2 Sep 1895: Chief of Staff, X. Army Corps:
30 Aug 1892: Promoted to *Major-General*
2 Sep 1895 - 22 Mar 1897: Head of Kharkov Military Hospital
22 Mar 1897 - 31 Jan 1898: Deputy Chief, Main Directorate of Cossack Troops
31 Jan 1898 - 14 Dec 1902: Deputy Chief of the General Staff
6 Dec 1899: Promoted to *Lieutenant-General*
14 Dec 1902 - 5 Dec 1905: Commanding General, II. Turkestan Army Corps, Commander, Trans-Caspian Region
5 Dec 1905 - 1 Jul 1906: Attached to the Ministry of War
1 Jul 1906: Promoted to *General of Infantry*
1 Jul 1906: Retired

Major-General Yury Konstantinovich **Ustimovich** (22 Nov 1873 - 1969)
23 Jan 1914 - 18 May 1915: Commander, 8th Hussar Regiment
18 May 1915 - 17 Jun 1915: Commander, 1st Brigade, 2nd Cavalry Division
25 May 1915: Promoted to *Major-General*
17 Jun 1915 - 2 Feb 1916: Commander, 2nd Brigade, 8th Cavalry Division
2 Feb 1916 - 1918: Commander, 1st Brigade, 8th Cavalry Division

Major-General Vladimir Semyonovich **Ustinov** (12 Jul 1855 - ?)
5 Apr 1909 - 30 Mar 1913: Commander of Gendarmerie, Terek Region
6 Dec 1912: Promoted to *Major-General*
30 Mar 1913 - 1917: Commander of Gendarmerie, Ufa Province

General of Infantry Lev Karlovich **Utgof** (24 Nov 1852 - 2 Aug 1918)
31 Oct 1905 - 25 Sep 1906: Commander of Gendarmerie, Warsaw Province
1906: Promoted to *Major-General*
25 Sep 1906 - 2 Dec 1914: Deputy Governor-General of Warsaw

8 Oct 1909:	Promoted to *Lieutenant-General*
2 Dec 1914:	Promoted to *General of Infantry*
2 Dec 1914:	Retired

Major-General Mikhail Alekseyevich **Utin** (6 Sep 1861 - Jul 1916)
7 Dec 1913 - Jul 1916:	Military Commander, St. Petersburg District
14 Jan 1915:	Promoted to *Major-General*

General of Artillery Aleksandr Vladimirovich **Utkevich** (7 Feb 1845 - ?)
13 Nov 1895:	Promoted to *Major-General*
13 Nov 1895 - 9 Feb 1901:	Commander, Life Guards 2nd Artillery Brigade
9 Feb 1901 - 7 Aug 1903:	Commander of Artillery, Guards Corps
6 Dec 1901:	Promoted to *Lieutenant-General*
7 Aug 1903 - 27 Nov 1910:	General for Special Assignments, Master-General of Ordnance
27 Nov 1910:	Promoted to *General of Artillery*
27 Nov 1910:	Retired

Major-General Mikhail Andreyevich **Uvarov** (28 Sep 1865 - ?)
18 Jul 1914 - 6 Nov 1914:	Commander, 159th Infantry Regiment
6 Nov 1914 - 16 Dec 1914:	Unassigned
16 Dec 1914:	Retired
21 Feb 1915:	Promoted to *Major-General*
Jun 1915:	Recalled with the rank of *Colonel*
Jun 1915 - 27 Dec 1915:	Commander, 414th Infantry Regiment
27 Dec 1915 - 3 Mar 1916:	Reserve officer, Minsk Military District
3 Mar 1916 - 2 Dec 1916:	Commander, 192nd Infantry Regiment
2 Dec 1916 - 28 Feb 1917:	Chief of Staff, 35th Infantry Division
6 Dec 1916:	Promoted to *Major-General*
28 Feb 1917 - 8 Oct 1917	Chief of Staff, 46th Infantry Division
8 Oct 1917 - 1918:	Commander, 46th Infantry Division

Lieutenant-General Vasily Nikolayevich **Uversky** (15 Mar 1862 - Dec 1916)
1 May 1907 - 9 Mar 1912:	Military Judge, Warsaw Military District Court
6 Dec 1907:	Promoted to *Major-General*
9 Mar 1912 - 31 Oct 1912:	Military Prosecutor, Caucasus Military District
31 Oct 1912 - 29 Jul 1914:	Military Prosecutor, Warsaw Military District
29 Jul 1914 - 18 Dec 1914:	Chief of Military Justice Service, Northwestern Front
18 Dec 1914 - 3 May 1915:	Chairman of the Military Tribunal, Galicia
3 May 1915 - Dec 1916:	Military Prosecutor, Minsk Military District
6 Dec 1915:	Promoted to *Lieutenant-General*

Major-General Artemy Solomonovich **Uzbashev** (30 Aug 1827 - ?)
14 Feb 1891 - 1903:	Deputy Military Governor of Dagestan
30 Aug 1892:	Promoted to *Major-General*

Major-General Prince Aleksandr Ivanovich **Vachnadze** (8 Aug 1855 - ?)
21 Feb 1915:	Promoted to *Major-General*

21 Feb 1915 - 1917: Commander, 2nd Trans-Caucasus Reserve Brigade

Lieutenant-General Prince Avraam Georgiyevich **Vachnadze** (4 Sep 1853 - Feb 1941)
12 May 1908: Promoted to *Major-General*
12 May 1908 - 31 Dec 1913: Commander, 2nd Brigade, 31st Infantry Division
31 Dec 1913 - Feb 1917: Commandant of Peterhof
6 Dec 1914: Promoted to *Lieutenant-General*
Feb 1917 - 29 May 1917: Unassigned
29 May 1917: Dismissed

Major-General Prince Leonty Tamozovich **Vachnadze** (2 May 1858 - ?)
26 Jul 1915 - 1917: Commander, 4th Caucasus Rifle Artillery Brigade
9 Aug 1916: Promoted to *Major-General*

Lieutenant-General Prince Nikolai Petrovich **Vadbolsky** (5 Dec 1869 - 1944)
18 Sep 1909 - 23 Aug 1914: At the disposal of the Chief of the General Staff
10 Apr 1911: Promoted to *Major-General*
23 Aug 1914 - 28 Mar 1915: Commander, 3rd Brigade, Caucasus Native Cavalry Division
28 Mar 1915 - 1 Jul 1915: Attached to the C-in-C, 8th Army
1 Jul 1915 - 25 Apr 1917: Commander, Consolidated Cavalry Division
6 Dec 1915: Promoted to *Lieutenant-General*
25 Apr 1917 - 1917: Commanding General, VII. Caucasus Army Corps

Lieutenant-General Torsten Karlovich **Vadensherna** (4 Jun 1861 - Feb 1920)
20 Apr 1910 - 4 Jul 1913: Commander, 12th Rifle Regiment
14 Apr 1913: Promoted to *Major-General*
4 Jul 1913 - 17 Aug 1913: Commander, 2nd Brigade, 48th Infantry Division
17 Aug 1913 - 20 May 1915: Commander, 2nd Brigade, 5th Infantry Division
20 May 1915 - 17 Jul 1915: Commander, 81st Infantry Division
17 Jul 1915 - 17 Oct 1917: Commander, 37th Infantry Division
10 Oct 1915: Promoted to *Lieutenant-General*
17 Oct 1917 - 27 Nov 1917: Reserve officer, Odessa Military District
27 Nov 1917 - 1918: Reserve officer, Kiev Military District

Major-General Aleksandr Nikolayevich **Vadin** (12 Jul 1866 - 1946)
18 Dec 1913 - 23 Jul 1916: Commander of Artillery, Fortess Kars
6 Dec 1914: Promoted to *Major-General*
23 Jul 1916 - 1917: Commander of Artillery & Fortifications, Erzurum

Major-General of the Fleet Pyotr Nikolayevich **Vagner** (10 May 1862 - 1932)
19 Apr 1904 - 1915: Lecturer, Naval Academy
6 Dec 1913: Promoted to *Major-General of the Fleet*
1915 - 1917: Head of Midshipmen Training Courses

Lieutenant-General Vsevolod Nikolayevich **Vakharlovsky** (21 Nov 1858 - 19 Jun 1939)
25 Jul 1906 - 28 Sep 1912: Commandant, Mikhailov Artillery School
6 Dec 1906: Promoted to *Major-General*

6 Dec 1911:	Promoted to *Lieutenant-General*
28 Sep 1912 - 17 Aug 1914:	Commander of Artillery, Turkestan Military District
17 Aug 1914 - 22 Dec 1915:	Inspector of Artillery, I. Turkestan Army Corps
22 Dec 1915 - 10 Oct 1916:	Inspector of Artillery, Moscow Military District
10 Oct 1916 - 20 Jan 1917:	Inspector of Artillery, I. Turkestan Army Corps
20 Jan 1917 - 5 Apr 1917:	Inspector of Artillery, 5. Army
5 Apr 1917 - 1917:	Reserve officer, Dvinsk Military District

Lieutenant-General Mikhail Nikolayevich **Vakhrushev** (5 Mar 1865 - 27 Nov 1934)

14 Dec 1914 - 30 Aug 1916:	Chief of Staff, II. Siberian Army Corps
6 Jan 1915:	Promoted to *Major-General*
30 Aug 1916 - 1 Jan 1917:	Quartermaster-General, 5th Army
1 Jan 1917 - 14 May 1917:	Chief of Staff, 5th Army
14 May 1917 - 19 Sep 1917:	Chief of Staff, Northern Front
16 Aug 1917:	Promoted to *Lieutenant-General*
19 Sep 1917 - 1918:	Reserve officer, Dvinsk Military District

Major-General Andrey Mikhailovich **Vaksmut** (13 Jan 1863 - 24 May 1934)

5 May 1906 - 1908:	Commander, Amur Cossack Regiment
1908:	Retired
1914:	Promoted to *Major-General*
1914 - 1916:	Recalled; Chief of Staff, VIII. Militia Corps
1916:	Retired

Major-General Arkady Arkadyevich **Vakulovsky-Doshchinsky** (15 Nov 1840 - ?)

25 Sep 1885 - 1896:	Subsection Chief, Main Intendant Directorate
30 Aug 1891:	Promoted to *Major-General*

General of Cavalry Viktor-Karl-Konrad-Vilhelm Vilgelmovich von **Val** (17 Jul 1840 - 7 Feb 1915)

4 Jun 1878 - 27 Feb 1879:	Governor of Grodno
9 Jan 1879:	Promoted to *Major-General*
27 Feb 1879 - 20 Apr 1880:	Governor of Kharkov
20 Apr 1880 - 24 Jul 1884:	Governor of Vitebsk
24 Jul 1884 - 5 Jun 1885:	Governor of Podolsky
5 Jun 1885 - 25 Feb 1889:	Governor of Volyn
25 Feb 1889 - 4 May 1892:	Governor of Kursk
4 May 1892 - 6 Dec 1895:	Mayor of St. Petersburg
30 Aug 1893:	Promoted to *Lieutenant-General*
6 Dec 1895 - 2 Oct 1901:	Honorary Trustee, Board of Trustees of His Imperial Majesty's Chancellery
2 Oct 1901 - 15 Sep 1902:	Governor of Vilnius
15 Sep 1902 - 10 Jan 1904:	Deputy Minister of the Interior, Commanding General, Corps of Gendarmerie
31 Dec 1903 - 7 Feb 1915:	Member of the State Council
28 Mar 1904:	Promoted to *General of Cavalry*

Lieutenant-General Ivan Ivanovich **Valberg** (4 Oct 1859 - 21 Sep 1918)
24 Nov 1908:	Promoted to *Major-General*
24 Nov 1908 - 2 Apr 1910:	Commander, 2nd Brigade, 41st Infantry Division
2 Apr 1910 - 26 Jan 1914:	Commander, 1st Brigade, 37th Infantry Division
26 Jan 1914 - 1 Oct 1917:	Commandant of Pavlovsk Military School
6 Dec 1914:	Promoted to *Lieutenant-General*
1 Oct 1917 - 25 Oct 1917:	Unassigned
25 Oct 1917 - 20 Feb 1918:	Attached to Main Directorate for Military Schools
20 Feb 1918:	Dismissed

Lieutenant-General Stepan Prokofievich **Valevachev** (13 Dec 1842 - 1913)
12 Aug 1892 - 13 May 1899:	Commandant, Artillery Officer School
30 Aug 1893:	Promoted to *Major-General*
13 May 1899 - 4 Jan 1900:	Commandant, Mikhailov Artillery School
4 Jan 1900 - 24 Sep 1903:	Commandant, Mikhailovsky Artillery Academy & Schools
1 Apr 1901:	Promoted to *Lieutenant-General*
24 Sep 1903 - 1 Sep 1905:	Member of the Artillery Committee, Main Artillery Administration
1 Sep 1905:	Retired

Lieutenant-General Mikhail Emerikovich **Valitsky** (27 Jul 1851 - 17 Oct 1910)
26 Oct 1892 - 10 Mar 1899:	Commandant, Main Artillery Polygon
6 Dec 1898:	Promoted to *Major-General*
10 Mar 1899 - 30 Mar 1902:	Commandant, Caucasus Siege Artillery Park
30 Mar 1902 - 1 Apr 1905:	Commander, Caucasus Siege Artillery Regiment
1 Apr 1905 - Jul 1910:	Commander of Artillery, I. Caucasus Army Corps
6 Dec 1906:	Promoted to *Lieutenant-General*
Jul 1910 - 17 Oct 1910:	Commander, 6th Infantry Division

Vice-Admiral Stepan Stanislavovich **Valitsky** (? - ?)
1888:	Promoted to *Rear-Admiral*
?:	Member, Naval Technical Committee
? - 1895:	Senior Flagman, Baltic Fleet
30 Dec 1895:	Promoted to *Vice-Admiral*

Rear-Admiral Konstantin Rostislavovich **Valrond** (20 Jul 1843 - 31 Dec 1899)
24 Jun 1896 - 31 Dec 1899:	Commandant, Port of Sevastopol
6 Nov 1895:	Promoted to *Rear-Admiral*

Major-General Leonid Vladimirovich **Valter** (29 Jul 1872 - ?)
19 Dec 1913 - 1917:	Deputy Director of Artillery Acceptance
22 Mar 1915:	Promoted to *Major-General*

Major-General Mechislav Konstantinovich **Valter** (22 Aug 1854 - 23 Feb 1907)
23 Feb 1903 - 23 Feb 1907:	Commander, 262nd Reserve Infantry Regiment
1906:	Promoted to *Major-General*

Lieutenant-General Rihard-Kirill Frantsevich **Valter** (15 Oct 1870 - Jan 1945)
11 Mar 1911 - 18 Jan 1915:	Military Attaché, China
14 Apr 1913:	Promoted to *Major-General*
18 Jan 1915 - 11 Oct 1915:	Commander, Brigade, 7th Infantry Division
11 Oct 1915 - 29 May 1916:	Chief of Staff, V. Army Corps
29 May 1916 - 18 Apr 1917:	Commander, 7th Infantry Division
21 Oct 1916:	Promoted to *Lieutenant-General*
18 Apr 1917 - 31 Aug 1917:	Chief of Staff, Special Army
31 Aug 1917 - 10 Sep 1917:	Commanding General, XLII. Army Corps
10 Sep 1917 - 7 Dec 1917:	Chief of Staff, Western Front

Major-General Vilyam Frantsevich **Valter** (17 Jul 1867 - ?)
29 Aug 1913 - 31 Oct 1915:	Chief of Construction, Fortress Kronstadt
31 Oct 1915 - 1917:	Commander of Engineers, Fortress Sveaborg
6 Dec 1915:	Promoted to *Major-General*

Lieutenant-General Arkady Mikhailovich **Valuev** (1 Feb 1861 - 1935)
20 Apr 1906 - 21 Aug 1909:	Military Governor of Sakhalin Island
1906:	Promoted to *Major-General*
21 Aug 1909 - 20 Oct 1910:	Governor of Sakhalin Region
20 Oct 1910 - 9 Aug 1913:	Military Governor of Amur Region, Ataman, Amur Cossack Army
9 Aug 1913:	Promoted to *Lieutenant-General*
9 Aug 1913:	Retired
20 Jun 1915 - 14 Sep 1915:	Recalled; Deputy Commanding General, Petrograd Military District, Acting Governor-General of Arkhangelsk
14 Sep 1915 - 22 Oct 1915:	Reserve officer, Petrograd Military District
22 Oct 1915 - 13 Jul 1916:	Inspector of Reserves, Northern Front
13 Jul 1916 - 21 Jan 1917:	Inspector of Reserves & Militias, Northern Front
12 Jan 1917 - 29 Apr 1917:	Commander, Brigade, 44th Infantry Division
29 Apr 1917 - 19 Aug 1917:	Commander, 116th Infantry Division
19 Aug 1917 - 9 Sep 1917:	Reserve officer, Dvinsk Military District
9 Sep 1917:	Retired

Lieutenant-General of the Admiralty Mikhail Ippolitovich **Van-Der-Shkruf** (7 Nov 1853 - ?)
6 Dec 1906:	Promoted to *Major-General of the Admiralty*
6 Dec 1906 - Jul 1911:	Inspector of Machinery, Baltic Fleet
1 Oct 1908 - Jul 1911:	Commander, 1st Baltic Naval Depot
18 Apr 1910:	Promoted to *Lieutenant-General of the Admiralty*

Major-General Semyon Nikolayevich **Vankov** (25 Jan 1858 - 21 Jun 1937)
27 Dec 1897 - 31 Dec 1913:	Commandant of Khabarovsk Arsenal
6 Dec 1911:	Promoted to *Major-General*
31 Dec 1913 - Apr 1915:	Commandant of Bryansk Arsenal
Apr 1915 - Apr 1918:	Commissioner for Shell Production, Main Artillery

Directorate

Lieutenant-General Boris Petrovich **Vannovsky** (26 Oct 1860 - ?)
15 Oct 1900 - 15 Feb 1904:	At the disposal of the Chief of the General Staff
6 Apr 1903:	Promoted to *Major-General*
15 Feb 1904 - 19 Nov 1904:	General for Special Assignments, C-in-C, Far East
19 Nov 1904 - 22 Dec 1905:	At the disposal of the Chief of the General Staff
22 Dec 1905 - 6 Mar 1906:	At the disposal of the Commanding General, St. Petersburg Military District
6 Mar 1906 - 1 May 1910:	General for Special Assignments, Commanding General, St. Petersburg Military District
1 May 1910:	Promoted to *Lieutenant-General*
1 May 1910 - 19 Jun 1912:	Commander, 4th Cavalry Division
19 Jun 1912:	Retired
15 Oct 1914 - 18 Apr 1917:	Recalled; Commander, 4th Cavalry Division
8 Sep 1917:	Retired

Lieutenant-General Gleb Mikhailovich **Vannovsky** (5 Mar 1862 - 17 Oct 1943)
12 Apr 1908:	Promoted to *Major-General*
12 Apr 1908 - 4 Aug 1908:	Commander, 1st Brigade, 2nd Cavalry Division
4 Aug 1908 - 19 Jul 1914:	Commander, 2nd Brigade, 13th Cavalry Division
19 Jul 1914 - 18 Apr 1917:	Commander, 5th Don Cossack Division
30 Jan 1915:	Promoted to *Lieutenant-General*
18 Apr 1917 - 7 Jul 1917:	Commanding General, XXXV. Army Corps
7 Jul 1917 - 26 Jul 1917:	Reserve officer, Minsk Military District
26 Jul 1917 - 31 Jul 1917:	Commanding General, XLII. Army Corps
31 Jul 1917 - 9 Sep 1917:	C-in-C, 1st Army

General of Infantry Pyotr Semyonovich **Vannovsky** (24 Nov 1822 - 16 Feb 1904)
18 Nov 1857 - 31 Oct 1861:	Commandant of the Infantry Officers School
30 Aug 1861:	Promoted to *Major-General*
31 Oct 1861 - 26 Sep 1863:	Director of Pavlovsky Cadet Corps
26 Sep 1863 - 13 Jul 1868:	Commandant of Pavlovsky Military College
13 Jul 1868 - 16 Oct 1868:	General for Special Assignments, Directorate-General for Military Schools
26 Oct 1868:	Promoted to *Lieutenant-General*
26 Oct 1868 - 31 Aug 1871:	Commander, 12th Infantry Division
31 Aug 1871 - 1 Nov 1876:	Commander, 33rd Infantry Division
1 Nov 1876 - 27 Jun 1877:	Commanding-General, XII. Army Corps
27 Jun 1877 - 24 Feb 1878:	Chief of Staff, Ruschuksk Detachment
24 Feb 1878 - 1 Aug 1879:	Commander, Eastern Detachment
26 Feb 1878:	Promoted to *General-Adjutant*
1 Aug 1879 - 22 May 1881:	Commanding-General, XII. Army Corps
22 May 1881 - 1 Jan 1882:	Deputy Minister of War
1 Jan 1882 - 1 Jan 1898:	Minister of War
15 May 1883:	Promoted to *General of Infantry*
1 Jan 1898 - 24 Mar 1901:	Member of the State Council
24 Mar 1901 - 11 Apr 1902:	Minister of Education

11 Apr 1902:   Retired

Lieutenant-General Sergey Petrovich **Vannovsky** (29 Jan 1869 - 10 Aug 1914)
12 May 1907 - 4 Sep 1910:   Commander, 20th Dragoon Regiment
4 Sep 1910:   Promoted to *Major-General*
4 Sep 1910 - 18 Jul 1914:   Deputy Chief of Staff, Don Cossack Army
18 Jul 1914 - 10 Aug 1914:   Commander, 3rd Independent Cavalry Brigade
11 May 1916:   Posthumously promoted to *Lieutenant-General*

Major-General Dmitry Nikolayevich **Vansovich** (10 Jun 1839 - ?)
7 May 1890:   Promoted to *Major-General*
7 May 1890 - 7 Feb 1901:   Commander, 2nd Brigade, 31st Infantry Division

Major-General Nikolai Afanasievich **Vansovich** (28 Oct 1862 - ?)
15 Mar 1916 - 1917:   Commander, Brigade, 70th Infantry Division
6 Dec 1916:   Promoted to *Major-General*

Major-General Nikolai Yevgenievich **Varaksin** (12 Nov 1862 - 28 Oct 1937)
2 Feb 1914 - 1916:   Deputy Chief of Billeting, Moscow Military District
6 Apr 1914:   Promoted to *Major-General*
1916 - 1917:   Deputy Chief of Billeting, Amur Military District

Major-General Pavel Aleksandrovich **Vargasov** (1 Jan 1862 - 25 Jun 1916)
1913 - 12 Oct 1916:   Attached to 11th Grenadier Regiment
12 Oct 1916:   Posthumously promoted to *Major-General*

Major-General Semyon Nikolayevich **Varlamov** (26 Apr 1845 - 1903)
4 Feb 1893 - 24 Feb 1895:   Commander, Life Guards Cossack Regiment
30 Aug 1893:   Promoted to *Major-General*
24 Feb 1895 - 1903:   Attached to the Don Cossack Army

Lieutenant-General of the Fleet Aleksandr Ivanovich **Varnek** (13 Jun 1858 - 10 Jun 1930)
31 Oct 1908 - 30 Sep 1912:   Member, Imperial Alexander Lyceum
29 Mar 1909:   Promoted to *Major-General of the Admiralty*
30 Sep 1912 - 24 Dec 1912:   Member, Naval Academy & Training Council of the
                                     Hydrographic Department
24 Dec 1912:   Promoted to *Lieutenant-General of the Admiralty*
24 Dec 1912:   Retired
1914 - 1916:   Recalled; Attached to the Central Office, Ministry of the
                                     Navy

Lieutenant-General Artemy Solomonovich **Vartanov** (15 Feb 1855 - 25 Oct 1937)
12 May 1907 - 3 Oct 1908:   Commander, 16th Artillery Brigade
31 May 1907:   Promoted to *Major-General*
3 Oct 1908 - 18 Feb 1912:   Commander, 27th Artillery Brigade
18 Feb 1912 - 16 Apr 1916:   Inspector of Artillery, XIV. Army Corps
31 May 1913:   Promoted to *Lieutenant-General*
16 Apr 1916 - 1917:   Inspector of Artillery, 1st Army

General of Cavalry Prince Sergei Illarionovich **Vasilchikov** (5 Aug 1849 - 27 Aug 1926)
10 Nov 1890:	Promoted to *Major-General*
10 Nov 1890 - 16 Aug 1896:	Commander, Life Guards Hussar Regiment
16 Aug 1896 - 17 Dec 1898:	Commander, 2nd Brigade, 2nd Guards Cavalry Division
17 Dec 1898 - 13 Jan 1899:	Commander, 12th Cavalry Division
13 Jan 1899 - 23 Dec 1901:	Commander, 1st Cavalry Division
6 Dec 1899:	Promoted to *Lieutenant-General*
23 Dec 1901 - 2 Nov 1902:	At the disposal of the Commanding General, St. Petersburg Military District
1902:	Promoted to *General-Adjutant*
2 Nov 1902 - 21 Jun 1906:	Commanding General, Guards Corps
21 Jun 1906 - Mar 1917:	Attached to the Imperial Court
18 Apr 1910:	Promoted to *General of Cavalry*

General of Cavalry Vasily Nikolayevich **Vasilchikov** (4 Oct 1840 - ?)
1 Apr 1892 - 28 Feb 1896:	Commander, 1st Labinsk Horse Regiment
28 Feb 1896:	Promoted to *Major-General*
28 Feb 1896 - 31 Oct 1900:	Commander, 2nd Brigade, 2nd Caucasus Cossack Division
31 Oct 1900 - 16 Nov 1904:	At the disposal of Grand Duke Mikhail Nikolayevich
16 Nov 1904 - 27 Nov 1905:	At the disposal of the C-in-C, 2nd Manchurian Army
27 Nov 1905 - 26 Aug 1911:	At the disposal of Grand Duke Mikhail Nikolayevich
6 Dec 1909:	Promoted to *Lieutenant-General*
26 Aug 1911:	Promoted to *General of Cavalry*
26 Aug 1911:	Retired

Major-General Aleksandr Pavlovich **Vasilenko** (23 Jul 1854 - ?)
1 Aug 1910:	Promoted to *Major-General*
1 Aug 1910 - 27 Sep 1912:	Commander, 2nd Siberian Rifle Artillery Brigade
27 Sep 1912:	Retired

Rear-Admiral Dmitry Nikolayevich **Vasilevsky** (4 Nov 1874 - 22 Aug 1947)
? - 1915:	Commander, Submarine Division, Baltic Fleet
1915:	Promoted to *Rear-Admiral*
1915:	Retired
Oct 1917:	Minister of the Navy, Provisional Government

Lieutenant-General Nikolai Aleksandrovich **Vasilevsky** (19 Feb 1852 - 6 Aug 1914)
11 Sep 1898:	Promoted to *Major-General*
11 Sep 1898 - 31 Jul 1900:	Special Assignments General, Amur Military District
31 Jul 1900 - 8 May 1901:	Chief of Staff, I. Siberian Army Corps
8 May 1901 - 24 Oct 1901:	At the disposal of the Commanding General, Warsaw Military District
24 Oct 1901 - 12 Feb 1904:	Commander, Warsaw Local Brigade
12 Feb 1904 - 25 Mar 1905:	At the disposal of the C-in-C, Far East
25 Mar 1905 - 16 May 1905:	Commander, East Siberian Replacement Battalion
16 May 1905 - 1906:	Chief of Sanatory Service, 3rd Manchurian Army
1906 - 7 Dec 1906:	At the disposal of the Commanding General, Warsaw

	Military District
7 Dec 1906:	Promoted to *Lieutenant-General*
7 Dec 1906:	Retired

Major-General Vladimir Andreyevich **Vasilevsky** (10 Jul 1862 - ?)
2 Oct 1909 - 15 Jan 1914:	Commander, 1st Railway Regiment
6 May 1913:	Promoted to *Major-General*
15 Jan 1914 - 1917:	Commander, Transcaucasus Railway

Major-General Aleksey Pavlovich **Vasiliev** (15 Jan 1867 - ?)
13 Apr 1910 - 1917:	Member of the Military Council, Irkutsk Military District
6 Dec 1916:	Promoted to *Major-General*

General of Infantry Fyodor Nikolayevich **Vasiliev** (5 Feb 1858 - 19 Nov 1923)
4 Apr 1902 - 31 Oct 1906:	Chief of Asian Section, General Staff
14 Apr 1902:	Promoted to *Major-General*
31 Oct 1906 - 24 Mar 1908:	Commander, 1st Rifle Brigade
24 Mar 1908 - 19 Jul 1914:	Chief of Staff, Odessa Military District
13 Apr 1908:	Promoted to *Lieutenant-General*
19 Jul 1914 - 26 Sep 1914:	Chief of Staff, 7th Army
26 Sep 1914 - 9 Sep 1917:	Commanding General, VI. Siberian Army Corps
22 Mar 1915:	Promoted to *General of Infantry*
9 Sep 1917:	Retired

Major-General Ivan Andreyevich **Vasiliev** (1 May 1860 - 9 Apr 1933)
1913 - 20 Feb 1917:	Commander, 7th Don Cossack Regiment
22 Sep 1916:	Promoted to *Major-General*
20 Feb 1917 - 14 Jun 1917:	Commander, 2nd Brigade, 2nd Turkestan Cossack Division
14 Jun 1917 - Nov 1917:	At the disposal of the High Command
Nov 1917 - 1918:	Commander, 6th Don Cossack Division

Major-General Ivan Fedorovich **Vasiliev** (3 Jan 1863 - May 1915)
1914 - May 1915:	Commander, 79th Infantry Regiment
17 Oct 1915:	Posthumously promoted to *Major-General*

Rear-Admiral Ivan Grigoryevich **Vasiliev** (23 Jan 1858 - 15 Feb 1918)
1910 - 31 Dec 1912:	Commander of Destroyers, Black Sea Fleet
31 Dec 1912:	Promoted to *Rear-Admiral*
31 Dec 1912:	Retired

Major-General Ivan Lvovich **Vasiliev** (12 Aug 1867 - 1914)
13 Apr 1913:	Promoted to *Major-General*
13 Apr 1913 - 1914:	Chief of Communications, Warsaw Military District

Lieutenant-General Konstantin Grigorievich **Vasiliev** (20 Apr 1847 - ?)
31 Dec 1900 - 30 Oct 1903:	At the disposal of the Commanding General, Amur

	Military District
25 Sep 1901:	Promoted to *Major-General*
30 Oct 1903 - 9 Mar 1905:	Commander, 2nd Brigade, 31st Infantry Division
9 Mar 1905 - Jun 1907:	Commander, 31st Infantry Division
13 May 1905:	Promoted to *Lieutenant-General*

Major-General Leonid Pavlovich **Vasiliev** (9 Apr 1856 - ?)
1 Feb 1897 - Feb 1917:	Master of the Household, Tsar's country palaces
18 Apr 1910:	Promoted to *Major-General*

Major-General Mikhail Nikolayevich **Vasiliev** (1 Jan 1872 - Dec 1941)
3 May 1915 - 15 Oct 1915:	Commander, 45th Siberian Rifle Regiment
15 Oct 1915:	Promoted to *Major-General*
15 Oct 1915 - 3 Feb 1916:	Commander, 1st Brigade, 12th Siberian Rifle Division
3 Feb 1916 - 1917:	Chief of Staff, XXXVII. Army Corps

Major-General Nikita Vasilievich **Vasiliev** (12 Sep 1855 - ?)
6 Dec 1905:	Promoted to *Major-General*
31 Dec 1905 - 1908:	Commander of Gendarmerie, Pskov Province

General of Artillery Nikolai Aleksandrovich **Vasiliev** (28 Nov 1842 - ?)
3 Mar 1891:	Promoted to *Major-General*
3 Mar 1891 - 14 Aug 1896:	Commander of Artillery, Transcaucasus Region
14 Aug 1896 - 24 Oct 1899:	Commander of Artillery, Amur Military District
24 Oct 1899 - 25 Feb 1905:	Deputy Chief, Main Artillery Directorate
6 Dec 1899:	Promoted to *Lieutenant-General*
25 Feb 1905 - 1 Jan 1911:	Member of the Military Council
27 May 1906 - 11 Apr 1907:	Commandant of Fortress Libau
6 Dec 1907:	Promoted to *General of Artillery*
1 Jan 1911:	Retired

Major-General Nikolai Petrovich **Vasiliev** (22 Mar 1865 - ?)
16 Nov 1913 - 30 May 1915:	Military Judge, Amur Military District Court
6 Dec 1913:	Promoted to *Major-General*
30 May 1915 - 8 Oct 1915:	Military Judge, Minsk Military District Court
8 Oct 1915 - 1917:	Chief of the Legal Section, Northern Front

Lieutenant-General Nikolai Vasilievich **Vasiliev** (30 Nov 1851 - ?)
12 Jun 1901 - 13 Jan 1906:	At the disposal of the Commanding General, Corps of Gendarmerie
28 Mar 1904:	Promoted to *Major-General*
13 Jan 1906 - 1909:	Commander of Gendarmerie, Poltava Province
1909:	Promoted to *Lieutenant-General*
1909:	Retired

Major-General of the Fleet Pyotr Ivanovich **Vasiliev** (26 Sep 1841 - 1914)
1890 - 30 Jan 1906:	Director of Lighthouses & Navigation, White Sea
1903:	Promoted to *Major-General of the Fleet*

30 Jan 1906:   Retired

Major-General Pyotr Konstantinovich **Vasiliev** (26 Jul 1851 - ?)
23 Jun 1896 - 9 Jun 1898:   Commander, 39th Infantry Regiment
9 Jun 1898:   Promoted to *Major-General*
9 Jun 1898 - 19 Jul 1900:   Special Assignments General, Caucasus Military District
19 Jul 1900 - 15 Mar 1906:   Commander, 65th Reserve Infantry Brigade
15 Mar 1906 - 1906:   Attached to the General Staff

Major-General Sergey Sergeyevich **Vasiliev** (2 May 1852 - ?)
21 Jul 1907:   Promoted to *Major-General*
21 Jul 1907 - 26 Jul 1910:   Commander, 7th East Siberian Rifle Artillery Brigade

Major-General Viktor Nikolayevich **Vasiliev** (10 Mar 1872 - 29 Aug 1917)
7 May 1915 - 8 Jul 1915:   Chief of Staff, X. Militia Corps
8 Jul 1915:   Promoted to *Major-General*
8 Jul 1915 - Jan 1917:   Chief of Staff, XLII. Army Corps
Jan 1917 - 29 Aug 1917:   Quartermaster-General, XLII. Army Corps

Lieutenant-General Vladimir Mikhailovich **Vasiliev** (17 Apr 1859 - 14 Dec 1922)
3 Aug 1900 - 21 Jul 1905:   Commander, 219th Infantry Regiment
29 Sep 1904:   Promoted to *Major-General*
21 Jul 1905 - 17 Aug 1906:   Commander, 2nd Brigade, 72nd Infantry Division
17 Aug 1906 - 28 Dec 1910:   Commander, 1st Brigade, 31st Infantry Division
28 Dec 1910 - 27 Sep 1914:   Commander, 1st Rifle Brigade
27 Sep 1914:   Promoted to *Lieutenant-General*
27 Sep 1914 - 15 Apr 1917:   Commander, 2nd Infantry Division
15 Apr 1917 - 7 May 1917:   Reserve officer, Odessa Military District
7 May 1917 - Oct 1917:   Reserve officer, Moscow Military District

Major-General Vladimir Nikolayevich **Vasiliev** (20 Jul 1853 - 29 May 1909)
17 Apr 1905:   Promoted to *Major-General*
17 Apr 1905 - Jul 1908:   Commander of Engineers, Fortress Brest-Litovsk
Jul 1908 - 1908:   Deputy Commander, Izhevsk Armory
1908:   Retired

Major-General Yevgeny Vladimirovich **Vasiliev** (4 Aug 1859 - ?)
30 May 1911 - 8 Dec 1914:   Deputy Intendant, Irkutsk Military District
6 Dec 1911:   Promoted to *Major-General*
8 Dec 1914:   Retired

Lieutenant-General Anton Stepanovich **Vasilkovsky** (6 Jun 1824 - 1 Sep 1895)
1 Jan 1878:   Promoted to *Major-General*
1 Jan 1878 - 21 Jan 1882:   Attached to the Tsar
21 Jan 1882 - 31 Jan 1883:   Deputy Court Marshal to the Tsar
31 Jan 1883 - 1 Sep 1895:   Chief of Administration of the Tsar's Court
30 Aug 1888:   Promoted to *Lieutenant-General*

Vice-Admiral Stanislav Frantsevich **Vasilkovsky** (27 Jul 1860 - 10 Feb 1918)
6 Dec 1911:	Promoted to *Rear-Admiral*
6 Dec 1911 - 24 Mar 1917:	Captain, Port of Sevastopol
30 Jul 1916:	Promoted to *Vice-Admiral*
24 Mar 1917 - 10 Feb 1918:	Naval Commander, Port of Sevastopol

Major-General Pyotr Nikolayevich **Vaskovsky** (29 Apr 1863 - ?)
1914 - 17 Jun 1916:	Deputy Chief, Lugansk Cartridge Factory
17 Jun 1916:	Promoted to *Major-General*
17 Jun 1916:	Retired

Lieutenant-General Georgy Robertovich **Vasmund** (25 Dec 1840 - 30 May 1904)
24 Oct 1877 - 12 Feb 1890:	Commander, 1st Life Guards Rifle Battalion
30 Aug 1886:	Promoted to *Major-General*
12 Feb 1890 - 30 Jan 1893:	Commander, Izmailovo Life Guards Regiment
17 Feb 1891 - 14 May 1893:	Commander, 2nd Brigade, 1st Guards Infantry Division
14 May 1893 - 29 Sep 1894:	Commander, 1st Brigade, 1st Guards Infantry Division
29 Sep 1894 - 7 Apr 1897:	Attached to the Commanding General, St. Petersburg Military District
15 Jul 1896:	Promoted to *Lieutenant-General*
7 Apr 1897 - 12 May 1898:	Commander, Guards Rifle Brigade
12 May 1898 - 24 Aug 1898:	Commander, 1st Guards Infantry Division
24 Aug 1898 - 30 May 1904:	Chief of Staff, St. Petersburg Military District

Lieutenant-General Vladimir Georgiyevich **Vasmund** (16 Jul 1872 - 13 Jan 1941)
26 Aug 1914 - 22 Jan 1915:	Commander, Life Guards 2nd Rifle Regiment
12 Dec 1914:	Promoted to *Major-General*
22 Jan 1915 - 5 Jan 1917:	First Chief Quartermaster, Main Directorate of the General Staff
5 Jan 1917:	Promoted to *Lieutenant-General*
5 Jan 1917:	Dismissed

Major-General Vladimir Ivanovich **Vasyanov** (22 Jul 1861 - ?)
11 Mar 1905 - 3 Oct 1907:	Commander, 40th Dragoon Regiment
3 Oct 1907:	Promoted to *Major-General*
3 Oct 1907 - 5 Nov 1908:	Commander, 2nd Brigade, 7th Cavalry Division

Lieutenant-General Leonid Konstantinovich **Vasyukinov** (11 Dec 1848 - ?)
29 Sep 1887 - 10 Jun 1911:	Artillery Inspector, Main Artillery Directorate
4 Dec 1904:	Promoted to *Major-General*
10 Jun 1911:	Promoted to *Lieutenant-General*
10 Jun 1911:	Retired

Major-General Vladimir Konstantinovich **Vasyukhnov** (19 Jun 1851 - ?)
22 Apr 1907 - 19 Jul 1911:	Commander, 17th Artillery Brigade
31 May 1907:	Promoted to *Major-General*
19 Jul 1911:	Retired

Lieutenant-General Aleksandr Aleksandrovich **Vatatsi** (16 Nov 1852 - 16 Sep 1933)
17 Feb 1903:	Promoted to *Major-General*
17 Feb 1903 - 8 Oct 1905:	Governor of St. Michelsky
8 Oct 1905 - 2 Nov 1905:	Governor of Kiev
2 Nov 1905 - 1906:	Governor of Kostroma
1906:	Promoted to *Lieutenant-General*
1906:	Retired

Lieutenant-General Vladimir Aleksandrovich **Vatatsi** (20 Apr 1860 - ?)
28 Mar 1912:	Promoted to *Major-General*
28 Mar 1912 - 12 May 1916:	Commander, 43rd Artillery Brigade
12 May 1916 - 22 Apr 1917:	Inspector of Artillery, XXX. Army Corps
28 Nov 1916:	Promoted to *Lieutenant-General*

Major-General Aleksandr Ivanovich **Vatropin** (23 Oct 1837 - ?)
6 Oct 1889 - 14 Mar 1894:	Commander, 3rd Infantry Regiment
26 Feb 1894:	Promoted to *Major-General*
14 Mar 1894 - 19 Jul 1895:	Commander, 2nd Brigade, 13th Infantry Division
19 Jul 1895 - 4 Jun 1899:	Commander, 1st Brigade, 22nd Infantry Division

Lieutenant-General Andrey Nikolayevich **Vaulin** (16 Oct 1860 - ?)
10 Jul 1900 - 1 Aug 1905:	Director of Khabarovsk Cadet Corps
28 Mar 1904:	Promoted to *Major-General*
1 Aug 1905 - 1 Aug 1908:	Director of Polotsk Cadet Corps
1 Aug 1908 - 1917:	Director, Suvorov Military School
18 Apr 1910:	Promoted to *Lieutenant-General*

Major-General Nikolai Nikolayevich **Vaulin** (24 Jul 1858 - ?)
8 Apr 1915 - 7 Nov 1916:	Commander, Warsaw Militia Brigade
26 Jul 1915:	Promoted to *Major-General*
7 Nov 1916 - 1917:	Reserve officer, Petrograd Military District

Major-General Vasily Grigoryevich **Vavilov** (6 Jan 1857 - 1915)
1 Apr 1911 - 1915:	Commander, 151st Infantry Regiment
28 May 1915:	Promoted to *Major-General*

General of Infantry Ferdinand Mavrikievich **Vebel** (24 Nov 1855 - 1919)
23 Feb 1904:	Promoted to *Major-General*
23 Feb 1904 - 11 Jun 1906:	Chief of Staff, IV. Siberian Army Corps
8 Mar 1905 - 20 Mar 1905:	Acting Quartermaster-General, 1st Manchurian Army
11 Jun 1906 - 28 Nov 1907:	Quartermaster-General of the General Staff
28 Nov 1907 - 20 Dec 1909:	Chief of Staff, Moscow Military District
13 Apr 1908:	Promoted to *Lieutenant-General*
20 Dec 1909 - 5 Dec 1914:	Commander, 13th Infantry Division
5 Dec 1914 - 27 Mar 1915:	Commanding General, XXX. Army Corps
27 Mar 1915 - 19 Apr 1915:	Reserve officer, Kiev Military District
19 Apr 1915:	Promoted to *General of Infantry*
19 Apr 1915 - 14 Feb 1916:	Commanding General, XXXIV. Army Corps

14 Feb 1916 - 16 Sep 1916:	Reserve officer, Minsk Military District
16 Sep 1916 - 1917:	Reserve officer, Petrograd Military District

Major-General Pyotr Nikandrovich **Vedenin** (12 Jan 1861 - 11 Jan 1920)
16 Jan 1911 - 1917:	Ataman, 3rd Military Division, Siberian Cossack Army
6 Dec 1913:	Promoted to *Major-General*

Major-General Vasily Stepanovich **Vedensky** (3 Dec 1851 - May 1911)
21 Sep 1907:	Promoted to *Major-General*
21 Sep 1907 - May 1911:	Commander, 6th East Siberian Rifle Artillery Brigade

General of Engineers Aleksandr Alekseyevich **Vedenyapin** (11 Aug 1845 - ?)
20 May 1895 - 13 Jan 1896:	Advisory Member of the Medical Council, Ministry of Internal Affairs
6 Dec 1895:	Promoted to *Major-General*
13 Jan 1896 - 28 Aug 1912:	Member of the Engineering Committee, Main Engineering Directorate
6 Dec 1902:	Promoted to *Lieutenant-General*
28 Aug 1912 - 21 Mar 1918:	Member of the Military Council
6 Dec 1912:	Promoted to *General of Engineers*
21 Mar 1918:	Retired

Major-General Orest Apollonovich **Vedenyapin** (12 Dec 1854 - ?)
18 Sep 1909 - 1911:	Commander, 4th Dragoon Regiment
1911:	Promoted to *Major-General*
1911:	Retired
26 Dec 1914 - 1917:	Recalled; General for Special Assignments, Main Directorate of Horse Breeding

Major-General Vladimir Georgiyevich **Vedenyayev** (15 Jul 1860 - 13 May 1915)
1 Mar 1913 - 4 May 1915:	Commander, 1st Battalion, 49th Artillery Brigade
May 1915:	Posthumously promoted to *Major-General*

Lieutenant-General of Naval Engineers Vladimir Petrovich **Vedernikov** (14 Jul 1859 - 13 Jan 1929)
1 Jan 1908 - 22 Nov 1911:	Chief Engineer, Port of St. Petersburg
6 Dec 1910:	Promoted to *Major-General of Naval Engineers*
22 Nov 1911 - 9 May 1917:	Chief of Mechanical Department, General Directorate of Shipbuilding
14 Apr 1913:	Promoted to *Lieutenant-General of Naval Engineers*
9 May 1917:	Dismissed

Lieutenant-General Avvakum Gerasimovich **Vekilov** (2 Dec 1846 - ?)
5 Aug 1902 - 12 Oct 1911:	Intendant, V. Army Corps
2 Apr 1906:	Promoted to *Major-General*
12 Oct 1911:	Promoted to *Lieutenant-General*
12 Oct 1911:	Retired

Lieutenant-General Nikolai Genrikhovich **Vekman** (22 May 1850 - 30 Sep 1906)
20 Dec 1892 - 8 Mar 1901:	Commander of Engineers, Fortress Ivangorod
6 Dec 1895:	Promoted to *Major-General*
8 Mar 1901 - 16 Jan 1906:	Deputy Commander of Engineers, Warsaw Military District
16 Jan 1906 - 30 Sep 1906:	Commander of Engineers, Vilnius Military District
2 Apr 1906:	Promoted to *Lieutenant-General*

Major-General Iosif Dmitriyevich **Velednitsky** (20 Mar 1858 - 9 Dec 1914)
6 Oct 1913 - 9 Dec 1914:	Commandant, Tiflis Railway Station
6 Dec 1914:	Promoted to *Major-General*

General of Infantry Filadelf Kirillovich **Velichko** (30 Aug 1833 - Oct 1898)
21 Mar 1866 - 13 May 1873:	Section Chief, General Staff
13 May 1873:	Promoted to *Major-General*
13 May 1873 - 7 Jul 1881:	Attached to the General Staff
7 Jul 1881 - 12 Mar 1894:	Deputy Chief of the General Staff
30 Aug 1882:	Promoted to *Lieutenant-General*
12 Mar 1894 - Oct 1898:	Member of the Military Council
14 May 1896:	Promoted to *General of Infantry*

General of Engineers Konstantin Ivanovich **Velichko** (20 May 1856 - 15 May 1927)
9 Jun 1891 - 6 Mar 1903:	Professor, Nikolai Academy of Engineering
6 Dec 1901:	Promoted to *Major-General*
6 Mar 1903 - 12 Feb 1904:	Deputy Chief of Main Engineering Directorate
12 Feb 1904 - 23 Feb 1904:	At the disposal of the C-in-C, Manchurian Army
23 Feb 1904 - 17 Dec 1904:	General for Special Assignments, Manchurian Army
17 Dec 1904 - 21 May 1905:	General for Special Assignments, Land & Naval Forces operating against Japan
21 May 1905 - 17 Nov 1910:	Deputy Chief of Main Engineering Directorate
6 Dec 1907:	Promoted to *Lieutenant-General*
17 Nov 1910 - Aug 1914:	Professor, Nikolai Academy of Engineering
Aug 1914 - Sep 1914:	Attached to the C-in-C, Southwestern Front
Sep 1914 - 4 Mar 1916:	Commander of Engineers, 11th Army
4 Mar 1916 - 10 May 1917:	Commander of Engineers, Southwestern Front
5 Nov 1916:	Promoted to *General of Engineers*
10 May 1917 - Feb 1918:	Inspector of Field Engineers, Supreme HQ

Major-General Ivan Ivanovich **Velikopolsky** (29 Aug 1835 - ?)
9 Feb 1897:	Promoted to *Major-General*
9 Feb 1897 - 29 Dec 1899:	Commander, 39th Artillery Brigade

Major-General Leonty Nikolayevich **Velikopolsky** (30 Jul 1866 - ?)
1 Nov 1911 - 25 Aug 1915:	Commander, 2nd Courland Uhlan Regiment
25 Aug 1915 - 19 Apr 1917:	Commander, 1st Brigade, 1st Cavalry Division
21 Jan 1916:	Promoted to *Major-General*
19 Apr 1917 - 1917:	Commander, 5th Cavalry Division

Major-General Baron Vladimir Ivanovich **Velio** (18 Feb 1877 - 4 Jan 1961)
3 Jul 1915 - 1917:	Commander, 1st Battalion, Guards Horse Artillery Brigade
1916:	Promoted to *Major-General*
1917:	Commander, Guards Horse Artillery Brigade

Lieutenant-General Andrey Karlovich **Velk** (9 Mar 1856 - ?)
20 Jul 1906 - 1913:	Chief of Gendarmerie, Tobolsk
6 Dec 1909:	Promoted to *Major-General*
1913:	Promoted to *Lieutenant-General*

Major-General Pyotr Yerofeyevich **Velyaminov** (30 Oct 1866 - 1 Jan 1914)
18 Jan 1913 - 1 Jan 1914:	Military Judge, St. Petersburg Military District Court
21 Jan 1914:	Posthumously promoted to *Major-General*

Lieutenant-General Mitrofan Alekseyevich **Velyaminov-Zernov** (16 Mar 1839 - 15 Oct 1903)
25 Jul 1879 - 12 Jul 1882:	Special Purposes General to the Ataman, Don Cossacks
30 Aug 1879:	Promoted to *Major-General*
12 Jul 1882 - 3 Dec 1894:	Commander, 1st Brigade, 14th Cavalry Division
3 Dec 1894 - 28 Nov 1901:	Commander, 3rd Reserve Cavalry Brigade
14 May 1896:	Promoted to *Lieutenant-General*
28 Nov 1901 - 15 Oct 1903:	Commander, 2nd Reserve Cavalry Brigade

Major-General Aleksandr Feliksovich **Velyamovich** (21 Aug 1844 - ?)
29 Dec 1899 - 13 Nov 1903:	Commander, 26th Artillery Brigade
1 Jan 1900:	Promoted to *Major-General*
13 Nov 1903 - 1906:	Commander of Artillery, II. Siberian Army Corps

General of Cavalry Leonid Nikolayevich **Velyashev** (7 Jul 1856 - 1 Apr 1940)
4 Jun 1901 - 1 Dec 1907:	Commander, 33rd Dragoon Regiment
1 Dec 1907:	Promoted to *Major-General*
1 Dec 1907 - 7 May 1910:	Commander, 2nd Brigade, 11th Cavalry Division
7 May 1910 - 23 Mar 1914:	Commander, 1st Brigade, 11th Cavalry Division
23 Mar 1914:	Promoted to *Lieutenant-General*
23 Mar 1914:	Retired
26 Sep 1914 - 22 Oct 1914:	Recalled; Reserve officer, Kiev Military District
22 Oct 1914 - 3 Nov 1915:	Commander, 11th Cavalry Division
3 Nov 1915 - Oct 1917:	Commanding General, V. Cavalry Corps
1917:	Promoted to *General of Cavalry*

Lieutenant-General Oskar Ignatyevich **Vendorf** (14 Jun 1849 - 7 Dec 1929)
6 Dec 1895 - 26 Jan 1904:	Chief of Police, St. Petersburg
6 Dec 1903:	Promoted to *Major-General*
26 Jan 1904 - Feb 1917:	Deputy Mayor of St. Petersburg
6 May 1911:	Promoted to *Lieutenant-General*

Lieutenant-General Alfred Alfredovich von **Vendrikh** (28 Oct 1845 - ?)
7 Mar 1893 - 1 Jan 1907:	Member of the Engineering Council, Ministry of Railways
14 May 1896:	Promoted to *Major-General*
6 Dec 1905:	Promoted to *Lieutenant-General*
1 Jan 1907 - 28 Jun 1907:	Chief of Railway Directorate, Ministry of Railways
28 Jun 1907 - 8 Oct 1908:	Deputy Minister of Railways
8 Oct 1908 - 1917:	Member of the State Council

General of Infantry Fyodor Khristianovich von **Vendt** (3 Jun 1857 - ?)
15 Dec 1904:	Promoted to *Major-General*
15 Dec 1904 - 15 Dec 1908:	Chief of Communications, Vilnius Military District
15 Dec 1908:	Promoted to *Lieutenant-General*
15 Dec 1908 - 27 Mar 1911:	Chief of Staff, Irkutsk Military District
27 Mar 1911 - 9 Jan 1915:	Commander, 32nd Infantry Division
9 Jan 1915 - 15 Jan 1915:	Reserve officer, Kiev Military District
15 Jan 1915:	Promoted to *General of Infantry*
15 Jan 1915:	Retired

General of Cavalry Stepan Alexandrovich **Venerovsky** (20 Dec 1828 - ?)
28 Sep 1872 - 30 Aug 1887:	Ataman, Temryuk Military Division, Kuban Cossack Army
26 Feb 1880:	Promoted to *Major-General*
30 Aug 1897 - 1 Jul 1888:	Ataman, Uman Military Division, Kuban Cossack Army
1 Jul 1888 - 1899:	Attached to the Caucasus Military District
17 May 1890:	Promoted to *Lieutenant-General*
1899:	Promoted to *General of Cavalry*
1899:	Retired

Major-General Grigory Ivanovich **Venevitinov** (8 Jan 1863 - ?)
1914 - 4 May 1915:	Commander, Infantry Regiment
1 Feb 1915:	Promoted to *Major-General*
4 May 1915 - 7 Aug 1915:	Commander, Brigade, 63rd Infantry Division
7 Aug 1915 - 1918:	POW

Major-General Anatoly Vasilievich **Venyukov** (5 Feb 1848 - 1918)
11 Aug 1900 - 2 Mar 1904:	Commander, 6th Artillery Brigade
6 Dec 1901:	Promoted to *Major-General*

Lieutenant-General Fyodor Semonovich **Verba** (25 Dec 1849 - ?)
1 Nov 1900:	Promoted to *Major-General*
1 Nov 1900 - 14 Apr 1901:	Commander, 2nd Brigade, 12th Cavalry Division
14 Apr 1901 - 18 Feb 1910:	Commander, 2nd Brigade, 3rd Cavalry Division
18 Feb 1910:	Promoted to *Lieutenant-General*
18 Feb 1910 - 25 Feb 1912:	Commander, 8th Cavalry Division

Lieutenant-General Pyotr Ivanovich **Verbitsky** (29 Jul 1863 - ?)
4 Aug 1909 - 23 Mar 1911:	Special Assignments General, Inspectorate-General of

	Engineers
6 Dec 1910:	Promoted to *Major-General*
23 Mar 1911 - 29 Nov 1912:	Inspector of Field Engineers, Kiev Military District
29 Nov 1912 - 1 Aug 1914:	Inspector of Engineers, Kiev Military District
1 Aug 1914 - 1917:	Chief of Engineering Logistics, Southwestern Front
6 Dec 1916:	Promoted to *Lieutenant-General*

Major-General of the Admiralty Pyotr Nikolayevich **Verbitsky** (16 Dec 1854 - 1917)
16 Jan 1899 - 1912:	Editor, "*Naval Digest*"
6 May 1908:	Promoted to *Major-General of the Admiralty*

Rear-Admiral Dmitry Nikolayevich **Verderevsky** (4 Nov 1873 - 22 Aug 1947)
10 Nov 1916 - Apr 1917:	Commander, Submarine Division, Baltic Fleet
6 Dec 1916:	Promoted to *Rear-Admiral*
Apr 1917 - May 1917:	Chief of Staff, Baltic Fleet
May 1917 - 5 Jul 1917:	C-in-C, Baltic Fleet
5 Jul 1917 - 30 Aug 1917:	Unassigned
30 Aug 1917 - 11 Nov 1917:	Minister of the Navy
22 Nov 1917:	Dismissed

Lieutenant-General Aleksandr Vasilievich **Vereshchagin** (14 Mar 1855 - 15 Sep 1910)
26 Jan 1902 - 20 Aug 1905:	Duty General, Caucasus Military District
14 Apr 1902:	Promoted to *Major-General*
20 Aug 1905 - 16 Mar 1906:	Commander, 63rd Replacement Infantry Brigade
16 Mar 1906 - 2 Dec 1908:	Commander, 65th Replacement Infantry Brigade
2 Dec 1908:	Promoted to *Lieutenant-General*
2 Dec 1908 - 13 Feb 1909:	Commander, 32nd Infantry Division
13 Feb 1909 - 15 Sep 1910:	Commander, 65th Infantry Division

Major-General Yakov Nikolayevich **Vereshchagin** (17 Aug 1838 - ?)
26 Feb 1894:	Promoted to *Major-General*
26 Feb 1894 - 19 Jun 1899:	Commander, 1st Brigade, 40th Infantry Division

Major-General Aleksei Porfiryevich **Veretennikov** (19 Mar 1860 - 1934)
25 Aug 1906:	Promoted to *Major-General*
25 Aug 1906 - 15 Dec 1906:	Governor of Kiev
15 Dec 1906 - 14 Feb 1910:	Governor of Kostroma
14 Feb 1910 - 1910:	Attached to the Ministry of the Interior
1910:	Retired
5 Apr 1916 - 1917:	Recalled; Reserve officer, Kiev Military District

Major-General Aleksandr Vasilievich **Verevkin** (1849 - Mar 1912)
27 Jun 1911:	Promoted to *Major-General*
27 Jun 1911 - Mar 1912:	Commander, Orenburg Regional Brigade

Major-General Ivan Avenirovitch **Verevkin** (18 Jan 1859 - ?)
12 Sep 1914 - 1917:	Duty General, 2nd Army
6 Dec 1915:	Promoted to *Major-General*

Lieutenant-General Mikhail Nikolayevich **Verevkin** (9 Jun 1851 - ?)
19 Aug 1896 - 25 Jan 1902:	Commander, 30th Dragoon Regiment
25 Jan 1902:	Promoted to *Major-General*
25 Jan 1902 - 5 Jun 1902:	Commander, 2nd Brigade, 7th Cavalry Division
5 Jun 1902 - 21 Aug 1907:	Commander, 2nd Brigade, 9th Cavalry Division
21 Aug 1907:	Promoted to *Lieutenant-General*
21 Aug 1907 - 9 Sep 1908:	Commander, 10th Cavalry Division

Major-General Nikolai Vasilyevich **Verevkin** (18 Feb 1842 - ?)
19 Jan 1881 - 15 Dec 1887:	Ataman, 1st Military Division, Transbaikal Cossack Army
6 May 1886:	Promoted to *Major-General*
15 Dec 1887 - 6 Dec 1888:	Ataman, 2nd Military Division, Transbaikal Cossack Army
6 Dec 1888 - 14 Aug 1889:	Military Commander, Irkutsk Province
14 Aug 1889 - 3 Mar 1891:	Transferred to the reserve
3 Mar 1891 - 8 Dec 1894:	Commander, 1st Brigade, 3rd Infantry Division

General of Infantry Vladimir Nikolayevich **Verevkin** (14 Jul 1821 - 13 Jan 1896)
20 May 1863:	Promoted to *Major-General*
20 May 1863 - 27 Jul 1867:	Governor of Grazhdansky
27 Jul 1867 - 21 Jan 1868:	Unassigned
21 Jan 1868 - 10 Apr 1868:	Commander, 16th Infantry Division
10 Apr 1868 - 1 Nov 1876:	Regional Commander, Vilnius Military District
28 Mar 1871:	Promoted to *Lieutenant-General*
1 Nov 1876 - 16 Apr 1878:	Commander, 36th Infnatry Division
16 Apr 1878 - 11 Jul 1878:	Commanding General, IV. Army Corps
11 Jul 1878 - 16 Jul 1885:	Commanding General, XIV. Army Corps
16 Jul 1885 - 13 Jan 1896:	Member, Committee for Wounded Veterans
30 Aug 1886:	Promoted to *General of Infantry*
14 Apr 1887 - 13 Jan 1896:	Commandant of Fortress St. Petersburg

Major-General Pavel Konstantinovich **Vergolich** (29 Oct 1852 - ?)
26 Mar 1901 - 1908:	Commander of Gendarmerie, Sedletsk Province
6 Dec 1906:	Promoted to *Major-General*

Major-General Sergey Ivanovich **Verkhovsky** (16 Oct 1865 - 1919)
9 Feb 1913:	Promoted to *Major-General*
9 Feb 1913 - 1915:	Chief of Staff, I. Caucasus Army Corps
1915 - 4 Dec 1915:	Commander, 3rd Brigade, Caucasus Rifle Division
4 Dec 1915 - 15 May 1916:	Chief of Staff, 3rd Finland Rifle Division
15 May 1916 - 18 Feb 1917:	Chief of Staff, XXXIII. Army Corps
18 Feb 1917 - 24 Jan 1918:	Commander, 4th Border Infantry Division

Major-General Sergey Zakharovich **Verkhovsky** (29 Aug 1862 - 21 Jan 1936)
30 Jan 1909 - 1 Apr 1915:	Commander, 99th Infantry Regiment
31 Dec 1914:	Promoted to *Major-General*

1 Apr 1915 - Nov 1916:	Commander, 102nd State Militia Brigade
Nov 1916 - Jan 1918:	Commander of Defenses, Gulf of Riga
Jan 1918:	Retired

Lieutenant-General Vasily Parfenyevich **Verkhovsky** (26 Jul 1838 - 5 May 1901)
21 Aug 1873 - 10 Jul 1886:	Inspector of Classes, 2nd Konstantinovsky School
6 May 1884:	Promoted to *Major-General*
10 Jul 1886 - 24 Nov 1887:	Director, Imperial Gatchina Orphan Institute
24 Nov 1887 - 15 Jan 1900:	Director, 1st Cadet Corps
15 Jan 1900 - 5 May 1901:	Member of the Artillery Committee, Main Artillery Directorate
9 Apr 1900:	Promoted to *Lieutenant-General*

Admiral Vladimir Pavlovich **Verkhovsky** (28 Apr 1838 - 23 Jun 1917)
1887:	Promoted to *Rear-Admiral*
1887 - 1889:	Commander, Ship Detachment, Naval Academy
1889 - 28 May 1890:	Deputy Chief of the Naval General Staff
28 May 1890 - 13 Jul 1896:	Commander, Port of St. Petersburg
28 Mar 1893:	Promoted to *Vice-Admiral*
13 Jul 1896 - 14 Apr 1902:	Chief of the Main Directorate of Shipbuilding & Logistics
14 Apr 1902 - 1908:	Member of the Admiralty Board
1904:	Promoted to *Admiral*
1908:	Retired

Major-General Fyodor-Aleksandr-Eduard-Adam Fyodorovich **Verman** (28 Feb 1868 - 25 Dec 1932)
6 Jan 1912 - 25 Mar 1914:	Commander, 15th Hussar Regiment
25 Mar 1914:	Promoted to *Major-General*
25 Mar 1914 - 29 Jul 1915:	Commander, Life Guards Cuirassier Regiment
29 Jul 1915 - 1917:	At the disposal of the C-in-C, Western Front

General of Engineers Aleksandr Petrovich **Vernander** (13 Jan 1844 - 1918)
20 Jan 1883 - 24 Dec 1890:	Supervisor of Fortress Construction, Warsaw
30 Aug 1890:	Promoted to *Major-General*
24 Dec 1890 - 28 Feb 1895:	Commander of Artillery, Fortress Warsaw
28 Feb 1895 - 28 Oct 1897:	Deputy Chief of Army Engineers
28 Oct 1897 - 11 Sep 1904:	Chief of Army Engineers
1 Jan 1898:	Promoted to *Lieutenant-General*
11 Sep 1904 - 6 Feb 1909:	Deputy Inspector-General of Engineers
6 Dec 1906:	Promoted to *General of Engineers*
1906 - 1908:	Permanent member of the Council of State for Defence
6 Feb 1909 - 2 May 1912:	Inspector-General of Engineers
2 May 1912 - 22 Mar 1915:	Deputy Minister of War
22 Mar 1915 - 1917:	Member of the State Council

General of Cavalry Aleksei Livovich **Vershinin** (12 Mar 1857 - 9 Apr 1922)
22 Jun 1904 - 4 Apr 1905:	Commander, 2nd Brigade, 5th Cavalry Division

1904:	Promoted to *Major-General*
4 Apr 1905 - 3 Apr 1907:	Commander, Life Guards Ataman Regiment
3 Apr 1907 - Jul 1914:	Commander, 1st Don Cossack Division
21 Jan 1909:	Promoted to *Lieutenant-General*
Jul 1914:	Promoted to *General of Cavalry*
Jul 1914:	Retired

Major-General Eduard Aleksandrovich **Vertsinsky** (5 Jan 1873 - 17 Apr 1941)
22 Jan 1915 - 21 Sep 1915:	Commander, 2nd Life Guards Infantry Regiment
22 Mar 1915:	Promoted to *Major-General*
21 Sep 1915 - 7 Sep 1916:	Chief of Staff, Guards Infantry Brigade
7 Sep 1916 - 19 Feb 1917:	Chief of Staff Guards Rifle Division
19 Feb 1917 - 10 Jun 1917:	Chief of Staff, XVIII. Army Corps
10 Jun 1917 - 15 Jul 1917:	Chief of Staff, 8th Army
15 Jul 1917 - Aug 1917:	Commander, Guards Rifle Division
Aug 1917 - 31 Jan 1918:	Reserve officer, Petrograd Military District
31 Jan 1918 - 15 Mar 1918:	Quartermaster-General of the General Staff
15 Mar 1918 - 13 Jul 1918:	At the disposal of the Chief of General Staff
13 Jul 1918:	Retired

Admiral Mikhail Gerasimovich **Veselago** (7 Nov 1843 - 20 Sep 1929)
1896:	Promoted to *Rear-Admiral*
1896 - 1898:	Chief of Staff, Port of Kronstadt
1898 - 1900:	Junior Flagman, Pacific Squadron
1900:	Commander, Pacific Squadron
1901 - 1902:	Junior Flagman, 1st Naval Division
1902:	Promoted to *Vice-Admiral*
1904 - 1905:	Senior Flagman, 1st Naval Division
1905 - 28 Aug 1909:	Member, Supreme Naval Tribunal
28 Aug 1909:	Promoted to *Admiral*
28 Aug 1909:	Retired

Lieutenant-General Valerian Gerasimovich **Veselago** (22 May 1847 - ?)
7 May 1910:	Promoted to *Major-General*
7 Mar 1910 - 31 Dec 1913:	Commander, Yaroslavl Regional Brigade
31 Dec 1913:	Promoted to *Lieutenant-General*
31 Dec 1913:	Retired
12 Jun 1915 - ?:	Recalled; Commander, Militia Brigade

Rear-Admiral Mikhail Mikhailovich **Veselkin** (13 Nov 1871 - 5 Jan 1918)
6 Dec 1915:	Promoted to *Rear-Admiral*
6 Dec 1915 - 1916:	Member of the Tsar's retinue
1916 - 4 Apr 1917:	Commandant of Fortress Sevastopol
4 Apr 1917 - 20 Aug 1917:	Reserve officer, Ministry of the Navy
20 Aug 1917:	Retired

Major-General Andrey Andreyevich **Veselovsky** (20 Feb 1862 - 11 Jun 1922)
26 Mar 1910 - 1 Jan 1916:	Commander, 21st Siberian Rifle Regiment

5 Oct 1915: Promoted to *Major-General*
1 Jan 1916 - 27 May 1917: Commander, 1st Brigade, 6th Siberian Rifle Division
27 May 1917 - 1917: Reserve officer, Kiev Military District

Lieutenant-General Antony Andreyevich **Veselovsky** (7 Mar 1866 - 1939)
5 Jul 1910 - 9 Feb 1915: Commander, 81st Infantry Regiment
9 Sep 1913: Promoted to *Major-General*
9 Feb 1915 - 21 Aug 1915: Commander, Brigade, 46th Infantry Division
12 Jul 1915: Promoted to *Lieutenant-General*
21 Aug 1915 - 16 Nov 1915: Commander, 44th Infantry Division
16 Nov 1915 - 8 Apr 1917: Commanding General, XIX. Army Corps
8 Apr 1917 - 12 Jul 1917: C-in-C, 2nd Army

Major-General Pavel Nikolayevich **Veselovsky** (1880 - 8 Jan 1942)
1917: Promoted to *Major-General*
1917: Commander, Brigade, 12th Infantry Division

Major-General Boris Petrovich **Veselovzorov** (28 Sep 1869 - 11 Apr 1944)
16 Feb 1911 - 22 Apr 1914: Commander, 84th Infantry Regiment
9 Oct 1913: Promoted to *Major-General*
22 Apr 1914 - 8 Nov 1914: Duty General, Caucasus Military District
8 Nov 1914 - 25 Sep 1916: Duty General, Caucasus Army
25 Sep 1916 - 24 Feb 1917: Chief of Staff, Caucasus Grenadier Division
24 Feb 1917 - 22 Apr 1917: Chief of Staff, IX. Army Corps
22 Apr 1917 - 1917: Commander, 1st Caucasus Grenadier Division

Lieutenant-General of Naval Engineers Pyotr Filimonovich **Veshkurtsov** (16 Dec 1858 - 1932)
18 Sep 1905 - 10 Dec 1913: Chief of the Baltic Shipyard
22 Apr 1907: Promoted to *Major-General of Naval Engineers*
6 Dec 1913: Promoted to *Lieutenant-General of Naval Engineers*
10 Dec 1913 - 1917: Chief of Shipbuilding Department, Ministry of the Navy

Major-General Yanuary Sergeyevich **Veshnyakov** (20 Jul 1869 - 30 Oct 1937)
28 May 1915 - 31 Mar 1917: Commander, 29th Artillery Brigade
27 Jun 1915: Promoted to *Major-General*
31 Mar 1917 - Oct 1917: Inspector of Artillery, XX. Army Corps

Lieutenant-General Aleksandr Ivanovich **Vestenrik** (5 Mar 1844 - 15 Jul 1906)
11 Mar 1894 - 19 Mar 1901: Commander, Crimea Borderguard Brigade
14 May 1896: Promoted to *Major-General*
19 Mar 1901 - 26 May 1906: Commander, 5th Borderguard District
6 Dec 1902: Promoted to *Lieutenant-General*
26 May 1906 - 15 Jul 1906: Commander, 3rd Borderguard District

Major-General Aleksandr Ivanovich **Vestfalen** (7 Aug 1866 - 3 Jul 1915)
31 Dec 1914 - 3 Jul 1915: Commander, 14th Hussar Regiment
9 Nov 1915: Posthumously promoted to *Major-General*

Major-General Ilya Vladimirovich **Vestman** (23 Sep 1849 - ?)
24 Oct 1899: Promoted to *Major-General*
24 Oct 1899 - 17 Feb 1905: Commander, 1st Brigade, 23rd Infantry Division
17 Feb 1905 - 1906: Commander, 50th Reserve Infantry Brigade

Major-General Ivan Ivanovich **Vetvenitsky** (22 Feb 1862 - 5 Apr 1942)
25 Dec 1908 - 9 Jun 1913: Commander, 171st Infantry Regiment
14 Apr 1913: Promoted to *Major-General*
9 Jun 1913 - 29 Jul 1914: Commander, 1st Brigade, 43rd Infantry Division
29 Jul 1914 - 27 Apr 1915: Commander, Brigade, 55th Infantry Division
27 Apr 1915 - 11 May 1915: Reserve officer, Dvinsk Military District
11 May 1915 - 24 Nov 1916: Commander, Brigade, 26th Infantry Division
Jun 1916 - Aug 1916: Acting Commander, 26th Infantry Division
24 Nov 1916 - 11 Mar 1917: General of Special Purposes, Moscow Military District
11 Mar 1917 - Nov 1917: Commander, 126th Infantry Division

Major-General Aleksandr Adamovich **Vevern** (4 Jul 1865 - ?)
8 Nov 1915: Promoted to *Major-General*
8 Nov 1915 - 29 Feb 1916: Commander, 50th Artillery Brigade
29 Feb 1916 - 9 Jun 1917: Commander, 31st Artillery Brigade
9 Jun 1917 - 1917: Inspector of Artillery, XXIII. Army Corps

Major-General Aleksandr Ioakimovich **Vevern** (6 Oct 1859 - ?)
27 Feb 1913 - 7 Oct 1913: Commander of Engineers, Fortress Kiev Depot
14 Apr 1913: Promoted to *Major-General*
7 Oct 1913 - 1917: Commander of Engineers, Fortress St. Petersburg

Major-General Viktor Adamovich **Vevern** (1858 - May 1912)
1 Aug 1910: Promoted to *Major-General*
1 Aug 1910 - May 1912: Commander, 31st Artillery Brigade

Major-General Aleksandr Aleksandrovich **Veykhler** (1851 - Sep 1913)
22 Mar 1910 - Sep 1913: Military Commander, Rybinsk District
1913: Promoted to *Major-General*

Major-General Georgy-Eduard Sigizmundovich von **Veyl** (1 Nov 1865 - 19 Apr 1916)
28 May 1915: Promoted to *Major-General*
28 May 1915 - 27 Dec 1915: Commander, Brigade, 27th Infantry Division
27 Dec 1915 - 19 Apr 1916: Chief of Staff, 43rd Infantry Division

Major-General Vladimir-Karl Sigizmundovich von **Veyl** (11 Jan 1868 - 18 Mar 1928)
1 Jun 1912: Promoted to *Major-General*
1 Jun 1912 - 24 Oct 1914: Chief of Staff, Fortress Brest-Litovsk
24 Oct 1914 - 19 Apr 1915: Chief of Staff, 11th Army
19 Apr 1915 - 11 Mar 1917: Chief of Staff, XXIV. Army Corps
11 Mar 1917 - 1917: Commander, 188th Infantry Division

General of Infantry Fyodor Petrovich **Veymarn** (16 Mar 1831 - 20 Apr 1913)
8 Jun 1866 - 29 Jun 1869:	Chief of Staff, Finland Military District
30 Aug 1867:	Promoted to *Major-General*
29 Jun 1869 - 30 Jul 1877:	General à la suite
30 Jul 1877 - 29 Jul 1879:	Commander, 7th Infantry Division
29 Jul 1879 - 27 Feb 1887:	Commander, 8th Infantry Division
30 Aug 1879:	Promoted to *Lieutenant-General*
27 Feb 1887 - 1899:	At the disposal of the Minister of War
1899:	Promoted to *General of Infantry*
1899:	Retired

General of Infantry Ivan Ivanovich **Veymarn** (8 Mar 1852 - Mar 1915)
8 Aug 1891 - 2 Jul 1896:	Commander, 11th Dragoon Regiment
2 Jul 1896:	Promoted to *Major-General*
2 Jul 1896 - 27 Mar 1901:	Chief of Staff, XIV. Army Corps
27 Mar 1901 - 11 Oct 1906:	Chief of Staff, Borderguard Corps
2 Jul 1902:	Promoted to *Lieutenant-General*
11 Oct 1906 - 21 May 1908:	Commanding General, XIV. Army Corps
21 May 1908:	Promoted to *General of Infantry*
21 May 1908:	Retired

General of Infantry Konstantin Aleksandrovich **Veys** (5 Aug 1839 - 22 Aug 1917)
30 Nov 1886 - 8 Feb 1895:	Commander, Lithuanian Life Guards Regiment
5 Apr 1887:	Promoted to *Major-General*
4 Feb 1891 - 8 Feb 1895:	Commander, 1st Brigade, 3rd Guards Infantry Division
8 Feb 1895 - 26 Mar 1898:	Commander, 11th Infantry Division
14 May 1896:	Promoted to *Lieutenant-General*
26 Mar 1898 - 8 May 1898:	Commander, 17th Infantry Division
8 May 1898 - 19 Mar 1901:	Commander, 3rd Guards Infantry Division
19 Mar 1901 - 30 Jun 1907:	Commanding General, XV. Army Corps
6 Dec 1906:	Promoted to *General of Infantry*
30 Jun 1907:	Retired

Rear-Admiral Aleksandr Konstantinovich **Veys** (6 Jul 1870 - ?)
6 Sep 1916 - Oct 1917:	Commander, Patrol Vessels Division
6 Dec 1916:	Promoted to *Rear-Admiral*

Major-General Vladimir Karlovich **Veysbakh** (9 Mar 1834 - ?)
20 Feb 1880 - 26 Dec 1890:	Commander, Kiev Railway Gendarmerie
30 Aug 1890:	Promoted to *Major-General*
26 Dec 1890 - 1894:	Deputy Chief of Staff, Independent Corps of Gendarmerie

Major-General Gotfrid Fyodorovich **Veyse** (17 Jan 1840 - ?)
1 Oct 1897:	Promoted to *Major-General*
1 Oct 1897 - 1900:	Commander, Caucasus Reserve Artillery Brigade

Major-General Vladislav Antonovich **Veytko** (1 Feb 1859 - 16 Nov 1933)
28 Feb 1914 - 1917:   Commander, 4th Pontoon Battalion
10 Apr 1916:   Promoted to *Major-General*

Major-General Sergey Aleksandrovich **Viberg** (4 Feb 1874 - ?)
1 Apr 1915 - 11 Apr 1916:   Commander, 18th Turkestan Rifle Regiment
2 Feb 1916:   Promoted to *Major-General*
11 Apr 1916 - 1917:   Chief of Staff, 5th Caucasus Rifle Division

Major-General Nikolai Karlovich von **Vidder**
1909:   At the disposal of the Chief of the General Staff
7 Dec 1913:   Promoted to *Major-General*

Major-General Boris-Otton Andreyevich **Vidnes** (12 May 1869 - 17 Sep 1950)
1 Sep 1910 - 6 Nov 1913:   Governor of Vaasa
6 Dec 1911:   Promoted to *Major-General*
6 Nov 1913 - 1917:   Governor of Nyuland

Major-General Arkady Karlovich **Vidovsky** (20 Sep 1858 - 16 Jul 1910)
7 Apr 1907 - 16 Jul 1910:   Military Commander, Kazan
1910:   Promoted to *Major-General*

Major-General Aleksandr Aleksandrovich **Vikhirev** (18 Nov 1869 - ?)
17 Dec 1915 - 8 Feb 1917:   Chief of Staff, 110th Infantry Division
20 Jul 1916:   Promoted to *Major-General*
8 Feb 1917 - 3 Jun 1917:   Chief of Staff, XXI. Army Corps
3 Jun 1917 - 10 Oct 1917:   Commander, 45th Infantry Division

Rear-Admiral Nikolai Emmanuilovich **Vikorst** (17 Sep 1873 - 4 Mar 1944)
2 Jun 1917 - 18 Jul 1919:   Commander, Arctic Ocean Flotilla
28 Jul 1917:   Promoted to *Rear-Admiral*
18 Jul 1919:   Retired

Major-General Konstantin Aleksandrovich **Viktorov** (13 Nov 1863 - 20 Sep 1915)
1915 - 20 Sep 1915:   Commander, 5th Siberian Rifle Regiment
13 Mar 1916:   Posthumously promoted to *Major-General*

Major-General Mikhail Mikhailovich **Viland** (20 Aug 1859 - 18 Aug 1914)
14 Apr 1913:   Promoted to *Major-General*
14 Apr 1913 - 18 Aug 1914:   At the disposal of the Minister of War

Major-General of the Naval Legal Corps Lyudovik Lyudovikovich **Vilchevsky** (15 Oct 1863 - ?)
14 Apr 1913:   Promoted to *Major-General of the Naval Legal Corps*
13 May 1913 - 1917:   Procurator, Kronstadt Naval Court

Major-General Avrelian-Mechislav Feliksovich **Vilchinsky** (9 Jul 1860 - 18 Nov 1914)
1914 - 18 Nov 1914:   Commander, 299th Infantry Regiment

1 Jun 1916: Posthumously promoted to *Major-General*

Major-General Vilgelm Vilgelmovich von **Vildeman-Klopman** (23 Mar 1853 - ?)
7 Aug 1901 - 1909: Commander of Railway Gendarmerie, Vilnius
1906: Promoted to *Major-General*

Rear-Admiral Alfred-Leonhard Karlovich **Vilgelms** (19 Dec 1854 - 8 Jul 1916)
27 Feb 1906 - 7 May 1906: Commander, 18th Naval Depot
7 May 1906: Promoted to *Rear-Admiral*
7 May 1906: Resigned

Vice-Admiral Viktor Yegorovich **Vilken** (14 Nov 1840 - ?)
30 Aug 1893: Promoted to *Rear-Admiral*
30 Aug 1893 - 1896: Director of Lighthouses & Navigation, Baltic Sea
1896 - 24 Nov 1900: Deputy Commander, Baltic Fleet
24 Nov 1900: Promoted to *Vice-Admiral*
24 Nov 1900: Retired

General of the Hydrographic Corps Andrey Ippolitovich **Vilkitsky** (1 Jun 1858 - 26 Feb 1913)
1901 - 12 Feb 1907: Deputy Chief of the Hydrographic Department, Ministry of the Navy
6 Dec 1903: Promoted to *Major-General of the Hydrographic Corps*
12 Feb 1907 - 26 Feb 1913: Chief of the Hydrographic Department, Ministry of the Navy
6 Dec 1909: Promoted to *Lieutenant-General of the Hydrographic Corps*
1913: Promoted to *General of the Hydrographic Corps*

General of Cavalry Nikolai Artemyevich **Villamov** (9 Jul 1850 - 27 Sep 1914)
22 Sep 1894 - 23 Feb 1899: Commander, 16th Dragoon Regiment
23 Feb 1899: Promoted to *Major-General*
23 Feb 1899 - 15 Mar 1906: Commander, 3rd Independent Cavalry Brigade, Consolidated Cavalry Division
15 Mar 1906: Promoted to *Lieutenant-General*
15 Mar 1906 - 22 Dec 1910: Commander, Caucasus Cavalry Division
22 Dec 1910: Promoted to *General of Cavalry*
22 Dec 1910: Retired
26 Jul 1913 - 27 Sep 1914: Recalled; Honorary Trustee, Empress Maria Institutions

Major-General Yevgeny Aleksandrovich **Villamov** (15 Jun 1866 - 1942)
21 Sep 1906 - 1917: Chief of the Lazarev State Horse Stud
14 Apr 1913: Promoted to *Major-General*
1917: Chairman of the Remount Commission, Poltava Region

General of Cavalry Viktor Fyodorovich **Vinberg** (16 Jun 1832 - ?)
16 Apr 1872: Promoted to *Major-General*
16 Apr 1872 - 28 Sep 1872: Attached to the 2nd Cavalry Division

28 Sep 1872 - 30 Aug 1873:	Deputy Commander, 2nd Cavalry Division
30 Aug 1873 - 10 Jan 1874:	Commander, 2nd Brigade, 2nd Cavalry Division
10 Jan 1874 - 2 Jan 1878:	Commandant of the Cavalry School
2 Jan 1878 - 22 Jun 1886:	Commander, 12th Cavalry Division
30 Aug 1881:	Promoted to *Lieutenant-General*
22 Jun 1886 - 2 Dec 1890:	Commander, 2nd Guards Cavalry Division
2 Dec 1890 - 15 Sep 1901:	Commanding General, X. Army Corps
6 Dec 1895:	Promoted to *General of Cavalry*
15 Sep 1901 - 1 Jan 1911:	Member of the Military Council
1 Jan 1911:	Retired

Major-General Baron Alexander Georgievich von **Vineken** (20 Mar 1868 - 12 Mar 1917)
3 Nov 1914 - 16 Feb 1916:	Commander, Life Guards Grodno Hussar Regiment
22 Mar 1915:	Promoted to *Major-General*
16 Feb 1916 - 5 Apr 1916:	Chief of Staff, Consolidated Cavalry Division
5 Apr 1916 - 12 Mar 1917:	Chief of Staff, Guards Cavalry Corps

Major-General Anton Sergeyevich **Vinogradov** (7 Dec 1860 - 1913)
24 Sep 1904 - 1913:	Commander of Gendarmerie, Kaluga District
1913:	Promoted to *Major-General*

Major-General Pyotr Alekseyevich **Vinogradov** (20 Jun 1847 - ?)
15 Feb 1905 - 12 Feb 1907:	Commander, 40th Artillery Brigade
12 Feb 1907 - 31 Oct 1907:	Commander, 5th Reserve Artillery Brigade
31 May 1907:	Promoted to *Major-General*
31 Oct 1907:	Retired

Major-General Aleksandr Nikolayevich **Vinogradsky** (24 Apr 1874 - 2 Dec 1935)
1 Dec 1912 - 18 Dec 1915:	Commander, 2nd Battalion, Life Guards Horse Artillery
30 Jul 1915:	Promoted to *Major-General*
18 Dec 1915 - Oct 1916:	Commander, 14th Artillery Brigade
Oct 1916 - Mar 1917:	Deputy Inspector of Artillery, Romanian Front

Major-General Viktor Ivanovich **Vinokurov** (24 Jul 1840 - ?)
12 May 1876 - 1898:	Inspector, Nizhny-Novgorod/Tyumen Displacement Region
30 Aug 1892:	Promoted to *Major-General*

Lieutenant-General David Frantsiskovich **Vinspier** (25 Feb 1830 - ?)
8 Nov 1877:	Promoted to *Major-General*
13 Jan 1878 - 9 Oct 1881:	At the disposal of the C-in-C, Caucasus Army
9 Oct 1881 - 1905:	Attached to Grand Duke Mikhail Nikolayevich
30 Aug 1886:	Promoted to *Lieutenant-General*

Lieutenant-General of Naval Engineers Viktor Andreyevich **Vinter** (12 Feb 1868 - ?)
11 Jan 1910 - 1917:	Chief Mechanical Engineer, Baltic Naval Command
27 Aug 1912:	Promoted to *Major-General of Naval Engineers*
30 Jul 1915:	Promoted to *Lieutenant-General of Naval Engineers*

Rear-Admiral Frants Andreyevich **Vinter** (18 Aug 1866 - 1 May 1917)
6 Dec 1916:	Promoted to *Rear-Admiral*
6 Dec 1916 - 17 Apr 1917:	Commander, Training Detachment, Black Sea Fleet
17 Apr 1917 - 1 May 1917:	Reserve officer, Black Sea Fleet

Lieutenant-General of Naval Engineers Viktor Genrikhovich **Vinter** (12 Feb 1868 - ?)
11 Jan 1910 - 1917:	Chief Engineer, Commanding Admiral, Naval Forces of the Baltic Sea
1912:	Promoted to *Major-General of Naval Engineers*
30 Jul 1915:	Promoted to *Lieutenant-General of Naval Engineers*

General of Cavalry Nikolai Aleksandrovich **Vintulov** (27 Jan 1845 - ?)
20 Dec 1889:	Promoted to *Major-General*
20 Dec 1889 - 27 Jul 1891:	Commander, 1st Brigade, 12th Cavalry Division
27 Jul 1891 - 15 Apr 1893:	Commander, 1st Brigade, 1st Cavalry Division
15 Apr 1893 - 20 Nov 1909:	General for Special Assignments, Inspectorate of Remounts
6 Dec 1899:	Promoted to *Lieutenant-General*
20 Nov 1909 - 1 Jan 1911:	General for Special Assignments, Army Remount Administration
6 Dec 1910:	Promoted to *General of Cavalry*
1 Jan 1911 - 7 Mar 1915:	Chief of the Army Remount Administration
7 Mar 1915:	Retired

Lieutenant-General Georgy Nikolayevich **Viranovsky** (1 Nov 1867 - 1920)
6 Jan 1911 - 12 Aug 1914:	Commander, 16th Infantry Regiment
12 Aug 1914:	Promoted to *Major-General*
12 Aug 1914 - 14 Dec 1914:	Commander, Brigade, 65th Infantry Division
3 Oct 1914 - 11 Oct 1914:	Acting Commander, 65th Infantry Division
14 Dec 1914 - 4 May 1916:	Chief of Staff, VIII. Army Corps
4 May 1916 - 6 Dec 1916:	Commander, 12th Infantry Division
6 Dec 1916 - 2 Apr 1917:	Chief of Staff, 6th Army
2 Apr 1917 - 19 Aug 1917:	Commanding General, II. Guards Corps
29 Apr 1917:	Promoted to *Lieutenant-General*
19 Aug 1917 - 8 Sep 1917:	Reserve officer, Kiev Military District
8 Sep 1917 - 9 Sep 1917:	Reserve officer, Odessa Military District
9 Sep 1917 - 23 Oct 1917:	Commanding General, XXV. Army Corps
23 Oct 1917 - 1918:	Deputy Chief of Staff, Romanian Front

Admiral Robert Nikolayevich **Viren** (25 Dec 1856 - 1 Mar 1917)
23 Aug 1904:	Promoted to *Rear-Admiral*
23 Aug 1904 - 20 Dec 1904:	Commander, Cruiser Squadron, Far East
Jan 1905 - Apr 1906:	POW, Japan
10 Apr 1906 - 7 Aug 1906:	Junior Flagman, Black Sea Naval Division
7 Aug 1906 - 2 Oct 1906:	Junior Flagman, Baltic Fleet
2 Oct 1906 - 26 Mar 1907:	Commander of Naval Artillery, Baltic Fleet
26 Mar 1907 - 15 Feb 1909:	C-in-C, Black Sea Fleet
24 Jul 1908 - 1 Mar 1917:	Member, Board of Admiralty

6 Dec 1909:	Promoted to *Vice-Admiral*
15 Feb 1909 - 1 Mar 1917:	Commandant of Kronstadt Port, Military Governor of Kronstadt
22 Mar 1915:	Promoted to *Admiral*

Vice-Admiral Andrei Andreyevich **Virenius** (17 Apr 1850 - 1919)
1901 - 31 Mar 1903:	Head of Scientific Department, General Staff
1902:	Promoted to *Rear-Admiral*
31 Mar 1903 - Apr 1904:	Deputy Chief of the Main Naval Staff
Apr 1904 - 29 Nov 1904:	Acting Chief of the Main Naval Staff
29 Nov 1904 - 1906:	Deputy Chief of the Main Naval Staff
1906 - 1908:	Chairman of the Naval Technical Committee
1908:	Promoted to *Vice-Admiral*
1908:	Dismissed

Rear-Admiral Fyodor Fyodorovich **Vishnevetsky** (21 Oct 1859 - ?)
1903:	Promoted to *Rear-Admiral*
1904 - 1 Aug 1905:	Junior Flagman, Black Sea Fleet
1 Aug 1905:	Retired

Major-General of Naval Engineers Iliodor Petrovich **Vishnevsky** (5 Feb 1859 - ?)
1910 - 1915:	Chief Engineer, Commander of Marine Corps Naval Vessels
16 Jul 1912 - 1917:	Senior Geometry Lecturer, Marine Corps
14 Apr 1913:	Promoted to *Major-General of Naval Engineers*

Lieutenant-General Nikolai Nikolayevich **Vishnevsky** (27 Nov 1838 - ?)
9 Jul 1891:	Promoted to *Major-General*
9 Jul 1891 - 9 Aug 1897:	Commander, 2nd Brigade, 3rd Infantry Division
9 Aug 1897 - 4 Dec 1900:	Commander, 66th Replacement Infantry Brigade
4 Dec 1900:	Promoted to *Lieutenant-General*
4 Dec 1900:	Retired

Major-General Aleksandr Mikhailovich **Vishnyakov** (3 Sep 1850 - ?)
9 Apr 1902 - 22 Dec 1908:	Section Chief, Electro-Technical Engineering Directorate
14 Apr 1902:	Promoted to *Major-General*
22 Dec 1908 - 1912:	At the disposal of the Main Engineering Directorate

Lieutenant-General of the Admiralty Nikolai Mikhailovich **Vishnyakov** (13 Jun 1843 - ?)
1892 - 1899:	Captain, Port of Sveaborg
1894:	Promoted to *Major-General of the Admiralty*
1899 - 7 Jul 1903:	Director, Tsar Pavel I Invalid Home
7 Jul 1903:	Promoted to *Lieutenant-General of the Admiralty*
7 Jul 1903:	Retired

Major-General Nikolai Petrovich **Vishnyakov** (3 Dec 1871 - 20 Dec 1937)
18 Nov 1916 - 1917:	Military Judge, Dvinsk Military District Court

6 Dec 1916:   Promoted to *Major-General*

General of Infantry Yevgeny Petrovich **Vishnyakov** (27 Dec 1841 - 13 Oct 1916)
29 Jan 1898:   Promoted to *Major-General*
29 Jan 1898 - 23 Jun 1899:   Commander, 2nd Brigade, 17th Infantry Division
23 Jun 1899 - 8 Apr 1902:   Commander, 2nd Brigade, 4th Infantry Division
8 Apr 1902 - 7 May 1903:   Commander, 53rd Replacement Infantry Brigade
7 May 1903 - 10 Jan 1909:   Commandant of Fortress Vyborg
6 Dec 1904:   Promoted to *Lieutenant-General*
10 Jan 1909 - 31 Dec 1913:   Commandant of Moscow
10 Apr 1911:   Promoted to *General of Infantry*
31 Dec 1913 - 13 Oct 1916:   Member, Committee for Wounded Veterans

Major-General Nikolai Ivanovich **Viskovsky** (29 Dec 1857 - ?)
31 Dec 1913 - 1917:   Commandant of Moscow Artillery Depot
6 Apr 1914:   Promoted to *Major-General*

Rear-Admiral Vilgelm Karlovich **Vitgeft** (14 Oct 1847 - 10 Aug 1904)
26 Oct 1899 - Feb 1903:   Commander, Kwantung Area, Pacific Fleet
6 Dec 1899:   Promoted to *Rear-Admiral*
Feb 1903 - 3 Mar 1904:   Chief of Staff to the Viceroy, Far East
3 Mar 1904 - 22 Apr 1904:   Chief of Naval Headquarters, Far East
22 Apr 1904 - 10 Aug 1904:   Acting Commander, 1st Pacific Squadron

Major-General Konstantin Vasilyevich **Vitkovsky** (8 Jul 1853 - ?)
10 Feb 1898 - 1906:   Military Judge, Kiev Military District Court
1 Jan 1901:   Promoted to *Major-General*

Lieutenant-General Vasily Vasilievich **Vitkovsky** (1 Sep 1856 - 20 Mar 1924)
1 Oct 1891 - 27 May 1905:   Professor of Geodesy & Topography, Military Topographic School
12 Nov 1897 - 27 Dec 1900:   Extraordinary Professor, General Staff Academy
6 Dec 1900:   Promoted to *Major-General*
27 Dec 1900 - 12 Sep 1907:   Ordinary Professor, General Staff Academy
12 Sep 1907 - 1918:   Honorary Ordinary Professor, General Staff Academy
6 Dec 1909:   Promoted to *Lieutenant-General*
Feb 1915 - Sep 1915:   Commandant, General Staff Academy

Major-General Aleksey Nikolayevich **Vitman** (20 May 1857 - ?)
19 Oct 1909 - 1914:   Chief of Yelisavetgrad Section, Military Billetting Directorate
1914:   Promoted to *Major-General*
1914:   Retired

Lieutenant-General Leopold Adolfovich **Vitovsky** (15 Jan 1833 - 1913)
10 Feb 1897:   Promoted to *Major-General*
10 Feb 1897 - 26 Jun 1902:   Deputy Commander of Engineers, Moscow Military District

26 Jun 1902: Promoted to *Lieutenant-General*
26 Jun 1902: Retired

Major-General Konstantin Aleksandrovich **Vitsnuda** (20 May 1872 - 6 Feb 1915)
19 Feb 1914 - 6 Feb 1915: Commander, 116th Infantry Regiment
11 Jul 1915: Posthumously promoted to *Major-General*

Lieutenant-General Adolf Vasilyevich von **Vitt** (10 Apr 1844 - ?)
13 Apr 1888 - 14 Apr 1904: Inspector, Courier Corps
30 Aug 1892: Promoted to *Major-General*
14 Apr 1904 - 1906: Member, General Staff Committee
6 Dec 1904: Promoted to *Lieutenant-General*

Lieutenant-General Bruno Albertovich **Vitte** (5 Jan 1846 - ?)
4 Jul 1898: Promoted to *Major-General*
4 Jul 1898 - 3 Aug 1900: Commander, 2nd Brigade, 7th Infantry Division
3 Aug 1900 - 21 Jun 1901: Commander, 60th Reserve Infantry Brigade
21 Jun 1901 - 15 Sep 1904: Commander, 1st Turkestan Reserve Brigade
15 Sep 1904 - 14 Aug 1905: Commander, 63rd Reserve Infantry Brigade
14 Aug 1905 - 1907: Commander, Vladikavkaz Regional Brigade
6 Dec 1906: Promoted to *Lieutenant-General*

Major-General Nikolai Mikhailovich von **Vittorf** (25 Apr 1869 - 1929)
2 Jul 1912 - 1918: Professor, Mikhailovsky Artillery Academy
6 Jul 1915: Promoted to *Major-General*

Lieutenant-General Vladimir Pavlovich von **Vittorf** (2 Jun 1835 - 1907)
10 Mar 1877 - 11 Mar 1880: Commander, Kexholm Grenadier Regiment
15 Jun 1877: Promoted to *Major-General*
11 Mar 1880 - 24 Sep 1881: Military Commander, Vladimir Region
24 Sep 1881 - 19??: Commander, 17th (Smolensk) Regional Brigade
30 Aug 1886: Promoted to *Lieutenant-General*

Lieutenant-General Nikolai Karlovich **Vitvitsky** (6 Aug 1855 - ?)
15 Jan 1909: Promoted to *Major-General*
15 Jan 1909 - 29 Jul 1914: Commander, 1st Brigade, 45th Infantry Division
29 Jul 1914 - 5 Sep 1914: Commander, Brigade, 80th Infantry Division
5 Sep 1914: Retired
16 Feb 1916 - 1917: Recalled; Attached to the Commanding General, Kazan Military District
10 Aug 1916: Promoted to *Lieutenant-General*

Major-General Iosif Iosifovich **Vivyen-de-Shatobren** (7 Apr 1859 - ?)
3 Mar 1909 - 6 Jul 1912: Commander, 14th Hussar Regiment
6 Jul 1912: Promoted to *Major-General*
6 Jul 1912 - 21 Aug 1915: Commander, 1st Brigade, Caucasus Cavalry Division
21 Aug 1915 - 7 Jan 1916: Reserve officer, Dvinsk Military District
7 Jan 1916 - 11 Mar 1917: Commander, 1st Brigade, 13th Cavalry Division

11 Mar 1917 - 23 Apr 1917:	Chief of Staff, IV. Siberian Army Corps
23 Apr 1917 - 8 Jun 1917:	Unassigned
8 Jun 1917 - 30 Jun 1917:	Commander, 7th Siberian Rifle Division
30 Jun 1917 - 12 Aug 1917:	Unassigned
12 Aug 1917 - 1918:	Chief of Staff, VII. Siberian Army Corps

Major-General Vladimir Aleksandrovich **Vladimirov** (25 Dec 1860 - ?)
1 Jan 1910 - 12 May 1917:	Deputy Chief of St. Petersburg Arsenal
6 Dec 1916:	Promoted to *Major-General*
12 May 1917:	Dismissed

Major-General Vladimir Grigorievich **Vladimirov** (8 Jul 1870 - ?)
13 Feb 1913 - 6 Jul 1915:	Commander, 174th Infantry Regiment
23 Apr 1915:	Promoted to *Major-General*
6 Jul 1915 - 17 Oct 1915:	Reserve officer, Kiev Military District
17 Oct 1915 - 20 Jan 1916:	Commander, Brigade, 35th Infantry Division
20 Jan 1916 - 12 Dec 1916:	Reserve officer, Kiev Military District
12 Dec 1916 - 20 Apr 1917:	Chief of Staff, V. Militia Corps
20 Apr 1917 - Oct 1917:	Chief of Staff, XXIV. Army Corps

Major-General Viktor Viktorovich **Vladimirsky** (3 Aug 1839 - 18 May 1901)
15 Nov 1889 - 18 May 1901:	Chief of Gendarmerie, Yaroslavl Province
21 Apr 1891:	Promoted to *Major-General*

Rear-Admiral Pyotr Petrovich **Vladislavlev** (20 Dec 1876 - 5 Oct 1917)
25 Apr 1917 - 5 Oct 1917:	Commander, Submarine Division, Baltic Fleet
28 Jul 1917:	Promoted to *Rear-Admiral*

Major-General Leonid Nikolayevich **Vladislavlevich** (5 Jun 1858 - ?)
2 Jun 1897 - 25 Jun 1901:	Commander, 24th Dragoon Regiment
25 Jun 1901:	Promoted to *Major-General*
25 Jun 1901 - 18 Dec 1901:	Chief of Communications, Amur Military District
18 Dec 1901 - 1906:	Special Assignments General, Siberian Military District

Major-General Aleksandr Akimovich **Vladychek** (1 Apr 1829 - ?)
12 Sep 1874 - 5 Jan 1897:	Military Commander of Revel County
14 May 1896:	Promoted to *Major-General*
5 Jan 1897 - 1899:	Commander, Arkhangelsk Regional Brigade

Major-General Adrian Vasilyevich **Vlasov** (30 Jul 1867 - ?)
3 Jul 1915 - 1917:	Chief of Technology, Gun Factory
10 Apr 1916:	Promoted to *Major-General*

Major-General Grigory Mikhailovich **Vlasov** (12 Oct 1839 - ?)
15 Dec 1887 - 1898:	Ataman, 1st Military Division, Trans-Baikal Cossack Army
14 May 1896:	Promoted to *Major-General*

Major-General Aleksandr Alekseyevich **Vlasyev** (10 Jul 1853 - ?)
10 Apr 1905 - 28 Aug 1912:	Chief of Gendarmerie, Orlov Province
10 Apr 1911:	Promoted to *Major-General*
28 Aug 1912:	Retired
1914 - 1916:	Recalled; Reserve officer, Kiev Military District

Lieutenant-General of the Admiralty Gennady Aleksandrovich **Vlasyev** (17 Apr 1844 - 23 Feb 1912)
1894 - 28 Nov 1905:	Chief, Obukhov Steel Factory, Ministry of the Navy
1895:	Promoted to *Major-General of the Admiralty*
1903:	Promoted to *Lieutenant-General of the Admiralty*
28 Nov 1905:	Retired

Major-General Iosif Nikolayevich **Vlasyev** (7 May 1861 - ?)
20 Jun 1916 - 1917:	Commander, 1st Siege Artillery Brigade
19 Oct 1916:	Promoted to *Major-General*

Major-General Leonty Nikolayevich **Vnorovsky** (2 Nov 1862 - ?)
12 May 1916 - 19 Sep 1917:	Commander, 21st Artillery Brigade
31 Dec 1916:	Promoted to *Major-General*
19 Sep 1917 - 1917:	Inspector of Artillery, III. Caucasus Army Corps

General of Infantry Aleksandr Karlovich **Vodar** (21 Sep 1836 - 18 Dec 1915)
23 Mar 1871 - 1 Dec 1878:	Chief of Staff, 24th Infantry Division
18 Dec 1877:	Promoted to *Major-General*
1 Dec 1878 - 20 Nov 1886:	Commander, Lithuanian Life Guards Regiment
20 Nov 1886 - 2 May 1891:	Commandant, 2nd Konstantinovsky Military College
30 Aug 1887:	Promoted to *Lieutenant-General*
2 May 1891 - 1 Jan 1898:	Commander, 1st Grenadier Division
1 Jan 1898 - 3 Feb 1903:	Commanding General, XXI. Army Corps
6 Dec 1899:	Promoted to *General of Infantry*
3 Feb 1903 - 18 Dec 1915:	Member of the Military Council

General of Cavalry Konstantin Ippolitovich **Vogak** (3 Aug 1859 - 10 Aug 1923)
17 Jan 1896 - 29 May 1903:	Military Attaché, China & Japan
24 Jul 1900:	Promoted to *Major-General*
29 May 1903 - 24 Mar 1905:	Military Attaché, Japan
24 Mar 1905 - 20 Feb 1907:	Military Attaché, United Kingdom
22 Apr 1907:	Promoted to *Lieutenant-General*
20 Feb 1907 - 30 Jan 1910:	Special Assignments General to the Chief of the General Staff
30 Jan 1910:	Promoted to *General of Cavalry*
30 Jan 1910:	Retired
10 Nov 1914 - 1 Mar 1917:	Recalled; Commanding General, I. Militia Corps
19 Jun 1915 - 2 Jul 1915:	Acting Commanding General, Moscow Military District

Major-General Sergey Konstantinovich **Vogak** (10 Jan 1833 - ?)
8 Aug 1891:	Promoted to *Major-General*

8 Aug 1891 - 14 Mar 1895:	Commander, Turkestan Artillery Brigade
14 Mar 1895 - 14 Jun 1899:	Commander, 3rd Grenadier Artillery Brigade

Major-General Vladimir Konstantinovich **Vogak** (5 Mar 1834 - 1909)

11 Oct 1879 - 18 May 1905:	Chief of Police, Peterhof
14 Apr 1902:	Promoted to *Major-General*
18 May 1905 - 1909:	Special Assignments General, Minister of the Imperial Court

Lieutenant-General Vladimir Aleksandrovich **Voinov** (3 Feb 1848 - ?)

27 Aug 1895:	Promoted to *Major-General*
27 Aug 1895 - 17 May 1900:	Special Purposes General, Kiev Military District
17 May 1900 - 24 Nov 1907:	Commander, Kiev Regional Brigade
1 Jan 1903:	Promoted to *Lieutenant-General*

Major-General Konstantin Mavrikievich von **Volf** (24 Jul 1856 - 1921)

24 Sep 1905 - 4 Sep 1907:	Commander, 21st Dragoon Regiment
4 Sep 1907:	Promoted to *Major-General*
4 Sep 1907 - 29 Mar 1908:	Commander, 1st Brigade, 6th Cavalry Division
29 Mar 1908 - 8 Jun 1912:	Commander, Life Guards Cuirassier Regiment
8 Jun 1912 - 21 Jun 1914:	Commander, 2nd Brigade, 1st Guards Cavalry Division
21 Jun 1914 - 13 Apr 1917:	General à la suite
13 Apr 1917 - Oct 1917:	Reserve officer, Petrograd Military District

Major-General Nikolai Khristoforovich **Volf** (3 Dec 1859 - ?)

5 Jul 1910 - 1917:	Commander, 5th Pontoon Battalion
5 Oct 1916:	Promoted to *Major-General*

Lieutenant-General Baron Otton Osipovic von **Volf** (12 Jul 1832 - ?)

23 Apr 1881 - 21 Sep 1884:	Commander, Life Guards Grodno Hussar Regiment
15 May 1883:	Promoted to *Major-General*
21 Sep 1884 - 13 Mar 1885:	Commander, 1st Brigade, 10th Cavalry Division
13 Mar 1855 - 11 Mar 1886:	Commander, 2nd Brigade, 2nd Cavalry Division
11 Mar 1886 - 13 May 1890:	Special Purposes General, V. Class, Ministry of War
13 May 1890 - 20 Nov 1899:	Special Purposes General, IV. Class, Ministry of War
30 Aug 1893:	Promoted to *Lieutenant-General*
20 Nov 1899 - 1901:	At the disposal of the Minister of War

Lieutenant-General Ivan Vasilyevich **Volkenau** (27 Sep 1848 - 12 Jun 1908)

23 Dec 1889 - 29 Jul 1891:	Commander, 40th Dragoon Regiment
29 Jul 1891:	Promoted to *Major-General*
29 Jul 1891 - 27 Jan 1895:	At the disposal of the Commanding General, Vilnius Military District
27 Jan 1895 - 24 Nov 1898:	Commander, 2nd Brigade, 1st Guards Cavalry Division
24 Nov 1898 - 12 Jan 1905:	Commander, 3rd Cavalry Division
6 Dec 1899:	Promoted to *Lieutenant-General*
12 Jan 1905 - 5 Dec 1906:	Commanding General, III. Army Corps
5 Dec 1906 - 12 Jun 1908:	At the disposal of the Minister of War

Major-General Konstantin Ivanovich **Volkenau** (4 Feb 1863 - 5 Nov 1937)
29 Dec 1914 - 28 Oct 1916: Commander, 198th Infantry Regiment
6 Dec 1915: Promoted to *Major-General*
28 Oct 1916 - 1917: Commander, Brigade, 80th Infantry Division

Major-General Mikhail Nikolayevich **Volkhovskoy** (20 Sep 1868 - 8 Mar 1944)
2 Nov 1914 - 13 Nov 1915: Commander, 35th Infantry Regiment
5 Oct 1915: Promoted to *Major-General*
13 Nov 1915 - 8 Feb 1916: Commander, Brigade, 31st Infantry Division
8 Feb 1916 - 18 Sep 1916: Chief of Staff, 112th Infantry Division
18 Sep 1916 - 20 May 1917: Chief of Staff, X. Army Corps
20 May 1917 - 3 Mar 1918: Commander, 31st Infantry Division

Lieutenant-General Pyotr Mironovich **Volkoboy** (26 Jun 1859 - 15 Oct 1918)
20 Apr 1910 - 19 Jul 1914: Commander, 147th Infantry Regiment
15 Apr 1914: Promoted to *Major-General*
19 Jul 1914 - 24 Sep 1914: Commander, 1st Finnish Rifle Brigade
24 Sep 1914 - 12 May 1915: Commander, 3rd Finnish Rifle Brigade
14 Feb 1915: Promoted to *Lieutenant-General*
12 May 1915 - 22 Apr 1917: Commander, 3rd Finnish Rifle Division
22 Apr 1917 - May 1917: Commanding General, XLIV. Army Corps

Major-General Prince Mikhail Viktorovich **Volkonsky** (22 Aug 1859 - 16 Mar 1908)
19 Apr 1906 - 16 Mar 1908: Commander of Railway Gendarmerie, Odessa
6 Dec 1906: Promoted to *Major-General*

Major-General Aleksandr Vasilyevich **Volkov** (22 Aug 1859 - 1 Mar 1917)
31 Oct 1914 - 1 Mar 1917: Commander, Fortress Kronstadt Sapper Brigade
6 Dec 1914: Promoted to *Major-General*

General of Infantry Arkady Nikolayevich **Volkov** (24 Nov 1854 - 11 Mar 1919)
1 Dec 1895 - 19 Oct 1904: Military Judge, Caucasus Military District Court
1 Jan 1901: Promoted to *Major-General*
19 Oct 1904 - 11 Nov 1905: Chief of the Military Justice Section, 2nd Manchurian Army
11 Nov 1905 - 14 Aug 1906: Military Prosecutor, Odessa Military District
14 Aug 1906 - 13 Feb 1907: Chairman of the Military Tribunal, Irkutsk Military District
13 Feb 1907 - 24 Oct 1908: Chairman of the Military Tribunal, Caucasus Military District
22 Apr 1907: Promoted to *Lieutenant-General*
24 Oct 1908 - 4 Aug 1911: Chairman of the Military Tribunal, Kiev Military District
4 Aug 1911 - 31 Mar 1917: Member, Supreme Military Tribunal
6 Dec 1915: Promoted to *General of Infantry*
31 Mar 1917: Dismissed

Major-General Dmitry Vladimirovich **Volkov** (10 Oct 1860 - 25 Sep 1918)
3 Jan 1906 - 6 Jan 1915: Chief of Bureau, Deputy Governor-General of Warsaw
6 Dec 1912: Promoted to *Major-General*
6 Jan 1915 - 9 Jan 1915: Attached to Warsaw Gendarmerie Command
9 Jan 1915 - 1917: Commander of Gendarmerie, Tambov Province

Lieutenant-General Ivan Dmitriyevich **Volkov** (12 Feb 1854 - 27 Feb 1917)
14 Jul 1903 - 9 Jan 1915: Commander of Gendarmerie, Livonia Province
6 Dec 1906: Promoted to *Major-General*
9 Jan 1915 - 27 Feb 1917: Commander of Gendarmerie, Petrograd
6 Dec 1915: Promoted to *Lieutenant-General*

Major-General Ivan Semyonovich **Volkov** (21 Jan 1850 - ?)
2 Nov 1883 - 1908: Chairman of the Board, Semirechensk Cossack Army
6 Apr 1903: Promoted to *Major-General*

Rear-Admiral Nikolai Aleksandrovich **Volkov** (7 Nov 1870 - 8 Mar 1954)
25 Jul 1913 - 1917: Naval Attaché, England
30 Jul 1916: Promoted to *Rear-Admiral*

Major-General Pavel Mikhailovich **Volkov** (1 Jan 1848 - 1907)
25 Apr 1901 - 10 Dec 1905: Commander of Artillery, Fortress Kars
6 Dec 1901: Promoted to *Major-General*
10 Dec 1905 - 1907: Commander of Artillery, Fortress Ivangorod

General of Cavalry Pyotr Nikolayevich **Volkov** (11 Sep 1817 - 6 Sep 1899)
7 Apr 1857: Promoted to *Major-General*
17 Apr 1857 - 26 Sep 1862: Commander, Life Guards Uhlan Regiment
26 Sep 1862 - 25 Aug 1864: Unassigned
25 Aug 1864 - 1 Apr 1879: Attached to Grand Duke Nikolai Nikolayevich
30 Aug 1864: Promoted to *Lieutenant-General*
6 Dec 1864: Promoted to *General-Adjutant*
16 Apr 1878: Promoted to *General of Cavalry*
1 Apr 1879 - 6 Sep 1899: Member of the Military Council

Lieutenant-General Vladimir Sergeyevich **Volkov** (17 Mar 1848 - 12 Feb 1912)
17 Apr 1896 - 12 Oct 1897: Chief of Staff, South Ussuri Sector
14 May 1896: Promoted to *Major-General*
12 Oct 1897 - 2 Apr 1898: At the disposal of the Commanding General, Amur Military District
2 Apr 1898 - 26 Jan 1899: Commander, 3rd East Siberian Rifle Brigade
26 Jan 1899 - 11 Jul 1900: Commander, 65th Replacement Infantry Brigade
11 Jul 1900 - 7 Feb 1901: Commander, 4th Rifle Brigade
31 Jan 1901: Promoted to *Lieutenant-General*
7 Feb 1901 - 4 Dec 1904: Deputy Commander, Kwantung District
4 Dec 1904 - 1906: Member of the Military Council
4 Dec 1904 - 4 Nov 1905: At the disposal of the C-in-C, Manchurian Army
4 Nov 1905 - 24 Apr 1906: Commanding General, XVII. Army Corps

3 Jan 1906: Retired (but continued in temporary command of XVII. Army Corps)

Lieutenant-General Yevgeny Nikolayevich **Volkov** (16 Jun 1864 - 1933)
17 Nov 1901 - 1 Jan 1905: Governor of Chernomorsk
1903: Promoted to *Major-General*
1 Jan 1905 - 18 Apr 1905: Mayor of Moscow
18 Apr 1905 - 3 Jan 1906: Governor of Taurida
3 Jan 1906 - 28 May 1906: Attached to the Ministry of the Imperial Court
28 May 1906 - 3 Jun 1906: Attached to the Ministry of Internal Affairs
3 Jun 1906 - 13 Aug 1909: Deputy Chief of the Tsar's Cabinet
13 Aug 1909 - 25 Apr 1917: Chief of the Tsar's Cabinet
1910: Promoted to *General-Adjutant*
6 Dec 1913: Promoted to *Lieutenant-General*
25 Apr 1917: Dismissed

Lieutenant-General Ilya Ildefonsovich **Volkovitsky** (5 Jul 1860 - 26 Jan 1918)
27 May 1907 - 26 Jul 1910: Commander, 3rd Reserve Artillery Brigade
31 May 1907: Promoted to *Major-General*
26 Jul 1910 - 10 Mar 1912: Commander, 46th Artillery Brigade
10 Mar 1912 - 22 Mar 1917: Inspector of Artillery, XXIV. Army Corps
31 May 1913: Promoted to *Lieutenant-General*

Lieutenant-General Viktor Mikhailovich **Volkovitsky** (26 Feb 1834 - ?)
15 Oct 1883 - 19 Mar 1888: Commander, 36th Artillery Brigade
6 May 1884: Promoted to *Major-General*
19 Mar 1888 - 4 Feb 1893: Commander, 1st Grenadier Artillery Brigade
4 Feb 1893 - 30 Jan 1900: Commander of Artillery, IV. Army Corps
30 Aug 1894: Promoted to *Lieutenant-General*

Lieutenant-General Vladimir Ildefonsovich **Volkovitsky** (25 May 1852 - 22 Sep 1909)
29 Dec 1899 - 15 Feb 1905: Commander, 7th Artillery Brigade
9 Apr 1900: Promoted to *Major-General*
15 Feb 1905 - 1 Mar 1906: Commander of Artillery, VI. Siberian Army Corps
1 Mar 1906 - 27 Jan 1907: Commander of Artillery, V. Army Corps
6 Dec 1906: Promoted to *Lieutenant-General*
27 Jan 1907 - 29 Jul 1907: Commander of Artillery, XVII. Army Corps
29 Jul 1907 - 22 Sep 1909: Commander, 31st Infantry Division

Major-General Grigory Afanasyevich **Volkovnyakov** (1 Mar 1857 - ?)
12 Sep 1905 - 1909: At the disposal of the Chief of the General Staff
1906: Promoted to *Major-General*

Major-General Anatoly Karlovich **Vollk** (26 Jun 1855 - ?)
2 Aug 1904 - 26 Jun 1913: Commandant of Irkutsk Railway Station
26 Jun 1913: Promoted to *Major-General*
26 Jun 1913: Retired

Lieutenant-General Nikolai Gerasimovich **Volodchenko** (20 Nov 1862 - 1945)
27 Oct 1905 - 2 Aug 1914:	Chief of Staff, Amur District Borderguards
14 Jul 1909:	Promoted to *Major-General*
2 Aug 1914 - 26 Apr 1915:	Commander, 3rd Brigade, Cossack Division
26 Apr 1915 - Apr 1917:	Commander, 16th Cavalry Division
13 Jun 1915:	Promoted to *Lieutenant-General*
Apr 1917 - 4 Jul 1917:	Commanding General, Cavalry Corps, 3rd Army
4 Jul 1917 - 9 Sep 1917:	Commanding General, XLIV. Army Corps
9 Sep 1917 - 24 Nov 1917:	C-in-C, Southwestern Front

Lieutenant-General Vladimir Mikhailovich **Volodimirov** (23 Dec 1840 - 5 Jul 1910)
1 Sep 1878 - 1899:	Professor, Military Law Academy
30 Aug 1888:	Promoted to *Major-General*
1899:	Promoted to *Lieutenant-General*
1899:	Retired

Major-General Aleksei Aleksandrovich **Volodkovsky** (1 Nov 1866 - ?)
9 Mar 1912 - 26 May 1914:	Military Judge, Caucasus Military District Court
25 Mar 1912:	Promoted to *Major-General*
26 May 1914 - 1917:	Military Judge, Odessa Military District Court

Major-General Fyodor Nikolayevich **Vologodsky** (20 Apr 1855 - ?)
20 Feb 1908 - 1911:	Chairman of the Board, Siberian Cossack Army
29 Mar 1909:	Promoted to *Major-General*

Lieutenant-General Yevgeny Mikhailovich **Volosatov** (2 Sep 1858 - ?)
27 May 1906 - 18 May 1911:	Deputy Commandant, St. Petersburg Arsenal
29 Mar 1909:	Promoted to *Major-General*
18 May 1911 - 1917:	Chief of St. Petersburg Pipe Factory
10 Apr 1916:	Promoted to *Lieutenant-General*

Major-General Fyodor Moiseyevich **Voloshin-Petrichenko** (20 Feb 1860 - ?)
4 Dec 1913 - 28 Dec 1915:	Commander, 155th Infantry Regiment
6 Dec 1915:	Promoted to *Major-General*
28 Dec 1915 - 12 Aug 1916:	Commander, Don Foot Brigade
12 Aug 1916 - 1917:	Commander, 6th Caucasus Rifle Division

Major-General Timofey Moiseyevich **Voloshin-Petrichenko** (22 Jan 1862 - ?)
16 Aug 1914 - Aug 1915:	Commander, 231st Infantry Regiment
1 May 1915:	Promoted to *Major-General*
Aug 1915 - 1918:	POW

General of Infantry Fyodor Afanasievich **Voloshinov** (26 Apr 1852 - 4 Oct 1919)
24 Apr 1902:	Promoted to *Major-General*
24 Apr 1902 - 13 Aug 1905:	Commander, 1st Brigade, 39th Infantry Division
13 Aug 1905 - 23 Oct 1908:	Commander, 2nd Caucasus Rifle Brigade
23 Oct 1908:	Promoted to *Lieutenant-General*
23 Oct 1908 - 9 Apr 1910:	Commander, 5th Siberian Rifle Division

9 Apr 1910 - 8 Apr 1911:	Unassigned
8 Apr 1911 - 1 May 1914:	Commander, 44th Infantry Division
1 May 1914:	Promoted to *General of Infantry*
1 May 1914:	Retired
20 Jul 1914 - 1 Nov 1914:	Recalled; Commander, 82nd Infantry Division
1 Nov 1914:	Retired

Lieutenant-General Pavel Lvovich **Volotskoy** (8 Sep 1826 - 23 Jun 1896)
14 Jul 1879 - 5 Sep 1885:	Commander, 28th Artillery Brigade
30 Aug 1882:	Promoted to *Major-General*
5 Sep 1885 - 13 Jul 1892:	Commander, 1st Artillery Brigade
13 Jul 1892 - 23 Jun 1896:	Commander of Artillery, II. Army Corps
30 Aug 1892:	Promoted to *Lieutenant-General*

Lieutenant-General Rudolf Adolfovich von **Volsky** (20 Jun 1852 - ?)
14 Oct 1903:	Promoted to *Major-General*
14 Oct 1903 - 24 Jan 1909:	Commander, 24th Artillery Brigade
24 Jan 1909:	Promoted to *Lieutenant-General*
24 Jan 1909 - 23 Apr 1910:	Commander of Artillery, XXI. Army Corps
23 Apr 1910 - 1912:	Commander of Artillery, IX. Army Corps

General of Infantry Sigizmund Viktorovich **Volsky** (30 Mar 1852 - ?)
21 Jun 1905:	Promoted to *Major-General*
21 Jun 1905 - 11 Mar 1906:	Commander, 1st Brigade, 38th Infantry Division
11 Mar 1906 - 8 Aug 1907:	Commander, 2nd Brigade, Caucasus Grenadier Division
8 Aug 1907 - 12 Mar 1908:	Commander, 1st Caucasus Rifle Brigade
12 Mar 1908 - 24 Jun 1908:	Military Governor of Kars Region
24 Jun 1908 - 17 Mar 1915:	Military Governor of Dagestan Region
6 Dec 1911:	Promoted to *Lieutenant-General*
17 Mar 1915 - 9 Apr 1917:	Commanding General, Caucasus Military District
9 Apr 1917:	Retired
26 May 1917:	Promoted to *General of Infantry*

Major-General Vladislav Valerianovich **Volyntsevich-Sidorovich** (2 Dec 1861 - ?)
1 Aug 1904 - Aug 1908:	Director, Tashkent Cadet Corps
13 Apr 1908:	Promoted to *Major-General*

Major-General Nikolai Nikolayevich **Volzhin** (6 Nov 1854 - ?)
17 Oct 1906 - 1909:	Commander, 6th Orenburg Cossack Regiment
1909:	Promoted to *Major-General*
1909:	Retired
23 Aug 1914 - 29 Jul 1917:	Recalled; Commander, 2nd Brigade, Siberian Cossack Division
29 Jul 1917:	Dismissed

General of Cavalry Nikolai Mikhailovich **Vonlyarlyarsky** (20 Mar 1846 - 15 Aug 1906)
14 Jul 1883 - 9 Jun 1885:	Commander, 9th Dragoon Regiment
9 Jun 1885:	Promoted to *Major-General*

9 Jun 1885 - 6 Nov 1891:	Commander, 2nd Brigade, 13th Cavalry Division
6 Nov 1891 - 4 Apr 1895:	Commander, 2nd Brigade, 6th Cavalry Division
4 Apr 1895 - 11 Aug 1900:	Commander, 14th Cavalry Division
6 Dec 1895:	Promoted to *Lieutenant-General*
11 Aug 1900 - 27 Jun 1902:	Commanding General, II. Cavalry Corps
27 Jun 1902 - 15 Aug 1906:	Commanding General, V. Army Corps
2 Apr 1906:	Promoted to *General of Cavalry*
1906 - 15 Aug 1906:	Acting Governor-General of Warsaw

Major-General Andrey Sergeyevich **Vorobyev** (30 Nov 1861 - 18 Jan 1917)
23 Jul 1916:	Promoted to *Major-General*
23 Jul 1916 - 18 Jan 1917:	Commander, Brigade, 65th Infantry Division

Lieutenant-General Nikolai Mikhailovich **Vorobyev** (15 Mar 1855 - ?)
1 Jun 1904 - 15 Jun 1905:	Commander, 242nd Infantry Regiment
30 Dec 1904:	Promoted to *Major-General*
15 Jun 1905 - 6 Jul 1905:	Commander, 1st Brigade, 10th East Siberian Rifle Division
6 Jul 1905 - 19 Oct 1906:	Commander, 2nd Brigade, 61st Infantry Division
19 Oct 1906 - 29 Mar 1915:	Commander, 2nd Brigade, 20th Infantry Division
12 Mar 1915:	Promoted to *Lieutenant-General*
29 Mar 1915 - 14 Sep 1915:	Commander, 4th Caucasus Rifle Brigade
14 Sep 1915 - 3 Jun 1917:	Commander, 4th Caucasus Rifle Division

General of Infantry Dmitry Nikolayevich **Voronets** (20 Oct 1852 - 26 May 1932)
22 Jun 1898:	Promoted to *Major-General*
22 Jun 1898 - 23 Oct 1899:	Chief of Staff, Fortress Modlin
23 Oct 1899 - 3 Aug 1900:	Deputy Chief of Staff, Warsaw Military District
3 Aug 1900 - 4 May 1902:	Commander, 6th East Siberian Rifle Brigade
4 May 1902 - 25 Jan 1905:	Commandant of Fortress Vladivostok
15 Oct 1904:	Promoted to *Lieutenant-General*
25 Jan 1905 - 24 May 1905:	At the disposal of the Minister of War
24 May 1905 - 19 Jul 1909:	Commander, 33rd Infantry Division
19 Jul 1909 - 19 Oct 1914:	General for Assignments to the Chief of the General Staff
19 Oct 1914 - 11 Aug 1916:	Chief of Staff, Turkestan Military District
11 Aug 1916 - 27 Apr 1917:	Attached to the Chief of the General Staff
27 Apr 1917:	Promoted to *General of Infantry*
27 Apr 1917:	Retired

Major-General Grigory Martinianovich **Voronets** (30 Jan 1867 - ?)
15 Sep 1915 - 1918:	Chairman of the Remount Commission, Penza Region
6 Dec 1915:	Promoted to *Major-General*

Major-General Yevstafy Grigoryevich **Voronets** (7 Nov 1846 - 1 Mar 1903)
6 Nov 1895 - 8 Jun 1899:	Commandant of Fortress Zegrze
14 May 1896:	Promoted to *Major-General*
8 Jun 1899 - 1 Mar 1903:	Commander, 1st Brigade, 35th Infantry Division

Major-General Vladimir Vladimirovich **Voronetsky** (26 Aug 1866 - 23 Jun 1916)
19 Apr 1914 - 14 May 1915:	Commander, 28th Siberian Rifle Regiment
18 Jan 1915:	Promoted to *Major-General*
14 May 1915 - 3 Feb 1916:	Chief of Staff, XXXVII. Army Corps
3 Feb 1916 - 23 Jun 1916:	Chief of Staff, XIII. Army Corps

Lieutenant-General Stepan Aleksandrovich **Voronin** (2 Aug 1858 - Aug 1926)
15 Aug 1900 - 30 Oct 1904:	Section Chief, Quartermaster-General Department, General Staff
28 Mar 1904:	Promoted to *Major-General*
30 Oct 1904 - 10 May 1907:	Quartermaster-General, Warsaw Military District
10 May 1907 - 25 Aug 1907:	Commander, 2nd Brigade, 3rd Guards Infantry Division
25 Aug 1907 - 4 Dec 1908:	Quartermaster-General, Warsaw Military District
4 Dec 1908 - 11 Jul 1910:	Commander, 47th Replacement Infantry Brigade
11 Jul 1910:	Promoted to *Lieutenant-General*
11 Jul 1910 - 18 Jun 1915:	Commander, 23rd Infantry Division
18 Jun 1915 - 30 Oct 1915:	Commanding General, XL. Army Corps
30 Oct 1915 - 5 Jul 1916:	At the disposal of the C-in-C, Southwestern Front
5 Jul 1916 - 1917:	At the disposal of the C-in-C, Northern Front

Major-General Aleksey Aleksandrovich **Voronov** (24 Feb 1850 - ?)
17 Oct 1904 - 1910:	Commander of Engineers, Fortress St. Petersburg
17 Apr 1905:	Promoted to *Major-General*
1910:	Retired

Major-General Nikolai Aleksandrovich **Voronov** (18 Sep 1851 - ?)
12 Dec 1905:	Promoted to *Major-General*
12 Dec 1905 - 13 Jul 1906:	Commander, 2nd Brigade, 3rd Infantry Division
13 Jul 1906 - 30 Jun 1907:	Commander, 2nd Brigade, 5th Infantry Division

Major-General Nikolai Aleksandrovich **Voronov** (5 Nov 1868 - 1920)
8 Sep 1910 - 1917:	Inspector of Classes, Pskov Cadet Corps
6 Dec 1913:	Promoted to *Major-General*

Major-General Nikolai Irakliyevich **Voronov** (12 Aug 1832 - ?)
19 Oct 1885 - 1900:	Commander of Gendarmerie, Vladimir Province
14 May 1896:	Promoted to *Major-General*

General of Infantry Nikolai Mikhailovich **Voronov** (5 Jul 1859 - ?)
13 Mar 1904 - 18 Jul 1905:	Commandant, Staff HQ to the C-in-C, Far East
18 Jun 1904:	Promoted to *Major-General*
18 Jul 1905 - 29 Dec 1908:	Commander, 1st Brigade, 14th Infantry Division
29 Dec 1908 - 21 Jul 1910:	Commander, 52nd Replacement Infantry Brigade
21 Jul 1910 - 12 Jun 1912:	Commander, 1st Turkestan Rifle Brigade
30 May 1912:	Promoted to *Lieutenant-General*
12 Jun 1912 - 31 Dec 1913:	Commander, 6th Siberian Rifle Division
31 Dec 1913 - 22 Dec 1914:	Commander, 51st Infantry Division
22 Dec 1914 - 12 Apr 1917:	Commanding General, V. Siberian Army Corps

12 Apr 1917 - Oct 1917:	Reserve officer, Kiev Military District
3 Jun 1917:	Promoted to *General of Infantry*
Oct 1917:	Retired

Lieutenant-General Pavel Nikolayevich **Voronov** (19 May 1851 - 5 Dec 1922)

30 Nov 1898:	Promoted to *Major-General*
30 Nov 1898 - 14 Aug 1904:	Special Assignments General, St. Petersburg Military District
14 Aug 1904 - 24 Dec 1905:	Commander, 23rd Infantry Division
6 Dec 1904:	Promoted to *Lieutenant-General*
24 Dec 1905 - 1 Jun 1908:	Reserve officer, General Staff
1 Jun 1908:	Retired

Major-General Pavel Pavlovich **Voronov** (26 Jul 1862 - ?)

7 Sep 1902 - 17 Apr 1906:	Commander, Primorsky Dragoon Regiment
1905:	Promoted to *Major-General*
17 Apr 1906 - 28 May 1907:	Attached to the General Staff
28 May 1907 - Nov 1907:	Commander, 2nd Brigade, 11th Cavalry Division

Major-General Vladimir Mikhailovich **Voronov** (19 Mar 1858 - ?)

6 Feb 1903 - 25 Jun 1907:	Commandant, Siberian Infantry Officer School
4 Feb 1906:	Promoted to *Major-General*
25 Jun 1907 - Dec 1908:	Commander, 2nd Brigade, 3rd Grenadier Division

Major-General Fyodor Vasilyevich **Vorontsov** (7 Apr 1857 - 1921)

5 Dec 1910 - 27 Sep 1914:	Duty General, Kazan Military District
1 Nov 1911:	Promoted to *Major-General*
27 Sep 1914 - 1917:	Duty General, 4th Army

General of Cavalry Count Illarion Ivanovich **Vorontsov-Dashkov** (27 May 1837 - 15 Jan 1916)

28 Oct 1866:	Promoted to *Major-General*
28 Oct 1866 - 15 Oct 1867:	Deputy Governor-General of Turkestan
15 Oct 1867 - 21 Oct 1874:	Commander, Life Guards Hussar Regiment
2 Oct 1873 - 21 Oct 1874:	Commander, 2nd Brigade, 2nd Guards Cavalry Division
21 Oct 1874 - 23 Jul 1878:	Chief of Staff, Guards Corps
1 Dec 19874 - 12 Oct 1878:	Member, Directorate-General for Remounts
19 Feb 1875:	Promoted to *General-Adjutant*
30 Aug 1876:	Promoted to *Lieutenant-General*
12 Oct 1878 - 8 Apr 1881:	Commander, 2nd Guards Infantry Division
1 Jun 1881 - 6 May 1897:	Director-General of State Horse Breeding
17 Aug 1881 - 6 May 1897:	Minister of the Imperial Court
30 Aug 1890:	Promoted to *General of Cavalry*
6 May 1897 - 27 Feb 1905:	Member of the State Council
27 Feb 1905 - 17 Mar 1915:	Commanding General, Caucasus Military District
27 Feb 1905 - 23 Aug 1915:	Governor-General of the Caucasus, Military Ataman of the Caucasus Cossacks
30 Aug 1914 - 23 Aug 1915:	C-in-C, Caucasus Army

23 Aug 1915 - 15 Jan 1916: Special Advisor to the Tsar

General of Engineers Aleksei Pavlovich **Vorontsov-Velyaminov** (23 Jul 1843 - 4 Oct 1912)
8 Aug 1882 - 12 Feb 1889: Deputy Commander of Engineers, Moscow Military District
5 May 1888: Promoted to *Major-General*
12 Feb 1889 - 18 Mar 1897: Commander of Engineers, Warsaw Military District
14 May 1896: Promoted to *Lieutenant-General*
18 Mar 1897 - 4 Jun 1910: Commander of Engineers, Moscow Military District
4 Jun 1910: Promoted to *General of Engineers*
4 Jun 1910: Retired

Lieutenant-General Ivan Vasilyevich **Vorontsov-Velyaminov** (5 Oct 1832 - 26 Mar 1904)
20 Jan 1892 - 1900: Member, Electrotechnical Committee, Main Engineering Directorate
30 Aug 1892: Promoted to *Major-General*
18 Oct 1900: Promoted to *Lieutenant-General*

Major-General Konstantin Vasilyevich **Vorontsov-Velyaminov** (13 Apr 1868 - 30 Aug 1915)
11 Sep 1913 - 30 Aug 1915: Commander, 184th Infantry Regiment
22 Oct 1915: Posthumously promoted to *Major-General*

Major-General Nikolai Petrovich **Voronyansky** (2 Aug 1842 - ?)
29 Dec 1899: Promoted to *Major-General*
29 Dec 1899 - 2 Jul 1902: Commander, Kuban Cossack Horse Artillery Brigade
2 Jul 1902 - 1905: Chief, Labinsky Group, Kuban Cossack Army

Lieutenant-General Nikolai Nikolayevich **Voropanov** (8 Sep 1854 - ?)
31 Dec 1901 - 9 Feb 1907: Commander, 5th Finnish Rifle Regiment
6 Dec 1906: Promoted to *Major-General*
9 Feb 1907 - 19 Jul 1911: Commander, 2nd Brigade, 37th Infantry Division
19 Jul 1911 - 24 Mar 1915: Commander, 2nd Caucasus Rifle Brigade
24 Mar 1915 - 21 Sep 1915: Commander, 66th Infantry Division
8 May 1915: Promoted to *Lieutenant-General*
21 Sep 1915 - 7 Dec 1915: Unassigned
7 Dec 1915 - 4 Sep 1917: Inspector of Reserve Forces, Caucasus Army
4 Sep 1917: Dismissed

Major-General Mikhail Petrovich **Voropayev** (2 Nov 1849 - ?)
22 Apr 1907 - 21 Sep 1907: Commander, 6th East Siberian Rifle Artillery Brigade
31 May 1907: Promoted to *Major-General*

Lieutenant-General Mark Semyonovich **Vorotnikov** (8 Mar 1843 - ?)
22 Mar 1895 - 9 Apr 1897: Commander, Turkestan Artillery Brigade
22 Mar 1895: Promoted to *Major-General*
9 Apr 1897 - 11 Aug 1900: Commander, 6th Artillery Brigade
11 Aug 1900 - 13 Aug 1905: Commander of Artillery, XV. Army Corps

6 Apr 1903: Promoted to *Lieutenant-General*
13 Aug 1905 - 3 May 1906: Commander of Artillery, XIX. Army Corps

Rear-Admiral Sergey Nikolayevich **Vorozheykin** (19 Jan 1867 - 26 Mar 1939)
3 Aug 1914 - Oct 1917: Director of Naval Construction Corps, Sevastopol
30 Jun 1916: Promoted to *Rear-Admiral*

Major-General Aleksandr Yevgafovich **Vorypayev** (23 Nov 1848 - ?)
2 Sep 1904 - 11 Apr 1907: Commander, 205th Reserve Infantry Regiment
6 Dec 1906: Promoted to *Major-General*
11 Apr 1907 - Jun 1910: Commander, 2nd Brigade, 9th Infantry Division

Major-General Nikolai Ivanovich **Voshchinin** (17 Jan 1854 - ?)
4 Mar 1910: Promoted to *Major-General*
4 Mar 1910 - 16 Feb 1911: Commander, 32nd Artillery Brigade
16 Feb 1911: Retired

Lieutenant-General of Naval Engineers Ivan Nikanorovich **Voskresensky** (21 Aug 1862 - 1943)
10 Nov 1908 - 1918: Chief of Izhorsky Factory
18 Apr 1910: Promoted to *Major-General of Naval Engineers*
14 Apr 1913: Promoted to *Lieutenant-General of Naval Engineers*

Major-General Vladimir Ivanovich **Voskresensky** (19 Feb 1867 - ?)
20 Aug 1915 - 30 Jan 1916: Commander, Brigade, Caucasus Grenadier Division
31 Oct 1915: Promoted to *Major-General*
30 Jan 1916 - 1 Jan 1917: Chief of Staff, 7th Siberian Rifle Division
1 Jan 1917 - 12 May 1917: Chief of Staff, XXVI. Army Corps
12 May 1917 - 1918: Quartermaster-General, 9th Army

Major-General of Naval Artillery Vyacheslav Ivanovich **Voskresensky** (20 Feb 1864 - ?)
25 Mar 1912: Promoted to *Major-General of Naval Artillery*
35 Oct 1912 - 17 Nov 1913: Chief of Marine Corps Artillery Factory
17 Nov 1913 - ?: Member of the Artillery Committee, Main Artillery Directorate

Lieutenant-General Aleksandr Pavlovich **Vostrosablin** (17 Aug 1857 - 1920)
23 Jan 1907 - 19 May 1910: Commander of Artillery, Sevastopol Garrison
31 May 1907: Promoted to *Major-General*
19 May 1910 - Sep 1918: Commandant of Fortress Kushka
6 Dec 1914: Promoted to *Lieutenant-General*

General of Infantry Nikolai Nikolayevich **Vostrosablin** (7 Aug 1854 - ?)
15 Feb 1903 - 24 Jan 1906: Military Judge, Vilnius Military District Court
6 Apr 1903: Promoted to *Major-General*
24 Jan 1906 - 21 May 1908: Military Procurator, Caucasus Military District
21 May 1908 - 4 Aug 1911: Chairman, Turkestan Military District Court
6 Dec 1909: Promoted to *Lieutenant-General*

4 Aug 1911 - 22 Apr 1917:	Chairman, Kiev Military District Court
22 Apr 1917:	Promoted to *General of Infantry*
22 Apr 1917:	Retired

Major-General Ivan Semyonovich **Vovk** (29 May 1860 - ?)
17 Sep 1912 - 10 Jul 1916:	Commander, 207th Infantry Regiment
27 Jan 1916:	Promoted to *Major-General*
10 Jul 1916 - 1917:	Commander, 1st Brigade, 52nd Infantry Division

General of Infantry Karl-Avgust-Fridrikh Mavrikievich **Voyde** (9 Jul 1833 - 1905)
15 Sep 1873 - 7 May 1878:	Deputy Chief of Staff, Warsaw Military District
29 Jun 1874:	Promoted to *Major-General*
7 May 1878 - 27 Sep 1881:	Chief of Staff, Orenburg Military District
27 Sep 1881 - 5 Aug 1882:	At the disposal of the Commanding General, Warsaw Military District
5 Aug 1882 - 14 Aug 1890:	Special Assignments General, Warsaw Military District
5 Aug 1882 - 1983:	Member, Commission for the Fortification of Warsaw
1883 - 30 Aug 1889:	Member, Commission on Troop Training
30 Aug 1889:	Promoted to *Lieutenant-General*
14 Aug 1890 - 31 Oct 1890:	Commander, 2nd Infantry Division
31 Oct 1890 - 3 Jun 1898:	Commander, 10th Infantry Division
3 Jun 1898 - 9 Mar 1903:	Member, Military Registration Committee, General Staff
9 Mar 1903:	Promoted to *General of Infantry*
9 Mar 1903 - 1905:	At the disposal of the Minister of War

Major-General Aleksandr Aleksandrovich **Voyevodin** (11 Dec 1849 - ?)
15 Feb 1908 - May 1910:	Military Commander, Bryansk District
May 1910:	Promoted to *Major-General*
May 1910:	Retired
1914 - 1916:	Recalled; Assigned to the State Militia
1916 - 1917:	Military Commander, Poltava

Lieutenant-General Aleksandr-Rokh Fyodorovich **Voyevodsky** (16 Aug 1855 - ?)
23 Jun 1901 - 9 Oct 1907:	Military Judge, Caucasus Military District Court
6 Dec 1901:	Promoted to *Major-General*
9 Oct 1907 - ?:	Military Judge, Moscow Military District Court
2 Mar 1911:	Promoted to *Lieutenant-General*

Lieutenant-General Iosif Fyodorovich **Voyevodsky** (23 Nov 1852 - 13 Apr 1917)
21 Oct 1904 - 23 Oct 1906:	Deputy Inspector of Engineers, 2nd Manchurian Army
22 Nov 1904:	Promoted to *Major-General*
23 Oct 1906 - 22 Oct 1912:	Commander of Engineers, Irkutsk Military District
10 Apr 1911:	Promoted to *Lieutenant-General*
22 Oct 1912 - 20 Mar 1914:	Chief of Troop Billeting, Irkutsk Military District
20 Mar 1914 - 13 Apr 1917:	Attached to the Main Directorate for Troop Billeting

Lieutenant-General of the Naval Legal Corps Platon Arkadyevich **Voyevodsky** (22 Oct 1861 - 14 Jan 1941)
6 Dec 1908:	Promoted to *Major-General of the Naval Legal Corps*
5 Oct 1909 - 13 May 1913:	Deputy Chief Naval Prosecutor
6 Dec 1912:	Promoted to *Lieutenant-General of the Naval Legal Corps*
13 May 1913 - 17 May 1917:	Member, Main Naval Tribunal
17 May 1917:	Dismissed

Admiral Stepan Arkadievich **Voyevodsky** (22 Mar 1859 - 18 Aug 1937)
Aug 1906 - 1908:	Commandant of the Imperial Naval Academy, Director of the Marine Corps
1907:	Promoted to *Rear-Admiral*
1908 - 8 Jan 1909:	Deputy Minister of the Navy, Member of the Admiralty Board
8 Jan 1909 - 18 Mar 1911:	Minister of the Navy, Chairman of the Admiralty Board
4 Sep 1909:	Promoted to *Vice-Admiral*
18 Mar 1911 - Oct 1917:	Member of the State Council
6 Dec 1913:	Promoted to *Admiral*

Major-General Aleksandr Nikolayevich **Voyeykov** (30 Oct 1865 - 26 Feb 1942)
6 May 1912:	Promoted to *Major-General*
6 May 1912 - 28 Aug 1915:	At the disposal of the Minister of War
28 Aug 1915 - 1917:	Attached to the Main Directorate of State Horse Breeding

General of Cavalry Nikolai Vasilyevich **Voyeykov** (6 Nov 1832 - 26 Sep 1898)
13 Oct 1866 - 1 May 1883:	Business Manager, Imperial Headquarters, Member of the Tsar's retinue
30 Aug 1867:	Promoted to *Major-General*
30 Aug 1876:	Promoted to *General-Adjutant*
30 Aug 1879:	Promoted to *Lieutenant-General*
1 May 1883 - 2 Apr 1895:	Deputy Commandant of the Imperial Headquarters
30 Aug 1893:	Promoted to *General of Cavalry*
2 Apr 1895 - 26 Sep 1898:	Chief Chamberlain of the Imperial Household

Major-General Pyotr Pavlovich **Voyeykov** (15 Jun 1850 - ?)
19 Jun 1905:	Promoted to *Major-General*
19 Jun 1905 - 28 Aug 1906:	Commander, 2nd Brigade, 2nd Rifle Division
28 Aug 1906 - 14 Feb 1909:	Commander, 2nd Brigade, 12th Infantry Division

Major-General Vladimir Nikolayevich **Voyeykov** (2 Aug 1868 - 8 Oct 1947)
11 Aug 1907 - 24 Dec 1913:	Commander, Life Guards Hussar Regiment
6 Dec 1909:	Promoted to *Major-General*
12 Dec 1913 - 7 Mar 1917:	Commandant of the Imperial Palace

Major-General Sergey Konstantinovich **Voyna-Panchenko** (4 Jul 1878 - 11 Jan 1920)
12 Feb 1915 - 1917:   Commander, Life Guards Heavy Artillery Battalion
9 Feb 1917:   Promoted to *Major-General*

Major-General Otton Lyudvigovich **Voynilovich** (22 Dec 1857 - 5 Nov 1940)
19 Jun 1910 - 1912:   Commander, 155th Infantry Regiment
1912:   Retired
1914 - 27 Jun 1916:   Recalled
26 Jun 1916:   Promoted to *Major-General*
27 Jun 1916 - 5 Jun 1917:   Deputy Commander, Airship Squadron
5 Jun 1917:   Dismissed

General of Engineers Genrikh Stanislavovich **Voynitsky** (15 Nov 1833 - ?)
1 Jan 1878:   Promoted to *Major-General*
1 Jan 1878 - 3 Sep 1887:   Attached to the Main Engineering Department
3 Sep 1887 - 9 Feb 1900:   Member of the Engineering Committee, Main Engineering Department
30 Aug 1889:   Promoted to *Lieutenant-General*
9 Feb 1900:   Promoted to *General of Engineers*
9 Feb 1900:   Retired

Major-General Sergey Arkadyevich **Voyno-Oransky** (9 Dec 1866 - 11 Feb 1915)
13 Jun 1910 - 24 Apr 1913:   Commander, 1st Battalion, Life Guards 3rd Artillery Brigade
14 Apr 1913:   Promoted to *Major-General*
24 Apr 1913 - 11 Feb 1915:   Commander, 5th Artillery Brigade

Major-General Illarion Markianovich **Voynov** (21 Oct 1830 - ?)
27 Feb 1891:   Promoted to *Major-General*
27 Feb 1891 - Nov 1898:   Commander, 35th Artillery Brigade

Major-General Genrikh-Oskar Bronislavovich **Voynovsky-Kriger** (17 Oct 1867 - 1 Jun 1920)
19 Mar 1914 - 1917:   Special Purposes General, Main Military Technical Directorate
10 Apr 1916:   Promoted to *Major-General*

General of Infantry Ippolit Paulinovich **Voyshin-Murdas-Zhilinsky** (6 Apr 1856 - 20 Jan 1926)
30 Apr 1900:   Promoted to *Major-General*
30 Apr 1900 - 20 May 1902:   Chief of Staff, XVIII. Army Corps
20 May 1902 - 26 Oct 1905:   Quartermaster-General, St. Petersburg Military District
26 Oct 1905 - 6 Apr 1907:   At the disposal of the Commanding General, St. Petersburg Military District
6 Apr 1907 - 15 May 1912:   Commander, 4th Infantry Division
22 Apr 1907:   Promoted to *Lieutenant-General*
15 May 1912 - 19 Apr 1917:   Commanding General, XIV. Army Corps
14 Apr 1913:   Promoted to *General of Infantry*

19 Apr 1917 - 4 May 1917:	Reserve officer, Dvinsk Military District
4 May 1917:	Retired

Lieutenant-General Leonid Paulinovich **Voyshin-Murdas-Zhilinsky** (1 Jun 1861 - 23 Feb 1924)

28 Sep 1904:	Promoted to *Major-General*
28 Sep 1904 - 10 Aug 1906:	Chief of Military Communications, 2nd Manchurian Army
10 Aug 1906 - 1917:	Director of Nizhny Novgorod Cadet Corps
10 Apr 1911:	Promoted to *Lieutenant-General*

Major-General Andrey Andreyevich **Voytsekhovich** (7 Sep 1840 - 8 Oct 1903)

17 Mar 1893 - 1899:	Engineer Inspector, Omsk Military District
30 Aug 1894:	Promoted to *Major-General*
1899:	Retired

Major-General Fyodor Pavlovich **Voytsekhovich** (8 Feb 1866 - ?)

3 May 1910 - 16 Nov 1913:	Military Judge, Omsk Military District Court
6 Dec 1910:	Promoted to *Major-General*
16 Nov 1913 - Aug 1914:	Military Judge, Moscow Military District Court
Aug 1914:	Chairman of the Military Court, XIII. Army Corps
Aug 1914 - 1916:	POW
10 Jul 1916 - 1917:	Military Judge, Moscow Military District Court

Lieutenant-General Aleksey Nikolayevich **Voytsekhovsky** (20 Feb 1863 - 26 Aug 1917)

3 Oct 1906 - 10 Jun 1909:	Ministry of War Representative, Irkutsk Military District Council
13 Apr 1908:	Promoted to *Major-General*
10 Jun 1909 - 1914:	Ministry of War Representative, Warsaw Military District Council
1913:	Promoted to *Lieutenant-General*
1914 - 26 Aug 1917:	At the disposal of the Commanding General, Minsk Military District

Major-General Mikhail Karlovich **Voytsekhovsky** (21 Jan 1854 - 4 Oct 1946)

25 May 1915:	Promoted to *Major-General*
14 Sep 1915 - 29 May 1916:	Commander, 29th Replacement Infantry Brigade
29 May 1916 - 18 Feb 1917:	Commander, Brigade, 7th Infantry Division
18 Feb 1917 - 30 Sep 1917:	Commander, 151st Infantry Division
30 Sep 1917 - 1918:	Commander, 28th Infantry Division

Major-General Nikolai Karlovich **Voytsekhovsky** (11 Feb 1857 - 1920)

5 Dec 1909 - 13 May 1913:	Commander, 11th Siberian Rifle Regiment
13 May 1913:	Promoted to *Major-General*
13 May 1913:	Retired
14 Nov 1914 - 1 Apr 1915:	Recalled; Reserve officer, Kiev Military District
1 Apr 1915 - 1917:	Commander, 85th Militia Brigade

Major-General Baron Anatoly-Nils Andreyevich **Vrangel** (28 Apr 1849 - 23 May 1931)
3 Aug 1879 - 1904: Chief of Police, Tsarskoye Selo
14 Apr 1902: Promoted to *Major-General*
1904: Retired

Major-General Baron Nikolai Aleksandrovich **Vrangel** (25 Aug 1869 - 7 Mar 1927)
10 Apr 1916: Promoted to *Major-General*
10 Apr 1916 - 19 Apr 1917: Attached to Grand Duke Mikhail Alexandrovich
19 Apr 1917 - Oct 1917: Reserve officer, Dvinsk Military District

Major-General Baron Pyotr Nikolayevich **Vrangel** (15 Aug 1878 - 25 Apr 1928)
24 Dec 1916 - 19 Jan 1917: Commander, 2nd Brigade, Ussuri Mounted Division
13 Jan 1917: Promoted to *Major-General*
19 Jan 1917 - 9 Jul 1917: Commander, 1st Brigade, Ussuri Mounted Division
23 Jan 1917 - Apr 1917: Acting Commander, Ussuri Mounted Division
9 Jul 1917 - 23 Aug 1917: Commander, 7th Cavalry Division
23 Aug 1917 - 9 Sep 1917: Commanding General, Consolidated Cavalry Corps

Lieutenant-General Baron Vladimir Lyudvigovich **Vrangel** (16 Jun 1820 - ?)
30 Aug 1873: Promoted to *Major-General*
30 Aug 1873 - 4 Dec 1873: Commander, 1st Brigade, 39th Infantry Division
4 Dec 1873 - 24 May 1892: Commander, 1st Brigade, 22nd Infantry Division
24 May 1892 - 1902: Commandant of Krasnoselsky
30 Aug 1892: Promoted to *Lieutenant-General*

Major-General Baron Vladimir Platonovich **Vrangel** (7 Feb 1864 - 10 Oct 1919)
17 Nov 1916: Promoted to *Major-General*
17 Nov 1916 - 1917: Commander, 1st Reserve Cavalry Brigade

General of Infantry Baron Aleksandr Borisovich **Vrevsky** (23 May 1834 - 9 Nov 1910)
30 Aug 1875: Promoted to *Major-General*
30 Aug 1875 - 1 Nov 1876: Deputy Chief of Staff, Moscow Military District
1 Nov 1876 - 25 Jul 1884: Chief of Staff, X. Army Corps
25 Jul 1884 - 28 Oct 1889: Chief of Staff, Odessa Military District
30 Aug 1885: Promoted to *Lieutenant-General*
28 Oct 1889 - 17 Mar 1898: Commanding General, Turkestan Military District, Governor-General of Turkestan
17 Mar 1898: Promoted to *General of Infantry*
17 Mar 1898 - 3 Jan 1906: Member of the Military Council
3 Jan 1906: Retired

Lieutenant-General Konstantin Vyacheslavovich **Vrotnovsky** (1 Apr 1852 - 1906)
18 Jan 1897 - 5 Sep 1905: Section Chief, Main Engineering Directorate
1 Jan 1901: Promoted to *Major-General*
5 Sep 1905 - 1906: Member of the Engineering Committee, Main Engineering Directorate
1906: Promoted to *Lieutenant-General*

Major-General Przhemyslav Ferdinandovich **Vrublevsky** (1 Apr 1831 - ?)
22 Oct 1883 - 3 Jun 1887: Deputy Commander of Engineers, Caucasus Military District
6 May 1884: Promoted to *Major-General*
3 Jun 1887 - 1894: Inspector of Engineering Works, Caucasus Military District

General of Artillery Mikhail Antonovich **Vrzheshch** (6 Sep 1847 - ?)
23 May 1899 - 17 May 1905: Ministry of War Representative, Vilnius Military District Council
6 Dec 1901: Promoted to *Major-General*
17 May 1905 - 13 Apr 1910: Ministry of War Representative, Caucasus Military District Council
6 Dec 1907: Promoted to *Lieutenant-General*
13 Apr 1910 - 1 Jan 1916: Ministry of War Representative, Odessa Military District Council
1 Jan 1916: Promoted to *General of Artillery*
1 Jan 1916: Retired

Lieutenant-General Andrei Dmitriyevich **Vsevolozhsky** (11 Jul 1851 - 16 May 1912)
7 Feb 1901: Promoted to *Major-General*
7 Feb 1901 - 22 Mar 1901: Commander, 2nd Brigade, 7th Infantry Division
22 Mar 1901 - 30 Apr 1903: Commander, Lithuanian Life Guards Regiment
30 Apr 1903 - 11 Dec 1903: Commander, 2nd Brigade, 2nd Infantry Division
11 Dec 1903 - 28 Jul 1905: Commander, 2nd Brigade, 30th Infantry Division
28 Jul 1905 - 1906: Commander, 4th Rifle Division
1906 - 7 Jul 1907: Commander, 4th Rifle Brigade
22 Apr 1907: Promoted to *Lieutenant-General*
7 Jul 1907: Dismissed
10 Aug 1909 - 16 May 1912: Recalled; Member, Board of Trustees, Empress Maria Institutions

Rear-Admiral Dmitry Dmitriyevich **Vsevolozhsky** (25 Sep 1854 - 1909)
1907: Promoted to *Rear-Admiral*
1907 - 1908: At the disposal of the Minister of the Navy
1908 - 1909: Commander, Port of Sveaborg

Major-General Dmitry Sergeyevich **Vsevolozhsky** (10 Jun 1874 - 24 Oct 1918)
30 Sep 1916 - 1917: Commander, Life Guards 2nd Rifle Regiment
6 Dec 1916: Promoted to *Major-General*
1917: Commander, Brigade, Guards Rifle Division

Lieutenant-General Sergey Sergeyevich **Vsevolozhsky** (8 Jul 1869 - 1950)
25 Jun 1905 - 19 Apr 1911: Section Chief, General Staff
6 Dec 1910: Promoted to *Major-General*
19 Apr 1911 - 5 Apr 1917: Deputy Chief of Military Communications, General Staff
1 Aug 1914 - 5 Apr 1917: Acting Chief of Military Communications, General

	Staff
6 Dec 1916:	Promoted to *Lieutenant-General*

Lieutenant-General Mikhail Ivanovich **Vukotich** (23 Dec 1847 - ?)
20 Oct 1892:	Promoted to *Major-General*
20 Oct 1892 - 5 Sep 1894:	Special Assignments General, Vilnius Military District
5 Sep 1894 - 23 Jan 1900:	Attached to the General Staff
23 Jan 1900 - 1905:	Commander, Kazan Regional Brigade
6 Dec 1902:	Promoted to *Lieutenant-General*

Vice-Admiral Pavel Nikolayevich **Vulf** (16 Jan 1843 - 10 Jul 1909)
1895:	Promoted to *Rear-Admiral*
Jan 1899 - Jan 1903:	Commander, Port of Revel
Jan 1903 - 16 Oct 1906:	Commander of Lighthouses & Navigation, Baltic Sea
16 Oct 1906:	Promoted to *Vice-Admiral*
16 Oct 1906:	Retired

Major-General Andrey Fyodorovich **Vyacheslov** (11 Sep 1859 - ?)
2 Aug 1898 - 1909:	Squadron Commander, Don Cadet Corps
1909:	Promoted to *Major-General*
1909:	Retired

Major-General Stepan Yefimovich **Vyalov** (30 Nov 1875 - Sep 1915)
1915 - Sep 1915:	Commander, 306th Infantry Regiment
16 Apr 1916:	Posthumously promoted to *Major-General*

Rear-Admiral Fyodor Alekseyevich **Vyatkin** (1 Jan 1864 - 3 Feb 1944)
19 Jan 1914:	Promoted to *Rear-Admiral*
19 Jan 1914 - Oct 1917:	Commandant, Port of Kronstadt

General of Cavalry Prince Leonid Dmitrievich **Vyazemsky** (19 Aug 1848 - 24 Nov 1909)
30 Aug 1887:	Promoted to *Major-General*
30 Aug 1887 - 31 Jul 1888:	Transferred to the reserve
31 Jul 1888 - 19 Apr 1890:	Governor of Astrakhan, Ataman of Astrakhan Cossack Army
19 Apr 1890 - 14 Dec 1899:	Chief of the Main Administration for Imperial Estates
14 May 1896:	Promoted to *Lieutenant-General*
14 Dec 1899 - 24 Nov 1909:	Member of the State Council
6 Dec 1906:	Promoted to *General of Cavalry*

Vice-Admiral Prince Nikolai Aleksandrovich **Vyazemsky** (14 Nov 1857 - 24 Jun 1925)
21 Apr 1908 - 15 Feb 1916:	Commander, Imperial Yacht "*Polar Star*"
22 Jul 1909:	Promoted to *Rear-Admiral*
15 Feb 1916:	Promoted to *Vice-Admiral*
15 Feb 1916 - 1917:	Member of Admiralty Board

Major-General Prince Pyotr Pavlovich **Vyazemsky** (12 May 1854 - 1931)
3 Nov 1900 - 1910:	Master of the Horse, Grand Duke Mikhail Nikolayevich

29 Mar 1909:   Promoted to *Major-General*
1910:   Retired

Rear-Admiral Sergey Sergeyevich **Vyazemsky** (1 Mar 1869 - 12 Sep 1915)
24 Dec 1914 - 12 Sep 1915:   Commander, Battleship "*Slava*"
12 Sep 1915:   Posthumously promoted to *Rear-Admiral*

Major-General Nikolai Fyodorovich **Vyazigin** (26 Jan 1858 - ?)
24 Mar 1910 - 1912:   Commander, 1st Semirechensk Cossack Regiment
1912:   Promoted to *Major-General*
1912:   Retired
18 Nov 1914 - 21 Oct 1917:   Recalled; Reserve officer, Caucasus Military District
21 Oct 1917:   Dismissed

Lieutenant-General Nikolai Ivanovich **Vygran** (7 May 1857 - ?)
6 Oct 1905 - 20 Dec 1908:   Commander, Kars Borderguard Brigade
20 Dec 1908 - 2 Aug 1914:   Commander, Khotyn Borderguard Brigade
25 Mar 1912:   Promoted to *Major-General*
2 Aug 1914 - 1917:   Commander, 5th Replacement Infantry Brigade
1917 - 3 Apr 1917:   Reserve officer, Odessa Military District
3 Apr 1917:   Dismissed
29 Apr 1917:   Promoted to *Lieutenant-General*

Major-General Nikolai Grigoryevich **Vysheslavtsev** (9 Nov 1853 - ?)
31 Jul 1898:   Promoted to *Major-General*
31 Jul 1898 - 12 Apr 1903:   Commander, 2nd Brigade, 2nd Consolidated Cossack Division
12 Apr 1903 - 11 Jun 1906:   Commander, 1st Caucasus Cossack Division

Major-General Yevgeny Yevgenievich **Vyshinsky** (19 Jul 1873 - 1919)
19 Apr 1915 - 26 Mar 1916:   Commander, 13th Life Grenadier Regiment
19 Feb 1916:   Promoted to *Major-General*
26 Mar 1916 - 25 Sep 1916:   Deputy Quartermaster-General, Caucasus Army
25 Sep 1916 - 9 Jun 1917:   Staff officer, Caucasus Army
9 Jun 1917 - 1917:   Acting Chief of Staff, Caucasus Army
1917 - 1918:   Quartermaster-General, Caucasus Army

Major-General Gavriil Ignatyevich **Vyshomirsky** (2 Aug 1856 - 1912)
21 Jul 1910 - 1912:   Commander, 19th Turkestan Rifle Regiment
1912:   Promoted to *Major-General*

Major-General Nikolai Fedorovich **Vysotsky** (20 May 1858 - 5 Jan 1939)
10 Oct 1916 - 1917:   Commander, 100th Artillery Brigade
30 Oct 1916:   Promoted to *Major-General*
1917:   Inspector of Artillery, XXXII. Army Corps

General of Infantry Viktor Viktorovich **Vysotsky** (17 Mar 1857 - ?)
8 Jun 1895 - 2 Dec 1905:   Military Judge, Warsaw Military District Court

1 Jan 1901:	Promoted to *Major-General*
2 Dec 1905 - 19 Feb 1908:	Prosecutor, Moscow Military District Court
22 Apr 1907:	Promoted to *Lieutenant-General*
19 Feb 1908 - 3 Oct 1912:	Chairman of the Military Court, Kazan Military District
3 Oct 1912:	Promoted to *General of Infantry*
3 Oct 1912:	Retired

Major-General Yevgeny Ivanovich **Vysotsky** (6 Jan 1846 - 26 Jul 1911)
7 Aug 1899 - 10 Dec 1903:	Intendant, II. Turkestan Army Corps
6 Dec 1903:	Promoted to *Major-General*
10 Dec 1903 - 13 Jan 1905:	Deputy Intendant, Turkestan Military District
13 Jan 1905 - 1 Mar 1908:	Deputy Intendant-General, Manchurian Army
1 Mar 1908 - 26 Jul 1911:	Deputy Intendant, Caucasus Military District

Major-General Rodzislav Eduardovich **Vyttek** (4 Oct 1849 - ?)
7 Aug 1895 - 3 Dec 1899:	Commander, 27th Dragoon Regiment
3 Dec 1899:	Promoted to *Major-General*
3 Dec 1899 - 2 Apr 1902:	Chief of Staff, I. Caucasus Army Corps

Admiral Kaiser **Wilhelm** II, Friedrich Wilhelm Viktor Albert von Preußen (27 Jan 1859 - 4 Jun 1941)
26 Jul 1897:	Promoted to *Admiral*

Lieutenant-General Vladimir Aleksandrovich **Yablochkin** (3 Apr 1864 - 3 May 1931)
10 Jul 1908 - 14 Dec 1913:	Commander, Life Guards Chasseurs Regiment
6 Dec 1908:	Promoted to *Major-General*
14 Dec 1913 - 30 Aug 1914:	Commander, 3rd Turkestan Rifle Brigade
30 Aug 1914 - 16 Feb 1915:	Commander, 2nd Rifle Brigade
16 Feb 1915 - 2 Apr 1916:	Commander, 32nd Infantry Division
10 Mar 1915:	Promoted to *Lieutenant-General*
2 Apr 1916 - 15 Apr 1917:	Commanding General, V. Caucasus Army Corps
15 Apr 1917 - Jul 1917:	Reserve officer, Petrograd Military District
Jul 1917 - 7 Oct 1917:	Commanding General, V. Caucasus Army Corps

Major-General Andrey Nikolayevich **Yablonsky** (9 Nov 1869 - 1918)
13 Nov 1914 - 6 Feb 1916:	Commander, 163rd Infantry Regiment
6 Feb 1916 - 25 Oct 1916:	Chief of Staff, 1st Finnish Rifle Division
10 Apr 1916:	Promoted to *Major-General*
25 Oct 1916 - 11 Mar 1917:	Chief of Staff, 47th Infantry Division
11 Mar 1917 - 27 Jun 1917:	Chief of Staff, XXIX. Army Corps
27 Jun 1917 - 1918:	Reserve officer, Kiev Military District

Major-General Feliks Vladislavovich **Yachevsky** (9 Jun 1844 - ?)
22 Jun 1880 - 1898:	Military Judge, Caucasus Military District Court
30 Aug 1890:	Promoted to *Major-General*

Major-General Nikolai Aleksandrovich **Yafimovich** (14 May 1850 - ?)
25 Apr 1897 - 11 Dec 1902:	Commander, Life Guards Dragoon Regiment

10 Apr 1899:	Promoted to *Major-General*
11 Dec 1902 - 13 Oct 1904:	At the disposal of the Commanding General, St. Petersburg Military District
13 Oct 1904 - 16 Feb 1906:	Commander, 2nd Brigade, 2nd Guards Cavalry Division

Major-General Vladimir Mikhailovich **Yafimovich** (5 Apr 1856 - ?)
4 Feb 1893 - 1906:	Chief of Police, Moscow 3rd District
6 Dec 1904:	Promoted to *Major-General*

Major-General Ferdinand-Ivan Avgustinovich **Yagimovsky** (30 May 1852 - ?)
6 Jul 1907:	Promoted to *Major-General*
6 Jul 1907 - 11 Dec 1908:	Commander, 1st Brigade, 41st Infantry Division

Lieutenant-General Nikolai Modestovich **Yagodin** (6 Apr 1844 - 14 Mar 1903)
26 Oct 1890:	Promoted to *Major-General*
26 Oct 1890 - 19 Aug 1899:	Commander, 2nd Brigade, 1st Don Cossack Division
19 Aug 1899 - 14 Mar 1903:	Commander, 1st Caucasus Cossack Division
6 Dec 1899:	Promoted to *Lieutenant-General*

Major-General Aleksandr Pavlovich **Yagodkin** (6 Oct 1838 - ?)
12 Dec 1901:	Promoted to *Major-General*
12 Dec 1901 - 1903:	Commander, Irkutsk Regional Brigade

Major-General Pavel Yakovlevich **Yagodkin** (2 Jun 1867 - ?)
28 Jul 1910 - 24 Apr 1913:	Commander, 1st Regiment, Kuban Cossack Army
24 Apr 1913:	Promoted to *Major-General*
24 Apr 1913 - 24 May 1914:	Commander, 2nd Brigade, 2nd Consolidated Cossack Division
24 May 1914 - 24 Mar 1917:	Deputy Ataman, Siberian Cossack Army
24 Mar 1917 - 1918:	Reserve officer, Moscow Military District

General of Infantry Aleksandr Alekseyevich **Yakimovich** (11 Aug 1929 - 17 Mar 1903)
7 Jul 1868 - 18 Aug 1881:	Deputy Chief of Chancellery, Ministry of War
30 Aug 1869:	Promoted to *Major-General*
1 Jan 1878:	Promoted to *Lieutenant-General*
18 Aug 1881 - 4 Jan 1884:	Chief of Chancellery, Ministry of War
4 Jan 1884 - 17 Mar 1903:	Member of the Military Council
Aug 1892:	Promoted to *General of Infantry*

Lieutenant-General Aleksey Aleksandrovich **Yakimovich** (15 Jan 1857 - ?)
23 Feb 1893 - 16 Feb 1909:	Member of the Artillery Committee, Main Artillery Directorate
6 Dec 1903:	Promoted to *Major-General*
16 Feb 1902 - 28 Sep 1914:	Head of Technical Artillery Institutions
6 Dec 1909:	Promoted to *Lieutenant-General*
28 Sep 1914 - 1 Oct 1915:	Chief of Technical Artillery Institutions Section, Main Artillery Directorate
1 Oct 1915 - Oct 1917:	Chief of Section 2, Artillery Committee, Main Artillery

Directorate

Major-General of Naval Engineering Leopold Yakovlevich **Yakobson** (2 Jul 1850 - ?)
28 Jul 1903 - 1909: Chief Engineer, Port of Sevastopol
10 Jan 1905: Promoted to *Major-General of Naval Engineering*

Major-General Georgy Stepanovich **Yakovenko** (26 Nov 1866 - 4 Sep 1915)
5 Feb 1915 - 4 Sep 1915: Commander, 168th Infantry Regiment
22 Oct 1915: Posthumously promoted to *Major-General*

Lieutenant-General Aleksandr Georgiyevich **Yakovlev** (6 Sep 1859 - 10 Feb 1940)
15 Oct 1910 - 29 Apr 1917: Chairman of the Remount Commission, Poltava Region
6 Dec 1910: Promoted to *Major-General*
29 Apr 1917: Promoted to *Lieutenant-General*
29 Apr 1917: Retired

Major-General Aleksandr Vasilyevich **Yakovlev** (27 Jul 1845 - ?)
9 Oct 1896 - 9 Feb 1905: Section Chief, Main Intendant Directorate
6 Apr 1903: Promoted to *Major-General*
9 Feb 1905 - 1905: Deputy Intendant, Vilnius Military District

Major-General Aleksey Nikolayevich **Yakovlev** (12 Feb 1859 - ?)
26 Oct 1910 - 22 Nov 1912: Commander, 1st Kronstadt Fortress Artillery Regiment
22 Nov 1912 - 27 Jul 1915: Commander of Artillery, Fortress Novogeorgiyevsk
6 Dec 1913: Promoted to *Major-General*
27 Jul 1915 - 1917: Reserve officer, Dvinsk Military District

General of Artillery Grigory Mikhailovich **Yakovlev** (30 Sep 1852 - 1922)
31 Jul 1900 - 1 Jul 1906: Director, Nikolayev Cadet Corps
1 Apr 1901: Promoted to *Major-General*
1 Jul 1906 - 10 Jun 1917: Deputy Chief, Main Directorate for Military Schools
22 Apr 1907: Promoted to *Lieutenant-General*
19 Jul 1914 - 27 Dec 1914: Acting Chief of the Main Directorate for Military Schools
22 Mar 1915: Promoted to *General of Artillery*
10 Jun 1917: Retired

Major-General Ivan Ivanovich **Yakovlev** (3 Feb 1859 - 5 Apr 1943)
11 May 1911 - 30 Jan 1916: Commander, 11th Dragoon Regiment
30 Jan 1916 - 22 May 1917: Commander, 2nd Brigade, Amur Cavalry Division
1916: Promoted to *Major-General*
22 May 1917 - 1918: Commander, Amur Cavalry Division

Lieutenant-General Mikhail Grigoryevich **Yakovlev** (2 Oct 1857 - ?)
24 Oct 1900 - 1 Jun 1904: Commander, 19th Dragoon Regiment
1 Jun 1904: Promoted to *Major-General*
1 Jun 1904 - 3 Dec 1904: Chief of Staff, V. Siberian Army Corps
3 Dec 1904 - 20 May 1905: At the disposal of the Chief of the General Staff

20 May 1905 - 9 Nov 1911:	Commander, 1st Brigade, 12th Cavalry Division
9 Nov 1911 - 30 Aug 1912:	Commander, 2nd Brigade, 12th Cavalry Division
30 Aug 1912:	Promoted to *Lieutenant-General*
30 Aug 1912:	Retired

Lieutenant-General Mikhail Mikhailovich **Yakovlev** (27 Sep 1857 - ?)

8 May 1902 - 14 Mar 1905:	Commander, 129th Infantry Regiment
14 Mar 1905:	Promoted to *Major-General*
14 Mar 1905 - 20 Jul 1910:	Chief of Kiev Military Hospital
20 Jul 1910 - 1915:	Commander, 1st Brigade, 33rd Infantry Division
1915 - 3 Apr 1915:	Commander, Brigade, 70th Infantry Division
3 Apr 1915 - 12 Jul 1915:	Commander, 44th Infantry Division
26 May 1915:	Promoted to *Lieutenant-General*
12 Jul 1915 - 15 Oct 1917:	Reserve officer, Kiev Military District
15 Oct 1917:	Retired

Admiral Nikolai Matveyevich **Yakovlev** (23 Mar 1856 - Sep 1919)

1906:	Promoted to *Rear-Admiral*
1906 - 1907:	Chief of Staff, Port of Kronstadt
1907 - 18 Apr 1911:	Chief of the Main Naval Staff
6 Dec 1909:	Promoted to *Vice-Admiral*
18 Apr 1911 - 28 Apr 1917:	Member, Board of Admiralty
30 Jul 1915:	Promoted to *Admiral*
28 Apr 1917:	Dismissed

Major-General Nikolai Mikhailovich **Yakovlev** (29 Oct 1852 - 1911)

26 Apr 1908 - 1911:	Commander of Gendarmerie, Estonia
29 Mar 1909:	Promoted to *Major-General*

Major-General of the Fleet Nikolai Nikiforovich **Yakovlev** (19 Mar 1859 - 1918)

29 Mar 1909 - 1917:	Commander, Nikolayev Naval Sub-Depot
29 Mar 1913:	Promoted to *Major-General of the Fleet*
1917:	Retired

General of Infantry Pyotr Petrovich **Yakovlev** (21 Nov 1852 - ?)

10 Mar 1898 - 27 Jul 1901:	Chief of Staff, XVII. Army Corps
14 Jun 1898:	Promoted to *Major-General*
27 Jul 1901 - 2 Oct 1903:	Commandant, Moscow Military School
2 Oct 1903 - 8 Jun 1905:	Commandant, Aleksandr Military School
6 Dec 1904:	Promoted to *Lieutenant-General*
8 Jun 1905 - 15 Apr 1909:	Commander, 3rd Grenadier Division
15 Apr 1909 - 2 Apr 1917:	Commanding General, XVII. Army Corps
6 Dec 1910:	Promoted to *General of Infantry*
Aug 1914:	Commanding General, Southern Group of Corps, 5th Army
2 Apr 1917 - 14 Jul 1917:	Reserve officer, Kiev Military District
14 Jul 1917:	Retired

Major-General Viktor Vasilyevich **Yakovlev** (30 Oct 1871 - 1945)
7 Oct 1916 - 6 Dec 1916:	Inspector of Classes, Nikolayev Engineering School
6 Dec 1916:	Promoted to *Major-General*
6 Dec 1916 - 11 Jan 1917:	Deputy Chief, Air Force Department
11 Jan 1917 - 1918:	Chief, Air Force Department

Lieutenant-General Pyotr Vasilyevich **Yakubinsky** (24 Jun 1864 - ?)
1 Sep 1906 - 3 Nov 1909:	Inspector of Classes, Vladimir-Kiev Cadet Corps
6 Dec 1908:	Promoted to *Major-General*
3 Nov 1909 - 15 Mar 1918:	Commandant of the Intendant Academy
6 Dec 1916:	Promoted to *Lieutenant-General*

Major-General Vladimir Petrovich **Yakubinsky** (4 Jul 1851 - ?)
2 Nov 1902:	Promoted to *Major-General*
2 Nov 1902 - 20 Aug 1905:	Commander, 2nd Brigade, 3rd Infantry Division
20 Aug 1905 - 14 Nov 1906:	Commander, Transbaikal Regional Brigade
14 Nov 1906 - 21 Dec 1908:	Commander, 2nd Brigade, 1st Infantry Division

Lieutenant-General Mikhail Andreyevich **Yakubovich** (26 Dec 1838 - ?)
7 May 1890 - 21 Jun 1894:	Commander of the Artillery Polygon, Odessa Military District
30 Aug 1890:	Promoted to *Major-General*
21 Jun 1894 - 1 Jan 1898:	Commander, 18th Artillery Brigade
1 Jan 1898 - 1902:	Artillery Inspector, Siberian Military District
6 Dec 1900:	Promoted to *Lieutenant-General*

Lieutenant-General Nikolai Andreyevich **Yakubovich** (7 Jan 1837 - 1914)
17 May 1878 - 6 Dec 1903:	Director, Simbirsk Cadet Corps
30 Aug 1881:	Promoted to *Major-General*
6 Apr 1903:	Promoted to *Lieutenant-General*
6 Dec 1903:	Retired

Major-General Ilya Lavrentyevich **Yakubovsky** (4 Jul 1824 - ?)
1 Jun 1888:	Promoted to *Major-General*
1 Jun 1888 - 26 May 1897:	Commander, 32nd Artillery Brigade

Major-General Iosif Stepanovich **Yakubovsky** (11 Oct 1853 - ?)
4 Jul 1907 - 6 Mar 1911:	At the disposal of the Intendant Department
6 Dec 1907:	Promoted to *Major-General*
6 Mar 1911 - Oct 1913:	Commander, 2nd Brigade, 16th Infantry Division

General of Infantry Ivan Iosifovich **Yakubovsky** (21 Jul 1838 - 1911)
1 Oct 1886 - 16 Apr 1891:	Commander, Life Guards Volyn Regiment
5 Apr 1887:	Promoted to *Major-General*
16 Apr 1891 - 13 Jan 1892:	Chief of Staff, XIII. Army Corps
13 Jan 1892 - 12 Dec 1892:	Deputy Chief of Staff, Moscow Military District
12 Dec 1892 - 15 Jan 1900:	Deputy Chief of Military Schools
26 May 1899 - 15 Jan 1900:	Acting Chief of the Main Directorate of Military

	Schools
14 May 1896:	Promoted to *Lieutenant-General*
15 Jan 1900 - 2 Jan 1911:	Member of the Military Council
6 Dec 1906:	Promoted to *General of Infantry*
2 Jan 1911:	Retired

Lieutenant-General Platon Filippovich **Yampolsky** (18 Nov 1826 - ?)
8 Apr 1877 - 15 Oct 1878:	Intendant, Odessa Military District
30 Aug 1878:	Promoted to *Major-General*
15 Oct 1878 - 5 May 1880:	Unassigned
5 May 1880 - 29 Jul 1891:	Deputy Intendant, Caucasus Military District
29 Jul 1891 - 1895:	Intendant, Caucasus Military District
30 Aug 1891:	Promoted to *Lieutenant-General*

Major-General Aleksandr Aleksandrovich **Yamshchikov** (14 Mar 1843 - ?)
14 Jan 1898:	Promoted to *Major-General*
14 Jan 1898 - 16 Mar 1903:	Commander, 1st Brigade, 45th Infantry Division

Lieutenant-General of Naval Engineers Nikolai Ivanovich **Yankovsky** (4 Apr 1866 - 6 Oct 1916)
18 Apr 1910:	Promoted to *Major-General of Naval Engineers*
24 May 1910 - 19 Oct 1911:	Senior Deputy Chief Inspector of Shipbuilding
19 Oct 1911 - 1 Jan 1915:	Deputy Chief of Shipbuilding Section, Main Shipbuilding Directorate
1 Jan 1915 - 6 Oct 1916:	Inspector of Factories, Ministry of the Navy
5 Oct 1916:	Promoted to *Lieutenant-General of Naval Engineers*

Major-General Viktor Osipovich **Yankovsky** (9 Jan 1828 - ?)
4 Aug 1884 - 6 Feb 1897:	Commander of Gendarmerie, Tiflis Province
24 Mar 1885:	Promoted to *Major-General*
6 Feb 1897 - 1898:	Commander of Gendarmerie, Tambov Province

Major-General Pavel Konstantinovich **Yannau** (6 Nov 1851 - ?)
25 Aug 1905:	Promoted to *Major-General*
25 Aug 1905 - 1906:	Duty General, Caucasus Military District

Major-General of the Fleet Aleksey Vladimirovich **Yanov** (7 Nov 1863 - ?)
21 Jan 1908 - 1916:	Section Chief, Ministry of the Navy
14 Apr 1913:	Promoted to *Major-General of the Fleet*
1916 - 1917:	Attached to 2nd Baltic Naval Depot

Lieutenant-General Dmitry Dmitriyevich **Yanov** (26 Sep 1831 - 26 Aug 1908)
Jan 1870 - 7 Oct 1875:	Squadron Commander, Life Guards Ataman Regiment
14 Aug 1872:	Promoted to *Major-General*
7 Oct 1875 - 1 Jul 1887:	Ataman, 2nd Military Division, Don Cossack Army
7 May 1887:	Promoted to *Lieutenant-General*
1 Jul 1887 - 8 Oct 1888:	Ataman, 1st Don Cossack District
8 Oct 1888 - 8 Aug 1899:	Attached to the Don Cossack Army

8 Aug 1899: Retired

Major-General Georgy Dmitriyevich **Yanov** (1 Apr 1864 - 21 Jul 1931)
10 Mar 1914: Promoted to *Major-General*
10 Mar 1914 - 19 Jul 1914: Chief of Communications, Vilnius Military District
19 Jul 1914 - 19 Oct 1914: Chief of Economic Section, 1st Army
19 Oct 1914 - Oct 1917: Chief of Economic Section, 10th Army

Major-General Pyotr Ivanovich **Yanov** (15 Jul 1864 - 17 Nov 1937)
7 Dec 1910 - 16 Nov 1915: Special Assignments General to the Ataman, Don Cossack Army
14 Apr 1913: Promoted to *Major-General*
16 Nov 1915 - 22 Jul 1917: Chief of Remounts, Don Cossack Army
22 Jul 1917: Dismissed

Major-General Pyotr Nikolayevich **Yanov** (31 Dec 1853 - 1921)
24 Jun 1904 - 28 May 1914: Head of Livadia Palace Buildings
5 Oct 1911: Promoted to *Major-General*
28 May 1914 - 7 Sep 1917: Chief of Administration, Massandra Livadia Palace
7 Sep 1917: Retired

Lieutenant-General Aleksandr Vasilyevich **Yanovsky** (30 May 1839 - ?)
26 Feb 1894: Promoted to *Major-General*
26 Feb 1894 - 16 Dec 1899: Chief of Staff, VIII. Army Corps
16 Dec 1899 - 20 Aug 1902: Commandant of Bobruisk
14 Apr 1902: Promoted to *Lieutenant-General*
20 Aug 1902 - Sep 1903: Commander, Smolensk Regional Brigade

Lieutenant-General Nikolai Kirillovich **Yanovsky** (24 Jul 1860 - ?)
13 May 1914: Promoted to *Major-General*
13 May 1914 - 7 Jul 1914: Commander, 1st Brigade, 28th Infantry Division
7 Jul 1914 - 29 Jul 1914: Commander, 1st Brigade, 27th Infantry Division
29 Jul 1914 - 20 May 1916: Commander, 1st Brigade, 73rd Infantry Division
20 May 1916 - 22 May 1917: Commander, 60th Infantry Division
22 May 1917 - 1 Jul 1917: Unassigned
1 Jul 1917: Promoted to *Lieutenant-General*
1 Jul 1917: Retired

General of Infantry Vasily Ivanovich **Yanovsky** (11 May 1828 - 9 Sep 1907)
23 Aug 1871 - 30 Aug 1873: Section Chief, General Staff
16 Apr 1872: Promoted to *Major-General*
30 Aug 1873 - 1 Nov 1876: Commander, 2nd Brigade, 13th Infantry Division
1 Nov 1876 - 31 Mar 1881: Chief of Staff, VII. Army Corps
31 Mar 1881 - 24 Jul 1885: Commander, 38th Infantry Division
30 Aug 1881: Promoted to *Lieutenant-General*
24 Jul 1885 - 17 Sep 1885: Acting Commanding General, I. Caucasus Army Corps
17 Sep 1885 - 7 Feb 1886: Commander, 38th Infantry Division
7 Feb 1886 - 22 Jun 1891: Intendant-General, Caucasus Military District

22 Jun 1891 - 14 Mar 1895:	Commanding General, VII. Army Corps
14 Mar 1895 - 7 Mar 1898:	Deputy Commanding General, Vilnius Military District
6 Dec 1895:	Promoted to *General of Infantry*
7 Mar 1898 - 3 Jan 1906:	Member of the Military Council
3 Jan 1906:	Retired

Lieutenant-General Vasily Minovich **Yanushev** (25 Mar 1852 - 1929)
21 Mar 1908:	Promoted to *Major-General*
21 Mar 1908 - 25 Jul 1910:	Commander, 18th Artillery Brigade
25 Jul 1910 - 24 Mar 1914:	Artillery Inspector, Omsk Military District
14 Apr 1913:	Promoted to *Lieutenant-General*
24 Mar 1914:	Retired
14 May 1916 - 29 Oct 1916:	Recalled; Commander of Evacuation Points, Siberian Military District
29 Oct 1916:	Retired

Major-General Aleksandr Ivanovich **Yanushevsky** (17 Apr 1850 - 1916)
12 Jul 1907 - 7 Dec 1913:	Military Commander, St. Petersburg District
6 Dec 1911:	Promoted to *Major-General*
7 Dec 1913:	Retired

Lieutenant-General Grigory Yefimovich **Yanushevsky** (18 Nov 1861 - ?)
19 Jun 1905:	Promoted to *Major-General*
19 Jun 1905 - 16 Dec 1906:	Commander, 1st Brigade, 1st Rifle Division
16 Dec 1906 - 16 Jul 1910:	Quartermaster-General, Moscow Military District
16 Jul 1910 - 27 Sep 1914:	Chief of Staff, IX. Army Corps
27 Sep 1914 - 29 Jul 1915:	Commander, 19th Infantry Division
13 Oct 1914:	Promoted to *Lieutenant-General*
29 Jul 1915 - 11 Sep 1916:	Commander, 1st Grenadier Division
11 Sep 1916 - 3 Apr 1917:	Commanding General, III. Army Corps
3 Apr 1917 - 15 Apr 1917:	Reserve officer, Minsk Military District
15 Apr 1917:	Retired

General of Infantry Khalil Aleksandrovich **Yanushevsky** (23 Dec 1845 - 1921)
12 Oct 1904:	Promoted to *Major-General*
12 Oct 1904 - 27 Dec 1912:	Commander, Vilnius Regional Brigade
18 Apr 1910:	Promoted to *Lieutenant-General*
27 Dec 1912:	Promoted to *General of Infantry*
27 Dec 1912:	Retired

Major-General of the Admiralty Konstantin Ivanovich **Yanushevsky** (? - ?)
?:	Promoted to *Major-General of the Admiralty*

General of Infantry Nikolai Nikolayevich **Yanushkevich** (1 May 1868 - Feb 1918)
25 Aug 1905 - 22 Feb 1911:	Chief of Legislative Affairs Office, Ministry of War
29 Mar 1909:	Promoted to *Major-General*
8 Jan 1910 - 8 Oct 1911:	Professor of Military Administration, Imperial Military Academy

22 Feb 1911 - 20 Jan 1913:	Deputy Chief of Staff, Ministry of War
20 Jan 1913:	Promoted to *Lieutenant-General*
20 Jan 1913 - 5 Mar 1914:	Commandant of the Imperial Military Academy
5 Mar 1914 - 1 Aug 1914:	Chief of the General Directorate of the General Staff
1 Aug 1914 - 18 Aug 1915:	Chief of Staff to the Supreme Commander-in-Chief
22 Oct 1914:	Promoted to *General of Infantry*
18 Aug 1915 - 31 Mar 1917:	Deputy Military Governor of the Caucasus
31 Mar 1917:	Dismissed

Lieutenant-General Vladislav Ignatyevich **Yanushkovsky** (5 Nov 1845 - ?)
15 Nov 1894 - 10 Feb 1897:	Deputy Commander of Engineers, Moscow Military District
25 Sep 1895:	Promoted to *Major-General*
10 Feb 1897 - 27 Mar 1903:	Commander of Engineers, Turkestan Military District
6 Oct 1901:	Promoted to *Lieutenant-General*
27 Mar 1903 - 22 May 1905:	Commander of Engineers, Vilnius Military District
22 May 1905 - 5 Mar 1907:	Commander of Engineers, Caucasus Military District

Lieutenant-General Nikolai Ivanovich **Yanzhul** (26 Nov 1852 - ?)
17 Jan 1896 - 18 Sep 1899:	Military Attaché, Japan
6 Dec 1897:	Promoted to *Major-General*
18 Sep 1899 - 30 Oct 1900:	Special Assignments General, Kiev Military District
30 Oct 1900 - 8 Apr 1904:	Chief of Staff, X. Army Corps
8 Apr 1904 - 15 Feb 1905:	Commander, 3rd Infantry Division
16 Aug 1904:	Promoted to *Lieutenant-General*

Lieutenant-General Vladimir Aleksandrovich von **Yarmershtedt** (9 Jan 1834 - ?)
9 Aug 1894:	Promoted to *Major-General*
9 Aug 1894 - Dec 1899:	Commander, 31st Artillery Brigade
Dec 1899:	Promoted to *Lieutenant-General*
Dec 1899:	Retired

Major-General Aleksandr Frantsevich **Yarminsky** (11 Aug 1869 - ?)
15 Sep 1913 - 6 Apr 1916:	Commander, 3rd Hussar Regiment
6 Sep 1915:	Promoted to *Major-General*
6 Apr 1916 - 26 Jun 1916:	Commander, 2nd Brigade, 13th Cavalry Division
26 Jun 1916 - 4 Jan 1917:	Commander, 1st Brigade, 3rd Cavalry Division
4 Jan 1917 - Oct 1917:	Commander, 2nd Brigade, 13th Cavalry Division

Lieutenant-General Vladimir Ivanovich **Yaron** (22 Dec 1872 - 11 Mar 1919)
29 Dec 1914 - 25 Dec 1915:	Commander, 4th Siberian Rifle Regiment
11 Feb 1915:	Promoted to *Major-General*
25 Dec 1915 - 29 Jul 1916:	Chief of Staff, 2nd Siberian Rifle Division
29 Jul 1916 - 9 Sep 1916:	Chief of Staff, XXXV. Army Corps
9 Sep 1916 - 18 Apr 1917:	Chief of Staff, I. Siberian Army Corps
18 Apr 1917 - 13 Aug 1917:	Commander, 2nd Siberian Rifle Division
13 Aug 1917 - 9 Sep 1917:	Chief of Staff, 8th Army
1917:	Promoted to *Lieutenant-General*

9 Sep 1917 - 21 Oct 1917: Commanding General, XLVI. Army Corps
21 Oct 1917 - 1918: Commanding General, XVI. Army Corps

Major-General Vladimir Nikolayevich **Yaroshev** (18 May 1834 - ?)
13 Jul 1892: Promoted to *Major-General*
13 Jul 1892 - 20 Nov 1897: Commander, 1st Artillery Brigade
20 Nov 1897 - 29 Dec 1899: Commander, 42nd Artillery Brigade

Major-General Makary Nikitich **Yaroshevsky** (26 Jul 1870 - ?)
7 Oct 1915 - 29 Apr 1917: Chief of Lines of Communications, 5th Army
28 Nov 1916: Promoted to *Major-General*
29 Apr 1917 - Oct 1917: Chief of Logistics, Western Front

Major-General Bogdan Ivanovich **Yarotsky** (11 Sep 1854 - 2 May 1913)
6 Apr 1903: Promoted to *Major-General*
6 Apr 1903 - 11 Sep 1903: At the disposal of the Chief of the General Staff
11 Sep 1903 - 23 Jul 1911: Commander, 2nd Brigade, 10th Infantry Division
23 Jul 1911 - 2 May 1913: Commander, 1st Brigade, 10th Infantry Division

Major-General Vladimir Dmitriyevich **Yartsev** (1 Jul 1846 - 12 Jan 1918)
3 Aug 1900: Promoted to *Major-General*
3 Aug 1900 - 7 Aug 1906: Commander, 1st Brigade, 28th Infantry Division
7 Aug 1906: Retired

Major-General Arkady Pavlovich **Yarygin** (23 May 1859 - ?)
6 Jan 1913: Promoted to *Major-General*
6 Jan 1913 - 9 Nov 1914: Commander, 45th Artillery Brigade
9 Nov 1914 - 7 Jul 1917: Reserve officer, Kiev Military District
7 Jul 1917: Retired

Lieutenant-General Nikolai Pavlovich **Yarygin** (24 Apr 1849 - ?)
29 Dec 1899 - 4 Jun 1904: Commander, 23rd Artillery Brigade
6 Dec 1900: Promoted to *Major-General*
4 Jun 1904 - 5 May 1905: Commander of Artillery, VI. Siberian Army Corps
5 May 1905 - Jun 1907: Commander of Artillery, XVIII. Army Corps
6 Dec 1906: Promoted to *Lieutenant-General*

Major-General Nikolai Nikolayevich **Yaryshkin** (17 Jan 1864 - 2 Dec 1914)
1914 - 8 Nov 1914: Commander, 4th Siberian Rifle Regiment
23 Apr 1915: Posthumously promoted to *Major-General*

General of Infantry Venedikt Aloiziyevich **Yasensky** (2 Feb 1851 - 13 Jul 1915)
24 Oct 1899: Promoted to *Major-General*
24 Oct 1899 - 8 Jul 1901: Commander, 1st Brigade, 9th Infantry Division
8 Jul 1901 - 4 Jul 1906: Commander, 1st Turkestan Rifle Brigade
4 Jul 1906 - 31 Dec 1913: Commander, 21st Infantry Division
6 Dec 1906: Promoted to *Lieutenant-General*
31 Dec 1913: Promoted to *General of Infantry*

31 Dec 1913:   Retired
19 Jul 1914 - 8 Oct 1914:   Recalled; Commander, 66th Infantry Division
8 Oct 1914:   Retired

Major-General Aleksandr Vasilyevich **Yasherov** (23 Jan 1869 - ?)
22 Nov 1912 - 1918:   Commander, Orenburg Cossack Artillery Brigade
22 Mar 1915:   Promoted to *Major-General*

Major-General Ivan Ivanovich **Yasnetsky** (15 May 1848 - 1 Apr 1904)
23 Feb 1898:   Promoted to *Major-General*
23 Feb 1898 - 16 Aug 1903:   Commander, 2nd Sapper Brigade
16 Aug 1903 - 1 Apr 1904:   At the disposal of the Main Engineering Directorate

Major-General Illarion Konstantinovich **Yastrebov** (6 Jun 1865 - 20 Oct 1930)
24 Dec 1910 - 18 Sep 1915:   Section Chief, Main Artillery Directorate
14 Apr 1913:   Promoted to *Major-General*
18 Sep 1915 - Oct 1917:   Deputy Chief of 2nd Economic Department, Main Artillery Directorate

Major-General Mikhail Stanislavovich **Yasyukovich** (27 Aug 1870 - ?)
22 Mar 1913 - 1917:   Extraordinary Professor, Nikolayev Engineering Academy
6 Dec 1916:   Promoted to *Major-General*

Lieutenant-General Stanislav Ignatyevich **Yasyukovich** (11 Apr 1839 - ?)
12 Jun 1886 - 1900:   Member of the Engineering Committee, Mian Engineering Directorate
30 Aug 1887:   Promoted to *Major-General*
5 Jul 1898:   Promoted to *Lieutenant-General*

Major-General Nikolai Ivanovich **Yatsenko** (13 May 1860 - ?)
17 Aug 1914 - 13 Sep 1916:   Commander, 4th Heavy Artillery Brigade
13 Sep 1916 - 10 Oct 1916:   Reserve officer, Kiev Military District
10 Oct 1916 - 1918:   Commander, 11th Heavy Field Artillery Brigade
19 Oct 1916:   Promoted to *Major-General*

General of Artillery Vladimir Avksentyevich **Yatskevich** (15 Nov 1839 - 8 Feb 1919)
24 Mar 1879 - 21 Mar 1890:   Commander, Horse Artillery Brigade, Kuban Cossack Army
6 May 1888:   Promoted to *Major-General*
21 Mar 1890 - 6 Jul 1898:   Deputy Commander, Kuban Region, Deputy Ataman, Kuban Cossack Army
6 Jul 1898:   Promoted to *Lieutenant-General*
6 Jul 1898 - 13 Dec 1903:   Commandant of Fortress Kars
13 Dec 1903 - 1 Jan 1910:   Commanding General, I. Caucasus Army Corps
6 Dec 1906:   Promoted to *General of Artillery*
1 Jan 1910 - 1 Jan 1916:   Member of the Military Council
1 Jan 1916:   Retired

Major-General of Naval Artillery Ivan Aleksandrovich **Yatsyna** (27 Dec 1861 - 1930)
19 Nov 1907 - 1917: Artillery Instructor, Marine Corps
6 Dec 1911: Promoted to *Major-General of Naval Artillery*

Major-General Nil Aleksandrovich **Yatsynin** (29 Oct 1849 - ?)
22 Feb 1904: Promoted to *Major-General*
22 Feb 1904 - 9 Mar 1905: Commander, 1st Brigade, 6th East Siberian Rifle Division
9 Mar 1905 - 1905: Attached to the General Staff

Major-General Sergey Georgiyevich **Yavlensky** (15 May 1860 - 14 May 1929)
9 Mar 1912 - Jul 1914: Military Judge, Warsaw Military District Court
25 Mar 1912: Promoted to *Major-General*
Jul 1914 - 7 Dec 1915: Military Judge, Minsk Military District Court
7 Dec 1915 - Oct 1917: Chief of Military Justice Section, Chief of Logistics, Western Front

Lieutenant-General Fyodor Konstantinovich **Yazvin** (17 Jul 1856 - 1920)
8 Apr 1899 - 9 Mar 1904: Commander, 139th Infantry Regiment
9 Mar 1904: Promoted to *Major-General*
12 Mar 1904 - 29 Apr 1907: Commander, 2nd Brigade, Corps of Borderguards, Amur Military District
29 Apr 1907 - 16 Nov 1911: Commander, 2nd Brigade, 3rd Infantry Division
16 Nov 1911: Promoted to *Lieutenant-General*
16 Nov 1911 - 22 Oct 1914: Commander, 41st Infantry Division
22 Oct 1914 - 1915: Reserve officer, Kiev Military District
1915 - Oct 1917: Special Assignments General, Kazan Military District

Major-General Gennady Konstantinovich **Yazvin** (30 Sep 1853 - ?)
22 Jan 1901 - 1904: Inspector of Classes, Pavlovsky Military School
6 Dec 1901: Promoted to *Major-General*

Major-General Aleksandr Petrovich **Yazykov** (29 May 1859 - ?)
8 Nov 1904 - 24 Apr 1906: Deputy Military Governor of Batum
2 Apr 1906: Promoted to *Major-General*
24 Apr 1906 - 28 Nov 1907: Governor of Kutaisi

Major-General Dmitry Aleksandrovich **Yazykov** (24 Jun 1852 - ?)
31 Mar 1896 - 19 Aug 1905: Member, Interim Administrative Commission for the Construction of Defensive Structures & Barracks, Amur Military District
19 May 1905: Promoted to *Major-General*
19 Aug 1905 - 10 Aug 1906: Special Assignments General, 1st Manchurian Army
10 Aug 1906 - 1909: Deputy Commander of Engineers, Amur Military District

Lieutenant-General Mikhail Konstantinovich **Yazykov** (1 Dec 1852 - ?)
6 Dec 1901: Promoted to *Major-General*
6 Dec 1901 - 8 Jan 1906: Attached to the Ministry of War
8 Jan 1906: Promoted to *Lieutenant-General*
8 Jan 1906: Retired

Lieutenant-General Nikolai Konstantinovich **Yazykov** (5 Jun 1842 - 22 Nov 1897)
20 Nov 1876 - 31 Aug 1881: Commander, 1st Life Dragoon Regiment
31 Aug 1881: Promoted to *Major-General*
31 Aug 1881 - 31 Oct 1881: Commander, 1st Brigade, 3rd Cavalry Division
31 Oct 1881 - 16 Jul 1891: Commander, 1st Brigade, 13th Cavalry Division
16 Jul 1891 - 22 Nov 1897: Commander, 2nd Replacement Cavalry Brigade
14 May 1896: Promoted to *Lieutenant-General*

Lieutenant-General Vasily Yefimovich **Yazykov** (6 Aug 1823 - 14 Feb 1901)
30 Nov 1877 - 1 Jan 1880: Military Commander & Governor of Yenisei
30 Aug 1878: Promoted to *Major-General*
1 Jan 1880 - 14 Oct 1880: Unassigned
14 Oct 1880 - 19 Jul 1889: Military Commander, Akmola Province
19 Jul 1889 - 25 Nov 1894: Commander, 26th Regional Brigade
30 Aug 1889: Promoted to *Lieutenant-General*
25 Nov 1894: Retired

Major-General Nikolai Pavlovich **Yefimov** (13 Jan 1872 - 19 Jan 1943)
22 Nov 1914 - 30 Jan 1916: Commander, 103rd Infantry Regiment
6 Dec 1915: Promoted to *Major-General*
30 Jan 1916 - 17 Nov 1916: Chief of Staff, 23rd Infantry Division
17 Nov 1916 - Oct 1917: Chief of Staff, V. Caucasus Army Corps

Major-General Aleksandr Fyodorovich **Yefimovich** (5 Jan 1866 - 24 Jan 1940)
14 Apr 1913: Promoted to *Major-General*
14 Apr 1913 - 15 Apr 1917: Member of retinue of Grand Duke Pavel Aleksandrovich
15 Apr 1917: Dismissed

Major-General Aleksandr Aleksandrovich **Yefremov** (14 May 1856 - ?)
25 Aug 1910 - 1913: Attached to the infantry
1913: Promoted to *Major-General*
1913: Retired
19 Dec 1915 - 1917: Recalled; Chief of Simferopol Evacuation Points

Lieutenant-General of the Fleet Pyotr Avraamovich **Yefremov** (18 Dec 1842 - ?)
1894 - 1900: Senior Deputy Commander, Port of Sebastopol
1897: Promoted to *Major-General of the Fleet*
1900 - 23 Dec 1902: At the disposal of the C-in-C, Black Sea Fleet
23 Dec 1902: Promoted to *Lieutenant-General of the Fleet*
23 Dec 1902: Retired

Major-General Vasily Pavlovich **Yefremov** (21 Mar 1868 - 11 Sep 1915)
13 Aug 1915 - 11 Sep 1915:   Commander, 239th Infantry Regiment
19 Jun 1915:   Promoted to *Major-General*

Lieutenant-General Veniamin Nikolayevich **Yefremov** (3 Sep 1853 - 11 Dec 1937)
21 Sep 1905:   Promoted to *Major-General*
21 Sep 1905 - 11 Jul 1908:   Commander, Kursk Artillery Depot
11 Jul 1908 - 31 Dec 1913:   Deputy Commander of Artillery, St. Petersburg Military District
31 Dec 1913:   Promoted to *Lieutenant-General*
31 Dec 1913:   Retired

Lieutenant-General of Naval Engineers Mikhail Mikhailovich **Yegipteos** (20 Jan 1861 - 1932)
10 Aug 1909 - 1917:   Chief of Shipbuilding Department, Ministry of the Navy
6 Dec 1911:   Promoted to *Major-General of Naval Engineers*
?:   Promoted to *Lieutenant-General of Naval Engineers*

Major-General Ivan Rodionovich **Yeglevsky** (8 Sep 1846 - ?)
16 Feb 1901 - Dec 1906:   Commander, 2nd Brigade, 1st Caucasus Cossack Division
6 Dec 1901:   Promoted to *Major-General*

Major-General of Naval Engineers Nikolai Ivanovich **Yegorov** (27 Feb 1870 - 16 Jun 1957)
1916 - 1917:   Chief Naval Engineer, Port of Odessa
1917:   Promoted to *Major-General of Naval Engineers*

Major-General of the Hydrographic Corps Vasily Ivanovich **Yegorov** (26 Apr 1861 - ?)
6 Dec 1915:   Promoted to *Major-General of the Hydrographic Corps*

Lieutenant-General Konstantin Nikolayevich **Yegoryev** (30 May 1870 - ?)
30 Jan 1911 - 20 Mar 1916:   Deputy Intendant-General, Ministry of War
10 Apr 1911:   Promoted to *Major-General*
1916:   Promoted to *Lieutenant-General*
20 Mar 1916 - 1917:   Intendant-General of the Field Army

Lieutenant-General Vladimir Nikolayevich **Yegoryev** (3 Mar 1869 - 20 Sep 1948)
1915 - 19 Nov 1915:   Commander, 5th Grenadier Regiment
29 Aug 1915:   Promoted to *Major-General*
19 Nov 1915 - 8 Feb 1917:   Chief of Staff, 1st Grenadier Division
8 Feb 1917 - 5 Apr 1917:   Chief of Staff, III. Army Corps
5 Apr 1917 - 9 Sep 1917:   Commander, 171st Infantry Division
9 Sep 1917 - Dec 1917:   Commanding General, XXXIX. Army Corps
12 Oct 1917:   Promoted to *Lieutenant-General*

Major-General Vasily Aleksandrovich **Yegupov** (22 Mar 1853 - 9 Jul 1907)
24 Sep 1901 - 9 Jul 1907:   Commander of Railway Gendarmerie, Kremenchug
6 Dec 1906:   Promoted to *Major-General*

Lieutenant-General Aleksandr Nikolayevich **Yelagin** (13 May 1851 - 1916)
5 Jan 1905 - Aug 1910: Section Chief, Main Directorate for Cossack Forces
31 May 1907: Promoted to *Major-General*
Aug 1910 - 3 Aug 1912: Chief of Cossack Section, General Staff
3 Aug 1912: Promoted to *Lieutenant-General*
3 Aug 1912: Retired
8 Feb 1915 - 1916: Recalled; Reserve officer, Minsk Military District

Lieutenant-General Andrei Georgievich **Yelchaninov** (7 Jun 1868 - 1918)
13 Apr 1909 - 5 Sep 1914: Professor, General Staff Academy
14 Sep 1910 - 27 Nov 1913: Chief of Fortress Section, General Staff
16 Nov 1910 - 27 Nov 1913: Member of the Artillery Committee, Main Artillery Directorate
6 Dec 1910: Promoted to *Major-General*
5 Sep 1914 - 18 May 1915: Chief of Staff, Fortress Modlin
18 May 1915 - 14 Jul 1917: Commander, 10th Siberian Rifle Division
11 May 1916: Promoted to *Lieutenant-General*
14 Jul 1917 - Oct 1917: Commanding General, VIII. Army Corps
Oct 1917 - 16 Dec 1917: Commanding General, Odessa Military District

Lieutenant-General Georgy Ivanovich **Yelchaninov** (11 Aug 1836 - 19 Nov 1897)
3 Aug 1884 - 16 May 1891: Director, Yaroslavl Military School
30 Aug 1886: Promoted to *Major-General*
16 May 1891 - 1897: Director, Polotsk Cadet Corps
1897: Promoted to *Lieutenant-General*
1897: Retired

Rear-Admiral Mikhail Ivanovich **Yelchaninov** (22 Aug 1842 - 1 Sep 1900)
1894: Promoted to *Rear-Admiral*
1894 - 1897: Junior Flagman, Baltic Fleet
1897 - 1898: Junior Flagman, Black Sea Fleet
1898 - 1 Sep 1900: Commander, 14th Naval Depot

Major-General of the Admiralty Yevgeny Panteleyevich **Yeliseyev** (2 Jan 1864 - ?)
1 Jan 1913: Promoted to *Major-General of the Admiralty*
1913 - Jan 1915: Section Chief, Main Shipbuilding Directorate

Lieutenant-General Konstantin Adolfovich **Yelita von Volsky** (23 Aug 1850 - ?)
27 Aug 1900: Promoted to *Major-General*
27 Aug 1900 - 16 Jul 1904: Commander, Life Guards Izmailovo Regiment
16 Jul 1904 - 2 Nov 1907: Commander, 2nd Brigade, 2nd Guards Infantry Division
2 Nov 1907: Promoted to *Lieutenant-General*
2 Nov 1907 - Nov 1908: Commander, 45th Infantry Division

Major-General Nikolai Adolfovich **Yelita von Volsky** (3 Feb 1855 - ?)
24 Dec 1907 - 3 Mar 1917: Commander of Gendarmerie, Tula Province
13 Apr 1908: Promoted to *Major-General*

Major-General Vilgelm Eduardovich **Yelita von Volsky** (1 Sep 1832 - ?)
3 May 1886 - 6 Sep 1896: Commander, 12th Grenadier Regiment
14 May 1896: Promoted to *Major-General*
6 Sep 1896 - 24 Oct 1899: Commander, 1st Brigade, 6th Infantry Division
24 Oct 1899: Retired

Lieutenant-General Aleksandr Yakovlevich **Yelshin** (13 Aug 1865 - 23 Sep 1951)
29 Mar 1909: Promoted to *Major-General*
29 Mar 1909 - 13 May 1911: Chief of Communications, Odessa Military District
13 May 1911 - 7 Oct 1913: Chief of Staff, XXII. Army Corps
7 Oct 1913 - 18 Dec 1913: Chief of Staff, XXV. Army Corps
18 Dec 1913 - 21 Jan 1915: Commandant of Fortress St. Michael
21 Jan 1915 - 18 Feb 1915: Reserve officer, Petrograd Military District
18 Feb 1915 - 4 Sep 1915: Commander, Brigade, 42nd Infantry Division
4 Sep 1915 - 18 Apr 1917: Commander, 42nd Infantry Division
19 Nov 1916: Promoted to *Lieutenant-General*
18 Apr 1917 - 1918: Commanding General, XX. Army Corps

Major-General Aleksandr Andreyevich **Yemelyanov** (28 Aug 1857 - ?)
12 Apr 1908: Promoted to *Major-General*
12 Apr 1908 - 1912: Duty General, Turkestan Military District
1912: Retired

Lieutenant-General Arian Alekseyevich **Yemelyanov** (20 Dec 1845 - 15 May 1908)
14 Jun 1899: Promoted to *Major-General*
14 Jun 1899 - 4 Sep 1903: Commander, 41st Artillery Brigade
4 Sep 1903 - 15 May 1908: Commander of Artillery, XII. Army Corps
6 Dec 1906: Promoted to *Lieutenant-General*

Lieutenant-General Marin Draganovich **Yenchevich** (1 Aug 1860 - 4 Jul 1934)
11 Jan 1912: Promoted to *Major-General*
11 Jan 1912 - 2 Apr 1915: Commander, 2nd Brigade, 2nd Siberian Rifle Division
2 Apr 1915 - 28 Aug 1917: Commander, 62nd Infantry Division
2 Jun 1916: Promoted to *Lieutenant-General*

Lieutenant-General Prince Nikolai Aleksandrovich **Yengalychev** (8 Oct 1862 - 1 Jan 1926)
12 Dec 1907 - 18 Aug 1912: Commander, 1st Life Dragoon Regiment
18 Aug 1912: Promoted to *Major-General*
18 Aug 1912 - 13 Jan 1915: Commander, Life Guards Grodno Hussar Regiment
14 Jul 1914 - 13 Jan 1915: Commander, 2nd Brigade, 1st Guards Cavalry Division
13 Jan 1915 - 8 Oct 1917: At the disposal of the C-in-C, Western Front
8 Oct 1917: Promoted to *Lieutenant-General*
8 Oct 1917: Retired

Lieutenant-General Prince Pavel Nikolayevich **Yengalychev** (19 Aug 1864 - 12 Aug 1944)
8 Jun 1902 - 6 Sep 1906: Commander, Life Guards Hussar Regiment
17 Apr 1905: Promoted to *Major-General*
6 Sep 1906 - 25 Oct 1906: Acting Commandant of the Imperial Palace

25 Oct 1906 - 22 Mar 1914:	Commandant of the Imperial Home Apartments
22 Mar 1914:	Promoted to *Lieutenant-General*
22 Mar 1914 - 8 Sep 1914:	Commandant of the Imperial Military Academy
8 Sep 1914 - 23 Dec 1914:	Chief of Staff, 6th Army
23 Dec 1914 - 8 Apr 1917:	Governor-General of Warsaw
9 Apr 1917 - 4 May 1917:	At the disposal of the Chief of Staff of the Supreme Commander-in-Chief
4 May 1917 - 19 Jul 1917:	Reserve officer, Kiev Military District
19 Jul 1917:	Retired

Rear-Admiral Nikolai Khristianovich **Yenish** (2 May 1848 - 25 Apr 1903)

12 Dec 1900 - 25 Apr 1903:	Chief of Staff, Black Sea Fleet
13 Jan 1901:	Promoted to *Rear-Admiral*

Admiral Aleksey Pavlovich **Yepanchin** (9 Feb 1823 - 28 Jun 1913)

1871 - 28 Jan 1877:	Commandant, Naval College
26 Feb 1873:	Promoted to *Rear-Admiral*
28 Jan 1877 - 27 Jun 1882:	Commandant, Nikolayev Naval Academy
27 Jun 1882 - 1 Jan 1904:	Admiral à la suite
26 Feb 1887:	Promoted to *Vice-Admiral*
1 Jan 1904:	Promoted to *General of the Admiralty*
1 Jan 1904 - 18 Dec 1909:	Attached to Grand Duke Alexey Aleksandrovich
18 Dec 1909:	Redesignated *Admiral*
18 Dec 1909:	Retired

Major-General of the Fleet Gavriil Alekseyevich **Yepanchin** (22 Nov 1863 - 1934)

6 Apr 1915:	Promoted to *Major-General of the Fleet*
1915 - 1917:	Member of the Izhorea Factory Economic Committee, Ministry of the Navy

General of Infantry Nikolai Alekseyevich **Yepanchin** (17 Jan 1857 - 12 Feb 1941)

11 Sep 1900 - 6 Jul 1907:	Director, Corps of Pages
1 Jan 1901:	Promoted to *Major-General*
22 Apr 1907:	Promoted to *Lieutenant-General*
6 Jul 1907 - 29 Jan 1913:	Commander, 42nd Infantry Division
29 Jan 1913 - 6 Feb 1915:	Commanding General, III. Army Corps
14 Apr 1913:	Promoted to *General of Infantry*
6 Feb 1915 - 5 Nov 1915:	Reserve officer, Dvinsk Military District
5 Nov 1915:	Retired
31 Jun 1916 - 9 Jan 1917:	Recalled; Reserve officer, Odessa Military District
9 Jan 1917 - 11 Apr 1917:	Commander, 5th Finnish Rifle Division
11 Apr 1917 - 24 Oct 1917:	Reserve officer, Kiev Military District
24 Oct 1917:	Retired

Major-General Viktor Nikolayevich **Yepanchin** (14 Aug 1845 - ?)

3 Sep 1901 - 1905:	Commander of Gendarmerie, St. Petersburg Railway
6 Dec 1902:	Promoted to *Major-General*
1905:	Retired

Lieutenant-General Ivan Nikolayevich **Yepaneshnikov** (31 Dec 1853 - ?)
18 Mar 1906 - 11 Nov 1907: Ataman, 1st Military Division, Orenburg Cossack Army
6 Dec 1906: Promoted to *Major-General*
11 Nov 1907 - 2 Nov 1912: Commander, Orenburg Cossack Horse Artillery Brigade
2 Nov 1912 - 21 Feb 1915: Inspector of Artillery, V. Army Corps
14 Apr 1913: Promoted to *Lieutenant-General*
21 Feb 1915 - 13 Aug 1915: Reserve officer, Dvinsk Military District
13 Aug 1915: Retired

Major-General Mikhail Semyonovich **Yepaneshnikov** (2 Nov 1855 - ?)
28 Jan 1913 - 24 Jun 1915: Commandant, St. Petersburg Ordnance Depot
14 Apr 1913: Promoted to *Major-General*
24 Jun 1915 - 25 Aug 1915: Reserve officer, 6th Army
25 Aug 1915: Retired

Major-General Pyotr Aleksandrovich **Yerekhovich** (3 Jun 1866 - ?)
23 Feb 1913 - 1917: Chief of Administration, Imperial Palace
14 Apr 1913: Promoted to *Major-General*

Major-General Aleksandr Mikhailovich **Yeremin** (21 Aug 1872 - ?)
1 Jun 1913 - 1917: Chief of Gendarmerie, Finland
6 Dec 1915: Promoted to *Major-General*

Lieutenant-General of the Fleet Konstantin Lvovich **Yergomyshev** (20 Apr 1856 - 9 Feb 1916)
18 Jun 1907 - 1 May 1914: Chief, St. Petersburg Naval Penitentiary
19 Apr 1910: Promoted to *Major-General of the Admiralty*
1 May 1914: Promoted to *Lieutenant-General of the Fleet*
1 May 1914: Retired

Lieutenant-General of the Fleet Vladimir Petrovich **Yermakov** (24 Jan 1867 - 9 Jul 1928)
6 Dec 1915: Promoted to *Major-General of the Fleet*
6 Dec 1915 - 1917: Senior Assistant Captain, Port of Kronstadt
1917: Promoted to *Lieutenant-General of the Fleet*
1917: Retired

Major-General Aleksey Mikhailovich **Yermakovsky** (17 Feb 1860 - 1913)
23 Feb 1907 - 26 Oct 1908: Military Judge, Vilnius Military District Court
22 Apr 1907: Promoted to *Major-General*
26 Oct 1908 - 9 Apr 1909: Military Judge, Odessa Military District Court
9 Apr 1909 - 4 Jun 1912: Military Judge, Moscow Military District Court
4 Jun 1912 - 1913: Military Judge, St. Petersburg Military District Court

General of Artillery Grigory Ivanovich **Yermolayev** (26 Dec 1838 - 3 Dec 1914)
29 Jul 1885 - 3 Dec 1914: Member of the Artillery Committee, Main Artillery Directorate
30 Aug 1885: Promoted to *Major-General*
6 Dec 1895: Promoted to *Lieutenant-General*

14 Apr 1913:   Promoted to *General of Artillery*

Major-General Nikolai Grigoryevich **Yermolayev** (8 May 1869 - ?)
18 Jan 1911 - 1915:   Duty General, St. Petersburg Military District
1911:   Promoted to *Major-General*
1915 - 6 Sep 1915:   Chief of Staff, St. Petersburg Military District
6 Sep 1915 - 1917:   Duty General, Northern Front

Vice-Admiral Platon Ivanovich **Yermolayev** (10 Oct 1832 - 6 Mar 1901)
1887:   Promoted to *Rear-Admiral*
31 Oct 1887 - 20 Dec 1888:   Military Governor, Port of Vladivostok
20 Dec 1888 - 1893:   Commander, Port of Vladivostok
1889 - 1897:   Junior Flagman, Pacific Squadron
1893:   Promoted to *Vice-Admiral*
1897 - 6 Mar 1901:   Attached to the Fleet

Major-General Georgy Stepanovich **Yermolin** (25 Apr 1843 - ?)
25 Jun 1885 - 20 Apr 1893:   Commander, 44th Dragoon Regiment
20 Apr 1893:   Promoted to *Major-General*
20 Apr 1893 - 20 May 1896:   Commander, 1st Brigade, Caucasus Cavalry Division
20 May 1896 - 30 Dec 1897:   At the disposal of the Commanding General, Caucasus Military District
30 Dec 1897 - 19 Dec 1901:   Commander, 2nd Reserve Cavalry Brigade
19 Dec 1901 - 1903:   At the disposal of the Commanding General, Moscow Military District

Major-General Nikolai Nikolayevich **Yermolinsky** (28 Oct 1869 - Feb 1919)
6 Dec 1911:   Promoted to *Major-General*
6 Dec 1911 - 27 Jul 1914:   Equerry to Grand Duke Konstantin Konstantinovich
27 Jul 1914 - Feb 1915:   Attached to the C-in-C, 1st Army
Feb 1915 - 2 Jun 1916:   Equerry to Grand Duke Konstantin Konstantinovich
2 Jun 1916 - 29 Jul 1917:   Equerry to Grand Duke Grand Duchess Elizaveta Mavrikievna
29 Jul 1917:   Discharged

Lieutenant-General Nikolai Sergeyevich **Yermolov** (28 Sep 1853 - 22 Jan 1924)
7 Jan 1891 - 2 Mar 1905:   Military Attaché, England
14 Apr 1902:   Promoted to *Major-General*
2 Mar 1905 - 25 Jun 1905:   Chief of Military Statistical Section, 2nd Quartermaster-General, General Staff
25 Jun 1905 - 10 May 1906:   Chief of Military Statistical Section, General Staff
10 May 1906 - 20 Feb 1907:   Duty General attached to the Chief of the General Staff
20 Feb 1907 - Oct 1917:   Military Attaché, England
29 Mar 1909:   Promoted to *Lieutenant-General*

Lieutenant-General Vladimir Viktorovich **Yermolov** (7 Jul 1870 - 14 Sep 1945)
8 Apr 1909 - 25 May 1915:   Chief of Bureau, Army Remount Administration
6 Dec 1911:   Promoted to *Major-General*

25 May 1915 - 5 Oct 1915:	Duty General, 13th Army
5 Oct 1915 - 28 Dec 1916:	Duty General, 12th Army
1916:	Promoted to *Lieutenant-General*
28 Dec 1916 - 1917:	Mililtary Governor of Dagestan

Lieutenant-General Aleksandr Gustavovich **Yernefelt** (21 Mar 1833 - 15 Apr 1896)

20 Mar 1870 - 1 Dec 1883:	Chief of the Finland Topographical Survey
17 Apr 1878:	Promoted to *Major-General*
1 Dec 1883 - 20 Jan 1884:	Commander, St. Mikhel Province
20 Jan 1884 - 6 Nov 1888:	Governor of Kuopio
30 Aug 1888:	Promoted to *Lieutenant-General*
6 Nov 1888 - 26 Oct 1894:	Governor of Vaasa Province
26 Oct 1894 - 15 Apr 1896:	Senator, Imperial Finnish Senate, Chief of Military Affairs, Imperial Finnish Senate

General of Infantry Mikhail Rodionovich **Yerofeyev** (1 Nov 1857 - 1941)

10 Mar 1903:	Promoted to *Major-General*
10 Mar 1903 - 8 Dec 1904:	Chief of Communications, Caucasus Military District
8 Dec 1904 - 30 Apr 1905:	Chief of Communications, 3rd Manchurian Army
30 Apr 1905 - 3 Jun 1906:	Commander, 2nd Brigade, 39th Infantry Division
3 Jun 1906 - 20 Jun 1907:	Commander, 1st Brigade, 21st Infantry Division
20 Jun 1907:	Promoted to *Lieutenant-General*
20 Jun 1907 - 2 Feb 1909:	Commandant of Fortress Kars
2 Feb 1909 - 15 Jan 1913:	Commander, Caucasus Grenadier Division
15 Jan 1913 - 5 Dec 1914:	Commanding General, I. Turkestan Army Corps
14 Apr 1913:	Promoted to *General of Infantry*
5 Dec 1914 - 17 Jun 1915:	Reserve officer, Dvinsk Military District
17 Jun 1915 - 12 Jul 1915:	Commanding General, VII. Siberian Army Corps
12 Jul 1915 - 1916:	Reserve officer, Dvinsk Military District
1916:	Acting Deputy Commanding General, Turkestan Military District
1916 - 5 May 1917:	Reserve officer, Dvinsk Military District
5 May1917 - Oct 1917:	Reserve officer, Kiev Military District

Lieutenant-General Vladimir Stepanovich **Yerofeyev** (30 Jan 1844 - ?)

31 Jul 1884 - 22 Apr 1900:	Commandant, St. Petersburg House of Detention
1 Jan 1895:	Promoted to *Major-General*
22 Apr 1900:	Promoted to *Lieutenant-General*
22 Apr 1900:	Retired

Major-General Mikhail Grigoryevich **Yerogin** (8 Nov 1856 - 8 Mar 1917)

14 Jan 1914:	Promoted to *Major-General*
14 Jan 1914 - 11 Feb 1914:	Commander, 2nd Brigade, 39th Infantry Division
11 Feb 1914 - 29 Jul 1914:	Commander, 1st Brigade, 17th Infantry Division
29 Jul 1914 - 10 Sep 1914:	Commander, 1st Brigade, 54th Infantry Division
10 Sep 1914 - 28 Mar 1915:	Commander, 1st Brigade, 28th Infantry Division
28 Mar 1915 - 4 Mar 1917:	Commander, Brigade, 30th Infantry Division
4 Mar 1917 -8 Mar 1917:	Reserve officer, Kiev Military District

Lieutenant-General Ippolit Alekseyevich **Yeropkin** (25 Jan 1852 - 30 Dec 1917)
6 Feb 1907:	Promoted to *Major-General*
6 Feb 1907 - 7 Apr 1907:	Commander, 2nd Brigade, 15th Cavalry Division
7 Apr 1907 - 25 Jan 1914:	Commander, 1st Reserve Cavalry Brigade
6 Dec 1911:	Promoted to *Lieutenant-General*
25 Jan 1914:	Retired
31 Jul 1915 - 26 Feb 1916:	Recalled; Reserve officer, 6th Army
26 Feb 1916 - 21 Aug 1917:	Commander, 1st Independent Baltic Mounted Brigade
21 Aug 1917:	Dismissed

Major-General Pyotr Konstantinovich **Yeroshevich** (4 Jul 1870 - 1945)
8 Feb 1915 - 29 Apr 1917:	Chief of Staff, VI. Siberian Army Corps
11 Feb 1915:	Promoted to *Major-General*
29 Apr 1917 - 27 Jul 1917:	Reserve officer, Petrograd Military District
27 Jul 1917 - 23 Oct 1917:	Chief of Staff, 12th Infantry Division
23 Oct 1917 - Dec 1917:	Commander, 12th Infantry Division

Lieutenant-General Aleksandr Pavlovich **Yershov** (6 Jul 1861 - 1922)
26 Jun 1910:	Promoted to *Major-General*
26 Jun 1910 - 17 Oct 1910:	Commander, 5th Sapper Brigade
17 Oct 1910 - 27 Apr 1911:	Inspector of Field Engineers, Odessa Military District
27 Apr 1911 - 29 Nov 1912:	Inspector of Field Engineers, Moscow Military District
29 Nov 1912 - 1917:	Inspector of Engineers, Moscow Military District
6 Dec 1916:	Promoted to *Lieutenant-General*

Major-General Vladimir Ivanovich **Yershov** (21 Jul 1844 - 4 Aug 1899)
30 Aug 1887:	Promoted to *Major-General*
30 Aug 1887 - 21 Jan 1892:	Transferred to the reserve
21 Jan 1892 - 4 Aug 1899:	Governor of Orenburg, Ataman, Orenburg Cossack Army

Major-General Aleksandr Alekseyevich **Yesaulov** (3 Dec 1859 - ?)
9 Apr 1910 - 11 Jun 1914:	Commander, 191st Infantry Regiment
11 Jun 1914:	Promoted to *Major-General*
11 Jun 1914 - 29 Jul 1914:	Commander, 2nd Brigade, 49th Infantry Division
29 Jul 1914 - 11 Mar 1917:	Commander, 1st Brigade, 84th Infantry Division
11 Mar 1917 - 26 May 1917:	Commander, 189th Infantry Division

Major-General of the Fleet Aleksey Alekseyevich **Yesaulov** (18 Feb 1865 - ?)
28 Sep 1909 - Jan 1915:	Chief of Naval Combat & Economic Section, Ministry of the Navy
14 Apr 1913:	Promoted to *Major-General of the Fleet*

Lieutenant-General Pavel Petrovich **Yesaulov** (7 Apr 1831 - ?)
13 Jan 1877 - 21 May 1881:	Commander, 25th Artillery Brigade
1 Jan 1878:	Promoted to *Major-General*
21 May 1881 - 8 Aug 1882:	Commander, 16th Artillery Brigade
8 Aug 1882 - 4 Dec 1888:	Commander, 25th Artillery Brigade

4 Dec 1888 - 1899:	Commander of Artillery, X. Army Corps
30 Aug 1889:	Promoted to *Lieutenant-General*

Lieutenant-General Vasily Filippovich **Yesimontovsky** (1 Mar 1851 - ?)
27 Nov 1904:	Promoted to *Major-General*
27 Nov 1904 - 6 Mar 1911:	Commander, 2nd Brigade, 16th Infantry Division
6 Mar 1911:	Promoted to *Lieutenant-General*
6 Mar 1911:	Retired

Major-General Leonid Nikolayevich **Yesipov** (16 Sep 1849 - ?)
10 Jan 1904 - 1907:	Commander of Engineers, Fortress Ochakov
2 Apr 1906:	Promoted to *Major-General*

Major-General Vladimir Nikolayevich **Yesipov** (25 Oct 1839 - ?)
10 Nov 1878 - 1900:	Chief of Police, St. Petersburg
14 May 1896:	Promoted to *Major-General*

Vice-Admiral Karl Petrovich **Yessen** (30 Jun 1852 - 30 Nov 1918)
1 Jan 1904:	Promoted to *Rear-Admiral*
24 Feb 1904 - 9 Nov 1904:	Commander, Cruiser Squadron, Pacific Fleet
9 Nov 1904 - 2 Jan 1905:	Commander, 1st Squadron, Pacific Fleet
2 Jan 1905 - 8 Apr 1906:	Commander of Cruisers, Pacific
8 Apr 1906 - 2 Nov 1906:	Unassigned
2 Nov 1906:	Promoted to *Vice-Admiral*
2 Nov 1906:	Retired

Privy Councillor Aleksandr Yakovlevich **Yevdokimov** (15 Aug 1854 - 13 Jul 1917)
?:	Promoted to *Actual State Councillor*
1906 - 23 May 1906:	Deputy Chief, Main Military Medical Directorate
23 May 1906 - Mar 1917:	Chief, Main Military Medical Directorate
?:	Promoted to *Privy Councillor*
Mar 1917:	Retired

Lieutenant-General Leonid Viktorovich **Yevdokimov** (8 Aug 1855 - 1 Sep 1928)
6 Dec 1902:	Promoted to *Major-General*
6 Dec 1902 - 12 Oct 1911:	General for Special Assignments, Main Engineering Directorate
12 Oct 1911:	Promoted to *Lieutenant-General*
12 Oct 1911:	Retired

Major-General Fyodor Osipovich **Yevgrafov** (5 Feb 1846 - ?)
30 May 1900:	Promoted to *Major-General*
30 May 1900 - 1901:	Ministry of War Representative, Military Council, Turkestan Military District

Lieutenant-General Aleksandr Aleksandrovich **Yevreinov** (24 Jan 1843 - 27 Jul 1905)
7 Sep 1887 - 30 Jan 1893:	Commander, Life Guards 4th Rifle Battalion
30 Aug 1889:	Promoted to *Major-General*

30 Jan 1893 - 21 May 1898:	Commander, Life Guards Izmailovo Regiment
14 May 1893 - 21 May 1898:	Commander, 2nd Brigade, 1st Guards Infantry Division
21 May 1898 - 15 Nov 1901:	Commander, Guards Rifle Brigade
6 Dec 1898:	Promoted to *Lieutenant-General*
15 Nov 1901 - 11 Dec 1902:	Commander, 1st Guards Infantry Division
11 Dec 1902 - 15 Apr 1904:	At the disposal of the Commanding General, St. Petersburg Military District
15 Apr 1904 - 27 Jul 1905:	Commanding General, XVIII. Army Corps

General of Infantry Aleksandr Iosafovich **Yevreinov** (16 Aug 1851 - 1929)

20 Nov 1899:	Promoted to *Major-General*
20 Nov 1899 - 26 Jun 1902:	Chief of Staff, XII. Army Corps
26 Jun 1902 - 17 Jan 1906:	Commander, 1st Brigade, 29th Infantry Division
17 Jan 1906 - 26 Oct 1907:	Commander, 45th Infantry Division
6 Dec 1906:	Promoted to *Lieutenant-General*
26 Oct 1907 - 31 Dec 1913:	Commander, 14th Infantry Division
31 Dec 1913:	Promoted to *General of Infantry*
31 Dec 1913:	Retired
29 Sep 1914 - 12 Mar 1915:	Recalled; Commander, 62nd Infantry Division
12 Mar 1915 - 18 Apr 1917:	Commanding General, XX. Army Corps
18 Apr 1917 - 11 Aug 1917:	Reserve officer, Odessa Military District
11 Aug 1917:	Retired

Lieutenant-General Ivan Ioasafovich **Yevreinov** (14 Aug 1848 - ?)

22 Jul 1902:	Promoted to *Major-General*
22 Jul 1902 - 20 Jan 1903:	Commander, 2nd Brigade, 4th Infantry Division
20 Jan 1903 - 5 Mar 1905:	Commander, 1st Brigade, 4th Infantry Division
5 Mar 1905 - 14 Mar 1906:	Commander, 2nd Brigade, 53rd Infantry Division
14 Mar 1906 - 4 Jul 1906:	Commander, 1st Brigade, 30th Infantry Division
4 Jul 1906 - 3 May 1910:	Commander, 55th Replacement Infantry Brigade
3 May 1910:	Promoted to *Lieutenant-General*
3 May 1910:	Retired

Major-General Konstantin Leonidovich **Yevreinov** (8 Jul 1872 - ?)

8 Jul 1916 - 17 Apr 1917:	Chief of Staff, 1st Caucasus Rifle Division
6 Dec 1916:	Promoted to *Major-General*
17 Apr 1917 - 1918:	Chief of Staff, XXVIII. Army Corps

General of Infantry Leonid Dmitrievich **Yevreinov** (15 Feb 1847 - ?)

22 Feb 1881 - 18 Sep 1890:	Chief of Clerk's Office, Ministry of War
30 Aug 1889:	Promoted to *Major-General*
18 Sep 1890 - 5 Jan 1891:	Manager of Apanage "Massandra"
5 Jan 1891 - 7 May 1892:	Manager of Livadsko-Massandra Estate
7 May 1892 - 12 Apr 1904:	Bailiff of "Livadia" Estate
12 Apr 1904 - 1917:	Honorary Trustee, Board of Trustees, Empress Maria Institutions
11 Sep 1904:	Promoted to *Lieutenant-General*
6 Dec 1914:	Promoted to *General of Infantry*

Lieutenant-General Mikhail Dmitryevich **Yevreinov** (6 Sep 1851 - ?)
20 Apr 1899 - 7 Jul 1899:	Deputy Chief of Staff, Turkestan Military District
26 Apr 1899:	Promoted to *Major-General*
7 Jul 1899 - 11 Oct 1904:	Quartermaster-General, Turkestan Military District
11 Oct 1904 - 15 Nov 1904:	Commander, 62nd Infantry Division
15 Nov 1904 - 20 Apr 1906:	Chief of Staff, Turkestan Military District
17 Apr 1905:	Promoted to *Lieutenant-General*
20 Apr 1906 - 10 Feb 1908:	Commander, Caucasus Grenadier Division
10 Feb 1908 - 26 Dec 1910:	Commanding General, II. Turkestan Army Corps, Commander, Trans-Caspian Region
26 Dec 1910:	Retired

Lieutenant-General Sergei Nikolayevich **Yevreinov** (14 Aug 1849 - Apr 1920)
30 Jul 1894 - 1906:	Estate Manager to Grand Duke Aleksandr Mikhailovich
10 Apr 1899:	Promoted to *Major-General*
1906:	Promoted to *Privy Councillor*
1906 - 1917:	Privy Councillor, Ministry of Estates & Principalities
1916:	Redesignated *Lieutenant-General*

Major-General Sergei Vladimirovich **Yevreinov** (14 Jul 1858 - 8 Sep 1914)
20 Apr 1907 - 20 Mar 1914:	Commander, Life Guards Ataman Regiment
13 Apr 1908:	Promoted to *Major-General*
20 Mar 1914 - 19 Jul 1914:	Attached to the Tsar's retinue
19 Jul 1914 - 23 Aug 1914:	Commander, 3rd Don Cossack Division
23 Aug 1914:	Dismissed

Major-General Nikolai Konstantinovich **Yevseyev** (18 Sep 1869 - ?)
22 Mar 1912 - 10 Mar 1916:	Military Judge, Omsk Military District Court
6 Dec 1912:	Promoted to *Major-General*
10 Mar 1916 - 1917:	Military Judge, Caucasus Military District Court

Major-General Aleksandr Ivanovich **Yevsky** (11 Nov 1842 - 10 Sep 1913)
1894 - 1901:	Battalion Commander, 34th Artillery Brigade
1901:	Promoted to *Major-General*
1901:	Retired

Major-General Nikolai Pavlovich **Yevstafyev** (27 Jul 1848 - ?)
14 Feb 1910:	Promoted to *Major-General*
14 Feb 1910 - 2 Jul 1913:	Commander, Omsk Regional Brigade
2 Jul 1913:	Retired

Major-General Nikolai Prokofyevich **Yevstafyev** (12 Sep 1842 - 19 Oct 1918)
29 Mar 1892 - 1901:	Commander of Gendarmerie, Terek Region
18 Apr 1899:	Promoted to *Major-General*
1901:	Retired

Major-General Nikolai Fyodorovich **Yevsyukov** (14 Jan 1866 - 5 Jul 1915)
Jul 1914 - 18 Jul 1915:	Commander, 121st Infantry Regiment

18 Jul 1915: Posthumously promoted to *Major-General*

Lieutenant-General Pavel Stepanovich **Yevtin** (22 Jun 1855 - ?)
19 May 1912: Promoted to *Major-General*
19 May 1912 - 12 May 1916: Commander, 41st Artillery Brigade
12 May 1916 - 1917: Inspector of Artillery, XLV. Army Corps
26 Aug 1916: Promoted to *Lieutenant-General*

Lieutenant-General Semyon Ivanovich **Yezersky** (1 Sep 1852 - 1921)
23 Dec 1902 - 13 Apr 1904: Ministry of War Representative, Military Council, Moscow Military District
1903: Promoted to *Major-General*
13 Apr 1904 - 14 Jul 1905: Inspector of Hospitals, Manchurian Army
14 Jul 1905 - 28 Dec 1906: Inspector of Hospitals, Fortress Vladivostok
28 Dec 1906 - 9 Jul 1912: Ministry of War Representative, Military Council, Amur Military District
6 Dec 1910: Promoted to *Lieutenant-General*
9 Jul 1912: Retired

Major-General Mikhail Semyonovich **Yudenich** (7 Nov 1867 - 1921)
1915 - 1917: Commander, 4th Caucasus Border Infantry Regiment
17 Dec 1916: Promoted to *Major-General*
1917 - 1918: Commander, Consolidated Border Infantry Brigade

General of Infantry Nikolai Nikolayevich **Yudenich** (18 Jul 1862 - 5 Oct 1933)
19 Jun 1905: Promoted to *Major-General*
19 Jun 1905 - 10 Feb 1907: Commander, 2nd Brigade, 5th Rifle Division
21 Nov 1905 - 3 Apr 1906: Acting Commander, 2nd Rifle Division
10 Feb 1907 - 6 Dec 1912: Quartermaster-General, Kazan Military District
6 Dec 1912: Promoted to *Lieutenant-General*
6 Dec 1912 - 25 Feb 1913: Chief of Staff, Kazan Military District
25 Feb 1913 - 2 Oct 1914: Chief of Staff, Caucasus Military District
2 Oct 1914 - 24 Jan 1915: Chief of Staff, Caucasus Army
24 Jan 1915: Promoted to *General of Infantry*
24 Jan 1915 - 3 Apr 1917: C-in-C, Caucasus Army
3 Apr 1917 - 31 May 1917: C-in-C, Caucasus Front
31 May 1917 - 1918: At the disposal of the Minister of War

Major-General Dmitry Aleksandrovich **Yudin** (22 Oct 1849 - ?)
2 Mar 1905 - 3 Aug 1908: Commander, 27th Artillery Brigade
1 Mar 1906: Promoted to *Major-General*
3 Aug 1908: Retired

Major-General Vladimir Parfenovich **Yudushkin** (6 Oct 1860 - 24 May 1915)
31 Mar 1912 - 24 May 1915: Commander, 2nd Battalion, 38th Artillery Brigade
26 Sep 1915: Posthumously promoted to *Major-General*

Major-General Faddey Yakovlevich **Yukhnitsky** (10 Jan 1861 - ?)
17 Feb 1916 - 1917:	Member, Committee for Permanent Radio Stations, Main Military-Technical Directorate
6 Dec 1916:	Promoted to *Major-General*

General of Infantry Leonty Avksentyevich **Yunakov** (19 Jun 1838 - 7 Dec 1905)
1880:	Promoted to *Major-General*
1 Mar 1880 - 11 Sep 1880:	Attached to the Commanding General, Kharkov Military District
11 Sep 1880 - 10 Aug 1882:	Deputy Chief of Staff, Kharkov Military District
10 Aug 1882 - 24 Jan 1890:	Chief of Staff, IX. Army Corps
24 Jan 1890 - 15 Jun 1892:	Chief of Staff, Amur Military District
15 Jun 1892 - 1 Dec 1892:	At the disposal of the Chief of the General Staff
1 Dec 1892 - 18 May 1894:	Commander, 47th Replacement Infantry Brigade
18 May 1894 - 11 Aug 1899:	Commander, 35th Infantry Division
30 Aug 1894:	Promoted to *Lieutenant-General*
11 Aug 1899 - 9 Sep 1900:	Commanding General, XII. Army Corps
9 Sep 1900 - 10 Feb 1904:	Commanding General, VII. Army Corps
10 Feb 1904:	Promoted to *General of Infantry*
10 Feb 1904:	Retired

Lieutenant-General Nikolai Leontievich **Yunakov** (6 Dec 1871 - 1 Aug 1931)
14 Jan 1911 - 9 Feb 1914:	Professor, Nikolaev Military Academy
6 Dec 1912:	Promoted to *Major-General*
9 Feb 1914 - 29 Jul 1914:	Commander, 1st Brigade, 37th Infantry Division
29 Jul 1914 - 4 Nov 1914:	Commander, Brigade, 74th Infantry Division
4 Nov 1914 - 4 Apr 1915:	Chief of Staff, XXV. Army Corps
4 Apr 1915 - 28 Apr 1917:	Chief of Staff, 4th Army
10 Apr 1916:	Promoted to *Lieutenant-General*
28 Apr 1917 - 25 Aug 1917:	Commanding General, VII. Army Corps
25 Aug 1917 - 18 Oct 1917:	Attached to the C-in-C, Romanian Front
18 Oct 1917 - 21 Dec 1917:	C-in-C, 8th Army
21 Dec 1917:	Dismissed

Major-General Andrey Ivanovich **Yunchis** (30 Nov 1848 - ?)
11 Oct 1904:	Promoted to *Major-General*
11 Oct 1904 - 16 Apr 1906:	Commander, 1st Brigade, 79th Infantry Division
16 Apr 1906 - 6 Oct 1906:	Commander, 2nd Brigade, 45th Infantry Division
6 Oct 1906 - 31 Jan 1907:	Commander, 1st Brigade, 45th Infantry Division
31 Jan 1907 - 1908:	Commander, 1st Turkestan Reserve Brigade

General of Infantry Pavel Stepanovich **Yuneyev** (6 Jun 1825 - 30 Jun 1907)
2 Nov 1867 - 4 Nov 1876:	Special Assignments Officer, Main Intendant Directorate
16 Apr 1872:	Promoted to *Major-General*
4 Nov 1876 - 27 Sep 1881:	Intendant, X. Army Corps
27 Sep 1881 - 1899:	Intendant, Omsk Military District
30 Aug 1882:	Promoted to *Lieutenant-General*

1887:	Acting Commander, Omsk Garrison
1890 - 1891:	Acting Commander, Omsk Garrison
1893 - 1894:	Acting Commander, Omsk Garrison
1895:	Acting Commanding General, Omsk Military District
1899:	Promoted to *General of Infantry*
1899:	Retired

Major-General Vladimir Gustavovich **Yunger** (28 Aug 1864 - ?)
16 Jun 1914 - 1917:	Commandant of Railway Officer School
6 Dec 1914:	Promoted to *Major-General*

Lieutenant-General Konstantin Danilovich **Yurgens** (9 Jun 1858 - ?)
15 Jan 1904:	Promoted to *Major-General*
15 Jan 1904 - 31 Dec 1905:	Commander, 1st Brigade, 30th Infantry Division
31 Dec 1905 - 21 Dec 1907:	Chief of Staff, III. Siberian Army Corps
21 Dec 1907 - 9 Jun 1913:	Commander, 1st Brigade, 43rd Infantry Division
9 Jun 1913:	Promoted to *Lieutenant-General*
9 Jun 1913:	Retired

Lieutenant-General Pyotr Semyonovich **Yurkevich** (26 Apr 1854 - ?)
27 Jul 1904 - 30 Jun 1907:	Commander, 101st Infantry Regiment
30 Jun 1907:	Promoted to *Major-General*
30 Jun 1907 - 8 Jan 1909:	Commander, 2nd Brigade, 28th Infantry Division
8 Jan 1909 - 26 Apr 1914:	Commander, 1st Brigade, 28th Infantry Division
26 Apr 1914:	Promoted to *Lieutenant-General*
26 Apr 1914:	Retired
13 Apr 1915 - 7 Apr 1916:	Recalled; Commander, Replacement Infantry Brigade
7 Apr 1916 - 1917:	Special Assignments General, Turkestan Military District

Major-General of the Naval Legal Corps Vladimir Andreyevich **Yurkovsky** (9 Jan 1867 - 1920)
1 Jan 1906 - 1917:	Judge, Kronstadt Naval Court
6 Dec 1913:	Promoted to *Major-General of the Naval Legal Corps*

General of Infantry Vladimir Ivanovich **Yurkovsky** (23 Apr 1857 - 1913)
11 Jan 1901:	Promoted to *Major-General*
11 Jan 1901 - 1 Nov 1902:	Special Assignments General to the Ataman, Don Cossack Army
1 Nov 1902 - 26 Jun 1906:	Chief of Staff, Fortress Georgiyevsk
26 Jun 1906 - 29 Mar 1907:	Commander, 48th Reserve Infantry Brigade
29 Mar 1907 - 15 Apr 1910:	Commandant of Fortress Ivangorod
31 May 1907:	Promoted to *Lieutenant-General*
15 Aug 1910 - 31 May 1913:	Commandant of Fortress Brest-Litovsk
31 May 1913:	Promoted to *General of Infantry*
31 May 1913:	Retired

Lieutenant-General Yevgeny Kornilyevich **Yurkovsky** (31 Jan 1833 - Jan 1899)
4 Apr 1881 - 16 Jan 1886: Deputy Commander, Terek Region
6 May 1884: Promoted to *Major-General*
16 Jan 1886 - 17 Jan 1887: Ataman, Terek Cossack Army
17 Jan 1887 - 27 Dec 1891: Chief of Police, Moscow
27 Dec 1891 - Jan 1899: Honorary Trustee, Moscow Board of Trustees, Empress Maria Institutions
14 May 1896: Promoted to *Lieutenant-General*

Lieutenant-General Nikolai Ivanovich **Yurlov** (25 Jan 1862 - ?)
12 Dec 1897 - 1912: Section Chief, Main Artillery Directorate
13 Apr 1908: Promoted to *Major-General*
1912: Promoted to *Lieutenant-General*
1912: Retired

Major-General Dmitry Vasilyevich **Yurov** (28 Sep 1855 - ?)
25 Apr 1900 - 22 Nov 1905: Commandant of Abas-Tuman
6 Apr 1903: Promoted to *Major-General*
22 Nov 1905 - 1908: Attached to Caucasus Military District

Major-General Ivan Andreyevich **Yurov** (24 Feb 1854 - ?)
14 Jun 1906 - 29 Sep 1907: Deputy Intendant-General, Moscow Military District
6 Dec 1906: Promoted to *Major-General*
29 Sep 1907 - 16 May 1910: Intendant-General, Odessa Military District
16 May 1910: Retired

Rear-Admiral Pyotr Fyodorovich **Yuryev** (16 Jan 1844 - ?)
1894: Promoted to *Rear-Admiral*
1896 - ?: Chairman of the Volunteer Fleet Committee

Major-General Vladimir Petrovich **Yuryev** (6 Oct 1861 - ?)
1 Jan 1916 - 1917: Commander, 2nd Brigade, 2nd Cavalry Division
11 May 1916: Promoted to *Major-General*

General of Engineers Vladimir Sergeyevich **Yuryev** (15 Nov 1854 - 23 Sep 1919)
2 Sep 1895 - 10 Aug 1911: Chairman, Main Selection Committee, Main Engineering Directorate
6 Dec 1902: Promoted to *Major-General*
29 Mar 1909: Promoted to *Lieutenant-General*
10 Aug 1911 - 16 Aug 1915: Chairman, Commission on Preparation of Engineering Assets
6 May 1915: Promoted to *General of Engineers*
16 Aug 1915 - Oct 1917: Member, Technical Committee, Main Engineering Directorate

Major-General Adrian Fomich **Yushkevich** (8 Oct 1861 - ?)
21 Sep 1913 - 1917: Deputy Chief of Engineering Section, Main Military-Technical Directorate

6 Dec 1916: Promoted to *Major-General*

Lieutenant-General Feliks Feliksovich Prince **Yusupov**, Count Sumarokov-Elston (5 Oct 1856 - Jun 1928)
22 Jul 1905:	Promoted to *Major-General*
22 Jul 1905- 28 Oct 1908:	Commander, Guards Cavalry Regiment
28 Oct 1908 - 13 Dec 1911:	Commander, 2nd Brigade, 2nd Guards Cavalry Division
13 Dec 1911 - 5 May 1915:	General à la suite
5 May 1915 - 19 Jun 1915:	Commanding General, Moscow Military District
5 May 1915 - 3 Sep 1915:	Commanding General, Moscow
6 May 1915:	Promoted to *Lieutenant-General*
6 May 1915:	Promoted to *General-Adjutant*
3 Sep 1915 - Mar 1917:	General à la suite

Lieutenant-General Yakov Davidovich **Yuzefovich** (12 Mar 1872 - 5 Jul 1929)
23 Aug 1914 - 22 Feb 1916:	Chief of Staff, Native Cavalry Division
10 Sep 1915:	Promoted to *Major-General*
22 Feb 1916 - 15 Apr 1917:	Chief of Staff, II. Cavalry Corps
15 Apr 1917 - 12 May 1917:	Quartermaster-General to the Supreme Commander-in-Chief
12 May 1917 - 15 Jun 1917:	1st Quartermaster-General to the Supreme Commander-in-Chief
15 Jun 1917 - 7 Sep 1917:	Commander, 12th Cavalry Division
7 Sep 1917:	Promoted to *Lieutenant-General*
7 Sep 1917 - 9 Sep 1917:	Commanding General, XXVI. Army Corps
9 Sep 1917 - 19 Nov 1917:	C-in-C, 12th Army
14 Nov 1917 - 1918:	C-in-C, Northern Front

Major-General Frants Ivanovich **Yuzvikevich** (1 Apr 1835 - ?)
14 May 1893:	Promoted to *Major-General*
14 May 1893 - 1898:	Commander of Kursk Artillery Depot, Kiev Military District

Major-General Aleksandr Alekseyevich **Yuzvitsky** (14 Nov 1854 - ?)
21 May 1911:	Promoted to *Major-General*
21 May 1911 - 19 Feb 1914:	Commander, 19th Artillery Brigade
19 Feb 1914:	Retired
3 Nov 1915 - 1917:	Recalled; Attached to Southwestern Front

Major-General Mikhail Zakharovich **Zaalov** (3 Jan 1858 - ?)
1 Mar 1912 - 3 Jan 1914:	Commander, 186th Infantry Regiment
3 Jan 1914:	Promoted to *Major-General*
3 Jan 1914:	Retired

General of Infantry Aleksandr Fyodorovich **Zabelin** (18 May 1856 - 22 Nov 1933)
19 Sep 1898 - 15 Mar 1904:	Deputy Chief of Staff. Ministry of War
6 Dec 1899:	Promoted to *Major-General*
15 Mar 1904 - 25 Jun 1905:	Chief of Communications, Manchurian Army

30 Nov 1904 - 25 Jun 1905:	Chief of Communications, Far East
5 Mar 1905:	Promoted to *Lieutenant-General*
25 Jun 1905 - 3 Mar 1910:	Chief of Staff, Ministry of War
3 Mar 1910 - 19 Jul 1914:	Chief of the Main Directorate for Military Schools
10 Apr 1911:	Promoted to *General of Infantry*
19 Jul 1914 - 27 Dec 1914:	Chief of Logistics, Southwestern Front
27 Dec 1914 - 2 Apr 1917:	Chief of Military Schools, Chief of the Main Directorate for Military Schools
2 Apr 1917:	Retired

Major-General Nikolai Lvovich **Zabello** (2 Feb 1857 - 15 May 1919)
25 Jan 1908 - 19 May 1913:	Commandant of Nerchinsk Prison
19 May 1913:	Promoted to *Major-General*
19 May 1913:	Retired
13 Jun 1916 - 1917:	Recalled; Commander, 245th Reserve Infantry Regiment
1917:	Deputy Commander, 33rd Replacement Infantry Brigade

Major-General Nikolai Nikolayevich **Zabello** (10 Feb 1870 - 27 Nov 1919)
10 Mar 1916 - 1917:	Military Judge, Omsk Military District Court
10 Apr 1916:	Promoted to *Major-General*

Major-General Vasily Silvestrovich **Zabolotny** (2 Mar 1860 - ?)
16 Aug 1914 - 9 Nov 1914:	Commander, 297th Infantry Regiment
9 Nov 1914 - 1917:	POW, Germany
18 Feb 1916:	Promoted to *Major-General*

Major-General of the Fleet Aleksey Andreyevich **Zaborovsky** (27 Feb 1862 - ?)
27 Sep 1911 - 9 Jul 1917:	Commander, Disciplinary Crew
10 Apr 1916:	Promoted to *Major-General of the Fleet*
9 Jul 1917:	Dismissed

Lieutenant-General Dmitry Stepanovich **Zabotkin** (15 Jan 1837 - 19 Dec 1894)
29 May 1872 - 25 Oct 1887:	Commander of Engineers, Fortress Kronstadt
8 Apr 1884:	Promoted to *Major-General*
25 Oct 1887 - 7 Oct 1890:	Member of the Engineering Committee, Main Engineering Directorate
7 Oct 1890 - 28 Apr 1891:	Deputy Inspector-General of Engineers
28 Apr 1891 - 19 Dec 1894:	Inspector-General of Engineers
30 Aug 1893:	Promoted to *Lieutenant-General*

Lieutenant-General Grigory Aleksandrovich **Zabudsky** (21 Jul 1854 - 1930)
12 Mar 1893 - 16 Aug 1909:	Commandant, Chemical Laboratory Academy
6 Apr 1903:	Promoted to *Major-General*
16 Aug 1909 - 23 Nov 1909:	At the disposal of the Minister of War
23 Nov 1909 - 7 May 1912:	Professor Emeritus, Mikhailovsky Artillery Academy
6 Dec 1909:	Promoted to *Lieutenant-General*
7 May 1912 - 3 Aug 1914:	Chairman, Commission for the Construction of Military Scientific and Engineering Laboratory

3 Aug 1914 - Oct 1917: Department Chief, Military Scientific and Engineering Laboratory

Lieutenant-General Nikolai Aleksandrovich **Zabudsky** (27 Jan 1853 - 27 Feb 1917)
11 Feb 1893 - 27 Feb 1917: Professor, Mikhailovsky Artillery Academy
30 Aug 1893 - 8 Oct 1914: Member of the Artillery Committee, Main Artillery Directorate
6 Dec 1901: Promoted to *Major-General*
6 Dec 1907: Promoted to *Lieutenant-General*
8 Oct 1914 - 27 Feb 1917: Chief of Section 1, Artillery Committee, Main Artillery Directorate

Lieutenant-General Nikolai Ivanovich **Zabusov** (6 Apr 1846 - 21 Sep 1914)
17 Jul 1900 - 9 Apr 1901: Commander, 45th Artillery Brigade
1 Jan 1901: Promoted to *Major-General*
9 Apr 1901 - 8 May 1905: Commander, 37th Artillery Brigade
8 May 1905 - 1910: Commander of Artillery, Don Cossack Army
22 Apr 1907: Promoted to *Lieutenant-General*
1910: Retired

Major-General Lyudvig Romualdovich **Zadarnovsky** (15 Nov 1835 - ?)
1 Oct 1878 - 1895: Military Judge, Kazan Military District Court
30 Aug 1889: Promoted to *Major-General*

Lieutenant-General Aleksandr Voinovich **Zadonsky** (7 Jul 1834 - 1912)
25 Jul 1884 - 25 Jun 1885: Commander of Gendarmerie, Warsaw Province
18 Nov 1884: Promoted to *Major-General*
25 Jun 1885 - 3 Jan 1895: Commander of Gendarmerie, Kursk Province
3 Jan 1895: Promoted to *Lieutenant-General*
3 Jan 1895: Retired

Lieutenant-General Pyotr Zakharovich **Zadorin** (8 Jun 1853 - 3 Aug 1906)
10 Mar 1903: Promoted to *Major-General*
10 Mar 1903 - 3 Aug 1906: Chief of Communications, Kiev Military District
Jul 1906: Promoted to *Lieutenant-General*

Rear-Admiral Andrey Sergeyevich **Zagoryansky-Kisel** (18 Aug 1858 - ?)
3 Jan 1911: Promoted to *Rear-Admiral*
3 Jan 1911 - 29 Oct 1914: Commander, Port of Emperor Aleksandr III (Libau)
29 Oct 1914: Retired

Vice-Admiral Apollinary Sergeyevich **Zagoryansky-Kisel** (2 Jul 1848 - ?)
6 Apr 1903: Promoted to *Rear-Admiral*
14 Apr 1903 - 5 Jan 1904: Commander, Emperor Aleksander III Naval Depot
22 Jul 1903 - 28 Jul 1903: Acting Commander, Port of Emperor Aleksandr III (Libau)
13 Oct 1903 - 28 Oct 1903: Acting Commander, Port of Emperor Aleksandr III (Libau)

5 Jan 1904 - 26 Apr 1904:	Junior Flagman, 1st Naval Division
26 Apr 1904 - 2 Jan 1906:	Commander, Port of Nikolayev, Mayor of Nikolayev
2 Jan 1906 - 23 Jan 1906:	Reserve officer, Ministry of the Navy
23 Jan 1906:	Promoted to *Vice-Admiral*
23 Jan 1906:	Retired

Major-General Mikhail Dmitriyevich **Zagoskin** (1 Oct 1857 - 28 Sep 1919)
2 Sep 1908 - 1912:	Commander of Gendarmerie, Vitebsk Province
18 Apr 1910:	Promoted to *Major-General*

General of Infantry Mikhail Nikolayevich **Zagoskin** (10 Jun 1851 - ?)
3 Jun 1901 - 30 Jul 1903:	Military Judge, Warsaw Military District Court
6 Dec 1901:	Promoted to *Major-General*
30 Jul 1903 - 15 Dec 1905:	Military Judge, Vilnius Military District Court
15 Dec 1905 - 19 May 1908:	Military Prosecutor, Vilnius Military District
6 Dec 1907:	Promoted to *Lieutenant-General*
19 May 1908 - 1912:	Chairman, Moscow Military District Court
1912:	Promoted to *General of Infantry*
1912:	Retired

Lieutenant-General Nikolai Mikhailovich **Zagyu** (24 Nov 1866 - ?)
15 Apr 1905 - 3 Feb 1917:	Commandant, Tiflis Military College
1 Sep 1910:	Promoted to *Major-General*
3 Feb 1917 - Oct 1917:	Commander, Caucasus Border Infantry Division
15 Aug 1917:	Promoted to *Lieutenant-General*

Major-General Ivan Aleksandrovich **Zakharchenko** (19 Mar 1862 - ?)
1916 - 8 Aug 1917:	Commander, 27th Artillery Brigade
24 Jul 1916:	Promoted to *Major-General*
8 Aug 1917:	Dismissed

Major-General Ivan Ivanovich **Zakhariyashevich** (22 Oct 1841 - 1909)
25 Jul 1900 - 1908:	Commander, Kiev Railway Gendarmerie
17 Apr 1905:	Promoted to *Major-General*
1908:	Retired

Major-General Agafangel Vasilyevich **Zakharov** (14 Jan 1856 - ?)
13 Jun 1910 - 1913:	Ataman, 2nd Don District, Don Cossack Army
6 Dec 1910:	Promoted to *Major-General*

Major-General Aleksandr Nikolayevich **Zakharov** (15 Jun 1847 - 1909)
10 Aug 1906 - 1909:	Chairman of the Economic Committee, St. Petersburg Regional Arsenal
1909:	Promoted to *Major-General*

Lieutenant-General Pyotr Matveyevich **Zakharov** (28 Jun 1866 - 11 Jul 1942)
26 Apr 1905 - 15 Mar 1907:	Chief of Military Communications, Manchurian Army

1906:	Promoted to *Major-General*
15 Mar 1907 - 11 Jan 1909:	Commander, 1st Brigade, 1st East Siberian Rifle Division
11 Jan 1909 - 19 Jul 1914:	Commander, 2nd Brigade, 3rd Grenadier Division
?:	Acting Commander, 3rd Grenadier Division
19 Jul 1914 - 17 Oct 1915:	Commander, 55th Infantry Division
8 May 1915:	Promoted to *Lieutenant-General*
17 Oct 1915:	Retired

Major-General Pavel Timofeyevich **Zakovenkin** (10 Dec 1849 - 31 Jan 1913)

21 Jun 1905:	Promoted to *Major-General*
21 Jun 1905 - 24 Dec 1908:	Commander, 2nd Brigade, 38th Infantry Division
24 Dec 1908:	Retired

General of Infantry Nikolai Iosifovich **Zakrzhevsky** (4 Sep 1853 - ?)

17 Jun 1896 - 26 Jul 1899:	Commander, 15th Grenadier Regiment
26 Jul 1899:	Promoted to *Major-General*
26 Jul 1899 - 29 Sep 1903:	Chief of Staff, V. Army Corps
29 Sep 1903 - 11 Oct 1904:	Commander, 1st Brigade, 38th Infantry Division
11 Oct 1904 - 8 Aug 1906:	Commander, 79th Infantry Division
8 Aug 1906 - 9 Jul 1910:	Commander, 17th Infantry Division
22 Apr 1907:	Promoted to *Lieutenant-General*
9 Jul 1910:	Promoted to *General of Infantry*
9 Jul 1910:	Retired

Lieutenant-General Ivan Andreyevich **Zakutovsky** (23 Jun 1855 - ?)

16 Jan 1909:	Promoted to *Major-General*
16 Jan 1909 - 16 Jan 1914:	Commander, 21st Artillery Brigade
16 Jan 1914 - 28 Apr 1917:	Inspector of Artillery, I. Siberian Army Corps
10 Mar 1915:	Promoted to *Lieutenant-General*
28 Apr 1917 - 25 Jul 1917:	Unassigned
25 Jul 1917:	Discharged

General of Infantry Nikolai Gavrilovich **Zalesov** (25 May 1828 - 23 Jan 1896)

6 Oct 1867 - 17 Nov 1870:	Chief of Staff, Orenburg Military District
20 Apr 1869:	Promoted to *Major-General*
17 Nov 1870 - 30 Aug 1873:	Attached to Finland Military District
30 Aug 1873 - 14 Mar 1875:	Commander, 2nd Brigade, 7th Infantry Division
14 Mar 1875 - 1 Nov 1876:	Member, Military Scientific Committee, General Staff
1 Nov 1876 - 8 Nov 1888:	Commander, 27th Infantry Division
30 Aug 1878:	Promoted to *Lieutenant-General*
8 Nov 1888 - 28 Nov 1892:	Commanding General, XVII. Army Corps
30 Aug 1892:	Promoted to *General of Infantry*
28 Nov 1892 - 23 Jan 1896:	Member of the Military Council

Major-General Andrian Ivanovich **Zalessky** (26 Aug 1866 - ?)

25 Jun 1903 - 1 May 1916:	Artillery Inspector, Main Artillery Directorate
14 Apr 1913:	Promoted to *Major-General*

1 May 1916 - 1917:	Deputy Chief of Artillery Acceptance, Main Artillery Directorate

Major-General Anton Stanislavovich **Zalessky** (13 Jun 1856 - ?)
? - 1913:	Attached to 26th Infantry Regiment
1913:	Promoted to *Major-General*
1913:	Retired
5 Oct 1914 - 1915:	Recalled; Commander, 274th Foot Detachment
1915 - 1916:	Commander, 106th State Militia Brigade
1916:	Retired

Lieutenant-General Ivan Petrovich **Zalessky** (6 Jan 1854 - ?)
6 Dec 1904:	Promoted to *Major-General*
6 Dec 1904 - 31 Jul 1905:	Attached to the Commanding General, Corps of Gendarmerie
31 Jul 1905 - 30 Jun 1913:	Deputy Chief of Staff, Corps of Gendarmerie
14 Apr 1913:	Promoted to *Lieutenant-General*
30 Jun 1913 - 23 Jun 1917:	At the disposal of the Minister of the Interior
23 Jun 1917:	Dismissed

Major-General Pyotr Ivanovich **Zalessky** (5 Oct 1867 - ?)
28 Aug 1914 - 16 Nov 1914:	Chief of Staff, VI. Army Corps
16 Nov 1914 - 25 Jun 1915:	Chief of Staff, I. Cavalry Corps
17 Nov 1914:	Promoted to *Major-General*
25 Jun 1915 - 26 Jun 1916:	Commander, 1st Brigade, 3rd Cavalry Division
26 Jun 1916 - 17 Dec 1916:	Commander, 2nd Brigade, 13th Cavalry Division
17 Dec 1916 - 16 Apr 1917:	Chief of Staff, XXVIII. Army Corps
30 Apr 1917 - Oct 1917:	Commander, 6th Cavalry Division

Major-General Pyotr Karlovich **Zalessky** (31 Jan 1850 - 22 Nov 1916)
6 Mar 1901 - 22 Nov 1916:	Attached to Military Topographical Section, Turkestan Military District
24 Jan 1917:	Posthumously promoted to *Major-General*

Major-General Pyotr Petrovich **Zalessky** (19 Jul 1863 - 10 Jan 1917)
29 Nov 1912 - Aug 1915:	Deputy Inspector of Engineers, Warsaw Military District
6 Dec 1912:	Promoted to *Major-General*
Aug 1915 - 16 Feb 1916:	Inspector of Engineers, Turkestan Military District
16 Feb 1916 - 10 Jan 1917:	Special Assignments General to the Chief of Staff to the Supreme Commander-in-Chief

Major-General Sigizmund Pavlovich **Zalessky** (1842 - Nov 1900)
1889 - Nov 1900:	At the disposal of the Main Directorate for Military Schools
1900:	Promoted to *Major-General*

Major-General Vasily Vasilyevich **Zalessky** (1 Oct 1844 - ?)
17 Jul 1885 - 15 Oct 1890:	Commander, Trans-Caspian Mounted Cossack Brigade
30 Aug 1889:	Promoted to *Major-General*
15 Oct 1890 - 1894:	Special Assignments General, Caucasus Military District

Major-General Adam Aleksandrovich **Zalivsky** (17 Oct 1862 - 24 Feb 1916)
5 Jun 1907 - 24 Oct 1908:	Military Judge, Odessa Military District Court
6 Dec 1907:	Promoted to *Major-General*
24 Oct 1908 - 24 Feb 1916:	Military Prosecutor, Odessa Military District Court

General of Infantry Baron Anton Yegorovich von **Zaltsa** (22 Oct 1843 - 9 Mar 1916)
8 Mar 1895:	Promoted to *Major-General*
8 Mar 1895 - 1 Nov 1895:	Commander, Caucasus Rifle Brigade
1 Nov 1895 - 30 Jan 1902:	Commander, 1st Caucasus Rifle Brigade
30 Jan 1902 - 14 Apr 1904:	Commander, 24th Infantry Division
14 Apr 1902:	Promoted to *Lieutenant-General*
14 Apr 1904 - 1 Aug 1905:	Commander, 1st Guards Infantry Division
1 Aug 1905 - 9 Nov 1906:	Commanding General, XXII. Army Corps
9 Nov 1906 - 8 Jun 1908:	Commanding General, I. Army Corps
13 Apr 1908:	Promoted to *General of Infantry*
8 Jun 1908 - 7 Feb 1912:	Deputy Commanding General, Kiev Military District
7 Feb 1912 - 19 Jul 1914:	Commanding General, Kazan Military District
19 Jul 1914 - 22 Aug 1914:	C-in-C, 4th Army
24 Aug 1914 - 18 Oct 1914:	Commanding General, Kazan Military District
18 Oct 1914 - 9 Mar 1916:	Commandant of Fortress Petrograd

Lieutenant-General Anatoly Petrovich **Zalyubovsky** (7 Oct 1859 - 30 Apr 1936)
5 Jul 1907 - 31 Dec 1913:	Deputy Chief of St. Petersburg Ammunition Factory
29 Mar 1909:	Promoted to *Major-General*
31 Dec 1913 - 1915:	Chief of Sestroretsk Arms Factory
1915 - Oct 1915:	Reserve officer, Petrograd Military District
Oct 1915 - May 1916:	Deputy Chief of Petrograd Pipe Plant
10 Apr 1916:	Promoted to *Lieutenant-General*
May 1916 - 1917:	Attached to the Russian Procurement Committee in the USA

Major-General of the Admiralty Apollony Viktorovich **Zamkov** (2 Aug 1856 - ?)
20 Feb 1906 - Mar 1913:	Chief of Libau Commercial Port
6 May 1910:	Promoted to *Major-General of the Admiralty*

Lieutenant-General Ivan Andreyevich **Zamshin** (24 May 1837 - ?)
23 Mar 1892:	Promoted to *Major-General*
23 Mar 1892 - 5 Jul 1895:	Commander, 1st Brigade, 14th Infantry Division
5 Jul 1895 - 11 Jan 1900:	Commander, 1st Brigade, 19th Infantry Division
11 Jan 1900:	Promoted to *Lieutenant-General*
11 Jan 1900:	Retired

Major-General Aleksandr Nikolayevich **Zamyatnin** (3 Sep 1857 - 12 Aug 1906)
6 Dec 1905: Promoted to *Major-General*
6 Dec 1905 - 12 Aug 1906: General for Special Assignments to the Minister of the Interior

Major-General Pyotr Dimitriyevich **Zamytsky** (19 Jan 1844 - ?)
10 Nov 1887 - 1902: Military Judge, Kiev Military District Court
30 Aug 1889: Promoted to *Major-General*

Major-General Andrey Aleksandrovich **Zander** (1916: **Zarin**) (6 Jul 1865 - ?)
2 Dec 1908 - 11 Oct 1911: Military Judge, Vilnius Military District Court
29 Mar 1909: Promoted to *Major-General*
11 Oct 1911 - 1917: Military Judge, St. Petersburg Military District Court

Lieutenant-General Georgy Aleksandrovich **Zander** (7 Jan 1858 - ?)
5 Nov 1904: Promoted to *Major-General*
5 Nov 1904 - 20 Dec 1909: Chief of Staff, XII. Army Corps
20 Dec 1909 - 29 May 1910: Chief of Staff, XXI. Army Corps
29 May 1910: Promoted to *Lieutenant-General*
29 May 1910 - 25 Feb 1912: Commander, 5th Cavalry Division
25 Feb 1912 - 5 Feb 1915: Commander, 8th Cavalry Division
12 May 1915 - 19 Aug 1915: Commander, 40th Infantry Division
19 Aug 1915 - 18 Feb 1916: Reserve officer, Dvinsk Military District
18 Feb 1916 - 1917: Chief of Horse Stocks, Minsk Military District

Lieutenant-General Oskar Yakovlevich **Zander** (25 Sep 1847 - Dec 1904)
7 Jan 1892: Promoted to *Major-General*
7 Jan 1892 - 29 May 1897: Commander, Life Guards Grodno Hussar Regiment
29 May 1897 - 26 Jan 1899: Commander, Independent Guards Cavalry Brigade
26 Jan 1899 - 23 Nov 1904: Chief of Staff, Kazan Military District
6 Dec 1899: Promoted to *Lieutenant-General*

Lieutenant-General Yakov-Iogan-Yevgeny Yakovlevich **Zander** (24 Jul 1854 - ?)
3 Feb 1898 - 14 Mar 1909: Chief of Mobilization Section, Main Artillery Directorate
6 Dec 1908: Promoted to *Major-General*
14 Mar 1909 - 17 May 1914: Chief of Bureau, Inspectorate-General of Artillery
17 May 1914 - 1917: Special Assignments General to the Inspector-General of Artillery
6 Dec 1914: Promoted to *Lieutenant-General*

Lieutenant-General Vladimir Viktorovich **Zanfirov** (22 Feb 1853 - ?)
18 Dec 1908: Promoted to *Major-General*
18 Dec 1908 - 27 Jan 1909: Commander, Perm Regional Brigade
27 Jan 1909 - 29 Jul 1914: Commander, Kazan Regional Brigade
29 Jul 1914 - 2 May 1915: Commander, 13th Replacement Infantry Brigade
26 Feb 1915: Promoted to *Lieutenant-General*
2 May 1915 - 1917: Commander, Kazan Regional Brigade

Major-General Mikhail Ippolitovich **Zankevich** (17 Sep 1872 - 14 Apr 1945)
7 Aug 1913 - 28 May 1915:	Commander, 146th Infantry Regiment
14 Jan 1915:	Promoted to *Major-General*
28 May 1915 - 22 Aug 1915:	Commander, Brigade, 37th Infantry Division
22 Aug 1915 - 20 May 1916:	Commander, Life Guards Pavlovsky Regiment
20 May 1916 - 11 Jul 1916:	Chief of Staff, 2nd Guards Infantry Division
11 Jul 1916 - Feb 1917:	Acting Quartermaster-General, General Staff
14 Jan 1917 - Feb 1917:	Acting Chief of the General Staff
Feb 1917 - Apr 1917:	Provost-Marshal, Petrograd
Apr 1917 - 4 May 1917:	Quartermaster-General, General Staff
4 May 1917 - Jul 1917:	At the disposal of the Chief of the General Staff
Jul 1917 - Dec 1918:	Representative of the Supreme Commander-in-Chief and Provisional Government in France, Military Attaché, France

Major-General Nikolai Ilyich **Zankovsky** (7 Dec 1859 - ?)
30 May 1915 - 1917:	Commander, 105th Militia Brigade
20 Jul 1915:	Promoted to *Major-General*

Major-General Mikhail Fyodorovich **Zapolsky** (16 Feb 1866 - ?)
30 Mar 1915 - 21 Aug 1916:	Commander, 15th Caucasus Rifle Regiment
2 Jun 1916:	Promoted to *Major-General*
21 Aug 1916 - Oct 1916:	Commander, Brigade, 4th Turkestan Rifle Division

Major-General Vladimir Fyodorovich **Zapolsky** (6 Feb 1865 - ?)
13 Aug 1911 - 13 Nov 1912:	Deputy Commander of Engineers, Amur Military District
6 Dec 1911:	Promoted to *Major-General*
13 Nov 1912 - 1 Oct 1914:	Deputy Chief of Billeting, Warsaw Military District
1 Oct 1914 - Feb 1915:	Reserve officer, Minsk Military District
Feb 1915 - 1917:	Chief of Billeting, Turkestan Military District

Major-General Pyotr Yegorovich **Zaporozhchenko** (16 Feb 1833 - ?)
26 Nov 1889:	Promoted to *Major-General*
26 Nov 1889 - 7 Feb 1894:	Commander, 1st Brigade, 13th Infantry Division
7 Feb 1894 - 23 Jun 1897:	Commander, 61st Reserve Infantry Brigade

Major-General Ivan Stepanovich **Zaporozhsky** (7 Sep 1842 - ?)
14 May 1898 - 1903:	Deputy Commander of Engineers, Kiev Military District
19 Jul 1898:	Promoted to *Major-General*

Lieutenant-General Ivan Ivanovich **Zarako-Zarakovsky** (8 Feb 1857 - 2 Jan 1930)
1 Jun 1904 - 18 Jun 1905:	Commander, 283rd Infantry Regiment
17 Feb 1905:	Promoted to *Major-General*
18 Jun 1905 - 8 Jan 1907:	Commander, 2nd Brigade, 71st Infantry Division
8 Jan 1907 - 4 Mar 1913:	Commander, 2nd Brigade, 8th Infantry Division
4 Mar 1913:	Promoted to *Lieutenant-General*

4 Mar 1913 - Jul 1917:				Commander, 11th Siberian Rifle Division

Major-General Ignaty Ivanovich **Zarakovsky** (15 Oct 1859 - ?)
24 Feb 1915 - 1917:				Deputy Chief of Troop Biletting, Governor-General of Galicia
6 Dec 1916:				Promoted to *Major-General*

Major-General of Naval Artillery Nikolai Viktorovich **Zarembo** (1 Feb 1875 - ?)
1914 - 1917:				Deputy Chief of Section 2, Main Artillery Directorate
30 Apr 1915:				Promoted to *Major-General of Naval Artillery*

Major-General Arkady Iosifovich **Zarembo-Ratsevich** (17 Apr 1856 - ?)
24 Feb 1911 - 17 Apr 1914:			Commander, 20th Infantry Regiment
17 Apr 1914:				Promoted to *Major-General*
17 Apr 1914:				Retired
15 Feb 1915 - 1917:				Recalled; Commander, 77th Militia Brigade

Major-General Georgy Karpovich **Zaretsky** (22 Jan 1856 - ?)
30 Aug 1913:				Promoted to *Major-General*
30 Aug 1913 - 9 Nov 1913:			Commander, 26th Artillery Brigade
9 Nov 1913 - 13 May 1916:			Commander, 7th Siberian Rifle Artillery Brigade
13 May 1916 - 31 Mar 1917:			Inspector of Artillery, XX. Army Corps

Major-General Nikolai Dmitriyevich **Zarin** (11 Mar 1872 - 28 Jun 1918)
5 Nov 1913 - 14 Nov 1914:			Commander, 100th Infantry Regiment
5 Oct 1914:				Promoted to *Major-General*
14 Nov 1914 - 18 Feb 1917:			Chief of Staff, XXII. Army Corps
18 Feb 1917 - 12 Apr 1917:			Commander, 19th Siberian Rifle Division
12 Apr 1917 - Jan 1918:			Reserve officer, Petrograd Military District
Jan 1918:				Dismissed

Major-General Pyotr Pavlovich **Zarnitsyn** (12 Dec 1852 - 13 Jun 1906)
15 Feb 1900:				Promoted to *Major-General*
15 Feb 1900 - 5 Jul 1903:			Commander, 2nd Brigade, 20th Infantry Division
5 Jul 1903 - 13 Jun 1906:			Commander, 64th Reserve Infantry Brigade

General of Infantry Nikolai Platonovich **Zarubayev** (6 Jan 1843 - 10 Jun 1912)
4 Sep 1890:				Promoted to *Major-General*
4 Sep 1890 - 25 Nov 1891:			Commander, 2nd Brigade, 13th Infantry Division
25 Nov 1891 - 25 Feb 1898:			Chief of Staff, VI. Army Corps
25 Feb 1898 - 28 Feb 1900:			Chief of Staff, Siberian Military District
6 Dec 1899:				Promoted to *Lieutenant-General*
28 Feb 1900 - 24 Dec 1903:			Commander, 9th Infantry Division
24 Dec 1903 - 9 Feb 1904:			Deputy Commanding General, Siberian Military District
9 Feb 1904 - 26 Oct 1905:			Commanding General, IV. Siberian Army Corps
26 Oct 1905 - 6 Aug 1906:			Deputy Commanding General, St. Petersburg Military District
1905:					Promoted to *General-Adjutant*

11 Jan 1906: Promoted to *General of Infantry*
6 Aug 1906 - 24 Dec 1909: Inspector General of Infantry
24 Dec 1909 - 10 Jun 1912: Commanding General, Odessa Military District

Rear-Admiral Sergey Valeriyanovich **Zarubayev** (22 Aug 1877 - 21 Oct 1921)
Jan 1917: Promoted to *Rear-Admiral*
Jan 1917 - Dec 1917: Commander, 1st Battleship Brigade

Lieutenant-General Nikolai Aleksandrovich **Zarubin** (25 Jul 1856 - 24 Mar 1927)
28 Jan 1900 - 4 Sep 1903: Commander, 13th Dragoon Regiment
4 Sep 1903: Promoted to *Major-General*
4 Sep 1903 - 14 Dec 1904: Commander, 1st Brigade, 11th Cavalry Division
14 Dec 1904 - 27 Mar 1906: Commander, 1st Brigade, 10th Cavalry Division
27 Mar 1906 - 26 May 1911: Chief of Staff, I. Siberian Army Corps
26 May 1911: Promoted to *Lieutenant-General*
26 May 1911: Retired

Lieutenant-General Iosif Iosifovich **Zashchuk** (25 Apr 1845 - 1918)
4 Jun 1897 - 14 May 1902: Duty General, Warsaw Military District
10 Apr 1899: Promoted to *Major-General*
14 May 1902 - 11 Oct 1904: Commander, 48th Reserve Infantry Brigade
11 Oct 1904 - 1906: Commander, 48th Infantry Division
17 Apr 1905: Promoted to *Lieutenant-General*
1906: Retired

Lieutenant-General Leonid Iosifovich **Zashchuk** (27 Mar 1847 - ?)
18 Jul 1900: Promoted to *Major-General*
18 Jul 1900 - 9 Feb 1901: Commander, 1st Brigade, 17th Infantry Division
9 Feb 1901 - 9 Mar 1905: Commander, 1st Brigade, 3rd Infantry Division
9 Mar 1905 - 30 May 1907: Commander, 49th Replacement Infantry Brigade
30 May 1907 - 21 Nov 1908: Commander, 11th Infantry Division
30 Jul 1907: Promoted to *Lieutenant-General*
21 Nov 1908: Retired

Major-General Ivan Ivanovich **Zaslavsky** (18 Jan 1856 - ?)
20 Jul 1910: Promoted to *Major-General*
20 Jul 1910 - 25 May 1915: Commander of Engineers, Fortress Kaunas
25 May 1915 - 1917: Reserve officer, Dvinsk Military District

Lieutenant-General Fridrikh Petrovich **Zass** (19 Sep 1827 - 18 Nov 1896)
12 Sep 1868 - 20 Sep 1876: Commander, 95th Infantry Regiment
30 Aug 1876: Promoted to *Major-General*
20 Sep 1876 - 20 Feb 1877: Transferred to the reserve
20 Feb 1877 - 11 Mar 1887: Commander, 1st Brigade, 8th Infantry Division
11 Mar 1887 - 23 Oct 1896: Commander, 33rd Infantry Division
30 Aug 1887: Promoted to *Lieutenant-General*

General of Infantry Mikhail Ivanovich **Zasulich** (24 Dec 1843 - 1910)
30 May 1894:	Promoted to *Major-General*
30 May 1894 - 30 Nov 1895:	Commander, 1st Brigade, 9th Infantry Division
30 Nov 1895 - 13 Sep 1899:	Commander, 1st Brigade, 2nd Grenadier Division
13 Sep 1899 - 13 Apr 1900:	Commandant of Fortress Osovets
13 Apr 1900 - 3 Feb 1903:	Commander, 6th Infantry Division
6 Dec 1900:	Promoted to *Lieutenant-General*
3 Feb 1903 - 9 Jun 1906:	Commanding General, II. Siberian Army Corps
9 Jun 1906:	Promoted to *General of Infantry*
9 Jun 1906:	Retired

Major-General Fyodor Andreyevich **Zasypkin** (27 Aug 1867 - ?)
25 Nov 1908 - 19 Aug 1914:	Chief of Police, Tiflis
6 Dec 1912:	Promoted to *Major-General*
19 Aug 1914 - 20 Aug 1916:	Military Commander, Sukhum District
20 Aug 1916:	Retired

Lieutenant-General Arseny Mikhailovich **Zatrapeznov** (6 May 1855 - ?)
2 Jan 1909 - 23 Mar 1913:	Commander, 2nd Battalion, 27th Artillery Brigade
2 Feb 1913:	Promoted to *Major-General*
23 Mar 1913 - 29 Oct 1915:	Commander, 14th Artillery Brigade
29 Oct 1915 - 9 May 1917:	Inspector of Artillery, VIII. Army Corps
8 Oct 1916:	Promoted to *Lieutenant-General*
9 May 1917 - 1 Aug 1917:	Unassigned
1 Aug 1917:	Dismissed

Admiral Vasily Maksimovich **Zatsarenny** (30 Jan 1852 - 1917)
2 Jan 1906 - 20 Oct 1907:	Commander, Port of Nikolayev
27 Jul 1906:	Promoted to *Rear-Admiral*
20 Oct 1907 - 16 Nov 1907:	Governor of Nikolayev
16 Nov 1907 - 22 Oct 1909:	Commander of Kherson Garrison
22 Oct 1909:	Promoted to *Vice-Admiral*
22 Oct 1909 - 21 Jul 1916:	Member, Board of Admiralty
14 Apr 1913:	Promoted to *Admiral*
21 Jul 1916:	Retired

Lieutenant-General Nikolai Antonovich **Zatvardnitsky** (14 Dec 1835 - 14 Dec 1911)
30 Aug 1891 - 11 Jul 1894:	Commander, Odessa Borderguard Brigade
28 Mar 1893:	Promoted to *Major-General*
11 Jul 1894 - Sep 1901:	Commander, Turkestan Customs District
Sep 1901:	Promoted to *Lieutenant-General*
Sep 1901:	Retired

Lieutenant-General Pyotr Timofeyevich **Zaushkevich** (12 May 1859 - ?)
12 Nov 1906 - 18 Jun 1908:	Intendant, Vilnius Military District
6 Dec 1906:	Promoted to *Major-General*
18 Jun 1908 - 15 Jun 1914:	Intendant, Moscow Military District
15 Jun 1914:	Promoted to *Lieutenant-General*

15 Jun 1914: Retired

Major-General Pyotr Fyodorovich **Zaustsinsky** (23 Mar 1866 - ?)
1 May 1903 - 1917: Chief of Tsarina Catherine the Great Military Publishing House
6 Dec 1913: Promoted to *Major-General*
1917 - 20 Apr 1917: Reserve officer, Petrograd Military District
20 Apr 1917: Dismissed

General of Artillery Iosif Ivanovich **Zavadovsky** (22 May 1836 - 7 Jul 1898)
16 May 1883 - 19 Sep 1886: Commander, Odessa Coastal Artillery Batteries
30 Aug 1885: Promoted to *Major-General*
19 Sep 1886 - 12 Oct 1892: Commander, 40th Artillery Brigade
12 Oct 1892 - 29 Nov 1893: Commander, 6th Reserve Artillery Brigade
29 Nov 1893 - 3 Jan 1896: Commander of Artillery, Grenadier Corps
14 Nov 1894: Promoted to *Lieutenant-General*
3 Jan 1896 - 7 Jul 1898: Commander of Artillery, Caucasus Military District
23 Mar 1898: Promoted to *General of Artillery*

Lieutenant-General Aleksandr Ignatyevich **Zavadsky** (26 Feb 1838 - ?)
23 Jun 1879 - 22 Aug 1884: Inspector of Classes, Corps of Pages
30 Aug 1882: Promoted to *Major-General*
22 Aug 1884 - 22 Oct 1892: Director, Nizhegorodsky Cadet Corps
22 Oct 1892 - 9 Apr 1904: Director, 1st Moscow Cadet Corps
6 Apr 1903: Promoted to *Lieutenant-General*
9 Apr 1904 - Sep 1905: Attached to the Directorate-General of Military Schools

Major-General Nikolai Nikolayevich **Zavadsky** (14 Aug 1858 - 16 Nov 1912)
4 Jan 1906 - 25 Mar 1910: Deputy Intendant, Kazan Military District
6 Dec 1908: Promoted to *Major-General*
25 Mar 1910 - 16 Nov 1912: Intendant, Odessa Military District

Major-General Viktor Valentiyevich **Zavadsky** (25 Dec 1833 - ?)
26 Feb 1894: Promoted to *Major-General*
26 Feb 1894 - 10 Apr 1901: Commander, 1st Brigade, 2nd Infantry Division
10 Apr 1901 - 1902: Commander, 48th Reserve Infantry Brigade

Major-General Yevgeny Konstantinovich **Zavadsky** (30 Dec 1863 - ?)
8 Jan 1909 - 12 Jul 1915: Commander, 5th Rifle Regiment
24 May 1915: Promoted to *Major-General*
12 Jul 1915 - 1917: Commander, Brigade, 2nd Rifle Division

Major-General of the Fleet Aleksandr Yevgenyevich **Zavalishin** (2 Mar 1867 - 8 Apr 1936)
2 Oct 1906 - 1916: Company Commander, Marine Corps
6 Dec 1915: Promoted to *Major-General of the Fleet*
1916 - 20 Aug 1917: Deputy Director of the Marine Corps
20 Aug 1917: Retired

Major-General Pavel Pavlovich **Zavarzin** (13 Feb 1868 - 10 Oct 1932)
3 Jun 1916 - 1917: Chief of Gendarmerie, Warsaw Province
1917: Promoted to *Major-General*

General of Artillery Vladimir Nikolayevich von **Zavatsky** (8 Apr 1850 - 14 Jul 1909)
29 Dec 1899 - 2 Mar 1905: Commander, 2nd Artillery Brigade
1 Jan 1901: Promoted to *Major-General*
2 Mar 1905 - 14 Jul 1909: Deputy Chief, Main Artillery Directorate
6 Dec 1906: Promoted to *Lieutenant -General*
1909: Promoted to *General of Artillery*

Major-General Stepan Konstantinovich **Zavernyayev** (24 Dec 1854 - ?)
4 Mar 1912: Promoted to *Major-General*
4 Mar 1912 - 27 Dec 1912: Commander, Minsk Regional Brigade
27 Dec 1912 - 1917: Commander, Vilnius Regional Brigade

Major-General Zakhary Ivanovich **Zaychenko** (5 Sep 1871 - ?)
17 Dec 1915 - 13 Nov 1916: Chief of Staff, 53rd Infantry Division
18 Feb 1916: Promoted to *Major-General*
13 Nov 1916 - 20 Jul 1917: Chief of Staff, XXXVIII. Army Corps
20 Jul 1917 - 1917: Commander, 59th Infantry Division
1917: Acting Commanding General, XXXIII. Army Corps

Major-General Nikolai Alekseyevich **Zayets** (6 Dec 1860 - ?)
22 Oct 1913: Promoted to *Major-General*
22 Oct 1913 - 9 Nov 1913: Unassigned
9 Nov 1913 - 25 Oct 1915: Commander, 26th Artillery Brigade
25 Oct 1915 - 26 Apr 1916: Unassigned
26 Apr 1916 - 1917: Commander, 4th Reserve Artillery Brigade

Major-General Mikhail Fyodorovich **Zaykovsky** (25 Apr 1859 - ?)
30 May 1915 - 31 Mar 1917: Commander, 44th Artillery Brigade
17 Mar 1916: Promoted to *Major-General*
31 Mar 1917 - Oct 1917: Inspector of Artillery, VII. Caucasus Army Corps

General of Infantry Andrei Medardovich **Zayonchkovsky** (8 Dec 1862 - 21 Mar 1926)
18 May 1904 - 9 Mar 1905: Commander, 85th Infantry Regiment
4 Jan 1905: Promoted to *Major-General*
9 Mar 1905 - 7 Sep 1905: Commander, 2nd Brigade, 3rd Siberian Infantry Division
7 Sep 1905 - 18 Feb 1906: Attached to St. Petersburg Military District
18 Feb 1906 - 10 Jul 1910: Commander, Life Guards Jaeger Regiment
10 Jul 1908 - 30 May 1912: Commander, 1st Brigade, 1st Guards Infantry Division
30 May 1912: Promoted to *Lieutenant-General*
30 May 1912 - 30 Jul 1912: Commander, 22nd Infantry Division
30 Jul 1912 - 27 Mar 1915: Commander, 37th Infantry Division
27 Mar 1915 - 12 Aug 1916: Commanding General, XXX. Army Corps
10 Apr 1916: Promoted to *General of Infantry*
12 Aug 1916 - 20 Oct 1916: Commanding General, XLVII. Army Corps

12 Aug 1916 - 20 Oct 1916:	C-in-C, Dobrudzha Army
22 Oct 1916 - 2 Apr 1917:	Commanding General, XVIII. Army Corps
2 Apr 1917 - 5 Jul 1917:	Reserve officer, Petrograd Military District
5 Jul 1917:	Retired

Major-General Vasily Vasilyevich **Zaytsev** (1 Jan 1859 - 7 May 1915)
31 Dec 1913 - 7 May 1915:	Commander, 206th Infantry Regiment
3 Apr 1915:	Promoted to *Major-General*

Lieutenant-General Ivan Moiseyevich **Zaytsov** (8 May 1834 - ?)
25 Apr 1876 - 1 May 1903:	Attached to the General Staff
1 Jan 1878:	Promoted to *Major-General*
30 Aug 1888:	Promoted to *Lieutenant-General*
1 May 1903 - 1906:	Member, General Staff Committee

Major-General Erast Grigoryevich **Zborovsky** (1 Nov 1840 - ?)
27 Feb 1898:	Promoted to *Major-General*
27 Feb 1898 - 14 Jul 1900:	Commander, 1st Brigade, 1st Caucasus Cossack Division
14 Jul 1900 - 1903:	Commander, 2nd Brigade, Siberian Cossack Division

Major-General of the Admiralty Ivan Ivanovich **Zborovsky** (27 Aug 1856 - ?)
1908 - 15 May 1911:	Commander, Port of Vladivostok
6 Dec 1910:	Promoted to *Major-General of the Admiralty*
15 May 1911 - Mar 1912:	Member, Volunteer Fleet Committee

Lieutenant-General Aleksandr Ivanovich **Zdanovich** (1 Mar 1849 - 18 Mar 1936)
8 May 1882 - 22 Nov 1905:	Chief of Derkul State Horse Stud
6 Apr 1903:	Promoted to *Major-General*
22 Nov 1905 - 4 Dec 1912:	Chief of the State Horse Stud
6 Dec 1909:	Promoted to *Lieutenant-General*
4 Dec 1912 - 1917:	Senator

General of Cavalry Mikhail Yulyanovich **Zdroyevsky** (5 Feb 1845 - ?)
19 Dec 1901 - 23 May 1905:	Commander, Guards Replacement Cavalry Regiment
6 Dec 1902:	Promoted to *Major-General*
23 May 1905 - 22 Mar 1907:	Commander, 1st Reserve Cavalry Brigade
22 Mar 1907 - 1917:	Special Assignments General, Inspectorate-General of Cavalry
6 Dec 1907:	Promoted to *Lieutenant-General*
6 Apr 1914:	Promoted to *General of Cavalry*

General of Infantry Baron Loggin Logginovich **Zeddeler** (10 Sep 1831 - 5 Apr 1899)
25 Jun 1872 - 24 Sep 1876:	Commander, Life Guards Grenadier Regiment
30 Aug 1872:	Promoted to *Major-General*
24 Sep 1876 - 27 Oct 1877:	Commander, 1st Brigade, 2nd Guards Infantry Division
27 Oct 1877 - 19 Feb 1881:	General à la suite
19 Feb 1881 - 28 Sep 1892:	Deputy Chief of Military Schools
30 Aug 1882:	Promoted to *Lieutenant-General*

28 Sep 1892 - 13 Aug 1895:	Commanding General, XVIII. Army Corps
13 Aug 1895 - 5 Apr 1899:	Member of the Military Council
14 May 1896:	Promoted to *General of Infantry*

Lieutenant-General Baron Nikolai Logginovich **Zeddeler** (2 Jan 1830 - ?)
15 Jun 1878:	Promoted to *Major-General*
15 Jun 1878 - 17 Oct 1881:	Military Commander, Estonia Province
17 Oct 1881 - 23 Dec 1881:	Unassigned
23 Dec 1881 - 4 May 1888:	Commander, 2nd Brigade, 22nd Infantry Division
4 May 1888 - 1895:	Commander, 14th Regional Brigade
30 Aug 1888:	Promoted to *Lieutenant-General*

Lieutenant-General Vladimir Albertovich **Zedergolm** (19 Apr 1861 - ?)
2 Sep 1907:	Promoted to *Major-General*
2 Sep 1907 - 9 Jul 1914:	Commander, 8th Artillery Brigade
30 Jul 1914:	Promoted to *Lieutenant-General*
30 Jul 1914:	Retired

General of Infantry Aleksandr Aleksandrovich **Zegelov** (31 Mar 1858 - 1939)
14 Mar 1904:	Promoted to *Major-General*
14 Mar 1904 - 10 Jan 1909:	Chief of Staff, XI. Army Corps
10 Jan 1909:	Promoted to *Lieutenant-General*
10 Jan 1909 - 21 Feb 1909:	Chief of Staff, Vilnius Military District
21 Feb 1909 - 22 Jul 1909:	Quartermaster-General, General Staff
22 Jul 1909 - 14 Feb 1915:	Commander, 33rd Infantry Division
14 Feb 1915 - 22 Aug 1915:	Commanding General, III. Army Corps
22 Mar 1915:	Promoted to *General of Infantry*
22 Aug 1915 - 10 Jun 1915:	Reserve officer, Dvinsk Military District
10 Jun 1915:	Retired

Lieutenant-General Aleksey Kondratyevich **Zeland** (**Ryndin**) (21 May 1860 - ?)
6 Jul 1904:	Promoted to *Major-General*
6 Jul 1904 - 20 Aug 1913:	Commander, 1st Brigade, 36th Infantry Division
20 Aug 1913:	Promoted to *Lieutenant-General*
20 Aug 1913:	Retired
29 Jul 1914 - 8 Aug 1914:	Recalled; Commander, 11th Replacement Infantry Brigade
8 Aug 1914 - 31 Aug 1915:	Commander, 7th Replacement Infantry Brigade
31 Aug 1915 - 1917:	Inspector of Replacements, Western Front

Major-General Mikhail Aleksandrovich **Zelenetsky** (1 Nov 1869 - 8 Feb 1917)
8 Sep 1912 - 19 Apr 1915:	Commander, 41st Infantry Regiment
16 Feb 1915:	Promoted to *Major-General*
19 Apr 1915 - 5 Jun 1916:	Chief of Staff, XXXI. Army Corps
5 Jun 1916 - 8 Feb 1917:	At the disposal of the Chief of the General Staff

Rear-Admiral Rostislav Dmitriyevich **Zelenetsky** (31 Jan 1865 - 18 Nov 1928)
17 Apr 1913 - 1916:	Commander of the Imperial Yacht "Standart"

30 Jul 1915: Promoted to *Rear-Admiral*
1915 - 1916: Deputy Commander, Naval Guards Depot

Lieutenant-General of the Admiralty Aleksandr Porfiryevich **Zelenoy** (16 Aug 1864 - ?)
1906: Promoted to *State Councillor*
1911 - 11 Oct 1911: Chief of Shipbuilding & Logistics, Ministry of the Navy
11 Oct 1911 - 1916: Chief of Naval Economic Administration, Ministry of the Navy
6 Dec 1911: Redesignated *Major-General of the Admiralty*
25 Mar 1912: Promoted to *Lieutenant-General of the Admiralty*

Admiral Nikolai Aleksandrovich **Zelenoy** (8 Jul 1844 - ?)
1895: Promoted to *Rear-Admiral*
1899 - 1901: Commander, 18th Naval Depot
1901 - 1903: Commander, Training Detachment, Black Sea Fleet
1903 - 1904: Junior Flagman, Baltic Fleet
1904: Promoted to *Vice-Admiral*
1904: Naval Attaché, London
1904 - 20 Oct 1908: Chairman, Committee for the Volunteer Fleet
20 Oct 1908: Promoted to *Admiral*
20 Oct 1908: Retired

General of the Admiralty Pavel Alekseyevich **Zelenoy** (5 Jan 1833 - 10 Jan 1909)
1882: Promoted to *Rear-Admiral*
1882 - 1885: Mayor of Taganrog
1885 - 1898: Mayor of Odessa
1891: Promoted to *Lieutenant-General of the Admiralty*
1898 - 10 Jan 1909: Honorary Trustee, Board of Trustees, Tsarina Maria Institutions
1902: Promoted to *General of the Admiralty*

Lieutenant-General of the Admiralty Sergey Aleksandrovich **Zelenoy** (30 Aug 1842 - ?)
1889 - 1902: Military Judge, Kronstadt Naval Court
1894: Promoted to *Major-General of the Admiralty*
1902 - 1904: Chairman, Sevastopol Naval Court
1903: Promoted to *Lieutenant-General of the Admiralty*
1904 - 1907: Chairman, Kronstadt Naval Court
1907 - 2 Jul 1907: Chairman, Sevastopol Naval Court
2 Jul 1907: Retired

Lieutenant-General Pyotr Aleksandrovich **Zelensky** (27 Sep 1835 - 31 Jul 1895)
22 Sep 1870 - 28 Aug 1885: Sub-section Chief, Main Artillery Directorate
28 Jan 1883: Promoted to *Major-General*
28 Aug 1885 - 12 Oct 1892: Commander, 6th Artillery Brigade
12 Oct 1892 - 31 Jul 1895: Commander of Artillery, XIII. Army Corps
30 Aug 1893: Promoted to *Lieutenant-General*

General of Infantry Aleksandr Semyonovich **Zeleny** (6 Nov 1839 - 1913)
5 Mar 1879 - 1 Feb 1885: At the disposal of the C-in-C, Caucasus Army
30 Aug 1880: Promoted to *Major-General*
1 Feb 1885 - 1913: Attached to the Caucasus Military District
30 Aug 1890: Promoted to *Lieutenant-General*
6 Mar 1909: Promoted to *General of Infantry*

Major-General Nikolai Gustavovich **Zelgeym** (16 Aug 1829 - ?)
4 Mar 1883 - 7 May 1892: Commander of Engineers, Fortress Brest-Litovsk
15 Mar 1887: Promoted to *Major-General*
7 May 1892 - 25 Jan 1893: Transferred to the reserve
25 Jan 1893 - 18 Oct 1896: Commander, 2nd Brigade, 2nd Infantry Division

Major-General Viktor Petrovich **Zelinsky** (13 Dec 1867 - 14 Dec 1940)
17 Jun 1911: Promoted to *Major-General*
17 Jun 1911 - 10 Nov 1914: Commander, 6th Siberian Rifle Artillery Brigade
10 Nov 1914 - 11 Nov 1914: Commander, 6th Siberian Rifle Division
11 Nov 1914 - 1918: POW
27 Feb 1915: Dismissed

Major-General Ivan Yevgenyevich **Zemlyanitsyn** (8 Sep 1855 - ?)
25 Oct 1903 - 12 Dec 1905: Commander, 3rd East Siberian Rifle Regiment
20 Feb 1905: Promoted to *Major-General*
12 Dec 1905 - 2 Aug 1906: Commander, 2nd Brigade, 1st Siberian Infantry Division
2 Aug 1906 - Nov 1908: Commander, 1st Brigade, 5th East Siberian Rifle Division

Major-General Mikhail Petrovich **Zenchenko** (2 Nov 1856 - ?)
11 Sep 1901 - 24 Aug 1913: Company Commander, Kiev Cadet Corps
24 Aug 1913: Promoted to *Major-General*
24 Aug 1913: Retired

Major-General Mikhail Vasilyevich **Zenchenko** (8 Nov 1851 - ?)
22 Jan 1910 - 1914: Military Commander, Chisinau District
1914: Retired
17 Feb 1915 - 1917: Recalled; Reserve officer, Dvinsk Military District
1916: Promoted to *Major-General*

Major-General Viktor Semyonovich **Zenkevich** (11 Nov 1857 - 27 Aug 1908)
27 Mar 1901 - 25 Mar 1905: Commander, 51st Dragoon Regiment
25 Mar 1905: Promoted to *Major-General*
25 Mar 1905 - 14 Apr 1906: Commander, 2nd Brigade, Trans-Baikal Cossack Division
14 Apr 1906 - 14 Aug 1908: Commander, 1st Brigade, 10th Cavalry Division

General of Infantry Nikolai Andreyevich **Zernets** (23 Feb 1852 - ?)
15 Feb 1900: Promoted to *Major-General*
15 Feb 1900 - 11 Jun 1904: Commander, 1st Brigade, 20th Infantry Division

11 Jun 1904 - 18 Dec 1906:	Commander, 2nd Turkestan Rifle Brigade
18 Dec 1906 - 12 Jun 1912:	Commander, 6th East Siberian Rifle Division
22 Apr 1907:	Promoted to *Lieutenant-General*
12 Jun 1912:	Promoted to *General of Infantry*
12 Jun 1912:	Retired

Major-General Yevstafy Karlovich **Zeyder** (10 Feb 1844 - 1899)

21 Jul 1894 - 20 May 1896:	Commander, 5th Infantry Regiment
14 Nov 1894:	Promoted to *Major-General*
20 May 1896 - 17 Dec 1898:	Commander, 2nd Turkestan Line Brigade
17 Dec 1898 - 1899:	Commander, 58th Reserve Infantry Brigade

Major-General Viktor Edvinovich **Zeydlits** (18 Jun 1866 - 23 Feb 1927)

28 Feb 1905 - 1917:	Senior Artillery Inspector, Main Artillery Directorate
14 Apr 1913:	Promoted to *Major-General*

General of Infantry Aleksandr Aleksandrovich **Zeyfart** (28 Apr 1835 - 28 Nov 1918)

14 Dec 1857 - 27 Nov 1909:	Professor, General Staff Academy
6 Dec 1894:	Promoted to *Major-General*
26 Nov 1907:	Promoted to *Lieutenant-General*
27 Nov 1909 - 24 May 1917:	Honorary Professor, General Staff Academy
1914 - 1915:	Acting Commandant of the General Staff Academy
24 May 1917:	Promoted to *General of Infantry*
24 May 1917:	Retired

Major-General Eduard Rudolfovich **Zeyme** (3 Mar 1864 - 29 Dec 1921)

16 Feb 1906 - 7 May 1917:	Deputy Chief of Administration, St. Petersburg Palace
6 Dec 1915:	Promoted to *Major-General*
7 May 1917:	Dismissed

Lieutenant-General Emmanuil Aleksandrovich **Zeyn** (11 Nov 1858 - ?)

21 Jun 1905:	Promoted to *Major-General*
21 Jun 1905 - 2 Jul 1913:	Commander, 2nd Brigade, 19th Infantry Division
2 Jul 1913 - 29 Apr 1916:	Commander, Omsk Local Brigade
6 Dec 1913:	Promoted to *Lieutenant-General*
29 Apr 1916 - 1917:	Commander, Tambov Local Brigade

Lieutenant-General Frants-Albert Aleksandrovich **Zeyn** (27 Jul 1862 - 1918)

9 Sep 1900 - 24 Jun 1906:	Chief of Chancellery, Governor-General of Finland
6 Dec 1905:	Promoted to *Major-General*
24 Jun 1906 - 16 Nov 1907:	Governor of Grodno
16 Nov 1907 - 11 Nov 1909:	Deputy Governor-General of Finland
11 Nov 1909:	Promoted to *Lieutenant-General*
11 Nov 1909 - 16 Mar 1917:	Governor-General of Finland
16 Mar 1917 - 27 Oct 1917:	Unassigned
27 Oct 1917:	Retired

Major-General Karl-Genrikh-Robert Florentinovich **Zeyts** (5 Nov 1866 - ?)
23 Apr 1916 - 1917: Commander, 13th Heavy Artillery Brigade
5 Nov 1916: Promoted to *Major-General*

General of Infantry Abunard-Vilgelm-Eduard Eduardovich **Zezeman** (17 Jun 1836 - 1902)
20 Oct 1877 - 20 Jul 1892: Commander, Caucasus Sapper Brigade
2 Oct 1877: Promoted to *Major-General*
30 Aug 1888: Promoted to *Lieutenant-General*
20 Jul 1892 - 31 Mar 1893: Commander, 30th Infantry Division
31 Mar 1893 - 11 Jun 1897: Commander, Caucasus Grenadier Division
11 Jun 1897 - 22 Mar 1899: Commanding General, Caucasus Army Corps
22 Mar 1899 - 27 Jun 1902: Commanding General, II. Caucasus Army Corps
9 Apr 1900: Promoted to *General of Infantry*

Major-General Viktor Kirillovich **Zhabyko** (15 Mar 1854 - Mar 1912)
25 Jul 1910: Promoted to *Major-General*
25 Jul 1910 - Mar 1912: Commander, 18th Artillery Brigade

Major-General Vladimir Anatolyevich **Zhadimerovsky** (12 Mar 1863 - 10 Jun 1916)
11 Jun 1901 - 10 Jun 1916: Head of Studies, Imperial Military Medical Academy
24 Jun 1916: Posthumously promoted to *Major-General*

Major-General Nikolai Izidorovich **Zhankolya** (6 Dec 1866 - ?)
12 Oct 1914 - 1917: Chief of the Legal Section, Main Artillery Directorate
6 Dec 1915: Promoted to *Major-General*
1917: Chief of Administrative Department, Main Artillery Directorate

Major-General Ivan Ivanovich **Zhavoronkov** (29 Aug 1859 - 1918)
8 Jul 1913: Promoted to *Major-General*
8 Jul 1913 - 29 Sep 1916: Commander, 3rd Artillery Brigade
29 Sep 1916 - 1917: Inspector of Artillery, XXI. Army Corps

Lieutenant-General of the Hydrographic Corps Nikolai Viktorovich **Zhavoronkov** (2 Dec 1857 - 28 Sep 1929)
19 Jan 1909 - 15 Nov 1911: Senior Clerk, Main Hydrographic Directorate
29 Mar 1909: Promoted to *Major-General of the Admiralty*
15 Nov 1911 - 1917: Chief of Pilotage, Main Hydrographic Directorate
4 Feb 1913: Redesignated *Major-General of the Hydrographic Corps*
1917: Promoted to *Lieutenant-General of the Hydrographic Corps*
1917: Retired

Lieutenant-General Iosif Petrovich **Zhaykovsky** (10 Sep 1841 - 12 Sep 1904)
7 Feb 1880 - 19 Jan 1896: Section Chief, Main Artillery Directorate
7 Feb 1880 - 12 Sep 1904: Member of the Artillery Committee, Main Artillery Directorate

6 May 1884: Promoted to *Major-General*
14 May 1896: Promoted to *Lieutenant-General*

Lieutenant-General Aleksandr Yefimovich **Zhdanko** (6 Jan 1858 - 8 Sep 1917)
28 Nov 1908: Promoted to *Major-General*
28 Nov 1908 - 19 Jul 1914: Commander, 2nd Brigade, 34th Infantry Division
19 Jul 1914 - 23 Nov 1916: Commander, 64th Infantry Division
1 May 1915: Promoted to *Lieutenant-General*
23 Nov 1916 - 31 Aug 1917: Reserve officer, Kiev Military District
31 Aug 1917: Retired

General of the Hydrographic Corps Mikhail Yefimovich **Zhdanko** (4 Nov 1855 - 16 Nov 1921)
5 Jan 1898 - 1913: Head of Hydrographic Expedition, Pacific
6 Dec 1907: Promoted to *Major-General of the Hydrographic Corps*
6 Dec 1912: Promoted to *Lieutenant-General of the Hydrographic Corps*
1913 - 4 Mar 1913: Representative of the Ministry of the Navy, Council of Merchant Shipping, Ministry of Trade and Industry
4 Mar 1913 - Feb 1917: Chief of the Hydrographic Department, Ministry of the Navy
1916: Promoted to *General of the Hydrographic Corps*
Feb 1917: Retired

Major-General Boris Petrovich **Zhdanov** (20 May 1831 - 8 Feb 1896)
28 Jun 1889: Promoted to *Major-General*
28 Jun 1889 - 29 Nov 1893: Commander, 19th Artillery Brigade
29 Nov 1893 - 8 Feb 1896: Artillery Inspector, Kazan Military District

Major-General Nikolai Aleksandrovich **Zhdanov** (21 Dec 1867 - ?)
1 Jul 1916 - Jul 1917: Chief of Staff, 65th Infantry Division
6 Dec 1916: Promoted to *Major-General*
Jul 1917 - 7 Aug 1917: Chief of Staff, 16th Siberian Rifle Division
7 Aug 1917 - 1918: Commander, 121st Infantry Division

Lieutenant-General Stepan Nikolayevich **Zhdanov** (15 Dec 1855 - 1928)
4 Dec 1909: Promoted to *Major-General*
4 Dec 1909 - 20 Dec 1911: Commander, Fortress Vladivostok Sapper Brigade
20 Dec 1911 - 29 Nov 1912: Inspector of Field Engineers, Irkutsk Military District
29 Nov 1912 - 1917: Inspector of Engineers, Irkutsk Military District
6 Dec 1916: Promoted to *Lieutenant-General*

Lieutenant-General Kondrat Nikitich **Zhdanovich** (8 Mar 1847 - 27 Aug 1917)
13 Feb 1903 - 15 Jun 1906: Military Commander, Samara District
2 Apr 1906: Promoted to *Major-General*
15 Jun 1906 - 16 Jul 1907: Military Commander, Saratov District
16 Jul 1907 - 27 Jun 1909: Commander, Kazan Regional Brigade
27 Jun 1909 - 31 Dec 1913: Commander, Poltava Regional Brigade

14 Apr 1913:	Promoted to *Lieutenant-General*
31 Dec 1913:	Retired
26 Mar 1916 - 26 Nov 1916:	Recalled; Reserve officer, Kiev Military District
26 Nov 1916 - 24 Jul 1917:	Commander, 35th Replacement Infantry Brigade
24 Jul 1917:	Dismissed

Lieutenant-General Nikolai Yakovlevich **Zhdanovich** (25 Dec 1854 - ?)
27 Nov 1902:	Promoted to *Major-General*
27 Nov 1902 - 19 Jul 1906:	Chief of Staff, Fortress Brest-Litovsk
19 Jul 1906 - 5 Jan 1907:	At the disposal of the Commanding General, Warsaw Military District
5 Jan 1907 - 5 Apr 1914:	Commander, 2nd Brigade, 7th Infantry Division
5 Apr 1914:	Promoted to *Lieutenant-General*
5 Apr 1914:	Retired

Major-General Konstantin Sakerdonovich **Zhdanovsky** (4 Jul 1859 - Feb 1918)
31 Dec 1904 - 15 Mar 1907:	Commander, 1st Brigade, 9th Infantry Division
10 Jan 1905:	Promoted to *Major-General*
15 Mar 1907:	Retired

Major-General Aleksandr Timofeyevich **Zhegalov** (27 Aug 1857 - 1911)
8 Nov 1906 - 1911:	Commander, 1st Battalion, 1st Artillery Brigade
1911:	Promoted to *Major-General*

Lieutenant-General Pyotr Timofeyevich **Zhegalov** (29 Jun 1838 - ?)
22 Nov 1894:	Promoted to *Major-General*
22 Nov 1894 - 1904:	Special Assignments General, Vilnius Military District
6 Dec 1902:	Promoted to *Lieutenant-General*

Major-General Boris Konstantinovich **Zhegochev** (7 Jun 1858 - ?)
21 May 1905 - Jan 1908:	Commander, 2nd Brigade, 14th Infantry Division
18 Jul 1905:	Promoted to *Major-General*

Protopresbyter Aleksandr Alekseyevich **Zhelobovsky** (28 Aug 1834 - 29 Apr 1910)
26 Mar 1888:	Promoted to *Protopresbyter*
26 Mar 1888 - 29 Apr 1910:	Chief, Directorate of the Orthodox Army and Naval Chaplaincy

Lieutenant-General Anton Nikolayevich **Zheltukhin** (26 Sep 1834 - ?)
2 Feb 1878 - 6 Sep 1891:	Commander, 2nd Life Dragoon Regiment
6 Sep 1891:	Promoted to *Major-General*
6 Sep 1891 - 12 May 1897:	Commander, 1st Brigade, 3rd Cavalry Division
12 May 1897 - Dec 1899:	Commander, 1st Brigade, 7th Cavalry Division
Dec 1899:	Promoted to *Lieutenant-General*
Dec 1899:	Retired

Major-General Konstantin Vasilyevich **Zheltukhin** (20 May 1870 - ?)
1914 - 3 Nov 1915:	Commander, Orenburg Cossack Division

19 Jul 1915: Promoted to *Major-General*
3 Nov 1915 - 1917: Commander, 1st Brigade, 15th Cavalry Division

Major-General Vladimir Aleksandrovich **Zheltyshev** (1 Nov 1867 - ?)
19 Jul 1914 - 13 Jan 1916: Commander, 98th Infantry Regiment
6 Dec 1915: Promoted to *Major-General*
13 Jan 1916 - 15 Mar 1916: Chief of Staff, 1st Turkestan Rifle Brigade
15 Mar 1916 - 14 Jul 1916: Chief of Staff, XXXV. Army Corps
14 Jul 1916 - 21 Mar 1917: At the disposal of the Chief of the General Staff
21 Mar 1917 - Oct 1917: Chief of Staff, XXXVI. Army Corps

Lieutenant-General Fyodor Ivanovich **Zherbin** (29 Mar 1836 - 30 Jan 1903)
26 Nov 1871: Promoted to *Major-General*
26 Nov 1871 - 3 Mar 1886: Transferred to the reserve
3 Mar 1886 - 30 Jan 1903: Attached to the Ministry of War
14 May 1896: Promoted to *Lieutenant-General*

General of Cavalry Aleksey Gerasimovich **Zherebkov** (30 Sep 1837 - 6 Sep 1922)
1 Nov 1878 - 16 Dec 1881: Commander, Don Guards Cossack Regiment
31 Oct 1881: Promoted to *Major-General*
16 Dec 1881 - 13 Mar 1884: Commander, Life Guards Consolidated Cossack Regiment
13 Mar 1884 - 26 Feb 1886: Commander, Life Guards Cossack Regiment
26 Feb 1886 - 7 Mar 1891: Commander, 3rd Brigade, 1st Guards Cavalry Division
7 Mar 1891 - 25 Jan 1893: Chief of Taganrog District, Don Cossack Region
30 Aug 1891: Promoted to *Lieutenant-General*
25 Jan 1893 - 26 Oct 1904: Commanding General, Finland Military District
26 Oct 1904 - 31 Jan 1906: At the disposal of the Minister of War
31 Jan 1906: Promoted to *General of Cavalry*
31 Jan 1906: Retired
24 Jan 1914: Promoted to *General-Adjutant*
24 Jan 1914 - 8 Sep 1917: Recalled; Attached to the Don Cossack Army
8 Sep 1917: Retired

Major-General Ivan Fyodorovich **Zherebyatyev** (22 May 1859 - ?)
15 Jan 1912 - 6 Feb 1913: Deputy Chief of Mikhailovsk-Shostka Gunpowder Factory
25 Mar 1912: Promoted to *Major-General*
6 Feb 1913 - 30 Apr 1915: Deputy Chief of Okhtenskaya Explosives Factory
30 Apr 1915 - 1917: Chief of Explosives Department, Sergiev-Samara Factory

Major-General Konstantin Vsevolodovich **Zherve** (29 May 1869 - ?)
17 Dec 1915 - 25 Aug 1917: Commander, 61st Artillery Brigade
12 Feb 1916: Promoted to *Major-General*
25 Aug 1917 - 1917: Inspector of Artillery, XLVII. Army Corps

General of Infantry Vladimir Konstantinovich **Zherve** (9 Nov 1833 - 29 Dec 1900)
24 Mar 1875 - 26 Jan 1886: Commander, 133rd Infantry Regiment
15 May 1883: Promoted to *Major-General*
26 Jan 1886 - 2 Oct 1892: Commander, 2nd Brigade, 15th Infantry Division
2 Oct 1892 - 20 Jan 1895: Commander, 12th Infantry Division
30 Aug 1893: Promoted to *Lieutenant-General*
20 Jan 1895 - 29 Dec 1900: Commander, Moscow Regional Brigade
22 Dec 1900: Promoted to *General of Infantry*

Major-General Aleksey Samsonovich **Zhgenti** (12 Jan 1860 - 16 Dec 1915)
11 May 1910 - 17 Nov 1915: Military Commander, Tiflis District
30 Jun 1915: Promoted to *Major-General*
17 Nov 1915 - 16 Dec 1915: Commander, 37th Militia Brigade

Major-General Ivan Timofeyevich **Zhidkov** (5 Jan 1855 - 7 Mar 1920)
17 Apr 1910 - 19 Apr 1912: Commander, 3rd Don Cossack Regiment
19 Apr 1912: Promoted to *Major-General*
19 Apr 1912: Retired
4 Jan 1914 - 24 Jul 1917: Recalled; Ataman, 2nd Don District, Don Cossack Army
24 Jul 1917: Dismissed

Lieutenant-General Leonid Ivanovich **Zhigalin** (9 Apr 1859 - 3 Oct 1926)
28 Jul 1906 - 22 Sep 1911: Commander, Life Guards Consolidated Cossack Regiment
31 May 1907: Promoted to *Major-General*
22 Sep 1911 - 31 Dec 1913: Commander, 3rd Brigade, 1st Guards Cavalry Division
31 Dec 1913: Promoted to *Lieutenant-General*
31 Dec 1913 - 24 Sep 1914: Commander, 2nd Consolidated Cossack Division
24 Sep 1914 - 10 Jan 1916: Reserve officer, Kiev Military District
10 Jan 1916 - 1917: Supervisor of Horse Recovery, Southwestern Front

Lieutenant-General Vladimir Ivanovich **Zhigalin** (24 Nov 1851 - ?)
25 Oct 1899: Promoted to *Major-General*
25 Oct 1899 - 22 Sep 1909: Commander, West Siberian Independent Cossack Brigade
11 Jul 1902 - 20 Feb 1903: Ataman, Semirechensky Cossack Troops
22 Sep 1909: Promoted to *Lieutenant-General*
22 Sep 1909 - 24 Nov 1911: Commander, Trans-Baikal Cossack Brigade
24 Nov 1911: Retired

Major-General Vatslav Ignatyevich **Zhigalkovsky** (22 Sep 1859 - ?)
14 Mar 1902 - 5 Mar 1910: Commander of Engineers, Fortress Vladivostok
29 Mar 1909: Promoted to *Major-General*
5 Mar 1910 - 8 Dec 1910: Commander of Engineers, Fortress Mikhailovsky
8 Dec 1910 - 1912: Attached to the Corps of Engineers

Major-General Pavel Lvovich **Zhigmont** (15 Jan 1859 - 15 Apr 1917)
15 Jan 1916 - 4 Sep 1916: Military Commander, Stavropol District

4 Sep 1916: Promoted to *Major-General*
4 Sep 1916: Retired

Major-General Nikolai Sergeyevich **Zhilin** (6 Aug 1852 - 23 Jun 1912)
21 Mar 1907: Promoted to *Major-General*
21 Mar 1907 - Apr 1908: Commander, 1st Brigade, 2nd Cavalry Division
Apr 1908: Retired

General of Infantry Iosif Ippolitovich **Zhilinsky** (8 Apr 1834 - 1916)
23 Feb 1877 - 7 Apr 1879: Member of the Military Academic Committee, General Staff
17 Apr 1877: Promoted to *Major-General*
7 Apr 1879 - Jan 1909: Member of the Board, Ministry of State Property
2 May 1881 - 26 Apr 1894: Chief of Survey, Western Border
30 Aug 1888: Promoted to *Lieutenant-General*
26 Apr 1894 - Jan 1909: Member of the Military Academic Committee, General Staff
Jan 1909: Promoted to *General of Infantry*
Jan 1909: Retired

General of Infantry Stanislav Ivanovich **Zhilinsky** (16 Dec 1838 - 23 Jan 1901)
10 Mar 1868 - 2 Sep 1900: Chief of Topographical Department, Turkestan Military District
15 May 1883: Promoted to *Major-General*
14 May 1896: Promoted to *Lieutenant-General*
2 Sep 1900: Promoted to *General of Infantry*
2 Sep 1900: Retired

General of Cavalry Yakov Grigoryevich **Zhilinsky** (15 Mar 1853 - 1918)
3 Aug 1900: Promoted to *Major-General*
3 Aug 1900 - 1 May 1903: Quartermaster-General, General Staff
1 May 1903 - 29 Jan 1904: 2nd Quartermaster-General, General Staff
29 Jan 1904: Promoted to *Lieutenant-General*
29 Jan 1904 - 9 Jan 1905: Chief of Staff to C-in-C, Far East
9 Jan 1905 - 27 Jan 1906: Attached to the Minister of War
27 Jan 1906 - 7 Jul 1907: Commander, 14th Cavalry Division
7 Jul 1907 - 22 Feb 1911: Commanding General, X. Army Corps
18 Apr 1910: Promoted to *General of Cavalry*
22 Feb 1911 - 4 Mar 1914: Chief of the General Directorate of the General Staff
4 Mar 1914 - 19 Jul 1914: Commanding General, Warsaw Military District
19 Jul 1914 - 3 Sep 1914: C-in-C, Northwestern Front
3 Sep 1914 - 19 Sep 1917: Attached to the Minister of War
19 Sep 1917: Retired

Lieutenant-General Viktor Ignatyevich **Zhilyay** (11 Nov 1844 - ?)
30 Jun 1897: Promoted to *Major-General*
30 Jun 1897 - 19 Jul 1901: Commander, 2nd Reserve Artillery Brigade
19 Jul 1901 - 7 Jan 1906: Commander of Artillery, II. Caucasus Army Corps

28 Mar 1904: Promoted to *Lieutenant-General*

Major-General Baron Lev Fyodorovich **Zhirar de Sukanton** (19 Jun 1855 - 1918)
14 Mar 1905: Promoted to *Major-General*
14 Mar 1905 - 24 May 1907: Commander, Life Guard Cuirassier Regiment
24 May 1907 - 7 Feb 1912: Commander, 1st Brigade, 2nd Guards Cavalry Division
7 Feb 1912 - 1917: General à la suite

Major-General Aleksandr Vladimirovich **Zhirkevich** (17 Nov 1857 - 13 Jul 1927)
28 Feb 1908 - 1908: Military Judge, Vilnius Military District
13 Apr 1908: Promoted to *Major-General*
1908: Resigned

Major-General Nikolai Aleksandrovich **Zhitkevich** (28 Sep 1868 - ?)
20 Apr 1905 - 1917: Professor, Nikolayev Military Engineering Academy
14 Apr 1913: Promoted to *Major-General*

Major-General Vladimir Aleksandrovich **Zhitkevich** (27 May 1865 - 1920)
30 Sep 1914 - 13 Jun 1916: Commander, Brigade, 80th Infantry Division
18 Jan 1915: Promoted to *Major-General*
13 Jun 1916 - 11 Mar 1917: Commander, Brigade, 80th 71st Infantry Division
11 Mar 1917 - 30 Jun 1917: Commander, 190th Infantry Division

Major-General Ilya Petrovich **Zhivkovich** (26 Oct 1853 - 25 Aug 1907)
1896 - 6 May 1907: Aide-de-Camp to the Tsar
6 May 1907: Promoted to *Major-General*
6 May 1907 - 25 Aug 1907: General à la suite

Major-General Aleksandr Ivanovich **Zhnov** (3 Dec 1865 - 20 Jan 1946)
4 Jul 1910 - 21 Jan 1915: Commander, 11th Finnish Rifle Regiment
24 Dec 1914: Promoted to *Major-General*
21 Jan 1915 - 20 Nov 1916: Duty General, 10th Army
20 Nov 1916 - 23 Jul 1917: Commander, 132nd Infantry Division
23 Jul 19017 - 1918: Reserve officer, Minsk Military District

Major-General Nikolai Agafangelovich **Zhogolev** (1 Jan 1830 - 7 Dec 1898)
17 Aug 1866 - 1 Feb 1898: Member, Committee for Revision of Cossack Regulations
6 May 1885: Promoted to *Major-General*
1 Feb 1898 - 7 Dec 1898: Attached to Astrakhan Cossack Army

Major-General Martyn Ignatyevich **Zholondziovsky** (7 Aug 1860 - ?)
7 Dec 1915 - 1917: Commander, 420th Infantry Regiment
12 Oct 1916: Promoted to *Major-General*

Major-General Vasily Petrovich **Zholtanovsky** (3 Jan 1854 - 23 Apr 1906)
12 Jul 1902: Promoted to *Major-General*
12 Jul 1902 - 18 Jun 1903: Commander, 2nd Brigade, 19th Infantry Division

18 Jun 1903 - 4 Jun 1904: Commander, 1st Brigade, 34th Infantry Division
4 Jun 1904 - 5 May 1905: Commander, 2nd Brigade, 34th Infantry Division

Major-General Vladimir Semyonovich **Zholtenko** (12 Jul 1867 - ?)
29 Oct 1915 - Apr 1917: Commander, 56th Infantry Regiment
21 Dec 1916: Promoted to *Major-General*
Apr 1917 - 1917: Reserve officer, Odessa Military District
1917: Garrison Commander, Bendery

Major-General Aleksandr Semyonovich **Zholtikov** (21 Aug 1863 - ?)
1 Aug 1908 - 2 Aug 1915: Inspector of Classes, Emperor Aleksandr II Cadet Corps
25 Mar 1912: Promoted to *Major-General*
2 Aug 1915 - 1918: Director, Simbirsk Cadet Corps

Major-General Gervasy Petrovich **Zhukov** (6 Oct 1861 - 14 Apr 1940)
22 Oct 1915: Promoted to *Major-General*
22 Oct 1915 - 28 Feb 1916: Commander, 1st Amur Cossack Brigade
28 Feb 1916 - 7 Sep 1917: Commander, 2nd Brigade, 12th Cavalry Division
7 Sep 1917 - 1918: Commander, 12th Cavalry Division

Major-General Grigory Andreyevich **Zhukov** (12 Dec 1863 - ?)
19 Jul 1906 - 19 Aug 1915: Inspector of Classes, Orenburg Neplyuyev Cadet Corps
6 Dec 1909: Promoted to *Major-General*
19 Aug 1915 - 1917: Director, Irkutsk Cadet Corps

Major-General Nikolai Nikolayevich **Zhukov** (28 Dec 1855 - ?)
17 Apr 1905: Promoted to *Major-General*
17 Apr 1905 - 29 Apr 1907: Commander, 2nd East Siberian Rifle Artillery Brigade
29 Apr 1907 - 2 Feb 1910: Commander, 32nd Artillery Brigade
2 Feb 1910: Retired
25 Jul 1915 - 1917: Recalled; Reserve officer, Kiev Military District

Major-General Pavel Aleksandrovich **Zhukov** (9 Jan 1852 - ?)
2 May 1904: Promoted to *Major-General*
2 May 1904 - 13 Jun 1906: At the disposal of the C-in-C, Far East
13 Jun 1906 - 1907: At the disposal of the Commanding General, Amur Military District

Major-General Sergey Vasilyevich **Zhukov** (4 Jan 1870 - 1915)
1915 - 1 Jul 1915: Commander, 196th Infantry Regiment
5 Jun 1915: Promoted to *Major-General*
1 Jul 1915: Missing in action

Major-General Vasily Sidorovich **Zhukov** (1 Jan 1838 - ?)
7 Apr 1894: Promoted to *Major-General*
7 Apr 1894 - 27 Feb 1898: Commander, 1st Brigade, 1st Caucasus Cossack Division
27 Feb 1898 - 1903: Attached to the Kuban Cossack Army

Major-General Vladimir Dmitriyevich **Zhukov** (19 Oct 1871 - 1920)
18 Jan 1916 - 1917: Commander, 1st Finnish Mountain Artillery Battalion
22 Jul 1916: Promoted to *Major-General*

Major-General Iosif Avgustinovich **Zhukovsky** (31 Mar 1860 - 12 Mar 1910)
4 Jun 1905 - 12 Mar 1910; Section Chief, Main Engineering Directorate
6 Dec 1906: Promoted to *Major-General*

Lieutenant-General Lev Vasilyevich **Zhukovsky** (19 Feb 1846 - 31 Mar 1913)
17 Feb 1900 - 3 Oct 1902: Commander, 10th Artillery Brigade
6 Dec 1900: Promoted to *Major-General*
3 Oct 1902 - 1905: Deputy Commander of Artillery, Warsaw Military District
1905: Promoted to *Lieutenant-General*
1905: Retired

General of Artillery Mikhail Mikhailovich **Zhukovsky** (25 Apr 1821 - Dec 1907)
20 Oct 1861 - 19 Jan 1864: Commander, 3rd Guards Regiment, Grenadier Artillery Brigade
8 Nov 1861: Promoted to *Major-General*
19 Jan 1864 - 6 Aug 1865: Commander of Artillery, Dagestan Region
6 Aug 1865 - 26 Nov 1869: Deputy Commander of Artillery, Caucasus Military District
26 Nov 1869: Promoted to *Lieutenant-General*
26 Nov 1869 - 18 Dec 1871: Commander of Artillery, Kiev Military District
18 Dec 1871 - 14 Sep 1874: Unassigned
14 Sep 1874 - 6 Nov 1876: Commander of Artillery, Guards Corps
1876: Promoted to *General-Adjutant*
6 Nov 1876 - 13 Jul 1878: Commander of Artillery, St. Petersburg Military District
13 Jul 1878 - Dec 1907: Member of the Tsar's Retinue
15 May 1883: Promoted to *General of Artillery*

Major-General Silvestr Konstantinovich **Zhukovsky** (31 Dec 1860 - 26 Nov 1937)
5 Apr 1916 - 18 May 1917: Commander, 1st Brigade, 1st Infantry Division
8 Nov 1916: Promoted to *Major-General*
18 May 1917 - Oct 1917: Commander, 1st Infantry Division

Major-General Vladimir Ivanovich **Zhukovsky** (12 Aug 1860 - 5 Oct 1914)
21 Jun 1912: Promoted to *Major-General*
21 Jun 1912 - 5 Oct 1914: Commander, 2nd Brigade, 1st Siberian Rifle Division

Major-General Yuri Nikolayevich **Zhuravsky** (23 Apr 1858 - Aug 1916)
1914 - Aug 1916: Attached to 13th Infantry Regiment
31 Dec 1916: Posthumously promoted to *Major-General*

Major-General Mikhail Mikhailovich **Ziborov** (13 Oct 1859 - 14 Nov 1912)
11 Dec 1904 - 14 Nov 1912: Professor, Nikolayev Engineering Academy
6 Dec 1906: Promoted to *Major-General*

Major-General Vyacheslav Ivanovich **Ziborov** (17 Aug 1868 - 19 Oct 1917)
14 Jul 1914:	Promoted to *Major-General*
14 Jul 1914 - 9 Sep 1916:	Chief of Staff, I. Siberian Army Corps
9 Sep 1916 - 8 Oct 1916:	Chief of Staff, XXXVIII. Army Corps
8 Oct 1916 - 11 Mar 1917:	Chief of Staff, XXIX. Army Corps
11 Mar 1917 - 19 Oct 1917:	Commander, 7th Infantry Division

Major-General Dmitry Mikhailovich von **Zigel** (14 Mar 1869 - 11 Jul 1922)
15 Jan 1914 - 31 May 1915:	Commander, 7th Grenadier Regiment
28 Oct 1914:	Promoted to *Major-General*
31 May 1915 - 2 Nov 1915:	Commander, Brigade, ? Infantry Division
2 Nov 1915 - 30 Jun 1916:	Chief of Staff, II. Turkestan Army Corps
30 Jun 1916 - 10 Oct 1917:	Commander, 127th Infantry Division
10 Oct 1917 - 1918:	Commanding General, VI. Caucasus Army Corps

Major-General Dmitry Ivanovich **Zilitinkevich** (20 Oct 1863 - ?)
26 Aug 1909 - 1917:	Inspector of Classes, Aleksandr Military School
6 Dec 1911:	Promoted to *Major-General*

Lieutenant-General of the Fleet Sergey Ilyich **Ziloti** (15 May 1862 - 27 Nov 1914)
30 May 1911 - 27 Nov 1914:	Deputy Chief of the Main Naval Staff
11 Oct 1911:	Promoted to *Major-General of the Admiralty*
8 Apr 1913:	Redesignated *Major-General of the Fleet*
1914:	Promoted to *Lieutenant-General of the Fleet*

Major-General Ivan Vladimirovich **Zimin** (23 Sep 1856 - ?)
7 May 1901 - 10 May 1904:	Commander, 10th Grenadier Regiment
10 May 1904:	Promoted to *Major-General*
10 May 1904 - 4 Aug 1907:	Deputy Chief of Staff, Kazan Military District
4 Aug 1907 - Jun 1908:	Chief of Staff, XV. Army Corps

Major-General Roman Mikhailovich **Zinchenko** (1 Oct 1851 - ?)
11 Apr 1908:	Promoted to *Major-General*
11 Apr 1908 - Oct 1911:	Commander, 4th East Siberian Rifle Artillery Brigade
Oct 1911:	Retired

Major-General Fyodor Yegorovich **Zinkovich** (21 Apr 1850 - 21 Jan 1917)
8 Nov 1908 - 1910:	Commander, 144th Infantry Regiment
1910:	Promoted to *Major-General*
1910:	Retired
16 Sep 1914 - 21 Jan 1917:	Recalled; Commander, 1st Replacement Infantry Brigade

Lieutenant-General Mikhail Alekseyevich **Zinovyev** (19 Feb 1838 - 2 Dec 1895)
6 Apr 1873 - 5 May 1873:	Commander, 4th Artillery Brigade
5 May 1873 - 5 Mar 1877:	Commander, 14th Artillery Brigade
5 Mar 1877 -?:	Commander, 3rd Guards Artillery Brigade

1878: Promoted to *Major-General*
? - 28 Dec 1884: Commander, Grenadier Artillery Brigade
28 Dec 1884 - 9 May 1885: Governor of Siedlce
9 May 1885 - 2 Dec 1895: Governor of Livonia
30 Aug 1887: Promoted to *Lieutenant-General*

Major-General Ivan Karlovich **Zisserman** (23 Sep 1863 - 28 Jan 1938)
10 Jan 1900 - 1917: Chief, Office of Peasant Affairs, Kutaisi Governorate
6 Dec 1915: Promoted to *Major-General*

Major-General Stefan Nikolayevich **Zlatarsky** (30 Nov 1862 - Nov 1912)
21 Nov 1907: Promoted to *Major-General*
21 Nov 1907 - Nov 1912: Commander, 22nd Artillery Brigade

Lieutenant-General Ivan Mikhailovich **Zlobin** (26 Sep 1854 - 30 Oct 1916)
16 Jan 1909: Promoted to *Major-General*
16 Jan 1909 - 16 Jan 1914: Commander, 13th Artillery Brigade
16 Jan 1914 - 9 Jan 1916: Inspector of Artillery, III. Siberian Army Corps
22 Mar 1915: Promoted to *Lieutenant-General*
9 Jan 1916 - 30 Oct 1916: Inspector of Artillery, Kazan Military District

General of Infantry Georgy Aleksandrovich **Zmetnov** (5 May 1859 - 20 Nov 1913)
20 Jan 1903: Promoted to *Major-General*
20 Jan 1903 - 30 Oct 1904: Chief of Staff, II. Army Corps
30 Oct 1904 - 7 May 1907: Chief of Staff, Kaunas Fortress
7 May 1907 - 8 May 1909: Commandant of Fortress Ochakov
31 May 1907: Promoted to *Lieutenant-General*
8 May 1909 - 9 Apr 1910: Commander, 6th Infantry Division
9 Apr 1910 - 29 Jun 1912: Commander, 9th Infantry Division
29 Jun 1912: Promoted to *General of Infantry*
29 Jun 1912: Retired

Lieutenant-General Andrey Petrovich **Znachko-Yavorsky** (5 Jul 1844 - 24 May 1904)
25 Apr 1893: Promoted to *Major-General*
25 Apr 1893 - 28 Dec 1896: Commander, 2nd Brigade, 2nd Cavalry Division
28 Dec 1896 - 20 Jun 1900: Commander, 2nd Brigade, 12th Cavalry Division
30 May 1900: Promoted to *Lieutenant-General*
20 Jun 1900: Transferred to the reserve

Major-General Fyodor Fedorovich **Znamensky** (30 May 1859 - ?)
29 Jun 1910 - 1915: Commander, 10th Finnish Rifle Regiment
1915 - 30 Mar 1916: Reserve status due to injuries
13 Jan 1916: Promoted to *Major-General*
30 Mar 1916 - 1917: Commander, Brigade, 116th Infantry Division

Lieutenant-General Nikolai Aleksandrovich **Znosko-Borovsky** (25 Aug 1850 - ?)
23 Apr 1901: Promoted to *Major-General*
23 Apr 1901 - 16 Jul 1901: Commander, 1st Brigade, 8th Infantry Division

16 Jul 1901 - 30 Sep 1904:	Commander, 1st Brigade, 12th Infantry Division
30 Sep 1904 - 23 Jun 1905:	Commander, 2nd Caucasus Rifle Brigade
23 Jun 1905 - Aug 1907:	Commander, 1st Caucasus Rifle Brigade
Aug 1907:	Promoted to *Lieutenant-General*
Aug 1907:	Retired
18 Oct 1914 - 25 Dec 1915:	Recalled; Commander, 19th Replacement Infantry Brigade
25 Dec 1915 - 1917:	Reserve officer, St. Petersburg Military District

Lieutenant-General Akim Mikhailovich **Zolotarev** (10 Jun 1853 - 19 May 1912)
1 Mar 1899 - 8 Jan 1904:	Member, Central Statistical Committee of the Ministry of Internal Affairs
6 Dec 1900:	Promoted to *Major-General*
8 Jan 1904 - 10 May 1911:	Director, Central Statistical Committee of the Ministry of Internal Affairs
22 Apr 1907:	Promoted to *Lieutenant-General*
10 May 1911 - 19 May 1912:	Professor, Nikolayev Military Academy

Major-General Ilya Petrovich **Zolotarev** (18 Jul 1853 - ?)
20 Nov 1904 - 1910:	Commander, 1st Regiment, Kuban Cossack Army
1910:	Promoted to *Major-General*
1910:	Retired
17 Mar 1915 - 23 Dec 1916:	Recalled; Commander, 1st Brigade, Consolidated Kuban Cossack Division
23 Dec 1916 - 1917:	Commander, 1st Brigade, 3rd Kuban Cossack Division

Major-General Ivan Vasilyevich **Zolotarev** (30 Jun 1855 - ?)
29 Oct 1903 - 31 Dec 1913:	Military Commander, Stavropol District
14 Apr 1913:	Promoted to *Major-General*
31 Dec 1913 - 1915:	Commander, Orenburg Regional Brigade
1915 - 1916:	Commander, 18th Replacement Infantry Brigade
1916 - 23 Sep 1917:	Commander, Orenburg Regional Brigade
23 Sep 1917:	Dismissed

Major-General Veniamin Nikolayevich **Zolotarev** (27 Dec 1850 - ?)
13 Feb 1906 - 6 Nov 1917:	Chief of Police, Moscow
6 Dec 1908:	Promoted to *Major-General*
6 Nov 1917:	Dismissed

Major-General Vladimir Pavlovich **Zolotov** (13 Aug 1854 - ?)
30 Aug 1894:	Promoted to *Major-General*
30 Aug 1894 - 1897:	Special Purposes Officer, 4th Class, Main Directorate for Military Schools

Major-General of Naval Artillery Sergey Kharlampiyevich **Zolotukhin** (22 Sep 1859 - ?)
1911 - 21 Jan 1913:	Chief of Artillery Design Section, Naval Technical Committee
25 Mar 1912:	Promoted to *Major-General of Naval Artillery*

21 Jan 1913 - 1917: Deputy Chief of Artillery Branch, Main Shipbuilding Directorate

Major-General Mikhail Karlovich **Zommer** (13 Dec 1841 - ?)
30 Dec 1889 - 6 Feb 1896: Commander, 97th Infantry Regiment
14 Nov 1894: Promoted to *Major-General*
6 Feb 1896 - 29 Jan 1898: Commander, 2nd Brigade, 17th Infantry Division

Lieutenant-General Aleksandr Sergeyevich **Zotov** (28 Apr 1835 - 1 Feb 1910)
28 Oct 1888 - 17 Dec 1900: Ataman, 1st Don District, Don Cossack Army
30 Aug 1893: Promoted to *Major-General*
17 Dec 1900: Promoted to *Lieutenant-General*
17 Dec 1900: Retired

Major-General of the Fleet Vladimir Grigoryevich **Zrazhevsky** (12 Mar 1867 - ?)
10 Sep 1906 - 7 Nov 1912: Chief Engineer, Battleship "Yevstafy"
7 Nov 1912: Promoted to *Major-General of the Fleet*
7 Nov 1912: Retired

Lieutenant-General Fyodor Ivanovich **Zubarev** (13 Nov 1868 - ?)
9 Jun 1906 - 31 Jul 1915: Inspector of Classes, Nikolayev Engineering Academy
18 Apr 1910: Promoted to *Major-General*
31 Jul 1915 - 9 Sep 1916: Deputy Commandant, Nikolayev Engineering Academy
9 Sep 1916 - 1917: Commandant, Nikolayev Engineering Academy
6 Dec 1916: Promoted to *Lieutenant-General*

General of Artillery Vladimir Stepanovich **Zubko** (24 Oct 1848 - ?)
12 May 1898 - 14 Jul 1906: Commander of Artillery, Fortress Warsaw
1 Jan 1901: Promoted to *Major-General*
14 Jul 1906 - 24 Oct 1911: Commander of Artillery, Irkutsk Military District
6 Dec 1906: Promoted to *Lieutenant-General*
24 Oct 1911: Promoted to *General of Artillery*
24 Oct 1911: Retired

Major-General of the Fleet Pyotr Aleksandrovich **Zubkov** (20 Dec 1858 - 1923)
3 Jan 1911 - 1913: Deputy Commander, Black Sea Naval Depot
1913: Promoted to *Major-General of the Fleet*
1913: Retired

Lieutenant-General Andrey Fedorovich **Zubkovsky** (15 Nov 1855 - 8 Oct 1915)
19 Jun 1905: Promoted to *Major-General*
19 Jun 1905 - 14 Mar 1906: Commander, 2nd Brigade, 1st Rifle Division
14 Mar 1906 - 5 Jan 1909: Commander, 2nd Brigade, 14th Infantry Division
5 Jan 1909 - 19 Jul 1914: Commander, 1st Brigade, 14th Infantry Division
19 Jul 1914 - 18 Apr 1915: Commander, 63rd Infantry Division
3 Feb 1915: Promoted to *Lieutenant-General*
18 Apr 1915 - 8 Oct 1915: Reserve officer, Dvinsk Military District

Lieutenant-General Sergei Aleksandrovich **Zubov** (26 Jan 1861 - ?)
8 Jun 1907:   Promoted to *Major-General*
8 Jun 1907 - 24 Apr 1912:   Chief of Staff, Fortress Kaunas
24 Apr 1912 - 13 Nov 1915:   Commandant of Fortress Kars
14 Apr 1913:   Promoted to *Lieutenant-General*
13 Nov 1915 - 19 Mar 1916:   Reserve officer, Dvinsk Military District
19 Mar 1916 - 2 Apr 1917:   Commander, 108th Infantry Division

Lieutenant-General Vladimir Kirillovich **Zubov** (24 Sep 1856 - ?)
14 Jan 1914:   Promoted to *Major-General*
14 Jan 1914 - 16 Jun 1914:   Commander, 1st Brigade, 7th Siberian Rifle Division
16 Jun 1914 - 1917:   Commander, 2nd Brigade, 5th Siberian Rifle Division
1917:   Promoted to *Lieutenant-General*

General of Infantry Vladimir Nikolayevich **Zubov** (22 May 1837 - 9 Nov 1912)
24 Feb 1878 - 9 Nov 1912:   Aide-de-Camp to Grand Duke Georgy
                                     Maksimilianovich
29 Apr 1879:   Promoted to *Major-General*
30 Aug 1889:   Promoted to *Lieutenant-General*
6 Dec 1911:   Promoted to *General of Infantry*

Major-General Aleksandr Oskarovich **Zundblad** (11 Oct 1872 - 11 Dec 1937)
Feb 1915 - 22 Oct 1915:   Commander, Brigade, 79th Infantry Division
21 Oct 1915:   Promoted to *Major-General*
22 Oct 1915 - 17 Jul 1916:   Chief of Staff, 120th Infantry Division
17 Jul 1916 - Jan 1917:   Chief of Staff, 12th Siberian Rifle Division
Jan 1917 - 15 Feb 1917:   Chief of Staff, 109th Infantry Division
15 Feb 1917 - Apr 1917:   Chief of Staff, XXVII. Army Corps
Apr 1917 - Oct 1917:   Deputy Section Chief, General Staff

Major-General Mikhail Nikolayevich **Zurabov** (1 Feb 1868 - ?)
30 Jun 1916 - 1917:   Deputy Chief, Lugansk Cartridge Factory
6 Dec 1916:   Promoted to *Major-General*

Lieutenant-General Aleksandr Aleksandrovich **Zurov** (13 Oct 1863 - 2 Jun 1945)
13 Jul 1907:   Promoted to *Major-General*
13 Jul 1907 - 21 Dec 1908:   Commander, Semenov Life Guards Regiment
21 Dec 1908:   Promoted to *Lieutenant-General*
21 Dec 1908:   Retired

General of Cavalry Aleksandr Yelpidiforovich **Zurov** (4 Nov 1837 - 14 Jan 1902)
15 Jul 1870:   Promoted to *Major-General*
15 Jul 1870 - 9 May 1878:   Governor of Grodno
19 Jul 1871:   Appointed *Major-General à la suite*
9 May 1878 - 8 May 1880:   Mayor of St. Petersburg
8 May 1880 - 11 Nov 1889:   Attached to the Ministry of Interior
30 Aug 1888:   Promoted to *Lieutenant-General*
11 Nov 1889 - 14 Jan 1902:   Trustee, Board of Trustees, Empress Maria Institutions

9 Apr 1900:	Promoted to *General of Cavalry*
Jan 1902 - 14 Jan 1902:	Deputy Minister of the Interior, Commanding General, Corps of Gendarmerie

General of Infantry Dmitry Petrovich **Zuyev** (11 Jun 1854 - Sep 1917)
27 Nov 1896 - 28 Oct 1903:	Chief of Staff, Independent Corps of Gendarmes
6 Dec 1897:	Promoted to *Major-General*
28 Oct 1903 - 21 Jun 1907:	At the disposal of the Chief of the General Staff
17 Apr 1905:	Promoted to *Lieutenant-General*
21 Jun 1907 - 16 Jun 1910:	Commander, 1st Infantry Division
16 Jun 1910 - 26 Sep 1914:	Commanding General, XXV. Army Corps
10 Apr 1911:	Promoted to *General of Infantry*
26 Sep 1914 - 16 Sep 1915:	Commanding General, XXIX. Army Corps
16 Sep 1915 - 25 Apr 1917:	Commanding General, Dvinsk Military District
25 Apr 1917 - Sep 1917:	Reserve officer, Petrograd Military District

Major-General Venedikt Grigoryevich **Zuyev** (25 Feb 1855 - ?)
4 Feb 1909 - 1917:	Inspector of Works, Troop Billeting Department, Turkestan Military District
29 Mar 1909:	Promoted to *Major-General*

General of Infantry Nikolai Yakovlevich **Zverev** (25 Oct 1830 - 22 May 1907)
14 Oct 1868 - 17 Nov 1870:	Section Chief, General Staff
17 Apr 1870:	Promoted to *Major-General*
17 Nov 1870 - 7 May 1878:	Chief of Staff, Orenburg Military District
7 May 1878 - 21 Mar 1881:	Chief of Staff, Vilnius Military District
19 Feb 1880:	Promoted to *Lieutenant-General*
21 Mar 1881 - 6 Jul 1884:	Chief of Staff, Warsaw Military District
6 Jul 1884 - 9 Apr 1889:	Commander, 3rd Grenadier Division
9 Apr 1889 - 13 Oct 1893:	Commanding General, XII. Army Corps
13 Oct 1893 - 5 Mar 1897:	Deputy Commanding General, Warsaw Military District
30 Aug 1894:	Promoted to *General of Infantry*
5 Mar 1897 - 22 May 1907:	Member of the Military Council

Lieutenant-General Aleksey Ivanovich **Zvonnikov** (20 Jan 1865 - Oct 1919)
29 Mar 1909:	Promoted to *Major-General*
29 Mar 1909 - 11 Sep 1910:	Deputy Chief, Department of Codification, Military Council
11 Sep 1910 - 12 Mar 1911:	Chief, Department of Codification, Military Council
12 Mar 1911 - 4 Jun 1912:	Chief Military Prosecutor
4 Jun 1912 - 8 Apr 1917:	Commandant, Military Law Academy
14 Apr 1913:	Promoted to *Lieutenant-General*
8 Apr 1917:	Retired

Lieutenant-General Ivan Nikolayevich **Zvorykin** (2 Jan 1861 - ?)
26 Jan 1907 - 3 Aug 1914:	Mayor of Rostov-on-Don
6 Dec 1910:	Promoted to *Major-General*
3 Aug 1914 - 16 Nov 1914:	Commandant, Rostov-on-Don Garrison

16 Nov 1914:	Promoted to *Lieutenant-General*
16 Nov 1914:	Retired
13 Feb 1915 - 8 Aug 1917:	Recalled; At the disposal of the Inspector-General of Artillery
8 Aug 1917:	Dismissed

Major-General Aleksandr Grigoryevich **Zyakin** (1837 - ?)
1894 - 1902:	Commander, 23rd (Odessa) Borderguard Brigade
1900:	Promoted to *Major-General*

Major-General Innokenty Andreyevich **Zybin** (24 Apr 1862 - 1 Nov 1942)
1 Sep 1901 - Dec 1917:	Inspector of Classes, Chuguev Military School
25 Mar 1912:	Promoted to *Major-General*

Lieutenant-General of the Admiralty Nikolai Nikolayevich **Zybin** (? - 9 Jul 1905)
1888:	Promoted to *Major-General of the Admiralty*
1888 - 1895:	Director of the Gatchina Orphan Institute
1895:	Promoted to *Lieutenant-General of the Admiralty*
1895 - 9 Jul 1905:	Honorary Trustee, Board of Trustees, Empress Maria Institutions

Major-General Sergey Aleksandrovich **Zybin** (9 Oct 1862 - 30 Jun 1942)
28 Sep 1913 - 1 Mar 1915:	Deputy Chief, Izhevsk Arms Factory
6 Dec 1913:	Promoted to *Major-General*
1 Mar 1915 - 1917:	Chief of Samara Pipe Factory

General of Cavalry Ivan Sergeyevich **Zykov** (24 Jun 1846 - ?)
27 Nov 1889 - 16 Mar 1893:	Commander, Life Guards Dragoon Regiment
30 Aug 1890:	Promoted to *Major-General*
16 Mar 1893 - 27 Jan 1895:	Commander, 1st Brigade, 2nd Guards Cavalry Division
27 Jan 1895 - 18 Dec 1895:	Commander, 2nd Brigade, 2nd Guards Cavalry Division
18 Dec 1895 - 19 Feb 1897:	Commander, 1st Brigade, 2nd Guards Cavalry Division
19 Feb 1897 - 13 Jan 1899:	Commander, 1st Cavalry Division
13 Jan 1899 - 29 Nov 1903:	Commander, 1st Guards Cavalry Division
6 Dec 1899:	Promoted to *Lieutenant-General*
29 Nov 1903 - 23 Dec 1906:	Commanding General, II. Cavalry Corps
23 Dec 1906 - 21 May 1908:	Commanding General, XVI. Army Corps
6 Dec 1907:	Promoted to *General of Cavalry*
21 May 1908 - 31 Jul 1908:	At the disposal of the Minister of War
31 Jul 1908:	Retired

General of Infantry Sergey Pavlovich **Zykov** (1831 - ?)
1 Jan 1869 - 30 Apr 1878:	Officer for Special Assignments to the Chief of the General Staff
30 Aug 1874:	Promoted to *Major-General*
30 Apr 1878 - 3 Aug 1878:	Chief of Staff, Kronstadt Naval & Coast Defenses
3 Aug 1878 - 5 May 1900:	Member of the Military Education Committee, General Staff

30 Aug 1885:	Promoted to *Lieutenant-General*
5 May 1900:	Promoted to *General of Infantry*
5 May 1900:	Retired

Lieutenant-General Viktor Pavlovich **Zykov** (19 Sep 1854 - ?)

26 Nov 1903 - 22 Feb 1904:	At the disposal of the Chief of the General Staff
1903:	Promoted to *Major-General*
22 Feb 1904 - 2 Jan 1905:	Commander, 2nd Brigade, 9th East Siberian Rifle Division
2 Jan 1905 - 2 Apr 1905:	Commander, 2nd Brigade, 7th Infantry Division
2 Apr 1905 - 20 Feb 1906:	Commander, 1st Brigade, 7th Infantry Division
20 Feb 1906 - 4 Oct 1908:	Commander, 1st Brigade, 29th Infantry Division
4 Oct 1908 - 4 Jul 1910:	Commander, 6th Turkestan Rifle Brigade
4 Jul 1910 - 5 Apr 1914:	Commander, 5th Turkestan Rifle Brigade
5 Apr 1914:	Promoted to *Lieutenant-General*
5 Apr 1914:	Retired

Nikolai II, Emperor and Autocrat of All the Russias

Tsar Nikolai II, in the uniform of a British *Admiral of the Fleet*

General-Field Marshals / General-Admiral / Supreme C-in-C of the Armed Forces

General-Field Marshal Archduke **Albrecht** von Österreich-Teschen

General-Field Marshal **Carol I**, King of Romania

General-Field Marshal Count Dmitry A. **Milyutin**

General-Field Marshal **Nikola I**, King of Montenegro

General-Field Marshal Grand Duke **Mikhail Nikolayevich**

General-Field Marshal Count Iosif V. **Romeyko-Gurko**

General-Field Marshal King **Albert of Saxony**

General-Admiral Grand Duke **Aleksei Aleksandrovich**

General of Cavalry Grand Duke **Nikolai Nikolayevich**

Ministers of War / Ministers of the Navy

General of Infantry Pyotr S. **Vannovsky**

General of Infantry Aleksei N. **Kuropatkin**

Lieutenant-General Viktor V. **Sakharov**

General of Infantry Aleksandr F. **Rediger**

General of Infantry Vladimir A. **Sukhomlinov**

General of Infantry Aleksey A. **Polivanov**

General of Infantry Dmitry S. **Shuvayev**

General of Infantry Mikhail A. **Belyayev**

Admiral Nikolai M. **Chikhachov**

Admiral Pavel P. **Tyrtov**

Admiral Fyodor K. **Avelan**

Admiral Aleksei A. **Birilev**

Admiral Ivan M. **Dikov**

Admiral Stepan A. **Voyevodsky**

Admiral Ivan K. **Grigorovich**

Chiefs of the General Staff / General Directorate of the General Staff / Main Naval Staff

General of Infantry Nikolai N. **Obruchev**

General of Infantry Pyotr A. **Frolov**

General of Infantry Aleksey Y. **Evert**

General of Infantry Aleksandr Z. **Myshlayevsky**

General of Infantry Nikolai P. **Mikhnevich**

General of Infantry Fyodor F. **Palitsyn**

Lieutenant-General Yevgeny A. **Gerngross**

General of Cavalry Yakov G. **Zhilinsky**

General of Infantry Nikolai N. **Yanushkevich**

Lieutenant-General Pyotr I. **Averyanov**

Admiral Oskar K. von **Kremer**

Vice-Admiral Zinovy P. **Rozhestvensky**

Vice-Admiral Andrei A. **Virenius**

Vice-Admiral Pyotr A. **Bezobrazov**

Vice-Admiral Aleksandr G. von **Nidermiller**

Admiral Nikolai M. **Yakovlev**

Admiral Mikhail V. **Knyazev**

Admiral Aleksandr I. **Rusin**

Vice-Admiral Lev A. **Brusilov**

Admiral Andrei A. **Ebergardt**

Vice-Admiral Prince Aleksandr A. **Liven**

Commanders-in-Chief of Fronts, Armies

General of Infantry Nikolai V. **Ruzsky**

General of Infantry Mikhail V. **Alekseyev**

General of Artillery Nikolai I. **Ivanov**

General of Cavalry Aleksei A. **Brusilov**

General of Cavalry Pavel A. **Pleve**

Marshal of Romania **Ferdinand I**, King of Romania

General of Cavalry Vladimir V. **Sakharov**

General of Cavalry Pavel K. von **Rennenkampf**

General of Cavalry Aleksandr I. **Litvinov**

General of Cavalry Aleksandr V. **Samsonov**

General of Cavalry Sergey M. **Sheydeman**

General of Infantry Radko D. **Radko-Dmitriev**

General of Infantry Leonid V. **Lesh**

General of Infantry Baron Anton Y. von **Zaltsa**

General of Infantry Aleksandr F. **Ragoza**

General of Infantry Aleksei Y. **Churin**

General of Infantry Vladislav N. **Klembovsky**

General of Cavalry Vasily I. **Romeyko-Gurko**

General of Cavalry Abram M. **Dragomirov**

General of Artillery Konstantin P. **Fan-der-Flit**

General of Infantry Vladimir N. **Gorbatovsky**

General of Cavalry Afanasy A. **Tsurikov**

General of Artillery Vladimir N. **Nikitin**

General of Infantry Dmitry G. **Shcherbachev**

General of Cavalry Aleksei M. **Kaledin**

General of Infantry Platon A. **Lechitsky**

General of Infantry Vasily Y. **Flug**

 *General of Infantry* Faddei V. **Sivers**

 *General of Infantry* Yevgeny A. **Radkevich**

 *General of Infantry* Andrei N. **Selivanov**

 *General of Infantry* Dmitry V. **Balanin**

 *General of Cavalry* Count Illarion I. **Vorontsov-Dashkov**

 *General of Infantry* Nikolai N. **Yudenich**

 *General of Infantry* Pyotr S. **Baluyev**

 *General of Infantry* Andrei M. **Zayonchkovsky**

Commanding Generals of Military Districts

General of Infantry Sergei M. **Dukhovskoy**

General of Infantry Nikolai I. **Grodekov**

General of Infantry Arkady S. **Benevsky**

Lieutenant-General Dean I. **Subbotich**

General of Infantry Nikolai P. **Lenevich**

General of Infantry Mikhail S. **Andreyev**

General of Cavalry Rostislav A. **Khreshchatitsky**

General of Engineers Pavel F. **Unterberger**

General of Infantry Nikolai N. **Martos**

General of Infantry Sergey S. **Savvich**

General of Artillery Arkady N. **Nishchenkov**

General of Cavalry Sergey A. **Sheremetev**

General of Infantry Prince Grigory S. **Golitsyn**

General of Cavalry Yakov D. **Malama**

General of Infantry Sigizmund V. **Volsky**

General of Engineers Prince Nikolai Y.**Tumanov**

General of Infantry Dmitry P. **Zuyev**

General of Infantry Aleksandr D. **Goremykin**

General of Infantry Aleksandr V.
Brilevich

General of Infantry Vladimir Y.
Bukholts

General of Infantry Yakov F.
Shkinsky

General of Infantry Grigory V.
Meshcherinov

General of Infantry Andrei I. **Kosych**

General of Infantry Aleksandr G.
Sandetsky

General of Infantry Aleksey A.
Mavrin

General of Infantry Platon A.
Geysman

General of Infantry Mikhail I.
Dragomirov

General of Cavalry Nikolai V. **Kleygels**

General of Infantry Vladimir I. **Trotsky**

General of Infantry Nikolai A. **Khodorovich**

General of Cavalry Baron Yevgeny A. **Raush von Traubenberg**

General of Artillery Apostol S. **Kostanda**

Lieutenant-General Grand Duke **Sergey Aleksandrovich**

General of Infantry Mikhail P. **Danilov**

General of Infantry Nikolai N. **Malakhov**

General of Infantry Sergey K. **Gershelman**

Lieutenant-General Feliks F. Prince **Yusupov**

General of Cavalry Konstantin I. **Vogak**

General of Infantry Pyotr D. **Olkhovsky**

General of Artillery Iosif I. **Mrozovsky**

General of Cavalry Count Aleksandr I. **Musin-Pushkin**

General of Cavalry Baron Aleksandr V. von **Kaulbars**

General of Cavalry Semyon V. **Kakhanov**

General of Infantry Nikolai P. **Zarubayev**

General of Infantry Mikhail I. **Ebelov**

General of Artillery Baron Maksim A.von **Taube**

General of Infantry Ivan P. **Nadarov**

General of Cavalry Yevgeny O. **Shmit**

Lieutenant-General Aleksandr F. **Karpov**

General of Cavalry Nikolai N. **Sukhotin**

General of Infantry Grand Duke **Vladimir Aleksandrovich**

General of Infantry Baron Nikolai P. von **Asheberg**

Lieutenant-General Sergey S. **Khabalov**

General of Infantry Baron Aleksandr B. **Vrevsky**

Lieutenant-General Nikolai A. **Ivanov**

General of Infantry Yevgeny O. **Matsiyevsky**

General of Cavalry Nikolai N. **Tevyashev**

General of Infantry Kiprian A. **Kondratovich**

General of Artillery Pavel I. **Mishchenko**

General of Infantry Fyodor V. **Martson**

General of Infantry Nikolai S. **Ganetsky**

General of Infantry Vitaly N. **Trotsky**

General of Infantry Pyotr T. **Perlik**

General of Infantry Aleksandr V. **Gurchin**

General of Infantry Oskar K. von **Grippenberg**

General of Infantry Aleksandr A. **Freze**

General of Infantry Count Pavel A. **Shuvalov**

General of Infantry Yakov S. **Krzhivoblotsky**

General of Infantry Prince Aleksandr K. **Imeretinsky**

General of Infantry Konstantin V. **Komarov**

General of Cavalry Mikhail I. **Chertkov**

General of Cavalry Georgy A. **Skalon**

Members of the Imperial family and princely houses

Admiral Grand Duke **Aleksandr Mikhailovich**

Major-General Grand Duke **Andrei Vladimirovich**

Major-General Grand Duke **Boris Vladimirovich**

General of Cavalry Grand Duke **Dmitry Konstantinovich**

Lieutenant-General Grand Duke **Georgy Mikhailovich**

Rear-Admiral Grand Duke **Kirill Vladimirovich**

General of Infantry Grand Duke **Konstantin Konstantinovich**

Lieutenant-General Grand Duke **Mikhail Alexandrovich**

General of Infantry Grand Duke **Nikolai Mikhailovich**

General of Cavalry Grand Duke
Pavel Aleksandrovich

Lieutenant-General Grand Duke
Pyotr Nikolayevich

General of Artillery Grand Duke
Sergey Mikhailovich

Lieutenant-General Prince Georgy M.
Romanovsky, Duke of Leuchtenberg

General of Infantry Prince Yevgeny M.
Romanovsky, Duke of Leuchtenberg

General of Infantry Prince
Aleksandr P. **Oldenburg**

General of Infantry Prince
Aleksandr P. **Barklay de Tolly**

Lieutenant-General of the Admiralty
Prince Ivan M. **Obolensky**

General of Cavalry Prince
Pyotr D. **Svyatopolk-Mirsky**

Order of Battle of the Imperial Russian Armed Forces
(20 October 1894 - 2 March 1917)

(*Ranks given are the final rank achieved by the officer in question, and not necessarily the rank held at the time of the respective command shown.)

Abbreviations:	
Gen. of Art.	*General of Artillery*
Gen. of Cav.	*General of Cavalry*
Gen. of Eng.	*General of Engineers*
Gen. of Inf.	*General of Infantry*
Lt.-Gen.	*Lieutenant-General*
Maj.-Gen.	*Major-General*

Supreme Commander-in-Chief of the Armed Forces
- 20 Oct 1894 - 20 Jul 1914: *Colonel* Tsar **Nikolai II**
- 20 Jul 1914 - 23 Aug 1915: *Gen. of Cav.* Grand Duke Nikolai Nikolayevich **Romanov**
- 23 Aug 1915 - 2 Mar 1917: *Colonel* Tsar **Nikolai II**

Chief of Staff to the Supreme Commander-in-Chief *(Position created in 1914)*
- 1 Aug 1914 - 18 Aug 1915: *Gen. of Inf.* Nikolai Nikolayevich **Yanushkevich**
- 18 Aug 1915 - 10 Nov 1916: *Gen. of Inf.* Mikhail Vasilievich **Alekseyev**
- 10 Nov 1916 - 17 Feb 1917: *Gen. of Cav.* Vasily Iosifovich **Romeyko-Gurko**

Commander, Imperial Headquarters
- 2 Sep 1881 - 13 Jun 1898: *Gen. of Inf.* Otton Borisovich **Rikhter**
- 14 Jun 1898 - 2 Mar 1917: *Gen. of Cav.* Count Vladimir Borisovich **Frederiks**

SECTION I: ARMY ADMINISTRATION

Minister of War
- 1 Jan 1882 - 1 Jan 1898: *Gen. of Inf.* Pyotr Semyonovich **Vannovsky**
- 1 Jan 1898 - 7 Feb 1904: *Gen. of Inf.* Aleksei Nikolayevich **Kuropatkin**
- 7 Feb 1904 - 21 Jun 1905: *Lt.-Gen.* Viktor Viktorovich **Sakharov**
- 21 Jun 1905 - 11 Mar 1909: *Gen. of Inf.* Aleksandr Fyodorovich **Rediger**
- 11 Mar 1909 - 13 Jun 1915: *Gen. of Inf.* Vladimir Aleksandrovich **Sukhomlinov**
- 13 Jun 1915 - 15 Mar 1916: *Gen. of Inf.* Aleksey Andreyevich **Polivanov**
- 15 Mar 1916 - 3 Jan 1917: *Gen. of Inf.* Dmitry Savelyevich **Shuvayev**
- 3 Jan 1917 - 2 Mar 1917: *Gen. of Inf.* Mikhail Alekseyevich **Belyayev**

Chief of the General Directorate of the General Staff *(Office created in 1905)*
- 28 Jun 1905 - 2 Dec 1908: *Gen. of Inf.* Fyodor Fyodorovich **Palitsyn**
- 2 Dec 1908 - 11 Mar 1909: *Gen. of Inf.* Vladimir Aleksandrovich **Sukhomlinov**
- 11 Mar 1909 - 19 Sep 1909: *Gen. of Inf.* Aleksandr Zakharyevich **Myshlayevsky**
- 19 Sep 1909 - 22 Feb 1911: *Lt.-Gen.* Yevgeny Aleksandrovich **Gerngross**
- 22 Feb 1911 - 4 Mar 1914: *Gen. of Cav.* Yakov Grigoryevich **Zhilinsky**

- 5 Mar 1914 - 1 Aug 1914: *Gen. of Inf.* Nikolai Nikolayevich **Yanushkevich**
- 2 Aug 1914 - 10 Aug 1916: *Gen. of Inf.* Mikhail Alekseyevich **Belyayev**
- 10 Aug 1916 - 9 May 1917: *Lt.-Gen.* Pyotr Ivanovich **Averyanov**

Chief of the Main General Staff of the Imperial Russian Army
- 10 Jun 1881 - 31 Dec 1897: *Gen. of Inf.* Nikolai Nikolayevich **Obruchev**
- 20 Jan 1898 - 11 Mar 1904: *Lt.-Gen.* Viktor Viktorovich **Sakharov**
- 11 Mar 1904 - 28 Jun 1905: *Gen. of Inf.* Pyotr Aleksandrovich **Frolov**
- 28 Jun 1905 - 14 Apr 1906: *Gen. of Inf.* Aleksey Andreyevich **Polivanov**
- 18 Apr 1906 - 21 May 1908: *Gen. of Inf.* Aleksey Yermolaevich **Evert**
- 22 May 1908 - 7 Mar 1909: *Gen. of Inf.* Aleksandr Zakharyevich **Myshlayevsky**
- 7 Mar 1911 - 2 Apr 1917: *Gen. of Inf.* Nikolai Petrovich **Mikhnevich**

Chief of the Main Artillery Directorate
- 16 Jun 1881 - 6 Dec 1896: *Gen. of Art.* Leonid Petrovich **Sofiano**
- 6 Dec 1896 - 19 Jun 1899: *Gen. of Art.* Aleksandr Andreyevich **Barsov**
- 3 Jul 1899 - 6 Dec 1904: *Gen. of Art.* Mikhail Georgievich **Altfater**
- 25 Feb 1905 - 24 May 1915: *Gen. of Art.* Dmitry Dmitrievich **Kuzmin-Korovayev**
- 24 May 1915 - 6 Mar 1917: *Gen. of Art.* Aleksei Alekseyevich **Manikovsky**

Chief of the Main Military Technical Directorate *(Office created in 1913)*
- 1 Dec 1913 - 29 Sep 1915: *Lt.-Gen.* Baron Yevgeny Eduardovich von der **Ropp**
- 29 Sep 1915 - 15 Mar 1917: *Lt.-Gen.* Gavriil Georgyevich **Mileant**

Chief of the Main Intendant Directorate
- 21 Jun 1879 - 25 Jun 1895: *Gen. of Inf.* Nikolai Nikolayevich **Skvortsov**
- 17 Oct 1895 - 14 Mar 1903: *Gen. of Cav.* Nikolai Nikolayevich **Tevyashev**
- 20 Mar 1903 - 6 Jun 1908: *Gen. of Inf.* Feliks Yakovlevich **Rostkovsky**
- 6 Jun 1908 - 7 Aug 1909: *Gen. of Inf.* Vladimir Alekseyevich **Polyakov**
- 8 Aug 1909 - 15 Mar 1916: *Gen. of Inf.* Dmitry Savelyevich **Shuvayev**
- 22 Mar 1916 - Oct 1917: *Lt.-Gen.* Nikolai Iosifovich **Bogatko**

Chief of the Main Directorate for Military Schools
- 4 Jul 1881 - 26 May 1899: *Gen. of Inf.* Nikolai Antonovich **Makhotin**
- 26 May 1899 - 15 Jan 1900: *Gen. of Inf.* Ivan Iosifovich **Yakubovsky**
- 15 Jan 1900 - 4 Mar 1900: *Lt.-Gen.* Konstantin Vasilyevich **Rudanovsky**
- 4 Mar 1900 - 13 Feb 1910: *Gen. of Inf.* Grand Duke Konstantin Konstantinovich **Romanov**
- 3 Mar 1910 - 19 Jul 1914: *Gen. of Inf.* Aleksandr Fyodorovich **Zabelin**
- 19 Jul 1914 - 27 Dec 1914: *Gen. of Art.* Grigory Mikhailovich **Yakovlev**
- 27 Dec 1914 - 2 Apr 1917: *Gen. of Inf.* Aleksandr Fyodorovich **Zabelin**

Chief of the Main Military Medical Directorate
- Sep 1887 - 26 Jul 1902: *Privy Councillor* Adolf Aleksandrovich **Remmert**
- 11 Aug 1902 - 23 May 1906: *Privy Councillor* Nikolai Vasilyevich **Speransky**
- 23 May 1906 - Mar 1917: *Privy Councillor* Aleksandr Yakovlevich **Yevdokimov**

Chief of the Main Military Justice Directorate
- 4 Jan 1892 - 14 Aug 1905:   *Gen. of Inf.* Nikolai Nikolayevich **Maslov**
- 14 Aug 1905 - 27 Dec 1906:   *Lt.-Gen.* Vladimir Petrovich **Pavlov**
- 27 Dec 1906 - 15 Jan 1907:   *Maj.-Gen.* Aleksandr Bogdanovich **Greym**
- 15 Jan 1907 - 8 Apr 1908:   *Gen. of Inf.* Genrikh Danilovich **Rylke**
- 30 Apr 1908 - 29 Mar 1909:   *Lt.-Gen.* Aleksandr Sergeyevich **Makarenko**
- 29 Mar 1909 - 12 Mar 1911:   *Gen. of Inf.* Ernest Rudolfovich von der **Osten-Sacken**
- 12 Mar 1911 - 27 Feb 1917:   *Lt.-Gen.* Aleksandr Sergeyevich **Makarenko**

Chief of the Main Directorate for Cossack Troops
- 12 Feb 1891 - 1 Jan 1897:   *Lt.-Gen.* Vasily Aleksandrovich **Bunakov**
- 21 Jan 1897 - 30 Jan 1907:   *Gen. of Inf.* Pavel Osipovich **Shcherbov-Nefedovich**
- 30 Jan 1907 - 3 Mar 1910:   *Lt.-Gen.* Yevgeny Georgiyevich **Garf**
- 16 Sep 1910:   DIRECTORATE ABOLISHED

Chief of the Main Directorate for Troop Billeting *(Office created in 1912)*
- 25 Aug 1912 - 1917:   *Gen. of Art.* Iosif Karlovich **Gausman**

Chief of the Army Veterinary Directorate *(Office created in 1910)*
- 1 Sep 1910 - Jul 1917:   *Lt.-Gen.* Andrey Matveyevich **Rudenko**

Chief of the Directorate of the Orthodox Army and Naval Chaplaincy
- 26 Mar 1888 - 29 Apr 1910:   *Protopresbyter* Aleksandr Alekseyevich **Zhelobovsky**
- 29 Apr 1910 - 30 Mar 1911:   *Protopresbyter* Yevgeny Petrovich **Akvilonov**
- 22 Apr 1911 - 2 Mar 1917:   *Protopresbyter* Georgy Ivanovich **Shavelsky**

Commanding General, Corps of Gendarmerie
- 6 Apr 1887 - 22 Jul 1895:   *Gen. of Cav.* Nikolai Ignatyevich **Shebeko**
- 22 Jul 1895 - 24 May 1896:   ?
- 24 May 1896 - 4 Feb 1897:   *Gen. of Inf.* Aleksandr Aleksandrovich **Freze**
- 4 Feb 1897 - 20 Apr 1900:   *Gen. of Inf.* Aleksandr Ilich **Panteleyev**
- 20 Apr 1900 - 15 Sep 1902:   *Gen. of Cav.* Pyotr Dmitriyevich **Svyatopolk-Mirsky**
- Jan 1902 - 14 Jan 1902:   *Gen. of Cav.* Aleksandr Yelpidiforovich **Zurov**
- 15 Sep 1902 - 10 Jan 1904:   *Gen. of Cav.* Viktor Vilgelmovich von **Val**
- 10 Jan 1904 - 28 Sep 1904:   ?
- 28 Sep 1904 - 24 May 1905:   *Gen. of Cav.* Konstantin Nikolayevich **Rydzevsky**
- 24 May 1905 - 26 Oct 1905:   *Maj.-Gen.* Dmitry Fyodorovich **Trepov**
- 26 Oct 1905 - 31 Dec 1905:   ?
- 31 Dec 1905 - 3 Sep 1906:   *Gen. of Cav.* Vladimir Aleksandrovich **Dedyulin**
- 3 Sep 1906 - 17 Nov 1906:   ?
- 17 Nov 1906 - 17 Mar 1909:   *Lt.-Gen.* Baron Fyodor Fyodorovich von **Taube**
- 24 Mar 1909 - 14 Oct 1911:   *Gen. of Inf.* Pavel Grigoriyevich **Kurlov**
- 14 Oct 1911 - 26 Jan 1912:   ?
- 26 Jan 1912 - 25 Jan 1913:   *Lt.-Gen.* Vladimir Aleksandrovich **Tolmachev**
- 25 Jan 1913 - 19 Aug 1915:   *Lt.-Gen.* Vladimir Fyodorovich **Dzhunkovsky**
- 20 Oct 1915 - 10 Jun 1917:   *Lt.-Gen.* Count Dmitry Nikolayevich **Tatishchev**

SECTION II: FIELD ARMY

FRONTS

C-in-C, Northwestern Front *(Formed in 1914)*
- 19 Jul 1914 - 3 Sep 1914: *Gen. of Cav.* Yakov Grigoryevich **Zhilinsky**
- 3 Sep 1914 - 17 Mar 1915: *Gen. of Inf.* Nikolai Vladimirovich **Ruzsky**
- 22 Mar 1915 - 8 Apr 1915: *Gen. of Inf.* Mikhail Vasilievich **Alekseyev**
- 8 Apr 1915: UNIT DISSOLVED

C-in-C, Southwestern Front *(Formed in 1914)*
- 19 Jul 1914 - 17 Mar 1916: *Gen. of Art.* Nikolai Iudovich **Ivanov**
- 17 Mar 1916 - 21 May 1917: *Gen. of Cav.* Aleksei Alekseyevich **Brusilov**

C-in-C, Northern Front *(Formed in 1915)*
- 18 Aug 1915 - 6 Dec 1915: *Gen. of Inf.* Nikolai Vladimirovich **Ruzsky**
- 6 Dec 1915 - 6 Feb 1916: *Gen. of Cav.* Pavel Adamovich **Pleve**
- 6 Feb 1916 - 22 Jul 1916: *Gen. of Inf.* Aleksei Nikolayevich **Kuropatkin**
- 1 Aug 1916 - 25 Apr 1917: *Gen. of Inf.* Nikolai Vladimirovich **Ruzsky**

C-in-C, Western Front *(Formed in 1915)*
- 8 Apr 1915 - 18 Aug 1915: *Gen. of Inf.* Mikhail Vasilievich **Alekseyev**
- 20 Aug 1915 - 11 Mar 1917: *Gen. of Inf.* Aleksey Yermolaevich **Evert**

C-in-C, Romanian Front *(Formed in 1916)*
- 3 Dec 1916 - 25 Mar 1918: *Marshal of Romania* **Ferdinand I**, King of Romania

Deputy C-in-C, Romanian Front
- 12 Dec 1916 - 2 Apr 1917: *Gen. of Cav.* Vladimir Viktorovich **Sakharov**

ARMIES

C-in-C, 1st Manchurian Army *(Formed in 1904)*
7 Feb 1904 - 13 Oct 1904: *Gen. of Inf.* Aleksei Nikolayevich **Kuropatkin**
22 Oct 1904 - 3 Mar 1905: *Gen. of Inf.* Nikolai Petrovich **Lenevich**
3 Mar 1905 - 3 Feb 1906: *Gen. of Inf.* Aleksei Nikolayevich **Kuropatkin**
3 Feb 1906: DISSOLVED

C-in-C, 2nd Manchurian Army *(Formed in 1904)*
11 Sep 1904 - 12 Mar 1905: *Gen. of Inf.* Oskar Kazimirovich von **Grippenberg**
13 Mar 1905 - 27 Aug 1905: *Gen. of Cav.* Aleksandr Vasiliyevich von **Kaulbars**
14 Sep 1905 - 4 Nov 1905: *Gen. of Cav.* Aleksandr Aleksandrovich von **Bilderling**
4 Nov 1905 - 3 Feb 1906: ?
3 Feb 1906: DISSOLVED

C-in-C, 3rd Manchurian Army *(Formed in 1904)*
22 Oct 1904 - 13 Mar 1905:   *Gen. of Cav.* Aleksandr Vasiliyevich von **Kaulbars**
13 Mar 1905 - 3 Feb 1906:   *Gen. of Inf.* Mikhail Ivanovich **Batyanov**
3 Feb 1906:   DISSOLVED

C-in-C, 1st Army *(Formed in 1914)*
- 19 Jul 1914 - 18 Nov 1914:   *Gen. of Cav.* Pavel Karlovich Edler von **Rennenkampf**
- 17 Nov 1914 - 2 Apr 1917:   *Gen. of Cav.* Aleksandr Ivanovich **Litvinov**

C-in-C, 2nd Army *(Formed in 1914)*
- 19 Jul 1914 - 17 Aug 1914:   *Gen. of Cav.* Aleksandr Vasilievich **Samsonov**
- 21 Aug 1914 - 5 Dec 1914:   *Gen. of Cav.* Sergey Mikhailovich **Sheydeman**
- 5 Dec 1914 - 8 Apr 1917:   *Gen. of Inf.* Vladimir Vasilievich **Smirnov**

C-in-C, 3rd Army *(Formed in 1914)*
- 19 Jul 1914 - 3 Sep 1914:   *Gen. of Inf.* Nikolai Vladimirovich **Ruzsky**
- 3 Sep 1914 - 20 May 1915:   *Gen. of Inf.* Radko Dmitrievich **Radko-Dmitriev**
- 3 Jun 1915 - 3 Apr 1917:   *Gen. of Inf.* Leonid Vilhelmovich **Lesh**

C-in-C, 4th Army *(Formed in 1914)*
- 19 Jul 1914 - 22 Aug 1914:   *Gen. of Inf.* Baron Anton Yegorovich von **Zaltsa**
- 22 Aug 1914 - 20 Aug 1915:   *Gen. of Inf.* Aleksey Yermolaevich **Evert**
- 30 Aug 1915 - 21 Nov 1917:   *Gen. of Inf.* Aleksandr Frantsevich **Ragoza**

C-in-C, 5th Army *(Formed in 1914)*
- 19 Jul 1914 - 14 Jan 1915:   *Gen. of Cav.* Pavel Adamovich **Pleve**
- 14 Jan 1915 - 8 Jun 1915:   *Gen. of Inf.* Aleksei Yevgrafovich **Churin**
- 8 Jun 1915 - 6 Dec 1915:   *Gen. of Cav.* Pavel Adamovich **Pleve**
- 6 Dec 1915 - 30 Jan 1916:   *Gen. of Inf.* Vladislav Napoleonovich **Klembovsky**
- 30 Jan 1916 - 6 Feb 1916:   *Gen. of Inf.* Aleksei Nikolayevich **Kuropatkin**
- 6 Feb 1916 - 14 Aug 1916:   *Gen. of Cav.* Vasily Iosifovich **Romeyko-Gurko**
- 14 Aug 1916 - 27 Apr 1917:   *Gen. of Cav.* Abram Mikhailovich **Dragomirov**

C-in-C, 6th Army *(Formed in 1914)*
- 19 Jul 1914 - 21 Jun 1915:   *Gen. of Art.* Konstantin Petrovich **Fan-der-Flit**
- 30 Jun 1915 - 18 Aug 1915:   *Gen. of Inf.* Nikolai Vladimirovich **Ruzsky**
- 20 Aug 1915 - 7 Mar 1916:   *Gen. of Inf.* Aleksei Yevgrafovich **Churin**
- 20 Mar 1916 - 12 Dec 1916:   *Gen. of Inf.* Vladimir Nikolayevich **Gorbatovsky**
- 12 Dec 1916 - Dec 1917:   *Gen. of Cav.* Afanasy Andreyevich **Tsurikov**

C-in-C, 7th Army *(Formed in 1914)*
- 19 Jul 1914 - 19 Oct 1915:   *Gen. of Art.* Vladimir Nikolayevich **Nikitin**
- 19 Oct 1915 - 11 Apr 1917:   *Gen. of Inf.* Dmitry Grigoriyevich **Shcherbachev**

C-in-C, 8th Army *(Formed in 1914)*
- 28 Jul 1914 - 17 Mar 1916:   *Gen. of Cav.* Aleksei Alekseyevich **Brusilov**
- 20 Mar 1916 - 29 Apr 1917:   *Gen. of Cav.* Aleksei Maksimovich **Kaledin**

C-in-C, 9th Army *(Formed in 1914)*
- 9 Aug 1914 - 18 Apr 1917: *Gen. of Inf.* Platon Alekseyevich **Lechitsky**

C-in-C, 10th Army *(Formed in 1914)*
- 10 Aug 1914 - 22 Aug 1914: *Gen. of Inf.* Aleksey Yermolaevich **Evert**
- 22 Aug 1914 - 23 Sep 1914: *Gen. of Inf.* Vasily Yegorovich **Flug**
- 23 Sep 1914 - 25 Apr 1915: *Gen. of Inf.* Faddei Vasilievich **Sivers**
- 25 Apr 1915 - 12 Oct 1916: *Gen. of Inf.* Yevgeny Aleksandrovich **Radkevich**
- 12 Oct 1916 - 12 Dec 1916: *Gen. of Cav.* Afanasy Andreyevich **Tsurikov**
- 12 Dec 1916 - 1 Apr 1917: *Gen. of Inf.* Vladimir Nikolayevich **Gorbatovsky**

C-in-C, 11th Army *(Formed in 1914)*
- 21 Oct 1914 - 5 Apr 1915: *Gen. of Inf.* Andrei Nikolayevich **Selivanov**
- 5 Apr 1915 - 19 Oct 1915: *Gen. of Inf.* Dmitry Grigoryevich **Shcherbachev**
- 25 Oct 1915 - 19 Oct 1916: *Gen. of Cav.* Vladimir Viktorovich **Sakharov**
- 19 Oct 1916 - 20 Dec 1916: *Gen. of Inf.* Vladislav Napoleonovich **Klembovsky**
- 20 Dec 1916 - 5 Apr 1917: *Gen. of Inf.* Dmitry Vasilievich **Balanin**

C-in-C, 12th Army *(Formed in 1915)*
- 14 Jan 1915 - 8 Jun 1915: *Gen. of Cav.* Pavel Adamovich **Pleve**
- 8 Jun 1915 - 20 Aug 1915: *Gen. of Inf.* Aleksei Yevgrafovich **Churin**
- 20 Aug 1915 - 20 Mar 1916: *Gen. of Inf.* Vladimir Nikolayevich **Gorbatovsky**
- 20 Mar 1916 - 20 Jul 1917: *Gen. of Inf.* Radko Dmitrievich **Radko-Dmitriev**

C-in-C, 13th Army *(Formed in 1915)*
- 12 Jun 1915 - 20 Aug 1915: *Gen. of Inf.* Vladimir Nikolayevich **Gorbatovsky**
- 20 Aug 1915: UNIT DISSOLVED

C-in-C, Caucasus Army *(Formed in 1914)*
- 30 Aug 1914 - 24 Jan 1915: *Gen. of Cav.* Illarion Ivanovich **Vorontsov-Dashkov**
- 24 Jan 1915 - 3 Apr 1917: *Gen. of Inf.* Nikolai Nikolayevich **Yudenich**

C-in-C, Special Army *(Formed in 1916)*
- 14 Aug 1916 - 10 Nov 1916: *Gen. of Cav.* Vasily Iosifovich **Romeyko-Gurko**
- 10 Nov 1916 - 17 Feb 1917: *Gen. of Inf.* Pyotr Semyonovich **Baluyev**
- 17 Feb 1917 - 31 Mar 1917: *Gen. of Cav.* Vasily Iosifovich **Romeyko-Gurko**

C-in-C, DobrudzhaArmy *(Formed in 1916)*
- 12 Aug 1916 - 20 Oct 1916: *Gen. of Inf.* Andrei Medardovich **Zayonchkovsky**
- 20 Oct 1916: UNIT DISSOLVED

C-in-C, Danube Army *(Formed in 1916)*
- 19 Oct 1916 - 12 Dec 1916: *Gen. of Cav.* Vladimir Viktorovich **Sakharov**

MILITARY DISTRICTS

Commanding General, Amur Military District
- 9 Mar 1893 - 28 Mar 1898: *Gen. of Inf.* Sergei Mikhailovich **Dukhovskoy**
- 28 Mar 1898 - 30 Aug 1902: *Gen. of Inf.* Nikolai Ivanovich **Grodekov**
- 30 Aug 1902 - 2 Nov 1902: *Gen. of Inf.* Arkady Semyonovich **Benevsky**
- 2 Nov 1902 - 7 Sep 1903: *Lt.-Gen.* Dean Ivanovich **Subbotich**
- 2 Oct 1903 - 22 Oct 1904: *Gen. of Inf.* Nikolai Petrovich **Lenevich**
- 22 Oct 1904 - 14 Nov 1904: *Gen. of Inf.* Mikhail Semyonovich **Andreyev**
- 14 Nov 1904 - 8 Nov 1905: *Gen. of Cav.* Rostislav Aleksandrovich **Khreshchatitsky**
- 8 Nov 1905 - 6 Dec 1910: *Gen. of Eng.* Pavel-Simon Fyodorovich **Unterberger**
- 6 Dec 1910 - 23 Dec 1910: *Gen. of Inf.* Nikolai Nikolayevich **Martos**
- 23 Dec 1910 - 9 Aug 1914: *Gen. of Inf.* Platon Alekseyevich **Lechitsky**
- 4 Sep 1914 - 10 Nov 1914: *Gen. of Inf.* Sergey Sergeyevich **Savvich**
- 10 Nov 1914 - 31 May 1917: *Gen. of Art.* Arkady Nikanorovich **Nishchenkov**

Commanding General, Caucasus Military District
- 3 Jun 1890 - 12 Dec 1896: *Gen. of Cav.* Sergey Alekseyevich **Sheremetev**
- 12 Dec 1896 - 1 Jan 1905: *Gen. of Inf.* Prince Grigory Sergeyevich **Golitsyn**
- 1 Jan 1905 - 27 Feb 1905: *Gen. of Cav.* Yakov Dmitriyevich **Malama**
- 27 Feb 1905 - 17 Mar 1915: *Gen. of Cav.* Illarion Ivanovich **Vorontsov-Dashkov**
- 17 Mar 1915 - 9 Apr 1917: *Gen. of Inf.* Sigizmund Viktorovich **Volsky**

Commanding General, Dvinsk Military District *(Formed in July 1914)*
- 19 Jul 1914 - 30 Aug 1914: *Gen. of Inf.* Aleksei Yevgrafovich **Churin**
- 30 Aug 1914 - 14 Sep 1915: *Gen. of Eng.* Prince Nikolai Yevseyevich **Tumanov**
- 16 Sep 1915 - 25 Apr 1917: *Gen. of Inf.* Dmitry Petrovich **Zuyev**

Commanding General, Irkutsk Military District
- 26 May 1889 - 9 Apr 1900: *Gen. of Inf.* Aleksandr Dmitrievich **Goremykin**
- 9 Apr 1900 - 25 Apr 1906: UNIT DISSOLVED
- 25 Apr 1906 - 21 Jul 1910: *Gen. of Inf.* Andrei Nikolayevich **Selivanov**
- 10 Aug 1910 - 10 Mar 1911: *Gen. of Inf.* Aleksandr Vasilyevich **Brilevich**
- 11 Mar 1911 - 13 Jun 1912: *Gen. of Art.* Vladimir Nikolayevich **Nikitin**
- 19 Jun 1912 - 10 Aug 1914: *Gen. of Inf.* Aleksey Yermolaevich **Evert**
- 10 Aug 1914 - 10 Nov 1914: *Gen. of Art.* Arkady Nikanorovich **Nishchenkov**
- 10 Nov 1914 - 7 Oct 1915: *Gen. of Inf.* Vladimir Yegorovich **Bukholts**
- 7 Oct 1915 - 31 Mar 1917: *Gen. of Inf.* Yakov Fyodorovich **Shkinsky**

Commanding General, Kazan Military District
- 25 May 1882 - 26 Aug 1901: *Gen. of Inf.* Grigory Vasilyevich **Meshcherinov**
- 15 Sep 1901 - 21 Oct 1905: *Gen. of Inf.* Andrei Ivanovich **Kosych**
- 7 Dec 1905 - 24 Sep 1907: *Gen. of Inf.* Ivan Aleksandrovich **Karass**
- 24 Sep 1907 - 7 Feb 1912: *Gen. of Inf.* Aleksandr Genrikhovich **Sandetsky**
- 7 Feb 1912 - 19 Jul 1914: *Gen. of Inf.* Baron Anton Yegorovich von **Zaltsa**

- 19 Jul 1914 - 24 Sep 1914:   *Gen. of Inf.* Aleksey Alekseyevich **Mavrin**
- 24 Aug 1914 - 18 Oct 1914:   *Gen. of Inf.* Baron Anton Yegorovich von **Zaltsa**
- 18 Oct 1914 - 3 Jan 1915:   *Gen. of Inf.* Aleksey Alekseyevich **Mavrin**
- 6 Jan 1915 - 8 Aug 1915:   *Gen. of Inf.* Platon Aleksandrovich **Geysman**
- 8 Aug 1915 - 5 Mar 1917:   *Gen. of Inf.* Aleksandr Genrikhovich **Sandetsky**

Commanding General, Kiev Military District
- 13 Aug 1889 - 24 Dec 1903:   *Gen. of Inf.* Mikhail Ivanovich **Dragomirov**
- 24 Dec 1903 - 19 Oct 1905:   *Gen. of Cav.* Nikolai Vasilyevich **Kleygels**
- Oct 1905:   *Gen. of Inf.* Ivan Aleksandrovich **Karass**
- 19 Oct 1905 - 2 Dec 1908:   *Gen. of Inf.* Vladimir Aleksandrovich **Sukhomlinov**
- 2 Dec 1908 - 19 Jul 1914:   *Gen. of Art.* Nikolai Iudovich **Ivanov**
- 19 Jul 1914 - 10 Nov 1914:   *Gen. of Inf.* Vladimir Yegorovich **Bukholts**
- 10 Nov 1914 - 8 Apr 1916:   *Gen. of Inf.* Vladimir Ioannikiyevich **Trotsky**
- 8 Apr 1916 - Oct 1917:   *Gen. of Inf.* Nikolai Aleksandrovich **Khodorovich**

Commanding General, Minsk Military District *(Formed in July 1914 from Warsaw Military District)*
- 19 Jul 1914 - 3 Mar 1917:   *Gen. of Cav.* Baron Yevgeny Aleksandrovich **Raush vonTraubenberg**

Commanding General, Moscow Military District
- 30 Aug 1888 - 26 May 1896:   *Gen. of Art.* Apostol Spiridonovich **Kostanda**
- 26 May 1896 - 4 Feb 1905:   *Lt.-Gen.* Grand Duke Sergey Aleksandrovich **Romanov**
- 4 Feb 1905 - 16 Feb 1905:   *Gen. of Inf.* Mikhail Pavlovich **Danilov**
- 16 Feb 1905 - 17 Jan 1906:   *Gen. of Inf.* Nikolai Nikolayevich **Malakhov**
- 17 Jan 1906 - 17 Mar 1909:   *Gen. of Inf.* Sergey Konstantinovich **Gershelman**
- 17 Mar 1909 - 19 Jul 1914:   *Gen. of Cav.* Pavel Adamovich **Pleve**
- 19 Jul 1914 - 5 May 1915:   *Gen. of Inf.* Aleksandr Genrikhovich **Sandetsky**
- 5 May 1915 - 19 Jun 1915:   *Lt.-Gen.* Feliks Feliksovich Prince **Yusupov**
- 19 Jun 1915 - 2 Jul 1915:   *Gen. of Cav.* Konstantin Ippolitovich **Vogak**
- 2 Jul 1915 - 2 Sep 1915:   *Gen. of Inf.* Pyotr Dmitriyevich **Olkhovsky**
- 2 Sep 1915 - 10 Mar 1917:   *Gen. of Art.* Iosif Ivanovich **Mrozovsky**

Commanding General, Odessa Military District
- 23 Oct 1890 - 19 Dec 1903:   *Gen. of Cav.* Aleksandr Ivanovich **Musin-Pushkin**
- 19 Dec 1903 - 22 Oct 1904:   *Gen. of Cav.* Aleksandr Vasiliyevich von **Kaulbars**
- 22 Oct 1904 - 27 Aug 1905:   *Gen. of Cav.* Semyon Vasilievich **Kakhanov**
- 27 Aug 1905 - 23 Dec 1909:   *Gen. of Cav.* Aleksandr Vasiliyevich von **Kaulbars**
- 24 Dec 1909 - 10 Jun 1912:   *Gen. of Inf.* Nikolai Platonovich **Zarubayev**
- 13 Jun 1912 - 19 Jul 1914:   *Gen. of Art.* Vladimir Nikolayevich **Nikitin**
- 19 Jul 1914 - 9 Aug 1917:   *Gen. of Inf.* Mikhail Isayevich **Ebelov**

Commanding General, Omsk Military District
- 24 Oct 1889 - 26 Dec 1897:   *Gen. of Art.* Baron Maksim Antonovich von **Taube**
- 26 Dec 1897 - 25 Apr 1906:   DISSOLVED

- 25 Apr 1906 - 8 Jun 1908: *Gen. of Inf.* Ivan Pavlovich **Nadarov**
- 8 Jun 1908 - 24 May 1915: *Gen. of Cav.* Yevgeny Ottovich **Shmit**
- 24 May 1915 - Mar 1917: *Gen. of Cav.* Nikolai Aleksandrovich **Sukhomlinov**

Commanding General, Siberian Military District *(Formed in 1897 from Omsk Military District)*
- 26 Dec 1897 - 11 Jul 1900: *Gen. of Art.* Baron Maksim Antonovich von **Taube**
- 28 Jul 1900 - 14 Apr 1901: *Lt.-Gen.* Aleksandr Fyodorovich **Karpov**
- 14 Apr 1901 - 24 Apr 1906: *Gen. of Cav.* Nikolai Nikolayevich **Sukhotin**
- 24 Apr 1906: DISSOLVED

Commanding General, St.-Petersburg (Petrograd) Military District
- 2 Mar 1881 - 26 Oct 1905: *Gen. of Inf.* Grand Duke Vladimir Aleksandrovich **Romanov**
- 26 Oct 1905 - 20 Jul 1914: *Gen. of Cav.* Grand Duke Nikolai Nikolayevich **Romanov**
- 27 Jul 1914 - 30 Aug 1914: *Gen. of Inf.* Pyotr Dmitriyevich **Olkhovsky**
- 30 Aug 1914 - 18 Nov 1914: *Gen. of Inf.* Baron Nikolai Pavlovich von **Asheberg**
- 18 Nov 1914 - 14 Sep 1915: *Gen. of Art.* Konstantin Petrovich **Fan-der-Flit**
- 14 Sep 1915 - 13 Jun 1916: *Gen. of Eng.* Prince Nikolai Yevseyevich **Tumanov**
- 13 Jun 1916 - 27 Feb 1917: *Lt.-Gen.* Sergey Semyonovich **Khabalov**
- 27 Feb 1917 - 2 Mar 1917: *Gen. of Art.* Nikolai Iudovich **Ivanov**

Commanding General, Turkestan Military District
- 28 Oct 1889 - 17 Mar 1898: *Gen. of Inf.* Baron Aleksandr Borisovich **Vrevsky**
- 28 Mar 1898 - 1 Jan 1901: *Gen. of Inf.* Sergei Mikhailovich **Dukhovskoy**
- 1 Jan 1901 - 18 May 1904: *Lt.-Gen.* Nikolai Aleksandrovich **Ivanov**
- 18 May 1904 - 22 Jun 1904: *Gen. of Inf.* Yevgeny Osipovich **Matsiyevsky**
- 22 Jun 1904 - 24 Nov 1905: *Gen. of Cav.* Nikolai Nikolayevich **Tevyashev**
- 24 Nov 1905 - 15 Aug 1906: *Lt.-Gen.* Dean Ivanovich **Subbotich**
- 15 Aug 1906 - 15 Dec 1906: *Gen. of Inf.* Yevgeny Osipovich **Matsiyevsky**
- 15 Dec 1906 - 8 Mar 1908: *Gen. of Inf.* Nikolai Ivanovich **Grodekov**
- 8 Mar 1908 - 2 May 1908: *Gen. of Inf.* Kiprian Antonovich **Kondratovich**
- 2 May 1908 - 17 Mar 1909: *Gen. of Art.* Pavel Ivanovich **Mishchenko**
- 17 Mar 1909 - 19 Jul 1914: *Gen. of Cav.* Aleksandr Vasilievich **Samsonov**
- 19 Jul 1914 - 4 Oct 1914: ?
- 4 Oct 1914 - 22 Jul 1916: *Gen. of Inf.* Fyodor Vladimirovich **Martson**
- 22 Jul 1916 - 5 Jul 1917: *Gen. of Inf.* Aleksei Nikolayevich **Kuropatkin**

Commanding General, Vilnius Military District
- 13 Mar 1886 - 11 Feb 1895: *Gen. of Inf.* Nikolai Stepanovich **Ganetsky**
- 25 Feb 1895 - 9 May 1901: *Gen. of Inf.* Vitaly Nikolayevich **Trotsky**
- 9 May 1901 - 13 Sep 1901: *Gen. of Inf.* Pyotr Timofeyevich **Perlik**
- 13 Sep 1901 - 15 Sep 1902: *Gen. of Inf.* Aleksandr Vikentyevich **Gurchin**
- 15 Sep 1902 - 11 Sep 1904: *Gen. of Inf.* Oskar Kazimirovich von **Grippenberg**
- 11 Sep 1904 - 12 Oct 1904: *Gen. of Cav.* Mikhail Vasilyevich von der **Launits**

- 12 Oct 1904 - 19 Dec 1905: *Gen. of Inf.* Aleksandr Aleksandrovich **Freze**
- 19 Dec 1905 - 13 Mar 1909: *Gen. of Inf.* Konstantin Faddeyevich **Krshivitsky**
- 17 Mar 1909 - 17 Nov 1910: *Gen. of Inf.* Sergey Konstantinovich **Gershelman**
- 17 Nov 1910 - 17 Jan 1913: *Gen. of Inf.* Fyodor Vladimirovich **Martson**
- 20 Jan 1913 - 19 Jul 1914: *Gen. of Cav.* Pavel Karlovich Edler von **Rennenkampf**
- 19 Jul 1914: DISSOLVED

Commanding General, Warsaw Military District
- 7 Jun 1883 - 6 Dec 1894: *General-Field Marshal* Count Iosif Vladimirovich **Romeyko-Gurko**
- 13 Dec 1894 - 12 Dec 1896: *Gen. of Inf.* Count Pavel Andreyevich **Shuvalov**
- 12 Dec 1896 - 1 Jan 1897: *Gen. of Inf.* Yakov Stepanovich **Krzhivoblotsky**
- 1 Jan 1897 - 17 Nov 1900: *Gen. of Inf.* Prince Aleksandr Konstantinovich **Imeretinsky**
- 17 Nov 1900 - 24 Mar 1901: *Gen. of Inf.* Konstantin Vissarionovich **Komarov**
- 24 Mar 1901 - 17 Feb 1905: *Gen. of Cav.* Mikhail Ivanovich **Chertkov**
- 19 Feb 1905 - 15 Aug 1905: *Gen. of Cav.* Konstantin Klavdyevich **Maksimovich**
- 15 Aug 1905 - 4 Mar 1914: *Gen. of Cav.* Georgy Antonovich **Skalon**
- 4 Mar 1914 - 19 Jul 1914: *Gen. of Cav.* Yakov Grigoryevich **Zhilinsky**
- 19 Jul 1914: DISSOLVED

CORPS

Commanding General, Guards Corps
- 11 Aug 1889 - 29 Mar 1897: *Gen. of Cav.* Konstantin Nikolayevich **Manzey**
- 29 Mar 1897 - 25 Aug 1898: *Lt.-Gen.* Prince Nikolai Nikolayevich **Obolensky**
- 25 Dec 1898 - 14 Oct 1902: *Gen. of Cav.* Grand Duke Pavel Aleksandrovich **Romanov**
- 2 Nov 1902 - 21 Jun 1906: *Gen. of Cav.* Prince Sergei Illarionovich **Vasilchikov**
- 21 Jun 1906 - 28 Jan 1912: *Gen. of Inf.* Vladimir Nikolayevich **Danilov**
- 29 Jan 1912 - 28 May 1915: *Gen. of Cav.* Vladimir Mikhailovich **Bezobrazov**
- 25 Aug 1915 - 8 Dec 1915: *Gen. of Inf.* Vladimir Apollonovich **Olokhov**
- 8 Dec 1915 - 27 May 1916: *Gen. of Cav.* Georgy Ottonovich von **Raukh**
- 27 May 1916 - 13 Sep 1916: *Gen. of Cav.* Grand Duke Pavel Aleksandrovich **Romanov**
- 13 Sep 1916 - 2 Apr 1917: *Gen. of Art.* Pavel Platonovich **Pototsky**

Commanding General, Grenadier Corps
- 11 Aug 1889 - 19 Jun 1904: *Gen. of Inf.* Nikolai Nikolayevich **Malakhov**
- 19 Jun 1904 - 15 Mar 1906: *Gen. of Art.* Mikhail Fyodorovich **Oreus**
- 15 Mar 1906 - 24 Sep 1907: *Gen. of Inf.* Aleksandr Genrikhovich **Sandetsky**
- 1 Oct 1907 - 15 May 1912: *Gen. of Inf.* Eduard Vladimirovich **Ekk**
- 21 May 1912 - 2 Sep 1915: *Gen. of Art.* Iosif Ivanovich **Mrozovsky**
- 12 Sep 1915 - 30 Jan 1916: *Gen. of Inf.* Aleksei Nikolayevich **Kuropatkin**
- 20 Feb 1916 - 20 Jul 1917: *Lt.-Gen.* Dmitry Pavlovich **Parsky**

Commanding General, I. Army Corps
- 19 Jan 1889 - 26 May 1896: *Gen. of Inf.* Mikhail Pavlovich **Danilov**
- 14 Jun 1896 - 19 Dec 1905: *Gen. of Cav.* Baron Feofil Yegorovich **Meyendorf**
- 19 Dec 1905 - 6 Nov 1906: *Gen. of Art.* Nikolai Iudovich **Ivanov**
- 9 Nov 1906 - 8 Jun 1908: *Gen. of Inf.* Baron Anton Yegorovich von **Zaltsa**
- 8 Jun 1908 - 11 Mar 1911: *Gen. of Art.* Vladimir Nikolayevich **Nikitin**
- 17 Mar 1911 - 18 Aug 1914: *Gen. of Inf.* Leonid Konstantinovich **Artamonov**
- 18 Aug 1914 - 30 Aug 1914: *Gen. of Inf.* Leonid-Otto Ottovich **Sirelius**
- 30 Aug 1914 - 13 Apr 1916: *Gen. of Inf.* Aleksandr Aleksandrovich **Dushkevich**
- 18 Apr 1916 - 14 Aug 1916: *Lt.-Gen.* Vasily Timofeyevich **Gavrilov**
- 14 Aug 1916 - 2 Apr 1917: *Gen. of Art.* Nikolai Ilyich **Bulatov**

Commanding General, II. Army Corps
- 18 Nov 1892 - 1 Jan 1898: *Gen. of Inf.* Vasily Nikolayevich **Maksimovich**
- 1 Jan 1898 - 4 Jul 1902: *Gen. of Inf.* Prince Aleksandr Petrovich **Shcherbatov**
- 4 Jul 1902 - 12 Mar 1903: *Lt.-Gen.* Nikolai Mikhailovich **Rogovsky**
- 12 Mar 1903 - 30 Dec 1906: *Gen. of Inf.* Ivan Maksimovich **Povolotsky**
- 2 Jan 1907 - 25 Jan 1907: *Gen. of Inf.* Kiprian Antonovich **Kondratovich**
- 30 Jan 1907 - 24 Jun 1908: *Gen. of Inf.* Mikhail Semyonovich **Andreyev**
- 24 Jun 1908 - 15 May 1912: *Gen. of Inf.* Aleksandr Aleksandrovich **Adlerberg**
- 15 May 1912 - 23 Aug 1914: *Gen. of Cav.* Sergey Mikhailovich **Sheydeman**

- 30 Aug 1914 - 14 Jan 1915: *Gen. of Inf.* Aleksei Yevgrafovich **Churin**
- 14 Jan 1915 - 30 May 1917: *Gen. of Inf.* Vasily Yegorovich **Flug**

Commanding General, III. Army Corps
- 28 Oct 1894 - 1 Jan 1898: *Gen. of Inf.* Viktor Ivanovich **Dmitrovsky**
- 1 Jan 1898 - 29 May 1899: *Gen. of Inf.* Vasily Nikolayevich **Maksimovich**
- 13 Jun 1899 - 25 Mar 1903: *Gen. of Inf.* Mitrofan Petrovich **Chaykovsky**
- 16 Apr 1903 - 22 Jul 1904: *Gen. of Inf.* Konstantin Iosifovich **Razgonov**
- 22 Jun 1904 - 16 Dec 1904: *Gen. of Inf.* Aleksandr Eduardovich **Preskott**
- 12 Jan 1905 - 5 Dec 1906: *Lt.-Gen.* Ivan Vasilyevich **Volkenau**
- 27 Dec 1906 - 20 Jan 1913: *Gen. of Cav.* Pavel Karlovich Edler von **Rennenkampf**
- 29 Jan 1913 - 6 Feb 1915: *Gen. of Inf.* Nikolai Alekseyevich **Yepanchin**
- 14 Feb 1915 - 22 Aug 1915: *Gen. of Inf.* Aleksandr Aleksandrovich **Zegelov**
- 22 Aug 1915 - 16 Apr 1916: *Gen. of Inf.* Vladimir Alekseyevich **Alftan**
- 16 Apr 1916 - 11 Sep 1916: *Gen. of Inf.* Pyotr Ivanovich **Oganovsky**
- 11 Sep 1916 - 3 Apr 1917: *Lt.-Gen.* Grigory Yefimovich **Yanushevsky**

Commanding General, IV. Army Corps
- 11 Dec 1891 - 8 Mar 1895: *Gen. of Inf.* Andrei Ivanovich **Kosych**
- 8 Mar 1895 - 30 Dec 1895: *Lt.-Gen.* Mikhail Lavrentyevich **Dukhonin**
- 30 Dec 1895 - 30 Mar 1896: *Gen. of Inf.* Vasily Danilovich **Skalon**
- 29 Apr 1896 - 16 Mar 1898: *Gen. of Inf.* Pyotr Timofeyevich **Perlik**
- 2 Apr 1898 - 1 Oct 1899: *Gen. of Inf.* Count Dmitry Yegorovich **Komarovsky**
- 1 Oct 1899 - 5 Dec 1906: *Gen. of Inf.* Ignaty Petrovich **Maslov**
- 27 Dec 1906 - 22 Nov 1908: *Gen. of Inf.* Nikolai Aleksandrovich **Kashtalinsky**
- 22 Nov 1908 - 2 Feb 1914: *Gen. of Cav.* Anton Vasilyevich **Novosiltsov**
- 8 Feb 1914 - 16 Nov 1917: *Gen. of Art.* Eris-Khan-Sultan-Girei **Aliyev**

Commanding General, V. Army Corps
- 7 Dec 1892 - 6 Apr 1895: *Lt.-Gen.* Karl Aleksandrovich **Timrot**
- 18 Apr 1895 - 1 Feb 1896: *Gen. of Cav.* Ivan Fyodorovich **Tutolmin**
- 27 Feb 1896 - 23 Jan 1901: *Gen. of Cav.* Konstantin Konstantinovich **Bodisko**
- 19 Mar 1901 - 5 Jun 1902: *Gen. of Inf.* Andrey Andreyevich **Bogolyubov**
- 27 Jun 1902 - 15 Aug 1906: *Gen. of Cav.* Nikolai Mikhailovich **Vonlyarlyarsky**
- 28 Aug 1906 - 17 Oct 1906: *Gen. of Inf.* Baron Aleksandr Nikolayevich **Meller-Zakomelsky**
- 2 Nov 1906 - 30 Apr 1910: *Gen. of Cav.* Nikolai Vasilyevich **Shutlevort**
- 30 Apr 1910 - 7 Mar 1911: *Gen. of Inf.* Nikolai Petrovich **Mikhnevich**
- 9 Mar 1911 - 17 Nov 1914: *Gen. of Cav.* Aleksandr Ivanovich **Litvinov**
- 6 Dec 1914 - 18 Mar 1917: *Gen. of Inf.* Pyotr Semyonovich **Baluyev**

Commanding General, VI. Army Corps
- 28 May 1889 - 3 May 1900: *Gen. of Cav.* Aleksey Petrovich **Kulgachev**
- 3 May 1900 - 7 Dec 1901: *Gen. of Inf.* Oskar Kazimirovich von **Grippenberg**
- 7 Dec 1901 - 27 Jun 1902: *Gen. of Inf.* Semyon Andreyevich **Faddeyev**
- 27 Jun 1902 - 3 Sep 1904: *Lt.-Gen.* Nikolai Aleksandrovich **Shepelev**

- 3 Sep 1904 - 25 Apr 1905:   *Gen. of Inf.* Arkady Platonovich **Skugarevsky**
- 21 May 1905 - 18 Mar 1906:   *Lt.-Gen.* Konstantin Nikolayevich **Gribsky**
- 18 Mar 1906 - 17 Nov 1909:   *Gen. of Art.* Nikolai Mikhailovich **Khitrovo**
- 5 Dec 1909 - 3 Jun 1910:   *Gen. of Inf.* Konstantin Mikhailovich **Alekseyev**
- 3 Jun 1910 - 1 Sep 1912:   *Gen. of Inf.* Leopold-Eduard Aleksandrovich **Shvank**
- 1 Sep 1912 - 26 Aug 1914:   *Gen. of Inf.* Aleksandr Aleksandrovich **Blagoveshchensky**
- 27 Aug 1914 - 30 Aug 1914:   *Gen. of Inf.* Gvido Kazimirovich **Rikhter**
- 30 Aug 1914 - 9 Nov 1914:   *Gen. of Inf.* Pyotr Semyonovich **Baluyev**
- 9 Nov 1914 - 6 Feb 1916:   *Gen. of Cav.* Vasily Iosifovich **Romeyko-Gurko**
- 6 Mar 1916 - 15 Apr 1917:   *Lt.-Gen.* Aleksei Yevgenyevich **Gutor**

Commanding General, VII. Army Corps
- 22 Jun 1891 - 14 Mar 1895:   *Gen. of Inf.* Vasily Ivanovich **Yanovsky**
- 17 Mar 1895 - 3 Jul 1900:   *Gen. of Inf.* Pavel Grigoryevich **Dukmasov**
- 11 Aug 1900 - 9 Sep 1900:   *Gen. of Inf.* Ivan Aleksandrovich **Karass**
- 9 Sep 1900 - 10 Feb 1904:   *Gen. of Inf.* Leonty Avksentyevich **Yunakov**
- 10 Feb 1904 - 5 Jul 1906:   *Gen. of Inf.* Baron Aleksandr Nikolayevich **Meller-Zakomelsky**
- 5 Jul 1906 - 10 Nov 1906:   *Gen. of Cav.* Yevgraf Vladimirovich **Shpitsberg**
- 10 Nov 1906 - 4 Nov 1911:   *Gen. of Cav.* Vladimir Viktorovich **Sakharov**
- 4 Nov 1911 - 15 May 1912:   ?
- 15 May 1912 - 19 Oct 1916:   *Gen. of Inf.* Eduard Vladimirovich **Ekk**
- 19 Oct 1916 - 5 Apr 1917:   *Gen. of Inf.* Arkady Valerianovich **Sychevsky**

Commanding General, VIII. Army Corps
- 17 Jul 1893 - 22 Aug 1897:   *Lt.-Gen.* Adolf Vilgelmovich von **Shak**
- 27 Sep 1897 - 23 Jan 1901:   *Gen. of Inf.* Vasily Danilovich **Skalon**
- 23 Jan 1901 - 7 May 1905:   *Gen. of Inf.* Sergey Nikolayevich **Mylov**
- 7 May 1905 - 30 Dec 1906:   *Gen. of Inf.* Arkady Platonovich **Skugarevsky**
- 9 Jan 1907 - 26 Jul 1914:   *Gen. of Inf.* Ivan Andreyevich **Romanenko**
- 26 Jul 1914 - 3 Sep 1914:   *Gen. of Inf.* Radko Dmitrievich **Radko-Dmitriev**
- 15 Sep 1914 - 16 Dec 1914:   *Gen. of Inf.* Nikolai Aleksandrovich **Orlov**
- 16 Dec 1914 - 23 Mar 1915:   *Lt.-Gen.* Vladimir Mikhailovich **Dragomirov**
- 23 Mar 1915 - 18 Aug 1915:   *Lt.-Gen.* Nikita Mikhailovich **Batashev**
- 18 Aug 1915 - 9 Sep 1916:   *Lt.-Gen.* Vladimir Mikhailovich **Dragomirov**
- 9 Sep 1916 - Feb 1917:   *Lt.-Gen.* Anton Ivanovich **Denikin**

Commanding General, IX. Army Corps
- 28 Sep 1892 - 6 Dec 1896:   *Gen. of Art.* Aleksandr Andreyevich **Barsov**
- 7 Jan 1897 - 6 Dec 1904:   *Gen. of Inf.* Yulian Viktorovich **Lyubovitsky**
- 16 Dec 1904 - 21 May 1908:   *Gen. of Cav.* Konstantin Pavlovich **De-Vitte**
- 21 May 1908 - 22 Oct 1912:   *Gen. of Inf.* Aleksey Alekseyevich **Mavrin**
- 14 Dec 1912 - 5 Apr 1915:   *Gen. of Inf.* Dmitry Grigoryevich **Shcherbachev**
- 6 Apr 1915 - 14 Aug 1916:   *Gen. of Cav.* Abram Mikhailovich **Dragomirov**
- 23 Aug 1916 - 9 Apr 1917:   *Lt.-Gen.* Nikolai Mikhailovich **Kiselevsky**

Commanding General, X. Army Corps
- 2 Dec 1890 - 15 Sep 1901: *Gen. of Cav.* Viktor Fyodorovich **Vinberg**
- 15 Sep 1901 - 30 Oct 1904: *Gen. of Eng.* Kapiton Konstantinovich **Sluchevsky**
- 30 Oct 1904 - 14 Nov 1905: *Lt.-Gen.* Konstantin Vikentyevich **Tserpitsky**
- 14 Nov 1905 - 17 Jan 1906: *Gen. of Inf.* Sergey Konstantinovich **Gershelman**
- 30 May 1906 - 7 Jul 1907: *Gen. of Inf.* Pavel Aleksandrovich von **Layming**
- 7 Jul 1907 - 22 Feb 1911: *Gen. of Cav.* Yakov Grigoryevich **Zhilinsky**
- 3 Mar 1911 - 23 Sep 1914: *Gen. of Inf.* Faddei Vasilievich **Sivers**
- 6 Oct 1914 - 28 May 1916: *Gen. of Inf.* Nikolai Ivanovich **Protopopov**
- 13 Jun 1916 - 12 Jul 1917: *Gen. of Inf.* Nikolai Aleksandrovich **Danilov**

Commanding General, XI. Army Corps
- 21 Jul 1894 - 17 Mar 1895: *Gen. of Inf.* Pavel Grigoryevich **Dukmasov**
- 17 Mar 1895 - 30 Apr 1900: *Gen. of Cav.* Dmitry Petrovich **Dokhturov**
- 3 May 1900 - 12 May 1903: *Lt.-Gen.* Vladimir Nikolayevich **Filipov**
- 22 May 1903 - 1 Jun 1905: *Gen. of Cav.* Aleksandr Yakovlevich von **Tal**
- 1 Jun 1905 - 7 Aug 1911: *Gen. of Inf.* Ivan Aleksandrovich **Fullon**
- 7 Aug 1911 - 13 Dec 1912: *Gen. of Inf.* Nikolai Ivanovich **Podvalnyuk**
- 13 Dec 1912 - 22 Aug 1915: *Gen. of Cav.* Vladimir Viktorovich **Sakharov**
- 3 Nov 1915 - 6 Apr 1917: *Gen. of Art.* Count Mikhail Aleksandrovich **Barantsov**

Commanding General, XII. Army Corps
- 3 Nov 1893 - 17 Feb 1896: *Gen. of Inf.* Mikhail Ivanovich **Batyanov**
- 21 Feb 1896 - 29 May 1899: *Gen. of Cav.* Nikolai Dementyevich **Novitsky**
- 11 Aug 1899 - 9 Sep 1900: *Gen. of Inf.* Leonty Avksentyevich **Yunakov**
- 9 Sep 1900 - 8 Nov 1904: *Gen. of Inf.* Ivan Aleksandrovich **Karass**
- 23 Nov 1904 - 12 Jan 1905: *Gen. of Cav.* Vladimir Aleksandrovich **Bekman**
- 12 Jan 1905 - 18 Mar 1906: *Gen. of Cav.* Yevgeny Ottovich **Shmit**
- 18 Mar 1906 - 21 May 1908: *Gen. of Inf.* Nikolai Fyodorovich **Meshetich**
- 21 May 1908 - 15 Aug 1913: *Gen. of Cav.* Adam Solomonovich **Karganov**
- 15 Aug 1913 - 19 Jul 1914: *Gen. of Cav.* Aleksei Alekseyevich **Brusilov**
- 19 Jul 1914 - 3 Jun 1915: *Gen. of Inf.* Leonid Vilhelmovich **Lesh**
- 3 Jun 1915 - 5 Jul 1915: *Gen. of Inf.* Vladimir Alekseyevich **Alftan**
- 5 Jul 1915 - 20 Mar 1916: *Gen. of Cav.* Aleksei Maksimovich **Kaledin**
- 30 Mar 1916 - 10 Apr 1917: *Gen. of Inf.* Nikolai Nikolayevich **Kaznakov**

Commanding General, XIII. Army Corps
- 9 Aug 1894 - 20 Mar 1897: *Gen. of Inf.* Pyotr Animpodistovich **Razgildeyev**
- 27 Mar 1897 - 21 Jun 1905: *Gen. of Cav.* Aleksandr Maksimovich **Rebinder**
- 4 Jul 1905 - 18 Mar 1906: *Gen. of Cav.* Pavel Adamovich **Pleve**
- 18 Mar 1906 - 21 May 1908: *Gen. of Art.* Pavel Karlovich **Lange**
- 21 May 1908 - 19 Jun 1912: *Gen. of Inf.* Aleksey Yermolaevich **Evert**
- 12 Jul 1912 - 19 Jul 1914: *Gen. of Inf.* Mikhail Vasilievich **Alekseyev**
- 19 Jul 1914 - 17 Aug 1914: *Lt.-Gen.* Nikolai Alekseyevich **Klyuyev**
- 17 Aug 1914 - 26 Jan 1916: DISSOLVED
- 26 Jan 1916 - 9 Sep 1917: *Lt.-Gen.* Polikarp Alekseyevich **Kuznetsov**

Commanding General, XIV. Army Corps
- 20 Dec 1890 - 14 Nov 1894: *Gen. of Inf.* Yakov Stepanovich **Krzhivoblotsky**
- 14 Nov 1894 - 29 May 1899: *Gen. of Inf.* Nikolai Grigoryevich **Stoletov**
- 13 Jun 1899 - 14 Nov 1904: *Gen. of Cav.* Rostislav Aleksandrovich **Khreshchatitsky**
- 23 Dec 1904 - 3 Oct 1906: *Lt.-Gen.* Yevgeny Nikolayevich **Kakurin**
- 11 Oct 1906 - 21 May 1908: *Gen. of Inf.* Ivan Ivanovich **Veymarn**
- 7 Jun 1908 - 29 Dec 1908: *Lt.-Gen.* Vladimir Mikhailovich **Kasherininov**
- 5 Jan 1909 - 15 May 1912: *Gen. of Cav.* Aleksei Alekseyevich **Brusilov**
- 15 May 1912 - 19 Apr 1917: *Gen. of Inf.* Ippolit Paulinovich **Voyshin-Murdas-Zhilinsky**

Commanding General, XV. Army Corps
- 3 Nov 1893 - 14 Nov 1894: *Gen. of Inf.* Nikolai Grigoryevich **Stoletov**
- 14 Nov 1894 - 29 May 1899: *Gen. of Cav.* Georgy Aleksandrovich **Borozdin**
- 29 May 1899 - 1 Oct 1899: ?
- 1 Oct 1899 - 9 Mar 1901: *Gen. of Inf.* Count Dmitry Yegorovich **Komarovsky**
- 19 Mar 1901 - 30 Jun 1907: *Gen. of Inf.* Konstantin Aleksandrovich **Veys**
- 30 Jun 1907 - 11 Apr 1909: *Gen. of Inf.* Fyodor Vladimirovich **Martson**
- 11 Apr 1909 - 20 Feb 1911: *Gen. of Inf.* Pavel Fyodorovich **Klauz**
- 28 Feb 1911 - 31 Oct 1914: *Gen. of Inf.* Nikolai Nikolayevich **Martos**
- 31 Oct 1914 - 16 Jan 1917: *Gen. of Inf.* Fyodor-Emily-Karl Ivanovich von **Torklus**
- 16 Jan 1917 - 12 Sep 1917: *Lt.-Gen.* Ilya Zurabovich **Odishelidze**

Commanding General, XVI. Army Corps
- 17 Feb 1891 - 31 Dec 1896: *Gen. of Inf.* Aleksandr Karlovich **Rikhter**
- 12 Jan 1897 - 1 Jan 1903: *Gen. of Inf.* Mikhail Ivanovich **Batyanov**
- 13 Jan 1903 - 19 Jun 1904: *Gen. of Art.* Mikhail Fyodorovich **Oreus**
- 22 Jul 1904 - 28 Sep 1904: *Gen. of Inf.* Konstantin Iosifovich **Razgonov**
- 28 Sep 1904 - 23 Dec 1906: *Gen. of Art.* Dmitry Andreyevich **Topornin**
- 23 Dec 1906 - 21 May 1908: *Gen. of Cav.* Ivan Sergeyevich **Zykov**
- 21 May 1908 - 21 Dec 1908: *Gen. of Inf.* Nikolai Fyodorovich **Meshetich**
- 21 Dec 1908 - 3 Mar 1911: *Gen. of Inf.* Faddei Vasilievich **Sivers**
- 5 Mar 1911 - 17 Mar 1911: *Gen. of Inf.* Leonid Konstantinovich **Artamonov**
- 31 Mar 1911 - 13 Oct 1914: *Gen. of Inf.* Platon Aleksandrovich **Geysman**
- 13 Oct 1914 - 13 Dec 1915: *Gen. of Inf.* Vladislav Napoleonovich **Klembovsky**
- 13 Dec 1915 - 8 Oct 1916: *Gen. of Inf.* Sergey Sergeyevich **Savvich**
- 8 Oct 1916 - 2 Apr 1917: *Lt.-Gen.* Vladimir Mikhailovich **Dragomirov**

Commanding General, XVII. Army Corps
- 20 Dec 1892 - 14 Jul 1899: *Gen. of Cav.* Stepan Stepanovich **Leonov**
- 14 Jul 1899 - 4 Nov 1905: *Gen. of Cav.* Aleksandr Aleksandrovich von **Bilderling**
- 4 Nov 1905 - 24 Apr 1906: *Lt.-Gen.* Vladimir Sergeyevich **Volkov**
- 24 Apr 1906 - 3 Apr 1909: *Gen. of Inf.* Vladimir Gavrilovich **Glazov**
- 15 Apr 1909 - Aug 1914: *Gen. of Inf.* Pyotr Petrovich **Yakovlev**

- Aug 1914: *Gen. of Inf.* Pyotr Platonovich **Pototsky**
- Aug 1914 - 2 Apr 1917: *Gen. of Inf.* Pyotr Petrovich **Yakovlev**

Commanding General, XVIII. Army Corps
- 28 Sep 1892 - 13 Aug 1895: *Gen. of Inf.* Baron Loggin Logginovich **Zeddeler**
- 17 Aug 1895 - 10 Jan 1902: *Gen. of Art.* Leonid Yefremovich **Adamovich**
- 16 Jan 1902 - 15 Apr 1904: *Lt.-Gen.* Fyodor Pavlovich **Laskovsky**
- 15 Apr 1904 - 27 Jul 1905: *Lt.-Gen.* Aleksandr Aleksandrovich **Yevreinov**
- 1 Aug 1905 - 6 Jul 1906: *Gen. of Cav.* Prince Ivan Makarovich **Dzhambakurian-Orbeliani**
- 8 Jul 1906 - 26 Aug 1908: *Gen. of Inf.* Baron Nikolai Pavlovich von **Asheberg**
- 26 Aug 1908 - 3 Dec 1910: *Gen. of Inf.* Platon Alekseyevich **Lechitsky**
- 23 Dec 1910 - 4 Oct 1916: *Gen. of Inf.* Nikolai Fyodorovich von **Kruzenshtern**
- 8 Oct 1916 - 22 Oct 1916: *Gen. of Inf.* Sergey Sergeyevich **Savvich**
- 22 Oct 1916 - 2 Apr 1917: *Gen. of Inf.* Andrei Medardovich **Zayonchkovsky**

Commanding General, XIX. Army Corps
- 17 Sep 1894 - 24 Oct 1900: *Gen. of Inf.* Aleksandr Vikentyevich **Gurchin**
- 24 Oct 1900 - 29 Nov 1903: *Gen. of Inf.* Grigory Vasilyevich **Kryukov**
- 11 Dec 1903 - 28 Sep 1904: *Gen. of Art.* Dmitry Andreyevich **Topornin**
- 9 Oct 1904 - 23 May 1905: *Gen. of Inf.* Dmitry Modestovich **Rezvy**
- 1 Jun 1905 - 4 Oct 1906: *Lt.-Gen.* Leonty Vasilyevich **Gaponov**
- 6 Oct 1906 - 9 May 1914: *Gen. of Eng.* Yevgraf Semyonovich **Saranchev**
- 9 May 1914 - 12 Jun 1915: *Gen. of Inf.* Vladimir Nikolayevich **Gorbatovsky**
- 24 Jun 1915 - 16 Nov 1915: *Gen. of Inf.* Dmitry Aleksandrovich **Dolgov**
- 16 Nov 1915 - 8 Apr 1917: *Lt.-Gen.* Antony Andreyevich **Veselovsky**

Commanding General, XX. Army Corps *(Formed in 1898)*
- 1 Jan 1898 - 4 Aug 1899: *Gen. of Inf.* Viktor Ivanovich **Dmitrovsky**
- 4 Aug 1899 - 22 Feb 1901: *Lt.-Gen.* Richard Troyanovich von **Meves**
- 1 Mar 1901 - 22 Oct 1904: *Gen. of Cav.* Semyon Vasilievich **Kakhanov**
- 22 Oct 1904 - 12 Jan 1905: ?
- 12 Jan 1905 - 9 Nov 1906: *Gen. of Cav.* Vladimir Aleksandrovich **Bekman**
- 11 Dec 1906 - 28 Jul 1908: *Lt.-Gen.* Ostap Andreyevich **Bertels**
- 28 Jul 1908 - 5 Dec 1914: *Gen. of Inf.* Vladimir Vasilievich **Smirnov**
- 6 Dec 1914 - 22 Feb 1915: *Gen. of Art.* Pavel Ilyich **Bulgakov**
- 12 Mar 1915 - 18 Apr 1917: *Gen. of Inf.* Aleksandr Iosafovich **Yevreinov**

Commanding General, XXI. Army Corps *(Formed in 1898)*
- 1 Jan 1898 - 3 Feb 1903: *Gen. of Inf.* Aleksandr Karlovich **Vodar**
- 4 Feb 1903 - 16 Dec 1904: *Gen. of Inf.* Pyotr Vikentyevich **Kononovich-Gorbatsky**
- 16 Dec 1904 - 2 Oct 1906: *Gen. of Inf.* Lyudvig Lyudvigovich **Drake**
- 6 Oct 1906 - 31 Jan 1909: *Gen. of Inf.* Nikolai Vladimirovich **Ruzsky**
- 4 Feb 1909 - 22 Apr 1914: *Gen. of Inf.* Aleksei Yevgrafovich **Churin**
- 22 Apr 1914 - 7 Oct 1915: *Gen. of Inf.* Yakov Fyodorovich **Shkinsky**

- 24 Oct 1915 - 2 Apr 1917:   *Lt.-Gen.* Viktor Pavlovich **Shirokov**

Commanding General, XXII. Army Corps *(Formed in 1905)*
- 18 Jul 1905 - 1 Aug 1905:   *Gen. of Cav.* Prince Ivan Makarovich **Dzhambakurian-Orbeliani**
- 1 Aug 1905 - 9 Nov 1906:   *Gen. of Inf.* Baron Anton Yegorovich von **Zaltsa**
- 9 Nov 1906 - 2 Feb 1908:   *Gen. of Cav.* Vladimir Aleksandrovich **Bekman**
- 2 Feb 1908 - 26 Aug 1912:   *Gen. of Inf.* Pyotr Dmitriyevich **Olkhovsky**
- 26 Aug 1912 - 25 Mar 1917:   *Gen. of Inf.* Baron Aleksandr Fridrikhovich von der **Brinken**

Commanding General, XXIII. Army Corps *(Formed in 1910)*
- 29 May 1910 - 15 Aug 1913:   *Gen. of Cav.* Baron Yevgeny Aleksandrovich **Raush von Traubenberg**
- 15 Aug 1913 - 30 Aug 1914:   *Gen. of Inf.* Kiprian Antonovich **Kondratovich**
- 30 Aug 1914 - 1 Nov 1914:   *Gen. of Inf.* Vladimir Nikolayevich **Danilov**
- 5 Nov 1914 - 28 Dec 1914:   *Gen. of Inf.* Leonid-Otto Ottovich **Sirelius**
- 28 Dec 1914 - 1 Jul 1915:   *Gen. of Inf.* Vladimir Apollonovich **Olokhov**
- 5 Sep 1915 - 12 Sep 1915:   *Gen. of Eng.* Nikolai Aleksandrovich **Tretyakov**
- 1 Oct 1915 - 19 Oct 1916:   *Gen. of Inf.* Arkady Valerianovich **Sychevsky**
- 19 Oct 1916 - 2 Apr 1917:   *Gen. of Inf.* Eduard Vladimirovich **Ekk**

Commanding General, XXIV. Army Corps *(Formed in 1910)*
- 7 Jun 1910 - 20 Jan 1913:   *Gen. of Inf.* Aleksandr Alekseyevich **Gerngross**
- 29 Jan 1913 - 2 Jan 1914:   *Gen. of Inf.* Georgy Eduardovich **Berkhman**
- 2 Jan 1914 - 12 Oct 1916:   *Gen. of Cav.* Afanasy Andreyevich **Tsurikov**
- 12 Oct 1916 - Aug 1917:   *Lt.-Gen.* Konstantin Gerasimovich **Nekrasov**

Commanding General, XXV. Army Corps *(Formed in 1910)*
- 16 Jun 1910 - 26 Sep 1914:   *Gen. of Inf.* Dmitry Petrovich **Zuyev**
- 27 Sep 1914 - 30 Aug 1915:   *Gen. of Inf.* Aleksandr Frantsevich **Ragoza**
- 30 Aug 1915 - 11 Aug 1916:   *Gen. of Inf.* Yuri Nikiforovitch **Danilov**
- 21 Aug 1916 - 13 Sep 1916:   *Gen. of Art.* Pavel Platonovich **Pototsky**
- 13 Sep 1916 - 2 Mar 1917:   *Gen. of Inf.* Lavr Georgievich **Kornilov**

Commanding General, XXVI. Army Corps *(Formed in 1914)*
- 15 Aug 1914 - 28 Dec 1916:   *Gen. of Inf.* Aleksandr Alekseyevich **Gerngross**
- 28 Dec 1916 - 7 Apr 1917:   *Lt.-Gen.* Yevgeny-Lyudvig Karlovich **Miller**

Commanding General, XXVII. Army Corps *(Formed in 1914)*
- 2 Sep 1914 - 20 Dec 1916:   *Gen. of Inf.* Dmitry Vasilievich **Balanin**
- 31 Dec 1916 - 14 May 1917:   *Lt.-Gen.* Aleksandr Nikolayevich **Kuzmin-Korovayev**

Commanding General, XXVIII. Army Corps *(Formed in 1914)*
- 26 Sep 1914 - 6 Oct 1915:   *Gen. of Inf.* Nikolai Aleksandrovich **Kashtalinsky**
- 24 Oct 1915 - Aug 1917:   *Gen. of Inf.* Vladimir Alekseyevich **Slyusarenko**

Commanding General, XXIX. Army Corps *(Formed in 1914)*
- 26 Sep 1914 - 16 Sep 1915: *Gen. of Inf.* Dmitry Petrovich **Zuyev**
- 16 Sep 1915 - 15 Apr 1917: *Lt.-Gen.* Nikolai Yakovlevich **Lisovsky**

Commanding General, XXX. Army Corps *(Formed in 1915)*
- 5 Dec 1914 - 27 Mar 1915: *Gen. of Inf.* Ferdinand Mavrikievich **Vebel**
- 27 Mar 1915 - 12 Aug 1916: *Gen. of Inf.* Andrei Medardovich **Zayonchkovsky**
- 14 Aug 1916 - 1917: *Lt.-Gen.* Vasily Timofeyevich **Gavrilov**

Commanding General, XXXI. Army Corps *(Formed in 1915)*
- 19 Mar 1915 - 16 Apr 1917: *Gen. of Art.* Pavel Ivanovich **Mishchenko**
- 16 Apr 1917 - 29 May 1917: *Lt.-Gen.* Sergey Matveyevich **Pospelov**

Commanding General, XXXII. Army Corps *(Formed in 1915)*
- 3 Apr 1915 - 23 Jun 1917: *Gen. of Inf.* Ivan Ivanovich **Fedotov**

Commanding General, XXXIII. Army Corps *(Formed in 1915)*
- 3 Apr 1915 - 14 Sep 1915: *Gen. of Inf.* Sergei Fyodorovich **Dobrotin**
- 23 Sep 1915 - 8 Jun 1917: *Gen. of Inf.* Konstantin Aleksandrovich **Krylov**

Commanding General, XXXIV. Army Corps *(Formed in 1915)*
- 19 Apr 1915 - 14 Feb 1916: *Gen. of Inf.* Ferdinand Mavrikievich **Vebel**
- 23 Feb 1916 - 22 Jan 1917: *Gen. of Inf.* Vladimir Pavlovich **Shatilov**
- 22 Jan 1917 - 2 Jul 1917: *Lt.-Gen.* Pavel Petrovich **Skoropadsky**

Commanding General, XXXV. Army Corps *(Formed in 1915)*
- 19 Apr 1915 - 15 May 1916: *Lt.-Gen.* Nikolai Petrovich **Reshchikov**
- 15 May 1916 - 13 Dec 1916: *Lt.-Gen.* Pavel Antonovich **Parchevsky**
- 13 Dec 1916 - 8 Jan 1917: *Lt.-Gen.* Sergey Vladimirovich **Pokatov**
- 8 Jan 1917 - 18 Apr 1917: *Lt.-Gen.* Pavel Antonovich **Parchevsky**

Commanding General, XXXVI. Army Corps *(Formed in 1915)*
- 28 Apr 1915 - 8 May 1915: *Lt.-Gen.* Nikolai Yakovlevich **Lisovsky**
- 8 May 1915 - 1917: *Lt.-Gen.* Nikolai Nikolayevich **Korotkevich**

Commanding General, XXXVII. Army Corps *(Formed in 1915)*
- 29 Apr 1915 - 3 Jun 1915: *Gen. of Inf.* Leonid-Otto Ottovich **Sirelius**
- 3 Jun 1915 - 16 Sep 1915: *Lt.-Gen.* Nikolai Yakovlevich **Lisovsky**
- 24 Oct 1915 - 26 Jan 1916: *Lt.-Gen.* Polikarp Alekseyevich **Kuznetsov**
- 26 Jan 1916 - 1 Mar 1916: *Gen. of Inf.* Dmitry Aleksandrovich **Dolgov**
- 20 Mar 1916 - 5 Feb 1917: *Gen. of Eng.* Nikolai Aleksandrovich **Tretyakov**

Commanding General, XXXVIII. Army Corps *(Formed in 1915)*
- 8 May 1915 - 31 Oct 1916: *Lt.-Gen.* Vasily Vasilievich **Artemyev**
- 31 Oct 1916 - 22 Apr 1917: *Lt.-Gen.* Mikhail Alekseyevich **Sokovnin**

Commanding General, XXXVIX. Army Corps *(Formed in 1915)*
- 18 Jun 1915 - 14 Sep 1917: *Gen. of Inf.* Stanislav Feliksovich **Stelnitsky**

Commanding General, XL. Army Corps *(Formed in 1915)*
- 20 Oct 1915 - 20 Apr 1916: *Lt.-Gen.* Baron Sergey Nikolayevich **Delvig**
- 20 Apr 1916 - 13 Nov 1916: *Gen. of Inf.* Nikolai Aleksandrovich **Kashtalinsky**
- 13 Nov 1916 - 5 Apr 1917: *Gen. of Inf.* Georgy Eduardovich **Berkhman**

Commanding General, XLI. Army Corps *(Formed in 1915)*
- 18 Jun 1915 - 5 Jul 1915: *Gen. of Cav.* Aleksei Maksimovich **Kaledin**
- 5 Jul 1915 - 13 Apr 1917: *Gen. of Inf.* Leonid Nikolayevich **Belkovich**

Commanding General, XLII. Army Corps *(Formed in 1915)*
- Dec 1915 - 20 Mar 1916: *Gen. of Eng.* Nikolai Aleksandrovich **Tretyakov**
- 20 Mar 1916 - 19 Apr 1917: *Lt.-Gen.* Arseny Anatolievich **Gulevich**

Commanding General, XLIII. Army Corps *(Formed in 1915)*
- 25 Jun 1915 - 2 Apr 1917: *Lt.-Gen.* Aleksandr Vasilyevich **Novikov**

Commanding General, XLIV. Army Corps *(Formed in 1916)*
- Jul 1916 - 22 Apr 1917: *Lt.-Gen.* Nikolai Aleksandrovich **Brzhozovsky**

Commanding General, XLV. Army Corps *(Formed in 1916)*
- 16 Mar 1916 - 5 Apr 1917: *Gen. of Inf.* Pavel Aleksandrovich von **Layming**

Commanding General, XLVI. Army Corps *(Formed in 1916)*
- 2 Apr 1916 - 6 Apr 1917: *Lt.-Gen.* Nikolai Mikhailovich **Istomin**

Commanding General, XLVII. Army Corps *(Formed in 1916)*
- 12 Aug 1916 - 20 Oct 1916: *Gen. of Inf.* Andrei Medardovich **Zayonchkovsky**
- 31 Oct 1916 - 14 Apr 1917: *Lt.-Gen.* Vasily Vasilievich **Artemyev**

Commanding General, XLVIII. Army Corps *(Formed in 1917)*
- 17 Jan 1917 - 5 Jun 1917: *Lt.-Gen.* Georgy Mikhailovich **Sheydeman**

Commanding General, Caucasus Army Corps
- 16 Jan 1893 - 11 Jun 1897: *Gen. of Cav.* Prince Ivan Yegorovich **Amilokhvarov**
- 11 Jun 1897 - 22 Mar 1899: *Gen. of Inf.* Abunard Eduardovich **Zezeman**
- 22 Mar 1899: SPLIT INTO I. and II. CAUCASUS ARMY CORPS

Commanding General, I. Caucasus Army Corps *(Formed 1899)*
- 22 Mar 1899 - 27 Nov 1903: *Lt.-Gen.* Prince Mikhail Kaikhosrovich **Amiradzhibov**
- 13 Dec 1903 - 1 Jan 1910: *Gen. of Art.* Vladimir Avksentyevich **Yatskevich**
- 1 Jan 1910 - 15 Aug 1913: *Gen. of Inf.* Kiprian Antonovich **Kondratovich**
- 15 Aug 1913 - 19 Jul 1914: *Lt.-Gen.* Nikolai Alekseyevich **Klyuyev**

- 19 Jul 1914 - 11 Dec 1914: ?
- 11 Dec 1914 - 4 Feb 1915: *Gen. of Inf.* Georgy Eduardovich **Berkhman**
- 4 Feb 1915 - 12 Mar 1917: *Gen. of Cav.* Pyotr Petrovich **Kalitin**

Commanding General, II. Caucasus Army Corps *(Formed 1899)*
- 22 Mar 1899 - 27 Jun 1902: *Gen. of Inf.* Abunard Eduardovich **Zezeman**
- 27 Jun 1902 - 21 Sep 1906: *Gen. of Inf.* Semyon Andreyevich **Faddeyev**
- 21 Sep 1906 - 2 May 1908: *Gen. of Art.* Pavel Ivanovich **Mishchenko**
- 21 May 1908 - 8 Aug 1909: *Gen. of Inf.* Dmitry Savelyevich **Shuvayev**
- 19 Sep 1909 - 24 Dec 1913: *Gen. of Inf.* Aleksandr Zakharyevich **Myshlayevsky**
- 2 Jan 1914 - 11 Dec 1914: *Gen. of Inf.* Georgy Eduardovich **Berkhman**
- 11 Dec 1914 - 18 Apr 1917: *Gen. of Art.* Samed-Bek-Sadyk-Bek-ogly **Mekhmandarov**

Commanding General, III. Caucasus Army Corps *(Formed 1910)*
- 3 Jun 1910 - 11 May 1912: *Gen. of Inf.* Konstantin Mikhailovich **Alekseyev**
- 11 May 1912 - 8 Jun 1917: *Gen. of Art.* Vladimir Aleksandrovich von **Irman**

Commanding General, IV. Caucasus Army Corps *(Formed 1915)*
- 24 Jan 1915 - 19 Dec 1915: *Gen. of Inf.* Pyotr Ivanovich **Oganovsky**
- 19 Dec 1915 - Jun 1917: *Gen. of Inf.* Vladimir Vladimirovich **De-Vitt**

Commanding General, V. Caucasus Army Corps *(Formed 1915)*
- 15 Mar 1915 - 2 Apr 1916: *Lt.-Gen.* Nikolai Mikhailovich **Istomin**
- 2 Apr 1916 - 15 Apr 1917: *Lt.-Gen.* Vladimir Aleksandrovich **Yablochkin**

Commanding General, VI. Caucasus Army Corps *(Formed 1916)*
- 14 Jun 1916 - 15 Sep 1917: *Lieutenant -General* Dmitry Konstantinovich **Abatsiev**

Commanding General, VII. Caucasus Army Corps *(Formed 1917)*
- 15 Feb 1917 - 25 Apr 1917: *Lt.-Gen.* Fyodor Grigoryevich **Chernozubov**

Commanding General, Siberian Army Corps *(Formed 1900)*
- 18 Jun 1900 - 31 Jul 1900: *Gen. of Inf.* Nikolai Petrovich **Lenevich**
- 31 Jul 1900: SPLIT INTO I. and II. SIBERIAN ARMY CORPS

Commanding General, I. Siberian Army Corps *(Formed 1900)*
- 31 Jul 1900 - 2 Oct 1903: *Gen. of Inf.* Nikolai Petrovich **Lenevich**
- 29 Nov 1903 - 5 Apr 1904: *Gen. of Cav.* Vladimir Viktorovich **Sakharov**
- 5 Apr 1904 - 17 Mar 1905: *Gen. of Cav.* Baron Georgy Karlovich von **Shtakelberg**
- 23 May 1905 - 7 Jun 1910: *Gen. of Inf.* Aleksandr Alekseyevich **Gerngross**
- 7 Jun 1910 - 11 Apr 1911: *Gen. of Inf.* Yakov Fyodorovich **Shkinsky**
- 26 Apr 1911 - 11 May 1912: *Gen. of Art.* Arkady Nikanorovich **Nishchenkov**
- 11 May 1912 - 3 Jul 1917: *Gen. of Cav.* Mikhail Mikhailovich **Pleshkov**

Commanding General, II. Siberian Army Corps *(Formed 1900)*
- 31 Jul 1900 - 14 Apr 1901:   *Gen. of Cav.* Aleksandr Vasiliyevich von **Kaulbars**
- 25 Apr 1901 - 2 Nov 1902:   *Gen. of Cav.* Baron Georgy Karlovich von **Shtakelberg**
- 3 Feb 1903 - 9 Jun 1906:   *Gen. of Inf.* Mikhail Ivanovich **Zasulich**
- 9 Jun 1906 - 28 Jul 1908:   *Gen. of Inf.* Vladimir Vasilievich **Smirnov**
- 14 Aug 1908 - 8 Feb 1914:   *Gen. of Art.* Eris-Khan-Sultan-Girei **Aliyev**
- 8 Feb 1914 - 8 May 1915:   *Gen. of Inf.* Arkady Valerianovich **Sychevsky**
- 8 May 1915 - 3 Jun 1915:   *Lt.-Gen.* Nikolai Yakovlevich **Lisovsky**
- 3 Jun 1915 - 11 Oct 1915:   *Gen. of Inf.* Radko Dmitrievich **Radko-Dmitriev**
- 20 Oct 1915 - 31 Mar 1917:   *Lt.-Gen.* Ivan Konstantinovich **Gandurin**

Commanding General, III. Siberian Army Corps *(Formed 1900)*
- 2 Aug 1900 - 23 Jan 1901:   *Gen. of Inf.* Sergey Nikolayevich **Mylov**
- 23 Jan 1901 - 20 Jan 1904:   DISSOLVED
- 30 Jan 1904 - 16 Jul 1905:   *Lt.-Gen.* Anatoly Mikhailovich **Stessel**
- 15 Sep 1905 - 19 Dec 1905:   *Gen. of Art.* Nikolai Iudovich **Ivanov**
- 19 Dec 1905 - 9 Jun 1906:   ?
- 9 Jun 1906 - 27 Dec 1906:   *Gen. of Cav.* Pavel Karlovich Edler von **Rennenkampf**
- 27 Dec 1906 - 30 Jul 1907:   *Lt.-Gen.* Nikolai Nikolayevich **Fleysher**
- 30 Jul 1907 - 14 Jun 1908:   ?
- 14 Jun 1908 - 1 Sep 1912:   *Gen. of Inf.* Yevgeny Aleksandrovich **Radkevich**
- 1 Sep 1912 - 21 Apr 1913:   *Gen. of Inf.* Vladimir Yegorovich **Bukholts**
- 24 Apr 1913 - 7 Aug 1914:   *Gen. of Inf.* Vladimir Petrovich **Korneyev**
- 7 Aug 1914 - 25 Apr 1915:   *Gen. of Inf.* Yevgeny Aleksandrovich **Radkevich**
- 25 Apr 1915 - 6 Apr 1917:   *Lt.-Gen.* Vladimir Onufriyevich **Trofimov**

Commanding General, IV. Siberian Army Corps *(Formed 1904)*
- 9 Feb 1904 - 26 Oct 1905:   *Gen. of Inf.* Nikolai Platonovich **Zarubayev**
- 26 Oct 1905 - 5 May 1906:   ?
- 5 May 1906 - 1910:   DISSOLVED
- Jun 1910 - 11 May 1912:   *Gen. of Art.* Vladimir Aleksandrovich von **Irman**
- 11 May 1912 - 7 Aug 1913:   *Gen. of Art.* Arkady Nikanorovich **Nishchenkov**
- 7 Aug 1913 - 8 May 1915:   *Gen. of Inf.* Sergey Sergeyevich **Savvich**
- 8 May 1915 - 1 Oct 1915:   *Gen. of Inf.* Arkady Valerianovich **Sychevsky**
- 2 Oct 1915 - 10 Apr 1917:   *Gen. of Inf.* Leonid-Otto Ottovich **Sirelius**

Commanding General, V. Siberian Army Corps *(Formed 1904)*
- 1 Jun 1904 - 5 May 1906:   *Gen. of Inf.* Leonid Matveyevich **Dembovsky**
- 5 May 1906 - 19 Jun 1910:   DISSOLVED
- 19 Jun 1910 - 7 Aug 1911:   *Gen. of Inf.* Nikolai Ivanovich **Podvalnyuk**
- 22 Sep 1911 - 28 Dec 1913:   *Gen. of Inf.* Pavel Sergeyevich **Savvich**
- 28 Dec 1913 - 8 Feb 1914:   *Gen. of Inf.* Arkady Valerianovich **Sychevsky**
- 8 Feb 1914 - 22 Dec 1914:   *Gen. of Inf.* Leonty Leontyevich **Sidorin**
- 22 Dec 1914 - 12 Apr 1917:   *Gen. of Inf.* Nikolai Mikhailovich **Voronov**

Commanding General, VI. Siberian Army Corps (Formed 1904)
- 1 Jun 1904 - 5 May 1906: *Gen. of Inf.* Leonid Nikolayevich **Sobolev**
- 5 May 1906 - 26 Sep 1914: DISSOLVED
- 26 Sep 1914 - 9 Sep 1917: *Gen. of Inf.* Fyodor Nikolayevich **Vasiliev**

Commanding General, VII. Siberian Army Corps (Formed 1905)
- 9 Nov 1905 - 9 Jun 1906: *Gen. of Cav.* Pavel Karlovich Edler von **Rennenkampf**
- 9 Jun 1905 - 17 Jun 1915: DISSOLVED
- 17 Jun 1915 - 12 Jul 1915: *Gen. of Inf.* Mikhail Rodionovich **Yerofeyev**
- 12 Jul 1915 - 11 Oct 1915: *Gen. of Inf.* Gotlib-Vilgelm Pavlovich **Rode**
- 11 Oct 1915 - 20 Mar 1916: *Gen. of Inf.* Radko Dmitrievich **Radko-Dmitriev**
- 20 Mar 1916 - Sep 1916: *Gen. of Inf.* Dmitry Aleksandrovich **Dolgov**
- 25 Oct 1916 - 18 Apr 1917: *Lt.-Gen.* Georgy Vladimirovich **Stupin**

Commanding General, I. Turkestan Army Corps (Formed 1899)
- 2 Jul 1899 - 1 Mar 1901: *Gen. of Cav.* Semyon Vasilievich **Kakhanov**
- 10 Apr 1901 - 11 Dec 1903: *Gen. of Art.* Dmitry Andreyevich **Topornin**
- 11 Dec 1903 - 14 Nov 1904: *Lt.-Gen.* Konstantin Vikentyevich **Tserpitsky**
- 14 Nov 1904 - 31 Aug 1906: *Gen. of Inf.* Yevgeny Osipovich **Matsiyevsky**
- 31 Aug 1906 - 2 Jul 1907: ?
- 2 Jul 1907 - 19 Jul 1912: *Gen. of Cav.* Pavel Aleksandrovich **Kozlovsky**
- 30 Jul 1912 - 15 Jan 1913: *Gen. of Inf.* Leonid Vilhelmovich **Lesh**
- 15 Jan 1913 - 5 Dec 1914: *Gen. of Inf.* Mikhail Rodionovich **Yerofeyev**
- 5 Dec 1914 - 4 Jun 1917: *Gen. of Cav.* Sergey Mikhailovich **Sheydeman**

Commanding General, II. Turkestan Army Corps (Formed 1899)
- 12 Jul 1899 - 19 Mar 1901: *Gen. of Inf.* Andrey Andreyevich **Bogolyubov**
- 10 Apr 1901 - 2 Nov 1902: *Lt.-Gen.* Dean Ivanovich **Subbotich**
- 14 Dec 1902 - 5 Dec 1905: *Gen. of Inf.* Yevgeny Yevgenyevich **Ussakovsky**
- 5 Dec 1905 - 16 Jun 1906: *Lt.-Gen.* Vladimir Andreyevich **Kosagovsky**
- 16 Jun 1906 - 1907: *Lt.-Gen.* Pyotr Aleksandrovich **Kartsev**
- 10 Feb 1908 - 26 Dec 1910: *Lt.-Gen.* Mikhail Dmitryevich **Yevreinov**
- 1 Jan 1911 - 1 Nov 1912: *Lt.-Gen.* Fyodor Aleksandrovich **Shostak**
- 15 Jan 1913 - 3 Feb 1915: *Gen. of Inf.* Leonid Vilhelmovich **Lesh**
- 3 Feb 1915 - 3 Apr 1917: *Gen. of Inf.* Mikhail Alekseyevich **Przhevalsky**

Commanding General, I. Cavalry Corps (Formed 1896)
- 23 Jul 1896 - 2 Nov 1902: *Gen. of Cav.* Aleksandr Mikhailovich **Lermantov**
- 2 Nov 1902 - 2 Mar 1904: *Gen. of Cav.* Baron Georgy Karlovich von **Shtakelberg**
- 11 Mar 1904 - 2 Nov 1906: *Gen. of Cav.* Nikolai Vasilyevich **Shutlevort**
- 2 Nov 1906 - Sep 1914: DISSOLVED
- 13 Oct 1914 - 31 Jan 1915: *Lt.-Gen.* Aleksandr Vasilyevich **Novikov**
- 31 Jan 1915 - 19 Apr 1917: *Gen. of Cav.* Vladimir Aloiziyevich **Oranovsky**

Commanding General, II. Cavalry Corps *(Formed 1897)*
- 28 Nov 1897 - 31 Jul 1900: *Gen. of Cav.* Aleksandr Vasiliyevich von **Kaulbars**
- 11 Aug 1900 - 27 Jun 1902: *Gen. of Cav.* Nikolai Mikhailovich **Vonlyarlyarsky**
- 27 Jun 1902 - 29 Nov 1903: ?
- 29 Nov 1903 - 23 Dec 1906: *Gen. of Cav.* Ivan Sergeyevich **Zykov**
- 23 Dec 1906 - 19 Oct 1914: DISSOLVED
- 19 Oct 1914 - 25 Oct 1915: *Gen. of Cav.* Khan Hussein **Nakhichevansky**
- 14 Nov 1915 - 8 Dec 1915: *Gen. of Cav.* Georgy Ottonovich von **Raukh**
- 4 Feb 1916 - 19 Jan 1917: *Lt.-Gen.* Grand Duke Mikhail Alexandrovich **Romanov**
- 8 Feb 1917 - 2 Apr 1917: *Lt.-Gen.* Vladimir Khristoforovich **Roop**

Commanding General, III. Cavalry Corps *(Formed 1915)*
- 3 Apr 1915 - 7 Apr 1917: *Gen. of Cav.* Count Fyodor Arturovich **Keller**

Commanding General, IV. Cavalry Corps *(Formed 1915)*
- 13 May 1915 - Jan 1918: *Lt.-Gen.* Yakov Fyodorovich von **Gillenshmidt**

Commanding General, V. Cavalry Corps *(Formed 1915)*
- 3 Nov 1915 - Oct 1917: *Gen. of Cav.* Leonid Nikolayevich **Velyashev**

Commanding General, VI. Cavalry Corps *(Formed 1915)*
- 17 Nov 1915 - 25 Apr 1917: *Lt.-Gen.* Aleksandr Aleksandrovich **Pavlov**

Commanding General, I. Caucasus Cavalry Corps *(Formed 1916)*
- 28 Apr 1916 - 24 Mar 1917: *Gen. of Cav.* Nikolai Nikolayevich **Baratov**

Commanding General, II. Caucasus Cavalry Corps *(Formed 1916)*
- 4 Jul 1916 - 15 Feb 1917: *Lt.-Gen.* Fyodor Grigoryevich **Chernozubov**

DIVISIONS & BRIGADES

(Infantry Divisions typically comprised two Infantry Brigades and an Artillery Brigade; Cavalry Divisions were composed of two Cavalry Brigades and a Horse Artillery Battalion. For the purposes of this section, Brigades that were assigned to Divisions are listed immediately below their parent Division.)

Commander, 1st Guards Infantry Division
- 11 Sep 1889 - 29 Mar 1897:   *Lt.-Gen.* Prince Nikolai Nikolayevich **Obolensky**
- 7 Apr 1897 - 12 May 1898:   *Gen. of Inf.* Oskar Kazimirovich von **Grippenberg**
- 12 May 1898 - 24 Aug 1898:   *Lt.-Gen.* Georgy Robertovich **Vasmund**
- 24 Aug 1898 - 15 Nov 1901:   *Gen. of Inf.* Georgy Ivanovich **Bobrikov**
- 15 Nov 1901 - 11 Dec 1902:   *Lt.-Gen.* Aleksandr Aleksandrovich **Yevreinov**
- 1 Feb 1903 - 14 Apr 1904:   *Lt.-Gen.* Count German Germanovich **Stenbok-Fermor**
- 14 Apr 1904 - 1 Aug 1905:   *Gen. of Inf.* Baron Anton Yegorovich von **Zaltsa**
- 9 Sep 1905 - 21 Jun 1906:   *Lt.-Gen.* Sergey Sergeyevich **Ozerov**
- 21 Jun 1906 - 26 Aug 1908:   *Gen. of Inf.* Platon Alekseyevich **Lechitsky**
- 26 Aug 1908 - 21 May 1912:   *Gen. of Art.* Iosif Ivanovich **Mrozovsky**
- 30 May 1912 - 28 Dec 1914:   *Gen. of Inf.* Vladimir Apollonovich **Olokhov**
- 16 Jan 1915 - 3 Jul 1915:   *Lt.-Gen.* Aleksandr Antonovich **Gertsyk**
- 3 Jul 1915 - 25 Apr 1917:   *Lt.-Gen.* Vladimir Vladimirovich von **Notbek**

Commander, 1st Brigade, 1st Guards Infantry Division
- 24 Nov 1894 - 2 Sep 1899:   *Gen. of Inf.* Ivan Sergeyevich **Maltsov**
- 2 Sep 1899 - 17 Feb 1900:   *Lt.-Gen.* Vladimir Vasilyevich **Pensky**
- 25 Apr 1900 - 18 Dec 1900:   *Lt.-Gen.* Andrey Ivanovich **Chekmarev**
- 7 Feb 1901 - 1902:   *Maj.-Gen.* Aleksandr Nikolayevich **Ogarev**
- 1902 - 20 Oct 1904:   ?
- 20 Oct 1904 - 6 Feb 1906:   *Gen. of Inf.* Baron Karl Fyodorovich **Langhoff**
- 18 Feb 1906 - 10 Jul 1908:   *Gen. of Inf.* Leonid-Otto Ottovich **Sirelius**
- 10 Jul 1908 - 30 May 1912:   *Gen. of Inf.* Andrei Medardovich **Zayonchkovsky**
- 30 May 1912 - 3 Apr 1915:   *Lt.-Gen.* Leopold Fridrikhovich von der **Brinken**
- 22 Apr 1915 - 21 Aug 1916:   *Maj.-Gen.* Konstantin Aleksandrovich **Goltgoyer**
- 21 Aug 1916 - 16 Apr 1917:   *Maj.-Gen.* Count Nikolai Nikolayevich **Ignatyev**

Commander, 2nd Brigade, 1st Guards Infantry Division
- 14 May 1893 - 21 May 1898: *Lt.-Gen.* Aleksandr Aleksandrovich **Yevreinov**
- 21 May 1898 - 25 Apr 1900: *Lt.-Gen.* Andrey Ivanovich **Chekmarev**
- 25 Apr 1900 - 27 Aug 1900: ?
- 27 Aug 1900 - 26 Mar 1903: *Gen. of Inf.* Nikolai Akimovich **Pavlovsky**
- 26 Mar 1903 - 23 Jan 1904: ?
- 23 Jan 1904 - Apr 1907: *Lt.-Gen.* Konstantin Adrianovich **Rudanovsky**
- 2 May 1907 - 10 Aug 1908: *Maj.-Gen.* Vladimir Vladimirovich **Belov**
- 10 Aug 1908 - 19 Jul 1914: *Lt.-Gen.* Aleksandr Antonovich **Gertsyk**
- 19 Jul 1914 - 2 Mar 1917: ?

Commander, Life Guards 1st Artillery Brigade
- 19 Dec 1890 - 9 Nov 1895: *Lt.-Gen.* Aleksandr Trofimovich **Baumgarten**
- 13 Nov 1895 - 14 Feb 1899: *Gen. of Art.* Timofey Mikhailovich **Belyayev**
- 16 Mar 1899 - 3 Mar 1904: *Maj.-Gen.* Nikolai Nikolayevich **Lyapunov**
- 3 Mar 1904 - 2 Jul 1908: *Lt.-Gen.* Mikhail Georgyevich Duke of **Mecklenburg-Strelitsky**
- 3 Jul 1908 - 25 Jul 1910: *Lt.-Gen.* Aleksei Dmitrievich **Golovachev**
- 25 Jul 1910 - 13 Nov 1914: *Lt.-Gen.* Nikolai Petrovich **Demidov**
- 22 Nov 1914 - 27 Feb 1917: *Maj.-Gen.* Yevgeny Vladimirovich **Ponomarevsky-Svidersky**

Commander, 2nd Guards Infantry Division
- 7 Mar 1891 - 21 Feb 1895: *Lt.-Gen.* Stepan Vasilyevich **Rykachev**
- 10 Mar 1895 - 7 Jan 1897: *Gen. of Inf.* Yulian Viktorovich **Lyubovitsky**
- 15 Jan 1897 - 4 Aug 1899: *Lt.-Gen.* Richard Troyanovich von **Meves**
- 13 Sep 1899 - 27 Sep 1900: *Lt.-Gen.* Yevgeny Mikhailovich **Bibikov**
- 20 Oct 1900 - 7 Jun 1904: *Gen. of Inf.* Nikolai Fyodorovich **Meshetich**
- 21 Jun 1904 - 25 Nov 1905: *Gen. of Inf.* Vladimir Ioannikiyevich **Trotsky**
- 25 Nov 1905 - 21 Jun 1906: *Gen. of Inf.* Vladimir Nikolayevich **Danilov**
- 21 Jun 1906 - 9 Jan 1907: *Gen. of Inf.* Ivan Andreyevich **Romanenko**
- 10 Jan 1907 - 24 Jun 1908: *Gen. of Inf.* Aleksandr Aleksandrovich **Adlerberg**
- 24 Jun 1908 - 30 Apr 1910: *Gen. of Inf.* Nikolai Petrovich **Mikhnevich**
- 3 May 1910 - 30 Jul 1912: *Gen. of Inf.* Leonid Vilhelmovich **Lesh**
- 30 Jul 1912 - 12 Jan 1913: *Gen. of Inf.* Vasily Yegorovich **Flug**
- 19 Jan 1913 - 4 Nov 1914: *Lt.-Gen.* Aleksandr Alekseyevich **Resin**
- 4 Nov 1914 - 16 Dec 1914: *Lt.-Gen.* Vladimir Mikhailovich **Dragomirov**
- 27 Dec 1914 - 21 Aug 1916: *Gen. of Art.* Pavel Platonovich **Pototsky**
- 21 Aug 1916 - 9 Apr 1917: *Maj.-Gen.* Konstantin Aleksandrovich **Goltgoyer**

Commander, 1st Brigade, 2nd Guards Infantry Division
- 22 Nov 1893 - 19 Jul 1895: *Lt.-Gen.* Pyotr Petrovich von **Enden**
- 2 Nov 1895 - 24 Nov 1899: *Gen. of Inf.* Pyotr Petrovich **Loginov**
- 31 Nov 1899 - 17 Feb 1900: *Gen. of Inf.* Aleksey Iosifovich **Dzichkanets**
- 17 Feb 1900 - 14 May 1901: ?
- 14 May 1901 - 1 Jun 1904: *Lt.-Gen.* Konstantin Petrovich **Tyrtov**
- 2 Jun 1904 - 23 Jan 1905: *Gen. of Inf.* Nikolai Appolonovich **Pykhachev**
- 18 Feb 1905 - 13 Nov 1907: *Lt.-Gen.* Baron Yevgeny Emilyevich **Fitingof**
- 13 Nov 1907 - 11 Feb 1908: ?
- 11 Feb 1908 - 24 Sep 1913: *Gen. of Inf.* Aleksandr Nikolayevich **Poretsky**
- 24 Sep 1913 - 24 Dec 1913: *Lt.-Gen.* Aleksandr Nestorovich **Chebykin**
- 24 Dec 1913 - 4 Nov 1914: *Lt.-Gen.* Nikolai Mikhailovich **Kiselevsky**
- 4 Nov 1914 - 9 Jan 1915: *Lt.-Gen.* Konstantin Gerasimovich **Nekrasov**
- 9 Jan 1915 - 2 Mar 1917: ?

Commander, 2nd Brigade, 2nd Guards Infantry Division
- 10 Jan 1894 - 14 Aug 1895: ?
- 14 Aug 1895 - 13 Sep 1899: *Lt.-Gen.* Yevgeny Mikhailovich **Bibikov**
- 13 Sep 1899 - 16 Feb 1900: ?
- 16 Feb 1900 - 4 Mar 1903: *Lt.-Gen.* Aleksandr Aleksandrovich von **Lizarkh-Kenigk**
- 10 May 1903 - 21 Jun 1904: *Gen. of Inf.* Vladimir Ioannikiyevich **Trotsky**
- 16 Jul 1904 - 2 Sep 1904: *Lt.-Gen.* Konstantin Adolfovich **Yelita von Volsky**
- 2 Sep 1904 - 23 May 1905: *Gen. of Inf.* Pavel Andreyevich **Smorodsky**
- 23 May 1905 - 8 Jun 1905: *Lt.-Gen.* Konstantin Adolfovich **Yelita von Volsky**
- 8 Jun 1905 - 1 Oct 1905: *Gen. of Inf.* Pavel Andreyevich **Smorodsky**
- 1 Oct 1905 - 2 Nov 1907: *Lt.-Gen.* Konstantin Adolfovich **Yelita von Volsky**
- 17 Nov 1907 - 19 Jan 1913: *Lt.-Gen.* Vladimir Dmitrievich **Bakulin**
- 19 Jan 1913 - 13 Apr 1913: *Lt.-Gen.* Pyotr Alekseyevich **Delsal**
- 13 Apr 1913 - 19 Jul 1914: *Lt.-Gen.* Vladimir Apollonovich **Kozlov**
- 19 Jul 1914 - 2 Mar 1917: ?

Commander, Life Guards 2nd Artillery Brigade
- 7 Aug 1888 - 29 Aug 1895: *Gen. of Art.* Aleksandr Vasilyevich **Onopriyenko**
- 29 Aug 1895 - 13 Nov 1895: *Gen. of Art.* Timofey Mikhailovich **Belyayev**
- 13 Nov 1895 - 9 Feb 1901: *Gen. of Art.* Aleksandr Vladimirovich **Utkevich**
- 9 Feb 1901 - 20 Jun 1901: *Lt.-Gen.* Aleksandr Ivanovich **Kolenkin**
- 20 Jun 1901 - 23 Oct 1904: *Gen. of Art.* Arkady Nikanorovich **Nishchenkov**
- 24 Oct 1904 - 14 Nov 1907: *Lt.-Gen.* Sergey Vasilyevich **Ivashentsov**
- 21 Nov 1907 - 14 Nov 1909: *Lt.-Gen.* Vladimir Andreyevich **Lyakhovich**
- 14 Nov 1909 - 27 May 1910: *Gen. of Art.* Ivan Karlovich **Baggovut**
- 30 May 1910 - 21 Mar 1913: *Lt.-Gen.* Aleksandr Fyodorovich von **Gillenshmidt**
- 21 Mar 1913 - 7 Apr 1915: *Lt.-Gen.* Aleksandr Mikhailovich **Sivers**
- 19 Apr 1915 - 27 Apr 1917: *Maj.-Gen.* Aleksandr Fyodorovich **Akkerman**

Commander, 3rd Guards Infantry Division
- 9 Aug 1894 - 2 Apr 1898: *Gen. of Inf.* Count Dmitry Yegorovich **Komarovsky**
- 8 May 1898 - 19 Mar 1901: *Gen. of Inf.* Konstantin Aleksandrovich **Veys**
- 16 Jun 1901 - 10 Feb 1904: *Gen. of Inf.* Baron Aleksandr Nikolayevich **Meller-Zakomelsky**
- 25 Jul 1904 - 2 Feb 1908: *Gen. of Inf.* Pyotr Dmitriyevich **Olkhovsky**
- 21 Feb 1908 - 7 Jun 1910: *Gen. of Inf.* Yakov Fyodorovich **Shkinsky**
- 11 Jun 1910 - 18 Aug 1914: *Gen. of Inf.* Leonid-Otto Ottovich **Sirelius**
- 16 Sep 1914 - 25 Aug 1917: *Lt.-Gen.* Vsevolod Vladimirovich **Chernavin**

Commander, 1st Brigade, 3rd Guards Infantry Division
- 4 Feb 1891 - 8 Feb 1895: *Gen. of Inf.* Konstantin Aleksandrovich **Veys**
- 5 Apr 1895 - 28 Oct 1899: *Gen. of Inf.* Dmitry Modestovich **Rezvy**
- 28 Oct 1899 - 1 Feb 1900: ?
- 1 Feb 1900 - 3 Aug 1900: *Lt.-Gen.* Prince David Luarsabovich **Argutinsky-**

- 3 Aug 1900 - 27 Jan 1901:   Dolgorukov
- 3 Aug 1900 - 27 Jan 1901:   *Lt.-Gen.* Mikhail Alekseyevich **Pashkov**
- 22 Mar 1901 - 2 May 1903:   *Lt.-Gen.* Prince David Luarsabovich **Argutinsky-Dolgorukov**
- 9 Jun 1903 - 24 Nov 1904:   *Lt.-Gen.* Vasily Aleksandrovich **Narbut**
- 10 Jan 1905 - 10 Oct 1909: *Lt.-Gen.* Viktor Aleksandrovich **Gedlund**
- 7 Nov 1909 - Aug 1914:   *Maj.-Gen.* Konstantin Andreyevich **Lyubarsky**
- 7 Oct 1914 - 12 May 1915:   *Lt.-Gen.* Baron Nikolai Andreyevich de **Bode**
- 24 Jun 1915 - 24 Jan 1916: *Lt.-Gen.* Konstantin Konstantinovich **Shildbakh**
- 24 Jan 1916 - 2 Mar 1917:   ?

Commander, 2nd Brigade, 3rd Guards Infantry Division
- 4 Feb 1891 - 15 Sep 1895:   *Gen. of Inf.* Yakov Aleksandrovich **Grebenshchikov**
- 12 Oct 1895 - 8 Jun 1899:   *Gen. of Inf.* Ivan Aleksandrovich **Fullon**
- 8 Jun 1899 - 3 Aug 1900:   ?
- 3 Aug 1900 - 22 Mar 1901:   *Lt.-Gen.* Prince David Luarsabovich **Argutinsky-Dolgorukov**
- 22 Mar 1901 - 7 Dec 1904:   *Gen. of Inf.* Aleksandr Mikhailovich **Butakov**
- 10 Jan 1905 - 22 Feb 1907: *Lt.-Gen.* Pyotr Petrovich **Domozhirov**
- 27 Feb 1907 - 10 May 1907: *Lt.-Gen.* Alfred-Stanislav Vasilievich von **Bekker**
- 10 May 1907 - 25 Aug 1907: *Lt.-Gen.* Stepan Aleksandrovich **Voronin**
- 25 Aug 1907 - 19 May 1908: *Lt.-Gen.* Alfred-Stanislav Vasilievich von **Bekker**
- 31 Aug 1908 - 13 Feb 1909: *Gen. of Inf.* Vladimir Apollonovich **Olokhov**
- 4 Mar 1909 - 3 May 1910:   *Lt.-Gen.* Aleksandr Alekseyevich **Resin**
- 3 May 1910 - 19 Jul 1914:   *Lt.-Gen.* Vsevolod Vladimirovich **Chernavin**
- 19 Jul 1914 - Aug 1915:   ?
- Aug 1915 - 5 Jan 1916:   *Lt.-Gen.* Boris Viktorovich **Adamovich**
- 5 Jan 1916 - 2 Mar 1917:   ?

Commander, Life Guards 3rd Artillery Brigade
- 30 Jan 1885 - 1 Feb 1895:   *Gen. of Art.* Vladimir Konstantinovich **Martyushev**
- 1 Feb 1895 - 16 Nov 1896:   *Lt.-Gen.* Gavriil Gavrilovich **Mikhailov**
- 30 Dec 1896 - 5 Dec 1899:   *Gen. of Art.* Vladimir Stepanovich **Usov**
- 29 Dec 1899 - 6 Jan 1903:   *Gen. of Art.* Vladimir Ivanovich **Gippius**
- 6 Apr 1903 - 8 Jun 1906:   *Gen. of Art.* Count Mikhail Aleksandrovich **Barantsov**
- 21 Jun 1906 - 13 Oct 1907: *Lt.-Gen.* Iosif Feliksovich **Mingin**
- 13 Oct 1907 - 12 Nov 1910: *Lt.-Gen.* Mikhail Dmitriyevich **Shreyder**
- 12 Nov 1910 - 18 Dec 1913: *Gen. of Art.* Count Viktor Viktorovich **Dolivo-Dobrovolsky-Yevdokimov**
- 18 Dec 1913 - 12 May 1916: *Maj.-Gen.* Andrey Vladimirovich **Burman**
- 12 May 1916 - 29 Apr 1917: *Maj.-Gen.* Mikhail Nikolayevich **Papa-Fedorov**

Commander, 1st Grenadier Division
- 2 May 1891 - 1 Jan 1898:   *Gen. of Inf.* Aleksandr Karlovich **Vodar**
- 10 Jan 1898 - 7 Jun 1898:   *Gen. of Inf.* Aleksandr Nikolayevich **Popov**

- 4 Jul 1898 - 16 Jan 1902: *Lt.-Gen.* Fyodor Pavlovich **Laskovsky**
- 23 Jan 1902 - 6 Feb 1903: *Gen. of Inf.* Konstantin Faddeyevich **Krshivitsky**
- 26 Mar 1903 - 19 May 1906: *Gen. of Inf.* Nikolai Akimovich **Pavlovsky**
- 19 May 1906 - 9 Nov 1912: *Gen. of Inf.* Nikolai Vasilyevich **Osipov**
- 17 Nov 1912 - 29 Jul 1915: *Lt.-Gen.* Aleksandr Ivanovich **Postovsky**
- 29 Jul 1915 - 11 Sep 1916: *Lt.-Gen.* Grigory Yefimovich **Yanushevsky**
- 18 Sep 1916 - 1 Oct 1917: *Maj.-Gen.* Pavel Stepanovich **Stayev**

Commander, 1st Brigade, 1st Grenadier Division
- 7 May 1893 - 29 Jan 1901: *Lt.-Gen.* Aleksandr Ignatyevich **Kossovich**
- 14 Feb 1901 - May 1904: *Maj.-Gen.* Nikolai Vasilyevich **Korshunov**
- 5 Jul 1904 - 2 Jul 1908: *Lt.-Gen.* Nikolai Ivanovich **Govorov**
- 12 Jul 1908 - 21 Dec 1908: *Maj.-Gen.* Ilya Yakovlevich **Kulnev**
- 15 Jan 1909 - 14 Jan 1913: *Lt.-Gen.* Aleksey Maksimovich **Rebinder**
- 14 Jan 1913 - 29 Jul 1914: *Maj.-Gen.* Ivan Alekseyevich **Kholmsen**
- 29 Jul 1914 - 2 Mar 1917: ?

Commander, 2nd Brigade, 1st Grenadier Division
- 14 Oct 1894 - 25 Apr 1901: *Lt.-Gen.* Baron Stepan Fyodorovich von **Rozen**
- 25 Apr 1901 - 14 Mar 1905: *Maj.-Gen.* Yakov Nikolayevich **Gukov**
- 22 Mar 1905 - 30 Apr 1905: *Gen. of Inf.* Vladimir Nikolayevich **Gorbatovsky**
- 7 Jun 1905 - 13 May 1910: *Lt.-Gen.* Matvey Nikolayevich **Frish**
- 13 May 1910 - 3 Apr 1915: *Lt.-Gen.* Boris Alekseyevich **Dzichkanets**
- 3 Apr 1915 - 19 Sep 1916: *Maj.-Gen.* Kaetan-Boleslav Vladislavovich **Olshevsky**
- 19 Sep 1916 - 2 Mar 1917: ?

Commander, 1st Grenadier Artillery Brigade
- 23 Feb 1893 - 30 Jan 1895: *Gen. of Art.* Konstantin Petrovich **Fan-der-Flit**
- 10 Mar 1895 - 31 Jan 1900: *Lt.-Gen.* Aleksey Pavlovich **Surazhevsky**
- 1 Mar 1900 - 31 Oct 1903: *Gen. of Art.* Andrei Adamovich **Atabekov**
- 13 Nov 1903 - 23 Apr 1907: *Maj.-Gen.* Nikolai Petrovich **Andreyev**
- 23 Apr 1907 - 3 Jul 1908: *Gen. of Art.* Nikolai Ilyich **Bulatov**
- 3 Jul 1908 - 16 Jan 1909: ?
- 16 Jan 1909 - 28 Jul 1913: *Lt.-Gen.* Ivan Vasilyevich **Kubarovsky**
- 7 Aug 1913 - 1 Oct 1914: *Gen. of Art.* Vladimir Petrovich **Mamontov**
- 11 Oct 1914 - 31 May 1917: *Maj.-Gen.* Nikolai Nikolayevich **Belkovich**

Commander, 2nd Grenadier Division
- 2 Aug 1894 - 31 May 1898: *Gen. of Inf.* Iosif-Ignatiy Onufriyevich **Kvitsinsky**
- 9 Jul 1898 - Jun 1906: *Gen. of Inf.* Sergey Sergeyevich **Buturlin**
- 4 Jul 1906 - 29 Dec 1908: *Lt.-Gen.* Lev Ivanovich **Ignatyev**
- 29 Dec 1908 - 26 Apr 1911: *Gen. of Art.* Arkady Nikanorovich **Nishchenkov**
- 1 May 1911 - 9 Dec 1915: *Lt.-Gen.* Nikolai Grigoryevich **Stavrovich**
- 9 Dec 1915 - 23 Jun 1917: *Gen. of Inf.* Vasily Yepifanovich **Sklyarevsky**

Commander, 1st Brigade, 2nd Grenadier Division
- 16 Feb 1894 - 6 Nov 1895:   *Maj.-Gen.* Aleksandr Yakovlevich **Lyapunov**
- 30 Nov 1895 - 13 Sep 1899:   *Gen. of Inf.* Mikhail Ivanovich **Zasulich**
- 31 Oct 1899 - 28 Dec 1904:   *Maj.-Gen.* Yevgeny Mikhailovich **Stolitsa**
- 14 Jan 1905 - 28 Mar 1907:   *Maj.-Gen.* Ivan Dmitriyevich **Khodnev**
- 28 Mar 1907 - 31 Dec 1913:   *Lt.-Gen.* Sergey Dmitriyevich **Mikhno**
- 31 Dec 1913 - 3 May 1914:   *Lt.-Gen.* Aleksandr Ivanovich **Chaplygin**
- 3 May 1914 - 2 Mar 1917:   ?

Commander, 2nd Brigade, 2nd Grenadier Division
- 18 Jan 1893 - 14 Apr 1902:   *Lt.-Gen.* Konstantin Ivanovich **Smirnsky**
- 10 Mar 1902 - 28 Apr 1906:   *Lt.-Gen.* Semyon Ivanovich **Nikonov**
- 5 May 1906 - 9 Nov 1907:   *Gen. of Inf.* Mikhail Nikiforovich **Kaygorodov**
- 28 Nov 1907 - 30 Jan 1915:   *Lt.-Gen.* Vladimir Ivanovich **Malinka**
- 30 Jan 1915 - 2 Mar 1917:   ?

Commander, 2nd Grenadier Artillery Brigade
- 19 Oct 1892 - Dec 1899:   *Maj.-Gen.* Leonid Nikolayevich **Platonov**
- 1 Jan 1900 - 27 Feb 1900:   *Maj.-Gen.* Vilgelm Kaetanovich **Ivanovsky**
- 29 Mar 1900 - 3 Oct 1902:   *Maj.-Gen.* Vladimir Yakovlevich **Chersky**
- 3 Oct 1902 - 20 May 1906:   *Maj.-Gen.* Georgy Aleksandrovich von **Glazenap**
- 20 May 1906 - 12 Sep 1907:   *Gen. of Inf.* Vladimir Alekseyevich **Slyusarenko**
- 12 Sep 1907 - 17 Dec 1908:   *Maj.-Gen.* Aleksey Nikolayevich **Tarkhov**
- 17 Dec 1908 - 25 Jul 1910:   *Lt.-Gen.* Aleksandr Yakovlevich **Petunin**
- 25 Jul 1910 - 31 May 1912:   *Maj.-Gen.* Aleksandr Ivanovich **Semenov**
- 31 May 1912 - 25 Mar 1914:   *Lt.-Gen.* Dmitry Alekseyevich **Davydov**
- 9 Apr 1914 - 19 Nov 1914:   *Maj.-Gen.* Ivan Grigoryevich **Kopestynsky**
- 19 Nov 1914 - 28 Dec 1914:   *Maj.-Gen.* Vasily Illarionovich **Levachev**
- 15 Jan 1915 - 18 May 1917:   *Maj.-Gen.* Vladimir Fyodorovich **Sozanovich**

Commander, 3rd Grenadier Division
- 30 Jul 1894 - 27 Dec 1894:   *Lt.-Gen.* Aleksandr Ivanovich **Manykin-Nevstruyev**
- 18 Jan 1895 - 3 Jun 1898:   *Gen. of Inf.* Mikhail Troyanovich von **Meves**
- 18 Aug 1898 - 25 Apr 1900:   *Lt.-Gen.* Dmitry Nikolayevich **Gets**
- 13 Oct 1900 - 1 Feb 1903:   *Lt.-Gen.* Count German Germanovich **Stenbok-Fermor**
- 10 Feb 1903 - 1 Jun 1905:   *Lt.-Gen.* Leonty Vasilyevich **Gaponov**
- 8 Jun 1905 - 15 Apr 1909:   *Gen. of Inf.* Pyotr Petrovich **Yakovlev**
- 8 May 1909 - 9 May 1914:   *Gen. of Inf.* Vladimir Nikolayevich **Gorbatovsky**
- 9 May 1914 - 19 Sep 1914:   *Lt.-Gen.* Filipp Nikolayevich **Dobryshin**
- 19 Sep 1914 - 4 Nov 1914:   *Lt.-Gen.* Vladislav Frantsevich **Baufal**
- 4 Nov 1914 - 23 Aug 1916:   *Lt.-Gen.* Nikolai Mikhailovich **Kiselevsky**
- 9 Sep 1916 - 29 May 1917:   *Lt.-Gen.* Aleksandr Ivanovich **Berezovsky**

Commander, 1st Brigade, 3rd Grenadier Division
- 18 Dec 1888 - 17 Sep 1896: *Lt.-Gen.* Orest Mikhailovich **Kislinsky**
- 27 Sep 1896 - 28 May 1899: *Lt.-Gen.* Fyodor Aleksandrovich **Dyubyuk**
- 4 Jun 1899 - 24 Oct 1899: *Gen. of Inf.* Dmitry Sergeyevich **Buturlin**
- 24 Oct 1899 - 3 Jun 1903: *Maj.-Gen.* Aleksandr Grigoryevich **Matveyenko**
- 3 Jun 1903 - 7 Mar 1905: *Maj.-Gen.* Georgy Yakovlevich **Meyer**
- 28 May 1905 - 4 Nov 1906: *Maj.-Gen.* Baron Nikolai Ottonovich **Rebinder**
- 4 Nov 1906 - 3 Feb 1907: *Maj.-Gen.* Aleksandr Yakovlevich **Mardanov**
- 3 Feb 1907 - 6 Jan 1911: *Lt.-Gen.* Nikolai Antonovich **Dumbadze**
- 13 Jan 1911 - 17 Sep 1911: *Maj.-Gen.* Aleksandr Vasilyevich **Bozheryanov**
- 14 Oct 1911 - 31 Dec 1913: *Lt.-Gen.* Aleksandr Ivanovich **Chaplygin**
- 14 Jan 1914 - 12 Mar 1915: *Maj.-Gen.* Mikhail Viktorovich **Khartulari**
- 12 Mar 1915 - 2 Mar 1917: ?

Commander, 2nd Brigade, 3rd Grenadier Division
- 20 Dec 1892 - 2 Apr 1899: *Lt.-Gen.* Fyodor Aleksandrovich **Avinov**
- 28 Apr 1899 - 22 May 1901: *Gen. of Inf.* Pyotr Timofeyevich **Redkin**
- 2 Jun 1901 - 7 Jun 1907: *Lt.-Gen.* Aksel Fridrikhovich von **Kruzenshtern**
- 25 Jun 1907 - Dec 1908: *Maj.-Gen.* Vladimir Mikhailovich **Voronov**
- 11 Jan 1909 - 19 Jul 1914: *Lt.-Gen.* Pyotr Matveyevich **Zakharov**
- 1 Aug 1914 - 13 Jan 1915: *Maj.-Gen.* Dmitry Petrovich **Kadomsky**
- 13 Jan 1915 - 3 Feb 1917: ?
- 3 Feb 1917 - 4 Sep 1917: *Maj.-Gen.* Viktor Ivanovich **Gavrilov**

Commander, 3rd Grenadier Artillery Brigade
- 7 Aug 1888 - 10 Mar 1895: *Lt.-Gen.* Aleksey Pavlovich **Surazhevsky**
- 14 Mar 1895 - 14 Jun 1899: *Maj.-Gen.* Sergey Konstantinovich **Vogak**
- 14 Jun 1899 - 22 Jun 1902: *Lt.-Gen.* Kondraty Kallistratovich **Kondratsky**
- 22 Jun 1902 - 30 Mar 1904: *Maj.-Gen.* Pyotr Petrovich **Potulov**
- 30 Mar 1904 - 2 May 1904: *Lt.-Gen.* Pyotr Vasilyevich **Sukhinsky**
- 2 May 1904 - Dec 1905: *Maj.-Gen.* Ivan Vasilievich **Bukin**
- 14 Jan 1906 - 16 Oct 1906: *Lt.-Gen.* Aleksandr Reyngoldovich **Meyster**
- 4 Nov 1906 - 24 May 1910: *Lt.-Gen.* Nikolai Ivanovich **Kurakin**
- 4 Jun 1910 - 11 Jul 1912: *Lt.-Gen.* Yevgeny Konstantinovich **Smyslovsky**
- 5 Aug 1912 - 24 Jun 1915: *Lt.-Gen.* Nikolai Andreyevich **Ilkevich**
- 24 Jun 1915 - 8 Jun 1917: *Maj.-Gen.* Sergey Vasilyevich **Rudnev**

Commander, 4th Grenadier Division *(Formed in 1917)*
- 1917 - 2 Mar 1917: ?

Commander, 5th Grenadier Division *(Formed in 1917)*
- 7 Feb 1917 - 12 May 1917: *Lt.-Gen.* Mikhail Mitrofanovich **Stavrov**

Commander, 6th Grenadier Division *(Formed in 1917)*
- 18 Feb 1917 - 23 Jul 1917: *Maj.-Gen.* Roman Ivanovich **Dubinin**

Commander, Caucasus Grenadier Division
- 31 Mar 1893 - 11 Jun 1897: *Gen. of Inf.* Abunard Eduardovich **Zezeman**
- 15 Sep 1897 - 30 Dec 1903: *Gen. of Inf.* Grand Duke Nikolai Mikhailovich **Romanov**
- 25 Jan 1904 - 11 Nov 1904: *Gen. of Inf.* Dmitry Aleksandrovich **Odintsov**
- 7 Dec 1904 - 15 Mar 1906: *Lt.-Gen.* Vasily Osipovich **Rylsky**
- 20 Apr 1906 - 10 Feb 1908: *Lt.-Gen.* Mikhail Dmitryevich **Yevreinov**
- 3 Mar 1908 - 7 Dec 1908: *Lt.-Gen.* Aleksandr Stepanovich **Mikheyev**
- 2 Feb 1909 - 15 Jan 1913: *Gen. of Inf.* Mikhail Rodionovich **Yerofeyev**
- 31 Jan 1913 - 24 Apr 1913: *Gen. of Inf.* Vladimir Petrovich **Korneyev**
- 1 May 1913 - 8 Jun 1915: *Gen. of Inf.* Vladimir Pavlovich **Shatilov**
- 5 Jul 1915 - 31 Aug 1916: *Lt.-Gen.* Vasily Davidovich **Gabayev**
- 9 Nov 1916 - 15 Apr 1917: *Lt.-Gen.* Aleksandr Fyodorovich **Dobryshin**

Commander, 1st Brigade, Caucasus Grenadier Division
- 26 Feb 1894 - 24 Nov 1899: *Lt.-Gen.* Ignaty Antonovich **Kozlovsky**
- 24 Nov 1899 - 4 Dec 1901: *Lt.-Gen.* Vasily Osipovich **Rylsky**
- 4 Jan 1902 - 20 Nov 1904: *Maj.-Gen.* Mikhail Vasilyevich **Martynov**
- 22 Nov 1904 - 19 Feb 1908: *Lt.-Gen.* Ivan Aleksandrovich **Snarsky**
- 19 Feb 1908 - 30 Mar 1913: *Lt.-Gen.* Vasily Davidovich **Gabayev**
- 3 Apr 1913 - 19 Jul 1914: *Lt.-Gen.* Konstantin Lukich **Gilchevsky**
- 19 Jul 1914 - 2 Mar 1917: ?

Commander, 2nd Brigade, Caucasus Grenadier Division
- 16 Feb 1894 - 24 Nov 1899: *Maj.-Gen.* Konstantin Fyodorovich **Starikov**
- 24 Nov 1899 - 17 Dec 1900: *Lt.-Gen.* Ignaty Antonovich **Kozlovsky**
- 17 Dec 1900 - 11 Mar 1906: *Maj.-Gen.* Aleksandr Akimovich **Sakhnovsky**
- 11 Mar 1906 - 8 Aug 1907: *Gen. of Inf.* Sigizmund Viktorovich **Volsky**
- 29 Sep 1907 - 3 Feb 1910: *Lt.-Gen.* Nikolai Ivanovich **Gavrilov**
- 3 Feb 1910 - 7 Dec 1912: *Lt.-Gen.* Aleksandr Nikolayevich **Kuzmin-Korovayev**
- 16 Jan 1913 - 22 Apr 1915: *Lt.-Gen.* Konstantin Nikolayevich **Bekov**
- 22 Apr 1915 - 2 Feb 1916: ?
- 2 Feb 1916 - 29 Nov 1916: *Maj.-Gen.* Lukyan Vasilievich **Afanasyev**
- 29 Nov 1916 - 2 Mar 1917: ?

Commander, Caucasus Grenadier Artillery Brigade
- 11 Oct 1889 - 9 Feb 1897: *Maj.-Gen.* Eduard Pavlovich von **Gering**
- 9 Feb 1897 - 13 Apr 1899: *Gen. of Art.* Prince Georgy Spiridonovich **Khimshiyev**
- 21 Apr 1899 - Aug 1904: *Maj.-Gen.* Nikolai Arkadyevich **Makarov**
- 3 Sep 1904 - 5 Jul 1910: *Lt.-Gen.* Vladimir Nikolayevich **Chikalin**
- 25 Jul 1910 - 23 Oct 1912: *Maj.-Gen.* Dmitry Pavlovich **Aseyev**
- 29 Nov 1912 - 7 May 1915: *Lt.-Gen.* Ivan Aleksandrovich **Karpovich**

- 27 Jun 1915 - 12 May 1916:   *Maj.-Gen.* Mikhail Nikolayevich **Papa-Fedorov**
- 12 May 1916 - 1917:   *Maj.-Gen.* Ivan Nikolayevich **Kazbek**

Commander, 1st Infantry Division
- 24 Aug 1892 - 9 Jan 1900:   *Lt.-Gen.* Mikhail Mikhailovich **Shulgin**
- 17 Feb 1900 - 12 Sep 1904:   *Lt.-Gen.* Vladimir Vasilyevich **Pensky**
- 28 Dec 1904 - 19 Jan 1906:   *Maj.-Gen.* Yevgeny Mikhailovich **Stolitsa**
- 19 Jan 1906 - 29 May 1907:   *Gen. of Inf.* Fyodor Kononovich **Bogutsky**
- 21 Jun 1907 - 16 Jun 1910:   *Gen. of Inf.* Dmitry Petrovich **Zuyev**
- 2 Jul 1910 - 17 Aug 1914:   *Lt.-Gen.* Andrey Aleksandrovich **Ugryumov**
- 2 Dec 1914 - 2 Jan 1915:   *Maj.-Gen.* Pyotr Nikolayevich **Kareyev**
- 2 Jan 1915 - 18 May 1917:   *Maj.-Gen.* Luka Lukich **Kondratovich**

Commander, 1st Brigade, 1st Infantry Division
- 12 Sep 1892 - 9 Oct 1899:   *Lt.-Gen.* Vasily Nikolayevich **Borodin**
- 24 Oct 1899 - 27 Aug 1903:   *Maj.-Gen.* Aleksandr Yegorovich **Dubyago**
- 11 Sep 1903 - 14 Jan 1905:   *Maj.-Gen.* Ivan Dmitriyevich **Khodnev**
- 14 Jan 1905 - 21 May 1910:   *Maj.-Gen.* Vladimir Petrovich **Devi**
- 21 May 1910 - 19 Jul 1914:   *Maj.-Gen.* Nikolai Ksenofontovich **Boldyrev**
- 4 Nov 1914 - 2 Dec 1914:   *Maj.-Gen.* Pyotr Nikolayevich **Kareyev**
- 2 Dec 1914 - 5 Apr 1916:   ?
- 5 Apr 1916 - 18 May 1917:   *Maj.-Gen.* Silvestr Konstantinovich **Zhukovsky**

Commander, 2nd Brigade, 1st Infantry Division
- 26 Feb 1894 - 12 Aug 1902:   *Lt.-Gen.* Aleksandr Karlovich **Pol**
- 16 Sep 1902 - 14 Nov 1906:   *Maj.-Gen.* Pyotr Aleksandrovich **Korvin-Piotrovsky**
- 14 Nov 1906 - 21 Dec 1908:   *Maj.-Gen.* Vladimir Petrovich **Yakubinsky**
- 7 Jan 1909 - 19 Jul 1914:   *Lt.-Gen.* Mikhail Ivanovich **Chizhov**
- 29 Jul 1914 - 18 Aug 1914:   *Maj.-Gen.* Afanasy Semyonovich **Saychuk**
- 18 Aug 1914 - 2 Mar 1917:   ?

Commander, 1st Artillery Brigade
- 13 Jul 1892 - 20 Nov 1897:   *Maj.-Gen.* Vladimir Nikolayevich **Yaroshev**
- 20 Nov 1897 - 19 Jan 1901:   *Maj.-Gen.* Lyudvig-Severin Ivanovich **Shukevich**
- 24 Feb 1901 - 12 Jun 1906:   *Lt.-Gen.* Vladimir Danilovich **Bodzento-Belyatsky**
- 27 Jun 1906 - 21 Nov 1907:   *Maj.-Gen.* Vladimir Petrovich **Mezentsov**
- 21 Nov 1907 - 30 Apr 1910:   *Lt.-Gen.* Dmitry Aleksandrovich **Razvadovsky**
- 30 Apr 1910 - 30 Apr 1912:   *Maj.-Gen.* Ivan Fyodorovich **Oguretsky**
- 19 May 1912 - Aug 1914:   *Lt.-Gen.* Pyotr Aleksandrovich **Polzikov**
- Aug 1914 - 18 Aug 1914:   *Colonel* Aleksandr Aleksandrovich **Khristinich**
- 18 Aug 1914 - 14 Mar 1916:   ?
- 14 Mar 1916 - 1917:   *Lt.-Gen.* Pyotr Aleksandrovich **Polzikov**

Commander, 2nd Infantry Division
- 5 Oct 1892 - 28 Feb 1897:   *Gen. of Inf.* Vasily Ivanovich **Markozov**
- 1 Mar 1897 - 8 May 1898:   *Lt.-Gen.* Baron Ferdinand Ferdinandovich von **Taube**
- 8 May 1898 - 27 Apr 1903:   *Gen. of Inf.* Nikolai Yulievich **Akerman**
- 4 May 1903 - 12 Aug 1903:   *Lt.-Gen.* Anatoly Mikhailovich **Stessel**
- 15 Sep 1903 - 2 Aug 1904:   *Gen. of Inf.* Pavel Aleksandrovich von **Layming**
- 2 Sep 1904 - 6 Feb 1907:   *Lt.-Gen.* Georgy Ivanovich **Peshchansky**
- 27 Feb 1907 - 1 Sep 1912:   *Gen. of Inf.* Aleksandr Aleksandrovich **Blagoveshchensky**
- 20 Sep 1912 - 17 Aug 1914:   *Lt.-Gen.* Iosif Feliksovich **Mingin**
- 27 Sep 1914 - 15 Apr 1917:   *Lt.-Gen.* Vladimir Mikhailovich **Vasiliev**

Commander, 1st Brigade, 2nd Infantry Division
- 26 Feb 1894 - 10 Apr 1901:   *Maj.-Gen.* Viktor Valentiyevich **Zavadsky**
- 23 Apr 1901 - 6 Apr 1907:   *Maj.-Gen.* Aleksey Aleksandrovich **Tyunegov**
- 6 Apr 1907 - 29 Nov 1911:   *Lt.-Gen.* Ivan Vasilyevich **Kolpikov**
- 2 Dec 1911 - 3 Aug 1914:   *Lt.-Gen.* Aleksandr Aleksandrovich **Arkhipov**
- 3 Aug 1914 - 7 Mar 1915:   *Lt.-Gen.* Iosif Ilich **Regulsky**
- 7 Mar 1915 - 2 Mar 1917:   ?

Commander, 2nd Brigade, 2nd Infantry Division
- 25 Jan 1893 - 18 Oct 1896:   *Maj.-Gen.* Nikolai Gustavovich **Zelgeym**
- 18 Oct 1896 - 23 Feb 1898:   *Maj.-Gen.* Aleksandr Aleksandrovich **Broterus**
- 4 Mar 1898 - 31 Oct 1899:   *Maj.-Gen.* Stepan Osipovich **Kurch**
- 31 Oct 1899 - 1 Feb 1900:   *Lt.-Gen.* Vasily Aleksandrovich **Narbut**
- 15 Feb 1900 - Apr 1903:   *Lt.-Gen.* Arseny Irodionovich **Aknov**
- 30 Apr 1903 - 11 Dec 1903:   *Lt.-Gen.* Andrei Dmitriyevich **Vsevolozhsky**
- 11 Dec 1903 - 15 Mar 1914:   *Lt.-Gen.* Iosif Ilich **Regulsky**
- 22 Mar 1914 - 13 Aug 1914:   *Maj.-Gen.* Germogen Semyonovich **Aksenov**
- 13 Aug 1914 - 2 Mar 1917:   ?

Commander, 2nd Artillery Brigade
- 5 Sep 1894 - 29 Oct 1899:   *Maj.-Gen.* Nikolai Stepanovich **Lazarev**
- 29 Dec 1899 - 2 Mar 1905:   *Gen. of Art.* Vladimir Nikolayevich von **Zavatsky**
- 8 Apr 1905 - 18 Mar 1906:   *Colonel* Nikolai Vasilyevich **Mikhailov**
- 18 Mar 1906 - 14 Nov 1906:   *Maj.-Gen.* Vladimir Afanasyevich **Prokhorovich**
- 14 Nov 1906 - 22 Apr 1907:   ?
- 22 Apr 1907 - 29 May 1910:   *Maj.-Gen.* Yevgeny Eduardovich **Gripenberg**
- 4 Jun 1910 - 17 Aug 1914:   *Maj.-Gen.* Lev Fedorovich **Gartung**
- 17 Aug 1914 - 22 Dec 1914:   ?
- 22 Dec 1914 - 26 Mar 1917:   *Maj.-Gen.* Vasily Nikolayevich **Danilov**

Commander, 3rd Infantry Division
- 29 Apr 1892 - 8 May 1900:   *Gen. of Inf.* Aleksey Fyodorovich **Ozerov**
- 19 May 1900 - 8 Apr 1904:   *Gen. of Inf.* Viktor Karlovich **Aspelund**

- 8 Apr 1904 - 15 Feb 1905:   Lt.-Gen. Nikolai Ivanovich **Yanzhul**
- 15 Feb 1905 - 11 Jan 1906:   ?
- 11 Jan 1906 - 22 Sep 1910:   Gen. of Inf. Nikolai Aleksandrovich **Orlov**
- 22 Sep 1910 - 13 Nov 1914:   Gen. of Inf. Pyotr Vladimirovich **Polzikov**
- 13 Nov 1914 - 17 Jun 1916:   Gen. of Art. Nikolai Ilyich **Bulatov**
- 13 Jul 1916 - 18 Apr 1917:   Maj.-Gen. Aleksandr Gustavovich **Sholp**

Commander, 1st Brigade, 3rd Infantry Division
- 3 Mar 1891 - 8 Dec 1894:   Maj.-Gen. Nikolai Vasilyevich **Verevkin**
- 8 Dec 1894 - 29 Jan 1901:   Gen. of Inf. Nikolai Pavlovich **Debogory-Mokriyevich**
- 9 Feb 1901 - 9 Mar 1905:   Lt.-Gen. Leonid Iosifovich **Zashchuk**
- 9 Mar 1905 - 18 Aug 1905:   Gen. of Inf. Vladimir Vladimirovich **De-Vitt**
- 18 Aug 1905 - 13 Jan 1906:   Lt.-Gen. Polikarp Alekseyevich **Kuznetsov**
- 14 Mar 1906 - 17 Feb 1907:   Gen. of Inf. Vladimir Vasilyevich **Bolotov**
- 12 Mar 1907 - 24 Apr 1909:   Maj.-Gen. Vladimir Nikolayevich **Snezhkov**
- 24 Apr 1909 - 19 Jul 1914:   Gen. of Inf. Leonid Nikolayevich **Belkovich**
- 19 Jul 1914 - 2 Mar 1917:   ?

Commander, 2nd Brigade, 3rd Infantry Division
- 9 Jul 1891 - 9 Aug 1897:   Lt.-Gen. Nikolai Nikolayevich **Vishnevsky**
- 18 Aug 1897 - 30 Mar 1900:   Lt.-Gen. Nikolai Emmanuilovich **Miloradovich**
- 4 Apr 1900 - 23 Jul 1902:   Lt.-Gen. Nikolai Fyodorovich **Rediger**
- 2 Nov 1902 - 20 Aug 1905:   Maj.-Gen. Vladimir Petrovich **Yakubinsky**
- 12 Dec 1905 - 13 Jul 1906:   Maj.-Gen. Nikolai Aleksandrovich **Voronov**
- 11 Aug 1906 - 28 Mar 1907:   Lt.-Gen. Sergey Dmitriyevich **Mikhno**
- 29 Apr 1907 - 16 Nov 1911:   Lt.-Gen. Fyodor Konstantinovich **Yazvin**
- 8 Dec 1911 - 3 May 1913:   Maj.-Gen. Nikolai Yakovlevich **Ivanov**
- 3 May 1913 - 19 Jul 1914:   Lt.-Gen. Aleksandr Semyonovich **Ogloblev**
- 19 Jul 1914 - 2 Mar 1917:   ?

Commander, 3rd Artillery Brigade
- 3 Mar 1891 - 27 Sep 1895:   Gen. of Art. Mikhail Karlovich **Mazing**
- 15 Oct 1895 - 5 Dec 1899:   Lt.-Gen. Yevgraf Yevgrafovich **Stogov**
- 29 Dec 1899 - 29 Dec 1900:   Maj.-Gen. Nikolai Ivanovich **Sokhansky**
- 4 Jan 1901 - 28 Apr 1903:   Maj.-Gen. Aleksandr Vladimirovich **Shashurin**
- 5 Jun 1903 - 2 Jul 1905:   Lt.-Gen. Ilya Petrovich **Gribunin**
- 2 Jul 1905 - 23 Nov 1908:   Gen. of Art. Valerian Mikhailovich **Gaitenov**
- 23 Nov 1908 - 24 Jan 1909:   Lt.-Gen. Nikolai Aloiziyevich **Oranovsky**
- 24 Jan 1909 - 27 Oct 1909:   Maj.-Gen. Aleksey Grigoryevich **Pashchenko**
- 23 Nov 1909 - 27 Jun 1913:   Lt.-Gen. Prince Mikhail Mikhailovich **Kantakuzen**
- 8 Jul 1913 - 29 Sep 1916:   Maj.-Gen. Ivan Ivanovich **Zhavoronkov**
- 29 Sep 1916 - 3 May 1917:   Maj.-Gen. Vladimir Aleksandrovich **Bankovsky**

Commander, 4th Infantry Division
- 11 Aug 1891 - 16 Feb 1896: *Lt.-Gen.* Mikhail Petrovich **Samokhvalov**
- 21 Feb 1896 - 26 Jul 1899: *Gen. of Inf.* Yakov Aleksandrovich **Grebenshchikov**
- 5 Aug 1899 - 9 Mar 1900: *Gen. of Inf.* Ivan Aleksandrovich **Fullon**
- 20 Mar 1900 - 24 Sep 1901: *Gen. of Inf.* Pyotr Nikolayevich **Bazhenov**
- 24 Nov 1901 - 10 Dec 1902: *Gen. of Inf.* Nikolai Pavlovich **Shatilov**
- 10 Dec 1902 - 18 Apr 1903: *Gen. of Inf.* Vladimir Yegorovich **Bukholts**
- 17 May 1903 - 6 Apr 1907: *Lt.-Gen.* Aleksey Vasiliyevich **Fedorov**
- 6 Apr 1907 - 15 May 1912: *Gen. of Inf.* Ippolit Paulinovich **Voyshin-Murdas-Zhilinsky**
- 7 Jun 1912 - 26 Aug 1914: *Gen. of Inf.* Nikolai Nikolayevich **Komarov**
- 6 Sep 1914 - 29 Sep 1915: *Lt.-Gen.* Gavriil Georgyevich **Mileant**
- 17 Oct 1915 - 9 Aug 1916: *Lt.-Gen.* Viktor Fyodorovich **Bauder**
- 12 Aug 1916 - 15 Apr 1917: *Lt.-Gen.* Avgust Aleksandrovich **Dmitriev**

Commander, 1st Brigade, 4th Infantry Division
- 21 Jun 1894 - 14 Oct 1894: *Lt.-Gen.* Baron Stepan Fyodorovich von **Rozen**
- 14 Oct 1894 - 24 Mar 1895: ?
- 24 Mar 1895 - 18 Sep 1897: *Lt.-Gen.* Nikolai Lvovich **Boltin**
- 18 Sep 1897 - 4 Mar 1898: *Maj.-Gen.* Stepan Osipovich **Kurch**
- 4 Mar 1898 - 28 Nov 1898: *Maj.-Gen.* Nikolai Petrovich **Ignatyev**
- 28 Nov 1898 - 9 Oct 1899: *Maj.-Gen.* Mikhail Nikitich **Mazyukevich**
- 24 Oct 1899 - 20 Dec 1899: *Maj.-Gen.* Ivan Fyodorovich **Levental**
- 18 Jan 1900 - 14 Dec 1902: *Maj.-Gen.* Aleksandr Georgiyevich **Nazarov**
- 20 Jan 1903 - 5 Mar 1905: *Lt.-Gen.* Ivan Ioasafovich **Yevreinov**
- 11 Apr 1905 - 1 Apr 1911: *Lt.-Gen.* Ivan Vladimirovich **Karpov**
- 1 Apr 1911 - 18 Sep 1912: *Lt.-Gen.* Nikolai Grigoryevich **Filimonov**
- 19 Sep 1912 - 29 Jul 1914: *Maj.-Gen.* Genrikh Aleksandrovich **Savich-Zablotsky**
- 29 Jul 1914 - Nov 1914: ?
- Nov 1914 - 22 Dec 1914: *Lt.-Gen.* Vilgelm-Karl Kasperovich von **Nordgeym**
- 22 Dec 1914 - 2 Mar 1917: ?

Commander, 2nd Brigade, 4th Infantry Division
- 28 Oct 1891 - 28 Nov 1898: *Maj.-Gen.* Mikhail Nikitich **Mazyukevich**
- 28 Nov 1898 - 23 Jun 1899: *Maj.-Gen.* Nikolai Petrovich **Ignatyev**
- 23 Jun 1899 - 8 Apr 1902: *Gen. of Inf.* Yevgeny Petrovich **Vishnyakov**
- 22 Jul 1902 - 20 Jan 1903: *Lt.-Gen.* Ivan Ioasafovich **Yevreinov**
- 20 Jan 1903 - Apr 1904: *Maj.-Gen.* Prokofy Semyonovich **Tyshkevich**
- 1 Jun 1904 - 12 Nov 1907: *Maj.-Gen.* Mikhail Alekseyevich **Tyumenkov**
- 12 Nov 1907 - 23 Jul 1911: *Lt.-Gen.* Vladimir Konstantinovich **Solonina**
- 23 Jul 1911 - 25 Aug 1915: *Lt.-Gen.* Aleksandr Dmitriyevich **Nechvolodov**
- 25 Aug 1915 - 2 Mar 1917: ?

Commander, 4th Artillery Brigade
- 7 Oct 1893 - 20 Jul 1899: *Maj.-Gen.* Nikolai Gustavovich **Enkel**
- 29 Dec 1899 - 15 Sep 1902: *Maj.-Gen.* Ivan Timofeyevich **Semplikevich**

- 5 Oct 1902 - 28 Oct 1906: *Maj.-Gen.* Aleksandr Yakovlevich **Lebedinets**
- 22 Apr 1907 - 27 Feb 1908: *Maj.-Gen.* Aleksandr Aleksandrovich **Krasyuk**
- 27 Feb 1908 - 21 Dec 1908: *Maj.-Gen.* Nikolai Petrovich **Shatilov**
- 16 Jan 1909 - 8 Jul 1913: *Maj.-Gen.* Konstantin Petrovich **Chervinov**
- 8 Jul 1913 - 27 Sep 1914: *Maj.-Gen.* Stepan Stepanovich **Chizh**
- 6 Nov 1914 - 18 Feb 1917: *Maj.-Gen.* Mikhail Mikhailovich **Sedelnikov**
- 18 Feb 1917 - 2 Mar 1917: ?

Commander, 5th Infantry Division
- 30 Nov 1892 - 17 Dec 1897: *Lt.-Gen.* Fyodor Fyodorovich **Golubev**
- 19 Dec 1897 - 30 May 1901: *Gen. of Inf.* Prince Georgy Yevseyevich **Tumanov**
- 4 Jul 1901 - 23 Dec 1904: *Lt.-Gen.* Yevgeny Nikolayevich **Kakurin**
- 10 Jan 1905 - 21 May 1908: *Gen. of Inf.* Dmitry Savelyevich **Shuvayev**
- 10 Jun 1908 - 31 Dec 1913: *Gen. of Inf.* Andrey Aleksandrovich **Perekrestov**
- 31 Dec 1913 - 15 May 1916: *Lt.-Gen.* Pavel Antonovich **Parchevsky**
- 21 May 1916 - 18 Aug 1916: *Lt.-Gen.* Pavel Andreyevich **Nikitin**
- 2 Sep 1916 - 15 Oct 1917: *Lt.-Gen.* Adam Ivanovich **Slavochinsky**

Commander, 1st Brigade, 5th Infantry Division
- 25 Oct 1889 - 6 Apr 1895: *Maj.-Gen.* Nikolai Dmitriyevich **Ivanov**
- 10 Apr 1895 - 4 Dec 1895: *Lt.-Gen.* Pavel Pavlovich **Dyagilev**
- 4 Dec 1895 - 4 Mar 1896: *Maj.-Gen.* Konstantin Mikhailovich **Akinfiyev**
- 4 Mar 1896 - 2 May 1896: *Lt.-Gen.* Aleksandr Aleksandrovich **Larionov**
- 2 May 1896 - 6 May 1901: *Lt.-Gen.* Lev Matveyevich **Baykov**
- 11 May 1901 - 28 Jun 1901: *Maj.-Gen.* Iosif Ivanovich **Gorsky**
- 28 Jun 1901 - 12 Nov 1907: *Maj.-Gen.* Andrey Andreyevich **Siversky**
- 12 Nov 1907 - 8 Jan 1909: *Maj.-Gen.* Mikhail Demyanovich **Fedotov**
- 15 Jan 1909 - 8 Oct 1913: *Lt.-Gen.* Aleksandr Andreyevich **Tsitsovich**
- 8 Oct 1913 - 5 Dec 1913: *Maj.-Gen.* Dmitry Petrovich **Kadomsky**
- 31 Dec 1913 - 29 Jul 1914: *Maj.-Gen.* Dmitry Ivanovich **Shevandin**
- 29 Jul 1914 - 9 Jul 1915: ?
- 9 Jul 1915 - 7 Feb 1917: *Maj.-Gen.* Konstantin Vladimirovich **Nikolsky**
- 8 Feb 1917 - 20 May 1917: *Maj.-Gen.* Konstantin Nikolayevich **Alyanchikov**

Commander, 2nd Brigade, 5th Infantry Division
- 19 Nov 1891 - 11 Oct 1899: *Maj.-Gen.* Karl Genrikhovich **Keller**
- 31 Oct 1899 - 14 Apr 1900: *Maj.-Gen.* Stepan Osipovich **Kurch**
- 26 Apr 1900 - 20 Jun 1906: *Maj.-Gen.* Sergey Nikolayevich **Urnizhevsky**
- 13 Jul 1906 - 30 Jun 1907: *Maj.-Gen.* Nikolai Aleksandrovich **Voronov**
- 30 Jun 1907 - 17 Aug 1913: *Lt.-Gen.* German Fyodorovich **Gershelman**
- 17 Aug 1913 - 20 May 1915: *Lt.-Gen.* Torsten Karlovich **Vadensherna**
- 20 May 1915 - 2 Mar 1917: ?

Commander, 5th Artillery Brigade
- 12 Oct 1892 - 9 Feb 1898:   *Maj.-Gen.* Slavomir Nikodimovich **Olshanovsky**
- 27 Feb 1898 - 13 May 1899:   *Maj.-Gen.* Dmitry Grigoryevich **Stoletov**
- 14 Jun 1899 - 15 Jun 1902:   *Maj.-Gen.* Nikolai Aleksandrovich **Studzitsky**
- 22 Jun 1902 - 26 Apr 1904:   *Lt.-Gen.* Kondraty Kallistratovich **Kondratsky**
- 26 Apr 1904 - 13 Aug 1905:   *Colonel* Sergey Yakovlevich **Zhelvinsky**
- 13 Aug 1905 - 15 Apr 1910:   *Maj.-Gen.* Vladimir Gavrilovich **Ivanovsky**
- 30 Apr 1910 - 24 Apr 1913:   *Lt.-Gen.* Dmitry Aleksandrovich **Razvadovsky**
- 24 Apr 1913 - 11 Feb 1915:   *Maj.-Gen.* Sergey Arkadyevich **Voyno-Oransky**
- 11 Feb 1915 - 11 Jan 1916:   *Maj.-Gen.* Vasily Aleksandrovich **Linevich**
- 11 Jan 1916 - 2 May 1916:   *Maj.-Gen.* Isai Isaevich **Akimov**
- 12 May 1916 - 1918:   *Maj.-Gen.* Mikhail Sergeyevich **Roslyakov**

Commander, 6th Infantry Division
- 2 Nov 1892 - 9 Jan 1900:   *Gen. of Inf.* Vladimir Petrovich **Golokhvastov**
- 13 Apr 1900 - 3 Feb 1903:   *Gen. of Inf.* Mikhail Ivanovich **Zasulich**
- 4 Mar 1903 - 8 Apr 1904:   *Lt.-Gen.* Aleksandr Aleksandrovich von **Lizarkh-Kenigk**
- 2 May 1904 - 11 Apr 1909:   *Gen. of Inf.* Pavel Fyodorovich **Klauz**
- 8 May 1909 - 9 Apr 1910:   *Gen. of Inf.* Georgy Aleksandrovich **Zmetnov**
- Jul 1910 - 17 Oct 1910:   *Lt.-Gen.* Mikhail Emerikovich **Valitsky**
- 17 Oct 1910 - 31 Oct 1914:   *Gen. of Inf.* Fyodor-Emily-Karl Ivanovich von **Torklus**
- 21 Dec 1914 - 25 Apr 1917:   *Lt.-Gen.* Konstantin Konstantinovich **Baiov**

Commander, 1st Brigade, 6th Infantry Division
- 23 Jul 1894 - 4 Sep 1896:   *Lt.-Gen.* Sergey Ivanovich **Klyucharev**
- 6 Sep 1896 - 24 Oct 1899:   *Maj.-Gen.* Vilgelm Eduardovich **Yelita von Volsky**
- 24 Oct 1899 - 16 Apr 1903:   *Gen. of Inf.* Vladimir Fyodorovich **Ozharovsky**
- 20 Apr 1903 - 8 Nov 1904:   *Lt.-Gen.* Ignaty Fyodorovich **Kazakevich**
- 27 Nov 1904 - 6 Jun 1907:   *Lt.-Gen.* Aleksandr Nikanorovich **Anikeyev**
- 6 Jul 1907 - 16 Jul 1913:   *Lt.-Gen.* Konstantin Ivanovich **Bussov**
- 16 Jul 1913 - 15 Aug 1914:   *Maj.-Gen.* Sergey Petrovich **Ilinsky**
- 6 Oct 1914 - 29 Jan 1917:   *Maj.-Gen.* Illarion Ivanovich **Gruzintsev**
- 29 Jan 1917 - 2 Mar 1917:   ?

Commander, 2nd Brigade, 6th Infantry Division
- 19 Oct 1892 - 21 Dec 1897:   *Maj.-Gen.* Aleksandr Alekseyevich **Rossysky**
- 14 Jan 1898 - 23 Jul 1898:   *Maj.-Gen.* Aleksandr Yevgrafovich **Baranov**
- 23 Jul 1898 - 16 Mar 1904:   *Maj.-Gen.* Konstantin Ivanovich **Chekmarev**
- 4 Apr 1904 - 13 May 1906:   *Maj.-Gen.* Aleksandr Khristianovich **Stradovsky**
- 15 May 1906 - 17 Oct 1910:   *Lt.-Gen.* Pavel Vladimirovich **Tarnagursky**
- 17 Oct 1910 - 31 Dec 1913:   *Lt.-Gen.* Pavel Antonovich **Parchevsky**
- 14 Jan 1914 - 29 Jul 1914:   *Maj.-Gen.* Prince Ilya Zakharovich **Makayev**
- 29 Jul 1914 - 2 Jan 1915:   ?
- 2 Jan 1915 - 11 Jan 1915:   *Maj.-Gen.* Aleksandr Ivanovich **Kamberg**

- 11 Jan 1915 - 2 Mar 1917: ?

Commander, 6th Artillery Brigade
- 30 Jan 1893 - 9 Apr 1897: *Maj.-Gen.* Ivan Vasilyevich **Rklitsky**
- 9 Apr 1897 - 11 Aug 1900: *Lt.-Gen.* Mark Semyonovich **Vorotnikov**
- 11 Aug 1900 - 2 Mar 1904: *Maj.-Gen.* Anatoly Vasilievich **Venyukov**
- 2 Mar 1904 - 25 Mar 1905: *Lt.-Gen.* Mikhail Mikhailovich **Krayevsky**
- 25 Mar 1905 - 24 Aug 1907: *Maj.-Gen.* Georgy Fyodorovich **Sergeyev**
- 24 Aug 1907 - 13 Jan 1910: *Lt.-Gen.* Aleksandr Valentinovich **De-Roberti**
- 5 Feb 1910 - 5 Sep 1912: *Maj.-Gen.* Koloman Ferdinandovich **Poganko**
- 23 Sep 1912 - 27 Jul 1913: *Lt.-Gen.* Sergey Apollonovich **Perfilyev**
- 30 Aug 1913 - 6 Nov 1914: *Maj.-Gen.* Filaret Lavrentyevich **Semenchuk**
- 6 Nov 1914 - 9 Feb 1915: *Lt.-Gen.* Karl-Nikolai Karlovich von **Lezedov**
- 13 Feb 1915 - 12 May 1916: *Maj.-Gen.* Ivan Grigoryevich **Kopestynsky**
- 12 May 1916 - Nov 1917: *Maj.-Gen.* Ruben Avetikovich **Pozoyev**

Commander, 7th Infantry Division
- 28 Apr 1894 - 7 Aug 1900: *Gen. of Inf.* Ivan Yakovlevich **Shelkovnikov**
- 10 Aug 1900 - 22 Jul 1902: *Gen. of Inf.* Ivan Platonovich **Pototsky**
- 12 Aug 1902 - 2 Nov 1904: *Lt.-Gen.* Aleksandr Karlovich **Pol**
- 7 Dec 1904 - 30 Dec 1913: *Gen. of Inf.* Aleksandr Mikhailovich **Butakov**
- 31 Dec 1913 - 29 May 1916: *Lt.-Gen.* Sergey Dmitriyevich **Mikhno**
- 29 May 1916 - 18 Apr 1917: *Lt.-Gen.* Rihard-Kirill Frantsevich **Valter**

Commander, 1st Brigade, 7th Infantry Division
- 10 Sep 1894 - 16 Jan 1901: *Maj.-Gen.* Allan Gustavovich **Ramzay**
- 7 Feb 1901 - 12 Mar 1905: *Maj.-Gen.* Nikolai Mikhailovich **Arbuzov**
- 2 Apr 1905 - 20 Feb 1906: *Lt.-Gen.* Viktor Pavlovich **Zykov**
- 27 Feb 1906 - 6 May 1910: *Lt.-Gen.* Mechislav Iosif Lyutsianovich **Sivitsky**
- 12 May 1910 - 16 Jan 1915: *Maj.-Gen.* Pyotr Andreyevich **Tikhonovich**
- 16 Jan 1915 - 2 Mar 1917: ?

Commander, 2nd Brigade, 7th Infantry Division
- 13 Jun 1891 - 22 Jun 1898: *Lt.-Gen.* Pyotr Yeremeyevich **Agapeyev**
- 4 Jul 1898 - 3 Aug 1900: *Lt.-Gen.* Bruno Albertovich **Vitte**
- 10 Aug 1900 - 7 Feb 1901: *Maj.-Gen.* Vladimir Ustinovich **Sollogub**
- 7 Feb 1901 - 22 Mar 1901: *Lt.-Gen.* Andrei Dmitriyevich **Vsevolozhsky**
- 23 Apr 1901 - 28 Jun 1901: *Maj.-Gen.* Andrey Andreyevich **Siversky**
- 28 Jun 1901 - 30 Nov 1904: *Maj.-Gen.* Iosif Ivanovich **Gorsky**
- 2 Jan 1905 - 2 Apr 1905: *Lt.-Gen.* Viktor Pavlovich **Zykov**
- 14 Jul 1905 - 5 Jan 1907: *Maj.-Gen.* Konstantin Porfirievich **Andreyev**
- 5 Jan 1907 - 5 Apr 1914: *Lt.-Gen.* Nikolai Yakovlevich **Zhdanovich**
- 25 Apr 1914 - 29 Jul 1914: *Lt.-Gen.* Yevgeny Matveyevich **Osipov**
- 29 Jul 1914 - 2 Mar 1917: ?

Commander, 7th Artillery Brigade
- 30 Jul 1888 - Apr 1897: *Maj.-Gen.* Mikhail Ilich **Butovich**
- 9 Apr 1897 - 29 Oct 1899: *Maj.-Gen.* Ivan Vasilyevich **Rklitsky**
- 29 Dec 1899 - 15 Feb 1905: *Lt.-Gen.* Vladimir Ildefonsovich **Volkovitsky**
- 15 Feb 1905 - 10 Oct 1908: *Gen. of Art.* Aleksandr Ivanovich **Teodorovich**
- 23 Nov 1908 - 13 May 1910: *Maj.-Gen.* Afanasy Vasilyevich **Brilevich**
- 13 May 1910 - 30 May 1910: *Lt.-Gen.* Andrey Vasilyevich **Ivashintsov**
- 30 May 1910 - 25 Jul 1910: *Lt.-Gen.* Nikolai Petrovich **Demidov**
- 25 Jul 1910 - 21 Feb 1915: *Lt.-Gen.* Aleksandr Yevstafyevich **Gorbachevich**
- 10 Mar 1915 - 29 Apr 1917: *Maj.-Gen.* Leonard-Vilgelm Genrikhovich **Skersky**

Commander, 8th Infantry Division
- 19 Aug 1894 - 29 Feb 1900: *Gen. of Inf.* Viktor Magnusovich **Kursel**
- 20 Mar 1900 - 9 Feb 1904: *Gen. of Inf.* German Berntovich **Prokope**
- 16 Mar 1904 - 3 Jun 1906: *Lt.-Gen.* Nikolai Grigoryevich **Mikhailov**
- 3 Jun 1906 - 1 Oct 1907: *Gen. of Inf.* Eduard Vladimirovich **Ekk**
- 13 Nov 1907 - 17 Aug 1914: *Lt.-Gen.* Baron Yevgeny Emilyevich **Fitingof**
- 21 Dec 1914 - 5 Jul 1915: *Lt.-Gen.* Eduard Arkadyevich **Kolyankovsky**
- 25 Aug 1915 - 18 Apr 1917: *Lt.-Gen.* Aleksey Alekseyevich **Prigorovsky**

Commander, 1st Brigade, 8th Infantry Division
- 26 Jan 1894 - 14 Jan 1898: *Maj.-Gen.* Aleksandr Yevgrafovich **Baranov**
- 14 Jan 1898 - 14 Jan 1900: *Maj.-Gen.* Leonid Andreyevich **Kokin**
- 15 Feb 1900 - 23 Apr 1901: *Maj.-Gen.* Aleksey Petrovich **Kashperov**
- 23 Apr 1901 - 16 Jul 1901: *Lt.-Gen.* Nikolai Aleksandrovich **Znosko-Borovsky**
- 23 Jul 1901 - 25 Jan 1904: *Maj.-Gen.* Mikhail Nilovich **Esaulov**
- 25 Jan 1904 - 14 Jan 1905: *Maj.-Gen.* Vladimir Petrovich **Devi**
- 21 May 1905 - 15 Dec 1908: *Lt.-Gen.* Nikolai Pavlovich **Gryaznov**
- 15 Jan 1909 - 7 Apr 1911: *Maj.-Gen.* Shaykhil-Islam-Mukhammed Gireyevich **Chanyshev**
- 7 Apr 1911 - 22 Aug 1914: *Maj.-Gen.* Adam Ivanovich **Bogatsky**
- 22 Aug 1914 - 2 Oct 1914: *Maj.-Gen.* Fyodor Fyodorovich **Novitsky**
- 2 Oct 1914 - 27 Aug 1915: ?
- 27 Aug 1915 - 6 Dec 1917: *Maj.-Gen.* Stanislav-Silvestr Onufriyevich **Surin**

Commander, 2nd Brigade, 8th Infantry Division
- 10 Feb 1891 - 4 Nov 1896: *Maj.-Gen.* Pyotr Petrovich **Printz**
- 11 Nov 1896 - 5 Feb 1897: *Lt.-Gen.* Nikolai Grigoryevich **Chernyayev**
- 12 Mar 1897 - 2 Feb 1900: *Lt.-Gen.* Zakhar Tselestinovich **Tarnovsky**
- 16 Mar 1900 - 17 Mar 1906: *Maj.-Gen.* Nikolai Mikhailovich **Dubrova**
- 17 Mar 1906 - 23 Dec 1906: *Maj.-Gen.* Viktor Nikolayevich **Mozgalevsky**
- 8 Jan 1907 - 4 Mar 1913: *Lt.-Gen.* Ivan Ivanovich **Zarako-Zarakovsky**
- 21 Mar 1913 - Aug 1914: *Lt.-Gen.* Dmitry Mikhailovich **Dernov**
- Aug 1914 - 12 Nov 1914: ?
- 12 Nov 1914 - 25 Aug 1915: *Lt.-Gen.* Aleksey Alekseyevich **Prigorovsky**

- 25 Aug 1915 - 2 Mar 1917:   ?

Commander, 8th Artillery Brigade
- 19 Oct 1893 - 29 Oct 1899:   *Maj.-Gen.* Pavel Arkadyevich **Sedletsky**
- 29 Dec 1899 - 11 Aug 1902:   *Maj.-Gen.* Pavel Grigoryevich **Lisunov**
- 11 Aug 1902 - 3 Mar 1904:   *Maj.-Gen.* Khristian Petrovich **Grenkvist**
- 3 Mar 1904 - 17 May 1905:   *Lt.-Gen.* Nikolai Vladimirovich **Bernikov**
- 17 May 1905 - 2 Sep 1907:   *Maj.-Gen.* Konstantin Nikolayevich **Rostovtsov**
- 2 Sep 1907 - 9 Jul 1914:   *Lt.-Gen.* Vladimir Albertovich **Zedergolm**
- 9 Jul 1914 - 15 Nov 1914:   *Colonel* Dmitry Georgiyevich **Savitsky**
- 15 Nov 1914 - 1917:   *Maj.-Gen.* Andrey Aleksandrovich **Enin**

Commander, 9th Infantry Division
- 2 Jun 1894 - 9 Jan 1900:   *Gen. of Inf.* Pavel Petrovich **Kazansky**
- 28 Feb 1900 - 24 Dec 1903:   *Gen. of Inf.* Nikolai Platonovich **Zarubayev**
- 12 Jan 1904 - 2 May 1904:   *Lt.-Gen.* Georgy Vasilyevich von **Poppen**
- 2 May 1904 - 17 Jan 1906:   *Gen. of Inf.* Sergey Konstantinovich **Gershelman**
- 27 Feb 1906 - 4 Nov 1906:   *Maj.-Gen.* Pyotr Vasilyevich **Polkovnikov**
- 22 Nov 1906 - 22 Feb 1907:   *Lt.-Gen.* Lev Ignatyevich **Kossovich**
- 22 Feb 1907 - 9 Apr 1910:   *Lt.-Gen.* Pyotr Petrovich **Domozhirov**
- 9 Apr 1910 - 29 Jun 1912:   *Gen. of Inf.* Georgy Aleksandrovich **Zmetnov**
- 29 Jun 1912 - 13 Oct 1914:   *Gen. of Inf.* Vladislav Napoleonovich **Klembovsky**
- 13 Oct 1914 - 28 Apr 1917:   *Lt.-Gen.* Iosif Semyonovich **Loshunov**

Commander, 1st Brigade, 9th Infantry Division
- 30 May 1894 - 30 Nov 1895:   *Gen. of Inf.* Mikhail Ivanovich **Zasulich**
- 30 Nov 1895 - 4 Mar 1896:   *Lt.-Gen.* Aleksandr Aleksandrovich **Larionov**
- 4 Mar 1896 - 24 Oct 1899:   *Maj.-Gen.* Konstantin Mikhailovich **Akinfiyev**
- 24 Oct 1899 - 8 Jul 1901:   *Gen. of Inf.* Venedikt Aloiziyevich **Yasensky**
- 21 Jul 1901 - 19 Sep 1902:   *Maj.-Gen.* Pyotr Ivanovich **Prilukov**
- 2 Nov 1902 - 1 Oct 1904:   *Maj.-Gen.* Konstantin Trofimovich **Ryabinkin**
- 31 Dec 1904 - 15 Mar 1907:   *Maj.-Gen.* Konstantin Sakerdonovich **Zhdanovsky**
- 15 Mar 1907 - 21 Nov 1908:   *Lt.-Gen.* Konstantin Romanovich **Dovbor-Musnitsky**
- 28 Nov 1908 - 17 Aug 1909:   *Maj.-Gen.* Iosif Mikhailovich **Bonch-Bogdanovsky**
- 11 Sep 1909 - 12 Feb 1911:   *Maj.-Gen.* Sergey Aleksandrovich **Bogdanovich**
- 12 Feb 1911 - 15 Aug 1911:   *Lt.-Gen.* Frants Feliksovich **Kublitsky-Piotukh**
- 14 Oct 1911 - 13 Oct 1914:   *Lt.-Gen.* Iosif Semyonovich **Loshunov**
- 17 Oct 1914 - 19 Dec 1914:   *Lt.-Gen.* Pavel Dmitriyevich **Shipov**
- 19 Dec 1914 - 10 Apr 1915:   *Lt.-Gen.* Ivan Yuryevich **Popovich-Lipovats**
- 19 Apr 1915 - 20 Jul 1915:   *Maj.-Gen.* Khristo Neykovich **Koychev**
- 9 Aug 1915 - 25 Jun 1916:   *Lt.-Gen.* Aleksey Martyanovich **Chizhikov**
- 10 Jul 1916 - Oct 1917:   *Maj.-Gen.* Nikolai Vladislavovich **Shatkovsky**

Commander, 2nd Brigade, 9th Infantry Division
- 26 Feb 1894 - 21 Dec 1896:   *Maj.-Gen.* Boleslav Konstantinovich **Kobordo**

- 21 Dec 1896 - 23 Oct 1897:   *Maj.-Gen.* Ivan Aleksandrovich **Rengarten**
- 23 Oct 1897 - 11 Oct 1899:   *Lt.-Gen.* Yevgeny Stepanovich **Spokoysky-Frantsevich**
- 24 Oct 1899 - 20 Apr 1903:   *Lt.-Gen.* Nikolai Petrovich **Engelke**
- 20 Apr 1903 - 15 Aug 1904:   *Maj.-Gen.* Leonty Vladimirovich **Martson**
- 22 Sep 1904 - 13 Dec 1906:   *Gen. of Inf.* Vladimir Pavlovich **Shatilov**
- 31 Dec 1906 - 11 Apr 1907:   *Maj.-Gen.* Eduard Renatovich **Kastellaz**
- 11 Apr 1907 - Jun 1910:   *Maj.-Gen.* Aleksandr Yevgafovich **Vorypayev**
- 14 Jul 1910 - 23 Jul 1912:   *Maj.-Gen.* Sergey Sergeyevich **Tishin**
- 23 Jul 1912 - 29 Jul 1914:   *Lt.-Gen.* Mikhail Lvovich **Matveyev**
- 29 Aug 1914 - 17 Oct 1914:   *Lt.-Gen.* Ivan Yuryevich **Popovich-Lipovats**
- 17 Oct 1914 - 2 Mar 1917:   ?

Commander, 9th Artillery Brigade
- 9 Jan 1890 - 9 Aug 1896:   *Gen. of Art.* Aleksandr Emmanuilovich **Budde**
- 9 Aug 1896 - 11 Aug 1900:   *Lt.-Gen.* Lyudvig Yustinovich **Lontkevich**
- 11 Aug 1900 - 20 Aug 1903:   *Lt.-Gen.* Yevgeny Vladimirovich **Buyakovich**
- 20 Aug 1903 - 2 May 1904:   *Maj.-Gen.* Adolf Aleksandrovich von **Shleyer**
- 2 May 1904 - 1 Jul 1908:   *Lt.-Gen.* Pyotr Vasilyevich **Sukhinsky**
- 16 Aug 1908 - 23 Nov 1909:   *Lt.-Gen.* Prince Mikhail Mikhailovich **Kantakuzen**
- 10 Dec 1909 - 22 Jun 1912:   *Maj.-Gen.* Nikolai Mikhailovich **Kuznetsov**
- 22 Jun 1912 - 18 Dec 1913:   *Maj.-Gen.* Andrey Vladimirovich **Burman**
- 18 Dec 1913 - 27 Aug 1914:   *Maj.-Gen.* Dmitry Dmitriyevich **Fedchenko**
- 11 Oct 1914 - 10 Oct 1916:   *Maj.-Gen.* Lev Alekseyevich **Bogayevsky**
- 10 Oct 1916 - 2 Mar 1917:   ?

Commander, 10th Infantry Division
- 31 Oct 1890 - 3 Jun 1898:   *Gen. of Inf.* Karl-Avgust-Fridrikh Mavrikievich **Voyde**
- 10 Jun 1898 - 16 Jun 1901:   *Gen. of Inf.* Baron Aleksandr Nikolayevich **Meller-Zakomelsky**
- 16 Jun 1901 - 21 Oct 1902:   *Lt.-Gen.* Pyotr Yeremeyevich **Agapeyev**
- 10 Dec 1902 - 29 Jan 1906:   *Gen. of Inf.* Nikolai Pavlovich **Shatilov**
- 3 Feb 1906 - 14 Jun 1908:   *Gen. of Inf.* Yevgeny Aleksandrovich **Radkevich**
- 10 Jul 1908 - 13 Mar 1915:   *Gen. of Inf.* Nikolai Yakovlevich **Lopushansky**
- 13 Mar 1915 - 18 Apr 1916:   *Lt.-Gen.* Vasily Timofeyevich **Gavrilov**
- 13 May 1916 - 7 Apr 1917:   *Lt.-Gen.* Dmitry Nikolayevich **Nadezhny**

Commander, 1st Brigade, 10th Infantry Division
- 20 Jul 1889 - Dec 1894:   *Maj.-Gen.* Aleksandr Dmitriyevich **Mikheyev**
- 5 Jan 1895 - 24 Oct 1900:   *Maj.-Gen.* Magis Karlovich **Kheykel**
- 17 Dec 1900 - 17 Mar 1906:   *Maj.-Gen.* Nikolai Aleksandrovich **Eksten**
- 17 Mar 1906 - 12 May 1910:   *Maj.-Gen.* Nikolai Mikhailovich **Dubrova**
- 12 May 1910 - 23 Jul 1911:   *Lt.-Gen.* Aleksandr Dmitriyevich **Nechvolodov**
- 23 Jul 1911 - 2 May 1913:   *Maj.-Gen.* Bogdan Ivanovich **Yarotsky**
- 2 May 1913 - 31 Jul 1915:   *Maj.-Gen.* Fyodor Vasilyevich **Butkov**

- 3 Aug 1915 - 20 Apr 1916:   *Lt.-Gen.* Dmitry Nikolayevich **Nadezhny**
- 29 May 1916 - 22 Jan 1917:   *Maj.-Gen.* Stepan Zakharovich **Potapov**
- 22 Jan 1917 - 2 Mar 1917:   ?

Commander, 2nd Brigade, 10th Infantry Division
- 22 Jan 1894 - 13 Dec 1897:   *Lt.-Gen.* Vyacheslav Mikhailovich **Duditsky-Lishin**
- 13 Dec 1897 - 10 Mar 1898:   *Maj.-Gen.* Ivan Ignatievich **Artsyshevsky**
- 23 Mar 1898 - 14 Jan 1900:   *Maj.-Gen.* Aleksandr Prokofievich **Baykovsky**
- 15 Feb 1900 - 26 Aug 1903:   *Gen. of Inf.* Viktor Konstantinovich **Grek**
- 11 Sep 1903 - 23 Jul 1911:   *Maj.-Gen.* Bogdan Ivanovich **Yarotsky**
- 23 Jul 1911 - 29 Oct 1913:   *Lt.-Gen.* Kornely Danilovich **Timkovsky**
- 5 Nov 1913 - 31 Dec 1913:   *Maj.-Gen.* Dmitry Ivanovich **Shevandin**
- 14 Jan 1914 - 29 Jul 1914:   *Maj.-Gen.* Nikolai Mitrofanovich **Remezov**
- 29 Jul 1914 - 2 Mar 1917:   ?

Commander, 10th Artillery Brigade
- 30 Nov 1892 - 17 Feb 1900:   *Maj.-Gen.* Leopold Valentinovich **Baranovsky**
- 17 Feb 1900 - 3 Oct 1902:   *Lt.-Gen.* Lev Vasilyevich **Zhukovsky**
- 3 Oct 1902 - 27 May 1905:   *Gen. of Inf.* Yevgeny Aleksandrovich **Radkevich**
- 5 Sep 1905 - 16 Aug 1908:   *Maj.-Gen.* Aleksandr Mikhailovich **Borukayev**
- 16 Aug 1908 - 8 May 1910:   *Maj.-Gen.* Pavel Aleksandrovich **Sokolsky**
- 18 May 1910 - 2 Apr 1913:   *Lt.-Gen.* Vasily Ivanovich **Masalitinov**
- 2 Apr 1913 - Jul 1914:   *Maj.-Gen.* Nikolai Vasilievich **Belikhov**
- 3 Aug 1914 - 13 Mar 1915:   *Lt.-Gen.* Vasily Timofeyevich **Gavrilov**
- 13 Mar 1915 - 16 May 1916:   *Maj.-Gen.* Nikolai Vladimirovich **Skrydlov**
- 3 Jun 1916 - 1917:   *Maj.-Gen.* Ivan Grigoryevich **Pashchenko**

Commander, 11th Infantry Division
- 6 Jun 1890 - 12 Jan 1895:   *Lt.-Gen.* Vsevolod Fyodorovich **Panyutin**
- 8 Feb 1895 - 26 Mar 1898:   *Gen. of Inf.* Konstantin Aleksandrovich **Veys**
- 26 Mar 1898 - 11 Feb 1900:   *Lt.-Gen.* Pavel Pavlovich **Matveyev**
- 17 Feb 1900 - 4 Jul 1901:   *Lt.-Gen.* Yevgeny Nikolayevich **Kakurin**
- 8 Jul 1901 - 3 Apr 1903:   *Gen. of Art.* Timofey Mikhailovich **Belyayev**
- 25 Apr 1903 - 21 May 1905:   *Lt.-Gen.* Konstantin Nikolayevich **Gribsky**
- 25 Jun 1905 - 4 Jul 1906:   *Lt.-Gen.* Lev Ivanovich **Ignatyev**
- 22 Jul 1906 - 2 May 1907:   *Lt.-Gen.* Vladimir Aleksandrovich **Romanov**
- 30 May 1907 - 21 Nov 1908:   *Lt.-Gen.* Leonid Iosifovich **Zashchuk**
- 21 Nov 1908 - 19 Jun 1910:   *Gen. of Inf.* Edmund Ferdinandovich **Svidzinsky**
- 2 Jul 1910 - 3 Apr 1915:   *Gen. of Inf.* Ivan Ivanovich **Fedotov**
- 18 Apr 1915 - 1917:   *Lt.-Gen.* Mikhail Lvovich **Bachinsky**

Commander, 1st Brigade, 11th Infantry Division
- 2 Nov 1888 - 14 Jun 1898:   *Lt.-Gen.* Gavriil Aristarkhovich **Galakhov**
- 2 Jul 1898 - 1 Nov 1901:   *Maj.-Gen.* Mikhail Vasilyevich **Mikhailov**
- 20 Nov 1901 - 7 Jan 1905:   *Maj.-Gen.* Anton Voytsekhovich-Adalbertovich

	Nemysky
• 7 Jan 1905 - 2 Jul 1913:	*Lt.-Gen.* Nil Nilovich **Putilov**
• 2 Jul 1913 - 29 Jul 1914:	*Maj.-Gen.* Nikolai Adolfovich **Abzholtovsky**
• 29 Jul 1914 - 16 Jan 1915:	?
• 16 Jan 1915 - 13 May 1915:	*Lt.-Gen.* Aleksandr Andreyevich **Tsitsovich**
• 13 May 1915 - 2 Mar 1917:	?

Commander, 2nd Brigade, 11th Infantry Division

- 20 Dec 1892 - 20 Oct 1899: *Lt.-Gen.* Pavel Aleksandrovich **Kamenogradsky**
- 20 Oct 1899 - 25 Apr 1901: ?
- 25 Apr 1900 - 9 Feb 1901: *Lt.-Gen.* Yevgeny Iosifovich **Grozmani**
- 23 Apr 1901 - 19 Nov 1908: *Lt.-Gen.* Alexey Sergeyevich **Bezsonov**
- 25 Nov 1908 - 15 Jun 1910: *Maj.-Gen.* Vladislav-Antony Teofilovich **Gaurilkevich**
- 15 Jun 1910 - 21 Dec 1910: *Lt.-Gen.* Nikolai Aleksandrovich **Babikov**
- 24 Feb 1911 - 28 Nov 1914: *Maj.-Gen.* Nikolai Matveyevich **Bratchikov**
- 28 Nov 1914 - 17 Dec 1915: *Maj.-Gen.* Vladimir Zenonovich **May-Mayevsky**
- 17 Dec 1915 - 2 Mar 1917: ?

Commander, 11th Artillery Brigade

- 30 Aug 1885 - 4 Nov 1894: *Lt.-Gen.* Dmitry Ivanovich **Mikhailov**
- 13 Nov 1894 - 30 Jan 1900: *Lt.-Gen.* Pavel Ippolitovich **Posnikov**
- 17 Feb 1900 - 5 Apr 1904: *Maj.-Gen.* Mitrofan Petrovich **Petrov**
- 5 Apr 1904 - 24 Jan 1909: *Lt.-Gen.* Pyotr Andreyevich **Kokhno**
- 24 Jan 1909 - 19 May 1912: *Lt.-Gen.* Aleksey Semyonovich **Sofiano**
- 19 May 1912 - 3 Aug 1915: *Maj.-Gen.* Vasily Dmitriyevich **Petunin**
- 3 Aug 1915 - 27 Feb 1917: *Maj.-Gen.* Aleksandr Vladimirovich **Nikitin**
- 27 Feb 1917 - 2 Mar 1917: ?

Commander, 12th Infantry Division

- 2 Oct 1892 - 20 Jan 1895: *Gen. of Inf.* Vladimir Konstantinovich **Zherve**
- 20 Jan 1895 - Jul 1895: *Maj.-Gen.* Pyotr Arkhipovich **Troitsky**
- 14 Aug 1895 - 11 Aug 1900: *Gen. of Inf.* Ivan Aleksandrovich **Karass**
- 31 Aug 1900 - 20 May 1901: *Lt.-Gen.* Nikolai Aleksandrovich **Avinov**
- 20 May 1901 - 12 Feb 1903: *Gen. of Inf.* Andrey Petrovich **Chaykovsky**
- 29 Mar 1903 - 18 Jun 1905: *Lt.-Gen.* Dmitry Semyonovich **Fursov**
- 18 Jun 1905 - 23 May 1906: *Lt.-Gen.* Aleksandr Davidovich **Tugan-Mirza-Baranovsky**
- 29 May 1906 - 22 Sep 1910: *Gen. of Inf.* Sergey Ivanovich **Rusanov**
- 22 Sep 1910 - 2 Oct 1914: *Gen. of Inf.* Nikolai Aleksandrovich **Orlov**
- 2 Oct 1914 - 31 Jul 1915: *Lt.-Gen.* Nikolai Aleksandrovich **Babikov**
- 31 Jul 1915 - 18 Apr 1916: *Lt.-Gen.* Mikhail Vasilyevich **Khanzhin**
- 4 May 1916 - 6 Dec 1916: *Lt.-Gen.* Georgy Nikolayevich **Viranovsky**
- 6 Dec 1916 - 21 Oct 1917: *Lt.-Gen.* Mikhail Savvich **Pustovoytenko**

Commander, 1st Brigade, 12th Infantry Division
- 4 Jul 1890 - 13 Sep 1895: *Maj.-Gen.* Pavel Avgustovich **Kotsebue**
- 13 Sep 1895 - 16 Jul 1901: *Maj.-Gen.* Eduard Eduardovich von **Shults**
- 16 Jul 1901 - 30 Sep 1904: *Lt.-Gen.* Nikolai Aleksandrovich **Znosko-Borovsky**
- 30 Sep 1904 - 6 Jul 1909: *Maj.-Gen.* Aleksandr Stepanovich **Chizh**
- 31 Jul 1909 - 9 May 1914: *Gen. of Inf.* Vladimir Alekseyevich **Alftan**
- 11 Jun 1914 - 3 Aug 1915: *Maj.-Gen.* Mikhail Ivanovich **Troitsky**
- 3 Aug 1915 - 22 Mar 1916: *Lt.-Gen.* Dmitry Nikolayevich **Parkhomov**
- 22 Mar 1916 - 2 Mar 1917: ?

Commander, 2nd Brigade, 12th Infantry Division
- 26 Feb 1894 - 11 Oct 1899: *Maj.-Gen.* Vilgelm Khristianovich **Okerman**
- 24 Oct 1899 - Jul 1906: *Maj.-Gen.* Viktor Aleksandrovich **Perebaskin**
- 28 Aug 1906 - 14 Feb 1909: *Maj.-Gen.* Pyotr Pavlovich **Voyeykov**
- 14 Feb 1909 - 12 Oct 1911: *Lt.-Gen.* Anatoly Nikolayevich **Rozenschild von Paulin**
- 22 Nov 1911 - 5 Jul 1915: *Lt.-Gen.* Dmitry Petrovich **Pavlov**
- 5 Jul 1915 - 2 Mar 1917: ?

Commander, 12th Artillery Brigade
- 25 Feb 1887 - 3 May 1895: *Lt.-Gen.* Aleksandr Aleksandrovich **Maksimov**
- 3 May 1895 - Oct 1900: *Maj.-Gen.* Arkady Ivanovich **Kartamyshev**
- 4 Nov 1900 - 27 Jun 1906: *Maj.-Gen.* Pyotr Petrovich **Not**
- 27 Jun 1906 - 4 Nov 1906: *Lt.-Gen.* Nikolai Ivanovich **Kurakin**
- 4 Nov 1906 - 20 Jul 1911: *Lt.-Gen.* Vladimir Georgiyevich **Konradi**
- 22 Jul 1911 - 15 Apr 1915: *Lt.-Gen.* Sergey Nikolayevich **Kolpakov**
- Apr 1915 - 1917: *Maj.-Gen.* Yevgraf Grigoryevich **Rybalchenko**

Commander, 13th Infantry Division
- 18 Sep 1892 - 17 Mar 1895: *Gen. of Cav.* Dmitry Petrovich **Dokhturov**
- 20 Mar 1895 - 28 Dec 1896: *Lt.-Gen.* Vladimir Nikolayevich **Filippov**
- 28 Dec 1896 - 22 Jan 1902: *Lt.-Gen.* Vasily Vasiliyevich **Khristiani**
- 20 Feb 1902 - 11 Dec 1903: *Lt.-Gen.* Konstantin Vikentyevich **Tserpitsky**
- 24 Dec 1903 - 23 Oct 1904: *Gen. of Inf.* Andrei Nikolayevich **Selivanov**
- 7 Nov 1904 - 26 Oct 1905: *Gen. of Inf.* Aleksandr Vasilyevich **Brilevich**
- 26 Oct 1905 - 8 Feb 1906: ?
- 8 Feb 1906 - 4 May 1907: *Lt.-Gen.* Apollon Yermolayevich **Evert**
- 5 May 1907 - 5 Dec 1909: *Gen. of Inf.* Konstantin Mikhailovich **Alekseyev**
- 20 Dec 1909 - 5 Dec 1914: *Gen. of Inf.* Ferdinand Mavrikievich **Vebel**
- 19 Dec 1914 - 21 Feb 1915: *Lt.-Gen.* Sergey Timofeyevich **Pogoretsky**
- 21 Feb 1915 - 5 May 1917: *Lt.-Gen.* Yevgeny Mikhailovich **Mikhelis de Genig**

Commander, 1st Brigade, 13th Infantry Division
- 26 Feb 1894 - 22 Jan 1896: *Lt.-Gen.* Prince Sergey Nikolayevich **Urusov**
- 22 Jan 1896 - 7 Feb 1901: *Maj.-Gen.* Konstantin Ivanovich **Engel**

- 7 Feb 1901 - 29 Apr 1904:   *Maj.-Gen.* Vladimir Ustinovich **Sollogub**
- 10 Jun 1904 - 1909:   *Maj.-Gen.* Vladimir Gavrilovich **Sidelnikov**
- 1909 - 12 May 1910:   ?
- 12 May 1910 - 19 Jul 1914:   *Lt.-Gen.* Anton Dmitriyevich **Lavrentyev**
- 19 Jul 1914 - 2 Mar 1917:   ?

Commander, 2nd Brigade, 13th Infantry Division
- 14 Mar 1894 - 19 Jul 1895:   *Maj.-Gen.* Aleksandr Ivanovich **Vatropin**
- 19 Jul 1895 - 10 May 1897:   *Lt.-Gen.* Pyotr Petrovich von **Enden**
- 13 May 1897 - 4 Dec 1901:   *Maj.-Gen.* Feliks Antonovich **Klimovich**
- 4 Dec 1901 - 27 Nov 1904:   *Lt.-Gen.* Nikolai Nikolayevich **Chetyrikin**
- 2 Dec 1904 - 5 May 1906:   *Lt.-Gen.* Fyodor Yemelyanovich **Pleshkov**
- 5 Jun 1906 - 21 Jun 1908:   *Maj.-Gen.* Ivan Nikolayevich **Davydov**
- 10 Jul 1908 - 23 Jul 1912:   *Maj.-Gen.* Ivan Antonovich **Dumbadze**
- 23 Jul 1912 - 6 Nov 1912:   *Maj.-Gen.* Sergey Sergeyevich **Tishin**
- 6 Nov 1912 - 3 Jan 1915:   *Lt.-Gen.* Iosif Aleksandrovich **Mikulin**
- 3 Jan 1915 - 2 Mar 1917:   ?

Commander, 13th Artillery Brigade
- 9 Aug 1894 - 30 Dec 1896:   *Lt.-Gen.* Aleksey Pavlovich **Litvinov**
- 30 Dec 1896 - 30 Jan 1900:   *Lt.-Gen.* Nikolai Nikiforovich **Syngayevsky**
- 17 Feb 1900 - 1905:   *Maj.-Gen.* Sergey Nikolayevich **Lyapunov**
- 1905 - May 1906:   *Maj.-Gen.* Georgy Vasilyevich **Osipov**
- 20 Jun 1906 - 16 Jan 1909:   *Lt.-Gen.* Ilya Petrovich **Gribunin**
- 16 Jan 1909 - 16 Jan 1914:   *Lt.-Gen.* Ivan Mikhailovich **Zlobin**
- 23 Jan 1914 - 12 May 1916:   *Maj.-Gen.* Konstantin Konstantinovich **Pilkin**
- 10 Jul 1916 - 12 Aug 1917:   *Maj.-Gen.* Pavel Vasilyevich **Shepelev**

Commander, 14th Infantry Division
- 24 Dec 1890 - 9 Apr 1898:   *Lt.-Gen.* Daniil Albertovich **Konarzhevsky**
- 22 Apr 1898 - 7 Dec 1901:   *Gen. of Inf.* Semyon Andreyevich **Faddeyev**
- 15 Jan 1902 - 6 Sep 1904:   *Lt.-Gen.* Vasily Ivanovich **Sendetsky**
- 8 Sep 1904 - 29 May 1906:   *Gen. of Inf.* Sergey Ivanovich **Rusanov**
- 6 Jun 1906 - 26 Oct 1907:   *Lt.-Gen.* Pavel Gavrilovich **Masalov**
- 26 Oct 1907 - 31 Dec 1913:   *Gen. of Inf.* Aleksandr Iosafovich **Yevreinov**
- 31 Dec 1913 - 27 Mar 1915:   *Lt.-Gen.* Nikolai Sergeyevich **Glinsky**
- 27 Mar 1915 - 30 Jul 1917:   *Lt.-Gen.* Vladimir Ivanovich **Sokolov**

Commander, 1st Brigade, 14th Infantry Division
- 23 Mar 1892 - 5 Jul 1895:   *Lt.-Gen.* Ivan Andreyevich **Zamshin**
- 5 Jul 1895 - 9 Oct 1899:   *Maj.-Gen.* Ivan Petrovich **Avramov**
- 31 Oct 1899 - 18 Jul 1905:   *Gen. of Inf.* Nikolai Ivanovich **Glebov**
- 18 Jul 1905 - 29 Dec 1908:   *Gen. of Inf.* Nikolai Mikhailovich **Voronov**
- 5 Jan 1909 - 19 Jul 1914:   *Lt.-Gen.* Andrey Fedorovich **Zubkovsky**
- 19 Jul 1914 - 2 Mar 1917:   ?

Commander, 2nd Brigade, 14th Infantry Division
- 13 May 1886 - 11 Oct 1899: *Lt.-Gen.* Pavel Petrovich **Dubelt**
- 24 Oct 1899 - 8 Jan 1901: *Maj.-Gen.* Aleksandr Mikhailovich **Artobolevsky**
- 7 Feb 1901 - 4 Jun 1901: *Maj.-Gen.* Baron Boris Borisovich **Kene**
- 18 Jun 1901 - 2 Sep 1904: *Maj.-Gen.* Vladimir Pavlovich **Aseyev**
- 2 Sep 1904 - 21 May 1905: ?
- *21 May 1905 - Jan 1908:* *Maj.-Gen.* Boris Konstantinovich **Zhegochev** *
- *14 Mar 1906 - 5 Jan 1909:* *Lt.-Gen.* Andrey Fedorovich **Zubkovsky** *
- 5 Jan 1909 - 28 May 1909: ?
- 28 May 1909 - 7 Nov 1909: *Maj.-Gen.* Aleksandr Aleksandrovich **Skopinsky-Shtrik**
- 14 Nov 1909 - 12 Feb 1914: *Lt.-Gen.* Kesar Vikentyevich **Russiyan**
- 19 Feb 1914 - 11 Nov 1914: *Lt.-Gen.* Mikhail Georgiyevich **Gorelov**
- 11 Nov 1914 - 7 Jan 1915: *Maj.-Gen.* Yakov Mikhailovich **Ofrosimov**
- 7 Jan 1915 - 17 Oct 1915: *Lt.-Gen.* Mikhail Georgiyevich **Gorelov**
- 17 Oct 1915 - 2 Mar 1917: ?

* The published 1906, 1907, 1908 Ministry of War rank lists show both these generals as commanders of this unit. Since all secondary sources are based on these official publications, it has not been possible to determine the correct situation.

Commander, 14th Artillery Brigade
- 7 May 1893 - 31 Oct 1899: *Maj.-Gen.* Feliks Vikentyevich **Roshkovsky**
- 31 Oct 1899 - 29 Dec 1899: ?
- 29 Dec 1899 - 24 Feb 1905: *Maj.-Gen.* Nikolai Izmaylovich **Sumarokov**
- 24 Feb 1905 - 29 Jul 1909: *Maj.-Gen.* Ivan Vladimirovich **Nepenin**
- 1 Aug 1909 - 7 Oct 1911: *Maj.-Gen.* Ivan Vladimirovich **Petrichenko**
- 7 Oct 1911 - 21 Mar 1913: *Lt.-Gen.* Aleksandr Mikhailovich **Sivers**
- 23 Mar 1913 - 29 Oct 1915: *Lt.-Gen.* Arseny Mikhailovich **Zatrapeznov**
- 29 Oct 1915 - 18 Dec 1915: ?
- 18 Dec 1915 - Oct 1916: *Maj.-Gen.* Aleksandr Nikolayevich **Vinogradsky**
- Oct 1916 - 20 Dec 1916: ?
- 20 Dec 1916 - 9 May 1917: *Maj.-Gen.* Fyodor Aleksandrovich **Kolodeyev**

Commander, 15th Infantry Division
- 31 Jul 1889 - 30 Dec 1895: *Gen. of Inf.* Vasily Danilovich **Skalon**
- 10 Jan 1896 - 8 Dec 1896: *Lt.-Gen.* Aleksandr Karlovich **Timler**
- 28 Dec 1896 - 3 May 1900: *Lt.-Gen.* Vladimir Nikolayevich **Filippov**
- 19 May 1900 - 6 Aug 1905: *Lt.-Gen.* Nikolai Martinovich **Ivanov**
- 6 Aug 1905 - 29 Dec 1907: *Gen. of Inf.* Nikolai Nikolayevich **Martos**
- 28 Jan 1908 - 26 Jul 1914: *Gen. of Inf.* Dmitry Nikolayevich **Bezradetsky**
- 26 Jul 1914 - 5 Jul 1915: *Gen. of Inf.* Leonid Nikolayevich **Belkovich**
- 17 Jul 1915 - 7 Apr 1917: *Lt.-Gen.* Pyotr Nikolayevich **Lomnovsky**

Commander, 1st Brigade, 15th Infantry Division
- 15 Mar 1890 - 10 Jan 1896: *Lt.-Gen.* Aleksandr Karlovich **Timler**
- 22 Jan 1896 - 23 Jun 1899: *Lt.-Gen.* Prince Sergey Nikolayevich **Urusov**
- 12 Jul 1899 - 25 Jan 1904: *Gen. of Inf.* Aleksandr Genrikhovich **Sandetsky**
- 4 Feb 1904 - 12 Sep 1905: *Lt.-Gen.* Sergey Petrovich **Nekrasov**
- 12 Sep 1905 - 13 Jan 1906: ?
- 13 Jan 1906 - 29 Jan 1907: *Lt.-Gen.* Polikarp Alekseyevich **Kuznetsov**
- 19 Feb 1907 - 19 Feb 1914: *Lt.-Gen.* Stanislav Konstantinovich **Abakanovich**
- 2 Mar 1914 - 1 Nov 1914: *Lt.-Gen.* Yakov Aleksandrovich **Fok**
- 1 Nov 1914 - 2 Mar 1917: ?

Commander, 2nd Brigade, 15th Infantry Division
- 2 Oct 1892 - 7 Apr 1898: *Lt.-Gen.* Nikolai Martinovich **Ivanov**
- 13 May 1898 - 1 Jun 1904: *Gen. of Inf.* Vikenty Vikentyevich **Sennitsky**
- 2 Jun 1904 - 11 Aug 1906: *Lt.-Gen.* Mikhail Grigoryevich **Golembatovsky**
- 11 Aug 1906 - 29 Jan 1907: *Lt.-Gen.* Aleksandr Nikolayevich **Stupin**
- 29 Jan 1907 - 21 Jul 1910: *Lt.-Gen.* Polikarp Alekseyevich **Kuznetsov**
- 21 Jul 1910 - 21 Dec 1910: *Lt.-Gen.* Frants-Martselian Vikentyevich **Bokshchanin**
- 21 Dec 1910 - 19 Jul 1914: *Lt.-Gen.* Nikolai Aleksandrovich **Babikov**
- 19 Jul 1914 - 6 Sep 1914: ?
- 6 Sep 1914 - 2 Oct 1914: *Lt.-Gen.* Nikolai Aleksandrovich **Babikov**
- 2 Oct 1914 - 2 Mar 1917: ?

Commander, 15th Artillery Brigade
- 24 Dec 1890 - 19 Nov 1898: *Maj.-Gen.* Nikolai Sergeyevich **Isakov**
- 23 Dec 1898 - 12 Feb 1903: *Lt.-Gen.* Vladimir Petrovich **Delsal**
- 4 Mar 1903 - 27 Nov 1904: *Gen. of Art.* Vladimir Frantsevich **Bandrovsky**
- 30 Nov 1904 - 10 Apr 1907: *Lt.-Gen.* Emmanuil Borisovich **Pokhvisnyev**
- 11 Apr 1907 - 1 Jul 1910: *Lt.-Gen.* Aleksandr Nikolayevich **Storozhenko**
- 25 Jul 1910 - 23 Sep 1912: *Lt.-Gen.* Sergey Apollonovich **Perfilyev**
- 23 Sep 1912 - 12 Dec 1914: *Maj.-Gen.* Ksenofont Nikolayevich **Ivanenko**
- 12 Dec 1914 - 23 Dec 1916: *Maj.-Gen.* Vitt Aleksandrovich **Dudin**
- 23 Dec 1916 - 2 Mar 1917: ?

Commander, 16th Infantry Division
- 3 Nov 1893 - 28 May 1895: *Gen. of Inf.* Pyotr Stepanovich **Lazarev**
- 14 Jun 1895 - 4 Jul 1901: *Lt.-Gen.* Nikolai Vasilyevich **Kopansky**
- 4 Jul 1901 - 24 Dec 1903: *Gen. of Inf.* Andrei Nikolayevich **Selivanov**
- 12 Jan 1904 - 1 May 1910: *Lt.-Gen.* Ivan Venediktovich **Bogayevsky**
- 1 May 1910 - 13 Aug 1914: *Gen. of Inf.* Gvido Kazimirovich **Rikhter**
- 13 Aug 1914 - 31 Jan 1915: *Lt.-Gen.* Viktor Fyodorovich **Bauder**
- 31 Jan 1915 - 16 Apr 1917: *Lt.-Gen.* Yevgeny Emmanuilovich **Tregubov**

Commander, 1st Brigade, 16th Infantry Division
- 26 Dec 1892 - 27 Apr 1900: *Gen. of Inf.* Alfons Ivanovich **Bush**

- 19 May 1900 - 16 Jan 1901: *Maj.-Gen.* Pavel Mikhailovich **Lisevich**
- 29 Jan 1901 - 16 Jun 1904: *Lt.-Gen.* Mikhail Pavlovich **Davydov**
- 6 Jul 1904 - 24 Feb 1905: *Lt.-Gen.* Aleksandr Alekseyevich **Resin**
- 25 Mar 1905 - Jun 1907: *Maj.-Gen.* Konstantin Lvovich **Sivers**
- 6 Jul 1907 - 19 Jul 1914: *Maj.-Gen.* Georgy Fyodorovich **Eykhe**
- 19 Jul 1914 - 17 Oct 1915: ?
- 17 Oct 1915 - 16 Apr 1917: *Maj.-Gen.* Aleksey Petrovich **Belyavsky**

Commander, 2nd Brigade, 16th Infantry Division
- 24 Apr 1889 - 18 Nov 1894: *Maj.-Gen.* Vladimir Mironovich **Sirotsynsky**
- 8 Dec 1894 - 30 Aug 1902: *Maj.-Gen.* Otton Lorentsovich **Tsetterman**
- 16 Sep 1902 - 5 Feb 1904: *Lt.-Gen.* Aleksandr Nikolayevich **Bykov**
- 19 Feb 1904 - 22 Oct 1904: *Gen. of Inf.* Pyotr Semyonovich **Baluyev**
- 27 Nov 1904 - 6 Mar 1911: *Lt.-Gen.* Vasily Filippovich **Yesimontovsky**
- 6 Mar 1911 - Oct 1913: *Maj.-Gen.* Iosif Stepanovich **Yakubovsky**
- 29 Oct 1913 - 31 Dec 1913: *Maj.-Gen.* Ivan Ivanovich **Kozlov**
- 14 Jan 1914 - 13 Aug 1914: *Lt.-Gen.* Viktor Fyodorovich **Bauder**
- 13 Aug 1914 - 31 Jan 1915: ?
- 31 Jan 1915 - 17 Oct 1915: *Lt.-Gen.* Viktor Fyodorovich **Bauder**
- 17 Oct 1916 - 2 Mar 1917: ?

Commander, 16th Artillery Brigade
- 2 Jan 1893 - 24 Oct 1896: *Lt.-Gen.* Ivan Vasilyevich **Kakhanov**
- 24 Oct 1896 - 31 Oct 1899: *Maj.-Gen.* Nikolai Kapitonovich **Shteynfeld**
- 31 Oct 1899 - 29 Dec 1899: ?
- 29 Dec 1899 - 24 Feb 1901: *Lt.-Gen.* Vladimir Zakharovich **Ivanov**
- 24 Feb 1901 - Dec 1904: *Maj.-Gen.* Mikhail Sergeyevich **Babikov**
- Dec 1904 - 9 Feb 1905: ?
- 9 Feb 1905 - 23 Apr 1907: *Gen. of Art.* Nikolai Ilyich **Bulatov**
- 12 May 1907 - 3 Oct 1908: *Lt.-Gen.* Artemy Solomonovich **Vartanov**
- 22 Oct 1908 - 18 Jan 1914: *Lt.-Gen.* Avksenty Dmitriyevich **Tsibulsky**
- 23 Jan 1914 - 1 May 1916: *Maj.-Gen.* Aleksandr Vasilyevich **Khomyakov**
- 12 May 1916 - 23 Jan 1917: *Maj.-Gen.* Vladimir Lyudvigovich **Drake**

Commander, 17th Infantry Division
- 2 Nov 1892 - 23 Mar 1898: *Gen. of Inf.* Aleksandr Fyodorovich **Kozen**
- 26 Mar 1898 - 8 May 1898: *Gen. of Inf.* Konstantin Aleksandrovich **Veys**
- 8 May 1898 - 8 Jan 1902: *Lt.-Gen.* Baron Ferdinand Ferdinandovich von **Taube**
- 30 Jan 1902 - 8 Aug 1906: *Lt.-Gen.* Pavel Yemelyanovich von **Essen**
- 8 Aug 1906 - 9 Jul 1910: *Gen. of Inf.* Nikolai Iosifovich **Zakrzhevsky**
- 9 Jul 1910 - 31 Oct 1914: *Gen. of Inf.* Pyotr Semyonovich **Baluyev**
- 31 Oct 1914 - 21 Mar 1915: *Lt.-Gen.* Nikolai Petrovich **Stremoukhov**
- 21 Mar 1915 - 19 Apr 1917: *Lt.-Gen.* Pyotr Dmitriyevich **Shreyder**

Commander, 1st Brigade, 17th Infantry Division
- 6 Sep 1891 - 5 Feb 1897: *Maj.-Gen.* Vasily Amfianovich **Polyansky**
- 5 Feb 1897 - 18 Jul 1900: *Lt.-Gen.* Kazimir Dominikovich **Nosarzhevsky**
- 18 Jul 1900 - 9 Feb 1901: *Lt.-Gen.* Leonid Iosifovich **Zashchuk**
- 7 Feb 1901 - 6 Nov 1902: *Lt.-Gen.* Ivan Karlovich **Peltser**
- 6 Nov 1902 - 21 Jul 1905: *Maj.-Gen.* Vonifaty Aleksandrovich **Kedrov**
- 21 Jul 1905 - 25 Jul 1906: *Maj.-Gen.* Vasily Fyodorovich **Orel**
- 25 Jul 1906 - 6 Feb 1914: *Lt.-Gen.* Eduard Arkadyevich **Kolyankovsky**
- 11 Feb 1914 - 29 Jul 1914: *Maj.-Gen.* Mikhail Grigoryevich **Yerogin**
- 29 Jul 1914 - 2 Mar 1917: ?

Commander, 2nd Brigade, 17th Infantry Division
- 13 Jun 1894 - 6 Feb 1896: *Maj.-Gen.* Vladimir Antonovich **Krasovsky**
- 6 Feb 1896 - 29 Jan 1898: *Maj.-Gen.* Mikhail Karlovich **Zommer**
- 29 Jan 1898 - 23 Jun 1899: *Gen. of Inf.* Yevgeny Petrovich **Vishnyakov**
- 23 Jun 1899 - 17 Nov 1899: *Lt.-Gen.* Prince Sergey Nikolayevich **Urusov**
- 17 Nov 1899 - May 1904: *Maj.-Gen.* Ivan Ignatievich **Artsyshevsky**
- 6 Jul 1904 - 3 Dec 1910: *Lt.-Gen.* Nikolai Vasilyevich **Novoselov**
- 13 Jan 1911 - 21 Jun 1915: *Maj.-Gen.* Viktor Brunovich **Kolshmidt**
- 21 Jun 1915 - 2 Mar 1917: ?

Commander, 17th Artillery Brigade
- 16 Mar 1892 - Sep 1899: *Maj.-Gen.* Baron Khristofor Germanovich von **Maydel**
- Sep 1899 - Apr 1900: *Maj.-Gen.* Pavel Moiseyevich **Chaplin**
- 14 Apr 1900 - 12 Jun 1906: *Lt.-Gen.* Yevgraf Nikolayevich **Kobozev**
- 12 Jun 1906 - 22 Apr 1907: ?
- 22 Apr 1907 - 19 Jul 1911: *Maj.-Gen.* Vladimir Konstantinovich **Vasyukhnov**
- 19 Jul 1911 - 25 Oct 1913: *Lt.-Gen.* Vasily Timofeyevich **Gavrilov**
- 25 Oct 1913 - 12 May 1916: *Maj.-Gen.* Pyotr Nikonovich **Fedorov**
- 27 Jun 1916 - Oct 1917: *Maj.-Gen.* Ivan Mikhailovich **Levandovsky**

Commander, 18th Infantry Division
- 22 Nov 1893 - 3 Oct 1899: *Lt.-Gen.* Semyon Afanasyevich **Shkurinsky**
- 20 Oct 1899 - 16 Jun 1901: *Lt.-Gen.* Pyotr Yeremeyevich **Agapeyev**
- 4 Jul 1901 - 9 Jun 1906: *Gen. of Inf.* Vladimir Vasilievich **Smirnov**
- 1 Jul 1906 - 19 Apr 1907: *Gen. of Inf.* Aleksei Yevgrafovich **Churin**
- 14 May 1907 - 21 Feb 1908: *Gen. of Inf.* Yakov Fyodorovich **Shkinsky**
- 21 Feb 1908 - 17 Jun 1908: ?
- 17 Jun 1908 - 2 Sep 1914: *Gen. of Inf.* Dmitry Vasilievich **Balanin**
- 16 Sep 1914 - 18 Apr 1917: *Lt.-Gen.* Pavel Oskarovich **Papengut**

Commander, 1st Brigade, 18th Infantry Division
- 26 Feb 1894 - 30 Jan 1901: *Lt.-Gen.* Eduard Eduardovich **Mendt**
- 7 Feb 1901 - 7 Nov 1907: *Lt.-Gen.* Vladimir Nikolayevich **Mufel**
- 12 Nov 1907 - 23 Jun 1914: *Lt.-Gen.* Andrey Vasilyevich **Romashev**

- 23 Jun 1914 - 11 Dec 1916:   *Maj.-Gen.* Mikhail Panteleymonovich **Mikhailov**
- 31 Dec 1916 - 14 Apr 1917:   *Maj.-Gen.* Lev Semyonovich **Novosiltsev**

Commander, 2nd Brigade, 18th Infantry Division
- 21 Mar 1888 - 14 Mar 1896:   *Lt.-Gen.* Dmitry Ivanovich **Larionov**
- 14 Mar 1896 - 23 Feb 1897:   *Maj.-Gen.* Prince Pavel Andreyevich **Kildishev**
- 11 Mar 1897 - 11 Mar 1900:   *Lt.-Gen.* Andrey Mikhailovich **Svechin**
- 4 Apr 1900 - 16 Sep 1902:   *Lt.-Gen.* Aleksandr Nikolayevich **Bykov**
- 6 Nov 1902 - 2 Sep 1904:   *Lt.-Gen.* Ivan Karlovich **Peltser**
- 15 Sep 1904 - 8 Oct 1908:   *Lt.-Gen.* Aleksandr Aleksandrovich **Remi**
- 27 Oct 1908 - 23 Jul 1911:   *Lt.-Gen.* Fyodor Yemelyanovich **Pleshkov**
- 23 Jul 1911 - 13 Aug 1914:   *Lt.-Gen.* Yevgeny Mikhailovich **Mikhelis de Genig**
- 13 Aug 1914 - 2 Mar 1917:   ?

Commander, 18th Artillery Brigade
- 21 Jun 1894 - 1 Jan 1898:   *Lt.-Gen.* Mikhail Andreyevich **Yakubovich**
- 1 Jan 1898 - 5 Dec 1900:   *Lt.-Gen.* Georgy Fyodorovich **Devel**
- 9 Dec 1900 - 5 Jan 1904:   *Maj.-Gen.* Nikolai Fyodorovich **Palitsyn**
- 5 Jan 1904 - 18 Feb 1904:   *Gen. of Art.* Iosif Ivanovich **Mrozovsky**
- 3 Mar 1904 - 21 Mar 1908:   *Lt.-Gen.* Andrey Robertovich **Musselius**
- 21 Mar 1908 - 25 Jul 1910:   *Lt.-Gen.* Vasily Minovich **Yanushev**
- 25 Jul 1910 - Mar 1912:   *Maj.-Gen.* Viktor Kirillovich **Zhabyko**
- 28 Mar 1912 - 3 Jul 1915:   *Maj.-Gen.* Dmitry Aleksandrovich **Kuchin**
- 8 Jul 1915 - 1917:   *Maj.-Gen.* Mikhail Leontyevich **Berg**

Commander, 19th Infantry Division
- 22 Dec 1887 - 16 Jun 1897:   *Gen. of Inf.* Nikolai Pavlovich **Lomakin**
- 23 Jun 1897 - 11 Oct 1900:   *Lt.-Gen.* Baron Nikolai Yegorovich von der **Khoven**
- 4 Dec 1900 - 5 Apr 1905:   *Lt.-Gen.* Nikolai Fyodorovich **Maryanov**
- 5 Apr 1905 - 12 Jun 1906:   ?
- 12 Jun 1906 - Mar 1909:   *Lt.-Gen.* Pyotr Petrovich **Fedorov**
- 17 Mar 1909 - 27 Sep 1914:   *Gen. of Inf.* Aleksandr Frantsevich **Ragoza**
- 27 Sep 1914 - 29 Jul 1915:   *Lt.-Gen.* Grigory Yefimovich **Yanushevsky**
- 25 Aug 1915 - 12 Apr 1917:   *Lt.-Gen.* Aleksandr Dmitriyevich **Nechvolodov**

Commander, 1st Brigade, 19th Infantry Division
- 22 Apr 1888 - 5 Jul 1895:   *Maj.-Gen.* Ivan Petrovich **Avramov**
- 5 Jul 1895 - 11 Jan 1900:   *Lt.-Gen.* Ivan Andreyevich **Zamshin**
- 15 Feb 1900 - 24 Apr 1900:   *Maj.-Gen.* Dmitry Aleksandrovich **Merkazin**
- 19 May 1900 - 16 Aug 1901:   *Gen. of Inf.* Edmund Ferdinandovich **Svidzinsky**
- 16 Aug 1901 - 24 Apr 1906:   *Lt.-Gen.* Nikolai Semyonovich **Kachura**
- 5 May 1906 - 27 Oct 1908:   *Lt.-Gen.* Fyodor Yemelyanovich **Pleshkov**
- 24 Nov 1908 - Jan 1909:   *Maj.-Gen.* Konstantin Vasilievich **Asseyev**
- 12 May 1909 - 16 May 1911:   *Maj.-Gen.* Boleslav Ioakimovich **Boyarsky**
- 26 May 1911 - 4 Nov 1911:   *Maj.-Gen.* Aleksandr Mikhailovich **Bykov**

- 4 Nov 1911 - 6 Mar 1913: *Maj.-Gen.* Konstantin Aleksandrovich **Mertsedin**
- 6 Mar 1913 - 16 Mar 1916: *Lt.-Gen.* Aleksandr Lvovich **Timchenko**
- 16 Mar 1916 - 2 Mar 1917: ?

Commander, 2nd Brigade, 19th Infantry Division
- 28 Aug 1889 - Oct 1897: *Maj.-Gen.* Ivan Nikolayevich **Nazansky**
- 1 Nov 1897 - 14 Jan 1898: *Maj.-Gen.* Aleksandr Karlovich **Nemysky**
- 14 Jan 1898 - Aug 1899: *Maj.-Gen.* Yegor Vasilyevich **Borisoglebsky**
- 6 Sep 1899 - 26 Jun 1902: *Lt.-Gen.* Lev Ignatyevich **Kossovich**
- 12 Jul 1902 - 18 Jun 1903: *Maj.-Gen.* Vasily Petrovich **Zholtanovsky**
- 30 Jun 1903 - 5 Mar 1905: *Maj.-Gen.* Aleksandr Severinovich **Przhetslavsky**
- 21 Jun 1905 - 2 Jul 1913: *Lt.-Gen.* Emmanuil Aleksandrovich **Zeyn**
- 2 Jul 1913 - 29 Jul 1914: *Lt.-Gen.* Pavel Andreyevich **Nikitin**
- 29 Jul 1914 - 2 Mar 1917: ?

Commander, 19th Artillery Brigade
- 29 Nov 1893 - 31 Oct 1899: *Lt.-Gen.* Grigory Kuzmich **Kazantsev**
- 31 Oct 1899 - 9 Ar 1900: ?
- 9 Apr 1900 - 22 Apr 1903: *Maj.-Gen.* Nikolai Aristarkhovich **Pichugin**
- 7 May 1903 - 2 May 1904: *Maj.-Gen.* Konstantin Mikhailovich **Dekinleyn**
- 2 May 1904 - 30 Nov 1904: *Maj.-Gen.* Adolf Aleksandrovich von **Shleyer**
- 30 Nov 1904 - 11 Apr 1908: *Maj.-Gen.* Iosaf Pavlovich **Kusakov**
- 11 Apr 1908 - 8 May 1911: *Lt.-Gen.* Aleksandr Andreyevich **Maksheyev**
- 21 May 1911 - 19 Feb 1914: *Maj.-Gen.* Aleksandr Alekseyevich **Yuzvitsky**
- 19 Feb 1914 - 31 Jul 1915: *Lt.-Gen.* Mikhail Vasilyevich **Khanzhin**
- 1 Aug 1915 - 8 May 1916: *Maj.-Gen.* Nikolai Vasilyevich **Rakovich**
- 8 May 1916 - 27 Feb 1917: *Maj.-Gen.* Aleksey Iosifovich **Bolkhovitinov**
- 27 Feb 1917 - 2 Mar 1917: ?

Commander, 20th Infantry Division
- 2 Aug 1884 - 12 Dec 1894: *Gen. of Inf.* Nikolai Ottovich **Duve**
- 15 Dec 1894 - 23 Jan 1901: *Gen. of Inf.* Sergey Nikolayevich **Mylov**
- 22 Feb 1901 - 10 Feb 1903: *Lt.-Gen.* Leonty Vasilyevich **Gaponov**
- 10 Feb 1903 - 10 Aug 1904: *Lt.-Gen.* Nikolai Nikolayevich **Fleysher**
- 24 Aug 1904 - 15 Mar 1906: *Lt.-Gen.* Nikolai Feofilovich **Shishkovsky**
- 19 Mar 1906 - 5 Dec 1911: *Gen. of Inf.* Nikolai Ivanovich **Glebov**
- 13 Dec 1911 - 1 May 1913: *Gen. of Inf.* Vladimir Pavlovich **Shatilov**
- 1 May 1913 - 15 Mar 1915: *Lt.-Gen.* Nikolai Mikhailovich **Istomin**
- 15 Mar 1915 - 22 Apr 1917: *Lt.-Gen.* Aleksandr Fyodorovich **Bauer**

Commander, 1st Brigade, 20th Infantry Division
- 18 Feb 1893 - 9 Oct 1899: *Maj.-Gen.* Karl Velyaminovich **Rostsius**
- 31 Oct 1899 - 15 Feb 1900: *Gen. of Inf.* Aleksandr Aleksandrovich **Adlerberg**
- 15 Feb 1900 - 11 Jun 1904: *Gen. of Inf.* Nikolai Andreyevich **Zernets**

- 6 Jul 1904 - 15 Dec 1908: *Lt.-Gen.* Nikolai Ilich **Sulimov**
- 15 Jan 1909 - 29 Jul 1914: *Lt.-Gen.* Vladimir Fyodorovich **Nevtonov**
- 29 Jul 1914 - 2 Mar 1917: ?

Commander, 2nd Brigade, 20th Infantry Division
- 4 May 1891 - Jul 1896: *Maj.-Gen.* Konstantin Onufriyevich **Silvestrovich**
- 16 Jul 1896 - 11 Jan 1900: *Lt.-Gen.* Eduard Ivanovich **Lents**
- 15 Feb 1900 - 5 Jul 1903: *Maj.-Gen.* Pyotr Pavlovich **Zarnitsyn**
- 12 Jul 1903 - 15 Sep 1904: *Lt.-Gen.* Aleksandr Aleksandrovich **Remi**
- 21 Sep 1904 - 8 Feb 1905: *Lt.-Gen.* Sergey Ivanovich **Samoylo**
- 4 Mar 1905 - 11 Sep 1906: *Lt.-Gen.* Aleksandr Fyodorovich **Bauer**
- 19 Oct 1906 - 29 Mar 1915: *Lt.-Gen.* Nikolai Mikhailovich **Vorobyev**
- 29 Mar 1915 - 2 Mar 1917: ?

Commander, 20th Artillery Brigade
- 8 Jul 1889 - 14 Nov 1899: *Lt.-Gen.* Fabian Osipovich **Rymashevsky**
- 29 Dec 1899 - 8 Feb 1904: *Gen. of Art.* Vladimir Nikolayevich **Nikitin**
- 3 Mar 1904 - 4 May 1907: *Lt.-Gen.* Vladimir Dmitriyevich **Afanasyev**
- 4 May 1907 - 19 Jul 1907: ?
- 19 Jul 1907 - 11 Jan 1913: *Lt.-Gen.* Mikhail Mikhailovich **Frolov**
- 2 Feb 1913 - 5 Apr 1915: *Maj.-Gen.* Mitrofan Vasilievich **Andrussky**
- 5 Apr 1915 - 10 Jun 1917: *Maj.-Gen.* Nikolai Alekseyevich **Dmitriev**

Commander, 21st Infantry Division
- 14 Jun 1883 - 12 Oct 1895: *Lt.-Gen.* Yuri Aleksandrovich von der **Borkh**
- 12 Oct 1895 - 5 Oct 1899: *Gen. of Inf.* Vasily Vasilyevich **Treyter**
- 28 Oct 1899 - 9 Oct 1904: *Gen. of Inf.* Dmitry Modestovich **Rezvy**
- 23 Nov 1904 - 29 Apr 1906: *Gen. of Inf.* Nikolai Yegorovich **Svetlov**
- 4 Jul 1906 - 31 Dec 1913: *Gen. of Inf.* Venedikt Aloiziyevich **Yasensky**
- 31 Dec 1913 - 11 Dec 1914: *Gen. of Art.* Samed-Bek-Sadyk-Bek-ogly **Mekhmandarov**
- 8 Jan 1915 - 8 Feb 1915: *Lt.-Gen.* Mikhail Fyodorovich **Kvetsinsky**
- 8 Feb 1915 - 2 May 1916: *Lt.-Gen.* Konstantin Gerasimovich **Nekrasov**
- 19 May 1916 - 27 Aug 1917: *Maj.-Gen.* Aleksandr Gavrilovich **Tuchapsky**

Commander, 1st Brigade, 21st Infantry Division
- 16 Jan 1890 - 23 Jul 1896: *Lt.-Gen.* Vladimir Lavrentyevich **Ober**
- 5 Aug 1896 - 10 Aug 1898: *Maj.-Gen.* Ivan Pavlovich **Fromandier**
- 18 Sep 1898 - 16 Sep 1902: *Maj.-Gen.* Viktor Vasilyevich **Popov**
- 16 Sep 1902 - 29 May 1906: *Maj.-Gen.* Vladimir Timofeyevich **Fofanov**
- 3 Jun 1906 - 20 Jun 1907: *Gen. of Inf.* Mikhail Rodionovich **Yerofeyev**
- 6 Jul 1907 - 3 Feb 1910: *Lt.-Gen.* Aleksandr Nikolayevich **Kuzmin-Korovayev**
- 3 Feb 1910 - 19 Jul 1914: *Lt.-Gen.* Nikolai Ivanovich **Gavrilov**
- 19 Jul 1914 - 2 Mar 1917: ?

Commander, 2nd Brigade, 21st Infantry Division
- 25 May 1888 - 3 Aug 1898: *Lt.-Gen.* Bala-Kishi-Ali-Bek **Arablinsky**
- 18 Sep 1898 - 17 Oct 1902: *Maj.-Gen.* Mitrofan Konstantinovich **Slonchevsky**
- 13 Nov 1902 - 1 Jul 1906: *Maj.-Gen.* Ivan Danilovich **Buslavsky**
- 21 Aug 1906 - 27 Oct 1906: *Maj.-Gen.* Vasily Nikolayevich **Levitsky**
- 27 Oct 1906 - 2 Dec 1906: ?
- 2 Dec 1906 - 19 Mar 1908: *Maj.-Gen.* Vatslav-Martsely Lavrentyevich **Prosinsky**
- 19 Mar 1908 - 3 Sep 1908: *Lt.-Gen.* Konstantin Lukich **Gilchevsky**
- 20 Sep 1908 - 18 Nov 1911: *Lt.-Gen.* Sergey Alekseyevich **Dobronravov**
- 18 Nov 1911 - 6 Jan 1914: *Lt.-Gen.* Ivan Adamovich **Genik**
- 14 Jan 1914 - 1 Jul 1915: *Lt.-Gen.* Nikolai Maksimovich **Ivanov**
- 1 Jul 1915 - 2 Mar 1917: ?

Commander, 21st Artillery Brigade
- 24 Aug 1888 - 18 Aug 1899: *Lt.-Gen.* Izrayel Agaporunovich **Sandzhanov**
- 18 Aug 1899 - Nov 1902: *Maj.-Gen.* Vladimir Yurevich **Gotsky-Danilovich**
- 4 Dec 1902 - 25 Jan 1905: *Maj.-Gen.* Aleksandr Pavlovich **Gurkovsky**
- 2 Mar 1905 - 31 Jul 1907: *Maj.-Gen.* Vladimir Iosifovich **Surin**
- 31 Jul 1907 - Dec 1908: *Maj.-Gen.* Konstantin-Karl Yulyevich **Tsumpfort**
- 16 Jan 1909 - 16 Jan 1914: *Lt.-Gen.* Ivan Andreyevich **Zakutovsky**
- 29 Jan 1914 - 12 May 1916: *Maj.-Gen.* Vladimir Andreyevich **Pryaslov**
- 12 May 1916 - 19 Sep 1917: *Maj.-Gen.* Leonty Nikolayevich **Vnorovsky**

Commander, 22nd Infantry Division
- 7 Aug 1892 - 27 Sep 1897: *Gen. of Inf.* Vladimir Andreyevich de **Latour de Berngardt**
- 5 Oct 1897 - 2 Oct 1901: *Gen. of Inf.* Aleksandr Savelyevich **Barmin**
- 15 Nov 1901 - 23 Oct 1904: *Lt.-Gen.* Viktor Konstantinovich **Affanasovich**
- 23 Oct 1904 - 12 Sep 1905: *Gen. of Inf.* Nikolai Borisovich **Kutnevich**
- 12 Sep 1905 - 7 Jul 1906: *Lt.-Gen.* Vladimir Mikhailovich **Novikov**
- 7 Jul 1906 - 14 Dec 1908: *Gen. of Inf.* Leonid Konstantinovich **Artamonov**
- 13 Feb 1909 - 30 May 1912: *Gen. of Inf.* Vladimir Apollonovich **Olokhov**
- 30 May 1912 - 30 Jul 1912: *Gen. of Inf.* Andrei Medardovich **Zayonchkovsky**
- 30 Jul 1912 - 6 Oct 1914: *Gen. of Inf.* Aleksandr Aleksandrovich **Dushkevich**
- 6 Oct 1914 - 11 Dec 1914: *Gen. of Inf.* Sergey Dmitriyevich **Markov**
- 11 Dec 1914 - 29 Oct 1916: *Lt.-Gen.* Mikhail Ivanovich **Shishkin**
- 29 Oct 1916 - Mar 1917: *Maj.-Gen.* Adrian Vladimirovich **Usov**
- Mar 1917 - 25 Apr 1917: *Maj.-Gen.* Fyodor Fyodorovich **Novitsky**
- 25 Apr 1917 - 22 Aug 1917: *Maj.-Gen.* Adrian Vladimirovich **Usov**

Commander, 1st Brigade, 22nd Infantry Division
- 4 Jun 1892 - Jul 1895: *Lt.-Gen.* Semyon Ivanovich **Butenko**
- 19 Jul 1895 - 4 Jun 1899: *Maj.-Gen.* Aleksandr Ivanovich **Vatropin**
- 23 Jun 1899 - 20 Jun 1900: *Maj.-Gen.* Nikolai Petrovich **Ignatyev**
- 3 Aug 1900 - 3 Jul 1905: *Lt.-Gen.* Vladimir Mikhailovich **Novikov**

- 3 Jul 1905 - 30 Sep 1905: *Lt.-Gen.* Mikhail Ivanovich **Shtegelman**
- 30 Sep 1905 - 17 Apr 1906: ?
- 17 Apr 1906 - 28 Nov 1907: *Lt.-Gen.* Adam Ivanovich **Slavochinsky**
- 4 Dec 1907 - Dec 1910: *Maj.-Gen.* Vladimir Aleksandrovich **Rayevsky**
- 30 Dec 1910 - 6 Mar 1913: *Lt.-Gen.* Aleksandr Aleksandrovich **Mikhelson**
- 10 Mar 1913 - 26 May 1915: *Lt.-Gen.* Pyotr Nikolayevich **Sivitsky**
- 5 Jun 1915 - 1917: *Maj.-Gen.* Dmitry Ivanovich **Solers**

Commander, 2nd Brigade, 22nd Infantry Division
- 26 May 1893 - 23 Jul 1899: *Maj.-Gen.* Vladimir Vasilyevich **Orzhevsky**
- 5 Aug 1899 - 21 Apr 1903: *Lt.-Gen.* Vasily Ignatyevich **Parutsky**
- 28 Apr 1903 - 19 Apr 1904: *Gen. of Inf.* Ivan Andreyevich **Romanenko**
- 2 May 1904 - 9 Mar 1905: *Lt.-Gen.* Matvey Nikolayevich **Frish**
- 9 Mar 1905 - 14 Jun 1905: *Gen. of Inf.* Sergey Dmitriyevich **Markov**
- 28 Jun 1905 - 2 Jul 1906: *Maj.-Gen.* Aleksandr Arsenyevich **Danilchuk**
- 7 Jul 1906 - 20 Sep 1908: *Lt.-Gen.* Sergey Petrovich **Lovtsov**
- 24 Nov 1908 - 19 Jul 1914: *Lt.-Gen.* Adam Yuryevich **Stankevich**
- 19 Jul 1914 - 2 Mar 1917: ?

Commander, 22nd Artillery Brigade
- 21 Jul 1885 - 1 Apr 1896: *Maj.-Gen.* Pavel Matveyevich **Limantov**
- 1 Apr 1896 - 9 Apr 1901: *Lt.-Gen.* Nikolai Gustavovich **Golmdorf**
- 9 Apr 1901 - 13 Feb 1904: *Gen. of Inf.* Nikolai Vasilyevich **Osipov**
- 3 Mar 1904 - 17 Nov 1904: *Gen. of Art.* Pavel Platonovich **Pototsky**
- 20 Nov 1904 - 21 Nov 1907: *Lt.-Gen.* Vladimir Andreyevich **Lyakhovich**
- 21 Nov 1907 - Nov 1912: *Maj.-Gen.* Stefan Nikolayevich **Zlatarsky**
- 29 Nov 1912 - 12 May 1916: *Lt.-Gen.* Nikolai Vasilyevich **Ivashintsov**
- 12 May 1916 - 1917: *Maj.-Gen.* Pyotr Dmitriyevich **Gladkov**

Commander, 23rd Infantry Division
- 10 Jan 1894 - 15 Jan 1897: *Lt.-Gen.* Richard Troyanovich von **Meves**
- 12 Feb 1897 - 2 Feb 1900: *Gen. of Art.* Count Mikhail Aleksandrovich **Sivers**
- 1 Mar 1900 - 9 Jun 1904: *Gen. of Inf.* Mikhail Semyonovich **Andreyev**
- 9 Jun 1904 - 14 Aug 1904: ?
- 14 Aug 1904 - 24 Dec 1905: *Lt.-Gen.* Pavel Nikolayevich **Voronov**
- 24 Dec 1905 - 6 Oct 1906: *Gen. of Eng.* Yevgraf Semyonovich **Saranchev**
- 9 Oct 1906 - 16 Apr 1908: *Gen. of Inf.* Nikolai Appolonovich **Pykhachev**
- 16 Apr 1908 - 10 Jul 1908: ?
- 10 Jul 1908 - 11 Jun 1910: *Gen. of Inf.* Leonid-Otto Ottovich **Sirelius**
- 11 Jul 1910 - 18 Jun 1915: *Lt.-Gen.* Stepan Aleksandrovich **Voronin**
- 1 Jul 1915 - 22 Apr 1917: *Lt.-Gen.* Pavel Alekseyevich **Kordyukov**

Commander, 1st Brigade, 23rd Infantry Division
- 16 Oct 1889 - 24 Nov 1895: *Maj.-Gen.* Dmitry Ivanovich **Kovalevsky**
- 4 Dec 1895 - 18 Sep 1897: *Lt.-Gen.* Pavel Pavlovich **Dyagilev**

- 18 Sep 1897 - 7 Oct 1899: *Lt.-Gen.* Nikolai Lvovich **Boltin**
- 24 Oct 1899 - 17 Feb 1905: *Maj.-Gen.* Ilya Vladimirovich **Vestman**
- 17 Feb 1905 - 25 May 1905: ?
- 25 May 1905 - 10 Mar 1912: *Lt.-Gen.* Aleksandr Aleksandrovich **Menchukov**
- 10 Mar 1912 - 1 Jul 1915: *Lt.-Gen.* Pavel Alekseyevich **Kordyukov**
- 1 Jul 1915 - 2 Mar 1917: ?

Commander, 2nd Brigade, 23rd Infantry Division
- 12 Apr 1892 - 20 Feb 1896: *Lt.-Gen.* Ivan Ivanovich **Maksimov**
- 14 Mar 1896 - 11 Jan 1900: *Lt.-Gen.* Dmitry Ivanovich **Larionov**
- 15 Feb 1900 - 27 Jun 1906: *Gen. of Inf.* Aleksandr Aleksandrovich **Adlerberg**
- 27 Jun 1906 - 30 Apr 1907: *Gen. of Inf.* Leonid Vilhelmovich **Lesh**
- 7 Jun 1907 - 10 Jun 1908: *Lt.-Gen.* Aksel Fridrikhovich von **Kruzenshtern**
- 10 Jun 1908 - 2 Aug 1914: *Lt.-Gen.* Eduard Rudolfovich von **Freyman**
- 2 Aug 1914 - 2 Mar 1917: ?

Commander, 23rd Artillery Brigade
- 16 Mar 1892 - 29 Aug 1895: *Gen. of Art.* Timofey Mikhailovich **Belyayev**
- 29 Aug 1895 - 30 Dec 1896: *Gen. of Art.* Vladimir Stepanovich **Usov**
- 30 Dec 1896 - 5 Dec 1899: *Lt.-Gen.* Aleksey Pavlovich **Litvinov**
- 29 Dec 1899 - 4 Jun 1904: *Lt.-Gen.* Nikolai Pavlovich **Yarygin**
- 4 Jun 1904 - 27 Jan 1907: *Maj.-Gen.* Pyotr Vasilyevich **Osipov**
- 22 Apr 1907 - 3 Jul 1908: *Lt.-Gen.* Aleksei Dmitrievich **Golovachev**
- 16 Aug 1908 - 30 May 1910: *Lt.-Gen.* Aleksandr Fyodorovich von **Gillenshmidt**
- 30 May 1910 - 18 Oct 1913: *Lt.-Gen.* Andrey Vasilyevich **Ivashintsov**
- 18 Oct 1913 - 16 Mar 1914: ?
- 16 Mar 1914 - 2 Oct 1916: *Maj.-Gen.* Mikhail Timofeyevich **Belyayev**

Commander, 24th Infantry Division
- 12 Feb 1890 - 12 Oct 1896: *Lt.-Gen.* Georgy Konstantinovich **Maklakov**
- 4 Nov 1896 - 12 Feb 1897: *Gen. of Art.* Count Mikhail Aleksandrovich **Sivers**
- 12 Feb 1897 - 10 Jan 1902: *Gen. of Inf.* Leonid Matveyevich **Dembovsky**
- 30 Jan 1902 - 14 Apr 1904: *Gen. of Inf.* Baron Anton Yegorovich von **Zaltsa**
- 19 Apr 1904 - 21 Jun 1906: *Gen. of Inf.* Ivan Andreyevich **Romanenko**
- 27 Jun 1906 - 10 Jan 1907: *Gen. of Inf.* Aleksandr Aleksandrovich **Adlerberg**
- 10 Jan 1907 - 24 Jun 1908: *Gen. of Inf.* Nikolai Petrovich **Mikhnevich**
- 2 Jul 1908 - 13 Oct 1908: *Lt.-Gen.* Nikolai Ivanovich **Govorov**
- 14 Oct 1908 - 21 Dec 1908: *Lt.-Gen.* Fyodor Aleksandrovich **Shostak**
- 16 Jan 1909 - 3 Jun 1910: *Gen. of Inf.* Leopold Aleksandrovich **Shvank**
- 12 Jul 1910 - 9 Nov 1914: *Lt.-Gen.* Nikolai Petrovich **Reshchikov**
- 9 Nov 1914 - 11 Dec 1914: *Lt.-Gen.* Mikhail Ivanovich **Shishkin**
- 11 Dec 1914 - 19 Apr 1915: *Lt.-Gen.* Nikolai Petrovich **Reshchikov**
- 22 Apr 1915 - 10 Jan 1917: *Lt.-Gen.* Aleksey Sergeyevich **Polyansky**
- 15 Feb 1917 - Jan 1918: *Maj.-Gen.* Vladislav-Aleksandr Eduardovich **Glyass**

Commander, 1st Brigade, 24th Infantry Division
- 31 Jul 1877 - Jan 1897: *Maj.-Gen.* Kazimir Iosifovich **Kononovich**
- 5 Feb 1897 - 11 Oct 1900: *Lt.-Gen.* Nikolai Grigoryevich **Chernyayev**
- 11 Oct 1900 - 18 Dec 1900: ?
- 18 Dec 1900 - 31 Dec 1901: *Gen. of Inf.* Konstantin Osipovich **Kurganovich**
- 31 Dec 1901 - 10 Mar 1902: ?
- 10 Mar 1902 - Jan 1906: *Maj.-Gen.* Pavel Aleksandrovich **Shiff**
- 27 Jan 1906 - 19 Jul 1914: *Lt.-Gen.* Aleksandr Nikolayevich **Apukhtin**
- 19 Jul 1914 - 2 Mar 1917: ?

Commander, 2nd Brigade, 24th Infantry Division
- 26 May 1893 - 30 Sep 1897: *Maj.-Gen.* Pyotr-Pavel Iosifovich **Garnovsky**
- 23 Oct 1897 - 25 Jan 1900: *Maj.-Gen.* Ivan Aleksandrovich **Rengarten**
- 15 Feb 1900 - 16 Apr 1903: *Maj.-Gen.* Pyotr Aleksandrovich **Stakhiyev**
- 20 Apr 1903 - 6 Oct 1910: *Lt.-Gen.* Pyotr Ivanovich **Klochenko**
- 6 Oct 1910 - 9 Nov 1914: *Lt.-Gen.* Mikhail Ivanovich **Shishkin**
- 9 Nov 1914 - 2 Mar 1917: ?

Commander, 24th Artillery Brigade
- 24 May 1893 - 5 Dec 1899: *Gen. of Art.* Konstantin Pavlovich **Prezhbyano**
- 29 Dec 1899 - 14 Oct 1903: *Lt.-Gen.* Georgy Konstantinovich **Meybaum**
- 14 Oct 1903 - 24 Jan 1909: *Lt.-Gen.* Rudolf Adolfovich von **Volsky**
- 24 Jan 1909 - 26 Jan 1914: *Lt.-Gen.* Baron Sergey Nikolayevich **Delvig**
- 11 Feb 1914 - 13 May 1916: *Maj.-Gen.* Iosif Ivanovich **Bogdanovich**
- 13 May 1016 - 2 Mar 1917: ?

Commander, 25th Infantry Division
- 17 Jun 1891 - 31 Mar 1896: *Gen. of Inf.* Nikolai Matveyevich **Turbin**
- 8 Apr 1896 - 27 Sep 1901: *Gen. of Inf.* Nikolai Fyodorovich Baron von der **Osten-Driesen**
- 13 Oct 1901 - 2 Aug 1906: *Gen. of Inf.* Vyacheslav Ivanovich **Pnevsky**
- 16 Aug 1906 - 7 Nov 1907: *Lt.-Gen.* Ivan Karlovich **Peltser**
- 7 Nov 1907 - 2 May 1910: *Lt.-Gen.* Vladimir Nikolayevich **Mufel**
- 2 May 1910 - 22 Sep 1911: *Gen. of Inf.* Pavel Sergeyevich **Savvich**
- 12 Oct 1911 - 6 Dec 1914: *Gen. of Art.* Pavel Ilyich **Bulgakov**
- 8 Jan 1915 - 23 Sep 1915: *Lt.-Gen.* Mikhail Alekseyevich **Sokovnin**
- 17 Oct 1915 - 7 Nov 1917: *Lt.-Gen.* Nikolai Grigoryevich **Filimonov**

Commander, 1st Brigade, 25th Infantry Division
- 31 May 1893 - 19 Sep 1898: *Maj.-Gen.* Nikita Grigoryevich **Shakhnazarov**
- 24 Sep 1898 - 30 Oct 1904: *Maj.-Gen.* Aleksey Fyodorovich **Lyutse**
- 3 Nov 1904 - 18 Jul 1905: *Maj.-Gen.* Kazimir-Aleksandr Ivanovich **Kley**
- 18 Jul 1905 - 12 May 1910: *Lt.-Gen.* Anton Dmitriyevich **Lavrentyev**
- 12 May 1910 - 12 Feb 1913: *Maj.-Gen.* Pyotr Pavlovich **Palibin**
- 17 Feb 1913 - 8 Feb 1915: *Lt.-Gen.* Gerbert Georgievich **Dzhonson**

- 8 Feb 1915 - 2 Mar 1917: ?

Commander, 2ⁿᵈ Brigade, 25ᵗʰ Infantry Division
- 30 Oct 1890 - 8 Apr 1896: *Gen. of Inf.* Nikolai Fyodorovich Baron von der **Osten-Driesen**
- 2 May 1896 - 6 Jul 1900: *Lt.-Gen.* Aleksandr Aleksandrovich **Larionov**
- 18 Jul 1900 - 11 Sep 1903: *Maj.-Gen.* Mily Kondratyevich **Mikhailov**
- 11 Sep 1903 - 17 Jan 1905: *Maj.-Gen.* Aleksandr Ivanovich **Luganin**
- 17 Jan 1905 - 18 Jul 1905: ?
- 18 Jul 1905 - 12 Jun 1912: *Lt.-Gen.* Pyotr Fyodorovich **Astanin**
- 21 Jun 1912 - 29 Jul 1914: *Maj.-Gen.* Aleksandr Vasilyevich **Orlov**
- 29 Jul 1914 - 2 Mar 1917: ?

Commander, 25ᵗʰ Artillery Brigade
- 26 Feb 1894 - 4 Jun 1899: *Maj.-Gen.* Aleksandr Petrovich **Engelke**
- 14 Jun 1899 - 11 Aug 1900: *Lt.-Gen.* Nikolai Arkadyevich **Koptev**
- 11 Aug 1900 - May 1903: *Maj.-Gen.* Vladimir Tarasovich **Slepushkin**
- 5 Jun 1903 - 24 Oct 1904: *Maj.-Gen.* Pyotr Ivanovich **Puzyrov**
- 17 Nov 1904 - 21 Nov 1907: *Gen. of Art.* Pavel Platonovich **Pototsky**
- 21 Nov 1907 - 15 Apr 1910: *Maj.-Gen.* Pyotr Dmitriyevich **Melnitsky**
- 27 Apr 1910 - 20 Nov 1913: *Lt.-Gen.* Grigory Fyodorovich **Chepurnov**
- 20 Nov 1913 - 19 Jan 1914: ?
- 19 Jan 1914 - 10 Oct 1916: *Maj.-Gen.* Vladimir Vasilyevich **Ivanov**
- 10 Oct 1816 - 2 Mar 1917: ?

Commander, 26ᵗʰ Infantry Division
- 20 Jan 1888 - 1 Jan 1898: *Gen. of Inf.* Prince Aleksandr Petrovich **Shcherbatov**
- 10 Jan 1898 - 12 Jun 1898: *Lt.-Gen.* Ivan Ivanovich **Maksimov**
- 20 Jun 1898 - 26 Sep 1898: *Gen. of Inf.* Konstantin Iosifovich **Razgonov**
- 26 Sep 1898 - 17 Dec 1898: ?
- 17 Dec 1898 - 10 Jul 1899: *Gen. of Inf.* Rudolf Samoylovich von **Raaben**
- 26 Jul 1899 - 14 Jul 1902: *Lt.-Gen.* Konstantin Akimovich **Stolitsa**
- 22 Jul 1902 - 17 Sep 1903: *Gen. of Inf.* Ivan Platonovich **Pototsky**
- 27 Sep 1903 - 17 Feb 1907: *Gen. of Inf.* Dmitry Sergeyevich **Buturlin**
- 17 Feb 1907 - 11 Sep 1907: *Lt.-Gen.* Vasily Vasilyevich **Shchagin**
- 9 Nov 1907 - 23 Aug 1913: *Gen. of Inf.* Mikhail Nikiforovich **Kaygorodov**
- 24 Sep 1913 - 18 Sep 1914: *Gen. of Inf.* Aleksandr Nikolayevich **Poretsky**
- 18 Sep 1914 - 16 Jan 1915: *Lt.-Gen.* Pyotr Nikolayevich **Turov**
- 16 Jan 1915 - 25 Aug 1915: *Maj.-Gen.* Pyotr Andreyevich **Tikhonovich**
- 25 Aug 1915 - 11 Aug 1916: *Lt.-Gen.* Fyodor Yevlampiyevich **Ogorodnikov**
- 11 Aug 1916 - 10 Apr 1917: *Lt.-Gen.* Pyotr Mikhailovich **Baranov**

Commander, 1ˢᵗ Brigade, 26ᵗʰ Infantry Division
- 10 May 1892 - 26 Jul 1899: *Lt.-Gen.* Konstantin Akimovich **Stolitsa**
- 26 Jul 1899 - 6 Sep 1899: ?

- 6 Sep 1899 - 3 Mar 1900: *Maj.-Gen.* Konstantin Iskrovich **Kesyakov**
- 4 Apr 1900 - 3 Dec 1902: *Maj.-Gen.* Nikolai Aleksandrovich **Stakhiyev**
- 28 Jan 1903 - 10 May 1910: *Lt.-Gen.* Ioann-Filipp-Vilgelm Aleksandrovich **Kannabikh**
- 10 May 1910 - 19 Jul 1914: *Lt.-Gen.* Feliks Dominikovich **Iozefovich**
- 19 Jul 1914 - 27 Aug 1914: *Maj.-Gen.* Konstantin Ivanovich **Druzhinin**
- 27 Aug 1914 - 13 May 1915: *Lt.-Gen.* Pyotr Nikolayevich **Turov**
- 13 May 1915 - 2 Mar 1917: ?

Commander, 2nd Brigade, 26th Infantry Division
- 4 May 1892 - 15 Sep 1900: *Lt.-Gen.* Andrey Konstantinovich **Gek**
- 13 Oct 1900 - Dec 1905: *Maj.-Gen.* Baron Maksimilian Vilgelmovich von **Funk**
- 30 Jan 1906 - 13 Dec 1908: *Gen. of Inf.* Nikolai Fridrikhovich **Krauze**
- 8 Jan 1909 - 9 Nov 1913: *Maj.-Gen.* Nikolai Nikolayevich **Przhetslavsky**
- 9 Nov 1913 - 10 Nov 1914: *Lt.-Gen.* Yakov Mikhailovich **Larionov**
- 10 Nov 1914 - 2 Mar 1917: ?

Commander, 26th Artillery Brigade
- 16 Mar 1892 - 16 Mar 1899: *Lt.-Gen.* Vladimir Osipovich **Bobrovsky**
- 16 Mar 1899 - 29 Dec 1899: *Gen. of Art.* Vladimir Ivanovich **Gippius**
- 29 Dec 1899 - 13 Nov 1903: *Maj.-Gen.* Aleksandr Feliksovich **Velyamovich**
- 13 Nov 1903 - 13 Aug 1905: *Gen. of Art.* Eris-Khan-Sultan-Girei **Aliyev**
- 13 Aug 1905 - 22 Apr 1907: *Colonel* Mikhail Konstantinovich **Zheltov**
- 22 Apr 1907 - 25 Jul 1910: *Lt.-Gen.* Modest Vladislavovich **Romishevsky**
- 25 Jul 1910 - 7 Aug 1913: *Gen. of Art.* Vladimir Petrovich **Mamontov**
- 30 Aug 1913 - 9 Nov 1913: *Maj.-Gen.* Georgy Karpovich **Zaretsky**
- 9 Nov 1913 - 25 Oct 1915: *Maj.-Gen.* Nikolai Alekseyevich **Zayets**
- 25 Oct 1915 - 19 Jan 1916: *Maj.-Gen.* Baron Ignaty Nikolayevich von **Maydel**
- 21 Feb 1916 - 1917: *Maj.-Gen.* Nikolai Antonovich **Pogrebnyakov**

Commander, 27th Infantry Division
- 9 Dec 1892 - 18 Jan 1896: *Lt.-Gen.* Ivan Ivanovich **Tyvalovich**
- 18 Jan 1896 - 18 Aug 1898: *Lt.-Gen.* Dmitry Nikolayevich **Gets**
- 26 Oct 1898 - 3 Sep 1904: *Gen. of Inf.* Arkady Platonovich **Skugarevsky**
- 19 Nov 1904 - 3 Dec 1906: *Gen. of Inf.* Faddei Vasilievich **Sivers**
- 6 Dec 1906 - 16 Jan 1909: *Gen. of Inf.* Leopold Aleksandrovich **Shvank**
- 27 Jan 1909 - 19 Feb 1914: *Gen. of Inf.* Rafail Nikolayevich **Fleysher**
- 19 Feb 1914 - 13 Mar 1914: *Lt.-Gen.* Stanislav Konstantinovich **Abakanovich**
- 2 Apr 1914 - 2 Feb 1915: *Lt.-Gen.* August-Karl-Mikhail Mikhailovich **Adaridi**
- 8 Feb 1915 - 4 Apr 1915: *Lt.-Gen.* Gerbert Georgievich **Dzhonson**
- 4 Apr 1915 - 22 Feb 1916: *Lt.-Gen.* Konstantin Vladimirovich **Asmus**
- 10 Mar 1916 - 18 Apr 1917: *Lt.-Gen.* Nikolai Grigoryevich **Stavrovich**

Commander, 1st Brigade, 27th Infantry Division
- 3 Mar 1891 - 7 Oct 1899: *Maj.-Gen.* Leopold Ivanovich **Rozhnov**

- 31 Oct 1899 - 29 May 1903: *Maj.-Gen.* Iosif Suleymanovich **Poltorzhitsky**
- 4 Jun 1903 - 2 Mar 1904: *Maj.-Gen.* Dmitry Lvovich **Shults**
- 2 Mar 1904 - 22 Oct 1904: *Gen. of Inf.* Aleksandr Frantsevich **Ragoza**
- 8 Nov 1904 - 4 Sep 1906: *Lt.-Gen.* Ignaty Fyodorovich **Kazakevich**
- 6 Oct 1906 - 17 Oct 1910: *Gen. of Inf.* Fyodor-Emily-Karl Ivanovich von **Torklus**
- 17 Oct 1910 - 29 Dec 1910: ?
- 29 Dec 1910 - Apr 1913: *Maj.-Gen.* Ivan Ignatyevich **Gursky**
- 2 May 1913 - 8 Feb 1914: *Lt.-Gen.* Mikhail Alekseyevich **Sokovnin**
- 8 Feb 1914 - 13 May 1914: *Maj.-Gen.* Pyotr Pavlovich **Palibin**
- 7 Jul 1914 - 29 Jul 1914: *Lt.-Gen.* Nikolai Kirillovich **Yanovsky**
- 29 Jul 1914 - 2 Mar 1917: ?

Commander, 2nd Brigade, 27th Infantry Division

- 4 Apr 1894 - 29 Jan 1898: *Maj.-Gen.* Vladimir Nikolayevich **Bazilevsky**
- 26 Feb 1898 - 4 Jun 1899: *Gen. of Inf.* Dmitry Sergeyevich **Buturlin**
- 4 Jun 1899 - 16 Aug 1900: *Lt.-Gen.* Aleksandr Davidovich **Tugan-Mirza-Baranovsky**
- 10 Sep 1900 - 22 Feb 1901: *Gen. of Inf.* Nikolai Dmitrievich **Butovsky**
- 22 Feb 1901 - 2 Aug 1901: *Gen. of Inf.* Vladimir Petrovich **Korneyev**
- 20 Sep 1901 - 23 Sep 1904: *Maj.-Gen.* Aleksandr Nikolayevich **Przhetslavsky**
- 3 Oct 1904 - 10 Aug 1910: *Lt.-Gen.* Fyodor Fyodorovich **Orlov**
- 10 Aug 1910 - Feb 1913: *Lt.-Gen.* Aleksey Alekseyevich **Prigorovsky**
- 12 Feb 1913 - 8 Feb 1914: *Maj.-Gen.* Pyotr Pavlovich **Palibin**
- 8 Feb 1914 - 24 May 1915: *Maj.-Gen.* Artur-Sevostyan Yemilyevich **Beymelburg**
- 24 May 1915 - 2 Mar 1917: ?

Commander, 27th Artillery Brigade

- 12 Oct 1890 - 1 Oct 1897: *Maj.-Gen.* Nikolai Adolfovich **Meynander**
- 1 Oct 1897 - 29 Dec 1899: *Maj.-Gen.* Nikolai Davydovich **Ivanov**
- 29 Dec 1899 - 17 Oct 1903: *Maj.-Gen.* Sergey Yevgenyevich **Kastorsky**
- 17 Oct 1903 - 24 Oct 1904: *Lt.-Gen.* Sergey Vasilyevich **Ivashentsov**
- 24 Oct 1904 - 24 Feb 1905: *Maj.-Gen.* Pyotr Ivanovich **Puzyrov**
- 2 Mar 1905 - 3 Aug 1908: *Maj.-Gen.* Dmitry Aleksandrovich **Yudin**
- 2 Aug 1908 - 3 Oct 1908: ?
- 3 Oct 1908 - 18 Feb 1912: *Lt.-Gen.* Artemy Solomonovich **Vartanov**
- 10 Mar 1912 - 31 Mar 1915: *Maj.-Gen.* Vladimir Nikolayevich **Folimonov**
- 31 Mar 1915 - 1916: ?
- 1916 - 8 Aug 1917: *Maj.-Gen.* Ivan Aleksandrovich **Zakharchenko**

Commander, 28th Infantry Division

- 8 Jan 1889 - 17 Feb 1896: *Lt.-Gen.* Otton Iosifovich **Nemira**
- 20 Feb 1896 - 10 Jan 1898: *Lt.-Gen.* Ivan Ivanovich **Maksimov**
- 10 Jan 1898 - 8 Jan 1902: *Lt.-Gen.* Orest Mikhailovich **Kislinsky**
- 30 Jan 1902 - 25 Nov 1906: *Lt.-Gen.* Dmitry Alekseyevich **Kamenetsky**
- 25 Nov 1906 - 15 Jun 1910: *Lt.-Gen.* Pavel Oskarovich **Papengut**

- 2 Jul 1910 - 23 Apr 1913:   *Gen. of Inf.* Pyotr Platonovich **Pototsky**
- 23 Apr 1913 - 31 Mar 1915:   *Gen. of Inf.* Nikolai Alekseyevich **Lashkevich**
- 3 Apr 1915 - 18 Apr 1917:   *Lt.-Gen.* Baron Leopold Fridrikhovich von der **Brinken**

Commander, 1st Brigade, 28th Infantry Division
- 28 Mar 1894 - 12 Oct 1895:   *Lt.-Gen.* Prince David Luarsabovich **Argutinsky-Dolgorukov**
- 25 Oct 1895 - 4 Dec 1895:   *Maj.-Gen.* Konstantin Mikhailovich **Akinfiyev**
- 4 Dec 1895 - 6 Nov 1897:   *Gen. of Inf.* Andrey Petrovich **Chaykovsky**
- 27 Nov 1897 - 12 Jul 1900:   *Lt.-Gen.* Ivan Venediktovich **Bogayevsky**
- 3 Aug 1900 - 7 Aug 1906:   *Maj.-Gen.* Vladimir Dmitriyevich **Yartsev**
- 7 Aug 1906 - 8 Jan 1909:   *Maj.-Gen.* Stepan Stepanovich **Morozov**
- 8 Jan 1909 - 26 Apr 1914:   *Lt.-Gen.* Pyotr Semyonovich **Yurkevich**
- 13 May 1914 - 7 Jul 1914:   *Lt.-Gen.* Nikolai Kirillovich **Yanovsky**
- 7 Jul 1914 - 29 Jul 1914:   *Lt.-Gen.* Pyotr Nikolayevich **Turov**
- 10 Sep 1914 - 28 Mar 1915:   *Maj.-Gen.* Mikhail Grigoryevich **Yerogin**
- 28 Mar 1915 - 2 Mar 1917:   ?

Commander, 2nd Brigade, 28th Infantry Division
- 26 Nov 1891 - 11 Jan 1900:   *Lt.-Gen.* Ivan Ivanovich **Radzishevsky**
- 15 Feb 1900 - 12 Apr 1906:   *Maj.-Gen.* Ivan Nikolayevich **Frezer**
- 12 Apr 1906 - 30 Jun 1907:   *Maj.-Gen.* Nikolai Seliverstovich **Koyshevsky**
- 30 Jun 1907 - 8 Jan 1909:   *Lt.-Gen.* Pyotr Semyonovich **Yurkevich**
- 8 Jan 1909 - 24 Mar 1909:   ?
- 24 Mar 1909 - 22 May 1910:   *Maj.-Gen.* Edmund-Boleslav Ivanovich **Rudnitsky**
- 22 May 1910 - 10 Aug 1910:   *Lt.-Gen.* Aleksey Alekseyevich **Prigorovsky**
- 10 Aug 1910 - 17 Feb 1913:   *Gen. of Inf.* Vladimir Vladimirovich **De-Vitt**
- 18 Mar 1913 - 26 Apr 1916:   *Maj.-Gen.* Yevgeny Aleksandrovich **Rossysky**
- 26 Apr 1916 - 2 Mar 1917:   ?

Commander, 28th Artillery Brigade
- 19 May 1894 - 23 Dec 1898:   *Lt.-Gen.* Pavel Ivanovich **Bedo**
- 23 Dec 1898 - 22 Jun 1902:   *Gen. of Art.* Aleksandr Nikolayevich **Petrakov**
- 22 Jun 1902 - 28 Mar 1903:   *Lt.-Gen.* Fyodor Petrovich **Falenberg**
- 28 Mar 1903 - 27 Sep 1906:   *Gen. of Art.* Pyotr Flegontovich **Putintsev**
- 27 Sep 1906 - 3 Oct 1908:   *Gen. of Art.* Aleksandr Vasilyevich **Sergeyev**
- 22 Oct 1908 - 27 Aug 1913:   *Lt.-Gen.* Nikolai Mikhailovich **Chelyustkin**
- 30 Aug 1913 - 9 Aug 1914:   *Maj.-Gen.* Vilgelm Fridrikhovich **Mallio**
- 9 Aug 1914 - 17 Oct 1914:   ?
- 17 Oct 1914 - 22 Jan 1917:   *Maj.-Gen.* Vladimir Yevgenyevich **Nasekin**
- 22 Jan 1917 - 2 Mar 1917:   ?

Commander, 29th Infantry Division
- 30 Aug 1890 - 17 Jan 1896:   *Gen. of Inf.* Count Nikolai Dmitriyevich **Tatishchev**

- 18 Jan 1896 - 13 Apr 1896: *Lt.-Gen.* Ivan Ivanovich **Tyvalovich**
- 19 Apr 1896 - May 1899: *Lt.-Gen.* Nikolai Vladimirovich **Cheremisinov**
- 13 May 1899 - 18 Jan 1900: *Gen. of Inf.* Pyotr Vikentyevich **Kononovich-Gorbatsky**
- 17 Feb 1900 - 17 Oct 1904: *Gen. of Inf.* Aleksey Iosifovich **Dzichkanets**
- 24 Nov 1904 - 11 Nov 1907: *Lt.-Gen.* Vasily Aleksandrovich **Narbut**
- 11 Nov 1907 - 24 Nov 1908: *Lt.-Gen.* Ivan Ivanovich **Kholodovsky**
- 24 Dec 1908 - 9 May 1914: *Gen. of Inf.* Vladimir Aleksandrovich **Arkhipov**
- 9 May 1914 - 3 Apr 1915: *Lt.-Gen.* Anatoly Nikolayevich **Rozenschild von Paulin**
- 3 Apr 1915 - 22 Apr 1917: *Lt.-Gen.* Boris Alekseyevich **Dzichkanets**

Commander, 1st Brigade, 29th Infantry Division
- 16 Sep 1885 - 7 Oct 1899: *Lt.-Gen.* Nikolai Antonovich **Tunzelman von Adlerflug**
- 31 Oct 1899 - 26 Jun 1902: *Maj.-Gen.* Kronid Pavlovich **Kondyrev**
- 26 Jun 1902 - 17 Jan 1906: *Gen. of Inf.* Aleksandr Iosafovich **Yevreinov**
- 20 Feb 1906 - 4 Oct 1908: *Lt.-Gen.* Viktor Pavlovich **Zykov**
- 27 Oct 1908 - 29 Jan 1909: *Maj.-Gen.* Aleksandr Andreyevich **Orel**
- 30 Jan 1909 - 9 Oct 1912: *Lt.-Gen.* Sergey Dmitriyevich **Chistyakov**
- 26 Oct 1912 - 29 Jul 1914: *Lt.-Gen.* Ivan Konstantinovich **Gandurin**
- 29 Jul 1914 - 2 Mar 1917: ?

Commander, 2nd Brigade, 29th Infantry Division
- 7 Jun 1890 - 7 Dec 1896: *Lt.-Gen.* Aleksandr Konstantinovich **Maklakov**
- 23 Dec 1896 - Dec 1900: *Maj.-Gen.* Eduard Iosifovich **Sassky**
- 22 Feb 1901 - 16 Jun 1904: *Gen. of Inf.* Nikolai Dmitrievich **Butovsky**
- 6 Jul 1904 - 29 Jan 1909: *Lt.-Gen.* Frants-Martselian Vikentyevich **Bokshchanin**
- 29 Jan 1909 - Sep 1914: *Maj.-Gen.* Aleksandr Andreyevich **Orel**
- 13 Oct 1914 - 24 May 1915: *Lt.-Gen.* Mikhail Ivanovich **Chizhov**
- 24 May 1915 - 2 Mar 1917: ?

Commander, 29th Artillery Brigade
- 16 Mar 1892 - 14 Feb 1899: *Lt.-Gen.* Vasily Vladimirovich **Tsilliakus**
- 14 Feb 1899 - 11 Aug 1900: *Lt.-Gen.* Nikolai Viktorovich **Tsvetkov**
- 11 Aug 1900 - 15 Feb 1905: *Gen. of Inf.* Vladimir Petrovich **Olshevsky**
- 15 Feb 1905 - 28 Sep 1911: *Lt.-Gen.* Khalil Mustafovich **Bazarevsky**
- 28 Sep 1911 - 31 Mar 1914: *Lt.-Gen.* Sergey Timofeyevich **Belyayev**
- 5 Apr 1914 - 18 May 1915: *Maj.-Gen.* Aleksandr Nikolayevich **Savich**
- 28 May 1915 - 31 Mar 1917: *Maj.-Gen.* Yanuary Sergeyevich **Veshnyakov**

Commander, 30th Infantry Division
- 11 Apr 1893 - 18 Apr 1895: *Lt.-Gen.* Ivan Semyonovich **Saranchov**
- 24 Apr 1895 - 1 Oct 1899: *Gen. of Inf.* Ignaty Petrovich **Maslov**
- 20 Oct 1899 - 10 Aug 1904: *Lt.-Gen.* Nikolai Nilovich **Lavrov**

- 8 Sep 1904 - 24 Apr 1908: *Gen. of Inf.* Aleksandr Prokhorovich **Shevtsov**
- 15 May 1908 - 28 Nov 1908: *Gen. of Inf.* Vikenty Vikentyevich **Sennitsky**
- 28 Nov 1908 - 6 Feb 1914: *Lt.-Gen.* Mikhail Nikitich **Ivanov**
- 6 Feb 1914 - 3 Oct 1914: *Lt.-Gen.* Eduard Arkadyevich **Kolyankovsky**
- 4 Nov 1914 - 1917: *Lt.-Gen.* Nikolai Nikolayevich **Karepov**

Commander, 1st Brigade, 30th Infantry Division
- 20 Nov 1886 - 24 Oct 1899: *Maj.-Gen.* Aleksandr Karlovich **Miller**
- 24 Oct 1899 - 12 Jul 1902: *Lt.-Gen.* Nikolai Prokofyevich **Pozhidayev**
- 12 Jul 1902 - 10 Sep 1902: ?
- 10 Sep 1902 - 7 Jan 1904: *Lt.-Gen.* Yevgeny Vasilyevich **Kolenko**
- 15 Jan 1904 - 31 Dec 1905: *Lt.-Gen.* Konstantin Danilovich **Yurgens**
- 31 Dec 1905 - 14 Mar 1906: ?
- 14 Mar 1906 - 4 Jul 1906: *Lt.-Gen.* Ivan Ioasafovich **Yevreinov**
- 4 Jul 1906 - 8 Oct 1908: *Gen. of Inf.* Nikolai Ivanovich **Timchenko-Ruban**
- 27 Oct 1908 - Dec 1909: *Maj.-Gen.* Aleksey Iosifovich **Tarasevich**
- 11 Feb 1910 - Mar 1911: *Maj.-Gen.* Aleksandr Karlovich **Sellinen**
- 6 Mar 1911 - 3 Sep 1913: *Maj.-Gen.* Sergey Gavrilovich **Leontovich**
- 3 Sep 1913 - 1 Aug 1914: *Maj.-Gen.* Vladimir Zakharovich **Gudima**
- 1 Aug 1914 - Sep 1914: *Lt.-Gen.* Vasily Fyodorovich **Novitsky**
- Sep 1914 - 2 Mar 1917: ?

Commander, 2nd Brigade, 30th Infantry Division
- 11 Dec 1892 - 2 Sep 1899: *Maj.-Gen.* Karl Konradovich **Shuld**
- 2 Sep 1899 - 6 Mar 1900: *Maj.-Gen.* Ivan Ivanovich **Reyman**
- 16 Mar 1900 - 15 Nov 1903: *Lt.-Gen.* Vasily Vasilyevich **Shchagin**
- 11 Dec 1903 - 28 Jul 1905: *Lt.-Gen.* Andrei Dmitriyevich **Vsevolozhsky**
- 28 Jul 1905 - 12 Dec 1905: ?
- 12 Dec 1905 - 17 Oct 1910: *Lt.-Gen.* Nikolai Nikolayevich **Korotkevich**
- 4 Nov 1910 - 8 Jul 1913: *Maj.-Gen.* Aleksandr Aleksandrovich **Skopinsky-Shtrik**
- 8 Jul 1913 - 29 Aug 1914: *Maj.-Gen.* Sergey Petrovich **Sokolov**
- 29 Aug 1914 - 2 Mar 1917: ?

Commander, 30th Artillery Brigade
- 2 Sep 1891 - 19 Sep 1895: *Maj.-Gen.* Vasily Petrovich **Bulayev**
- 15 Oct 1895 - 1 Apr 1896: *Lt.-Gen.* Nikolai Gustavovich **Golmdorf**
- 25 Apr 1896 - 30 May 1901: *Lt.-Gen.* Aleksey Stepanovich **Shepilov**
- 30 May 1901 - 24 Oct 1904: *Lt.-Gen.* Stepan Ivanovich **Sobolevsky**
- 24 Oct 1904 - 13 Mar 1906: *Colonel* Ivan Sergeyevich **Polikarpov**
- 13 Mar 1906 - 22 Oct 1908: *Maj.-Gen.* Ivan Nikolayevich **Lyapunov**
- 22 Oct 1908 - 12 Nov 1910: *Gen. of Art.* Count Viktor Viktorovich **Dolivo-Dobrovolsky**
- 12 Nov 1910 - 19 Nov 1914: *Lt.-Gen.* Leopold Fyodorovich **Gilferding**
- 19 Nov 1914 - 15 Jan 1915: ?
- 15 Jan 1915 - 28 May 1915: *Lt.-Gen.* Leopold Fyodorovich **Gilferding**

- 28 May 1915 - 18 Jan 1916:   *Maj.-Gen.* Dmitry Yakovlevich **Milovich**
- 12 Feb 1916 - 1917:   *Maj.-Gen.* Sergey Nikolayevich **Boyarsky**

Commander, 31st Infantry Division
- 19 Feb 1890 - 18 Dec 1900:   *Gen. of Inf.* Viktor Emmanuilovich **Budde**
- 18 Dec 1900 - 22 Feb 1901:   ?
- 22 Feb 1901 - 8 Mar 1903:   *Gen. of Inf.* Pyotr Sofronovich **Kublitsky**
- 3 Apr 1903 - 9 Mar 1905:   *Lt.-Gen.* Nikolai Ivanovich **Mau**
- 9 Mar 1905 - Jun 1907:   *Lt.-Gen.* Konstantin Grigorievich **Vasiliev**
- 29 Jul 1907 - 22 Sep 1909:   *Lt.-Gen.* Vladmir Ildefonsovich **Volkovitsky**
- 3 Oct 1909 - 1 Sep 1912:   *Gen. of Inf.* Vladimir Yegorovich **Bukholts**
- 23 Sep 1912 - 6 Oct 1914:   *Gen. of Inf.* Nikolai Ivanovich **Protopopov**
- 6 Oct 1914 - 24 Oct 1915:   *Lt.-Gen.* Polikarp Alekseyevich **Kuznetsov**
- 24 Oct 1915 - 18 Apr 1917:   *Lt.-Gen.* Leonid Vasilyevich **Fedyay**

Commander, 1st Brigade, 31st Infantry Division
- 9 Nov 1892 - 30 Dec 1897:   *Maj.-Gen.* Vasily Mitrofanovich **Gulyayev**
- 30 Dec 1897 - 17 May 1903:   *Lt.-Gen.* Konstantin Ivanovich **Radzishevsky**
- 17 May 1903 - 9 Mar 1905:   *Maj.-Gen.* Georgy Vladislavovich **Chizhevich**
- 9 Mar 1905 - 17 Aug 1906:   *Maj.-Gen.* Gavriil Vikentyevich **Rzhesniovetsky**
- 17 Aug 1906 - 28 Dec 1910:   *Lt.-Gen.* Vladimir Mikhailovich **Vasiliev**
- 28 Dec 1910 - 31 Mar 1912:   ?
- 31 Mar 1912 - 19 Jul 1914:   *Lt.-Gen.* Aleksandr Petrovich **Gavrilov**
- 19 Jul 1914 - 6 Sep 1914:   ?
- 6 Sep 1914 - 4 Nov 1914:   *Lt.-Gen.* Aleksandr Sergeyevich **Savvich**
- 4 Nov 1914 - 2 Mar 1917:   ?

Commander, 2nd Brigade, 31st Infantry Division
- 7 May 1890 - 7 Feb 1901:   *Maj.-Gen.* Dmitry Nikolayevich **Vansovich**
- 7 Feb 1901 - 30 Oct 1903:   *Gen. of Inf.* Leonid Konstantinovich **Artamonov**
- 30 Oct 1903 - 9 Mar 1905:   *Lt.-Gen.* Konstantin Grigorievich **Vasiliev**
- 18 Jul 1905 - 14 Aug 1905:   *Maj.-Gen.* Nikolai Aleksandrovich **Myuller**
- 14 Aug 1905 - 12 Dec 1905:   *Lt.-Gen.* Nikolai Nikolayevich **Korotkevich**
- 12 Dec 1905 - 12 May 1908:   *Maj.-Gen.* Nikolai Aleksandrovich **Myuller**
- 12 May 1908 - 31 Dec 1913:   *Lt.-Gen.* Prince Avraam Georgiyevich **Vachnadze**
- 31 Dec 1913 - 13 Aug 1914:   *Maj.-Gen.* Fyodor Konstantinovich **Khitrovo**
- 13 Aug 1914 - 4 Nov 1914:   ?
- 4 Nov 1914 - 27 Aug 1915:   *Lt.-Gen.* Aleksandr Sergeyevich **Savvich**
- 27 Aug 1915 - 2 Mar 1917:   ?

Commander, 31st Artillery Brigade
- 9 Aug 1894 - Dec 1899:   *Lt.-Gen.* Vladimir Aleksandrovich von **Yarmershtedt**
- 29 Dec 1899 - 5 Aug 1903:   *Maj.-Gen.* Konstantin Georgiyevich **Kuzminsky**
- 5 Aug 1903 - 2 May 1904:   *Maj.-Gen.* Ivan Vasilievich **Bukin**
- 2 May 1904 - 22 Feb 1905:   *Maj.-Gen.* Konstantin Mikhailovich **Dekinleyn**

- 1 Mar 1905 - Jun 1907: *Maj.-Gen.* Iosif Fedotovich **Kosinsky**
- 20 Jul 1907 - 26 Jul 1910: *Lt.-Gen.* Vladimir Dmitriyevich **Turov**
- 1 Aug 1910 - May 1912: *Maj.-Gen.* Viktor Adamovich **Vevern**
- 19 May 1912 - 4 Jan 1914: *Lt.-Gen.* Aleksey Semyonovich **Sofiano**
- 23 Jan 1914 - 29 Feb 1916: *Maj.-Gen.* Igor Konstantinovich **Teleshev**
- 29 Feb 1916 - 9 Jun 1917: *Maj.-Gen.* Aleksandr Adamovich **Vevern**

Commander, 32nd Infantry Division
- 6 Jun 1890 - 2 Sep 1895: *Gen. of Inf.* Vadim Vasilyevich **Plaksin**
- 15 Sep 1895 - 21 Feb 1896: *Gen. of Inf.* Yakov Aleksandrovich **Grebenshchikov**
- 21 Feb 1896 - 19 Dec 1897: *Gen. of Inf.* Prince Georgy Yevseyevich **Tumanov**
- 19 Dec 1897 - 27 Jun 1902: *Lt.-Gen.* Nikolai Aleksandrovich **Shepelev**
- 22 Jul 1902 - 28 Dec 1905: *Lt.-Gen.* Aleksandr Semyonovich **Pisarenko**
- 16 Jan 1906 - 15 May 1908: *Gen. of Inf.* Vikenty Vikentyevich **Sennitsky**
- 19 May 1908 - 2 Dec 1908: *Lt.-Gen.* Alfred-Stanislav Vasilievich von **Bekker**
- 2 Dec 1908 - 13 Feb 1909: *Lt.-Gen.* Aleksandr Vasilievich **Vereshchagin**
- 13 Feb 1909 - 21 Jul 1910: *Lt.-Gen.* Nikolai Sergeyevich **Berdyayev**
- 21 Jul 1910 - 25 Mar 1911: *Gen. of Inf.* Nikolai Dmitrievich **Butovsky**
- 27 Mar 1911 - 9 Jan 1915: *Gen. of Inf.* Fyodor Khristianovich von **Vendt**
- 9 Jan 1915 - 8 Feb 1915: *Lt.-Gen.* Konstantin Gerasimovich **Nekrasov**
- 16 Feb 1915 - 2 Apr 1916: *Lt.-Gen.* Vladimir Aleksandrovich **Yablochkin**
- 2 Apr 1916 - 14 Oct 1916: *Lt.-Gen.* Aleksandr Sergeyevich **Lukomsky**
- 14 Oct 1916 - 18 Apr 1917: *Lt.-Gen.* Ivan Ivanovich **Popov**

Commander, 1st Brigade, 32nd Infantry Division
- 17 Jul 1893 - 21 Sep 1895: *Maj.-Gen.* Vasily Aleksandrovich **Brandorf**
- 21 Sep 1895 - 18 Oct 1896: *Maj.-Gen.* Aleksandr Aleksandrovich **Broterus**
- 18 Oct 1896 - 2 Feb 1902: *Maj.-Gen.* Valentin Mikhailovich **Baranovsky**
- 2 Feb 1902 - 31 May 1903: *Lt.-Gen.* Pavel Kaetanovich **Dombrovsky**
- 9 Jun 1903 - 14 Feb 1907: *Maj.-Gen.* Vladimir Ivanovich **Bubnov**
- 8 Mar 1907 - 2 Jul 1907: *Gen. of Inf.* Stanislav Feliksovich **Stelnitsky**
- 6 Jul 1907 - 7 Dec 1912: *Maj.-Gen.* Vladimir Ampliyevich **Odintsov**
- 7 Dec 1912 - 21 Jan 1916: *Lt.-Gen.* Baron Sergey Ernestovich von **Ber**
- 21 Jan 1916 - 2 Mar 1917: ?

Commander, 2nd Brigade, 32nd Infantry Division
- 12 Jun 1891 - Oct 1899: *Maj.-Gen.* Dmitry Vasilyevich **Messarosh**
- 24 Oct 1899 - 29 Mar 1906: *Maj.-Gen.* Valerian Aleksandrovich **Kishinets**
- 29 Mar 1906 - 28 Feb 1907: *Maj.-Gen.* Konstantin Ilich **Krichinsky**
- 28 Feb 1907 - 12 Nov 1907: *Maj.-Gen.* Konstantin-Gugo Kasparovich **Peterov**
- 12 Nov 1907 - 21 Nov 1908: *Lt.-Gen.* Pavel Konstantinovich **Abakanovich**
- 22 Nov 1908 - 2 May 1913: *Lt.-Gen.* Pyotr Mikhailovich **Baranov**
- 23 Jun 1913 - 29 Jul 1914: *Lt.-Gen.* Aleksandr Mikhailovich **Khvostov**
- 29 Jul 1914 - 10 Nov 1914: ?
- 10 Nov 1914 - 16 Jan 1915: *Lt.-Gen.* Aleksandr Andreyevich **Tsitsovich**

- 16 Jan 1915 - 2 Mar 1917: ?

Commander, Consolidated Brigade, 32nd Infantry Division *(Formed 1916)*
- 6 Feb 1916 - 12 Jul 1916: *Gen. of Inf.* Vladimir Andreyevich **Cheremisov**

Commander, 32nd Artillery Brigade
- 1 Jun 1888 - 26 May 1897: *Maj.-Gen.* Ilya Lavrentyevich **Yakubovsky**
- 26 May 1897 - Jan 1899: *Maj.-Gen.* Nikolai Nikolayevich **Martynov**
- 16 Mar 1899 - 8 Nov 1902: *Maj.-Gen.* Ivan Mikhailovich **Dovgilevich**
- 11 Nov 1902 - 29 Apr 1907: *Maj.-Gen.* Mikhail Kornilovich **Kozlovsky**
- 29 Apr 1907 - 2 Feb 1910: *Maj.-Gen.* Nikolai Nikolayevich **Zhukov**
- 4 Mar 1910 - 16 Feb 1911: *Maj.-Gen.* Nikolai Ivanovich **Voshchinin**
- 16 Feb 1911 - 2 Nov 1914: *Lt.-Gen.* Mikhail Nikolayevich **Promtov**
- 2 Nov 1914 - Jan 1915: ?
- Jan 1915 - 31 Mar 1915: *Lt.-Gen.* Leonid Nikolayevich **Gobyato**
- 31 Mar 1915 - 4 Dec 1915: *Maj.-Gen.* Vasily Vasilyevich **Mirovich**
- 4 Dec 1915 - 1917: *Maj.-Gen.* Aleksandr Konstantinovich **Obrucheshnikov**

Commander, 33rd Infantry Division
- 11 Mar 1887 - 23 Oct 1896: *Lt.-Gen.* Fridrikh Petrovich **Zass**
- 30 Oct 1896 - 13 May 1899: *Gen. of Inf.* Pyotr Vikentyevich **Kononovich-Gorbatsky**
- 13 May 1899 - 2 Jul 1899: *Lt.-Gen.* Yevgeny Stanislavovich **Shimanovsky**
- 5 Aug 1899 - 16 Dec 1904: *Gen. of Inf.* Lyudvig Lyudvigovich **Drake**
- 25 Jan 1905 - 16 May 1905: *Gen. of Inf.* Viktor Konstantinovich **Grek**
- 24 May 1905 - 19 Jul 1909: *Gen. of Inf.* Dmitry Nikolayevich **Voronets**
- 22 Jul 1909 - 14 Feb 1915: *Gen. of Inf.* Aleksandr Aleksandrovich **Zegelov**
- 26 Feb 1915 - 27 Feb 1917: *Lt.-Gen.* Matvey Aleksandrovich **Sulkevich**

Commander, 1st Brigade, 33rd Infantry Division
- 16 Apr 1889 - 18 Aug 1895: *Maj.-Gen.* Nikolai Maksimovich **Sidorenko**
- 18 Aug 1895 - 6 Feb 1896: ?
- 6 Feb 1896 - 11 Feb 1902: *Maj.-Gen.* Vladimir Antonovich **Krasovsky**
- 11 Feb 1902 - 21 May 1903: *Gen. of Inf.* Nikolai Aleksandrovich **Kashtalinsky**
- 31 May 1903 - 15 Sep 1904: *Lt.-Gen.* Pavel Kaetanovich **Dombrovsky**
- 15 Sep 1904 - 9 Oct 1906: *Maj.-Gen.* Ivan Filippovich **Alekseyev**
- 9 Oct 1906 - Jun 1908: *Maj.-Gen.* Georgy Vladislavovich **Chizhevich**
- 12 Jul 1908 - 20 Jul 1910: *Maj.-Gen.* Ivan Yegorovich **Bychinsky**
- 20 Jul 1910 - 1915: *Lt.-Gen.* Mikhail Mikhailovich **Yakovlev**
- 3 Apr 1915 - 25 May 1917: *Lt.-Gen.* Konstantin Konstantinovich **Kolen**

Commander, 2nd Brigade, 33rd Infantry Division
- 26 Feb 1894 - 29 Apr 1898: *Lt.-Gen.* Vasily Ivanovich **Sendetsky**

- 13 May 1898 - May 1905: *Maj.-Gen.* Nikolai Aleksandrovich von **Fokht**
- 9 Jul 1905 - 19 Jul 1914: *Lt.-Gen.* Nikolai Vasilievich **Belov**
- 24 Jul 1914 - 31 Oct 1915: *Maj.-Gen.* Ivan Ivanovich **Efirov**
- 23 Dec 1915 - 31 Mar 1917: *Maj.-Gen.* Nikolai Pavlovich **Chernov**

Commander, 33rd Artillery Brigade
- 2 Apr 1888 - 17 May 1895: *Gen. of Art.* Vasily Yakovlevich **Fride**
- 17 May 1895 - 5 Dec 1899: *Lt.-Gen.* Nikolai Dmitriyevich **Tikhobrazov**
- 29 Dec 1899 - 4 Jun 1904: *Gen. of Art.* Nikolai Vladimirovich **Stoyanov**
- 14 Jun 1904 - Jun 1910: *Maj.-Gen.* Nikolai Nikolayevich **Diterikhs**
- 26 Jul 1910 - 19 Mar 1915: *Lt.-Gen.* Pyotr Aleksandrovich **Derevitsky**
- 19 Mar 1915 - 31 May 1916: *Lt.-Gen.* Georgy Mikhailovich **Sheydeman**
- 31 May 1916 - 2 Mar 1917: ?

Commander, 34th Infantry Division
- 9 Sep 1894 - 21 Jun 1899: *Gen. of Eng.* Nikolai Venediktovich **Bogayevsky**
- 4 Aug 1899 - 17 Feb 1900: *Lt.-Gen.* Aleksandr Fyodorovich **Plyutsinsky**
- 17 Feb 1900 - 27 Apr 1900: ?
- 27 Apr 1900 - 10 Jan 1904: *Gen. of Inf.* Alfons Ivanovich **Bush**
- 25 Jan 1904 - 15 Mar 1906: *Gen. of Inf.* Aleksandr Genrikhovich **Sandetsky**
- 15 Mar 1906 - 5 Sep 1906: *Lt.-Gen.* Vasily Osipovich **Rylsky**
- 5 Sep 1906 - 8 Jun 1907: *Lt.-Gen.* Mikhail Pavlovich **Davydov**
- 14 Jul 1907 - Mar 1909: *Lt.-Gen.* Fyodor Dmitryevich **Domozhirov**
- 20 Mar 1909 - 14 Sep 1911: *Gen. of Inf.* Mikhail Isayevich **Ebelov**
- 12 Oct 1911 - 25 Aug 1914: *Lt.-Gen.* Mikhail Mikhailovich **Dobrovolsky**
- 25 Aug 1914 - 23 Mar 1915: *Lt.-Gen.* Nikita Mikhailovich **Batashev**
- 1 Apr 1915 - 6 Mar 1916: *Lt.-Gen.* Aleksei Yevgenyevich **Gutor**
- 10 Mar 1916 - 4 Sep 1917: *Lt.-Gen.* Nikolai Petrovich **Stremoukhov**

Commander, 1st Brigade, 34th Infantry Division
- 14 Feb 1888 - 23 Jun 1897: *Lt.-Gen.* Vladimir Nikolayevich **Klevezal**
- 7 Jul 1897 - 18 Jun 1903: *Maj.-Gen.* Anatoly Rafailovich **Krizhanovsky**
- 18 Jun 1903 - 4 Jun 1904: *Maj.-Gen.* Vasily Petrovich **Zholtanovsky**
- 10 Jun 1904 - 14 Jan 1905: *Maj.-Gen.* Yakov Gennadyevich **Dudyshkin**
- 14 Jan 1905 - 19 Jul 1914: *Lt.-Gen.* Nikita Mikhailovich **Batashev**
- 19 Jul 1914 - 2 Mar 1917: ?

Commander, 2nd Brigade, 34th Infantry Division
- 21 Jan 1894 - 7 Jul 1897: *Maj.-Gen.* Anatoly Rafailovich **Krizhanovsky**
- 7 Jul 1897 - 11 Mar 1898: *Maj.-Gen.* Nikolai Andreyevich **Suvorov**
- 11 Mar 1898 - 12 Oct 1902: *Maj.-Gen.* Ivan Yevteyevich **Nechayev**
- 12 Oct 1902 - 2 Jun 1904: *Lt.-Gen.* Mikhail Grigoryevich **Golembatovsky**
- 4 Jun 1904 - 5 May 1905: *Maj.-Gen.* Vasily Petrovich **Zholtanovsky**
- 5 May 1906 - 7 Jul 1907: *Lt.-Gen.* Vladislav Frantsevich **Baufal**
- 7 Jul 1907 - 15 Oct 1907: ?

- 15 Oct 1907 - 10 Jul 1908: *Maj.-Gen.* Ivan Antonovich **Dumbadze**
- 10 Jul 1908 - 28 Nov 1908: ?
- 28 Nov 1908 - 19 Jul 1914: *Lt.-Gen.* Aleksandr Yefimovich **Zhdanko**
- 19 Jul 1914 - 2 Mar 1917: ?

Commander, 34th Artillery Brigade
- 24 Aug 1888 - 9 Sep 1895: *Maj.-Gen.* Aleksandr Ivanovich **Kornilovich**
- 9 Sep 1895 - 29 Dec 1899: *Maj.-Gen.* Grigory Moiseyevich **Beletsky**
- 29 Dec 1899 - 4 Mar 1903: *Lt.-Gen.* Aleksandr Stepanovich **Mikheyev**
- 4 Mar 1903 - 4 Jun 1904: *Maj.-Gen.* Pyotr Vasilyevich **Osipov**
- 4 Jun 1904 - 16 Jan 1909: *Lt.-Gen.* Konstantin Vasilyevich **Kolokoltsov**
- 16 Jan 1909 - 25 Jul 1910: *Lt.-Gen.* Sergey Apollonovich **Perfilyev**
- 25 Jul 1910 - 24 Jan 1914: *Lt.-Gen.* Vladimir Yakovlevich **Gusev**
- 29 Jan 1914 - 8 Aug 1916: *Maj.-Gen.* Leonid Vitalyevich **Nishchinsky**
- 8 Aug 1916 - 2 Mar 1917: ?

Commander, 35th Infantry Division
- 18 May 1894 - 11 Aug 1899: *Gen. of Inf.* Leonty Avksentyevich **Yunakov**
- 6 Sep 1899 - 23 Jan 1902: *Gen. of Inf.* Konstantin Faddeyevich **Krshivitsky**
- 23 Jan 1902 - 14 Apr 1902: ?
- 14 Apr 1902 - 12 Apr 1904: *Lt.-Gen.* Konstantin Ivanovich **Smirnsky**
- 19 Apr 1904 - Dec 1908: *Lt.-Gen.* Ksavery Antonovich **Dobrzhinsky**
- 21 Dec 1908 - 1 Jan 1911: *Lt.-Gen.* Fyodor Aleksandrovich **Shostak**
- 15 Feb 1911 - 19 Feb 1913: *Gen. of Inf.* Arkady Valerianovich **Sychevsky**
- 19 Feb 1913 - 13 Apr 1913: *Lt.-Gen.* Yevgeny Ivanovich **Martynov**
- 23 Apr 1913 - 22 Oct 1914: *Gen. of Inf.* Pyotr Platonovich **Pototsky**
- 22 Oct 1914 - 23 Sep 1915: *Gen. of Inf.* Konstantin Aleksandrovich **Krylov**
- 4 Oct 1915 - 29 Sep 1916: *Maj.-Gen.* Vladimir Pavlovich **Talgren**
- 8 Oct 1916 - 18 Apr 1917: *Maj.-Gen.* Vladimir Zenonovich **May-Mayevsky**

Commander, 1st Brigade, 35th Infantry Division
- 26 Dec 1892 - 25 May 1899: *Gen. of Inf.* Viktor Karlovich **Aspelund**
- 8 Jun 1899 - 1 Mar 1903: *Maj.-Gen.* Yevstafy Grigoryevich **Voronets**
- 31 Mar 1903 - 20 Feb 1910: *Lt.-Gen.* Iosif Aloizovich **Glinsky**
- 21 Feb 1910 - 19 Jul 1914: *Maj.-Gen.* Dmitry Dmitriyevich **Orlov**
- 29 Jul 1914 - 1915: *Maj.-Gen.* Nikolai Mitrofanovich **Remezov**
- 1915 - 20 Jan 1916: ?
- 20 Jan 1916 - 30 Oct 1916: *Maj.-Gen.* Nikolai Mitrofanovich **Remezov**
- 30 Oct 1916 - 2 Mar 1917: ?

Commander, 2nd Brigade, 35th Infantry Division
- 21 Dec 1893 - 11 Aug 1899: *Maj.-Gen.* Baron Sergey Nikolayevich **Meller-Zakomelsky**
- 11 Aug 1899 - 31 Oct 1899: ?
- 31 Oct 1899 - 14 Jul 1905: *Lt.-Gen.* Aleksandr Stepanovich **Glasko**

- 14 Jul 1905 - 7 Sep 1905: ?
- 7 Sep 1905 - 7 Oct 1905: *Gen. of Inf.* Leonid Nikolayevich **Belkovich**
- 7 Oct 1905 - 30 Jan 1908: ?
- 30 Jan 1908 - 21 Feb 1910: *Maj.-Gen.* Dmitry Dmitriyevich **Orlov**
- 24 Mar 1910 - 19 Jul 1914: *Lt.-Gen.* Panteleymon Nikolayevich **Simansky**
- 19 Jul 1914 - 2 Mar 1917: ?

Commander, 35th Artillery Brigade
- 27 Feb 1891 - Nov 1898: *Maj.-Gen.* Illarion Markianovich **Voynov**
- 17 Nov 1898 - 18 Jan 1902: *Lt.-Gen.* Konstantin Yegorovich **Tsvetkovsky**
- 22 Jan 1902 - 23 Aug 1905: *Maj.-Gen.* Feliks Feliksovich **Terpilovsky**
- 23 Aug 1905 - 21 Nov 1907: *Maj.-Gen.* Leonid Yulievich von **Akerman**
- 21 Nov 1907 - 23 Nov 1908: *Lt.-Gen.* Nikolai Aloiziyevich **Oranovsky**
- 23 Nov 1908 - Aug 1909: *Maj.-Gen.* Pyotr Antonovich **Narkovich**
- 30 Aug 1909 - 26 Jul 1910: *Lt.-Gen.* Kaspar Nikolayevich **Blyumer**
- 26 Jul 1910 - 31 Mar 1915: *Lt.-Gen.* Viktor Voldemarovich **Meysner**
- 31 Mar 1915 - 21 May 1915: *Lt.-Gen.* Leonid Nikolayevich **Gobyato**
- 21 May 1915 - 23 Jul 1916: ?
- 23 Jul 1916 - 23 Aug 1916: *Maj.-Gen.* Vladimir Andreyevich **Lerkam**
- 23 Aug 1916 - 7 Aug 1917: *Maj.-Gen.* Ivan Petrovich **Mikhailovsky**

Commander, 36th Infantry Division
- 16 Aug 1894 - 16 Jan 1901: *Gen. of Inf.* Aleksandr Nikolayevich **Shulgin**
- 29 Jan 1901 - 7 Mar 1904: *Lt.-Gen.* Aleksandr Ignatyevich **Kossovich**
- 7 Mar 1904 - 11 Dec 1906: *Lt.-Gen.* Ostap Andreyevich **Bertels**
- 27 Dec 1906 - 23 Apr 1913: *Gen. of Inf.* Nikolai Alekseyevich **Lashkevich**
- 29 Apr 1913 - 17 Aug 1914: *Lt.-Gen.* Aleksandr Bogdanovich **Prezhentsov**
- 17 Aug 1914 - 12 Dec 1914: ?
- 12 Dec 1914 - 2 Jan 1915: *Maj.-Gen.* Aleksandr Ivanovich **Kamberg**
- 2 Jan 1915 - 17 Oct 1915: ?
- 17 Oct 1915 - 19 Jun 1916: *Lt.-Gen.* Mikhail Georgiyevich **Gorelov**
- 6 Jul 1916 - 19 Apr 1917: *Lt.-Gen.* Vladimir Vasilievich **Antipov**

Commander, 1st Brigade, 36th Infantry Division
- 2 May 1894 - 9 Oct 1899: *Maj.-Gen.* Fyodor Osipovich **Goncharov**
- 24 Oct 1899 - Jan 1903: *Lt.-Gen.* Mikhail Nikolayevich **Bazilevsky**
- Jan 1903 - 7 Apr 1903: ?
- 7 Apr 1903 - 5 Jul 1904: *Lt.-Gen.* Nikolai Ivanovich **Govorov**
- 6 Jul 1904 - 20 Aug 1913: *Lt.-Gen.* Aleksey Kondratyevich **Zeland**
- 20 Aug 1913 - 19 Jul 1914: *Lt.-Gen.* Georgy Aleksandrovich **Levitsky**
- 19 Jul 1914 - 4 Nov 1914: ?
- 4 Nov 1914 - 12 Dec 1914: *Maj.-Gen.* Aleksandr Ivanovich **Kamberg**
- 12 Dec 1914 - 2 Mar 1917: ?

Commander, 2nd Brigade, 36th Infantry Division
- 13 Jun 1894 - 29 Jul 1899: *Lt.-Gen.* Aleksandr Fyodorovich **Korobka**
- 29 Jul 1899 - 29 Sep 1900: *Maj.-Gen.* Arnold Aleksandrovich von **Remlingen**
- 24 Oct 1900 - 7 Feb 1901: *Maj.-Gen.* Nikolai Mikhailovich **Arbuzov**
- 7 Feb 1901 - 11 Jul 1902: *Gen. of Inf.* Kiprian Antonovich **Kondratovich**
- 11 Jul 1902 - 12 Aug 1907: *Maj.-Gen.* Ivan Ivanovich **Kudryavtsev**
- 12 Aug 1907 - 8 Dec 1907: ?
- 8 Dec 1907 - 5 Aug 1911: *Lt.-Gen.* Lev Stepanovich **Baranovsky**
- 5 Aug 1911 - 20 Aug 1913: *Lt.-Gen.* Georgy Aleksandrovich **Levitsky**
- 27 Sep 1913 - 16 Aug 1914: *Maj.-Gen.* Andrey Andreyevich **Kalyuzhny**
- 16 Aug 1914 - 2 Mar 1917: ?

Commander, 36th Artillery Brigade
- 15 Jul 1891 - Dec 1899: *Lt.-Gen.* Nikolai Georgiyevich **Petrakov**
- 29 Dec 1899 - 18 Jan 1902: *Lt.-Gen.* Aleksandr Mikhailovich **Khitrovo**
- 22 Jan 1902 - 2 Oct 1903: *Maj.-Gen.* Aleksandr Mikhailovich **Shepelev-Voronovich**
- 2 Oct 1903 - 28 May 1907: *Lt.-Gen.* Aleksandr Nikolayevich **Popov**
- 10 Jul 1907 - 3 Oct 1908: *Lt.-Gen.* Mikhail Grigoryevich **Malkovsky**
- 3 Oct 1908 - 24 Jan 1909: ?
- 24 Jan 1909 - 13 Jun 1914: *Lt.-Gen.* Konstantin Ivanovich **Tikhonravov**
- 17 Jun 1914 - 1 Sep 1914: *Maj.-Gen.* Aleksandr Aleksandrovich von **Den**
- 1 Sep 1914 - 23 Aug 1916: ?
- 23 Aug 1916 - 17 Mar 1917: *Maj.-Gen.* Dmitry Vasilievich **Altfater**

Commander, 37th Infantry Division
- 10 Jan 1894 - 30 Dec 1899: *Lt.-Gen.* Aleksey Andreyevich **Tillo**
- 5 Jan 1900 - 15 Nov 1901: *Lt.-Gen.* Nikolai Dmitriyevich **Skaryatin**
- 15 Nov 1901 - 16 Mar 1903: *Gen. of Inf.* Ivan Sergeyevich **Maltsov**
- 18 Apr 1903 - 23 Oct 1904: *Lt.-Gen.* Andrey Ivanovich **Chekmarev**
- 23 Oct 1904 - 18 Aug 1905: *Gen. of Inf.* Andrei Nikolayevich **Selivanov**
- 24 Aug 1905 - 30 Apr 1907: *Maj.-Gen.* Mikhail Stepanovich **Stolitsa**
- 30 Apr 1907 - Jul 1909: *Gen. of Inf.* Konstantin Osipovich **Kurganovich**
- Jul 1909 - 19 Nov 1909: ?
- 19 Nov 1909 - 30 Jul 1912: *Gen. of Inf.* Vasily Yegorovich **Flug**
- 30 Jul 1912 - 27 Mar 1915: *Gen. of Inf.* Andrei Medardovich **Zayonchkovsky**
- 27 Mar 1915 - 2 Jun 1915: *Lt.-Gen.* Aleksandr Konstantinovich **Freyman**
- 7 Jun 1915 - 17 Jul 1915: *Lt.-Gen.* Mikhail Lvovich **Matveyev**
- 17 Jul 1915 - 17 Oct 1917: *Lt.-Gen.* Torsten Karlovich **Vadensherna**

Commander, 1st Brigade, 37th Infantry Division
- 20 Feb 1890 - 6 Sep 1899: *Lt.-Gen.* Sigizmund Faddeyevich **Serzhpinsky**
- 24 Oct 1899 - 16 Jul 1904: *Lt.-Gen.* Aleksey Semyonovich **Kamensky**
- 16 Jul 1904 - 2 Apr 1910: *Lt.-Gen.* Ivan Akimovich **Mandryka**
- 2 Apr 1910 - 26 Jan 1914: *Lt.-Gen.* Ivan Ivanovich **Valberg**

- 9 Feb 1914 - 29 Jul 1914:   Lt.-Gen. Nikolai Leontievich **Yunakov**
- 29 Jul 1914 - 2 Mar 1917:   ?

Commander, 2nd Brigade, 37th Infantry Division
- 26 May 1893 - 23 Aug 1897:   *Maj.-Gen.* Matvey Mikhailovich **Polivanov**
- 18 Sep 1897 - 5 Jul 1901:   *Lt.-Gen.* Pavel Pavlovich **Dyagilev**
- 5 Jul 1901 - 8 Sep 1901:   *Gen. of Inf.* Platon Aleksandrovich **Geysman**
- 8 Sep 1901 - 28 Apr 1904:   *Lt.-Gen.* Pavel Pavlovich **Dyagilev**
- 15 May 1904 - 30 Jan 1907:   *Gen. of Inf.* Pyotr Vladimirovich **Polzikov**
- 15 Feb 1907 - 1 May 1907:   *Lt.-Gen.* Aleksandr Konstantinovich **Freyman**
- 1 May 1907 - 19 Jul 1911:   *Lt.-Gen.* Nikolai Nikolayevich **Voropanov**
- 15 Aug 1911 - 4 Nov 1914:   *Lt.-Gen.* Frants Feliksovich **Kublitsky-Piotukh**
- 4 Nov 1914 - 2 Mar 1917:   ?

Commander, 37th Artillery Brigade
- 1 Aug 1888 - 1 Feb 1895:   *Lt.-Gen.* Gavriil Gavrilovich **Mikhailov**
- 1 Feb 1895 - 29 Aug 1895:   *Gen. of Art.* Vladimir Stepanovich **Usov**
- 29 Aug 1895 - 5 Dec 1899:   *Gen. of Art.* Konstantin Petrovich **Fan-der-Flit**
- 29 Dec 1899 - 9 Apr 1901:   *Gen. of Inf.* Nikolai Vasilyevich **Osipov**
- 9 Apr 1901 - 8 May 1905:   *Lt.-Gen.* Nikolai Ivanovich **Zabusov**
- 17 May 1905 - 13 Jun 1907:   *Lt.-Gen.* Nikolai Vladimirovich **Bernikov**
- 13 Jun 1907 - 14 Nov 1909:   *Gen. of Art.* Ivan Karlovich **Baggovut**
- 23 Nov 1909 - 25 Jul 1910:   *Lt.-Gen.* Aleksandr Yevstafyevich **Gorbachevich**
- 8 Sep 1910 - Mar 1912:   *Maj.-Gen.* Ivan Aleksandrovich von **Shults**
- 10 Mar 1912 - 20 Jun 1915:   *Lt.-Gen.* Aleksandr Ivanovich **Dobrov**
- 3 Jul 1915 - 18 Feb 1917:   *Maj.-Gen.* Mikhail Ivanovich **Repyev**
- 18 Feb 1917 - 2 Mar 1917:   ?

Commander, 38th Infantry Division
- 9 Oct 1894 - 24 Oct 1900:   *Gen. of Inf.* Grigory Vasilyevich **Kryukov**
- 24 Oct 1900 - 5 Dec 1900:   ?
- 5 Dec 1900 - 24 Jun 1903:   *Lt.-Gen.* Viktor Fyodorovich **Ilinsky**
- 24 Jun 1903 - 4 Sep 1903:   *Gen. of Eng.* Prince Nikolai Yevseyevich **Tumanov**
- 4 Sep 1903 - 16 May 1905:   *Lt.-Gen.* Viktor Fyodorovich **Ilinsky**
- 16 May 1905 - 11 Mar 1912:   *Gen. of Inf.* Viktor Konstantinovich **Grek**
- 11 Mar 1912 - 13 May 1915:   *Lt.-Gen.* Vladimir Porfiryevich **Prasalov**
- 13 May 1915 - 10 Oct 1915:   *Lt.-Gen.* Pyotr Nikolayevich **Turov**
- 10 Oct 1915 - 31 Oct 1916:   *Lt.-Gen.* Aleksandr Vladimirovich **Gerua**
- 7 Nov 1916 - 17 Jan 1917:   *Lt.-Gen.* Iosif Romanovich **Dovbor-Musnitsky**
- 17 Jan 1917 - 19 Jun 1917:   *Maj.-Gen.* Aleksandr Petrovich **Bukovsky**

Commander, 1st Brigade, 38th Infantry Division
- 26 Feb 1894 - 30 Jan 1897:   *Lt.-Gen.* Vladimir Vladimirovich **Sergeyevsky**
- 30 Jan 1897 - 6 Mar 1900:   *Lt.-Gen.* Aleksey Vasiliyevich **Fedorov**
- 16 Mar 1900 - 29 Sep 1903:   *Maj.-Gen.* Nikolai Nikolayevich **Sherfer**

- 29 Sep 1903 - 11 Oct 1904: *Gen. of Inf.* Nikolai Iosifovich **Zakrzhevsky**
- 23 Oct 1904 - 21 Jun 1905: *Maj.-Gen.* Anton Ferdinandovich **Brokhotsky**
- 21 Jun 1905 - 11 Mar 1906: *Gen. of Inf.* Sigizmund Viktorovich **Volsky**
- 11 Mar 1906 - 18 May 1906: ?
- 18 May 1906 - 16 Dec 1906: *Maj.-Gen.* Aleksandr Severinovich **Przhetslavsky**
- 21 Dec 1906 - 13 Dec 1908: *Maj.-Gen.* Vladimir Alekseyevich **Myasoyedov**
- 15 Jan 1909 - 9 Jul 1910: *Lt.-Gen.* Georgy Mikhailovich **Nekrashevich**
- 9 Jul 1910 - 7 Apr 1911: *Maj.-Gen.* Adam Ivanovich **Bogatsky**
- 8 Apr 1911 - 9 Oct 1915: *Maj.-Gen.* Mikhail Antonovich **Bem**
- 9 Oct 1915 - 2 Mar 1917: ?

Commander, 2nd Brigade, 38th Infantry Division
- 12 Mar 1887 - 8 Jan 1897: *Lt.-Gen.* Lyudvig Fyodorovich **Savitsky**
- 30 Jan 1897 - 9 Feb 1900: *Lt.-Gen.* Vladimir Vladimirovich **Sergeyevsky**
- 16 Mar 1900 - 21 Jun 1905: *Maj.-Gen.* Ivan Aleksandrovich **Gazenkampf**
- 21 Jun 1905 - 24 Dec 1908: *Maj.-Gen.* Pavel Timofeyevich **Zakovenkin**
- 15 Jan 1909 - 19 Jan 1912: *Lt.-Gen.* Pyotr Ivanovich **Melnikov**
- 20 Feb 1912 - 19 Jul 1914: *Lt.-Gen.* Mikhail Ivanovich **Shtegelman**
- 19 Jul 1914 - 2 Mar 1917: ?

Commander, 38th Artillery Brigade
- 7 Oct 1893 - 11 Jun 1897: *Maj.-Gen.* Anton Lvovich **Moravsky**
- 11 Jun 1897 - 14 Jun 1899: *Lt.-Gen.* Nikolai Arkadyevich **Koptev**
- 14 Jun 1899 - 27 Feb 1904: *Maj.-Gen.* Nikolai Mikhailovich **Rozov**
- 27 Feb 1904 - 30 Nov 1904: ?
- 30 Nov 1904 - 25 Jul 1910: *Maj.-Gen.* Andrey Lvovich **Grigorovich**
- 25 Jul 1910 - 25 Sep 1910: ?
- 25 Sep 1910 - 1 Aug 1911: *Maj.-Gen.* Semyon Dmitriyevich **Muratov**
- 1 Aug 1911 - 7 May 1915: *Maj.-Gen.* Sergey Leonidovich **Fufayevsky**
- 18 May 1915 - 26 Sep 1916: *Maj.-Gen.* Anatoly Semyonovich **Fedorov**
- 26 Sep 1916 - 17 Dec 1916: *Maj.-Gen.* Ivan Petrovich **Astakhov**
- 17 Dec 1916 - 2 Mar 1917: ?

Commander, 39th Infantry Division
- 21 Jul 1893 - 22 Mar 1899: *Lt.-Gen.* Prince Mikhail Kaikhosrovich **Amiradzhibov**
- 8 Jun 1899 - 5 Aug 1899: *Gen. of Inf.* Ivan Aleksandrovich **Fullon**
- 6 Oct 1899 - 17 Oct 1902: *Lt.-Gen.* Vyacheslav Mikhailovich **Duditsky-Lishin**
- 17 Oct 1902 - 11 Jan 1903: ?
- 11 Jan 1903 - 19 Mar 1906: *Lt.-Gen.* Zakhar Tselestinovich **Tarnovsky**
- 19 Mar 1906 - 2 Jan 1907: *Gen. of Inf.* Valerian Pavlovich **Tikhmenev**
- 8 Mar 1907 - 31 Jan 1913: *Gen. of Inf.* Vladimir Petrovich **Korneyev**
- 17 Feb 1913 - 19 Dec 1915: *Gen. of Inf.* Vladimir Vladimirovich **De-Vitt**
- 2 Jan 1916 - 22 May 1916: *Lt.-Gen.* Fyodor Trofimovich **Ryabinkin**
- 22 May 1916 - 12 Mar 1917: *Lt.-Gen.* Vladimir Platonovich **Lyakhov**

Commander, 1st Brigade, 39th Infantry Division
- 29 Oct 1889 - 28 Dec 1899: *Maj.-Gen.* Yemelyan Mikhailovich **Drozdovich**
- 18 Jan 1900 - 6 May 1901: *Maj.-Gen.* Konstantin Vladimirovich **Gershelman**
- 2 Jun 1901 - 9 Mar 1902: *Gen. of Art.* Pavel Ivanovich **Mishchenko**
- 24 Apr 1902 - 13 Aug 1905: *Gen. of Inf.* Fyodor Afanasievich **Voloshinov**
- 25 Aug 1905 - 25 Sep 1907: *Maj.-Gen.* Yevgeny Aleksandrovich **Poray-Koshits**
- 25 Sep 1907 - 19 Jul 1908: *Maj.-Gen.* Vasily Vasilyevich **Kukuran**
- 3 Sep 1908 - 3 Apr 1913: *Lt.-Gen.* Konstantin Lukich **Gilchevsky**
- 26 Apr 1913 - 2 May 1913: *Maj.-Gen.* Fyodor Vasilyevich **Butkov**
- 23 Jun 1913 - 29 Jul 1914: *Maj.-Gen.* Nikolai Ivanovich **Navrotsky**
- 29 Jul 1914 - 2 Mar 1917: ?

Commander, 2nd Brigade, 39th Infantry Division
- 20 Jun 1888 - 5 Aug 1896: *Maj.-Gen.* Ivan Pavlovich **Fromandier**
- 14 Aug 1896 - 28 Apr 1899: *Gen. of Inf.* Pyotr Timofeyevich **Redkin**
- 28 Apr 1899 - 6 Sep 1899: *Maj.-Gen.* Konstantin Iskrovich **Kesyakov**
- 6 Sep 1899 - 30 Apr 1905: *Maj.-Gen.* Aleksey Matveyevich **Pokrovsky**
- 30 Apr 1905 - 3 Jun 1906: *Gen. of Inf.* Mikhail Rodionovich **Yerofeyev**
- 28 Jul 1906 - 7 Mar 1908: *Gen. of Inf.* Ernest-Yakov Kasparovich **Peterov**
- 7 Mar 1908 - 19 Jul 1908: ?
- 19 Jul 1908 - 11 Sep 1912: *Maj.-Gen.* Konstantin Stepanovich **Solonenko**
- 11 Sep 1912 - 31 Dec 1913: *Gen. of Inf.* Vasily Yepifanovich **Sklyarevsky**
- 14 Jan 1914 - 11 Feb 1914: *Maj.-Gen.* Mikhail Grigoryevich **Yerogin**
- 25 Mar 1914 - 2 Apr 1916: *Lt.-Gen.* Filipp-Stanislav Iosifovich **Dubissky**
- 2 Apr 1916 - 2 Mar 1917: ?

Commander, 39th Artillery Brigade
- 30 Jan 1893 - 9 Feb 1897: *Gen. of Art.* Prince Georgy Spiridonovich **Khimshiyev**
- 9 Feb 1897 - 29 Dec 1899: *Maj.-Gen.* Ivan Ivanovich **Velikopolsky**
- 29 Dec 1899 - 22 Jan 1902: *Maj.-Gen.* Ivan Yakovlevich **Kanevsky**
- 22 Jan 1902 - 7 Jun 1906: *Maj.-Gen.* Yakov Ivanovich **Kovtunovich**
- 7 Jun 1906 - 21 Nov 1907: *Maj.-Gen.* Mikhail Semyonovich **Paskevich**
- 21 Nov 1907 - 18 Jun 1908: *Maj.-Gen.* Vladimir Vladimirovich **Saltykov**
- 16 Aug 1908 - 25 Jul 1910: *Maj.-Gen.* Dmitry Pavlovich **Aseyev**
- 1 Aug 1910 - 21 Feb 1915: *Lt.-Gen.* Vladimir Dmitriyevich **Kalin**
- 4 Mar 1915 - 1917: *Maj.-Gen.* Ivan Spiridonovich **Gamchenko**

Commander, 40th Infantry Division
- 9 Apr 1889 - 3 Jun 1896: *Gen. of Inf.* Nikolai Veniaminovich **Ellis**
- 3 Jun 1896 - 17 Dec 1898: *Lt.-Gen.* Mikhail Pavlovich **Khoroshkhin**
- 21 Jan 1899 - 23 Apr 1902: *Gen. of Inf.* Konstantin Alekseyevich **Baiov**
- 13 Jun 1902 - 7 Oct 1906: *Lt.-Gen.* Viktor Adamovich **Sokolovsky**
- 7 Oct 1906 - 19 Nov 1908: *Lt.-Gen.* Pavel Kaetanovich **Dombrovsky**
- 18 Nov 1908 - 13 May 1914: *Gen. of Inf.* Yevgeny Aleksandrovich **Fersman**
- 13 May 1914 - 8 May 1915: *Lt.-Gen.* Nikolai Nikolayevich **Korotkevich**

- 12 May 1915 - 19 Aug 1915: *Lt.-Gen.* Georgy Aleksandrovich **Zander**
- 19 Aug 1915 - 21 Oct 1915: *Lt.-Gen.* Baron Aleksei Pavlovich von **Budberg**
- 21 Oct 1915 - 6 Jul 1916: *Lt.-Gen.* Nikolai Vasilievich **Belov**
- 6 Jul 1916 - 30 Apr 1917: *Maj.-Gen.* Anatoly Anatolyevich **Rezvoy**

Commander, 1st Brigade, 40th Infantry Division
- 26 Feb 1894 - 19 Jun 1899: *Maj.-Gen.* Yakov Nikolayevich **Vereshchagin**
- 30 Jun 1899 - 10 Feb 1903: *Maj.-Gen.* Nikolai Pavlovich **Ralgin**
- 19 Mar 1903 - 20 Aug 1905: *Lt.-Gen.* Dmitry Ivanovich **Perlik**
- 20 Aug 1905 - 14 Mar 1906: ?
- 14 Mar 1906 - 17 Dec 1908: *Lt.-Gen.* Mikhail Andreyevich **Pryaslov**
- 15 Jan 1909 - 4 Nov 1914: *Lt.-Gen.* Nikolai Nikolayevich **Karepov**
- 4 Nov 1914 - 2 Mar 1917: ?

Commander, 2nd Brigade, 40th Infantry Division
- 30 Jun 1893 - 20 Jul 1895: *Lt.-Gen.* Prince Almaskhan Otiyevich **Mikeladze**
- 20 Jul 1895 - 16 Oct 1898: *Maj.-Gen.* Vladimir Kuzmich **Nikitin**
- 20 Nov 1898 - 2 Feb 1902: *Maj.-Gen.* Nikolai Aleksandrovich **Gorbatovsky**
- 2 Feb 1902 - 28 Jul 1905: *Maj.-Gen.* Ozv Alfredovich **Modl**
- 28 Jul 1905 - 23 Jan 1906: ?
- 23 Jan 1906 - 31 Dec 1913: *Lt.-Gen.* Oskar Aleksandrovich von **Gennings**
- 9 Feb 1914 - 29 Jul 1914: *Lt.-Gen.* Anatoly Mikhailovich von **Galberg**
- 29 Jul 1914 - 2 Mar 1917: ?

Commander, 40th Artillery Brigade
- 30 Nov 1892 - 15 Oct 1895: *Lt.-Gen.* Yevgraf Yevgrafovich **Stogov**
- 15 Oct 1895 - 14 Feb 1899: *Lt.-Gen.* Nikolai Viktorovich **Tsvetkov**
- 14 Feb 1899 - 16 Mar 1899: *Lt.-Gen.* Valerian Petrovich **Dobuzhinsky**
- 16 Mar 1899 - 2 May 1900: *Lt.-Gen.* Vladimir Aleksandrovich **Boye**
- 2 May 1900 - 6 Dec 1900: ?
- 6 Dec 1900 - 15 Feb 1905: *Lt.-Gen.* Aleksey Mikhailovich **Slezkin**
- 15 Feb 1905 - 12 Feb 1907: *Maj.-Gen.* Pyotr Alekseyevich **Vinogradov**
- 21 Feb 1907 - 17 Dec 1908: *Lt.-Gen.* Aleksandr Yakovlevich **Petunin**
- 16 Jan 1909 - 4 May 1911: *Maj.-Gen.* Vladimir Fyodorovich **Apushkin**
- 4 May 1911 - 3 Jun 1911: ?
- 3 Jun 1911 - 7 May 1915: *Lt.-Gen.* Nikolai Aleksandrovich **Romanovsky**
- 7 May 1915 - 26 Jun 1916: ?
- 26 Jun 1916 - 1917: *Maj.-Gen.* Leonid Ivanovich **Milostanov**

Commander, 41st Infantry Division
- 12 Jun 1891 - 17 May 1896: *Gen. of Inf.* Ivan Fyodorovich **Nevadovsky**
- 3 Jun 1896 - 26 Aug 1898: *Gen. of Inf.* Nikolai Veniaminovich **Ellis**
- 26 Sep 1898 - 16 Apr 1903: *Gen. of Inf.* Konstantin Iosifovich **Razgonov**
- 4 May 1903 - 4 Jun 1905: *Lt.-Gen.* Aleksandr Karlovich **Birger**
- 4 Jun 1905 - 1 Aug 1905: ?

- 1 Aug 1905 - 27 Feb 1906: *Lt.-Gen.* Nikolai Nikolayevich **Chetyrikin**
- 3 Mar 1906 - 19 Jun 1910: *Gen. of Inf.* Nikolai Ivanovich **Podvalnyuk**
- 19 Jun 1910 - 16 Nov 1911: *Gen. of Inf.* Edmund Ferdinandovich **Svidzinsky**
- 16 Nov 1911 - 22 Oct 1914: *Lt.-Gen.* Fyodor Konstantinovich **Yazvin**
- 22 Oct 1914 - 24 Oct 1915: *Lt.-Gen.* Viktor Pavlovich **Shirokov**
- 30 Oct 1915 - 10 Oct 1917: *Lt.-Gen.* Vladimir Aleksandrovich **Chagin**

Commander, 1st Brigade, 41st Infantry Division
- 21 Jun 1894 - 13 Sep 1899: *Lt.-Gen.* Dmitry Semyonovich **Fursov**
- 1 Oct 1899 - 15 Feb 1900: *Maj.-Gen.* Pyotr Aleksandrovich **Stakhiyev**
- 15 Feb 1900 - 7 Dec 1902: *Maj.-Gen.* Yevgeny Viktorovich **Fetter**
- 18 Dec 1902 - 16 Jun 1906: *Maj.-Gen.* Fridrikh Ivanovich **Elliot**
- 13 Jul 1906 - 2 Jul 1907: *Lt.-Gen.* Dmitry Ivanovich **Avramov**
- 6 Jul 1907 - 11 Dec 1908: *Maj.-Gen.* Ferdinand Avgustinovich **Yagimovsky**
- 11 Dec 1908 - 31 Mar 1912: *Lt.-Gen.* Aleksandr Petrovich **Gavrilov**
- 31 Mar 1912 - 1 Oct 1912: *Maj.-Gen.* Nikolai Petrovich **Kuchin**
- 17 Nov 1912 - 1 Nov 1913: *Lt.-Gen.* Ivan Ivanovich **Popov**
- 5 Nov 1913 - 13 Jul 1916: *Maj.-Gen.* Aleksandr Gustavovich **Sholp**
- 13 Jul 1916 - 2 Mar 1917: ?

Commander, 2nd Brigade, 41st Infantry Division
- 30 May 1888 - 24 Oct 1899: *Maj.-Gen.* Aleksandr Andreyevich von **Tsurmilen**
- 24 Oct 1899 - 22 Nov 1902: *Maj.-Gen.* Nikolai Ivanovich **Mikhael**
- 1 Dec 1902 - 18 Jul 1905: *Gen. of Inf.* Rafail Nikolayevich **Fleysher**
- 28 Jul 1905 - 24 Nov 1908: *Maj.-Gen.* Nikolai Ivanovich **Krinitsky**
- 24 Nov 1908 - 2 Apr 1910: *Lt.-Gen.* Ivan Ivanovich **Valberg**
- 2 Apr 1910 - 23 Jul 1911: *Lt.-Gen.* Yevgeny Mikhailovich **Mikhelis de Genig**
- 5 Aug 1911 - 19 Jul 1914: *Lt.-Gen.* Lev Stepanovich **Baranovsky**
- 19 Jul 1914 - 2 Mar 1917: ?

Commander, 41st Artillery Brigade
- 3 Mar 1894 - May 1899: *Maj.-Gen.* Vasily Vasilyevich **Lysenko**
- 14 Jun 1899 - 4 Sep 1903: *Lt.-Gen.* Arian Alekseyevich **Yemelyanov**
- 4 Sep 1903 - 13 Aug 1905: *Lt.-Gen.* Iosif Feliksovich **Mingin**
- 23 Aug 1905 - 12 May 1907: *Maj.-Gen.* Vladimir Kazimirovich **Tutsevich**
- 12 May 1907 - Dec 1908: *Maj.-Gen.* Mikhail Yefimovich **Grumm-Grzhimaylo**
- 16 Jan 1909 - 27 Apr 1910: *Lt.-Gen.* Grigory Fyodorovich **Chepurnov**
- 27 Apr 1910 - 27 Apr 1912: *Maj.-Gen.* Nikolai Mikhaylovich **Lyashenko**
- 19 May 1912 - 12 May 1916: *Lt.-Gen.* Pavel Stepanovich **Yevtin**
- 12 May 1916 - 1917: *Maj.-Gen.* Leonid Gavrilovich **Podgoretsky**

Commander, 42nd Infantry Division *(Formed in 1898)*
- 1 Jan 1898 - 22 Jun 1904: *Gen. of Inf.* Aleksandr Eduardovich **Preskott**
- 22 Jun 1904 - 10 Aug 1904: ?
- 10 Aug 1904 - 8 Feb 1906: *Lt.-Gen.* Apollon Yermolayevich **Evert**

- 26 Feb 1906 - 30 Jun 1907:   *Gen. of Inf.* Fyodor Vladimirovich **Martson**
- 6 Jul 1907 - 29 Jan 1913:   *Gen. of Inf.* Nikolai Alekseyevich **Yepanchin**
- 29 Jan 1913 - 23 Apr 1915:   *Gen. of Inf.* Gotlib-Vilgelm Pavlovich **Rode**
- 23 Apr 1915 - 10 May 1915:   *Gen. of Art.* Valerian Mikhailovich **Gaitenov**
- 5 Jun 1915 - 12 Jul 1915:   *Gen. of Inf.* Gotlib-Vilgelm Pavlovich **Rode**
- 4 Sep 1915 - 18 Apr 1917:   *Lt.-Gen.* Aleksandr Yakovlevich **Yelshin**

Commander, 1st Brigade, 42nd Infantry Division
- 14 Jan 1898 - 31 Dec 1899:   *Lt.-Gen.* Nikolai Aleksandrovich **Rekhenberg**
- 8 Jan 1900 - 18 Jan 1901:   *Lt.-Gen.* Prince Aleksey Petrovich **Putyatin**
- 9 Feb 1901 - 25 Jan 1907:   *Lt.-Gen.* Yevgeny Iosifovich **Grozmani**
- 14 Feb 1907 - 3 Oct 1907:   *Maj.-Gen.* Vladimir Ivanovich **Bubnov**
- 14 Oct 1907 - 19 Dec 1908:   *Gen. of Inf.* Sergey Sergeyevich **Savvich**
- 8 Jan 1909 - Oct 1911:   *Maj.-Gen.* Mikhail Demyanovich **Fedotov**
- 12 Oct 1911 - 9 May 1914:   *Lt.-Gen.* Anatoly Nikolayevich **Rozenschild von Paulin**
- 9 May 1914 - 19 Jul 1914:   *Gen. of Inf.* Vladimir Alekseyevich **Alftan**
- 19 Jul 1914 - 2 Mar 1917:   ?

Commander, 2nd Brigade, 42nd Infantry Division
- 14 Jan 1898 - 16 Aug 1901:   *Maj.-Gen.* Aleksandr Karlovich **Nemysky**
- 16 Aug 1901 - 21 Nov 1908:   *Gen. of Inf.* Edmund Ferdinandovich **Svidzinsky**
- 21 Nov 1908 - 2 May 1913:   *Lt.-Gen.* Pavel Konstantinovich **Abakanovich**
- 2 May 1913 - 19 Jul 1914:   *Lt.-Gen.* Pyotr Mikhailovich **Baranov**
- 19 Jul 1914 - 2 Mar 1917:   ?

Commander, 42nd Artillery Brigade
- 20 Nov 1897 - 29 Dec 1899:   *Maj.-Gen.* Vladimir Nikolayevich **Yaroshev**
- 29 Dec 1899 - 27 Feb 1903:   *Lt.-Gen.* Aleksandr Feofilaktinovich **Babakin**
- 28 Mar 1903 - 18 Jan 1905:   *Lt.-Gen.* Fyodor Petrovich **Falenberg**
- 2 Mar 1905 - Apr 1907   *Colonel* Pyotr Mikhailovich **Arbuzov**
- 13 Jun 1907 - 7 Jul 1910:   *Maj.-Gen.* Yustinian Leopoldovich **Gasparini**
- 7 Jul 1910 - 19 Apr 1915:   *Lt.-Gen.* Ivan Yulyevich **Kleynenberg**
- 19 Apr 1915 - 28 Apr 1917:   *Maj.-Gen.* Aleksandr Mikhailovich **Benua**

Commander, 43rd Infantry Division *(Formed in 1898)*
- 1 Jan 1898 - 14 Oct 1900:   *Lt.-Gen.* Vladimir Petrovich **Makeyev**
- 14 Oct 1900 - 18 Dec 1900:   ?
- 18 Dec 1900 - 18 Apr 1903:   *Lt.-Gen.* Andrey Ivanovich **Chekmarev**
- 28 Apr 1903 - 15 May 1910:   *Gen. of Inf.* Vladimir Aleksandrovich **Orlov**
- 15 May 1910 - 24 Oct 1915:   *Gen. of Inf.* Vladimir Alekseyevich **Slyusarenko**
- 30 Oct 1915 - 17 Mar 1917:   *Lt.-Gen.* Dmitry Ivanovich **Gnida**

Commander, 1st Brigade, 43rd Infantry Division
- 14 Jan 1898 - 22 May 1902:   *Maj.-Gen.* Vladimir Vladimirovich **Aleksandrov**

- 22 May 1902 - Dec 1907: *Maj.-Gen.* Pyotr Platonovich **Lastochkin**
- 21 Dec 1907 - 9 Jun 1913: *Lt.-Gen.* Konstantin Danilovich **Yurgens**
- 9 Jun 1913 - 29 Jul 1914: *Maj.-Gen.* Ivan Ivanovich **Vetvenitsky**
- 29 Jul 1914 - 2 Mar 1917: ?

Commander, 2nd Brigade, 43rd Infantry Division
- 14 Jan 1898 - 15 Feb 1907: *Lt.-Gen.* Yevstafy Aleksandrovich **Skupio**
- 15 Feb 1907 - 17 Nov 1912: *Lt.-Gen.* Baron Karl Fyodorovich **Forseles**
- 17 Nov 1912 - 19 Apr 1917: *Maj.-Gen.* Leonid Prokofyevich **Ternavsky**

Commander, 43rd Artillery Brigade
- 1 Jan 1898 - 2 Mar 1899: *Maj.-Gen.* Nikolai Adolfovich **Meynander**
- 16 Mar 1899 - 28 Mar 1903: *Lt.-Gen.* Valerian Petrovich **Dobuzhinsky**
- 28 Mar 1903 - 12 Feb 1908: *Gen. of Art.* Nikolai Vasilyevich **Kokhanov**
- 25 Feb 1908 - 28 Mar 1912: *Maj.-Gen.* Aleksandr Nikolayevich **Dirin**
- 28 Mar 1912 - 12 May 1916: *Lt.-Gen.* Vladimir Aleksandrovich **Vatatsi**
- 12 May 1916 - 2 Mar 1917: ?

Commander, 44th Infantry Division *(Formed in 1898)*
- 1 Jan 1898 - 28 Feb 1900: *Lt.-Gen.* Sergey Ivanovich **Klyucharev**
- 13 Apr 1900 - 23 Oct 1904: *Gen. of Inf.* Nikolai Borisovich **Kutnevich**
- 7 Dec 1904 - 14 Dec 1906: *Gen. of Inf.* Vladimir Fyodorovich **Ozharovsky**
- 15 Jan 1907 - 31 Mar 1911: *Gen. of Inf.* Platon Aleksandrovich **Geysman**
- 8 Apr 1911 - 1 May 1914: *Gen. of Inf.* Fyodor Afanasievich **Voloshinov**
- 3 May 1914 - 3 Apr 1915: *Gen. of Inf.* Sergei Fyodorovich **Dobrotin**
- 3 Apr 1915 - 12 Jul 1915: *Lt.-Gen.* Mikhail Mikhailovich **Yakovlev**
- 21 Aug 1915 - 16 Nov 1915: *Lt.-Gen.* Antony Andreyevich **Veselovsky**
- 17 Dec 1915 - 12 Jul 1917: *Lt.-Gen.* Yanuary Kazimirovich **Tsikhovich**

Commander, 1st Brigade, 44th Infantry Division
- 14 Jan 1898 - 22 Jan 1901: *Lt.-Gen.* Aleksandr Yakovlevich **Ivanitsky**
- 7 Feb 1901 - 11 May 1907: *Maj.-Gen.* Nikolai Nikolayevich **Troitsky**
- 6 Jul 1907 - 12 Aug 1907: *Lt.-Gen.* Lev Stepanovich **Baranovsky**
- 12 Aug 1907 - 16 Jan 1913: *Lt.-Gen.* Stepan Iosifovich **Danovsky**
- 16 Jan 1913 - 29 Jul 1914: *Lt.-Gen.* Dmitry Pavlovich **Trotsky**
- 29 Jul 1914 - 2 Mar 1917: ?

Commander, 2nd Brigade, 44th Infantry Division
- 14 Jan 1898 - 14 Jan 1900: *Maj.-Gen.* Georgy Gustavovich **Leydenius**
- 15 Feb 1900 - 6 Oct 1903: *Gen. of Inf.* Nikolai Ivanovich **Podvalnyuk**
- 9 Oct 1903 - 25 Jan 1904: *Maj.-Gen.* Avgust Vasilievich **Aurenius**
- 25 Jan 1904 - 20 Feb 1906: *Maj.-Gen.* Adolf Ottovich **Shreder**
- 29 Mar 1906 - 10 Dec 1908: *Lt.-Gen.* Sergey Timofeyevich **Pogoretsky**
- 15 Jan 1909 - 14 Oct 1912: *Lt.-Gen.* Vladimir Yemelyanovich **Przhilutsky**
- 26 Oct 1912 - 27 Nov 1915: *Lt.-Gen.* Vladimir Nikolayevich **Svyatsky**

- 27 Nov 1915 - 2 Mar 1917: ?

Commander, 44th Artillery Brigade
- 1 Jan 1898 - 29 Dec 1899: *Maj.-Gen.* Pyotr Aloizovich **Dzyubandovsky**
- 29 Dec 1899 - 5 Jun 1903: *Maj.-Gen.* Vasily Alekseyevich **Sornev**
- 5 Jun 1903 - 25 Aug 1906: *Maj.-Gen.* Nikolai Mikhailovich **Chizhev**
- 25 Aug 1906 - Jun 1907: *Maj.-Gen.* Aleksandr Dmitriyevich **Firsov**
- *13 Jun 1907 - 18 Feb 1912:* *Lt.-Gen. Nikolai Pavlovich* ***Kostylev*** *
- *13 May 1911 - 1 Nov 1913:* *Lt.-Gen. Konstantin Andreyevich* ***Piradov*** *
- 1 Nov 1913 - 23 Jan 1914: ?
- 23 Jan 1914 - 1 Apr 1915: *Maj.-Gen.* Dmitry Dmitriyevich **Popov**
- 1 Apr 1915 - 30 May 1915: ?
- 30 May 1915 - 31 Mar 1917: *Maj.-Gen.* Mikhail Fyodorovich **Zaykovsky**

* *The published 1911 and 1912 Ministry of War rank lists show both these generals as commanders of this unit. Since all secondary sources are based on these official publications, it has not been possible to determine the correct situation.*

Commander, 45th Infantry Division *(Formed in 1898)*
- 1 Jan 1898 - 8 Apr 1904: *Lt.-Gen.* Lyudvig Fyodorovich **Savitsky**
- 2 May 1904 - 17 Jan 1906: *Lt.-Gen.* Georgy Vasilyevich von **Poppen**
- 17 Jan 1906 - 26 Oct 1907: *Gen. of Inf.* Aleksandr Iosafovich **Yevreinov**
- 2 Nov 1907 - Nov 1908: *Lt.-Gen.* Konstantin Adolfovich **Yelita von Volsky**
- 11 Nov 1908 - 2 May 1910: *Gen. of Inf.* Pavel Sergeyevich **Savvich**
- 24 May 1910 - 5 Sep 1914: *Lt.-Gen.* Ivan Romanovich **Gershelman**
- 27 Sep 1914 - 24 Jan 1916: *Lt.-Gen.* Pavel Timofeyevich **Nikolayev**
- 25 Feb 1916 - 7 Dec 1916: *Lt.-Gen.* Lev Stepanovich **Baranovsky**
- 13 Dec 1916 - 20 May 1917: *Lt.-Gen.* Veniamin Veniaminovich **Rychkov**

Commander, 1st Brigade, 45th Infantry Division
- 14 Jan 1898 - 16 Mar 1903: *Maj.-Gen.* Aleksandr Aleksandrovich **Yamshchikov**
- 16 Mar 1903 - 1 Aug 1906: *Maj.-Gen.* Pyotr Vladimirovich **Nepenin**
- 1 Aug 1906 - 6 Oct 1906: *Gen. of Inf.* Fyodor Ivanovich von **Torklus**
- 6 Oct 1906 - 31 Jan 1907: *Maj.-Gen.* Andrey Ivanovich **Yunchis**
- 19 Feb 1907 - 12 Nov 1907: *Lt.-Gen.* Vladimir Konstantinovich **Solonina**
- 12 Nov 1907 - 11 Dec 1908: *Maj.-Gen.* Aleksandr Lvovich **Karlevich**
- 11 Dec 1908 - 7 Jan 1909: *Lt.-Gen.* Mikhail Ivanovich **Chizhov**
- 15 Jan 1909 - 29 Jul 1914: *Lt.-Gen.* Nikolai Karlovich **Vitvitsky**
- 29 Jul 1914 - 27 Nov 1914: ?
- 27 Nov 1914 - 7 Apr 1916: *Lt.-Gen.* Adam Ivanovich **Slavochinsky**
- 7 Apr 1916 - 29 Jan 1917: *Maj.-Gen.* Fyodor Matveyevich **Ivanov**
- 29 Jan 1917 - 2 Mar 1917: ?

Commander, 2nd Brigade, 45th Infantry Division
- 14 Jan 1898 - Jan 1902: *Maj.-Gen.* Stepan Alekseyevich **Fedorov**
- 2 Feb 1902 - 16 Apr 1906: *Maj.-Gen.* Aleksandr Aleksandrovich **Khorunzhenkov**

- 16 Apr 1906 - 6 Oct 1906:   *Maj.-Gen.* Andrey Ivanovich **Yunchis**
- 2 Nov 1906 - 20 Feb 1912:   *Lt.-Gen.* Mikhail Ivanovich **Shtegelman**
- 3 Mar 1912 - 22 Jan 1913:   *Maj.-Gen.* Viktor Viktorovich **Eggert**
- 27 Jan 1913 - 5 Sep 1914:   *Maj.-Gen.* Ivan Ivanovich **Gordeyev**
- 30 Sep 1914 - 19 Jan 1915:   *Lt.-Gen.* Sergey Nikolayevich **Rozanov**
- 19 Jan 1915 - 2 Mar 1917:   ?

Commander, 45th Artillery Brigade
- 1 Oct 1897 - 17 Jul 1900:   *Lt.-Gen.* Eleazar Stepanovich **Bobrikov**
- 17 Jul 1900 - 9 Apr 1901:   *Lt.-Gen.* Nikolai Ivanovich **Zabusov**
- 9 Apr 1901 - 27 Nov 1904:   *Maj.-Gen.* Nikolai Aleksandrovich **Kovanko**
- 27 Nov 1904 - 13 Aug 1905:   *Gen. of Art.* Vladimir Frantsevich **Bandrovsky**
- 23 Aug 1905 - 20 May 1906:   *Gen. of Inf.* Vladimir Alekseyevich **Slyusarenko**
- 20 May 1906 - 27 Sep 1906:   ?
- 27 Sep 1906 - 16 Jan 1909:   *Maj.-Gen.* Mikhail Ippolitovich **Sulin**
- 16 Jan 1909 - 16 Jan 1911:   *Maj.-Gen.* Nikolai Sergeyevich **Somov**
- 16 Feb 1911 - 6 Jan 1913:   *Lt.-Gen.* Aleksandr Reyngoldovich **Meyster**
- 6 Jan 1913 - 9 Nov 1914:   *Maj.-Gen.* Arkady Pavlovich **Yarygin**
- 16 Dec 1914 - 18 Feb 1917:   *Maj.-Gen.* Ivan Nikanorovich **Andreyev**
- 18 Feb 1917 - 28 Apr 1917:   *Maj.-Gen.* Mikhail Vasilyevich **Lekarev**

Commander, 46th Infantry Division *(Formed in 1905)*
- 28 Jun 1905 - 29 Apr 1906:   *Lt.-Gen.* Nikolai Petrovich **Engelke**
- 29 Apr 1906 - 3 Jul 1910:   DISSOLVED
- 3 Jul 1910 - 24 Jun 1915:   *Gen. of Inf.* Dmitry Aleksandrovich **Dolgov**
- 24 Jun 1915 - 6 Apr 1917:   *Lt.-Gen.* Nikolai Andreyevich **Ilkevich**

Commander, 1st Brigade, 46th Infantry Division
- 1905 - 1906:   ?
- 1906 - 1910:   DISSOLVED
- 3 Jun 1910 - Apr 1912:   *Lt.-Gen.* Mikhail Mikhaylovich **Grigoryev**
- 25 Apr 1912 - Oct 1912:   *Maj.-Gen.* Vikenty Logginovich **Raykovsky**
- 9 Oct 1912 - 19 Jul 1914:   *Lt.-Gen.* Sergey Dmitriyevich **Chistyakov**
- 19 Jul 1914 - 2 Mar 1917:   ?

Commander, 2nd Brigade, 46th Infantry Division
- 1905 - 1906:   ?
- 1906 - 1910:   DISSOLVED
- 17 Jun 1910 - 31 Jan 1915:   *Lt.-Gen.* Dmitry Pavlovich **Parsky**
- 31 Jan 1915 - 2 Mar 1917:   ?

Commander, 46th Artillery Brigade
- 1905 - 1906:   ?
- 1906 - 1910:   DISSOLVED
- 26 Jul 1910 - 10 Mar 1912:   *Lt.-Gen.* Ilya Ildefonsovich **Volkovitsky**

- 10 Mar 1912 - 22 Dec 1915:   *Lt.-Gen.* Aleksandr Aleksandrovich **Fogel**
- 11 Jan 1916 - 23 Jun 1917:   *Maj.-Gen.* Georgy Avetikovich **Pozoyev**

Commander, 47th Infantry Division *(Formed in 1905)*
- 28 Jun 1905 - 5 Sep 1906:   *Lt.-Gen.* Mikhail Pavlovich **Davydov**
- 5 Sep 1906 - 9 Jul 1910:   DISSOLVED
- 9 Jul 1910 - 1 Apr 1917:   *Gen. of Inf.* Vladimir Vasilyevich **Bolotov**

Commander, 1st Brigade, 47th Infantry Division
- 28 Jun 1905 - 15 Oct 1905:   *Maj.-Gen.* Vladimir Mikhailovich **Savitsky**
- 15 Oct 1905 - 1906:   ?
- 1906 - 1910:   DISSOLVED
- 12 Jun 1910 - 8 Jun 1913:   *Maj.-Gen.* Ivan Aleksandrovich **Mikhailov**
- 8 Jun 1913 - 29 Jul 1914:   *Lt.-Gen.* Anton Petrovich **Symon**
- 29 Jul 1914 - 1915:   ?
- 1915 - 26 Apr 1916:   *Lt.-Gen.* Anton Petrovich **Symon**
- 26 Apr 1916 - 2 Mar 1917:   ?

Commander, 2nd Brigade, 47th Infantry Division
- 1905 - 1906:   ?
- 1906 - 1910:   DISSOLVED
- 25 Jun 1910 - 1915:   *Maj.-Gen.* Pavel Petrovich **Ryabkov**
- 1915 - 2 Mar 1917:   ?

Commander, 47th Artillery Brigade
- 1905 - 1906:   ?
- 1906 - 1910:   DISSOLVED
- 1 Aug 1910 - 24 Jul 1912:   *Lt.-Gen.* Vladimir Aleksandrovich **Gaaz de Gryunenvald**
- 3 Aug 1912 - 12 May 1916:   *Maj.-Gen.* Konstantin Georgievich **Abashidze**
- 3 Jun 1916 - 1918:   *Maj.-Gen.* Vladimir Lyudvigovich **Shlegel**

Commander, 48th Infantry Division *(Formed in 1905)*
- 11 Oct 1904 - 1906:   *Lt.-Gen.* Iosif Iosifovich **Zashchuk**
- 1906 - 1910:   DISSOLVED
- 5 Jul 1910 - 24 Aug 1914:   *Lt.-Gen.* Sergey Timofeyevich **Pogoretsky**
- 24 Aug 1914 - 11 Sep 1914:   *Gen. of Inf.* Lavr Georgievich **Kornilov**
- 11 Sep 1914 - 30 Dec 1914:   ?
- 30 Dec 1914 - 12 May 1915:   *Gen. of Inf.* Lavr Georgievich **Kornilov**
- 12 May 1915 - 22 Apr 1917:   *Lt.-Gen.* Yevgeny Fyodorovich **Novitsky**

Commander, 1st Brigade, 48th Infantry Division
- 11 Oct 1904 - 17 Mar 1906:   *Maj.-Gen.* Viktor Nikolayevich **Mozgalevsky**
- 1906 - 1910:   DISSOLVED

- 7 Jun 1910 - 29 Jul 1914: *Maj.-Gen.* Boris Aleksandrovich **Rudakov**
- 29 Jul 1914 - 18 Nov 1914: ?
- 18 Nov 1914 - 22 Nov 1914: *Maj.-Gen.* Boris Aleksandrovich **Rudakov**
- 22 Nov 1914 - 2 Mar 1917: ?

Commander, 2nd Brigade, 48th Infantry Division
- 1905 - 1906: ?
- 1906 - 1910: DISSOLVED
- 3 Jun 1910 - 4 Jul 1913: *Lt.-Gen.* Apollon Ivanovich **Burov**
- 4 Jul 1913 - 17 Aug 1913: *Lt.-Gen.* Torsten Karlovich **Vadensherna**
- 27 Sep 1913 - 10 Apr 1915: *Maj.-Gen.* Khristo Neykovich **Koychev**
- 10 Apr 1915 - Jun 1915: *Lt.-Gen.* Ivan Yuryevich **Popovich-Lipovats**

Commander, 48th Artillery Brigade
- 1905 - 1906: ?
- 1906 - 1910: DISSOLVED
- 31 Mar 1911 - 2 Apr 1913: *Maj.-Gen.* Nikolai Vasilievich **Belikhov**
- 2 Apr 1913 - 23 Apr 1915: *Maj.-Gen.* Arnold Khristoforovich **Shulman**
- 10 Jun 1915 - 23 Jul 1916: *Maj.-Gen.* Nikolai Grigoryevich **Sineokov**
- 27 Jul 1916 - 4 Dec 1917: *Maj.-Gen.* Mikhail Mikhailovich **Chelyustkin**

Commander, 49th Infantry Division *(Formed in 1905)*
- 1905 - 1906: ?
- 1906 - 1910: DISSOLVED
- 6 Jul 1910 - 8 May 1915: *Lt.-Gen.* Mikhail Andreyevich **Pryaslov**
- 8 May 1915 - 25 Jun 1915: *Maj.-Gen.* Semyon Yegorovich **Molchanov**
- 25 Jun 1915 - 5 Jul 1915: *Lt.-Gen.* Mikhail Andreyevich **Pryaslov**
- 5 Jul 1915 - 1917: *Lt.-Gen.* Dmitry Petrovich **Pavlov**

Commander, 1st Brigade, 49th Infantry Division
- 28 Jun 1905 - 1906: *Maj.-Gen.* Sergey Yakolevich **Timofeyev**
- 1906 - 1910: DISSOLVED
- 15 Jul 1910 - 26 Oct 1912: *Lt.-Gen.* Ivan Konstantinovich **Gandurin**
- 26 Oct 1912 - 11 Sep 1914: *Maj.-Gen.* Nikolai Fyodorovich **Domelunksen**
- 11 Sep 1914 - 30 Dec 1914: *Gen. of Inf.* Lavr Georgievich **Kornilov**
- 3 Feb 1915 - 28 Apr 1915: *Maj.-Gen.* Semyon Yegorovich **Molchanov**
- 28 Apr 1915 - 25 Jun 1915: ?
- 25 Jun 1915 - 10 Mar 1917: *Maj.-Gen.* Semyon Yegorovich **Molchanov**

Commander, 2nd Brigade, 49th Infantry Division
- 1905 - 1906: ?
- 1906 - 1910: DISSOLVED
- 25 Jun 1910 - 18 Aug 1912: *Maj.-Gen.* Nikolai Ivanovich **Semenov**
- 18 Aug 1912 - 1914: *Lt.-Gen.* Ivan Aleksandrovich **Fotengauer**

Commander, 49th Artillery Brigade
- 1905 - 1906: ?
- 1906 - 1910: DISSOLVED
- 30 Jul 1910 - 26 Mar 1915: *Lt.-Gen.* Andrey Panteleymonovich **Kotovsky**
- 26 Mar 1915 - 2 Mar 1917: ?

Commander, 50th Infantry Division *(Formed in 1910)*
- 21 Jul 1910 - 22 Dec 1914: *Lt.-Gen.* Nikolai Sergeyevich **Berdyayev**
- 22 Dec 1914 - 20 Sep 1916: *Lt.-Gen.* Vilgelm-Karl Kasperovich von **Nordgeym**
- 25 Sep 1916 - 15 Apr 1917: *Lt.-Gen.* Vladimir Aleksandrovich **Lavdovsky**

Commander, 1st Brigade, 50th Infantry Division
- 11 Jun 1910 - 29 Jul 1914: *Maj.-Gen.* Vilgelm Vilgelmovich **Malm**
- 29 Jul 1914 - 2 Mar 1917: ?

Commander, 2nd Brigade, 50th Infantry Division
- 14 Jul 1910 - 13 Feb 1913: *Maj.-Gen.* Nikolai Ivanovich **Tikhomirov**
- 3 Feb 1913 - 1915: *Maj.-Gen.* Mikhail Favstovich **Pigulevsky**
- 1915 - 2 Mar 1917: ?

Commander, 50th Artillery Brigade
- 25 Jul 1910 - 18 Feb 1912: *Lt.-Gen.* Vladimir Aleksandrovich **Krasilnikov**
- 10 Mar 1912 - 8 Nov 1915: *Maj.-Gen.* Mikhail Nikanorovich **Andreyev**
- 8 Nov 1915 - 29 Feb 1916: *Maj.-Gen.* Aleksandr Adamovich **Vevern**
- 29 Feb 1916 - 1917: *Maj.-Gen.* Pyotr Vasilyevich **Polyakov**

Commander, 51st Infantry Division *(Formed in 1904)*
- 1 Jun 1904 - 1906: *Lt.-Gen.* Nikolai Ivanovich **Nechayev**
- 1906 - 1910: DISSOLVED
- 24 Oct 1910 - 31 Dec 1913: *Gen. of Inf.* Pyotr Ivanovich **Oganovsky**
- 31 Dec 1913 - 22 Dec 1914: *Gen. of Inf.* Nikolai Mikhailovich **Voronov**
- 22 Dec 1914 - 2 Apr 1917: *Lt.-Gen.* Vladimir Onufrievich **Beneskul**

Commander, 1st Brigade, 51st Infantry Division
- 1 Jun 1904 - 13 Jul 1906: *Lt.-Gen.* Dmitry Ivanovich **Avramov**
- 1906 - 1910: DISSOLVED
- 7 Sep 1910 - 4 Nov 1911: *Maj.-Gen.* Konstantin Aleksandrovich **Mertsedin**
- 4 Nov 1911 - 4 Jun 1913: *Maj.-Gen.* Aleksandr Mikhailovich **Bykov**
- 4 Jun 1913 - 14 Nov 1915: *Maj.-Gen.* Ivan Avgustovich **Bergau**
- 14 Nov 1915 - 2 Mar 1917: ?

Commander, 2nd Brigade, 51st Infantry Division
- 1904 - 1906: ?
- 1906 - 1910: DISSOLVED
- 15 Jun 1910 - 29 Jul 1914: *Lt.-Gen.* Aleksandr Nikolayevich **Skornyakov**

- 29 Jul 1914 - 2 Mar 1917: ?

Commander, 51st Artillery Brigade
- 4 Jun 1904 - 1905: *Maj.-Gen.* Georgy Vasilyevich **Osipov**
- 1905 - 1906: ?
- 1906 - 1910: DISSOLVED
- 25 Jul 1910 - 26 Oct 1910: *Lt.-Gen.* Meyngard Antonovich **Shifner**
- 12 Nov 1910 - 29 Nov 1912: *Lt.-Gen.* Ivan Aleksandrovich **Karpovich**
- 29 Nov 1912 - 9 Jan 1916: *Lt.-Gen.* Aleksandr Vladimirovich **Martynov**
- 24 Jan 1916 - 1917: *Maj.-Gen.* Nikolai Aleksandrovich **Krutikov**

Commander, 52nd Infantry Division *(Formed in 1904)*
- 2 Sep 1904 - 29 Jan 1907: *Lt.-Gen.* Nikolai Emmanuilovich **Miloradovich**
- 1907 - 1910: DISSOLVED
- 29 May 1910 - 24 Oct 1910: *Gen. of Inf.* Pyotr Ivanovich **Oganovsky**
- 4 Nov 1910 - 18 Oct 1911: *Lt.-Gen.* Ivan Aleksandrovich **Snarsky**
- 16 Nov 1911 - 31 Dec 1913: *Gen. of Inf.* Ernest-Yakov Kasparovich **Peterov**
- 31 Dec 1913 - 8 May 1915: *Lt.-Gen.* Vasily Vasilievich **Artemyev**
- 1 Jul 1915 - Jul 1917: *Lt.-Gen.* Nikolai Maksimovich **Ivanov**

Commander, 1st Brigade, 52nd Infantry Division
- 2 Sep 1904 - 12 Jan 1905: *Maj.-Gen.* Vladimir Pavlovich **Aseyev**
- 12 Jan 1905 - 11 Aug 1906: *Lt.-Gen.* Aleksandr Nikolayevich **Stupin**
- 1906 - 1910: DISSOLVED
- 16 Jun 1910 - 18 Nov 1911: *Lt.-Gen.* Ivan Adamovich **Genik**
- 18 Nov 1911 - 30 Nov 1913: *Lt.-Gen.* Sergey Alekseyevich **Dobronravov**
- 31 Dec 1913 - 21 Oct 1914: *Gen. of Inf.* Vasily Yepifanovich **Sklyarevsky**
- 21 Oct 1914 - 18 Dec 1914: ?
- 18 Dec 1914 - 9 Dec 1915: *Gen. of Inf.* Vasily Yepifanovich **Sklyarevsky**
- 9 Dec 1915 - 10 Jul 1916: ?
- 10 Jul 1916 - 1917: *Maj.-Gen.* Ivan Semyonovich **Vovk**

Commander, 2nd Brigade, 52nd Infantry Division
- 1904 - 1906: ?
- 1906 - 1910: DISSOLVED
- 7 Sep 1910 - 25 Dec 1913: *Lt.-Gen.* Anton Stanislavovich **Bleshinsky**
- 31 Dec 1913 - 3 Jul 1916: *Maj.-Gen.* Vasily Alekseyevich **Kvanchkhadze**
- 3 Jul 1916 - 2 Mar 1917: ?

Commander, 52nd Artillery Brigade
- 3 Sep 1904 - 13 Mar 1906: *Maj.-Gen.* Ivan Nikolayevich **Lyapunov**
- 1906 - 1910: DISSOLVED
- Jul 1910 - 15 Oct 1910: *Lt.-Gen.* Ilya Sakvarelovich **Makarashvili**
- 12 Nov 1910 - 20 Jun 1915: *Lt.-Gen.* Mikhail Grigoryevich **Kardinalovsky**
- 25 Jul 1915 - 1917: *Maj.-Gen.* Asad-Bek **Talyshkhanov**

Commander, 53rd Infantry Division *(Formed in 1905)*
- 5 Mar 1905 - 1906: *Maj.-Gen.* Iosif Suleymanovich **Poltorzhitsky**
- 1906 - 1914: DISSOLVED
- 19 Jul 1914 - Feb 1915: *Lt.-Gen.* Semyon Ivanovich **Fedorov**
- 3 Apr 1915 - 11 Aug 1915: *Lt.-Gen.* Pavel Konstantinovich **Abakanovich**
- 11 Aug 1915 - 25 Aug 1915: *Lt.-Gen.* Dmitry Pavlovich **Trotsky**
- 28 Aug 1915 - 9 Sep 1917: *Lt.-Gen.* David Konstantinovich **Guntsadze**

Commander, 1st Brigade, 53rd Infantry Division
- 5 Mar 1905 - 18 May 1906: *Maj.-Gen.* Aleksandr Severinovich **Przhetslavsky**
- 1906 - 1914: DISSOLVED
- 29 Jul 1914 - Feb 1915: *Maj.-Gen.* Ivan Alekseyevich **Kholmsen**
- Feb 1915 - 13 Apr 1916: ?
- 13 Apr 1916 - 31 Jul 1917: *Maj.-Gen.* Konstantin Grigorievich **Girshfeld**

Commander, 2nd Brigade, 53rd Infantry Division
- 5 Mar 1905 - 14 Mar 1906: *Lt.-Gen.* Ivan Ioasafovich **Yevreinov**
- 1906 - 1914: DISSOLVED
- 29 Jul 1914 - 2 Mar 1917: ?

Commander, 53rd Artillery Brigade
- 1905 - 1906: ?
- 1906 - 1914: DISSOLVED
- 29 Jul 1914 - 8 Feb 1915: *Maj.-Gen.* Andrey Vladimirovich **Kislyakov**
- 8 Feb 1915 - 1915: ?
- 1915 - 6 Nov 1916: *Maj.-Gen.* Aleksandr Nikolayevich **Malkovsky**
- 6 Nov 1916 - ?: ?

Commander, 54th Infantry Division *(Formed in 1904)*
- 1 Jun 1904 - 21 Sep 1904: *Gen. of Inf.* Nikolai Aleksandrovich **Orlov**
- 17 Oct 1904 - 4 Jul 1906: *Gen. of Inf.* Leonid Konstantinovich **Artamonov**
- 1906 - 1914: DISSOLVED
- 19 Jul 1914 - 13 Oct 1914: *Lt.-Gen.* Mikhail Ivanovich **Chizhov**
- 13 Oct 1914: DISSOLVED

Commander, 1st Brigade, 54th Infantry Division
- 1 Jun 1904 - 28 Jul 1906: *Gen. of Inf.* Ernest-Yakov Kasparovich **Peterov**
- 1906 - 1914: DISSOLVED
- 19 Jul 1914 - 10 Sep 1914: *Maj.-Gen.* Mikhail Grigoryevich **Yerogin**
- 10 Sep 1914 - 13 Oct 1914: ?

Commander, 2nd Brigade, 54th Infantry Division
- *1 Jun 1904 - 1906:* *Maj.-Gen.* Mikhail Nazarovich **Fomin** *
- *5 Oct 1904 - 29 Jul 1905:* *Lt.-Gen.* Nikolai Yakovlevich **Lisovsky** *
- 1906 - 1914: DISSOLVED

- 19 Jul 1914 - 13 Oct 1914: ?
- 13 Oct 1914: DISSOLVED

The published 1904, 1905 and 1906 Ministry of War rank lists show both these generals as commanders of this unit. Since all secondary sources are based on these official publications, it has not been possible to determine the correct situation.

Commander, 54th Artillery Brigade
- Aug 1914 - 12 Nov 1914: *Maj.-Gen.* Vladimir Fyodorovich **Sozanovich**
- 12 Nov 1914: DISSOLVED

Commander, 55th Infantry Division *(Formed in 1904)*
- 1 Jun 1904 - 2 Aug 1904: *Maj.-Gen.* Nikolai Petrovich **Ignatyev**
- 2 Aug 1904 - 10 Apr 1906: *Gen. of Inf.* Pavel Aleksandrovich von **Layming**
- 1906 - 1914: DISSOLVED
- 19 Jul 1914 - 10 Sep 1915: *Lt.-Gen.* Pyotr Matveyevich **Zakharov**
- 10 Sep 1915 - 28 Oct 1915: *Maj.-Gen.* Yakov Yakovlevich **Lyubitsky**
- 28 Oct 1915 - 20 Feb 1916: *Lt.-Gen.* Dmitry Pavlovich **Parsky**
- 26 Feb 1916 - 4 May 1917: *Lt.-Gen.* Sergey Vladimirovich **Pokatov**

Commander, 1st Brigade, 55th Infantry Division
- 1 Jun 1904 - ?: *Maj.-Gen.* Rafail Fomich **Frankovsky**
- ? - 1906: ?
- 1906 - 1914: DISSOLVED
- 1914 - 2 Mar 1917: ?

Commander, 2nd Brigade, 55th Infantry Division
- 1 Apr 1904 - 22 Dec 1905: *Lt.-Gen.* Mikhail Mikhailovich **Dobrovolsky**
- 22 Dec 1905 - 1906: ?
- 1906 - 1914: DISSOLVED
- 1914 - 2 Mar 1917: ?

Commander, 55th Artillery Brigade
- 24 Oct 1904 - 24 Dec 1905: *Lt.-Gen.* Stepan Ivanovich **Sobolevsky**
- 24 Dec 1905 - 1906: ?
- 1906 - 1914: DISSOLVED
- 1914 - 23 May 1915: ?
- 23 May 1915 - 28 Aug 1917: *Maj.-Gen.* Anton Viktorovich **Kachinsky**

Commander, 56th Infantry Division *(Formed in 1904)*
- 1 Jun 1904 - 3 Apr 1906: *Lt.-Gen.* Konstantin Petrovich **Tyrtov**
- 1906 - 19 Jul 1914: DISSOLVED
- 19 Jul 1914 - 8 Oct 1914: *Maj.-Gen.* Nikolai Ksenofontovich **Boldyrev**
- 8 Oct 1914 - 31 Mar 1915: *Lt.-Gen.* Feliks Dominikovich **Iozefovich**
- 3 Apr 1915 - 26 Apr 1916: *Lt.-Gen.* Aleksandr Semyonovich **Madritov**
- 26 Apr 1916 - 22 Jan 1917: *Maj.-Gen.* Yevgeny Aleksandrovich **Rossysky**

- 22 Jan 1917 - 7 Sep 1917: *Maj.-Gen.* Stepan Zakharovich **Potapov**

Commander, 1st Brigade, 56th Infantry Division
- 1 Jun 1904 - 9 Mar 1906: *Lt.-Gen.* Sergey Evstafievich **Debesh**
- 1906 - 1914: DISSOLVED
- 29 Jul 1914 - 23 Sep 1917: *Maj.-Gen.* Prince Ilya Zakharovich **Makayev**

Commander, 2nd Brigade, 56th Infantry Division
- 1904 - 1906: ?
- 1906 - 1914: DISSOLVED
- 1914 - 1 Apr 1915: ?
- 1 Apr 1915 - 25 Jun 1915: *Colonel* Pyotr Pavlovich **Kramarenko**
- 25 Jun 1915 - 2 Mar 1917: ?

Commander, 56th Artillery Brigade
- 23 Oct 1904 - 1906: *Colonel* Ivan Ivanovich **Likhachev**
- 1906 - 1914: DISSOLVED
- 25 Jul 1914 - 29 Mar 1917: *Maj.-Gen.* Yevgeny Yulyevich **Kleynenberg**

Commander, 57th Infantry Division *(Formed in 1914)*
- 19 Jul 1914 - 26 Jul 1914: *Gen. of Inf.* Leonid Nikolayevich **Belkovich**
- 26 Jul 1914 - 19 Nov 1914: *Gen. of Inf.* Dmitry Nikolayevich **Bezradetsky**
- 19 Nov 1914 - 7 May 1915: *Maj.-Gen.* Nikolai Ivanovich **Omelyanovich**
- 12 May 1915 - 1917: *Lt.-Gen.* Baron Nikolai Andreyevich de **Bode**

Commander, 1st Brigade, 57th Infantry Division
- 19 Jul 1914 - 3 Aug 1914: ?
- 3 Aug 1914 - 16 Apr 1916: *Lt.-Gen.* Aleksandr Aleksandrovich **Arkhipov**
- 16 Apr 1916 - 2 Mar 1917: ?

Commander, 2nd Brigade, 57th Infantry Division
- 19 Jul 1914 - 2 Mar 1917: ?

Commander, 57th Artillery Brigade
- 25 Jul 1914 - 1917: *Maj.-Gen.* Aleksandr Ksenofontovich **Lipkin**

Commander, 58th Infantry Division *(Formed in 1914)*
- 19 Jul 1914 - 16 Sep 1914: *Lt.-Gen.* Vsevolod Vladimirovich **Chernavin**
- 24 Sep 1914 - 18 Jun 1915: *Gen. of Inf.* Stanislav Feliksovich **Stelnitsky**
- 24 Jun 1915 - Aug 1915: *Lt.-Gen.* Lev Vladimirovich **De-Vitt**
- Aug 1915: *Maj.-Gen.* Porfiry Grigoryevich **Chebotarev**
- Aug 1915: DISSOLVED

Commander, 1st Brigade, 58th Infantry Division
- 19 Jul 1914 - Aug 1915: ?

Commander, 2nd Brigade, 58th Infantry Division
- 19 Jul 1914 - Aug 1915:   ?

Commander, 58th Artillery Brigade
- 19 Jul 1914 - Aug 1915:   *Maj.-Gen.* Porfiry Grigoryevich **Chebotarev**

Commander, 59th Infantry Division *(Formed in 1914)*
- 19 Jul 1914 - Jul 1917:   *Lt.-Gen.* Aleksandr Semyonovich **Ogloblev**

Commander, 1st Brigade, 59th Infantry Division
- 19 Jul 1914 - 2 Mar 1917:   ?

Commander, 2nd Brigade, 59th Infantry Division
- 19 Jul 1914 - 2 Mar 1917:   ?

Commander, 59th Artillery Brigade *(Formed 1904)*
- 23 Oct 1904 - 1906:   *Colonel* Georgy Yemelyanovich **Pavlovsky**
- 1906 - 1914:   DISSOLVED
- 25 Jul 1914 - 1917:   *Maj.-Gen.* Pavel Florovich **Maksimov**

Commander, 60th Infantry Division *(Formed in 1914)*
- 19 Jul 1914 - 29 Jul 1914:   *Lt.-Gen.* Pyotr Mikhailovich **Baranov**
- 29 Jul 1914 - 17 Oct 1914:   *Lt.-Gen.* Mikhail Lvovich **Matveyev**
- 17 Oct 1914 - 30 Apr 1915:   *Lt.-Gen.* Pyotr Mikhailovich **Baranov**
- 17 May 1915 - 18 Apr 1916:   *Gen. of Art.* Vladimir Petrovich **Mamontov**
- 20 May 1916 - 22 May 1917:   *Lt.-Gen.* Nikolai Kirillovich **Yanovsky**

Commander, 1st Brigade, 60th Infantry Division
- 19 Jul 1914 - 2 Mar 1917:   ?

Commander, 2nd Brigade, 60th Infantry Division
- 19 Jul 1914 - 2 Mar 1917:   ?

Commander, 60th Artillery Brigade
- 19 Jul 1914 - 9 Nov 1915:   ?
- 9 Nov 1915 - 1917:   *Maj.-Gen.* Vasily Grigoryevich **Tovstoles**

Commander, 61st Infantry Division *(Formed in 1904)*
- 1 Jun 1904 - 3 Mar 1906:   *Gen. of Inf.* Nikolai Ivanovich **Podvalnyuk**
- 3 Mar 1906 - 19 Jul 1914:   DISSOLVED
- 19 Jul 1914 - 7 Jul 1917:   *Lt.-Gen.* Panteleymon Nikolayevich **Simansky**

Commander, 1st Brigade, 61st Infantry Division
- 25 May 1904 - 14 Mar 1906: *Lt.-Gen.* Mikhail Andreyevich **Pryaslov**
- 1906 - 1914: DISSOLVED
- 19 Jul 1914 - 2 Mar 1917: ?

Commander, 2nd Brigade, 61st Infantry Division
- 1 Jun 1904 - 3 Dec 1904: *Lt.-Gen.* Nikolai Grigoryevich **Stavrovich**
- 9 Mar 1905 - 6 Jul 1905: *Lt.-Gen.* Aleksandr Nikolayevich **Apukhtin**
- 6 Jul 1905 - 19 Oct 1906: *Lt.-Gen.* Nikolai Mikhailovich **Vorobyev**
- 1906 - 1914: DISSOLVED
- 19 Jul 1914 - 2 Mar 1917: ?

Commander, 61st Artillery Brigade
- 4 Jun 1904 - 11 Mar 1906: *Lt.-Gen.* Vladimir Ivanovich **Plotnikov**
- 1906 - 1914: DISSOLVED
- 19 Jul 1914 - 17 Dec 1914: ?
- 17 Dec 1915 - 25 Aug 1917: *Maj.-Gen.* Konstantin Vsevolodovich **Zherve**

Commander, 62nd Infantry Division *(Formed in 1904)*
- 11 Oct 1904 - 15 Nov 1904: *Lt.-Gen.* Mikhail Dmitryevich **Yevreinov**
- 21 Jan 1905 - 19 Mar 1906: *Gen. of Inf.* Valerian Pavlovich **Tikhmenev**
- 1906 - 1914: DISSOLVED
- 19 Jul 1914 - 26 Aug 1914: *Lt.-Gen.* Anton Dmitriyevich **Lavrentyev**
- 29 Sep 1914 - 12 Mar 1915: *Gen. of Inf.* Aleksandr Iosafovich **Yevreinov**
- 2 Apr 1915 - 3 Dec 1915: *Lt.-Gen.* Marin Draganovich **Yenchevich**
- 3 Dec 1915 - 22 Jan 1916: *Lt.-Gen.* Aleksandr Mikhailovich **Khvostov**
- 22 Jan 1916 - 28 Aug 1917: *Lt.-Gen.* Marin Draganovich **Yenchevich**

Commander, 1st Brigade, 62nd Infantry Division
- 11 Oct 1904 - 1 Aug 1906: *Gen. of Inf.* Fyodor-Emily-Karl Ivanovich von **Torklus**
- 1906 - 1914: DISSOLVED
- 19 Jul 1914 - 2 Mar 1917: ?

Commander, 2nd Brigade, 62nd Infantry Division
- 1904 - 1906: ?
- 1906 - 1914: DISSOLVED
- 19 Jul 1914 - 2 Mar 1917: ?

Commander, 62nd Artillery Brigade
- 1904 - 1906: ?
- 1906 - 1914: DISSOLVED
- 19 Jul 1914 - 10 Jul 1916: *Maj.-Gen.* Pavel Vasilyevich **Shepelev**
- 10 Jul 1916 - 1917: *Maj.-Gen.* Mikhail Vasilyevich **Gurzhin**

Commander, 63rd Infantry Division *(Formed in 1914)*
- 19 Jul 1914 - 18 Apr 1915: *Lt.-Gen.* Andrey Fedorovich **Zubkovsky**
- 18 Apr 1915 - 18 May 1915: *Lt.-Gen.* Vladimir Vasilievich **Antipov**
- 21 Jun 1915 - 20 Aug 1915: *Maj.-Gen.* Viktor Brunovich **Kolshmidt**
- 1915: DISSOLVED

Commander, 1st Brigade, 63rd Infantry Division
- 1914 - 1915: ?
- 1915: DISSOLVED

Commander, 2nd Brigade, 63rd Infantry Division
- 1914 - 1915: ?
- 1915: DISSOLVED

Commander, 63rd Artillery Brigade
- 1914 - 23 Apr 1915: ?
- 23 Apr 1915 - 1915: *Colonel* Aleksandr Nikolayevich **Yandolovsky**
- 1915: DISSOLVED

Commander, 64th Infantry Division *(Formed in 1914)*
- 19 Jul 1914 - Sep 1916: *Lt.-Gen.* Aleksandr Yefimovich **Zhdanko**
- Sep 1916 - 23 Nov 1916: *Lt.-Gen.* Andrey Yevgenyevich **Snesarev**
- 23 Nov 1916 - 6 Apr 1917: *Lt.-Gen.* Ivan Georgievich **Erdeli**

Commander, 1st Brigade, 64th Infantry Division
- 19 Jul 1914 - 2 Mar 1917: ?

Commander, 2nd Brigade, 64th Infantry Division
- 19 Jul 1914 - 2 Mar 1917: ?

Commander, 64th Artillery Brigade
- 25 Jul 1914 - 25 Sep 1916: *Maj.-Gen.* Konstantin Gavrilovich **Aleksinsky**
- 25 Sep 1916 - 1917: *Maj.-Gen.* Konstantin Georgievich **Gorelov**

Commander, 65th Infantry Division *(Formed in 1914)*
- 19 Jul 1914 - 11 Oct 1914: *Maj.-Gen.* Georgy Fyodorovich **Eykhe**
- 3 Oct 1914 - 11 Oct 1914: *Lt.-Gen.* Georgy Nikolayevich **Viranovsky**
- 11 Oct 1914 - 28 Oct 1914: *Maj.-Gen.* Georgy Fyodorovich **Eykhe**
- 11 Nov 1914 - 5 Jul 1915: *Lt.-Gen.* Pyotr Ivanovich **Postovsky**
- 5 Jul 1915 - 22 Aug 1915: *Gen. of Inf.* Vladimir Alekseyevich **Alftan**
- 25 Aug 1915 - Oct 1917: *Lt.-Gen.* Dmitry Pavlovich **Trotsky**

Commander, 1st Brigade, 65th Infantry Division
- 19 Jul 1914 - 2 Mar 1917: ?

Commander, 2nd Brigade, 65th Infantry Division
- 19 Jul 1914 - 2 Mar 1917: ?

Commander, 65th Artillery Brigade
- 25 Jul 1914 - 6 Aug 1917: *Maj.-Gen.* Arseny Ivanovich **Chaplygin**

Commander, 66th Infantry Division *(Formed in 1914)*
- 19 Jul 1914 - 8 Oct 1914: *Gen. of Inf.* Venedikt Aloiziyevich **Yasensky**
- 8 Oct 1914 - 24 Jan 1915: *Gen. of Inf.* Pyotr Ivanovich **Oganovsky**
- 24 Jan 1915 - 24 Mar 1915: ?
- 24 Mar 1915 - 21 Sep 1915: *Lt.-Gen.* Nikolai Nikolayevich **Voropanov**
- 26 Oct 1915 - 12 Oct 1917: *Lt.-Gen.* Ippolit Viktorovich **Savitsky**

Commander, 1st Brigade, 66th Infantry Division
- 19 Jul 1914 - 2 Mar 1917: ?

Commander, 2nd Brigade, 66th Infantry Division
- 19 Jul 1914 - 2 Mar 1917: ?

Commander, 66th Artillery Brigade
- 25 Jul 1914 - 1916: *Colonel* Nikolai Nestorovich **Yazhinsky**
- 1916 - 2 Mar 1917: ?

Commander, 67th Infantry Division *(Formed in 1914)*
- 19 Jul 1914 - 14 Nov 1914: *Lt.-Gen.* Adam Yuryevich **Stankevich**
- 14 Nov 1914 - 26 Aug 1916: *Lt.-Gen.* Vladimir Yemelyanovich **Przhilutsky**
- 26 Aug 1916 - 31 Jul 1917: *Lt.-Gen.* Anatoly Vladimirovich **Khrostitsky**

Commander, 1st Brigade, 67th Infantry Division
- 19 Jul 1914 - 16 Sep 1915: ?
- 16 Sep 1915 - 7 Feb 1917: *Maj.-Gen.* Vladimir Aleksandrovich **Chermoyev**
- 7 Feb 1917 - 2 Mar 1917: ?

Commander, 2nd Brigade, 67th Infantry Division
- 19 Jul 1914 - 2 Mar 1917: ?

Commander, 67th Artillery Brigade *(Formed 1904)*
- 4 Jun 1904 - 30 Sep 1904: *Lt.-Gen.* Ilya Sakvarelovich **Makarashvili**
- 23 Oct 1904 - 17 May 1905: *Maj.-Gen.* Konstantin Nikolayevich **Rostovtsov**
- 17 May 1905 - 1906: ?
- 19 Jul 1914 - 25 Jul 1915: ?
- 25 Jul 1915 - 28 Apr 1917: *Maj.-Gen.* Nikolai Nikolayevich **Malkovsky**

Commander, 68th Infantry Division *(Formed in 1904)*
- 1 Jun 1904 - 16 Jan 1906:   *Gen. of Inf.* Vikenty Vikentyevich **Sennitsky**
- 1906 - 1914:   DISSOLVED
- 19 Jul 1914 - 15 Apr 1917:   *Lt.-Gen.* Aleksandr Nikolayevich **Apukhtin**

Commander, 1st Brigade, 68th Infantry Division
- 1 Jun 1904 - 1906:   *Maj.-Gen.* Polikarp-Genrikh Osipovich **Lunkevich**
- 1906 - 1914:   DISSOLVED
- 1914 - 2 Mar 1917:   ?

Commander, 2nd Brigade, 68th Infantry Division
- 1904 - 1906:   ?
- 1906 - 1914:   DISSOLVED
- 1914 - 2 Mar 1917:   ?

Commander, 68th Artillery Brigade
- 4 Jun 1904 - 30 Sep 1904:   *Maj.-Gen.* Vladimir Petrovich **Mezentsov**
- 30 Sep 1904 - 25 Jan 1906:   *Lt.-Gen.* Aleksandr Aleksandrovich **Dolgov**
- 1906 - 1914:   DISSOLVED
- 25 Jul 1914 - 19 Apr 1915:   *Maj.-Gen.* Aleksandr Fyodorovich **Akkerman**
- 24 Jun 1915 - 17 Mar 1917:   *Maj.-Gen.* Leonid Yakovlevich **Simonov**

Commander, 69th Infantry Division *(Formed in 1904)*
- 4 Oct 1904 - 6 Jun 1906:   *Lt.-Gen.* Pavel Gavrilovich **Masalov**
- 1906 - 1914:   DISSOLVED
- 19 Jul 1914 - 3 Jun 1917:   *Lt.-Gen.* Aleksandr Petrovich **Gavrilov**

Commander, 1st Brigade, 69th Infantry Division
- 6 Sep 1904 - 12 Jan 1905:   *Lt.-Gen.* Aleksandr Nikolayevich **Stupin**
- 12 Jan 1905 - 1906:   ?
- 1906 - 1914:   DISSOLVED
- 29 Jul 1914 - 22 Oct 1915:   *Lt.-Gen.* Aleksandr Mikhailovich **Khvostov**
- 22 Oct 1915 - 2 Mar 1917:   ?

Commander, 2nd Brigade, 69th Infantry Division
- 1904 - 1906:   ?
- 1906 - 1914:   DISSOLVED
- 1914 - 2 Mar 1917:   ?

Commander, 69th Artillery Brigade
- 1904 - 1906:   ?
- 1906 - 1914:   DISSOLVED
- 25 Jul 1914 - 29 Sep 1916:   *Maj.-Gen.* Konstantin Vladislavovich **Lomikovsky**
- 29 Sep 1916 - 2 Mar 1917:   ?

Commander, 70th Infantry Division (Formed in 1905)
- 7 Mar 1905 - 19 Jan 1906:   Gen. of Inf. Fyodor Kononovich **Bogutsky**
- 1906 - 1914:   DISSOLVED
- 19 Jul 1914 - 21 Oct 1915:   Lt.-Gen. Nikolai Vasilievich **Belov**
- 21 Oct 1915 - 22 Apr 1917:   Lt.-Gen. Baron Aleksei Pavlovich von **Budberg**

Commander, 1st Brigade, 70th Infantry Division
- 12 Mar 1905 - Jul 1906:   Maj.-Gen. Nikolai Mikhailovich **Arbuzov**
- 1906 - 1914:   DISSOLVED
- 11 Sep 1914 - 17 Nov 1914:   Lt.-Gen. Ivan Nikolayevich **Tolmachev**
- 17 Nov 1914 - 15 Mar 1915:   Maj.-Gen. Prince Nikolai Pavlovich **Stokasimov**
- 15 Mar 1015 - 2 Mar 1917:   ?

Commander, 2nd Brigade, 70th Infantry Division
- 1905 - 1906:   ?
- 1906 - 1914:   DISSOLVED
- 1914 - 2 Mar 1917:   ?

Commander, 70th Artillery Brigade
- 1905 - 1906:   ?
- 1906 - 1914:   DISSOLVED
- 1914 - 12 May 1916:   Maj.-Gen. Fyodor Ivanovich **Gorelov**
- 12 May 1916 - 2 Mar 1917:   ?

Commander, 71st Infantry Division (Formed in 1904)
- 1 Jun 1904 - 3 Jun 1906:   Gen. of Inf. Eduard Vladimirovich **Ekk**
- 1906 - 1914:   DISSOLVED
- 19 Jul 1914 - 25 Aug 1914:   Lt.-Gen. Nikita Mikhailovich **Batashev**
- 26 Aug 1914 - 21 Apr 1915:   Lt.-Gen. Anton Dmitriyevich **Lavrentyev**
- 21 Apr 1915 - 5 Jun 1916:   Lt.-Gen. Konstantin Nikolayevich **Desino**
- 5 Jun 1916 - 25 Sep 1916:   Lt.-Gen. Nikolai Avgustovich **Monkevits**
- 25 Sep 1916 - 25 Oct 1916:   ?
- 25 Oct 1916 - 12 May 1917:   Lt.-Gen. Nikolai Avgustovich **Monkevits**

Commander, 1st Brigade, 71st Infantry Division
- 1 Jun 1904 - 29 Mar 1906:   Lt.-Gen. Sergey Timofeyevich **Pogoretsky**
- 1906 - 1914:   DISSOLVED
- 1914 - 2 Mar 1917:   ?

Commander, 2nd Brigade, 71st Infantry Division
- 1 Jun 1904 - 18 Jul 1905:   Lt.-Gen. Mitrofan Yefimovich **Nudzhevsky**
- 18 Jun 1905 - 8 Jan 1907:   Lt.-Gen. Ivan Ivanovich **Zarako-Zarakovsky**
- 1907 - 1914:   DISSOLVED
- 1914 - 14 Jan 1915:   ?
- 14 Jan 1915 - 1 Apr 1915:   Maj.-Gen. Lev Lvovich **Baykov**

- 1 Apr 1915 - 2 Mar 1917: ?

Commander, 71st Artillery Brigade
- 4 Jun 1904 - 18 Mar 1906: *Maj.-Gen.* Vladimir Afanasyevich **Prokhorovich**
- 1906 - 1914: DISSOLVED
- 1914 - 25 Jul 1915: ?
- 25 Jul 1915 - 4 Nov 1916: *Maj.-Gen.* Nikolai Petrovich **Ivanov**
- 4 Nov 1916 - 2 Mar 1917: ?

Commander, 72nd Infantry Division *(Formed in 1904)*
- 1 Jun 1904 - 27 May 1905: *Lt.-Gen.* Aleksandr Davidovich **Tugan-Mirza-Baranovsky**
- 27 May 1905 - 3 Feb 1906: *Gen. of Inf.* Yevgeny Aleksandrovich **Radkevich**
- 1906 - 1914: DISSOLVED
- 19 Jul 1914 - 31 May 1915: *Maj.-Gen.* Dmitry Dmitriyevich **Orlov**
- 1915: DISSOLVED

Commander, 1st Brigade, 72nd Infantry Division
- 1 Jun 1904 - 14 Mar 1906: *Gen. of Inf.* Vladimir Vasilyevich **Bolotov**
- 1906 - 1914: DISSOLVED
- 1914 - 1915: ?
- 1915: DISSOLVED

Commander, 2nd Brigade, 72nd Infantry Division
- 1 Jun 1904 - 19 Jun 1905: *Maj.-Gen.* Aleksandr Aleksandrovich **Kusov**
- 21 Jul 1905 - 17 Aug 1906: *Lt.-Gen.* Vladimir Mikhailovich **Vasiliev**
- 1906 - 1914: DISSOLVED
- 1914 - 1915: ?
- 1915: DISSOLVED

Commander, 72nd Artillery Brigade
- 4 Jun 1904 - 1906: *Colonel* Nikolai Vladimirovich **Vykhodtsevksy**
- 1906 - 1914: DISSOLVED
- 1914 - 14 Feb 1915: *Maj.-Gen.* Vladimir Konstantinovich **Bodisko**
- 1915: DISSOLVED

Commander, 73rd Infantry Division *(Formed in 1904)*
- 1 Jun 1904 - 1906: *Lt.-Gen.* Konstantin Ivanovich **Smirnsky**
- 1906 - 1914: DISSOLVED
- 19 Jul 1914 - 8 Oct 1915: *Lt.-Gen.* Georgy Aleksandrovich **Levitsky**
- 22 Oct 1915 - 20 Mar 1917: *Lt.-Gen.* Vasily Fyodorovich **Novitsky**

Commander, 1st Brigade, 73rd Infantry Division
- 1 Jun 1904 - 4 Jul 1906: *Gen. of Inf.* Nikolai Ivanovich **Timchenko-Ruban**
- 1906 - 1914: DISSOLVED

- 29 Jul 1914 - 20 May 1916: *Lt.-Gen.* Nikolai Kirillovich **Yanovsky**
- 20 May 1916 - 2 Mar 1917: ?

Commander, 2nd Brigade, 73rd Infantry Division
- 1904 - 1906: ?
- 1906 - 1914: DISSOLVED
- 1914 - 2 Mar 1917: ?

Commander, 73rd Artillery Brigade
- 4 Jun 1904 - 25 Sep 1904: *Gen. of Art.* Prince Vladimir Nikolayevich **Masalsky**
- 23 Oct 1904 - 13 Dec 1905: *Gen. of Art.* Nikolai Konstantinovich **Tomashevsky**
- 1906 - 1914: DISSOLVED
- 25 Jul 1914 - 2 Sep 1916: *Maj.-Gen.* Ipaty Ivanovich **Klochenko**
- 2 Sep 1916 - 1 Feb 1917: *Maj.-Gen.* Pyotr Mikhailovich **Konopchansky**
- 1 Feb 1917 - 2 Mar 1917: ?

Commander, 74th Infantry Division *(Formed in 1914)*
- 19 Jul 1914 - 19 Dec 1914: *Gen. of Art.* Ivan Karlovich **Baggovut**
- 19 Dec 1914 - 29 May 1917: *Lt.-Gen.* Pavel Dmitriyevich **Shipov**

Commander, 1st Brigade, 74th Infantry Division
- 1914 - 2 Mar 1917: ?

Commander, 2nd Brigade, 74th Infantry Division
- 1914 - 2 Mar 1917: ?

Commander, 74th Artillery Brigade
- 25 Jul 1914 - 27 Feb 1917: *Maj.-Gen.* Aleksandr Fridrikhovich **Iordan**
- 27 Feb 1917 - 2 Mar 1917: ?

Commander, 75th Infantry Division *(Formed in 1905)*
- 19 Jul 1914 - 28 Apr 1917: *Lt.-Gen.* Mikhail Ivanovich **Shtegelman**

Commander, 1st Brigade, 75th Infantry Division
- 1914 - 2 Mar 1917: ?

Commander, 2nd Brigade, 75th Infantry Division
- 1914 - 24 Jan 1915: ?
- 24 Jan 1915 - 26 Jun 1915: *Maj.-Gen.* Iosif Kazimirovich **Kononovich**
- 26 Jun 1915 - 2 Mar 1917: ?

Commander, 75th Artillery Brigade
- 25 Jul 1914 - 22 Jan 1917: *Lt.-Gen.* Konstantin Konstantinovich **Egger**
- 23 Jan 1917 - 1918: *Maj.-Gen.* Fyodor Alekseyevich **Snessorev**

Commander, 76th Infantry Division *(Formed in 1914)*
- 19 Jul 1914 - 8 Oct 1914: *Lt.-Gen.* Feliks Dominikovich **Iozefovich**
- 8 Oct 1914 - 11 Nov 1914: *Lt.-Gen.* Pyotr Ivanovich **Postovsky**
- 11 Nov 1914 - 31 Dec 1916: *Lt.-Gen.* Aleksandr Nikolayevich **Kuzmin-Korovayev**
- 31 Dec 1916 - 2 Mar 1917: ?

Commander, 1st Brigade, 76th Infantry Division
- 1914 - 2 Mar 1917: ?

Commander, 2nd Brigade, 76th Infantry Division
- 1914 - 2 Mar 1917: ?

Commander, 76th Artillery Brigade
- 1914 - 1915: ?
- 1915 - 1917: *Maj.-Gen.* Ivan Aleksandrovich **Maksheyev**

Commander, 77th Infantry Division *(Formed in 1904)*
- 28 Dec 1904 - 4 Jul 1906: *Gen. of Inf.* Aleksandr Nikolayevich **Lebedev**
- 1906 - 1914: DISSOLVED
- 19 Jul 1914 - 25 Aug 1915: *Lt.-Gen.* Lev Stepanovich **Baranovsky**
- 25 Aug 1915 - 30 Sep 1917: *Lt.-Gen.* Vladimir Georgiyevich **Leontyev**

Commander, 1st Brigade, 77th Infantry Division
- 1904 - 1906: ?
- 1906 - 1914: DISSOLVED
- 1914 - 2 Mar 1917: ?

Commander, 2nd Brigade, 77th Infantry Division
- 1904 - 1906: ?
- 1906 - 1914: DISSOLVED
- 1914 - 2 Mar 1917: ?

Commander, 77th Artillery Brigade
- 1904 - 1906: ?
- 1906 - 1914: DISSOLVED
- 25 Jul 1914 - 13 Apr 1916: *Maj.-Gen.* Prince Aleksandr Vladimirovich **Ukhtomsky**
- 12 May 1916 - 1917: *Maj.-Gen.* Vladimir Pavlovich **Starov**

Commander, 78th Infantry Division *(Formed in 1904)*
- 1 Jun 1904 - 2 Jan 1906: *Lt.-Gen.* Valerian Yakovlevich **Lisovsky**
- 1906 - 1914: DISSOLVED
- 19 Jul 1914 - 3 Jun 1915: *Gen. of Inf.* Vladimir Alekseyevich **Alftan**
- 3 Jun 1915 - 17 Jul 1917: *Lt.-Gen.* Sergey Konstantinovich **Dobrorolsky**

Commander, 1st Brigade, 78th Infantry Division
- 1 Jun 1904 - 1906:   *Lt.-Gen.* Vasily Ignatyevich **Parutsky**
- 1906 - 1914:   DISSOLVED
- 29 Jul 1914 - 26 Apr 1916:   *Maj.-Gen.* Nikolai Adolfovich **Abzholtovsky**
- 26 Apr 1916 - 2 Mar 1917:   *Colonel* Mikhail Aleksandrovich **Vasiliev**

Commander, 2nd Brigade, 78th Infantry Division
- 1 Jun 1904 - 18 Jul 1905:   *Lt.-Gen.* Aleksandr Pavlovich von **Ganenfeldt**
- 18 Jul 1905 - 1906:   ?
- 1906 - 1914:   DISSOLVED
- 1914 - 14 Jan 1915:   ?
- 14 Jan 1915 - 3 Feb 1915:   *Maj.-Gen.* Semyon Yegorovich **Molchanov**
- 3 Feb 1915 - 7 Jun 1915:   *Lt.-Gen.* Mikhail Lvovich **Matveyev**
- 5 Jul 1915 - 6 Mar 1917:   *Maj.-Gen.* Mikhail Petrovich **Losyev**

Commander, 78th Artillery Brigade
- 1904 - 1906:   ?
- 1906 - 1914:   DISSOLVED
- 25 Jul 1914 - 1917:   *Maj.-Gen.* Ivan Yevgrafovich **Lukin**

Commander, 79th Infantry Division *(Formed in 1904)*
- 11 Oct 1904 - 8 Aug 1906:   *Gen. of Inf.* Nikolai Iosifovich **Zakrzhevsky**
- 1906 - 1914:   DISSOLVED
- 19 Jul 1914 - 22 Apr 1917:   *Lt.-Gen.* Nikolai Ivanovich **Gavrilov**

Commander, 1st Brigade, 79th Infantry Division
- 11 Oct 1904 - 16 Apr 1906:   *Maj.-Gen.* Andrey Ivanovich **Yunchis**
- 1906 - 1914:   DISSOLVED
- 1914 - 2 Mar 1917:   ?

Commander, 2nd Brigade, 79th Infantry Division
- 1904 - 1906:   ?
- 1906 - 1914:   DISSOLVED
- 1914 - 2 Mar 1917:   ?

Commander, 79th Artillery Brigade
- 1904 - 1906:   ?
- 1906 - 1914:   DISSOLVED
- 1914 - 8 Jul 1916:   ?
- 8 Jul 1916 - 17 Oct 1917:   *Maj.-Gen.* Pavel Pavlovich **Sytin**

Commander, 80th Infantry Division *(Formed in 1914)*
- 19 Jul 1914 - 16 Jan 1915:   *Lt.-Gen.* Aleksandr Antonovich **Gertsyk**
- 31 Jan 1915 - 9 Aug 1915:   *Lt.-Gen.* Dmitry Pavlovich **Parsky**
- 7 Sep 1915 - 4 May 1917:   *Lt.-Gen.* Mikhail Dmitriyevich **Kitchenko**

Commander, 1st Brigade, 80th Infantry Division
- 1914 - 2 Mar 1917: ?

Commander, 2nd Brigade, 80th Infantry Division
- 1914 - 2 Mar 1917: ?

Commander, 80th Artillery Brigade
- 25 Jun 1914 - 28 Apr 1917: *Maj.-Gen.* Mikhail Ivanovich **Pyzhevsky**

Commander, 81st Infantry Division *(Formed in 1914)*
- 19 Jul 1914 - 20 Apr 1915: *Lt.-Gen.* Sergey Dmitriyevich **Chistyakov**
- 20 May 1915 - 17 Jul 1915: *Lt.-Gen.* Torsten Karlovich **Vadensherna**
- 27 Aug 1915 - 1917: *Lt.-Gen.* Aleksandr Sergeyevich **Savvich**

Commander, 1st Brigade, 81st Infantry Division
- 1914 - 2 Mar 1917: ?

Commander, 2nd Brigade, 81st Infantry Division
- 1914 - 2 Mar 1917: ?

Commander, 81st Artillery Brigade
- 1914 - 27 Dec 1915: ?
- 27 Dec 1915 - 1917: *Maj.-Gen.* Vasily Nikolayevich **Borisov**

Commander, 82nd Infantry Division *(Formed in 1914)*
- 20 Jul 1914 - 1 Nov 1914: *Gen. of Inf.* Fyodor Afanasievich **Voloshinov**
- 2 Nov 1914 - 7 Apr 1917: *Lt.-Gen.* Mikhail Nikolayevich **Promtov**

Commander, 1st Brigade, 82nd Infantry Division
- 1914 - 2 Mar 1917: ?

Commander, 2nd Brigade, 82nd Infantry Division
- 1914 - 2 Mar 1917: ?

Commander, 82nd Artillery Brigade
- 1914 - 22 Oct 1915: ?
- 22 Oct 1915 - 1917: *Maj.-Gen.* Mikhail Lvovich **Makarov**

Commander, 83rd Infantry Division *(Formed in 1914)*
- 19 Jul 1914 - 9 Nov 1914: *Lt.-Gen.* Konstantin Lukich **Gilchevsky**
- 9 Nov 1914 - 19 Jun 1915: *Lt.-Gen.* Vladimir Vasilievich **Belyayev**
- 26 Jun 1915 - 7 Apr 1917: *Lt.-Gen.* Vasily Vasilievich **Butovich**

Commander, 1ˢᵗ Brigade, 83ʳᵈ Infantry Division
- 1914 - 2 Mar 1917: ?

Commander, 2ⁿᵈ Brigade, 83ʳᵈ Infantry Division
- 1914 - 2 Mar 1917: ?

Commander, 83ʳᵈ Artillery Brigade
- 1914 - 2 Mar 1917: ?

Commander, 84ᵗʰ Infantry Division *(Formed in 1914)*
- 19 Jul 1914 - 15 Apr 1917: *Lt.-Gen.* Vladimir Apollonovich **Kozlov**

Commander, 1ˢᵗ Brigade, 84ᵗʰ Infantry Division
- 29 Jul 1914 - 11 Mar 1917: *Maj.-Gen.* Aleksandr Alekseyevich **Yesaulov**

Commander, 2ⁿᵈ Brigade, 84ᵗʰ Infantry Division
- 1914 - 2 Mar 1917: ?

Commander, 84ᵗʰ Artillery Brigade
- 1914 - 12 May 1916: *Maj.-Gen.* Vladimir Pavlovich **Starov**
- 12 May 1916 - 1917: *Maj.-Gen.* Aleksandr Dormidontovich **Morozov**

85ᵗʰ - 98ᵗʰ Infantry Divisions not formed

During the period 1915 - early 1917, Infantry Divisions numbered 99 - 138 and 151 - 194 were formed on an ad hoc basis. What little information that is available about the commanders of these units is presented below. Divisions 188 - 194 were formed in the weeks following the Tsar's abdication, and therefore are not included in this listing.

Commander, 99ᵗʰ Infantry Division *(Formed in 1916)*
- 1916 - 2 Mar 1917: ?

Commander, 100ᵗʰ Infantry Division *(Formed in 1916)*
- 11 Mar 1916 - 29 May 1917: *Maj.-Gen.* Sergey Ivanovich **Gavrilov**

Commander, 101ˢᵗ Infantry Division *(Formed in 1915)*
- 3 Jul 1915 - 6 Apr 1917: *Lt.-Gen.* Konstantin Lukich **Gilchevsky**

Commander, 102ⁿᵈ Infantry Division *(Formed in 1915)*
- 3 Jul 1915 - 20 Oct 1915: *Lt.-Gen.* Ivan Konstantinovich **Gandurin**
- 25 Oct 1915 - 26 May 1916: *Lt.-Gen.* Iosif Aleksandrovich **Mikulin**
- 17 Jun 1916 - 10 Oct 1916: *Gen. of Inf.* Karl-Avgust Aleksandrovich **Shulman**

- 14 Oct 1916 - 10 Apr 1917:   *Lt.-Gen.* Konstantin Konstantinovich **Shildbakh**

Commander, 103rd Infantry Division *(Formed in 1915)*
- 3 Jul 1915 - 26 Apr 1917:   *Lt.-Gen.* Ivan Konstantinovich **Sarafov**

Commander, 104th Infantry Division *(Formed in 1915)*
- 20 Jul 1915 - 23 Jul 1916:   *Lt.-Gen.* Aleksandr Andreyevich **Tsitsovich**
- 23 Jul 1916 - 7 Mar 1917:   *Lt.-Gen.* Sergey Nikolayevich **Lyupov**

Commander, 105th Infantry Division *(Formed in 1915)*
- 15 Jul 1915 - 22 Apr 1917:   *Lt.-Gen.* Aleksandr Nikolayevich **Skornyakov**

Commander, 106th Infantry Division *(Formed in 1915)*
- 19 Jun 1915 - 1917:   *Lt.-Gen.* Adam Yuryevich **Stankevich**

Commander, 107th Infantry Division *(Formed in 1915)*
- 6 Jun 1915 - 15 Apr 1917:   *Lt.-Gen.* Pavel Mitrofanovich **Samgin**

Commander, 108th Infantry Division *(Formed in 1915)*
- 6 Jun 1915 - 16 Mar 1916:   *Lt.-Gen.* Selvin Severinovich **Lassky**
- 19 Mar 1916 - 2 Apr 1917:   *Lt.-Gen.* Sergei Aleksandrovich **Zubov**

Commander, 109th Infantry Division *(Formed in 1915)*
- 5 Jul 1915 - 4 Nov 1915:   *Lt.-Gen.* Mikhail Andreyevich **Pryaslov**
- 10 Nov 1915 - 18 Apr 1917:   *Lt.-Gen.* Nikolai Ilich **Sulimov**

Commander, 110th Infantry Division *(Formed in 1915)*
- 6 Jun 1915 - 9 Mar 1917:   *Lt.-Gen.* Mikhail Pavlovich **Ganenfeldt**

Commander, 111th Infantry Division *(Formed in 1915)*
- 12 Jul 1915 - 22 Apr 1917:   *Lt.-Gen.* Mikhail Nikolayevich **Maslov**

Commander, 112th Infantry Division *(Formed in 1916)*
- 22 Jan 1916 - 6 Apr 1917:   *Lt.-Gen.* Aleksandr Mikhailovich **Khvostov**

Commander, 113th Infantry Division *(Formed in 1916)*
- 16 Mar 1916 - 17 Mar 1917: *Lt.-Gen.* Aleksandr Lvovich **Timchenko**

Commander, 114th Infantry Division *(Formed in 1915)*
- 12 Jul 1915 - 20 Aug 1915: *Lt.-Gen.* Genrikh Gustavovich **Liliyental**
- Aug 1915: DISSOLVED

Commander, 115th Infantry Division *(Formed in 1916)*
- 21 Feb 1916 - 1 Nov 1916: *Lt.-Gen.* Aleksandr Konstantinovich **Freyman**
- 2 Nov 1916 - 19 Apr 1917: *Maj.-Gen.* Lev Lvovich **Baykov**

Commander, 116th Infantry Division *(Formed in 1916)*
- 20 Mar 1916 - 5 Apr 1917: *Maj.-Gen.* Vyacheslav Frantsevich **Poboyevsky**

Commander, 117th Infantry Division *(Formed in 1916)*
- 26 Apr 1916 - 4 May 1917: *Lt.-Gen.* Anton Petrovich **Symon**

Commander, 118th Infantry Division *(Formed in 1916)*
- 25 Jun 1916 - 1917: *Maj.-Gen.* Semyon Petrovich **Bylim-Kolosovsky**

Commander, 119th Infantry Division *(Formed in 1915)*
- 22 Jul 1915 - 20 Aug 1915: *Lt.-Gen.* Vladimir Porfiryevich **Prasalov**
- Aug 1915: DISSOLVED

Commander, 120th Infantry Division *(Formed in 1916)*
- 1 Jan 1916 - 18 Apr 1917: *Lt.-Gen.* Eduard Arkadyevich **Kolyankovsky**

Commander, 121st Infantry Division *(Formed in 1916)*
- 1 Jan 1916 - 25 Mar 1916: *Lt.-Gen.* Baron Aleksandr Aleksandrovich von **Taube**
- 19 Mar 1916 - 14 Jul 1917: *Lt.-Gen.* Anastas Fyodorovich **Benderev**

Commander, 122nd Infantry Division *(Formed in 1916)*
- 21 Oct 1916 - 1917: *Lt.-Gen.* Gavriil Aleksandrovich **Likhachev**

Commander, 123rd Infantry Division *(Formed in 1916)*
- 25 Feb 1916 - 7 Nov 1916: *Lt.-Gen.* Iosif Romanovich **Dovbor-Musnitsky**
- 10 Nov 1916 - 16 Sep 1917: *Lt.-Gen.* Mikhail Nikolayevich **Kalnitsky**

Commander, 124th Infantry Division *(Formed in 1915)*
- 12 Jul 1915 - 13 Apr 1917: *Gen. of Inf.* Nikolai Yakovlevich **Lopushansky**

Commander, 125th Infantry Division *(Formed in 1915)*
- 25 Aug 1915 - 21 Jan 1916: *Lt.-Gen.* Yevgeny Yakovlevich **Kotyuzhinsky**
- 21 Jan 1916 - 11 Aug 1916: *Lt.-Gen.* Baron Sergey Ernestovich von **Ber**
- 11 Aug 1916 - 2 Apr 1917: *Lt.-Gen.* Fyodor Yevlampiyevich **Ogorodnikov**

Commander, 126th Infantry Division *(Formed in 1916)*
- 7 Jan 1916 - 11 Mar 1917: *Lt.-Gen.* Georgy Aleksandrovich **Levitsky**

Commander, 127th Infantry Division *(Formed in 1916)*
- 7 Jan 1916 - 9 Jun 1916: *Lt.-Gen.* Pyotr Mikhailovich **Baranov**
- 30 Jun 1916 - 10 Oct 1917: *Maj.-Gen.* Dmitry Mikhailovich von **Zigel**

Commander, 128th Infantry Division *(Formed in 1916)*
- 9 Nov 1916 - 9 Jun 1917: *Maj.-Gen.* Pyotr Andreyevich **Tikhonovich**

Commander, 129th Infantry Division *(Formed in 1916)*
- 29 Nov 1916 - 4 May 1917: *Maj.-Gen.* Pyotr Petrovich **Karpov**

Commander, 130th Infantry Division *(Formed in 1916)*
- 29 Nov 1916 - 19 May 1917: *Maj.-Gen.* Georgy Alekseyevich **Danilov**

Commander, 131st Infantry Division *(Formed in 1916)*
- 29 Nov 1916 - 10 Jan 1917: *Lt.-Gen.* Vladimir Fyodorovich **Dzhunkovsky**
- 10 Jan 1917: REDESIGNATED 15th SIBERIAN RIFLE DIVISION

Commander, 132nd Infantry Division *(Formed in 1916)*
- 20 Nov 1916 - 23 Jul 1917: *Maj.-Gen.* Aleksandr Ivanovich **Zhnov**

Commander, 133rd Infantry Division *(Formed in 1916)*
- 29 Nov 1916 - 30 Apr 1917: *Maj.-Gen.* Prince Dmitry Alekseyevich **Kropotkin**

Commander, 134th Infantry Division *(Formed in 1916)*
- 29 Nov 1916 - 1917: *Maj.-Gen.* Lukyan Vasilievich **Afanasyev**

Commander, 135th Infantry Division *(Formed in 1917)*
- 21 Jan 1917 - 1917: *Maj.-Gen.* David Petrovich **Simonson**

Commander, 136th Infantry Division *(Formed in 1916)*
- 2 Dec 1916 - 4 May 1917: *Maj.-Gen.* Nikolai Maksimovich **Ostryansky**

Commander, 137th Infantry Division *(Formed in 1916)*
- 2 Dec 1916 - 20 May 1917: *Maj.-Gen.* Nikolai Denisovich **Liventsev**

Commander, 138th Infantry Division *(Formed in 1916)*
- 11 Dec 1916 - 20 May 1917: *Maj.-Gen.* Mikhail Panteleymonovich **Mikhailov**

139th - 150th Infantry Divisions not formed

Commander, 151st Infantry Division *(Formed in 1917)*
- 18 Feb 1917 - 30 Sep 1917: *Maj.-Gen.* Mikhail Karlovich **Voytsekhovsky**

Commander, 152nd Infantry Division *(Formed in 1917)*
- 1917 - 2 Mar 1917: ?

Commander, 153rd Infantry Division *(Formed in 1917)*
- 1917 - 2 Mar 1917: ?

Commander, 154th Infantry Division *(Formed in 1917)*
- 18 Feb 1917 - 6 Apr 1917: *Maj.-Gen.* Nikolai Petrovich **Kuchin**

Commander, 155th Infantry Division *(Formed in 1917)*
- 18 Feb 1917 - 25 Apr 1917: *Maj.-Gen.* Yulian Vasilyevich **Prokopenko**

Commander, 156th Infantry Division *(Formed in 1917)*
- 18 Feb 1917 - 22 Apr 1917: *Lt.-Gen.* Sergey Dmitriyevich **Chistyakov**

Commander, 157th Infantry Division *(Formed in 1917)*
- 18 Feb 1917 - 23 Apr 1917: *Maj.-Gen.* Maksimilian Nikolayevich **Munte von Morgenstyern**

Commander, 158th Infantry Division *(Formed in 1917)*
- 1917 - 2 Mar 1917: ?

Commander, 159th Infantry Division *(Formed in 1917)*
- 1917 - 2 Mar 1917: ?

Commander, 160th Infantry Division *(Formed in 1917)*
- 1917 - 2 Mar 1917: ?

Commander, 161st Infantry Division *(Formed in 1917)*
- 1917 - 2 Mar 1917: ?

Commander, 162nd Infantry Division *(Formed in 1917)*
- 18 Feb 1917 - 25 Aug 1917: *Lt.-Gen.* Sergey Nikolayevich **Rozanov**

Commander, 163rd Infantry Division *(Formed in 1917)*
- 1917 - 2 Mar 1917: ?

Commander, 164th Infantry Division *(Formed in 1917)*
- 21 Feb 1917 - Oct 1917: *Maj.-Gen.* Konstantin Fodorovich **Shchedrin**

Commander, 165th Infantry Division *(Formed in 1917)*
- 18 Feb 1917 - 1918: *Lt.-Gen.* Valentin Yevgrafovich **Lukin**

Commander, 166th Infantry Division *(Formed in 1917)*
- 18 Feb 1917 - 1917: *Maj.-Gen.* Mikhail Ivanovich **Repyev**

Commander, 167th Infantry Division *(Formed in 1917)*
- 18 Feb 1917 - 1918: *Maj.-Gen.* Konstantin Konstantinovich **Pilkin**

Commander, 168th Infantry Division *(Formed in 1917)*
- 7 Feb 1917 - 5 May 1917: *Lt.-Gen.* Yevgeny Andreyevich **Iskritsky**

Commander, 169th Infantry Division *(Formed in 1917)*
- 7 Feb 1917 - 6 Aug 1917: *Maj.-Gen.* Vladimir Aleksandrovich **Dobrzhansky**

Commander, 170th Infantry Division *(Formed in 1917)*
- 7 Feb 1917 - 6 Aug 1917:   *Maj.-Gen.* Vladimir Aleksandrovich **Chermoyev**

Commander, 171st Infantry Division *(Formed in 1917)*
- 7 Feb 1917 - 28 Apr 1917:   *Maj.-Gen.* Nikolai Dmitriyevich **Chausov**

Commander, 172nd Infantry Division *(Formed in 1917)*
- 7 Feb 1917 - 1918:   *Maj.-Gen.* Mikhail Ivanovich **Merro**

Commander, 173rd Infantry Division *(Formed in 1917)*
- 7 Jan 1917 - 23 Nov 1917:   *Maj.-Gen.* Viktor Vladimirovich **Nagayev**

Commander, 174th Infantry Division *(Formed in 1917)*
- 7 Feb 1917 - 22 Aug 1917:   *Maj.-Gen.* Prince Georgy Davidovich **Tsulukidze**

Commander, 175th Infantry Division *(Formed in 1917)*
- 7 Feb 1917 - 1917:   *Maj.-Gen.* Vasily Stepanovich **Smirnov**

Commander, 176th Infantry Division *(Formed in 1917)*
- 1917 - 2 Mar 1917:   ?

Commander, 177th Infantry Division *(Formed in 1917)*
- 7 Feb 1917 - 29 May 1917:   *Maj.-Gen.* Yakov Yakovlevich **Lyubitsky**

Commander, 178th Infantry Division *(Formed in 1917)*
- 20 Feb 1917 - 5 Sep 1917:   *Maj.-Gen.* Pyotr Nikitich **Burov**

Commander, 179th Infantry Division *(Formed in 1917)*
- 1917 - 2 Mar 1917:   ?

Commander, 180th Infantry Division *(Formed in 1917)*
- 29 Jan 1917 - Mar 1917:   *Maj.-Gen.* Fyodor Matveyevich **Ivanov**

Commander, 181st Infantry Division *(Formed in 1917)*
- 29 Jan 1917 - 18 Apr 1917:   *Maj.-Gen.* Illarion Ivanovich **Gruzintsev**

Commander, 182ⁿᵈ Infantry Division *(Formed in 1917)*
- 29 Jan 1917 - 20 Sep 1917: *Maj.-Gen.* Viktor Lukich **Popov**

Commander, 183ʳᵈ Infantry Division *(Formed in 1917)*
- 29 Jan 1917 - 25 Apr 1917: *Maj.-Gen.* Ivan Dmitriyevich **Chistyakov**

Commander, 184ᵗʰ Infantry Division *(Formed in 1917)*
- 29 Jan 1917 - 27 May 1917: *Maj.-Gen.* Pyotr Alekseyevich **Noskov**

Commander, 185ᵗʰ Infantry Division *(Formed in 1917)*
- 29 Jan 1917 - Jan 1918: *Maj.-Gen.* Mikhail Antonovich **Dorman**

Commander, 186ᵗʰ Infantry Division *(Formed in 1917)*
- 29 Jan 1917 - Oct 1917: *Maj.-Gen.* Viktor Viktorovich **Eggert**

Commander, 187ᵗʰ Infantry Division *(Formed in 1917)*
- 29 Jan 1917 - 31 Jan 1918: *Maj.-Gen.* Aleksandr Mikhailovich **Ivanov**

Commander, 1ˢᵗ Special Infantry Division *(Formed in 1916)*
- 1916 - 2 Mar 1917: ?

Commander, 2ⁿᵈ Special Infantry Division *(Formed in 1916)*
- 2 Nov 1916 - 27 Jan 1917: *Maj.-Gen.* Vladimir Zakharovich **Gudima**
- 27 Jan 1917 - Oct 1917: *Maj.-Gen.* Viktor Petrovich **Taranovsky**

Commander, 3ʳᵈ Special Infantry Division *(Formed in 1917)*
27 Jan 1917 - 20 May 1917: *Maj.-Gen.* Vladimir Zakharovich **Gudima**

Commander, 4ᵗʰ Special Infantry Division *(Formed in 1917)*
29 Jan 1917 - 30 Jun 1917: *Maj.-Gen.* Yevgeny Vasilievich **Lebedinsky**

Commander, Guards Rifle Division *(Formed in 1915 from Guards Rifle Brigade)*
- 17 Feb 1915 - 16 Apr 1917: *Lt.-Gen.* Pyotr Alekseyevich **Delsal**

   Commander, 1ˢᵗ Brigade, Guards Rifle Division
   - 17 Dec 1915 - 29 Oct 1916: *Maj.-Gen.* Adrian Vladimirovich **Usov**
   - 29 Oct 1916 - 7 Apr 1917: *Maj.-Gen.* Iosif Kazimirovich **Kononovich**

Commander, 2nd Brigade, Guards Rifle Division
- 30 Dec 1915 - 24 Apr 1917: *Maj.-Gen.* Prince Anatoly Vladimirovich **Baryatinsky**

Commander, 1st Rifle Division *(Formed in 1905 from 1st Rifle Brigade)*
- 13 Aug 1905 - 7 Oct 1906: *Lt.-Gen.* Pavel Kaetanovich **Dombrovsky**
- 1906 - 1916: REVERTED TO BRIGADE
- 17 Jan 1916 - 14 May 1917: *Lt.-Gen.* Pavel Aristovich von **Kotsebue**

Commander, 1st Brigade, 1st Rifle Division
- 19 Jun 1905 - 16 Dec 1906: *Lt.-Gen.* Grigory Yefimovich **Yanushevsky**
- 1906 - 1916: DISSOLVED
- 1916 - 2 Mar 1917: ?

Commander, 2nd Brigade, 1st Rifle Division
- 19 Jun 1905 - 14 Mar 1906: *Lt.-Gen.* Andrey Fedorovich **Zubkovsky**
- 1906 - 1916: DISSOLVED
- 1916 - 2 Mar 1917: ?

Commander, 2nd Rifle Division *(Formed in 1905 from 2nd Rifle Brigade)*
- 21 Nov 1905 - 3 Apr 1906: *Gen. of Inf.* Nikolai Nikolayevich **Yudenich**
- 1906 - 1915: REVERTED TO BRIGADE
- 12 Jul 1915 - 7 Apr 1917: *Lt.-Gen.* Yulian Yulianovich **Belozor**

Commander, 1st Brigade, 2nd Rifle Division
- 19 Jun 1905 - 31 Dec 1906: *Maj.-Gen.* Eduard Renatovich **Kastellaz**
- 1906 - 1916: DISSOLVED
- 1916 - 2 Mar 1917: ?

Commander, 2nd Brigade, 2nd Rifle Division
- 19 Jun 1905 - 28 Aug 1906: *Maj.-Gen.* Pyotr Pavlovich **Voyeykov**
- 1906 - 1916: DISSOLVED
- 1916 - 2 Mar 1917: ?

Commander, 3rd Rifle Division *(Formed in 1905 from 3rd Rifle Brigade)*
- 18 Jul 1905 - 19 Mar 1906: *Gen. of Inf.* Nikolai Ivanovich **Glebov**
- 1906 - 1915: REVERTED TO BRIGADE
- 6 Aug 1915 - 6 Apr 1916: *Lt.-Gen.* Yakov Aleksandrovich **Fok**
- 26 Apr 1916 - Oct 1917: *Maj.-Gen.* Nikolai Adolfovich **Abzholtovsky**

Commander, 1st Brigade, 3rd Rifle Division
- 19 Jun 1905 - 2 Dec 1906: *Maj.-Gen.* Vatslav-Martsely Lavrentyevich **Prosinsky**
- 1906 - 1916: DISSOLVED
- 1916 - 2 Mar 1917: ?

Commander, 2nd Brigade, 3rd Rifle Division
- 19 Jun 1905 - 1906:   *Maj.-Gen.* Gilyary Stanislavovich **Pashkovsky**
- 1906 - 1916:   DISSOLVED
- 1916 - 2 Mar 1917:   ?

Commander, 4th Rifle Division *(Formed in 1905 from 4th Rifle Brigade)*
- 28 Jul 1905 - 7 Jul 1907:   *Lt.-Gen.* Andrei Dmitriyevich **Vsevolozhsky**
- 1907 - 1915:   REVERTED TO BRIGADE
- 6 Aug 1915 - 9 Sep 1916:   *Lt.-Gen.* Anton Ivanovich **Denikin**
- 9 Sep 1916 - 25 Aug 1917:   *Lt.-Gen.* Silvestr Lvovich **Stankevich**

Commander, 1st Brigade, 4th Rifle Division
- 1905 - 1906:   ?
- 1906 - 1915:   DISSOLVED
- 7 Aug 1915 - 9 Sep 1916:   *Lt.-Gen.* Silvestr Lvovich **Stankevich**

Commander, 2nd Brigade, 4th Rifle Division
- 19 Jun 1905 - 5 May 1906:   *Lt.-Gen.* Vladislav Frantsevich **Baufal**
- 1906 - 1916:   DISSOLVED
- 1916 - 2 Mar 1917:   ?

Commander, 5th Rifle Division *(Formed in 1905 from 5th Rifle Brigade)*
- 13 Aug 1905 - 1 Jul 1906:   *Gen. of Inf.* Aleksei Yevgrafovich **Churin**
- 1906 - 1915:   REVERTED TO BRIGADE
- 22 Oct 1915 - 26 Apr 1916:   *Maj.-Gen.* Vladimir Stepanovich **Ivanov**
- 26 Apr 1916 - 27 Jan 1917:   *Maj.-Gen.* Viktor Petrovich **Taranovsky**
- 27 Jan 1917 - 2 Mar 1917:   ?

Commander, 1st Brigade, 5th Rifle Division
- 19 Jun 1905 - 30 Dec 1906:   *Lt.-Gen.* Fyodor Trofimovich **Ryabinkin**
- 1906 - 1916:   DISSOLVED
- 1916 - 2 Mar 1917:   ?

Commander, 2nd Brigade, 5th Rifle Division
- 19 Jun 1905 - 10 Feb 1907:   *Gen. of Inf.* Nikolai Nikolayevich **Yudenich**
- 1907 - 1916:   DISSOLVED
- 1916 - 2 Mar 1917:   ?

Commander, 1st Caucasus Rifle Division *(Formed in 1915)*
- 3 Nov 1915 - 1917:   *Lt.-Gen.* Konstantin Nikolayevich **Bekov**

Commander, 1st Brigade, 1st Caucasus Rifle Division
- 1915 - 2 Mar 1917:   ?

Commander, 2nd Brigade, 1st Caucasus Rifle Division
- 1915 - 2 Mar 1917: ?

Commander, 2nd Caucasus Rifle Division *(Formed in 1915)*
- 19 Nov 1915 - Jan 1917: *Maj.-Gen.* Foma Ivanovich **Nazarbekov**
- Jan 1917 - 2 Mar 1917: ?

Commander, 1st Brigade, 2nd Caucasus Rifle Division
- 1915 - 2 Mar 1917: ?

Commander, 2nd Brigade, 2nd Caucasus Rifle Division
- 1915 - 2 Mar 1916: ?
- 2 Mar 1916 - 1917: *Colonel* Vsevolod Ivanovich **Obraztsov**

Commander, 3rd Caucasus Rifle Division *(Formed in 1915)*
- 1915 - 13 Jun 1916: ?
- 13 Jun 1916 - 14 Nov 1916: *Lt.-Gen.* Feliks Dominikovich **Iozefovich**
- 21 Nov 1916 - 25 Mar 1917: *Maj.-Gen.* Boris Iosifovich **Shchutskoy**

Commander, 1st Brigade, 3rd Caucasus Rifle Division
- 1915 - 2 Mar 1917: ?

Commander, 2nd Brigade, 3rd Caucasus Rifle Division
- 1915 - 2 Mar 1917: ?

Commander, 4th Caucasus Rifle Division *(Formed in 1915)*
- 14 Sep 1915 - 3 Jun 1917: *Lt.-Gen.* Nikolai Mikhailovich **Vorobyev**

Commander, 1st Brigade, 4th Caucasus Rifle Division
- 1915 - 2 Mar 1917: ?

Commander, 2nd Brigade, 4th Caucasus Rifle Division
- 1915 - 2 Mar 1917: ?

Commander, 5th Caucasus Rifle Division *(Formed in 1916)*
- 2 Apr 1916 - 16 Sep 1917: *Lt.-Gen.* Filipp-Stanislav Iosifovich **Dubissky**

Commander, 1st Brigade, 5th Caucasus Rifle Division
- 1915 - 2 Mar 1917: ?

Commander, 2nd Brigade, 5th Caucasus Rifle Division
- 1915 - 2 Mar 1917: ?

Commander, 6ᵗʰ Caucasus Rifle Division *(Formed in 1916)*
- 12 Aug 1916 - 1917: *Maj.-Gen.* Fyodor Moiseyevich **Voloshin-Petrichenko**

   Commander, 1ˢᵗ Brigade, 6ᵗʰ Caucasus Rifle Division
   - 1915 - 2 Mar 1917: ?

   Commander, 2ⁿᵈ Brigade, 6ᵗʰ Caucasus Rifle Division
   - 1915 - 2 Mar 1917: ?

Commander, 7ᵗʰ Caucasus Rifle Division *(Formed in 1916)*
- 7 Oct 1916 - 9 Jun 1917: *Maj.-Gen.* Yakov Vasilievich **Amasysky**

   Commander, 1ˢᵗ Brigade, 7ᵗʰ Caucasus Rifle Division
   - 1915 - 2 Mar 1917: ?

   Commander, 2ⁿᵈ Brigade, 7ᵗʰ Caucasus Rifle Division
   - 1915 - 2 Mar 1917: ?

Commander, 1ˢᵗ Finnish Rifle Division *(Formed in 1915)*
- 12 May 1915 - 31 Mar 1917: *Lt.-Gen.* Nikolai Afanasyevich **Obruchev**

   Commander, 1ˢᵗ Brigade, 1ˢᵗ Finnish Rifle Division
   - 5 Aug 1915 - 25 Aug 1915: *Maj.-Gen.* Vladimir Georgiyevich **Shevelev**
   - 25 Aug 1915 - 12 Apr 1917: *Maj.-Gen.* Ivan Ivanovich **Geshtovt**

   Commander, 2ⁿᵈ Brigade, 1ˢᵗ Finnish Rifle Division
   - 1915 - 2 Mar 1917: ?

Commander, 2ⁿᵈ Finnish Rifle Division *(Formed in 1915)*
- 21 Aug 1915 - 15 Apr 1917: *Lt.-Gen.* Frants Feliksovich **Kublitsky-Piotukh**

   Commander, 1ˢᵗ Brigade, 2ⁿᵈ Finnish Rifle Division
   - 1915 - 2 Mar 1917: ?

   Commander, 2ⁿᵈ Brigade, 2ⁿᵈ Finnish Rifle Division
   - 1915 - 2 Mar 1917: ?

Commander, 3ʳᵈ Finnish Rifle Division *(Formed in 1915)*
- 12 May 1915 - 22 Apr 1917: *Lt.-Gen.* Pyotr Mironovich **Volkoboy**

   Commander, 1ˢᵗ Brigade, 3ʳᵈ Finnish Rifle Division
   - 1915 - 2 Mar 1917: ?

Commander, 2nd Brigade, 3rd Finnish Rifle Division
- 1915 - 2 Mar 1917: ?

Commander, 4th Finnish Rifle Division *(Formed in 1915)*
- 12 May 1915 - 6 Apr 1917: *Lt.-Gen.* Vladimir Ivanovich **Selivachev**

Commander, 1st Brigade, 4th Finnish Rifle Division
- 1915 - 2 Mar 1917: ?

Commander, 2nd Brigade, 4th Finnish Rifle Division
- 1915 - 2 Mar 1917: ?

Commander, 1st Siberian Rifle Division *(Formed in 1904; until 1910 East-Siberian)*
- 22 Feb 1904 - 23 May 1905: *Gen. of Inf.* Aleksandr Alekseyevich **Gerngross**
- 17 Jun 1905 - 8 Feb 1914: *Gen. of Inf.* Leonty Leontyevich **Sidorin**
- 5 Mar 1914 - 11 Aug 1914: *Gen. of Inf.* Sergey Dmitriyevich **Markov**
- 12 Aug 1914 - 5 Sep 1915: *Gen. of Eng.* Nikolai Aleksandrovich **Tretyakov**
- 5 Sep 1915 - Nov 1917: *Lt.-Gen.* Fyodor Aleksandrovich **Podgursky**

Commander, 1st Brigade, 1st Siberian Rifle Division
- 22 Feb 1904 - 15 Aug 1904: *Maj.-Gen.* Ivan Stanislavovich **Rutkovsky**
- 5 Oct 1904 -15 Mar 1907: *Lt.-Gen.* Konstantin Romanovich **Dovbor-Musnitsky**
- 15 Mar 1907 - 11 Jan 1909: *Lt.-Gen.* Pyotr Matveyevich **Zakharov**
- 19 Jan 1909 - 22 Apr 1915: *Lt.-Gen.* Aleksey Nikolayevich **Bunin**
- 11 May 1915 - 8 Sep 1915: *Maj.-Gen.* Yakov Yakovlevich **Lyubitsky**
- 8 Sep 1915 - 28 Oct 1915: ?
- 28 Oct 1915 - 7 Feb 1917: *Maj.-Gen.* Yakov Yakovlevich **Lyubitsky**
- 7 Feb 1917 - 2 Mar 1917: ?

Commander, 2nd Brigade, 1st Siberian Rifle Division
- 22 Feb 1904 - 9 Mar 1905: *Maj.-Gen.* Anatoly Aleksandrovich **Maksimovich**
- 9 Mar 1905 - 7 Sep 1905: ?
- 7 Sep 1905 - 24 May 1906: *Gen. of Inf.* Leonid Vilhelmovich **Lesh**
- 6 Jul 1906 - Sep 1908: *Maj.-Gen.* Makary-Tselestin Petrovich **Tomashevsky**
- 6 Sep 1908 - 12 Jun 1912: *Maj.-Gen.* Dydan-Stanislav Mikhailovich **Morzhitsky**
- 21 Jun 1912 - 5 Oct 1914: *Maj.-Gen.* Vladimir Ivanovich **Zhukovsky**
- 5 Oct 1914 - 20 Jul 1915: ?
- 20 Jul 1915 - 11 Sep 1916: *Lt.-Gen.* Yakov Mikhailovich **Larionov**

Commander, 1st Siberian Rifle Artillery Brigade
- 22 Feb 1904 - 20 Aug 1905: *Maj.-Gen.* Aleksey Antonovich **Luchkovsky**
- 20 Aug 1905 - 9 May 1906: ?
- 9 May 1906 - Apr 1909: *Maj.-Gen.* Aleksandr Aleksandrovich **Ovsyany**
- 5 May 1909 - 10 Apr 1910: *Maj.-Gen.* Valentin Fyodorovich **Mokhov**
- 13 May 1910 - 14 Feb 1915: *Lt.-Gen.* Nikolai Aleksandrovich **Mikhailov**

- 14 Feb 1915 - 28 Apr 1917:   *Maj.-Gen.* Vladimir Konstantinovich **Bodisko**

Commander, 2nd Siberian Rifle Division *(Formed in 1904; until 1910 East-Siberian)*
- 22 Feb 1904 - 3 Dec 1908:   *Lt.-Gen.* Konstantin Andreyevich **Anisimov**
- 3 Dec 1908 - 13 Dec 1911:   *Gen. of Inf.* Vladimir Pavlovich **Shatilov**
- 23 Dec 1911 - 16 Apr 1917:   *Lt.-Gen.* Sergey Matveyevich **Pospelov**

Commander, 1st Brigade, 2nd Siberian Rifle Division
- 22 Feb 1904 - Jul 1907:   *Maj.-Gen.* Viktor Pavlovich **Aseyev**
- Jul 1907 - 1 Nov 1907:   ?
- 1 Nov 1907 - Aug 1908:   *Maj.-Gen.* Kirill Ivanovich **Perepechin**
- 21 Aug 1908 - 28 Jul 1913:   *Lt.-Gen.* Mikhail Ivanovich **Stavsky**
- 28 Jul 1913 - 11 Sep 1917:   *Maj.-Gen.* Iosif Lyudvigovich **Shamota**

Commander, 2nd Brigade, 2nd Siberian Rifle Division
- 22 Feb 1904 - Sep 1905:   *Maj.-Gen.* Pavel Andreyevich **Shupinsky**
- 7 Sep 1905 - 23 Aug 1906:   *Lt.-Gen.* Aleksey Yefimovich **Redko**
- 23 Aug 1906 - 20 Jan 1907:   ?
- 20 Jan 1907 - 29 Jun 1910:   *Lt.-Gen.* Konstantin Aleksandrovich **Danich**
- 16 Jul 1910 - 8 Dec 1911:   *Maj.-Gen.* Nikolai Yakovlevich **Ivanov**
- 11 Jan 1912 - 2 Apr 1915:   *Lt.-Gen.* Marin Draganovich **Yenchevich**
- 2 Apr 1915 - 2 Mar 1917:   ?

Commander, 2nd Siberian Rifle Artillery Brigade
- 22 Feb 1904 - 17 Apr 1905:   ?
- 17 Apr 1905 - 29 Apr 1907:   *Maj.-Gen.* Nikolai Nikolayevich **Zhukov**
- 29 Apr 1907 - 14 Nov 1907:   ?
- 14 Nov 1907 - 6 Nov 1908:   *Lt.-Gen.* Nikanor Nikanorovich **Nishchenkov**
- 23 Nov 1908 - 25 Jul 1910:   *Lt.-Gen.* Vladimir Yakovlevich **Gusev**
- 1 Aug 1910 - 27 Sep 1912:   *Maj.-Gen.* Aleksandr Pavlovich **Vasilenko**
- 2 Oct 1912 - 7 Jan 1916:   *Maj.-Gen.* Prince Aleksey Gavrilovich **Gantimurov**
- 7 Jan 1916 - 2 Mar 1917:   ?

Commander, 3rd Siberian Rifle Division *(Formed in 1904; until 1910 East-Siberian)*
- 22 Feb 1904 - 4 Jul 1906:   *Gen. of Inf.* Nikolai Aleksandrovich **Kashtalinsky**
- 4 Jul 1906 - 21 Sep 1906:   ?
- 21 Sep 1906 - 3 May 1910:   *Gen. of Inf.* Vladimir Petrovich **Olshevsky**
- 3 May 1910 - 13 Jul 1910:   ?
- 13 Jul 1910 - 12 Oct 1911:   *Lt.-Gen.* Mikhail Mikhailovich **Dobrovolsky**
- 12 Oct 1911 - 12 Aug 1914:   *Gen. of Eng.* Nikolai Aleksandrovich **Tretyakov**
- 12 Aug 1914 - 24 Oct 1914:   ?
- 24 Oct 1914 - 29 Sep 1915:   *Lt.-Gen.* Mikhail Aleksandrovich **Folbaum**
- 29 Sep 1915 - 2 Mar 1917:   ?

Commander, 1st Brigade, 3rd Siberian Rifle Division
- 22 Feb 1904 - 18 Jun 1905: *Maj.-Gen.* Aleksandr Yakovlevich **Mardanov**
- 5 Aug 1905 - 2 Jul 1908: *Lt.-Gen.* Selvin Severinovich **Lassky**
- 21 Oct 1908 - Oct 1910: *Maj.-Gen.* Aleksandr Konstantinovich **Turkov**
- 17 Oct 1910 - 2 May 1913: *Lt.-Gen.* Mikhail Alekseyevich **Sokovnin**
- 24 May 1913 - 25 Apr 1915: *Maj.-Gen.* Prince Dmitry Alekseyevich **Kropotkin**
- 25 Apr 1915 - 2 Mar 1917: ?

Commander, 2nd Brigade, 3rd Siberian Rifle Division
- 22 Feb 1904 - 7 Jan 1905: *Maj.-Gen.* Mikhail Stepanovich **Stolitsa**
- 9 Mar 1905 - 25 Apr 1905: *Lt.-Gen.* Mikhail Lvovich **Bachinsky**
- 18 Jul 1905 - 8 Oct 1907: *Lt.-Gen.* Sergey Matveyevich **Pospelov**
- 12 Nov 1907 - 1909: *Maj.-Gen.* Dmitriy Nilovich **Kazin**
- 1909 - 18 Aug 1912: ?
- 18 Aug 1912 - 29 Jul 1914: *Maj.-Gen.* Fyodor Nikolayevich **Trankovsky**
- 29 Jul 1914 - 2 Mar 1917: ?

Commander, 3rd Siberian Rifle Artillery Brigade
- 18 Feb 1904 - 16 Apr 1904: *Maj.-Gen.* Konstantin Konstantinovich **Shverin**
- 16 Apr 1904 - 13 Dec 1905: ?
- 13 Dec 1905 - 29 May 1908: *Gen. of Art.* Nikolai Konstantinovich **Tomashevsky**
- 11 Jun 1908 - 4 Jul 1912: *Lt.-Gen.* Karl-Nikolai Karlovich von **Lezedov**
- 18 Aug 1912 - 25 Jul 1914: *Maj.-Gen.* Vladimir Petrovich **Sagatovsky**
- 25 Jul 1914 - 3 Apr 1915: *Maj.-Gen.* Pavel Pavlovich **Lagunov**
- 3 Apr 1915 - 2 Aug 1916: *Maj.-Gen.* Ivan Almaskhanovich **Gogoberidze**
- 2 Aug 1916 - 2 Mar 1917: ?

Commander, 4th Siberian Rifle Division *(Formed in 1904; until 1910 East-Siberian)*
- 22 Feb 1904 - 19 Aug 1906: *Lt.-Gen.* Aleksandr Viktorovich **Fok**
- 19 Aug 1906 - 12 Apr 1907: *Gen. of Inf.* Konstantin Mikhailovich **Alekseyev**
- 11 May 1907 - Dec 1907: *Maj.-Gen.* Nikolai Nikolayevich **Troitsky**
- 2 Jan 1908 - Dec 1908: *Lt.-Gen.* Sigizmund Feliksovich **Sulikovsky**
- 13 Dec 1908 - 22 Apr 1915: *Gen. of Inf.* Nikolai Fridrikhovich **Krauze**
- 22 Apr 1915 - 29 Oct 1915: *Lt.-Gen.* Aleksey Nikolayevich **Bunin**
- 11 Nov 1915 - 24 Apr 1917: *Lt.-Gen.* Yevgeny Petrovich **Kartsov**

Commander, 1st Brigade, 4th Siberian Rifle Division
- 22 Feb 1904 - 15 Oct 1905: ?
- 15 Oct 1905 - 17 Apr 1907: *Maj.-Gen.* Vladimir Mikhailovich **Savitsky**
- 15 May 1907 - 24 Apr 1909: *Gen. of Inf.* Leonid Nikolayevich **Belkovich**
- 20 May 1909 - May 1912: *Maj.-Gen.* Boris Aleksandrovich **Makhatadze**
- 8 May 1912 - 10 May 1915: *Maj.-Gen.* Ferdinand Aleksandrovich **Karlstedt**
- 10 May 1915 - 2 Mar 1917: ?

Commander, 2nd Brigade, 4th Siberian Rifle Division
- 22 Feb 1904 - 15 Oct 1905: *Lt.-Gen.* Mitrofan Aleksandrovich **Nadein**
- 15 Oct 1905 - 9 Jan 1906: ?
- 9 Jan 1906 - 19 Jun 1906: *Maj.-Gen.* Sergey Aleksandrovich **Danilovich**
- 19 Jun 1906 - 23 Aug 1906: ?
- 23 Aug 1906 - 27 Nov 1906: *Lt.-Gen.* Aleksey Yefimovich **Redko**
- 15 Jan 1907 - 21 May 1910: *Maj.-Gen.* Nikolai Ksenofontovich **Boldyrev**
- 21 May 1910 - 10 Aug 1910: ?
- 10 Aug 1910 - 23 Jul 1912: *Lt.-Gen.* Mikhail Lvovich **Matveyev**
- 3 Aug 1912 - 26 Oct 1912: *Maj.-Gen.* Nikolai Fyodorovich **Domelunksen**
- 29 Oct 1912 - 27 Jan 1913: *Maj.-Gen.* Ivan Ivanovich **Gordeyev**
- 6 Feb 1913 - 1915: *Maj.-Gen.* Vladimir Nikitich **Kolbe**
- 1915 - 2 Mar 1917: ?

Commander, 4th Siberian Rifle Artillery Brigade
- 18 Feb 1904 - 7 Mar 1906: *Gen. of Art.* Vladimir Aleksandrovich von **Irman**
- 7 Mar 1906 - 11 Apr 1908: ?
- 11 Apr 1908 - Oct 1911: *Maj.-Gen.* Roman Mikhailovich **Zinchenko**
- 22 Oct 1911 - 28 Dec 1915: *Gen. of Art.* Kuzma Yevstafyevich **Muntyanov**
- 28 Dec 1915 - 21 Nov 1916: *Maj.-Gen.* Vladimir Nilovich **Lakhtionov**
- 21 Nov 1916 - 1917: *Maj.-Gen.* Maksimilian Emilianovich **Malyshchitsky**

Commander, 5th Siberian Rifle Division *(Formed in 1904; until 1910 East-Siberian)*
- 22 Feb 1904 - 21 Jun 1905: *Gen. of Inf.* Konstantin Mikhailovich **Alekseyev**
- 16 Jul 1905 - 27 Feb 1906: *Maj.-Gen.* Pyotr Vasilyevich **Polkovnikov**
- 27 Feb 1906 - 16 May 1906: ?
- 16 May 1906 - 14 Aug 1908: *Gen. of Art.* Eris-Khan-Sultan-Girei **Aliyev**
- 14 Aug 1908 - 23 Oct 1908: ?
- 23 Oct 1908 - 9 Apr 1910: *Gen. of Inf.* Fyodor Afanasievich **Voloshinov**
- 9 Apr 1910 - 23 Jan 1913: *Lt.-Gen.* Sergey Evstafievich **Debesh**
- 13 Feb 1913 - 24 Jan 1915: *Lt.-Gen.* Genrikh Gustavovich **Liliyental**
- 31 Jan 1915 - 26 Jul 1915: *Lt.-Gen.* Baron Aleksandr Aleksandrovich von **Taube**
- 3 Aug 1915 - 19 Sep 1917: *Maj.-Gen.* Yevgeny Aleksandrovich **Milodanovich**

Commander, 1st Brigade, 5th Siberian Rifle Division
- 22 Feb 1904 - 19 Jul 1906: *Maj.-Gen.* Stanislav Antonovich **Okulich**
- 2 Aug 1906 - Nov 1908: *Maj.-Gen.* Ivan Yevgenyevich **Zemlyanitsyn**
- 24 Nov 1908 - 16 Jun 1912: *Maj.-Gen.* Mikhail Vladimirovich **Lindeström**
- 16 Jul 1912 - 20 Aug 1913: *Maj.-Gen.* Pyotr Ivanovich **Suvorov**
- 20 Aug 1913 - 3 Apr 1915: *Lt.-Gen.* Aleksandr Semyonovich **Madritov**
- 4 Apr 1915 - 1917: *Maj.-Gen.* Grigory Grigoryevich **Khilchenko**

Commander, 2nd Brigade, 5th Siberian Rifle Division
- 22 Feb 1904 - 9 Mar 1905: *Lt.-Gen.* Pavel Nikolayevich **Putilov**
- 25 Apr 1905 - 16 May 1906: *Lt.-Gen.* Mikhail Lvovich **Bachinsky**

- 16 May 1906 - 28 Nov 1907: ?
- 28 Nov 1907 - May 1910: *Maj.-Gen.* Vladimir Fyodorovich **Elsh**
- 13 May 1910 - 16 Jun 1914: *Lt.-Gen.* Valentin Yevgrafovich **Lukin**
- 16 Jun 1914 - 1917: *Lt.-Gen.* Vladimir Kirillovich **Zubov**

Commander, 5th Siberian Rifle Artillery Brigade
- 22 Feb 1904 - 26 Nov 1904: ?
- 26 Nov 1904 - Dec 1906: *Maj.-Gen.* Nikolai Aleksandrovich **De-Bryuks**
- 18 Feb 1907 - 21 Dec 1907: *Lt.-Gen.* Kaspar Nikolayevich **Blyumer**
- 10 Jan 1908 - 2 Feb 1913: *Lt.-Gen.* Dmitry Andreyevich **Goryachev**
- 15 Feb 1913 - 1915: *Maj.-Gen.* Nikolai Aleksandrovich **Ivanov**
- 1915 - 25 Jul 1915: *Maj.-Gen.* Nikolai Petrovich **Ivanov**
- 11 Nov 1915 - 1917: *Maj.-Gen.* Mikhail Mikhailovich **Radkevich**

Commander, 6th Siberian Rifle Division *(Formed in 1904; until 1910 East-Siberian)*
- 22 Feb 1904 - 16 Jul 1904: *Maj.-Gen.* Aleksey Aleksandrovich **Trusov**
- 16 Apr 1904 - 21 Sep 1904: *Lt.-Gen.* Vladimir Aleksandrovich **Romanov**
- 21 Sep 1904 - 25 Nov 1905: *Gen. of Inf.* Vladimir Nikolayevich **Danilov**
- 25 Nov 1905 - 10 Mar 1906: ?
- 10 Mar 1906 - 21 Jun 1906: *Gen. of Inf.* Platon Alekseyevich **Lechitsky**
- 21 Jun 1906 - 18 Dec 1906: ?
- 18 Dec 1906 - 12 Jun 1912: *Gen. of Inf.* Nikolai Andreyevich **Zernets**
- 12 Jun 1912 - 31 Dec 1913: *Gen. of Inf.* Nikolai Mikhailovich **Voronov**
- 31 Dec 1913 - 4 Dec 1914: *Lt.-Gen.* Oskar Aleksandrovich von **Gennings**
- 4 Dec 1914 - 30 Oct 1915: *Lt.-Gen.* Vladimir Aleksandrovich **Chagin**
- 30 Oct 1915 - 12 Apr 1917: *Lt.-Gen.* Aleksandr Fedorovich **Turbin**

Commander, 1st Brigade, 6th Siberian Rifle Division
- 22 Feb 1904 - 9 Mar 1905: *Maj.-Gen.* Nil Aleksandrovich **Yatsynin**
- 9 Mar 1905 - 14 Jul 1905: *Lt.-Gen.* Selvin Severinovich **Lassky**
- 14 Jul 1905 - 10 Mar 1906: *Gen. of Inf.* Platon Alekseyevich **Lechitsky**
- 29 May 1906 - 28 Oct 1906: *Lt.-Gen.* Pavel Nikolayevich **Putilov**
- 28 Oct 1906 - 12 Jan 1907: ?
- 12 Jan 1907 - 20 Sep 1908: *Lt.-Gen.* Sergey Alekseyevich **Dobronravov**
- 5 Nov 1908 - Sep 1913: *Lt.-Gen.* Pyotr Nikolayevich **Korovin**
- 28 Sep 1913 - 18 Dec 1914: *Maj.-Gen.* Leonid Nikolayevich **Bykov**
- 18 Dec 1914 - 1 Jan 1916: ?
- 1 Jan 1916 - 27 May 1917: *Maj.-Gen.* Andrey Andreyevich **Veselovsky**

Commander, 2nd Brigade, 6th Siberian Rifle Division
- 22 Feb 1904 - 29 Mar 1906: *Lt.-Gen.* Konstantin Ilich **Krichinsky**
- 29 Mar 1906 - Oct 1906: *Maj.-Gen.* Apollon Apollonovich **Ostolopov**
- 28 Oct 1906 - 15 Aug 1911: *Lt.-Gen.* Pavel Nikolayevich **Putilov**
- 15 Aug 1911 - 18 Feb 1917: *Lt.-Gen.* Aleksandr Semyonovich **Sulevich**
- 18 Feb 1917 - 2 Mar 1917: ?

Commander, 6th Siberian Rifle Artillery Brigade
- 22 Feb 1904 - 23 Aug 1905: ?
- 23 Aug 1905 - 25 Aug 1906: *Maj.-Gen.* Aleksandr Dmitriyevich **Firsov**
- 25 Aug 1906 - 22 Apr 1907: ?
- 22 Apr 1907 - 21 Sep 1907: *Maj.-Gen.* Mikhail Petrovich **Voropayev**
- 21 Sep 1907 - May 1911: *Maj.-Gen.* Vasily Stepanovich **Vedensky**
- 17 Jun 1911 - 10 Nov 1914: *Maj.-Gen.* Viktor Petrovich **Zelinsky**
- 10 Nov 1914 - 27 Feb 1915: ?
- 27 Feb 1915 - 9 Sep 1917: *Maj.-Gen.* Vilgelm Fridrikhovich **Mallio**

Commander, 7th Siberian Rifle Division *(Formed in 1904; until 1910 East-Siberian)*
- 10 Feb 1904 - 2 Dec 1904: *Lt.-Gen.* Roman Isidorovich **Kondratenko**
- 2 Dec 1904 - 15 Oct 1905: DISSOLVED
- 15 Oct 1905 - 21 Feb 1907: *Lt.-Gen.* Mitrofan Aleksandrovich **Nadein**
- 22 Mar 1907 - 21 Jul 1910: *Gen. of Inf.* Nikolai Dmitrievich **Butovsky**
- 21 Jul 1910 - 30 Jul 1912: *Gen. of Inf.* Aleksandr Aleksandrovich **Dushkevich**
- 13 Aug 1912 - 8 Aug 1914: *Lt.-Gen.* Nikolai Ilich **Sulimov**
- 8 Aug 1914 - 25 Apr 1915: *Lt.-Gen.* Vladimir Onufriyevich **Trofimov**
- 25 Apr 1915 - 6 Apr 1917: *Lt.-Gen.* Vasily Nikolayevich **Bratanov**

Commander, 1st Brigade, 7th Siberian Rifle Division
- 22 Feb 1904 - 22 Mar 1905: *Gen. of Inf.* Vladimir Nikolayevich **Gorbatovsky**
- 22 Mar 1905 - 15 Oct 1905: DISSOLVED
- 15 Oct 1905 - 6 Jul 1906: *Maj.-Gen.* Vladimir Grigoryevich **Semenov**
- 6 Jul 1906 - 2 Oct 1906: ?
- 2 Oct 1906 - 14 Jan 1914: *Lt.-Gen.* Vladimir Onufriyevich **Trofimov**
- 14 Jan 1914 - 16 Jun 1914: *Lt.-Gen.* Vladimir Kirillovich **Zubov**
- 29 Jul 1914 - 25 Jul 1916: *Maj.-Gen.* Vasily Yemelyanovich **Myasnikov**
- 25 Jul 1916 - 2 Mar 1917: ?

Commander, 2nd Brigade, 7th Siberian Rifle Division
- 22 Feb 1904 - 1905: *Maj.-Gen.* Valerian Kazimirovich **Tserpitsky**
- 1905 - 9 Jan 1906: DISSOLVED
- 9 Jan 1906 - 25 Feb 1909: *Lt.-Gen.* Olgerd Viktorovich **Radvan-Rypinsky**
- 25 Feb 1909 - 8 Apr 1909: ?
- 8 Apr 1909 - 14 Jul 1910: *Maj.-Gen.* Adam Adamovich **Boyarovsky**
- 14 Jul 1910 - 14 Jan 1914: *Lt.-Gen.* Nikolai Maksimovich **Ivanov**
- 14 Jan 1914 - 19 Jul 1914: *Lt.-Gen.* Vladimir Onufriyevich **Trofimov**
- 19 Jul 1914 - 2 Mar 1917: ?

Commander, 7th Siberian Rifle Artillery Brigade *(Formed in 1905)*
- 13 Dec 1905 - 12 Jun 1906: ?
- 12 Jun 1906 - 15 Jul 1907: *Gen. of Art.* Samed-Bek-Sadyk-Bek **Mekhmandarov**
- 21 Jul 1907 - 26 Jul 1910: *Maj.-Gen.* Sergey Sergeyevich **Vasiliev**
- 26 Jul 1910 - 22 Oct 1913: *Lt.-Gen.* Sergey Ivanovich **Razumov**

- 9 Nov 1913 - 13 May 1916: *Maj.-Gen.* Georgy Karpovich **Zaretsky**
- 13 May 1916 - 1917: *Maj.-Gen.* Yevgeny Semyonovich **Stepantsov**

Commander, 8th Siberian Rifle Division *(Formed in 1904; until 1910 East-Siberian)*
- 22 Feb 1904 - 17 Oct 1904: *Gen. of Inf.* Leonid Konstantinovich **Artamonov**
- 8 Nov 1904 - 27 Dec 1906: *Gen. of Inf.* Nikolai Alekseyevich **Lashkevich**
- 25 Jan 1907 - 10 Sep 1907: *Lt.-Gen.* Yevgeny Iosifovich **Grozmani**
- 10 Sep 1907 - 11 Nov 1908: *Lt.-Gen.* Aleksandr Nikolayevich **Ragozin**
- 29 Nov 1908 - 7 Aug 1914: *Gen. of Inf.* Eduard Karlovich von **Klodt**
- 7 Aug 1914 - 6 Apr 1917: *Lt.-Gen.* Aleksey Yefimovich **Redko**

Commander, 1st Brigade, 8th Siberian Rifle Division
- 22 Feb 1904 - 25 Aug 1905: *Maj.-Gen.* Valerian Kazimirovich **Furs-Zhirkevich**
- 25 Aug 1905 - 1 Nov 1907: *Maj.-Gen.* Kirill Ivanovich **Perepechin**
- 6 Dec 1907 - 19 Jul 1914: *Lt.-Gen.* Pyotr Andreyevich **Andreyev**
- 19 Jul 1914 - 2 Mar 1917: ?

Commander, 2nd Brigade, 8th Siberian Rifle Division
- 22 Feb 1904 - 30 Sep 1906: ?
- 30 Sep 1906 - 21 Aug 1908: *Maj.-Gen.* Aleksandr Aleksandrovich **Kusov**
- 21 Aug 1908 - 1910: *Maj.-Gen.* Konstantin Ivanovich **Bachevksy**
- 1910 - 18 Oct 1911: *Maj.-Gen.* Konstantin Ivanovich **Bachevksy**
- 18 Oct 1911 - 11 May 1915: *Lt.-Gen.* Nikolai Mikhailovich **Pepelyayev**
- 11 May 1915 - 2 Mar 1917: ?

Commander, 8th Siberian Rifle Artillery Brigade *(Formed in 1906)*
- 6 Jun 1906 - 20 Jul 1907: ?
- 20 Jul 1907 - May 1910: *Maj.-Gen.* Mikhail Mikhailovich **Chistyakov**
- 5 May 1910 - 5 Jun 1914: *Maj.-Gen.* Viktor Alekseyevich **Slyusarenko**
- 15 Jun 1914 - 22 Aug 1915: *Maj.-Gen.* Aleksey Vasilyevich **Nesterenko**
- 1 Sep 1915 - 26 May 1917: *Maj.-Gen.* Pavel Grigoryevich **Meshcherinov**

Commander, 9th Siberian Rifle Division *(Formed in 1904; until 1910 East-Siberian)*
- 22 Feb 1904 - 4 Jul 1906: *Gen. of Inf.* Kiprian Antonovich **Kondratovich**
- 4 Jul 1906 - 3 May 1910: *Gen. of Inf.* Aleksandr Nikolayevich **Lebedev**
- 3 May 1910 - 26 Feb 1915: *Lt.-Gen.* Aleksey Mikhailovich **Slezkin**
- 7 Mar 1915 - 13 Apr 1917: *Lt.-Gen.* Iosif Ilich **Regulsky**

Commander, 1st Brigade, 9th Siberian Rifle Division
- 22 Feb 1904 - 30 Jan 1906: *Gen. of Inf.* Nikolai Fridrikhovich **Krauze**
- 30 Jan 1906 - 24 May 1906: ?
- 24 May 1906 - 27 Jun 1906: *Gen. of Inf.* Leonid Vilhelmovich **Lesh**
- 28 Jul 1906 - Sep 1908: *Maj.-Gen.* Nikolai Ilich **Kvyatkovsky**
- 6 Sep 1908 - Dec 1912: *Lt.-Gen.* Vladimir Gustavovich **Pogoretsky**

- 16 Jan 1913 - 4 Jul 1913: *Lt.-Gen.* Mikhail Konstantinovich **Samoylov**
- 4 Jul 1913 - 24 Aug 1914: *Gen. of Inf.* Lavr Georgievich **Kornilov**
- 24 Aug 1914 - 2 Mar 1917: ?

Commander, 2nd Brigade, 9th Siberian Rifle Division
- 22 Feb 1904 - 2 Jan 1905: *Lt.-Gen.* Viktor Pavlovich **Zykov**
- 2 Jan 1905 - 19 Jun 1906: ?
- 19 Jun 1906 - Jul 1907: *Maj.-Gen.* Sergey Aleksandrovich **Danilovich**
- 6 Jul 1907 - 21 Oct 1908: *Maj.-Gen.* Aleksandr Konstantinovich **Turkov**
- 5 Nov 1908 - 3 May 1913: *Lt.-Gen.* Aleksandr Semyonovich **Ogloblev**
- 7 May 1913 - 1917: *Maj.-Gen.* Konstantin Aleksandrovich **Fleming**

Commander, 9th Siberian Rifle Artillery Brigade
- 18 Feb 1904 - 23 Aug 1905: *Gen. of Art.* Iosif Ivanovich **Mrozovsky**
- 23 Aug 1905 - 17 Jun 1906: ?
- 17 Jun 1906 - 4 Nov 1906: *Lt.-Gen.* Vladimir Georgiyevich **Konradi**
- 4 Nov 1906 - 22 Apr 1907: ?
- 22 Apr 1907 - 9 Sep 1907: *Maj.-Gen.* Georgy Aleksandrovich **Grigoryev**
- 9 Sep 1907 - 6 Nov 1908: *Maj.-Gen.* Konstantin Iosifovich **Mamatsev**
- 6 Nov 1908 - 26 Jul 1910: *Lt.-Gen.* Nikanor Nikanorovich **Nishchenkov**
- 1 Aug 1910 - 20 Nov 1913: *Lt.-Gen.* Aleksandr Petrovich **Andreyev**
- 20 Nov 1913 - 23 Jan 1914: ?
- 23 Jan 1914 - 13 May 1916: *Maj.-Gen.* Ivan Levanovich **Muskhelov**
- 13 May 1916 - 1 Feb 1917: ?
- 1 Feb 1917 - 1917: *Maj.-Gen.* Nikolai Grigorievich **Gruzevich-Nechay**

Commander, 10th Siberian Rifle Division *(Formed in 1905; until 1910 East-Siberian)*
- 28 Jul 1905 - 1906: *Maj.-Gen.* Ozv Alfredovich **Modl**
- 1906 - 1910: DISSOLVED
- 23 Jul 1910 - 15 Feb 1911: *Gen. of Inf.* Arkady Valerianovich **Sychevsky**
- 28 Feb 1911 - 12 Oct 1911: *Gen. of Eng.* Nikolai Aleksandrovich **Tretyakov**
- 16 Nov 1911 - 28 Apr 1915: *Lt.-Gen.* Nikolai Yakovlevich **Lisovsky**
- 18 May 1915 - 14 Jul 1917: *Lt.-Gen.* Andrei Georgievich **Yelchaninov**

Commander, 1st Brigade, 10th Siberian Rifle Division
- 15 Jun 1905 - 6 Jul 1905: *Lt.-Gen.* Nikolai Mikhailovich **Vorobyev**
- 6 Jul 1905 - 29 May 1906: *Lt.-Gen.* Pavel Nikolayevich **Putilov**
- 1906 - 1910: DISSOLVED
- 3 Jul 1910 - 28 Feb 1911: *Lt.-Gen.* Mikhail Mikhailovich **Manakin**
- 28 Feb 1911 - 27 Sep 1913: *Maj.-Gen.* Pavel Ustinovich **Tolochko**
- 27 Sep 1913 - 3 Aug 1914: *Maj.-Gen.* Semyon Petrovich **Bylim-Kolosovsky**
- 3 Aug 1914 - 11 Jan 1915: ?
- 11 Jan 1915 - 1917: *Maj.-Gen.* Aleksandr Ivanovich **Kamberg**

Commander, 2nd Brigade, 10th Siberian Rifle Division
- 15 Jul 1905 - 19 Nov 1905: *Lt.-Gen.* Anatoly Nikolayevich **Rozenschild von Paulin**
- 19 Nov 1905 - 1906: ?
- 1906 - 1910: DISSOLVED
- 16 Jul 1910 - 5 Sep 1915: *Lt.-Gen.* Fyodor Aleksandrovich **Podgursky**
- 5 Sep 1915 - 12 Jul 1916: ?
- 12 Jul 1916 - 10 Apr 1917: *Maj.-Gen.* Pavel Petrovich **Klimovsky**

Commander, 10th Siberian Rifle Artillery Brigade
- 28 May 1905 - 2 Jul 1905: *Gen. of Art.* Valerian Mikhailovich **Gaitenov**
- 28 Aug 1905 - 19 May 1906: *Maj.-Gen.* Ivan Vladimirovich **Petrichenko**
- 19 May 1906 - 1907: ?
- 1907 - 1910: DISSOLVED
- 1 Aug 1910 - May 1912: *Maj.-Gen.* Yevgeny Rudolfovich **Kister**
- 31 May 1912 - 23 Apr 1915: *Maj.-Gen.* Dmitry Grigorovich **Gavrishev**
- 23 Apr 1915 - 5 Apr 1917: *Maj.-Gen.* Boris Ivanovich **Stolbin**

Commander, 11th Siberian Rifle Division *(Formed in 1910)*
- 11 Jun 1910 - 4 Mar 1913: *Lt.-Gen.* Sergey Petrovich **Nekrasov**
- 4 Mar 1913 - Jul 1917: *Lt.-Gen.* Ivan Ivanovich **Zarako-Zarakovsky**

Commander, 1st Brigade, 11th Siberian Rifle Division
- 5 Jul 1910 - 31 Mar 1912: *Maj.-Gen.* Nikolai Petrovich **Kuchin**
- 31 Mar 1912 - 19 Apr 1915: *Maj.-Gen.* Nikolai Nikiforovich **Raspopov**
- 19 Apr 1915 - 2 Mar 1917: ?

Commander, 2nd Brigade, 11th Siberian Rifle Division
- 15 Jul 1910 - 23 Jul 1914: *Lt.-Gen.* Aleksey Sergeyevich **Polyansky**
- 23 Jul 1914 - 2 Mar 1917: ?

Commander, 11th Siberian Rifle Artillery Brigade
- 1 Aug 1910 - 2 Oct 1912: *Maj.-Gen.* Rudolf Khristoforovich **Ivanovich**
- 2 Oct 1912 - 13 May 1916: *Maj.-Gen.* Aleksandr Nikolayevich **Kozlovsky**
- 13 May 1916 - 2 Mar 1917: ?

Commander, 12th Siberian Rifle Division *(Formed in 1914)*
- 19 Jul 1914 - 8 Aug 1914: *Lt.-Gen.* Vladimir Onufriyevich **Trofimov**
- 8 Aug 1914 - 12 Jul 1915: *Lt.-Gen.* Nikolai Ilich **Sulimov**
- 17 Jul 1915 - 25 Oct 1916: *Maj.-Gen.* Viktor Viktorovich **Eggert**
- 25 Oct 1916 - 7 Jul 1917: *Maj.-Gen.* Nikolai Georgievich **Arkhipovich**

Commander, 1st Brigade, 12th Siberian Rifle Division
- 19 Jul 1914 - 15 Oct 1915: ?
- 15 Oct 1915 - 3 Feb 1916: *Maj.-Gen.* Mikhail Nikolayevich **Vasiliev**

- 3 Feb 1916 - 2 Mar 1917: ?

Commander, 2nd Brigade, 12th Siberian Rifle Division
- 19 Jul 1914 - 2 Mar 1917: ?

Commander, 12th Siberian Rifle Artillery Brigade
- 25 Jun 1914 - 1917: *Maj.-Gen.* Aleksey Flegontovich **Fialkovsky**

Commander, 13th Siberian Rifle Division *(Formed in 1914)*
- 19 Jul 1914 - 20 Oct 1915: *Lt.-Gen.* Pyotr Andreyevich **Andreyev**
- 31 Oct 1915 - 25 Oct 1916: *Maj.-Gen.* Ivan Ivanovich **Efirov**
- 25 Oct 1916 - 22 Apr 1917: *Maj.-Gen.* Pyotr Stepanovich **Osovsky**

Commander, 1st Brigade, 13th Siberian Rifle Division
- 19 Jul 1914 - 2 Mar 1917: ?

Commander, 2nd Brigade, 13th Siberian Rifle Division
- 19 Jul 1914 - 2 Mar 1917: ?

Commander, 13th Siberian Rifle Artillery Brigade
- 25 Jul 1914 - 29 Apr 1917: *Maj.-Gen.* Vasily Timofeyevich **Chumakov**

Commander, 14th Siberian Rifle Division *(Formed in 1914)*
- 19 Jul 1914 - 7 Aug 1914: *Lt.-Gen.* Aleksey Yefimovich **Redko**
- 8 Aug 1914 - 11 Sep 1914: *Gen. of Inf.* Eduard Karlovich von **Klodt**
- 11 Sep 1914 - 22 Jan 1917: *Lt.-Gen.* Konstantin Romanovich **Dovbor-Musnitsky**
- 22 Jan 1917 - 10 Sep 1917: *Lt.-Gen.* Mikhail Ivanovich **Shishkin**

Commander, 1st Brigade, 14th Siberian Rifle Division
- 19 Jul 1914 - 3 Aug 1914: ?
- 3 Aug 1914 - 25 Jun 1916: *Maj.-Gen.* Semyon Petrovich **Bylim-Kolosovsky**
- 25 Jun 1916 - 2 Mar 1917: ?

Commander, 2nd Brigade, 14th Siberian Rifle Division
- 19 Jul 1914 - 2 Mar 1917: ?

Commander, 14th Siberian Rifle Artillery Brigade
- 25 Jul 1914 - 9 Mar 1917: *Maj.-Gen.* Anton Antonovich **Martusevich**

Commander, 15th Siberian Rifle Division *(Formed in 1917)*
- 10 Jan 1917 - 4 Oct 1917: *Lt.-Gen.* Vladimir Fyodorovich **Dzhunkovsky**

Commander, 1st Brigade, 15th Siberian Rifle Division
- 10 Jan 1917 - 2 Mar 1917: ?

Commander, 2ⁿᵈ Brigade, 15ᵗʰ Siberian Rifle Division
- 10 Jan 1917 - 2 Mar 1917:   ?

Commander, 15ᵗʰ Siberian Rifle Artillery Brigade
- 10 Jan 1917 - 2 Mar 1917:   ?

Commander, 1ˢᵗ Turkestan Rifle Division *(Formed in 1916)*
- 12 Mar 1916 - Aug 1916:   *Maj.-Gen.* Dydan Mikhailovich **Morzhitsky**
- Aug 1916 - 9 Sep 1916:   *Maj.-Gen.* Aleksandr Petrovich **Bukovsky**
- 9 Sep 1916 - 22 Mar 1917:   *Lt.-Gen.* Georgy Mikhailovich **Nekrashevich**

Commander, 1ˢᵗ Brigade, 1ˢᵗ Turkestan Rifle Division
- 1916 - 2 Mar 1917:   ?

Commander, 2ⁿᵈ Brigade, 1ˢᵗ Turkestan Rifle Division
- 1916 - 2 Mar 1917:   ?

Commander, 2ⁿᵈ Turkestan Rifle Division *(Formed in 1916)*
- 12 Mar 1916 - 26 Feb 1917:   *Lt.-Gen.* Ivan Vasilyevich **Kolpikov**
- 26 Feb 1917 - 2 Mar 1917:   ?

Commander, 1ˢᵗ Brigade, 2ⁿᵈ Turkestan Rifle Division
- 1916 - 2 Mar 1917:   ?

Commander, 2ⁿᵈ Brigade, 2ⁿᵈ Turkestan Rifle Division
- 1916 - 2 Mar 1917:   ?

Commander, 3ʳᵈ Turkestan Rifle Division *(Formed in 1916)*
- 11 Mar 1916 - 15 Apr 1917:   *Lt.-Gen.* Adrian Ivanovich **Tumsky**

Commander, 1ˢᵗ Brigade, 3ʳᵈ Turkestan Rifle Division
- 1916 - 2 Mar 1917:   ?

Commander, 2ⁿᵈ Brigade, 3ʳᵈ Turkestan Rifle Division
- 1916 - 2 Mar 1917:   ?

Commander, 4ᵗʰ Turkestan Rifle Division *(Formed in 1915)*
- 20 May 1915 - 1917:   *Maj.-Gen.* Nikolai Nikolayevich **Azaryev**

Commander, 1ˢᵗ Brigade, 4ᵗʰ Turkestan Rifle Division
- 1916 - 2 Mar 1917:   ?

Commander, 2nd Brigade, 4th Turkestan Rifle Division
- 1916 - 2 Mar 1917: ?

Commander, 5th Turkestan Rifle Division *(Formed in 1915)*
- 19 Nov 1915 - 25 Apr 1917: *Lt.-Gen.* Aleksandr Ivanovich **Chaplygin**

Commander, 1st Brigade, 5th Turkestan Rifle Division
- 1916 - 2 Mar 1917: ?

Commander, 2nd Brigade, 5th Turkestan Rifle Division
- 1916 - 2 Mar 1917: ?

Commander, 6th Turkestan Rifle Division *(Not formed)*

Commander, 7th Turkestan Rifle Division *(Formed in 1916)*
- 13 Mar 1916 - 11 Sep 1916: *Gen. of Inf.* Rafail Nikolayevich **Fleysher**
- 11 Sep 1916 - 14 Aug 1917: *Lt.-Gen.* Yakov Mikhailovich **Larionov**

Commander, 1st Brigade, 7th Turkestan Rifle Division
- 1916 - 2 Mar 1917: ?

Commander, 2nd Brigade, 7th Turkestan Rifle Division
- 1916 - 2 Mar 1917: ?

Commander, 1st Guards Cavalry Division
- 24 Feb 1893 - 11 Aug 1896: *Gen. of Cav.* Nikolai Nikolayevich **Shipov**
- 11 Aug 1896 - 25 Dec 1898: *Gen. of Cav.* Grand Duke Pavel Aleksandrovich **Romanov**
- 13 Jan 1899 - 29 Nov 1903: *Gen. of Cav.* Ivan Sergeyevich **Zykov**
- 7 Jan 1904 - 1 Mar 1905: *Gen. of Cav.* Prince Nikolai Nikolayevich **Odoyevsky-Maslov**
- 31 Mar 1905 - 10 Feb 1907: *Lt.-Gen.* Aleksandr Nikolayevich **Dubensky**
- 10 Feb 1907 - 23 Dec 1910: *Gen. of Inf.* Nikolai Fyodorovich von **Kruzenshtern**
- 23 Dec 1910 - 30 Mar 1916: *Gen. of Inf.* Nikolai Nikolayevich **Kaznakov**
- 2 Apr 1916 - 22 Jan 1917: *Lt.-Gen.* Pavel Petrovich **Skoropadsky**
- 22 Jan 1917 - 2 Mar 1917: ?

Commander, 1st Brigade, 1st Guards Cavalry Division
- 20 Oct 1894 - 11 Aug 1896: ?
- 11 Aug 1896 - 12 Jun 1897: *Gen. of Cav.* Artur Aleksandrovich von **Grinvald**
- 12 Jun 1897 - 2 Aug 1897: ?
- 2 Aug 1897 - 2 Apr 1899: *Gen. of Cav.* Georgy Antonovich **Skalon**
- 7 Apr 1899 - 17 Feb 1902: *Lt.-Gen.* Otto Yegorovich von **Tranzege**

- 17 Feb 1902 - 11 Apr 1902: ?
- 11 Apr 1902 - 28 Dec 1903: *Lt.-Gen.* Aleksandr Nikolayevich **Nikolayev**
- 28 Dec 1903 - 18 Feb 1904: *Gen. of Cav.* Konstantin Antonovich **Shirma**
- 18 Feb 1904 - 6 Apr 1904: ?
- 6 Apr 1904 - 6 Nov 1906: *Gen. of Cav.* Vladimir Mikhailovich **Bezobrazov**
- 6 Nov 1906 - 12 Nov 1907: *Maj.-Gen.* Georgy Georgyevich Duke of **Mecklenburg-Strelitsky**
- 30 Nov 1907 - 22 Apr 1910: *Maj.-Gen.* Boris Mikhailovich **Petrovo-Sololovo**
- 22 Apr 1910 - 30 Apr 1910: *Lt.-Gen.* Count Georgy Georgyevich **Mengden**
- 30 Apr 1910 - 24 Jan 1914: *Maj.-Gen.* Boris Mikhailovich **Petrovo-Sololovo**
- 4 Feb 1914 - 23 Jul 1914: *Maj.-Gen.* Prince Vasily Aleksandrovich **Dolgorukov**
- 23 Jul 1914 - 3 Oct 1914: ?
- 3 Oct 1914 - 29 Jul 1915: *Lt.-Gen.* Pavel Petrovich **Skoropadsky**
- 9 Aug 1915 - 27 Jun 1916: *Lt.-Gen.* Pyotr Ivanovich **Arapov**
- 7 May 1916 - 14 May 1917: *Lt.-Gen.* Prince Aleksandr Nikolayevich **Eristov**

Commander, 2nd Brigade, 1st Guards Cavalry Division
- 21 May 1892 - 15 Dec 1894: *Gen. of Cav.* Aleksandr Yakovlevich von **Tal**
- 27 Jan 1895 - 24 Nov 1898: *Lt.-Gen.* Ivan Vasilyevich **Volkenau**
- 24 Nov 1898 - 2 Mar 1899: ?
- 2 Mar 1899 - 17 May 1900: *Lt.-Gen.* Aleksandr Nikolayevich **Dubensky**
- 17 May 1900 - 11 Apr 1902: *Lt.-Gen.* Aleksandr Nikolayevich **Nikolayev**
- 21 Apr 1902 - 7 Feb 1905: *Gen. of Cav.* Konstantin Varfolomeyevich **Dembsky**
- 14 Mar 1905 - 23 Feb 1907: *Maj.-Gen.* Baron Khristofor Platonovich von **Derfelden**
- 24 Feb 1907 - 19 Mar 1912: *Lt.-Gen.* Baron Nikolai Aleksandrovich **Budberg**
- 19 Mar 1912 - 8 Jun 1912: ?
- 8 Jun 1912 - 21 Jun 1914: *Maj.-Gen.* Konstantin Mavrikievich von **Volf**
- 14 Jul 1914 - 13 Jan 1915: *Lt.-Gen.* Prince Nikolai Aleksandrovich **Yengalychev**
- 13 Jan 1915 - 9 Aug 1915: *Lt.-Gen.* Pyotr Ivanovich **Arapov**
- 9 Aug 1915 - 30 Aug 1915: *Maj.-Gen.* Dmitry Maksimovich **Knyazhevich**
- 30 Aug 1915 - 11 Sep 1915: *Maj.-Gen.* Count Fyodor Maksimilianovich **Nirod**
- 11 Sep 1915 - 1 Nov 1915: ?
- 1 Nov 1915 - 19 Dec 1915: *Maj.-Gen.* Mikhail Fyodorovich **Dabich**
- 19 Dec 1915 - 8 Oct 1916: *Maj.-Gen.* Vasily Aleksandrovich **Kruglevsky**
- 8 Oct 1916 - 1917: *Maj.-Gen.* Stepan Stepanovich **Dzhunkovsky**

Commander, 3rd Brigade, 1st Guards Cavalry Division
- 22 Jan 1894 - 20 Feb 1899: *Maj.-Gen.* Vasily Nikolayevich **Turchaninov**
- 4 Mar 1899 - 18 Feb 1904: *Gen. of Cav.* Anton Vasilyevich **Novosiltsov**
- 18 Feb 1904 - 24 May 1905: *Gen. of Cav.* Konstantin Antonovich **Shirma**
- 19 Jun 1905 - 10 Feb 1907: *Gen. of Cav.* Pyotr Robertovich von **Nettelgorst**
- 10 Feb 1907 - 14 Sep 1911: *Gen. of Cav.* Aleksey Viktorovich **Rodionov**
- 22 Sep 1911 - 31 Dec 1913: *Lt.-Gen.* Leonid Ivanovich **Zhigalin**
- 31 Dec 1913 - 14 Jan 1915: *Lt.-Gen.* Georgy Logginovich **Ponomarev**
- 14 Jan 1915 - 24 Jan 1915: *Lt.-Gen.* Count Mikhail Nikolayevich von **Grabbe**

- 24 Jan 1915 - 22 Dec 1915: *Maj.-Gen.* Ivan Davydovich **Orlov**
- 26 Dec 1915 - 27 Jun 1916: *Maj.-Gen.* Pyotr Petrovich **Orlov**
- 27 Jun 1916 - 2 Mar 1917: ?

Commander, 2nd Guards Cavalry Division
- 11 Dec 1890 - 6 May 1895: *Gen. of Cav.* Grand Duke Nikolai Nikolayevich **Romanov**
- 30 May 1895 - 14 Mar 1901: *Gen. of Cav.* Vsevolod Matveyevich **Ostrogradsky**
- 4 Apr 1901 - 15 May 1905: *Gen. of Cav.* Georgy Antonovich **Skalon**
- 24 May 1905 - 19 Apr 1906: *Gen. of Cav.* Konstantin Antonovich **Shirma**
- 19 Apr 1906 - 5 Jan 1909: *Gen. of Cav.* Aleksei Alekseyevich **Brusilov**
- 5 Jan 1909 - 29 Jan 1912: *Gen. of Cav.* Vladimir Mikhailovich **Bezobrazov**
- 29 Jan 1912 - 11 Oct 1914: *Gen. of Cav.* Georgy Ottonovich von **Raukh**
- 11 Oct 1914 - 13 May 1915: *Lt.-Gen.* Yakov Fyodorovich von **Gillenshmidt**
- 13 May 1915 - 23 Nov 1916: *Lt.-Gen.* Ivan Georgievich **Erdeli**
- 3 Dec 1916 - 1917: *Lt.-Gen.* Aleksandr Aleksandrovich **Abaleshev**

Commander, 1st Brigade, 2nd Guards Cavalry Division
- 16 Mar 1893 - 27 Jan 1895: *Gen. of Cav.* Ivan Sergeyevich **Zykov**
- 27 Jan 1895 - 18 Dec 1895: ?
- 18 Dec 1895 - 19 Feb 1897: *Gen. of Cav.* Ivan Sergeyevich **Zykov**
- 6 Mar 1897 - 1 Feb 1898: *Gen. of Cav.* Pyotr Petrovich **Baranov**
- 7 Feb 1898 - 26 Apr 1900: *Gen. of Cav.* Yevgeny Ottovich **Shmit**
- 17 May 1900 - 30 Jan 1902: *Lt.-Gen.* Aleksandr Nikolayevich **Dubensky**
- 30 Jan 1902 - 11 Apr 1902: ?
- 11 Apr 1902 - 28 Dec 1903: *Gen. of Cav.* Konstantin Antonovich **Shirma**
- 28 Dec 1903 - 23 Mar 1905: *Gen. of Cav.* Grand Duke Dmitry Konstantinovich **Romanov**
- 4 Apr 1905 - 19 Jun 1905: *Gen. of Cav.* Pyotr Robertovich von **Nettelgorst**
- 19 Jun 1905 - 23 May 1907: *Gen. of Cav.* Daniil Fyodorovich **Devel**
- 24 May 1907 - 7 Feb 1912: *Maj.-Gen.* Baron Lev Fyodorovich **Zhirar de Sukanton**
- 3 Mar 1912 - 20 Nov 1913: *Lt.-Gen.* Yevgeny Ivanovich **Bernov**
- 24 Dec 1913 - Aug 1914: *Lt.-Gen.* Prince Sergey Konstantinich **Beloselsky-Belozersky**
- Aug 1914 - 23 Nov 1914: *Maj.-Gen.* Dmitry Aleksandrovich **Lopukhin**
- 23 Nov 1914 - 11 Jul 1915: *Lt.-Gen.* Prince Sergey Konstantinich **Beloselsky-Belozersky**
- 11 Jul 1915 - 21 Nov 1915: *Maj.-Gen.* Georgy Ivanovich **Shevich**
- 10 Dec 1915 - 18 Apr 1917: *Maj.-Gen.* Dmitry Maksimovich **Knyazhevich**

Commander, 2nd Brigade, 2nd Guards Cavalry Division
- 15 Apr 1891 - 8 Dec 1894: *Gen. of Cav.* Sergey Prokofyevich **Chervonny**
- 27 Jan 1895 - 18 Dec 1895: *Gen. of Cav.* Ivan Sergeyevich **Zykov**
- 18 Dec 1895 - 16 Aug 1896: ?

- 16 Aug 1896 - 17 Dec 1898: *Gen. of Cav.* Prince Sergei Illarionovich **Vasilchikov**
- 17 Dec 1898 - 2 Mar 1899: ?
- 2 Mar 1899 - 7 May 1901: *Lt.-Gen.* Sergey Ilyich **Bibikov**
- 25 May 1901 - 25 May 1903: *Gen. of Cav.* Prince Nikolai Nikolayevich **Odoyevsky-Maslov**
- 25 May 1903 - 12 Oct 1904: *Gen. of Cav.* Yakov Bogdanovich **Prezhentsov**
- 13 Oct 1904 - 16 Feb 1906: *Maj.-Gen.* Nikolai Aleksandrovich **Yafimovich**
- 16 Feb 1906 - 10 Feb 1907: *Gen. of Inf.* Nikolai Fyodorovich von **Kruzenshtern**
- 10 Feb 1907 - 3 Sep 1907: *Gen. of Cav.* Pyotr Robertovich von **Nettelgorst**
- 4 Sep 1907 - Oct 1908: *Maj.-Gen.* Aleksandr Afinogenovich **Orlov**
- 28 Oct 1908 - 13 Dec 1911: *Lt.-Gen.* Feliks Feliksovich Prince **Yusupov**
- 13 Dec 1911 - 14 Nov 1912: *Maj.-Gen.* Nikolai Nikolayevich **Komstadius**
- 14 Nov 1912 - 11 Oct 1914: *Lt.-Gen.* Count Georgy Georgyevich **Mengden**
- 12 Nov 1914 - 13 Jan 1915: *Lt.-Gen.* Pyotr Ivanovich **Arapov**
- 13 Jan 1915 - 30 Aug 1915: *Maj.-Gen.* Count Fyodor Maksimilianovich **Nirod**
- 30 Aug 1915 - 19 Dec 1915: *Maj.-Gen.* Dmitry Maksimovich **Knyazhevich**
- 19 Dec 1915 - 10 Mar 1917: *Lt.-Gen.* Yevgeny Konstantinovich **Arsenyev**

Commander, 3rd Brigade, 2nd Guards Cavalry Division
- 4 May 1892 - 24 Nov 1894: *Gen. of Cav.* Nikolai Stepanovich **Khrulev**
- 15 Dec 1894 - 4 May 1897: *Gen. of Cav.* Aleksandr Yakovlevich von **Tal**
- 1897: DISSOLVED

Commander, 3rd Guards Cavalry Division *(Formed in 1916)*
- 27 Jun 1916 - Oct 1917: *Lt.-Gen.* Pyotr Ivanovich **Arapov**

Commander, 1st Brigade, 3rd Guards Cavalry Division
- 1916 - 2 Mar 1917: ?

Commander, 2nd Brigade, 3rd Guards Cavalry Division
- 1916 - 2 Mar 1917: ?

Commander, 1st Cavalry Division
- 1 Sep 1888 - 18 Feb 1897: *Gen. of Cav.* Mikhail Vasilyevich von der **Launits**
- 19 Feb 1897 - 13 Jan 1899: *Gen. of Cav.* Ivan Sergeyevich **Zykov**
- 13 Jan 1899 - 23 Dec 1901: *Gen. of Cav.* Prince Sergei Illarionovich **Vasilchikov**
- 31 Dec 1901 - 9 Oct 1906: *Gen. of Cav.* Aleksandr Vladimirovich **Bartolomey**
- 9 Oct 1906 - 9 Mar 1911: *Gen. of Cav.* Aleksandr Ivanovich **Litvinov**
- 12 Mar 1911 - 20 Aug 1914: *Gen. of Cav.* Vasily Iosifovich **Romeyko-Gurko**
- 20 Aug 1914 - 9 Sep 1914: *Lt.-Gen.* Yevgeny Aleksandrovich **Leontovich**
- 9 Sep 1914 - 9 Nov 1914: *Gen. of Cav.* Vasily Iosifovich **Romeyko-Gurko**
- 9 Nov 1914 - 5 Dec 1914: ?
- 5 Dec 1914 - 21 Aug 1915: *Maj.-Gen.* Baron Vladimir Nikolayevich von **Maydel**
- 21 Aug 1915 - Dec 1917: *Maj.-Gen.* Aleksei Kirillovich **Grekov**

Commander, 1st Brigade, 1st Cavalry Division
- 2 Mar 1894 - Jul 1902: *Lt.-Gen.* Aleksey Tikhonovich **Kanshin**
- 3 Jul 1902 - Sep 1907: *Maj.-Gen.* Yevgeny Petrovich **Golubkov**
- 28 Sep 1907 - 17 Oct 1910: *Maj.-Gen.* Grigory Ivanovich **Kartashevsky**
- 17 Oct 1910 - 23 Dec 1911: *Lt.-Gen.* Baron Nikolai Arkadyevich von **Shtempel**
- 23 Dec 1911 - 25 Aug 1915: *Lt.-Gen.* Nikolai Nikolayevich **Leo**
- 25 Aug 1915 - 19 Apr 1917: *Maj.-Gen.* Leonty Nikolayevich **Velikopolsky**

Commander, 2nd Brigade, 1st Cavalry Division
- 10 Aug 1885 - 10 Apr 1896: *Lt.-Gen.* Yakov Aleksandrovich **Gardenin**
- 25 Apr 1896 - Nov 1901: *Maj.-Gen.* Pyotr Nikolayevich **Kolesnikov**
- 1 Dec 1901 - 19 Jun 1905: *Gen. of Cav.* Daniil Fyodorovich **Devel**
- 19 Jun 1905 - 4 Oct 1905: ?
- 4 Oct 1905 - 18 Aug 1908: *Lt.-Gen.* Vasily Ivanovich **Kosov**
- 18 Aug 1908 - 21 May 1912: *Gen. of Cav.* Mikhail Stepanovich **Tyulin**
- 21 May 1912 - 25 Aug 1915: *Lt.-Gen.* Ivan Dmitriyevich **Nilov**
- 25 Aug 1915 - Feb 1917: *Lt.-Gen.* Nikolai Nikolayevich **Leo**
- Feb 1917 - 2 Mar 1917: ?

Commander, 2nd Cavalry Division
- 22 Apr 1892 - Mar 1897: *Lt.-Gen.* Baron Aleksandr Fyodorovich **Offenberg**
- 18 Mar 1897 - 23 Jun 1899: *Gen. of Inf.* Pyotr Nikolayevich **Bazhenov**
- 30 Jun 1899 - 20 Nov 1901: *Gen. of Cav.* Pavel Adamovich **Pleve**
- 30 Jan 1902 - 31 Mar 1905: *Lt.-Gen.* Aleksandr Nikolayevich **Dubensky**
- 11 Apr 1905 - 8 Mar 1907: *Lt.-Gen.* Nikolai Nikolayevich **Gulkovsky**
- 8 Mar 1907 - 2 Jan 1914: *Gen. of Cav.* Afanasy Andreyevich **Tsurikov**
- 16 Jan 1914 - 18 Oct 1914: *Gen. of Cav.* Khan Hussein **Nakhichevansky**
- 18 Oct 1914 - 18 Apr 1917: *Lt.-Gen.* Prince Georgy Ivanovich **Trubetskoy**

Commander, 1st Brigade, 2nd Cavalry Division
- 13 Jul 1890 - 7 Jun 1895: *Maj.-Gen.* Nikolai Fyodorovich **Ilin**
- 7 Jun 1895 - 3 Jun 1896: ?
- 3 Jun 1896 - 16 Dec 1899: *Maj.-Gen.* Aleksandr Sergeyevich **Ambrazantsev-Nechayev**
- 16 Dec 1899 - 8 Mar 1907: *Lt.-Gen.* Nikolai Georgiyevich **Papa-Afanasopulo**
- 21 Mar 1907 - Apr 1908: *Maj.-Gen.* Nikolai Sergeyevich **Zhilin**
- 12 Apr 1908 - 4 Aug 1908: *Lt.-Gen.* Gleb Mikhailovich **Vannovsky**
- 11 Sep 1908 - 20 Aug 1914: *Lt.-Gen.* Yevgeny Aleksandrovich **Leontovich**
- 10 Aug 1914 - 24 Jun 1915: *Lt.-Gen.* Nikolai Aloiziyevich **Oranovsky**
- 24 Jun 1915 - 29 Feb 1916: *Maj.-Gen.* Mikhail Mikhailovich **Makhov**
- 25 Mar 1916 - 1917: *Maj.-Gen.* Pavel Nikolayevich **Pavlishchev**

Commander, 2nd Brigade, 2nd Cavalry Division
- 25 Apr 1893 - 28 Dec 1896: *Lt.-Gen.* Andrey Petrovich **Znachko-Yavorsky**
- 28 Dec 1896 - Dec 1901: *Maj.-Gen.* Viktor Ignatyevich **Kardashevsky**

- 25 Jan 1902 - 15 Jun 1907: *Gen. of Cav.* Mikhail Mikhailovich **Pleshkov**
- 15 Jun 1907 - 23 Dec 1911: *Lt.-Gen.* Nikolai Nikolayevich **Leo**
- 25 Jan 1912 - 15 Aug 1914: *Lt.-Gen.* Grigory Ivanovich **Choglokov**
- 28 Oct 1914 - 1 Jan 1916: *Maj.-Gen.* Prince Arseny Aleksandrovich **Karageorgiyevich**
- 1 Jan 1916 - 1917: *Maj.-Gen.* Vladimir Petrovich **Yuryev**

Commander, 3rd Cavalry Division
- 12 Apr 1880 - Nov 1894: *Lt.-Gen.* Konstantin Stanislavovich **Krayevsky**
- 24 Nov 1894 - 17 Aug 1898: *Gen. of Cav.* Nikolai Nikolayevich **Sukhotin**
- 17 Aug 1898 - 24 Nov 1898: ?
- 24 Nov 1898 - 12 Jan 1905: *Lt.-Gen.* Ivan Vasilyevich **Volkenau**
- 8 Mar 1905 - 29 Dec 1906: *Lt.-Gen.* Baron Aleksandr Nikolayevich **Bistrom**
- 29 Dec 1906 - Jul 1908: *Gen. of Cav.* Aleksandr Dmitriyevich **Oboleshev**
- 31 Aug 1908 - 15 May 1912: *Gen. of Cav.* Sergey Mikhailovich **Sheydeman**
- 21 May 1912 - 18 Aug 1914: *Lt.-Gen.* Vladimir Karlovich **Belgardt**
- 9 Sep 1914 - 13 Apr 1917: *Lt.-Gen.* Yevgeny Aleksandrovich **Leontovich**

Commander, 1st Brigade, 3rd Cavalry Division
- 6 Sep 1891 - 12 May 1897: *Lt.-Gen.* Anton Nikolayevich **Zheltukhin**
- 26 May 1897 - 2 Apr 1899: *Gen. of Cav.* Konstantin Varfolomeyevich **Dembsky**
- 28 Apr 1899 - 3 Feb 1904: *Gen. of Cav.* Adam Solomonovich **Karganov**
- 4 Feb 1904 - 3 May 1908: *Maj.-Gen.* Dmitry Dmitriyevich **Kolomnin**
- 3 May 1908 - 21 Feb 1915: *Maj.-Gen.* Baron Aleksandr Georgiyevich **Tornau**
- 21 Feb 1915 - 20 May 1915: *Maj.-Gen.* Gavriil Mikhailovich **Ladyzhensky**
- 20 May 1915 - 25 Jun 1915: *Maj.-Gen.* Baron Aleksandr Georgiyevich **Tornau**
- 25 Jun 1915 - 26 Jun 1916: *Maj.-Gen.* Pyotr Ivanovich **Zalessky**
- 26 Jun 1916 - 4 Jan 1917: *Maj.-Gen.* Aleksandr Frantsevich **Yarminsky**
- 15 Jan 1917 - 16 May 1917: *Maj.-Gen.* Vasily Viktorovich **Biskupsky**

Commander, 2nd Brigade, 3rd Cavalry Division
- 26 Nov 1890 - 7 Nov 1895: *Maj.-Gen.* Ivan Vasilyevich **Ilovaysky**
- 20 Nov 1895 - 14 Apr 1901: *Maj.-Gen.* Aleksandr Aleksandrovich **Tregubov**
- 14 Apr 1901 - 18 Feb 1910: *Lt.-Gen.* Fyodor Semonovich **Verba**
- 23 Feb 1910 - 22 Jun 1912: *Lt.-Gen.* Aleksandr Nikolayevich **Ivanov**
- 22 Jun 1912 - 9 Nov 1913: *Lt.-Gen.* Andrey Mikhailovich **Nikolayev**
- 9 Nov 1913 - 11 Oct 1914: *Maj.-Gen.* Baron Vladimir Nikolayevich von **Maydel**
- 11 Oct 1914 - 27 Dec 1914: ?
- 27 Dec 1914 - 1917: *Maj.-Gen.* Pavel Georgiyevich **Khandakov**

Commander, 4th Cavalry Division
- 22 Jan 1892 - 3 Aug 1897: *Gen. of Cav.* Nikolai Arkadyevich **Timiryazev**
- 12 Sep 1897 - 2 Mar 1899: *Maj.-Gen.* Pyotr Vladimirovich **Charkovsky**
- 2 Apr 1899 - 4 Apr 1901: *Gen. of Cav.* Georgy Antonovich **Skalon**

- 7 May 1901 - 29 Nov 1903: *Gen. of Cav.* Vladimir Viktorovich **Sakharov**
- 24 Dec 1903 - Dec 1906: *Lt.-Gen.* Edmund Karlovich von **Bader**
- 6 Dec 1906 - 1 May 1910: *Lt.-Gen.* Aleksandr Leontievich **Garnak**
- 1 May 1910 - 19 Jun 1912: *Lt.-Gen.* Boris Petrovich **Vannovsky**
- 22 Jun 1912 - 15 Oct 1914: *Lt.-Gen.* Anton Aleksandrovich **Tolpygo**
- 15 Oct 1914 - 18 Apr 1917: *Lt.-Gen.* Boris Petrovich **Vannovsky**

Commander, 1st Brigade, 4th Cavalry Division
- 17 Feb 1891 - 2 May 1895: *Maj.-Gen.* Aleksandr Mechislavovich **Pilsudsky**
- 3 Mar 1895 - 30 Jan 1902: *Lt.-Gen.* Edmund Karlovich von **Bader**
- 30 Jan 1902 - 10 Mar 1902: ?
- 10 Mar 1902 - 3 Feb 1904: *Gen. of Inf.* Nikolai Fyodorovich von **Kruzenshtern**
- 4 Feb 1904 - 2 Dec 1904: *Lt.-Gen.* Prince Pyotr Nikolayevich **Myshetsky**
- 9 Dec 1904 - Dec 1907: *Maj.-Gen.* Fyodor Andreyevich **Savenkov**
- 6 Dec 1907 - 31 Dec 1913: *Lt.-Gen.* Bronislav Ivanovich **Krasovsky**
- 31 Dec 1913 - 13 Feb 1918: *Maj.-Gen.* Yevgeny Fyodorovich **Kayander**

Commander, 2nd Brigade, 4th Cavalry Division
- 28 Apr 1885 - 31 Jul 1895: *Maj.-Gen.* Aleksandr Antonovich **Baronch**
- 31 Jul 1895 - 19 Aug 1896: *Lt.-Gen.* Aleksandr Aleksandrovich **Benkendorf**
- 19 Aug 1896 - 13 Nov 1896: *Maj.-Gen.* Vladimir Aleksandrovich **Pakhalen**
- 14 Nov 1896 - 29 May 1897: *Lt.-Gen.* Aleksandr Nikolayevich **Dubensky**
- 12 Jun 1897 - 11 Apr 1905: *Lt.-Gen.* Nikolai Nikolayevich **Gulkovsky**
- 20 May 1905 - 20 Apr 1906: *Maj.-Gen.* Valter Valterovich **Meynard**
- 20 Apr 1906 - 30 Oct 1906: *Gen. of Cav.* Vasily Iosifovich **Romeyko-Gurko**
- 30 Oct 1906 - 4 Jul 1907: *Lt.-Gen.* Nikolai Aleksandrovich **Medvedev**
- 4 Jul 1907 - 6 Dec 1907: ?
- 6 Dec 1907 - 29 May 1910: *Lt.-Gen.* Anton Aleksandrovich **Tolpygo**
- 29 May 1910 - 1 Aug 1913: *Lt.-Gen.* Ivan Amvrosiyevich **Falkovsky**
- 30 Aug 1913 - 6 Jun 1915: *Lt.-Gen.* Anatoly Ivanovich **Martynov**
- 6 Jun 1915 - 24 Jul 1917: *Maj.-Gen.* Baron Andrey Romanovich **Budberg**

Commander, 5th Cavalry Division
- 9 Nov 1892 - 30 May 1895: *Gen. of Cav.* Vsevolod Matveyevich **Ostrogradsky**
- 11 Jun 1985 - 11 Jun 1901: *Gen. of Cav.* Prince David Evstafiyevich **Eristov**
- 11 Jun 1901 - 2 Jul 1907: *Gen. of Cav.* Pavel Aleksandrovich **Kozlovsky**
- 12 Sep 1907 - 29 May 1910: *Gen. of Cav.* Baron Yevgeny Aleksandrovich **Raush von Traubenberg**
- 29 May 1910 - 25 Feb 1912: *Lt.-Gen.* Georgy Aleksandrovich **Zander**
- 25 Feb 1912 - 28 Jan 1915: *Lt.-Gen.* Aleksandr Arnoldovich **Morits**
- 28 Jan 1915 - 29 Jul 1915: *Maj.-Gen.* Nikolai Ivanovich **Chaykovsky**
- 29 Jul 1915 - 2 Apr 1916: *Lt.-Gen.* Pavel Petrovich **Skoropadsky**
- 26 Apr 1916 - 18 Apr 1917: *Lt.-Gen.* Ivan Dmitriyevich **Nilov**

Commander, 1st Brigade, 5th Cavalry Division
- 20 Sep 1894 - 12 Dec 1900: *Gen. of Cav.* Baron Reyngold Aleksandrovich von **Shtempel**
- 18 Dec 1900 - 28 Aug 1907: *Lt.-Gen.* Dmitry Petrovich **Ofrosimov**
- 28 Aug 1907 - 4 Feb 1910: *Gen. of Inf.* Nikolai Nikolayevich **Kaznakov**
- 23 Feb 1910 - 17 Oct 1910: *Lt.-Gen.* Baron Nikolai Arkadyevich von **Shtempel**
- 17 Oct 1910 - 18 Jul 1914: *Lt.-Gen.* Aglay Dmitriyevich **Kuzmin-Korovayev**
- 29 Jul 1914 - 13 May 1915: *Maj.-Gen.* Vladimir Nikolayevich **Peters**
- 15 May 1915 - 10 Nov 1915: *Maj.-Gen.* Ivan Andreyevich **Nikulin**
- 9 Dec 1915 - 19 Apr 1917: *Maj.-Gen.* Nikolai Pavlovich **Luchov**

Commander, 2nd Brigade, 5th Cavalry Division
- 14 Oct 1891 - Jan 1895: *Maj.-Gen.* Porfiry Petrovich **Grekov**
- 5 Jan 1895 - 5 Jan 1900: *Lt.-Gen.* Nikolai Ivanovich **Dutkin**
- 26 Jan 1900 - 16 Apr 1904: *Gen. of Cav.* Vladimir Pavlovich **Grekov**
- 22 Jun 1904 - 4 Apr 1905: *Gen. of Cav.* Aleksei Livovich **Vershinin**
- 15 Apr 1905 - 28 Aug 1907: *Gen. of Inf.* Nikolai Nikolayevich **Kaznakov**
- 28 Aug 1907 - 15 Jun 1910: *Lt.-Gen.* Dmitry Petrovich **Ofrosimov**
- 15 Jun 1910 - 8 Oct 1913: *Lt.-Gen.* Aleksandr Vasilyevich **Novikov**
- 19 Nov 1913 - 31 Jan 1915: *Maj.-Gen.* Fyodor Nikolayevich **Mikhailov**
- 31 Jan 1915 - 13 Nov 1915: *Maj.-Gen.* Vasily Matveyevich **Rodionov**
- 13 Nov 1915 - 1917: *Maj.-Gen.* Vladimir Nikolayevich **Popov**

Commander, 6th Cavalry Division
- 19 Feb 1890 - 7 Dec 1898: *Gen. of Inf.* Pyotr Dmitriyevich **Parensov**
- 13 Jan 1899 - 9 Jun 1903: *Gen. of Cav.* Nikolai Vasilyevich **Shutlevort**
- 10 Jun 1903 - 23 May 1907: *Lt.-Gen.* Konstantin Yefimovich **Przhevlotsky**
- 23 May 1907 - 13 Nov 1913: *Gen. of Cav.* Daniil Fyodorovich **Devel**
- 15 Nov 1913 - 8 Feb 1917: *Lt.-Gen.* Vladimir Khristoforovich **Roop**
- 26 Feb 1917 - 16 Apr 1917: *Lt.-Gen.* Vladimir Aleksandrovich **Moshnin**

Commander, 1st Brigade, 6th Cavalry Division
- 5 Nov 1890 - Apr 1899: *Maj.-Gen.* Aleksandr Lukich **Bogushevich**
- 31 May 1899 - 26 Mar 1901: *Gen. of Cav.* Baron Nikolai Vasilyevich von der **Ropp**
- 26 Mar 1901 - Sep 1907: *Lt.-Gen.* Vladimir Aleksandrovich **Kovalevsky**
- 4 Sep 1907 - 29 Mar 1908: *Maj.-Gen.* Konstantin Mavrikievich von **Volf**
- 29 Mar 1908 - 11 May 1908: ?
- 11 May 1908 - 20 May 1913: *Lt.-Gen.* Yuly Maksimilianovich von **Kube**
- 29 May 1913 - 4 May 1915: *Maj.-Gen.* Nikolai Nikolayevich **Maksimovsky**
- 27 May 1915 - 1917: *Maj.-Gen.* Baron Sesil Arturovich von **Korf**

Commander, 2nd Brigade, 6th Cavalry Division
- 6 Nov 1891 - 4 Apr 1895: *Gen. of Cav.* Nikolai Mikhailovich **Vonlyarlyarsky**
- 24 Apr 1895 - Dec 1899: *Maj.-Gen.* Feofil Nikolayevich **Gotovsky**
- 25 Jan 1900 - 19 Feb 1904: *Gen. of Cav.* Sergey Alekseyevich **Kareyev**

- 25 Mar 1904 - 14 Apr 1906: *Maj.-Gen.* Mikhail Ivanovich **Mezentsov**
- 17 Apr 1906 - 12 May 1910: *Lt.-Gen.* Yevgeny Alekseyevich **Panchulidzev**
- 13 May 1910 - 24 Nov 1910: *Maj.-Gen.* Prince Nikolai Valeryevich **Urusov**
- 1 Jan 1911 - 10 Feb 1913: *Maj.-Gen.* Erast Alekseyevich **Shlyakhtin**
- 10 Feb 1913 - 1917: *Lt.-Gen.* Baron Nikolai Arkadyevich von **Shtempel**

Commander, 7th Cavalry Division
- 16 Sep 1894 - 4 Jul 1902: *Lt.-Gen.* Nikolai Mikhailovich **Rogovsky**
- 4 Jul 1902 - 15 Jun 1907: *Gen. of Cav.* Leonid Petrovich **Fomin**
- 15 Jun 1907 - 11 May 1912: *Gen. of Cav.* Mikhail Mikhailovich **Pleshkov**
- 21 May 1912 - 23 Nov 1914: *Gen. of Cav.* Mikhail Stepanovich **Tyulin**
- 23 Nov 1914 - 6 Apr 1917: *Lt.-Gen.* Fyodor Sergeyevich **Rerberg**

Commander, 1st Brigade, 7th Cavalry Division
- 14 Nov 1888 - 12 May 1897: *Maj.-Gen.* Yegor Ivanovich von **Brevern**
- 12 May 1897 - Dec 1899: *Lt.-Gen.* Anton Nikolayevich **Zheltukhin**
- 25 Jan 1900 - 10 Jun 1903: *Lt.-Gen.* Konstantin Yefimovich **Przhevlotsky**
- 3 Jul 1903 - 1 Dec 1907: *Maj.-Gen.* Valerian Aleksandrovich **Karandeyev**
- 1 Dec 1907 - Nov 1910: *Maj.-Gen.* Sergey Petrovich **Demor**
- 5 Dec 1910 - 5 May 1912: *Maj.-Gen.* Yevgraf Yevgrafovich **Lavrov**
- 21 May 1912 - 12 Apr 1917: *Maj.-Gen.* Nikolai Nikolayevich **Durov**

Commander, 2nd Brigade, 7th Cavalry Division
- 6 Aug 1894 - 1 Mar 1895: *Lt.-Gen.* Vasily Petrovich **Korochentsov**
- 14 Mar 1895 - 25 Jan 1900: *Lt.-Gen.* Konstantin Yefimovich **Przhevlotsky**
- 25 Jan 1900 - 1 Dec 1901: *Gen. of Cav.* Daniil Fyodorovich **Devel**
- 25 Jan 1902 - 5 Jun 1902: *Lt.-Gen.* Mikhail Nikolayevich **Verevkin**
- 5 Jun 1902 - 3 Jul 1903: *Maj.-Gen.* Valerian Aleksandrovich **Karandeyev**
- 9 Jul 1903 - 3 Oct 1907: *Maj.-Gen.* Vladimir Grigoryevich **Mandryko**
- 3 Oct 1907 - 5 Nov 1908: *Maj.-Gen.* Vladimir Ivanovich **Vasyanov**
- 5 Nov 1908 - 17 Nov 1910: *Lt.-Gen.* Ivan Zakharovich **Shirokov**
- 17 Nov 1910 - 1 Dec 1913: *Lt.-Gen.* Nikolai Vasilyevich **Savoysky**
- 14 Dec 1913 - 2 Aug 1914: *Lt.-Gen.* Nikolai Lvovich **Sveshnikov**
- 7 Sep 1914 - 8 Oct 1915: *Lt.-Gen.* Fyodor Vasilyevich **Rubets-Masalsky**
- 8 Oct 1915 - 1917: *Maj.-Gen.* Pyotr Nikolayevich **Kolzakov**

Commander, 8th Cavalry Division
- 30 Aug 1885 - 14 Nov 1894: *Gen. of Cav.* Georgy Aleksandrovich **Borozdin**
- 24 Nov 1894 - 28 Nov 1897: *Gen. of Cav.* Nikolai Stepanovich **Khrulev**
- 30 Dec 1897 - 25 Jan 1899: *Maj.-Gen.* Mikhail Illarionovich **Markov**
- 25 Jan 1899 - 2 Mar 1899: ?
- 2 Mar 1899 - 23 Nov 1904: *Gen. of Cav.* Vladimir Aleksandrovich **Bekman**
- 23 Nov 1904 - 7 Feb 1905: ?
- 7 Feb 1905 - 18 Feb 1910: *Gen. of Cav.* Konstantin Varfolomeyevich **Dembsky**

- 18 Feb 1910 - 25 Feb 1912: *Lt.-Gen.* Fyodor Semonovich **Verba**
- 25 Feb 1912 - 5 Feb 1915: *Lt.-Gen.* Georgy Aleksandrovich **Zander**
- 5 Feb 1915 - 2 Jan 1916: *Maj.-Gen.* Leonid Petrovich **Kiselev**
- 2 Jan 1916 - 16 Apr 1917: *Maj.-Gen.* Aleksandr Apollinariyevich **Krasovsky**

Commander, 1st Brigade, 8th Cavalry Division
- 20 Oct 1894 - 31 Jul 1898: ?
- 31 Jul 1898 - 21 Jul 1899: *Maj.-Gen.* Daniil Grigoryevich **Dukmasov**
- 16 Aug 1899 - 15 Jun 1902: *Gen. of Cav.* Vladislav Ksaveryevich **Topchevsky**
- 15 Jun 1902 - 8 Sep 1902: *Gen. of Inf.* Dmitry Nikolayevich **Bezradetsky**
- 8 Sep 1902 - 18 Jan 1907: *Gen. of Cav.* Vladislav Ksaveryevich **Topchevsky**
- 18 Jan 1907 - 24 Aug 1907: *Lt.-Gen.* Bronislav Lyudvigovich **Chernota-de-Boyary-Boyarsky**
- 4 Sep 1907 - 15 May 1908: *Maj.-Gen.* Vasily Trofimovich **Kartashev**
- 15 May 1908 - 29 Jun 1912: *Maj.-Gen.* Baron Anatoly Aleksandrovich **Budberg**
- 29 Jun 1912 - 30 Aug 1912: ?
- 30 Aug 1912 - 27 Nov 1915: *Maj.-Gen.* Aleksandr Apollinariyevich **Krasovsky**
- 27 Nov 1915 - 2 Feb 1916: *Maj.-Gen.* Ferdinand Yulyevich **Bush**
- 2 Feb 1916 - 1918: *Maj.-Gen.* Yury Konstantinovich **Ustimovich**

Commander, 2nd Brigade, 8th Cavalry Division
- 17 Oct 1891 - 17 Jun 1899: *Gen. of Cav.* Erast Ksenofontovich **Kvitnitsky**
- 21 Jul 1899 - 10 Dec 1903: *Maj.-Gen.* Daniil Grigoryevich **Dukmasov**
- 16 Dec 1903 - 23 Jul 1907: *Maj.-Gen.* Konstantin Adamovich **Karangozov**
- 24 Aug 1907 - 9 Oct 1912: *Lt.-Gen.* Bronislav Lyudvigovich **Chernota-de-Boyary-Boyarsky**
- 9 Oct 1912 - 14 Nov 1914: *Maj.-Gen.* Nikolai Antonovich **Knyazhevich**
- 14 Nov 1914 - 17 Jun 1915: *Lt.-Gen.* Nikolai Aleksandrovich **Radkevich**
- 17 Jun 1915 - 2 Feb 1916: *Maj.-Gen.* Yury Konstantinovich **Ustimovich**
- 2 Feb 1916 - 1917: *Maj.-Gen.* Ferdinand Yulyevich **Bush**

Commander, 9th Cavalry Division
- 30 Aug 1885 - 21 Feb 1896: *Gen. of Cav.* Nikolai Dementyevich **Novitsky**
- 18 Mar 1896 - 17 Mar 1900: *Lt.-Gen.* Aleksandr Aleksandrovich **Lesli**
- 26 Apr 1900 - 16 Dec 1904: *Gen. of Cav.* Konstantin Pavlovich **De-Vitte**
- 10 Jan 1905 - 21 May 1908: *Gen. of Cav.* Adam Solomonovich **Karganov**
- 21 May 1908 - 30 Dec 1908: *Gen. of Cav.* Yakov Bogdanovich **Prezhentsov**
- 7 Jan 1909 - 4 Sep 1911: *Gen. of Cav.* Nikolai Aleksandrovich **Sukhomlinov**
- 4 Sep 1911 - 6 Apr 1917: *Lt.-Gen.* Prince Konstantin Sergeyevich **Begildeyev**

Commander, 1st Brigade, 9th Cavalry Division
- 12 Aug 1892 - 18 Feb 1899: *Gen. of Cav.* Konstantin Pavlovich **De-Vitte**
- 1 Mar 1899 - 16 Jan 1901: *Maj.-Gen.* Nikolai Petrovich **Stepanov**
- 6 Feb 1901 - 2 Dec 1901: *Lt.-Gen.* Konstantin Aleksandrovich **Nazarov**
- 2 Dec 1901 - 13 Dec 1902: *Maj.-Gen.* Vasily Mikhailovich **Sakharov**

- 13 Dec 1902 - 3 Feb 1903: ?
- 3 Feb 1903 - 7 Jan 1909: *Gen. of Cav.* Nikolai Aleksandrovich **Sukhomlinov**
- 11 Feb 1909 - 27 Nov 1912: *Lt.-Gen.* Vladimir Aleksandrovich **Moshnin**
- 5 Dec 1912 - 28 Feb 1916: *Lt.-Gen.* Prince Konstantin Aleksandrovich **Tumanov**
- 28 Feb 1916 - 13 Apr 1917: *Maj.-Gen.* Konstantin Konstantinovich **Kuzmin-Korovayev**

Commander, 2nd Brigade, 9th Cavalry Division
- 10 Dec 1886 - 17 Dec 1896: *Gen. of Cav.* Nikolai Ivanovich **Merkling**
- 24 Dec 1896 - 5 Jun 1902: *Maj.-Gen.* Prince Archil Gulbatovich **Chavchavadze**
- 5 Jun 1902 - 21 Aug 1907: *Lt.-Gen.* Mikhail Nikolayevich **Verevkin**
- 31 Aug 1907 - 23 May 1909: *Lt.-Gen.* Apollinary Aleksandrovich **Alymov**
- 23 May 1909 - 8 Sep 1909: *Lt.-Gen.* Lev Vladimirovich **De-Vitt**
- 8 Sep 1909 - 22 Oct 1910: *Lt.-Gen.* Apollinary Aleksandrovich **Alymov**
- 24 Nov 1910 - 7 Aug 1912: *Maj.-Gen.* Prince Nikolai Valeryevich **Urusov**
- 7 Aug 1912 - 27 Nov 1912: *Gen. of Cav.* Abram Mikhailovich **Dragomirov**
- 27 Nov 1912 - 27 Nov 1912: *Maj.-Gen.* Prince Nikolai Valeryevich **Urusov**
- 27 Nov 1912 - 26 Feb 1917: *Lt.-Gen.* Vladimir Aleksandrovich **Moshnin**

Commander, 10th Cavalry Division
- 23 Nov 1887 - 27 Mar 1897: *Gen. of Cav.* Aleksandr Maksimovich **Rebinder**
- 16 Apr 1897 - 25 May 1899: *Gen. of Inf.* Vladimir Aleksandrovich **Sukhomlinov**
- 31 May 1899 - 25 Apr 1901: *Gen. of Cav.* Baron Georgy Karlovich von **Shtakelberg**
- 7 May 1901 - 7 May 1903: *Lt.-Gen.* Sergey Ilyich **Bibikov**
- 25 May 1903 - 7 Jan 1904: *Gen. of Cav.* Prince Nikolai Nikolayevich **Odoyevsky-Maslov**
- 3 Feb 1904 - 14 Aug 1907: *Lt.-Gen.* Pyotr Aleksandrovich **Mashin**
- 21 Aug 1907 - 9 Sep 1908: *Lt.-Gen.* Mikhail Nikolayevich **Verevkin**
- 9 Sep 1908 - 29 Jan 1912: *Gen. of Cav.* Georgy Ottonovich von **Raukh**
- 25 Feb 1912 - 3 Apr 1915: *Gen. of Cav.* Count Fyodor Arturovich **Keller**
- 21 Apr 1915 - 1917: *Lt.-Gen.* Vasily Yevgenyevich **Markov**

Commander, 1st Brigade, 10th Cavalry Division
- 13 Mar 1885 - Nov 1896: *Maj.-Gen.* Nikolai Fyodorovich **Glavatsky**
- 25 Nov 1896 - 28 Nov 1897: *Gen. of Cav.* Leonty Nikolayevich von **Baumgarten**
- 3 Dec 1897 - 26 Mar 1901: *Maj.-Gen.* Mikhail Aleksandrovich **Kozlovsky**
- 26 Mar 1901 - 9 Dec 1904: *Maj.-Gen.* Fyodor Andreyevich **Savenkov**
- 14 Dec 1904 - 27 Mar 1906: *Lt.-Gen.* Nikolai Aleksandrovich **Zarubin**
- 14 Apr 1906 - 14 Aug 1908: *Maj.-Gen.* Viktor Semyonovich **Zenkevich**
- 14 Aug 1908 - 1 May 1910: *Lt.-Gen.* Aleksandr Konstantinovich **Rutkovsky**
- 13 May 1910 - 21 Apr 1915: *Lt.-Gen.* Vasily Yevgenyevich **Markov**
- 21 Apr 1915 - 2 Mar 1917: ?

Commander, 2nd Brigade, 10th Cavalry Division
- 14 Nov 1888 - 17 Feb 1895: *Gen. of Cav.* Sergey Ivanovich **Sannikov**

- 1 Mar 1895 - 3 Feb 1900: *Lt.-Gen.* Vasily Petrovich **Korochentsov**
- 6 Mar 1900 - 19 Nov 1907: *Gen. of Cav.* Nikolai Vasilievich **Avdeyev**
- 19 Nov 1907 - 11 Feb 1908: ?
- 11 Feb 1908 - 19 Jul 1914: *Maj.-Gen.* Vladimir Mikhailovich **Khitrovo**
- 19 Jul 1914 - 25 Jul 1915: ?
- 25 Jul 1915 - 24 Mar 1917: *Maj.-Gen.* Leonid Petrovich **Timashev**

Commander, 11th Cavalry Division
- 10 Oct 1884 - 8 Feb 1895: *Lt.-Gen.* Dmitry Bogdanovich **Ter-Asaturov**
- 17 Feb 1895 - 25 Oct 1901: *Gen. of Cav.* Sergey Ivanovich **Sannikov**
- 25 Oct 1901 - 30 Jan 1902: ?
- 30 Jan 1902 - 24 Dec 1903: *Lt.-Gen.* Edmund Karlovich von **Bader**
- 24 Dec 1903 - 3 Feb 1904: ?
- 3 Feb 1904 - 10 Jan 1905: *Gen. of Cav.* Adam Solomonovich **Karganov**
- 10 Jan 1905 - 21 Aug 1906: *Lt.-Gen.* Dmitry Viktorovich **Kryzhanovsky**
- 21 Aug 1906 - 17 Oct 1906: ?
- 17 Oct 1906 - 3 May 1910: *Gen. of Cav.* Pyotr Konstantinovich **Rutkovsky**
- 3 May 1910 - 22 Oct 1914: *Lt.-Gen.* Lev Vladimirovich **De-Vitt**
- 22 Oct 1914 - 3 Nov 1915: *Gen. of Cav.* Leonid Nikolayevich **Velyashev**
- 3 Nov 1915 - 1918: *Lt.-Gen.* Baron Nikolai Aleksandrovich von **Disterlo**

Commander, 1st Brigade, 11th Cavalry Division
- 23 Mar 1884 - 18 Mar 1896: *Lt.-Gen.* Aleksandr Aleksandrovich **Lesli**
- 1 Apr 1896 - 14 Nov 1896: *Lt.-Gen.* Aleksandr Nikolayevich **Dubensky**
- 13 Nov 1896 - 2 Aug 1903: *Maj.-Gen.* Vladimir Aleksandrovich **Pakhalen**
- 4 Sep 1903 - 14 Dec 1904: *Lt.-Gen.* Nikolai Aleksandrovich **Zarubin**
- 14 Jan 1905 - 7 May 1910: *Lt.-Gen.* Vasily Pavlovich **Debogory-Mokriyevich**
- 7 May 1910 - 23 Mar 1914: *Gen. of Cav.* Leonid Nikolayevich **Velyashev**
- 23 Mar 1914 - 9 May 1917: *Maj.-Gen.* Aleksandr Vladimirovich **Monomakhov**

Commander, 2nd Brigade, 11th Cavalry Division
- 17 Aug 1892 - Mar 1901: *Maj.-Gen.* Nikolai Pavlovich **Nazimov**
- 26 Mar 1901 - 1 Nov 1902: *Gen. of Cav.* Afanasy Andreyevich **Tsurikov**
- 19 Dec 1902 - 3 Apr 1907: *Lt.-Gen.* Vladimir Andreyevich **Tsurikov**
- 28 May 1907 - Nov 1907: *Maj.-Gen.* Pavel Pavlovich **Voronov**
- 1 Dec 1907 - 7 May 1910: *Gen. of Cav.* Leonid Nikolayevich **Velyashev**
- 2 Jun 1910 - 6 Dec 1912: *Gen. of Cav.* Aleksei Maksimovich **Kaledin**
- 10 Jan 1913 - 3 Nov 1915: *Lt.-Gen.* Georgy Petrovich **Rozalion-Soshalsky**
- 20 Nov 1915 - 14 Aug 1916: *Maj.-Gen.* Aleksandr Sergeyevich **Danilov**
- 14 Aug 1916 - 2 Mar 1917: ?

Commander, 12th Cavalry Division
- 19 Jul 1886 - 23 Jul 1896: *Gen. of Cav.* Aleksandr Mikhailovich **Lermantov**
- 23 Jul 1896 - 11 Sep 1896: ?

- 11 Sep 1896 - 10 Nov 1898: *Lt.-Gen.* David Ivanovich **Orlov**
- 17 Dec 1898 - 13 Jan 1899: *Gen. of Cav.* Prince Sergei Illarionovich **Vasilchikov**
- 18 Feb 1899 - 26 Apr 1900: *Gen. of Cav.* Konstantin Pavlovich **De-Vitte**
- 26 Apr 1900 - 12 Jan 1905: *Gen. of Cav.* Yevgeny Ottovich **Shmit**
- 12 Jan 1905 - 7 Mar 1905: ?
- 7 Mar 1905 - 12 Jan 1907: *Lt.-Gen.* Aleksandr Aleksandrovich **Benkendorf**
- 12 Jan 1907 - 1 May 1910: *Gen. of Cav.* Vladislav Ksaveryevich **Topchevsky**
- 1 May 1910 - 6 Dec 1912: *Lt.-Gen.* Aleksandr Konstantinovich **Rutkovsky**
- 6 Dec 1912 - 18 Jun 1915: *Gen. of Cav.* Aleksei Maksimovich **Kaledin**
- 24 Jun 1915 - 31 May 1917: *Lt.-Gen.* Baron Karl Karlovich **Mannerheim**

Commander, 1st Brigade, 12th Cavalry Division
- 6 Sep 1891 - Dec 1896: *Maj.-Gen.* Mikhail Yefremovich **Adamovich**
- 28 Dec 1896 - 7 Mar 1905: *Lt.-Gen.* Aleksandr Aleksandrovich **Benkendorf**
- 7 Mar 1905 - 20 May 1905: ?
- 20 May 1905 - 9 Nov 1911: *Lt.-Gen.* Mikhail Grigoryevich **Yakovlev**
- 9 Nov 1911 - 8 Sep 1913: *Maj.-Gen.* Nikolai Konstantinovich **Benua**
- 8 Sep 1913 - 17 Jun 1916: *Maj.-Gen.* Boris Aleksandrovich **Kuzmin-Korovayev**
- 17 Jun 1916 - 23 Aug 1916: ?
- 23 Aug 1916 - 14 Oct 1917: *Maj.-Gen.* Grigory Grigoryevich **Chertkov**

Commander, 2nd Brigade, 12th Cavalry Division
- 11 Mar 1892 - 2 Oct 1895: *Maj.-Gen.* Aleksandr Petrovich **Dobromyslov**
- 18 Oct 1895 - 23 Jul 1896: *Lt.-Gen.* Aleksandr Nikolayevich **Ovodov**
- 19 Aug 1896 - 28 Dec 1896: *Lt.-Gen.* Aleksandr Aleksandrovich **Benkendorf**
- 28 Dec 1896 - 20 Jun 1900: *Lt.-Gen.* Andrey Petrovich **Znachko-Yavorsky**
- 21 Jun 1900 - 1 Nov 1900: *Lt.-Gen.* Nikolai Aleksandrovich **Kovalkov**
- 1 Nov 1900 - 14 Apr 1901: *Lt.-Gen.* Fyodor Semonovich **Verba**
- 7 May 1901 - 30 Apr 1910: *Gen. of Cav.* Yevgeny Zakharovich **Korbut**
- 2 Jun 1910 - 10 Dec 1910: *Maj.-Gen.* Aleksandr Petrovich **Arakantsev**
- 1 Jan 1911 - 9 Nov 1911: *Maj.-Gen.* Ignaty Oktavievich **Balinsky**
- 9 Nov 1911 - 30 Aug 1912: *Lt.-Gen.* Mikhail Grigoryevich **Yakovlev**
- 30 Aug 1912 - 8 Sep 1913: *Maj.-Gen.* Boris Aleksandrovich **Kuzmin-Korovayev**
- 8 Sep 1913 - 28 Feb 1916: *Maj.-Gen.* Vladislav Ignatyevich **Frankovsky**
- 28 Feb 1916 - 7 Sep 1917: *Maj.-Gen.* Gervasy Petrovich **Zhukov**

Commander, 13th Cavalry Division
- 24 Nov 1886 - 25 Apr 1897: *Gen. of Cav.* Baron Nikolai Yegorovich **Meyendorf**
- 4 May 1897 - 22 May 1903: *Gen. of Cav.* Aleksandr Yakovlevich von **Tal**
- 9 Jun 1903 - 11 Mar 1904: *Gen. of Cav.* Nikolai Vasilyevich **Shutlevort**
- 11 Mar 1904 - 22 May 1904: ?
- 22 May 1904 - 23 May 1907: *Lt.-Gen.* Yevgeny Aleksandrovich **Sykalov**
- 23 May 1907 - 1 May 1910: *Gen. of Cav.* Baron Nikolai Vasilyevich von der **Ropp**
- 1 May 1910 - 8 Mar 1916: *Gen. of Cav.* Prince Georgy Aleksandrovich **Tumanov**
- 13 Mar 1916 - 22 Apr 1917: *Maj.-Gen.* Nikolai Ivanovich **Chaykovsky**

Commander, 1st Brigade, 13th Cavalry Division
- 30 Jul 1891 - 1 Dec 1899: *Lt.-Gen.* Nikolai Zinovyevich **Likhtansky**
- 25 Jan 1900 - 10 Jan 1905: *Lt.-Gen.* Dmitry Viktorovich **Kryzhanovsky**
- 15 Jan 1905 - Jul 1908: *Maj.-Gen.* Aleksey-Ebert Karlovich von **Kruzenshtern**
- 4 Aug 1908 - 12 May 1910: *Lt.-Gen.* Prince Pyotr Nikolayevich **Myshetsky**
- 12 May 1910 - 17 Sep 1912: *Lt.-Gen.* Yevgeny Alekseyevich **Panchulidzev**
- 17 Sep 1912 - 7 Jan 1916: *Maj.-Gen.* Viktor Platonovich von **Krug**
- 7 Jan 1916 - 11 Mar 1917: *Maj.-Gen.* Iosif Iosifovich **Vivyen-de-Shatobren**

Commander, 2nd Brigade, 13th Cavalry Division
- 6 Nov 1891 - 11 Jun 1895: *Gen. of Cav.* Prince David Evstafiyevich **Eristov**
- 28 Jun 1895 - 20 Jan 1901: *Lt.-Gen.* Nikolai Karlovich **Klaver**
- 20 Jan 1901 - 26 Mar 1901: ?
- 26 Mar 1901 - 8 Feb 1903: *Gen. of Cav.* Baron Nikolai Vasilyevich von der **Ropp**
- 8 Feb 1903 - 23 Mar 1904: ?
- 23 Mar 1904 - 13 Nov 1904: *Gen. of Cav.* Aleksandr Rudolfovich **Eykhgolts**
- 2 Dec 1904 - 4 Aug 1908: *Lt.-Gen.* Prince Pyotr Nikolayevich **Myshetsky**
- 4 Aug 1908 - 19 Jul 1914: *Lt.-Gen.* Gleb Mikhailovich **Vannovsky**
- 19 Jul 1914 - 25 Jun 1915: ?
- 25 Jun 1915 - 2 Jul 1915: *Maj.-Gen.* Sergey Pavlovich **Tovarishchev**
- 2 Jul 1915 - 6 Apr 1916: ?
- 6 Apr 1916 - 26 Jun 1916: *Maj.-Gen.* Aleksandr Frantsevich **Yarminsky**
- 26 Jun 1916 - 17 Dec 1916: *Maj.-Gen.* Pyotr Ivanovich **Zalessky**
- 4 Jan 1917 - Oct 1917: *Maj.-Gen.* Aleksandr Frantsevich **Yarminsky**

Commander, 14th Cavalry Division
- 27 Jul 1891 - 20 Mar 1895: *Lt.-Gen.* Count Georgy Fyodorovich **Mengden**
- 4 Apr 1895 - 11 Aug 1900: *Gen. of Cav.* Nikolai Mikhailovich **Vonlyarlyarsky**
- 13 Oct 1900 - Dec 1905: *Lt.-Gen.* Fyodor Nilovich **Bobylev**
- 27 Jan 1906 - 7 Jul 1907: *Gen. of Cav.* Yakov Grigoryevich **Zhilinsky**
- 7 Jul 1907 - 3 Sep 1907: ?
- 3 Sep 1907 - 1 May 1910: *Gen. of Cav.* Pyotr Robertovich von **Nettelgorst**
- 1 May 1910 - 23 Aug 1913: *Gen. of Cav.* Vladimir Aloiziyevich **Oranovsky**
- 8 Oct 1913 - 13 Oct 1914: *Lt.-Gen.* Aleksandr Vasilyevich **Novikov**
- 18 Oct 1914 - 13 May 1915: *Lt.-Gen.* Ivan Georgiyevich **Erdeli**
- 13 May 1915 - 4 Feb 1916: *Maj.-Gen.* Vladimir Nikolayevich **Peters**
- 4 Feb 1916 - 5 Apr 1917: *Lt.-Gen.* Anton Aleksandrovich **Tolpygo**

Commander, 1st Brigade, 14th Cavalry Division
- 12 Jul 1882 - 3 Dec 1894: *Lt.-Gen.* Mitrofan Alekseyevich **Velyaminov-Zernov**
- 15 Dec 1894 - 13 Oct 1900: *Lt.-Gen.* Fyodor Nilovich **Bobylev**
- 1 Nov 1900 - Oct 1907: *Lt.-Gen.* Nikolai Aleksandrovich **Kovalkov**
- 3 Oct 1907 - 21 May 1912: *Lt.-Gen.* Vladimir Karlovich **Belgardt**
- 21 May 1912 - 2 Aug 1914: *Maj.-Gen.* Nikolai Ivanovich **Chaykovsky**
- 16 Aug 1914 - 7 Sep 1914: *Lt.-Gen.* Fyodor Vasilyevich **Rubets-Masalsky**

- 7 Sep 1914 - 28 Jan 1915: *Maj.-Gen.* Nikolai Ivanovich **Chaykovsky**
- 28 Jan 1915 - 18 May 1915: ?
- 18 May 1915 - 24 Jun 1915: *Maj.-Gen.* Mikhail Mikhailovich **Makhov**
- 26 Jul 1915 - 14 Apr 1917: *Maj.-Gen.* Mikhail Pavlovich **Perevoshchikov**

Commander, 2nd Brigade, 14th Cavalry Division
- 21 Sep 1891 - 11 Sep 1895: *Maj.-Gen.* Fyodor Nikolayevich von **Kridener**
- 25 Sep 1895 - 9 Aug 1897: *Lt.-Gen.* Baron Aleksandr Nikolayevich **Bistrom**
- 23 Aug 1897 - 2 Jul 1898: *Lt.-Gen.* Aleksandr Leontievich **Garnak**
- 2 Jul 1898 - 25 Jan 1900: ?
- 25 Jan 1900 - Feb 1904: *Maj.-Gen.* Leonid Fyodorovich **Baumgarten**
- 23 Feb 1904 - 17 Jul 1912: *Lt.-Gen.* Nikolai Patrikeyevich **Martynov**
- 17 Jul 1912 - 19 Jul 1914: *Lt.-Gen.* Mikhail Grigoryevich **Mikheyev**
- 19 Jul 1914 - 2 Dec 1914: ?
- 2 Dec 1914 - 29 Jul 1915: *Maj.-Gen.* Aleksei Georgievich von **Byunting**
- 29 Jul 1915 - Dec 1915: ?
- Dec 1915 - 1917: *Maj.-Gen.* Aleksandr Alekseyevich **Karneyev**

Commander, 15th Cavalry Division
- 23 Jul 1891 - 28 Nov 1897: *Gen. of Cav.* Aleksandr Vasiliyevich von **Kaulbars**
- 3 Dec 1897 - 31 May 1899: *Gen. of Cav.* Georgy Karlovich von **Shtakelberg**
- 17 Jun 1899 - 14 Jan 1907: *Gen. of Cav.* Erast Ksenofontovich **Kvitnitsky**
- 18 Jan 1907 - 8 Mar 1907: *Gen. of Cav.* Afanasy Andreyevich **Tsurikov**
- 8 Mar 1907 - 1 May 1910: *Lt.-Gen.* Nikolai Georgiyevich **Papa-Afanasopulo**
- 1 May 1910 - 29 Jul 1915: *Lt.-Gen.* Pavel Petrovich **Lyubomirov**
- 29 Jul 1915 - 12 Sep 1915: *Maj.-Gen.* Aleksei Georgievich von **Byunting**
- 12 Sep 1915 - 21 Nov 1916: *Maj.-Gen.* Fyodor Fyodorovich **Abramov**
- 8 Dec 1916 - 1918: *Lt.-Gen.* Anatoly Ivanovich **Martynov**

Commander, 1st Brigade, 15th Cavalry Division
- 14 Apr 1894 - Jun 1896: *Maj.-Gen.* Baron Aleksandr Karlovich **Korf**
- 11 Jun 1896 - 11 Aug 1896: *Lt.-Gen.* Aleksandr Nikolayevich **Nikolayev**
- 19 Aug 1896 - 22 May 1904: *Lt.-Gen.* Yevgeny Aleksandrovich **Sykalov**
- 18 Jun 1904 - 29 Jan 1913: *Lt.-Gen.* Vladimir Ivanovich **Kotsurik**
- 29 Jan 1913 - 30 Mar 1915: *Lt.-Gen.* Pyotr Nikolayevich **Ryzhov**
- 30 Mar 1915 - 22 Oct 1915: *Lt.-Gen.* Pyotr Pavlovich **Kanshin**
- 3 Nov 1915 - 1917: *Maj.-Gen.* Konstantin Vasilyevich **Zheltukhin**

Commander, 2nd Brigade, 15th Cavalry Division
- 23 Jul 1891 - 18 Mar 1897: *Gen. of Inf.* Pyotr Nikolayevich **Bazhenov**
- 28 Mar 1897 - 18 Sep 1900: *Gen. of Cav.* Ippolit Apollonovich **Pozdeyev**
- 1 Nov 1900 - 20 Jul 1904: *Maj.-Gen.* Mikhail Nikolayevich **Teleshev**
- 20 Jul 1904 - 9 Sep 1904: ?
- 9 Sep 1904 - 6 Feb 1907: *Maj.-Gen.* Aleksandr Aleksandrovich Baron von der **Osten-Driesen**

- 6 Feb 1907 - 7 Apr 1907: *Lt.-Gen.* Ippolit Alekseyevich **Yeropkin**
- 22 Apr 1907 - 18 Aug 1912: *Lt.-Gen.* Mikhail Anzelmovich **Lyshchinsky**
- 18 Aug 1912 - 2 Dec 1914: *Maj.-Gen.* Aleksei Georgievich von **Byunting**
- 2 Dec 1914 - 1915: *Maj.-Gen.* Sergey Frantsevich **Foss**
- 1915 - 4 Jul 1916: ?
- 4 Jul 1916 - 1918: *Maj.-Gen.* Sergey Lvovich **Gamzagurdi**

Commander, 16th Cavalry Division *(Formed in 1914)*
- 12 Dec 1914 - 6 Apr 1915: *Gen. of Cav.* Abram Mikhailovich **Dragomirov**
- 26 Apr 1915 - Apr 1917: *Lt.-Gen.* Nikolai Gerasimovich **Volodchenko**

Commander, 1st Brigade, 16th Cavalry Division
- 19 Jan 1915 - 4 Mar 1915: *Maj.-Gen.* Nikolai Sergeyevich **Blokhin**
- 4 Mar 1915 - 17 Oct 1915: *Maj.-Gen.* Pyotr Iosafovich **Sukovkin**
- 17 Oct 1915 - 2 Feb 1916: *Maj.-Gen.* Aleksandr Ivanovich **Linitsky**
- 2 Feb 1916 - 1 Oct 1916: ?
- 1 Oct 1916 - 1917: *Maj.-Gen.* Count Pyotr Mikhailovich **Stenbok**

Commander, 2nd Brigade, 16th Cavalry Division
- 6 Jan 1915 - 1917: *Maj.-Gen.* Vyacheslav Aleksandrovich **Konstantinov**

Commander, Caucasus Cavalry Division
- 16 Jan 1893 - 18 Apr 1895: *Gen. of Cav.* Ivan Fyodorovich **Tutolmin**
- 10 May 1895 - Dec 1896: *Maj.-Gen.* Yefim Yefimovich **Rynkevich**
- 19 Jan 1897 - 2 Jul 1902: *Lt.-Gen.* Vladimir Nikolayevich **Ivashkin**
- 2 Jul 1902 - 3 Mar 1906: *Lt.-Gen.* Prince Lyudovik Karlovich **Lyudovik-Napoleon**
- 15 Mar 1906 - 22 Dec 1910: *Gen. of Cav.* Nikolai Artemyevich **Villamov**
- 22 Dec 1910 - 29 Dec 1915: *Lt.-Gen.* Klaas Robertovich **Charpentier**
- 29 Dec 1915 - 15 Apr 1917: *Lt.-Gen.* Prince Sergey Konstantinich **Beloselsky-Belozersky**

Commander, 1st Brigade, Caucasus Cavalry Division
- 20 Apr 1893 - 20 May 1896: *Maj.-Gen.* Georgy Stepanovich **Yermolin**
- 17 Jun 1896 - 19 May 1898: *Gen. of Cav.* Pavel Aleksandrovich **Kozlovsky**
- 19 May 1898 - 1 Jan 1907: *Maj.-Gen.* Vladimir Nikolayevich **Goloshchapov**
- 1 Jan 1907 - 22 Jun 1907: ?
- 22 Jun 1907 - 14 Jun 1910: *Lt.-Gen.* Vladimir Aleksandrovich **Kartsov**
- 14 Jun 1910 - 25 Feb 1912: *Gen. of Cav.* Count Fyodor Arturovich **Keller**
- 25 Feb 1912 - 21 May 1912: ?
- 21 May 1912 - 8 Jun 1912: *Lt.-Gen.* Yakov Fyodorovich von **Gillenshmidt**
- 6 Jul 1912 - 21 Aug 1915: *Maj.-Gen.* Iosif Iosifovich **Vivyen-de-Shatobren**
- 21 Aug 1915 - 1917: *Maj.-Gen.* Nikolai Nikolayevich **Kopachev**

Commander, 2ⁿᵈ Brigade, Caucasus Cavalry Division
- 20 Oct 1894 - 20 Feb 1895: ?
- 20 Feb 1895 - Nov 1901: *Maj.-Gen.* Vasily Andreyevich **Nudzhevsky**
- 2 Dec 1901 - 4 Jun 1904: *Lt.-Gen.* Konstantin Aleksandrovich **Nazarov**
- 18 Jun 1904 - 9 Feb 1914: *Lt.-Gen.* Aleksandr Nikolayevich **Gorchakov**
- 2 Apr 1914 - 20 Aug 1916: *Maj.-Gen.* Iosif Lukich **Isarlov**
- 1 Sep 1916 - 1918: *Maj.-Gen.* Eduard Oskarovich **Kharten**

Commander, Consolidated Cavalry Division *(Formed in 1897)*
- 28 Nov 1897 - 18 Feb 1904: *Gen. of Cav.* Nikolai Stepanovich **Khrulev**
- 18 Feb 1904 - 22 Nov 1908: *Gen. of Cav.* Anton Vasilyevich **Novosiltsov**
- 1908 - 1915: DISSOLVED
- 1 Jul 1915 - 25 Apr 1917: *Lt.-Gen.* Prince Nikolai Petrovich **Vadbolsky**

Commander, 1ˢᵗ Brigade, Consolidated Cavalry Division
- 1897 - 1908: ?
- 1908 - 1915: DISSOLVED
- 1915 - 2 Mar 1917: ?

Commander, 2ⁿᵈ Brigade, Consolidated Cavalry Division
- 1897 - 1908: ?
- 1908 - 1915: DISSOLVED
- 1915 - 2 Mar 1917: ?

Commander, 3ʳᵈ Brigade, Consolidated Cavalry Division
- 28 Nov 1897 - 10 Feb 1899: *Gen. of Cav.* Leonty Nikolayevich von **Baumgarten**
- 23 Feb 1899 - 15 Mar 1906: *Gen. of Cav.* Nikolai Artemyevich **Villamov**
- 1906: DISSOLVED

Commander, 2ⁿᵈ Consolidated Cossack Division
- 10 Mar 1893 - 13 Jun 1899: *Gen. of Cav.* Rostislav Aleksandrovich **Khreshchatitsky**
- 28 Jul 1899 - 14 Sep 1904: *Gen. of Cav.* Aleksey Ivanovich **Domantovich**
- 13 Oct 1904 - Oct 1906: *Lt.-Gen.* Aleksey Seliverstovich **Melyanin**
- 14 Oct 1906 - Nov 1907: *Lt.-Gen.* Mikhail Pavlovich **Stoyanov**
- 19 Nov 1907 - 14 Sep 1911: *Gen. of Cav.* Nikolai Vasilievich **Avdeyev**
- 14 Sep 1911 - 31 Dec 1913: *Gen. of Cav.* Aleksey Viktorovich **Rodionov**
- 31 Dec 1913 - 24 Sep 1914: *Lt.-Gen.* Leonid Ivanovich **Zhigalin**
- 24 Sep 1914 - 10 Sep 1915: *Lt.-Gen.* Aleksandr Aleksandrovich **Pavlov**
- 10 Sep 1915 - 4 May 1917: *Maj.-Gen.* Pyotr Nikolayevich **Krasnov**

Commander, 1ˢᵗ Brigade, 2ⁿᵈ Consolidated Cossack Division
- 23 Mar 1889 - 15 Jan 1901: *Lt.-Gen.* Varlaam Aleksandrovich **Denisov**
- 29 Mar 1901 - 20 Jul 1904: *Lt.-Gen.* Mikhail Pavlovich **Stoyanov**
- 29 Jul 1904 - 20 Jan 1906: ?

- 20 Jan 1906 - 19 Jun 1908: *Maj.-Gen.* Pyotr Petrovich **Grekov**
- 19 Jun 1908 - 6 Jan 1913: *Lt.-Gen.* Vasily Ivanovich **Filenkov**
- 6 Jan 1913 - 27 Aug 1913: *Maj.-Gen.* Sergey Aleksandrovich **Platov**
- 27 Aug 1913 - 21 Jul 1917: *Lt.-Gen.* Pyotr Lukich **Guslavsky**

Commander, 2nd Brigade, 2nd Consolidated Cossack Division
- 23 Mar 1894 - 18 May 1898: *Gen. of Cav.* Aleksey Ivanovich **Domantovich**
- 31 Jul 1898 - 12 Apr 1903: *Maj.-Gen.* Nikolai Grigoryevich **Vysheslavtsev**
- 28 May 1903 - 8 Aug 1906: *Gen. of Cav.* Pyotr Petrovich **Kalitin**
- 31 Aug 1906 - 18 Jul 1907: *Maj.-Gen.* Grigory Nikitich **Milashevich**
- 23 Jul 1907 - 16 Mar 1913: *Lt.-Gen.* Vasily Andreyevich **Akulov**
- 24 Apr 1913 - 24 May 1914: *Maj.-Gen.* Pavel Yakovlevich **Yagodkin**
- 6 Jun 1914 - 27 Aug 1914: *Maj.-Gen.* Vasily Ivanovich **Goloshchapov**
- 27 Aug 1914 - 14 Nov 1914: ?
- 14 Nov 1914 - 29 Apr 1917: *Maj.-Gen.* Nikolai Sergeyevich **Plautin**

Commander, 1st Caucasus Cossack Division
- 31 Jul 1893 - 20 Apr 1898: *Gen. of Cav.* Stepan Mironovich **Prozorkevich**
- 18 May 1898 - 28 Jul 1899: *Gen. of Cav.* Aleksey Ivanovich **Domantovich**
- 19 Aug 1899 - 14 Mar 1903: *Lt.-Gen.* Nikolai Modestovich **Yagodin**
- 12 Apr 1903 - 11 Jun 1906: *Maj.-Gen.* Nikolai Grigoryevich **Vysheslavtsev**
- 11 Jun 1906 - Oct 1908: *Lt.-Gen.* Inal Tegoyevich **Kusov**
- 24 Oct 1908 - Nov 1912: *Lt.-Gen.* Nikolai Ivanovich **Mikhailov**
- 26 Nov 1912 - 28 Apr 1916: *Gen. of Cav.* Nikolai Nikolayevich **Baratov**
- 25 May 1916 - 1918: *Lt.-Gen.* Ernest-Avgust Ferdinandovich **Raddats**

Commander, 1st Brigade, 1st Caucasus Cossack Division
- 7 Apr 1894 - 27 Feb 1898: *Maj.-Gen.* Vasily Sidorovich **Zhukov**
- 27 Feb 1898 - 14 Jul 1900: *Maj.-Gen.* Erast Grigoryevich **Zborovsky**
- 14 Jul 1900 - 3 Nov 1900: ?
- 3 Nov 1900 - 11 Jun 1906: *Lt.-Gen.* Inal Tegoyevich **Kusov**
- 19 Jul 1906 - 15 Mar 1911: *Lt.-Gen.* Aleksandr Petrovich **Logvinov**
- 13 May 1911 - Jun 1915: *Lt.-Gen.* Zaurbek Dzhambulatovich **Turgiyev**
- 4 Jul 1915 - 29 Feb 1916: *Maj.-Gen.* Mikhail Georgiyevich **Fisenko**
- 29 Feb 1916 - 5 May 1916: ?
- 5 May 1916 - 1 Jul 1916: *Colonel* Aleksandr Vasilyevich **Perepelovsky**
- 1 Jul 1916 - 1918: *Colonel* Nikolai Kosmich **Fedyushkin**

Commander, 2nd Brigade, 1st Caucasus Cossack Division
- 3 Aug 1891 - Dec 1899: *Lt.-Gen.* Anton Filippovich **Pedin**
- 10 Jan 1900 - 31 Oct 1900: *Maj.-Gen.* Ali Davletovich **Sheikhaliev**
- 16 Feb 1901 - Dec 1906: *Maj.-Gen.* Ivan Rodionovich **Yeglevsky**
- 6 Jan 1907 - 9 Oct 1912: *Lieutenant-General* Dmitry Konstantinovich **Abatsiev**
- 5 Nov 1912 - 29 Jul 1914: *Lt.-Gen.* Tigran Danilovich **Aryutinov**
- 29 Jul 1914 - May 1915: ?

- May 1915 - 1 Jul 1916: *Maj.-Gen.* Aleksandr Ferdinandovich **Rafalovich**
- 1 Jul 1916 - 2 Mar 1917: ?

Commander, 2nd Caucasus Cossack Division
- 14 Jan 1893 - 16 Nov 1895: *Lt.-Gen.* Ilya Ivanovich **Safonov**
- 16 Nov 1895 - 15 Jan 1899: *Lt.-Gen.* Sergey Nikolayevich **Panin**
- 15 Jan 1899 - 18 Jul 1905: *Gen. of Cav.* Prince Ivan Makarovich **Dzhambakurian-Orbeliani**
- 2 Sep 1905 - Nov 1906: *Maj.-Gen.* Konstantin Maksimovich **Shvedov**
- 28 Nov 1906 - 3 Jul 1907: *Lt.-Gen.* Maksud **Alikhanov-Avarsky**
- 3 Aug 1907 - 1 May 1910: *Gen. of Cav.* Lyudomir Aleksandrovich **Rzhevusky**
- 22 Jun 1910 - 16 Sep 1912: *Gen. of Cav.* Sergey Nikolayevich **Fleysher**
- 9 Oct 1912 - 14 Jun 1916: *Lieutenant-General* Dmitry Konstantinovich **Abatsiev**
- Jul 1916 - 1917: *Lt.-Gen.* Aleksandr Parfentyevich **Kulebyakin**

Commander, 1st Brigade, 2nd Caucasus Cossack Division
- 1 Mar 1893 - 12 Sep 1897: *Maj.-Gen.* Pyotr Vladimirovich **Charkovsky**
- 24 Oct 1897 - 15 Jan 1899: *Gen. of Cav.* Prince Ivan Makarovich **Dzhambakurian-Orbeliani**
- 15 Jan 1899 - 2 Apr 1899: ?
- 2 Apr 1899 - 18 Jun 1899: *Lt.-Gen.* Pyotr Ivanovich **Kosyakin**
- 18 Jun 1899 - 27 Oct 1899: ?
- 27 Oct 1899 - Nov 1900: *Maj.-Gen.* Konstantin Maksimovich **Shvedov**
- Nov 1900 - 16 Feb 1901: *Gen. of Cav.* Sergey Nikolayevich **Fleysher**
- 16 Feb 1901 - 2 Sep 1905: *Maj.-Gen.* Konstantin Maksimovich **Shvedov**
- 2 Sep 1905 - 2 Nov 1905: ?
- 2 Nov 1905 - 22 May 1910: *Lt.-Gen.* Aleksandr Alekseyevich **Gramotin**
- 22 May 1910 - 23 Jul 1910: ?
- 23 Jul 1910 - 31 Dec 1913: *Lt.-Gen.* Konstantin Nikitich **Stoyanovsky**
- 9 Jan 1914 - 20 Jan 1916: *Maj.-Gen.* Aleksandr Leontyevich **Pevnev**
- 14 Feb 1916 - 1917: *Lt.-Gen.* Elbert Asmurziyevich **Nalgiyev**

Commander, 2nd Brigade, 2nd Caucasus Cossack Division
- 26 Feb 1894 - Feb 1896: *Maj.-Gen.* Aleksandr Frantsevich **Klyuki von Klugenau**
- 28 Feb 1896 - 31 Oct 1900: *Gen. of Cav.* Vasily Nikolayevich **Vasilchikov**
- 31 Oct 1900 - 16 Feb 1901: ?
- 16 Feb 1901 - 22 Jun 1910: *Gen. of Cav.* Sergey Nikolayevich **Fleysher**
- 23 Jul 1910 - 2 Aug 1913: *Lt.-Gen.* Afako Patsiyevich **Fidarov**
- 14 Aug 1913 - 4 Jun 1915: *Maj.-Gen.* Malakhy Kvadzhiyevich **Marganiya**
- 4 Jun 1915 - 21 Jan 1917: *Maj.-Gen.* Aleksandr Vasilyevich **Potto**
- 21 Jan 1917 - 2 Mar 1917: ?

Commander, 3rd Caucasus Cossack Division *(Formed in 1910)*
- 5 Jul 1910 - 16 Apr 1917: *Gen. of Cav.* Pavel Lyudvigovich **Khelmitsky**

Commander, 1st Brigade, 3rd Caucasus Cossack Division
- 22 Jul 1910 - 19 Jul 1914: *Maj.-Gen.* Nikolai Ivanovich **Fisenko**
- 19 Jul 1914 - 4 Jun 1915: ?
- 4 Jun 1915 - 30 Oct 1916: *Maj.-Gen.* Malakhy Kvadzhiyevich **Marganiya**
- 10 Dec 1916 - 1918: *Maj.-Gen.* Safar-Bey Tausultanovich **Malsagov**

Commander, 2nd Brigade, 3rd Caucasus Cossack Division
- 22 Jul 1910 - 26 Jun 1913: *Maj.-Gen.* Andrey Onisimovich **Mayboroda**
- 26 Jun 1913 - 27 Aug 1913: ?
- 27 Aug 1913 - 25 Aug 1916: *Maj.-Gen.* Fyodor Petrovich **Filimonov**
- 25 Aug 1916 - Mar 1917: ?

Commander, 4th Caucasus Cossack Division *(Formed in 1915)*
- 1 Apr 1915 - 4 Jul 1916: *Lt.-Gen.* Fyodor Grigoryevich **Chernozubov**
- 25 Aug 1916 - 1918: *Maj.-Gen.* Fyodor Petrovich **Filimonov**

Commander, 1st Brigade, 4th Caucasus Cossack Division
- 4 Jun 1915 - 24 Jan 1917: *Maj.-Gen.* Aleksandr Grigoryevich **Rybalchenko**
- 24 Jan 1917 - 2 Mar 1917: ?

Commander, 2nd Brigade, 4th Caucasus Cossack Division
- 4 Jun 1915 - Jul 1916: *Lt.-Gen.* Aleksandr Parfentyevich **Kulebyakin**
- Jul 1916 - 2 Mar 1917: ?

Commander, 5th Caucasus Cossack Division *(Formed in 1915)*
- 14 Nov 1915 - 15 Nov 1916: *Lt.-Gen.* Andrey Mikhailovich **Nikolayev**
- 15 Nov 1916 - 2 Sep 1917: *Lt.-Gen.* Sergey Vladimirovich **Tomashevsky**

Commander, 1st Brigade, 5th Caucasus Cossack Division
- 1915 - 31 Aug 1916: ?
- 31 Aug 1916 - 1917: *Maj.-Gen.* Pyotr Grigoryevich **Filippov**

Commander, 2nd Brigade, 5th Caucasus Cossack Division
- 1915 - 8 Feb 1916: ?
- 8 Feb 1916 - 26 Sep 1917: *Maj.-Gen.* Ivan Nikiforovich **Kolesnikov**

Commander, 1st Don Cossack Division
- 9 Dec 1893 - 20 Aug 1898: *Gen. of Cav.* Mitrofan Ilyich **Grekov**
- 20 Aug 1898 - 10 Nov 1898: ?
- 10 Nov 1898 - 5 Aug 1900: *Lt.-Gen.* David Ivanovich **Orlov**
- 18 Sep 1900 - Apr 1907: *Gen. of Cav.* Ippolit Apollonovich **Pozdeyev**

- 3 Apr 1907 - Jul 1914: *Gen. of Cav.* Aleksei Livovich **Vershinin**
- 18 Jul 1914 - 15 Aug 1914: *Lt.-Gen.* Aglay Dmitriyevich **Kuzmin-Korovayev**
- 15 Aug 1914 - 20 May 1916: *Lt.-Gen.* Grigory Ivanovich **Choglokov**
- 13 Jun 1916 - 1917: *Maj.-Gen.* Pyotr Ivanovich **Grekov**

Commander, 1st Brigade, 1st Don Cossack Division
- 22 Jan 1894 - 24 Jan 1900: *Maj.-Gen.* Nikolai Matveyevich **Kalinin**
- 24 Jan 1900 - 9 Mar 1900: ?
- 9 Mar 1900 - 25 Nov 1904: *Lt.-Gen.* Nikolai Petrovich **Ilovaysky**
- 7 Dec 1904 - 20 Jan 1906: *Maj.-Gen.* Pyotr Petrovich **Grekov**
- 20 Jan 1906 - 18 May 1906: ?
- 18 May 1906 - 17 Jan 1910: *Lt.-Gen.* Fyodor Fyodorovich **Abramov**
- 17 Feb 1910 - Jul 1911: *Maj.-Gen.* Nikolai Yakovlevich **Dyakov**
- 12 Jul 1911 - 11 Sep 1913: *Maj.-Gen.* Ivan Ivanovich **Kamennov**
- 11 Sep 1913 - 9 Nov 1913: *Maj.-Gen.* Nikandr Arkadyevich **Lashchilin**
- 18 Dec 1913 - 15 Feb 1915: *Lt.-Gen.* Yefim Fedorovich **Kunakov**
- 15 Feb 1915 - 2 Mar 1917: ?

Commander, 2nd Brigade, 1st Don Cossack Division
- 26 Oct 1890 - 19 Aug 1899: *Lt.-Gen.* Nikolai Modestovich **Yagodin**
- 20 Nov 1899 - 12 Jun 1904: *Lt.-Gen.* Ivan Andreyevich **Luizov**
- 25 Jun 1904 - Dec 1911: *Lt.-Gen.* Stepan Alekseyevich **Boldyrev**
- 14 Jan 1912 - 18 Dec 1913: *Lt.-Gen.* Yefim Fedorovich **Kunakov**
- 18 Dec 1913 - 6 Oct 1914: *Maj.-Gen.* Konstantin Semyonovich **Polyakov**
- 6 Oct 1914 - 13 Jun 1916: *Maj.-Gen.* Pyotr Ivanovich **Grekov**
- 13 Jun 1916 - 9 Sep 1916: ?
- 9 Sep 1916 - 22 Oct 1917: *Maj.-Gen.* Boris Rostislavovich **Khreshchatitsky**

2nd Don Cossack Division
Unit not formed

Commander, 3rd Don Cossack Division *(Formed in 1914)*
- 19 Jul 1914 - 23 Aug 1914: *Maj.-Gen.* Sergei Vladimirovich **Yevreinov**
- 29 Sep 1914 - 11 Oct 1914: *Lt.-Gen.* Yakov Fyodorovich von **Gillenshmidt**
- 10 Nov 1914 - 7 Jul 1915: *Lt.-Gen.* Prince Aleksandr Nikolayevich **Dolgorukov**
- 7 Jul 1915 - 11 Jul 1915: *Maj.-Gen.* Pyotr Nikolayevich **Krasnov**
- 11 Jul 1915 - 29 Dec 1915: *Lt.-Gen.* Prince Sergey Konstantinich **Beloselsky-Belozersky**
- 11 Jan 1916 - 19 Apr 1917: *Lt.-Gen.* Prince Aleksandr Nikolayevich **Dolgorukov**

Commander, 1st Brigade, 3rd Don Cossack Division
- 19 Jul 1914 - 15 Feb 1915: ?
- 15 Feb 1915 - 24 Mar 1917: *Lt.-Gen.* Yefim Fedorovich **Kunakov**

Commander, 2nd Brigade, 3rd Don Cossack Division
- 19 Jul 1914 - 27 Apr 1915: ?
- 27 Apr 1915 - 3 Jun 1916: *Maj.-Gen.* Vasily Maksimovich **Kaledin**
- 3 Jun 1915 - 2 Mar 1917: ?

Commander, 4th Don Cossack Division *(Formed in 1904)*
- 20 Jul 1904 - 11 Aug 1905: *Maj.-Gen.* Mikhail Nikolayevich **Teleshev**
- 2 Sep 1905 - 18 May 1906: *Lt.-Gen.* Mikhail Pavlovich **Stoyanov**
- 1906 - 1914: DISSOLVED
- 19 Jul 1914 - 18 Dec 1914: *Maj.-Gen.* Vladimir Mikhailovich **Khitrovo**
- 24 Jan 1915 - 6 May 1916: *Lt.-Gen.* Count Mikhail Nikolayevich von **Grabbe**
- 3 Jun 1916 - Oct 1917: *Maj.-Gen.* Vasily Maksimovich **Kaledin**

Commander, 1st Brigade, 4th Don Cossack Division
- 20 Jul 1904 - 2 Sep 1905: *Lt.-Gen.* Mikhail Pavlovich **Stoyanov**
- 2 Sep 1905 - 1906: ?
- 1906 - 1914: DISSOLVED
- 19 Jul 1914 - 21 May 1915: ?
- 21 May 1915 - 21 Aug 1915: *Maj.-Gen.* Aleksei Kirillovich **Grekov**
- 21 Aug 1915 - 13 Nov 1915: ?
- 13 Nov 1915 - 28 Aug 1917: *Maj.-Gen.* Vasily Matveyevich **Rodionov**

Commander, 2nd Brigade, 4th Don Cossack Division
- 20 Jul 1904 - 18 May 1906: *Lt.-Gen.* Fyodor Fyodorovich **Abramov**
- 1906 - 1914: DISSOLVED
- 19 Jul 1914 - 2 Mar 1917: ?

Commander, 5th Don Cossack Division *(Formed in 1914)*
- 19 Jul 1914 - 18 Apr 1917: *Lt.-Gen.* Gleb Mikhailovich **Vannovsky**

Commander, 1st Brigade, 5th Don Cossack Division
- 19 Jul 1914 - 6 Oct 1914: ?
- 6 Oct 1914 - 4 May 1917: *Maj.-Gen.* Konstantin Semyonovich **Polyakov**

Commander, 2nd Brigade, 5th Don Cossack Division
- 19 Jul 1914 - 22 Nov 1915: *Lt.-Gen.* Prince Pyotr Nikolayevich **Myshetsky**
- 22 Nov 1915 - 23 Dec 1915: ?
- 23 Dec 1915 - 7 May 1917: *Maj.-Gen.* Kiprian Yakovlevich **Usachev**

Commander, 6th Don Cossack Division *(Formed in 1916)*
- 18 Apr 1916 - Nov 1917: *Lt.-Gen.* Georgy Logginovich **Ponomarev**

Commander, 1st Brigade, 6th Don Cossack Division
- 23 Apr 1916 - 8 Jun 1917: *Maj.-Gen.* Ivan Danilovich **Popov**

Commander, 2nd Brigade, 6th Don Cossack Division
- 5 May 1916 - 31 Dec 1916:   *Maj.-Gen.* Vladimir Nikolayevich **Shishkin**
- 31 Dec 1916 0 2 Mar 1917:   ?

Commander, Trans-Baikal Cossack Division *(Formed in 1915)*
- 22 Dec 1915 - 24 Mar 1917:   *Maj.-Gen.* Ivan Davydovich **Orlov**

Commander, 1st Brigade, Trans-Baikal Cossack Division
- 1 Jan 1916 - 28 Aug 1917:   *Maj.-Gen.* Prince Nikolai Aleksandrovich **Kekuatov**

Commander, 2nd Brigade, Trans-Baikal Cossack Division
- Dec 1915 - 2 Mar 1917:   ?

Commander, 1st Turkestan Cossack Division *(Formed in 1900)*
- 14 Sep 1900 - 5 Jul 1906:   *Gen. of Cav.* Yevgraf Vladimirovich **Shpitsberg**
- 1 Aug 1906 - 18 Jul 1913:   *Gen. of Cav.* Vladimir Pavlovich **Grekov**
- 2 Aug 1913 - Dec 1917:   *Lt.-Gen.* Afako Patsiyevich **Fidarov**

Commander, 1st Brigade, 1st Turkestan Cossack Division
- 14 Sep 1900 - 13 Oct 1904:   *Lt.-Gen.* Aleksey Seliverstovich **Melyanin**
- 13 Oct 1904 - 18 Jul 1905:   ?
- 18 Jul 1905 - 18 Nov 1905:   *Maj.-Gen.* Ilya Petrovich **Dutov**
- 17 Nov 1905 - 30 Jan 1906:   *Lt.-Gen.* Sheikh Il-Islam Abdul-Vaganovich **Kochurov**
- 30 Jan 1906 - 1908:   *Maj.-Gen.* Aleksandr Dmitriyevich **Naumov**
- 1908 - 9 Mar 1910:   ?
- 9 Mar 1910 - 18 Feb 1914:   *Lt.-Gen.* Anastas Fyodorovich **Benderev**
- 16 Mar 1914 - 1917:   *Maj.-Gen.* Aleksandr Matveyevich **Loginov**

Commander, 2nd Brigade, 1st Turkestan Cossack Division
- 14 Sep 1900 - 30 Apr 1905:   *Maj.-Gen.* Pyotr Sergeyevich **Shcherbakov**
- 30 Apr 1905 - 30 Jan 1906:   *Maj.-Gen.* Aleksandr Dmitriyevich **Naumov**
- 30 Jan 1906 - 4 May 1910:   *Lt.-Gen.* Sheikh Il-Islam Abdul-Vaganovich **Kochurov**
- 2 Jun 1910 - 22 Jun 1912:   *Lt.-Gen.* Andrey Mikhailovich **Nikolayev**
- 16 Jul 1912 - 16 Mar 1914:   *Maj.-Gen.* Aleksandr Matveyevich **Loginov**
- 16 Mar 1914 - 2 Aug 1914:   *Maj.-Gen.* Mikhail Apollonovich **Perfilyev**
- 2 Aug 1914 - 2 Mar 1917:   ?

Commander, 2nd Turkestan Cossack Division *(Formed in 1916)*
- 20 May 1916 - 22 Apr 1917:   *Lt.-Gen.* Grigory Ivanovich **Choglokov**

Commander, 1st Brigade, 2nd Turkestan Cossack Division
- 1916 - 2 Mar 1917:   ?

Commander, 2nd Brigade, 2nd Turkestan Cossack Division
- 1916 - 20 Feb 1917: ?
- 20 Feb 1917 - 14 Jun 1917: *Maj.-Gen.* Ivan Andreyevich **Vasiliev**

Commander, Ussuri Mounted Division *(Formed in 1915)*
- 18 Dec 1915 - 23 Jan 1917: *Lt.-Gen.* Aleksandr Mikhailovich **Krymov**
- 23 Jan 1917 - Apr 1917: *Maj.-Gen.* Baron Pyotr Nikolayevich **Vrangel**

Commander, 1st Brigade, Ussuri Mounted Division
- 18 Dec 1915 - 19 Jan 1917: ?
- 19 Jan 1917 - 9 Jul 1917: *Maj.-Gen.* Baron Pyotr Nikolayevich **Vrangel**

Commander, 2nd Brigade, Ussuri Mounted Division
- 18 Dec 1915 - 24 Dec 1916: ?
- 24 Dec 1916 - 19 Jan 1917: *Maj.-Gen.* Baron Pyotr Nikolayevich **Vrangel**
- 19 Jan 1917 - 2 Mar 1917: ?

INDEPENDENT BRIGADES

Commander, Black Sea Infantry Brigade *(Formed in 1915)*
- 17 Dec 1915 - 11 Mar 1916:   *Maj.-Gen.* Sergey Ivanovich **Gavrilov**
- 11 Mar 1916:   UPGRADED TO 100st INFANTRY DIVISION

Commander, Guards Rifle Brigade
- 11 Sep 1889 - 7 Apr 1897:   *Gen. of Inf.* Oskar Kazimirovich von **Grippenberg**
- 7 Apr 1897 - 12 May 1898:   *Lt.-Gen.* Georgy Robertovich **Vasmund**
- 21 May 1898 - 15 Nov 1901:   *Lt.-Gen.* Aleksandr Aleksandrovich **Yevreinov**
- 15 Nov 1901 - 8 Nov 1903:   *Lt.-Gen.* Nikolai Dmitriyevich **Skaryatin**
- 8 Nov 1903 - 7 Jun 1908:   *Lt.-Gen.* Vladimir Mikhailovich **Kasherininov**
- 19 Jun 1908 - 3 May 1910:   *Gen. of Inf.* Leonid Vilhelmovich **Lesh**
- 3 May 1910 - 19 Jan 1913:   *Lt.-Gen.* Aleksandr Alekseyevich **Resin**
- 19 Jan 1913 - 13 Apr 1913:   *Lt.-Gen.* Vladimir Dmitrievich **Bakulin**
- 13 Apr 1913 - 17 Feb 1915:   *Lt.-Gen.* Pyotr Alekseyevich **Delsal**
- 1915:   UPGRADED TO DIVISION

Commander, 1st Rifle Brigade
- 10 Nov 1886 - 2 Jun 1900:   *Gen. of Inf.* Mikhail Khristoforovich **Leo**
- 12 Jul 1900 - 12 Jan 1904:   *Lt.-Gen.* Ivan Venediktovich **Bogayevsky**
- 12 Jan 1904 - 12 Aug 1904:   *Gen. of Inf.* Sergey Ivanovich **Rusanov**
- 12 Aug 1904 - 8 Sep 1904:   *Gen. of Inf.* Aleksandr Prokhorovich **Shevtsov**
- 15 Sep 1904 - 13 Aug 1905:   *Lt.-Gen.* Pavel Kaetanovich **Dombrovsky**
- 1905 - 1906:   UPGRADED TO DIVISION
- 31 Oct 1906 - 24 Mar 1908:   *Gen. of Inf.* Fyodor Nikolayevich **Vasiliev**
- 3 Apr 1908 - 7 Dec 1910:   *Lt.-Gen.* Yevgeny Ivanovich **Martynov**
- 28 Dec 1910 - 27 Sep 1914:   *Lt.-Gen.* Vladimir Mikhailovich **Vasiliev**
- 22 Oct 1914 - 14 Dec 1914:   *Lt.-Gen.* Nikolai Grigoryevich **Filimonov**
- 24 Dec 1914 - 11 Nov 1915:   *Lt.-Gen.* Yevgeny Petrovich **Kartsov**
- 11 Nov 1915 - 27 Jan 1916:   *Lt.-Gen.* Pavel Aristovich von **Kotsebue**
- 27 Jan 1916:   UPGRADED TO DIVISION

Commander, 2nd Rifle Brigade
- 8 Jul 1891 - 1 Mar 1897:   *Lt.-Gen.* Baron Ferdinand Ferdinandovich von **Taube**
- 3 Mar 1897 - 13 Jul 1900:   *Lt.-Gen.* Iosif Ivanovich **Nikolev**
- 13 Jul 1900 - 2 Feb 1904:   *Lt.-Gen.* Konstantin Nikolayevich **Smirnov**
- 17 Feb 1904 - 17 Sep 1905:   *Lt.-Gen.* Aleksandr Konstantinovich **Petrov**
- 1905 - 1906:   UPGRADED TO DIVISION
- 10 Mar 1906 - 11 Jun 1910:   *Lt.-Gen.* Aleksandr Konstantinovich **Petrov**
- 11 Jun 1910 - 31 Dec 1913:   *Lt.-Gen.* Vasily Vasilievich **Artemyev**
- 31 Dec 1913 - 30 Aug 1914:   *Lt.-Gen.* Aleksandr Vasilyevich **Sheremetov**
- 30 Aug 1914 - 16 Feb 1915:   *Lt.-Gen.* Vladimir Aleksandrovich **Yablochkin**

- 26 Feb 1915 - 12 Jul 1915: *Lt.-Gen.* Yulian Yulianovich **Belozor**
- 1915: UPGRADED TO DIVISION

Commander, 3rd Rifle Brigade
- 8 Jul 1891 - 11 Aug 1899: *Lt.-Gen.* Andrey Afanasiyevich **Nemirovich-Danchenko**
- 11 Aug 1899 - 13 Apr 1900: *Gen. of Inf.* Nikolai Borisovich **Kutnevich**
- 13 Apr 1900 - 28 Feb 1901: ?
- 28 Feb 1901 - 19 Apr 1904: *Lt.-Gen.* Ksavery Antonovich **Dobrzhinsky**
- 29 Apr 1904 - 18 Jul 1905: *Maj.-Gen.* Vladimir Ustinovich **Sollogub**
- 1905 - 1906: UPGRADED TO DIVISION
- 30 May 1906 - 3 May 1914: *Gen. of Inf.* Sergei Fyodorovich **Dobrotin**
- 13 May 1914 - 1 Nov 1914: *Maj.-Gen.* Pyotr Pavlovich **Palibin**
- 1 Nov 1914 - 6 Aug 1915: *Lt.-Gen.* Yakov Aleksandrovich **Fok**
- 1915: UPGRADED TO DIVISION

Commander, 4th Rifle Brigade
- 4 Feb 1891 - 20 Mar 1895: *Lt.-Gen.* Vladimir Nikolayevich **Filippov**
- 20 Mar 1895 - 28 Apr 1896: *Gen. of Inf.* Arkady Platonovich **Skugarevsky**
- 27 May 1896 - 29 Feb 1900: *Lt.-Gen.* Vladimir Korneyevich **Khudyakov**
- 14 Mar 1900 - 19 May 1900: *Lt.-Gen.* Nikolai Martinovich **Ivanov**
- 11 Jul 1900 - 7 Feb 1901: *Lt.-Gen.* Vladimir Sergeyevich **Volkov**
- 28 Feb 1901 - 9 Mar 1905: *Maj.-Gen.* Pyotr Vasilyevich **Polkovnikov**
- 9 Mar 1905 - 6 Jul 1905: *Lt.-Gen.* Pavel Nikolayevich **Putilov**
- 1905 - 1906: UPGRADED TO DIVISION
- 1906 - 7 Jul 1907: *Lt.-Gen.* Andrei Dmitriyevich **Vsevolozhsky**
- 7 Jul 1907 - 19 Sep 1914: *Lt.-Gen.* Vladislav Frantsevich **Baufal**
- 19 Sep 1914 - 6 Aug 1915: *Lt.-Gen.* Anton Ivanovich **Denikin**
- 1915: UPGRADED TO DIVISION

Commander, 5th Rifle Brigade
- 10 Feb 1891 - Sep 1896: *Lt.-Gen.* Nikolai Faddeyevich **Krshivitsky**
- 17 Sep 1896 - 10 Jan 1898: *Lt.-Gen.* Orest Mikhailovich **Kislinsky**
- 11 Feb 1898 - 23 Jun 1899: *Lt.-Gen.* Konstantin Vikentyevich **Tserpitsky**
- 26 Jul 1899 - Jul 1902: *Maj.-Gen.* Stanislav Stanislavovich **Novogrebelsky**
- 8 Jul 1902 - 13 Aug 1905: *Gen. of Inf.* Aleksei Yevgrafovich **Churin**
- 1905 - 1906: UPGRADED TO DIVISION
- 4 Jun 1906 - 13 Feb 1909: *Lt.-Gen.* Nikolai Sergeyevich **Berdyayev**
- 13 Feb 1909 - 13 Aug 1912: *Lt.-Gen.* Nikolai Ilich **Sulimov**
- 13 Aug 1912 - 14 Oct 1912: ?
- 14 Oct 1912 - 15 Nov 1913: *Lt.-Gen.* Vladimir Yemelyanovich **Przhilutsky**
- 15 Nov 1913 - 21 Mar 1915: *Lt.-Gen.* Pyotr Dmitriyevich **Shreyder**
- 21 Mar 1915 - 22 Oct 1915: *Lt.-Gen.* Vasily Fyodorovich **Novitsky**

- 1915: UPGRADED TO DIVISION

Commander, 1ˢᵗ Caucasus Rifle Brigade *(Formed in 1900 from Caucasus Native Rifle Brigade)*
- 1 Nov 1895 - 30 Jan 1902: *Gen. of Inf.* Baron Anton Yegorovich von **Zaltsa**
- 10 Feb 1902 - 23 Nov 1904: *Gen. of Inf.* Nikolai Yegorovich **Svetlov**
- 30 Nov 1904 - Jun 1905: *Maj.-Gen.* Iosif Ivanovich **Gorsky**
- 23 Jun 1905 - Aug 1907: *Lt.-Gen.* Nikolai Aleksandrovich **Znosko-Borovsky**
- 8 Aug 1907 - 12 Mar 1908: *Gen. of Inf.* Sigizmund Viktorovich **Volsky**
- 12 Mar 1908 - 4 Nov 1910: *Lt.-Gen.* Ivan Aleksandrovich **Snarsky**
- 21 Dec 1910 - 9 Apr 1913: *Lt.-Gen.* Frants-Martselian Vikentyevich **Bokshchanin**
- 9 Apr 1913 - 19 Jul 1914: *Lt.-Gen.* Pyotr Ivanovich **Postovsky**
- 23 Jul 1914 - 22 Apr 1915: *Lt.-Gen.* Aleksey Sergeyevich **Polyansky**
- 22 Apr 1915 - 3 Nov 1915: *Lt.-Gen.* Konstantin Nikolayevich **Bekov**
- 1915: UPGRADED TO DIVISION

Commander, 2ⁿᵈ Caucasus Rifle Brigade *(Formed in 1900 from Caucasus Native Rifle Brigade)*
- 1 Nov 1895 - 4 Dec 1901: *Maj.-Gen.* Ivan Yakovlevich **Ushakov**
- 4 Dec 1901 - 23 Sep 1904: *Lt.-Gen.* Vasily Osipovich **Rylsky**
- 30 Sep 1904 - 23 Jun 1905: *Lt.-Gen.* Nikolai Aleksandrovich **Znosko-Borovsky**
- 13 Aug 1905 - 23 Oct 1908: *Gen. of Inf.* Fyodor Afanasievich **Voloshinov**
- 21 Nov 1908 - 19 Jul 1911: *Lt.-Gen.* Konstantin Romanovich **Dovbor-Musnitsky**
- 19 Jul 1911 - 24 Mar 1915: *Lt.-Gen.* Nikolai Nikolayevich **Voropanov**
- 24 Mar 1915 - 19 Nov 1915: *Maj.-Gen.* Foma Ivanovich **Nazarbekov**
- 1915: UPGRADED TO DIVISION

Commander, 3ʳᵈ Caucasus Rifle Brigade *(Formed in 1914)*
- 3 Sep 1914 - 5 Jul 1915: *Lt.-Gen.* Vasily Davidovich **Gabayev**
- 5 Jul 1915 - 19 Nov 1915: *Lt.-Gen.* Eduard Arkadyevich **Kolyankovsky**
- 1915: UPGRADED TO DIVISION

Commander, 4ᵗʰ Caucasus Rifle Brigade *(Formed in 1915)*
- 29 Mar 1915 - 14 Sep 1915: *Lt.-Gen.* Nikolai Mikhailovich **Vorobyev**
- 1915: UPGRADED TO DIVISION

Commander, 1ˢᵗ Finnish Rifle Brigade *(Formed in 1902)*
- 24 Oct 1902 - 10 Aug 1904: *Lt.-Gen.* Apollon Yermolayevich **Evert**
- 4 Sep 1904 - Jun 1906: *Lt.-Gen.* Pavel Grigoryevich **Sakhnovsky**
- 23 Jun 1906 - 24 Jan 1907: *Gen. of Inf.* Dmitry Grigoryevich **Shcherbachev**
- 30 Jan 1907 - 22 Sep 1910: *Gen. of Inf.* Pyotr Vladimirovich **Polzikov**
- 17 Oct 1910 - 13 May 1914: *Lt.-Gen.* Nikolai Nikolayevich **Korotkevich**

- 17 May 1914 - 19 Jul 1914:   *Lt.-Gen.* Nikolai Afanasyevich **Obruchev**
- 19 Jul 1914 - 24 Sep 1914:   *Lt.-Gen.* Pyotr Mironovich **Volkoboy**
- 24 Sep 1914 - 12 May 1915:   *Lt.-Gen.* Nikolai Afanasyevich **Obruchev**
- 1915:   UPGRADED TO DIVISION

Commander, 2nd Finnish Rifle Brigade *(Formed in 1902)*
- 31 Dec 1901 - 30 Apr 1907:   *Gen. of Inf.* Konstantin Osipovich **Kurganovich**
- 30 Apr 1907 - 19 Jun 1908:   *Gen. of Inf.* Leonid Vilhelmovich **Lesh**
- 2 Jul 1908 - 31 Dec 1910:   *Lt.-Gen.* Selvin Severinovich **Lassky**
- 31 Dec 1910 - 3 Jul 1915:   *Lt.-Gen.* Vladimir Vladimirovich von **Notbek**
- 1915:   UPGRADED TO DIVISION

Commander, 3rd Finnish Rifle Brigade *(Formed in 1910)*
- 8 Jun 1910 - 24 Sep 1914:   *Gen. of Inf.* Stanislav Feliksovich **Stelnitsky**
- 24 Sep 1914 - 12 May 1915:   *Lt.-Gen.* Pyotr Mironovich **Volkoboy**
- 1915:   UPGRADED TO DIVISION

Commander, 4th Finnish Rifle Brigade *(Formed in 1914)*
- 2 Apr 1914 - 12 May 1915:   *Lt.-Gen.* Vladimir Ivanovich **Selivachev**
- 1915:   UPGRADED TO DIVISION

Commander, 1st Turkestan Rifle Brigade *(Formed in 1900)*
- 23 Jul 1900 - 8 Jul 1901:   *Maj.-Gen.* Aleksandr Aleksandrovich **Broterus**
- 8 Jul 1901 - 4 Jul 1906:   *Gen. of Inf.* Venedikt Aloiziyevich **Yasensky**
- 17 Jul 1906 - 3 Oct 1907:   *Maj.-Gen.* Vitaly Yevgenievich **Andro-de-Byui-Ginglyatt**
- 3 Oct 1907 - 8 Aug 1908:   *Maj.-Gen.* Vladimir Ivanovich **Bubnov**
- 8 Aug 1908 - 21 Jul 1910:   *Gen. of Inf.* Aleksandr Aleksandrovich **Dushkevich**
- 21 Jul 1910 - 12 Jun 1912:   *Gen. of Inf.* Nikolai Mikhailovich **Voronov**
- 12 Jun 1912 - 12 Mar 1916:   *Maj.-Gen.* Dydan-Stanislav Mikhailovich **Morzhitsky**
- 1916:   UPGRADED TO DIVISION

Commander, 2nd Turkestan Rifle Brigade *(Formed in 1900)*
- 23 Jul 1900 - 1 Jul 1903:   *Lt.-Gen.* Aleksandr Fyodorovich **Korobka**
- 30 Jul 1903 - 1 Jun 1904:   *Lt.-Gen.* Aleksandr Davidovich **Tugan-Mirza-Baranovsky**
- 11 Jun 1904 - 18 Dec 1906:   *Gen. of Inf.* Nikolai Andreyevich **Zernets**
- 26 Feb 1907 - 15 Jul 1910:   *Lt.-Gen.* Aleksandr Pavlovich von **Ganenfeldt**
- 15 Jul 1910 - 16 Nov 1911:   *Gen. of Inf.* Ernest-Yakov Kasparovich **Peterov**
- 29 Nov 1911 - 12 Mar 1916:   *Lt.-Gen.* Ivan Vasilyevich **Kolpikov**
- 1916:   UPGRADED TO DIVISION

Commander, 3rd Turkestan Rifle Brigade *(Formed in 1900)*
- 23 Jul 1900 - 18 Jun 1906: *Lt.-Gen.* Pyotr Mikhailovich **Shorokhov**
- 24 Jul 1906 - 23 Jul 1910: *Lt.-Gen.* Mikhail Nikolayevich **Maslov**
- 23 Jul 1910 - 13 Dec 1913: *Lt.-Gen.* Olgerd-Antony Viktorovich **Radvan-Rypinsky**
- 14 Dec 1913 - 30 Aug 1914: *Lt.-Gen.* Vladimir Aleksandrovich **Yablochkin**
- 1 Oct 1914 - 24 Mar 1915: *Lt.-Gen.* Mikhail Nikolayevich **Maslov**
- 29 Mar 1915 - 11 Mar 1916: *Lt.-Gen.* Adrian Ivanovich **Tumsky**
- 1916: UPGRADED TO DIVISION

Commander, 4th Turkestan Rifle Brigade *(Formed in 1900)*
- 16 Aug 1900 - 30 Jul 1903: *Lt.-Gen.* Aleksandr Davidovich **Tugan-Mirza-Baranovsky**
- 26 Aug 1903 - 25 Jan 1905: *Gen. of Inf.* Viktor Konstantinovich **Grek**
- 8 Feb 1905 - 10 Feb 1909: *Lt.-Gen.* Sergey Ivanovich **Samoylo**
- 25 Feb 1909 - 23 Jul 1910: *Lt.-Gen.* Olgerd-Antony Viktorovich **Radvan-Rypinsky**
- 23 Jul 1910 - 19 Jul 1914: *Lt.-Gen.* Aleksey Yefimovich **Redko**
- 19 Jul 1914 - 22 Nov 1915: ?
- 1915: UPGRADED TO DIVISION

Commander, 5th Turkestan Rifle Brigade *(Formed in 1900)*
- 23 Jul 1900 - May 1903: *Lt.-Gen.* Pavel Nikolayevich **Tishevsky**
- 26 May 1903 - 12 May 1910: *Lt.-Gen.* Ivan Gavrilovich **Motorny**
- 4 Jul 1910 - 5 Apr 1914: *Lt.-Gen.* Viktor Pavlovich **Zykov**
- 3 May 1914 - 19 Nov 1915: *Lt.-Gen.* Aleksandr Ivanovich **Chaplygin**
- 1915: UPGRADED TO DIVISION

Commander, 6th Turkestan Rifle Brigade *(Formed in 1900)*
- 23 Jun 1900 - 24 Oct 1902: *Lt.-Gen.* Apollon Yermolayevich **Evert**
- 24 Oct 1902 - 14 Dec 1907: *Maj.-Gen.* Gugo Gustavovich von **Khakevits**
- 14 Dec 1907 - Sep 1908: *Maj.-Gen.* Vladimir Grigoryevich **Semenov**
- 4 Oct 1908 - 4 Jul 1910: *Lt.-Gen.* Viktor Pavlovich **Zykov**
- 4 Jul 1910 - 23 Dec 1911: *Lt.-Gen.* Sergey Matveyevich **Pospelov**
- 19 Jan 1912 - Oct 1913: *Lt.-Gen.* Pyotr Ivanovich **Melnikov**
- 5 Nov 1913 - 13 Sep 1914: *Maj.-Gen.* Nikolai Ivanovich **Omelyanovich**
- 13 Sep 1914 - 1915: ?
- 1915: UPGRADED TO DIVISION

Commander, 7th Turkestan Rifle Brigade *(Formed in 1900)*
- 23 Jul 1900 - 12 Jan 1904: *Gen. of Inf.* Sergey Ivanovich **Rusanov**
- 7 Feb 1904 - 13 Dec 1906: *Maj.-Gen.* Sergey Sergeyevich **Khatov**
- 13 Dec 1906 - 3 Dec 1908: *Gen. of Inf.* Vladimir Pavlovich **Shatilov**
- 15 Dec 1908 - 1 Jun 1910: *Lt.-Gen.* Nikolai Pavlovich **Gryaznov**

- 1910: DISSOLVED

Commander, 8th Turkestan Rifle Brigade (Formed in 1900)
- 23 Jul 1900 - 18 May 1902: *Lt.-Gen.* Pyotr Petrovich **Fedorov**
- 18 May 1902 - 17 Apr 1905: ?
- 17 Apr 1905 - 8 Oct 1907: *Maj.-Gen.* Aleksey Aleksandrovich **Fok**
- 8 Oct 1907 - 4 Jul 1910: *Lt.-Gen.* Sergey Matveyevich **Pospelov**
- 1910: DISSOLVED

Commander, Independent Guards Cavalry Brigade (Formed in 1897)
- 29 May 1897 - 26 Jan 1899: *Lt.-Gen.* Oskar Yakovlevich **Zander**
- 11 Mar 1899 - 26 Jan 1904: *Lt.-Gen.* Baron Aleksandr Nikolayevich **Bistrom**
- 26 Jan 1904 - 9 Jun 1907: ?
- 9 Jun 1907 - 22 Dec 1910: *Lt.-Gen.* Klaas Gustav Robert Robertovich **Charpentier**
- 22 Dec 1910 - 18 Feb 1912: *Maj.-Gen.* Esper Aleksandrovich **Feldman**
- 3 Mar 1912 - 15 Nov 1913: *Lt.-Gen.* Vladimir Khristoforovich **Roop**
- 24 Dec 1913 - 24 Jun 1915: *Lt.-Gen.* Baron Karl Karlovich **Mannerheim**
- 1915: REDESIGNATED 1st BRIGADE, CONSOLIDATED CAVALRY DIVISION

Commander, 1st Independent Cavalry Brigade (Formed in 1895)
- 15 Sep 1895 - May 1898: *Maj.-Gen.* Baron Fyodor Nikolayevich von **Kridener**
- 19 May 1898 - 11 Jun 1901: *Gen. of Cav.* Pavel Aleksandrovich **Kozlovsky**
- 24 Jul 1901 - 1 Feb 1904: *Gen. of Cav.* Pavel Karlovich Edler von **Rennenkampf**
- 19 Feb 1904 - 6 Nov 1906: *Gen. of Cav.* Sergey Alekseyevich **Kareyev**
- 31 Dec 1906 - Apr 1912: *Lt.-Gen.* Yevgeny Georgiyevich **Trambitsky**
- 18 Apr 1912 - 16 Jan 1914: *Gen. of Cav.* Khan Hussein **Nakhichevansky**
- 25 Mar 1914 - 10 Aug 1914: *Lt.-Gen.* Nikolai Aloiziyevich **Oranovsky**
- 11 Oct 1914 - 5 Dec 1914: *Maj.-Gen.* Baron Vladimir Nikolayevich von **Maydel**
- 5 Dec 1914 - 19 Mar 1916: *Lt.-Gen.* Anastas Fyodorovich **Benderev**
- Apr 1916: DISSOLVED

Commander, 2nd Independent Cavalry Brigade (Formed in 1896)
- 16 Sep 1896 - 12 Dec 1900: *Lt.-Gen.* Aleksandr Nikolayevich **Ovodov**
- 16 Jan 1901 - 13 Jun 1905: *Maj.-Gen.* Nikolai Petrovich **Stepanov**
- 28 Jun 1905 - 5 Sep 1905: *Maj.-Gen.* Emmanuil Ivanovich **Bernov**
- 2 Oct 1905 - 24 Jul 1907: *Gen. of Cav.* Leonty Nikolayevich von **Baumgarten**
- 21 Aug 1907 - 11 Jul 1908: *Gen. of Cav.* Vladimir Aloiziyevich **Oranovsky**
- 11 Jul 1908 - 4 Oct 1908: ?
- 4 Oct 1908 - 27 Nov 1912: *Lt.-Gen.* Pavel Aleksandrovich **Stakhovich**
- 27 Nov 1912 - 12 Dec 1914: *Gen. of Cav.* Abram Mikhailovich **Dragomirov**
- 12 Dec 1914: REDESIGNATED 1st BRIGADE, 16th CAVALRY

DIVISION

Commander, 3rd Independent Cavalry Brigade *(Formed in 1897)*
- 28 Nov 1897 - 10 Feb 1899: *Gen. of Cav.* Leonty Nikolayevich von **Baumgarten**
- 23 Feb 1899 - 15 Mar 1906: *Gen. of Cav.* Nikolai Artemyevich **Villamov**
- 14 Apr 1906 - 29 May 1910: *Maj.-Gen.* Mikhail Ivanovich **Mezentsov**
- 29 May 1910 - 22 Jun 1912: *Lt.-Gen.* Anton Aleksandrovich **Tolpygo**
- 29 Jun 1912 - 18 Jul 1914: *Maj.-Gen.* Baron Anatoly Aleksandrovich **Budberg**
- 18 Jul 1914 - 10 Aug 1914: *Lt.-Gen.* Sergey Petrovich **Vannovsky**
- Aug 1914: REDESIGNATED 2nd BRIGADE, 16th CAVALRY DIVISION

Commander, 4th Independent Cavalry Brigade *(Formed in 1914)*
- 15 Aug 1914 - 4 Jul 1915: *Lt.-Gen.* Vasily Aleksandrovich **Khimets**
- 4 Jul 1915 - 22 Oct 1915: ?
- 22 Oct 1915 - 22 Jan 1917: *Lt.-Gen.* Pyotr Pavlovich **Kanshin**
- 22 Jan 1917 - 2 Mar 1917: ?

Commander, Trans-Caspian Cossack Brigade
- 1894 - 3 Dec 1897: *Gen. of Cav.* Baron Georgy Karlovich von **Shtakelberg**
- 17 Dec 1897 - 3 May 1904: *Maj.-Gen.* Viktor Semyonovich **Kovalev**
- 3 May 1904 - 5 Jul 1910: *Gen. of Cav.* Pavel Lyudvigovich **Khelmitsky**
- 5 Jul 1910 - 9 Nov 1913: *Lt.-Gen.* Prince Georgy Ilich **Orbeliani**
- 9 Nov 1913 - 14 Nov 1914: *Lt.-Gen.* Andrey Mikhailovich **Nikolayev**
- 14 Nov 1915: UPGRADED TO 5th CAUCASUS COSSACK DIVISION

Commander, Siberian Cossack Brigade *(Formed in 1909)*
- 22 Sep 1909 - 4 Feb 1915: *Gen. of Cav.* Pyotr Petrovich **Kalitin**
- 4 Feb 1915 - 25 May 1916: *Lt.-Gen.* Ernest-Avgust Ferdinandovich **Raddats**
- 1 Jul 1916 - 21 Oct 1916: *Maj.-Gen.* Aleksandr Ferdinandovich **Rafalovich**
- 21 Oct 1916 - 23 Oct 1917: *Maj.-Gen.* Vladimir Antonovich **Levandovsky**

Commander, Trans-Baikal Cossack Brigade *(Formed in 1903; until 1906 Independent Brigade)*
- 23 Mar 1903 - 17 Feb 1905: *Gen. of Art.* Pavel Ivanovich **Mishchenko**
- 17 Feb 1905 - 20 Jul 1906: UPGRADED TO DIVISION
- 20 Jul 1906 - 10 Jul 1907: *Lt.-Gen.* Vladimir Aleksandrovich **Tolmachev**
- 10 Jul 1907 - 22 Sep 1909: *Gen. of Cav.* Pyotr Petrovich **Kalitin**
- 22 Sep 1909 - 24 Nov 1911: *Lt.-Gen.* Vladimir Ivanovich **Zhigalin**
- 23 Dec 1911 - 21 Oct 1915: *Lt.-Gen.* Sergey Vladimirovich **Tomashevsky**
- 21 Oct 1915 - 22 Dec 1915: *Maj.-Gen.* Ivan Davydovich **Orlov**

- 22 Dec 1915: UPGRADED TO 1st TRANS-BAIKAL COSSACK DIVISION

Commander, 2nd Trans-Baikal Cossack Brigade *(Formed in 1916)*
- 4 Feb 1916 - 24 Mar 1917: *Maj.-Gen.* Anatoly Mikhailovich **Nazarov**

Commander, Ussuri Mounted Brigade *(Formed in 1897)*
- 26 May 1897 - 15 Mar 1904: *Maj.-Gen.* Nikolai Nikolayevich **Kryzhanovsky**
- 15 Mar 1904 - 2 Sep 1904: *Gen. of Cav.* Aleksandr Vasilievich **Samsonov**
- 5 Nov 1904 - 8 Aug 1906: *Maj.-Gen.* Georgy Aleksandrovich **Pavlov**
- 8 Aug 1906 - 10 Jul 1907: *Gen. of Cav.* Pyotr Petrovich **Kalitin**
- 10 Jul 1907 - 26 Jan 1912: *Lt.-Gen.* Vladimir Aleksandrovich **Tolmachev**
- 19 Feb 1912 - 5 Feb 1915: *Maj.-Gen.* Leonid Petrovich **Kiselev**
- 27 Mar 1915 - 18 Dec 1915: *Lt.-Gen.* Aleksandr Mikhailovich **Krymov**
- 18 Dec 1915: UPGRADED TO DIVISION

SECTION III: NAVAL ADMINISTRATION

Minister of the Navy
- 28 Nov 1888 - 13 Jul 1896: *Admiral* Nikolai Matveyevich **Chikhachov**
- 13 Jul 1896 - 4 Mar 1903: *Admiral* Pavel Petrovich **Tyrtov**
- 4 Mar 1903 - 29 Jun 1905: *Admiral* Fyodor Karlovich **Avelan**
- 29 Jun 1905 - 11 Jan 1907: *Admiral* Aleksei Alekseyevich **Birilev**
- 11 Jan 1907 - 8 Jan 1909: *Admiral* Ivan Mikhailovich **Dikov**
- 8 Jan 1909 - 18 Mar 1911: *Admiral* Stepan Arkadievich **Voyevodsky**
- 19 Mar 1911 - 28 Feb 1917: *Admiral* Ivan Konstantinovich **Grigorovich**

Chief of the Main Naval Staff
- 28 Nov 1888 - 14 May 1896: *Admiral* Oskar Karlovich von **Kremer**
- 14 May 1896 - 4 Mar 1903: *Admiral* Fyodor Karlovich **Avelan**
- 4 Mar 1903 - Apr 1904: *Vice-Admiral* Zinovy Petrovich **Rozhestvensky**
- Apr 1904 - 29 Nov 1904: *Vice-Admiral* Andrei Andreyevich **Virenius**
- 29 Nov 1904 - Nov 1905: *Vice-Admiral* Pyotr Alekseyevich **Bezobrazov**
- Nov 1905 - Feb 1906: *Vice-Admiral* Zinovy Petrovich **Rozhestvensky**
- Feb 1906 - 1907: *Vice-Admiral* Aleksandr Georgievich von **Nidermiller**
- 1907 - 18 Apr 1911: *Admiral* Nikolai Matveyevich **Yakovlev**
- 6 Dec 1911 - 17 Sep 1913: *Admiral* Mikhail Valerianovich **Knyazev**
- 17 Sep 1913 - Apr 1917: *Admiral* Aleksandr Ivanovich **Rusin**

Chief of the Naval General Staff *(Office created in 1906)*
- Jun 1906 - 14 Jul 1908: *Vice-Admiral* Lev Alekseyevich **Brusilov**
- 14 Jul 1908 - 11 Oct 1911: *Admiral* Andrei Augustovich **Ebergardt**
- 11 Oct 1911 - 23 Feb 1914: *Vice-Admiral* Prince Aleksandr Aleksandrovich **Liven**
- 23 Feb 1914 - Apr 1917: *Admiral* Aleksandr Ivanovich **Rusin**

Chief of the Main Directorate of Shipbuilding & Logistics
- 1893 - 13 Jul 1896: *Admiral* Pavel Petrovich **Tyrtov**
- 13 Jul 1896 - 14 Apr 1902: *Admiral* Vladimir Pavlovich **Verkhovsky**
- Apr 1902 - 1906: *Lieutenant-General of the Admiralty* Lev Alekseyevich **Lyubimov**
- 1906 - 26 Feb 1907: *Vice-Admiral* Aleksandr Rostislavovich **Rodionov**
- 26 Feb 1907 - 9 Mar 1909: *Vice-Admiral* Ivan Petrovich **Uspensky**
- 9 Mar 1909 - 18 Apr 1911: *General of the Fleet* Sergey Petrovich **Dyushen**
- 15 Nov 1911 - 25 May 1915: *Admiral* Pyotr Petrovich **Muravyev**
- 1 Jun 1915 - 27 Jun 1916: *Vice-Admiral* Aleksey Petrovich **Ugryumov**
- 27 Jun 1916 - 15 Dec 1917: *Vice-Admiral* Vladimir Konstantinovich **Girs**

SECTION IV: NAVAL UNITS

Commander-in-Chief, Baltic Fleet (Formed in 1909)
- 3 Dec 1909 - 14 May 1915:   *Admiral* Nikolai Ottovich von **Essen**
- 14 May 1915 - 6 Aug 1916:   *Admiral* Vasily Aleksandrovich **Kanin**
- 6 Aug 1916 - 4 Mar 1917:   *Vice-Admiral* Adrian Ivanovich **Nepenin**

Commander-in-Chief, Black Sea Fleet
- 1 Jan 1891 - 1898:   *Vice-Admiral* Nikolai Vasilyevich **Kopytov**
- 1898 - 6 May 1898:   *Admiral* Yevgeny Ivanovich **Alekseyev**
- 6 May 1898 - 4 Mar 1903:   *Vice-Admiral* Sergey Petrovich **Tyrtov**
- 4 Mar 1903 - 1 Apr 1904:   *Admiral* Nikolai Illarionovich **Skrydlov**
- 2 Apr 1904 - 1 Jun 1905:   *Vice-Admiral* Grigory Pavlovich **Chukhnin**
- 1 Jun 1905 - 1 Aug 1905:   *Vice-Admiral* Aleksandr Khristianovich **Kriger**
- 1 Aug 1905 - 28 Jun 1906:   *Vice-Admiral* Grigory Pavlovich **Chukhnin**
- 28 Jun 1906 - 26 Mar 1907:   *Admiral* Nikolai Illarionovich **Skrydlov**
- 26 Mar 1907 - 15 Feb 1909:   *Admiral* Robert Nikolayevich **Viren**
- 15 Feb 1909 - 9 Oct 1909:   *Vice-Admiral* Ivan Fyodorovich **Bostrem**
- 9 Oct 1909 - 7 Jun 1911:   *Admiral* Vladimir Simonovich **Sarnavsky**
- 7 Jun 1911 - 8 Aug 1911:   *Vice-Admiral* Pavel Ivanovich **Novitsky**
- 11 Oct 1911 - 28 Jun 1916:   *Admiral* Andrei Augustovich **Ebergardt**
- 28 Jun 1916 - 7 Jun 1917:   *Admiral* Aleksandr Vasilievich **Kolchak**

Commander-in-Chief, Pacific Fleet/Squadron
- 6 Jan 1895 - 11 Aug 1897:   *Admiral* Yevgeny Ivanovich **Alekseyev**
- Aug 1897 - 6 Dec 1899:   *Admiral* Fyodor Vasilyevich **Dubasov**
- 1899 - 1900:   *Admiral* Yakov Apollonovich **Giltebrandt**
- 1900 - 7 Feb 1902:   *Admiral* Nikolai Illarionovich **Skrydlov**
- 7 Feb 1902 - 24 Feb 1904:   *Admiral* Oskar Viktorovich **Stark**
- 1 Feb 1904 - 31 Mar 1904:   *Vice-Admiral* Stepan Osipovich **Makarov**
- 31 Mar 1904 - 3 Apr 1904:   *Vice-Admiral* Prince Pavel Petrovich **Ukhtomsky**
- 4 Apr 1904 - 7 Jan 1905:   *Admiral* Nikolai Illarionovich **Skrydlov**
- 8 May 1905 - 29 Jun 1905:   *Admiral* Aleksei Alekseyevich **Birilev**
- Jun 1905:   DISSOLVED

Primary Sources:

- Генералитет российской императорской армии и флота (http://www.rusgeneral.ru)
  [*Generals of the Imperial Russian Army and Navy*]

- Генералов, Штабъ и Обер-офицеров, Корпусов Морского Ведомства, Чинов по Адмиралтейству и Числящихся по Корпусам
  [*Generals, Staff- and Senior Officers of the Naval Office, Officials of the Admiralty*]

- Русская армия в Первой мировой войне (http://www.grwar.ru)
  [*The Russian Army in World War I*]

- Список генералам по старшинству 1894 - 1916
  [*Seniority list of generals*]

- Список личного состава судов флота, строевых и административных учреждений Морского ведомства
  [*List of fleet personnel, combat and administrative institutions of the Naval Office*]

- Список полковникам по старшинству 1894 - 1916
  [*Seniority list of colonels*]

- Suomalaiset kenraalit ja amiraalit Venäjän sotavoimissa 1809 - 1917
  (http://www.kansallisbiografia.fi/kenraalit/)
  [*Finnish generals and admirals of the Russian armed forces 1809 - 1917*]

- Участники первой мировой войны (http://1914ww.ru/biograf/index.php)
  [*Participants of World War I*]

ACKNOWLEDGEMENTS

Of all the writing projects that I have undertaken during the last twenty years, this has by far been the most labor-intensive and time-consuming. I must thank my wife, Rosemarie, for her patience, support and encouragement during this project.

Other books by Andris J. Kursietis:

The Fallen Generals
La Regia Marina 1919 - 1945
The Wehrmacht at War
The Armed Forces of Latvia 1918 - 1940
The Hungarian Army & Its Military Leadership in World War II
The Luftwaffe 1935 - 1945
Generals & Admirals of the Spanish Armed Forces 1900 - 1945
A Lifetime for Hungary
The Imperial Japanese Navy (Nihon Kaigun) 1900 - 1945
Under Three Flags

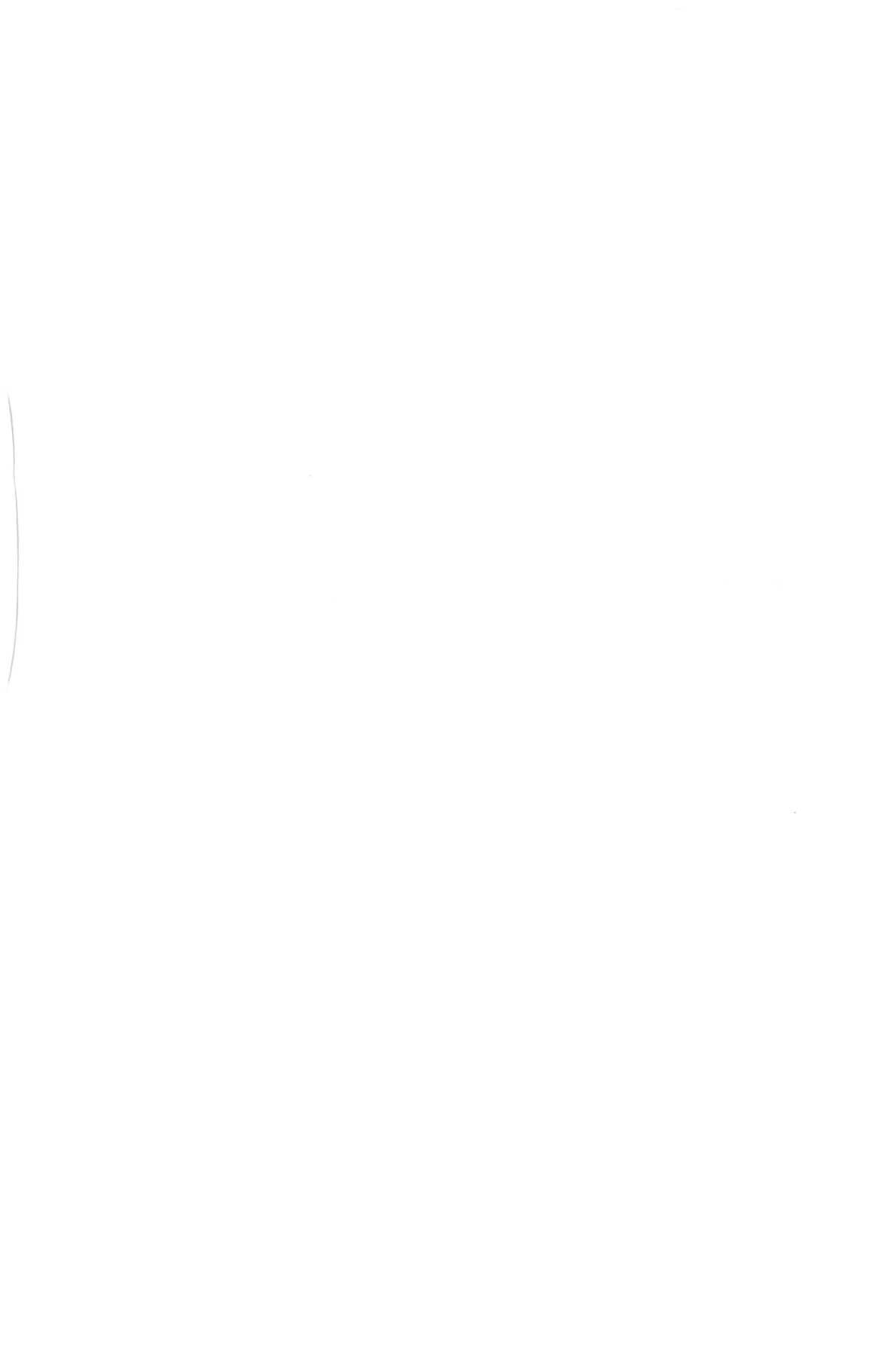